T0180307

Lecture Notes in Computer Science 13090

Founding Editors

Gerhard Goos
Karlsruhe Institute of Technology, Karlsruhe, Germany
Juris Hartmanis
Cornell University, Ithaca, NY, USA

Editorial Board Members

Elisa Bertino
Purdue University, West Lafayette, IN, USA
Wen Gao
Peking University, Beijing, China
Bernhard Steffen
TU Dortmund University, Dortmund, Germany
Gerhard Woeginger
RWTH Aachen, Aachen, Germany
Moti Yung
Columbia University, New York, NY, USA

More information about this subseries at https://link.springer.com/bookseries/7410

Mehdi Tibouchi · Huaxiong Wang (Eds.)

Advances in Cryptology – ASIACRYPT 2021

27th International Conference on the Theory
and Application of Cryptology and Information Security
Singapore, December 6–10, 2021
Proceedings, Part I

 Springer

Editors
Mehdi Tibouchi 🆔
NTT Corporation
Tokyo, Japan

Huaxiong Wang 🆔
Nanyang Technological University
Singapore, Singapore

ISSN 0302-9743   ISSN 1611-3349   (electronic)
Lecture Notes in Computer Science
ISBN 978-3-030-92061-6   ISBN 978-3-030-92062-3   (eBook)
https://doi.org/10.1007/978-3-030-92062-3

LNCS Sublibrary: SL4 – Security and Cryptology

© International Association for Cryptologic Research 2021
This work is subject to copyright. All rights are reserved by the Publisher, whether the whole or part of the material is concerned, specifically the rights of translation, reprinting, reuse of illustrations, recitation, broadcasting, reproduction on microfilms or in any other physical way, and transmission or information storage and retrieval, electronic adaptation, computer software, or by similar or dissimilar methodology now known or hereafter developed.
The use of general descriptive names, registered names, trademarks, service marks, etc. in this publication does not imply, even in the absence of a specific statement, that such names are exempt from the relevant protective laws and regulations and therefore free for general use.
The publisher, the authors and the editors are safe to assume that the advice and information in this book are believed to be true and accurate at the date of publication. Neither the publisher nor the authors or the editors give a warranty, expressed or implied, with respect to the material contained herein or for any errors or omissions that may have been made. The publisher remains neutral with regard to jurisdictional claims in published maps and institutional affiliations.

This Springer imprint is published by the registered company Springer Nature Switzerland AG
The registered company address is: Gewerbestrasse 11, 6330 Cham, Switzerland

Preface

Asiacrypt 2021, the 27th Annual International Conference on Theory and Application of Cryptology and Information Security, was originally planned to be held in Singapore during December 6–10, 2021. Due to the COVID-19 pandemic, it was shifted to an online-only virtual conference.

The conference covered all technical aspects of cryptology, and was sponsored by the International Association for Cryptologic Research (IACR).

We received a total of 341 submissions from all over the world, and the Program Committee (PC) selected 95 papers for publication in the proceedings of the conference. The two program chairs were supported by a PC consisting of 74 leading experts in aspects of cryptology. Each submission was reviewed by at least three PC members (or their sub-reviewers) and five PC members were assigned to submissions co-authored by PC members. The strong conflict of interest rules imposed by IACR ensure that papers are not handled by PC members with a close working relationship with the authors. The two program chairs were not allowed to submit a paper, and PC members were limited to two submissions each. There were approximately 363 external reviewers, whose input was critical to the selection of papers.

The review process was conducted using double-blind peer review. The conference operated a two-round review system with a rebuttal phase. After the reviews and first-round discussions the PC selected 233 submissions to proceed to the second round and the authors were then invited to provide a short rebuttal in response to the referee reports. The second round involved extensive discussions by the PC members.

Alongside the presentations of the accepted papers, the program of Asiacrypt 2021 featured an IACR distinguished lecture by Andrew Chi-Chih Yao and two invited talks by Kazue Sako and Yu Yu. The conference also featured a rump session which contained short presentations on the latest research results of the field.

The four volumes of the conference proceedings contain the revised versions of the 95 papers that were selected, together with the abstracts of the IACR distinguished lecture and the two invited talks. The final revised versions of papers were not reviewed again and the authors are responsible for their contents.

Via a voting-based process that took into account conflicts of interest, the PC selected the three top papers of the conference: "On the Hardness of the NTRU problem" by Alice Pellet-Mary and Damien Stehlé (which received the best paper award); "A Geometric Approach to Linear Cryptanalysis" by Tim Beyne (which received the best student paper award); and "Lattice Enumeration for Tower NFS: a 521-bit Discrete Logarithm Computation" by Gabrielle De Micheli, Pierrick Gaudry, and Cécile Pierrot. The authors of all three papers were invited to submit extended versions of their manuscripts to the Journal of Cryptology.

Many people have contributed to the success of Asiacrypt 2021. We would like to thank the authors for submitting their research results to the conference. We are very grateful to the PC members and external reviewers for contributing their knowledge and expertise, and for the tremendous amount of work that was done with reading papers and contributing to the discussions. We are greatly indebted to Jian Guo, the General Chair, for his efforts and overall organization. We thank San Ling and Josef Pieprzyk, the advisors of Asiacrypt 2021, for their valuable suggestions. We thank Michel Abdalla, Kevin McCurley, Kay McKelly, and members of IACR's emergency pandemic team for their work in designing and running the virtual format. We thank Chitchanok Chuengsatiansup and Khoa Nguyen for expertly organizing and chairing the rump session. We are extremely grateful to Zhenzhen Bao for checking all the LaTeX files and for assembling the files for submission to Springer. We also thank Alfred Hofmann, Anna Kramer, and their colleagues at Springer for handling the publication of these conference proceedings.

December 2021

Mehdi Tibouchi
Huaxiong Wang

Organization

General Chair

Jian Guo   Nanyang Technological University, Singapore

Program Committee Co-chairs

Mehdi Tibouchi   NTT Corporation, Japan
Huaxiong Wang   Nanyang Technological University, Singapore

Steering Committee

Masayuki Abe	Dingyi Pei
Lynn Batten	Duong Hieu Phan
Jung Hee Cheon	Raphael Phan
Steven Galbraith	Josef Pieprzyk (Vice Chair)
D. J. Guan	C. Pandu Rangan
Jian Guo	Bimal Roy
Khalid Habib	Leonie Simpson
Lucas Hui	Huaxiong Wang
Nassar Ikram	Henry B. Wolfe
Kwangjo Kim	Duncan Wong
Xuejia Lai	Tzong-Chen Wu
Dong Hoon Lee	Bo-Yin Yang
Satya Lokam	Siu-Ming Yiu
Mitsuru Matsui (Chair)	Yu Yu
Tsutomu Matsumoto	Jianying Zhou
Phong Nguyen	

Program Committee

Shweta Agrawal	IIT Madras, India
Martin R. Albrecht	Royal Holloway, University of London, UK
Zhenzhen Bao	Nanyang Technological University, Singapore
Manuel Barbosa	University of Porto (FCUP) and INESC TEC, Portugal
Lejla Batina	Radboud University, The Netherlands
Sonia Belaïd	CryptoExperts, France
Fabrice Benhamouda	Algorand Foundation, USA
Begül Bilgin	Rambus - Cryptography Research, The Netherlands
Xavier Bonnetain	University of Waterloo, Canada
Joppe W. Bos	NXP Semiconductors, Belgium

Wouter Castryck	KU Leuven, Belgium
Rongmao Chen	National University of Defense Technology, China
Jung Hee Cheon	Seoul National University, South Korea
Chitchanok Chuengsatiansup	The University of Adelaide, Australia
Kai-Min Chung	Academia Sinica, Taiwan
Dana Dachman-Soled	University of Maryland, USA
Bernardo David	IT University of Copenhagen, Denmark
Benjamin Fuller	University of Connecticut, USA
Steven Galbraith	The University of Auckland, New Zealand
María Isabel González Vasco	Universidad Rey Juan Carlos, Spain
Robert Granger	University of Surrey, UK
Alex B. Grilo	CNRS, LIP6, Sorbonne Université, France
Aurore Guillevic	Inria, France
Swee-Huay Heng	Multimedia University, Malaysia
Akinori Hosoyamada	NTT Corporation and Nagoya University, Japan
Xinyi Huang	Fujian Normal University, China
Andreas Hülsing	Eindhoven University of Technology, The Netherlands
Tetsu Iwata	Nagoya University, Japan
David Jao	University of Waterloo and evolutionQ, Inc., Canada
Jérémy Jean	ANSSI, France
Shuichi Katsumata	AIST, Japan
Elena Kirshanova	I. Kant Baltic Federal University, Russia
Hyung Tae Lee	Chung-Ang University, South Korea
Dongdai Lin	Institute of Information Engineering, Chinese Academy of Sciences, China
Rongxing Lu	University of New Brunswick, Canada
Xianhui Lu	Institute of Information Engineering, Chinese Academy of Sciences, China
Mary Maller	Ethereum Foundation, UK
Giorgia Azzurra Marson	NEC Labs Europe, Germany
Keith M. Martin	Royal Holloway, University of London, UK
Daniel Masny	Visa Research, USA
Takahiro Matsuda	AIST, Japan
Krystian Matusiewicz	Intel Corporation, Poland
Florian Mendel	Infineon Technologies, Germany
Nele Mentens	Leiden University, The Netherlands, and KU Leuven, Belgium
Atsuko Miyaji	Osaka University, Japan
Michael Naehrig	Microsoft Research, USA
Khoa Nguyen	Nanyang Technological University, Singapore
Miyako Ohkubo	NICT, Japan
Emmanuela Orsini	KU Leuven, Belgium
Jiaxin Pan	NTNU, Norway
Panos Papadimitratos	KTH Royal Institute of Technology, Sweden

Alice Pellet–Mary	CNRS and University of Bordeaux, France
Duong Hieu Phan	Télécom Paris, Institut Polytechnique de Paris, France
Francisco Rodríguez-Henríquez	CINVESTAV, Mexico
Olivier Sanders	Orange Labs, France
Jae Hong Seo	Hanyang University, South Korea
Haya Shulman	Fraunhofer SIT, Germany
Daniel Slamanig	AIT Austrian Institute of Technology, Austria
Ron Steinfeld	Monash University, Australia
Willy Susilo	University of Wollongong, Australia
Katsuyuki Takashima	Waseda University, Japan
Qiang Tang	The University of Sydney, Australia
Serge Vaudenay	EPFL, Switzerland
Damien Vergnaud	Sorbonne Université and Institut Universitaire de France, France
Meiqin Wang	Shandong University, China
Xiaoyun Wang	Tsinghua University, China
Yongge Wang	UNC Charlotte, USA
Wenling Wu	Institute of Software, Chinese Academy of Sciences, China
Chaoping Xing	Shanghai Jiao Tong University, China
Sophia Yakoubov	Aarhus University, Denmark
Takashi Yamakawa	NTT Corporation, Japan
Bo-Yin Yang	Academia Sinica, Taiwan
Yu Yu	Shanghai Jiao Tong University, China
Hong-Sheng Zhou	Virginia Commonwealth University, USA

Additional Reviewers

Behzad Abdolmaleki
Gorjan Alagic
Orestis Alpos
Miguel Ambrona
Diego Aranha
Victor Arribas
Nuttapong Attrapadung
Benedikt Auerbach
Zeta Avarikioti
Melissa Azouaoui
Saikrishna Badrinarayanan
Joonsang Baek
Karim Baghery
Shi Bai
Gustavo Banegas
Subhadeep Banik

James Bartusek
Balthazar Bauer
Rouzbeh Behnia
Yanis Belkheyar
Josh Benaloh
Ward Beullens
Tim Beyne
Sarani Bhattacharya
Rishiraj Bhattacharyya
Nina Bindel
Adam Blatchley Hansen
Olivier Blazy
Charlotte Bonte
Katharina Boudgoust
Ioana Boureanu
Markus Brandt

Anne Broadbent
Ileana Buhan
Andrea Caforio
Eleonora Cagli
Sébastien Canard
Ignacio Cascudo
Gaëtan Cassiers
André Chailloux
Tzu-Hsien Chang
Yilei Chen
Jie Chen
Yanlin Chen
Albert Cheu
Jesús-Javier Chi-Domíguez
Nai-Hui Chia
Ilaria Chillotti
Ji-Jian Chin
Jérémy Chotard
Sherman S. M. Chow
Heewon Chung
Jorge Chávez-Saab
Michele Ciampi
Carlos Cid
Valerio Cini
Tristan Claverie
Benoît Cogliati
Alexandru Cojocaru
Daniel Collins
Kelong Cong
Craig Costello
Geoffroy Couteau
Daniele Cozzo
Jan Czajkowski
Tianxiang Dai
Wei Dai
Sourav Das
Pratish Datta
Alex Davidson
Lauren De Meyer
Elke De Mulder
Claire Delaplace
Cyprien Delpech de Saint Guilhem
Patrick Derbez
Siemen Dhooghe
Daniel Dinu
Christoph Dobraunig

Samuel Dobson
Luis J. Dominguez Perez
Jelle Don
Benjamin Dowling
Maria Eichlseder
Jesse Elliott
Keita Emura
Muhammed F. Esgin
Hulya Evkan
Lei Fan
Antonio Faonio
Hanwen Feng
Dario Fiore
Antonio Florez-Gutierrez
Georg Fuchsbauer
Chaya Ganesh
Daniel Gardham
Rachit Garg
Pierrick Gaudry
Romain Gay
Nicholas Genise
Adela Georgescu
David Gerault
Satrajit Ghosh
Valerie Gilchrist
Aron Gohr
Junqing Gong
Marc Gourjon
Lorenzo Grassi
Milos Grujic
Aldo Gunsing
Kaiwen Guo
Chun Guo
Qian Guo
Mike Hamburg
Ben Hamlin
Shuai Han
Yonglin Hao
Keisuke Hara
Patrick Harasser
Jingnan He
David Heath
Chloé Hébant
Julia Hesse
Ryo Hiromasa
Shiqi Hou

Lin Hou
Yao-Ching Hsieh
Kexin Hu
Jingwei Hu
Zhenyu Huang
Loïs Huguenin-Dumittan
Arnie Hung
Shih-Han Hung
Kathrin Hövelmanns
Ilia Iliashenko
Aayush Jain
Yanxue Jia
Dingding Jia
Yao Jiang
Floyd Johnson
Luke Johnson
Chanyang Ju
Charanjit S. Jutla
John Kelsey
Taechan Kim
Myungsun Kim
Jinsu Kim
Minkyu Kim
Young-Sik Kim
Sungwook Kim
Jiseung Kim
Kwangjo Kim
Seungki Kim
Sunpill Kim
Fuyuki Kitagawa
Susumu Kiyoshima
Michael Klooß
Dimitris Kolonelos
Venkata Koppula
Liliya Kraleva
Mukul Kulkarni
Po-Chun Kuo
Hilder Vitor Lima Pereira
Russell W. F. Lai
Jianchang Lai
Yi-Fu Lai
Virginie Lallemand
Jason LeGrow
Joohee Lee
Jooyoung Lee
Changmin Lee

Hyeonbum Lee
Moon Sung Lee
Keewoo Lee
Dominik Leichtle
Alexander Lemmens
Gaëtan Leurent
Yannan Li
Shuaishuai Li
Baiyu Li
Zhe Li
Shun Li
Liang Li
Jianwei Li
Trey Li
Xiao Liang
Chi-Chang Lin
Chengjun Lin
Chao Lin
Yao-Ting Lin
Eik List
Feng-Hao Liu
Qipeng Liu
Guozhen Liu
Yunwen Liu
Patrick Longa
Sebastien Lord
George Lu
Yuan Lu
Yibiao Lu
Xiaojuan Lu
Ji Luo
Yiyuan Luo
Mohammad Mahzoun
Monosij Maitra
Christian Majenz
Ekaterina Malygina
Mark Manulis
Varun Maram
Luca Mariot
Loïc Masure
Bart Mennink
Simon-Philipp Merz
Peihan Miao
Kazuhiko Minematsu
Donika Mirdita
Pratyush Mishra

Tomoyuki Morimae
Pratyay Mukherjee
Alex Munch-Hansen
Yusuke Naito
Ngoc Khanh Nguyen
Jianting Ning
Ryo Nishimaki
Anca Nitulescu
Kazuma Ohara
Cristina Onete
Jean-Baptiste Orfila
Michele Orrù
Jong Hwan Park
Jeongeun Park
Robi Pedersen
Angel L. Perez del Pozo
Léo Perrin
Thomas Peters
Albrecht Petzoldt
Stjepan Picek
Rafael del Pino
Geong Sen Poh
David Pointcheval
Bernardo Portela
Raluca Posteuca
Thomas Prest
Robert Primas
Chen Qian
Willy Quach
Md Masoom Rabbani
Rahul Rachuri
Srinivasan Raghuraman
Sebastian Ramacher
Matthieu Rambaud
Shahram Rasoolzadeh
Krijn Reijnders
Joost Renes
Elena Reshetova
Mélissa Rossi
Mike Rosulek
Yann Rotella
Joe Rowell
Arnab Roy
Partha Sarathi Roy
Alexander Russell
Carla Ráfols

Paul Rösler
Yusuke Sakai
Amin Sakzad
Yu Sasaki
Or Sattath
John M. Schanck
Lars Schlieper
Martin Schläfer
Carsten Schmidt
André Schrottenloher
Jacob Schuldt
Jean-Pierre Seifert
Yannick Seurin
Yaobin Shen
Yixin Shen
Yu-Ching Shen
Danping Shi
Omri Shmueli
Kris Shrishak
Hervais Simo Fhom
Luisa Siniscalchi
Daniel Smith-Tone
Fang Song
Pratik Soni
Claudio Soriente
Akshayaram Srinivasan
Douglas Stebila
Damien Stehlé
Bruno Sterner
Christoph Striecks
Patrick Struck
Adriana Suarez Corona
Ling Sun
Shi-Feng Sun
Koutarou Suzuki
Aishwarya T
Erkan Tairi
Akira Takahashi
Atsushi Takayasu
Abdul Rahman Taleb
Younes Talibi Alaoui
Benjamin Hong Meng Tan
Syh-Yuan Tan
Titouan Tanguy
Alexander Tereshchenko
Adrian Thillard

Emmanuel Thomé
Tyge Tiessen
Radu Titiu
Ivan Tjuawinata
Yosuke Todo
Junichi Tomida
Bénédikt Tran
Jacques Traoré
Ni Trieu
Ida Tucker
Michael Tunstall
Dominique Unruh
Thomas Unterluggauer
Thomas van Himbeeck
Daniele Venturi
Jorge Villar
Mikhail Volkhov
Christine van Vredendaal
Benedikt Wagner
Riad Wahby
Hendrik Waldner
Alexandre Wallet
Junwei Wang
Qingju Wang
Yuyu Wang
Lei Wang
Senpeng Wang
Peng Wang
Weijia Wang
Yi Wang

Han Wang
Xuzi Wang
Yohei Watanabe
Florian Weber
Weiqiang Wen
Nils Wisiol
Mathias Wolf
Harry H. W. Wong
Keita Xagawa
Zejun Xiang
Jiayu Xu
Luyao Xu
Yaqi Xu
Shota Yamada
Hailun Yan
Wenjie Yang
Shaojun Yang
Masaya Yasuda
Wei-Chuen Yau
Kazuki Yoneyama
Weijing You
Chen Yuan
Tsz Hon Yuen
Runzhi Zeng
Cong Zhang
Zhifang Zhang
Bingsheng Zhang
Zhelei Zhou
Paul Zimmermann
Lukas Zobernig

Probabilistic Reasoning in Cryptography and Machine Learning (IACR Distinguished Lecture)

Andrew Chi-Chih Yao

Tsinghua University, China

Abstract. Distributed protocols occupy a key position in cryptography as well as in machine learning. Yet their analysis, especially in the probabilistic setting, can be quite involved. Simple statements regarding a protocol's behavior often take sophisticated analysis to affirm. In this talk we present several new results along this line in cryptography and machine learning.

The first result concerns *information complexity* which specifies, for a given task, the amount of information that any protocol must leak. We determine the information complexity for a natural problem, using information theory to show why certain loss of privacy in inputs is inevitable.

The second result concerns machine learning. Traditional algorithms are designed to solve a specific problem with performance guarantees. The rise of powerful machine learning algorithms (ML) is a paradigm shift. Yet to show what problems can be solved by ML can be challenging; even seemingly obvious conjectures are often hard to establish rigorously. In this talk we give a proof for some cases where ML is known to demonstrate poor performance experimentally.

Invited Talks

Cryptography For a Secure, Privacy-Respecting and Fair Society: What More Can We Do?

Kazue Sako

Waseda University, Japan

Abstract. Cryptographic protocols such as electronic voting schemes, auction schemes, lottery schemes and many others, are designed to bring more security, privacy and fairness to society. In this talk, I will discuss some further steps we could take towards achieving this goal using our expertise in cryptography, together with lessons I learned along my ongoing journey.

Learning Parity with Noise: Constructions, Reductions, and Analyses

Yu Yu

Shanghai Jiao Tong University, China

Abstract. In this talk, I will introduce my recent works on the learning parity with noise (LPN) problem. In particular, we consider the LPN problem under the constant rate noise regime. First, we show how to construct public-key encryptions and collision-resistant hash functions from the LPN assumption with sufficient hardness. Second, we discuss whether such (average-case) hardness can be reducible from its worst-case analog, i.e., the promise-NCP problem (on specific codes). Finally, we study the asymptotic hardness of LPN by reviewing the BKW algorithm. We introduce ways to optimize the BKW with fine-grained trade-offs between time, space, and sample complexities without heuristics.

Contents – Part I

Quantum Security

Best Paper Awards

On the Hardness of the NTRU Problem

Alice Pellet-Mary[1]([⊠]) and Damien Stehlé[2,3]([⊠])

[1] CNRS, Inria and Université de Bordeaux, Bordeaux, France
alice.pellet-mary@math.u-bordeaux.fr
[2] ENS de Lyon, Lyon, France
damien.stehle@ens-lyon.fr
[3] Institut Universitaire de France, Paris, France

Abstract. The 25 year-old NTRU problem is an important computational assumption in public-key cryptography. However, from a reduction perspective, its relative hardness compared to other problems on Euclidean lattices is not well-understood. Its decision version reduces to the search Ring-LWE problem, but this only provides a hardness upper bound.

We provide two answers to the long-standing open problem of providing reduction-based evidence of the hardness of the NTRU problem. First, we reduce the worst-case approximate Shortest Vector Problem over ideal lattices to an average-case search variant of the NTRU problem. Second, we reduce another average-case search variant of the NTRU problem to the decision NTRU problem.

1 Introduction

In the NTRU encryption scheme [HPS98], the public key is an element h of a polynomial ring R_q that can be chosen as $\mathbb{Z}_q[x]/\Phi$ for some degree d monic irreducible polynomial Φ and some integer $q \geq 2$. This public key h is far from uniform in R_q, as it can be written as $h = f/g \bmod q$ where the secret key polynomials $f, g \in R = \mathbb{Z}[x]/\Phi$ have coefficients with small magnitudes compared to $\sqrt{q}$. In most concrete instantiations, such as the original scheme and the NTRU and NTRU Prime Round-3 candidates to the NIST post-quantum cryptography standardization project [CDH20, BBC20], the coefficients of f and g even belong to $\{-1, 0, 1\}$ and q grows as a small degree polynomial in d. As a result, the set of such h's is very sparse in R_q. The tasks of distinguishing h from uniform and recovering a sufficiently short pair (f, g) from h are respectively known as the decision and search variants of the NTRU problem.

The search NTRU problem can be solved with lattice reduction algorithms (such as [Sch87]), but to succeed for the most usual setting of $q \leq \mathrm{poly}(d)$, they require a computational effort growing as $\exp(O(d))$. In [KF15], Kirchner and Fouque described a heuristic algorithm with slightly subexponential cost $\exp(O(d/\log\log d))$ for the usual setting of $q \leq \mathrm{poly}(d)$ and $\|f\|_\infty, \|g\|_\infty \leq O(1)$. If the magnitude bound grows as $\Omega(\sqrt{d})$, then the cost of this algorithm is $\exp(O(d))$. In the completely different regime of very large q (but with $\|f\|$ and $\|g\|$ growing at a much smaller pace), recent works [ABD16, CJL16, KF17]

© International Association for Cryptologic Research 2021
M. Tibouchi and H. Wang (Eds.): ASIACRYPT 2021, LNCS 13090, pp. 3–35, 2021.
https://doi.org/10.1007/978-3-030-92062-3_1

have shown that the NTRU problem is significantly easier than previously thought. For example, one can recover appropriately distributed f, g with $\|f\|, \|g\| \leq \text{poly}(d)$ from h in quantum polynomial time when $q \geq \exp(\Omega(\sqrt{d}))$. Prior to those works, it was believed that $q \geq \exp(\widetilde{\Omega}(d))$ was necessary for polynomial cost. This range of modulus q is far from the one used for the NTRU encryption scheme. However, NTRU instances with a large modulus q can occur in more advanced cryptographic constructions such as [LTV12] and [GGH13].

On the lower-bound front, it was shown in [SS11] for Φ a power-of-2 cyclotomic and extended in [WW18] to all cyclotomics that if f, g are Gaussian over R (restricted to elements that are invertible modulo q) with standard deviation that is a little larger than $\sqrt{q}$, then the distribution of $h = f/g \bmod q$ is within $2^{-\Omega(d)}$ statistical distance from the uniform distribution over invertible elements of R_q. This variant of decision NTRU is therefore vacuously hard. This parameter regime is relevant to the NTRU signature algorithm [HHP03, SS13]. It also allows to obtain an NTRU-like public-key encryption scheme, but less efficient than with smaller secret key polynomials f, g.

Despite 25 years of study, little is known about the relationships between the NTRU problem variants and between them and other well-studied problems over Euclidean lattices. To our knowledge, the only exceptions are the direct reduction from decision NTRU to search NTRU and a reduction from decision NTRU to the search version of the Ring-LWE problem [SSTX09, LPR10], sketched in [Pei16, Se. 4.4.4]. Note that this only provides an *upper bound* to the hardness of the NTRU problem. Given this state of affairs, Peikert asked the following question in [Pei16, Se. 7.1]:

Is there a worst-case hardness reduction, or a search-to-decision reduction, for an NTRU-like problem?

CONTRIBUTIONS. We provide positive answers to both components of the above question.

First, we give a reduction from the approximate Shortest Vector Problem restricted to ideal lattices (ideal-SVP) to a worst-case variant of the search NTRU problem. Combining the latter with the recent worst-case to average-case reduction for ideal-SVP from [dBDPW20] leads to a reduction from worst-case ideal-SVP to an average-case version of the search NTRU problem. The instance distribution is inherited from the distribution over ideal lattices considered in [dBDPW20]. We also show that this distribution over NTRU instances h can be efficiently sampled from, together with a corresponding trapdoor (f, g), if one has access to a quantum computer or if the modulus q is sufficiently large: this property allows to sample an NTRU encryption public key along with a corresponding secret key.

Second, we exhibit a reduction from another (average-case) variant of the search NTRU problem (see below) to the decision NTRU problem. The reduction works for a wide set of distributions for the search NTRU instances, and the decision NTRU instance distribution is directly derived from the considered search NTRU distribution. A sufficient condition on the search NTRU distribution is that it produces with overwhelming probability an h with trapdoor (f, g) such that f and g have balanced coefficients (in canonical embedding) and f

or g is coprime to q. This covers in particular the standard ternary distribution for f and g (i.e., $f, g \leftarrow \mathcal{U}(\{-1, 0, 1\}^d)$) provided we reject (f, g) when they are not balanced enough or not coprime to q (heuristically, this should happen with probability $\leq 1/2$). On the other hand, the choice of the decision NTRU distribution is much less flexible: even if we start with a ternary distribution for the search NTRU instances, it is very unlikely that the decision NTRU distribution we obtain is ternary. Similarly to the first reduction, we show that if the samples h from the search NTRU distribution can be efficiently sampled along with a corresponding trapdoor (f, g), then so can the samples from the resulting decision NTRU instance.

TECHNICAL OVERVIEW. For the sake of simplicity, in the forthcoming discussion, we restrict ourselves to power-of-2 cyclotomic defining polynomials, i.e., $\Phi = x^d + 1$ for d a power of 2. In this case, the ring $R = \mathbb{Z}[x]/(x^d + 1)$ matches the ring of integers of the degree-d cyclotomic number field. Moreover, the coefficient embedding (which is the one usually considered in the NTRU literature) and the canonical embedding (used in this article) define the same geometry, up to scaling and rotation. (In the core of the paper, the results are presented for arbitrary number fields.)

To state the above contributions formally, we consider several variants of the NTRU problem. We say that $h \in R_q = \mathbb{Z}_q[x]/(x^d + 1)$ is an NTRU instance with gap γ if there exists $(f, g) \in R^2 \setminus \{(0, 0)\}$ such that $g \cdot h = f \bmod q$ and $\|f\|, \|g\| \leq \sqrt{q}/\gamma$. Note that writing $g \cdot h = f \bmod q$ rather than the more standard $h = f/g \bmod q$ allows one to consider g's that are not invertible modulo q and suffices for cryptographic applications. The norm $\|f\|$ is the Euclidean norm of the vector made of the coefficients of f, and the comparison to $\sqrt{q}$ is justified by the fact that for a uniformly chosen h, one expects the smallest such pair (f, g) to have Euclidean norm around $\sqrt{q}$, up to a small polynomial in d (in the core of the paper, we consider the Euclidean norm induced by the canonical embedding, which leads to a slightly different definition, differing by another $\sqrt{d}$ factor). In the literature, the bound on $\|f\|, \|g\|$ is often absolute rather than relative to $\sqrt{q}$: our definition variant stresses the distance to the uniform h regime. For a distribution $\mathcal{D}$ over NTRU instances with gap γ, the decision problem $(\mathcal{D}, \gamma, q)$-dNTRU consists in distinguishing between $\mathcal{D}$ and the uniform distribution over R_q. On the search NTRU side, the situation is more complex. We consider two variants of search NTRU, both of which with a worst-case and an average-case version. For $\gamma \geq \gamma'$, the worst-case vector NTRU problem wcNTRU$_{\text{vec}}$ consists, given as input an NTRU instance h with gap γ, in recovering $(f, g) \neq (0, 0)$ such that $g \cdot h = f \bmod q$ and $\|f\|, \|g\| \leq \sqrt{q}/\gamma'$. Note that if $h \in R_q$ has a trapdoor (f, g), then $(t \cdot f, t \cdot g)$ is another NTRU trapdoor of a possibly larger Euclidean norm, for any non-zero $t \in R$. The wcNTRU$_{\text{vec}}$ definition allows solutions whose norms are within an approximation factor γ/γ' from the norms of the promise. Even though there may be plenty of solutions of the form $(t \cdot f, t \cdot g)$ for $t \in R$, the pair ratio $h_{\mathbb{R}} = (tf)/(tg) = f/g$ over $K := \mathbb{Q}[x]/(x^d + 1)$ is an invariant. This motivates the definition of the worst-case module NTRU problem wcNTRU$_{\text{mod}}$, which consists in recovering $h_{\mathbb{R}}$

from h. This is equivalent to recovering the rank-1 submodule $(f, g)^T \cdot K \cap M_h$ of the rank-2 R-module $M_h = \{(f', g')^T \in R^2 : g' \cdot h = f' \bmod q\}$, hence justifying the name. The average-case counterparts to wcNTRU$_{\text{vec}}$ and wcNTRU$_{\text{mod}}$ are defined analogously.

We now sketch the reduction from ideal-SVP to wcNTRU$_{\text{vec}}$. Let us consider the worst-case variants, and the restriction of ideal-SVP to principal ideals with a known generator: we are given as input a generator z of a principal ideal $I = \langle z \rangle$ of R, and want to use a wcNTRU$_{\text{vec}}$ oracle to find a short non-zero vector in I. Any element $g \in I$ is of the form $g = z \cdot r$ for some $r \in R$. Consider a short non-zero $g \in I$. Multiplying it by q/z, we obtain that $g \cdot (q/z) = 0 \bmod q$. This already looks like an NTRU equation with a candidate q/z for h. But note that q/z is in $K = \mathbb{Q}[x]/(x^d + 1)$ and has no a priori reason to belong to $R = \mathbb{Z}[x]/(x^d + 1)$, whereas the element h of an NTRU instance must belong to R. To handle this difficulty, we can round q/z to R (coefficient-wise). This leads to $g \cdot \lfloor q/z \rceil = -g \cdot \{q/z\} \bmod q$, where both g and $f := -g \cdot \{q/z\}$ are small elements of R. We obtain the existence of a small pair $(f, g) \in R^2 \setminus \{(0,0)\}$ such that $g \cdot \lfloor q/z \rceil = f \bmod q$. We can then provide the element $h := \lfloor q/z \rceil$ to the wcNTRU$_{\text{vec}}$ oracle. The latter returns a pair $(f', g') \in R^2 \setminus \{(0,0)\}$ such that $g' \cdot \lfloor q/z \rceil = f' \bmod q$, and it can be proved that for any such sufficiently short pair, we have that g' is a short non-zero element of I. To handle possibly non-principal ideals (and also principal ideals with unknown generator), we rely on the 2-element representation of ideals.

If we forget polynomial factors and rely on a wcNTRU$_{\text{vec}}$ oracle with parameters q, γ and γ', the above allows to find γ_{svp} approximations to a shortest non-zero vector of an arbitrary ideal of volume $\leq N$ for $N^{1/d} \approx \sqrt{q}/\gamma$ and $\gamma_{\text{svp}} \approx \gamma/\gamma'$. Note that the reduction is worst-case to worst-case and handles bounded-volume ideals. To handle both limitations, we rely on the recent worst-case to average-case reduction for ideal-SVP from de Boer et al. [dBDPW20]. By using the reduction with ideals from the average-case distribution from [dBDPW20], we obtain a reduction from worst-case ideal-SVP to average-case NTRU$_{\text{vec}}$. Further, the ideals from the average-case distribution from [dBDPW20] have volumes bounded as $\exp(O(d^2))$. This leads to q of the order of $\exp(O(d))$, which is significantly larger than in many applications. We refine the analysis of [dBDPW20] to show that by allowing the worst-case to average-case ideal-SVP reduction to run in time higher than polynomial in d, the average-case ideals from [dBDPW20] can be chosen with smaller volumes. The resulting NTRU modulus q is still slightly larger than polynomial, but it can be chosen as small as $d^{\omega(1)}$ if one considers sub-exponential time reductions.

We now provide an overview of our second main result, which is a reduction from average-case NTRU$_{\text{mod}}$ to dNTRU. This one is applicable for q larger than some moderate poly(d). At the core of the reduction is an NTRU rerandomization process. Assume we are given some $h \in R_q$ for which there exists a short pair $(f, g) \neq (0,0)$ with $g \cdot h = f \bmod q$. Now, for any $x_1, x_2 \in R$, we have $g \cdot (x_1 h + x_2) = x_1 f + x_2 g \bmod q$, which may be rewritten as $g \cdot h' = f' \bmod q$ with $h' = x_1 h + x_2$ and $f' = x_1 f + x_2 g$. Further, if x_1 and x_2 are short, then so is f'. This hence gives a way to produce arbitrarily many NTRU samples with a common denominator g, from a single one. Our aim is to query the dNTRU oracle on many such samples, and gather relevant information to solve NTRU$_{mod}$. Concretely, we define the dNTRU distribution and show how to tweak the rerandomization process to be able to use the Oracle Hidden Center Problem (OHCP) framework from [PRS17]. At a high level, in the OHCP framework, one is given access to a decision oracle whose acceptance probabilities on a family of distributions $(\mathcal{D}_z)_{z \in \mathbb{C}}$ is a function of the distance $|z - c|$ to a hidden center $c \in \mathbb{C}$. Under some conditions on the oracle behaviour, there exists an efficient algorithm that recovers an arbitrarily accurate approximation $\tilde{c}$ to c, by querying the OHCP oracle on samples from $\mathcal{D}_z$ for well-chosen values of z. Prior to this work, the OHCP framework has been used to provide a reduction from ideal-SVP to the decision version of Ring-LWE [PRS17], and a search to decision reduction for Ring-LWE [RSW18].

Let us now look more closely at the rerandomization of f. It was shown in [LSS14] that by sampling x_1 and x_2 from spherical Gaussians over R with standard deviation sufficiently above $\max(\|f\|, \|g\|)$, the distribution of $x_1 f + x_2 g$ is Gaussian over the ideal $\langle f \rangle + \langle g \rangle$ with a covariance matrix that is a function of f and g. This spherical Gaussian rerandomization defines our dNTRU distribution. We extend the proof of [LSS14] to show that if instead we sample x_1 and x_2 from correlated non-spherical Gaussians over R, then the distribution of $x_1 f + x_2 g$ is Gaussian over $\langle f \rangle + \langle g \rangle$ with a covariance matrix that can be made to depend solely on $|f(\zeta) - z \cdot g(\zeta)|$ for ζ an arbitrary complex root of $\Phi = x^d + 1$, and $z \in \mathbb{C}$ arbitrary. The center of the OHCP instance is $c = f(\zeta)/g(\zeta) = h_{\mathbb{R}}(\zeta)$ (recall that $h_{\mathbb{R}} = f/g$ belongs to $K = \mathbb{Q}[x]/(x^d + 1)$). Using the dNTRU oracle within the OHCP framework hence allows us to recover an approximation to $h_{\mathbb{R}}(\zeta)$. In the applications from [PRS17, RSW18] of the OHCP framework, one recovers a vector $\mathbf{c}$ of OHCP centers from an approximation $\tilde{\mathbf{c}}$ by observing that $\mathbf{c}$ belongs to a lattice: the exact center $\mathbf{c}$ can hence be obtained by simply rounding a sufficiently precise approximation $\tilde{\mathbf{c}}$. In our case, we cannot proceed similarly, as $h_{\mathbb{R}}$ has rational coordinates. We instead show that the LLL algorithm [LLL82] can be used in a manner similar to [KLL84] to recover $h_{\mathbb{R}} = f/g \in K$ from a sufficiently precise approximation to $h_{\mathbb{R}}(\zeta)$, given an a priori upper bound to $\max(\|f\|, \|g\|)$.

DISCUSSION. The two reductions put forward in this work provide some evidence towards supporting the conjectured hardness of the search vectorial NTRU problem and the decision NTRU problem. They may give the impression that the hardness of the NTRU problems lies somewhere between the hardness of the ideal-SVP and that of Ring-LWE. This is however neglecting the fact that there are several NTRU problem variants, and it is unclear whether they are computationally equivalent. In particular, the reductions are incompatible, in that the first one reduces to NTRU$_{vec}$ and the second one from NTRU$_{mod}$. NTRU$_{mod}$ reduces to NTRU$_{vec}$, but it is a reduction from NTRU$_{vec}$ to NTRU$_{mod}$ that we would need to obtain a chain of reductions from ideal-SVP to Ring-LWE via the computationally equivalent NTRU problems. Note that if we assume that ideal-SVP is easy, then these problems are computationally equivalent (see Subsect. 3.4), but the reduction from ideal-SVP to NTRU_{vec} becomes vacuous. In fact, it seems that NTRU_{vec} and NTRU_{mod} could even be of different natures: when attempting to solve NTRU_{vec} using an NTRU_{mod} oracle, it is unclear how to make the approximation factor γ/γ' appear, as NTRU_{mod} is only parametrized by the promise gap γ. Better understanding the differences between the NTRU variants seems important to better capture the NTRU hardness. In this direction, note that the known attacks specific to NTRU [ABD16,CJL16,KF17] are mostly relevant for NTRU_{mod}: they can also be used to solve NTRU_{vec}, but the quality of the solution obtained for NTRU_{vec} is the same as the one we would obtain by running the attack to solve NTRU_{mod}, and then running an ideal-SVP solver on the dense rank-1 sub-module to obtain a somehow short vector.

Despite the apparent uncomposability of our two reductions, it would be interesting to have NTRU instance distributions that are compatible with both of them. The second reduction is very permissive with respect to the NTRU_{mod} instance distribution, but the latter still has to satisfy some properties (see Definition 5.1). In particular, the canonical embedding of f and g should be bounded from below and above, and the ideal $\langle f \rangle + \langle g \rangle$ should be coprime with $\langle q \rangle$. We note that in the reduction from ideal-SVP to $\text{wcNTRU}_{\text{vec}}$, the element g is an element of the ideal-SVP instance ideal, which could be chosen Gaussian. Using standard properties of lattice Gaussians, it is not unlikely that one can prove the desired property on its canonical embedding. There seems to be less flexibility in the choice of $f = -g \cdot \{q/z\}$. However, one could replace the deterministic rounding by a Gaussian rounding, to then use a similar approach as the one for g. Concerning the co-primality with $\langle g \rangle$, one could hope to use an inclusion-exclusion argument for Gaussian sums like the one in [SS11].

Concerning the hardness of the NTRU problems relatively to ideal-SVP and Ring-LWE, note that the state of the art suggests that ideal-SVP might be strictly easier than Ring-LWE, as ideal-SVP is known to reduce to Ring-LWE [SSTX09,LPR10,PRS17] but no reduction from Ring-LWE to ideal-SVP is known. In fact, Ring-LWE seems less related to ideal-SVP than to finding two short linearly independent vectors in rank-2 modules over R (SIVP): for an appropriate parametrisation, Ring-LWE reduces to the latter problem [LS15, Se. 5] and, although for some other parametrisation, the latter problem reduces to Ring-LWE (by combining [LS15, Se. 4] and [AD17]). From a lattice perspective, NTRU is a generalization of the unique Shortest Vector Problem to rank-2 modules. At this stage, it is unclear whether its complexity matches the one of ideal-SVP (i.e., SVP for rank-1 modules) or the one of SIVP restricted to rank-2 modules. It could also be strictly in between.

2 Preliminaries

The notations log and ln respectively denote the logarithms in bases 2 and e. For n an integer, we let $[n]$ denote the set $\{1, 2, \ldots, n\}$. Vectors and matrices are denoted with bold lower-case and upper-case letters, respectively. The statistical distance between two distributions D_1 and D_2 with compatible countable supports is defined as $\mathrm{dist}(D_1, D_2) = \frac{1}{2} \sum_x |D_1(x) - D_2(x)|$. We write $D_1 \approx_\varepsilon D_2$ if $\mathrm{dist}(D_1, D_2) \leq \varepsilon$ for some $\varepsilon > 0$. If X is a finite set, then we let $U(X)$ denote the uniform distribution over X. If $\mathbf{b}_1, \ldots, \mathbf{b}_n \in \mathbb{R}^m$ are linearly independent vectors, then the notation $(\widetilde{\mathbf{b}}_1, \ldots, \widetilde{\mathbf{b}}_n)$ refers to their Gram-Schmidt orthogonalization. The notation $\|\|\cdot\|\|$ refers to the matrix norm induced by the Euclidean norm. Finally, we define $\widetilde{O}(d^t)$ as $O(d^t \mathrm{poly}(\log d))$ for any $t \geq 0$ including $t = 0$.

2.1 Euclidean Lattices

A lattice $L \subset \mathbb{R}^m$ is a set of the form $L = \mathbf{B} \cdot \mathbb{Z}^{m \times n}$ for some full column-rank matrix $\mathbf{B} \in \mathbb{R}^{m \times n}$ (for some $m \geq n \geq 1$). The columns of $\mathbf{B}$ are said to form a basis of L. For $i \in [n]$, the ith lattice minimum is defined as $\lambda_i(L) = \min(r : \dim L \cap \mathcal{B}(r) \geq i)$, where $\mathcal{B}(r)$ denotes the closed ball of $\mathbb{R}^m$ of radius r. The determinant $\det(L)$ is defined as $\sqrt{\det(\mathbf{B}^T \mathbf{B})}$, which is independent of the particular choice of basis $\mathbf{B}$ of L. Minkowski's (second) theorem states that $\prod_{i \in [n]} \lambda_i(L) \leq \sqrt{n}^n \cdot \det(L)$.

In this article, we will be interested in the ideal Hermite Shortest vector problem. We first recall below the definition of the Hermite Shortest Vector Problem (HSVP) for arbitrary lattices, and we will instantiate it for ideal lattices in Sect. 2.4.

Definition 2.1 (γ-HSVP). *Let $\gamma \geq 1$. Given as input a lattice $L \subset \mathbb{Q}^n$ (represented by an arbitrary $\mathbb{Z}$-basis), the γ-HSVP problem asks to find a vector $\mathbf{w} \in L \setminus \{\mathbf{0}\}$ such that $\|\mathbf{w}\| \leq \gamma \cdot \sqrt{n} \cdot \det(L)^{1/n}$.*

By Minkowski's theorem, this problem is well-defined for any $\gamma \geq 1$.

2.2 Discrete Gaussian Distributions

Let $\mathbf{S} \in \mathrm{GL}_n(\mathbb{R})$ be an invertible matrix. The Gaussian density function with parameter $\mathbf{S}$ is defined over $\mathbb{R}^n$ by

$$\rho_{\mathbf{S}}(\mathbf{x}) = e^{-\pi \|\mathbf{S}^{-1}\mathbf{x}\|^2}.$$

When the matrix $\mathbf{S}$ is diagonal with diagonal coefficients all equal to some $\sigma > 0$, we also use the notation $\rho_\sigma = \rho_{\mathbf{S}}$. Let $L \subset \mathbb{R}^n$ be a full rank lattice, and $\mathbf{c} \in \mathbb{R}^n$. The discrete Gaussian distribution $D_{L,\mathbf{S},\mathbf{c}}$ over L with center $\mathbf{c}$ and parameter $\mathbf{S}$ is the distribution for which the probability of any $\mathbf{v} \in L$ is $\rho_{\mathbf{S}}(\mathbf{v} - \mathbf{c})/\rho_{\mathbf{S}}(L - \mathbf{c})$, where $\rho_{\mathbf{S}}(T) = \sum_{t \in T} \rho_{\mathbf{S}}(t)$ for any countable $T \subset \mathbb{R}^n$. Again, we will use the notation $D_{L,\sigma,\mathbf{c}}$ when $\mathbf{S} = \mathrm{diag}(\sigma)$ for some $\sigma > 0$. When $\mathbf{c} = \mathbf{0}$, we omit the subscript $\mathbf{c}$.

If $L \subset \mathbb{R}^n$ is a lattice, its smoothing parameter $\eta_\varepsilon(L)$ is defined as the smallest $\sigma > 0$ such that $\rho_{1/\sigma}(L^\star \setminus \{\mathbf{0}\}) \leq \varepsilon$, where $L^\star = \{\mathbf{c} \in \mathrm{span}(L) : \forall \mathbf{b} \in L : \langle \mathbf{b}^\star, \mathbf{b} \rangle \in \mathbb{Z}\}$ is the dual of L. For any n-dimensional lattice L and $\varepsilon > 0$, we have the following upper bound on the smoothing parameter (see [MR07, Le. 3.3]):

$$\eta_\varepsilon(L) \leq \sqrt{\frac{\ln(2n(1 + 1/\varepsilon))}{\pi}} \cdot \lambda_n(L). \tag{2.1}$$

The following Lemma (adapted from [GPV08, Th. 4.1]) shows that one can efficiently sample (bounded) elements from a distribution that is statistically close to a discrete Gaussian distribution. A proof can be found in the full version.

Lemma 2.2. *There exists a* ppt *algorithm that takes as input a basis* $\mathbf{B} = (\mathbf{b}_1, \ldots, \mathbf{b}_n)$ *of an* n*-dimensional lattice* L*, a parameter* $\sigma \geq \sqrt{n} \cdot \max_i \|\mathbf{b}_i\|$ *and a center* $\mathbf{c} \in \mathrm{Span}(L)$ *and outputs a sample from a distribution* $\widetilde{D}_{\mathbf{B},\sigma,\mathbf{c}}$ *such that*

- $D_{L,\sigma,\mathbf{c}} \approx_{2^{-\Omega(n)}} \widetilde{D}_{\mathbf{B},\sigma,\mathbf{c}}$;
- *for all* $\mathbf{v} \leftarrow \widetilde{D}_{\mathbf{B},\sigma,\mathbf{c}}$, *it holds that* $\|\mathbf{v} - \mathbf{c}\| \leq \sqrt{n} \cdot \sigma$ *and* $\mathbf{v} \neq \mathbf{0}$.

The following lemma bounds the statistical distance between two discrete Gaussian distributions over the same lattice L, depending on the distance between their centers and their parameter matrices. Similar results were already present in previous works, such as in [Reg09, Claim 2.2] for 1-dimensional continuous Gaussian distributions, and in the proof of [dBDPW20, Th. 4.4] for the case of ideal lattices with specific parameters and centers. Since the following precise statement seems new, we provide a proof in the full version for the sake of completeness.

Lemma 2.3. *Let* $L \subset \mathbb{R}^n$ *be a full rank lattice,* $\mathbf{S}_1, \mathbf{S}_2 \in \mathrm{GL}_n(R)$ *be two invertible matrices and* $\mathbf{c}_1, \mathbf{c}_2 \in \mathbb{R}^n$ *be two vectors. If* $\eta_{1/2}(\mathbf{S}_1^{-1}L), \eta_{1/2}(\mathbf{S}_2^{-1}L) \leq 1/2$, *then it holds that*

$$\mathrm{dist}\left(D_{L,\mathbf{S}_1,\mathbf{c}_1}, D_{L,\mathbf{S}_2,\mathbf{c}_2}\right) \leq 4\sqrt{n} \cdot \left(\sqrt{\|\mathbf{S}_2^{-1}\mathbf{S}_1 - \mathbf{I}_n\|} + \sqrt{\|\mathbf{S}_2^{-1}(\mathbf{c}_1 - \mathbf{c}_2)\|}\right).$$

The next lemma states that a lattice Gaussian distribution with sufficiently large standard deviation is almost uniform when reduced modulo a sublattice.

Lemma 2.4 ([GPV08], Cor. 2.8). *Let* $L_1 \subseteq L_2$ *be two lattices of rank* n*. If* $1 \geq \eta_\varepsilon(L_1)$ *for some* $\varepsilon < 1/2$, *then* $(D_{L_2,1} \bmod L_1) \approx_{2\varepsilon} U(L_2 \bmod L_1)$.

2.3   Number Fields

Let K be a number field of degree $d \geq 2$ and $K_\mathbb{R} = K \otimes_\mathbb{Q} \mathbb{R}$. We let R denote its ring of integers. We identify any element of K with its canonical embedding vector $\sigma : x \mapsto (\sigma_1(x), \ldots, \sigma_d(x))^T \in \mathbb{C}^d$. This leads to an identification of $K_\mathbb{R}$ with $\{\mathbf{y} \in \mathbb{C}^d : \forall i \in [r_\mathbb{R}], y_i \in \mathbb{R} \text{ and } \forall i \in [r_\mathbb{C}], \overline{y_{r_\mathbb{R}+2(i+1)}} = y_{r_\mathbb{R}+2i+1}\}$, where $r_\mathbb{R}$ and $r_\mathbb{C}$ respectively denote the number of real and complex embeddings. Via this identification, the set $K_\mathbb{R}$ is a real vector subspace of dimension d embedded in $\mathbb{C}^d$. In the following, for any element $x \in R, K$ or $K_\mathbb{R}$, we will let $\|x\|$ (resp. $\|x\|_\infty$) denote the Hermitian norm (resp. infinity norm) of the vector $\sigma(x) \in \mathbb{C}^d$. The set $\sigma(R)$ is a lattice, and the absolute field discriminant Δ_K is defined as $\Delta_K = |\det(\sigma(R))^2|$.[1] We have $\Delta_K \geq (\pi/4)^d \cdot (d^d/d!)^2$, which implies that we have $d = O(\log \Delta_K)$, for Δ_K growing to infinity.

---

[1] Note that in order to avoid having absolute values everywhere in the rest of the article, we define Δ_K as the absolute value of the discriminant of K.

The (absolute value of the) algebraic norm of $x \in K_{\mathbb{R}}$ is defined as $\mathcal{N}(x) = \prod_i |\sigma_i(x)|$. Any non-zero element $r \in R$ has algebraic norm ≥ 1, which implies in particular that $\|r\|_\infty \geq 1$.

In this work, we assume that we know a monic polynomial $\Phi \in \mathbb{Z}[X]$ defining K and a $\mathbb{Z}$-basis $(r_1, \ldots, r_d)$ of R, where the r_i's are represented by polynomials modulo Φ (of degree $< d$) with rational coefficients. Let $D_\Phi > 0$ be the smallest integer such that $D_\Phi \cdot r_i$ has integral coefficients for all i (i.e., D_Φ is the common denominator to all the r_i polynomials), then the bit-size of D_Φ is polynomial in d and $\|\Phi\|$, where $\|\Phi\|$ is the Euclidean norm of the vector of coefficients of Φ (see for instance [Sut16, Se. 12.4]).

We will assume that this basis has been LLL-reduced [LLL82]. We define $\delta_K = \max_i \|r_i\|_\infty$. Since $\|r\|_\infty \geq 1$ for all $r \in R \setminus \{0\}$, we know that $\delta_K \geq 1$. Using Minkowski's second theorem and the LLL-reducedness of $(r_1, \ldots, r_d)$, we have that $\delta_K \leq \Delta_K^{O(1)}$. In the case of cyclotomic number fields, taking the power basis gives $\delta_K = 1$. For an element $x = \sum_i x_i r_i \in K_{\mathbb{R}}$, define $\lfloor x \rceil = \sum_i \lfloor x_i \rceil r_i$. We will also use the notation $\{x\} = x - \lfloor x \rceil$. It holds that $\|\{x\}\|_\infty \leq d/2 \cdot \delta_K$, and hence that $\|\{x\}\| \leq d^{3/2} \cdot \delta_K$.

For a rational $x = x_1/x_2$ with $x_1, x_2 \in \mathbb{Z}$ and $\gcd(x_1, x_2) = 1$, we define $\text{size}(x) = 1 + \log|x_1| + \log|x_2|$. For an element $x = \sum_i x_i r_i \in K$, we define $\text{size}(x) = \sum_i \text{size}(x_i)$. The following lemma shows that if we have a sufficiently precise approximation to an embedding of $x \in K$, then one can recover x exactly. This seems folklore, but as we were unable to find a proof, we provide one in the full version. The result and the proof strategy are mentioned in [Coh00, Se. 6.2.4] in the context of quadratic fields and in Roblot's PhD thesis [Rob97] (just after Lemma 2.14). But both references are very brief on the topic. We note that a detailed study was done on a $\mathfrak{p}$-adic counterpart in [Bel04a].

Lemma 2.5. *Let $k \leq d$ arbitrary. There exists an algorithm that, given $\widetilde{y}$ such that $|\widetilde{y} - \sigma_k(x)| \leq 2^{-p}$ for some $x \in K$ and some $p \geq \text{poly}(d, \log \delta_K, \log \|\Phi\|, \text{size}(x))$, recovers x as a rational linear combination of the basis $(r_1, \ldots, r_d)$ of R in* ppt *with respect to p.*

2.4 Ideals and Modules

Ideals. An integral ideal I is a subset of R that is stable by addition and by multiplication with any element of R. A fractional ideal is a subset of K of the form $x \cdot I$ for some $x \in K$ and some integral ideal $I \subseteq R$. We write $\langle z \rangle$ the principal (fractional) ideal generated by $z \in K$. Using the canonical embedding, any non-zero fractional ideal of K is identified to a d-dimensional lattice, called ideal lattice. The algebraic norm of an integral ideal $I \subseteq R$ is defined by $\mathcal{N}(I) = |R/I|$. We extend the notation to a fractional ideal xI with $x \in K$ and I an integral ideal, by setting $\mathcal{N}(xI) = \mathcal{N}(x) \cdot \mathcal{N}(I)$. For a non-zero fractional ideal $I = I_1/2$ with $I_1, I_2 \subseteq R$ and $\gcd(I_1, I_2) = R$, we define the quantity $\text{size}(I) := \log(\mathcal{N}(I_1)) + \log(\mathcal{N}(I_2))$.

Two-Element Representation of an Ideal. Any fractional ideal I can be generated by only two elements, i.e., there exist $x, y \in K$ such that $I = \langle x \rangle + \langle y \rangle$ (see, e.g., [Coh95, Prop. 4.7.7]). In fact, for any $x \in I \setminus \{0\}$, there exists $y \in I$ such that $I = \langle x \rangle + \langle y \rangle$. The lemma below states that computing such a y, given as input (I, x), can be done in probabilistic polynomial time.

Lemma 2.6 (Adapted from [Bel04b], Alg. 6.15 and [FS10], Th. 3). *There exists a probabilistic algorithm taking a fractional ideal $I \subset K$ and a non-zero $x \in I$ as inputs, computing $y \in I$ such that $I = \langle x \rangle + \langle y \rangle$, and whose run-time is polynomial in $\mathrm{size}(x)$, $\mathrm{size}(I)$ and $\log(\Delta_K)$.*

Proof. Wlog, we can restrict the study to non-zero integral ideals. The algorithm is the same as the one given in [FS10, Fig. 1], except that in Step 1, the element x_1 is chosen to be x, rather than the first vector of a reduced basis. The correctness proof is unchanged. The upper bounds on the bit-sizes of the elements appearing during the algorithm execution do change, but one can check that all these bit-sizes stay polynomial in $\mathrm{size}(x)$, as well as the other quantities related to I and K that were already present in [FS10] (which are all polynomial in $\mathrm{size}(I)$ and $\log \Delta_K$). So overall, the run-time remains polynomial in $\mathrm{size}(x)$, $\mathrm{size}(I)$ and $\log \Delta_K$.   □

Algorithmic Problems Over Ideal Lattices. The ideal-HSVP (or id-HSVP for short) problem is the HSVP problem restricted to lattices that are (fractional) ideal lattices. Using the fact that for an ideal lattice $I \subset K$ we have $\det(I) = \sqrt{|\Delta_K|} \cdot \mathcal{N}(I)$, the problem admits the following equivalent formulation.

Definition 2.7 (γ-id-HSVP). *Let $\gamma \geq 1$. Given as input a non-zero fractional ideal $I \subset K$ (represented by an arbitrary $\mathbb{Z}$-basis), the γ-id-HSVP problem asks to find an element $\mathbf{w} \in I \setminus \{0\}$ such that $\|\mathbf{w}\| \leq \gamma \cdot \sqrt{d} \cdot \Delta_K^{1/(2d)} \cdot \mathcal{N}(I)^{1/d}$.*

Observe that γ-id-HSVP is equivalent to γ'-SVP in ideal lattices, up to polynomial losses $\leq \sqrt{d} \cdot \Delta_K^{1/(2d)}$ in the approximation factors γ and γ', thanks to the inequalities

$$\mathcal{N}(I)^{1/d} \leq \lambda_1(I) \leq \sqrt{d} \cdot \Delta_K^{1/(2d)} \cdot \mathcal{N}(I)^{1/d},$$

which hold for any non-zero fractional ideal I. The approximation factor loss is polynomial when $\Delta_K^{1/(2d)} \leq \mathrm{poly}(d)$.

If $\gamma = \exp(\widetilde{O}(d^\alpha))$ for $\alpha \in [0, 1]$, then Id-HSVP can be solved using lattice reduction algorithms [Sch87], in time $\exp(\widetilde{O}(d^{1-\alpha}))$. In [CDW21], Cramer, Ducas and Wesolowski obtained a heuristic quantum polynomial-time algorithm for $\gamma = \exp(\widetilde{O}(d^{1/2}))$ for cyclotomic fields. In [PHS19], Pellet-Mary, Hanrot and Stehlé gave a quantum heuristic algorithm for $\gamma = \exp(\widetilde{O}((\log \Delta_K)^{\alpha+1})/d)$ running in time $\exp(\widetilde{O}((\log \Delta_K)^{1-2\alpha}))$ for any field K, where $\alpha \in [0, 1/2]$ is arbitrary. They also propose a classical variant of their algorithm, achieving the same approximation factor γ in time $\exp(\widetilde{O}((\log \Delta_K)^{\max(2/3, 1-2\alpha)}))$ for any field K; and in time $\exp(\widetilde{O}(d^{\max(1/2, 1-2\alpha)}))$ for cyclotomic fields. Both the classical and the quantum algorithms require an advice depending only on the field K, whose bit-length is bounded as $\exp(\widetilde{O}((\log \Delta_K)^{1-2\alpha}))$.

Smoothing Ideals. The following lemma from [PRS17] provides a sufficient condition for a diagonal matrix $\mathbf{S}$ to be above the smoothing parameter of an ideal lattice.

Lemma 2.8 ([PRS17], **Le. 6.9**). *Let $I \subset K$ be a fractional ideal and $\mathbf{S} \in \mathbb{R}^{d \times d}$ be a diagonal matrix with positive diagonal coefficients. Assume that*

$$c := \left(\prod_i S_{ii} \right)^{1/d} \cdot (\mathcal{N}(I) \Delta_K)^{-1/d} \geq 1,$$

then $1 \geq \eta_\varepsilon(\mathbf{S}^{-1}I)$, where $\varepsilon = \exp(-c^2 d)$.

Modules. For $\ell \geq k \geq 1$, a rank-k module $M \subset K_{\mathbb{R}}^\ell$ is a set of the form $M = \mathbf{b}_1 I_1 + \ldots + \mathbf{b}_k I_k$ for some non-zero ideals $(I_i)_i$ and some $K_{\mathbb{R}}$-linearly independent vectors $(\mathbf{b}_i)_i$ (i.e., if $\sum_i y_i \mathbf{b}_i = \mathbf{0}$, then all y_i's must be 0). The tuple $((I_i, \mathbf{b}_i))_i$ is called a pseudo-basis of M. If M admits a pseudo-basis for which all the I_i's are equal to R, then M is called free. We define $\det(M)$ as the determinant of M when identified with a kd-dimensional lattice via the canonical embedding σ. For any pseudo-basis $((I_i, \mathbf{b}_i))_i$ of M, we have

$$\det(M)^2 = \Delta_K^k \cdot \mathcal{N}\left(\det_{K_{\mathbb{R}}}(\overline{\mathbf{B}}^T \mathbf{B}) \prod_i I_i^2 \right), \tag{2.2}$$

where $\det_{K_{\mathbb{R}}}$ is the determinant of a square matrix over $K_{\mathbb{R}}$.

2.5   Oracle Hidden Center Problem

In the search to decision reduction from Sect. 5, we will make use of the OHCP technique from [PRS17]. The proof of Proposition 2.10 is provided in the full version.

Definition 2.9 (Oracle Hidden Center Problem [PRS17], Def. 4.3). *Let $\varepsilon, \delta \in (0, 1)$ and $\beta \geq 1$. An OHCP instance consists in a scale parameter $D > 0$ and a randomized oracle $\mathcal{O} : \mathbb{R}^k \times \mathbb{R}_{\geq 0} \to \{0, 1\}$ such that, for all $\mathbf{z} \in \mathbb{R}^k$ with $\|\mathbf{z} - \mathbf{z}^*\| \leq \beta D$ and $t \in \mathbb{R}_{\geq 0}$, it holds that $\Pr(\mathcal{O}(\mathbf{z}, t) = 1) = p(t + \log \|\mathbf{z} - \mathbf{z}^*\|)$, where $\mathbf{z}^* \in \mathbb{R}^k$ is an unknown center satisfying $\delta D \leq \|\mathbf{z}^*\| \leq D$ and $p(\cdot)$ is an unknown function. The goal of the OHCP is to recover $\tilde{\mathbf{z}} \in \mathbb{R}^k$ such that $\|\tilde{\mathbf{z}} - \mathbf{z}^*\| \leq \varepsilon D$.*

Proposition 2.10 (Adapted from [PRS17], Prop. 4.4). *There exists an algorithm that takes as input a parameter $\kappa \geq 20 \log(k + 1)$, the scaling parameter D and the oracle $\mathcal{O}$ of a $(\exp(-\kappa), \exp(-\kappa), 1 + 1/\kappa)$-OHCP instance in dimension k, and solves it with probability $\geq 1 - \exp(-\kappa)$, in time $\mathrm{poly}(\kappa, k)$, provided the oracle $\mathcal{O}$ satisfies the extra following conditions. For some $p_\infty \in [0, 1]$ and $t^* \geq 0$ we have*

1. *$p(s^*) - p_\infty \geq 1/\kappa$;*
2. *$|p(t) - p_\infty| \leq 2 \exp(-t/\kappa)$ for any $t \geq 0$;*
3. *for any $t_1, t_2 \geq 0$, it holds that $|p(t_1) - p(t_2)| \leq \kappa \sqrt{|t_1 - t_2|}$;*

where $p(t) = \Pr(\mathcal{O}(\mathbf{0}, t) = 1)$.

3 Different Variants of the NTRU Problem

In this section, we define the three variants of the NTRU problem that we will consider in this work.

3.1 NTRU Instances

We first define NTRU instances, which will be the inputs to the NTRU problem variants. We also consider the less standard case of tuple NTRU instances, which has also been considered in cryptographic constructions (see, e.g., the variant of the candidate cryptographic multilinear map from [GGH13] proposed in [LSS14, Se. 6]). All definitions of this section readily extend to the tuple setting, in a manner that is consistent with the second part of Definition 3.1.

Definition 3.1 ((γ, q)-NTRU instance). *Let $q \geq 2$ an integer and $\gamma > 0$ a real number. A (γ, q)-NTRU instance is an element $h \in R_q$ such that there exists $(f, g) \in R^2 \setminus \{(0, 0)\}$ with $g \cdot h = f \mod q$ and $\|f\|, \|g\| \leq \sqrt{q}/\gamma$. The pair (f, g) is called a trapdoor of the NTRU instance h.*

For $t \geq 1$ and γ and q as above, a (γ, q, t)-tuple-NTRU instance is a tuple $(h_i)_{i \leq t} \in R_q$ such that there exists $((f_i)_{i \leq t}, g) \in R^{t+1} \setminus \{(0, \ldots, 0)\}$ with $g \cdot h_i = f_i \mod q$ and $\max_i \|f_i\|, \|g\| \leq \sqrt{q}/\gamma$.

For a uniform h in R_q, we will see below that the expected norm of a smallest trapdoor (f, g) is of the order of $\sqrt{q}$ (up to factors depending on the field). Hence, the quantity γ of an NTRU instance measures the gap between the size of a short trapdoor of h and the size of a smallest trapdoor of h we would have expected if h was uniform modulo q. Note also that any (γ, q)-NTRU instance is also a (γ', q)-NTRU instance for any $\gamma' \leq \gamma$ (the quantity γ is only a lower bound on the promised gap).

We now consider distributions over NTRU instances. To be useful for constructing cryptosystems, these distributions must be efficiently samplable and we also need to be able to sample, together with the NTRU instance h, a trapdoor (f, g) for h. This motivates the following definition.

Definition 3.2 ($(\mathcal{D}, \gamma, q)$-NTRU setup). *Let $q \geq 2$, $\gamma > 0$ and $\mathcal{D}$ a distribution over (γ, q)-NTRU instances. A $(\mathcal{D}, \gamma, q)$-NTRU setup is a ppt algorithm (with respect to $\log q$ and $\log \Delta_K$) sampling triples $(h, f, g) \in R_q \times R^2$ such that*

- *the marginal distribution of h is $\mathcal{D}$,*
- *$(f, g) \neq (0, 0)$ and $\|f\|, \|g\| \leq \sqrt{q}/\gamma$,*
- *$g \cdot h = f \mod q$.*

It was shown in [SS11] that for power-of-2 cyclotomic fields, there exists a $(\mathcal{D}, \gamma, q)$-NTRU setup with $\mathcal{D} \approx_{2^{-\Omega(d)}} U(R_q^\times)$ for any prime $q \geq 5$ and some $\gamma = 1/\text{poly}(d)$. This was extended to any cyclotomic field in [WW18]. In such cases, the decision NTRU problem introduced below is information-theoretically hard, if we replace $U(R_q)$ by $U(R_q^\times)$. In this work, we rather focus on the case of $\gamma \geq 1$.

3.2 Decision NTRU Problem

We can now define the decision variant of the NTRU problem.

Definition 3.3 $((\mathcal{D}, \gamma, q)\text{-}\textbf{dNTRU})$. *Let $q \geq 2$, $\gamma \geq 1$ and $\mathcal{D}$ a distribution over (γ, q)-NTRU instances. The $(\mathcal{D}, \gamma, q)$ decisional NTRU problem $((\mathcal{D}, \gamma, q)$-dNTRU for short) asks to distinguish between samples from $\mathcal{D}$ and from $U(R_q)$. The advantage of an algorithm $\mathcal{A}$ against the $(\mathcal{D}, \gamma, q)$-dNTRU problem is defined as*

$$\text{Adv}(\mathcal{A}) := \left| \Pr_{h \leftarrow \mathcal{D}} \left(\mathcal{A}(h) = 1 \right) - \Pr_{u \leftarrow U(R_q)} \left(\mathcal{A}(u) = 1 \right) \right|,$$

where the probabilities are also over the internal randomness of $\mathcal{A}$.

A reduction from dNTRU to sRLWE is sketched in [Pei16, Se. 4.4.4].

3.3 Search NTRU Problems

We consider two different search variants for the NTRU problem. The first one consists in finding a trapdoor (f, g) for an NTRU instance h such that $\|f\|$ and $\|g\|$ are as small as possible, whereas the second variant only asks to recover any multiple (xf, xg) (with $x \in K$) of a small trapdoor (f, g). We explain below why both variants may be of interest. Further, for both variants, the definition comes with worst-case and average-case flavours.

Definition 3.4 $((\mathcal{D}, \gamma, \gamma', q)\text{-}\textbf{NTRU}_{\text{vec}}$ **and** $(\gamma, \gamma', q)\text{-}\textbf{wcNTRU}_{\text{vec}})$. *Let $q \geq 2$, $\gamma \geq \gamma' > 0$ and $\mathcal{D}$ a distribution over (γ, q)-NTRU instances. The $(\mathcal{D}, \gamma, \gamma', q)$ average-case search NTRU vector problem $((\mathcal{D}, \gamma, \gamma', q)$-NTRU$_{\text{vec}}$ for short) asks, given as input some h sampled from $\mathcal{D}$, to compute a pair $(f, g) \in R^2 \setminus \{(0,0)\}$ such that $g \cdot h = f \bmod q$ and $\|f\|, \|g\| \leq \sqrt{q}/\gamma'$. The advantage of an algorithm $\mathcal{A}$ against the $(\mathcal{D}, \gamma, \gamma', q)$-NTRU$_{\text{vec}}$ problem is defined as*

$$\text{Adv}(\mathcal{A}) = \Pr_{h \leftarrow \mathcal{D}} \left(\mathcal{A}(h) = (f, g) \text{ with } \begin{vmatrix} g \cdot h = f \bmod q \\ (f, g) \neq (0, 0) \\ \|f\|, \|g\| \leq \sqrt{q}/\gamma' \end{vmatrix} \right),$$

where the probability is also over the internal randomness of $\mathcal{A}$.

The (γ, γ', q) worst-case search NTRU vector problem $((\gamma, \gamma', q)$-wcNTRU$_{\text{vec}}$ for short) asks, given as input a (γ, q)-NTRU instance h, to compute a pair $(f, g) \in R^2 \setminus \{(0,0)\}$ such that $g \cdot h = f \bmod q$ and $\|f\|, \|g\| \leq \sqrt{q}/\gamma'$.

Before describing the second search variant of the NTRU problem, we prove the following lemma, which states that all short trapdoors (f, g) of an NTRU instance h are K-multiples of one another.

Lemma 3.5. *Let $q \geq 2$, $\gamma > \sqrt{2}$ and h be a (γ, q)-NTRU instance. Then, for all trapdoors $(f, g), (f', g') \in R^2 \setminus \{(0,0)\}$ with $\|f\|, \|g\|, \|f'\|, \|g'\| \leq \sqrt{q}/\gamma$ and $g \cdot h = f \bmod q$, $g' \cdot h = f' \bmod q$, it holds that $(f, g) = x \cdot (f', g')$ for some $x \in K$.*

Equivalently, there exists a unique field element $h_K \in K$ such that, for all trapdoors $(f, g) \in R^2 \setminus \{(0,0)\}$ with $\|f\|, \|g\| \leq \sqrt{q}/\gamma$ and $g \cdot h = f \bmod q$, it holds that $f/g = h_K$ (where the division is performed in K and not modulo q).

Proof. Let (f, g) and (f', g') be as in the lemma statement. Then

$$g' \cdot f = g' \cdot (g \cdot h) = g \cdot (g' \cdot h) = g \cdot f' \bmod q.$$

This implies that $g'f - gf' \in qR$. Moreover, we know that $\|g'f - gf'\| \leq \|g'\| \cdot \|f\| + \|g\| \cdot \|f'\| \leq 2q/\gamma^2 < q$ by assumption on γ. Since any non-zero element of R has euclidean norm at least 1, we conclude that all non-zero elements of qR have norm at least q, and so $g'f - gf' = 0$ in K as desired. The equivalent formulation follows immediately by taking $h_K = f/g$ for any short trapdoor (f, g). Note that g must be invertible in K because otherwise $g = 0$, which implies that $f \in qR$ and so f cannot satisfy $\|f\| \leq \sqrt{q}/\gamma$. □

We now describe our second search variant of the NTRU problem. Since we have seen in Lemma 3.5 that recovering a K-multiple of a short trapdoor is equivalent to recovering the (unique) element h_K, we will use this second approach in the description of the problem.

Definition 3.6 (($\mathcal{D}, \gamma, q$)-NTRU$_{\text{mod}}$ and (γ, q)-wcNTRU$_{\text{mod}}$). *Let $q \geq 2$, $\gamma > \sqrt{2}$ and $\mathcal{D}$ a distribution over (γ, q)-NTRU instances. The $(\mathcal{D}, \gamma, q)$ search NTRU module problem $((\mathcal{D}, \gamma, q)$-NTRU$_{\text{mod}}$ for short) asks, given as input an NTRU instance h sampled from $\mathcal{D}$, to recover the unique field element $h_K \in K$ associated to h (as defined in Lemma 3.5). The advantage of an algorithm $\mathcal{A}$ against the $(\mathcal{D}, \gamma, q)$-NTRU$_{\text{mod}}$ problem is defined as*

$$\text{Adv}(\mathcal{A}) = \Pr_{h \leftarrow \mathcal{D}} \left(\mathcal{A}(h) = h_K \right),$$

where the probability is also over the internal randomness of $\mathcal{A}$.

The (γ, q) worst-case search NTRU module problem $((\gamma, q)$-wcNTRU$_{\text{mod}}$ for short) asks, given as input a (γ, q)-NTRU instance h, to recover the unique field element $h_K \in K$ associated to h.

We note that NTRU$_{\text{mod}}$ is definitionally convenient in that the quantity h_K that we are looking for is unique. In NTRU$_{\text{vec}}$, on the contrary, the short trapdoor (f, g) that we are looking for is far from being unique: it can always be multiplied by small elements of R to obtain other trapdoors.

Given a (γ, q)-NTRU instance h, one can construct the following free rank-2 module M_h:

$$M_h := \begin{pmatrix} 1 & 0 \\ h & q \end{pmatrix} \cdot R^2 = \{(g, f)^T \in R^2 \,|\, g \cdot h = f \bmod q\}.$$

This module is called the NTRU-module associated to h. As a lattice, it has determinant $\det M_h = \Delta_K \cdot q^d$ and dimension $2d$. If it were a generic lattice with such determinant and dimension, we would heuristically expect that its minimum is $\Theta(\sqrt{d} \cdot \Delta_K^{1/(2d)} \cdot \sqrt{q})$. However, since h is a (γ, q)-NTRU instance with $\gamma > \sqrt{2}$, we know that there exists an unexpectedly short vector $(g, f)^T$ in the module M_h. This short vector is not unique, any small multiple $(rg, rf)^T$

with $r \in R$ small is also a short vector of M_h. However, Lemma 3.5 implies that the module spanned by all these short vectors has rank 1 and is unique. Moreover, since this module contains unexpectedly short vectors, it will have an unexpectedly small volume. Summing up, the rank-2 module M_h has multiple unexpectedly short vectors and a unique unexpectedly short rank-1 sub-module. NTRU_{vec} asks to find any of the unexpectedly short non-zero vectors of M_h, whereas NTRU_{mod} asks to recover the unique short rank-1 sub-module (hence the names "NTRU vector" and "NTRU module").

3.4   Elementary Relations Between the Different NTRU Problems

NTRU_{mod} and NTRU_{vec} respectively reduce to their worst-case counterparts. The proof of the following lemma is similarly direct.

Lemma 3.7. *Let* $q \geq 2$, $\gamma \geq \gamma' > \sqrt{2}$. *Then there exists a* ppt *reduction from* (γ, q)-wcNTRU$_{\text{mod}}$ *to* (γ, γ', q)-wcNTRU$_{\text{vec}}$. *In the average-case setup, the reduction preserves the distribution of instances.*

If one assumes that ideal-HSVP is easy, then the latter admits a converse result. The proof of the following lemma is available in the full version.

Lemma 3.8. *Let* $q \geq 2$, $\gamma \geq \gamma' > \sqrt{2}$ *and* $\varepsilon > 0$. *Then there exists a* ppt *reduction from* $(\gamma, \gamma_{\text{vec}}, q)$-wcNTRU$_{\text{vec}}$ *to* (γ, q)-wcNTRU$_{\text{mod}}$ *and* γ_{hsvp}-id-HSVP, *where*

$$\gamma_{\text{vec}} = \frac{1}{(1 + \varepsilon)\sqrt{2}\Delta_K^{1/(2d)}} \cdot \frac{\gamma}{\gamma_{\text{hsvp}}}.$$

In the average-case setup, the NTRU$_{\text{mod}}$ *and* NTRU$_{\text{vec}}$ *instance distributions are identical.*

To reduce dNTRU to NTRU_{mod}, it suffices to show that for a uniform h, we do not expect an unexpectedly short non-zero vector (or short rank-1 submodule) in M_h. The proof of the following lemma is available in the full version.

Lemma 3.9. *Let* $q \geq 2$ *be a prime that does not divide* Δ_K, $\gamma > 16 \cdot \sqrt{d} \cdot \Delta_K^{1/(2d)}$ *and* $\mathcal{D}$ *a distribution over* (γ, q)-NTRU *instances. Then there exists a* ppt *reduction from* $(\mathcal{D}, \gamma, q)$-dNTRU *to* $(\mathcal{D}, \gamma, q)$-NTRU$_{\text{mod}}$. *Further, the reduction makes a single call to the* NTRU$_{\text{mod}}$ *oracle, and if the advantage of the* NTRU$_{\text{mod}}$ *solver is* ε, *then the advantage of the resulting* dNTRU *solver is* $\geq \varepsilon - 2^{-d}$.

The objective of the next two sections is to (partly) complete the picture by giving two more sophisticated reductions: a reduction from id-HSVP to NTRU$_{\text{vec}}$ and a reduction from NTRU$_{\text{mod}}$ to dNTRU.

4   Reduction from Ideal-HSVP to NTRU_vec

This section is devoted to reducing worst-case id-HSVP to average-case NTRU$_{\text{vec}}$. For this purpose, we first exhibit a Karp reduction from worst-case id-HSVP to wcNTRU$_{\text{vec}}$. This reduction is then enhanced by using the worst-case to average-case reduction for id-HSVP from [dBDPW20], resulting in a reduction from worst-case id-HSVP to average-case NTRU$_{\text{vec}}$, where the NTRU$_{\text{vec}}$ average-case distribution is defined as the distribution obtained by applying the worst-case to worst-case reduction to the distribution on ideals from [dBDPW20]. In the process, we improve the reduction of [dBDPW20] to better suit our needs. We extend it to regimes in which it is not polynomial-time anymore, but allows to reach smaller values for the NTRU modulus q, and we show that it allows to sample from the average-case id-HSVP distribution along with a short non-zero element of the ideal (provided q is sufficiently large, or we have access to a quantum computer). The latter is important to allow to sample from the average-case distribution over NTRU instances, along with a trapdoor.

4.1   Transforming an Ideal Lattice into an NTRU Module

In this section, we show how to efficiently 'embed' an ideal lattice into an NTRU module such that any sufficiently short vector of the NTRU module provides a short vector of the embedded ideal lattice. We first give an efficient reduction from ideal-HSVP to worst-case vectorial NTRU.

Theorem 4.1. *Let $q \geq 2$ and $\gamma \geq \gamma' > 0$ with $\gamma \cdot \gamma' \cdot \sqrt{d} > 1$. Let $\gamma_{\text{hsvp}} = 4d\delta_K \cdot \gamma/\gamma'$. There is a* ppt *(Karp) reduction from γ_{hsvp}-id-HSVP to (γ, γ', q)-wcNTRU$_{\text{vec}}$ for ideals $I \subseteq R$ satisfying $\mathcal{N}(I) \in [N/2^d, N]$, with*

$$
N = \left\lfloor \left(\frac{\sqrt{q}}{\gamma \cdot d^{1.5} \cdot \delta_K \cdot \Delta_K^{\frac{1}{2d}}} \right)^d \right\rfloor .
$$

Note that the reduction is restricted to integral ideals of bounded norms. The lower bound is not restrictive: given a non-zero integral ideal I such that $\mathcal{N}(I) \leq N$, we can scale it to the non-zero integral ideal $I' = \lfloor (N/\mathcal{N}(I))^{1/d} \rfloor \cdot I$, which satisfies $\mathcal{N}(I') \in [N/2^d, N]$ and for which a γ_{hsvp}-id-HSVP solution directly leads to a γ_{hsvp}-id-HSVP solution for I. Concerning the upper bound restriction, the id-HSVP worst-case to average-case reduction from [dBDPW20] (as refined in Subsect. 4.2) shows that we can wlog focus on integral ideals I of norms $N \approx 2^{d^{1+\alpha}}$ for some $\alpha \in (0,1]$. This impacts the choice of the NTRU modulus q.

Let us now focus on the problem parameters. If we put aside factors that depend only on the number field, we can set $N^{1/d} \approx \sqrt{q}/\gamma$, and we then obtain that $\gamma_{\text{hsvp}} \approx \gamma/\gamma'$. This means that the approximation factor (which is γ/γ' in the NTRU case) stays roughly the same, and that the root determinant of the NTRU module is γ times larger than the one of the ideal lattice.

Algorithm 4.1. Transforming an ideal lattice into an NTRU instance

---

Input: A $\mathbb{Z}$-basis of a non-zero ideal $I \subseteq R$ and a modulus q.
Output: An NTRU instance h.
 1: Compute $z \in K$ such that $I = R \cap \langle z \rangle$ (see Lemma 4.2).
 2: Let $h = \lfloor q/z \rceil \bmod q \in R_q$.
 3: **return** h

The transformation that embeds an ideal lattice into an NTRU module is described in Algorithm 4.1. In Lemma 4.3, we show some properties of Algorithm 4.1, which will be used to prove Theorem 4.1.

Lemma 4.2. *There exists a* ppt *algorithm (in* size(I) *and* $\log \Delta_K$) *which, given a non-zero integral ideal I as input, computes $z \in K$ such that $I = R \cap \langle z \rangle$.*

Proof. If $I = 0$, then the algorithm returns $z = 0$. If $I = R$, it returns $z = 1$. We now assume that I is neither 0 nor R. Since $I \subseteq R$, it holds that $1 \in I^{-1}$. Let $y \in I^{-1}$ be the output of the algorithm of Lemma 2.6, given $(I^{-1}, 1)$ as input: we have $I^{-1} = \langle 1 \rangle + \langle y \rangle$. Note that $I \neq R$ implies that $y \neq 0$. We then define $z = 1/y$, which fulfills our needs as $J_1 \cap J_2 = (J_1^{-1} + J_2^{-1})^{-1}$ for any non-zero fractional ideals J_1 and J_2. $\qquad\square$

When using Lemma 4.2 in Algorithm 4.1, the element z is necessarily non-zero, as I is non-zero. The analysis of Algorithm 4.1 follows the intuition provided by the case of principal ideals (with a known generator) described in the introduction.

Lemma 4.3. *Let $q \geq 2$ and $I \subseteq R$ a non-zero integral ideal. On input (I, q), Algorithm 4.1 outputs $h \in R_q$ such that*

- *there exists a pair $(f, g) \in R^2 \setminus \{(0,0)\}$ with $g \cdot h = f \bmod q$ and $\|f\|, \|g\| \leq d^{1.5} \cdot \delta_K \cdot \Delta_K^{1/(2d)} \cdot \mathcal{N}(I)^{1/d}$;*
- *for any pair $(f', g') \in R^2 \setminus \{(0,0)\}$ with $g' \cdot h = f' \bmod q$ and $\|f'\|_\infty, \|g'\|_\infty < q/(d \cdot \delta_K \cdot \Delta_K^{1/(2d)} \cdot \mathcal{N}(I)^{1/d})$, we have $g' \in I \setminus \{0\}$.*

Moreover, Algorithm 4.1 runs in time polynomial in size(I), $\log q$ *and* $\log \Delta_K$.

Proof. The run-time of the algorithm follows from Lemma 4.2. For the proofs of the two main statements, we consider $g \in I \setminus \{0\}$ with minimal infinity norm. By Minkowski's bound, we have that $\|g\|_\infty \leq \Delta_K^{1/(2d)} \cdot \mathcal{N}(I)^{1/d}$.

We now prove the existence of f such that (f, g) is a short trapdoor for h. By multiplying g with h, we obtain

$$g \cdot h = g \cdot \lfloor q/z \rceil = g \cdot q/z + f,$$

with $f := -g \cdot \{q/z\}$. Since $g \in I$ and $z^{-1} \in I^{-1}$ (because $I \subseteq \langle z \rangle$), we have that $g \cdot q/z \in qR$. This implies that $f \in R$ and $gh = f \bmod q$, as desired. Let us now compute an upper bound on the norm of f (we already know that $\|g\| \leq$

$\sqrt{d} \cdot \Delta_K^{1/(2d)} \cdot \mathcal{N}(I)^{1/d})$. We know from the preliminaries that $\|\{q/z\}\|_\infty \le d/2 \cdot \delta_K$, from which we obtain:

$$\|f\| \le \|g\| \cdot (d \cdot \delta_K) \le d^{3/2} \cdot \delta_K \cdot \Delta_K^{\frac{1}{2d}} \cdot \mathcal{N}(I)^{\frac{1}{d}}.$$

Let us now prove the second property of the lemma. Let $(g', f') \in R^2 \setminus \{(0,0)\}$ be such that $g' \cdot h = f' \bmod q$ and

$$\|f'\|_\infty, \|g'\|_\infty < \frac{q}{d \cdot \delta_K \cdot \Delta_K^{\frac{1}{2d}} \cdot \mathcal{N}(I)^{\frac{1}{d}}}.$$

We first show that $g' \ne 0$. Assume by contradiction that $g' = 0$. Then $f' = 0 \bmod q$, i.e., $f' \in qR$. But any non-zero element of qR has infinity norm $\ge q$ (using the fact that any non-zero element of R has infinity norm ≥ 1). Since we know that $\|f'\|_\infty < q$, we conclude that $f' = 0$, which contradicts the assumption that $(f', g') \ne (0,0)$.

We now show that $g' \in I$. Recall that z is such that $I = R \cap \langle z \rangle$. Since we already know that $g' \in R$, it suffices to prove that $g' \in \langle z \rangle$, i.e., that $g'/z \in R$. By definition of h, we have:

$$g' \cdot q/z = g' \cdot h + g' \cdot \{q/z\} = f' + g' \cdot \{q/z\} + q \cdot r,$$

for some $r \in R$. Multiplying this equation by g/q (recall that g is a shortest non-zero vector of I for the infinity norm), we obtain

$$g' \cdot g/z = (f' + g' \cdot \{q/z\}) \cdot g/q + g \cdot r.$$

We have seen that $g/z \in R$, so that both terms $g' \cdot g/z$ and $g \cdot r$ are in R. We hence have that the term $(f' + g' \cdot \{q/z\}) \cdot g/q$ must also belong to R. Further, we know that

$$\|(f' + g' \cdot \{q/z\}) \cdot g/q\|_\infty \le (\|f'\|_\infty + \|g'\|_\infty \cdot \|\{q/z\}\|_\infty) \cdot \|g\|_\infty/q$$

$$\le \max(\|f'\|_\infty, \|g'\|_\infty) \cdot (1 + d/2 \cdot \delta_K) \cdot \Delta_K^{\frac{1}{2d}} \cdot \mathcal{N}(I)^{\frac{1}{d}}/q.$$

By assumption, the above is < 1. Since no non-zero element of R has infinity norm < 1, we conclude that $f' + g' \cdot \{q/z\} = 0$. This implies that $g' \cdot q/z = q \cdot r$. Dividing this equality by q, we obtain that $g'/z \in R$, as desired.   □

We are now ready to prove Theorem 4.1.

Proof (Theorem 4.1). The reduction consists in calling Algorithm 4.1 on I and q to obtain some $h \in R_q$, then calling the wcNTRU$_{\text{vec}}$ oracle on h and returning the oracle output.

Let $I \subseteq R$ be a γ_{hsvp}-id-HSVP instance satisfying $\mathcal{N}(I) \in [N/2^d, N]$, with N as in the theorem statement. The first statement of Lemma 4.3 ensures that the element h computed by the reduction is a valid (γ, γ', q)-wcNTRU$_{\text{vec}}$ instance. The wcNTRU$_{\text{vec}}$ oracle hence outputs a pair $(f', g') \in R^2 \setminus \{(0,0)\}$

such that $g' \cdot h = f' \bmod q$ and $\|f'\|, \|g'\| \leq \sqrt{q}/\gamma'$. By the parameter conditions, the assumption of the second statement of Lemma 4.3 holds. We hence have that $g' \in I \setminus \{0\}$. Further, by definition of N, the lower bound on $\mathcal{N}(I)$ and definition of γ_{hsvp}, we have

$$\|g'\| \leq \frac{\sqrt{q}}{\gamma'} \leq \frac{2^{1/d} \cdot N^{\frac{1}{d}} \cdot \gamma \cdot d^{1.5} \cdot \delta_K \cdot \Delta_K^{\frac{1}{2d}}}{\gamma'} \leq \gamma_{\text{hsvp}} \cdot \sqrt{d} \cdot \Delta_K^{\frac{1}{2d}} \cdot \mathcal{N}(I)^{\frac{1}{d}}.$$

Note that we used the inequality $\lfloor x \rfloor \geq x/2$, which holds for any $x \geq 1$. □

4.2 From Worst-Case id-HSVP to Average-Case id-HSVP

In [dBDPW20], the authors gave a worst-case to average-case reduction for id-HSVP, for a certain average-case distribution of ideals. We adapt [dBDPW20, Th. 4.5] to Theorem 4.4 below, so that it better fits with our application. We explain in the full version how to adapt the proof.

Theorem 4.4 (Adapted from [dBDPW20], Th. 4.5, ERH). *Let K a number field of degree d and $N \geq (12d^{1.5} \log d \cdot \delta_K \cdot \Delta_K^{1/(2d)})^d$ an integer. Let $\gamma > 0$. There exist $\gamma' = \gamma \cdot O(d^{1.5} \Delta_K^{1/d})$, a distribution $\mathcal{D}_N^{\text{id-HSVP}}$ over non-zero integral ideals of K of norm $\leq N$ and a reduction:*

- *from worst-case γ'-id-HSVP for all fractional ideals of K,*
- *to average-case γ-id-HSVP for integral ideals distributed from $\mathcal{D}_N^{\text{id-HSVP}}$.*

The reduction decreases the success probability by at most $2^{-\Omega(d)}$, makes a single call to the average-case γ-id-HSVP oracle, and runs in time $T_\beta^{\text{id-HSVP}} + \text{poly}(\log N, \text{size}(I), \log \Delta_K)$ where

- *I is the input (worst-case) ideal;*
- *$T_\beta^{\text{id-HSVP}}$ is the time needed to solve id-HSVP with approximation factor $2^{d/\beta}$ and*

$$\beta = \left\lceil \frac{d}{\log \left(N^{1/d}/(6d^{1.5} \log d \cdot \delta_K \cdot \Delta_K^{1/(2d)}) \right)} \right\rceil.$$

Moreover, there exist $N_0 = \text{poly}(\Delta_K^{1/d}, \delta_K, d)^d$ and a ppt algorithm $\mathcal{A}$ (with respect to $\log N$ and $\log \Delta_K$) such that, for all $N \geq N_0$, algorithm $\mathcal{A}$ samples pairs (J, w) such that:

- *the ideal J is a non-zero integral ideal of norm $\leq N$;*
- *the distribution $\widetilde{\mathcal{D}}_N^{\text{id-HSVP}}$ of J satisfies $\widetilde{\mathcal{D}}_N^{\text{id-HSVP}} \approx_{2^{-\Omega(d)}} \mathcal{D}_N^{\text{id-HSVP}}$;*
- *the element $w \in J \setminus \{0\}$ satisfies $\|w\| \leq \text{poly}(d, \delta_K, \Delta_K^{1/d}, 2^{\sqrt{\log \Delta_K + d \log d}}) \cdot \mathcal{N}(J)^{1/d}$.*

If we have access to a factoring oracle or if $N \geq N_0' = N_0 \cdot 2^{O(d\sqrt{\log \Delta_K + d \log d})}$, then we can reduce the size of w down to $\|w\| \leq \text{poly}(d, \delta_K, \Delta_K^{1/d}) \cdot \mathcal{N}(J)^{1/d}$.

Note that even though the reduction relies on a worst-case id-HSVP solver, the latter is with an approximation factor $2^{d/\beta}$ which is typically much larger than γ'. This implies that $T_\beta^{\text{id-HSVP}}$ is expected to be much smaller than the time needed to solve γ'-id-HSVP. Assume that $\Delta_K^{1/(2d)}$ and δ_K are both poly(d) and that we use the lattice reduction algorithm from [Sch87] with block size β to solve $2^{d/\beta}$-id-HSVP. It runs in time $T_\beta^{\text{id-HSVP}} = 2^{O(\beta)}$ (up to a poly($\log N, \log \Delta_K$) factor). Then, it can be seen that the reduction is polynomial-time when $N = 2^{\Omega(d^2)}$; it becomes more expensive when N is below this bound; and it ends up being $2^{O(d)}$ when $N \approx \text{poly}(d)^d$. The run-time of the reduction can be improved using id-HSVP algorithms such as those mentioned in Subsect. 2.3. In all cases, we note that one can sample ideals J from $\mathcal{D}_N^{\text{id-HSVP}}$, together with a short vector of J in quantum polynomial time even for small N, and in classical polynomial time for larger N's (of the order of $2^{O(d^{1.5}\sqrt{\log d})}$ if $\Delta_K^{1/(2d)}$ and δ_K are both poly(d)).

All the ingredients for the proof of Theorem 4.4 are present in [dBDPW20], however the latter only considered the case of $N \geq (2^d \cdot 6d^{1.5} \log d \cdot \Delta_K^{1/(2d)} \cdot \delta_K)^d$, since this is the range of parameters for which the reduction runs in polynomial time. The generalization to smaller N and larger run-time is relatively immediate and is provided in the full version. A further difference with [dBDPW20] is that the distribution $\mathcal{D}_N^{\text{id-HSVP}}$ in [dBDPW20] is over the inverses of integral ideals (see [dBDPW20, Le. 4.1]) whereas here it is more convenient to have a distribution over integral ideals. Finally, we also explain in the full version how to sample ideals from $\mathcal{D}_N^{\text{id-HSVP}}$ with a somehow short vector.

4.3 An Average-Case Distribution of NTRU Instances

In this subsection, we define a distribution $\mathcal{D}_{q,\gamma}^{\text{NTRU}}$ over (γ, q)-NTRU instances. This distribution is defined as the one being produced by Algorithm 4.2. In fact, Algorithm 4.2 actually provides a $(\widetilde{\gamma}, q)$-NTRU setup for some $\widetilde{\gamma} \geq \gamma$, i.e., the instance h can be sampled along with a trapdoor (f, g) that may be a little larger than a shortest one.

Algorithm 4.2. Sampling h from $\mathcal{D}_{q,\gamma}^{\text{NTRU}}$ together with a trapdoor

---

Input: An integer $q \geq 2$ and a real $\gamma \geq 1$
Output: A triple $(h, f, g) \in R_q \times R^2$.

1: Let $N = \left\lfloor \left(\dfrac{\sqrt{q}}{\gamma \cdot d^{1.5} \cdot \delta_K \cdot \Delta_K^{1/(2d)}} \right)^d \right\rfloor$.

2: Sample I from $\widetilde{\mathcal{D}}_N^{\text{id-HSVP}}$ with $v \in I \setminus \{0\}$ such that $\|v\| \leq \text{poly}(d, \delta_K, \Delta_K^{1/d}) \cdot \mathcal{N}(I)^{1/d}$ (see Theorem 4.4).

3: Let $I' = \lfloor (N/\mathcal{N}(I))^{1/d} \rfloor \cdot I$ and $v' = \lfloor (N/\mathcal{N}(I))^{1/d} \rfloor \cdot v$.

4: Run Algorithm 4.1 on I'; let $h \in R_q$ be the output and z as in Algorithm 4.1.

5: Compute $g = v'$ and $f = -g \cdot \{q/z\}$.

6: **return** (h, f, g).

Lemma 4.5. *There exist $\Gamma = \mathrm{poly}(d, \delta_K, \Delta_K^{1/d})$ and $\Gamma' = \Gamma \cdot 2^{O(\sqrt{\log \Delta_K + d \log d})}$ such that if $\sqrt{q}/\gamma \geq \Gamma$ (resp. $\sqrt{q}/\gamma \geq \Gamma'$), then Algorithm 4.2 runs in quantum (resp. classical) polynomial time (with respect to $\log q$ and $\log \Delta_K$).*

Proof. Let $\Gamma = 2d^{1.5} \cdot \delta_K \cdot \Delta_K^{1/(2d)} \cdot N_0^{1/d}$ (resp. $\Gamma' = 2d^{1.5} \cdot \delta_K \cdot \Delta_K^{1/(2d)} \cdot (N_0')^{1/d}$), where N_0 (resp. N_0') is as in the second part of Theorem 4.4. Note that we have $\Gamma = \mathrm{poly}(d, \delta_K, \Delta_K^{1/d})$ (resp. $\Gamma' = \Gamma \cdot 2^{O(\sqrt{\log \Delta_K + d \log d})}$) as desired. Moreover, by definition of N and using the fact that $\sqrt{q}/\gamma \geq \Gamma$ (resp. $\sqrt{q}/\gamma \geq \Gamma'$), we have $N \geq N_0$ (resp. $N \geq N_0'$). Hence, by Theorem 4.4, one can sample (I, v) in Step 2 in quantum (resp. classical) time $\mathrm{poly}(\log N, \log \Delta_K) = \mathrm{poly}(\log \Delta_K, \log q)$.

By Theorem 4.4, we also know that the ideal I is non-zero and satisfies $\mathcal{N}(I) \leq N$, hence $\lfloor (N/\mathcal{N}(I))^{1/d} \rfloor \neq 0$. Therefore, the ideal I' computed at Step 3 is also non-zero, and v' is a non-zero element of I'. Thanks to Lemma 4.3, we know that Algorithm 4.1 can be run on I' in time $\mathrm{poly}(\mathrm{size}(I'), \log q, \log \Delta_K)$. Since I' is integral and $\mathcal{N}(I') \leq N \leq q^d$, we conclude that $\mathrm{size}(I') \leq \mathrm{poly}(\log q, \log \Delta_K)$. Finally, computing f using the formula $-g \cdot \{q/z\}$ can also be done in time $\mathrm{poly}(\log q, \log \Delta_K)$, since the rounding operation in R is efficient. $\square$

Now that it is established that Algorithm 4.2 terminates, we can formally define $\mathcal{D}_{\gamma,q}^{\mathrm{NTRU}}$ as the distribution produced by the algorithm.

Definition 4.6 (Distribution $\mathcal{D}_{q,\gamma}^{\mathrm{NTRU}}$). *Let q, γ as in Algorithm 4.2. The distribution $\mathcal{D}_{\gamma,q}^{\mathrm{NTRU}}$ over R_q is defined as the distribution of the element h produced by Algorithm 4.2 on input (q, γ).*

Lemma 4.7. *The support of the distribution $\mathcal{D}_{q,\gamma}^{\mathrm{NTRU}}$ is contained in the set of (γ, q)-NTRU instances.*

Proof. Let h be computed by Algorithm 4.2 on input (q, γ). By the first property of Lemma 4.3, there exists a trapdoor $(f^\star, g^\star) \neq (0, 0)$ for h, with $\|f^\star\|, \|g^\star\| \leq d^{1.5} \cdot \delta_K \cdot \Delta_K^{1/(2d)} \cdot \mathcal{N}(I')^{1/d}$. We have $\mathcal{N}(I') = \lfloor (N/\mathcal{N}(I))^{1/d} \rfloor^d \cdot \mathcal{N}(I) \leq N$. Using the definition of N, we conclude that $\|f^\star\|, \|g^\star\| \leq \sqrt{q}/\gamma$. $\square$

Algorithm 4.2 gives a way to sample from $\mathcal{D}_{q,\gamma}^{\mathrm{NTRU}}$ together with a trapdoor.

Lemma 4.8. *Let q, γ as in Algorithm 4.2 and Γ (resp. Γ') as in Lemma 4.5. If $\sqrt{q}/\gamma \geq \Gamma$ (resp. $\sqrt{q}/\gamma \geq \Gamma'$), then there exist $\widetilde{\gamma} = \gamma/\mathrm{poly}(d, \delta_K, \Delta_K^{1/d})$ such that Algorithm 4.2 is a $(\mathcal{D}_{q,\gamma}^{\mathrm{NTRU}}, \widetilde{\gamma}, q)$-NTRU quantum (resp. classical) setup.*

Proof. We have already seen in Lemma 4.5 that Algorithm 4.2 is quantum (resp. classical) ppt. We have seen in Lemma 4.7 that $\mathcal{D}$ is a distribution over (γ, q)-NTRU instances. It is hence a distribution over $(\widetilde{\gamma}, q)$-NTRU instances, as $\widetilde{\gamma} \leq \gamma$. We now show that the sampled pair $(f, g) \neq (0, 0)$ satisfies $g \cdot h = f \mod q$ and $\|f\|, \|g\| \leq \sqrt{q}/\gamma \cdot \mathrm{poly}(d, \delta_K, \Delta_K^{1/d})$.

We have already seen that $g = v'$ is non-zero. Moreover, by definitions of $f = -g \cdot \{q/z\}$ and $h = \lfloor q/z \rceil$, is holds that $f = g \cdot h \mod q$ (see the proof of

Lemma 4.3). Further, we have (successively using Theorem 4.4, the definition of I' and the definition of N):

$$\|g\| = \|v'\| \leq \mathrm{poly}(d, \delta_K, \Delta_K^{1/d}) \cdot \mathcal{N}(I')^{1/d} \leq \mathrm{poly}(d, \delta_K, \Delta_K^{1/d}) \cdot N^{1/d}$$
$$\leq \mathrm{poly}(d, \delta_K, \Delta_K^{1/d}) \cdot \frac{\sqrt{q}}{\gamma}.$$

Moreover, by definition of f, we know that $\|f\| \leq \|g\| \cdot (d \cdot \delta_K)$. Hence, there exists some $\widetilde{\gamma} = \gamma/\mathrm{poly}(d, \delta_K, \Delta_K^{1/d})$ such that $\|f\|, \|g\| \leq \sqrt{q}/\widetilde{\gamma}$, as desired.   □

4.4   From Average-Case id-HSVP to Average-Case NTRU

By combining the results from Subsects. 4.1 and 4.3, we obtain that, for well-chosen parameters, average-case id-HSVP for distribution $\mathcal{D}_N^{\mathrm{id\text{-}HSVP}}$ reduces to average-case $\mathrm{NTRU}_{\mathrm{vec}}$ for distribution $\mathcal{D}_{q,\gamma}^{\mathrm{NTRU}}$. The proof of Theorem 4.9 is available in the full version. This theorem can in turn be combined with Theorem 4.4 to obtain a reduction from worst-case id-HSVP to average-case $\mathrm{NTRU}_{\mathrm{vec}}$.

Theorem 4.9. *Let $q \geq 2$, $\gamma \geq 1$ and $\gamma' > 0$ such that $\gamma \cdot \gamma' \cdot \sqrt{d} > 1$ and $\sqrt{q}/\gamma \geq 13 \cdot d^3 \log d \cdot \delta_K^2 \cdot \Delta_K^{1/d}$. Define:*

$$N = \left\lfloor \left(\frac{\sqrt{q}}{\gamma \cdot d^{1.5} \cdot \delta_K \cdot \Delta_K^{1/(2d)}} \right)^d \right\rfloor \quad and \quad \gamma_{\mathrm{hsvp}} = \frac{\gamma}{\gamma'} \cdot 4d\delta_K.$$

There is a ppt *reduction (with respect to $\log \Delta_K$ and $\log q$) from average-case γ_{hsvp}-id-HSVP for ideals sampled from $\widetilde{\mathcal{D}}_N^{\mathrm{id\text{-}HSVP}}$ to $(\mathcal{D}_{q,\gamma}^{\mathrm{NTRU}}, \gamma, \gamma', q)$-$\mathrm{NTRU}_{\mathrm{vec}}$. The reduction makes a single call to the $\mathrm{NTRU}_{\mathrm{vec}}$ oracle and preserves the success probability.*

5   A Search to Decision Reduction for NTRU

In this section, we provide a reduction from average-case search-$\mathrm{NTRU}_{\mathrm{mod}}$ with distribution $\mathcal{D}^{\mathrm{s}}$ to average-case dec-NTRU with distribution $\mathcal{D}^{\mathrm{d}}$. The distribution $\mathcal{D}^{\mathrm{s}}$ can be chosen from a large class of distributions (it only has to be bounded and to have an invertible denominator, as per Definition 5.1 below) and the distribution $\mathcal{D}^{\mathrm{d}}$ is a function of $\mathcal{D}^{\mathrm{s}}$. Moreover, we show that if the distribution $\mathcal{D}^{\mathrm{s}}$ enjoys an NTRU setup, then so does $\mathcal{D}^{\mathrm{d}}$.

5.1   Choice of the Distributions

We start by describing a property of distributions that we will need for our search to decision reduction. We also describe the distribution $\mathcal{D}^{\mathrm{d}}$ as a function of $\mathcal{D}^{\mathrm{s}}$, and explain how one can sample h with a trapdoor (f, g) from $\mathcal{D}^{\mathrm{d}}$, provided there is an efficient algorithm doing it for $\mathcal{D}^{\mathrm{s}}$.

Definition 5.1 (Well-behaved elements and distributions). *Let $q \geq 2$ be an integer and $B > 1$ be a real number. An element $h \in R_q$ is said to be B-well-behaved if there exists $f, g \in R$ such that $gh = f \bmod q$; $\langle f \rangle + \langle g \rangle + \langle q \rangle = R$; and for all $1 \leq i \leq d$ we have $1/B \leq |\sigma_i(f)|, |\sigma_i(g)| \leq B$.*

A distribution $\mathcal{D}$ over R_q is said to be (B, ε)-well-behaved for some $\varepsilon \geq 0$ if the probability that $h \leftarrow \mathcal{D}$ is B-well-behaved is $\geq 1 - \varepsilon$.

Observe that any $(B, 0)$-well-behaved distribution over R_q is a distribution over (γ, q)-NTRU instances, where $\gamma = \sqrt{q}/(B\sqrt{d})$. Observe also that the condition $\langle f \rangle + \langle g \rangle + \langle q \rangle = R$ is equivalent to asking that g is invertible modulo q. Indeed, since $gh = f \bmod q$, then any prime factor dividing both $\langle g \rangle$ and $\langle q \rangle$ would also be a prime factor of $\langle f \rangle$, contradicting the coprimality condition. Let us now define a randomized mapping ϕ_B over R_q.

Definition 5.2 (Function ϕ_B). *Let $q \geq 2$ and $B > 1$. We define the randomized mapping ϕ_B over R_q as follows*

$$\phi_B : \quad R_q \to R_q$$
$$h \mapsto xh + y \bmod q \quad \text{where } x, y \leftarrow D_{R, 2Bd\delta_K}.$$

We extend ϕ_B to distributions over R_q: for a distribution $\mathcal{D}$, we let $\phi_B(\mathcal{D})$ be the distribution over R_q obtained by sampling $h \leftarrow \mathcal{D}$ and then outputting $\phi_B(h)$.

Finally, we show that if $\mathcal{D}$ enjoys an NTRU setup, then so does $\phi_B(\mathcal{D})$.

Lemma 5.3. *Let $B \geq 1$, $q \geq 2$, $\gamma > 0$ and $\mathcal{D}$ a distribution over (γ, q)-NTRU instances. If there exists a $(\mathcal{D}, \gamma, q)$-NTRU setup, then there exists a $(\mathcal{D}', \gamma', q)$-NTRU setup where $\mathcal{D}'$ is a distribution over R_q such that $\mathcal{D}' \approx_{2^{-\Omega(d)}} \phi_B(\mathcal{D})$ and $\gamma' = \gamma/(4Bd^{1.5}\delta_K)$.*

Proof. Let $\mathcal{A}$ be a ppt algorithm (with respect to $\log q$ and $\log \Delta_K$) sampling triples $(h, f, g) \in R_q \times R^2$ such that the marginal distribution of h is $\mathcal{D}$, $(f, g) \neq (0, 0)$, $\|f\|, \|g\| \leq \sqrt{q}/\gamma$ and $g \cdot h = f \bmod q$.

We consider the following algorithm $\mathcal{B}$:

- run $\mathcal{A}$; let (h, f, g) be the output;
- use the algorithm from Lemma 2.2 with parameters $\sigma = 2Bd\delta_K$ and $\mathbf{c} = \mathbf{0}$ to sample x and y (using the basis $(r_1, \ldots, r_d)$ of R);
- return $(h', f', g') = (xh + y, xf + yg, g)$.

Note that $\mathcal{B}$ is ppt and that (f', g') is non-zero and satisfies $g' \cdot h' = f' \bmod q$. By Lemma 2.2, we also have

$$\|f'\| \leq 2Bd^{1.5}\delta_K \cdot (\|f\| + \|g\|) \leq 4Bd^{1.5}\delta_K \cdot \frac{\sqrt{q}}{\gamma}.$$

Finally, as the residual distribution of h is $\mathcal{D}$, Lemma 2.2 also implies that the residual distribution of h' is within statistical distance $2^{-\Omega(d)}$ from $\phi_B(\mathcal{D})$. $\qquad \square$

We can now state the main result of this section: a reduction from NTRU_{mod} to dNTRU, for well-chosen distributions. This theorem follows from Lemmas 2.5, 5.6 and 5.7, which are stated and proved in the following subsections. The proof of Theorem 5.4 is provided in the full version.

Theorem 5.4. *Let $q \geq 2$, $B \in (1, q]$, $\varepsilon \geq 0$ and $\mathcal{D}^s$ be a (B, ε)-well-behaved distribution over R_q. Assume that $\log q, \log \Delta_K, \log \|\Phi\| \leq 2^{o(d)}$ (recall that Φ is a defining polynomial of K). Define $\gamma' := \frac{\sqrt{q}}{4B^2 d^2 \delta_K}$ and assume that $\gamma \geq 1$. Let $\mathcal{A}$ be an algorithm solving $(\phi_B(\mathcal{D}^s), \gamma', q)$-dNTRU with advantage $\text{Adv}(\mathcal{A}) \geq 2^{-o(d)}$. Then, there exists an algorithm $\mathcal{B}$ solving $(\mathcal{D}^s, \gamma, q)$-$\text{NTRU}_{\text{mod}}$ with $\gamma = \sqrt{q}/(B\sqrt{d})$ and advantage $\text{Adv}(\mathcal{B}) \geq (\text{Adv}(\mathcal{A}) - 2\varepsilon)/4$. Algorithm $\mathcal{B}$ is ppt (with respect to $\log q$, $\log \Delta_K$, $\log \|\Phi\|$ and $\text{Adv}(\mathcal{A})^{-1}$) and makes (possibly that many) oracle queries to $\mathcal{A}$.*

Observe that up to polynomial factors depending on the number field K, we have $\gamma \approx \sqrt{q}/B$ and $\gamma' \approx \sqrt{q}/B^2$. Said differently, the Euclidean norm of the short trapdoor is squared when we go from $\mathcal{D}^s$ (which has short trapdoors of size roughly B) to $\phi_B(\mathcal{D}^s)$ (which has short trapdoors of size roughly B^2). Hence, one should consider $B \leq q^{1/4}$ for the dNTRU instances to have short trapdoors of norm $\geq \sqrt{q}$.

5.2   Creating New NTRU Instances

In this section, we give a lemma which will allow us to rerandomize an NTRU instance h so that the distribution of the new NTRU instance depends on $c_1 \sigma_1(f) + c_2 \sigma_1(g)$ for some parameters c_1 and c_2 that we can customize. This lemma will be used to prove Lemma 5.7, in the next subsection.

Lemma 5.5. *Let $(f, g) \in R^2 \setminus \{(0, 0)\}$ and $I = \langle f \rangle + \langle g \rangle$. Let $c_1, c_2 \in \sigma_1(K_\mathbb{R})$ (which is either $\mathbb{R}$ or $\mathbb{C}$), $s_0 > 0$ and $s \geq \sqrt{d}\delta_K \cdot (\|f\| + \|g\|)$.*

Given $t \in \sigma_1(K_\mathbb{R})$, we define $\psi(t) \in K_\mathbb{R}$ as $(t, 0, \ldots, 0)^T \in K_\mathbb{R}$ if σ_1 is a real embedding and as $(t/\sqrt{2}, \bar{t}/\sqrt{2}, 0, \ldots, 0)^T \in K_\mathbb{R}$ if σ_1 is a complex embedding with $\sigma_2 = \overline{\sigma_1}$.[2]

Let $\mathcal{D}$ be the output distribution of the following algorithm:

- *sample $c_0 \leftarrow D_{\sigma_1(K_\mathbb{R}), s_0, 0}$;*
- *sample $x \leftarrow D_{R, s, \psi(c_0 \cdot c_1)}$ and $y \leftarrow D_{R, s, \psi(c_0 \cdot c_2)}$;*
- *return $x \cdot f + y \cdot g \in I$.*

Then it holds that $\mathcal{D} \approx_{2^{-\Omega(d)}} D_{I, \mathbf{S}, 0}$, where $\mathbf{S}$ is a diagonal matrix with

$$S_{11} = \sqrt{s_0^2 \cdot |c_1 \sigma_1(f) + c_2 \sigma_1(g)|^2 + s^2 \cdot (|\sigma_1(f)|^2 + |\sigma_1(g)|^2)}$$

$$S_{22} = \begin{cases} S_{11} & \text{if } \sigma_1 \text{ is a complex embedding} \\ s \cdot \sqrt{|\sigma_2(f)|^2 + |\sigma_2(g)|^2} & \text{if } \sigma_1 \text{ is a real embedding} \end{cases}$$

$$S_{ii} = s \cdot \sqrt{|\sigma_i(f)|^2 + |\sigma_i(g)|^2} \qquad \text{for } i \geq 3.$$

---

[2] The scaling by a factor $1/\sqrt{2}$ in the complex case ensures that the norm of $\psi(t)$ is still equal to $|t|$, which allows simpler expressions.

The above can be obtained by combining the convolution result of [Pei10, Th. 3.1] and the discrete Gaussian leftover hash lemma from [LSS14, Th. 5.1]. Unfortunately, the statements of [Pei10, Th. 3.1] and [LSS14, Th. 5.1] do not exactly match what we need (in particular, non-zero centers are not considered in [LSS14, Th. 5.1] and the convolution result of [Pei10, Th. 3.1] does not consider c_0 being sampled from a smaller space and extended with zeros). In the full version, we prove some slight variants of these results, in order to prove Lemma 5.5.

Observe that by taking $s = 2Bd\delta_K$ and $c_1 = c_2 = 0$, then the distribution of $x \cdot f + y \cdot g$ is exactly the distribution of the numerator of $\phi_B(h)$, over the randomness of ϕ_B (i.e., when h, f and g are fixed). Note that for Lemma 5.5 to be applicable, we need $s = 2Bd\delta_K \geq \sqrt{d}\delta_K \cdot (\|f\| + \|g\|)$, which holds true if $\|f\|_\infty, \|g\|_\infty \leq B$. This is the source of the 'standard deviation squaring' in Theorem 5.4. Finally, note that by using the lemma multiple times with the same h, we obtain tuple NTRU instances (as defined in Definition 3.1), implying that the dNTRU and NTRU_{vec} problem variants reduce to their tuple counterparts (under proper parametrization).

5.3   Using the OHCP Framework

We now prove two lemmas for the core of the proof of Theorem 5.4. Lemma 5.6 essentially states that when sampling h from $\mathcal{D}^s$, then one should get a "good" h with non-negligible probability. Lemma 5.7 then shows that when h is "good", it is possible to recover a very accurate approximation of $\sigma_1(h_K)$ using the dNTRU oracle. Combining these two lemmas with Lemma 2.5 (which states that one can recover an element $x \in K$ exactly from a sufficiently good approximation of $\sigma_1(x)$) then yields Theorem 5.4 (whose proof is provided in the full version).

Lemma 5.6. *Let $q \geq 2$, $B \in (1, q]$, $\varepsilon \geq 0$ and $\mathcal{D}^s$ be a (B, ε)-well-behaved distribution over R_q. Let $\mathcal{A}$ be an algorithm solving $(\phi_B(\mathcal{D}^s), \gamma, q)$-dNTRU for some $\gamma \geq 1$. Then, there exists a set $H \subset R_q$ such that every h in H is B-well-behaved; $\Pr_{h \leftarrow \mathcal{D}^s}(h \in H) \geq \text{Adv}(\mathcal{A})/2 - \varepsilon$; and for all $h \in H$*

$$\left| \Pr\left(\mathcal{A}(\phi_B(h)) = 1\right) - \Pr\left(\mathcal{A}(u) = 1\right) \right| \geq \text{Adv}(\mathcal{A})/2,$$

where the probabilities are taken over the internal randomness of $\mathcal{A}$, the randomness of ϕ_B and the random choice of $u \leftarrow U(R_q)$ (but not over the choice of h).

Proof. There exists $H_0 \subset R_q$ of weight $\geq \text{Adv}(\mathcal{A})/2$ under $\mathcal{D}^s$ such that for all $h \in H_0$, the advantage of $\mathcal{A}$ on $\phi_B(h)$ is at least $\text{Adv}(\mathcal{A})/2$. We define H as the subset of the h's in H_0 that are B-well-behaved. The result follows from the definition of (B, ε)-well-behavedness and the union bound. □

Lemma 5.7. *Let $q \geq 2$, $B \in (1, q]$, $\varepsilon \geq 0$ and $\mathcal{D}^s$ be a (B, ε)-well-behaved distribution over R_q. Let $\mathcal{D}^d = \phi_B(\mathcal{D}^s)$. Let $\mathcal{A}$ and H as in Lemma 5.6. Assume* that $\mathrm{Adv}(\mathcal{A})^{-1}, \log q, \log \Delta_K \leq 2^{o(d)}$. Then, there exists a probabilistic algorithm $\mathcal{B}$ that, given an integer $\ell \leq 2^{o(d)}$ and any $h \in H$, recovers $\sigma_1(h_K)$ with ℓ bits of absolute precision[3] with probability $\geq 1 - 2^{-\Omega(d)}$ (where h_K is defined as in Lemma 3.5). Moreover, algorithm $\mathcal{B}$ runs in time polynomial in $\ell, \mathrm{Adv}(\mathcal{A})^{-1}, \log q$ and $\log \Delta_K$ and makes (possibly that many) oracle queries to $\mathcal{A}$.

Proof. In order to prove the lemma, we will express our problem as an instance of the Oracle Hidden Center Problem (see Definition 2.9) and then use Proposition 2.10 to conclude.

Let $h \in H$ be fixed once and for all, and given to $\mathcal{B}$. Let us also fix some (unknown) $(f, g) \in R^2$ such that $g \cdot h = f \bmod q$; g is invertible modulo q; and $|\sigma_i(f)|, |\sigma_i(g)| \in [1/B, B]$ for all embeddings σ_i (we know that such f and g exist since h is B-well-behaved by definition of H). We write $I = \langle f \rangle + \langle g \rangle$, which is also fixed once and for all (and is coprime to $\langle q \rangle$).

Let $k = 1$ if σ_1 is a real embedding and $k = 2$ if σ_1 is a complex embedding. In the following, we will identify $\mathbb{R}^k$ with $\sigma_1(K_\mathbb{R})$. Note that in both cases, the Euclidean norm of a vector in $\mathbb{R}^k$ corresponds to the absolute value of the element seen in $\mathbb{R}$ or $\mathbb{C}$.

In order to fit the OHCP framework, we need to describe a randomized oracle $\mathcal{O}$ that takes as input a pair $(z, t) \in \mathbb{R}^k \times \mathbb{R}^{\geq 0}$ and outputs 0 or 1 such that $\Pr_\mathcal{O}(\mathcal{O}(z, t) = 1) = P(t + \ln|z - \sigma_1(h_K)|)$, for some (unknown) function P (that may depend on h). In other words, we want that the acceptance probability of the oracle $\mathcal{O}$ only depends on $t + \ln|z - \sigma_1(h_K)|$ (when t and z vary).

We start by considering an oracle $\mathcal{O}^{\mathrm{ideal}}$ that we do not know how to implement efficiently, but which is more convenient for the analysis. We will later replace it by an oracle $\mathcal{O}^{\mathrm{approx}}$ that can be implemented efficiently and whose behavior is very close to the one of $\mathcal{O}^{\mathrm{ideal}}$. Oracle $\mathcal{O}^{\mathrm{ideal}}$ is as follows. On input $(z, t) \in \mathbb{R}^k \times \mathbb{R}^{\geq 0}$, it first samples $f' \leftarrow D_{I, \mathbf{S}}$, where $\mathbf{S}$ is a diagonal matrix with

$$S_{11} = \sqrt{\exp(t - d)^2 |\sigma_1(f) - z\sigma_1(g)|^2 + 4B^2 d^2 \delta_K^2 (|\sigma_1(f)|^2 + |\sigma_1(g)|^2)}$$

$$S_{22} = \begin{cases} S_{11} & \text{if } \sigma_1 \text{ is a complex embedding} \\ 2Bd\delta_K \sqrt{(|\sigma_2(f)|^2 + |\sigma_2(g)|^2)} & \text{if } \sigma_1 \text{ is a real embedding} \end{cases}$$

$$S_{ii} = 2Bd\delta_K \sqrt{(|\sigma_i(f)|^2 + |\sigma_i(g)|^2)} \qquad \text{if } i \geq 3.$$

The astute reader will observe that sampling such an f' may be difficult: this is why we will later introduce $\mathcal{O}^{\mathrm{approx}}$. Oracle $\mathcal{O}^{\mathrm{ideal}}$ then defines $h' = f'/g \bmod q$ (recall that g is invertible modulo q) and returns $\mathcal{A}(h')$.

Note that z and t only appear in S_{11} (and $S_{22} = S_{11}$ if σ_1 is a complex embedding). Since $|\sigma_1(f) - z\sigma_1(g)|/|\sigma_1(g)| = |\sigma_1(h_K) - z|$, we obtain that the success probability of the oracle depends only on $t + \ln|z - \sigma_1(h_K)|$ when t and z vary, as required (recall that h, f and g are fixed once and for all).

---

[3] The term "absolute precision" refers here to $|\tilde{x} - x| \leq 2^{-\ell}$, as opposed to the "relative precision" which would be $\frac{|\tilde{x} - x|}{|x|} \leq 2^{-\ell}$.

In Claim 5.8 below, we show that the oracle $\mathcal{O}^{\text{ideal}}$ satisfies all the desired conditions to be an OHCP oracle and the conditions of Proposition 2.10. This will imply that one can efficiently recover an approximation of $\sigma_1(h_K)$ by using the oracle $\mathcal{O}^{\text{ideal}}$ as a black box.

Claim 5.8. There exist a parameter $\kappa_0 = \text{poly}(\text{Adv}(\mathcal{A})^{-1}, \log q, \log \Delta_K)$ and an algorithm $\mathcal{B}'$ that takes as input any parameter $\kappa \geq \kappa_0$ and outputs $\widetilde{\sigma_1(h_K)} \in \sigma_1(K_{\mathbb{R}})$ such that $|\widetilde{\sigma_1(h_K)} - \sigma_1(h_K)| \leq B^2 \cdot \exp(-\kappa)$ with probability $\geq 1 - \exp(-\kappa)$. Algorithm $\mathcal{B}'$ runs in time $\text{poly}(\kappa)$ and makes (possibly that many) oracle queries to the OHCP oracle $\mathcal{O}^{\text{ideal}}$ described above.

The difficulty with algorithm $\mathcal{B}'$ from Claim 5.8 is that it makes oracle calls to $\mathcal{O}^{\text{ideal}}$, which we do not know how to run in polynomial time given only access to h and $\mathcal{A}$ (in order to run $\mathcal{O}^{\text{ideal}}$ efficiently, we would probably need to know f and g). To handle this difficulty, we describe another oracle $\mathcal{O}^{\text{approx}}$, whose behavior is very close to the one of $\mathcal{O}^{\text{ideal}}$, but which can be run efficiently.

On input $(z, t) \in \mathbb{R}^k \times \mathbb{R}^{\geq 0}$, the randomized oracle $\mathcal{O}^{\text{approx}}$ proceeds as follows. It first samples c_0 in $\mathbb{R}^k$ from the continuous Gaussian distribution $D_{\mathbb{R}^k, \exp(t-d), 0}$; it then defines $\mathbf{c}_1 = \psi(c_0) \in K_{\mathbb{R}}$ and $\mathbf{c}_2 = \psi(-c_0 \cdot z) \in K_{\mathbb{R}}$ (where ψ is as defined in Lemma 5.5); the oracle then samples $x \leftarrow \widetilde{D}_{R, 2Bd \cdot \delta_K, \mathbf{c}_1}$ and $y \leftarrow \widetilde{D}_{R, 2Bd \cdot \delta_K, \mathbf{c}_2}$ (see Lemma 2.2); finally, the oracle runs $\mathcal{A}$ on input $\hat{h} = x \cdot h + y \bmod q$, and outputs $\mathcal{A}(\hat{h})$.

Oracle $\mathcal{O}^{\text{approx}}$ can indeed be run in polynomial time from h. Let us now write $\hat{f} = x \cdot f + y \cdot g$, so that $\hat{h} = \hat{f}/g \bmod q$. Observe that $\Pr(\mathcal{O}^{\text{approx}}(z, t) = 1) = \Pr(\mathcal{A}(\hat{h}) = 1)$, and $\Pr(\mathcal{O}^{\text{ideal}}(z, t) = 1) = \Pr(\mathcal{A}(h') = 1)$, where $\hat{h}$ and h' are two random variables. So $|\Pr(\mathcal{O}^{\text{approx}}(z, t) = 1) - \Pr(\mathcal{O}^{\text{ideal}}(z, t) = 1)| \leq \text{dist}(\hat{h}, h')$. Since g is fixed, we have $\text{dist}(\hat{h}, h') = \text{dist}(\hat{f}, f')$, and we obtain that

$$|\Pr(\mathcal{O}^{\text{approx}}(z, t) = 1) - \Pr(\mathcal{O}^{\text{ideal}}(z, t) = 1)| \leq \text{dist}(\hat{f}, f') \leq 2^{-\Omega(d)}.$$

The last inequality comes from Lemma 5.5 and Lemma 2.2.

To conclude, algorithm $\mathcal{B}$ is obtained by taking algorithm $\mathcal{B}'$ of Claim 5.8, but replacing its oracle calls to $\mathcal{O}^{\text{ideal}}$ by oracle calls to $\mathcal{O}^{\text{approx}}$, and taking $\kappa = \max(\kappa_0, d, \ell + 2\ln(B))$. By assumption on $\log q, \text{Adv}(\mathcal{A}), \ell$ and $\log \Delta_K$, we know that $\kappa \leq 2^{o(d)}$ (recall that $B \leq q$), so that algorithm $\mathcal{B}$ makes at most $2^{o(d)}$ oracle calls to $\mathcal{O}^{\text{approx}}$. Hence, we obtain that

$$|\Pr(\mathcal{B} \text{ succeeds}) - \Pr(\mathcal{B}' \text{ succeeds})| \leq 2^{o(d)} \cdot 2^{-\Omega(d)} = 2^{-\Omega(d)}.$$

This completes the proof of Lemma 5.7. $\square$

Proof (Claim 5.8). First, we need to check that the oracle $\mathcal{O}^{\text{ideal}}$ is a valid OHCP oracle. Let us write $z^* = \sigma_1(h_K)$. Since $\sigma_1(h_K) = \sigma_1(f)/\sigma_1(g)$, we know by choice of f and g that $\|z^*\| \in [1/B^2, B^2]$. Hence, the oracle $\mathcal{O}^{\text{ideal}}$ and scale parameter $D = B^2$ form a valid instance of the $(\varepsilon, \delta, \beta)$-OHCP problem (cf Definition 2.9), for any $\varepsilon \in (0,1)$, any $\delta \in (0, 1/B^4]$ and any $\beta \geq 1$.

We will show below that for all $\kappa \geq \kappa_0$ with

$$\kappa_0 := \max\left(4\mathrm{Adv}(\mathcal{A})^{-1}, 8d(1 + \ln(q\Delta_K^{1/d})), 4\ln(B)\right),$$

the OHCP oracle satisfies the conditions of Proposition 2.10, with

$$p_\infty = \Pr_{u \leftarrow U(R_q)} (\mathcal{A}(u) = 1) \quad \text{and} \quad s^* = 0.$$

More formally, letting $p(t)$ denote $\Pr(\mathcal{O}^{\mathrm{ideal}}(\mathbf{0}, t) = 1)$ as in Proposition 2.10, we prove that

1. $p(s^*) - p_\infty \geq 1/\kappa$;
2. $|p(t) - p_\infty| \leq 2\exp(-t/\kappa)$ for any $t \geq 0$;
3. for any $t_1, t_2 \geq 0$, it holds that $|p(t_1) - p(t_2)| \leq \kappa\sqrt{|t_1 - t_2|}$.

Using Proposition 2.10, we the conclude that there exists an algorithm $\mathcal{B}'$ solving the $(\exp(-\kappa), \exp(-\kappa), 1 + 1/\kappa)$-OHCP problem in time $\mathrm{poly}(\kappa)$ by making oracle calls to $\mathcal{O}^{\mathrm{ideal}}$. Thanks to the condition $\kappa \geq 4\ln(B)$, it holds that $\exp(-\kappa) \leq 1/B^4$ is a valid choice of δ. Moreover, using the fact that $B \leq q$, we see that $\kappa_0 = \mathrm{poly}(\mathrm{Adv}(\mathcal{A})^{-1}, \log q, \log \Delta_K)$, which proves Claim 5.8. We now proceed to prove the three properties above.

Property 1. We want to show that $p(s^*)$ is very close to $\Pr(\mathcal{A}(\phi_B(h)) = 1)$, which will allow us to conclude with Lemma 5.6. Observe that by definition of the OHCP oracle $\mathcal{O}^{\mathrm{ideal}}$, we know that $p(s^*) = \Pr(\mathcal{A}(h') = 1)$, where $h' = f'/g \bmod q$. So in order to bound the difference between $\Pr\left(\mathcal{A}(\phi_B(h) = 1\right)$ and $p(s^*)$, it suffices to bound the statistical distance between the two random variables $\phi_B(h)$ and h', which is equivalent to bounding $\mathrm{dist}(g \cdot \phi_B(h), f')$ (i.e., it suffices to consider the numerator since the denominator is g in both cases).

Using Lemma 5.5 with $c_1 = c_2 = 0$ and $s = 2Bd\delta_K$, we know that the distribution of $g \cdot \phi_B(h)$ is within $2^{-\Omega(d)}$ statistical distance from $D_{I,\mathbf{S}_2,\mathbf{0}}$, where $\mathbf{S}_2$ is a diagonal matrix with i-th diagonal entry equal to $2Bd\delta_K \cdot \sqrt{|\sigma_i(f)|^2 + |\sigma_i(g)|^2}$. Moreover, by definition of $\mathcal{O}^{\mathrm{ideal}}$, the distribution of f' is $D_{I,\mathbf{S}_1,\mathbf{0}}$, where $\mathbf{S}_1$ is identical to $\mathbf{S}_2$, except for first diagonal coefficient (or first two diagonal coefficients if σ_1 is complex), which is equal to

$$\sqrt{(2Bd\delta_K)^2(|\sigma_1(f)|^2 + |\sigma_1(g)|^2) + \exp(-2d) \cdot |\sigma_1(f)|^2}.$$

We now apply Lemma 2.3 to show that these two Gaussian distributions are statistically close. We first check that $\eta_{1/2}(\mathbf{S}_i^{-1}I) \leq 1/2$, for $i \in \{1, 2\}$. We know from Eq. (2.1) that

$$\eta_{1/2}(\mathbf{S}_i^{-1}I) \leq \sqrt{\frac{\ln(2d(1+2))}{\pi}} \cdot \lambda_d(\mathbf{S}_i^{-1}I)$$

$$\leq \sqrt{d} \cdot \lambda_d(\mathbf{S}_i^{-1}I)$$

Recall that $I = \langle f \rangle + \langle g \rangle$, so that $f \in I$. Hence, we know that the $\mathbf{S}_i^{-1} \cdot f \cdot r_j$'s are linearly independent vectors of $\mathbf{S}_i^{-1} \cdot I$ (recall that the r_j's form a basis of R). For every j, it holds that $\|\mathbf{S}_i^{-1} \cdot f \cdot r_j\| \le \delta_K \cdot \|\mathbf{S}_i^{-1} \cdot f\| \le \delta_K \cdot \sqrt{d}/(2Bd\delta_K)$ (since every diagonal coefficient of $\mathbf{S}_i$ is no smaller than the corresponding coefficient of f multiplied by $2Bd\delta_K$). Hence, we conclude that $\lambda_d(\mathbf{S}_i^{-1}I) \le 1/(2\sqrt{d})$ and that $\eta_{1/2}(\mathbf{S}_i^{-1}I) \le 1/2$, as desired. We can apply Lemma 2.3 and we obtain that

$$\mathrm{dist}(D_{I,\mathbf{S}_1,0}, D_{I,\mathbf{S}_2,0}) \le 4\sqrt{d} \cdot \sqrt{\left\|\mathbf{S}_2^{-1}\mathbf{S}_1 - \mathbf{I}_d\right\|}.$$

The matrix $\mathbf{S}_2^{-1}\mathbf{S}_1 - \mathbf{I}_d$ is zero, except for the top-left coefficient (or for the first two top-left coefficients if σ_1 is a complex embedding), which is equal to $\sqrt{1+\eta} - 1$ where $\eta = \exp(-2d) \cdot |\sigma_1(f)|^2/((2Bd\delta_K)^2 \cdot (|\sigma_1(f)|^2 + |\sigma_1(g)|^2))$. Since $\eta \le \exp(-2d)$, we conclude that $|\sqrt{1+\eta} - 1| \le \exp(-2d)$, and so $\left\|\mathbf{S}_2^{-1}\mathbf{S}_1 - \mathbf{I}_d\right\| \le \exp(-2d)$ (or $\le 2\exp(-2d)$ in case we had two non-zero coefficients). We finally obtain that $D_{I,\mathbf{S}_1,0} \approx_{2^{-\Omega(d)}} D_{I,\mathbf{S}_2,0}$, which in turn shows that

$$|p(s^*) - \Pr\left(\mathcal{A}(\phi_B(h)) = 1\right)| \le 2^{-\Omega(d)}.$$

Finally, since $h \in H$, we know from Lemma 5.6 that $|\Pr(\mathcal{A}(\phi_B(h)) = 1) - p_\infty| \ge \mathrm{Adv}(\mathcal{A})/2$. Wlog, we can assume that $\Pr(\mathcal{A}(\phi_B(h)) = 1) - p_\infty \ge 0$ (otherwise we can simply consider $\mathcal{A}' = 1 - \mathcal{A}$), from which we obtain that

$$p(s^*) - p_\infty \ge \mathrm{Adv}(\mathcal{A})/2 - 2^{-\Omega(d)} \ge \mathrm{Adv}(\mathcal{A})/4,$$

where the last inequality holds asymptotically when d tends to infinity, since we assumed that $1/\mathrm{Adv}(\mathcal{A}) \le 2^{o(d)}$. By choice of κ, this implies that $p(s^*) - p_\infty \ge 1/\kappa$.

Property 2. To prove this second property, we want to show that when t is sufficiently large, then the distribution of $f' \bmod q$ (where f' is implicitly computed by the oracle $\mathcal{O}^{\mathrm{ideal}}$ as defined above) is statistically close to uniform in $R \bmod qR$. Recall that the support of f' is I, which may be a strict subset of R. However, we know that $I = \langle f \rangle + \langle g \rangle$ is coprime to $\langle q \rangle$. So if $\widetilde{f} \in I$ is uniform in $I/(qI)$, then $\widetilde{f} + qR$ is a uniform class of $R/(qR)$. Hence, it suffices to show that f' is statistically close to uniform in $I/(qI)$.

Recall that f' is sampled from the distribution $D_{I,\mathbf{S}}$, where $\mathbf{S}$ is a diagonal matrix with positive diagonal coefficients, with $S_{11} \ge \exp(t - d) \cdot |\sigma_1(f)|$ (we consider $z = 0$ here) and $S_{ii} \ge |\sigma_i(f)|$ for $i \ge 2$. Taking the product, we conclude that $\prod_i S_{ii} \ge \exp(t - d) \cdot \mathcal{N}(f)$. Let us call c the quantity $c = (\exp(t - d)\mathcal{N}(f)/(\mathcal{N}(qI) \cdot \Delta_K))^{1/d}$. Using Lemma 2.8, we know that when t is sufficiently large so that $c \ge 1$, then it holds that $1 \ge \eta_\varepsilon(\mathbf{S}^{-1} \cdot (qI))$ for $\varepsilon = \exp(-c^2d)$. Moreover, applying Lemma 2.4 to $L_1 = \mathbf{S}^{-1} \cdot (qI)$ and $L_2 = \mathbf{S}^{-1} \cdot I$, we see that

$$\mathrm{dist}\left(D_{\mathbf{S}^{-1} \cdot I,1} \bmod \mathbf{S}^{-1} \cdot (qI), U(\mathbf{S}^{-1} \cdot I \bmod \mathbf{S}^{-1} \cdot (qI))\right) \le 2\exp(-c^2d).$$

Multiplying the outputs of these two distributions by $\mathbf{S}$, we finally obtain

$$\text{dist}\Big(D_{I,\mathbf{S}} \bmod qI, U(I \bmod qI)\Big) \leq 2\exp(-c^2 d).$$

Using the fact that $c^2 \geq c$ (as $c \geq 1$), that $\exp(x) \geq x$ for all $x \in \mathbb{R}$, and that $\mathcal{N}(I) \leq \mathcal{N}(f)$, we obtain the upper bound

$$2\exp(-c^2 d) \leq 2\exp(-cd) \leq 2\exp\big(-e^{(t-d-\ln(q^d \Delta_K))/d} \cdot d\big)$$
$$\leq 2\exp\big(-(t - d(1 + \ln(q\Delta_K^{1/d})))\big).$$

If $t \geq 2d(1 + \ln(q\Delta_K^{1/d}))$, then $(t - d(1 + \ln(q\Delta_K^{1/d})) \geq t/2$ and $c \geq 1$, which implies that

$$|p(t) - p_\infty| \leq 2\exp(-t/2) \leq 2\exp(-t/\kappa).$$

For smaller t, note that $t \leq \kappa/2$. In this case, the upper bound $2\exp(-t/\kappa)$ is at least 1, and so the property is also satisfied.

Property 3. Let us fix some $t_1 \geq t_2 \geq 0$. We want to show that $|p(t_1) - p(t_2)| \leq \kappa \cdot \sqrt{|t_1 - t_2|}$. Observe first that since p takes values in $[0, 1]$ and $\kappa \geq 1$, then the condition is always satisfied when $|t_1 - t_2| \geq 1$. We will hence assume wlog that $0 \leq t_1 - t_2 \leq 1$.

We know from the definition of $\mathcal{O}^{\text{ideal}}$ that $|p(t_1) - p(t_2)| \leq \text{dist}(D_{I,\mathbf{S}_1}, D_{I,\mathbf{S}_2})$, where $\mathbf{S}_1$ and $\mathbf{S}_2$ are diagonal and equal, except for their for top-left coefficient (or two top-left coefficients if σ_1 is a complex embedding):

$$(S_1)_{11} = \sqrt{c + (\exp(t_1 - d)|\sigma_1(f)|)^2} \quad \text{and} \quad (S_2)_{11} = \sqrt{c + (\exp(t_2 - d)|\sigma_1(f)|)^2},$$

for some $c \geq 0$. As when proving Property 1, one can check that $\eta_{1/2}(\mathbf{S}_1^{-1}I)$, $\eta_{1/2}(\mathbf{S}_2^{-1}I) \leq 1/2$. Therefore, we can apply Lemma 2.3 to obtain that

$$\text{dist}\big(D_{I,\mathbf{S}_1}, D_{I,\mathbf{S}_2}\big) \leq 4\sqrt{d} \cdot \sqrt{\big\|\mathbf{S}_2^{-1}\mathbf{S}_1 - \mathbf{I}_d\big\|}.$$

Once again, the matrix $\mathbf{S}_2^{-1}\mathbf{S}_1 - \mathbf{I}_d$ is zero, except for its top-left coefficient (or two top-left coefficients) which is equal to

$$\sqrt{\frac{c + (\exp(t_1 - d)|\sigma_1(f)|)^2}{c + (\exp(t_2 - d)|\sigma_1(f)|)^2}} - 1 \leq \sqrt{\frac{(\exp(t_1 - d)|\sigma_1(f)|)^2}{(\exp(t_2 - d)|\sigma_1(f)|)^2}} - 1 = \exp(t_1 - t_2) - 1.$$

The first inequality comes from the fact that $t_1 \geq t_2$ (and c and $(\exp(t_2 - d)|\sigma_1(f)|)^2$ are non-negative). Finally, since $0 \leq t_1 - t_2 \leq 1$, we conclude that $\exp(t_1 - t_2) - 1 \leq 2|t_1 - t_2|$. This in turns implies that $|p(t_1) - p(t_2)| \leq 8\sqrt{d}\sqrt{|t_1 - t_2|} \leq \kappa\sqrt{|t_1 - t_2|}$, as desired. $\qquad\square$

Acknowledgment. The authors thank Koen de Boer, Léo Ducas, Guillaume Hanrot, Miruna Rosca aux Adeline Roux-Langlois for insightful discussions. The first author was supported in part by CyberSecurity Research Flanders with reference number VR20- 192203 and by the Research Council KU Leuven grant C14/18/067 on Cryptanalysis of Post-quantum Cryptography. The second author was supported in part by European Union Horizon 2020 Research and Innovation Program Grant 780701 and BPI-France in the context of the national project RISQ (P141580).

References

[ABD16] Albrecht, M., Bai, S., Ducas, L.: A subfield lattice attack on overstretched NTRU assumptions. In: Robshaw, M., Katz, J. (eds.) CRYPTO 2016. LNCS, vol. 9814, pp. 153–178. Springer, Heidelberg (2016). https://doi.org/10.1007/978-3-662-53018-4_6

[AD17] Albrecht, M.R., Deo, A.: Large modulus ring-LWE $\geq$ module-LWE. In: Takagi, T., Peyrin, T. (eds.) ASIACRYPT 2017. LNCS, vol. 10624, pp. 267–296. Springer, Cham (2017). https://doi.org/10.1007/978-3-319-70694-8_10

[BBC20] Bernstein, D.J., et al.: NTRU Prime round-3 candidate to the NIST post-quantum cryptography standardisation project (2020). https://ntruprime.cr.yp.to/

[Bel04a] Belabas, K.: A relative van Hoeij algorithm over number fields. J. Symb. Comput. **37**(5), 641–668 (2004)

[Bel04b] Belabas, K.: Topics in computational algebraic number theory. J. théorie des nombres de Bordeaux **16**, 19–63 (2004)

[CDH20] Chen, C., et al.: NTRU round-3 candidate to the NIST post-quantum cryptography standardisation project (2020). https://ntru.org/

[CDW21] Cramer, R., Ducas, L., Wesolowski, B.: Mildly short vectors in cyclotomic ideal lattices in quantum polynomial time. J. ACM **68**(2), 1–26 (2021)

[CJL16] Cheon, J.H., Jeong, J., Lee, C.: An algorithm for NTRU problems and cryptanalysis of the GGH multilinear map without an encoding of zero. LMS J. Comput. Math. **19**(A), 255–266 (2016)

[Coh95] Cohen, H.: A Course in Computational Algebraic Number Theory. Springer, Heidelberg (1995). https://doi.org/10.1007/978-3-662-02945-9

[Coh00] Cohen, H.: Advanced Topics in Computational Number Theory. Springer, Heidelberg (2000). https://doi.org/10.1007/978-1-4419-8489-0

[dBDPW20] de Boer, K., Ducas, L., Pellet-Mary, A., Wesolowski, B.: Random self-reducibility of ideal-SVP via arakelov random walks. In: Micciancio, D., Ristenpart, T. (eds.) CRYPTO 2020. LNCS, vol. 12171, pp. 243–273. Springer, Cham (2020). https://doi.org/10.1007/978-3-030-56880-1_9

[FS10] Fieker, C., Stehlé, D.: Short bases of lattices over number fields. In: Hanrot, G., Morain, F., Thomé, E. (eds.) ANTS 2010. LNCS, vol. 6197, pp. 157–173. Springer, Heidelberg (2010). https://doi.org/10.1007/978-3-642-14518-6_15

[GGH13] Garg, S., Gentry, C., Halevi, S.: Candidate multilinear maps from ideal lattices. In: Johansson, T., Nguyen, P.Q. (eds.) EUROCRYPT 2013. LNCS, vol. 7881, pp. 1–17. Springer, Heidelberg (2013). https://doi.org/10.1007/978-3-642-38348-9_1

[GPV08] Gentry, C., Peikert, C., Vaikuntanathan, V.: Trapdoors for hard lattices and new cryptographic constructions. In: STOC (2008)

[HHP03] Hoffstein, J., Howgrave-Graham, N., Pipher, J., Silverman, J.H., Whyte, W.: NTRUSign: digital signatures using the NTRU lattice. In: Joye, M. (ed.) CT-RSA 2003. LNCS, vol. 2612, pp. 122–140. Springer, Heidelberg (2003). https://doi.org/10.1007/3-540-36563-X_9

[HPS98] Hoffstein, J., Pipher, J., Silverman, J.H.: NTRU: a ring-based public key cryptosystem. In: Buhler, J.P. (ed.) ANTS 1998. LNCS, vol. 1423, pp. 267–288. Springer, Heidelberg (1998). https://doi.org/10.1007/BFb0054868

[KF15] Kirchner, P., Fouque, P.-A.: An improved BKW algorithm for LWE with applications to cryptography and lattices. In: Gennaro, R., Robshaw, M. (eds.) CRYPTO 2015. LNCS, vol. 9215, pp. 43–62. Springer, Heidelberg (2015). https://doi.org/10.1007/978-3-662-47989-6_3

[KF17] Kirchner, P., Fouque, P.-A.: Revisiting lattice attacks on overstretched NTRU parameters. In: Coron, J.-S., Nielsen, J.B. (eds.) EUROCRYPT 2017. LNCS, vol. 10210, pp. 3–26. Springer, Cham (2017). https://doi.org/10.1007/978-3-319-56620-7_1

[KLL84] Kannan, R., Lenstra, A.K., Lovász, L.: Polynomial factorization and nonrandomness of bits of algebraic and some transcendental numbers. In: STOC (1984)

[LLL82] Lenstra, A.K., Lenstra, H.W., Jr., Lovász, L.: Factoring polynomials with rational coefficients. Math Ann 261, 515–534 (1982)

[LPR10] Lyubashevsky, V., Peikert, C., Regev, O.: On ideal lattices and learning with errors over rings. In: Gilbert, H. (ed.) EUROCRYPT 2010. LNCS, vol. 6110, pp. 1–23. Springer, Heidelberg (2010). https://doi.org/10.1007/978-3-642-13190-5_1

[LS15] Langlois, A., Stehlé, D.: Worst-case to average-case reductions for module lattices. Des Codes Cryptogr. 75, 565–599 (2015)

[LSS14] Langlois, A., Stehlé, D., Steinfeld, R.: GGHLite: more efficient multilinear maps from ideal lattices. In: Nguyen, P.Q., Oswald, E. (eds.) EUROCRYPT 2014. LNCS, vol. 8441, pp. 239–256. Springer, Heidelberg (2014). https://doi.org/10.1007/978-3-642-55220-5_14

[LTV12] López-Alt, A., Tromer, E., Vaikuntanathan, V.: On-the-fly multiparty computation on the cloud via multikey fully homomorphic encryption. In: STOC (2012)

[MR07] Micciancio, D., Regev, O.: Worst-case to average-case reductions based on gaussian measures. SIAM J. Comput. 37(1), 267–302 (2007)

[Pei10] Peikert, C.: An efficient and parallel gaussian sampler for lattices. In: Rabin, T. (ed.) CRYPTO 2010. LNCS, vol. 6223, pp. 80–97. Springer, Heidelberg (2010). https://doi.org/10.1007/978-3-642-14623-7_5

[Pei16] Peikert, C.: A decade of lattice cryptography. Found. Trends Theor. Comput. Sci. 10(4) 2016

[PHS19] Pellet-Mary, A., Hanrot, G., Stehlé, D.: Approx-SVP in ideal lattices with pre-processing. In: Ishai, Y., Rijmen, V. (eds.) EUROCRYPT 2019. LNCS, vol. 11477, pp. 685–716. Springer, Cham (2019). https://doi.org/10.1007/978-3-030-17656-3_24

[PRS17] Peikert, C., Regev, O., Stephens-Davidowitz, N.: Pseudorandomness of ring-LWE for any ring and modulus. In: STOC (2017)

[Reg09] Regev, O.: On lattices, learning with errors, random linear codes, and cryptography. J. ACM 56, 1–40 (2009)

[Rob97]   Roblot, F.-X.: Algorithmes de factorisation dans les extensions relatives et applications de la conjecture de Stark à la construction des corps de classes de rayon. PhD thesis, Université Bordeaux 1 (1997). http://math. univ-lyon1.fr/~roblot/resources/these.pdf

[RSW18]   Rosca, M., Stehlé, D., Wallet, A.: On the ring-LWE and polynomial-LWE problems. In: Nielsen, J.B., Rijmen, V. (eds.) EUROCRYPT 2018. LNCS, vol. 10820, pp. 146–173. Springer, Cham (2018). https://doi.org/10.1007/ 978-3-319-78381-9_6

[Sch87]   Schnorr, C.-P.: A hierarchy of polynomial lattice basis reduction algorithms. Theor. Comput. Sci. **53**, 201–224 (1987)

[SS11]   Stehlé, D., Steinfeld, R.: Making NTRU as secure as worst-case problems over ideal lattices. In: Paterson, K.G. (ed.) EUROCRYPT 2011. LNCS, vol. 6632, pp. 27–47. Springer, Heidelberg (2011). https://doi.org/10. 1007/978-3-642-20465-4_4

[SS13]   Stehlé, D., Steinfeld, R.: Making NTRUEncrypt and NTRUSign as secure as standard worst-case problems over ideal lattices. IACR ePrint 2013/004 (2013)

[SSTX09]   Stehlé, D., Steinfeld, R., Tanaka, K., Xagawa, K.: Efficient public key encryption based on ideal lattices. In: Matsui, M. (ed.) ASIACRYPT 2009. LNCS, vol. 5912, pp. 617–635. Springer, Heidelberg (2009). https:// doi.org/10.1007/978-3-642-10366-7_36

[Sut16]   Sutherland, A.: Lecture notes of Number Theory I, taught at MIT (2016). https://math.mit.edu/classes/18.785/2016fa/LectureNotes12.pdf

[WW18]   Wang, Y., Wang, M.: Provably secure NTRUEncrypt over any cyclotomic field. In: SAC (2018)

A Geometric Approach to Linear Cryptanalysis

Tim Beyne[(✉)]

Imec-COSIC, ESAT, KU Leuven, Leuven, Belgium
tim.beyne@esat.kuleuven.be

Abstract. A new interpretation of linear cryptanalysis is proposed. This 'geometric approach' unifies all common variants of linear cryptanalysis, reveals links between various properties, and suggests additional generalizations. For example, new insights into invariants corresponding to non-real eigenvalues of correlation matrices and a generalization of the link between zero-correlation and integral attacks are obtained. Geometric intuition leads to a fixed-key motivation for the piling-up principle, which is illustrated by explaining and generalizing previous results relating invariants and linear approximations. Rank-one approximations are proposed to analyze cell-oriented ciphers, and used to resolve an open problem posed by Beierle, Canteaut and Leander at FSE 2019. In particular, it is shown how such approximations can be analyzed automatically using Riemannian optimization.

Keywords: Linear cryptanalysis · Nonlinear cryptanalysis · Piling-up lemma · Correlation matrices · Block cipher invariants

1 Introduction

At EUROCRYPT 1993, Matsui [31] introduced linear cryptanalysis as a new known-plaintext attack on the block cipher DES. Linear cryptanalysis is based on probabilistic linear relations or *linear approximations*, a concept introduced by Tardy-Corfdir and Gilbert [36].

The success of Matsui's attack led to the development of a myriad of extensions and variants of linear approximations, and to more advanced techniques for their analysis [16,32]. Despite significant advances, many questions related to linear cryptanalysis and its theoretical foundations remain unresolved.

Kaliski and Robshaw [25] suggested using multiple linear approximations. Hermelin, Cho and Nyberg [23] proposed the related multidimensional linear attack. Both extensions are widely used. Generalizations of linear cryptanalysis to groups other than $\mathbb{F}_2^n$ were proposed by Granboulan, Levieil and Piret [20] and Baignères, Stern and Vaudenay [3]. The use of nonlinear approximations is another natural extension, and has been attempted by Knudsen and Robshaw [26], Harpes, Kramer and Massey [21] with I/O sums, Harpes and Massey [22] with partitioning attacks and recently by Beierle, Canteaut and Leander [4].

© International Association for Cryptologic Research 2021
M. Tibouchi and H. Wang (Eds.): ASIACRYPT 2021, LNCS 13090, pp. 36–66, 2021.
https://doi.org/10.1007/978-3-030-92062-3_2

All of the above techniques rely on heuristic methods to glue together several approximations over multiple rounds of a cipher. These methods will be collectively referred to as the *piling-up principle*. This principle has traditionally been justified using independence or Markov chain assumptions [2,31,42], which can be related to earlier work on Markov ciphers in the context of differential cryptanalysis [28]. However, such assumptions are hard to reconcile with the key-dependence of approximations and the increased importance of cryptographic permutations. In fact, key-dependence is one of the fundamental difficulties of nonlinear cryptanalysis. Alternatively, the correlation matrix framework of Daemen *et al.* [16] is more suitable for the fixed-key setting. It motivates the piling-up principle using the dominant trail hypothesis. Beierle *et al.* [4] extend this approach by applying linear cryptanalysis to a nonlinearly transformed variant of the cipher.

In a different direction, Rijmen and Bogdanov [13] introduced zero-correlation linear cryptanalysis to exploit unbiased linear approximations. The construction of zero-correlation approximations relies on the miss-in-the-middle technique as opposed to the piling-up principle. At ASIACRYPT 2012, Bogdanov *et al.* [12] established a link between multidimensional zero-correlation approximations and integral distinguishers [27].

Finally, several lightweight block ciphers have been found vulnerable to weak-key attacks based on invariant subspaces [30] and nonlinear invariants [39]. These attacks have led to renewed interest in linear cryptanalysis and its generalizations. Abdelraheem *et al.* [1] found links between invariant subspaces and linear cryptanalysis. Moreover, nonlinear invariants provide one of the most compelling examples of nonlinearity in cryptanalysis, with applications including the analysis of SCREAM, iSCREAM, Midori-64 and MANTIS [5,39]. At ASIACRYPT 2018, it was shown that invariant subspaces and nonlinear invariants can be described as eigenvectors of correlation matrices [5]. Furthermore, one of the invariants discovered in [5] corresponds to a perfect linear approximation. These results established a strong link between nonlinear invariants and linear cryptanalysis, but a true statistical generalization of the nonlinear invariant attack was left open. Lastly, Beierle *et al.* [4] extended the links discovered by Abdelraheem *et al.* to some classes of nonlinear invariants.

Contribution. A conceptually new way of thinking about linear cryptanalysis is introduced. It provides an alternative viewpoint for the foundations of linear cryptanalysis and has a number of concrete benefits. Firstly, it results in a systematized and unified description of the above-mentioned variants of linear cryptanalysis. Secondly, it leads to generalizations of the connections between these attacks, such as the link between integral and zero-correlation cryptanalysis and the links between invariants and linear approximations. Some of these results are illustrated in Table 1, and are discussed in more detail below. Thirdly, it suggests a general form of the piling-up principle. Finally, to illustrate the relevance for the working cryptanalyst, the approach is used to solve a problem posed by Beierle *et al.* [4].

Section 3 introduces a correspondence between cryptanalytic properties and vector spaces of complex-valued functions on the domain of a primitive. This

Table 1. Approximations for a function F from the geometric viewpoint. Here, U and V are vector spaces (of dimension d) of functions. The notation follows Sects. 3 to 5.

	Zero-correlation $C^F U \perp V$	$\xrightarrow{\text{Thm. 4.2}}$ $\xleftarrow{}$ Perfect $C^F U \subseteq V$	$\xrightarrow{\text{Sect. 5.3}}$ General $\langle V, U \rangle_F$
$d = 1$	Linear zero-correlation [13] Nonlinear zero-correlation (Ex. 4.3)	Invariant subspaces [30] Nonlinear invariants [39] Eigenvectors of C^F [5]	Linear cryptanalysis [31] Abelian groups [3] I/O sums [21] Beierle et al. [4] Rank-one (Section 6)
$d \geq 1$	Multidimensional zero-correlation [12]	Integral attacks [27] General invariants (Def. 4.3, Ex. 4.2)	Multiple linear [9,25] Multidim. linear [23] Partitioning [22] Projection, χ^2 [2,41,42]

results in a uniform description of the properties (sets, linear and nonlinear Boolean functions, ...) that are used in different variants of linear cryptanalysis. The correspondence generalizes the idea introduced in [5] that invariant subspaces and nonlinear invariants can be represented by complex vectors, which led to their characterization as eigenvectors of correlation matrices.

Definition 4.1 characterizes an approximation of a cipher as a pair of vector spaces (U, V), corresponding to input and output properties as sketched above. This results in a systematization of many variants of linear cryptanalysis, as summarized in Table 1. It will be shown that the type and quality of approximations is related to the geometric properties of the spaces U and V. Section 4.1 illustrates how this results in new insight into block cipher invariants and gives a realistic example of invariants related to non-real eigenvalues of correlation matrices, a problem that was left open at ASIACRYPT 2018 [5]. Theorem 4.2 generalizes the links between zero-correlation and integral attacks discovered by Bogdanov et al. [12]. For general approximations, *principal correlations* are introduced as a natural extension of the correlation of a linear approximation and it is shown how they relate to the complexity of optimal distinguishers discussed by Baignères, Junod and Vaudenay [2].

A general piling-up principle is given in Theorem 5.1. Its motivation is the result of geometric intuition. This avoids independence and Markov chain assumptions and simplifies working with fixed keys. Furthermore, the result evades the issues that are encountered when the dominant-trail approach of Daemen et al. is extended to the nonlinear case. Theorem 5.1 allows for much greater flexibility than previous formulations of the piling-up principle. In particular, it becomes possible to build trails that combine diverse cryptanalytic properties. This is illustrated in Sect. 5.3 by strengthening the links between linear approximations and invariants, extending previous work by Abdelraheem et al. [1] and Beierle et al. [4].

Finally, Sect. 6 introduces rank-one approximations to analyze cell-oriented ciphers. A tool to find optimal rank-one trails is introduced, and its application to searching for invariants is discussed. Perhaps surprisingly, the tool is based on numerical optimization on a Riemannian manifold. This is enabled by the generality of Sects. 3 to 5, which relaxes the search space by introducing many new types of approximations. The tool is provided as supplementary material. Rank-one approximations and the aforementioned tool are used in Sect. 7.3 to resolve a problem introduced by Beierle *et al.* [4], who describe it as "a major open problem". It is representative of other concrete problems, and its solution relies on the general techniques that are introduced in Sects. 3 to 5.

2 Functions on Abelian Groups

The goal of this section is to introduce several concepts that will be used to develop a general theory of linear cryptanalysis in Sects. 3 to 5. These concepts provide the setting for the proposed geometric approach. It is assumed that the reader is familiar with finite Abelian groups and linear algebra in finite-dimensional inner product spaces.

It will be shown in Sect. 3 that many cryptanalytic properties can be described by complex-valued functions on the domain of a primitive. Section 2.1 discusses preliminaries related to the set of such functions. Section 2.2 introduces the Fourier transformation on finite Abelian groups. This will be an important tool to simplify the effect of constant (including key) additions. Finally, Sect. 2.3 discusses the geometry of subspaces of an inner product space.

2.1 Inner Product Space of Functions

Let G be a finite Abelian group, for example the domain of a block cipher. In fact, all of the properties in this section are valid for any *set* G. However, the results in Sect. 2.2 will require the assumption that G is a finite Abelian group. The $\mathbb{C}$-vector space of all functions from G to $\mathbb{C}$, with the usual pointwise addition and scalar multiplication, will be denoted by $\mathbb{C}G$. The standard inner product between two functions $f, g \in \mathbb{C}G$ is defined by $\langle f, g \rangle = \sum_{x \in G} \overline{f(x)} g(x)$, where $\overline{f(x)}$ denotes the complex-conjugate of $f(x)$. Hence, the vector space $\mathbb{C}G$ is a finite-dimensional inner product space. One also has a norm $\|f\|_2 = \sqrt{\langle f, f \rangle}$, which carries the geometric interpretation of length. The modulus of the inner product between two normalized vectors can be interpreted as the cosine of the smallest angle enclosed by them – although for non-real vectors, several definitions of angles are plausible. The theory developed in Sects. 4 and 5 will draw on these geometric concepts for intuition.

The functions δ_x, which are equal to one at $x \in G$ and zero everywhere else, clearly form an orthonormal basis for $\mathbb{C}G$. This basis will be referred to as the *standard basis*. It follows that $\mathbb{C}G$ is isomorphic to $\mathbb{C}^{|G|}$ as an inner product space.

Recall that the tensor product of $\mathbb{C}$-vector spaces $V_1, \ldots, V_n$ is another $\mathbb{C}$-vector space $V_1 \otimes \cdots \otimes V_n$ of dimension $\prod_{i=1}^{n} \dim V_i$ together with a multilinear map $\otimes : \prod_{i=1}^{n} V_i \to \bigotimes_{i=1}^{n} V_i$, which has the universal property that it uniquely linearizes arbitrary multilinear maps. Specifically, for any $T : \prod_{i=1}^{n} V_i \to W$ linear in each variable (multilinear), there exists a unique *linear* map $L : \bigotimes_{i=1}^{n} V_i \to W$ such that $T(v_1, \ldots, v_n) = L(v_1 \otimes \cdots \otimes v_n)$.

For the purposes of this paper, readers who are not familiar with tensor products may take the following characterization as a definition. Let $G = A \oplus B$ be a direct sum of Abelian groups A and B. That is, the group G consists of all pairs (a, b) with $a \in A$ and $b \in B$. The tensor product of $\mathbb{C}A$ and $\mathbb{C}B$ can then be characterized by $\mathbb{C}A \otimes \mathbb{C}B \cong \mathbb{C}G$. Indeed, the linear map defined by $\delta_{(a,b)} \mapsto \delta_a \otimes \delta_b$ for all $a \in A$ and $b \in B$ is an isomorphism. In this paper, $\mathbb{C}G$ and $\mathbb{C}A \otimes \mathbb{C}B$ will always be identified through this isomorphism. Hence, for $f \in \mathbb{C}A$ and $g \in \mathbb{C}B$, it can be said that $f \otimes g \in \mathbb{C}G$ with $(f \otimes g)(a, b) = f(a) g(b)$.

A rank-one vector $v \in \bigotimes_{i=1}^{n} V_i$ is a vector of the form $v = v_1 \otimes \cdots \otimes v_n$. Given bases for $V_1, \ldots, V_n$, the set of all their tensor products is a basis of rank-one vectors for $\bigotimes_{i=1}^{n} V_i$. More generally, for any vector v there exists an integer $r \geq 0$ such that $v = \sum_{i=1}^{r} \lambda_i \bigotimes_{j=1}^{n} v_{i,j}$, for some vectors $v_{i,j} \in V_j$ and scalars $\lambda_i \in \mathbb{C}$. The smallest r for which such a decomposition exists is called the tensor rank of v.

2.2 Fourier Analysis

Given a function $f \in \mathbb{C}G$ and a constant $t \in G$, one can define a new function by $x \mapsto f(x + t)$. The effect of translations on the coordinates of functions in the standard basis of $\mathbb{C}G$ is inconvenient: the basis vectors are shuffled around by the permutation $\delta_x \mapsto \delta_{x+t}$, which corresponds to multiplication by a Toeplitz matrix. It would be more convenient if the effect of translation would be a simple scaling of the coordinates, *i.e.* multiplication by a diagonal matrix. This can be achieved by working with respect to a different basis.

To achieve the goal of diagonalization, the new basis vectors should be eigenvectors of the set of translation operations. This is achieved for any homomorphism $\chi : G \to \mathbb{C}^\times$ from G to the multiplicative group of complex numbers $\mathbb{C}^\times = \mathbb{C} \setminus \{0\}$, since $\chi(x + t) = \chi(t)\chi(x)$ for any $x, t \in G$. This leads to the following definition.

Definition 2.1 (Group characters [37]). *Let G be a finite Abelian group. A (complex) character of G is a group homomorphism $G \to \mathbb{C}^\times$. The (Pontryagin) dual of G is the group $\widehat{G}$ of all characters of G with respect to the pointwise product.*

It is not hard to see that $\widehat{G}$ is indeed an Abelian group. For example, the inverse of $\chi \in \widehat{G}$ is the character $x \mapsto \chi(-x)$. That is, $\chi(-x) = \overline{\chi(x)}$.

Example 2.1. The dual of the additive group $\mathbb{F}_2$ is $\widehat{\mathbb{F}}_2 = \{x \mapsto 1, x \mapsto (-1)^x\}$. Indeed, these are the only two group homomorphisms $\mathbb{F}_2 \to \mathbb{C}^\times$. ▷

The functions in the dual group $\widehat{G}$ form a basis for $\mathbb{C}G$ that behaves well with respect to translation. Further properties of the dual group are given in Theorem 2.1 below. In particular, property (2) shows that the basis of characters is orthogonal.

Theorem 2.1 (Properties of dual groups [37]**).** *If G is a finite Abelian group with dual $\widehat{G}$, then*

(1) The dual group $\widehat{G}$ is isomorphic to G.
(2) For all $\chi, \psi \in \widehat{G}$, it holds that $\langle \chi, \psi \rangle = |G|\, \delta_\chi(\psi)$.
(3) If $G = H_1 \oplus H_2$ with $\oplus$ the internal direct sum, then $\widehat{G} = \widehat{H}_1 \oplus \widehat{H}_2$.

By Theorem 2.1 (1), $\widehat{G}$ can be identified with G. In general, this identification is not unique. However, there is a *functorial* isomorphism between the double dual of G and G itself, which identifies $g \in G$ with the evaluation map $\chi \mapsto \chi(g)$ in the dual of $\widehat{G}$ [37]. This result justifies the term 'dual group'. In order to avoid arbitrary choices, isomorphisms between $\widehat{G}$ and G will be avoided throughout this paper. This makes no difference in specific calculations, but it is theoretically more elegant.

Example 2.2. Since the additive group $\mathbb{F}_2^n$ is the direct sum of n copies of $\mathbb{F}_2$, it follows from Theorem 2.1 (3) that the dual group is essentially the direct sum of n copies of $\widehat{\mathbb{F}}_2$. Specifically, $\widehat{\mathbb{F}}_2^n = \{x \mapsto \prod_{i=1}^n (-1)^{u_i x_i} = (-1)^{u^\top x} \mid u \in \mathbb{F}_2^n\}$. Note that identifying $\widehat{\mathbb{F}}_2^n$ and $\mathbb{F}_2^n$ requires choosing a basis for $\mathbb{F}_2^n$.

The Fourier transformation $\mathcal{F}$ is essentially a change of basis from the standard basis to the character basis. However, in order to avoid identifying $\widehat{G}$ and G, we shall define $\mathcal{F}$ as a transformation from $\mathbb{C}G$ to $\mathbb{C}\widehat{G}$. With this definition, the Fourier transformation maps a character $\chi \in \widehat{G} \subset \mathbb{C}G$ directly to a multiple of the standard basis vector $\delta_\chi \in \mathbb{C}\widehat{G}$. Since group characters are orthogonal, Definition 2.2 achieves the desired basis transformation.

Definition 2.2 (Fourier transformation [37]**).** *Let $f : G \to \mathbb{C}$ be a function. The Fourier transformation of f is the function $\widehat{f} : \widehat{G} \to \mathbb{C}$ defined by*

$$\widehat{f}(\chi) = \langle \chi, f \rangle = \sum_{x \in G} \overline{\chi(x)} f(x).$$

The Fourier transformation is the map $\mathcal{F} : \mathbb{C}G \to \mathbb{C}\widehat{G}$ such that $\mathcal{F}f = \widehat{f}$.

The transformation $\mathcal{F}$ is a vector space isomorphism. In fact, since $\mathbb{C}G$ and $\mathbb{C}\widehat{G}$ are algebras with either the pointwise product or convolution, $\mathcal{F}$ is an isomorphism of algebras which swaps the pointwise product and convolution. This is by construction, since the set of convolution operators is generated by translations.

The vector space $\mathbb{C}\widehat{G}$ is also an inner product space. In fact, due to the orthogonality of characters, the inner product between $f_1, f_2 \in \mathbb{C}G$ coincides with the inner product of their Fourier transforms up to a constant factor: $\langle \widehat{f}_1, \widehat{f}_2 \rangle = |G| \langle f_1, f_2 \rangle$. In other words, $\mathcal{F}/\sqrt{|G|}$ is a unitary map and $\mathcal{F}^{-1} = \mathcal{F}^*/|G|$ with $\mathcal{F}^*$ the adjoint (conjugate transpose) of $\mathcal{F}$.

To end this section, consider the case $G = A \oplus B$. As mentioned above, one has $\mathbb{C}G = \mathbb{C}A \otimes \mathbb{C}B$ (technically up to isomorphism). By Theorem 2.1 (3), the dual group satisfies $\widehat{G} = \widehat{A} \oplus \widehat{B}$. Hence, one also has $\mathbb{C}\widehat{G} = \mathbb{C}\widehat{A} \otimes \mathbb{C}\widehat{B}$. Consequently, the Fourier transformation on $\mathbb{C}G$ is given by $\mathcal{F}_A \otimes \mathcal{F}_B$. Equivalently, the matrix representation of $\mathcal{F}$ in the standard basis is the Kronecker product of the matrix representations of $\mathcal{F}_A$ and $\mathcal{F}_B$ in the standard basis.

2.3 Subspaces of $\mathbb{C}G$ and $\mathbb{C}\widehat{G}$

Sections 3 and 4 will demonstrate that subspaces of $\mathbb{C}G$ and $\mathbb{C}\widehat{G}$ are often more interesting for cryptanalysis than individual functions. For this reason, it will be convenient to extend the inner product notation $\langle \cdot, \cdot \rangle$ to subspaces of $\mathbb{C}G$. For subspaces $U \subseteq \mathbb{C}G$ and $V \subseteq \mathbb{C}G$, define the linear map $\langle V, U \rangle : U \to V$ by $\langle V, U \rangle = \pi_V \iota_U$, where $\iota_U : U \to \mathbb{C}G$ is the inclusion map and $\pi_V : \mathbb{C}G \to V$ is the orthogonal projection on V. A similar definition can be given for subspaces of $\mathbb{C}\widehat{G}$. Note that $\langle V, U \rangle = \langle U, V \rangle^*$ since projection and inclusion are adjoint.

Example 2.3. Let U and V be one-dimensional subspaces of $\mathbb{C}G$ spanned by unit-norm vectors u and v respectively. By definition, $\iota_U(\lambda u) = \lambda u$ and $\pi_V(x) = v\langle v, x \rangle$. Consequently, $\langle V, U \rangle : U \to V$ is the map $\lambda u \mapsto \langle v, u \rangle \lambda v$. The matrix representation of this map is thus simply the 1×1 matrix containing the inner product $\langle v, u \rangle$.

The transformation $\langle V, U \rangle$ comes with a geometric interpretation, which will be important in Sects. 4 and 5. Due to standard properties of orthogonal projection, $\langle V, U \rangle$ maps any $u \in U$ to the nearest vector $v \in V$. In addition, no other vector in V of the same length makes a smaller angle to u than v. This suggests that $\langle V, U \rangle$ encodes all information about the 'angles' between U and V. This can be made precise using the notion of principal angles between subspaces, which is due to Jordan [24]. The characterization below follows Björck and Golub [10].

Definition 2.3 (Principal angles). *Let U and V be subspaces of an inner product space over $\mathbb{C}$ of finite dimension and let $d = \min\{\dim U, \dim V\}$. The principal angles $0 \le \theta_1 \le \ldots \le \theta_d \le \pi/2$ between U and V are recursively defined by (for $i = 1, 2, \ldots, d$)*

$$\cos \theta_i = \frac{\langle u_i, v_i \rangle}{\|u_i\|_2 \|v_i\|_2} = \max_{\substack{u \in U_i \setminus \{0\} \\ v \in V_i \setminus \{0\}}} \frac{|\langle u, v \rangle|}{\|u\|_2 \|v\|_2},$$

where $u_i \in U_i$ and $v_i \in V_i$ are nonzero vectors for which the maximum on the right is achieved with $\langle u_i, v_i \rangle$ a non-negative real number, $U_i = U \cap \{u_1, \ldots, u_{i-1}\}^{\perp}$ and $V_i = V \cap \{v_1, \ldots, v_{i-1}\}^{\perp}$.

The cosines of the principal angles are precisely the singular values of $\langle V, U \rangle$, and the singular vectors are the directions along which these angles are to be measured. This follows directly from the variational characterization of singular values. Further details may be found in [10].

3 Cryptanalytic Properties

Many cryptanalytic techniques rely only on partial information about the inputs and outputs of a primitive, such as membership of a set or the value taken by a Boolean function. Below, the structure of the inputs (or outputs) will be informally referred to as cryptanalytic input (or output) properties.

One of the obstacles to a more general approach to linear cryptanalysis and its variants, is the fact that different cryptanalytic properties are often described by disparate mathematical objects (such as sets, linear or nonlinear functions, ...). In a few cases, overcoming this difficulty has resulted in new or generalized results. Examples include the projection function approach of Wagner [42] and Baignères *et al.* [2], which enables unifying the data-complexity analysis of several attacks, and the observation that both invariant subspaces and nonlinear invariants correspond to eigenvectors of correlation matrices [5].

Section 3.1 introduces a general correspondence between cryptanalytic properties and subspaces of the inner product space $\mathbb{C}G$. It works for all properties relevant to linear cryptanalysis and its variants, and in particular generalizes both examples just mentioned above. Section 3.2 describes how properties change when a function is applied to the state. This leads to a more general perspective on correlation matrices.

3.1   Correspondence Between Properties and Subspaces

The purpose of this section is to show that the cryptanalytic properties used in linear cryptanalysis and its variants are naturally described by functions $G \to \mathbb{C}$, *i.e.* functions in the inner product space $\mathbb{C}G$ from Sect. 2.1. This will be motivated from two viewpoints, which are dual to one another. Specifically, the following two perspectives will be advanced:

(i) Cryptanalytic properties correspond to functions in $\mathbb{C}G$.
(ii) Cryptanalytic properties corrsepond to linear functions $\mathbb{C}G \to \mathbb{C}$.

From viewpoint (i), a cryptanalytic property characterizes the state of a collection of inputs or outputs. For instance, probability distributions on G can be represented by functions $G \to [0,1] \subset \mathbb{C}$. Similarly, any subset S of G has an indicator function $\mathbb{1}_S \in \mathbb{C}G$. It will be shown below that the general idea of associating not just positive numbers, but also arbitrary complex-valued weights, to the elements of G is necessary to describe other types of properties.

According to (ii), properties describe a measurement or observation of the state of a collection of inputs or outputs. Importantly, only *linear* functions of the state vector are considered in the present framework. The set of linear functions $\mathbb{C}G \to \mathbb{C}$ is itself a vector space $\mathbb{C}G^*$, *i.e.* the dual vector space of $\mathbb{C}G$. However, the explicit choice of the inner product in Sect. 2.1 identifies $\mathbb{C}G$ and $\mathbb{C}G^*$. Indeed, $f \in \mathbb{C}G$ corresponds to the function $g \mapsto \langle f, g \rangle$ in $\mathbb{C}G^*$. This correspondence will be used throughout this paper, and both (i) and (ii) will be represened by elements of $\mathbb{C}G$. For example, for a subset S, the indicator function $\mathbb{1}_S$ is dual to the function $f \mapsto \langle \mathbb{1}_S, f \rangle = \sum_{x \in S} f(x)$.

More generally, consider a subspace V of $\mathbb{C}G$. Any function in V can then be interpreted according to either (i) or (ii). The assumption that the property must correspond to a *subspace* of $\mathbb{C}G$ implies that it is possible to make arbitrary linear combinations of these functions.

Representing properties as subspaces of $\mathbb{C}G$ comes with a geometric interpretation. Specifically, the inner product yields the observed outcome when a pair of properties with interpretations (i) and (ii) are combined. This aspect will be discussed in detail in Sect. 4. The remainder of this section is intended as a dictionary between conventional cryptanalytic properties and their corresponding subspaces.

A short summary for $G = \mathbb{F}_2^n$ is given in Table 2. The table includes both the subspaces of $\mathbb{C}G$ and their Fourier transforms, which are subspaces of $\mathbb{C}\widehat{G}$. Importantly, there are other useful subspaces which do not correspond to any of the constructions discussed below. One example will be discussed in Sect. 6.

Table 2. Commonly used cryptanalytic properties and their corresponding subspaces. The characters of $\mathbb{F}_2^n$ are denoted by $\chi_u(x) = (-1)^{u^\top x}$, where $u \in \mathbb{F}_2^n$.

Property	Basis for subspace		Applications
	$V \subseteq \mathbb{C}G$	$\mathcal{F}(V) \subseteq \mathbb{C}\widehat{G}$	
Affine space $a + U \subseteq \mathbb{F}_2^n$	$\{\mathbb{1}_{a+U}\}$	$\{\chi_a \mathbb{1}_{U^\perp}\}$	Invariant subspaces
Affine spaces $a_1 + U_1, \ldots \subseteq \mathbb{F}_2^n$	$\{\mathbb{1}_{a_1+U_1}, \ldots\}$	$\{\chi_{a_1} \mathbb{1}_{U_1^\perp}, \ldots\}$	Integral cryptanalysis
Probability distribution $p : \mathbb{F}_2^n \to [0,1]$	$\{p\}$	$\{\widehat{p}\}$	Statistical saturation
Linear $Mask\ u \in \mathbb{F}_2^n$	$\{\chi_u\}$	$\{\delta_{\chi_u}\}$	Linear approximations
Multidimensional linear $Subspace\ U \subseteq \mathbb{F}_2^n$	$\{\chi_u \mid u \in U\}$	$\{\delta_{\chi_u} \mid u \in U\}$	Multidimensional linear approximations
Multiple linear $Subset\ U \subseteq \mathbb{F}_2^n$	$\{\chi_u \mid u \in U\}$	$\{\delta_{\chi_u} \mid u \in U\}$	Multiple linear approximations
Nonlinear $Function\ \mathsf{F} : \mathbb{F}_2^n \to \mathbb{F}_2$	$\{(-1)^\mathsf{F}\}$	$\{\mathcal{F}[(-1)^\mathsf{F}]\}$	Nonlinear invariants I/O sums
Projection $Function\ \mathsf{F} : \mathbb{F}_2^n \to X$	$\{\delta_x \circ \mathsf{F} \mid x \in X\}$	$\{\widehat{\delta_x \circ \mathsf{F}} \mid x \in X\}$	Partitioning attacks χ^2 distinguishers

Probability Distributions. Several properties correspond to subspaces spanned by one or more probability distributions. Subspaces and sets are one example, since any set corresponds to the uniform distribution on that set (equivalently, its indicator function). Affine spaces are an important example and are used in the invariant subspace attack of Leander *et al.* [30].

Integral and division properties [17,38] are also examples[1], but their analysis is not the main focus of this paper. In this case, the corresponding vector space could be spanned by the indicator function of a set which is balanced on certain

---

[1] The present framework only describes zero-sum properties.

bits. However, the intermediate and output properties typically correspond to higher-dimensional vector spaces because they express several possible sets in which the state could be contained. Equivalently, following (ii), one observes the marginal (but *not necessarily* joint) distribution of several state bits.

Not many variants of linear cryptanalysis are directly based on non-uniform probability distributions. The statistical saturation attack of Collard and Standaert [15], in its original form, may be considered an example. In this attack, one estimates the key-dependent probability distribution of the state of a block cipher when some of the plaintext bits are constant and the others are uniform random. However, depending on how the estimated distribution is used, it may be more appropriate to approach this attack using the projection functions discussed below.

Projection Functions. Let $\mathsf{F} : G \to H$ be a function between finite Abelian groups G and H, with H typically much smaller than G. In fact, H need not be a group for the construction below to work, but this will be assumed for simplicity. Such functions play an important role in Wagner's framework of 'commutative diagram cryptanalysis', where they are called *projections* [42]. Baignères *et al.* [2] analyze the statistical properties of distinguishers based on balanced projections, such as χ^2-attacks [41], partitioning cryptanalysis [22] and multidimensional linear attacks [23].

From the viewpoint of (ii), a projection property gives access to the evaluation of F on the state. Equivalently, the property allows observing any linear combination of the functions $\delta_h \circ \mathsf{F}$, where $\{\delta_h \mid h \in H\}$ is the standard basis of $\mathbb{C}H$. More generally, any function on H can be 'pulled back' to G along the projection function F and the projection property corresponds to the vector space of all such functions. This leads to Definition 3.1 below.

Definition 3.1 (Pullback). *Let $\mathsf{F} : G \to H$ be a function. The pullback operator along F is the linear operator $T^{\mathsf{F}^*} : \mathbb{C}H \to \mathbb{C}G$ defined by $f \mapsto f \circ \mathsf{F}$. The pullback space of $\mathbb{C}H$ along F is the image of T^{F^*}: $\operatorname{im} T^{\mathsf{F}^*} = \{f \circ \mathsf{F} \mid f \in \mathbb{C}H\} \subseteq \mathbb{C}G$. Similarly, the Fourier transformation $\mathfrak{F}(\operatorname{im} T^{\mathsf{F}^*})$ of $\operatorname{im} T^{\mathsf{F}^*}$ will be called the pullback of $\mathbb{C}H$ to $\mathbb{C}\widehat{G}$ along F.*

Let V be the vector space corresponding to the projection property defined by F, *i.e.* the pullback of $\mathbb{C}H$ along F. It was already mentioned above that $\{\delta_h \circ \mathsf{F} \mid h \in H\}$ is a basis for V. However, it is often more convenient to use the basis of functions $\chi \circ \mathsf{F}$ where $\chi \in \widehat{H}$. This choice behaves particularly well for homomorphisms $\mathsf{F} : G \to H$ when working with the Fourier transformation of V, since $\widehat{\chi \circ \mathsf{F}} = \delta_{\chi \circ \mathsf{F}}$ in that case.

The following example describes the vector space corresponding to a Boolean projection function in more detail. Such properties are closely related to classical linear cryptanalysis, and more generally the I/O-sums of Harpes *et al.* [21] and the nonlinear approximations considered by Beierle *et al.* [4]. However, as discussed below, there is subtle difference.

Example 3.1. Let $\mathsf{F} : \mathbb{F}_2^n \to \mathbb{F}_2$ be a Boolean function. Denote the characters of $\mathbb{F}_2^n$ by $\chi_u(x) = (-1)^{u^\top x}$. The pullback space V of $\mathbb{C}\mathbb{F}_2$ along F is equal to $V = \mathrm{span}\{\delta_0 \circ \mathsf{F}, \delta_1 \circ \mathsf{F}\} = \mathrm{span}\{\mathbb{1}, (-1)^{\mathsf{F}}\}$, with $\mathbb{1} = \chi_0$ the trivial character of $\mathbb{F}_2^n$. Hence, the Fourier transformation of V is given by $\mathcal{F}(V) = \mathrm{span}\{\delta_{\mathbb{1}}, \mathcal{F}[(-1)^{\mathsf{F}}]\}$. The function $\mathcal{F}[(-1)^{\mathsf{F}}]$ is often called the Walsh-Hadamard transform of F. If F is a linear function, then $\mathsf{F}(x) = u^\top x$ for some $u \in \mathbb{F}_2^n$. Hence, $(-1)^{\mathsf{F}} = \chi_u$ and consequently $\mathcal{F}(V) = \mathrm{span}\{\delta_{\mathbb{1}}, \delta_{\chi_u}\}$.

Example 3.1 suggests that ordinary linear properties correspond to a vector space $V = \mathrm{span}\{\delta_{\mathbb{1}}, \delta_\chi\}$, where χ is a character of the additive group $\mathbb{F}_2^n$. Table 2 instead lists the one-dimensional space $\mathrm{span}\{\delta_\chi\} \subset V$. For the analysis of permutations, there is no significant difference since $\delta_{\mathbb{1}}$ corresponds to a trivial invariant for any permutation (its domain). However, for general functions, the vector space V represents a strictly stronger property.

In general, many commonly used cryptographic properties correspond to subspaces of pullback spaces. This difference is not easily expressed in the formalism of Baignères *et al.* [2] and Wagner [42]. The next paragraph discusses several important examples.

Subspaces of Pullbacks. Example 3.1 generalizes to other finite Abelian groups. Let $\mathsf{F} : G \to H$ be a homomorphism. Since $\chi \circ \mathsf{F} \in \widehat{G}$ for any character χ of H, the pullback V of $\mathbb{C}H$ to $\mathbb{C}\widehat{G}$ is spanned by the functions $\delta_{\chi \circ \mathsf{F}}$ with $\chi \in \widehat{H}$. Hence, $\dim V = |H|$. However, the dimension could be reduced by one for permutations. This is essentially the generalization of linear cryptanalysis proposed by Granboulan *et al.* [20, §3]. However, it is also reasonable to consider only one of the functions $\delta_{\chi \circ \mathsf{F}}$. Since this results in one-dimensional subspaces and is closer to the spirit of ordinary linear cryptanalysis. This is essentially the generalization of linear cryptanalysis proposed by Baignères *et al.* [3]. The approach of Baignères *et al.* and its multidimensional generalization were recently used in the cryptanalysis of FF3.1 [8].

The difference between *multiple* and *multidimensional* linear cryptanalysis is of the same nature. For multiple linear properties, one uses a subspace spanned by one or more standard basis vectors δ_χ. In multidimensional linear cryptanalysis, the considered characters form a subgroup of $\widehat{G}$ and consequently the subspace is the pullback of a homomorphism to some subgroup of G.

3.2   Transformations on $\mathbb{C}G$ and $\mathbb{C}\widehat{G}$

This section investigates how properties, *i.e.* subspaces of $\mathbb{C}G$, change when a function $\mathsf{F} : G \to H$ is applied to the state of the primitive under analysis.

Definition 3.2 (Transition matrix). *Let* $\mathsf{F} : G \to H$ *be a function. Define* $T^{\mathsf{F}} : \mathbb{C}G \to \mathbb{C}H$ *as the unique linear operator defined by* $\delta_x \mapsto \delta_{\mathsf{F}(x)}$ *for all* $x \in G$. *The transition matrix of* F *is the coordinate representation of* T^{F} *with respect to the standard bases of* $\mathbb{C}G$ *and* $\mathbb{C}H$.

Definition 3.2 only specifies the action of T^F on the standard basis of $\mathbb{C}G$, but this uniquely defines T^F on all of $\mathbb{C}G$. The choice of the notations $T^{\mathsf{F}*}$ and T^F for pullback (Definition 3.1) and transition (Definition 3.2) operators respectively is not arbitrary: these operators are indeed represented by conjugate-transposed matrices. In fact, T^F could also be called the *pushforward* operator.

Note that the notation T^F will be overloaded, referring to both the operator and its standard matrix representation. The coordinates of the matrix T^F will be indexed by elements of G and H rather than by integers, since this avoids choosing an arbitrary ordering of the standard basis. In particular,

$$T^\mathsf{F}_{y,x} = \langle \delta_y, T^\mathsf{F}\delta_x \rangle = \langle \delta_y, \delta_{\mathsf{F}(x)} \rangle = \delta_y(\mathsf{F}(x)).$$

An analog of Definition 3.2 for $\mathbb{C}\widehat{G}$ is given in Definition 3.3. It generalizes the definition of correlation matrices given in [5] to arbitrary finite Abelian groups. The term *correlation matrix* is due to Daemen *et al.* [16], who defined these matrices in terms of their coordinates.

Definition 3.3 (Correlation matrix). *Let* $\mathsf{F} : G \to H$ *be a function between finite Abelian groups* G *and* H. *Define* $C^\mathsf{F} : \mathbb{C}\widehat{G} \to \mathbb{C}\widehat{H}$ *as the Fourier transformation of* T^F. *That is,* $C^\mathsf{F} = \mathcal{F}_H\, T^\mathsf{F}\, \mathcal{F}_G^{-1}$, *with* $\mathcal{F}_H$ *and* $\mathcal{F}_G$ *the Fourier transformation on* $\mathbb{C}H$ *and* $\mathbb{C}G$ *respectively. The correlation matrix of* F *is the coordinate representation of* C^F *with respect to the standard bases of* $\mathbb{C}\widehat{G}$ *and* $\mathbb{C}\widehat{H}$.

The notation C^F will refer to both the linear operator and its standard matrix representation. Contrary to [5,16], the coordinates will be indexed by elements of $\widehat{G}$ in order to avoid arbitrary choices. Since $T^\mathsf{F}_{y,x} = \delta_y(\mathsf{F}(x))$, the coordinates are given by

$$C^\mathsf{F}_{\chi,\psi} = \langle \delta_\chi, C^\mathsf{F}\delta_\psi \rangle = \frac{1}{|G|}\langle \chi, T^\mathsf{F}\psi \rangle = \frac{1}{|G|}\sum_{x\in G}\overline{\chi(\mathsf{F}(x))}\psi(x).$$

For $G = \mathbb{F}_2^n$ and $H = \mathbb{F}_2^m$, and after identifying these groups with their dual, the expression above coincides with the original definition of correlation matrices given by Daemen *et al.* [16]. The following two theorems list the main properties of transition and correlation matrices that will be used throughout this paper. The last two properties in Theorem 3.1 also apply to correlation matrices. For (2), this follows from the fact that $\mathcal{F}_{G_1\oplus G_2}$ is essentially the same as $\mathcal{F}_{G_1} \otimes \mathcal{F}_{G_2}$.

Theorem 3.1 (Properties of transition matrices). *Let* $\mathsf{F} : G \to H$ *be a function. The transition matrix of* T^F *of* F *has the following properties:*

(1) If F *is a bijection, then* T^F *is a permutation matrix.*
(2) If $\mathsf{F} = (\mathsf{F}_1, \ldots, \mathsf{F}_n)$ *with* $\mathsf{F}_i : G_i \to H_i$, *then* $T^\mathsf{F} = \bigotimes_{i=1}^n T^{\mathsf{F}_i}$.
(3) If $\mathsf{F} = \mathsf{F}_2 \circ \mathsf{F}_1$, *then* $T^\mathsf{F} = T^{\mathsf{F}_2}T^{\mathsf{F}_1}$.

Proof. The first two claims directly follow from $T^\mathsf{F}_{y,x} = \delta_y(\mathsf{F}(x))$. The third property is an immediate consequence of Definition 3.2. □

Theorem 3.2 (Properties of correlation matrices). *Let* $\mathsf{F} : G \to H$ *be a function between finite Abelian groups G and H. The correlation matrix C^{F} of F has the following properties:*

(1) If F is a bijection, then C^{F} is a unitary matrix.
(2) If F is a group homomorphism, then $C^{\mathsf{F}}_{\chi,\psi} = \delta_{\chi \circ \mathsf{F}}(\psi)$.
(3) If $G = H$ and $\mathsf{F}(x) = x - t$ for some constant $t \in G$, then C^{F} is a diagonal matrix with $C^{\mathsf{F}}_{\chi,\chi} = \chi(t)$.

Proof. By Theorem 3.1 (1), if F is a permutation, then T^{F} is a permutation matrix and thus unitary. Furthermore, since $|G| = |H|$, both $\mathcal{F}^*_H / \sqrt{|G|}$ and $\mathcal{F}_G / \sqrt{|G|}$ are unitary matrices. Property (1) follows since the product of unitary matrices is unitary and $C^{\mathsf{F}} = \mathcal{F}_H T^{\mathsf{F}} \mathcal{F}_G^{-1}$.

For (2), note that if F is a group homomorphism, then so is $\chi \circ \mathsf{F} : G \to \mathbb{C}^\times$. Hence, by the orthogonality of group characters, $C^{\mathsf{F}}_{\chi,\psi} = \delta_{\chi \circ \mathsf{F}}(\psi)$. As discussed in Sect. 2.2, property (3) holds by construction of the Fourier transformation. Indeed, note that the action of F corresponds to a translation by t.   □

4   Approximations

An approximation of a function $\mathsf{F} : G \to H$ is essentially a pair consisting of an input and an output property. By the correspondence in Sect. 3, these properties can be represented by subspaces U and V. As discussed in Sect. 3, $u \in U$ represents a state and $v \in V$ corresponds to a linear measurement function or observation. The inner product $\langle v, T^{\mathsf{F}} u \rangle$ gives the outcome of such an observation. This leads to Definition 4.1 below, where the *approximation map* represents all such inner products without relying on the choice of a specific basis. Given orthonormal bases $u_1, u_2, \ldots$ and $v_1, v_2, \ldots$ for U and V respectively, the coordinates of the matrix representing the approximation map are given by the inner products $\langle v_i, T^{\mathsf{F}} u_i \rangle$.

Definition 4.1 (Approximation). *Let G and H be finite Abelian groups. An approximation of a function $\mathsf{F} : G \to H$ is a pair (U, V) of subspaces $U \subseteq \mathbb{C}\widehat{G}$ and $V \subseteq \mathbb{C}\widehat{H}$. The approximation map of (U, V) is a linear transformation $\langle V, U \rangle_{\mathsf{F}} : U \to V$ defined by $\langle V, U \rangle_{\mathsf{F}} = \pi_V C^{\mathsf{F}} \iota_U$, with $\iota_U : U \to \mathbb{C}\widehat{G}$ the inclusion map and $\pi_V : \mathbb{C}\widehat{H} \to V$ the orthogonal projection on V.*

Definition 4.1 refers to subspaces of $\mathbb{C}\widehat{G}$ and $\mathbb{C}\widehat{H}$. An equivalent definition could be given for the subspaces $\mathcal{F}^*_G(U) \subseteq \mathbb{C}G$ and $\mathcal{F}^*_H(V) \subseteq \mathbb{C}H$, taking into account that C^{F} should be replaced by T^{F}. The same remark applies to all definitions in this section and Sect. 5.

Note that the notation $\langle V, U \rangle_{\mathsf{F}}$ is intentionally similar to the 'inner product of subspaces' notation $\langle V, U \rangle$ from Sect. 2.3. It will be shown in Sect. 4.1 that the maps $\langle V, U \rangle_{\mathsf{F}}$ and $\langle V, C^{\mathsf{F}} U \rangle$ are indeed closely related and encode the same geometric information.

Example 4.1. Consider a linear approximation for a function $F : \mathbb{F}_2^n \to \mathbb{F}_2^m$. As listed in Table 2, linear properties correspond to one-dimensional spaces $U = \mathrm{span}\{\delta_{\chi_u}\}$ and $V = \mathrm{span}\{\delta_{\chi_v}\}$ with masks $u \in \mathbb{F}_2^n$ and $v \in \mathbb{F}_2^m$. As in Example 2.3, one has the inclusion map $\iota_U(x) = x$ and the orthogonal projection $\pi_V(x) = \langle \delta_{\chi_v}, x \rangle \delta_{\chi_v}$. Hence, $\langle V, U \rangle_F$ is given by $\lambda \delta_{\chi_u} \mapsto \langle \delta_{\chi_v}, C^F \delta_{\chi_u} \rangle \lambda \delta_{\chi_v} = C^F_{\chi_v, \chi_u} \lambda \delta_{\chi_v}$. The same result holds for any pair of finite Abelian groups.

The main purpose of this section is to show that Definition 4.1 indeed encompasses all variants of linear cryptanalysis mentioned in Sect. 1, and leads to new insights for several of them.

As illustrated in Fig. 1, two geometrically intuitive edge cases of Definition 4.1 can be identified: parallel or orthogonal spaces V and $C^F U$. Approximations in the former category will be called 'perfect'. This includes the important case of invariants. The latter case corresponds to a broad generalization of zero-correlation linear approximations. In the remaining cases, the vector spaces V and $C^F U$ are neither completely parallel nor fully orthogonal. All three cases are discussed in detail in Sects. 4.1 to 4.3.

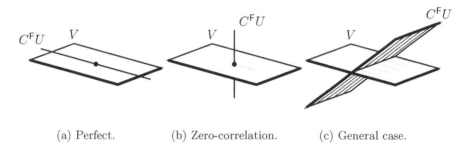

(a) Perfect.   (b) Zero-correlation.   (c) General case.

Fig. 1. Geometric interpretation of Definition 4.1.

The geometric intuitions illustrated in Fig. 1 can be quantified using the concept of principal angles that was introduced in Sect. 2.3. This leads to the following definition of 'principal correlations'. For linear approximations, the unique principal correlation coincides with the ordinary absolute correlation. Further aspects of principal correlations, such as their relation to the 'capacity' in multiple linear cryptanalysis, are discussed in Sect. 4.3.

Definition 4.2 (Principal correlations). *Let (U, V) be an approximation for a function $F : G \to H$ between finite Abelian groups G and H. Let $d = \min\{\dim U, \dim V\}$. The principal correlations of the approximation (U, V) are the d largest singular values of the approximation map $\langle V, U \rangle_F$.*

The geometric interpretation of the principal correlations is due to the following result, which relates them to the principal angles between the subspaces $C^F U$ and V.

Theorem 4.1. *Let* (U, V) *be an approximation for a function* $\mathsf{F} : G \to H$ *between finite Abelian groups* G *and* H. *Let* $d = \min\{\dim U, \dim V\}$. *If* F *is injective, then the principal correlations of the approximation* (U, V) *are equal to the cosines of the* d *smallest principal angles between the subspaces* $C^{\mathsf{F}}U$ *and* V.

Proof. By Theorem 3.2 (1), C^{F} is a unitary matrix if F is a permutation. More generally, $[C^{\mathsf{F}}]^* C^{\mathsf{F}}$ is a nonzero multiple of the identity map if F is an injection. That is, C^{F} preserves the inner product up to multiplication by a constant. To prove this, show that the result holds for T^{F} (by direct calculation) and then apply the same argument as in the proof of Theorem 3.2 (1).

If C^{F} preserves the inner product up to multiplication by a nonzero constant, then $u_{i+1} \perp u_i$ implies $C^{\mathsf{F}} u_{i+1} \perp C^{\mathsf{F}} u_i$. Hence, the result follows from the fact that the variational characterization of singular values is then equivalent to the definition of principal angles (Definition 2.3).   □

4.1   Invariants and Perfect Approximations

If the subspaces U and V are aligned as in Fig. 1a, the approximation (U, V) will be called perfect. More formally, (U, V) is perfect if $C^{\mathsf{F}}U \subseteq V$. Alternatively, an approximation *over a permutation* F is perfect if its principal correlations are equal to one.

Integral and division properties are of this type, but these traditionally 'algebraic' properties are not the main focus of this work. However, the case $U = V$ is of particular interest since it leads to a class of approximations that will be called *invariants*, and which includes the invariant subspaces of Leander *et al.* [30] and the nonlinear invariants of Todo *et al.* [39].

Definition 4.3 (Invariant). *Let* $\mathsf{F} : G \to G$ *be a function. An approximation* (V, V) *such that* $C^{\mathsf{F}}V \subseteq V$ *will be called an invariant for* F.

If F is a permutation, all principal correlations of an invariant (V, V) are equal to one. For general functions, this is not necessarily true. For example, if two distinct input distributions result in the same output distribution, it is natural to consider the difference of their probability mass functions as invariant.

Since transition matrices and correlation matrices of permutations have finite multiplicative order, they are diagonalizable. Consequently, by a standard linear algebra result for algebraically closed fields, any invariant V splits into one-dimensional invariant subspaces spanned by the eigenvectors of C^{F}. Hence, Definition 4.3 reduces to the characterization of invariants introduced in [5, Definition 2]

Despite the fact that the eigenvectors of C^{F} determine all possible invariants, the more general characterization of invariants in Definition 4.3 sometimes leads to additional insight. This will be illustrated using the following example, which involves eigenvectors whose corresponding eigenvalue is imaginary – thereby addressing a problem left as future work by [5].

Example 4.2. Consider the following 4-bit S-box, defined in cycle notation:

$$S = (0\ 7\ b\ 3\quad d\ 5\ 9\ 6\quad 8\ 2\ 1\ e\quad a\ f\ c\ 4).$$

Further details about this S-box, including a lookup table representation, are given as supplementary material in the extended version [7]. From a cryptanalytic perspective, the properties of S are seemingly excellent: the linear and differential properties are optimal, and it does not have any fixed points since it is a cyclic permutation. The last property implies that all eigenspaces of C^S are one-dimensional, see for instance [5, §4.2]. An immediate consequence of this is that S does not have any nontrivial invariant subspaces.

Denote the ring of integers modulo four by $\mathbb{Z}_4$ and let $f : \mathbb{F}_2^4 \to \mathbb{Z}_4$ be the function defined by $f(\{0, \mathsf{d}, 8, \mathsf{a}\}) = 0$, $f(\{\mathsf{b}, 9, 1, \mathsf{c}\}) = 2$, $f(\{7, 5, 2, \mathsf{f}\}) = 1$ and $f(\{3, 6, \mathsf{e}, 4\}) = 3$. By inspection of the cycle structure of S, one can see that $f(\mathsf{S}(x)) = f(x) + 1$ for all $x \in \mathbb{F}_2^4$. This property is reminiscent of nonlinear invariants, and in fact yields a nonlinear invariant for S when reduced modulo two. Nevertheless, the property is more powerful than a nonlinear invariant since its defining function takes values in $\mathbb{Z}_4$ rather than $\mathbb{F}_2$. In fact, the use of $\mathbb{Z}_4$-approximations has been previously suggested by Parker and Raddum [33]. Properties such as f are to nonlinear invariants as nonlinear invariants are to invariant sets: just as a nonlinear invariant can be interpreted as a pair of sets that are potentially swapped by S, f can be interpreted as a pair of nonlinear invariants that are swapped by S.

To obtain a subspace V of $\mathbb{C}\widehat{\mathbb{F}}_2^4$ from f, the pullback construction from Sect. 3.1 can be applied. Since $\mathbb{Z}_4$ is cyclic of order four, one can deduce from Theorem 2.1 that $\widehat{\mathbb{Z}}_4 = \{x \mapsto \zeta_4^{kx}\ k \in \mathbb{Z}_4\}$ with ζ_4 a primitive fourth root of unity such as $\sqrt{-1}$. Hence, using the basis of functions $\widehat{\chi \circ f}$ where $\chi \in \widehat{\mathbb{Z}}_4$, yields

$$
\begin{aligned}
V = \operatorname{span}\big\{&\widehat{\zeta_4^0}, \widehat{\zeta_4^f}, \widehat{\zeta_4^{2f}}, \widehat{\zeta_4^{3f}}\big\}\\
= \operatorname{span}\big\{&(1,\ 0,0,0,0,\quad 0,0,\ 0,\quad 0,0,0,\ 0,0,\quad 0,0,0)^\top,\\
&(0,\overline{\zeta_8},0,0,0,2\zeta_8,0,\overline{\zeta_8},\ 0,0,0,\overline{\zeta_8},0,-\overline{\zeta_8},0,0)^\top/\sqrt{8},\\
&(0,\ 0,1,0,1,\quad 0,0,\ 0,-1,0,0,\ 0,0,\quad 0,1,0)^\top/2,\\
&(0,\zeta_8,0,0,0,2\overline{\zeta_8},0,\zeta_8,\ 0,0,0,\zeta_8,0,-\zeta_8,0,0)^\top/\sqrt{8}\big\}.
\end{aligned}
$$

The choice of $\widehat{\chi \circ f}$ (up to a scalar multiple) as a basis is not arbitrary: since $\chi(f(\mathsf{S}(x))) = \chi(1)\chi(f(x))$, it ensures that each basis vector is an eigenvector of C^S. Consequently, it is immediately clear that V is indeed an invariant. Note that the first vector listed above is the trivial eigenvector with eigenvalue one. The second and fourth vectors are complex-conjugate eigenvectors corresponding to the conjugate eigenvalues ζ_4 and $\overline{\zeta_4}$. Finally, the third vector is an eigenvector with eigenvalue $\zeta_4^2 = -1$. It corresponds to the nonlinear invariant obtained by reduction modulo two that was mentioned above.

For the purpose of obtaining an interesting example, the S-box S was carefully chosen. In particular, by taking appropriate linear combinations of the two complex-conjugate eigenvectors above, one can see that V is spanned by four real vectors $v_1, \ldots, v_4$ such that $v_1^{\otimes 16}, \ldots, v_4^{\otimes 16}$ are all eigenvectors of C^{L}, where L is the linear layer of Midori-64. Furthermore, these vectors are invariant under the round-constant and key-additions for 2^{32} weak keys. In fact, $v_3^{\otimes 16}$ is itself a nonlinear invariant for the same number of weak keys, but it has been shown that there exists a stronger four-dimensional invariant.

Moreover, there is a larger set of 2^{96} weak keys for which $v_1^{\otimes 16}$ and $v_2^{\otimes 16}$ are still invariants for the whole cipher. This is due to the fact that Midori-64 alternates round keys, and because $C^{\mathsf{S}}v_2 = -v_4$ and $C^{\mathsf{S}}v_4 = v_2$. However, neither v_2 nor v_4 corresponds to a nonlinear invariant for S. One can think of the invariant obtained here as a 'remnant' of the stronger – yet valid for fewer keys – invariant described above. The supplementary material of the extended version [7] contains additional details regarding the preceding claims.   ▷

In general, a one-dimensional periodically repeating perfect approximation for a function F must be an eigenvector of $[C^{\mathsf{F}}]^l$ with eigenvalue one for some positive integer l. These eigenvectors are linear combinations of the eigenvectors of C^{F} with eigenvalues of order divisible by l.

4.2   Zero-Correlation Approximations

Zero-correlation linear approximations were introduced by Bogdanov and Rijmen [13]. They correspond to linear approximations $(\text{span}\{\delta_\psi\}, \text{span}\{\delta_\chi\})$ such that $C^{\mathsf{F}}_{\chi,\psi} = 0$. That is, δ_χ is orthogonal to $C^{\mathsf{F}}\delta_\psi$. This corresponds to the geometric situation sketched in Fig. 1b, motivating the following definition.

Definition 4.4 (Zero-correlation approximation). *Let* $\mathsf{F} : G \to H$ *be a function. An approximation* (U, V) *such that* $V \perp C^{\mathsf{F}}U$ *will be called a zero-correlation approximation for* F. *Equivalently, all principal correlations of a zero-correlation approximation* (U, V) *are zero.*

Zero-correlation and perfect approximations are closely related, despite being opposite extremes. In fact, this is clear from a geometrical point of view, see for instance Figs. 1a and 1b.

Theorem 4.2. *If* (U, V) *is a zero-correlation approximation, then* $(U, V^\perp)$ *is a perfect approximation and conversely.*

Proof. Since (U, V) is a zero-correlation approximation, any $v \in C^{\mathsf{F}}U$ is orthogonal to V. Hence, $C^{\mathsf{F}}U \subseteq V^\perp$. The proof of the converse result is analogous.   □

The statement and proof of Theorem 4.2 are deceptively simple, but the result is powerful. Indeed, it generalizes the well-known correspondence between multidimensional linear zero-correlation approximations and integral properties, first noted by Bogdanov *et al.* at ASIACRYPT 2012 [12][2] and discussed futher by Sun *et al.* [35].

---

[2] For the case of multidimensional zero-correlation approximations with 'coupled masks', apply Theorem 4.2 to the function $x \mapsto (x, \mathsf{F}(x))$ to obtain their result.

Definition 4.4 leads to a useful generalization of the miss-in-the-middle approach that is commonly used to find zero-correlation linear approximations. Suppose $F = F_2 \circ F_1$. Let (U_1, V_1) and (U_2, V_2) be approximations such that

$$C^{F_1} U_1 \subseteq V_1 \perp V_2 \supseteq [C^{F_2}]^* U_2.$$

It then follows that (U_1, U_2) is a zero-correlation approximation for $F_2 \circ F_1$. Recall from Theorem 3.2 (1) that if F_2 is invertible, then $[C^{F_2}]^* = C^{F_2^{-1}}$.

Example 4.3. The key-recovery attacks on Midori-64 and MANTIS from ASIACRYPT 2018 [5] are based on a one-dimensional *nonlinear* zero-correlation approximation, and this property was obtained by connecting an ordinary integral property with a nonlinear invariant using the miss-in-the-middle approach discussed above. For completeness, a fully worked out version of this approximation is provided as supplementary material in the extended version [7].

The zero-correlation approximation in Example 4.3 can still be explained by mismatching activity patterns in the middle. The benefit of the geometric approach here is mainly that it clarifies that the combination of integral properties with invariants is a natural example of a more general principle, rather than just a 'trick'. However, in some cases, a more refined and possibly key-dependent analysis is necessary to establish the orthogonality of the subspaces V_1 and V_2. Such an example will be encountered in Sect. 7.3.

4.3   General Approximations

It follows from Example 4.1 that the unique principal correlation for an ordinary linear approximation equals the absolute value of the (conventional) correlation of the linear approximation. For a fixed advantage, the data-complexity of a linear distinguisher is inversely proportional to the square of the correlation.

More generally, Baignères *et al.* [2] discuss the optimal data-complexity of distinguishers for a permutation $F : G_1 \to G_2$ based on balanced projections $P_1 : G_1 \to H_1$ and $P_2 : G_2 \to H_2$. As discussed in Sect. 3.1, these projections correspond to subspaces $U = \mathrm{span}\{\delta_x \circ P_1 \mid x \in H_1\} \subseteq \mathbb{C}G_1$ and $V = \mathrm{span}\{\delta_x \circ P_2 \mid x \in H_2\} \subseteq \mathbb{C}G_2$ by the pullback construction. The approximation map $\langle V, U \rangle_F$ can be represented by a matrix M with coordinates

$$M_{y,x} = \frac{\langle \delta_y \circ P_2, T^F[\delta_x \circ P_1]\rangle}{\|\delta_y \circ P_2\|_2 \, \|\delta_x \circ P_1\|_2}$$

$$= \sqrt{\frac{|G_1|}{|G_2|} \frac{\Pr[P_1(z_1) = x]}{\Pr[P_2(z_2) = y]}} \; \Pr[P_2(F(z_1)) = y \mid P_1(z_1) = x],$$

where z_1 is uniform random on G_1 and z_2 is uniform random on G_2. Since the approximations considered by Baignères *et al.* are balanced, $\Pr[P_1(z_1) = x] = |H_1|/|G_1|$ and $\Pr[P_2(z_2) = y] = |H_2|/|G_2|$, so the prefactor simplifies to $\sqrt{|H_1|}/\sqrt{|H_2|}$. Recall that the Frobenius norm $\|\cdot\|_F$ of a linear operator is the square

root of the sum of its squared singular values. Equivalently, its square equals
the sum of all squared coordinates of an arbitrary matrix representation with
respect to an orthonormal basis. It follows that the Frobenius norm of $\langle V, U \rangle_\mathsf{F}$
is given by

$$\|\langle U, V \rangle_\mathsf{F}\|_F^2 = \frac{|H_1|}{|H_2|} \sum_{\substack{x \in H_1 \\ y \in H_2}} \Pr\left[\mathsf{P}_2(\mathsf{F}(z_1)) = y \mid \mathsf{P}_1(z_1) = x\right]^2.$$

In particular, $\|\langle U, V \rangle_\mathsf{F}\|_F^2 - 1$ is equal to the *squared Euclidean imbalance* as
defined by Baignères *et al.* [2, Definition 7]. The term -1 is due to the triv-
ial invariant corresponding to the uniform distribution. If this is omitted, one
obtains that the data-complexity of an optimal distinguisher is inversely proportional to the sum of the squared principal correlations. This generalizes to
multiple linear distinguishers (which are not necessarily of projection type), in
which case the squared Frobenius norm corresponds to the fixed-key capacity.

5   Trails

Most cryptographic primitives F do not allow for a direct computation of the
approximation map $\langle V, U \rangle_\mathsf{F}$, even when U and V are low-dimensional. Indeed, if
F is devoid of structure, one is forced to estimate the approximation map empir-
ically. Consequently, finding good approximations of the general type discussed
in Sect. 4.3 is nontrivial.

However, cryptographic primitives are often a composition of highly struc-
tured round functions. That is, $\mathsf{F} = \mathsf{F}_r \circ \mathsf{F}_{r-1} \circ \cdots \circ \mathsf{F}_1$. By exploiting the structure of the functions F_i, one can often find approximations (V_i, V_{i+1}) such that
$\langle V_{i+1}, V_i \rangle_{\mathsf{F}_i}$ can be efficiently computed. This is for instance the case for linear cryptanalysis, and Sect. 6 will introduce rank-one approximations as another
example for cell-oriented ciphers. The remaining task is to combine or 'pile-up'
the individual approximations (V_i, V_{i+1}) for F_i in order to obtain an approximation (V_1, V_{r+1}) for F. The purpose of the piling-up principle, which will
be discussed in Sect. 5.1, is to obtain an estimate of the approximation map
$\langle V_{r+1}, V_1 \rangle_\mathsf{F}$.

Definition 5.1 (Trail). *Let $G_1, G_2, \ldots, G_{r+1}$ be finite Abelian groups. A trail
of vector spaces for a function $\mathsf{F} = \mathsf{F}_r \circ \cdots \circ \mathsf{F}_1$ with $\mathsf{F}_i : G_i \to G_{i+1}$ is a tuple
$(V_1, V_2, \ldots, V_{r+1})$ of subspaces $V_1 \subseteq \mathbb{C}\widehat{G}_1, \ldots, V_{r+1} \subseteq \mathbb{C}\widehat{G}_{r+1}$.*

Similarly to ordinary linear trails, Definition 5.1 defines a sequence of compatible intermediate approximations. In particular, if all vector spaces V_i are
spanned by a standard basis vector $\delta_{\chi_i} \in \mathbb{C}\widehat{G}_i$, one obtains ordinary linear trails
as defined by Matsui [31] and generalized to other groups by Baignères *et al.* [3].
Note that the compatibility requirement does not exclude taking one or more of
the functions F_i as the identity map.

5.1   Piling-Up Principle

As discussed in Sect. 1, methods for piling-up the approximations within a trail are often motivated by Markov chain assumptions, or a dominant trail hypothesis. Unfortunately, when the former assumption fails, it is often hard to understand why or how to resolve the problem. The latter approach has been mostly limited to the case of simple linear cryptanalysis.

Theorem 5.1 below provides an alternative motivation for the piling-up principle. The premise is that each approximation in a trail corresponds to a transformation of its input space, followed by an orthogonal projection on the input space of the next approximation. Each of these successive projections introduces an error, but orthogonal projection is optimal in the sense that it keeps the inner product between the state and its approximation maximal and the norm of the error minimal (see Sect. 2.3).

Theorem 5.1 (Piling-up principle). *Let $(V_1, V_2, \ldots, V_{r+1})$ be a trail for a function $\mathsf{F} = \mathsf{F}_r \circ \cdots \circ \mathsf{F}_1$. The approximation map of the approximation (V_{r+1}, V_1) for F can be written as*

$$\langle V_{r+1}, V_1 \rangle_\mathsf{F} = \langle V_{r+1}, V_r \rangle_{\mathsf{F}_r} \cdots \langle V_2, V_1 \rangle_{\mathsf{F}_1} + E \,,$$

where the error term E is the transformation given by

$$E = \sum_{i=1}^{r-1} \langle V_{r+1}, V_{i+1} \rangle_{\mathsf{F}_r \circ \cdots \circ \mathsf{F}_{i+1}} \langle V_{i+1}^{\perp}, V_i \rangle_{\mathsf{F}_i} \cdots \langle V_2, V_1 \rangle_{\mathsf{F}_1} \,.$$

Proof. The proof follows the above intuition of successive orthogonal projection, but keeps track of the error term. Recall from Definition 4.1 that $\langle V, U \rangle_\mathsf{F} = \pi_V C^\mathsf{F} \iota_U$ where π_V is the orthogonal projector on V and ι_U the inclusion map. Since $\pi_V + \pi_{V^\perp}$ is equal to the identity map, one has the following decomposition for $i = 1, \ldots, r - 1$:

$$\langle V_{r+1}, V_i \rangle_{\mathsf{F}_r \circ \cdots \circ \mathsf{F}_i}$$
$$= \pi_{V_{r+1}} C^{\mathsf{F}_r \circ \cdots \circ \mathsf{F}_{i+1}} (\pi_{V_{i+1}} + \pi_{V_{i+1}^{\perp}}) C^{\mathsf{F}_i} \iota_{V_i}$$
$$= \langle V_{r+1}, V_{i+1} \rangle_{\mathsf{F}_r \circ \cdots \circ \mathsf{F}_{i+1}} \langle V_{i+1}, V_i \rangle_{\mathsf{F}_i} + \langle V_{r+1}, V_{i+1} \rangle_{\mathsf{F}_r \circ \cdots \circ \mathsf{F}_{i+1}} \langle V_{i+1}^{\perp}, V_i \rangle_{\mathsf{F}_i}.$$

The result follows by successively decomposing the factor $\langle V_{r+1}, V_{i+1} \rangle_{\mathsf{F}_r \circ \cdots \circ \mathsf{F}_{i+1}}$ using the same expression.   □

Theorem 5.1 generalizes the piling-up principle as used in many variants of linear cryptanalysis. This will be demonstrated in Sect. 5.2. Furthermore, allowing arbitrary subspaces V_i increases flexibility. Even if the spaces V_1 and V_{r+1} correspond to a specific type of property, the intermediate vector spaces can represent seemingly unrelated properties. This will be illustrated in Theorem 5.3, and again in Sect. 6. In addition, since the formulation of Theorem 5.1 is basis-free, the choice of basis for these spaces can be arbitrary[3]. This may have computational benefits.

---

[3] If B_i is a matrix whose columns form a basis for V_i, then the matrix-representation of $\langle V_{i+1}, V_i \rangle_{\mathsf{F}_i}$ with respect to these bases is $(B_{i+1}^* B_{i+1})^{-1} B_{i+1}^* C^{\mathsf{F}_i} B_i (B_i^* B_i)^{-1}$. Note the normalization factors for non-orthonormal bases.

5.2   Discussion of Theorem 5.1

In the one-dimensional case with V_i spanned by δ_{χ_i}, Theorem 5.1 reduces to

$$C^{\mathsf{F}}_{\chi_{r+1},\chi_1} = \prod_{i=1}^{r} C^{\mathsf{F}_i}_{\chi_{i+1},\chi_i} + e,$$

where the error term e can be written as a sum over all other linear trails. This is the fixed-key piling-up principle as stated in [16, §6.1] for $\mathbb{F}_2^n$. It also implies the piling-up lemma as stated by Matsui [31] and generalized by Baignères et al. [3] to other groups (after taking the variance with respect to independent round keys). The composition result of Beierle et al. [4, Theorem 3] for one-dimensional nonlinear approximations is another special case.

A few examples of the higher-dimensional case can be found in the literature. Consider the case where all spaces V_i are pullbacks of $\mathbb{C}H_i$ along balanced projection functions $\mathsf{P}_i : G_i \to H_i$, as in Baignères et al. [2] and Wagner [42]. Like all results in this paper, Theorem 5.1 is basis-free and also applies to the spaces $U_i = \mathcal{F}^{-1}(V_i) \subseteq \mathbb{C}G$ provided that one replaces C^{F_i} by T^{F_i}. As shown in Sect. 4.3, relative to the bases $\{\delta_x \circ \mathsf{P}_i / \|\delta_x \circ \mathsf{P}_i\|_2 \mid x \in H_i\}$ for U_i, the map $\langle U_{i+1}, U_i \rangle_{\mathsf{F}_i}$ can be represented by a matrix M with coordinates

$$M_{y,x} = \sqrt{\frac{|H_i|}{|H_{i+1}|}} \; \Pr\left[\mathsf{P}_{i+1}(\mathsf{F}(z)) = y \mid \mathsf{P}_i(z) = x\right],$$

where z is uniform random on $|G_i|$. That is, there exist diagonal matrices D_i and D_{i+1} such that $D_{i+1} M D_i^{-1}$ is the transition matrix considered in [2,42]. These works follow the Markov chain assumption, which leads to using the product of round transition matrices as an approximation for the true transition matrix. The factors D_i and D_{i+1} indeed cancel out, so that Theorem 5.1 yields the same result up to initial and final multiplication by D_{r+1} and D_1^{-1} respectively.

In the case of multiple linear cryptanalysis [9,25], it is common practice to combine many individual linear trails by adding their correlations. Alternatively, the squared correlations are added in order to estimate the variance of the correlation under the assumption of independent round keys. However, in general, strong approximations can often be found by taking into account the correlations between all pairs of approximations. Theorem 5.1 reflects this because, for multiple linear approximations, the coordinate representation of $\langle V_{i+1}, V_i \rangle_{\mathsf{F}_i}$ in the standard basis is a submatrix of the correlation matrix C^{F_i}. This approach has been (sometimes implicitly) used in several works, notably in analyses of Present [14], Puffin [29] and Spongent [11]. Note that this is often combined with key-averaging, but a careful analysis of the key-dependency would be both feasible and preferable in many cases.

5.3   Clustering and Linear Approximations from Invariants

A minimal condition for the applicability of the piling-up approximation is that one chooses the best trail from within a predetermined class of candidates, where the principal correlations can be used as a measure of quality. Indeed, by decomposing the error term in Theorem 5.1, one can see that it can be large if other trails result in better or comparable approximations.

However, it is also possible that the class of candidate trails is too limited to obtain a good estimate for $\langle V_{r+1}, V_1 \rangle_F$. In the context of linear cryptanalysis, this phenomenon has been called *clustering* by Daemen and Rijmen [18]. In some cases, clustering can be explained by broadening the set of candidate trails. At ASIACRYPT 2018, an example of a perfect linear approximation over full Midori-64 (with modified round constants) was presented [5]. However, full-round Midori-64 does not admit any high-correlation linear *trails*. This observation can be thought of as an extreme case of a more general phenomenon. At CRYPTO 2012, Abdelraheem *et al.* [1] showed that invariant subspaces give rise to linear approximations with higher-than-expected correlation. The same observation was later generalized to plateaued nonlinear invariants by Beierle *et al.* [4]. Plateaued nonlinear invariants are characterized by a flat Walsh-Hadamard transform, taking only two values up to sign. The results of Beierle *et al.* [4] can be summarized and generalized as follows.

Theorem 5.2. *Let* $F : G \to G$ *be a function on a finite Abelian group G. Let* $v \in \mathbb{C}\widehat{G}$ *be any function such that* $|v(\chi)| = 1/\sqrt{|\text{supp } v|}$ *for all $\chi \in \text{supp } v$ and zero elsewhere. If* $\text{span}\{v\}$ *is an invariant of* F *in the sense of Definition 4.3, then there exist characters* $\chi, \psi \in \text{supp } v$ *such that* $|C_{\chi,\psi}^F| \geq 1/|\text{supp } v|$.

Proof. By Definition 4.3, it holds that (the sum is over $\chi, \psi \in \text{supp } v$)

$$1 = |\langle v, C^F v \rangle| = \left| \sum_{\chi,\psi} \overline{v(\chi)} v(\psi) C_{\chi,\psi}^F \right| \leq |\text{supp } v| \max_{\chi,\psi} |C_{\chi,\psi}^F|.$$

It follows that $|C_{\chi,\psi}^F| \geq 1/|\text{supp } v|$ for at least one pair (χ, ψ). □

Note that the same result is spread over two theorems in previous work [4, Theorem 4 and 5]: one for invariant subspaces, and one for plateaued nonlinear invariants. This illustrates the convenience of the general definitions in Sect. 4. To apply the results to the case of invariant subspaces, one only needs to know that the Fourier transformation of the indicator function of a subgroup $H \subseteq G$ is flat with support size $|G|/|H|$. This follows from the Poisson-summation formula [37, Theorem 1]. See also the first entry of Table 2 for $G = \mathbb{F}_2^n$.

Theorem 5.2 and the results above illustrate that a strong approximation using one kind of property tends to result in unexpectedly good approximations using other properties. This can be understood using Theorem 5.1. For example, let $\text{span}\{v\}$ with $\|v\|_2 = 1$ be any one-dimensional invariant for C^F. Consider an ordinary linear approximation, *i.e.* a pair $(\text{span}\{\delta_\psi\}, \text{span}\{\delta_\chi\})$ where ψ, χ are characters. Assuming $\delta_\psi \not\perp v$ and $\delta_\chi \not\perp v$, the correlation of the linear approximation over F can be estimated using the following trail:

$$\delta_\psi \xrightarrow[\langle v, \delta_\psi \rangle]{I} v \xrightarrow[1]{C^F} v \xrightarrow[\langle \delta_\chi, v \rangle]{I} \delta_\chi.$$

Theorem 5.1 yields the estimate $|\langle v, \delta_\psi \rangle \langle \delta_\chi, v \rangle| = |v(\psi)v(\chi)|$ for the absolute correlation. If v is flat as in Theorem 5.2, then the piling-up approximation suggests that all approximations with $\psi, \chi \in \operatorname{supp} v$ will have a correlation of roughly $1/|\operatorname{supp} v|$. In fact, this resolves a problem of Beierle $et\ al.$, who note that "our arguments are non-constructive and therefore, we are not able to identify those highly-biased linear approximations" [4, §1]. In fact, it is easy to identify the highly-biased approximations in practice: generically, any approximation with $\psi, \chi \in \operatorname{supp} v$ will do.

6   Rank-One Approximations

It is often convenient to represent the domain of a cipher as an array of m cells of n-bit vectors, because most of the operations in the cipher act on the cells in an independent way. In fact, in ciphers such as the AES, only the linear layer results in diffusion between cells. That is, let $G = (\mathbb{F}_2^n)^m$. Recall from Sect. 2 that $\mathbb{C}(\mathbb{F}_2^n)^m \cong [\mathbb{C}\mathbb{F}_2^n]^{\otimes m}$ and similarly for the dual group. For example, the probability distribution of a state with independent cells having distributions $p_1, \dots, p_m$, is represented by the rank-one tensor $p_1 \otimes \cdots \otimes p_m \in [\mathbb{C}\mathbb{F}_2^n]^{\otimes m}$ (see Sect. 2.1 for definitions).

A rank-one approximation (U, V) is any approximation such that U and V are spanned by a rank-one tensor. No further conditions are imposed on U and V. An important class of rank-one approximations is obtained from balanced Boolean functions $f : (\mathbb{F}_2^n)^m \to \mathbb{F}_2$ such that $f(x_1, \dots, x_m) = \sum_{i=1}^m f_i(x_i)$. As shown in Table 2, the corresponding vector space for such a property is spanned by the function $(-1)^f = \bigotimes_{i=1}^m (-1)^{f_i}$. Equivalently, the Fourier transformation of the corresponding vector space is spanned by

$$\mathcal{F}[(-1)^f] = \bigotimes_{i=1}^m \mathcal{F}[(-1)^{f_i}],$$

where $\mathcal{F}[(-1)^{f_i}]$ is precisely the Walsh-Hadamard transform of f_i. The invariants discussed in [5] and the nonlinear approximations considered by Beierle $et\ al.$ [4] are of this type.

6.1   Theoretical Analysis of Rank-One Trails

By Theorem 3.1 (2), the correlation matrix of a layer of m identical S-boxes S is equal to $(C^{\mathsf{S}})^{\otimes m}$. Indeed, correlation matrices are themselves tensors and the tensor rank (not to be confused with matrix rank) of $(C^{\mathsf{S}})^{\otimes m}$ is one. This expresses the fact that the S-box layer preserves independence of cells. A similar result holds for the key-addition step. Whereas the S-box layer preserves the rank-one structure of approximations, the linear layer tends to increase the rank. In fact, it is reasonable to interpret the rank as a measure of diffusion between the state cells. The correlation matrix of any function $\mathsf{F} : (\mathbb{F}_2^n)^m \to (\mathbb{F}_2^n)^m$ is itself a tensor and can be decomposed as $C^{\mathsf{F}} = \sum_{i=1}^r \lambda_i \bigotimes_{j=1}^m C_{i,j}$, where $C_{i,j}$ are $2^n \times 2^n$ matrices and r is the tensor rank of C^{F}.

Lemma 6.1. *Let* $F : (\mathbb{F}_2^n)^m \to (\mathbb{F}_2^n)^m$ *be a function such that* $F = (G, G, \ldots, G)$ *for some* $G : \mathbb{F}_2^n \to \mathbb{F}_2^n$. *If* $C^G = \sum_{i=1}^r \lambda_i \bigotimes_{j=1}^n C_{i,j}$, *then*

$$C^F = \sum_{i_1,\ldots,i_m \in [r]} \left(\prod_{k=1}^m \lambda_{i_k} \right) \bigotimes_{k=1}^m \bigotimes_{j=1}^n C_{i_k,j},$$

where $[r] = \{1, \ldots, r\}$. *In particular, the tensor rank of* C^F *is at most* r^m.

Proof. By Theorem 3.1 (2), it holds that $C^F = (C^G)^{\otimes m}$. The result follows by expanding this expression using the multilinearity of tensor products. □

Lemma 6.1 can be used to obtain a decomposition of the correlation matrix of the `MixColumn` map of Midori-64 and MANTIS into 2^8 rank-one terms. This map $M : (\mathbb{F}_2^4)^4 \to (\mathbb{F}_2^4)^4$ can be represented by the following matrix over $\mathbb{F}_{2^4}$:

$$\begin{pmatrix} 0 & 1 & 1 & 1 \\ 1 & 0 & 1 & 1 \\ 1 & 1 & 0 & 1 \\ 1 & 1 & 1 & 0 \end{pmatrix}.$$

Up to a reordering of the input bits, one can think of M as a map $\widetilde{M} = (L, L, L, L)$ where L corresponds to the same matrix as above, but over $\mathbb{F}_2$. Specifically, $\widetilde{M} = \sigma M \sigma$ where $\sigma : (\mathbb{F}_2^4)^4 \to (\mathbb{F}_2^4)^4$ is the bit permutation defined by $\sigma_i(x_1, \ldots, x_4) = (x_{1,i}, \ldots, x_{4,i})$. Since C^L is a 16×16 matrix, one can check that

$$C^L = \frac{1}{2}\left[\begin{pmatrix} 1 & 0 \\ 0 & 1 \end{pmatrix}^{\otimes 4} + \begin{pmatrix} 0 & 1 \\ 1 & 0 \end{pmatrix}^{\otimes 4} + \begin{pmatrix} 1 & 0 \\ 0 & -1 \end{pmatrix}^{\otimes 4} - \begin{pmatrix} 0 & 1 \\ -1 & 0 \end{pmatrix}^{\otimes 4} \right].$$

To see this, it is helpful to observe that C^L is symmetric as a tensor. Since $\widetilde{M} = \sigma M \sigma$ where σ is a linear map corresponding to a reordering of bits, it follows from Theorem 3.2 (2) and Lemma 6.1 that

$$C^M = 2^{-4} \sum_{i_1,i_2,i_3,i_4 \in [4]^4} \left(\prod_{j=1}^4 \lambda_{i_j} \right) \left[\bigotimes_{j=1}^4 C_{i_j} \right]^{\otimes 4}.$$

with $\lambda_1 = \lambda_2 = \lambda_3 = 1$ and $\lambda_4 = -1$ and

$$C_1 = \begin{pmatrix} 1 & 0 \\ 0 & 1 \end{pmatrix}, \quad C_2 = \begin{pmatrix} 0 & 1 \\ 1 & 0 \end{pmatrix}, \quad C_3 = \begin{pmatrix} 1 & 0 \\ 0 & -1 \end{pmatrix}, \quad C_4 = \begin{pmatrix} 0 & 1 \\ -1 & 0 \end{pmatrix}.$$

Hence, the tensor rank of C^M is at most 2^8. This is significantly lower than the worst-case of 2^{16}. Practically speaking, this enables a detailed analysis of rank-one approximations for Midori-64 in Sect. 7.3. In fact, one can show that this decomposition is minimal *i.e.* the rank of C^M is equal to 2^8.

Lemma 6.2. (Lemma 3.5 in [19]). *Let* $V_1, \ldots, V_d$ *be finite-dimensional vector spaces over* $\mathbb{C}$. *If* $x_{i,1}, \ldots, x_{i,r} \in V_i$ *are linearly independent for* $i = 1, \ldots, d$, *then the vector* $\sum_{i=1}^r x_{1,i} \otimes x_{2,i} \otimes \cdots \otimes x_{d,i}$ *in* $\bigotimes_{i=1}^r V_i$ *has tensor rank* r.

To see why Lemma 6.2 implies the result, let V_i be the vector space of 16×16 matrices over $\mathbb{C}$. This is an inner product space under the Frobenius inner product $\mathrm{Tr}\,(A^*B)$ between matrices A and B. It is easy to check that the matrices C_i defined above are mutually orthogonal with respect to this inner product. This implies the mutual orthogonality of the matrices $\left[\bigotimes_{j=1}^{4} C_{i_j}\right]^{\otimes 4}$. The result follows by the linear independence of orthogonal vectors.

6.2   Automated Analysis of Rank-One Trails

Let $\mathsf{F} = \mathsf{F}_r \circ \cdots \circ \mathsf{F}_1$ be a permutation on $(\mathbb{F}_2^n)^m$. By Theorem 5.1, an optimal rank-one trail for F can be found by solving the following optimization problem:

$$\text{maximize } \sum_{i=1}^{r} \log_2 \left| \left\langle \bigotimes_{j=1}^{m} v_{i+1,j}, \, C^{\mathsf{F}_i} \bigotimes_{j=1}^{m} v_{i,j} \right\rangle \right|$$

$$\text{subject to } \|v_{i,j}\|_2 = 1 \text{ for } i = 1, \ldots, r+1, \, j = 1, \ldots, m$$

$$v_{i,j}(\mathbb{1}) = 0 \text{ for } (i,j) \in A \text{ and } v_{i,j} = \delta_{\mathbb{1}} \text{ otherwise,}$$

where the last condition ensures that the vectors $v_{i,j}$ are active and balanced, *i.e.* orthogonal to $\delta_{\mathbb{1}}$, on a predetermined pattern of cells A. Clearly, at least one cell must be active to obtain a nontrivial result. In practice, it is better to take the logarithm of the objective function in order to avoid vanishing gradients.

Restricting to real-valued $v_{i,j}$, the above is an optimization problem over the product of several copies of the $(2^n - 1)$-dimensional unit sphere. This domain is a Riemannian manifold, and common iterative numerical optimization techniques such as steepest descent and conjugate gradient have been generalized to this setting [34]. This is the basic approach behind the automated method proposed in this section. The source code of the tool is provided as supplementary material and relies on the PYMANOPT library [40].

The power of this method lies in the fact that it enables iterative convergence to an optimal trail. This is made possible because the general nature of rank-one approximations results in a relaxed, continuous optimization problem rather than a discrete one. Although it is sometimes necessary to ensure that the outermost vectors of the trail correspond to (for example) a Boolean function, there is no reason to impose the same condition on vectors which are internal to the trail.

Example 6.1. The tool can be applied to find rank-one invariants of arbitrary functions with a limited number of input and output bits, which is a difficult problem in general [5]. For example, Fig. 2 shows the iterative convergence towards an invariant of the Midori-64 linear layer. This process takes about a second on an ordinary computer. By optimizing over the ellipsoid of unit-norm vectors in the eigenspaces $E_\lambda(C^{\mathsf{S}})$ of the correlation matrix C^{S}, joint invariants for the linear and S-box layer can be found. Instructions to reproduce this example are included as supplementary material in the supplementary material of the extended version [7]. The tool also implements a barrier method to find *all* rank-one invariants for a given linear layer.   ▷

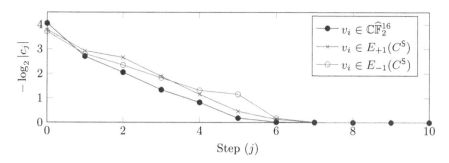

Fig. 2. Correlation c_j at each step of the optimization process for finding invariants of the form $v_1 \otimes v_2 \otimes v_3 \otimes v_4$ with $v_i(\mathbb{1}) = 0$ for the Midori-64 linear layer.

A number of challenges remain for larger problems. These include addressing key-dependence, which is simplified due to the use of the Fourier transform, and convergence issues. For completeness, the supplementary material of the extended version [7] summarizes the (somewhat technical) steps that were taken to address these challenges.

7   Open Problem of Beierle *et al.*

This section explains observations of Beierle *et al.* [4] regarding a nonlinear approximation for two rounds of Midori-64. More broadly, the results in this section lead to a deeper understanding of many nonlinear approximations of the Midori-64 round function.

7.1   Problem Statement

Beierle *et al.* [4, Section 4.4] consider a nonlinear approximation over two rounds of Midori-64, restricted to a single column of the state. Denote this function by F. Its correlation matrix is equal to $C^F = C^M [C^S]^{\otimes 4} C^{K_2} C^M [C^S]^{\otimes 4} C^{K_1}$, where K_1 and K_2 are key-addition maps, S is the S-box and M the matrix defined in Sect. 6.1. Recall from Sect. 1 that Beierle *et al.* [4] describe nonlinear approximations using linear properties of a nonlinearly transformed representation of the cipher. The details of their approach will not be discussed here; the geometric framework developed in Sects. 4 and 5 will be used instead. The nonlinear functions considered by Beierle *et al.* are of the form $\sum_{i=1}^{4} f_i(x)$ with $f_i : \mathbb{F}_2^4 \to \mathbb{F}_2$ and consequently, as discussed in Sect. 6 on page 23, correspond to approximations spanned by rank-one vectors. Specifically, the pair of nonlinear functions considered in [4, Section 4.4] corresponds to a one-dimensional approximation $(\text{span}\{u \otimes v^{\otimes 3}\}, \text{span}\{u \otimes v^{\otimes 3}\})$ for F with

$$u = 1/4 \cdot (0, 1, 0, -1, 0, 1, 0, -1, 0, -1, 0, 1, 0, -1, 0, -3)^\top$$
$$v = 1/2 \cdot (0, 0, 0, -1, 0, 0, 0, -1, 0,\ \ 0, 0, 1, 0,\ \ 0, 0, -1)^\top.$$

The coordinates above are given for the character basis δ_{χ_w} with lexicographic ordering of w. Note that v is an eigenvector of C^S. Beierle *et al.* estimate the correlation of the above approximation by (from the perspective of this paper) the following one-round trail, which has absolute correlation at least $9/32$:

$$u \otimes v \otimes v \otimes v \xrightarrow[\pm 1 \text{ or } \pm 1/2]{[C^S]^{\otimes 4} C^{K_i}} u \otimes v \otimes v \otimes v \xrightarrow[9/16]{C^M} u \otimes v \otimes v \otimes v. \tag{1}$$

The computation of the correlation over C^M was done by a direct evaluation of the inner product $\langle u \otimes v^{\otimes 3}, C^M u \otimes v^{\otimes 3} \rangle$. This trail was believed to hold whenever $K_i \in \mathbb{F}_2^4 \times \mathcal{K}^3$ for $i = 1, 2$, with $\mathcal{K} = \{(0, 0, x, y) \mid x, y \in \mathbb{F}_2\}$. The weak key set $\mathcal{K}$ ensures the invariance of the tensor product factor v under key addition. Based on the above, one estimates an absolute correlation of at least $(9/32)^2$ over F. However, Beierle *et al.* experimentally observe that this estimate is not accurate:

(i) When $K_2 \in (\mathbb{F}_2^4 \setminus \mathcal{K}) \times \mathcal{K}^3$, the correlation is found to equal zero.
(ii) For other keys, the correlation takes on various values, but is always significantly larger than the estimated minimum of $81/1024$. Specifically, for $K_1, K_2 \in \mathcal{K}^4$, the correlation ranges from $35/64$ to $40/64 = 5/8$. For other keys, it lies between $39/256$ and $65/256$.

In their conclusion, the authors remark that understanding this phenomenon is "a major open problem". Sections 7.2 and 7.3 completely explains the above observations using the methods developed in Sects. 4 and 5.

7.2 Optimal Rank-One Trail

As shown in Sect. 6.1, the effect of the linear layer is nontrivial and this makes finding an optimal rank-one trail difficult. Hence, a simple explanation for observation (ii) could be that the trail (1) proposed by Beierle *et al.* is not a good guess. Using the tool from Sect. 6.2, it is easy to find the optimal rank-one trail – ignoring the effect of key-addition for now. Running the tool (the configuration is given in the extended version [7]) yields the following trail with absolute correlation at most $9/16$:

$$u \otimes v^{\otimes 3} \xrightarrow[\pm 3/4 \text{ or } \pm 1/4]{[C^S]^{\otimes 4} C^{K_1}} v^{\otimes 4} \xrightarrow[1]{C^M} v^{\otimes 4} \xrightarrow[\pm 1]{[C^S]^{\otimes 4} C^{K_2}} v^{\otimes 4} \xrightarrow[3/4]{C^M} u \otimes v^{\otimes 3}.$$

A short calculation shows that the third step requires $K_2 \in \mathcal{K}$, otherwise the trail has correlation zero. Furthermore, the correlation $3/4$ in the first step occurs if and only if $K_1 \in \mathcal{K}^4$. In hindsight, one might have guessed the above trail without detailed analysis: the choice of $v^{\otimes 4}$ as an intermediate step is natural, since $v^{\otimes 4}$ is an invariant for the round function. This is an instance of the general phenomenon discussed in the last paragraph of Sect. 5.3.

7.3 Theoretical Analysis of the Problem

The correlations predicted by the rank-one trail obtained in Sect. 7.2 are within 10 to 30% of the observed correlations reported by Beierle *et al.* [4, Tables 1–4].

However, the trail does not yet explain the zero-correlation approximation. In this section, the results from Sect. 6.1 will be used to find a *minimal and complete* set of rank-one trails for the approximation.

The propagation of $u \otimes v^{\otimes 3}$ under the Midori-64 round function will first be analyzed. For the zero-correlation case, the miss-in-the-middle strategy from Sect. 4.2 will be used. It will then be shown that a relatively short formula for the exact key-dependent correlation of the approximation can be computed.

Let $K_1 = (k_1, k_2, \ldots, k_{16}) \in \mathbb{F}_2^{16}$ and $K_2 = (k'_1, k'_2, \ldots, k'_{16}) \in \mathbb{F}_2^{16}$. The results in Sect. 6.1 can be used to compute the image of $u \otimes v^{\otimes 3}$ under one round:

$$C^{\mathsf{M}}[C^{\mathsf{S}}]^{\otimes 4} C^{K_1} u \otimes v^{\otimes 3} = -\nu\, C^{\mathsf{M}}(C^{\mathsf{S}} C^{k_1 \| \cdots \| k_4} u) \otimes v^{\otimes 3} = \nu\, v \otimes \left(\textstyle\sum_{i=1}^{16} c_i\, v_i^{\otimes 3}\right),$$

where $\nu = -\prod_{i=2}^{4}(-1)^{k_{4i-1}+k_{4i}}$. The coefficients c_i and the vectors v_i are listed in the supplementary material of the extended version [7]. Note that, because C^{M} has rank 2^8, one initially obtains 2^8 terms. However, this can be reduced to 16 by grouping terms appropriately. This can be done manually by exploiting the structure of the rank-decomposition, but SAGE code to automate this is also provided as supplementary material. Since the vectors v_i are mutually orthogonal and this is preserved when multiplied with (the same) orthogonal matrices, Lemma 6.2 implies that the above decomposition is minimal. Interestingly, not all of the vectors v_i correspond to Boolean functions or probability distributions.

A similar computation can be performed for the inverse of the second round. Specifically, recalling that S and M are involutions,

$$C^{K_2}[C^{\mathsf{S}}]^{\otimes 4} C^{\mathsf{M}} u \otimes v^{\otimes 3} = \nu'\, C^{k'_1 \| \cdots \| k'_4} v \otimes \left(\textstyle\sum_{i=1}^{8} c'_i \bigotimes_{j=1}^{3}(C^{k'_{4j} \| \cdots \| k'_{4j+4}} v'_i)\right).$$

The coefficients c'_i and the vectors v'_i are listed in the supplementary material of the extended version [7] and $\nu' = (-1)^{k'_3 + k'_4 + 1}$. The minimality of the above decomposition can again be established using Lemma 6.2.

Zero-Correlation Approximation. Let $U = \operatorname{span}\{v\} \otimes (\mathbb{C}\widehat{\mathbb{F}}_2^4)^{\otimes 3}$ and $V = \operatorname{span}\{C^{k'_1 \| \cdots \| k'_4} v\} \otimes (\mathbb{C}\widehat{\mathbb{F}}_2^4)^{\otimes 3}$. The decompositions above clearly imply the following inclusions:

$$C^{\mathsf{M}}[C^{\mathsf{S}}]^{\otimes 4} C^{K_1} u \otimes v^{\otimes 3} \in U \quad \text{and} \quad C^{K_2}[C^{\mathsf{S}}]^{\otimes 4} C^{\mathsf{M}} u \otimes v^{\otimes 3} \in V.$$

Consequently, if $U \perp V$, the general miss-in-the-middle principle discussed in Sect. 4.2 implies that the approximation has correlation zero. This happens whenever $\langle v, C^{k'_1 \| \cdots \| k'_4} v \rangle = 0$. That is,

$$\begin{aligned}
&\langle (0,0,0,1,0,0,0,1,0,0,0,-1,0,0,0,1)^{\top}, \\
&\quad (0,0,0,1,0,0,0,(-1)^{k'_2},0,0,0,(-1)^{1+k'_1},0,0,0,(-1)^{k'_1+k'_2})^{\top} \rangle \\
&= 1 + (-1)^{k'_1} + (-1)^{k'_2} + (-1)^{k'_1+k'_2},
\end{aligned}$$

which equals zero unless $k'_1 = k'_2 = 0$. This explains the condition $K_2 \in (\mathbb{F}_2^4 \setminus \mathcal{K}) \times \mathcal{K}^3$ observed by Beierle *et al.* [4].

Refining the Correlation Estimate. Now assume $K_2 \in \mathcal{K}^4$, so that the correlation is nonzero. A closer inspection of the vectors v_i and v'_j reveals that $|\langle v_i, C^{k'_{4j}\|\cdots\|k'_{4j+4}} v'_j\rangle| \le 1/2$ unless $i = 3$ and $j = 1$. That is, when the inner product $\langle C^{\mathsf{K}_2}[C^\mathsf{S}]^{\otimes 4} C^\mathsf{M} u \otimes v^{\otimes 3}, C^{\mathsf{K}_2}[C^\mathsf{S}]^{\otimes 4} C^\mathsf{M} u \otimes v^{\otimes 3}\rangle$ is expanded using the decomposition above, the term corresponding to $c_3 c'_1$ has a weight of one whereas all other terms have weight at most 2^{-3}. Since $v_3 = v'_1 = v$, this term corresponds to the trail from Sect. 7.2.

The correlation estimate can be improved by including additional trails. In principle, all 128 terms in the expanded inner product between the forward and backward expressions can be computed. The supplementary material contains a SAGE script that computes a short formula for the exact key-dependent correlation of the approximation, which is also listed in the extended version [7].

In fact, due to the low rank of C^M, the same technique can be used to analyze *any* rank-one approximation of F. This includes all linear approximations. In general, the minimal number of rank-one trails can be higher or lower than 16×8 (depending on the choice of the input and output property).

Acknowledgments. This work is based on my master's thesis "Linear Cryptanalysis in the Weak-Key Model" [6]. I'm grateful to Vincent Rijmen for supervising this thesis, and for comments on a draft of this paper. I also thank Gregor Leander and Christof Beierle for interesting discussions about this work at Ruhr-University Bochum. The author is supported by a PhD Fellowship from the Research Foundation – Flanders (FWO).

References

1. Abdelraheem, M.A., Ågren, M., Beelen, P., Leander, G.: On the distribution of linear biases: three instructive examples. In: Safavi-Naini, R., Canetti, R. (eds.) CRYPTO 2012. LNCS, vol. 7417, pp. 50–67. Springer, Heidelberg (2012). https://doi.org/10.1007/978-3-642-32009-5_4

2. Baignères, T., Junod, P., Vaudenay, S.: How far can we go beyond linear cryptanalysis? In: Lee, P.J. (ed.) ASIACRYPT 2004. LNCS, vol. 3329, pp. 432–450. Springer, Heidelberg (2004). https://doi.org/10.1007/978-3-540-30539-2_31

3. Baignères, T., Stern, J., Vaudenay, S.: Linear cryptanalysis of non binary ciphers. In: Adams, C., Miri, A., Wiener, M. (eds.) SAC 2007. LNCS, vol. 4876, pp. 184–211. Springer, Heidelberg (2007). https://doi.org/10.1007/978-3-540-77360-3_13

4. Beierle, C., Canteaut, A., Leander, G.: Nonlinear approximations in cryptanalysis revisited. IACR Trans. Symm. Cryptol. **4**, 80–101 (2018)

5. Beyne, T.: Block cipher invariants as eigenvectors of correlation matrices. In: Peyrin, T., Galbraith, S. (eds.) ASIACRYPT 2018. LNCS, vol. 11272, pp. 3–31. Springer, Cham (2018). https://doi.org/10.1007/978-3-030-03326-2_1

6. Beyne, T.: Linear Cryptanalysis in the Weak Key Model. Master's thesis, KU Leuven (2019). https://homes.esat.kuleuven.be/~tbeyne/masterthesis/thesis.pdf

7. Beyne, T.: A geometric approach to linear cryptanalysis. Cryptology ePrint Archive, Report 2021/1247 (2021). https://ia.cr/2021/1247

8. Beyne, T.: Linear cryptanalysis of FF3-1 and FEA. In: Malkin, T., Peikert, C. (eds.) CRYPTO 2021. LNCS, vol. 12825, pp. 41–69. Springer, Cham (2021). https://doi.org/10.1007/978-3-030-84242-0_3

9. Biryukov, A., De Cannière, C., Quisquater, M.: On multiple linear approximations. In: Franklin, M. (ed.) CRYPTO 2004. LNCS, vol. 3152, pp. 1–22. Springer, Heidelberg (2004). https://doi.org/10.1007/978-3-540-28628-8_1

10. Björck, Å., Golub, G.H.: Numerical methods for computing angles between linear subspaces. Math. Comput. **27**(123), 579–594 (1973)

11. Bogdanov, A., Knežević, M., Leander, G., Toz, D., Varıcı, K., Verbauwhede, I.: SPONGENT: a lightweight hash function. In: Preneel, B., Takagi, T. (eds.) CHES 2011. LNCS, vol. 6917, pp. 312–325. Springer, Heidelberg (2011). https://doi.org/10.1007/978-3-642-23951-9_21

12. Bogdanov, A., Leander, G., Nyberg, K., Wang, M.: Integral and multidimensional linear distinguishers with correlation zero. In: Wang, X., Sako, K. (eds.) ASIACRYPT 2012. LNCS, vol. 7658, pp. 244–261. Springer, Heidelberg (2012). https://doi.org/10.1007/978-3-642-34961-4_16

13. Bogdanov, A., Rijmen, V.: Linear hulls with correlation zero and linear cryptanalysis of block ciphers. Des. Codes Cryptogr. **70**(3), 369–383 (2014)

14. Cho, J.Y.: Linear cryptanalysis of reduced-round PRESENT. In: Pieprzyk, J. (ed.) CT-RSA 2010. LNCS, vol. 5985, pp. 302–317. Springer, Heidelberg (2010). https://doi.org/10.1007/978-3-642-11925-5_21

15. Collard, B., Standaert, F.-X.: A statistical saturation attack against the block cipher PRESENT. In: Fischlin, M. (ed.) CT-RSA 2009. LNCS, vol. 5473, pp. 195–210. Springer, Heidelberg (2009). https://doi.org/10.1007/978-3-642-00862-7_13

16. Daemen, J., Govaerts, R., Vandewalle, J.: Correlation matrices. In: Preneel, B. (ed.) FSE 1994. LNCS, vol. 1008, pp. 275–285. Springer, Heidelberg (1995). https://doi.org/10.1007/3-540-60590-8_21

17. Daemen, J., Knudsen, L., Rijmen, V.: The block cipher square. In: Biham, E. (ed.) FSE 1997. LNCS, vol. 1267, pp. 149–165. Springer, Heidelberg (1997). https://doi.org/10.1007/BFb0052343

18. Daemen, J., Rijmen, V.: The wide trail design strategy. In: Honary, B. (ed.) Cryptography and Coding 2001. LNCS, vol. 2260, pp. 222–238. Springer, Heidelberg (2001). https://doi.org/10.1007/3-540-45325-3_20

19. De Silva, V., Lim, L.H.: Tensor rank and the ill-posedness of the best low-rank approximation problem. SIAM J. Matrix Anal. Appl. **30**(3), 1084–1127 (2008)

20. Granboulan, L., Levieil, É., Piret, G.: Pseudorandom permutation families over abelian groups. In: Robshaw, M. (ed.) FSE 2006. LNCS, vol. 4047, pp. 57–77. Springer, Heidelberg (2006). https://doi.org/10.1007/11799313_5

21. Harpes, C., Kramer, G.G., Massey, J.L.: A generalization of linear cryptanalysis and the applicability of matsui's piling-up lemma. In: Guillou, L.C., Quisquater, J.-J. (eds.) EUROCRYPT 1995. LNCS, vol. 921, pp. 24–38. Springer, Heidelberg (1995). https://doi.org/10.1007/3-540-49264-X_3

22. Harpes, C., Massey, J.L.: Partitioning cryptanalysis. In: Biham, E. (ed.) FSE 1997. LNCS, vol. 1267, pp. 13–27. Springer, Heidelberg (1997). https://doi.org/10.1007/BFb0052331

23. Hermelin, M., Cho, J.Y., Nyberg, K.: Multidimensional linear cryptanalysis of reduced round serpent. In: Mu, Y., Susilo, W., Seberry, J. (eds.) ACISP 2008. LNCS, vol. 5107, pp. 203–215. Springer, Heidelberg (2008). https://doi.org/10.1007/978-3-540-70500-0_15

24. Jordan, C.: Essai sur la géométrie à n dimensions. Bull. de la Société mathématique de France **3**, 103–174 (1875)

25. Kaliski, B.S., Robshaw, M.J.B.: Linear cryptanalysis using multiple approximations. In: Desmedt, Y.G. (ed.) CRYPTO 1994. LNCS, vol. 839, pp. 26–39. Springer, Heidelberg (1994). https://doi.org/10.1007/3-540-48658-5_4

26. Knudsen, L.R., Robshaw, M.J.B.: Non-linear approximations in linear cryptanalysis. In: Maurer, U. (ed.) EUROCRYPT 1996. LNCS, vol. 1070, pp. 224–236. Springer, Heidelberg (1996). https://doi.org/10.1007/3-540-68339-9_20

27. Knudsen, L., Wagner, D.: Integral cryptanalysis. In: Daemen, J., Rijmen, V. (eds.) FSE 2002. LNCS, vol. 2365, pp. 112–127. Springer, Heidelberg (2002). https://doi.org/10.1007/3-540-45661-9_9

28. Lai, X., Massey, J.L., Murphy, S.: Markov ciphers and differential cryptanalysis. In: Davies, D.W. (ed.) EUROCRYPT 1991. LNCS, vol. 547, pp. 17–38. Springer, Heidelberg (1991). https://doi.org/10.1007/3-540-46416-6_2

29. Leander, G.: On linear hulls, statistical saturation attacks, PRESENT and a cryptanalysis of PUFFIN. In: Paterson, K.G. (ed.) EUROCRYPT 2011. LNCS, vol. 6632, pp. 303–322. Springer, Heidelberg (2011). https://doi.org/10.1007/978-3-642-20465-4_18

30. Leander, G., Abdelraheem, M.A., AlKhzaimi, H., Zenner, E.: A cryptanalysis of PRINTCIPHER: the invariant subspace attack. In: Rogaway, P. (ed.) CRYPTO 2011. LNCS, vol. 6841, pp. 206–221. Springer, Heidelberg (2011). https://doi.org/10.1007/978-3-642-22792-9_12

31. Matsui, M.: Linear cryptanalysis method for DES cipher. In: Helleseth, T. (ed.) EUROCRYPT 1993. LNCS, vol. 765, pp. 386–397. Springer, Heidelberg (1994). https://doi.org/10.1007/3-540-48285-7_33

32. Nyberg, K.: Linear approximation of block ciphers. In: De Santis, A. (ed.) EUROCRYPT 1994. LNCS, vol. 950, pp. 439–444. Springer, Heidelberg (1995). https://doi.org/10.1007/BFb0053460

33. Parker, M., Raddum, H.: $\mathbb{Z}_4$-linear cryptanalysis. Tech. rep., NESSIE Internal Report: NES/DOC/UIB/WP5/018/1 (2020)

34. Smith, S.T.: Optimization techniques on riemannian manifolds. Fields Inst. Commun. **3**(3), 113–135 (1994)

35. Sun, B., et al.: Links among impossible differential, integral and zero correlation linear cryptanalysis. In: Gennaro, R., Robshaw, M. (eds.) CRYPTO 2015. LNCS, vol. 9215, pp. 95–115. Springer, Heidelberg (2015). https://doi.org/10.1007/978-3-662-47989-6_5

36. Tardy-Corfdir, A., Gilbert, H.: A known plaintext attack of FEAL-4 and FEAL-6. In: Feigenbaum, J. (ed.) CRYPTO 1991. LNCS, vol. 576, pp. 172–182. Springer, Heidelberg (1992). https://doi.org/10.1007/3-540-46766-1_12

37. Terras, A.: Fourier Analysis on Finite Groups and Applications. Cambridge University Press, Cambridge (1999)

38. Todo, Y.: Structural evaluation by generalized integral property. In: Oswald, E., Fischlin, M. (eds.) EUROCRYPT 2015. LNCS, vol. 9056, pp. 287–314. Springer, Heidelberg (2015). https://doi.org/10.1007/978-3-662-46800-5_12

39. Todo, Y., Leander, G., Sasaki, Yu.: Nonlinear invariant attack. In: Cheon, J.H., Takagi, T. (eds.) ASIACRYPT 2016. LNCS, vol. 10032, pp. 3–33. Springer, Heidelberg (2016). https://doi.org/10.1007/978-3-662-53890-6_1

40. Townsend, J., Koep, N., Weichwald, S.: Pymanopt: a python toolbox for optimization on manifolds using automatic differentiation. J. Mach. Learn. Res. **17**(137), 1–5 (2016)

41. Vaudenay, S.: An experiment on DES statistical cryptanalysis. In: ACM CCS 96, pp. 139–147

42. Wagner, D.: Towards a unifying view of block cipher cryptanalysis. In: Roy, B., Meier, W. (eds.) FSE 2004. LNCS, vol. 3017, pp. 16–33. Springer, Heidelberg (2004). https://doi.org/10.1007/978-3-540-25937-4_2

Lattice Enumeration for Tower NFS: A 521-Bit Discrete Logarithm Computation

Gabrielle De Micheli[✉], Pierrick Gaudry[✉], and Cécile Pierrot[✉]

Université de Lorraine, CNRS, Inria, Nancy, France
{gabrielle.de-micheli,cecile.pierrot}inria.fr, pierrick.gaudry@loria.fr

Abstract. The Tower variant of the Number Field Sieve (TNFS) is known to be asymptotically the most efficient algorithm to solve the discrete logarithm problem in finite fields of medium characteristics, when the extension degree is composite. A major obstacle to an efficient implementation of TNFS is the collection of algebraic relations, as it happens in dimension greater than 2. This requires the construction of new sieving algorithms which remain efficient as the dimension grows. In this article, we overcome this difficulty by considering a lattice enumeration algorithm which we adapt to this specific context. We also consider a new sieving area, a high-dimensional sphere, whereas previous sieving algorithms for the classical NFS considered an orthotope. Our new sieving technique leads to a much smaller running time, despite the larger dimension of the search space, and even when considering a larger target, as demonstrated by a record computation we performed in a 521-bit finite field $\mathbb{F}_{p^6}$. The target finite field is of the same form than finite fields used in recent zero-knowledge proofs in some blockchains. This is the first reported implementation of TNFS.

1 Introduction

Context. While the post-quantum competition is ongoing, the discrete logarithm problem is still at the basis of the security of many currently-deployed public key protocols. Given a cyclic group G, a generator $g \in G$ and a target $h \in G$, solving the discrete logarithm problem in G means finding an integer $x \mod |G|$ such that $g^x = h$. The hardness of this problem depends on the group G and the two usual choices are the group of the invertible elements in a finite field and the group of points of an elliptic curve. This article deals with discrete logarithms in finite fields. In particular, as small characteristics finite fields are no longer considered because of the advent of quasipolynomial time algorithms [3,12,25]. We focus on medium and large characteristics. For a finite field $\mathbb{F}_{p^n}$ we recall that the characteristic p is of medium size if $L_{p^n}(1/3) < p < L_{p^n}(2/3)$ and of large size if $p > L_{p^n}(2/3)$.[1] Equivalently, it means that the extension degree n is of bounded size with respect to the finite field order.

---

[1] We use the usual notation $L_Q(\alpha, c) = \exp((c + o(1))(\log Q)^\alpha (\log \log Q)^{1-\alpha})$, where $o(1)$ tends to 0 when Q tends to infinity.

© International Association for Cryptologic Research 2021
M. Tibouchi and H. Wang (Eds.): ASIACRYPT 2021, LNCS 13090, pp. 67–96, 2021.
https://doi.org/10.1007/978-3-030-92062-3_3

NFS and TNFS. The Number Field Sieve (NFS) algorithm and its variants are the fastest known algorithms to solve the discrete logarithm problem in finite fields of medium and large characteristics. One of these variants is the Tower Number Field Sieve (TNFS), known to be asymptotically more efficient than a classical NFS for some fields when the extension degree is composite. TNFS exploits the algebraic structure of towers of number fields: the main difference with NFS comes from the representation of the target field $\mathbb{F}_{p^n}$. Whereas in the classical NFS setup, the finite field $\mathbb{F}_{p^n}$ is represented as the quotient field $\mathbb{F}_p[x]/(f)$ where f is a polynomial of degree n over $\mathbb{F}_p$, in the TNFS setup, we have $\mathbb{F}_{p^n} \cong \mathcal{R}/p\mathcal{R}$ where $\mathcal{R}$ is the ring defined as the quotient $\mathbb{Z}[t]/h(t)$, and $h \in \mathbb{Z}[t]$ is a degree n polynomial that remains irreducible modulo p.

Originally proposed by Schirokauer [32], TNFS was reinvestigated by Barbulescu, Gaudry, and Kleinjung [4] in 2015. They showed that the asymptotic complexity of TNFS in large characteristics is $L_{p^n}(1/3, \sqrt[3]{64/9})$, the same as for the NFS. In medium characteristics, the complexity of TNFS is greater than $L_{p^n}(1/3)$ and thus this algorithm is only considered in the large case.

This algorithm was then modified by Kim, Barbulescu [23] and Jeong [24] to form the extended Tower Number Field Sieve (exTNFS), the variant being dedicated to composite extension degrees, *i.e.*, when $n = \eta\kappa$. This extended variant has an $L_{p^n}(1/3)$ complexity also in medium characteristics. In this case, the overall complexity of exTNFS can be as low as $L_{p^n}(1/3, \sqrt[3]{48/9})$ if there is a factor of n of the appropriate size (see Table 1). Both TNFS and exTNFS can be coupled with a multiple field variant – for any finite field – and a special variant – for some sparse characteristics only – giving each time a lower asymptotic complexity. We do not address these variants in this article.

Table 1. Medium and large characteristics complexities of various algorithms, expressed as $L_{p^n}(1/3, \sqrt[3]{c/9})$, where c is the reported value in this table.

Algorithm	Medium characteristic	Boundary	Large characteristic
NFS	96	48	64
TNFS	–	–	64
exTNFS	≥ 48	48	64

Towards an Implementation of ExTNFS. One can see from the complexities given in Table 1 that for NFS, medium characteristics are harder than large characteristics. This remains true for the multiple and special variants. However, a noticeable exception to this observation lies in the exTNFS algorithm. Indeed, when the degree n is composite, *i.e.*, $n = \eta\kappa$, the target finite field $\mathbb{F}_{p^n} = \mathbb{F}_{p^{\eta\kappa}}$ can be viewed as $\mathbb{F}_{P^\kappa}$ where P is a prime power of the same bitsize as p^η. Thus, the complexity of exTNFS in medium characteristics can be viewed similarly as the complexity of NFS at the boundary case between medium and large characteristics, leading to a smaller c constant in the L_{p^n}-notation. Hence we find a lower complexity in medium characteristics than in large ones with exTNFS, which makes it a promising candidate for computational records in this area.

Let us assume we want to evaluate the security of a family of finite fields with fixed composite extension degree (for instance $n = 6$). These families often arise in pairing-based protocols. Evaluating the security of a concrete finite field in such a family is not an easy task, as we are not even able to tell beforehand whether NFS or exTNFS would be the fastest algorithm. Indeed, using a fixed extension degree asymptotically defines the characteristic as large, an area where the best discrete logarithm algorithm is NFS (not exTNFS). However, let us keep in mind that medium and large characteristics are notions defined for asymptotic sizes; as soon as we set a concrete target finite field it is not well understood how we should qualify its characteristic. In this work we underline that exTNFS shows real improvements with regards to current NFS computations for this family. Current record computations (e.g. for 400 or 500-bit finite fields) deal with areas where asymptotic analysis are not yet the relevant ones. We cannot easily extrapolate on current and deployed sizes (e.g. for more than 2000-bit finite fields) but our implementation of exTNFS provides practical insight on security parameters by showing its incredibly good behavior at lower sizes.

In the rest of this article, to simplify notations and to be coherent with the recent literature, we use TNFS as a short hand for ex-TNFS[2]. We do however assume the degree n of our target finite field is composite, thus considering specifically the extended variant.

Lattice Enumeration for TNFS. Despite the fact that TNFS is promising, no implementation was done using this variant of NFS, up to this work. Indeed, so far, excluding the very small characteristics 2 and 3, all discrete logarithm record computations were performed using NFS, the special variant of NFS, or the Function Field Sieve – a method for small characteristics only.

A major obstacle to an efficient implementation of TNFS is the collection of algebraic relations where equations between small elements of number fields must be found. Indeed, whereas NFS requires sieving through $(a, b) \in \mathbb{Z}^2$ pairs, the tower setup sieves through $(a(\iota), b(\iota))$-pairs, *i.e.*, degree $\eta - 1$ polynomials with bounded coefficients. This requires the construction of sieving algorithms in a space of dimension $2\eta \geq 4$, which remain efficient as the dimension grows.

In dimension 2, Franke and Kleinjung [10] proposed in 2005 an efficient algorithm used in all previous records. For higher dimensions, after the pioneer work in $\mathbb{F}_{p^{12}}$ by Hayasaka et al. [19], the transition vectors method from Grémy [13] and a recursive plane method proposed by McGuire and Robinson [27] were tested in dimension 3 and used for record computations using NFS. However, the efficiency of their algorithms for even higher dimensions is questionable.

Our Work. In this article, we introduce an efficient sieving algorithm for higher dimensions which allows us to implement TNFS and perform the first record computation with it. More specifically, we propose the following contributions.

---

[2] We use the same abuse in the abstract and title too.

1. *Sieving in a high dimensional sphere instead of an orthotope.* All siev-
   ·ing algorithms so far considered a product of intervals as search space $\mathcal{S}$.
   Indeed, whether a candidate relation is characterized by an (a, b)-pair or an
   $(a(\iota), b(\iota))$-pair with more than two coefficients, every coefficient is bounded
   separately in an interval $[-H_1^i, H_2^i]$ for $i = 1, 2, \cdots, d$ where d is the total
   number of coefficients. Hence, the search space considered is a d-orthotope of
   the form $\mathcal{S} = [-H_1^1, H_2^1] \times \cdots \times [-H_1^d, H_2^d]$. We argue that when $d \geq 3$, the
   shape of $\mathcal{S}$ must be adequately chosen. More precisely, we consider a d-sphere
   instead of a d-orthotope and explain why we believe this choice leads to a
   more efficient algorithm when the dimension grows.
2. *Adapting a lattice enumeration algorithm to the context of TNFS.* In order
   to fully exploit the new search space, we adapt a known lattice algorithm
   to the context of TNFS: Schnorr-Euchner's enumeration algorithm [33], that
   outputs the shortest vector of a lattice. We modify this algorithm in order to
   list all the vectors of a lattice $\mathcal{L}$ within a d-dimensional sphere S_d. Furthermore, a part of the common coefficients of the enumerated vectors are kept
   in memory during the algorithm, leading to a 10% reduction in the execution
   time. This algorithm remains competitive when the dimension grows and also
   provides an exhaustive search of all the vectors in $\mathcal{L} \cap S_d$, contrary to previous
   approaches.
3. *Analysis of the relation collection step in TNFS and duplicate relations.* We
   place this sieving algorithm in the context of the entire relation collection step.
   Sieving algorithms are usually combined with batch algorithms and ECM to
   provide the most efficient relation collection. We give details on this relation
   collection step, and give new insight on how to define and remove duplicate
   relations that arise in the context of TNFS.
4. *A 521-bit finite field record.* Our new lattice enumeration for the sieving step
   led to the first record computation of a discrete logarithm with TNFS, reaching a 521-bit finite field $\mathbb{F}_{p^6}$. Previous record on a finite field of the same shape
   reached a 423-bit finite field in January 2020. The choice of the extension
   degree was motivated by the use of such finite fields in pairing-based protocols, in particular in recent zero-knowledge proofs in some blockchains [5,8].
   Ultimately, as shown in Table 2, our algorithm is much faster than existing high-dimensional sieving algorithms, despite the larger dimension of the
   search space and the larger finite field.

Table 2. Comparison of the relation collection step in core hours with [14] and [27]
for finite fields of the form $\mathbb{F}_{p^6}$.

Parameters	[14]	[27]	This work
Algorithm	NFS	NFS	TNFS
Field size (bits)	422	423	521
Sieving dimension	3	3	6
Sieving time	201,600	69,120	**23,300**

Outline. In Sect. 2, we recall the general setup of TNFS and in particular we concentrate on the steps that differ the most from the classical NFS setup. In Sect. 3, we focus on the relation collection step with the special-q method, and explain how to deal with duplicate relations. In Sect. 4, we describe our adaptation of Schnorr-Euchner's enumeration algorithm to the context of TNFS. We justify why we choose a d-sphere as sieving area and introduce an efficient way to compute the desired vectors of coefficients for the relations. Section 5 analyses the complexity of our sieving algorithm and compares the latter with pre-existing algorithms. Finally, in Sect. 6 we detail our complete discrete logarithm computation in a 521-bit finite field with extension degree 6.

2   The Tower Number Field Sieve

2.1   Mathematical Setup

The classical tower of number fields that illustrates the TNFS setup considers the intermediate number field $\mathbb{Q}(\iota)$ where ι is a root of h, a polynomial over $\mathbb{Z}$ that remains irreducible modulo p. Above this number field are set the two number fields $K_1 = \mathbb{Q}(\iota)[x]/f_1(x)$ and $K_2 = \mathbb{Q}(\iota)[x]/f_2(x)$ where f_1, f_2 are irreducible polynomials over $\mathcal{R} = \mathbb{Z}[\iota]$ that share an irreducible factor φ modulo the unique ideal $\mathfrak{p}$ over p in $\mathbb{Q}(\iota)$. We write $\mathcal{O}_i$ the ring of integers of K_i and α_i a root of f_i in K_i for $i = 1, 2$. This construction is illustrated in the left part of Fig. 1. Because of the conditions on the polynomials h, f_1 and f_2, there exist two ring homomorphisms from $\mathcal{R}[x] = \mathbb{Z}[\iota][x]$ to the target finite field $\mathbb{F}_{p^n}$ through the number fields K_1 and K_2. This allows to build a commutative diagram as shown in the right part of Fig. 1. The extension degree n is assumed to be composite, and we write $n = \eta\kappa$. In this setting, h is of degree η, and f_1 and f_2 have degree at least κ, so that the degree of their common factor φ is exactly κ. For simplicity, we will assume that f_1 and f_2 are defined over $\mathbb{Z}$, since it is the case in our record computation; this is only possible when κ and η are coprime.

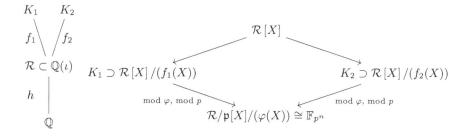

Fig. 1. Commutative diagram of Tower NFS.

2.2 A Step by Step Walk Through TNFS

The TNFS algorithm follows similar steps as any index calculus algorithm.

Polynomial Selection. Unlike NFS which uses only two polynomials f_1 and f_2 to define the number fields, three polynomials must be selected for this algorithm, namely h, f_1 and f_2. The polynomial h must be of degree η and irreducible modulo p to ensure the uniqueness of the ideal $\mathfrak{p}$ over p in $\mathcal{R}$. Ideally one would choose a unitary h with small coefficients and such that the inverse of the Dedekind zeta function evaluated at 2 (implemented in Sage for example) is close to 1. Indeed, as we will see in Sect. 3.4, this is related to non-coprime ideals that produce equivalent relations which are useless for the linear algebra step.

The polynomials f_1 and f_2 are selected to fit the mathematical setting of Sect. 2.1. One can use NFS polynomial selections such as the Conjugation, JLSV or Sarkar-Singh's methods [2,20,31], not recalled here. The polynomials we use for our 521-bit computation come from the Conjugation method. In NFS, the quality of the polynomials can be refined with a quantity known as the Murphy-α value. See [17] for details about Murphy-α adapted to TNFS.

Relation Collection. The goal of the relation collection step is to select among the set of linear polynomials $\phi(x, \iota) = a(\iota) - b(\iota)x \in \mathcal{R}[x]$ at the top of the diagram the candidates which produce a relation. A relation is found if the polynomial $\phi(x, \iota)$ mapped to K_1 and K_2 factors into products of ideals of small norms in both number fields. The ideals of small norms that occur in these factorizations constitute the factor basis $\mathcal{F}$. More precisely, we define it as $\mathcal{F} = \mathcal{F}_1 \cup \mathcal{F}_2$ with

$$\mathcal{F}_i(B) = \{\text{prime ideals of } \mathcal{O}_i \text{ of norm} \leq B, \text{ whose inertia degree over } \mathbb{Q}(\iota) \text{ is } 1\},$$

for $i = 1, 2$. The representation of these ideals of degree 1 in the context of TNFS is summarized in [4, Proposition 1].

To verify the B-smoothness on each side, one needs to evaluate the norms $N_i(a(\iota) - b(\iota)\alpha_i)$ for $i = 1, 2$. To do so we recall that when the polynomials f_i are monic, these norms are integers that can be computed thanks to resultants as $N_i(a(\iota) - b(\iota)\alpha_i) = \text{Res}_t(\text{Res}_x(a(t) - b(t)x, f_i(x)), h(t))$. The relation collection step stops when we have enough relations to construct a system of linear equations that may be full rank. The unknowns of these equations are the *virtual* logarithms of the ideals of the factor basis.

Linear Algebra. A good feature of the linear system created is that the number of non-zero coefficients per line is very low. This allows to use sparse linear algebra algorithms such as the block variant of Wiedemann's algorithm [34], for which parallelization is partly possible. The output of this step is a kernel vector corresponding to the virtual logarithms of the ideals in the factor basis. There is no difference for this step between TNFS and NFS.

Individual Discrete Logarithm. The final step of TNFS consists in finding the discrete logarithm of the target element. This step is subdivided into two sub-steps: a smoothing step and a descent step. The smoothing step is an iterative process where the target element t is randomized by considering $s = g^e t \in \mathbb{F}_{p^n}^*$ for an exponent e chosen uniformly at random.

The second step consists in decomposing every factor of the lifted value of s, in our case prime ideals with norms less than a smoothness bound B_i (but usually greater than B) into elements of the factor basis for which we now know the virtual logarithms. This process creates descent trees where the root is an ideal coming from the smoothing step and the nodes are ideals that get smaller and smaller as they go deeper. The leaves are ultimately elements of the factor basis. The edges of the tree are defined as follows: for every node, there exists an equation between the ideal of the node and all the ideals of its children.

In this work, we consider an improvement given by Guillevic in [16, Algorithm 5] for the smoothing step, that is useful in the context of TNFS only. The goal is to improve the smoothness probability of the lift of $s \in \mathbb{F}_{p^n}^*$ to K_i by constructing an adequate lattice whose reduced vectors define elements of K_i with potentially small norms which is precisely the potential lifts of s we are looking for.

3   Focus on the Relation Collection

In TNFS the relation collection step requires sieving in dimension $2\eta \geq 4$, which is the number of coefficients involved in ϕ. We start by dividing the set of polynomials ϕ into multiple subsets and then we present different algorithms to successively select the candidates in each of these subsets.

3.1   The Special-q Setup

The relation collection phase looks at a set of linear polynomials $\phi(x, \iota) = a(\iota) - b(\iota)x \in \mathcal{R}[x]$ where a, b are polynomials of degree $\deg h - 1$ with $\deg h = \eta$ and bounded coefficients, and tries to identify which are going to produce doubly-smooth norms, *i.e.,* for which pair $(a(\iota), b(\iota))$ the norms $N_1(a(\iota) - b(\iota)\alpha_1)$ and $N_2(a(\iota) - b(\iota)\alpha_2)$ factor into small primes. To reduce the time of the siev-ing stage, Pollard [30] suggested to divide the set of all polynomials ϕ, com-monly called the search space, into multiple subsets. This corresponds to the so-called *special-q method.* This method regroups polynomials into groups such that $\phi(\alpha_1, \iota)$ (or $\phi(\alpha_2, \iota)$ depending on whether we put the special-q on the f_1-side or the f_2-side) share a common factor: the ideal $\mathfrak{Q}$, above a prime q, hence the name. Thus, when talking about a sieving algorithm, we usually consider a fixed special-q ideal $\mathfrak{Q}$, and select good polynomials ϕ in the corresponding subset. This idea of using special-q's increases the smoothness probability on the side where divisibility by $\mathfrak{Q}$ is forced, since the norm is already divisible by q. Furthermore this provides a natural parallelization where each work-unit corresponds to a special-q.

Let ϕ denote the (row-) vector of coefficients of the polynomial $\phi(x, \iota)$, *i.e.* the vector $\underline{\phi} = (a_0, \cdots, a_{\eta-1}, b_0, \cdots, b_{\eta-1}) \in \mathbb{Z}^{2\eta}$. Let us consider a special-q ideal $\mathfrak{Q}$ of degree 1 in K_i of the form $\mathfrak{Q} = \langle q, \iota - \rho_\iota, x - \rho_x \rangle$, where q is a prime number, ρ_ι is a root of h modulo q, and ρ_x is a root of f_i modulo q. One could also consider ideals of degree greater than 1, but special-q of degree 1 are the most common among ideals of bounded norms and thus we restrict to this case.

Proposition 1. *The set of polynomials ϕ such that the corresponding principal ideal in K_i is divisible by $\mathfrak{Q}$ form a lattice that we call the $\mathfrak{Q}$-lattice $\mathcal{L}_{\mathfrak{Q}}$.*

The latter can be made explicit as follows.

$$\mathcal{L}_{\mathfrak{Q}} = \{(a_0, \cdots, a_{\eta-1}, b_0, \cdots, b_{\eta-1}) \in \mathbb{Z}^{2\eta} : \sum_{k=0}^{\eta-1} \left(a_k \iota^k - b_k \iota^k \alpha_i\right) \equiv 0 \pmod{\mathfrak{Q}}\}$$

where $i = 1, 2$ depending on the side we consider. A basis $B_{\mathfrak{Q}}$ of this lattice can be expressed as follows.

$$
\begin{array}{cc}
(a, b) &
\begin{array}{ccccc|cccc}
a_0 & a_1 & \cdots & a_{\eta-2} & a_{\eta-1} & b_0 & b_1 & \cdots & b_{\eta-1}
\end{array}
\\
\begin{array}{c}
(q, 0) \\
(\iota - \rho_\iota, 0) \\
(\iota(\iota - \rho_\iota), 0) \\
\vdots \\
(\iota^{\eta-2}(\iota - \rho_\iota), 0) \\
(\rho_x, 1) \\
(\iota \rho_x, \iota) \\
\vdots \\
(\iota^{\eta-1} \rho_x, \iota^{\eta-1})
\end{array}
&
\left(
\begin{array}{ccccc|cccc}
q & 0 & & & 0 & & & & \\
-\rho_\iota & 1 & 0 & & & & & & \\
0 & -\rho_\iota & 1 & 0 & & & & & \\
& & \ddots & \ddots & & & & & \\
& & & -\rho_\iota & 1 & & & & \\
\rho_x & 0 & & & & 1 & & & \\
0 & \rho_x & 0 & & & & 1 & & \\
& & \ddots & & & & & \ddots & \\
& & & & \rho_x & & & & 1
\end{array}
\right) = B_{\mathfrak{Q}}.
\end{array}
$$

The determinant of this lattice is $q^{\deg \phi_h}$, where ϕ_h is an irreducible factor of h (mod p). In our case $\phi_h = \iota - \rho_\iota$ because we only consider special-q ideals of degree 1 and so the determinant is simply q. The lattice dimension is 2η.

Each unit of computation targets one special-q ideal $\mathfrak{Q}$ and searches for polynomials $\phi(x, \iota)$ with $\underline{\phi} \in \mathcal{L}_{\mathfrak{Q}}$ leading to relations, *i.e.*, for which both sides are smooth. In order to explore the lattice $\mathcal{L}_{\mathfrak{Q}}$, we first LLL-reduce the basis $B_{\mathfrak{Q}}$, and then consider linear combinations with small coefficients of these new basis elements. This allows us to focus on polynomials where one of the norms on one side is known to be divisible by q, thus increasing the probability of it being smooth. More precisely, let $M_{\mathfrak{Q}}$ be an LLL-reduced basis of $\mathcal{L}_{\mathfrak{Q}}$. We study the (row-) vectors $\mathbf{c}$ of coefficients such that $\underline{\phi} = \mathbf{c} \cdot M_{\mathfrak{Q}}$, potentially leads to a relation. This is done using sieving algorithms.

3.2 Constructing the Double-Divisibility Lattice $\mathcal{L}_{\mathfrak{Q},\mathfrak{p}}$

We concentrate on vectors $\mathbf{c}$ that belong to a sieving region $\mathcal{S}$. Traditionally, $\mathcal{S}$ is an ℓ_∞-ball, however in this work we consider the ℓ_2-norm. Section 4.2 explains this preference. In order to efficiently detect the vectors $\mathbf{c}$ giving elements of smooth norms, one can perform an Eratosthenes-like sieving, quickly marking all vectors $\mathbf{c}$ in S leading to a norm on the f_1-side (or the f_2-side) that is divisible by a small prime p. Repeating this sieve for many primes p allows to detect the most promising vectors $\underline{\phi}$, those for which the norm is divisible by many small primes. To do so, we proceed as for the divisibility by $\mathfrak{Q}$.

Let $\mathfrak{p}$ be a prime ideal of norm p in K_i of the form $\mathfrak{p} = \langle p, \iota - r_\iota, x - r_x \rangle$, where r_ι is a root of h modulo p and r_x is a root of f_i modulo p. The second statement of [4, Proposition 1] can be reformulated for this specific context.

Proposition 2. *The principal ideal generated by $\phi(x, \iota)$ in K_i is divisible by $\mathfrak{p}$ if and only if $\phi(r_x, r_\iota) \equiv 0 \mod p$.*

Let $\mathbf{U}_\mathfrak{p}$ be the (row-) vector of size 2η defined by

$$\mathbf{U}_\mathfrak{p} = \left(1, r_\iota \bmod p, \cdots, r_\iota^{\eta-1} \bmod p, r_x, r_x r_\iota \bmod p, \cdots, r_x r_\iota^{\eta-1} \bmod p\right).$$

Then similarly as before, we can translate the divisibility property of the ideal of Proposition 2: the divisibility by $\mathfrak{p}$ is equivalent to the condition $\underline{\phi} \cdot \mathbf{U}_\mathfrak{p}^\mathsf{T} \equiv 0$ mod p. Recall that $\underline{\phi}$ is taken in a subset of the search space so that the ideal generated by $\underline{\phi}$ is divisible by $\mathfrak{Q}$, namely its coefficients are written as $\underline{\phi} = \mathbf{c} \cdot M_\mathfrak{Q}$. Taking into account the divisibility by $\mathfrak{Q}$ and by $\mathfrak{p}$ yields the condition on $\mathbf{c}$:

$$\mathbf{c} \cdot M_\mathfrak{Q} \mathbf{U}_\mathfrak{p}^\mathsf{T} \equiv 0 \mod p. \tag{1}$$

The product $M_\mathfrak{Q} \mathbf{U}_\mathfrak{p}^\mathsf{T}$, reduced modulo p and normalized so that its first coordinate is 1, is expressed as $M_\mathfrak{Q} \mathbf{U}_\mathfrak{p}^\mathsf{T} \equiv \lambda \left(1, \alpha_1, \alpha_2, \ldots, \alpha_{\eta-1}\right)^\mathsf{T} \mod p$, with $\lambda > 0$. Since $M_\mathfrak{Q}$ and $\mathbf{U}_\mathfrak{p}$ are known, we explicitly compute the values α_i. This assumes the first coordinate is non-zero. Otherwise, one must either adapt the construction of $M_{\mathfrak{Q},\mathfrak{p}}$ below or skip the ideal $\mathfrak{p}$ during sieving. Finally, the set of vectors $\mathbf{c}$ verifying Eq. (1) is the lattice $\mathcal{L}_{\mathfrak{Q},\mathfrak{p}}$ generated by the rows of the matrix

$$M_{\mathfrak{Q},\mathfrak{p}} = \begin{pmatrix} p & 0 & 0 & 0 & \cdots & 0 \\ -\alpha_1 & 1 & 0 & 0 & \cdots & 0 \\ -\alpha_2 & 0 & \ddots & 0 & \cdots & 0 \\ \vdots & & 0 & 0 & \ddots & 0 \\ -\alpha_{\eta-1} & 0 & 0 & 0 & \cdots & 1 \end{pmatrix}.$$

In the end, since $M_{\mathfrak{Q},\mathfrak{p}}$ is explicitly known, we can compute the coefficients $\underline{\phi} = \mathbf{c} \cdot M_\mathfrak{Q}$ of the polynomials ϕ. This is possible as soon as we are able to enumerate the short vectors $\mathbf{c}$ in this lattice which is the aim of Sect. 4. This procedure, which is called enumeration, is done for all prime p from 2 up to a predefined bound $p_{\max}$, forming a so called sieving algorithm. Sieving allows to detect quickly vectors $\mathbf{c}$ that belong to several $M_{\mathfrak{Q},\mathfrak{p}}$ for various $\mathfrak{p}$. The corresponding polynomials ϕ are good candidates that potentially give relations as they provide by construction ideals that are already divisible by $\mathfrak{Q}$ and several ideals $\mathfrak{p}$. Hence we keep them for the next selection phase.

3.3   Combining Three Algorithms

Other algorithms are used, either to directly detect polynomials leading to doubly-smooth norms, or to work as complementary algorithms one after another as a sequence of filters to determine and only keep the promising candidates at each step (as done with the enumeration above). These algorithms either find and extract smooth parts of the norms, or completely factor them. The family of sieving algorithms [13,27], batch algorithms [6, Algorithm 2.1] and ECM [7,26] are examples of such methods used in factorization and DLP computations.

They all have different complexities and properties and thus cannot be used on the same amount of input norms N_i. ECM is for example much more costly than sieving. Hence, applying it to all norms N_i is far from optimal. On the other hand, sieving is a much less costly algorithm per candidate, and thus can be used to find the small factors (up to p_{max}) of a large number of norms of structured candidates. This is why the relation collection step usually starts with a sieving algorithm with input all candidates $(a(\iota), b(\iota))$ pairs. ECM is then used to guarantee that the norms of promising candidates are indeed B-smooth by checking the larger prime factors. Batch smoothness can be added in between sieving and ECM or as a substitution of one of them to further optimize the overall cost. It is less costly than ECM and thus can be used to pre-select promising candidates but more costly than sieving and thus cannot be run on the entire set of candidates. It extracts prime factors up to a bound p_{batch} such that $p_{max} < p_{batch} < B$. Table 3 describes the properties of these algorithms.

Table 3. Properties of the different relation collection algorithms

Properties	Sieving	Batch	ECM
Input candidates	Numerous and structured	Numerous	Few
Prime factors extracted	Small	Small or medium	Large
RAM	Very large	Large	Tiny
Cost per candidate	Small	Medium	High

The relation collection is thus seen as a sequence of filters, each taking a certain amount of candidates as input, and selecting *survivors* based on a criterion. These survivors are then the input to the next filter. The selection of survivors is usually based on the size of the cofactor, which we now define.

Definition 1. ($\mathcal{A}$-cofactor). *Let N be a positive integer and consider $P = \prod_i p_i$ where the p_i are the prime factors of N extracted by Algorithm $\mathcal{A}$. Then the $\mathcal{A}$-cofactor of N is $C_{\mathcal{A}}(N) = N/P$.*

For a fixed $\mathcal{A}$-cofactor threshold $\mathcal{T}_{\mathcal{A}}$, the survivors are the candidates selected if their norm N satisfies $C_{\mathcal{A}}(N) \leq \mathcal{T}_{\mathcal{A}}$ (there can be such a condition on both sides if sieving is done on both of them). Finally, the complete relation collection is given in Algorithm 1. Note that on line 7, we remove duplicate relations, as explained in the next Section.

Algorithm 1. Relation collection for a given special-q with sieving, batch and ECM

Input: A prime ideal $\mathfrak{Q}$, a sieving region $\mathcal{S}$
Output: A list of relations.

1: Construct the lattice $\mathcal{L}_\mathfrak{Q}$ and LLL-reduce it.
2: **for** each prime ideal $\mathfrak{p}$ in $\mathcal{O}_1$ (or $\mathcal{O}_2$) up to norm $p_{\max}$ **do**
3:     Construct the lattice $\mathcal{L}_{\mathfrak{Q},\mathfrak{p}}$
4:     Enumerate all vectors $\mathbf{c}$ in $\mathcal{L}_{\mathfrak{Q},\mathfrak{p}} \cap \mathcal{S}$.
5:     For each $\mathbf{c}$, keep track of the size of the factor p with a sieving table.
6: For promising $\mathbf{c}$, for which the product of the factors p is large, compute approximations of the norms N_1, N_2 and identify vectors with sieve-cofactor smaller than T_{siev}. They are called sieve-survivors.
7: Remove duplicates.
8: Run batch algorithm with input the (exact) norms N_1 and N_2 of the sieve-survivors and primes up to p_{batch}. Keep batch-survivors whose batch-cofactor is smaller than $T_{\mathrm{batch}} < T_{\mathrm{siev}}$.
9: Run ECM on the batch-survivors to identify all the doubly-B-smooth norms.
10: **return** Vectors with doubly-B-smooth norms

3.4 Filtering Through Equivalent Relations

When sieving through all the pairs of candidates it is sometimes the case that two pairs $(a(\iota), b(\iota))$ and $(a'(\iota), b'(\iota))$ provide the same relation, *i.e.*, they correspond to two linear equations that provide the same information on the virtual logarithms of the elements of the factor basis involved.

Removing duplicates is common in factoring and DLP computations. Let us start by identifying three different types of duplicates. Because these definitions apply in both NFS and TNFS, we use the terminology (a, b) to either define a classical $(a, b) \in \mathbb{Z}^2$ pair in NFS or $(a(\iota), b(\iota)) \in \mathcal{R}[x]$ in TNFS.

Definition 2 (Duplicates). *A duplicate relation refers to a pair (a, b) such that there exists another pair (a', b') that leads to the same relation. We distinguish three types of duplicates:*

- *We refer to **special-q-duplicates** when a relation with ideal factorization $(a - b\alpha_i)\mathcal{O}_i = \prod_j \mathfrak{Q}_j^{e_j}$ involves several prime ideals $\mathfrak{Q}_j$ that occur in the set of special-q's considered. In other words, more than one special-q units of computation provide the same relation.*
- *If (a, b) generates a relation for a fixed special-q, then a K_h-**unit-duplicate** refers to the pair (ua, ub), for $u \in \mathcal{O}_{K_h}^*$, where u is a small enough unit of K_h.*
- *If (a, b) generates a relation for a fixed special-q, then a ζ_2-**duplicate** refers to the pair $(\lambda a, \lambda b)$, for $\lambda \in \mathcal{O}_{K_h} \setminus \mathcal{O}_{K_h}^*$, where λ is small enough.*

Duplicate relations generate identical or nearly identical lines in the linear system of equations. As the cost of solving the system grows with its dimension, we want to get rid of all the unnecessary lines. The related matrix is encoded as a list of prime ideal factors for each relation. So in theory, a simple solution would be to remove identical lines in this file before the linear algebra step.

However, in practice generating duplicate relations is costly. Indeed, they generate more hits during the enumeration of the vectors in $\mathcal{L}_{\mathfrak{Q},\mathfrak{p}} \cap \mathcal{S}$ (line 4 in Algorithm 1), they imply more sieve-survivors for which we must compute exact norms (line 8), and this finally results in more batch-survivors and hence a more costly ECM algorithm (line 9). To minimize these extra computations, it is thus convenient to get rid of the duplicates that can be identified as fast as possible. However, the same strategy cannot be applied for each type of duplicates.

Indeed, the special-q duplicates can only be detected once we know the entire factorization of the norms, meaning after running ECM. Moreover, special-q computation units are often run in parallel and thus there is little hope to be able to detect any special-q duplicates before the end of the relation collection phase. These duplicates are thus removed just before the linear algebra step.

On the other hand, K_h-unit-duplicates and ζ_2-duplicates are *local* to a special-q and can be detected at an earlier stage. Yet there is a trade-off between the extra cost of having duplicates and the cost of analyzing whether a pair (a, b) yields a duplicate relation. In our Algorithm 1, we chose to remove duplicates before running the batch algorithm. Let us now explain how to remove them.

Classical Strategy for Removing Duplicates. A classical trick used in NFS is to reduce the search space by enforcing a positive sign to the first coordinate a. Indeed, when looking at K_h-unit-duplicates, we are concerned with elements $u \in \mathcal{O}_{K_h}^*$ and in the classical NFS setup, $\mathcal{O}_{K_h}^* = \mathbb{Z}^* = \{-1, 1\}$. Enforcing $a > 0$ reduces the search space by a factor 2 and avoids all unit-duplicates.

The situation is more complicated in TNFS as the number of units to consider is greater than 2. It is still possible to restrict to positive coefficients in order to avoid duplicates resulting from the units $\{\pm 1\}$ and we see in Sect. 4 that the enumeration algorithm indeed only considers half of the vectors in $\mathcal{L}_{\mathfrak{Q},\mathfrak{p}} \cap \mathcal{S}$. However, we are left with the following open question. Is there a systematic way to identify and thus remove duplicates generated from units other than ± 1? The difficulty of answering this question comes not only from the large number of units but also from the fact that the units must be small enough in order to produce a relation. Indeed, if u is too large, then (ua, ub) will be outside the sieving region and we do not have to worry about it.

Our Strategy to Identify K_h-Unit-Duplicates and ζ_2-Duplicates. For each pair (a, b) that is a sieve-survivor, we compute the value $k := a/b \pmod{h} \in K_h$, and store it in a hash table. If (a, b) and (a', b') are either K_h-unit-duplicates or ζ_2-duplicates, then they have the same index k. The hash table allows us to quickly identify if a given pair (a', b') is a duplicate of a previously seen (a, b) pair. This method also justifies the choice of where in Algorithm 1 we test for duplicates. Indeed, computing k is not cost-free thus we want to avoid this computation for every pair (a, b) outputted by the enumeration algorithm. It is however less costly than computing an exact norm, so we compute it before.

However, the method brings forth the following issue. Duplicates can be seen as an equivalence class from which we want to select a unique representative. This representative of the class should be the "smallest" pair (a, b), meaning the (a, b)-pair which leads to the smallest norms. Indeed, a larger (a, b)-pair adds non-zero coefficients in the matrix of the linear system of relations and thus slows down the linear algebra step. For example, considering the $(\lambda a, \lambda b)$-pair, we have $N_i(\lambda a, \lambda b) = N_i(a, b)N_{K_h}(\lambda)$ for $i = 1, 2$ with the additional term $N_{K_h}(\lambda)$ with respect to the (a, b)-pair. This additional term yields extra ideals in the prime ideal decomposition, thus non-zero coefficients in the matrix. Our method does not necessarily keep the smallest pair. Indeed, if $(\lambda a, \lambda b)$ for $\lambda \in \mathcal{O}_{K_h}$ is already in the hash table, and if the algorithm sees the pair (a, b) afterwards, it will discard it and keep $(\lambda a, \lambda b)$.

The removal of special-q duplicates is easier when the representative of a duplicate class is in its canonical form. Indeed, special-q duplicates are removed by simply comparing the lines in the file that encodes the relations. Thus if different special-q's produce the same relation but each keep a different representative, say (a, b) for one and $(\lambda a, \lambda b)$ for the other, then their prime ideal decomposition will differ by some factors corresponding to $N_{K_h}(\lambda)$ and thus the duplicate will be kept. To identify the "smallest" (a, b)-pair in a ζ_2-duplicates class of equivalence, the most intuitive idea is to consider the notion of a primitive pair.

Definition 3. *A pair (a, b) is primitive if there exists no $\lambda \in \mathcal{O}_{K_h} \setminus \mathcal{O}_{K_h}^*$ such that $a = \lambda a'$ and $b = \lambda b'$ with $a', b' \in \mathcal{O}_{K_h}$.*

In NFS, we simply keep the (a, b)-pairs such that $\gcd(a, b) = 1$. The situation is more problematic in TNFS as the notion of gcd exists at the level of ideals, but not for $a(\iota)$ and $b(\iota)$. Consequently we propose to detect non-primitive pairs by computing the gcd of their norms: if $\gcd(N_1(a, b), N_2(a, b)) = 1$, then the (a, b)-pair is primitive. Indeed if one considers $(\lambda a, \lambda b)$ which is clearly non-primitive, we have $\gcd(N_1(\lambda a, \lambda b), N_2(\lambda a, \lambda b)) \geq N_{K_h}(\lambda)^{\min(\deg f_1, \deg f_2)} \neq 1$.

Hence, on line 7 of Algorithm 1, if an (a, b)-pair survives the K_h-unit duplicates and ζ_2-duplicates elimination, we check whether our representative is primitive and if not, try to make it so, using Algorithm 2.

Remark 1. In Algorithm 2 we use the fact that if $\gcd(N_1(a, b), N_2(a, b)) = 1$, then the (a, b)-pair is primitive. We actually have an equivalence if the number field K_h is principal. In particular, in our computation, the field K_h is principal which ensures we do not throw away too many relations by using Algorithm 2.

We have presented how to detect ζ_2-duplicates and K_h-unit duplicates. For ζ_2-duplicates we can keep a unique representative and make sure that representative is in a primitive form. Unfortunately, Algorithm 2 does not work for finding a unique representative with respect to K_h-unit duplicates. Indeed, if γ is a unit, then $N_{K_h}(\gamma) = 1$. In this case, we simply rely on the prime ideal decomposition which is unique in an equivalence class of K_h-unit duplicates.

Algorithm 2. Primitive representative for each class of duplicates

---

Input: (a, b)-pair corresponding to a sieve-survivor
Output: primitive (a, b)-pair corresponding to the same sieve-survivor, or Fail

  1: Compute $\gcd(N_1(a, b), N_2(a, b))$
  2: **if** $\gcd(N_1(a, b), N_2(a, b)) = 1$ **then**
  3:      Return (a, b)-pair.
  4: **else**
  5:      **for** each prime $\ell |\gcd(N_1(a, b), N_2(a, b))$ **do**
  6:            Try to find β in $\mathcal{O}_{K_h}$ of norm ℓ such that a/β and b/β are in $\mathcal{O}_{K_h}$.
  7:            **if** Such a value β is found **then**
  8:                 $a \leftarrow a/\beta$ and $b \leftarrow b/\beta$
  9:                 Recompute $\gcd(N_1(a, b), N_2(a, b))$
10:                 **if** $\gcd(N_1(a, b), N_2(a, b)) = 1$ **then**
11:                     Return new (a, b)-pair
12:            **else**
13:                 Return Fail

---

4   Relation Collection with Lattice Enumeration

Recall we can select polynomials ϕ that are good candidates that lead to potential relations as soon as we enumerate all vectors **c** in $\mathcal{L}_{\mathfrak{Q},\mathfrak{p}} \cap \mathcal{S}$. Different enumeration techniques exist in the literature which depend on the shape of the sieving region $\mathcal{S}$ and the dimension d of the lattice $\mathcal{L}_{\mathfrak{Q},\mathfrak{p}}$. For NFS, usually $d = 2$ since $(a, b) \in \mathbb{Z}^2$ are not polynomials. Higher dimensions can also be considered in theory to target medium characteristics finite fields. When $d = 2$, thus for previous records using NFS, the sieving method of Franke and Kleinjung [10] is very efficient. However, in this article, we focus on methods that can be used in higher dimensions. Indeed, as shown above, for TNFS we have $d = \dim M_{\mathfrak{Q},\mathfrak{p}}$. Taking the polynomials $a(\iota)$ and $b(\iota)$ of degree $\deg h - 1$ leads to $d = 2 \times \deg h$ hence $d \geq 4$. There exist two competitive algorithms that can be used when $d \geq 3$: the transition vectors method [13] and the recursive hyperplane one [27], see Sect. 4.1 for these algorithms. They both use as a sieving space a d-orthotope whereas in this work we consider a d-sphere. Section 4.2 justifies our choice. We use the notation $\mathcal{S} = S_d(R)$ to indicate we are working in a d-sphere of radius R or simply S_d to lighten the notation when possible. Section 4.3 describes our new algorithm adapted for TNFS.

4.1   Existing Algorithms to Enumerate Vectors in $\mathcal{L}_{\mathfrak{Q},\mathfrak{p}} \cap \mathcal{S}$

Transition Vectors for Lattice Sieving in [13]. In 2018, Grémy suggested a sieving algorithm inspired by Franke-Kleinjung's algorithm in dimension 2 but extended to higher dimensions. Let $\mathcal{S}$ be the sieving space considered, in this case, a d-orthotope defined as the product of intervals $\mathcal{S} = [H_0^m, H_0^M[\times \cdots, [H_{d-1}^m, H_{d-1}^M[$ for fixed bounds H_k^m, H_k^M. The key notion used by Grémy to enumerate vectors of a lattice $\mathcal{L}$ is the notion of transition-vectors, allowing to jump from vector to vector in order to reach all elements in $\mathcal{L}_{\mathcal{Q},\mathfrak{p}} \cap \mathcal{S}$. The transition-vectors are divided into d subsets $T_1, \cdots, T_d$, with T_k the set of k-transition-vectors for $k = 1, \cdots, d$. The latter have at least a non-zero k-coordinate and the last $d - k$ coordinates all equal to 0. The algorithm starts from $(0, 0, \cdots, 0) \in \mathcal{L}_{\mathfrak{Q},\mathfrak{p}}$ and enumerates all vectors in $\mathcal{L}_{\mathfrak{Q},\mathfrak{p}} \cap \mathcal{S}$ by adding or subtracting transition-vectors. It starts with vectors of T_1 until it reaches the edges of $\mathcal{S}$, then looks at additions (or subtractions) of vectors of T_2 etc., increasing from 1 to d step by step.

In most cases, producing the entire set T is not possible, and thus the notion of transition-vectors is relaxed into nearly-transition-vectors. This variant is effective, but no longer reaches all vectors. A fall-back strategy is then considered when the algorithm fails to find an appropriate nearly-transition vector.

In dimension 4, this method seems to have sufficient prospects of success. However, even with the relaxed variant, experiments ran in dimension 6 in [13] point to the limits of this method due to the poor quality of the nearly-transition-vectors and the number of calls required to the dedicated fall-back strategy. [13] concluded that *"using cuboid search is probably a too hard constraint that implies the hardness or even an impossibility for the sieving process"*.

Recursive Lattice Sieving through Hyperplanes in [27]. In 2020, McGuire and Robinson also proposed an enumeration algorithm in dimension 3 or higher. The sieving area is again a d-orthotope $\mathcal{S} = [0, H[\times[-H, H] \cdots \times [-H, H[$ for a fixed bound H. To enumerate all the vectors in $\mathcal{L}_{\mathfrak{Q},\mathfrak{p}} \cap \mathcal{S}$ the main idea consists in dividing the search space into hyperplanes, and enumerating in each of them. Minimizing the number of hyperplanes to visit is done by adequately choosing a "ground" hyperplane and then considering translations of it.

More precisely, in dimension 3 the "ground" plane G_0 is defined as a plane spanned by the two shortest vectors $\mathbf{c}_1, \mathbf{c}_2$ of $\mathcal{L}_{\mathfrak{Q},\mathfrak{p}}$ through the origin. Because of the small dimension of $\mathcal{L}_{\mathfrak{Q},\mathfrak{p}}$, these shortest vectors are easily found with LLL. One then enumerates every point in $G_0 \cap \mathcal{S}$ before moving to the next translated plane: $G_1 = G_0 + \mathbf{c}_3, G_2 = G_0 + 2\mathbf{c}_3, \cdots, G_k = G_0 + k\mathbf{c}_3$ until a k is reached such that $G_k \cap \mathcal{S} = \emptyset$. For each translated plane, one enumerates points in $G_k \cap \mathcal{S}$.

As we understand it, these short vectors serve a similar purpose as Grémy's transition-vectors: the aim is to choose relevant vectors to add (or subtract) to others while being as exhaustive as possible. Similarly to [13], the enumeration here is not completely exhaustive. Indeed, in [27], the authors report consistently missing around 1.8 % of the lattice points per special-q due to corner cases.

Pseudo-code for dimension 3 (only) is given in [27]. Although the authors state their algorithm can be extended to higher dimension, we wonder whether it remains efficient when $d \geq 3$. We write in Algorithm 3 a pseudo-code of our understanding of how their method can be adapted for any dimension d. One difficulty we see is finding $e_{\max}$ when enumerating in $G_k \cap \mathcal{S}$, which increases with d and the task can become too expensive very quickly. Indeed, finding $e_{\max}$ can be done using integer linear programming, which is doable in low dimension but should be very hard (or at least more costly than desired) as d grows.

Algorithm 3. Recursive version of enumeration algorithm from [27]

Input: the basis of a lattice $\mathcal{L}$ of dimension d, a sieving region $\mathcal{S}$.
Output: list L of vectors in $\mathcal{L} \cap \mathcal{S}$

def enum(d, $\mathcal{S}$, $[b_1, b_2, \cdots, b_d]$)
  1: $L = \{\}$
  2: **if** $d \neq 1$ **then**
  3:     $k = 0$
  4:     $P = \text{plane}(\mathbf{0}, \mathbf{b}_1, \mathbf{b}_2, \cdots, \mathbf{b}_{d-1})$
  5:     $e_{\max} = \max\{e \in \mathbb{N} : \mathcal{S} \cap (P - e \cdot \mathbf{b}_d) \neq \emptyset\}$
  6:     $G_0 = P - e_{\max} \cdot \mathbf{b}_d$
  7:     **while** $G_k \cap \mathcal{S} \neq \emptyset$ **do**
  8:         $L' \leftarrow \text{enum}(d - 1, G_k \cap \mathcal{S}, [\mathbf{b}_1, \mathbf{b}_2, \cdots, \mathbf{b}_{d-1}])$
  9:         Append L' to L
10:         $k = k + 1$
11:         $G_{k+1} = G_k + \mathbf{b}_d$
12: **if** $d = 1$ **then**
13:     Find $p_0 \in \text{plane}(\mathbf{0}, \mathbf{b}_1) \cap \mathcal{S}$ with linear programming
14:     Add p_0 to L
15:     $e_{\max} = \max\{e \in \mathbb{N} : \mathcal{S} \cap (p_0 - e \cdot \mathbf{b}_1) \neq \emptyset\}$
16:     Define $P_0 = p_0 - e_{\max} \cdot \mathbf{b}_1$
17:     **while** $P_0 \cap \mathcal{S} \neq \emptyset$ **do**
18:         $P_0 = P_0 + \mathbf{b}_1$
19:         Add P_0 to L
20: **return** L.

4.2   Why Do We Choose a d-sphere?

Let d be the dimension of the sieving space. Consider a d-sphere S_d and a d-orthotope C_d of equal volume. The number of vectors $\mathbf{c}$ of $\mathcal{L}_{\mathfrak{Q}, \mathfrak{p}} \cap \mathcal{S}$ to enumerate is thus approximately the same if we consider $\mathcal{S}$ to be S_d or C_d. Let us assume that the size of the norms is only dependent on the size of the coordinates of the vectors $\mathbf{c}$. We now argue that using S_d instead of C_d leads to smaller norms.

Recall that the volume of a d-sphere is given by $V_d(R) = \frac{\pi^{d/2} R^d}{\Gamma(d/2+1)}$, and the volume of a d-hypercube of fixed length L is L^d. We use a d-hypercube instead of a d-orthotope to simplify the presentation. In order to have the same sieving volume, i.e., $V_d(R) = L^d$ we must have $R = L \cdot \Gamma(d/2 + 1)^{1/d} \cdot \pi^{-1/2}$. For the hypercube, the length of half the diagonal (from the center) is given by $D = L \cdot \sqrt{d}/2$. The distance between the vertices of the hypercube and the sphere is expressed as $D - R = L \cdot \sqrt{d}/2 - L \cdot \Gamma(d/2 + 1)^{1/d} \cdot \pi^{-1/2}$ and from this last equality we see $\lim_{d \to \infty}(D - R) = \infty$. Let $P_d = C_d \setminus S_d$ and $Q_d = S_d \setminus C_d$. The quantity $D - R$ represents an upper bound on the distance from the origin to points in P_d, which would correspond to the largest norms. Hence, if we want to consider smaller norms, when $d \to \infty$ it is more advantageous to consider points in Q_d, and thus choosing S_d rather than C_d is a more suitable choice.

4.3   Schnorr-Euchner's Enumeration Algorithm for TNFS

In order to find potential relations, recall that we enumerate all the vectors of bounded norms in the lattice $\mathcal{L}_{\mathfrak{Q},\mathfrak{p}}$, where $\mathcal{L}_{\mathfrak{Q},\mathfrak{p}}$ translates the notion of divisibility by an ideal $\mathfrak{p}$ and a special-q ideal $\mathfrak{Q}$. By enumerating vectors in $\mathcal{L}_{\mathfrak{Q},\mathfrak{p}} \cap S_d(R)$ for many different $\mathfrak{p}$ (each generating a different $\mathcal{L}_{\mathfrak{Q},\mathfrak{p}}$) one can identify vectors divisible by many $\mathfrak{p}$'s and thus more likely to correspond to B-smooth norms.

Let us fix $\mathfrak{p}$ and a special-q ideal $\mathfrak{Q}$. Given an LLL-reduced basis $\{\mathbf{b}_1, \cdots, \mathbf{b}_d\}$ of $\mathcal{L}_{\mathfrak{Q},\mathfrak{p}}$ and the radius R of a d-sphere S_d which corresponds to the sieving area, we propose to find these vectors thanks to an adaptation of Schnorr-Euchner's enumeration algorithm [33]. We choose to follow [33] instead of Fincke-Pohst-Kannan's algorithm [9,22] as it appears more efficient operation-wise.

Description of the Algorithm. Schnorr-Euchner's algorithm constructs an enumeration tree of depth d in order to find the vectors $\mathbf{c} = \sum_{i=1}^{d} v_i \mathbf{b}_i$ that satisfy $||\mathbf{c}|| \leq R$. To construct the tree, the algorithm considers projections of the lattice $\mathcal{L}_{\mathfrak{Q},\mathfrak{p}}$. Since the norm of vectors cannot increase under orthogonal projections, the enumeration algorithm proceeds recursively by looking at the orthogonal projections π_k on the set $\{\mathbf{b}_1, \cdots, \mathbf{b}_{k-1}\}^{\perp}$ for decreasing values of k (we set π_1 to be the identity). The projection of the vector $\mathbf{c}$ for a given $k = 1, 2, \cdots, d$ is

$$\pi_k(\mathbf{c}) = \sum_{j=1}^{d} \left(\left(v_j + \sum_{i=j+1}^{d} (\mu_{i,j} v_i) \pi_k(\mathbf{b}_j^*) \right) \right) = \sum_{j=k}^{d} \left(\left(v_j + \sum_{i=j+1}^{d} (\mu_{i,j} v_i) \mathbf{b}_j^* \right) \right),$$

where the vectors $\mathbf{b}_i^*$ correspond to the Gram-Schmidt orthogonalization of the basis vectors $\mathbf{b}_i$ and the $\mu_{i,j}$ are the Gram-Schmidt coefficients.

At each level k of the tree, the algorithm verifies that $||\pi_k(\mathbf{c})|| \leq R$ which can be reduced to enumerating admissible values of v_k that lie in a bounded interval. The leaves of the tree then correspond to the desired vectors in $\mathcal{L}_{\mathfrak{Q},\mathfrak{p}} \cap S_d(R)$. The algorithm visits half the nodes since if $\mathbf{c} \in \mathcal{L}_{\mathfrak{Q},\mathfrak{p}}$ then $-\mathbf{c} \in \mathcal{L}_{\mathfrak{Q},\mathfrak{p}}$.

Efficiently Computing the Vectors $\mathbf{c} = \mathbf{v} \cdot M_{\mathfrak{Q},\mathfrak{p}}$. The algorithm works with the coefficient vectors $\mathbf{v} = (v_1, \cdots, v_d)$. However, in the end, we do not want the combinations $\mathbf{v}$, but the vectors $\mathbf{c} = \mathbf{v} \cdot M_{\mathfrak{Q},\mathfrak{p}} = \sum_{i=1}^{d} v_i \mathbf{b}_i$. Computing these vectors $\mathbf{c}$ can either be done naively, at the leaf level by explicitly computing $\mathbf{c} = \sum_{i=1}^{d} v_i \mathbf{b}_i$ for each leaf, or one can keep track of a partial sum $\sum_{i=t}^{d} v_i \mathbf{b}_i$ for a fixed value t chosen as input to the algorithm and update the quantity $v_i \mathbf{b}_i$ once a v_i is changed during the algorithm, *i.e.*, once the algorithm visits a new internal node in levels t to d. We opt for the second option as it reduces the overall cost of enumeration.

More precisely, let `common_part` $= \sum_{i=t}^{d} v_i \mathbf{b}_i$, where each $v_i \mathbf{b}_i$ is stored in a variable. Each time the algorithm visits a new internal node, thus updates v_i for a given $i = t, \cdots, d$, the algorithm updates `common_part` by subtracting the current $v_i \mathbf{b}_i$, computing the new $v_i \mathbf{b}_i$ with the new value of v_i and adding it back to `common_part`. Once at the leaf, in order to compute the vector $\mathbf{c}$, it remains to compute $\mathbf{c} = \sum_{i=1}^{t-1} v_i \mathbf{b}_i +$ `common_part`.

For most values of p we are concerned about, we use this optimized code with $t = 2$, thus updating all values $v_i \mathbf{b}_i$ during the algorithm, except at the leaf level, and finally computing $\mathbf{c} = v_1 \mathbf{b}_1 + \texttt{common\_part}$. When p becomes large and few leaves are found, it can be less efficient to choose $t = 2$, and thus one selects the appropriate $t > 2$ in order to optimize the number of operations performed for this computation. More details are given in the Sect. 5 below and the pseudo-code for the optimized enumeration algorithm is given in Algorithm 4.

Remark 2. This optimization makes sense in this specific context where our lattices are of small dimension and often dense (in particular for small primes). This would not translate well for general lattices of larger dimensions or if only a handful of small vectors were output.

5 Analysis of the Enumeration Algorithm

5.1 Number of Leaves, Nodes and Enumeration Cost

We now estimate the cost of our enumeration algorithm. This implies having an estimate of the number of nodes and leaves in the enumeration tree. This estimate is derived using the Gaussian heuristic. In order to do so, it is necessary to analyze the geometry of the input lattice $\mathcal{L}_{\mathfrak{Q},\mathfrak{p}}$. In particular, we are interested in the ratio between the norms of two consecutive Gram-Schmidt vectors of the (reduced) lattice. Indeed, to count the number of nodes in the enumeration tree, we need to compute the volume of the projected lattices which is given by the product of the norms of the Gram-Schmidt vectors.

The dimension of the lattices we consider is small, *i.e.*, precisely 6 in our computation but plausible dimensions are 4, 6 or 8 for other realistic targets. Because of these small dimensions, we observe that classical analyses of lattice reduction algorithms do not hold. For example, an expected lower bound β on the ratio $||\mathbf{b}_{i+1}^*||^2/||\mathbf{b}_i^*||^2$ was observed in [29] for vectors outputted from a reduction algorithm. The constant β depends on the reduction algorithm considered and in the case of LLL, we have $\beta = 1/(\delta - \eta^2)$. Sage's default LLL implementation uses $\delta = 0.99$ and $\eta = 0.501$, thus $\beta = 1.35$. This value is obtained for random bases. Our lattices $\mathcal{L}_{\mathfrak{Q},\mathfrak{p}}$ are however not random. We thus experimentally measured that for 6-dimensional lattices, the ratio $||\mathbf{b}_{i+1}^*||/||\mathbf{b}_i^*||$ is smaller than expected, hence we introduce the following heuristic.

Heuristic 1. *For 6-dimensional lattices $\mathcal{L}_{\mathfrak{Q},\mathfrak{p}}$, $||\boldsymbol{b}_{i+1}^*||/||\boldsymbol{b}_i^*|| \approx 1.09$ on average.*

In what follows, we need to estimate the number of lattice vectors in a sphere. For this, we rely on the Gaussian heuristic, which tells us that the number of points belonging to the intersection of a lattice $\mathcal{L}$ and a set $\mathcal{S}$ is roughly the ratio of the volumes, *i.e.*, $\text{vol}(\mathcal{S})/\text{vol}(\mathcal{L})$. This heuristic was suggested to analyze enumeration algorithms in [18] and experimentally confirmed to be accurate in [11] for random lattices.

Algorithm 4. Optimized enumerating $\mathcal{L}_{\mathfrak{Q},\mathfrak{p}} \cap S_d$

Input: LLL-reduced basis $\{\mathbf{b}_1, \cdots, \mathbf{b}_d\}$ of $\mathcal{L}_{\mathfrak{Q},\mathfrak{p}}$, radius R of d-sphere S_d, variable t for optimization.

Output: List K of vectors $\mathbf{c} \in \mathcal{L}_{\mathfrak{Q},\mathfrak{p}} \cap S_d(R)$.

1: Pre-computation: compute all Gram-Schmit coefficients $\mu_{i,j}$ for $i < j$ and the norms of the Gram-Schmidt vectors $||\mathbf{b}_i^*||^2$ for all $i \leq d$.

2: $K \leftarrow \{\}$, $\sigma \leftarrow (0)_{(d+1) \times d}$, $r_0 = 0, r_1 = 1, \cdots, r_d = d$, $v_1 = 1, v_2 = \cdots = v_d = 0$.

3: $\rho_1 = \rho_2 = \rho_{d+1} = 0$ ▷ with $\rho_k = ||\pi_k(\mathbf{c})||^2$

4: $c_1 = \cdots = c_d = 0$ ▷ with $c_k = \sum_{i=k+1}^{d} \mu_{i,k} v_i$

5: $w_1 = \cdots = w_d = 0$

6: last_nonzero $= 1$, common_part $= v_t \mathbf{b}_t + \cdots + v_d \mathbf{b}_d$

7: $k = 1$

8: **while** true **do**

9:      $\rho_k = \rho_{k+1} + (v_k - c_k)^2 ||\mathbf{b}_k^*||^2$

10:      **if** $\rho_k \leq R^2$ **then**

11:          **if** $k = 1$ **then**

12:              $\mathbf{c} = \sum_{i=1}^{t-1} v_i \mathbf{b}_i +$ common_part   ▷ opt. computation of $\mathbf{c}$

13:              $K \leftarrow K \cup \mathbf{c}$

14:              **if** last_nonzero $= 1$ **then**

15:                  Skip   ▷ this generates ζ_2-duplicates

16:              **else**

17:                  **if** $v_k > c_k$ **then** $v_k \leftarrow v_k - w_k$

18:                  **else**

19:                      $v_k \leftarrow v_k + w_k$

20:                  $w_k \leftarrow w_k + 1$

21:          **else**

22:              $k \leftarrow k - 1$ ▷ we go down the tree

23:              $r_k \leftarrow \max(r_k, r_{k+1})$

24:              **for** $i = r_{k+1}$ to $k + 2$ **do**

25:                  $\sigma_{i,k} \leftarrow \sigma_{i+1,k} + v_i \mu_{i,k}$

26:              $c_k \leftarrow -\sigma_{k+1,k}$

27:              $v_k = \lceil c_k \rfloor$, $w_k = 1$.

28:              **if** $k = \ell$ for $\ell = t, \cdots, d$ **then**

29:                  Re-compute common_part by updating $v_\ell \mathbf{b}_\ell$.

30:      **else**

31:          $k \leftarrow k + 1$ ▷ going back up the tree.

32:          **if** $k = d + 1$ **then**

33:              **return** K ▷ we find no more solutions

34:          $r_k \leftarrow k$

35:          **if** $k \geq$ last_nonzero **then**

36:              last_nonzero $\leftarrow k$

37:              $v_k \leftarrow v_k + 1$

38:              **if** $k = \ell$ for $\ell = t, \cdots, n$ **then**

39:                  Re-compute common_part by updating $v_\ell b_\ell$.

40:          **else**

41:              **if** $v_k > c_k$ **then** $v_k \leftarrow v_k - w_k$

42:                  **if** $k = \ell$ for $\ell = t, \cdots, n$ **then**

43:                      Re-compute common_part by updating $v_\ell b_\ell$.

44:              **else**

45:                  $v_k \leftarrow v_k + w_k$

46:                  **if** $k = \ell$ for $\ell = t, \cdots, n$ **then**

47:                      Re-compute common_part by updating $v_\ell b_\ell$.

48:          $w_k \leftarrow w_k + 1$

Number of Leaves. The volume of a full-rank d-dimensional lattice $\mathcal{L}$ is given by $\det(\mathcal{L}) = \prod_{i=1}^{d} ||\mathbf{b}_i^*||$ and in our case the volume of $\mathcal{L}_{\mathfrak{Q},\mathfrak{p}}$ is p. Using the Gaussian heuristic, and taking into account the fact that we visit only half of the tree, the number of leaves is thus given by

$$\Xi_{\text{leaves}} \approx \frac{1}{2} \frac{\text{vol}(\mathrm{S}_d(\mathrm{R}))}{\det(\mathcal{L}_{\mathfrak{Q},\mathfrak{p}})} = \frac{R^d \pi^{d/2}}{2\Gamma(d/2+1)p}.$$

Number of Nodes. Let Ξ_k denote the number of nodes at level k which corresponds to the number of points in $\pi_k(\mathcal{L}_{\mathfrak{Q},\mathfrak{p}}) \cap S_k(R)$. From the Gaussian heuristic and dividing by 2 for the half-tree, we have $\Xi_k = |\pi_k(\mathcal{L}_{\mathfrak{Q},\mathfrak{p}}) \cap S_{d-k+1}(R)|$ and

$$\Xi_k = \text{vol}(\mathrm{S}_{d-k+1}(\mathrm{R}))/(2 \cdot \text{vol}(\pi_k(\mathcal{L}_{\mathfrak{Q},\mathfrak{p}}))).$$

The volume of the projected lattice $\pi_k(\mathcal{L}_{\mathfrak{Q},\mathfrak{p}})$ is $\prod_{i=k}^{d} ||\mathbf{b}_i^*||$, and we can use Heuristic 1 to estimate it. We get

$$\text{vol}(\pi_k(\mathcal{L}_{\mathfrak{Q},\mathfrak{p}})) \approx ||\mathbf{b}_1||^{d-k+1}(1.09)^{\sum_{i=k-1}^{d-1} i} \approx ||\mathbf{b}_1||^{d-k+1}(1.09)^{0.5(d-k+1)(d+k-2)}.$$

Since for $k = 1$ we have $\text{vol}(\pi_1(\mathcal{L}_{\mathfrak{Q},\mathfrak{p}})) = \mathrm{p}$, we can set $||\mathbf{b}_1|| \approx p^{1/d}/(1.09)^{(\sum_{i=1}^{d-1} i)/d}$. We then have

$$\text{vol}(\pi_k(\mathcal{L}_{\mathfrak{Q},\mathfrak{p}})) \approx \mathrm{p}^{(d-k+1)/d}(1.09)^{\sum_{i=k-1}^{d-1} i-((d-k+1)/d)\sum_{i=1}^{d-1} i}$$

that leads to $\text{vol}(\pi_k(\mathcal{L}_{\mathfrak{Q},\mathfrak{p}})) = \mathrm{p}^{(d-k+1)/d}(1.09)^{0.5(d-k+1)(k-1)}$. We therefore get

$$\Xi_k \approx \frac{R^{d-k+1}\pi^{(d-k+1)/2}}{2 \cdot \Gamma((d-k+1)/2+1) \cdot p^{(d-k+1)/d} \cdot (1.09)^{0.5(d-k+1)(k-1)}}.$$

Finally, the total number of nodes is $\Xi = \sum_{k=1}^{d} \Xi_k$. Experimental verification of these formulae are provided in Sect. 6.

Running Time of Enumeration. The running time of our enumeration algorithm is given by the number of nodes Ξ times the number of operations per node. At each node, the algorithm performs 7 arithmetic operations on average to compute and update the linear combinations $\mathbf{v}$. In addition, one must also compute the vector $\mathbf{c} = \mathbf{v} \cdot M_{\mathfrak{Q},\mathfrak{p}} = \sum_{i=1}^{d} v_i \mathbf{b}_i$. As mentioned above, this can either be done naively at the leaf level by explicitly computing $\mathbf{c} = \sum_{i=1}^{d} v_i \mathbf{b}_i$ for each leaf, which costs $2d^2 - 1$ extra operations per leaf.

Or, one uses `common_part` $= \sum_{i=t}^{d} v_i \mathbf{b}_i$. Each time the algorithm visits a new internal node in the levels t up to d, thus updates v_i for a given $i = t, \cdots, d$, the algorithm performs $4d - 1$ operations: in order to update `common_part`, we subtract the current $v_i \mathbf{b}_i$ (d operations), compute the new $v_i \mathbf{b}_i$ ($2d - 1$ operations) with the new value of v_i and add it back to `common_part` (again, d operations).

Once at the leaf, in order to compute the vector $\mathbf{c}$, it remains to perform $(t - 1)(2d - 1) + t - 1$ operations, $\mathbf{c} = v_1 \mathbf{b}_1 + \cdots + v_{t-1}\mathbf{b}_{t-1} + $ `common_part`. In summary, we have for the additional cost of computing the vector $\mathbf{c}$

$$\texttt{Comp c naively} = \Xi_{\text{leaves}} \times (2d^2 - 1)$$

but using `common_part`, the cost of computing the vector **c** is $\texttt{Comp\,c\,opt} =$ # int. $\text{nodes}_{t \to d} \times (4d - 1) + \Xi_{\text{leaves}} \times ((t - 1)(2d - 1) + t - 1)$ so

$$\texttt{Comp c opt} = \left(\sum_{i=t}^{d} \Xi_i \right)(4d - 1) + \Xi_{\text{leaves}}((t - 1)(2d - 1) + t - 1).$$

We experimentally verify that the optimized code results in less operations than the naive one to compute all the vectors c for all but too large values of p when choosing $t = 2$. When p becomes too large and there aren't many leaves, the optimized code uses more operations than the naive one. One easy way to resolve this is to increase the value of t in the definition of `common_part`. However, this occurs when p is large enough that the predominant cost is in generating the lattice $\mathcal{L}_{\mathfrak{Q},\mathfrak{p}}$ and not in the enumeration algorithm. Finally, the total cost of enumeration on average is thus equal to $\texttt{Cost enum} = 7 \times \Xi + \texttt{Compcopt}$.

Number of Leaves Per Node. The number of leaves per node is given by $r = \Xi_{\text{leaves}}/\Xi$ as a function of p. This ratio r captures the behavior of our algorithm. The higher r is, the more efficient our algorithm becomes: we want this ratio to remain high as internal nodes correspond to (necessary) operations which do not produce any information as lattice vectors are seen only at the leaf level. When p increases, r decreases, as illustrated in Fig. 2 for parameters specific to our computation. Indeed, the probability of a norm being divisible by a small prime is higher than for larger primes. Hence for small primes, r is close to 1. This explains why we enumerate on small primes first, and switch to batch algorithms for larger primes.

Comparing Enumeration and Construction of the Lattice. When p is small, the enumeration algorithm is more costly (in terms of number of operations) than constructing the lattice itself. However, when p becomes large enough, constructing the basis $M_{\mathfrak{Q},\mathfrak{p}}$ becomes much more costly. The intersection point varies depending on the radius R and can be chosen to be close to $p_{\max}$.

5.2   Overall Complexity of Relation Collection

The total cost of Algorithm 1 is the sum of the cost of constructing $\mathcal{L}_{\mathfrak{Q},\mathfrak{p}}$, the cost of enumerating in $\mathcal{L}_{\mathfrak{Q},\mathfrak{p}} \cap S$, and the costs of batch algorithm on the sieve-survivors and ECM on the batch-survivors. In order to optimize the overall complexity, it is important to correctly set the many parameters that come into play during this step. In particular, one must decide the size of (many) fixed parameters: the radius R, the smoothness bound B, the range of special-q's to consider, the bounds $p_{\max}$, p_{batch} and the balance between sieving, batch smoothness and ECM based and the size of the cofactors.

5.3   Comparison with Previous Methods

Our Enumeration Algorithm vs. [13]. Grémy's algorithm uses a d-orthotope as sieving space, whereas we consider a d-sphere. As explained previously, we believe that as the dimension increases, it is more efficient to sieve in a d-sphere as opposed to a d-orthotope. The number of nearly-transition vectors required in [13] for the algorithm to enumerate most of the vectors also increases with the dimension. These nearly-transition vectors are generated during the initialization of the enumeration procedure using various strategies. Moreover, [13] indicates that in dimension 6, the number of calls to the fall-back strategy is important, indicating that the nearly-transition-vectors are of poor quality, and thus the algorithm requires the use of skew-small-vectors (also to be computed). Finally, Grémy's algorithm is not exhaustive in its search of vectors in $\mathcal{L}_{\mathcal{Q},\mathfrak{p}} \cap \mathcal{S}$, and as the dimension increases, in addition to what was mentioned just before, we suspect the percentage of missing vectors increases as well.

Our Enumeration Algorithm vs [27]. Similarly as Grémy's algorithm, this algorithm also uses a d-orthotope as sieving space. Moreover, the algorithm presented in [27] is very similar to the classical enumeration algorithm of Fincke-Pohst-Kannan (FPK) [9,22] adapted to a rectangular sieving region. One important cost in both FPK and this algorithm is finding the initial point in each plane from which the enumeration starts. In [27], this is done with linear programming. Every time the algorithm changes hyperplane, an integer linear programming problem must be solved. This does not add much complexity to the algorithm, but its cost is non-negligible with respect to the rest of the operations performed, and increases with the dimension. Our algorithm is based on Schnorr-Euchner's variant which starts its enumeration of a given interval at its center. This avoids the computation of the edge of the interval at each level as required in FPK or the linear programming cost.

Moreover, as the dimension grows, so does the number of hyperplanes. Thus, we believe that the algorithm would struggle to be competitive when this number becomes too large and a linear program must be solved for each hyperplane.

Finally, our algorithm is exhaustive by construction, and thus enumerates every single vector in $\mathcal{L}_{\mathcal{Q},\mathfrak{p}} \cap S$. As mentioned previously, the algorithm in [27] encounters boundary issues when the planes intersect only the corners of the sieving region. The loss is reasonable in dimension 3 but may become more and more problematic as the dimension grows.

6   A 521-Bit Computation

6.1   A Target from the Pairing World

Considering finite fields with composite extensions is highly motivated by pairing-based cryptography. The security of pairing-based protocols relies on both the discrete logarithm problem in the curve and in the finite field. MNT curves [28] are pairing-friendly elliptic curves with small embedding degree 6, meaning that the security of the related pairing-based protocols relies on the discrete logarithm problem in $\mathbb{F}_{p^6}^*$ for a prime p. Our target is precisely $\mathbb{F}_{p^6}^*$ with a 87-bit prime. MNT curves were introduced in the early 2000's but are back into the spotlight due to the recent arising of zk-SNARKS within the zero-knowledge community, that brings other needs and other uses. For instance, the need of cycles of curves[3] in zk-SNARKS, that are currently only available with MNT curves explains why MNT-6 curves are so useful, as explained in Guillevic's blog-post [15]. Two of them are widely deployed: one with a 298-bit prime [5] and the other with a 753-bit prime [5,8]. With our 87-bit prime we are still far from these concrete parameters, but our work shows that in order to evaluate the security of these curves the right threat to consider is TNFS.

More precisely, we consider the 521-bit finite field $\mathbb{F}_{p^n}$ where $n = 6$ and $p = \texttt{0x6fb96ccdf61c1ea3582e57}$ is a 87-bit prime. The extension degree n is composite with factors $\eta = 3$ and $\kappa = 2$. The prime p is "random" in the sense that it is the closest prime to the 87 first bits of RSA-1024, the 1024-bit integer coming from the RSA Factoring Challenge, such that $p^2 - p + 1$ is also prime. Moreover, we choose as target an element in $\mathbb{F}_{p^6}$ whose decimal digits are taken from π:

$$\texttt{target} = (31415926535897932384626433 + 83279502884197169399375105\iota$$
$$+\ 82097494459230781640628620\iota^2) + x(89986280348253421170679821$$
$$+\ 48086513282306647093844609\iota + 55058223172535940812848111\iota^2).$$

This does not fully define the element since this depends on the representation taken for $\mathbb{F}_{p^6}$. For this, we will simply choose the one that follows from the polynomial selection below. Because the computation of a discrete logarithm in a group can be reduced to its computation in one of its prime subgroups by Pohlig-Hellman's reduction, we work modulo $\ell = p^2 - p + 1 = \texttt{30c252a90b588491be0a93f6fd11924531a80adb333b}$, the 174-bit prime order of the 6-th cyclotomic subgroup of the multiplicative group.

6.2 Polynomial Selection

Three polynomials with specific characteristics must be chosen for TNFS. The polynomial h is of degree $\eta = 3$, monic and irreducible modulo p. In our computation, we use $h(\iota) = \iota^3 - \iota + 1$. The polynomials f_1, f_2 are selected thanks to the Conjugation method [2]. We recall that this method looks for polynomials of degree κ and 2κ. We get $f_1 = x^4 + 1$, and $f_2 = 11672244015875x^2 + 1532885840586x + 11672244015875$.

6.3 Relation Collection

Many parameters have to be balanced in practice in Algorithm 1 to optimise the relation collection step. In our computation, we chose the parameters

$$q_{min} = 5,000,113 \approx 2^{22.2}, \quad q_{max} = 26,087,683 \approx 2^{24.6}, \quad B = 2^{27}, \quad R = 21,$$

---

[3] A cycle of curves is a pair of pairing-friendly elliptic curves $\mathcal{E}_1, \mathcal{E}_2$ such that $\mathcal{E}_1$ is defined over a finite prime field $\mathbb{F}_{p_1}$ with prime order p_2, and $\mathcal{E}_2$ is defined over the finite field $\mathbb{F}_{p_2}$ with order p_1.

$$p_{\max} = 10^7, \quad \mathcal{T}_{\text{sieve}} = 60, \quad p_{\text{batch}} = 2^{27}, \quad \mathcal{T}_{\text{batch}} = 0.$$

This results in a total of 1,280,000 special-q's subsets of polynomials to sieve on.

Sieving and Enumeration. For each special-q, the first step in relation collection is to run a sieving algorithm to collect promising relations. This is done using Algorithm 4 which enumerates all vectors in $\mathcal{L}_{\mathfrak{Q},\mathfrak{p}} \cap S_6(21)$, for each prime ideal up to $p_{\max}$. In our implementation, we used this algorithm only on the f_2-side. On the f_1-side, the norms are much smaller, and the cost of enumerating is too high compared to the information it gives about the probability of being smooth.

All in all, we collect approximately 76,401 million sieve-survivors. Note that these survivors are dealt with on-the-fly: in order to avoid storing all of them, they are removed just after the batch algorithm. Recall that at this stage of the algorithm, we also remove the K_h-unit duplicates and the ζ_2-duplicates.

Number of Leaves and Nodes in the Enumeration Trees. We analyze our enumeration algorithm by computing the expected number of leaves and nodes for a fixed special-q as the value of p increases. As seen in Fig. 2, the output of our enumeration algorithm matches the expected values given by the formulae in Sect. 5. Both the amount of nodes and leaves decrease when p increases. The ratio r between the amount of leaves and nodes also decreases with p. We see that the estimation of the number of internal node is not precise. However, it gives a good idea of the general behavior of the algorithm. Furthermore r indeed remains high, which is a good indication that we do not spend too much computation for each divisibility information gathered by the process.

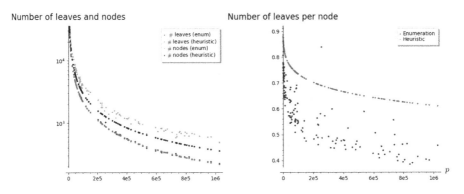

Fig. 2. Number of leaves and nodes (left) and number of leaves per node (right) as a function of p for a fixed 24-bit special-q. We see that as p increases, both the number of nodes visited by the enumeration algorithm and the number of leaves decreases, as expected. We compare the output of our code with the formulae given in Sect. 5 using the Gaussian heuristic.

Balancing Sieving, Batch and ECM. The sieve-survivors outputted by the enumeration algorithm are now the inputs to the batch algorithm implemented in CADO-NFS [1]. Running batch and ECM is done sequentially in CADO-NFS. Here we choose not to run ECM as the computation is efficient enough for the record to finish in reasonable time. Further optimizing the parameters including the ECM algorithm is left for future work. We therefore select the batch-survivors with $p_{\text{batch}} = B = 2^{27}$ and $T_{\text{batch}} = 0$. Indeed, we want the batch-survivors to correspond to our relations which is equivalent to saying that all the norms have no cofactor left, *i.e.*, they completely factor into primes up to the smoothness bound $p_{\text{batch}} = B$. Removing all the possible duplicates further reduces the final amount of relations. This is described in Table 4.

The relation collection was run with an early version of our code, and took the equivalent of 25,300 core-hours. After the optimization given in Algorithm 4, it was going 10% faster, and would have taken only 23,300 core-hours. On our sample computations, the relations were strictly identical to the one computed with the previous code, so we did not run again the whole computation.

Table 4. Number of survivors after each step of the relation collection algorithm. The percentage is given with respect to the previous step. The percentage of sieve-survivors is taken with respect to $\text{vol}(S_6(21)) \times$ #special-q's.

	Sieve-survivors	Batch-survivors (removing K_h/ζ_2-dup.)	Removing special-q duplicates
# survivors	76 401M	18.69M	13.63M
% kept	0.013%	0.02%	73%

6.4 Linear Algebra

Before starting the linear algebra step, the matrix must undergo a few modifications in order to speed up the resolution of the system. This is done by a step called filtering. More precisely, the aim of filtering is to reduce the size of the matrix of relations without modifying its kernel.

Dealing with Special-q Duplicates. As mentioned in Sect. 3.4, only ζ_2-duplicates and K_h-unit duplicates can be dealt with prior to constructing the matrix. To remove special-q duplicates, we compare the ideal factorizations of each relation and remove identical lines in the file containing all our relations. Before eliminating special-q duplicates we had 18.25M batch-survivors. Removing these duplicates decreased the amount of survivors to 13.63M, a loss of 27%.

Filtering. The matrix of relations is now ready to be sent to CADO-NFS's filter. We have 15.21M ideals in the factor basis, and thus the input matrix to CADO-NFS's filter is a matrix of size 13.63M $\times$ 15.21M. Note that not all the ideals intervene in the relations. The goal of filtering is to reduce the size of the matrix and make it square. Filtering in CADO-NFS uses two steps: purge and merge.

The purge step consists in removing columns that only contain zero coefficients. Indeed only 87% of the ideals of the factor basis appear in relations. The rest leading to zero-columns are deleted. Besides, the purge step removes columns (and corresponding lines) that contain a unique element. These columns correspond to prime ideals, called *singletons*, that occur only once in all the relations. We start with 13.63M lines in the matrix. After removing the singletons, we are left with only 5.21M lines. Hence, purge reduces the number of lines in our matrix by approximately 62%. Thus even if the purge step and more generally filtering is not present in the complexity analysis of TNFS, it is of significant importance in practice for the feasibility of the linear algebra step.

The next step of filtering is merge, which corresponds to a structured Gaussian elimination. It aims at further reducing the matrix size by performing linear combinations of the rows of the input matrix. In our computation, the merge takes as input a square matrix of dimension 5.21M and, after Gaussian elimination up to a density of 100 coefficients per line, its size is decreased to 1.73M. If we eliminate up to 150 coefficients per line, the size is decreased to 1.51M.

Finally, after filtering, we have 1.51M relations and a $(1.51\text{M} + 7) \times 1.51\text{M}$ dimension matrix. The entire filtering step removes 89% of the relations (or 92% if we count before the removal of the duplicates). The 7 extra columns come from the Schirokauer maps, as we see now.

Schirokauer Maps. In order to easily use CADO-NFS implementation of Schirokauer maps, we propose a rather simple trick: represent the tower of number fields as an absolute (non-tower) extension field. More precisely, recall that a Schirokauer maps is any surjective morphism from $K_i^*/(K_i^*)^\ell \to (\mathbb{Z}/\ell\mathbb{Z})^{r_i}$ where K_i is a number field and r_i its unit rank. In the classical NFS setup, K_i is simply an extension of $\mathbb{Q}$, whereas in the Tower setup, K_i is an extension of $\mathbb{Q}(\iota)$.

It is then possible to define a Schirokauer map in TNFS by first defining an isomorphism from the intermediate fields $K_i = \mathbb{Q}(\iota, \alpha_i)$ to a number field K_{F_i} of degree $\deg h \times \deg f_i$ and then using a classical Schirokauer map $\Lambda_{\text{classical}}$ from the latter to $(\mathbb{Z}/\ell\mathbb{Z})^{r_i}$. In other words, we define the map Λ_i as

$$\Lambda_i : K_i^*/(K_i)^{*\ell} \xrightarrow{\simeq} K_{F_i}^*/(K_{F_i})^{*\ell} \to (\mathbb{Z}/\ell\mathbb{Z})^{r_i}.$$

A polynomial F_i and the corresponding isomorphism

$$\Phi_i : K_i \to K_{F_i}$$

are easy to find, and can be represented by the images of each base elements. Thereafter, the map from K_i to K_{F_i} is seen as a linear map and applying it to an element is essentially free.

There are as many Schirokauer maps as the rank of units in K_i. For our computation, this means 2 on the f_1-side and 5 on the f_2-side. Computing Schirokauer maps, *i.e.*, filling seven columns, takes 40 core-hours.

Remark 3. In general, and also true in our computation, the values $\Phi_i(1), \Phi_i(\iota), \cdots$ have denominators. As Schirokauer maps, as implemented in

CADO-NFS, only require integers, we directly multiply the coefficients by the least common multiplier of these denominators. This denominator-clearing can be made completely transparent by choosing Schirokauer maps Λ_i that evaluate to zero over $\mathbb{Q}$. This is the `legacy` mode in CADO-NFS's implementation of Schirokauer maps.

Solving the System. Solving the linear system with 1.51M rows and columns, including the 7 dense columns of Schirokauer maps is done with the block-Wiedemann algorithm, as implemented in CADO-NFS. We used the default behavior which is to run 7 sequences, each one taking one of the heavy columns as input (see [21]). Therefore, the large number of Schirokauer maps does not induce an increase in the running time of this step.

All the sequences can be run in parallel, for a total cost of 1,210 core hours. The reconstruction of the linear generator and the final sum-up leading to the kernel vector must be added up, and the overall cost of linear algebra is 1,403 core hours. We emphasize that the most expensive steps of the linear algebra part are the computation of the sequences and the solution step where the sparse matrix-vector multiplication is the most costly operation.

Un-Filtering. The kernel vector gives the virtual logarithms of 1.51M ideals belonging to the factor basis. Using the relations that were deleted during the purge and merge process, many more can be deduced. This can be seen as reverting the filtering, where each time a relation is re-added, we check if it involves a (unique) ideal for which the virtual logarithm is not yet known. If so, we can deduce it. After this process, we know the virtual logarithms of 12M ideals, corresponding to 79.4% of the factor bases elements.

6.5   Descent Step and Discrete Logarithm of the Target

Now that we know the virtual logarithms of (a large proportion of) the factor basis elements, we are ready for the descent step. We choose as generator the element $g = x + \iota$. This element g lifted in the field defined by f_1 is a unit (of infinite order). This allows us to easily compute its virtual logarithm as it is found using the virtual logarithms outputted by the linear algebra step and an additional Schirokauer map computation.

As mentioned in Sect. 2.2, we use Guillevic's algorithm [16] to optimize the initial splitting step. The descent starts by a smoothing step which required 45 core hours to generate 64M candidates and 10 core hours to identify an element $s \in \mathbb{F}_{p^6}^*$ such that its lift to K_1 has a 35-bit smooth norm. The factors of s greater than 27-bit for which we do not have the virtual logarithms yet are descended in a single special-q step. This descent is done with the same strategy as for the relation collection, namely enumeration and batch, but using a larger radius $R = 33$. Because of the small amount of factors concerned, the time is negligible. The descent step takes 55 core hours. The overall time in core hours of the computation is reported in Table 5.

We finally find the discrete logarithm of our target element:

Table 5. Overall time of our record computation in core hours.

Relation Collection	Linear algebra	Schirokauer maps	Descent	Overall time
23,300	1,403	40	55	24,798

$\log(\texttt{target}) = 762728081687532229776674797013837853035385297631 5498.$

To confirm the validity of our computation, we verify that $g^{\log(\texttt{target})} = \texttt{target}$ is true, modulo ℓ-th powers, as we computed the discrete logarithm only modulo ℓ.

Concluding Remarks

We recall the data from Table 1 in the introduction: the time for collecting relations in our 521-bit computation is only 23,300 core-hours, much less that the 69,120 core-hours of McGuire and Robinson for a 423-bit computation, also in a field of the form $\mathbb{F}_{p^6}$; and this was already much faster than Grémy's work.

This huge improvement is mostly due to the fact that our efficient sieving technique allows to work in large dimensions, and therefore enables the use of Tower NFS. While asymptotic complexities can hardly lead to definitive statements about the performance of TNFS for such "small" target finite fields, the norms that it produces are indeed quite small.

In an attempt to quantify this smallness, we compare them to the norms obtained for equivalent target sizes with the classical NFS algorithm for factoring or for DLP in prime fields. For those, CADO-NFS can serve as a reference, since parameters are provided that are reasonably well optimized (we use 512-bit targets instead of 521-bits, since these are standard sizes for CADO-NFS). The result of this comparison is that, while in our computation we encountered norms, the product of which is around 250 bits, the equivalent for a 512-bit factorisation is around 280 bits, and for a 512-bit prime field DLP with Joux-Lercier polynomial selection, this is around 270 bits. We therefore consider that even if $\mathbb{F}_{p^6}$ is not a high degree extension, and even if 521 bits is still far from a secure cryptographic size, the "tower" effect is already pretty impactful.

Furthermore, we would like to emphasize that our experiment was merely a first demonstration, but there is still much room for improvement in the tuning of the various parameters and the use of the explicit Galois action that is available with the Conjugation method. These will be required for working with Tower NFS on larger sized finite fields.

Acknowledgements. We are indebted to Léo Ducas and Wessel van Woerden for insightful discussions about the lattice points enumeration aspect of this work. Many thanks to Aurore Guillevic, for numerous discussions, in particular about polynomial selection and the blockchain ecosystem. Experiments in this paper were carried out using the Grid'5000 testbed, supported by a scientific interest group hosted by Inria and including CNRS, RENATER and several Universities as well as other organizations (see https://www.grid5000.fr).

References

1. The CADO-NFS Development Team. CADO-NFS, An Implementation of the Number Field Sieve Algorithm. Found at https://gitlab.inria.fr/cado-nfs/cado-nfs, development version of January 2021
2. Barbulescu, R., Gaudry, P., Guillevic, A., Morain, F.: Improving NFS for the discrete logarithm problem in non-prime finite fields. In: Oswald, E., Fischlin, M. (eds.) EUROCRYPT 2015. LNCS, vol. 9056, pp. 129–155. Springer, Heidelberg (2015). https://doi.org/10.1007/978-3-662-46800-5_6
3. Barbulescu, R., Gaudry, P., Joux, A., Thomé, E.: A heuristic quasi-polynomial algorithm for discrete logarithm in finite fields of small characteristic. In: Nguyen, P.Q., Oswald, E. (eds.) EUROCRYPT 2014. LNCS, vol. 8441, pp. 1–16. Springer, Heidelberg (2014). https://doi.org/10.1007/978-3-642-55220-5_1
4. Barbulescu, R., Gaudry, P., Kleinjung, T.: The tower number field sieve. In: Iwata, T., Cheon, J.H. (eds.) ASIACRYPT 2015. LNCS, vol. 9453, pp. 31–55. Springer, Heidelberg (2015). https://doi.org/10.1007/978-3-662-48800-3_2
5. Ben-Sasson, E., Chiesa, A., Tromer, E., Virza, M.: Scalable zero knowledge via cycles of elliptic curves. In: Garay, J.A., Gennaro, R. (eds.) CRYPTO 2014, Part II. LNCS, vol. 8617, pp. 276–294. Springer, Heidelberg, August 2014. https://doi.org/10.1007/s00453-016-0221-0
6. Bernstein, D.J.: How to find smooth parts of integers (2004). http://cr.yp.to/factorization/smoothparts-20040510.pdf
7. Bouvier, C., Imbert, L.: Faster cofactorization with ECM using mixed representations. In: Kiayias, A., Kohlweiss, M., Wallden, P., Zikas, V. (eds.) PKC 2020, Part II. LNCS, vol. 12111, pp. 483–504. Springer, Heidelberg, May 2020. https://doi.org/10.1007/978-3-030-45374-9
8. CODA: MNT-6 curve with parameter 753 for Snark prover. Webpage at https://coinlist.co/build/coda/pages/MNT6753
9. Fincke, U., Pohst, M.: Improved methods for calculating vectors of short length in a lattice, including a complexity analysis. Math. Comput. **44**, 463–471 (1985)
10. Franke, J., Kleinjung, T.: Continued Fractions and Lattice Sieving. Special-Purpose Hardware for Attacking Cryptographic Systems-SHARCS, p. 40 (2005)
11. Gama, N., Nguyen, P.Q., Regev, O.: Lattice enumeration using extreme pruning. In: Gilbert, H. (ed.) EUROCRYPT 2010. LNCS, vol. 6110, pp. 257–278. Springer, Heidelberg (2010). https://doi.org/10.1007/978-3-642-13190-5_13
12. Granger, R., Kleinjung, T., Zumbrägel, J.: On the discrete logarithm problem in finite fields of fixed characteristic. Trans. Am. Math. Soc. **370**(5), 3129–3145 (2018)
13. Grémy, L.: Higher dimensional sieving for the number field sieve algorithms. In: ANTS 2018 - Thirteenth Algorithmic Number Theory Symposium, pp. 1–16, Jul 2018
14. Grémy, L., Guillevic, A., Morain, F., Thomé, E.: Computing discrete logarithms in $\mathbb{F}_{p^6}$. In: Adams, C., Camenisch, J. (eds.) SAC 2017. LNCS, vol. 10719, pp. 85–105. Springer, Heidelberg, August 2017. https://doi.org/10.1007/978-3-319-72565-9_5
15. Guillevic, A.: Pairing-friendly curves. Blogpost found at https://members.loria.fr/AGuillevic/pairing-friendly-curves
16. Guillevic, A.: Faster individual discrete logarithms in finite fields of composite extension degree. Math. Comput. **88**(317), 1273–1301 (2019). https://doi.org/10.1090/mcom/3376
17. Guillevic, A., Singh, S.: On the alpha value of polynomials in the tower number field sieve algorithm. Math. Cryptol. **1**(1), 39 (2021)

18. Hanrot, G., Stehlé, D.: Improved analysis of Kannan's shortest lattice vector algorithm. In: Menezes, A. (ed.) CRYPTO 2007. LNCS, vol. 4622, pp. 170–186. Springer, Heidelberg (2007). https://doi.org/10.1007/978-3-540-74143-5_10

19. Hayasaka, K., Aoki, K., Kobayashi, T., Takagi, T.: An experiment of number field sieve for discrete logarithm problem over GF(p^n). JSIAM Lett. **6**, 53–56 (2014)

20. Joux, A., Lercier, R., Smart, N., Vercauteren, F.: The number field sieve in the medium prime case. In: Dwork, C. (ed.) CRYPTO 2006. LNCS, vol. 4117, pp. 326–344. Springer, Heidelberg (2006). https://doi.org/10.1007/11818175_19

21. Joux, A., Pierrot, C.: Nearly sparse linear algebra and application to discrete logarithms computations. In: Contemporary Developments in Finite Fields and Applications (2016)

22. Kannan, R.: Improved algorithms for integer programming and related lattice problems. In: Proceedings of the Fifteenth Annual ACM Symposium on Theory of Computing, pp. 193–206. STOC 1983. Association for Computing Machinery, New York, NY, USA (1983)

23. Kim, T., Barbulescu, R.: Extended tower number field sieve: a new complexity for the medium prime case. In: Robshaw, M., Katz, J. (eds.) CRYPTO 2016. LNCS, vol. 9814, pp. 543–571. Springer, Heidelberg (2016). https://doi.org/10.1007/978-3-662-53018-4_20

24. Kim, T., Jeong, J.: Extended tower number field sieve with application to finite fields of arbitrary composite extension degree. In: Fehr, S. (ed.) PKC 2017. LNCS, vol. 10174, pp. 388–408. Springer, Heidelberg (2017). https://doi.org/10.1007/978-3-662-54365-8_16

25. Kleinjung, T., Wesolowski, B.: Discrete logarithms in quasi-polynomial time in finite fields of fixed characteristic (2019), https://eprint.iacr.org/2019/751, cryptology ePrint Archive, Report 2019/751, to appear in Journal of the AMS

26. Lenstra, H.W.: Factoring integers with elliptic curves. Ann. Mathem. **126**(3), 649–673 (1987)

27. McGuire, G., Robinson, O.: Lattice sieving in three dimensions for discrete log in medium characteristic. J. Math. Cryptol. **15**(1), 223–236 (2021)

28. Miyaji, A., Nakabayashi, M., Nonmembers, S.: New explicit conditions of elliptic curve traces for FR-reduction. IEICE Trans. Fundam. Electron. Commun. Comput. Sci. **84**, 1234–1243 (2001)

29. Nguyen, P.Q., Stehlé, D.: LLL on the average. In: Hess, F., Pauli, S., Pohst, M. (eds.) ANTS 2006. LNCS, vol. 4076, pp. 238–256. Springer, Heidelberg (2006). https://doi.org/10.1007/11792086_18

30. Pollard, J.M.: The lattice sieve. In: Lenstra, A.K., Lenstra, H.W. (eds.) The development of the number field sieve. LNM, vol. 1554, pp. 43–49. Springer, Heidelberg (1993). https://doi.org/10.1007/BFb0091538

31. Sarkar, P., Singh, S.: New complexity trade-offs for the (multiple) number field sieve algorithm in non-prime fields. In: Fischlin, M., Coron, J.-S. (eds.) EUROCRYPT 2016. LNCS, vol. 9665, pp. 429–458. Springer, Heidelberg (2016). https://doi.org/10.1007/978-3-662-49890-3_17

32. Schirokauer, O.: Using number fields to compute logarithms in finite fields. Math. Comput. **69**, 1267–1283 (2000)

33. Schnorr, C.P., Euchner, M.: Lattice basis reduction: improved practical algorithms and solving subset sum problems. Math. Programm. **66**(2), 181–199 (1994). https://doi.org/10.1007/BF01581144

34. Wiedemann, D.H.: Solving sparse linear equations over finite fields. IEEE Trans. Inf. Theory **32**(1), 54–62 (1986). https://doi.org/10.1109/TIT.1986.1057137

Public-Key Cryptanalysis

Partial Key Exposure Attack on Short Secret Exponent CRT-RSA

Alexander May[1(✉)] ⓘ, Julian Nowakowski[1] ⓘ, and Santanu Sarkar[1,2]

[1] Ruhr-University Bochum, Bochum, Germany
{alex.may,julian.nowakowski}@rub.de
[2] Indian Institute of Technology Madras, Chennai, India
santanu@iitm.ac.in

Abstract. Let (N, e) be an RSA public key, where $N = pq$ is the product of equal bitsize primes p, q. Let d_p, d_q be the corresponding secret CRT-RSA exponents.

Using a Coppersmith-type attack, Takayasu, Lu and Peng (TLP) recently showed that one obtains the factorization of N in polynomial time, provided that $d_p, d_q \leq N^{0.122}$. Building on the TLP attack, we show the first *Partial Key Exposure* attack on short secret exponent CRT-RSA. Namely, let $N^{0.122} \leq d_p, d_q \leq N^{0.5}$. Then we show that a constant known fraction of the least significant bits (LSBs) of both d_p, d_q suffices to factor N in polynomial time.

Naturally, the larger d_p, d_q, the more LSBs are required. E.g. if d_p, d_q are of size $N^{0.13}$, then we have to know roughly a $\frac{1}{5}$-fraction of their LSBs, whereas for d_p, d_q of size $N^{0.2}$ we require already knowledge of a $\frac{2}{3}$-LSB fraction. Eventually, if d_p, d_q are of full size $N^{0.5}$, we have to know all of their bits. Notice that as a side-product of our result we obtain a heuristic deterministic polynomial time factorization algorithm on input (N, e, d_p, d_q).

Keywords: CRT-RSA · Coppersmith's method · Partial key exposure

1 Introduction

The RSA cryptosystem has the remarkable property that it admits polynomial time attacks for small secrets. Since Wiener's attack [29] for secret exponents $d \leq N^{\frac{1}{4}}$ and Coppersmith's seminal work [6] on factoring $N = pq$ given half of the bits of p, there has been a long line of research on RSA cryptanalysis.

Using Coppersmith's method, Wiener's bound has been improved by Boneh and Durfee [5] to $d \leq N^{0.284}$, respectively $N^{0.292}$, which despite some efforts [16, 26] remains the best known small secret RSA exponent bound. Coron

A. May—Funded by DFG under Germany's Excellence Strategy - EXC-2092 CASA - 390781972.
S. Sarkar—Funded by a Humboldt Research Fellowship for experienced researchers, while visiting Ruhr-University Bochum.

ⓒ International Association for Cryptologic Research 2021
M. Tibouchi and H. Wang (Eds.): ASIACRYPT 2021, LNCS 13090, pp. 99–129, 2021.
https://doi.org/10.1007/978-3-030-92062-3_4

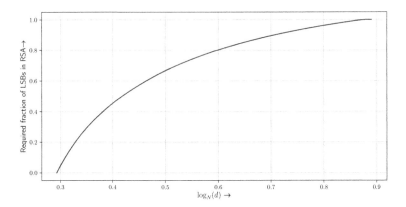

Fig. 1. Required fraction of LSBs for the best known Partial Key Exposure attacks on RSA.

and May [8,22] proved that on input (N, e, d) the factorization of N can be found in polynomial time.

Afterwards, Ernst, Jochemsz, May, and de Weger [9] showed that both latter results can be linked by a Partial Key Exposure attack. Namely in the range $N^{0.284} \le d \le N$, there exists an RSA Partial Key Exposure attack on the most significant bits (MSBs) of d. More precisely, for all d's in this range there is a constant fraction of MSBs whose knowledge allows to factor N in polynomial time. As one would expect, if d is slightly larger than $N^{0.284}$ then one needs only a small MSB bit fraction, whereas for d tending to N (or more precisely $\phi(N)$) one needs all of d's bits.

Later this Partial Key Exposure attack was improved by Takayasu and Kunihiro [24] to cover the range $N^{0.292} \le d \le N$ of the superior Boneh-Durfee bound. Notice that for Partial Key Exposure attacks a smaller range is indeed an improvement. Whereas in the range $d \in [N^{0.284}, N^{0.292}]$ the attack of [9] requires some known bits, the attack of Takayasu and Kunihiro [24] succeeds in this range without any bit-knowledge. The fact that the superior Boneh-Durfee bound $d \le N^{0.292}$ extrapolates smoothly to full size $d \le N$ gives us some indication that [24] might be optimal.

Takayasu and Kunihiro [24] also presented an LSB attack, based on a result by Aono [1], that works in the range $N^{0.292} \le d \le N^{0.89}$, see Fig. 1. Somewhat surprisingly, it is open whether there exists an LSB-type Partial Key Exposure attack up to full size d.

In practice, RSA Partial Key Exposure attacks led to a wide range of devastating attacks [2,11,23] on real-world RSA implementations that leaked private key bits.

CRT-RSA. As opposed to small secret d, the case of small CRT exponents seems to be notoriously harder to analyze. The existence of such attacks was initially raised as an open problem in Wiener [29]. The first result was achieved in [20] only for primes p, q of imbalanced bitsize, and later improved in [3].

The first bound for the standard RSA setting with balanced primes was given by Jochemsz and May [15], who showed a Coppersmith-type polynomial time attack for $d_p, d_q \leq N^{0.073}$. This was recently improved by Takayasu, Lu and Peng [27] to $N^{0.091}$ and shortly after [28] to a remarkably large bound $N^{0.122}$. We refer to the latter bound as the TLP attack.

However, several natural questions remain unanswered. First, the optimality of the TLP attack is unclear, especially since TLP is a highly involved application of Coppersmith's method to a system of three polynomials. Second, it remained open whether small CRT exponents admit Partial Key Exposure attacks at all. Partial Key Exposure attacks on CRT exponents where so far only known for the special setting of small public exponents e, see [4,18,25]. And third, even if small CRT exponent Partial Key Exposure attacks exist, do they interpolate to the natural bound $d_p, d_q \leq N^{0.5}$? For this bound, i.e. known CRT-exponents, Maitra and Sarkar [19] showed a deterministic Coppersmith-type factorization attack on input (N, e, d_p, d_q).

Our Results. As our main result, we give the first Partial Key Exposure attack on CRT exponents in the full range $N^{0.122} \leq d_p, d_q \leq N^{0.5}$, see Fig. 2 for an illustration. Since we achieve a smooth interpolation from the TLP result $N^{0.122}$ to the natural upper bound $N^{0.5}$, this gives some indication of optimality. Our upper bound provides a *heuristic* deterministic polynomial time factorization algorithm on input (N, e, d_p, d_q), different from the one of Maitra and Sarkar [19]. For our results, we require the typical well-studied Coppersmith heuristic for multivariate polynomials, as e.g. used in [1,3–5,9,12,15,16,19,28].

On the way to achieving our main result, we make some contributions that might be of independent interest. First, we give a geometric interpretation of the TLP attack in terms of Newton polytopes that helps to gain a deeper structural insight. Second, we show a simplified LSB Partial Key Exposure attack in the range $N^{0.083} \leq d_p, d_q \leq N^{0.5}$, see Fig. 2.

This attack admits an elegant formula as follows. Assume that d_p, d_q are of size N^β and write $d_p = d_p^* 2^k + \widetilde{d_p}$, $d_q = d_q^* 2^k + \widetilde{d_q}$ for some k, known LSBs $\widetilde{d_p}, \widetilde{d_q}$, and unknown MSBs $d_p^*, d_q^* \leq N^\delta$. Then we can find the factorization of N in polynomial time under the usual Coppersmith-type heuristic, provided that $\delta \leq \frac{1}{10} - \frac{1}{5}\beta$.

Notice that our formula already has the desired end point $d_p, d_q \leq N^{\frac{1}{2}}$. For any $\beta \leq \frac{1}{2}$, i.e., for any d_p, d_q up to full size, we obtain a non-negative bound for δ. For $\beta = \delta$, in which case we do not know any LSBs, we achieve $\delta \leq \frac{1}{12} \approx 0.083$.

Eventually, we optimize our attack such that it works in the range $N^{0.122} \leq d_p, d_q \leq N^{1/2}$, i.e., building on top of the TLP bound. This improves on our simplified Partial Key Exposure attack, since it requires no key-knowledge in the range $d_p, d_q \in [N^{0.083}, N^{0.122}]$. Moreover, for any secret exponent size in the range $N^{0.083} \leq d_p, d_q \leq N^{1/2}$ it requires less key-knowledge of d_p, d_q, see Fig. 2 for a comparison of the required LSB fraction.

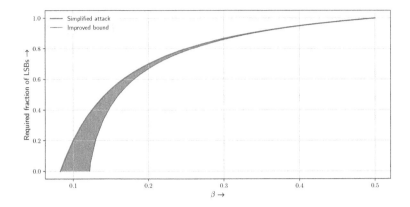

Fig. 2. Comparison between our simplified attack and our m ain result.

We find it somewhat remarkable that our CRT-RSA LSB attack works for full size d_p, d_q, whereas the best known RSA LSB Partial Key Exposure attack [24] from Fig. 1 does not reach full size d.

Since RSA Partial Key Exposure attacks already found many real-world applications [2,11,23], we hope that our CRT-RSA counterpart also stimulates further research in this area. We believe that in practice bits of d_p, d_q might be easier to get via side-channel attacks than bits of d, since almost all standard RSA implementations for efficiency reasons actually use CRT exponents.

Our paper is structured as follows. In Sect. 2, we recall the basics of Coppersmith's method. In Sect. 3, we revisit the TLP attack, and thoroughly analyze TLP using our new geometric approach. This reformulation then in turn allows us to easily prove our simplified small CRT exponent attack in Sect. 4. To show our main result for the improved CRT attack in the range $N^{0.122} \leq d_p, d_q \leq N^{0.5}$ in Sect. 4.1, we again heavily reuse our results from Sect. 3. We conclude by providing experimental evidence of our standard Coppersmith-type heuristic in Sect. 5.

2   Coppersmith's Method

Like in many other attacks on RSA, we base our attack on Coppersmith's method for finding small modular roots of multivariate polynomials [7]. For that, we model the problem of factoring an RSA modulus as a problem of finding a small root of multivariate polynomials modulo some large integer M. In particular, we use the RSA key generation equations to derive n polynomials $f_1, \ldots, f_n$ in k variables $x_1, \ldots, x_k$, which share a small root $r = (r_1, \ldots, r_k)$ modulo M. Small means here that we know for $j = 1, \ldots, k$ upper bounds X_j with $|r_j| \leq X_j$. Then, we choose an $m \in \mathbb{N}$ and define so-called *shift polynomials*

$$p_i := f_1^{i_1} \cdot \ldots \cdot f_n^{i_n} \cdot x_1^{j_1} \cdot \ldots \cdot x_k^{j_k} \cdot M^{m-(i_1+\ldots+i_n)},$$

with appropriately chosen exponents. Notice that by construction the shift polynomials have the root r modulo M^m.

Our goal is to compute integer linear combinations

$$h_j(x_1, \ldots, x_k) := \sum_i \alpha_{j,i} p_i(x_1, \ldots, x_k) \qquad (\alpha_{j,i} \in \mathbb{Z})$$

of the shift polynomials, to obtain k polynomials $h_1, \ldots, h_k$, such that for every $j = 1, \ldots, k$ the coefficient vector of $h_j(X_1 x_1, \ldots, X_k x_k)$ has sufficiently small Euclidean norm. A lemma by Howgrave-Graham (as stated below) then guarantees us that $h_1, \ldots, h_k$ have the root r not just modulo M^m, but also over the integers. If the variety of the ideal $(h_1, \ldots, h_k)$ is zero-dimensional, this allows us to recover their root by using a Groebner basis – which in our case means that we can efficiently factor the RSA modulus.

Lemma 1 (Howgrave-Graham, [14]). *Let* $h(x_1, \ldots, x_k) \in \mathbb{Z}[x_1, \ldots, x_k]$ *be a polynomial in at most* ω *monomials. Suppose that* $h(r_1, \ldots, r_k) \equiv 0 \bmod M^m$ *for some positive integer* m. *Also let* $|r_i| < X_i$ *for* $1 \leq i \leq k$ *and*

$$\|h(x_1 X_1, \ldots, x_k X_k)\| < \frac{M^m}{\sqrt{\omega}}.$$

Then $h(r_1, \ldots, r_k) = 0$ *holds over the integers.*

To find suitable polynomials h_j, we use lattice-based techniques.

Definition 1. *Let* $\{\mathbf{b_1}, \ldots, \mathbf{b_\omega}\} \subset \mathbb{Z}^n$ *be linearly independent row vectors. The lattice* $\mathcal{L}$ *generated by these vectors is defined by*

$$\mathcal{L} = \{z_1 \mathbf{b_1} + \ldots + z_\omega \mathbf{b_\omega} \mid z_i \in \mathbb{Z}, \forall i \in \{1, \ldots, \omega\}\}.$$

$\{\mathbf{b_1}, \ldots, \mathbf{b_\omega}\}$ *is called a* basis *of* $\mathcal{L}$. *The parameter* n *is called the* dimension *of* $\mathcal{L}$, ω *is called the rank of* $\mathcal{L}$. *If* $\omega = n$, *then we call* $\mathcal{L}$ *a* full-rank *lattice.*

We often associate a lattice with a *basis matrix* $\mathbf{B}$. Two lattice bases generate the same lattice if and only if their basis matrices $\mathbf{B}_1$ and $\mathbf{B}_2$ satisfy $\mathbf{B}_1 = \mathbf{U}\mathbf{B}_2$ for some unimodular matrix $\mathbf{U}$. As unimodular square matrices have determinant ± 1, one can define the *determinant of a full-rank lattice* $\mathcal{L}$ as

$$\det \mathcal{L} := |\det \mathbf{B}|.$$

Notice that the coefficient vectors of the polynomials $h_j(X_1 x_1, \ldots, X_k x_k)$, as defined above, are elements of a lattice $\mathcal{L}_S$, which is generated by the coefficient vectors of the polynomials $p_i(X_1 x_1, \ldots, X_k x_k)$. Hence, the problem of finding polynomials h_j with short norm boils down to finding short non-zero vectors in $\mathcal{L}_S$. This can be achieved in polynomial time using the well-known LLL algorithm [17].

Lemma 2. *Let* $\mathcal{L}$ *be an integer lattice of dimension* ω. *The LLL algorithm applied to* $\mathcal{L}$ *outputs a reduced basis* $\{\mathbf{v_1}, \ldots, \mathbf{v_\omega}\}$ *of* $\mathcal{L}$ *with*

$$\|\mathbf{v_1}\| \leq \|\mathbf{v_2}\| \leq \cdots \leq \|\mathbf{v_i}\| \leq 2^{\frac{\omega(\omega-1)}{4(\omega+1-i)}} \det(\mathcal{L})^{\frac{1}{\omega+1-i}}, \quad \textit{for } i = 1, \ldots, \omega,$$

in time polynomial in the dimension ω *and the bit size of the entries of* $\mathcal{L}$.

For a proof of Lemma 2, we refer to [21, Theorem 4].

As a consequence of Lemma 2, if the condition

$$2^{\frac{\omega(\omega-1)}{4(\omega+1-\ell)}} \det(\mathcal{L}_s)^{\frac{1}{\omega+1-\ell}} < \frac{M^m}{\sqrt{\omega}},$$

holds for all $\ell \leq k$, we can obtain the required k polynomials h_j, which satisfy the condition of Lemma 1, by simply applying LLL to the lattice $\mathcal{L}_S$. Since in our case the values of the determinant and of M grow significantly faster than the other terms (as usual in these types of attacks), we can also use the simplified *enabling condition*

$$\det \mathcal{L}_S < (M^m)^{\dim \mathcal{L}_S}. \tag{1}$$

To keep the calculation of the determinant simple, we require that the basis matrix of $\mathcal{L}_S$ is of a triangular shape. For that, we need to ensure that the shift polynomial p_1 has exactly one monomial and moreover that for every $i > 1$ the set

$$\{\lambda \mid \lambda \text{ is a monomial of } p_i \text{ but not of } p_1, \ldots, p_{i-1}\}$$

contains exactly one element. Calculating the determinant then becomes particularly easy, as we simply have to keep track for every i, which monomial λ_i the polynomial p_i adds to the basis matrix' diagonal. Denoting the coefficient of λ_i by c_i, the determinant then can be calculated as

$$\det \mathcal{L}_S = \prod_i |c_i \cdot \lambda_i(X_1, \ldots, X_k)|.$$

For constructing our basis matrix, we will often make use of a powerful tool, the so called *Newton polytope* of a polynomial.

Definition 2. *The* Newton polytope *of a k-variate polynomial $p(x_1, \ldots, x_k)$ is defined as the convex hull of the set*

$$N(p) := \left\{ (i_1, \ldots, i_k) \in \mathbb{N}^k \mid x_1^{i_1} \cdot \ldots \cdot x_k^{i_k} \text{ is a monomial of } p \right\}.$$

Notice that for two polynomials p_1, p_2 the sets $N(p_1)$, $N(p_2)$ as defined above have the useful property that $N(p_1 p_2) = N(p_1) + N(p_2)$, where $+$ denotes the Minkowski sum. Hence, the Newton polytope of some polynomial $x_i^a \cdot p$ (where $a \in \mathbb{N}$) is obtained by moving the Newton polytope of p up a units on the axis corresponding to x_i. Similarly, the Newton polytope of p^a is obtained by scaling the Newton polytope of p by a factor of a. (See Fig. 3 for examples.)

It is worth to note that we have no provable guarantee that the LLL gives us polynomials, which generate an ideal with zero-dimensional variety. Thus, our approach relies on the standard Coppersmith-type heuristic assumption.

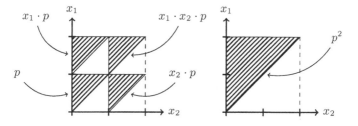

Fig. 3. The Newton polytopes of $p(x_1, x_2) := x_1 x_2 + x_1 + 1$ and related polynomials.

Assumption 1. *In this work, the lattice based constructions yield polynomials, that generate an ideal with zero-dimensional variety.*

In Sect. 5 we verify Assumption 1 experimentally.

3 The TLP Attack Revisited

As our attack is strongly based on the Takayasu-Lu-Peng attack (TLP) [28] on CRT-RSA, we describe it in this section in detail. We deviate from the original algebraic TLP formulation, with the hope that our geometric view helps to gain a deeper understanding. We first present a simplified construction and after that optimize it to obtain TLP.

3.1 A Simplified Construction

Let us recall the CRT-RSA key generation equations

$$ed_p = k(p - 1) + 1, \tag{2}$$
$$ed_q = \ell(q - 1) + 1, \tag{3}$$

where $N = pq$ is an RSA modulus, e is a public exponent, d_p, d_q are the corresponding CRT-exponents and $k, \ell \in \mathbb{N}$. Writing $e = N^\alpha$ and upper bounding $d_p, d_q \leq N^\delta$ for some $\alpha, \delta \in \mathbb{R}$, the values of k and ℓ can be bounded as

$$k = \frac{ed_p - 1}{p - 1} < \frac{ed_p}{p - 1} = \Theta\left(\frac{ed_p}{N^{1/2}}\right) = \Theta(N^{\alpha + \delta - 1/2}),$$
$$\ell = \frac{ed_q - 1}{q - 1} < \frac{ed_q}{q - 1} = \Theta\left(\frac{ed_q}{N^{1/2}}\right) = \Theta(N^{\alpha + \delta - 1/2}),$$

since in the usual RSA setting we have $p, q = \Theta(N^{1/2})$. By that, we find an $X = \Theta(N^{\alpha + \delta - 1/2})$, which is an upper bound for both k and ℓ.

We use Eq. (2) to derive a polynomial

$$f(x_p, y_p) := x_p(y_p - 1) + 1 = x_p y_p - x_p + 1,$$

which has the root (k, p) modulo e. Similarly, we could also use Eq. (3) to derive another polynomial, which in turn has the root (ℓ, q) modulo e. Takayasu, Lu and Peng, however, advise to first multiply Eq. (3) with p and rearrange terms as suggested by Bleichenbacher and May [3]:

$$ped_q = p\ell(q - 1) + p = N\ell - p\ell + p = N(\ell - 1) + N - p(\ell - 1).$$

Then, the equation yields a polynomial

$$g(y_p, z_p) := y_p z_p - N z_p - N,$$

which has the root $(p, \ell - 1)$ modulo e.

The multiplication with p has the advantage that we can get rid of the unknown q and by that treat f and g as three-variate polynomials in the variables x_p, y_p, z_p, which have a common root $(k, p, \ell - 1)$. Using $\ell - 1$ instead of ℓ, gives g a superior Newton polytope, since f and g then share a monomial (see Fig. 4).

With f, we now have a polynomial, which relates the unknowns k and p, while g relates ℓ and p. To obtain a third polynomial, that relates k and ℓ, one can use an idea by Galbraith, Heneghan and McKee [10]. First, we rewrite Eqs. (2) and (3) as

$$kp = k - 1 + ed_p,$$
$$\ell q = \ell - 1 + ed_q.$$

Then, multiplying kp with ℓq, we obtain

$$k\ell N = (k - 1)(\ell - 1) + (k - 1)ed_q + ed_p(\ell - 1) + e^2 d_p d_q$$

and equivalently

$$(N - 1)k(\ell - 1) + Nk + (\ell - 1) = e\left(d_q(k - 1) + d_p(\ell - 1) + ed_p d_q\right),$$

from which we can derive a polynomial

$$h(x_p, z_p) := (N - 1)x_p z_p + N x_p + z_p$$

with the root $(k, \ell - 1)$ modulo e.

Now, we have the following system of polynomial equations

$$f(x_p, y_p, z_p) = x_p y_p - x_p + 1 = 0,$$
$$g(x_p, y_p, z_p) = y_p z_p - N z_p - N = 0,$$
$$h(x_p, y_p, z_p) = (N - 1)x_p z_p + N x_p + z_p = 0,$$

with the solution $(x_0, y_0, z_0) = (k, p, \ell - 1)$ modulo e, which can be upper bounded as

$$x_0, z_0 \leq X = \Theta(N^{\alpha + \delta - 1/2}),$$
$$y_0 \leq Y = \Theta(N^{1/2}).$$

If we can efficiently compute (x_0, y_0, z_0), we factor the RSA modulus N.

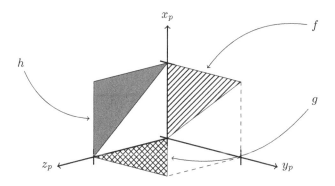

Fig. 4. The Newton polytopes of f, g and h.

We want to use Coppersmith's method to compute (x_0, y_0, z_0). For that, we define shift polynomials, which have the root (x_0, y_0, z_0) modulo e^{2m} for some $m \in \mathbb{N}$. The polynomials will form a lattice with triangular lattice basis matrix whose columns correspond to the elements of the set

$$\mathcal{M} := \left\{ x_p^a y_p^b z_p^c \mid x_p^a y_p^b z_p^c \text{ is a monomial of } f^m g^m \right\}.$$

Notice that by Fig. 4 we may equivalently define $\mathcal{M}$ as

$$\mathcal{M} = \left\{ x_p^a y_p^b z_p^c \mid 0 \le a \le m, 0 \le c \le m, 0 \le b \le a + c \right\}. \tag{4}$$

We partition $\mathcal{M}$ into four subsets

$$\mathcal{M}_1 := \left\{ x_p^a y_p^b z_p^c \in \mathcal{M} \mid a \le c, b \le c - a \right\},$$
$$\mathcal{M}_2 := \left\{ x_p^a y_p^b z_p^c \in \mathcal{M} \mid a > c, b < a - c \right\},$$
$$\mathcal{M}_3 := \left\{ x_p^a y_p^b z_p^c \in \mathcal{M} \mid x_p^a y_p^b z_p^c \notin (\mathcal{M}_1 \cup \mathcal{M}_2), a + b + c \equiv 0 \mod 2 \right\},$$
$$\mathcal{M}_4 := \left\{ x_p^a y_p^b z_p^c \in \mathcal{M} \mid x_p^a y_p^b z_p^c \notin (\mathcal{M}_1 \cup \mathcal{M}_2 \cup \mathcal{M}_3) \right\}.$$

These partitions are used to define a collection of functions, which we call the *exponent functions*.

$$E_f(a, b, c) := \begin{cases} 0, & x_p^a y_p^b z_p^c \in \mathcal{M}_1 \\ b, & x_p^a y_p^b z_p^c \in \mathcal{M}_2 \\ (a + b - c)/2, & x_p^a y_p^b z_p^c \in \mathcal{M}_3 \\ (a + b - c + 1)/2, & x_p^a y_p^b z_p^c \in \mathcal{M}_4 \end{cases},$$

$$E_g(a, b, c) := \begin{cases} b, & x_p^a y_p^b z_p^c \in \mathcal{M}_1 \\ 0, & x_p^a y_p^b z_p^c \in \mathcal{M}_2 \\ (-a + b + c)/2, & x_p^a y_p^b z_p^c \in \mathcal{M}_3 \\ (-a + b + c - 1)/2, & x_p^a y_p^b z_p^c \in \mathcal{M}_4 \end{cases},$$

$$E_h(a,b,c) := \begin{cases} a, & x_p^a y_p^b z_p^c \in \mathcal{M}_1 \\ c, & x_p^a y_p^b z_p^c \in \mathcal{M}_2 \\ (a-b+c)/2, & x_p^a y_p^b z_p^c \in \mathcal{M}_3 \\ (a-b+c-1)/2, & x_p^a y_p^b z_p^c \in \mathcal{M}_4 \end{cases},$$

$$E_x(a,b,c) := \begin{cases} a-b-c, & x_p^a y_p^b z_p^c \in \mathcal{M}_2 \\ 0, & x_p^a y_p^b z_p^c \in \mathcal{M}_1 \cup \mathcal{M}_3 \cup \mathcal{M}_4 \end{cases},$$

$$E_z(a,b,c) := \begin{cases} -a-b+c, & x_p^a y_p^b z_p^c \in \mathcal{M}_1 \\ 0, & x_p^a y_p^b z_p^c \in \mathcal{M}_2 \cup \mathcal{M}_3 \\ 1, & x_p^a y_p^b z_p^c \in \mathcal{M}_4 \end{cases}.$$

One can easily verify that the exponent functions satisfy the following properties.

Lemma 3. *Let $x_p^a y_p^b z_p^c \in \mathcal{M}$. Then the following holds:*

1. $E_f(a,b,c), E_g(a,b,c), E_h(a,b,c), E_x(a,b,c), E_z(a,b,c) \in \mathbb{N}$.
2. $E_f(a,b,c) + E_g(a,b,c) + E_h(a,b,c) \leq 2m$.
3. $E_f(a,b,c) + E_h(a,b,c) + E_x(a,b,c) = a$.
4. $E_f(a,b,c) + E_g(a,b,c) = b$.
5. $E_g(a,b,c) + E_h(a,b,c) + E_z(a,b,c) = c$.

Proof. Simply compare the definitions of $\mathcal{M}_1, \mathcal{M}_2, \mathcal{M}_3, \mathcal{M}_4$ with those of the exponent functions. □

For a given monomial $x_p^a y_p^b z_p^c \in \mathcal{M}$ we use the exponent functions to define a shift polynomial as follows:

$$p_{[a,b,c]}(x_p, y_p, z_p) := f^{E_f(a,b,c)} \cdot g^{E_g(a,b,c)} \cdot h^{E_h(a,b,c)}.$$
$$x_p^{E_x(a,b,c)} \cdot z_p^{E_z(a,b,c)}.$$
$$e^{2m-(E_f(a,b,c)+E_g(a,b,c)+E_h(a,b,c))}.$$

Notice that the first two statements in Lemma 3 ensure that every exponent in $p_{[a,b,c]}$ has a non-negative value. Further notice that $p_{[a,b,c]}$ has the root $(k, p, \ell - 1)$ modulo e^{2m}.

We equip our shift polynomials with the *lexicographic monomial order on* (z_p, x_p, y_p), which in the following we simply call the (z_p, x_p, y_p)-*order*.

Definition 3 ((z_p, x_p, y_p)-**order**). *The monomial order*

$$x_p^{a_1} y_p^{b_1} z_p^{c_1} < x_p^{a_2} y_p^{b_2} z_p^{c_2} :\Longleftrightarrow \begin{cases} c_1 < c_2 \\ c_1 = c_2, a_1 < a_2 \\ c_1 = c_2, a_1 = a_2, b_1 < b_2 \end{cases}$$

is called the (z_p, x_p, y_p)-order.

The shift polynomials have the following nice properties.

Lemma 4. *Let $x_p^a y_p^b z_p^c \in \mathcal{M}$. Then the following holds:*

1. *The leading monomial of $p_{[a,b,c]}$ in the (z_p, x_p, y_p)-order is $x_p^a y_p^b z_p^c$.*
2. *The monomials of $p_{[a,b,c]}$ form a subset of $\mathcal{M}$.*

Proof. Every shift polynomial is of the form $p_{[a,b,c]} = f^{i_1} g^{i_2} h^{i_3} x_p^{j_1} z_p^{j_2} e^{j_3}$, where the exponents are defined by our exponent functions. From Fig. 4, we conclude that the leading monomials of f^{i_1}, g^{i_2} and h^{i_3} are $x_p^{i_1} y_p^{i_1}$, $y_p^{i_2} z_p^{i_2}$ and $x_p^{i_3} z_p^{i_3}$ respectively. Thus, $p_{[a,b,c]}$ has leading monomial

$$x_p^{i_1+i_3+j_1} y_p^{i_1+i_2} z_p^{i_2+i_3+j_2}.$$

Since from Lemma 3 it follows that the exponent functions are defined in such a way that $a = i_1 + i_3 + j_1$, $b = i_1 + i_2$ and $c = i_2 + i_3 + j_2$ always holds, this proves the first statement in the lemma.

To prove the second statement, we conclude from Fig. 4 that the set of the monomials $p_{[a,b,c]}$ is a subset of

$$\mathcal{M}' := \left\{ x_p^{a'} y_p^{b'} z_p^{c'} \mid 0 \leq a' \leq i_1 + i_3 + j_1, 0 \leq c' \leq i_2 + i_3 + j_2, 0 \leq b' \leq a' + c' \right\}.$$

Thus, it suffices to show that $\mathcal{M}' \subseteq \mathcal{M}$.

From the above, we conclude

$$x_p^{i_1+i_3+j_1} y_p^{i_1+i_2} z_p^{i_2+i_3+j_2} = x_p^a y_p^b z_p^c \in \mathcal{M}.$$

Hence, from (4) it follows that $i_1 + i_3 + j_1 \leq m$ and $i_2 + i_3 + j_2 \leq m$. Comparing the definition of $\mathcal{M}'$ with (4), the statement $\mathcal{M}' \subseteq \mathcal{M}$ easily follows. □

Using Lemma 4 we now prove the following important proposition.

Proposition 1. *Order the monomials in $\mathcal{M}$ according to the (z_p, x_p, y_p)-order. Define a lattice basis matrix $\mathbf{B}$, in which the i-th column corresponds to the i-th smallest monomial $x_p^a y_p^b z_p^b \in \mathcal{M}$ and the i-th row corresponds to the coefficient vector of the polynomial $p_{[a,b,c]}(Xx_p, Yy_p, Xz_p)$. Then $\mathbf{B}$ is triangular.*

Proof. If $p_{[a,b,c]}$ has a monomial $x_p^{a'} y_p^{b'} z_p^{c'} \neq x_p^a y_p^b z_p^c$, then with Lemma 4 it follows that $x_p^{a'} y_p^{b'} z_p^{c'} < x_p^a y_p^b z_p^c$ and furthermore $x_p^{a'} y_p^{b'} z_p^{c'} \in \mathcal{M}$. Therefore, when adding $p_{[a,b,c]}$ to $\mathbf{B}$, $x_p^{a'} y_p^{b'} z_p^{c'}$ already is included, as it is the leading monomial of some polynomial $p_{[a',b',c']}$, which, by construction, is added before $p_{[a,b,c]}$ to $\mathbf{B}$. Conversely, no polynomial $p_{[a',b',c']}$, which is added before $p_{[a,b,c]}$ to $\mathbf{B}$, has the monomial $x_p^a y_p^b z_p^c$, since all its monomials are strictly smaller than $x_p^a y_p^b z_p^c$. Hence, $p_{[a,b,c]}$ has with $x_p^a y_p^b z_p^c$ exactly one monomial, which is not added priorly to the basis. □

In Fig. 5 we give an example of the lattice construction as described in Proposition 1 for the case $m = 2$. The table on the left shows the polynomials, that are included in the lattice. The table on the right shows the corresponding leading

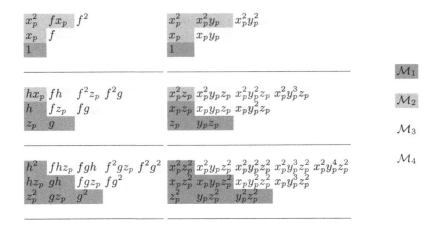

Fig. 5. The lattice construction as described in Proposition 1 for $m = 2$.

monomials. The cell colours indicate, in which set $\mathcal{M}_i$ the leading monomials lie. For the sake of a simpler notation, we omit the powers of e that are multiplied to the shift polynomials.

The entry in the a-th row of the b-th column in the c-th block corresponds to the shift polynomial $p_{[m-a,b,c]}$. (We chose to use $m-a$ instead of a, as the shape of the tables then matches the shape of the Newton polytope of $f^m g^m$.) Notice that the monomials in $\mathcal{M}_1$ and $\mathcal{M}_2$ are added to the lattice by polynomials, which contain only powers of g, h and z_p or f, h and x_p respectively. The monomials in $\mathcal{M}_3$ and $\mathcal{M}_4$ are added by multiplying powers of f to the polynomials, that lie on the right border of the lower triangles corresponding to $\mathcal{M}_1$.

Remark 1. We would like to explain the optimization process, that led us to the definitions of the exponent functions. To keep the lattice's determinant as small as possible, the sum

$$E_f(a,b,c) + E_g(a,b,c) + E_h(a,b,c)$$

should be maximized for every shift polynomial $p_{[a,b,c]}$. (The larger the sum, the smaller the power of e in the shift polynomial and by that the value of the determinant.) If one wants to use shift polynomials, which satisfy the useful properties of Lemma 4, then with Fig. 4 it is not hard to see that the optimal values for the exponent functions are obtained by maximizing the sum under the constraints

$$E_f(a,b,c) + E_h(a,b,c) \leq a,$$
$$E_f(a,b,c) + E_g(a,b,c) \leq b,$$
$$E_g(a,b,c) + E_h(a,b,c) \leq c.$$

This suggests that the problem of selecting optimal exponent functions can be modelled as an integer programming problem. We solved the integer programming problem for efficiently solvable instances of a, b and c, looked for patterns in its solutions and then based the definitions of the exponent functions on those.

For all instances of a, b and c, that we checked, our definitions perfectly match the optimal solution of the corresponding integer programming problem. This gives some evidence for the optimality of our definitions.

Unfortunately, our lattice construction so far does not result in a successful attack, as for any value of m it does not satisfy the enabling condition (1). In fact, no shift polynomial in our lattice is *helpful*, since no polynomial adds a factor smaller than e^{2m} to the lattice's determinant. However, as we will see below, by only slightly enhancing the construction with some clever tricks as suggested by Takayasu, Lu and Peng in [28], we immediately obtain their lattice, which then yields the attack that works whenever $\delta < 0.122$.

3.2   Improving the Construction via Unravelled Linearization

Instead of using three-variate shift polynomials in the variables x_p, y_p, z_p, we now want to use six-variate polynomials in the variables $x_p, x_q, y_p, y_q, z_p, z_q$, which have the root $r := (k, k - 1, p, q, \ell - 1, \ell)$ modulo e^{2m}. With these new variables, we can apply *unravelled linearization* as introduced by Hermann and May [12,13] to our polynomials. That is, we can interchange terms in our polynomials as shown below, while preserving their root r:

$$y_p y_q \longleftrightarrow N,$$
$$x_p - 1 \longleftrightarrow x_q,$$
$$x_q + 1 \longleftrightarrow x_p,$$
$$z_p + 1 \longleftrightarrow z_q,$$
$$z_q - 1 \longleftrightarrow z_p.$$

With the above replacement rules, we linearize our polynomials as

$$f(x_p, x_q, y_p, y_q, z_p, z_q) := x_p y_p - x_q,$$
$$g(x_p, x_q, y_p, y_q, z_p, z_q) := y_p z_p - N z_q,$$
$$h(x_p, x_q, y_p, y_q, z_p, z_q) := N x_p z_q - x_q z_p.$$

By that, all three polynomials have the root r modulo e.

In the following we want to apply the replacement rules to our shift polynomials by using an operator $\mathsf{trans}(\cdot)$ as defined below.

Definition 4. *Let F be a polynomial in the variables $x_p, x_q, y_p, y_q, z_p, z_q$. Then $\mathsf{trans}(F)$ denotes the polynomial, that is obtained by transforming the monomials of F as follows:*

1. *In every monomial replace every $y_p y_q$ by N.*
2. *In every monomial, that has no factor of y_p, replace every x_p by $x_q + 1$ and every z_p by $z_q - 1$.*

3. *In every monomial, that has a factor of y_p, replace every x_q by $x_p - 1$ and every z_q by $z_p + 1$.*

Notice that $\mathsf{trans}(F)$ only has monomials of the form $x_p^a y_p^b z_p^c$ and $x_q^a y_q^b z_q^c$, i.e., variables with subscripts p and q never appear together in one monomial.

As the following lemma shows, polynomials of the form $f^{i_1} y_q^{i_2}$ have a rather nice shape after application of $\mathsf{trans}(\cdot)$.

Lemma 5. *Let $F := f^{i_1} y_q^{i_2}$ with $i_1 > i_2 \geq 1$ and let $F^* := \mathsf{trans}(F)$. Then the following holds:*

1. *The monomials of F^* are of the form $x_p^a y_p^b$ and $x_q^a y_q^b$.*
2. *The absolute value of the coefficient of $x_p^{i_1} y_p^{i_1 - i_2}$ in F^* is N^{i_2}.*
3. *The absolute value of the coefficient of $x_q^{i_2} y_q^{i_2}$ in F^* is 1.*
4. *If $x_p^a y_p^b$ is a monomial of F^*, then $a \geq b + i_2$.*
5. *If $x_q^a y_q^b$ is a monomial of F^*, then $a \geq b + i_1 - i_2$.*

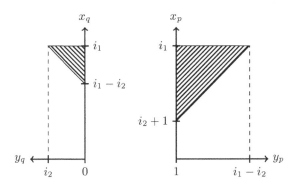

Fig. 6. The Newton polytope of $\mathsf{trans}(f^{i_1} y_q^{i_2})$.

Before we prove Lemma 5, let us give a geometrical interpretation. The Newton polytope of F^* consists of two upper triangles, as shown in Fig. 6. Hence, F^* may be written as

$$F^*(x_p, x_q, z_p, z_q) = F_p^*(x_p, y_p) + F_q^*(x_q, y_q),$$

such that the monomials of F_p^* are the elements of the set

$$\left\{ x_p^a y_p^b \mid b > 0, x_p^a y_p^b \text{ is a monomial of } f^{i_1} y_p^{-i_2} \right\},$$

where f has the shape it had before linearization, and similarly the monomials of F_q^* are the elements of the set

$$\left\{ x_q^a y_q^b \mid b \geq 0, x_p^a y_p^b \text{ is a monomial of } f^{i_1} y_p^{i_2 - i_1} \right\}.$$

Proof (Lemma 5). From the equation

$$f^{i_1} = (x_p y_p - x_q)^{i_1} = \sum_{j_1=0}^{i_1} \binom{i_1}{j_1} (x_p y_p)^{i_1 - j_1} (-x_q)^{j_1},$$

we conclude that the monomials of F are of the form $y_p^{i_1 - j_1} y_q^{i_2} x_p^{i_1 - j_1} x_q^{j_1}$, where $0 \leq j_1 \leq i_1$. By Definition 4, every monomial with $i_1 - j_1 > i_2$ gets transformed via trans as

$$
\begin{aligned}
& y_p^{i_1 - j_1} y_q^{i_2} x_p^{i_1 - j_1} x_q^{j_1} \\
\mapsto & N^{i_2} y_p^{i_1 - j_1 - i_2} x_p^{i_1 - j_1} x_q^{j_1} \\
\mapsto & N^{i_2} y_p^{i_1 - j_1 - i_2} x_p^{i_1 - j_1} (x_p - 1)^{j_1} \\
= & N^{i_2} y_p^{i_1 - j_1 - i_2} x_p^{i_1 - j_1} \sum_{j_2=0}^{j_1} \binom{j_1}{j_2} (-1)^{j_2} x_p^{j_1 - j_2} \\
= & N^{i_2} y_p^{i_1 - j_1 - i_2} \sum_{j_2=0}^{j_1} \binom{j_1}{j_2} (-1)^{j_2} x_p^{i_1 - j_2}.
\end{aligned}
$$

Similarly, every monomial with $i_1 - j_1 \leq i_2$ gets transformed as

$$
\begin{aligned}
& y_p^{i_1 - j_1} y_q^{i_2} x_p^{i_1 - j_1} x_q^{j_1} \\
\mapsto & N^{i_1 - j_1} y_q^{i_2 - (i_1 - j_1)} x_p^{i_1 - j_1} x_q^{j_1} \\
\mapsto & N^{i_1 - j_1} y_q^{i_2 - (i_1 - j_1)} (x_q + 1)^{i_1 - j_1} x_q^{j_1} \\
= & N^{i_1 - j_1} y_q^{i_2 - (i_1 - j_1)} x_q^{j_1} \sum_{j_3=0}^{i_1 - j_1} \binom{i_1 - j_1}{j_3} x_q^{i_1 - j_1 - j_3} \\
= & N^{i_1 - j_1} y_q^{i_2 - (i_1 - j_1)} \sum_{j_3=0}^{i_1 - j_1} \binom{i_1 - j_1}{j_3} x_q^{i_1 - j_3}.
\end{aligned}
$$

Notice that this already proves the first three statements.

Statements four and five now follow easily. For every monomial $x_p^a y_p^b$ we find values $j_1 = 0, \ldots, i_1$ and $j_2 = 0, \ldots, j_1$, such that $a = i_1 - j_2$ and $b = i_1 - j_1 - i_2$. As this yields the inequality

$$a = i_1 - j_2 \geq i_1 - j_1 = b + i_2,$$

this proves the fourth statement. Similarly, for every every monomial $x_q^a y_q^b$ we find values $j_1 = 0, \ldots, i_1$ and $j_3 = 0, \ldots, i_1 - j_1$, such that $a = i_1 - j_3$ and $b = i_2 - (i_1 - j_1)$. This yields the inequality

$$a = i_1 - j_3 \geq i_1 - (i_1 - j_1) = b + i_1 - i_2$$

and thus concludes the proof of the lemma. □

One can generalize Lemma 5 with a completely analogous proof to the statement of Lemma 6.

Lemma 6. Let $F := f^{i_1} g^{i_2} h^{i_3} x_p^{i_4} z_p^{i_5} y_q^{i_6}$ with $i_1 + i_2 > i_6 \geq 1$ and let $F^* := \mathsf{trans}(F)$. Then the following holds:

1. The monomials of F^* are of the form $x_p^a y_p^b z_p^c$ and $x_q^a y_q^b z_q^c$.
2. The absolute value of the coefficient of

$$x_p^{i_1+i_3+i_4} y_p^{i_1+i_2-i_6} z_p^{i_2+i_3+i_5}$$

   in F^* is $N^{j_1}(N-1)^{i_3}$ for some $j_1 \in \mathbb{N}$.
3. The absolute value of the coefficient of

$$x_q^{i_1+i_3+i_4} y_q^{i_6} z_q^{i_2+i_3+i_5}$$

   in F^* is $N^{j_2}(N-1)^{i_3}$ for some $j_2 \in \mathbb{N}$.
4. If $x_p^a y_p^b z_p^c$ is a monomial of F^*, then $a + c \geq b + i_3 + i_4 + i_5 + i_6$.
5. If $x_q^a y_q^b z_q^c$ is a monomial of F^*, then $a + c \geq b + i_1 + i_2 + i_3 - i_6$.

Lemma 6 can be interpreted geometrically analogous to Lemma 5. That is, F^* may be written as

$$F^*(x_p, x_q, y_p, y_q, z_p, z_q) = F_p^*(x_p, y_p, z_p) + F_q^*(x_q, y_q, z_q),$$

such that the monomials of F_p^* are the elements of the set

$$\left\{ x_p^a y_p^b z_p^c \mid b > 0, x_p^a y_p^b z_p^c \text{ is a monomial of } f^{i_1} g^{i_2} h^{i_3} x_p^{i_4} z_p^{i_5} y_p^{-i_6} \right\}, \quad (5)$$

where f, g and h have the shape they had before the linearization, and similarly the monomials of F_q^* are the elements of the set

$$\left\{ x_q^a y_q^b z_q^c \mid b \geq 0, x_p^a y_p^b z_p^c \text{ is a monomial of} \right.$$
$$\left. f^{i_1} g^{i_2} h^{i_3} (x_p + 1)^{i_4} (z_p - 1)^{i_5} y_p^{i_6 - i_1 - i_2} \right\}. \quad (6)$$

Thus, geometrically, the $\mathsf{trans}(\cdot)$ operator creates two copies of the Newton polytope of $f^{i_1} g^{i_2} h^{i_3} x_p^{i_4} z_p^{i_5}$, where one lies in the (x_p, y_p, z_p)-plane and the other one in the (x_q, y_q, z_q)-plane. The larger the exponent of y_q, the larger is the polytope in the (x_q, y_q, z_q)-plane and the smaller is the polytope in the (x_p, y_p, z_p)-plane. In particular, for $i_6 = i_1 + i_2$ the Newton polytope of F^* lies completely in the (x_q, y_q, z_q)-plane, whereas for $i_6 = 0$ it lies completely in the (x_p, y_p, z_p)-plane (except for some monomials $x_q^a y_q^b z_q^c$ with $b = 0$). For $i_6 = (i_1 + i_2)/2$, both components become equally sized. (See also Fig. 6.)

Based on this interpretation, we now enhance in the following Proposition 2 our lattice construction from Proposition 1, such that the Newton polytopes of the shift polynomials are equally balanced in both the (x_q, y_q, z_q)-plane and the (x_p, y_p, z_p)-plane.

Proposition 2. *Order the monomials in $\mathcal{M}$ according to the (z_p, x_p, y_p)-order. Define a lattice basis matrix $\mathbf{B}$, in which the i-th column corresponds to the monomial*

$$\lambda_{[a,b,c]} := \begin{cases} x_q^a y_q^{b/2} z_q^c, & \text{if } b \text{ is even} \\ x_p^a y_p^{\lceil b/2 \rceil} z_p^c, & \text{if } b \text{ is odd} \end{cases}$$

and the i-th row corresponds to the coefficient vector of

$$p^*_{[a,b,c]} := \mathsf{trans}\left(p_{[a,b,c]} \cdot y_q^{\lfloor b/2 \rfloor}\right)(Xx_p, Xx_q, Yy_p, Yy_q, Xz_p, Xz_q),$$

where $x_p^a y_p^b z_p^c$ is the i-th smallest element in $\mathcal{M}$. Then $\mathbf{B}$ is triangular.

Proof. The proof is similar to that of Proposition 1. We need to show that the i-th polynomial $p^*_{[a,b,c]}$ has with $\lambda_{[a,b,c]}$ exactly one monomial, which is not included in $\mathbf{B}$, before adding $p^*_{[a,b,c]}$ to $\mathbf{B}$. We prove this by induction over i.

Let us first prove the statement for $i = 1$. The smallest element in $\mathcal{M}$ is the monomial $x_p^0 y_p^0 z_p^0 = 1$. Hence, the first column corresponds to $\lambda_{[0,0,0]} = 1$ and the first row corresponds to

$$p^*_{[0,0,0]} = e^{2m} = e^{2m} \cdot \lambda_{[0,0,0]}.$$

As $p^*_{[0,0,0]}$ therefore has with $\lambda_{[0,0,0]}$ exactly one monomial, this proves the statement for $i = 1$.

Now fix an arbitrary $i < |\mathcal{M}|$ and suppose that the statement is true for all $j \le i$. We show that it then holds for $i+1$. With (5), (6) and Lemma 4 it follows that the $(i + 1)$-th polynomial $p^*_{[a,b,c]}$ may be written as

$$p^*_{[a,b,c]}(x_p, x_q, y_p, y_q, z_p, z_q) = p^*_{[a,b,c],p}(x_p, y_p, z_p) + p^*_{[a,b,c],q}(x_q, y_q, z_q),$$

such that:

1. The monomials of $p^*_{[a,b,c],p}$ form a subset of $\mathcal{M}$.
2. The monomials of $p^*_{[a,b,c],q}$ form a subset of $\{x_q^a y_q^b z_q^c \mid x_p^a y_p^b z_p^c \in \mathcal{M}\}$.
3. The leading monomial of $p^*_{[a,b,c],p}$ (according to the (x_p, y_p, z_p)-order) is

$$x_p^a y_p^{b-\lfloor b/2 \rfloor} z_p^c = x_p^a y_p^{\lceil b/2 \rceil} z_p^c.$$

4. The leading monomial of $p^*_{[a,b,c],q}$ (according to a similarly defined (x_q, y_q, z_q)-order) is

$$x_q^a y_q^{b+\lfloor b/2 \rfloor - E_f(a,b,c) - E_g(a,b,c)} z_q^c = x_q^a y_q^{\lfloor b/2 \rfloor} z_q^c.$$

Notice that the equality above follows from the fourth statement in Lemma 3.

Now arguing analogous to the proof of Proposition 1, Proposition 2 easily follows by induction. □

When compared to Proposition 1, the advantage of the lattice construction in Proposition 2 is that we can effectively halve the exponent of Y in the lattice's determinant and by that significantly reduce the determinant's value. One can show (see Remark 3) that the enabling condition (1) now becomes

$$\delta < \frac{5}{56} \approx 0.089. \tag{7}$$

Proposition 2 therefore yields an attack, that already outperforms the Jochemsz-May attack [15].

$$
\begin{array}{llllll}
x_p^2 y_q^0 & f x_p y_q^0 & f^2 y_q^1 & f^2 y_q^1 y_q^1 & f^2 y_q^1 y_p^1 \\
x_p y_q^0 & f y_q^0 & f y_q^0 y_q^1 \\
1 y_q^0
\end{array}
$$

$$
\begin{array}{llllll}
h x_p y_q^0 & f h y_q^0 & f^2 z_p y_q^1 & f^2 g y_q^1 & f^2 g y_q^1 y_q^1 & f^2 g y_q^1 y_q^2 & f^2 g y_q^1 y_p^1 \\
h y_q^0 & f z_p y_q^0 & f g y_q^1 & f g y_q^1 y_q^1 & f g y_q^1 y_p^1 \\
z_p y_q^0 & g y_q^0 & g y_q^0 y_q^1
\end{array}
$$

$$
\begin{array}{lllllll}
h^2 y_q^0 & f h z_p y_q^0 & f g h y_q^1 & f^2 g z_p y_q^1 & f^2 g^2 y_q^2 & f^2 g^2 y_q^2 y_q^1 & f^2 g^2 y_q^2 y_q^2 & f^2 g^2 y_q^2 y_p^2 1 & f^2 g^2 y_q^2 y_p^2 \\
h z_p y_q^0 & g h y_q^0 & f g z_p y_q^1 & f g^2 y_q^1 & f g^2 y_q^1 y_q^1 & f g^2 y_q^1 y_q^2 & f g^2 y_q^1 y_p^1 \\
z_p^2 y_q^0 & g z_p y_q^0 & g^2 y_q^1 & g^2 y_q^1 y_q^1 & g^2 y_q^1 y_p^1
\end{array}
$$

Fig. 7. The polynomials in the TLP lattice for $m = 2$ and $\tau = 1$.

To further improve the bound on δ to 0.122, Takayasu, Lu and Peng use in [28] basically the lattice construction from Proposition 2, but add extra shifts in the variables y_p and y_q to the lattice, i.e., they include additional polynomials of the form

$$p_{[a,b,c,i],q}^* := \mathsf{trans}\left(p_{[a,b,c]} \cdot y_q^{\lfloor b/2 \rfloor} \cdot y_q^i\right)(X x_p, X x_q, Y y_p, Y y_q, X z_p, X z_q),$$

$$p_{[a,b,c,i],p}^* := \mathsf{trans}\left(p_{[a,b,c]} \cdot y_q^{\lfloor b/2 \rfloor} \cdot y_p^i\right)(X x_p, X x_q, Y y_p, Y y_q, X z_p, X z_q).$$

More precisely, whenever adding a polynomial $p_{[a,b,c]}^*$ with $b = a+c$, they include additional rows corresponding to the polynomials

$$
\begin{aligned}
& p_{[a,b,c,1],q}^*, p_{[a,b,c,2],q}^*, \dots, p_{[a,b,c,\lfloor \tau b \rfloor - \lfloor b/2 \rfloor],q}^* \\
& p_{[a,b,c,1],p}^*, p_{[a,b,c,2],p}^*, \dots, p_{[a,b,c,\lfloor \tau b \rfloor - \lceil b/2 \rceil],p}^*
\end{aligned} \tag{8}
$$

as well as additional columns corresponding to the monomials

$$
\begin{aligned}
& x_q^a y_q^{\lfloor b/2 \rfloor + 1} z_q^c, x_q^a y_q^{\lfloor b/2 \rfloor + 2} z_q^c, \dots, x_q^a y_q^{\lfloor \tau b \rfloor} z_q^c, \\
& x_p^a y_p^{\lceil b/2 \rceil + 1} z_p^c, x_p^a y_p^{\lceil b/2 \rceil + 2} z_p^c, \dots, x_p^a y_p^{\lfloor \tau b \rfloor} z_p^c,
\end{aligned} \tag{9}
$$

for some parameter $\tau \geq 1/2$, which has to be optimized as a function of δ. Notice that by (4) it follows that none of these monomials are already included in the lattice basis from Proposition 2.

In Fig. 7 we give an example of the polynomials in the TLP lattice. The polynomials $p^*_{[a,b,c]}$ with $b = a + c$ are coloured in a light gray tone. The additional polynomials $p^*_{[a,b,c,i],q}$, $p^*_{[a,b,c,i],p}$ are coloured in a dark gray tone. As in Fig. 5, we omit the powers of e. We interpret the additional polynomial geometrically as follows. We take in $p^*_{[a,a+c,c]}$ the polynomials with the outer most Newton polytopes and push these further into the (x_q, y_q, z_q)-plane, respectively the (x_p, y_p, z_p)-plane, by using $p^*_{[a,a+c,c,i],q}$ and $p^*_{[a,a+c,c,i],p}$.

With this interpretation, it is not hard to see that the basis matrix still remains triangular: The polynomial $p^*_{[a,b,c,i],q}$ adds the monomial $x_q^a y_q^{\lfloor b/2 \rfloor + i} z_q^c$ to the lattice basis and $p^*_{[a,b,c,i],p}$ adds $x_p^a y_p^{\lceil b/2 \rceil + i} z_p$. Using this observation, we finally prove the TLP attack.

Theorem 1 (Takayasu, Lu, Peng). *Let $N = pq$ be a sufficiently large RSA modulus, where p and q have the same bit-size. Let $e < \phi(N)$ be a public exponent with $\gcd(e, N - 1) = \mathcal{O}(1)$. Suppose the corresponding CRT exponents d_p, d_q are upper bounded by $d_p, d_q \leq N^\delta$, where*

$$\delta < \frac{1}{2} - \frac{1}{\sqrt{7}} \approx 0.122.$$

Given (N, e), we can factor N in polynomial time (under Assumption 1).

Proof. We build a lattice basis matrix $\mathbf{B}$ as in Proposition 2 and add the additional polynomials (8) and monomials (9) as described above. The diagonal elements of $\mathbf{B}$ are products of powers of e, X, Y and (due to statements two and three in Lemma 6) N and $(N - 1)$. To reduce the value of the determinant of $\mathbf{B}$, we remove the powers of N and $(N - 1)$ as follows. Let

$$\mathbf{B}_{i,i} = e^{E_{1,i}} X^{E_{2,i}} Y^{E_{3,i}} N^{E_{4,i}} (N - 1)^{E_{5,i}}$$

denote the i-th diagonal element of $\mathbf{B}$. We replace for every i the value of $\mathbf{B}_{i,i}$ by

$$e^{E_{1,i}} X^{E_{2,i}} Y^{E_{3,i}} \gcd(N - 1, e)^{E_{5,i}}$$

and then multiply every other entry in the i-th row of $\mathbf{B}$ by

$$\left(N^{E_{4,i}} \left(\frac{N - 1}{\gcd(N - 1, e)} \right)^{E_{5,i}} \right)^{-1} \mod e^{2m}.$$

By that, the i-th row still corresponds to a polynomial with the root r modulo e^{2m}.

Notice that we can assume without loss of generality that N is invertible modulo e. If it was not, we could easily obtain a prime factor of N in $\gcd(e, N)$. For $(N - 1)$ on the other hand, we of course can not make this assumption and therefore have to use $(N-1)/\gcd(N-1,e)$. Since we have $\gcd(N-1,e) = \mathcal{O}(1)$, we can asymptotically neglect the remaining powers of $\gcd(N-1,e)$ on the diagonal. This allows us to asymptotically calculate the determinant of $\mathbf{B}$ as $\det \mathbf{B} = e^{s_e} X^{s_x} Y^{s_y}$, where

$$s_e = \sum_{x_p^a y_p^b z_p^c \in \mathcal{M}} E(a,b,c) + \sum_{\substack{x_p^a y_p^b z_p^c \in \mathcal{M}, \\ b=a+c}} 2 \cdot \sum_{i=1}^{\tau b - b/2} E(a,b,c) = \frac{1+5\tau}{3} m^4 + o(m^4),$$

$$s_X = \sum_{x_p^a y_p^b z_p^c \in \mathcal{M}} (a+c) + \sum_{\substack{x_p^a y_p^b z_p^c \in \mathcal{M}, \\ b=a+c}} 2 \cdot \sum_{i=1}^{\tau b - b/2} (a+c) = \frac{7\tau}{3} m^4 + o(m^4),$$

$$s_Y = \sum_{x_p^a y_p^b z_p^c \in \mathcal{M}} \frac{b}{2} + \sum_{\substack{x_p^a y_p^b z_p^c \in \mathcal{M}, \\ b=a+c}} 2 \cdot \sum_{i=1}^{\tau b - b/2} \left(\frac{b}{2}+i\right) = \frac{7\tau^2}{6} m^4 + o(m^4)$$

and

$$E(a,b,c) := 2m - E_f(a,b,c) - E_g(a,b,c) - E_h(a,b,c).$$

Then, calculating the dimension n of the lattice as

$$n = \sum_{x_p^a y_p^b z_p^c \in \mathcal{M}} 1 + \sum_{\substack{x_p^a y_p^b z_p^c \in \mathcal{M}, \\ b=a+c}} 2 \cdot \sum_{i=1}^{\tau b - b/2} 1 = 2\tau m^3 + o(m^3),$$

and plugging in the values $e = N^\alpha$, $X = \Theta(N^{\alpha+\delta-1/2})$ and $Y = \Theta(N^{1/2})$, we find that the enabling condition $\det \mathbf{B} < e^{2mn}$ becomes

$$\alpha \cdot \frac{1+5\tau}{3} m^4 + \left(\alpha + \delta - \frac{1}{2}\right) \cdot \frac{7\tau}{3} m^4 + \frac{1}{2} \cdot \frac{7\tau^2}{6} m^4 < \alpha \cdot 4\tau m^4 + o(m^4). \quad (10)$$

To maximize the bound on δ, we set $\tau := \max\{1-2\delta, 1/2\}$, which simplifies the above to

$$\delta < \frac{1}{2} - \sqrt{\frac{\alpha}{7}} + o(1).$$

Notice, the smaller α, the better the bound on δ becomes. Since we have $e < \phi(N)$ and consequently $\alpha < 1$, we can therefore also use the simpler bound

$$\delta < \frac{1}{2} - \frac{1}{\sqrt{7}} + o(1).$$

Consequently, we find for every $\delta < 1/2 - 1/\sqrt{7}$ an m, such that the enabling condition becomes satisfied, which proves the theorem. □

Remark 2. The condition $\gcd(N-1,e) = \mathcal{O}(1)$ does not appear in the original formulation of the theorem in [28]. However, we do not see how to avoid this.

If $\gcd(N-1, e)$ becomes large, then we can no longer asymptotically ignore the additional factors on the determinant, and by that obtain a worse bound in the enabling condition. This would imply an inferior bound on δ.

Remark 3. The proof of Theorem 1 can be easily modified to prove the previously mentioned bound (7) of $\delta < 5/56$ for the construction from Proposition 2. If one sets $\tau = 1/2$ in the proof, then no additional polynomials $p^*_{[a,b,c,i],q}$ and $p^*_{[a,b,c,i],p}$ are added to the lattice. Thus, the construction in that case is exactly the same as in Proposition 2. The enabling condition (10) then simplifies to

$$\delta < \frac{3}{8} - \frac{2\alpha}{7} + o(1),$$

which one can further simplify to

$$\delta < \frac{3}{8} - \frac{2}{7} + o(1) = \frac{5}{56} + o(1)$$

by using $\alpha < 1$ as before.

4 Our Small CRT-exponent Attacks

Our geometrical interpretation of the TLP attack from Sect. 3 now allows us to easily explain our Partial Key Exposure attack.

As before, let $N = pq$ be an RSA modulus, let $e = N^\alpha$ be a public exponent and let d_p, d_q be the corresponding CRT exponents. We assume that both d_p and d_q are upper bounded by $d_p, d_q \leq N^\beta$ for some $\beta \in \mathbb{R}$. Additionally, we assume that we know integers $\tilde{d}_p, \tilde{d}_q, M \approx N^{\beta-\delta}$ (for some $\delta \leq \beta$), such that we can write $d_p = d^*_p M + \tilde{d}_p$, $d_q = d^*_q M + \tilde{d}_q$ for some unknown integers $d^*_p, d^*_q \leq N^\delta$. In practice, M might, for instance, be a power of 2 and therefore d^*_p, d^*_q the MSBs of d_p and d_q respectively and $\tilde{d}_p, \tilde{d}_q$ the LSBs.

In the previous section, we used the equations

$$kp - (k-1) = ed_p,$$
$$p(\ell-1) - N\ell = -ed_q p,$$
$$k\ell N - (k-1)(l-1) = e^2 d_p d_q + e(d_p(\ell-1) + d_q(k-1))$$

to derive polynomials

$$f(x_p, x_q, y_p, y_q, z_p, z_q) = x_p y_p - x_q,$$
$$g(x_p, x_q, y_p, y_q, z_p, z_q) = y_p z_p - N z_q,$$
$$h(x_p, x_q, y_p, y_q, z_p, z_q) = N x_p z_q - x_q z_p,$$

which all have the root $r = (k, k-1, p, q, \ell-1, \ell)$ modulo e. With the additional information given by $\tilde{d}_p$ and $\tilde{d}_q$, we can similarly define polynomials

$$\tilde{f}(x_p, x_q, y_p, y_q, z_p, z_q) := x_p y_p - x_q - e\tilde{d}_p,$$

$$\widetilde{g}(x_p, x_q, y_p, y_q, z_p, z_q) := y_p z_p - N z_q + e\widetilde{d}_q y_p,$$
$$\widetilde{h}(x_p, x_q, y_p, y_q, z_p, z_q) := N x_p z_q - x_q z_p - e^2 \widetilde{d}_p \widetilde{d}_q - e\widetilde{d}_p z_p - e\widetilde{d}_q x_q,$$

which in turn have the root r modulo eM. Notice that for increasing M, the polynomials $\widetilde{f}$, $\widetilde{g}$ and $\widetilde{h}$ are in terms of Coppersmith's method superior to f, g and h, as they have the same small root r modulo a larger modulus. At the same time they are, however, also inferior, since they have more monomials. As we will see below, we therefore obtain our best results, when carefully balancing the use of $\widetilde{f}$, $\widetilde{g}$ and $\widetilde{h}$ with that of f, g and h.

We now use $\widetilde{f}$, $\widetilde{g}$ and $\widetilde{h}$ to build a lattice basis matrix and then apply Coppersmith's method to compute r. We closely follow the construction as described in Proposition 2. However, some modifications are necessary. If we would simply build the lattice exactly as described in Proposition 2, but construct the shift polynomials using $\widetilde{f}$, $\widetilde{g}$ and $\widetilde{h}$ instead of f, g and h, we would not obtain a triangular matrix. For instance, the polynomial $\widetilde{g}$ would add with y_p a new monomial, which does not appear in the lattice from Proposition 2. Overall, we would obtain many additional monomials, as the trans$(\cdot)$ operator does not work as good with $\widetilde{f}$, $\widetilde{g}$ and $\widetilde{h}$ as it does with f, g and h. Let us illustrate this with an example.

When instantiating the lattice from Proposition 2 with $m = 2$, the shift polynomial $p^*_{[2,2,0]}$ is obtained by multiplying $p_{[2,2,0]} = f^2 e^2$ by a factor of $y_q^{\lfloor 2/2 \rfloor} = y_q$ and transforming it using trans$(\cdot)$ as shown below. (For better readability we omit the factor e^2.)

$$f^2 y_q = (x_p y_p - x_q)^2 y_q$$
$$= x_p^2 y_p^2 y_q - 2 x_p x_q y_p y_q + x_q^2 y_q$$
$$\mapsto N x_p^2 y_p - 2 N x_p x_q + x_q^2 y_q$$
$$\mapsto N x_p^2 y_p - 2 N (x_q + 1) x_q + x_q^2 y_q$$
$$= N x_p^2 y_p - 2 N x_q^2 - 2 N x_q + x_q^2 y_q.$$

Applying the same transformations to $\widetilde{f}^2$, we obtain

$$\widetilde{f}^2 y_q = (x_p y_p - x_q - e\widetilde{d}_p)^2 y_q$$
$$= x_p^2 y_p^2 y_q - 2 x_p x_q y_p y_q - 2 e\widetilde{d}_p x_p y_p y_q - x_q^2 y_q + 2 e\widetilde{d}_p x_q y_q + e^2 \widetilde{d}_p^2 y_q$$
$$\mapsto N x_p^2 y_p - 2 N x_p x_q - 2 N e\widetilde{d}_p x_p - x_q^2 y_q + 2 e\widetilde{d}_p x_q y_q + e^2 \widetilde{d}_p^2 y_q$$
$$\mapsto N x_p^2 y_p - 2 N (x_q + 1) x_q - 2 N e\widetilde{d}_p (x_q + 1) - x_q^2 y_q + 2 e\widetilde{d}_p x_q y_q + e^2 \widetilde{d}_p^2 y_q$$
$$= N x_p^2 y_p - 2 N x_q^2 - 2 N (1 + e\widetilde{d}_p) x_q - 2 N e\widetilde{d}_p - x_q^2 y_q + 2 e\widetilde{d}_p x_q y_q + e^2 \widetilde{d}_p^2 y_q.$$

Comparing the monomials in the variables x_q and y_q of both polynomials in Fig. 8, they form a small triangle for the former polynomial, whereas they form a rather large rectangle for the latter.

One can show with a proof analogous to that of Lemma 5 that the shape of the shift polynomials overall becomes more rectangular, when using $\widetilde{f}$, $\widetilde{g}$, $\widetilde{h}$, instead of f, g and h. More precisely, one can easily show that

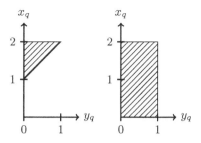

Fig. 8. Parts of the Newton polytopes of $f^2 y_q$ and $\tilde{f}^2 y_q$ after applying trans($\cdot$).

$$F^*(x_p, x_q, y_p, y_q, z_p, z_q) := \text{trans}\left(\tilde{f}^{i_1} \tilde{g}^{i_2} \tilde{h}^{i_3} x_p^{i_4} z_p^{i_5} y_q^{i_6}\right)$$

can be written as

$$F^*(x_p, x_q, y_p, y_q, z_p, z_q) = F_p^*(x_p, y_p, z_p) + F_q^*(x_q, y_q, z_q),$$

such that the monomials of F_p^* form a subset of

$$\left\{x_p^a y_p^b z_p^b \mid 0 \le a \le i_1 + i_3 + i_4, 0 < b \le i_1 + i_2 - i_6, 0 \le c \le i_2 + i_3 + i_5\right\}$$

and the monomials of F_q^* form a subset of

$$\left\{x_q^a y_q^b z_q^b \mid 0 \le a \le i_1 + i_3 + i_4, 0 \le b \le i_6, 0 \le c \le i_2 + i_3 + i_5\right\}.$$

See Fig. 9 for an example.

Additionally, one can show that (as before) the coefficients of

$$x_p^{i_1+i_3+i_4} y_p^{i_1+i_2-i_6} z_p^{i_2+i_3+i_5}$$

and

$$x_q^{i_1+i_3+i_4} y_q^{i_6} z_q^{i_2+i_3+i_5}$$

are non-zero, or more precisely that they are products of powers of N and $(N-1)$. Notice that these monomials correspond to the outer most points in Fig. 9, i.e., the points with the largest $\|\cdot\|_1$-norm.

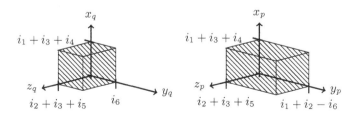

Fig. 9. The effect of trans($\cdot$) on F^*.

As a consequence, we suggest instead of using the set $\mathcal{M}$ for selecting the shift polynomials, to use a different set, which itself has a rectangular shape. For that, we define

$$\widetilde{\mathcal{M}} := \left\{ x_p^a y_p^b z_p^c \mid 0 \le a \le m, 0 \le c \le m, 0 \le b \le 2m \right\}.$$

Notice that the set of tuples (a, b, c) with $x_p^a y_p^b z_p^c \in \widetilde{\mathcal{M}}$ forms a rectangular cuboid of size $m \times 2m \times m$ in $\mathbb{Z}^3$. Also notice that $\mathcal{M} \subseteq \widetilde{\mathcal{M}}$.

We enhance our exponent functions, such that for monomials $x_p^a y_p^b z_p^c \in \widetilde{\mathcal{M}} \setminus \mathcal{M}$ they take the values

$$
\begin{aligned}
E_f(a, b, c) &:= a, \\
E_g(a, b, c) &:= c, \\
E_h(a, b, c) &:= E_x(a, b, c) := E_z(a, b, c) := 0.
\end{aligned}
$$

Further, we redefine our shift polynomials as follows:

$$
\begin{aligned}
\widetilde{p}_{[a,b,c]}(x_p, x_q, y_p, y_q, z_p, z_q) := \; & \widetilde{f}^{E_f(a,b,c)} \cdot \widetilde{g}^{E_g(a,b,c)} \cdot \widetilde{h}^{E_h(a,b,c)} \cdot \\
& x_p^{E_x(a,b,c)} \cdot z_p^{E_z(a,b,c)} \cdot \\
& (eM)^{2m - (E_f(a,b,c) + E_g(a,b,c) + E_h(a,b,c))}.
\end{aligned}
$$

Now, to obtain a triangular matrix, our basic idea is to include sufficiently many extra-shifts in y_p and y_q to the lattice, such that for every shift polynomial F^*, every monomial in the cuboids in Fig. 9 is included in the basis. We make this strategy more precise in Proposition 3.

Proposition 3. *Order the monomials in $\widetilde{\mathcal{M}}$ according to the (z_p, x_p, y_p)-order. Define a lattice basis matrix $\mathbf{B}$, in which the i-th column corresponds to the monomial*

$$
\lambda_{[a,b,c]} :=
\begin{cases}
x_q^a y_q^{b/2} z_q^c, & \text{if } b \text{ is even} \\
x_p^a y_p^{\lceil b/2 \rceil} z_p^c, & \text{if } b \text{ is odd}.
\end{cases}
$$

where $x_p^a y_p^b z_p^c$ is the i-th smallest element in $\widetilde{\mathcal{M}}$. For $x_p^a y_p^b z_p^c \in \mathcal{M}$, the i-th row of $\mathbf{B}$ corresponds to the coefficient vector of

$$\text{trans}\left(\widetilde{p}_{[a,b,c]} \cdot y_q^{\lfloor b/2 \rfloor} \right) (X x_p, X x_q, Y y_p, Y y_q, X z_p, X z_q).$$

For $x_p^a y_p^b z_p^c \in \widetilde{\mathcal{M}} \setminus \mathcal{M}$ with even b, the i-th row of $\mathbf{B}$ corresponds to the coefficient vector of

$$\text{trans}\left(\widetilde{p}_{[a,b,c]} \cdot y_q^{\lfloor (a+c)/2 \rfloor} \cdot y_q^{\lceil (b-a-c)/2 \rceil} \right) (X x_p, X x_q, Y y_p, Y y_q, X z_p, X z_q).$$

For $x_p^a y_p^b z_p^c \in \widetilde{\mathcal{M}} \setminus \mathcal{M}$ with odd b, the i-th row of $\mathbf{B}$ corresponds to the coefficient vector of

$$\text{trans}\left(\widetilde{p}_{[a,b,c]} \cdot y_q^{\lfloor (a+c)/2 \rfloor} \cdot y_p^{\lceil (b-a-c)/2 \rceil} \right) (X x_p, X x_q, Y y_p, Y y_q, X z_p, X z_q).$$

Then $\mathbf{B}$ is triangular.

As the proof for Proposition 3 is completely analogous to that of Proposition 2, we omit it here.

We are now ready to prove our main theorem.

Theorem 2. *Let $N = pq$ be a sufficiently large RSA modulus, where p and q have the same bit-size. Let $e < \phi(N)$ be a public exponent. Suppose the corresponding CRT exponents d_p, d_q are upper bounded by $d_p, d_q \leq N^\beta$. Write $d_p = d_p^* 2^k + \tilde{d}_p$, $d_q = d_q^* 2^k + \tilde{d}_p$, for some $k \in \mathbb{N}$, MSBs $d_p^*, d_q^* \leq N^\delta$ and LSBs $\tilde{d}_p, \tilde{d}_q$. If we are given (N, e) and $\tilde{d}_p, \tilde{d}_q$, such that*

$$\delta < \frac{1 - -2\beta}{10}$$

and $\gcd(e \cdot 2^k, N - 1) = \mathcal{O}(1)$, then we can factor N in polynomial time (under Assumption 1).

Proof. The proof is very similar to that of Theorem 1. We build a lattice basis matrix $\mathbf{B}$ as described in Proposition 3 with $M = 2^k$. As before, we remove the powers of N and $N - 1$ from the diagonal of $\mathbf{B}$ and multiply the other entries in the matix appropriately with the inverses. Notice that as opposed to Theorem 1 here we need the slightly stronger assumption $\gcd(e \cdot 2^k, N - 1) = \mathcal{O}(1)$, as we now have to take inverses modulo eM.

We can asymptotically compute the determinant as $\det \mathbf{B} = (eM)^{s_{eM}} X^{s_X} Y^{s_Y}$, where

$$s_{eM} = \sum_{x_p^a y_p^b z_p^c \in \widetilde{\mathcal{M}}} (2m - E_f(a, b, c) - E_g(a, b, c) - E_h(a, b, c)) = \frac{7}{3} m^4 + o(m^4),$$

$$s_X = \sum_{x_p^a y_p^b z_p^c \in \widetilde{\mathcal{M}}} (a + c) = 2m^4 + o(m^4),$$

$$s_Y = \sum_{x_p^a y_p^b z_p^c \in \widetilde{\mathcal{M}}} \frac{b}{2} = m^4 + o(m^4).$$

Then, calculating the lattice's dimension as $n = |\widetilde{\mathcal{M}}| = 2m^3$, our enabling condition becomes

$$(\alpha + \beta - \delta) \cdot \frac{7}{3} m^4 + \left(\alpha + \beta - \frac{1}{2}\right) \cdot 2m^4 + \frac{1}{2} \cdot m^4 < (\alpha + \beta - \delta) \cdot 4m^4 + o(m^4).$$

By incorporating $\alpha < 1$ as before, the above simplifies to

$$\delta < \frac{1 - -2\beta}{10} + o(1),$$

which concludes the proof of the theorem.   □

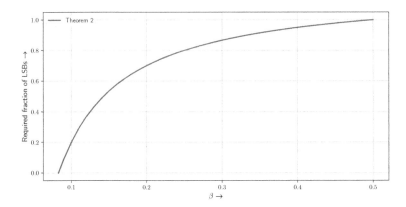

Fig. 10. Required fraction of LSBs to make the attack from Theorem 2 work.

In Fig. 10 we show for a given value of β, how large of a fraction of key bits is required for the attack to work. That, is on the vertical axis we plot the value $(\beta - \delta)/\beta$.

Notice that the graph in Fig. 10 has with $(1/2, 1)$ a very natural ending point. The result strongly suggests that for a maximum level of security, full size CRT-exponents must be used – as only then Partial Key Exposure attacks can be prevented. Additionally, it shows that regardless of the key size, we can always factor the modulus, once all key bits are exposed.

Unfortunately, the ending point $(1/12,0)$ on the left side of the graph, however, clearly is non-optimal, as it tells us that for any $\beta > 1/12 \approx 0.083$, at least some key bits have to be exposed to yield the factorization of N. This is contradictory to Theorem 1, by which for any $\beta < 0.122$ no additional key bits are required to factor N.

Intuitively this might be explained with the fact that for $\delta \to \beta$ (i.e., when almost all key bits are unknown) the value eM tends to e. By that, the benefit of using the larger modulus in the lattice construction shrinks more and more as δ grows to β. At a certain point, the inferior shape of the polynomials then outweighs said benefit and therefore gives us an inferior bound. To fill this gap, we propose in the following an alternative lattice construction, inspired by ideas of Aono [1].

4.1 Improved Attack by Linking Our First Attack and TLP

The main idea behind the improved construction is to use our lattice from Theorem 2 *together* with the TLP lattice. For that, we define a new set

$$\widetilde{\mathcal{M}}_\sigma := \left\{ x_p^a y_p^b z_p^c \mid 0 \le a \le m, 0 \le c \le m, 0 \le b \le 2\sigma m \right\} \subseteq \widetilde{\mathcal{M}}$$

for some parameter $0 \le \sigma \le 1$, that allows us to interpolate between the TLP lattice and the construction from Proposition 3 and Theorem 2.

When now constructing a lattice exactly as described in Proposition 3, but using the set $\widetilde{\mathcal{M}}_\sigma$ instead of $\widetilde{\mathcal{M}}$, one obtains the same basis matrix $\mathbf{B}_\sigma$, that one would obtain, when removing all polynomials, which add monomials $x_p^a y_p^b z_p^c$ and $x_q^a y_q^b z_q^c$ with $b > \sigma m$ to the lattice from Proposition 3. Notice that from Fig. 9 it follows that the remaining polynomials in $\mathbf{B}_\sigma$ do not have monomials $x_p^a y_p^b z_p^c$ or $x_q^a y_q^b z_q^c$ with $b > \sigma m$. Hence, $\mathbf{B}_\sigma$ is still triangular.

Next, we build another lattice basis matrix $\mathbf{B}_{TLP}$ exactly as described in the TLP attack from Theorem 1, but apply two minor changes:

1. Instead of using the polynomials f, g and h for defining the shift polynomials, we use

$$f^* := Mf, \qquad g^* := Mg, \qquad h^* := Mh.$$

2. We multiply powers of eM to the shift polynomials, instead of powers of e.

Clearly, this does not weaken the TLP attack, as all additional powers of M in the enabling condition cancel out. With these changes, the shift polynomials now have the root r not only modulo e, but also modulo eM. This allows us to combine $\mathbf{B}_\sigma$ and $\mathbf{B}_{TLP}$ as follows.

We remove all polynomials from $\mathbf{B}_{TLP}$ that add monomials $x_p^a y_p^b z_p^c$ and $x_q^a y_q^b z_q^c$ with $b \leq \sigma m$ to the diagonal. After that, we add all polynomials from the matrix $\mathbf{B}_\sigma$ to $\mathbf{B}_{TLP}$. Since in $\mathbf{B}_\sigma$ all monomials $x_p^a y_p^b z_p^c$ and $x_q^a y_q^b z_q^c$ with $a \leq m$, $c \leq m$ and $b \leq \sigma m$ appear, it follows that in particular all monomials that we have just removed, reappear in our matrix. Hence, we can rearrange the rows of the newly obtained matrix, such that it is again triangular.

With the above, we thus obtain a triangular lattice basis matrix which nicely incorporates the advantages of the lattice construction from Theorems 1 and 2 at the same time. Similar as in the proofs of both theorems, the enabling condition for the construction becomes

$$e^{s_e} M^{s_M} X^{s_X} Y^{s_Y} < (eM)^{2mn},$$

with analogously defined exponents s_e, s_M, s_X, s_Y and n. (Here we sum over the monomials in $\mathbf{B}_\sigma$ as well as over those in $\mathbf{B}_{TLP}$, except for those that we remove from $\mathbf{B}_{TLP}$.)

For $\sigma \leq \tau$, we have

$$n = \frac{\sigma^3 + 6\tau^3}{3\tau^2} m^3 + o(m^3),$$

$$s_X = \frac{\sigma^4 + 14\tau^4}{6\tau^3} m^4 + o(m^4),$$

$$s_Y = \frac{3\sigma^4 \tau + 14\tau^5}{12\tau^3} m^4 + o(m^4),$$

$$s_e = -\frac{\sigma^4 - 4\sigma^3 \tau - 10\tau^4 - 2\tau^3}{6\tau^3} m^4 + o(m^4),$$

Table 1. Values of β, $(\beta - \delta)/\beta$ and σ for our improved lattice construction.

β	0.122	0.123	0.124	0.125	0.13	0.14	0.15	0.16	0.17	0.18	0.19	0.20	0.21	0.22
$(\beta - \delta)/\beta$	0	0.053	0.084	0.110	0.205	0.332	0.423	0.492	0.549	0.595	0.635	0.0668	0.698	0.723
σ	0	0.328	0.392	0.434	0.548	0.655	0.716	0.757	0.787	0.811	0.830	0.846	0.859	0.869
β	0.23	0.24	0.25	0.26	0.27	0.28	0.29	0.30	0.31	0.32	0.33	0.34	0.35	0.36
$(\beta - \delta)/\beta$	0.746	0.767	0.786	0.803	0.819	0.833	0.847	0.859	0.871	0.882	0.892	0.902	0.911	0.919
σ	0.878	0.885	0.891	0.897	0.902	0.907	0.912	0.917	0.922	0.927	0.931	0.935	0.940	0.944
β	0.37	0.38	0.39	0.40	0.41	0.42	0.43	0.44	0.45	0.46	0.47	0.48	0.49	0.50
$(\beta - \delta)/\beta$	0.927	0.934	0.942	0.948	0.955	0.961	0.966	0.972	0.977	0.982	0.987	0.991	0.995	1
σ	0.948	0.952	0.956	0.960	0.964	0.968	0.972	0.976	0.980	0.984	0.988	0.992	0.996	1

$$s_M = -\frac{\sigma^4 \tau^2 - 4\sigma^3 \tau^2 + 6\sigma^2 \tau^2 - 2\sigma^3 + 2\sigma\tau^2 - 12\tau^3}{3\tau^2} m^4 + o(m^4)$$

and for $\tau \leq \sigma \leq 2\tau$

$$n = -\frac{\sigma^3 - 6\sigma^2\tau + 6\sigma\tau^2 - 8\tau^3}{3\tau^2} m^3 + o(m^3),$$

$$s_X = -\frac{\sigma^4 - 4\sigma^3\tau + 4\sigma\tau^3 - 16\tau^4}{6\tau^3} m^4 + o(m^4),$$

$$s_Y = -\frac{3\sigma^4\tau - 16\sigma^3\tau^2 + 12\sigma^2\tau^3 - 16\tau^5}{12\tau^3} m^4 + o(m^4),$$

$$s_e = \frac{\sigma^4 - 8\sigma^3\tau + 24\sigma^2\tau^2 - 20\sigma\tau^3 + 16\tau^4 + 2\tau^3}{6\tau^3} m^4 + o(m^4),$$

$$s_M = -\frac{\sigma^4\tau^2 - 4\sigma^3\tau^2 + 6\sigma^2\tau^2 + 2\sigma^3 - 12\sigma^2\tau + 14\sigma\tau^2 - 16\tau^3}{3\tau^2} m^4 + o(m^4).$$

Unfortunately, we can not give a closed formula on β and δ as in Theorem 2, because there seems to be no way for analytically maximizing σ. Therefore, we can only present numerical results.

When setting $\tau := \max\{1/2, 1 - 2\beta\}$ (as in the proof of Theorem 1) and then numerically optimizing σ, we obtain the results shown in Table 1. These results have been used to plot the graph in Fig. 2.

Since we reach the lower bound of 0.122, we fully close the gap between Theorems 1 and 2. Notice how the table shows that for $\beta = 0.122$ it is best to use the TLP lattice (i.e., setting $\sigma = 0$) and for $\beta = 0.5$ to use the lattice construction from Proposition 3 (i.e., setting $\sigma = 1$).

5   Experimental Results

The main purpose of our experiments is to verify the validity of Assumption 1.

Although our results theoretically hold in the range $N^{0.122} \leq d_p, d_q \leq N^{0.5}$, we cannot expect to provide experimental data for large d_p, d_q in practice. The reason is that for small exponent CRT-RSA attacks like TLP and our Partial Key Exposure attack the lattice dimension grows as a cubic function in m. Thus, the convergence to the theoretical bounds is quite slow. E.g. for the TLP attack with its theoretical bound $d_p, d_q \leq N^{0.122}$, the original authors provide in [28] practical experiments only up to $N^{0.062}$.

Hence, in order to demonstrate that our attack naturally extends the TLP attack to the Partial Key scenario, we provide some data points with $\beta \geq 0.062$.

We implemented our experiments in SAGE 9.2 using Linux Ubuntu 18.04.4 on a laptop with Intel(R) Core(TM) i7-7920HQ CPU 3.67 GHz. The results are given in Table 2.

Assumption 1 was valid in all experiments. In every run we were able to recover the unknown secrets via Groebner basis computation.

Table 2. Experimental results of our Partial Key Exposure attack.

β	Bit-size of N	Bit-size of d_p, d_q	Unknown key-bits	Dimension	LLL Time (sec.)
0.040	1,000	40	2×15	53	4
0.040	5,000	200	2×80	53	196
0.040	10,000	400	2×175	53	1,179
0.065	1,000	65	2×20	132	1,242
0.065	5,000	325	2×100	132	9,505
0.070	1,000	70	2×30	263	51,181
0.100	1,000	100	2×30	434	786,423
0.110	1,000	110	2×30	434	841,310

References

1. Aono, Y.: A new lattice construction for partial key exposure attack for RSA. In: Jarecki, S., Tsudik, G. (eds.) PKC 2009. LNCS, vol. 5443, pp. 34–53. Springer, Heidelberg (2009). https://doi.org/10.1007/978-3-642-00468-1_3

2. Bernstein, D.J., et al.: Factoring RSA keys from certified smart cards: coppersmith in the wild. In: Sako, K., Sarkar, P. (eds.) ASIACRYPT 2013. LNCS, vol. 8270, pp. 341–360. Springer, Heidelberg (2013). https://doi.org/10.1007/978-3-642-42045-0_18

3. Bleichenbacher, D., May, A.: New attacks on RSA with small secret CRT-exponents. In: Yung, M., Dodis, Y., Kiayias, A., Malkin, T. (eds.) PKC 2006. LNCS, vol. 3958, pp. 1–13. Springer, Heidelberg (2006). https://doi.org/10.1007/11745853_1

4. Blömer, J., May, A.: New partial key exposure attacks on RSA. In: Boneh, D. (ed.) CRYPTO 2003. LNCS, vol. 2729, pp. 27–43. Springer, Heidelberg (2003). https://doi.org/10.1007/978-3-540-45146-4_2

5. Boneh, D., Durfee, G.: Cryptanalysis of RSA with private key d less than $N^{0.292}$. IEEE Trans. Inf. Theory **46**(4), 1339–1349 (2000)

6. Coppersmith, D.: Finding a small root of a bivariate integer equation; factoring with high bits known. In: Maurer, U. (ed.) EUROCRYPT 1996. LNCS, vol. 1070, pp. 178–189. Springer, Heidelberg (1996). https://doi.org/10.1007/3-540-68339-9_16

7. Coppersmith, D.: Small solutions to polynomial equations, and low exponent RSA vulnerabilities. J. Cryptol. **10**(4), 233–260 (1997)
8. Coron, J.S., May, A.: Deterministic polynomial-time equivalence of computing the RSA secret key and factoring. J. Cryptol. **20**(1), 39–50 (2007)
9. Ernst, M., Jochemsz, E., May, A., de Weger, B.: Partial key exposure attacks on RSA up to full size exponents. In: Cramer, R. (ed.) EUROCRYPT 2005. LNCS, vol. 3494, pp. 371–386. Springer, Heidelberg (2005). https://doi.org/10.1007/11426639_22
10. Galbraith, S.D., Heneghan, C., McKee, J.F.: Tunable balancing of RSA. In: Boyd, C., González Nieto, J.M. (eds.) ACISP 2005. LNCS, vol. 3574, pp. 280–292. Springer, Heidelberg (2005). https://doi.org/10.1007/11506157_24
11. Heninger, N., Durumeric, Z., Wustrow, E., Halderman, J.A.: Mining your Ps and Qs: detection of widespread weak keys in network devices. In: 21st USENIX Security Symposium USENIX Security 12, pp. 205–220 (2012)
12. Herrmann, M., May, A.: Attacking power generators using unravelled linearization: when do we output too much? In: Matsui, M. (ed.) ASIACRYPT 2009. LNCS, vol. 5912, pp. 487–504. Springer, Heidelberg (2009). https://doi.org/10.1007/978-3-642-10366-7_29
13. Herrmann, M., May, A.: Maximizing small root bounds by linearization and applications to small secret exponent RSA. In: Nguyen, P.Q., Pointcheval, D. (eds.) PKC 2010. LNCS, vol. 6056, pp. 53–69. Springer, Heidelberg (2010). https://doi.org/10.1007/978-3-642-13013-7_4
14. Howgrave-Graham, N.: Finding small roots of univariate modular equations revisited. In: Darnell, M. (ed.) Cryptography and Coding 1997. LNCS, vol. 1355, pp. 131–142. Springer, Heidelberg (1997). https://doi.org/10.1007/BFb0024458
15. Jochemsz, E., May, A.: A polynomial time attack on RSA with private CRT-exponents smaller than $N^{0.073}$. In: Menezes, A. (ed.) CRYPTO 2007. LNCS, vol. 4622, pp. 395–411. Springer, Heidelberg (2007). https://doi.org/10.1007/978-3-540-74143-5_22
16. Kunihiro, N., Shinohara, N., Izu, T.: A unified framework for small secret exponent attack on RSA. In: Miri, A., Vaudenay, S. (eds.) SAC 2011. LNCS, vol. 7118, pp. 260–277. Springer, Heidelberg (2012). https://doi.org/10.1007/978-3-642-28496-0_16
17. Lenstra, A.K., Lenstra, H.W., Lovász, L.: Factoring polynomials with rational coefficients. Mathematische Annalen **261**, 515–534 (1982)
18. Lu, Y., Zhang, R., Lin, D.: New partial key exposure attacks on CRT-RSA with large public exponents. In: Boureanu, I., Owesarski, P., Vaudenay, S. (eds.) ACNS 2014. LNCS, vol. 8479, pp. 151–162. Springer, Cham (2014). https://doi.org/10.1007/978-3-319-07536-5_10
19. Maitra, S., Sarkar, S.: On deterministic polynomial-time equivalence of computing the CRT-RSA secret keys and factoring. Def. Sci. J. **62**(2), 122–126 (2012)
20. May, A.: Cryptanalysis of unbalanced RSA with small CRT-exponent. In: Yung, M. (ed.) CRYPTO 2002. LNCS, vol. 2442, pp. 242–256. Springer, Heidelberg (2002). https://doi.org/10.1007/3-540-45708-9_16
21. May, A.: New RSA vulnerabilities using lattice reduction methods. Ph.D. thesis, University of Paderborn (2003)
22. May, A.: Computing the RSA secret key is deterministic polynomial time equivalent to factoring. In: Franklin, M. (ed.) CRYPTO 2004. LNCS, vol. 3152, pp. 213–219. Springer, Heidelberg (2004). https://doi.org/10.1007/978-3-540-28628-8_13

23. Nemec, M., Sys, M., Svenda, P., Klinec, D., Matyas, V.: The return of Copper-smith's attack: Practical factorization of widely used RSA moduli. In: Proceedings of the 2017 ACM SIGSAC Conference on Computer and Communications Security, pp. 1631–1648 (2017)
24. Takayasu, A., Kunihiro, N.: Partial key exposure attacks on RSA: achieving the Boneh-Durfee bound. In: Joux, A., Youssef, A. (eds.) SAC 2014. LNCS, vol. 8781, pp. 345–362. Springer, Cham (2014). https://doi.org/10.1007/978-3-319-13051-4_21
25. Takayasu, A., Kunihiro, N.: Partial key exposure attacks on CRT-RSA: better cryptanalysis to full size encryption exponents. In: Malkin, T., Kolesnikov, V., Lewko, A.B., Polychronakis, M. (eds.) ACNS 2015. LNCS, vol. 9092, pp. 518–537. Springer, Cham (2015). https://doi.org/10.1007/978-3-319-28166-7_25
26. Takayasu, A., Kunihiro, N.: How to generalize RSA cryptanalyses. In: Cheng, C.-M., Chung, K.-M., Persiano, G., Yang, B.-Y. (eds.) PKC 2016. LNCS, vol. 9615, pp. 67–97. Springer, Heidelberg (2016). https://doi.org/10.1007/978-3-662-49387-8_4
27. Takayasu, A., Lu, Y., Peng, L.: Small CRT-exponent RSA revisited. In: Coron, J.-S., Nielsen, J.B. (eds.) EUROCRYPT 2017. LNCS, vol. 10211, pp. 130–159. Springer, Cham (2017). https://doi.org/10.1007/978-3-319-56614-6_5
28. Takayasu, A., Lu, Y., Peng, L.: Small CRT-exponent RSA revisited. J. Cryptol. **32**(4), 1337–1382 (2019)
29. Wiener, M.J.: Cryptanalysis of short RSA secret exponents. IEEE Trans. Inf. theory **36**(3), 553–558 (1990)

A Formula for Disaster: A Unified Approach to Elliptic Curve Special-Point-Based Attacks

Vladimir Sedlacek[1,2]($\boxtimes$) (ID), Jesús-Javier Chi-Domínguez[3,4] (ID), Jan Jancar[1] (ID), and Billy Bob Brumley[4] (ID)

[1] Masaryk University, Brno, Czech Republic
{vlada.sedlacek,j08ny}@mail.muni.cz
[2] Ca'Foscari University, Venice, Italy
[3] Cryptography Research Centre, Technology Innovation Institute, Abu Dhabi, UAE
jesus.dominguez@tii.ae
[4] Tampere University, Tampere, Finland
billy.brumley@tuni.fi

Abstract. The Refined Power Analysis, Zero-Value Point, and Exceptional Procedure attacks introduced side-channel techniques against specific cases of elliptic curve cryptography. The three attacks recover bits of a static ECDH key adaptively, collecting information on whether a certain multiple of the input point was computed. We unify and generalize these attacks in a common framework, and solve the corresponding problem for a broader class of inputs. We also introduce a version of the attack against windowed scalar multiplication methods, recovering the full scalar instead of just a part of it. Finally, we systematically analyze elliptic curve point addition formulas from the Explicit-Formulas Database, classify all non-trivial exceptional points, and find them in new formulas. These results indicate the usefulness of our tooling, which we released publicly, for unrolling formulas and finding special points, and potentially for independent future work.

Keywords: Elliptic curve cryptography · ECC · Elliptic curve Diffie-Hellman · ECDH · Side-channel analysis · Refined Power Analysis · RPA · Zero-value point attack · ZVP · Exceptional procedure attack · EPA · Exceptional points

1 Introduction

Since the initial proposal of elliptic curve cryptography (ECC) by Koblitz [28] and Miller [31], the main building block of most elliptic curve cryptosystems has been scalar point multiplication, which involves a plethora of different formulas. There are several side-channel attacks targeting the formulas, either via forcing an intermediate value to be zero or by causing the computation to fail. However,

© International Association for Cryptologic Research 2021
M. Tibouchi and H. Wang (Eds.): ASIACRYPT 2021, LNCS 13090, pp. 130–159, 2021.
https://doi.org/10.1007/978-3-030-92062-3_5

these attacks are only described in special cases, specific to a small number of formulas. In this work, we unify and generalize the attacks, and systematically classify exceptional points in many widely used formulas.

Related Work. In 2003, Goubin [20] introduced a new side-channel attack against implementations of ECC. Titled Refined Power Analysis (RPA), it uses a power side channel and the existence of points with a zero coordinate to steer an adaptive attack on implementations of the static elliptic curve Diffie-Hellman (ECDH) protocol. Smart [35] described effective countermeasures against RPA. Subsequently, Akishita and Takagi [1] proposed a slightly different method named the Zero-Value Point (ZVP) attack. It focuses on forcing zeros into intermediate values inside a given point addition formula, and not only in the point coordinate. Several extensions followed: Zhang, Lin, and Liu [40] modified the ZVP attack to target genus 2 curves, and Crépeau and Kazmi [14] proposed ZVP for elliptic curves over binary extension fields. Danger, Guilley, Hoogvorst, Murdica, and Naccache [15] gave new countermeasures against ZVP and RPA, while Tena, Tomàs, and Valls [29] analyzed Edwards curves with regards to ZVP attacks, showing that some addition formulas on Edwards curves are resistant to ZVP attacks. Finally, Murdica, Guilley, Danger, Hoogvorst, and Naccache [33] proposed the Same Value Analysis (SVA) attack, which tries to detect the repeated use of some finite field value via a side channel.

Izu and Takagi [26] analyzed the Brier and Joye [8] addition formulas and presented an Exceptional Procedure Attack (EPA). It uses a similar adaptive mechanism as the aforementioned attacks, but relies on an error side channel by inducing incorrect computations, without the use of fault induction. To avoid EPAs, it is best to use complete addition formulas that always compute the sum of two points correctly for all inputs. Costello, and Batina [34] credit Bosma and Lenstra [7] for the only known complete formulas for prime order short Weierstrass curves, while Bernstein, Birkner, Joye, Lange, and Peters [3] and Hisil, Wong, Carter, and Dawson [24] proposed complete formulas for Twisted Edwards curves. The Explicit-Formulas Database (EFD) by Bernstein and Lange [4] contains formulas for many different curve models and coordinate systems.

What Could Possibly Go Wrong? Most of the current public EC libraries do not use complete formulas for short Weierstrass curves, with the exception of ECCKiila [2]. This includes production libraries:

- Mozilla issued two security advisories for unimplemented exceptions in NSS's projective addition, leading to incorrect (degenerate) multiplication results;
- OpenSSL had unimplemented exceptions during its projective ladder step addition, leading to incorrect (degenerate) results;
- BoringSSL's check for exceptional projective inputs was not constant time, leaking critical algorithm state;
- Python's `fastecdsa` module had an unimplemented exception during affine point doubling, leading to incorrect (degenerate) results.

Contributions and Outline. In this work, we present a novel formal framework to unify the ZVP, RPA, and EPA attacks as instances of a more

general problem, which we solve for some cases (Sect. 3). Our approach leads
to a new attack on windowed scalar multiplication algorithms (Sect. 3.5), and
allows for clearer analysis of the attacks. Next, we develop a semi-automated
methodology to discover non-trivial exceptional points, applying it to systematically analyze EFD formulas, completely classifying all such points (Sect. 4). We
then survey widely deployed software libraries, gaining insight into the practical implications of our analysis (Sect. 5). Finally, we draw our concluding
remarks in Sect. 6. We released our code and data under an open-source license
at github.com/crocs-muni/formula-for-disaster.

2 Background

We define an elliptic curve E in the short Weierstrass model over a prime field
$\mathbb{F}_p$, $p \geq 3$ by the following equation:

$$E/\mathbb{F}_p \colon y^2 = x^3 + ax + b, \quad a, b \in \mathbb{F}_p, \quad 4a^3 + 27b^2 \neq 0. \tag{1}$$

The group $E(\mathbb{F}_p)$ consists of affine points $(x, y) \in \mathbb{F}_p^2$ satisfying (1) together with
the neutral element $\mathcal{O}$, corresponding to the point at infinity. For any positive
integer k, we define the scalar multiplication $[k]P$ as the sum of k copies of P
and also define $[-k]P$ by $-[k]P$. The *order of a point* $P \in E(\mathbb{F}_p)$ is defined as
the smallest positive integer k such that $[k]P = \mathcal{O}$. We refer to points of order
dividing k as the k-torsion points. For typical cryptographic applications, $E(\mathbb{F}_p)$
has cardinality $n = h \cdot q$, where q is prime and $h \in \{1, 2, 4, 8\}$; h is called the
cofactor.

The scalar point multiplication mapping $P \mapsto [k]P$ can also be computed by
using the *division polynomial* ψ_k [38]: that is,

$$[k](x, y) = \left(\frac{\phi_k(x)}{\psi_k^2(x)}, \frac{\omega_k(x, y)}{\psi_k^3(x, y)} \right),$$

where

$$\psi_0 = 0,$$
$$\psi_1 = x,$$
$$\psi_2 = 2y,$$
$$\psi_3 = 3x^4 + 6ax^2 + 12bx - a^2,$$
$$\psi_4 = 4y(x^6 + 5ax^4 + 20bx^3 - 5a^2x^2 - 4abx - 8b^2 - a^3),$$
$$\psi_{2k+1} = \psi_{k+2}\psi_k^3 - \psi_{k-1}\psi_{k+1}^3 \qquad \text{for } k \geq 2,$$
$$\psi_{2k} = (2y)^{-1}\psi_k(\psi_{k+2}\psi_{k-1}^2 - \psi_{k-2}\psi_{k+1}^2) \qquad \text{for } k \geq 3,$$
$$\phi_k = x\psi_c^2 - \psi_{k+1}\psi_{k-1},$$
$$\omega_k = (4y)^{-1}(\psi_{k+2}\psi_{k-1}^2 - \psi_{k-2}\psi_{k+1}^2).$$

All of these polynomials are considered modulo the curve Eq. (1). For simplicity,
we denote $m_k(x) := \frac{\phi_k(x)}{\psi_k^2(x)}$, then for all $k_1, k_2, i \in \mathbb{Z}$, we have $(m_{k_1} \circ m_{k_2})(x) = m_{k_1 \cdot k_2}(x)$, $m_{k_1}(x) = m_{-k_1}(x)$ and $m_{k_1}(x) = m_{\pm k_1 + in}(x)$.

2.1   Curve Models and Their Zero-Coordinate Points

For a short Weierstrass curve E_W over $\mathbb{F}_p$ given by Eq. (1), the points with zero y-coordinate are exactly the points of order 2. Points with zero x-coordinate exist iff b is a square in $\mathbb{F}_p$, in which case $(0, \pm\sqrt{b}) \in E_W/\mathbb{F}_p$ [21]. Any elliptic curve can be converted to the short Weierstrass model.

Montgomery. The Montgomery model of an elliptic curve [13,32] is

$$E_M/\mathbb{F}_p \colon By^2 = x^3 + Ax^2 + x \quad A, B \in \mathbb{F}_p, \quad B(A^2 - 4) \neq 0.$$

Similar to the short Weierstrass model, the neutral element $\mathcal{O}$ does not have an affine representation. Points of order 2 are $(0,0)$ and $(\frac{1}{2}(-A \pm \sqrt{A^2 - 4}), 0)$, though the latter two might not be defined over $\mathbb{F}_p$. All the other affine points have non-zero coordinates.

Twisted Edwards. The twisted Edwards model of an elliptic curve [3] is

$$E_T/\mathbb{F}_p \colon a_T x^2 + y^2 = 1 + d_T x^2 y^2 \quad a_T, d_T \in \mathbb{F}_p, \quad a_T d_T (a_T - d_T) \neq 0.$$

Typically, we also require a_T to be a square in $\mathbb{F}_p$ and d_T a non-square in $\mathbb{F}_p$. The neutral element is the affine point $(0, 1)$, the point $(0, -1)$ has order 2, and the points $(\pm 1/\sqrt{a}, 0)$ have order 4. All the other affine points have non-zero coordinates.

Edwards. The Edwards model of an elliptic curve [5,17] is

$$E_E/\mathbb{F}_p \colon x^2 + y^2 = c^2(1 + dx^2 y^2) \quad c, d \in \mathbb{F}_p, \quad cd(1 - dc^4) \neq 0.$$

When using yz or yzsquared coordinates, we also require d to be a square in $\mathbb{F}_p$, though in other cases, we may require it to be non-square. The neutral element is the affine point $(0, c)$, the point $(0, -c)$ has order 2, and the points $(\pm c, 0)$ have order 4. All the other affine points have non-zero coordinates.

For any Edwards curve $E_E/\mathbb{F}_p$, we can rescale $c \mapsto 1$ by taking $d \mapsto dc^4$, $x \mapsto cx$, $y \mapsto cy$ (thus also obtaining a twisted Edwards curve with $a_T = 1$).

2.2   Point Coordinates and Addition Formulas

In practice, we mostly work with non-affine coordinates[1], as they delay the costly field inversion required in affine computations. For example, (x, y) can be represented with standard projective coordinates as $(x : y : 1)$, from the set of points $\{(\lambda x, \lambda y, \lambda) | \lambda \in \mathbb{F}_p^*\}$ (that is, projective points are lines in $\mathbb{F}_p^3$, without the zero vector). Some curve models allow performing point additions with either x-only (short Weierstrass and Montgomery models [32]) or y-only (Edwards models [9]) coordinates, assuming the difference of the input points is known. Table 1 lists the non-affine coordinates present in EFD.

---

[1] We use the name *non-affine* for coordinate systems other than affine coordinates and *projective* to denote the standard projective coordinates.

Table 1. Non-affine coordinates analyzed in this work, and the quantity of corresponding EFD formulas. Note that the conversion from xz, yz, and yzsquared coordinates to affine is not unique, and that both yz and yzsquared assume $c = 1$.

Model	Coordinates	(x, y) representation	$\mathcal{O}$ representation	#
E_W	Projective [4,8,11,34]	$(xZ : yZ : Z)$	$(0 : 1 : 0)$	21
	Jacobian [10,11,21,22,30]	$(xZ^2 : yZ^3 : Z)$	$(1 : 1 : 0)$	36
	Modified [4,11]	$(xZ^2 : yZ^3 : Z : aZ^4)$	$(1 : 1 : 0 : 0)$	4
	w12 with $b = 0$ [12]	$(xZ : yZ^2 : Z)$	$(1 : 0 : 0)$	2
	xyzz	$(xZ^2 : yZ^3 : Z^2 : Z^3)$	$(1 : 1 : 0 : 0)$	6
	xz [8,25]	$(xZ : Z)$	$(1 : 0)$	22
E_M	xz [32]	$(xZ : Z)$	$(1 : 0)$	8
E_T	Projective [3]	$(xZ : yZ : Z)$	$(0 : 1 : 1)$	3
	Extended [23]	$(xZ : yZ : xyZ : Z)$	$(0 : 1 : 0 : 1)$	18
	Inverted [3,24]	$\left(\frac{Z}{x} : \frac{Z}{y} : Z\right)$	None	3
E_E	Projective [5,23,24]	$(xZ : yZ : Z)$	$(0 : c : 1)$	12
	Inverted [6,24]	$\left(\frac{Z}{x} : \frac{Z}{y} : Z\right)$	None	6
	yz [19]	$\left(yZ\sqrt{d} : Z\right)$	$\left(\sqrt{d} : 1\right)$	6
	yzsquared [19]	$\left(y^2 Z\sqrt{d} : Z\right)$	$\left(\sqrt{d} : 1\right)$	6

A point addition formula (w.r.t. a given curve model and coordinate system) is an explicit way of computing the sum of two points on an elliptic curve. It takes the coordinates of the two points as inputs and returns the coordinates of their sum, depending on the used representation. There are also formulas for doubling or tripling a point, or for computing the simultaneous doubling of a point and an addition of a different point, known as ladder formulas.

An addition formula is called *unified* if it correctly computes $P + P$ and *complete* if it correctly computes $P + Q$ for any P and Q on any curve satisfying the assumptions of the formula. Unified and complete formulas are important as they do not require exceptions and encourage secure constant-time implementations, where point doubling is indistinguishable from point addition. Any complete formula is also unified, but the converse is not true. For prime order short Weierstrass curves, only a single complete formula is known [34].

2.3 Explicit-Formulas Database

The Explicit-Formulas Database (EFD) by Bernstein and Lange [4] is the largest publicly available database of formulas for different coordinate systems and curve models. It provides the formulas in a 3-operand notation, breaking down the computation into individual binary and unary operations on intermediate values. This machine readable format mimics the computations in real software and hardware. We exported the EFD data and provide it in a repository[2] with some cleanups and added missing information. The EFD contains addition formulas (i.e. $P+Q = \mathbf{add}(P,Q)$), doubling formulas (i.e. $[2]P = \mathbf{dbl}(P)$), tripling formulas, differential addition formulas (i.e. $P+Q = \mathbf{dadd}(P-Q,P,Q)$) and ladder formulas (i.e. $([2P], P+Q) = \mathbf{ladd}(P-Q,P,Q)$).

The EFD also includes automated formula verification in SageMath, though it only compares the expressions as rational functions. This means the results are correct globally, but not necessarily locally – there might be exceptions for points where the denominators equal zero and the quotient is undefined. We investigate these cases in Sect. 4.

2.4   Scalar Multiplication Algorithms

During an ECDH key exchange, all scalar multiplications use a single scalar and the multiplied point is the public key of the other party, which is unknown before the computation. This excludes the use of heavy pre-computations like comb-based methods. Following Jancar [27], we divide the applicable scalar multiplication algorithms into three rough categories:

– *Basic* ones (often called *double-and-add*) that scan the scalar bit by bit, and perform either doubling or addition based on the bit value [21]. During the scalar multiplication, a basic multiplier executes the formulas:

$$[2k]P = \mathbf{dbl}([k]P) \qquad \text{or}$$
$$[k+1]P = \mathbf{add}(P,[k]P),$$

depending on the iteration; k is equal to some part of the scalar.

– *Ladder* ones that resemble the basic ones, but use a ladder formula [32] with two temporary variables maintaining a constant difference. This ensures the computations are uniform and take the same time, regardless of the scalar. The formula executions in this scalar multiplier are:

$$([2(k+1)]P, [2k+1]P) = \mathbf{ladd}(P, [k+1]P, [k]P) \qquad \text{or}$$
$$([2k]P, [2k+1]P) = \mathbf{ladd}(P, [k]P, [k+1]P),$$

depending on the iteration.

– *Window* ones that divide the scalar into blocks of digits (called windows) of a given width and precompute the corresponding multiples of the point. The precomputation is cheap enough to be possible even for variable points. If zero digits are skipped, the window is called *sliding* [21]. The formula executions in this scalar multiplier are:

$$[2k]P = \mathbf{dbl}([k]P) \qquad \text{or}$$
$$[k+e]P = \mathbf{add}([e]P, [k]P),$$

depending on the iteration; $[e]P$ is a precomputed point.

---

[2] https://github.com/crocs-muni/efd.

Scalar multiplication algorithms can also use signed digit representations of the scalar, most often the binary Non-Adjacent Form (NAF), or in the window case window NAF.

In the rest of this work, we refer to the *accumulator point* that represents the point variable to which points are added in scalar multiplication, and which stores the current multiple of the input point through the iterations of the algorithm. Note that a ladder-based scalar multiplier has two accumulator points which have a constant difference.

2.5   Side-Channel Attack Countermeasures

To mitigate side-channel attacks on ECC, including those discussed in this work, several countermeasures were developed. Here we show those relevant to our attacks, which are based on randomization and target the scalar multiplication with a secret scalar.

Scalar Randomization. The first possibility of randomization lies in the secret scalar itself. There are several techniques which randomize the scalar and compute either one scalar multiplication (group scalar randomization) or several (additive, multiplicative, or Euclidean scalar splitting) [16]. For us, it is important that this countermeasure leads to randomized multiples of the input point, stored in the accumulator point, as the algorithm proceeds. Thus, if the attacker learns that a particular multiple of the input point was computed during some scalar multiplication, they learn almost nothing about the secret scalar used.

Point Randomization. Another possibility of randomizing values inside the scalar multiplication lies in the use of non-affine point representations and their scaling property. As one affine point corresponds to an entire class of non-affine points, one can select a random representative out of the class when converting the affine input point for scalar multiplication. This randomizes almost all intermediate values in the scalar multiplication [16]. It does not randomize zero values in one of the coordinates of the affine point like $(x, 0)$ or $(0, y)$, as their projective representatives are $(xZ : 0 : Z)$ or $(0 : yZ : Z)$ for some $Z \in \mathbb{F}_p^*$.

Curve Randomization. Finally, it is possible to randomize the curve over which the computations are performed. This also randomizes almost all intermediate values in the scalar multiplication. Such randomization uses either an isomorphic or an isogenous curve [16,35].

2.6   The Refined Power Analysis and Zero-Value Point Attacks

Goubin's Refined Power Analysis (RPA) [20] is a side-channel attack against ECC implementations using a static secret, such as ECDH or X25519, together with basic or ladder scalar multiplication. It is based on the assumption that adding[3] a point P_0 with a zero x- or y-coordinate to another can be distinguished from adding a general point, at least over several measured traces. We

---

[3] The attack also applies to doubling. For simplicity, we only consider addition in this paper, but our results easily extend to doubling.

discussed the existence of zero coordinate points in Sect. 2.1. The side channel is usually based on power or electromagnetic emanation, where one can distinguish the multiplication with a zero field element from the general case (see e.g. Fig. 1 in [15]) due to the dependency of power consumption of a device on the data and instructions that are being executed. The attacker measures the power consumption of a device using an oscilloscope and a current probe.

In each iteration, the attacker makes a guess $k' \in \mathbb{Z}_n^*$ for the partial secret key k, and then checks the guess by querying the implementation using the public key $P_1 = [k'^{-1} \bmod n]P_0$. The guess was correct iff the implementation computes $[k']P_1 = P_0$, detectable using a side channel. Since the scalar multiplication is iterative in nature, the attacker adaptively guesses the bits of the key one by one, building upon the previous guesses. All scalar randomization countermeasures successfully thwart the RPA attack, as well as Smart's curve randomization via isogenies [35], while point randomization or curve randomization via isomorphisms do not, since the zero point coordinate does not get randomized. Unlike [18], the attack does not require fault injection.

More generally, Akishita's and Takagi's Zero-Value Point (ZVP) attack [1] considers intermediate scalar values computed during point addition (as a subroutine of scalar multiplication). The intermediate values can be expressed as a polynomial expression in the input coordinates (see Algorithm 1 for an example of the intermediate values and Fig. 4 for the unrolled version). If the attacker can select a point P such that $P + [k']P$ produces a zero scalar intermediate value during the formula's execution (not necessarily at the end), the attacker can detect the zero using a side channel. Then they can deduce which multiples of the input were computed during the scalar multiplication, and thus recover the secret scalar. Unlike RPA, ZVP does not assume the existence of points with a zero coordinate; in particular, it applies to prime-order curves.

The value of the input point P depends on k', the used formulas, the particular intermediate value that is being zeroed out, as well as the curve. It seems that finding these points for even a mildly large k' is an open problem, claimed to be as difficult as computing the k'-th division polynomial. The maximal k' required for key recovery is in the same range as the secret scalar, approaching n. For some coordinate systems and formulas for (twisted) Edwards curves, the intermediate expressions can be classified [29], but the general case is not settled. The ZVP attack can be thought of as a generalization of the RPA attack, and the same countermeasures prevent it.

2.7 Exceptional Procedure Attacks

In practice, scalar multiplication uses non-affine point representations (shown in Table 1), only mapping the non-affine result into its unique affine representation at the end. This final conversion is the only part of the computation requiring field inversions, usually of the Z-coordinate. Exceptional Procedure Attacks (EPA) are based on finding a pair of points P and Q such that the final conversion of $P + Q = \mathbf{add}(P, Q)$ fails, because the expression being inverted is zero. The implementation then either throws an error, or produces an obviously detectable output [26]. Such points are called exceptional w.r.t. a given formula; see Sect. 4 for a more precise definition and classification of all non-trivial exceptional points for EFD formulas.

3   A Unified Approach to the Attacks

The attacks introduced in Sect. 2.6 and Sect. 2.7 have a lot in common. In this section, we build a common framework that captures them as special cases.

3.1   Attack Setting

Let $S : (k, P) \mapsto [k]P$ be a scalar point multiplication algorithm on a curve. Assume k is a fixed secret input, and P is an arbitrary affine point. This scalar multiplication with a fixed secret scalar and chosen input point is the target in our setting. The evaluation of $S(k, P)$ consists of a sequence of formula executions. As described in Sect. 2.4 and displayed in Fig. 1, the formulas take as input some multiples of P, which depend on k and S.

Let us define $\mathcal{O}^{\mathcal{F}}_{B,U} : \mathbb{I}^m \to \{0, 1, \bot\}$, the *boolean special point oracle for formula* $\mathcal{F}$:

$$
\mathcal{O}^{\mathcal{F}}_{B,U}(I) := \begin{cases} 1 \text{ if } I \text{ was input into } \mathcal{F} \text{ during the } S(k, P) \text{ computation;} \\ 0 \text{ if } I \text{ was not input into } \mathcal{F}; \\ \bot \text{ if the oracle could not determine the result,} \end{cases}
$$

where $\mathcal{O}^{\mathcal{F}}_{B,U}(I) \in \{0, 1\}$ for $I \in U$, and $\mathbb{I} = \{[i] | i \in \mathbb{Z}\} \cup \{\_\}$ is the set of symbolic multiples of the input point P, (with $[i]$ representing the point $[i]P$ and $\_$ representing any multiple of the point P). When $U = \mathbb{I}^m$, we omit the subscript, and we also simply write I instead of $\{I\}$. The arity m of the oracle is the same as the arity of $\mathcal{F}$, e.g., 2 for **add**.

We also define the *temporal special point oracle* $\mathcal{O}^{\mathcal{F}}_{T,U} : \mathbb{I}^m \to \{0, 1, \bot\} \times \mathcal{P}(\mathbb{N})$ as $\mathcal{O}^{\mathcal{F}}_{T,U}(I) = (\mathcal{O}^{\mathcal{F}}_{B,U}(I), \mathcal{T})$, where $\mathcal{T}$ is a set of iteration indices when $\mathcal{F}$ took I as an input. If the oracle cannot distinguish between a multiple $[i]$ and its negative $[-i]$, we add $\pm$ to its notation and obtain $\mathcal{O}^{\mathcal{F}}_{\pm B,U}$ and $\mathcal{O}^{\mathcal{F}}_{\pm T,U}$.

An example instance of the boolean oracle is $\mathcal{O}^{\mathbf{add}}_B$, which given $I = (\_, [3])$ returns 1 iff the formula **add** ever received as its second input $[3]P$ during the $S(k, P)$ computation. A different example of an oracle, useful in the case of a windowed S, is $\mathcal{O}^{\mathbf{add}}_T$ with input $I = ([5], \_)$. It returns all of the iterations in which the **add** formula took $[5]P$ as its first input. We assume an instance of the oracle makes a constant amount of queries to the implementation performing the scalar multiplication, with chosen input points.

Section 3.4 shows how to construct instances of the boolean and temporal special point oracles using the techniques of RPA, ZVP, and EPA attacks, as well as how to use these oracles in an attack.

$\mathcal{O}_B^{\mathrm{add}}\left(I\right)$

1. Create P.
2. Give P to implementation.
3. Receive $[k]P$ and observe side-channel.
4. Repeat a constant amount of times.
5. Evaluate and return.

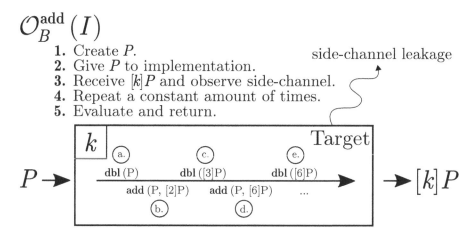

Fig. 1. An example of the boolean special point oracle, with a target performing the $S(k, P)$ scalar multiplication execution using a basic double-and-add-always algorithm. The scalar k has MSBs 110.

3.2   The Dependent Coordinates Problem

To unify the attacks, we first introduce an abstract problem and analyze it.

Following the notation introduced in Sect. 2, for the rest of this section we fix a prime $p \geq 3$ and an elliptic curve $E/\mathbb{F}_p$ given[4] by $Y^2 = f_E(X)$, where $f_E(X) = X^3 + aX + b$ and $a, b \in \mathbb{F}_p$. Let $\mathbb{G}$ be a subgroup of $E(\mathbb{F}_p)$ with prime order q. Recall that m_k is the x-coordinate of the rational multiplication-by-k function on E. Furthermore, let

$$R_E := \mathbb{F}_p[X_1, X_2, Y_1, Y_2]/(Y_1^2 - f_E(X_1), Y_2^2 - f_E(X_2))$$

be the coordinate ring of E, and for a multivariate polynomial g, let $\deg g$ denote its multi-degree, given as the sum of its degrees with respect to all individual variables. Finally, note that lower case letters denote scalar values, whereas upper case letters denote either free variables or curve points.

Definition 1 (DCP: the dependent coordinates problem). *Given a polynomial* $f \in \mathbb{F}_p[X_1, X_2, Y_1, Y_2]$ *and an integer* k*, find a pair of points (if they exist)* $P, Q \in \mathbb{G}$ *such that* $Q = [k]P$ *and* $f(X_1, X_2, Y_1, Y_2) = 0$*, where* $P = (X_1, Y_1), Q = (X_2, Y_2)$*. If* $f \in \mathbb{F}_p[X_1, X_2]$*, we call the problem the x-only dependent coordinates problem, or xDCP.*

Without loss of generality, we can also consider $k \in \mathbb{Z}_q$ instead of $k \in \mathbb{Z}$, and replace f by any of its representatives from R_E.

Solving DCP via xDCP. The following lemma cancels the occurrences of Y_1 and Y_2 (if any) thanks to squarings and reductions modulo the curve equation.

---

[4] In principle, our techniques apply to other curves models as well, but we use the short Weierstrass model for simplicity, as it represents all curves.

Lemma 1. *Let $f \in \mathbb{F}_p[X_1, X_2, Y_1, Y_2]$, $k \in \mathbb{Z}$ and let (P, Q) be a solution to the DCP determined by f and c. Then there exists a polynomial $f' \in \mathbb{F}_p[X_1, X_2]$ such that (P, Q) is also a solution to the xDCP determined by f' and k and $\deg f' \leq 6 \cdot \deg f + 12$.*

Proof. Working in R_E, we replace all even powers of Y_1 and Y_2 by powers of $f_E(X_1)$ and $f_E(X_2)$, respectively; representing f as $f_0 + f_1 Y_1 + f_2 Y_2 + f_{12} Y_1 Y_2$ for some $f_0, f_1, f_2, f_{12} \in \mathbb{F}_p[X_1, X_2]$. Next, we eliminate Y_1 and Y_2:

$$f_0 + f_1 Y_1 + f_2 Y_2 + f_{12} Y_1 Y_2 = 0$$
$$Y_1(f_1 + f_{12} Y_2) = -(f_0 + f_2 Y_2)$$
$$f_E(X_1)(f_1 + f_{12} Y_2)^2 = (f_0 + f_2 Y_2)^2$$
$$f_E(X_1)(f_1^2 + f_{12}^2 f_E(X_2) + 2 f_1 f_{12} Y_2) = f_0^2 + f_2^2 f_E(X_2) + 2 f_0 f_2 Y_2$$
$$Y_2(f_E(X_1) \cdot 2 f_1 f_{12} - 2 f_0 f_2) = f_0^2 + f_2^2 f_E(X_2)$$
$$\qquad - f_E(X_1)(f_1^2 + f_{12}^2 f_E(X_2))$$
$$f_E(X_2)(f_E(X_1) \cdot 2 f_1 f_{12} - 2 f_0 f_2)^2 = (f_0^2 + f_2^2 f_E(X_2)$$
$$\qquad - f_E(X_1)(f_1^2 + f_{12}^2 f_E(X_2))^2 .$$

Thus, instead of finding the roots of f, we find the roots of f', where

$$f' = f_E(X_2)(f_E(X_1) \cdot 2 f_1 f_{12} - 2 f_0 f_2)^2$$
$$- \left(f_0^2 + f_2^2 f_E(X_2) - f_E(X_1)(f_1^2 + f_{12}^2 f_E(X_2)) \right)^2 .$$

To conclude the proof, it suffices to estimate

$$\deg f' = \max\{ 2 \cdot \max\{\deg f_1 f_{12} + 3, \deg f_0 f_2\} + 3,$$
$$2 \cdot \max\{2 \cdot \deg f_0, 2 \cdot \deg f_2 + 3, \max\{2 \cdot \deg f_1, 2 \cdot \deg f_{12} + 3\} + 3\}\}$$
$$\leq 4 \cdot \max\{\deg f_0, \deg f_1, \deg f_2, \deg f_{12}\} + 12$$
$$\leq 4 \cdot \deg(f_0 + f_1 Y_1 + f_2 Y_2 + f_{12} Y_1 Y_2) + 12$$
$$\leq 4 \cdot \frac{3}{2} \cdot \deg f + 12.$$

$\square$

Indeed, Lemma 1 allows us to only consider xDCP instead of DCP for the remainder of the paper. Yet with care: we lost the information about the signs of Y_1 and Y_2 during the squaring procedure in the proof, so the resulting xDCP also has solutions with incorrect signs (note that xDCP is always sign-agnostic).

The multi-degree bound is loose and might be much lower in many instances. When solving ZVP or EPA, the multi-degree of f is typically between 1 and 8, so the reduction to xDCP is still practical. Furthermore, we can often factor the expressions and take only a single factor as f.

An Easy Case. If $f \in \mathbb{F}_p[X_2, Y_2]$, then the DCP becomes easy whenever a solution exists. Using Lemma 1, we instead solve xDCP with $f' \in \mathbb{F}_p[X_2]$, finding the roots algorithmically. If there is a root corresponding to the x-coordinate of some point Q, we simply compute $P = [k^{-1} \bmod q]Q$ and we are done. Note that this approach relies heavily on ignoring the relationship between P and Q until the very end. In particular, the solvability of DCP does not depend on the size of k in this case. This contrasts the claims of Akishita and Takagi [1], who found constructing ZVP points for addition (which amounts to solving an instance of the DCP) as hard as computing the k-th division polynomial.

The Number of Solutions. We now estimate the number of k's such that the xDCP has a solution. If f is linear in one of its variables, say X_1, then for any $x_2 \in \mathbb{F}_p$, there is exactly one x_1 such that $f(x_1, x_2) = 0$ (except for rare cases when $F(X_1, x_2)$ is a constant polynomial). The probability that both x_1 and x_2 are the x-coordinates of $P, Q \in \mathbb{G}$ is roughly $\frac{1}{4} \cdot \frac{q}{n}$. For any such point pairs, there is exactly one $k \in \mathbb{Z}_q$ such that $Q = [k]P$, corresponding to the two possible solutions k, $q - k$. Even though such k's can overlap, we estimate the number of k's for which xDCP has a solution as $2 \cdot p \cdot \frac{1}{4} \cdot \frac{q}{n} \approx \frac{p}{2}$ when $\mathbb{G}$ is a large subgroup. The same heuristic applies when the degree D of at least one variable in f is coprime to $\varphi(p) = p - 1$, since taking the D-th power is an invertible operation in $\mathbb{F}_p$. In general, the correspondence between the roots of f is more problematic, but based on our empirical results, the above heuristic still seems to be reasonably accurate.

3.3   Solving xDCP

The basic strategy to solve xDCP described in [1] is setting $X_2 = m_k(X_1)$ and then finding the roots of $f(X_1, X_2) \in \mathbb{F}_p[X_1]$. If any of the roots is an x-coordinate of a point $P' \in \mathbb{G}$, we take $P = P', Q = [k]P$. The main limitation is that m_k is very hard to compute for large $k \geq B$. In practice, $B \approx 2^{20}$, mainly due to memory requirements.

Shifting the Scalar. Suppose that both l and kl are small modulo q for some $l \in \mathbb{Z}$. Then we set $X_1 = m_l(X), X_2 = m_{kl}(X)$, and find the roots of $f(X_1, X_2) \in \mathbb{F}_p[X_1]$. If any of them is an x-coordinate of a point $P' \in \mathbb{G}$, we take $P = [l]P'$, $Q = [k]P$.

In practice, we find the shortest vector in the lattice generated by $\left(\begin{smallmatrix} 1 & k \\ 0 & q \end{smallmatrix}\right)$ using the Lagrange-Gauss algorithm, and take l as its first coordinate. Indeed, this increases the size of the set of all k's for which we can solve the xDCP to almost B^2, compared to B for the basic approach.

Using the Greatest Common Divisor. To avoid expensive root-finding of a large polynomial, we suggest to construct another polynomial with the same roots, and compute the greatest common divisor (gcd). Replacing m_{kl} with $m_{|q-kl|}$ in the above method offers such a polynomial. Since $m_{|q-kl|}$ might not be directly computable, we reduce both its numerator and its denominator modulo the first polynomial at every step. This does not influence the gcd. Finally, we perform a final reduction after substituting it into f.

More precisely, let $\mathrm{num}(g)$ denote the numerator of a rational function g. Let $X_1 = m_l(X), X_2 = m_{kl}(X)$, and define $F_1 = \mathrm{num}(f(X_1, X_2))$. Furthermore, let $X_2' \equiv m_{|q-kl|}(X) \bmod F_1$ and $F_2 = \mathrm{num}(f(X_1, X_2'))$. Then we efficiently compute $F = \gcd(F_1, F_2)$ using Euclid's algorithm. If any of the roots of F is an x-coordinate of a point $P' \in \mathbb{G}$, we take $P = [l]P', Q = [k]P$. Heuristically, it seems that F is always linear.

Minor Scalar Optimizations. The symmetry between P and Q, and the fact that $m_k(x) = m_{-k}(x)$ for all $x \in \mathbb{F}_p$, allows us to replace k with $\pm k^{\pm 1} \bmod q$. This saves up to two bits.

3.4   The Full Attack

We now show that RPA, ZVP, and EPA are all special cases of the same attack, utilizing different side channels and the dependent coordinates problem to build an instance of the special point oracle.

The Adaptive Approach. As mentioned in Sect. 3.1, the multiples which are input into the formulas during a scalar multiplication operation depend on the scalar. These multiples allow us to reconstruct the scalar, as they determine the corresponding addition chain. For example, step e) in Fig. 1 computes either **dbl**($[6]P$) or **dbl**($[7]P$), depending on the third most significant bit of the scalar.

During the attack, we have a known part of the scalar. It starts empty, and we recover it in the same way the scalar multiplication algorithm processes it. Given a known part, we make a guess on the next subpart, either a single bit or a window of bits, then use some special point oracle to determine whether the guess was true. This implies some multiples derived from the known part and next subpart were input into a formula. This way, we recover the scalar in logarithmically many queries to the oracle.

The type of oracle we have access to, and the scalar multiplication algorithm used, both affect the attack. For example, if a fixed window scalar multiplication algorithm is used and we have access to an $\mathcal{O}^{\mathbf{add}}_{T,([e],\_)}$ for e ranging over all of the precomputed multiples of the input point, we can recover the window digits directly and assemble the scalar afterwards. If on the other hand a basic scalar multiplication algorithm is used and we have an $\mathcal{O}^{\mathbf{dbl}}_{B,([e])}$ for e ranging over all possible scalars, we recover the scalar adaptively. Given a known part of the scalar k', we can gain the next bit based on the output of $\mathcal{O}^{\mathbf{dbl}}_{B,([k'])}$ or $\mathcal{O}^{\mathbf{dbl}}_{B,([k'+1])}$.

All of the RPA, ZVP, and EPA attacks utilize this adaptive approach, differing only in how they construct a special point oracle (i.e. which side channel and property of the curve, formula, or implementation they use).

Constructing Oracles from ZVP. Given a point addition formula, we consider the intermediate polynomials, and pick any one of them as f. A solution to the dependent coordinates problem for some k then allows us to construct a point P such that f will evaluate to zero during the computation of $P + [k]P$. Now using a suitable side channel, we can detect whether this zero appears during the scalar multiplication, and potentially localize it into an iteration of the scalar multiplication algorithm [1]. Thus we can construct an instance of the

$\mathcal{O}_{T,([1],[k])}^{\text{add}}$ oracle for all k for which we can solve the (x)DCP[5]. Similarly, considering the intermediate polynomials in a doubling formula and zeroing out some of them for an input of $[k]P$ allows us to construct an instance of the $\mathcal{O}_{T,([k])}^{\text{dbl}}$ oracle. Note that in the case of the addition formula, if the chosen intermediate polynomial f depends only on one of the input points, it is possible to construct the $\mathcal{O}_{T,(\_,[k])}^{\text{add}}$ and $\mathcal{O}_{T,([1],\_)}^{\text{add}}$ oracles.

Constructing Oracles from RPA. This is a special case of ZVP in which the intermediate value to zero out is a coordinate of an input point [20]. This leads to an easy case of the (x)DCP, discussed in Sect. 3.2, as $f = X_2$ or $f = Y_2$. Because this oracle construction approach leads to an easy case of the (x)DCP, there is no bound on the multiple k in the constructed oracle instances $\mathcal{O}_{T,(\_,[k])}^{\text{add}}$. One can also construct oracle instances such as $\mathcal{O}_{T,([1],\_)}^{\text{add}}$ or $\mathcal{O}_{T,([k])}^{\text{dbl}}$, but not $\mathcal{O}_{T,([1],[k])}^{\text{add}}$ as the appearance of a zero in one of the input points necessarily does not depend on the other point.

Whether these RPA oracles can be constructed depends on the properties of the curve, i.e. whether it has the points $(x, 0)$ or $(0, y)$. Note that if both a point and its negative have a zero-coordinate (as is the case of the $(0, y)$ point on short Weierstrass curves), one can only use it to construct $\mathcal{O}_{\pm T}^{\mathcal{F}}$ and $\mathcal{O}_{\pm B}^{\mathcal{F}}$ oracles.

Constructing Oracles from EPA. In this case, the side channel used to construct the oracle is an error one. The oracle detects whether a computation fails because of an undefined inversion. As explained in Sect. 2.7, this can only happen at the very end of the scalar multiplication, when mapping the result back to affine coordinates, so we can take f to be the expression by which we divide. If we can solve the (x)DCP for this f and some k, we can input this point[6] into the scalar multiplication, which will fail if it computes $P + [k]P$, enabling us to construct an $\mathcal{O}_{B,([1],[k])}^{\text{add}}$. Note that this is a boolean oracle, as with the error side channel we can only detect that the mapping back to affine coordinates failed, and not during which iteration the zero was introduced.

3.5   Window Method Attack

The main limitation of the ZVP-based attacks compared to RPA-like attacks is that they allow the attacker to recover only a limited number of secret scalar bits. This is due to the need for solving a hard case of the (x)DCP with large k. We show that these attacks can extract the full scalar when the target algorithm is window-based, or more generally adds points to the accumulator point from a set of precomputed input point multiples, conditionally on secret scalar bits.

The attack requires that the addition formula in question has an intermediate value which depends only on one of the operands, so that zeroing it out leads to an easy case of the DCP as mentioned in Sect. 3.2. Together with an appropriate side channel, this allows the attacker to construct an $\mathcal{O}_{T,([e],\_)}^{\text{add}}$ oracle. Note that

---

[5] We cannot always consider affine representations as f might not be homogeneous, but in practice this is not a problem, as we have freedom in choosing f.

[6] The homogeneity of f allows us to only consider affine representations.

the attacker needs a temporal special point oracle, and not a boolean one, as the event that the e-th multiple was added to the accumulator point somewhere in the scalar multiplication is insufficient to extract information on the secret scalar. Once the attacker is able to detect the iterations where the e-th multiple was added, the attacker varies over all values e in the set of precomputed multiples, based on the algorithm. In this way, the attacker recovers the window digits and thus the full secret scalar. This attack works even if the curve has no RPA points $(0, y)$, $(x, 0)$, and thus RPA does not apply.

4 Classifying the Exceptional Points

While many EFD formulas [4] are not complete, we are not aware of any systematic overview of the respective pairs of exceptional points. To rectify this, we implemented tooling for unrolling the formulas and tracing their intermediate values. The tooling is an extension of **pyecsca** [27] (**Py**thon **E**lliptic **C**urve cryptography **S**ide-**C**hannel **A**nalysis) – a Python toolkit that aims to extract information from black-box implementations of ECC through side channels and offers extensive simulations of ECC implementations.

Our methodology loosely combines two very different, yet complementary, techniques: fuzzing and manual analysis.

Fuzzing. To quickly identify possible exceptional points (and later verify our findings heuristically), an automated approach is useful. We fuzzed small curves (e.g., over 5-bit fields) of all relevant types, trying all input point pairs for all the analyzed addition formulas, comparing the result to the correct affine output. This approach scales well, but at the cost of an inherently high number of false positives (and possibly false negatives). The results for small curves do not always generalize to large ones (though they can reveal patterns for manual analysis).

Manual Analysis. To find the sufficient and necessary conditions that classify all the exceptional points, we resort to manual inspection. Compared to breadth-focused fuzzing, it dives deeper, taking much more effort, argumentation, and attention to detail. But in the end, it provides more insight, and is applicable to all relevant curves of all sizes.

We carefully went through all 111 addition formulas and 42 differential addition/ladder formulas for the E_W, E_M, E_T, E_E models in the EFD[7], and investigated when the expressions by which we divide during the conversion to affine coordinates could be zero[8]; we present the results in Table 3. Namely, for addition this amounted to studying the conditions $X_3 = 0$ or $Y_3 = 0$ for (twisted) inverted Edwards coordinates, $ZZ_3 = 0$ or $ZZZ_3 = 0$ for short Weierstrass **xyzz** coordinates[9], and $Z_3 = 0$ for all other coordinates. The variable's subscript

---

[7] Some of the formulas are just adaptations for specific coefficients (e.g. $a = -3$ for E_W), mixed additions, etc.

[8] Occasionally omitting the cases where the result is the neutral element.

[9] ZZ_i and ZZZ_i are variables whose values equal Z_i^2 and Z_i^3 throughout the computation, respectively.

denotes its index in the addition formula with 1 and 2 being the inputs and 3 being the output. Similarly, for differential addition and/or ladders, we instead study when the outputs Z_4 and Z_5 were equal to zero. Furthermore, the unrolled expressions could be studied to see which formulas are unified, though we did not pursue this path further.

The rest of this section describes the details of our manual analysis. The expressions we refer to are present in our data release (see Sect. 5.3), though we also provide example expressions that illustrate the process in Table 2.

Coordinates	Formula	Expression
jacobian jacobian-0 jacobian-3	add-1986-cc	$Z3 = Z2 * Z1 * (X2 * Z1^2 - X1 * Z2^2)$
	add-1998-cmo-2	$Z3 = Z2 * Z1 * (X2 * Z1^2 - X1 * Z2^2)$
	add-1998-cmo	$Z3 = Z2 * Z1 * (X2 * Z1^2 - X1 * Z2^2)$
	add-1998-hnm	$Z3 = (-1) * Z2 * Z1 * (X2 * Z1^2 - X1 * Z2^2)$
	add-2001-b	$Z3 = Z2 * Z1 * (X2 * Z1^2 - X1 * Z2^2)$
	add-2007-bl	$Z3 = 2 * Z2 * Z1 * (X2 * Z1^2 - X1 * Z2^2)$
	madd-2004-hmv	$Z3 = Z1 * (X2 * Z1^2 - X1)$
	madd-2007-bl	$Z3 = 2 * Z1 * (X2 * Z1^2 - X1)$
	madd-2008-g	$Z3 = (-1) * Z1 * (X2 * Z1^2 - X1)$
	madd	$Z3 = 2 * Z1 * (X2 * Z1^2 - X1)$
	mmadd-2007-bl	$Z3 = (-1) * 2 * (X1 - X2)$
	zadd-2007-m	$Z3 = (-1) * Z1 * (X1 - X2)$

Table 2. Jacobian coordinate outputs on short Weierstrass curves.

4.1   Exceptional Points for Addition

We call a pair of points P, Q *exceptional* (w.r.t. some representation) for an addition formula $\mathcal{F}$ if $\mathcal{F}(P, Q) \neq P + Q$. If moreover $P \neq \pm Q$, and both P and Q have odd prime order, we say that P, Q are *non-trivial*. This also implies that $\mathcal{F}(P, Q)$ should always have an affine representation for all $\mathcal{F}$ we discuss.

Short Weierstrass: Projective, Jacobian, Modified, w12, xyzz Coords. For short Weierstrass curves, non-triviality implies $x_1 \neq x_2$. Moreover, we do not need to consider the expression corresponding to Z_3 in the formulas by Renes et al. [34], as Bosma and Lenstra [7] prove their completeness. Since none of the Z_3 expressions depend on a particular representation of a point, we can (without loss of generality) assume

$$Z_1 = Z_2 = ZZ_1 = ZZ_2 = ZZZ_1 = ZZZ_2 = 1$$

when searching for non-trivial exceptional points, which implies $x_i = X_i, y_i = Y_i$. With this in mind, there is only a single factor that could possibly be zero in the studied Z_3 expressions, namely $(y_1 + y_2)^3$. This factor is present in all variants of the Brier-Joye [8] formulas (add-2002-bj) and Bernstein-Lange [4] formulas (add-2007-bl), illustrated in Algorithm 1. Note that $(y_1 + y_2)^3 = 0$ is equivalent to $y_1 = -y_2$, which implies

$$x_1^3 + ax_1 + b = y_1^2 = y_2^2 = x_2^3 + ax_2 + b$$
$$(x_1^2 + x_1 x_2 + x_2^2 + a)(x_1 - x_2) = 0$$
$$x_1^2 + x_1 x_2 + x_2^2 + a = 0, \quad \text{since } x_1 \neq x_2.$$

Thus, we get a family of non-trivial exceptional points

$$P = (x, y) \text{ and } Q = (x', -y) \text{ with } x \neq x',$$

equivalently characterized by $x^2 + xx' + x'^2 + a = 0$, which is a possible input to the xDCP. Izu and Takagi [26] previously identified this family for the add-2002-bj case, but not for the add-2007-bl one.

Algorithm 1. Point addition formula add-2007-bl in projective coordinates

$E/\mathbb{F}_p \colon y^2 = x^3 + ax + b,$

Require: $\quad P = (X_1 \colon Y_1 \colon Z_1),$
$\qquad\qquad Q = (X_2 \colon Y_2 \colon Z_2)$

Ensure: $(X_3 \colon Y_3 \colon Z_3) = P + Q$

1: $U_1 = X_1 \cdot Z_2$
2: $U_2 = X_2 \cdot Z_1$
3: $S_1 = Y_1 \cdot Z_2$
4: $S_2 = Y_2 \cdot Z_1$
5: $ZZ = Z_1 \cdot Z_2$
6: $T = U_1 + U_2$
7: $TT = T^2$
8: $M = S_1 + S_2$
9: $t_0 = ZZ^2$
10: $t_1 = a \cdot t_0$
11: $t_2 = U_1 \cdot U_2$
12: $t_3 = TT - t_2$
13: $R = t_3 + t_1$
14: $F = ZZ \cdot M$

15: $L = M \cdot F$
16: $LL = L^2$
17: $t_4 = T + L$
18: $t_5 = t_4^2$
19: $t_6 = t_5 - TT$
20: $G = t_6 - LL$
21: $t_7 = R^2$
22: $t_8 = 2 \cdot t_7$
23: $W = t_8 - G$
24: $t_9 = F \cdot W$
25: $X_3 = 2 \cdot t_9$
26: $t_{10} = 2 \cdot W$
27: $t_{11} = G - t_{10}$
28: $t_{12} = 2 \cdot LL$
29: $t_{13} = R \cdot t_{11}$
30: $Y_3 = t_{13} - t_{12}$
31: $t_{14} = F^2$
32: $t_{15} = F \cdot t_{14}$
33: $Z_3 = 4 \cdot t_{15}$

(Twisted) Edwards: Projective, Extended, Inverted Coords. Let $E_{a,d} \colon ax^2 + y^2 = 1 + dx^2 y^2$ be a (twisted) Edwards curve[10] (cf. Sect. 2; note that we do not impose any (non-)square restrictions on $a, d \in \mathbb{F}_p$). In order to go through all the Z_3 expressions and see when they are equal to zero, we introduce the following lemma.

---

[10] We only consider Edwards curves with $c = 1$, since the others can be isomorphically rescaled to this case without affecting the nullity of the Z_3 expressions.

Lemma 2. *Let* $P = (x_1, y_1), Q = (x_2, y_2)$ *be a pair of non-trivial exceptional points on* $E_{a,d}$. *Then the following holds:*

$$x_1 x_2 y_1 y_2 \neq 0, \tag{2}$$

$$dx_1 x_2 y_1 y_2 \neq \pm 1, \tag{3}$$

$$y_1 y_2 \neq -a x_1 x_2, \tag{4}$$

$$x_1 y_2 \neq x_2 y_1, \tag{5}$$

$$x_1 y_2 \neq -x_2 y_1, \tag{6}$$

$$y_1 y_2 \neq a x_1 x_2. \tag{7}$$

$$x_1 y_1 \neq \pm x_2 y_2. \tag{8}$$

Proof. (2) follows from the fact that neither P nor Q are 4-torsion. Hisil et al. [24] (Theorem 1, Corollary 1) prove (3), (4) and (5).

Now consider the addition law from [3]:

$$(x_1, y_1) + (y_1, y_2) = \left(\frac{x_1 y_2 + y_1 x_2}{1 + d x_1 x_2 y_1 y_2}, \frac{y_1 y_2 - a x_1 x_2}{1 - d x_1 x_2 y_1 y_2} \right).$$

Assume that either (6) or (7) is false. Since the denominators are nonzero by (3), one of the coordinates of $P + Q$ is zero, which implies $P + Q$ is a 4-torsion point. This is impossible, since both P and Q have odd order and $P \neq -Q$.

Finally, consider the addition law from [24]:

$$(x_1, y_1) + (y_1, y_2) = \left(\frac{x_1 y_1 + x_2 y_2}{y_1 y_2 + a x_1 x_2}, \frac{x_1 y_1 - x_2 y_2}{x_1 y_2 - y_1 x_2} \right).$$

Assume that (8) is false. Since the denominators are nonzero by (4) and (5), one of the coordinates of $P + Q$ is zero, which implies $P + Q$ is a 4-torsion point. This is impossible, since both P and Q have odd prime order and $P \neq -Q$. □

After factoring all the Z_3 expressions, we can (without loss of generality) set $Z_1 = Z_2 = 1$. Then we have $x_i = 1/X_i, y_i = 1/Y_i$ for inverted coordinates, and $x_i = X_i, y_i = Y_i$ for all others. Lemma 2 handles all the possible zero factors, which means that there are no non-trivial exceptional points.

4.2   Exceptional Points for Differential Addition and Ladders

Recall from Sect. 2.3 that differential addition and ladder formulas take representations of three input points $(P - Q, P, Q)$ and return the representation of $P + Q$ or $([2]P, P + Q)$, respectively.

We call a triplet of points $(P - Q, P, Q)$ *exceptional* (w.r.t. a representation) for a differential addition or ladder formula $\mathcal{F}$ if $\mathcal{F}(P - Q, P, Q) \neq P + Q$ or $\mathcal{F}(P - Q, P, Q) \neq ([2]P, P + Q)$, respectively. If moreover $P \neq \pm Q$, and both P and Q have odd prime order, we say that $(P - Q, P, Q)$ are *non-trivial*. This also implies that $\mathcal{F}(P - Q, P, Q)$ should always have an affine representation for all $\mathcal{F}$ we discuss (hence Z_4 and Z_5 should be nonzero).

Table 3. Formulas [4,8,25] with non-trivial exceptional points. The projective coordinates apply to all formula versions: $a = -1$, $a = -3$ and general a.

Curve model	Coordinates	Formula name
E_W	Projective	add-2007-bl
		add-2002-bj
	xz	dadd-2002-it, mdadd-2002-it
		ladd-2002-it, mladd-2002-it
		dadd-2002-it-3, mdadd-2002-it-3
		ladd-2002-it-3, mladd-2002-it-3
		mdadd-2002-bj, mladd-2002-bj
		mdadd-2002-bj-2, mladd-2002-bj-2
		mladd-2002-bj-3

Short Weierstrass: xz Coords. In this case, the inputs are $P - Q = (X_1, Z_1)$, $P = (X_2, Z_2)$, $Q = (X_3, Z_3)$ on $E_W/\mathbb{F}_p : y^2 = x^3 + ax + b$; the outputs are (X_4, Z_4) for diff. addition and $(X_4, Z_4), (X_5, Z_5)$ for ladders.

Setting $Z_1 = Z_2 = Z_3 = 1$ and $x_1 = X_1, x_2 = X_2, x_3 = X_3$, the only possibilities for $Z_4 = 0$ or $Z_5 = 0$ that arise in the formulas are $x_2 = x_3$, $x_2^3 + ax_2 + b = 0$, and $x_1 = 0$. Only the latter corresponds[11] to a triplet of non-trivial exceptional points $((0 : 1) - Q, (0 : 1), Q)$, whenever b is a square in $\mathbb{F}_p$. The impacted formulas are {d/l}add-2002-it, {d/l}add-2002-it-3, and their mixed variants, as well as mdadd-2002-bj, m{l/d}add-2002-bj-2, and mladd-2002-bj-3.

Montgomery: xz Coords. Here, the inputs are $P - Q = (X_1, Z_1)$, $P = (X_2, Z_2)$, $Q = (X_3, Z_3)$ on $E_M/\mathbb{F}_p : By^2 = x^3 + Ax^2 + x$; the outputs are (X_4, Z_4) for diff. addition and $(X_4, Z_4), (X_5, Z_5)$ for ladders.

Setting $Z_1 = Z_2 = Z_3 = 1$ and $x_1 = X_1, x_2 = X_2, x_3 = X_3$, the only possibilities for $Z_4 = 0$ or $Z_5 = 0$ that arise in the formulas are $x_1 = 0$, $x_2 = 0$, $x_2 = 1/2 \cdot (-a \pm \sqrt{a^2 - 4})$, $x_2 = x_3$ and $(x_2 - 1)(x_3 + 1) = (x_2 + 1)(x_3 - 1)$. Section 2 shows that the former three correspond to points of order 2 (though $\sqrt{a^2 - 4}$ might not exist over $\mathbb{F}_p$). The last one implies either $x_2 - 1 = x_3 - 1 = 0$, or $x_2 + 1 = x_3 + 1 = 0$, or else

$$1 - \frac{2}{x_2 + 1} = \frac{x_2 - 1}{x_2 + 1} = \frac{x_3 - 1}{x_3 + 1} = 1 - \frac{2}{x_3 + 1}.$$

In all of these cases, we have $x_2 = x_3$, hence the corresponding points are trivial.

Edwards: yz, yzsquared Coords. Recall that in these cases, $d = r^2$ for some $r \neq \pm 1$ in $\mathbb{F}_p^*$. The inputs are $P - Q = (Y_1, Z_1)$, $P = (Y_2, Z_2)$, $Q = (Y_3, Z_3)$ on $E_E/\mathbb{F}_p : x^2 + y^2 = 1 + r^2 x^2 y^2$; the outputs are (Y_4, Z_4) for diff. addition and

---

[11] Note that x_1 does not directly affect X_4 nor X_5.

$(Y_4, Z_4), (Y_5, Z_5)$ for ladders. In fact, (Y_4, Z_4) for ladders is just a special case of (Y_5, Z_5) with $Y_2 = Y_3, Z_2 = Z_3$, so we may ignore it.

Setting $Z_1 = Z_2 = Z_3 = 1$, we get $y_1 = Y_1/r, y_2 = Y_2/r, y_3 = Y_3/r$ for the yz coordinates, and $y_1^2 = Y_1/r, y_2^2 = Y_2/r, y_3^2 = Y_3/r$ for the yzsquared coordinates, the ladder Z_5 and diff. addition Z_4 coincide for all of these formulas. The only conditions to analyze are $y_1 = 0$ (which is a trivial case as it corresponds to 4-torsion $P - Q$) and

$$(1 + ry_2^2)(1 + ry_3^2) = \frac{r+1}{r-1}\left(1 - ry_2^2\right)\left(1 - ry_3^2\right),$$

which implies

$$(r - 1)(1 + ry_2^2 + ry_3^2 + r^2y_2^2y_3^2) = (r + 1)(1 - ry_2^2 - ry_3^2 + r^2y_2^2y_3^2)$$
$$-2 + 2r^2y_2^2 + 2r^2y_3^2 - 2r^2y_2^2y_3^2 = 0$$
$$r^2y_3^2(1 - y_2^2) = 1 - r^2y_2^2. \tag{9}$$

If $1 - r^2y_2^2 = 0$, then either $y_3 = 0$ or $y_2^2 = 1$, implying Q or P being 4-torsion. In the other case, we get

$$y_3^2 = \frac{1 - r^2y_2^2}{r^2(1 - y_2^2)} = \frac{1}{r^2x_2^2},$$

and since (9) is symmetric, analogical arguments yield

$$y_2^2 = \frac{1 - r^2y_3^2}{r^2(1 - y_3^2)} = \frac{1}{r^2x_3^2}.$$

Thus the only case left to consider is $x_2^2y_3^2 = x_3^2y_2^2 = \frac{1}{r^2}$. But then we have $(1 + dx_2x_3y_2y_3)(1 - dx_2x_3y_2y_3) = 1 - r^4x_2^2x_3^2y_2^2y_3^2 = 0$, which is impossible for non-trivial exceptional points by (3) in Lemma 2.

5   Practical Implications

This work has several practical implications, stemming from (i) its findings on exceptional points for EFD formulas; (ii) its development of a ZVP-like attack on windowed scalar multiplication methods; and (iii) improvements to the techniques used in the ZVP and EPA attacks.

5.1   Impact on Cryptographic Libraries

We examined the EC arithmetic implementations in 15 popular open-source cryptographic libraries. Table 4 lists their scalar multiplication algorithm, coordinates, and addition formulas. The focus of our analysis was on ECDH operations over E_W, and in case the library implements several algorithms, we list the one used for generic curves. Most analyzed libraries use Jacobian coordinates, for which we report no classes of non-trivial exceptional points in any of the formulas on EFD. One could conclude that the impact of the new classes of exceptional points is thus negligible. However, these libraries represent only a fraction of the uses of addition formulas. Implementations of EC arithmetic, potentially using one of the addition formulas with non-trivial exceptional points, are found in pairing-based cryptography, password-authenticated key exchange, or many zero-knowledge proof system implementations, which we did not examine.

The discovered classes of exceptional points are unexpected from the point-of-view of a developer. While many developers know that formulas which are not complete or unified need special handling, they do not expect seemingly unrelated points causing issues in the formula. There is thus nothing stopping the developer from misusing the formulas, as the formula papers or the EFD give no warning. We illustrate this by presenting a history of issues surrounding exceptional cases in formulas used by cryptographic libraries.

NSS: Unimplemented Exceptions. For generic E_W, NSS has three different implementations of EC arithmetic. The first is pure affine, which we disregard. The second is mixed point addition using an implementation of `madd-2004-hmv`, optimized for $a = -3$. However, the code failed to account for the $P = \pm Q$ cases. Furthermore, the corresponding point doubling is an implementation of `dbl-1998-cmo-2`, and failed to account for the $2P = \mathcal{O}$ case. Mozilla issued CVE-2015-2730[12] to track these issues.

NSS: More Unimplemented Exceptions. The last, and most generic E_W arithmetic in NSS, is mixed point addition using a `madd-2004-hmv` implementation, with no optimizations for curve coefficients. Two years after the previous issue, Valenta, Sullivan, Sanso, and Heninger [37, Section 7.2] uncovered the analogous flaw in this code. There were no corresponding flaws in point doubling. Mozilla issued CVE-2017-7781[13] to track this issue.

OpenSSL: Broken Ladder. In 2018, OpenSSL switched to a ladder implementation for generic E_W scalar multiplications. Work by Tuveri et al. [36] prompted the change. For the ladder step, the initial code, merged to the development branch, was an implementation of `ladd-2002-it-3`. Unfortunately, this code fails in the case of a particular x-coordinate being zero (Sect. 4.2). One month passed between merging the broken implementation and the fix[14], switching to `ladd-2002-it-4`. The discovery[15] was mostly luck – during standardization, GOST curves utilized generators with the smallest possible x-coordinate.

BoringSSL: Untaken Exceptions Leak. Historically, Google's BoringSSL only supports a very narrow subset of curves: P-224, P-256, P-384, P-521, and Curve25519. Weiser et al. [39] discovered timing leaks in BoringSSL's point addition formulas, affecting the legacy NIST curves in the aforementioned list. The

---

[12] https://cve.mitre.org/cgi-bin/cvename.cgi?name=CVE-2015-2730.

[13] https://cve.mitre.org/cgi-bin/cvename.cgi?name=CVE-2017-7781.

[14] https://github.com/openssl/openssl/pull/7000.

[15] https://github.com/openssl/openssl/issues/6999.

leaks were in three distinct implementations: P-224 and P-256 have dedicated EC arithmetic stacks, while P-384 and P-521 share a single stack. In all cases, the root cause is short circuit logic: a snippet from the vulnerabilities follows.

```
if (x_equal && y_equal && !z1_is_zero && !z2_is_zero)
```

The first two variables are booleans tracking whether the two x-coordinates are equal (resp. y), and the last two ensure neither operand is $\mathcal{O}$ by checking if the z-coordinates are zero. This C statement is not constant-time. For instance:

- if the first branch fails, this tells the attacker the x-coordinates are not equal;
- if the second branch fails, this tells the attacker the x-coordinates are equal, but the y-coordinates are not;
- if the third branch fails, this tells the attacker the x- and y-coordinates are equal, and the first operand is $\mathcal{O}$;
- if the fourth branch fails, this tells the attacker the x- and y-coordinates are equal, the first operand is not $\mathcal{O}$, yet the last operand is $\mathcal{O}$;
- if no branch fails, this tells the attacker the x- and y-coordinates are equal, and neither operand is $\mathcal{O}$ (subsequently early exiting to point doubling).

For example, this leak is relevant at the beginning of scalar multiplication, in various cases where the accumulator takes the value $\mathcal{O}$. These (probabilistically) small leaks are often sufficient for lattice-based cryptanalysis of nonce-based digital signature schemes, such as ECDSA. We feel this case is particularly interesting, since it is not the exception itself that usually leaks, but rather the *check* for the exception. Google fixed[16] the issues in 2019.

Python fastecdsa: Division by Zero. The Python module `fastecdsa` is an extension module, backed by GNU MP, a multiprecision arithmetic library written in C. It implements the ECDSA signature scheme[17], also providing flexible EC arithmetic with affine coordinates. The module supports generic E_W curves, as well as several standardized curves with fixed parameters, and E_W versions of modern E_E and E_T curves such as Curve25519 and Curve448. Using our Sect. 4 methodology, we discovered[18] that the point doubling code does not handle the $2P = \mathcal{O}$ case properly. The C code ignores the return code from GNU MP's modular inversion function. In the $y = 0$ case, this leads to a silent division by zero, and incorrect results for points with even order. While this naturally affected generic `fastecdsa` curves, the E_W versions of Curve25519 and Curve448 were impacted the most. This is because all other standardized curves built into `fastecdsa` have large prime order.

5.2   Attack Improvements

Previous ZVP attacks targeting addition formulas on different scalar multiplication methods required the computation of large degree division polynomials.

---

[16] https://boringssl.googlesource.com/boringssl/+/12d9ed670da3edd64ce8175c.

[17] https://pypi.org/project/fastecdsa/.

[18] https://github.com/AntonKueltz/fastecdsa/pull/58.

Table 4. Libraries analyzed in this work, in the context of ECDH over E_W, i.e. both key generation (KEYGEN) and shared secret derivation (DERIVE). For libraries supporting multiple choices of coordinates or formulas, we report the most generic and default setting.

Library	Operation	Scalar multiplier	Coordinates	Formulas
BouncyCastle	KEYGEN	Comb	Modified	add-1998-cmo-2
1.68	DERIVE	Window NAF	Modified	add-1998-cmo-2
BoringSSL	KEYGEN	Fixed window	Jacobian	add-2007-bl
9f55d97	DERIVE	Fixed window	Jacobian	add-2007-bl
Botan	KEYGEN	Fixed window	Jacobian-3	add-1998-cmo-2
2.18.0	DERIVE	Fixed window	Jacobian-3	add-1998-cmo-2
Crypto++	KEYGEN	Sliding window	Affine	textbook[a]
8.5.0	DERIVE	Sliding window	Affine	textbook[a]
fastecdsa	KEYGEN	Ladder	Affine	textbook[a]
2.2.1	DERIVE	Ladder	Affine	textbook[a]
libgcrypt	KEYGEN	Basic left-to-right	Jacobian	add-1998-hnm
1.9.3	DERIVE	Basic left-to-right	Jacobian	add-1998-hnm
LibreSSL	KEYGEN	Ladder	Jacobian	add-1998-hnm
3.3.3	DERIVE	Ladder	Jacobian	add-1998-hnm
libtomcrypt	KEYGEN	Sliding window	Jacobian	add-1998-hnm
0.18.2	DERIVE	Sliding window	Jacobian	add-1998-hnm
IPP-crypto	KEYGEN	Window NAF	Jacobian	add-1998-cmo-2
2021.2	DERIVE	Window NAF	Jacobian	add-1998-cmo-2
Microsoft CNG	KEYGEN	Fixed window	Jacobian	add-2007-bl
6d019ce	DERIVE	Fixed window	Jacobian	add-2007-bl
NSS	KEYGEN	Window NAF	Jacobian	madd-2004-hmv
3.65	DERIVE	Window NAF	Jacobian	madd-2004-hmv
OpenSSL	KEYGEN	Ladder	xz	mladd-2002-it-4
1.1.1k	DERIVE	Ladder	xz	mladd-2002-it-4
wolfSSL	KEYGEN	Sliding window	Jacobian	add-1998-hnm
4.7.0	DERIVE	Sliding window	Jacobian	add-1998-hnm
MatrixSSL	KEYGEN	Sliding window	Jacobian	add-1998-hnm
4.3.0	DERIVE	Sliding window	Jacobian	add-1998-hnm
Go 1.16.4	KEYGEN	Basic left-to-right	Jacobian	add-2007-bl
crypto/elliptic	DERIVE	Basic left-to-right	Jacobian	add-2007-bl

[a]Using textbook chord-and-tangent addition formulas.

This limited the attack to only recover a small amount of secret scalar bits. On the other hand, our proposed attack on windowed scalar multiplication methods from Sect. 3.5 allows the attacker to recover the full scalar. Thus, this shows that windowed methods of scalar multiplication are somewhat more vulnerable to ZVP-like attacks. We simulated the attack using the **pyecsca** toolkit, and were able to recover the full secret scalar from a window NAF algorithm with `add-2016-rcb` formulas on the P-224 curve. In the attack, we do not observe a real power or EM side channel, but the toolkit simulates the computation down to individual finite field operations, and produces the side-channel output (i.e., whether a zero occurred during computation). Appendix A shows the attack code snippets. Note that the P-224 curve does not have any zero-coordinate point suitable for the RPA attack, and the used formulas are complete, disallowing the possibility of an EPA attack.

We also expanded the range of scalars for which the (x)DCP can be solved. While this increases the number of recovered bits only slightly, our improvements are quite general and might be combined with future ones.

5.3 Tooling

We released all of our code and data under an open-source license, as an extension to the **pyecsca** project[19]. This includes tooling for unrolling EFD formulas, helping analyze exceptional cases, and automatically construct ZVP points (note that Akishita and Takagi [1] construct them manually), as well as improvements to (x)DCP solving (Sect. 3.3). These tools can be used proactively in the future, analyzing formulas about to be used in new implementations, rather than analyzing existing implementations and finding vulnerabilities.

5.4 Reverse Engineering

Another application of our techniques is in reverse engineering black-box implementations of ECC, as suggested in [27]. Many side-channel attacks critically depend on the attacker having detailed knowledge of the target's implementation, such as the scalar multiplication algorithm, coordinates, or even specific formulas used. In practice (e.g., smartcards), vendors keep this information secret; de facto using security-by-obscurity.

In our unified framework, reverse engineering is an easier problem than attacking. Indeed, it suffices to choose f as an intermediate value of a point addition formula, then solve the (x)DCP problem for several small values of k. Our methodology allows us to choose f in a manner that allows us to identify the target addition formulas, after confirming one of our guesses (e.g., using $k = 1$ and $k = 2$). Furthermore, as the sequence of formula executions during scalar multiplication with a fixed scalar depends on the scalar multiplication algorithm used, we can apply our technique to identify this algorithm as well.

6 Conclusion

In this work, we presented a unified framework for the RPA, ZVP, and EPA attacks, and demonstrated its utility by mounting an attack on window-based

---

[19] https://github.com/crocs-muni/formula-for-disaster.

scalar multiplication methods (Sect. 3.5). We were also able to push the ZVP and EPA attacks further: introducing the dependent coordinates problem, and solving it for new cases. We created automated tooling that unrolls formulas and constructs ZVP points, which was only possible manually before. We released all our code and data as an open-source extension of the **pyecsca** toolkit, with the hope that they can serve as a basis for future work.

As a result of our systematic classification, we uncovered new classes of exceptional points in EFD formulas. These formulas are, however, currently not used by any of the open-source cryptographic libraries we analyzed, which we see more as happenstance than competence – for example, OpenSSL was using `ladd-2002-it-3` not that long ago.

Lessons Learned. Our Sect. 5 results demonstrate Murphy's law, in action, (sometimes) in real code, with (at least) billions of deployments. Furthermore, they highlight our failure as a research community. We know of these exceptions for over two decades, yet we are still unable to eradicate legacy theoretical constructs and code from real-world standards, products, and systems. This is exacerbated by the fact that, again as a research community, we often prioritize speed over security, in the name of establishing novelty for scientific contributions. These are often then left in dubious hands, without diligent technology transfer, and with little to no knowledge of how to apply them safely. This is precisely where our Sect. 4 results help, by providing feedback on the type and nature of failures in various EC arithmetic formulas. All of these results are enabled by our unified attack framework in Sect. 3.

We believe that in order to prevent future vulnerabilities, we should start paying more attention to the properties of the formulas and their assumptions, and clearly document them in libraries, papers, and the EFD.

Acknowledgments. The authors would like thank Marek Sys for helpful consultations. This project has initially received funding from the European Research Council (ERC) under the European Union's Horizon 2020 research and innovation programme (grant agreement No 804476), and it has been made possible in part by a grant from the Cisco University Research Program Fund, an advised fund of Silicon Valley Community Foundation. This project started when J. J. Chi-Domínguez was a postdoctoral researcher at Tampere University. V. Sedlacek and J. Jancar were supported by Czech Science Foundation project GA20-03426S. J. Jancar was also supported by Red Hat Czech and V. Sedlacek by the Ph.D. Talent Scholarship - funded by the Brno City Municipality.

A   Example: ZVP Attack on Window NAF Scalar Multiplication

To demonstrate the ZVP attack on a window NAF scalar multiplication algorithm (window size of 5), we used the **pyecsca** toolkit. We demonstrate the attack on NIST's P-224 curve, which has no points suitable for RPA. Figure 2 shows the basic setup of the attack, with `zvp_p0` being a point which zeros out an intermediate value when input into the `add-2016-rcb` formulas in projective coordinates, regardless of the second input point (Fig. 3).

B   Example: Unrolled Formula

To analyze the ZVP and EPA attacks, we developed tooling for "unrolling" EFD formulas. The tooling expresses all the intermediate values in the formula as polynomials in the input variables. Figure 4 gives an excerpt of the unrolled `add-2007-bl` formula in projective coordinates on short Weierstrass curves.

```
x = Mod(0xd83d7049c30873afc4893bf229d1c1ccb9eefd30f62ec71504b65fdc, p)
y = Mod(0x27c28fb63cf78c503b76c40dd62e3e32461102cf09d138eafb49a025, p)
z = Mod(1, p)
zvp_p0 = Point(coords, X=x, Y=y, Z=z)

def zvp_c(c):
    """Compute [c^-1]P_0"""
    return params.curve.affine_multiply(zvp_p0.to_affine(),
            int(Mod(c, params.order).inverse())).to_model(coords, params.curve)

def query(pt: Point) -> Tuple[int, List[int]]:
    """Query the implementation and observe the ZVP side-channel,
        i.e. at which iterations a zero in the intermediate value appeared.
        Returns the total number of formula applications and indexes
        where a zero in the intermediate value appeared."""
    with local(DefaultContext()) as ctx:
        mult.init(params, pt)
        mult.multiply(scalar)
    smult, subtree = ctx.actions.get_by_index([1])
    iterations = []
    for i, formula_action in enumerate(subtree):
        for intermediate in formula_action.intermediates.values():
            if 0 in [j.value for j in intermediate]:
                iterations.append(i)
                break
    return len(subtree), iterations

def try_guess(guess) -> bool:
    """Test if we have the right private key."""
    return params.curve.affine_multiply(g, guess) == pubkey
```

Fig. 2. Setup for the ZVP window NAF attack.

```
wnaf_multiples = [1, 3, 5, 7, 9, 11, 13, 15, -1, -3, -5, -7, -9, -11, -13, -15]
all_iters = {}
for multiple in wnaf_multiples:
    rpa_point = zvp_c(multiple)
    num_iters, iters = query(rpa_point)
    all_iters[multiple] = iters
full = [0 for _ in range(num_iters)]
for multiple, iters in all_iters.items():
    for i in iters:
        full[i] = multiple
full_wnaf = [e for i, e in enumerate(full) if (not full[i - 1] != 0) or i in (0, 1)]
full_wnaf[0] = 1
```

Fig. 3. ZVP attack demonstration on window NAF scalar multiplication algorithm.

```
U1 = Z2 * X1
U2 = Z1 * X2
S1 = Z2 * Y1
S2 = Z1 * Y2
ZZ = Z2 * Z1
T  = X2*Z1 + X1*Z2
TT = (X2*Z1 + X1*Z2)^2
M  = Y2*Z1 + Y1*Z2
t0 = Z2^2 * Z1^2
t1 = a * Z2^2 * Z1^2
t2 = Z2 * Z1 * X2 * X1
t3 = X2^2*Z1^2 + X1*X2*Z1*Z2 + X1^2*Z2^2
R  = a*Z1^2*Z2^2 + X2^2*Z1^2 + X1*X2*Z1*Z2 + X1^2*Z2^2
F  = Z2 * Z1 * (Y2*Z1 + Y1*Z2)
L  = Z2 * Z1 * (Y2*Z1 + Y1*Z2)^2
LL = Z2^2 * Z1^2 * (Y2*Z1 + Y1*Z2)^4
t4 = Y2^2*Z1^3*Z2 + 2*Y1*Y2*Z1^2*Z2^2 + Y1^2*Z1*Z2^3 + X2*Z1 + X1*Z2
...
X3 = 2^2 * Z2 * Z1 * (Y2*Z1 + Y1*Z2) * (a^2*Z1^4*Z2^4 + 2*a*X2^2*Z1^4*Z2^2 +
     2*a*X1*X2*Z1^3*Z2^3 + 2*a*X1^2*Z1^2*Z2^4 + X2^4*Z1^4 + 2*X1*X2^3*Z1^3*Z2 -
     X2*Y2^2*Z1^4*Z2 + 3*X1^2*X2^2*Z1^2*Z2^2 - 2*X2*Y1*Y2*Z1^3*Z2^2 -
     X1*Y2^2*Z1^3*Z2^2 + 2*X1^3*X2*Z1*Z2^3 - X2*Y1^2*Z1^2*Z2^3 -
     2*X1*Y1*Y2*Z1^2*Z2^3 + X1^4*Z2^4 - X1*Y1^2*Z1*Z2^4)
...
```

Fig. 4. An excerpt of an unrolled formula, `add-2007-bl` in projective coordinates on short Weierstrass curves.

References

1. Akishita, T., Takagi, T.: Zero-value point attacks on elliptic curve cryptosystem. In: Boyd, C., Mao, W. (eds.) ISC 2003. LNCS, vol. 2851, pp. 218–233. Springer, Heidelberg (2003). https://doi.org/10.1007/10958513_17
2. Belyavsky, D., Brumley, B.B., Chi-Domínguez, J., Rivera-Zamarripa, L., Ustinov, I.: Set it and forget it! Turnkey ECC for instant integration. In: ACSAC 2020: Annual Computer Security Applications Conference, Virtual Event/Austin, TX, USA, 7–11 December 2020, pp. 760–771. ACM (2020). https://doi.org/10.1145/3427228.3427291

3. Bernstein, D.J., Birkner, P., Joye, M., Lange, T., Peters, C.: Twisted Edwards curves. In: Vaudenay, S. (ed.) AFRICACRYPT 2008. LNCS, vol. 5023, pp. 389–405. Springer, Heidelberg (2008). https://doi.org/10.1007/978-3-540-68164-9_26

4. Bernstein, D.J., Lange, T.: Explicit-Formulas database (EFD) (2007). https://www.hyperelliptic.org/EFD/

5. Bernstein, D.J., Lange, T.: Faster addition and doubling on elliptic curves. In: Kurosawa, K. (ed.) ASIACRYPT 2007. LNCS, vol. 4833, pp. 29–50. Springer, Heidelberg (2007). https://doi.org/10.1007/978-3-540-76900-2_3

6. Bernstein, D.J., Lange, T.: Inverted Edwards coordinates. In: Boztaş, S., Lu, H.-F.F. (eds.) AAECC 2007. LNCS, vol. 4851, pp. 20–27. Springer, Heidelberg (2007). https://doi.org/10.1007/978-3-540-77224-8_4

7. Bosma, W., Lenstra, H.W., Jr.: Complete systems of two addition laws for elliptic curves. J. Number Theory **53**(2), 229–240 (1995). https://doi.org/10.1006/jnth.1995.1088

8. Brier, É., Joye, M.: Weierstraß elliptic curves and side-channel attacks. In: Naccache, D., Paillier, P. (eds.) PKC 2002. LNCS, vol. 2274, pp. 335–345. Springer, Heidelberg (2002). https://doi.org/10.1007/3-540-45664-3_24

9. Castryck, W., Galbraith, S.D., Farashahi, R.R.: Efficient arithmetic on elliptic curves using a mixed Edwards-Montgomery representation. IACR Cryptol. ePrint Arch. 2008(218) (2008). http://eprint.iacr.org/2008/218

10. Chudnovsky, D.V., Chudnovsky, G.V.: Sequences of numbers generated by addition in formal groups and new primality and factorization tests. Adv. Appl. Math. **7**(4), 385–434 (1986). https://doi.org/10.1016/0196-8858(86)90023-0

11. Cohen, H., Miyaji, A., Ono, T.: Efficient elliptic curve exponentiation using mixed coordinates. In: Ohta, K., Pei, D. (eds.) ASIACRYPT 1998. LNCS, vol. 1514, pp. 51–65. Springer, Heidelberg (1998). https://doi.org/10.1007/3-540-49649-1_6

12. Costello, C., Lange, T., Naehrig, M.: Faster pairing computations on curves with high-degree twists. In: Nguyen, P.Q., Pointcheval, D. (eds.) PKC 2010. LNCS, vol. 6056, pp. 224–242. Springer, Heidelberg (2010). https://doi.org/10.1007/978-3-642-13013-7_14

13. Costello, C., Smith, B.: Montgomery curves and their arithmetic - the case of large characteristic fields. J. Cryptogr. Eng. **8**(3), 227–240 (2018). https://doi.org/10.1007/s13389-017-0157-6

14. Crépeau, C., Kazmi, R.A.: An analysis of ZVP-attack on ECC cryptosystems. IACR Cryptol. ePrint Arch. 2012(329) (2012). https://eprint.iacr.org/2012/329

15. Danger, J., Guilley, S., Hoogvorst, P., Murdica, C., Naccache, D.: Dynamic countermeasure against the zero power analysis. In: IEEE International Symposium on Signal Processing and Information Technology, Athens, Greece, 12–15 December 2013, pp. 140–147. IEEE Computer Society (2013). https://doi.org/10.1109/ISSPIT.2013.6781869

16. Danger, J.-L., Guilley, S., Hoogvorst, P., Murdica, C., Naccache, D.: A synthesis of side-channel attacks on elliptic curve cryptography in smart-cards. J. Cryptogr. Eng. **3**(4), 241–265 (2013). https://doi.org/10.1007/s13389-013-0062-6

17. Edwards, H.M.: A normal form for elliptic curves. Bull. Amer. Math. Soc. (N.S.) **44**(3), 393–422 (2007). https://doi.org/10.1090/S0273-0979-07-01153-6

18. Fan, J., Gierlichs, B., Vercauteren, F.: To infinity and beyond: combined attack on ECC using points of low order. In: Preneel, B., Takagi, T. (eds.) CHES 2011. LNCS, vol. 6917, pp. 143–159. Springer, Heidelberg (2011). https://doi.org/10.1007/978-3-642-23951-9_10

19. Gaudry, P.: Variants of the Montgomery form based on Theta functions. Toronto, November 2006

20. Goubin, L.: A refined power-analysis attack on elliptic curve cryptosystems. In: Desmedt, Y.G. (ed.) PKC 2003. LNCS, vol. 2567, pp. 199–211. Springer, Heidelberg (2003). https://doi.org/10.1007/3-540-36288-6_15

21. Hankerson, D., Menezes, A., Vanstone, S.: Guide to Elliptic Curve Cryptography. Springer Professional Computing, Springer, New York (2004). https://doi.org/10.1016/s0012-365x(04)00102-5

22. Hasegawa, T., Nakajima, J., Matsui, M.: A practical implementation of elliptic curve cryptosystems over $GF(p)$ on a 16-bit microcomputer. In: Imai, H., Zheng, Y. (eds.) PKC 1998. LNCS, vol. 1431, pp. 182–194. Springer, Heidelberg (1998). https://doi.org/10.1007/BFb0054024

23. Hisil, H., Carter, G., Dawson, E.: New formulae for efficient elliptic curve arithmetic. In: Srinathan, K., Rangan, C.P., Yung, M. (eds.) INDOCRYPT 2007. LNCS, vol. 4859, pp. 138–151. Springer, Heidelberg (2007). https://doi.org/10.1007/978-3-540-77026-8_11

24. Hisil, H., Wong, K.K.-H., Carter, G., Dawson, E.: Twisted Edwards curves revisited. In: Pieprzyk, J. (ed.) ASIACRYPT 2008. LNCS, vol. 5350, pp. 326–343. Springer, Heidelberg (2008). https://doi.org/10.1007/978-3-540-89255-7_20

25. Izu, T., Takagi, T.: A fast parallel elliptic curve multiplication resistant against side channel attacks. In: Naccache, D., Paillier, P. (eds.) PKC 2002. LNCS, vol. 2274, pp. 280–296. Springer, Heidelberg (2002). https://doi.org/10.1007/3-540-45664-3_20

26. Izu, T., Takagi, T.: Exceptional procedure attack on elliptic curve cryptosystems. In: Desmedt, Y.G. (ed.) PKC 2003. LNCS, vol. 2567, pp. 224–239. Springer, Heidelberg (2003). https://doi.org/10.1007/3-540-36288-6_17

27. Jancar, J.: PYECSCA: reverse-engineering black-box elliptic curve cryptography implementations via side-channels. Master's thesis, Masaryk University, Brno, Czechia (2020). https://is.muni.cz/th/fjgay/

28. Koblitz, N.: Elliptic curve cryptosystems. Math. Comput. **48**(177), 203–209 (1987). https://doi.org/10.2307/2007884

29. Martínez, S., Sadornil, D., Tena, J., Tomàs, R., Valls, M.: On Edwards curves and ZVP-attacks. Appl. Algebra Eng. Commun. Comput. **24**(6), 507–517 (2013). https://doi.org/10.1007/s00200-013-0211-2

30. Meloni, N.: New point addition formulae for ECC applications. In: Carlet, C., Sunar, B. (eds.) WAIFI 2007. LNCS, vol. 4547, pp. 189–201. Springer, Heidelberg (2007). https://doi.org/10.1007/978-3-540-73074-3_15

31. Miller, V.S.: Use of elliptic curves in cryptography. In: Williams, H.C. (ed.) CRYPTO 1985. LNCS, vol. 218, pp. 417–426. Springer, Heidelberg (1986). https://doi.org/10.1007/3-540-39799-X_31

32. Montgomery, P.L.: Speeding the Pollard and elliptic curve methods of factorization. Math. Comput. **48**(177), 243–264 (1987). https://doi.org/10.2307/2007888

33. Murdica, C., Guilley, S., Danger, J.-L., Hoogvorst, P., Naccache, D.: Same values power analysis using special points on elliptic curves. In: Schindler, W., Huss, S.A. (eds.) COSADE 2012. LNCS, vol. 7275, pp. 183–198. Springer, Heidelberg (2012). https://doi.org/10.1007/978-3-642-29912-4_14

34. Renes, J., Costello, C., Batina, L.: Complete addition formulas for prime order elliptic curves. In: Fischlin, M., Coron, J.-S. (eds.) EUROCRYPT 2016. LNCS, vol. 9665, pp. 403–428. Springer, Heidelberg (2016). https://doi.org/10.1007/978-3-662-49890-3_16

35. Smart, N.P.: An analysis of Goubin's refined power analysis attack. In: Walter, C.D., Koç, Ç.K., Paar, C. (eds.) CHES 2003. LNCS, vol. 2779, pp. 281–290. Springer, Heidelberg (2003). https://doi.org/10.1007/978-3-540-45238-6_23

36. Tuveri, N., ul Hassan, S., Pereida García, C., Brumley, B.B.: Side-channel analysis of SM2: a late-stage featurization case study. In: Proceedings of the 34th Annual Computer Security Applications Conference, ACSAC 2018, San Juan, PR, USA, 03–07 December 2018, pp. 147–160. ACM (2018). https://doi.org/10.1145/3274694.3274725
37. Valenta, L., Sullivan, N., Sanso, A., Heninger, N.: In search of CurveSwap: measuring elliptic curve implementations in the wild. In: 2018 IEEE European Symposium on Security and Privacy, EuroS&P 2018, London, United Kingdom, 24–26 April 2018, pp. 384–398. IEEE (2018). https://doi.org/10.1109/EuroSP.2018.00034
38. Washington, L.C.: Elliptic Curves: Number Theory and Cryptography. Discrete Mathematics and Its Applications, 2nd edn. Chapman and Hall/CRC (2008). https://doi.org/10.1201/9781420071474
39. Weiser, S., Schrammel, D., Bodner, L., Spreitzer, R.: Big numbers - big troubles: systematically analyzing nonce leakage in (EC)DSA implementations. In: Capkun, S., Roesner, F. (eds.) 29th USENIX Security Symposium, USENIX Security 2020, 12–14 August 2020, pp. 1767–1784. USENIX Association (2020). https://www.usenix.org/conference/usenixsecurity20/presentation/weiser
40. Zhang, F., Lin, Q., Liu, S.: Zero-value point attacks on Kummer-based cryptosystem. In: Bao, F., Samarati, P., Zhou, J. (eds.) ACNS 2012. LNCS, vol. 7341, pp. 293–310. Springer, Heidelberg (2012). https://doi.org/10.1007/978-3-642-31284-7_18

Cryptanalysis of an Oblivious PRF from Supersingular Isogenies

Andrea Basso[1(✉)], Péter Kutas[1,6(✉)], Simon-Philipp Merz[2(✉)],
Christophe Petit[1,3(✉)], and Antonio Sanso[4,5(✉)]

[1] University of Birmingham, Birmingham, UK
a.basso@cs.bham.ac.uk, p.kutas@bham.ac.uk
[2] Royal Holloway, University of London, Egham, UK
simon-philipp.merz.2018@rhul.ac.uk
[3] Université Libre de Bruxelles, Brussels, Belgium
christophe.petit@ulb.be
[4] Ethereum Foundation, Zug, Switzerland
antonio.sanso@ethereum.org
[5] Ruhr Universität Bochum, Bochum, Germany
[6] Eötvös Loránd University, Budapest, Hungary

Abstract. We cryptanalyse the SIDH-based oblivious pseudorandom function from supersingular isogenies proposed at Asiacrypt'20 by Boneh, Kogan and Woo. To this end, we give an attack on an assumption, the auxiliary one-more assumption, that was introduced by Boneh et al. and we show that this leads to an attack on the oblivious PRF itself. The attack breaks the pseudorandomness as it allows adversaries to evaluate the OPRF without further interactions with the server after some initial OPRF evaluations and some offline computations. More specifically, we first propose a polynomial-time attack. Then, we argue it is easy to change the OPRF protocol to include some countermeasures, and present a second subexponential attack that succeeds in the presence of said countermeasures. Both attacks break the security parameters suggested by Boneh et al. Furthermore, we provide a proof of concept implementation as well as some timings of our attack. Finally, we examine the generation of one of the OPRF parameters and argue that a trusted third party is needed to guarantee provable security.

1 Introduction

An oblivious pseudorandom function (OPRF) is a two-party protocol between a client and a server that computes a pseudorandom function (PRF) on a client's input with the server's key. At the end, the server does not learn anything about the client's input or the output of the function and the client learns the evaluation of the OPRF but nothing about the server's key. In particular, a client should not be able to compute the OPRF on any input without the server's participation.

Moreover, a *verifiable* oblivious pseudo random function (VOPRF) is an OPRF, where a server commits to some key and the client is ensured that the server

© International Association for Cryptologic Research 2021
M. Tibouchi and H. Wang (Eds.): ASIACRYPT 2021, LNCS 13090, pp. 160–184, 2021.
https://doi.org/10.1007/978-3-030-92062-3_6

used this key to evaluate the OPRF. In particular, the client is guaranteed that a server does not change their secret key across different executions of the protocol.

Oblivious pseudorandom functions are an important building block in many cryptographic applications. They can be used for private set intersection [23], which in turn has many applications such as private contact discovery for messaging services [14] or checking for compromised credentials [25]. Further applications of (V)OPRFs include password-authenticated key exchange [22], password-management systems [16], adaptive oblivious transfer [24], password-protected secret sharing [21] and privacy-preserving CAPTCHA systems [10].

Apart from their theoretical relevance in cryptography, OPRFs have had significant real-world impact recently. The password-authenticated key exchange OPAQUE [22] which is built on an OPRF is intended for use in TLS 1.3 [33].

The privacy-preserving authorisation mechanism known as Privacy Pass by Davidson et al. [10] is also based entirely on the security of a VOPRF. Privacy Pass is currently used at scale by Cloudflare. There is an ongoing effort to standardise OPRFs at the Crypto Forum Research Group (CFRG) [11].

Generic techniques from two-party computation and zero-knowledge proofs can be used to construct verifiable OPRFs. However, the resulting protocols might be inefficient. Therefore, all of the real-world use-cases of (V)OPRFs are currently instantiated with performant (V)OPRFs which are based on classical security assumptions. Practical constructions are currently based either on the hardness of the decisional Diffie-Hellman problem, called DH-OPRF [21], or they are derived from RSA blind signatures [8,11].

For quantum-secure OPRFs, there are only few proposals. Indeed, only three such solutions appear in the literature to date. In 2019, Albrecht et al. proposed a lattice-based VOPRF [1] based on the ring learning with errors problem and the short integer solution problem in one dimension. Seres et al. constructed an OPRF based on the shifted Legendre symbol problem [31] and Boneh et al. presented two isogeny-based (V)OPRFs at ASIACRYPT 2020 [3].

Isogeny-based cryptography is one of the branches of post-quantum cryptography that are currently being explored. The particularly small key sizes required by isogeny-based cryptosystems make them very attractive in some areas of information security. Isogeny-based cryptography was first proposed by Couveignes in 1997 [9]. However, his ideas were not published at the time and they were independently rediscovered by Rostovtsev and Stolbunov [30]. The idea of Couveignes and Rostovtsev-Stolbunov (CRS) was to build a Diffie-Hellman type key exchange using the class group of the endomorphism ring of ordinary elliptic curves. However, neither of the suggested schemes was efficient enough to be considered practical. Meanwhile, supersingular elliptic curves were first used in cryptography by Charles, Lauter and Goren [7] to build a hash function.

Jao and De Feo took a different approach to isogeny-based cryptography when they introduced the *supersingular isogeny Diffie-Hellman* (SIDH) key exchange [20]. Instead of computing class group actions as in the case of CRS, Jao and De Feo use the following observation. Two subgroups of an elliptic curve of coprime cardinality are only intersecting at the point at infinity. Independent of the order in which two such subgroups are divided out of an elliptic curve, the resulting curve will be equal up to isomorphism. The only isogeny-based cryptosystem submitted to NIST's ongoing post-quantum standardization process is the SIDH-based candidate SIKE [2,19] which has been selected as one of the alternate finalists.

Later, the idea of CRS-type schemes was resurrected, when Castryck et al. adapted it to supersingular elliptic curves and managed to eliminate most of its performance issues [5]. The resulting scheme is called CSIDH.

In their ASIACRYPT 2020 paper [3], Boneh et al. propose an augmentable commitment framework that can be used to build an OPRF and is instantiated with both an SIDH-based scheme that can be made verifiable, and with a CSIDH-based one. The SIDH-based variant relies on the hardness of the decisional supersingular isogeny problem, a standard assumption in the area, and a novel 'one-more' isogeny assumption.

Our Contributions. In this paper, we cryptanalyse the SIDH-based 'one-more' assumption introduced by Boneh, Kogan and Woo. We first give multiple variants of an attack on the assumption itself. A first variant leads to a polynomial-time attack against the proposed SIDH-based OPRF protocol. We then argue that a simple modification of the (V)OPRF protocol prevents such an attack. Then, we show that a second variant of the attack leads to an attack on the protocol even in the presence of those countermeasures. This attack has a subexponential complexity, but there appear to be no simple countermeasures. Developing countermeasures is left as an open problem. As a result of our attack, the parameters suggested by Boneh et al. fall short of their estimated security level.

The attacks on the OPRF allow malicious clients to evaluate the OPRF on arbitrary inputs after some initial queries to the server, without even interacting with the server any further. This breaks the pseudorandomness property of the OPRF and could lead to significant attacks on OPRF-based protocols. In the context of private set intersection based on oblivious PRFs, the proposed attack allows the attacker to brute-force the other party's set elements and break the privacy requirement. In the Privacy Pass protocol used to guarantee privacy-preserving CAPTCHAs, our attack allows the attacker to generate unlimited tokens, thus avoiding solving CAPTCHAs and fully breaking the security of the system.

Furthermore, we discuss how one of the parameters of the SIDH-based OPRF by Boneh et al. is generated and which party should compute it. We argue there are security implications if the server, the client or any third party maliciously generates this parameter. The client or a third party can introduce a backdoor through this parameter to recover the secret key of the server, whereas if the server is malicious, they can break the supersingular-isogeny collision assumption on which Boneh et al.'s security proofs are built. We suggest that a trusted setup may be needed to guarantee provable security.

Finally, we want to emphasise that the CSIDH-based OPRF proposal by Boneh et al. is not affected by our attacks.

Outline. In Sect. 2, we introduce some background on isogeny-based cryptography, the security properties of (verifiable) oblivious PRFs and Boneh et al.'s construction. The attacks against the 'one-more' assumption are presented in Sect. 3, while their application to the OPRF protocol by Boneh et al. is discussed in Sect. 4. We present our implementation of the attack and discuss its results in Sect. 5. In Sect. 6, we argue that a trusted setup should be used for the OPRF and briefly sketch two attacks that follow a lack of trusted setup before concluding the paper in Sect. 7.

2   Preliminaries

In this section we introduce the necessary mathematical background on isogenies and the SIDH key exchange, we summarize the security properties of OPRFs and we briefly recall Boneh et al.'s OPRF construction [3].

2.1   Mathematical Background on Isogenies

Let $\mathbb{F}_q$ be a finite field of characteristic p. In the following, we assume $p \geq 3$ and therefore an elliptic curve E over $\mathbb{F}_q$ can be defined by its short Weierstrass form

$$E(\mathbb{F}_q) = \{(x, y) \in \mathbb{F}_q^2 \mid y^2 = x^3 + Ax + B\} \cup \{\mathcal{O}_E\}$$

with $A, B \in \mathbb{F}_q$ such that the discriminant is non-zero and $\mathcal{O}_E$ denotes the point $(X : Y : Z) = (0 : 1 : 0)$ on the associated projective curve $Y^2 Z = X^3 + AXZ^2 + BZ^3$. The *j-invariant* of an elliptic curve is $j(E) = 1728 \frac{4A^3}{4A^3 + 27B^2}$.

A non-constant rational map $\phi : E_1 \to E_2$ between two elliptic curves is an *isogeny* if it sends the point at infinity of E_1 to the point at infinity of E_2. Equivalently, an isogeny is a rational map which is also a group homomorphism. Thus an isogeny is the natural morphism of the category of elliptic curves. An isogeny ϕ induces a field extension between the function fields of E_1 and E_2. The degree of this extension is the degree of the isogeny. We call an isogeny *separable* if this field extension is separable. The kernel of a separable isogeny as a group homomorphism is finite and is equal to the degree of the isogeny. If $\phi : E_1 \to E_2$ is an isogeny of degree d, then there exists a unique isogeny $\hat{\phi}$ of degree d such that $\phi \circ \hat{\phi} = [d]$, where $[d]$ denotes multiplication by d. The isogeny $\hat{\phi}$ is called the *dual isogeny* of ϕ. An isomorphism of elliptic curves is an isogeny of degree 1 and there is an isomorphism of curves $f : E_0 \to E_1$ if and only if $j(E_0) = j(E_1)$.

An *endomorphism* of E is an isogeny from E to itself. Endomorphisms of E form a ring under composition and addition denoted by $\mathrm{End}(E)$. The endomorphism ring of an elliptic curve over a finite field is either an order in an imaginary quadratic field (in which case the curve is called *ordinary*) or a maximal order in the quaternion algebra ramified at infinity and p (in which case the curve is called *supersingular*).

The *j*-invariant of any supersingular elliptic curve defined over $\mathbb{F}_q$ lies in $\mathbb{F}_{p^2}$.

For a thorough introduction to elliptic curves and isogeny-based cryptography, we refer to Silverman [32] and De Feo [12], respectively.

2.2 SIDH

We briefly recall the *supersingular isogeny Diffie-Hellman* key exchange introduced by Jao and De Feo [20].

Let E_0 be a supersingular elliptic curve defined over $\mathbb{F}_{p^2}$, where p is a prime of the form $f \cdot N_1 N_2 \pm 1$. Here $f \in \mathbb{Z}$ is a small cofactor and N_1, N_2 are two coprime smooth integers (e.g. a power of 2 and 3 respectively). Furthermore, fix two bases P_A, Q_A and P_B, Q_B such that $\langle P_A, Q_A \rangle = E_0[N_1]$ and $\langle P_B, Q_B \rangle = E_0[N_2]$. To agree on a secret key over an insecure channel, Alice and Bob proceed as follows:

1. Alice chooses a random cyclic subgroup of $E_0[N_1]$ generated by a point of the form $A = P_A + [x_A]Q_A$ as her secret. Similarly, Bob chooses his secret as $\langle B \rangle := \langle P_B + [x_B]Q_B \rangle \subset E_0[N_2]$.
2. Then, Alice and Bob compute their secret isogeny $\varphi_A : E_0 \to E_0/\langle A \rangle$ and $\varphi_B : E_0 \to E_0/\langle B \rangle$, respectively.
3. Alice sends the curve $E_A := E_0/\langle A \rangle$ and the points $\varphi_A(P_B), \varphi_A(Q_B)$ to Bob. Mutatis mutandis, Bob sends $E_B := E_0/\langle B \rangle$, $\varphi_B(P_A)$ and $\varphi_B(Q_A)$ to Alice.
4. Both Alice and Bob can compute the shared secret curve $E_{AB} := E_0/\langle A, B \rangle$ up to isomorphism as

$$E_{AB} \cong E_B/\langle \varphi_B(P_A) + [x_A]\varphi_B(Q_A) \rangle \cong E_A/\langle \varphi_A(P_B) + [x_B]\varphi_A(Q_B) \rangle.$$

Since isomorphic curves have the same j-invariant, Alice and Bob use $j(E_{AB})$ as their shared secret.

2.3 Security Properties of (V)OPRFs

In the following, we will call a function $\mu : \mathbb{N} \to \mathbb{R}$ *negligible* if for every positive polynomial $\mathsf{poly}(\cdot)$ there exists an integer $N_{\mathsf{poly}} > 0$ such that for all $x > N_{\mathsf{poly}}$, we have $|\mu(x)| < 1/\mathsf{poly}(x)$.

The security properties of an oblivious pseudorandom function (OPRF) include those of a standard pseudorandom function (PRF).

Definition 1. *Let $F : K \times X \to Y$ be an efficiently computable function. F is a* pseudorandom function *(PRF) if for all probabilistic polynomial-time distinguishers D, there is a negligible function* **negl** *such that*

$$\mathbb{P}[D^{F(k,\cdot)}(1^n) = 1] - \mathbb{P}[D^{f(\cdot)}(1^n) = 1] \leq \mathsf{negl}(n),$$

where the first probability is taken over uniform choices of $k \in \{0, 1\}^n$ and the randomness of D, and the second probability is taken over uniform choices of functions $f : X \to Y$ and the randomness of D.

A consequence of pseudorandomness is that one cannot compute a new evaluation of $F(k, \cdot)$ from existing evaluations. However, our attack on Boneh et al.'s OPRF will allow adversaries to evaluate $F(k, \cdot)$ on arbitrary inputs after some initial evaluations.

Furthermore, an OPRF is oblivious in the following sense.

Definition 2 ([17]). *Let $F : K \times X \to Y$ be a PRF. A protocol between a client with input $x \in X$ and a server with key $k \in K$ is called* oblivious *PRF, if the client learns $F(k, x)$ and nothing else and the server learns nothing about x or $F(k, x)$ at the end of the protocol.*

In particular, the server will learn nothing about the input x of the client and the client will learn nothing about the server's key k. Additionally, an OPRF can be verifiable.

Definition 3. *An OPRF is said to be* verifiable *if the evaluation y that the client obtains at the end of the protocol is correct, i.e. if it satisfies $y = F(k, x)$, where $x \in X$ is the client's input and $k \in K$ is the server's private key.*

In practice, verifiability is ensured by the server committing to a key k prior to the execution of the verifiable OPRF (VOPRF) and providing a zero-knowledge proof that the VOPRF execution uses the same key as the committed value.

2.4 An Isogeny-Based OPRF by Boneh, Kogan and Woo

We provide a simplified description of Boneh et al.'s OPRF based on the SIDH key exchange protocol.

Let λ be the security parameter and let $p = f N_K N_M N_V N_R N_S - 1$ be a prime where $f \in \mathbb{Z}$ is a small cofactor and N_i are powers of distinct small primes such that N_K, N_M, N_V, N_R are roughly of size $2^{5\lambda/2}$ and $N_S \approx 2^{2\lambda}$. To prevent an attack by Merz et al. [27], the factors N_K, N_M, N_V, N_R are of size $2^{5\lambda/2}$ instead of the more common size $2^{2\lambda}$ in the SIDH setting. Moreover, let $H_1 : \{0,1\}^* \to \mathbb{Z}_{N_M}$ be a cryptographic hash function. In their proofs, Boneh et al. treat H_1 as a random oracle. Finally, let E_0 be a randomly chosen supersingular elliptic curve over $\mathbb{F}_{p^2}$ and let $\{P_i, Q_i\}$ denote a basis of $E_0[N_i]$ for $i = K, M, V, R, S$. While Boneh et al. only require E_0 to be a randomly chosen elliptic curve, we will discuss how it is generated in Sect. 6 and argue that this choice should be done by a trusted third party.

First, the server chooses their private key k which is the PRF key and publishes a commitment to this key. To evaluate the OPRF at an input x in the input space, a client computes the hash $H_1(x) = m \in \mathbb{Z}_{N_M}$. Furthermore, the client randomly chooses an element $r \in \mathbb{Z}_{N_R}$.

The client computes the isogenies $\phi_m : E_0 \to E_m := E_0/\langle P_M + [m]Q_M\rangle$ and $\phi_r : E_m \to E_{mr} := E_m/\langle \phi_m(P_R) + [r]\phi_m(Q_R)\rangle$. Then, the client sends E_{mr} together with the torsion point images of P_i, Q_i for $i = V, K, S$ to the server as well as a basis of $E_{mr}[N_R]$. To avoid active attacks like the GPST attack [18], where a malicious client tries to recover information about the server's private key by sending manipulated torsion point information, the client proves to the server in a non-interactive zero-knowledge proof that they know the kernel of the isogeny from E_0 to E_{mr} and that the provided torsion point images are indeed the images under this isogeny. For full details about the zero-knowledge proof we refer to Sect. 5 of [3].

Subsequently, the server computes their secret isogeny $\phi_k : E_{mr} \to E_{mrk}$, where $E_{mrk} := E_{mr}/\langle \phi_r \circ \phi_m(P_K) + [k]\phi_r \circ \phi_m(Q_K)\rangle$. Moreover, the server computes the images of the order N_V torsion points and the basis of $E_{mr}[N_R]$ provided by the client. The server sends E_{mrk} together with the torsion point information to the client. Using an interactive zero-knowledge proof with a cut-and-choose approach between server and client, the server can prove to the client that it computed the isogeny and the torsion point images correctly. This proof uses the torsion point images of order N_V and the server's initial commitment to the key k. Details about this zero-knowledge proof can be found in Sect. 6 of [3].

After executing the zero-knowledge proof with the server to convince itself of the correctness of the server's reply, the client uses the images of the $E_{mr}[N_R]$ torsion to "unblind" E_{mrk}. The unblinding isogeny $\hat{\phi}'_r$ is a translation of the dual of ϕ_r starting from E_{mrk}. This allows the client to compute a curve isomorphic to $E_{mk} := E_m/\langle \phi_m(P_K) + k\phi_m(Q_K)\rangle$ without knowing k at any point in time. Hashing the input together with the j-invariant of E_{mk} and the server's initial commitment to his key k yields the output of the VOPRF. The entire evaluation is sketched in Fig. 1.

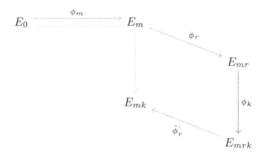

Fig. 1. Sketch of Boneh et al.'s isogeny-based VOPRF. The isogenies computed by the client are marked in red (ϕ_m, ϕ_r, and $\hat{\phi}'_r$) while the server's isogeny is noted in blue (ϕ_k). The green isogenies represent the PRF which is jointly evaluated by the client and the server. The output of the OPRF is computed as $F(k, x) = H(x, j(E_{mk}), \mathsf{pk})$, where H is a cryptographic hash function and pk is the server's (public) commitment to his key k.

3 Attacks on the Auxiliary One-More SIDH Assumption

In [3], Boneh et al. introduce the auxiliary one-more SIDH assumption. This is a new security assumption to prove the unpredictability of their isogeny-based VOPRF. In this section we challenge the validity of this assumption and we present multiple attacks on the corresponding computational problem.

All of the attacks follow a similar strategy. First, an attacker recovers certain torsion point images up to a scalar under the secret isogeny using queries in the security game. Having recovered these torsion point images, an attacker is capable of answering any challenge set by the challenger correctly. This breaks the security assumption and also leads to an attack on Boneh et al.'s (V)OPRF.

We start by recalling the security assumption introduced by Boneh et al. [3]. Then, we show that recovering said torsion point images up to a scalar is sufficient to compute the correct answer to arbitrary challenges in the corresponding security game. Subsequently, we give multiple approaches to recover these torsion point images. In Sect. 4, we will show how the attack on the security assumption translates to an attack on the (V)OPRF itself.

3.1   The Auxiliary One-More SIDH Assumption

First, we recall the game underlying the auxiliary one-more SIDH assumption as defined by Boneh et al. [3]. While Boneh et al. use the "decision queries" defined in the following game in their security proofs, our attacks will not make use of decision queries and a reader may ignore this additional ability of an adversary.

Game 1 (Auxiliary One-More SIDH). Let $p = f \cdot N_1 \cdots N_n - 1$ be a prime depending on the security level λ and n, where N_i are smooth coprime integers and f is a small cofactor, and let $\mathsf{M}, \mathsf{K} \in \{1, \dots, n\}$ be two distinct indices. Consider the following game between a challenger and an adversary:

- The challenger chooses a random supersingular curve $E_0/\mathbb{F}_{p^2}$ and a basis $\{P, Q\}$ of $E_0[(p+1)/(N_\mathsf{M} \cdot N_\mathsf{K})]$. Moreover, it chooses $K \in E_0$ of order N_K, computes $\phi_K : E_0 \to E_K := E_0/\langle K \rangle$, and sends E_0, P, Q, and E_K to the adversary.
- The adversary can make a sequence of queries of the following types to the challenger:
  - Challenge query: The challenger chooses $M \in E_0[N_\mathsf{M}]$ randomly and sends it to the adversary
  - Solve query: The adversary submits $V \in E_0[(p+1)/N_\mathsf{K}]$ to the challenger[1], who computes $\phi_{KV} : E_0 \to E_0/\langle K, V \rangle$ and sends $j(E_0/\langle K, V \rangle)$, $\phi_{KV}(P)$, and $\phi_{KV}(Q)$ to the adversary.
  - Decision query: The adversary submits a pair (i, j) to the challenger, where i is a positive integer bounded by the number of challenge queries made so far, and $j \in \mathbb{F}_{p^2}$. The challenger responds true if $j = j(E_0/\langle K, M \rangle)$, where M is the challenger's response to the ith challenge query, and false otherwise.
- The adversary outputs a list of distinct pairs of the form (i, j), where i is a positive integer bounded by the number of challenge queries made and $j \in \mathbb{F}_{p^2}$.

We call an output-pair (i, j) correct, if j is the j-invariant of $E_0/\langle K, M \rangle$, where M is the challenger's response to the ith challenge query. An adversary wins the game, if the number of correct pairs exceeds the number of Solve queries.

Assumption 2 (Auxiliary One-More SIDH [3]). For every constant n and every distinct $\mathsf{M}, \mathsf{K} \in \{1, \ldots, n\}$, every efficient adversary wins the above game with probability negligible in λ.

In the following, we will show that the auxiliary one-more SIDH assumption does not hold. We will give different attacks on the security problem underlying Assumption 2 that follow a similar strategy. Let K be the server's secret, determining the isogeny $\phi_K : E_0 \to E_0/\langle K \rangle$. The idea is to use a number of solve queries to subsequently predict $E_0/\langle K, M \rangle$ for any $M \in E_0[N_\mathsf{M}]$. To this end, we will derive a method to extract the subgroup generated by $\phi_K(P)$ for any $P \in E_0[N_\mathsf{M}]$ with a number of solve queries. Using this procedure, an adversary can extract the subgroups generated by $\phi_K(P_M)$, $\phi_K(Q_M)$ and $\phi_K(P_M + Q_M)$, where $\{P_M, Q_M\}$ is a basis of $E_0[N_\mathsf{M}]$.

Knowing these subgroups allows the adversary to compute the subgroups generated by $\phi_K(M)$ for arbitrary $M \in E_0[N_\mathsf{M}]$ without any further solve queries. Given a generator of $\langle \phi_K(M) \rangle$, the adversary can compute the j-invariant of $E_0/\langle K, M \rangle$ as $E_0/\langle K, M \rangle \cong E_K/\langle \phi_K(M) \rangle$. In particular, the adversary can produce arbitrarily many correct output-pairs and win the security game underlying the auxiliary one-more SIDH assumption (Assumption 2).

3.2   Winning the Security Game Given Torsion Point Images

In this section, we show how mapping three different N_M-order subgroups to $E_K := E_0/\langle K \rangle$ is enough to recover sufficient information to compute a generator of $\langle \phi_K(M) \rangle \in E_K$ for any point $M \in E_0[N_\mathsf{M}]$.

Lemma 1. *Let $P_V, Q_V, R_V := P_V + Q_V \in E_0$ be pairwise linearly independent points of smooth order N_M and let $\phi_K : E_0 \to E_K$ be an unknown isogeny of degree coprime to N_M. Given the points P_V, Q_V, R_V and the subgroups $\langle \phi_K(P_V) \rangle$, $\langle \phi_K(Q_V) \rangle$ and $\langle \phi_K(R_V) \rangle$, an adversary can compute $\langle \phi_K(M) \rangle$ for arbitrary $M \in E_0[N_\mathsf{M}]$.*

Proof. Fix P', Q', and R' to be generators of $\langle \phi_K(P_V) \rangle$, $\langle \phi_K(Q_V) \rangle$ and $\langle \phi_K(R_V) \rangle$ respectively. Note that the given information $\langle \phi_K(P_V) \rangle$, $\langle \phi_K(Q_V) \rangle$ and $\langle \phi_K(R_V) \rangle$ is the same as knowing $\phi_K(P_V)$, $\phi_K(Q_V)$, $\phi_K(R_V)$ up to a scalar multiple. There are many different generators for the groups $\langle \phi_K(P_V) \rangle$, $\langle \phi_K(Q_V) \rangle$ and $\langle \phi_K(R_V) \rangle$ but for any fixed choice we have

$$P' = \alpha \phi_K(P_V),$$
$$Q' = \beta \phi_K(Q_V),$$
$$R' = \gamma \phi_K(R_V)$$

---

[1] In Algorithm 1, we will describe how an adversary can win the game in polynomial time, if the point V is not required to be of full order.

for some (unknown) integers α, β, γ coprime to N_M. As isogenies are homomorphisms, we have $\phi_K(R_V) = \phi_K(P_V) + \phi_K(Q_V)$. One finds a, b such that $R' = aP' + bQ'$, which can be done efficiently as computing discrete logarithms is easy in a group of smooth order N_M. We have $\gamma = a\alpha = b\beta$. Thus, it is possible for the attacker to recover the ratio $\alpha/\beta = b/a$.

Given any $M \in E_0[N_M]$, an adversary can compute integers k_1, k_2 such that $M = k_1 P_V + k_2 Q_V$ (which again is possible because N_M is smooth) and obtain $\langle \phi_K(M) \rangle$ by computing $\langle k_1 \phi_K(P) + k_2 \phi_K(Q) \rangle = \langle k_1 P' + k_2 \frac{\alpha}{\beta} Q' \rangle$. $\square$

In particular, an adversary who knows $\phi_K(P_V)$, $\phi_K(Q_V)$ and $\phi_K(R_V)$ up to a scalar and $E_K := E_0/\langle K \rangle$ can compute $E_0/\langle K, M \rangle \cong E_K/\langle \phi_K(M) \rangle$ for any $M \in E_0[N_M]$.

3.3   Recovering Points in $\phi_K(E_0[N_M])$ Up to a Scalar

The previous subsection shows that $E_0/\langle K, M \rangle$ can be computed by an adversary for arbitrary $M \in E_0[N_M]$ as long as they can recover images of points in $E_0[N_M]$ under the secret isogeny ϕ_K up to scalar. In this section, we will present multiple ways an adversary can recover this information. For didactic purposes, we include not only a polynomial and a subexponential attack (in case countermeasures to prevent the former one are put in place) but also an exponential attack in our exposition.

Query points of arbitrary order. Let $M \in E_0[N_M]$. We are interested in recovering $\phi_K(M)$ up to a scalar, given access to the oracle provided by the "solve queries" in Game 1. Note that our attack will not use "decision queries" as defined in the same game.

There is a simple procedure to compute an isogeny between E_K and $E_M := E_K/\langle \phi_K(M) \rangle$ and therefore $\phi_K(M)$ up to scalar, if "solve queries" are allowed for points of arbitrary order. Recall that during a solve query in Game 1, an adversary gets to submit points $V \in E_0[(p + 1)/N_K]$ to the challenger, who replies with the j-invariant of $E_0/\langle K, V \rangle$ and some additional torsion point images. Algorithm 1 describes how an adversary can recover $\phi_K(M)$ up to a scalar for arbitrary $M \in E_0[N_M]$. The Algorithm recovers the isogeny from E_K to $E_K/\langle \phi_K(M) \rangle$ by using solve queries to obtain all intermediate curves. This allows to recover the isogeny $E_K \to E_K/\langle \phi_K(M) \rangle$ one step at a time and therefore its kernel $\langle \phi_K(M) \rangle$.

Algorithm 1: Computation of $\langle \phi_K(M) \rangle$ using solve queries on points of arbitrary order

---

Let $\{l_i\}_{i=0}^n$ be an integer sequence of all divisors of N_M such that l_{i+1}/l_i is a prime, $l_i < l_{i+1}$, with $l_0 := 1$, $l_n := N_M$.
Input: E_K, $M \in E_0[N_M]$ and access to an oracle answering solve queries as defined in Game 1.
Output: A generator of $\langle \phi_K(M) \rangle$

---

1 $E^{(n)} \leftarrow E_0/\langle K \rangle$;
2 **for** $i = n-1, \ldots, 0$ **do**
3   Query the oracle with the point $V_i := [l_i]M$ and obtain the curve
       $E^{(i)} := E_0/\langle K, V_i \rangle = E_0/\langle K, [l_i]M \rangle = E_K/\langle [l_i]\phi_K(M) \rangle$;
4   Find l_{i+1}/l_i-isogeny ϕ_i from $E^{(i+1)}$ to $E^{(i)}$;
5 **return** A generator of $\ker(\phi_0 \circ \cdots \circ \phi_{n-1})$;

Lemma 2. *Algorithm 1 returns $\lambda \phi_K(M)$, where $\lambda \in \mathbb{Z}$ is coprime to N_M.*

Proof. Let ψ_M be the isogeny from E_K to $E_K/\phi_K(M)$. Then the claim follows from the observation that $E_0/\langle K, [l_i]M \rangle \cong E_0/\langle [l_i]K, [l_i]M \rangle$, since l_i is coprime to the order of K. □

Remark 1. Note that an attacker can easily change the attack to require fewer queries. Instead of using one query for each intermediate curve, an attacker can choose any factorisation $f_1 \cdots f_t$ of N_M such that f_i are roughly of equal size and query the oracle with $\left[\prod_{j=1}^b f_i \right] M$ for $b = 1, \ldots, t$. Then, the attacker is left to recover the isogeny between any two consecutive queries, i.e. the isogenies of degree f_i for $i = 1, \ldots, t$, using a meet-in-the-middle attack.

In Game 1, Boneh et al. did not specify any restrictions on the points of $E_0[(p+1)/N_K]$ that can be submitted to the solve queries. However, in the context of the game, this attack can be easily thwarted by answering to a solve query only if the submitted point is of order $(p+1)/N_K$. This property can be checked efficiently by the challenger. In Sect. 4, we discuss how this polynomial-time attack and its countermeasures translate to the VOPRF protocol.

Query Points of Order $(p+1)/N_K$. Next, we present how an attacker can retrieve the necessary information even if they are only allowed to send solve queries on points of order $(p+1)/N_K$, i.e. if the challenger checks the order of a submitted point and only replies to a query if the point is of order $(p+1)/N_K$.

Let ϕ_V denote the isogeny $E_K \rightarrow E_0/\langle V, K \rangle$ of degree $(p+1)/N_K$ and let $\phi_V = \phi_{V'} \circ \phi_M$ be its decomposition into a degree $(p+1)/(N_K N_M)$ and a degree N_M isogeny. Our attack aims to recover the image of multiple subgroups of $E_0[N_M]$ under the isogeny ϕ_K, i.e. we are interested in the kernel of the isogeny ϕ_M for different points V. The isogenies are depicted in Fig. 2.

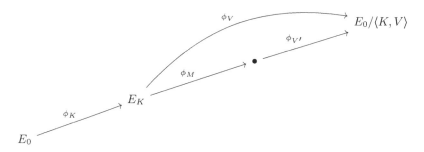

Fig. 2. Depiction of the isogenies of a solve query

Recovering $\phi_{V'}$ from torsion point information. Let $P, Q \in E_0[(p + 1)/N_M N_K]$ be the torsion point basis provided by the challenger and let $V \in E_0[(p + 1)/N_K]$ be linearly independent of P or Q. Then, we can use the torsion point images provided during a solve queries to compute $\hat{\phi}_V$ as follows.

Let $P' := \phi_V \circ \phi_K(P)$, $Q' := \phi_V \circ \phi_K(Q)$ be the images of the torsion points provided by the challenger. The adversary can compute $\hat{\phi}_{V'}$ as the isogeny from $E_0/\langle K, V \rangle$ with kernel $\langle P', Q' \rangle$. Note that $\langle P', Q' \rangle \subset \ker(\hat{\phi}_{V'})$, because $\hat{\phi}_{V'} \circ \phi_{V'} = [(p + 1)/N_M N_K]$ is the order of the points P, Q. As V is linearly independent to at least one of P and Q, the other inclusion follows from $\langle P', Q' \rangle$ spanning a subgroup of size $(p + 1)/N_M N_K$.

Choosing P_V, Q_V as a basis of $E_0[(p + 1)/N_K]$ such that $[N_M]P_V = P + [(p + 1)/N_M N_K]Q$ and $[N_M]Q_V = [(p + 1)/N_M N_K]P + Q$, every point of the form $P_V + [i]Q_V$ or $[i]P_V + Q_V$ will be linearly independent of P or Q.

As a consequence of $\phi_{V'}$ being easy to recover, we may assume that during a solve query an attacker can send a point M of order N_M to the challenger who returns $E_0/\langle K, M \rangle$. We are left to recover the kernel of ϕ_M.

Naïve attack to recover ϕ_M. Next we describe an exponential attack that recovers $\hat{\phi}_M$ using meet-in-the-middle (MITM) computations of increasing size. In the subsequent part, we will introduce a trade-off between queries and computation costs that reduces the complexity of the attack to subexponential.

Let P_M, Q_M denote a basis of $E_0[N_M]$. For simplicity of exposition we treat N_M as a prime power and we write $N_M = \ell_M^{e_M}$. The attack recovers $\phi_M : E_K \to E_K/\langle P_M \rangle$ by recovering each of the e_M intermediate curves one at a time.

The attacker starts by querying the solve oracle with two points $V_0 := P_M$ and $V_1 := P_M + [\ell_M^{e_M-1}]Q_M$. Note that the curves $E_K/\langle \phi_K(V_0) \rangle$ and $E_K/\langle \phi_K(V_1) \rangle$ are ℓ_M^2-isogenous, since they are both ℓ_M-isogenous to $E_K/\langle [\ell_M]\phi_K(V_0) \rangle = E_K/\langle [\ell_M]\phi_K(V_1) \rangle$. The attacker recovers the curve $E_K/\langle [\ell_M]\phi_K(V_0) \rangle$, which is the first intermediate curve on the ϕ_M isogeny path by computing the common neighbour of $E_K/\langle \phi_K(V_0) \rangle$ and $E_K/\langle \phi_K(V_1) \rangle$.

The rest of the attacks proceeds similarly. The attacker queries with the points $V_i := P_M + [\ell_M^{e_M-i}]Q_M$, $i = 1, \ldots, e_M/2$ and runs a MITM attack to recover $E_K/\langle [\ell_M^i]\phi_K(V_0) \rangle$ given $E_K/\langle \phi_K(V_i) \rangle$ and $E_K/\langle [\ell_M^{i-1}]\phi_K(V_0) \rangle$. This could be repeated e_M times to recover the entire isogeny ϕ_M. However, the attacker does not need to recover the last part of the isogeny through this strategy, since it is faster to directly compute the MITM between $E_K/\langle[\ell_M^{e_M/2}]V_0\rangle$ and the starting curve E_K. The attack with the required meet-in-the-middle computations is shown in Fig. 3.

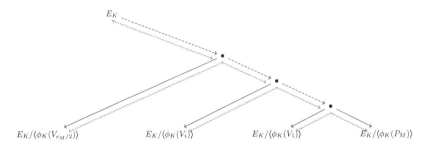

Fig. 3. Naïve attack where isogenies of increasing length need to be recovered. The blue lines represent the meet-in-the-middle computations. (Color figure online)

Note that the isogenies that need to be recovered using MITM grow at each step. To recover the i-th intermediate curve, the attacker needs to compute an isogeny between two curves that are $\ell_M^{(i+1)}$-isogenous, which takes roughly $O(\ell_M^{(i+1)/2})$.

Clearly, this attack can be optimised by recovering multiple steps of ϕ_M at a time, and by making sure that the different MITM attacks that need to be executed have similar complexity. We will discuss these improvements in the following.

Full attack with query-time trade-off. We can reduce the complexity of the naïve attack by introducing a trade-off between queries and the cost of MITM computations. This is because the attacker recovers the whole path between two isogenies during a MITM computation. Thus, it is possible to recover more than one intermediate curve with a single (longer) MITM computation. Moreover, the queries can be spaced out more in order to reduce the length of the isogenies that have to be recovered using MITM strategies.

More formally, let 2^q denote the number of queries that an attacker can (or wants to) send to the challenger. For simplicity of this exposition, assume that $2e_m$ is divisible by $q+2$. The attacker chooses the V_i such that $E_0/\langle K, V_i\rangle$ correspond to curves that are the leaves of a binary isogeny tree. The V_i should be chosen such that there is an $\ell_M^{2e_M/(q+2)}$ isogeny between any two siblings in the binary tree and the curve that is $\ell_M^{e_M/(q+2)}$-isogenous to both leaves is their parent in the tree. Again, the parent and its sibling should be $\ell_M^{2e_M/(q+2)}$-isogenous, etc.

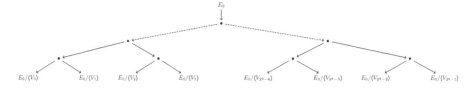

Fig. 4. The attacker queries the challenger on points corresponding to isogeny kernels leading to the leaves of this binary tree

Remark 2. Note that it is easy to choose such a set of points V_i. Let P_M, Q_M be a basis of $E_0[\ell_M^{e_M}]$. The attacker can choose

$$V_0 := P_M$$

$$V_i := V_{i-2^{\lfloor \log i \rfloor}} + [\ell_M^{e_M - (\lfloor \log i \rfloor + 1) 2 e_M / (q+2)}] Q_M$$

Lemma 3. *Let* $E_0/\langle V_i \rangle$ *and* $E_0/\langle V_j \rangle$ *be* ℓ_M^k *isogenous curves. Then* $E_K/\langle \phi_K(V_i) \rangle$ *and* $E_K/\langle \phi_K(V_j) \rangle$ *are* ℓ_M^k-*isogenous curves too.*

Proof. This follows from $N_K = \deg(\phi_K)$ being coprime to ℓ_M^k. □

In particular, $\{\phi_K(P_M), \phi_K(Q_M)\}$ is a basis of $E_K[N_M]$ and $E_K/\langle \phi_K(V_i) \rangle$ are the leaves in a binary tree where all siblings are $\ell_M^{2e_M/(q+2)}$ isogenous.

After querying the oracle to obtain $E_K/\langle \phi_K(V_i) \rangle = E_0/\langle K, V_i \rangle$, an attacker recovers iteratively parent nodes in the binary tree using a meet-in-the-middle approach. Any siblings in the tree correspond to curves that are $\ell_M^{2e_M/(q+2)}$-isogenous, thus this can be done in $O(\ell_M^{e_M/(q+2)})$. Note that the root of the binary tree is recovered after $2^q - 1$ such meet-in-the-middle instances, i.e. the number of internal nodes in the binary tree. This root of the binary tree is then by construction $\ell_M^{2e_M/(q+2)}$-isogenous to E_0. This final isogeny can be recovered using meet-in-the-middle again. An attacker recovers and saves the intermediate nodes and isogenies from E_K to the leaf $E_K/\phi_K(V_0)$. Clearly, the kernel of this isogeny is $\phi_K(V_0)$.

In summary, we can recover the isogeny from $E_K \to E_K/\langle \phi_K(P_M) \rangle$ for any P_M with 2^q queries to the challenger and 2^q instances of meet-in-the-middle isogeny computations with cost of $O(\ell_M^{e_M/(q+2)})$ each.

Remark 3. If $\ell_M = 2$, we get q bits for free, i.e. one additional bit per layer of the binary tree. This is because every parent node in the binary tree has three outgoing edges: two edges leading to its children and one edge leading towards the root. Thus, having recovered both paths to the children an attacker gets one step towards the root for free.

3.4 Attack Analysis

The proposed attack is composed of two stages: firstly the generators of $\langle \phi_K(P_V) \rangle$, $\langle \phi_K(Q_V) \rangle$, and $\langle \phi_K(R_V) \rangle$ are recovered, and then these points are used to recover $\phi_K(M)$ for any possibly challenge $M \in E_0[N_M]$.

The second part consists mostly of pairing evaluations and discrete log computations in groups of smooth order. Thus, it runs in polynomial time. The complexity of the attack is dominated by the complexity of recovering the subgroups in the first step.

The algorithm proposed in Sect. 3.3 offers different trade-offs between computation costs and solve queries. As little as two solve queries can be enough to recover ϕ_M with two meet-in-the-middle computations. If we write $N_M \approx 2^m$, each meet-in-the-middle requires $O(2^{m/3})$ operations. This is already an improvement over the standard meet-in-the-middle attack that requires $O(2^{m/2})$ time. The OPRF protocol targets 128 bits of security, which corresponds to $m \approx 5\lambda/2 = 320$. Thus six queries (two per generator) are enough to reduce the security to $m/3 = 106$ bits. The number of solve queries can be significantly increased to obtain a faster attack. Note that OPRF protocols are usually used for applications such as private set intersection, that support a large number of queries. Thus, common scenarios where the OPRF may be used would easily lend themselves to an attack with many queries.

Since OPRFs are used in protocols where the clients interact several times with the server, we can expect the attacker to be able to run several OPRF instances. Thus, we model a solve query as an oracle query, where it has a unitary complexity. Then, the overall complexity of recovering a generator of $\langle \phi_K(P_V) \rangle$ with 2^q solve queries is $O(2^{m/(q+2)+q})$ operations, since the attacker needs to compute 2^q meet-in-the-middle instances between curves which are $2^{2m/(q+2)}$-isogenous. In terms of the security parameter, that complexity is equivalent to $O(2^{5\lambda/2(q+2) + q})$, since the OPRF protocol suggests using $m \approx 5\lambda/2$. If the number of solve queries is unrestricted, the complexity of the attack is minimized for $q = \sqrt{5\lambda/2} - 2$, which gives an overall complexity of $O(2^{\sqrt{10\lambda}-2})$, or using the L-notation $L[1/2, c]$, for some constant c. This shows the attack is subexponential, assuming that the solve query complexity is $O(1)$.

At 128-bit of security, our attack becomes feasible with around 64 solve queries, when it requires 64 meet-in-the-middle computations between curves which are 2^{80}-isogenous, i.e. each MITM has a complexity of 2^{40} operations. If the number of solve queries is unrestricted, an attacker can use 2^{18} solve queries to reduce the overall complexity of the attack to 2^{18} MITM computations, where each MITM operations has a complexity of 2^{16} operations.

The high-level attack does not generally require much memory. Storing the isogeny tree in memory is not particularly demanding, especially if the tree is traversed depth-first. In particular, memory is used only to store the part of the recovered isogeny, together with the two curves between which the meet-in-the-middle needs to be computed. However, a more significant amount of memory is used by the meet-in-the-middle computations, and indeed we see that the memory used by a single meet-in-the-middle generally outweighs the memory used by the rest of the attack. Meet-in-the-middle computations between curves which are 2^n-isogenous require to store $2^{n/2}$ curves. Thus, their memory requirements are given by $2 \cdot 2^{n/2} \log p$, since each curve can be represented by its j-invariant in $\mathbb{F}_{p^2}$. For common security levels, such as those proposed by Boneh et al. [3], the memory requirements remain moderate. In Sect. 5, we show that indeed our attack requires about 3 GB of memory to break 128 bits of security. However, for a more complete asymptotical analysis, we note that the memory requirements may become a bottleneck for the attack against higher security levels. In those instances, it may be preferable to substitute the meet-in-the-middle approach with the van Oorschot-Wiener algorithm [28]. This reduces the memory consumption at the cost of higher asymptotic complexity. In particular, the vOW algorithm requires $O(2^{3n/4})$ computations (compared to $O(2^{n/2})$ of MITM) to recover the halfway curve between curves which are 2^n-isogenous. Thus, while the concrete performance of the attack may differ, its asymptotic complexity remains subexponential.

Future improvements. A natural question to ask is whether the proposed attack that queries points of the correct order may be improved to achieve a polynomial running time. Consider that an attacker chooses an isogeny ϕ_V : $E_0 \to E_0/\langle V \rangle$ and he is given the curve $E_0/\langle K, V \rangle$. Since the attacker knows the entire isogeny ϕ_V, backtracking from $E_0/\langle K, V \rangle$ to E_K to recover $\phi_K(V)$ in polynomial time does not seem too far fetched, since the attacker knows the entire isogeny ϕ_V. A possible strategy may start by retrieving $E_0/\langle K, V \rangle$ and $E_0/\langle K, V + \ell_M^{e_M} V' \rangle$, for a point V' linearly independent of V. Their common ℓ_M-neighbour is the first curve on the isogeny path. Then, the attacker may use the knowledge of ϕ_V starting from E_0 to distinguish between the ℓ_M possible candidates for the next curve on the isogeny path. Unfortunately, our efforts to develop such an attack did not succeed. It remains an open problem whether such an attack is possible.

4   Attack on the OPRF

Having presented an attack on one of the security assumptions underlying the isogeny-based OPRF by Boneh et al., we investigate how an adversary can use the same method to attack the OPRF itself.

We will show that a malicious client can send carefully crafted queries to the server for which it can produce all necessary NIZK proofs required by the protocol that was summarized in Sect. 2.4. However, after some offline computation analogously to the attack on the auxiliary one-more SIDH assumption outlined in the previous section, the malicious client can evaluate the OPRF on any input without the help of the server. Even though the malicious client does not recover the server's secret key k, this breaks the "pseudorandomness", Definition 1, of the OPRF. We will use the same notation as in Sect. 2.4 to refer to different isogenies of the OPRF.

A malicious client will not use a hashed input to obtain the kernel for the first isogeny $\phi_m : E_0 \to E_m$ but rather choose the kernel of this first isogeny maliciously. The choice is analogous to the points from $E_0[N_M]$ that the attacker submitted to the solve queries in the attack of the previous section. In other words, instead of computing E_m as $E_0/\langle P + H(x)Q \rangle$ for some input x, the malicious client chooses a point V_i and computes E_m as $E_0/\langle V_i \rangle$ in the i-th evaluation of the OPRF.

The rest of the protocol is executed honestly. The malicious client can pick some $r \in N_R$ to blind his maliciously chosen E_m. And it can compute the torsion point information for the server honestly since it knows the kernel of the isogeny $E_0 \to E_{mr} = E_m/\langle \phi_m(P_R) + [r]\phi_m(Q_R) \rangle$. In particular, the malicious client will always be able to produce the valid non-interactive zero-knowledge proof of knowledge for the kernel of $E_0 \to E_{mr}$ and the correct computation of the torsion point information.

Following through with the rest of the OPRF protocol, the malicious client obtains the j-invariant of the curve $E_0/\langle V_i, K \rangle$ after unblinding. Here K denotes the server's secret $P_K + [k]Q_K$. This is exactly what corresponds to a "solve query" in the auxiliary one-more SIDH game, Game 1.

Now the malicious client can proceed as in the attacks on the auxiliary one-more SIDH assumption.

In the attack using points of arbitrary order dividing N_M, the malicious client recovers the isogeny $E_K \to E_K/\langle \phi_K(P) \rangle = E_0/\langle K, P \rangle$ and therefore $\langle \phi_K(P) \rangle$ for any $P \in E_0[N_M]$ in polynomial time. This is done by submitting points of lower order, i.e. choosing the isogeny $E_0 \to E_m$ shorter, to recover the isogeny stepwise. After recovering three such isogenies corresponding to pairwise linearly independent points $P, Q, P + Q$, the malicious client can compute $E_0/\langle M, K \rangle$ for any $M \in E_0[N_M]$ as was shown in Sect. 3.2.

Then, the malicious client can evaluate the OPRF on arbitrary inputs x as follows: They compute the point $M := P_M + H_1(x)Q_M$ as in the honest evaluation and then they compute $j(E_0/\langle M, K \rangle)$ directly. Hashing this j-invariant together with the input x and public information of the server yields the output of the OPRF. Note that the malicious client does not even need to interact with the server to evaluate the OPRF on arbitrary inputs.

Clearly, this breaks the pseudorandomness property of an OPRF, see Definition 1, as a malicious client will be able to predict the output of the OPRF for any input after the initial queries.

Remark 4. The SIDH-based OPRF protocol by Boneh et al. does not prohibit malicious clients from using points of smaller order dividing N_M, i.e. from using a shorter isogeny $E_0 \to E_m$. However, this attack could be thwarted if the server checked that the submitted curve is of correct distance from the starting curve. A simple test using pairing computations on the provided torsion point information may be tricked, but the NIZK of the client could be extended to include a proof that the client's witness, i.e. the kernel of the isogeny $E_0 \to E_{mr}$, is of full order $N_M N_R$.

Even if countermeasures for this polynomial-time attack are put in place, we are left with the following subexponential attack when points of full order are used.

The client evaluates the OPRF on a certain number of inputs that correspond to solve queries in the auxiliary one-more game. More precisely, the client chooses the kernel of his first isogeny as in the subexponential attack of the previous section. After blinding, evaluation of the server and unblinding, the client obtains what would have been the result of a "solve query" in the previous section. After the offline computation which, using meet-in-the-middle routines, recovers the binary tree described in Sect. 5, the client obtains torsion point images of $E_0[N_M]$ up to scalar under the isogeny $E_0 \rightarrow E_K := E_0/\langle P_K + [k]Q_K \rangle$. Again this is enough to compute $E_0/\langle M, K \rangle$ for any $M \in E_0[N_M]$ by Sect. 3.2, allowing the client to compute the OPRF on arbitrary inputs and therefore breaking the pseudorandomness property.

Possible countermeasures. In the case where the degree of the client's isogeny is forced to be $N_M N_R$, the proposed attack has subexponential complexity, and thus possible countermeasures may include increasing the parameter sizes. However, the solve queries to time trade-off may reduce the feasibility of such an approach. If the number of possible solve queries is unrestricted, to get 128-bit security one would need the isogeny degree N_M to be $\approx 2^{(128^2)}$. This can be partially mitigated by guaranteeing security only up to a certain number of queries. Given a limit of 2^Q queries, the exponent m needs to guarantee that $\min\{2^{\sqrt{m}-2}, 2^{m/(Q+2)+Q}\}$ is at least 2^λ. Thus, for 128-bit security, with $Q = 64$ the isogeny degree N_M would have to be increased to $\approx 2^{4224}$, whereas $Q = 32$ would require a degree $N_M \approx 2^{3264}$. Note that handling 2^{32} queries may well be within the scope of several OPRF applications, and isogenies of such a size may become impractically large. Their feasibility, however, depends on the specifics of the OPRF application and its time and bandwidth requirements. Thus, while the attack is subexponential (assuming $O(1)$ complexity for solve queries), increasing the parameter size comes at a significant performance and communication cost.

Therefore, it is important to consider possible algorithmic countermeasures. Firstly, note that the attacker submits seemingly valid requests, so the server cannot stop such interactions. Even if the server did want to prevent these requests, it may not be able to detect them. This is because the attacker only submits the image curve and some torsion point images under an isogeny with chosen kernel.

However, the attack strongly depends on the attacker choosing the point V. If the input points V were randomized, the attack as such could not work. The OPRF protocol requires that such points are obtained via hashing the client's PRF input x, but it does not enforce it. Hence, a possible countermeasure to the proposed attack would be requiring the client to provide a zero-knowledge proof that the curve E_{mr} is not only the result of honest isogeny computations, but also that the kernel of ϕ_m is the result of some hash function. However, developing an ad-hoc and efficient proof that can prove such statements remains an open problem.

5   Attack Implementation

We implemented the subexponential attack of Sect. 3.3 in SageMath to demonstrate the correctness of the algorithm and prove its feasibility. The source code is freely available at https://github.com/isogenists/isogeny-OPRF. We remark that this implementation is to be regarded only as a proof-of-concept and that several subroutines can be further optimized. Improving their performance and using lower-level languages, such as C, as well as platform-specific instructions, such as AVX, could significantly reduce the running time of the attack.

The proposed attack has two distinguishing features that help its implementation: it can be easily parallelized, and it has very low memory requirements. Indeed, the computations to recover the generators of $\langle \phi_K(P_V) \rangle$, $\langle \phi_K(Q_V) \rangle$ and $\langle \phi_K(P_V + Q_V) \rangle$ are independent of each other. It is also possible to achieve a higher degree of parallelization. Within each computation to recover a single generator, the meet-in-the-middle operations within each layer of the tree are also independent of each other, and they can thus be parallelized. In this case, the tree is generated layer-by-layer in a breadth-first manner. Note that while this may require a sizeable amount of memory to fully store an entire layer, the memory requirements are hardly the bottleneck. An attack with 2^{20} queries requires to store, at most, 2^{19} curves. Since an elliptic curve can be represented by its j-invariant, the memory limit is $2^{19} \cdot 2 \log p$. With a prime of size $\approx 2^{1500}$, as proposed in the OPRF protocol, the memory limit is about 196 MB. Alternatively, it is possible to traverse the tree in a depth-first manner to further lower the memory requirement, but this may limit the degree of parallelization. We remark that while parallelization only provides a linear speed-up, its effects can be significant. Our implementation provides parallelized meet-in-the-middle computations with a configurable number of cores in parallel.

Results. The majority of the attack's subroutines have polynomial complexity and they are optimized enough that their performance does not affect the overall running time. The building block that most affects the performance of the attack is the meet-in-the-middle computation. Indeed, the timings of the attack are directly correlated to the timing of a single meet-in-the-middle and the total number of queries. The memory requirements of the attack are given by the amount of memory needed for a single meet-in-the-middle, which in turn depends on the distance between the two curves. For parallelized implementations of the attack, the memory requirements correspond to as many meet-in-the-middle computations as there are parallel instances.

Table 1 shows the running times at different security levels on an Apple M1 CPU clocked at 3.20 GHz with 4 CPUs running in parallel. Up to 32 bits of security, the results come from running the entire attack, whereas for higher security levels the results are estimated based on those of a single MITM computation. The estimated time t is computed as

$$t = \frac{3(M+Q)2^q}{C}, \tag{1}$$

where M is the average running time of a MITM computation, Q is the average running time of a solve query computation, 2^q is the number of queries and C is the number of CPUs running in parallel. This formula follows from the fact that there are 2^q MITM computations and 2^q solve queries for each generator recovery, and three of those are needed. Moreover, parallelization gives a linear speed-up, and the remaining computations (such as those of Sect. 3.2) are extremely fast when compared to the rest of the attack, and thus negligible. Running computations at lower security levels and computing Eq. 1 does indeed estimate the running time accurately. It should be noted that this remains an estimate and the real results may vary to some degree.

We estimate that our non-optimized implementation running on a laptop with 4 CPUs can break 64 bits[2] of security in less than two days and 128 bits of security in about 5 years. If the same attack was performed with more powerful hardware and an optimized implementation, the running time could easily be reduced to a matter of months, if not weeks. We remark that if a server rotates its keys often, an attack that breaks the server one-more unpredictability after the key has changed still leads to significant attacks. For instance, in the case of OPRF-based private set intersection protocols, breaking the one-more unpredictability property allows the attacker to break the privacy property of the server's set at the time when that specific key was used.

Lastly, note that in the implementation solve queries are simulated locally. A real attack would interact with the server, and thus the "correct" attack time should not include the query computation times. For completeness, Table 1 reports the running time of the entire implementation, including the solve queries.

6 Trusted Setup

In the OPRF protocol of Boneh et al., the authors suggest using a random supersingular elliptic curve as starting curve. However, there is currently no known algorithm to generate a random supersingular elliptic curve such that its endomorphism ring is unknown to the person who generated it. Some attempts to solve this problem have been proposed in [26] and further studied in [6]. This motivates the following question:

---

[2] We report the results for $e_M = 169$, which corresponds to $\lambda = 67$. That is because our implementation requires $(q + 2) \mid e_M$, and 169 allows choosing $q = 11$. Using $e_M = 160$ would have required using significantly more queries or a longer MITM, thus resulting in worse performance. Note that the requirement that $(q + 2) \mid e_M$ is a limitation of the implementation and not of the attack itself.

Table 1. Results of our proof-of-concept implementation of the attack, running on an Apple M1 CPU clocked at 3.20 GHz with 4 CPUs in parallel and SageMath version 9.2. Results for $\lambda = 128$ are estimated based on the average running time of a meet-in-the-middle computation. Parameters include the size of the prime p, the security level λ, the degree of the isogeny written as $N_M = 2^{e_M}$, and the number of queries 2^q. The MITM section reports the distance between the curves and memory needed to compute a single meet-in-the-middle.

Parameters				MITM		Running time
$\log p$	λ	e_M	q	Distance	Memory (kB)	(s)
112	8	20	3	8	3.5	15
216	16	40	6	10	13.8	212 (3.53 m)
413	32	80	8	16	211.4	1,371 (22.85 m)
859	67	169	11	26	14,073	163,869 (1.89 d)
1,614	128	320	18	40	3,384,803	174,709,440 (5.54 y)

Is a trusted third party needed to generate the starting curve E_0?

Phrased differently, would choosing the starting curve E_0 and therefore knowledge of its endomorphism ring allow a malicious server, client or third party to break security properties of the (V)OPRF?

We first discuss whether a server may know the endomorphism ring of the starting curve E_0. The security proof by Boneh et al.'s OPRF relies on the hardness of finding two distinct isogenies (up to isomorphism) of the same degree from E_0 to a second curve [3, Lemma 29]. If the server chooses the starting curve and therefore knows its endomorphism ring, they are able to produce such collisions by breaking the collision resistance of the CGL hash function as in [15,29]. To guarantee provable security, a server should therefore not choose the starting curve.

However, breaking the verifiability insured by the zero-knowledge proof [3, Protocol 17] or the weak binding property [3, Game 3] of the protocol seems harder than finding collisions. Indeed, the server would need to produce two isogenies of degree dividing N_K such that both isogenies have the same action on the N_V-torsion for a chosen starting curve. We leave adapting the security proofs or finding an attack on the zero-knowledge proof for future work.

We now argue that any other party, either the client or a third party, cannot choose the curve E_0 either without compromising the security of the protocol. In [13], the authors describe algorithms for finding a secret isogeny when torsion information is provided. Their algorithms can be split into two categories: one where the starting curve has j-invariant 1728 and one where the starting curve is a trapdoor curve from which one can solve the isogeny problem faster than generic meet-in-the-middle algorithms. Trapdoor curves are parameterized by a pair (A, B) where A corresponds to the degree of the secret isogeny and B to the order of torsion points whose image under the secret isogeny is known. When $B \approx A^2$ or larger, then one can construct (A, B) trapdoor curves from which one can retrieve secret isogenies of degree A in polynomial time, if the action on the B-torsion is known [13, Theorem 15].

Attacks from the special starting curve with j-invariant 1728 do not apply here, since the starting curve cannot have j-invariant 1728 because the endomorphism ring needs to be unknown to the server. However, trapdoor curves have the property that without extra information they are difficult to distinguish from a random supersingular curve.

Suppose that a malicious party generates the starting curve E_0 in the following way. They generate a curve E' which is a trapdoor $(N_K, N_V N_R)$-curve and then perform a random walk of length $N_M N_R$ to obtain E_0 which is sent to the server. Now the malicious party poses as a client and instead of honestly complying with the protocol, they use E' as E_{mr}. They can prove knowledge of a suitable isogeny and torsion point images as they know an isogeny of the correct degree from E_0. Then the server computes E_{mrk} and reveals the action of the $N_V N_R$-torsion. Since E_{mr} was chosen to be a trapdoor curve and $N_V N_R \approx N_K^2$, the malicious party can retrieve this isogeny in polynomial time.

Such an attack can be thwarted by applying a trusted setup in which E_0 is a truly random curve. In [4, §4], an efficient way to perform a distributed trusted setup is described, ensuring that, if at least one participant is honest, the setup can be trusted. In that case, torsion point attacks are not applicable. The attack can also be weakened by substantially increasing N_K. However, this might be susceptible to future improvements of trapdoor curve constructions.

7 Conclusion

In this paper, we perform a thorough cryptanalysis of Boneh et al.'s SIDH-based oblivious pseudorandom function. The security of this OPRF is based on a new hardness assumption, the auxiliary one-more assumption. We investigate this assumption and we show how an attacker can win the corresponding security game in polynomial time, or with the appropriate countermeasures in subexponential time.

The attack on the underlying hardness assumption leads to an attack on the pseudorandomness of the OPRF itself. We show how a malicious client can extract enough information from a number of initial executions of the OPRF protocol to subsequently evaluate the OPRF on arbitrary inputs without further interaction with the server. In particular, this attack breaks the security parameters provided by Boneh et al. As a proof of concept, we implement the attack in SageMath, verified its correctness and give timings for various security levels.

Furthermore, we discuss the security implications following from a lack of a trusted setup when generating the starting curve parameter in the SIDH-based OPRF. Note that Boneh et al. do not explicitly require a trusted setup. We show how a client or a third party generating the starting curve can backdoor it to retrieve the server's secret key, while a malicious server could generate the starting curve to break the supersingular-isogeny collision assumption.

This work leads to some open problems. On one hand, one could improve and extend the proposed attack, with a particular focus on reducing the complexity of the subexponential attack to polynomial time, as well as extending it to the CSIDH-based OPRF. On the other hand, further work is needed to develop efficient countermeasures against the subexponential attack or to design a novel SIDH-based VOPRF. Future research will also focus on understanding the implications of breaking the supersingular-isogeny collision assumption on the OPRF protocol itself, and whether it is possible to avoid a trusted setup.

Acknowledgments. We would like to thank Dan Boneh, Jesús Javier Chi Domínguez, Luca De Feo, Enric Florit, Dmitry Kogan and Simon Masson for fruitful discussions. Péter Kutas, Simon-Philipp Merz and Christophe Petit were supported by EPSRC and the UK government as part of the grant EP/S01361X/1 for Péter Kutas and Christophe Petit and the grant EP/P009301/1 for Simon-Philipp Merz. Further, Péter Kutas was supported by the Ministry of Innovation and Technology and the National Research, Development and Innovation Office within the Quantum Information National Laboratory of Hungary.

References

1. Albrecht, M.R., Davidson, A., Deo, A., Smart, N.P.: Round-optimal verifiable oblivious pseudorandom functions from ideal lattices. In: Garay, J.A. (ed.) PKC 2021. LNCS, vol. 12711, pp. 261–289. Springer, Cham (2021). https://doi.org/10.1007/978-3-030-75248-4_10
2. Azarderakhsh, R., et al.: Supersingular isogeny key encapsulation. Updated parameters for round 2 of NIST Post-Quantum Standardization project (2019)
3. Boneh, D., Kogan, D., Woo, K.: Oblivious pseudorandom functions from isogenies. In: Moriai, S., Wang, H. (eds.) ASIACRYPT 2020. LNCS, vol. 12492, pp. 520–550. Springer, Cham (2020). https://doi.org/10.1007/978-3-030-64834-3_18
4. Burdges, J., Feo, L.D.: Delay encryption. Cryptology ePrint Archive, Report 2020/638 (2020). https://eprint.iacr.org/2020/638
5. Castryck, W., Lange, T., Martindale, C., Panny, L., Renes, J.: CSIDH: an efficient post-quantum commutative group action. In: Peyrin, T., Galbraith, S. (eds.) ASIACRYPT 2018. LNCS, vol. 11274, pp. 395–427. Springer, Cham (2018). https://doi.org/10.1007/978-3-030-03332-3_15
6. Castryck, W., Panny, L., Vercauteren, F.: Rational isogenies from irrational endomorphisms. In: Canteaut, A., Ishai, Y. (eds.) EUROCRYPT 2020. LNCS, vol. 12106, pp. 523–548. Springer, Cham (2020). https://doi.org/10.1007/978-3-030-45724-2_18
7. Charles, D.X., Lauter, K.E., Goren, E.Z.: Cryptographic hash functions from expander graphs. J. Cryptology **22**(1), 93–113 (2009)
8. Chaum, D.: Blind signatures for untraceable payments. In: Advances in Cryptology: Proceedings of CRYPTO 1982, Santa Barbara, California, USA, 23–25 August 1982, pp. 199–203 (1982)
9. Couveignes, J.M.: Hard homogeneous spaces. IACR Cryptology ePrint Archive **2006**, 291 (1999)
10. Davidson, A., Goldberg, I., Sullivan, N., Tankersley, G., Valsorda, F.: Privacy pass: bypassing internet challenges anonymously. Proc. Priv. Enhancing Technol. **2018**(3), 164–180 (2018)

11. Davidson, A., Sullivan, N., Wood, C.A.: Oblivious Pseudorandom Functions (OPRFs) using Prime-Order Groups. Internet-Draft draft-sullivan-cfrg-voprf-03, Internet Engineering Task Force (2019), work in Progress
12. De Feo, L.: Mathematics of isogeny based cryptography. arXiv preprint: arXiv:1711.04062 (2017)
13. de Quehen, V., et al.: Improved torsion point attacks on SIDH variants. arXiv e-prints arXiv:2005.14681 (May 2020)
14. Demmler, D., Rindal, P., Rosulek, M., Trieu, N.: PIR-PSI: scaling private contact discovery. Proc. Priv. Enhancing Technol. **2018**(4), 159–178 (2018)
15. Eisenträger, K., Hallgren, S., Lauter, K., Morrison, T., Petit, C.: Super singular isogeny graphs and endomorphism rings: reductions and solutions. In: Nielsen, J.B., Rijmen, V. (eds.) EUROCRYPT 2018. LNCS, vol. 10822, pp. 329–368. Springer, Cham (2018). https://doi.org/10.1007/978-3-319-78372-7_11
16. Everspaugh, A., Chatterjee, R., Scott, S., Juels, A., Ristenpart, T.: The pythia PRF service. In: Jung, J., Holz, T. (eds.) 24th USENIX Security Symposium, USENIX Security 15, Washington, D.C., USA, 12–14 August 2015, pp. 547–562. USENIX Association (2015)
17. Freedman, M.J., Ishai, Y., Pinkas, B., Reingold, O.: Keyword search and oblivious pseudorandom functions. In: Kilian, J. (ed.) TCC 2005. LNCS, vol. 3378, pp. 303–324. Springer, Heidelberg (2005). https://doi.org/10.1007/978-3-540-30576-7_17
18. Galbraith, S.D., Petit, C., Shani, B., Ti, Y.B.: On the security of super singular isogeny cryptosystems. In: Advances in Cryptology - ASIACRYPT 2016, pp. 63–91 (2016). https://doi.org/10.1007/978-3-662-53887-6_3
19. Jao, D., et al.: SIKE: Supersingular isogeny key encapsulation http://sike.org/ (2017)
20. Jao, D., De Feo, L.: Towards quantum-resistant cryptosystems from supersingular elliptic curve isogenies. In: Yang, B.-Y. (ed.) PQCrypto 2011. LNCS, vol. 7071, pp. 19–34. Springer, Heidelberg (2011). https://doi.org/10.1007/978-3-642-25405-5_2
21. Jarecki, S., Kiayias, A., Krawczyk, H.: Round-optimal password-protected secret sharing and T-PAKE in the password-only model. In: Sarkar, P., Iwata, T. (eds.) ASIACRYPT 2014. LNCS, vol. 8874, pp. 233–253. Springer, Heidelberg (2014). https://doi.org/10.1007/978-3-662-45608-8_13
22. Jarecki, S., Krawczyk, H., Xu, J.: OPAQUE: an asymmetric PAKE protocol secure against pre-computation attacks. In: Nielsen, J.B., Rijmen, V. (eds.) EURO-CRYPT 2018. LNCS, vol. 10822, pp. 456–486. Springer, Cham (2018). https://doi.org/10.1007/978-3-319-78372-7_15
23. Jarecki, S., Liu, X.: Efficient oblivious pseudorandom function with applications to adaptive OT and secure computation of set intersection. In: Theory of Cryptography, 6th Theory of Cryptography Conference, TCC 2009, San Francisco, CA, USA, 15–17 March 2009. Proceedings, pp. 577–594 (2009)
24. Jarecki, S., Liu, X.: Efficient oblivious pseudorandom function with applications to adaptive OT and secure computation of set intersection. In: Reingold, O. (ed.) TCC 2009. LNCS, vol. 5444, pp. 577–594. Springer, Heidelberg (2009). https://doi.org/10.1007/978-3-642-00457-5_34
25. Li, L., Pal, B., Ali, J., Sullivan, N., Chatterjee, R., Ristenpart, T.: Protocols for checking compromised credentials. In: Cavallaro, L., Kinder, J., Wang, X., Katz, J. (eds.) Proceedings of the 2019 ACM SIGSAC Conference on Computer and Communications Security, CCS 2019, London, UK, 11–15 November 2019, pp. 1387–1403. ACM (2019)
26. Love, J., Boneh, D.: Supersingular curves with small noninteger endomorphisms. Open Book Ser. **4**(1), 7–22 (2020)

27. Merz, S.-P., Minko, R., Petit, C.: Another look at some isogeny hardness assumptions. In: Jarecki, S. (ed.) CT-RSA 2020. LNCS, vol. 12006, pp. 496–511. Springer, Cham (2020). https://doi.org/10.1007/978-3-030-40186-3_21
28. van Oorschot, P.C., Wiener, M.J.: Parallel collision search with cryptanalytic applications. J. Cryptology **12**(1), 1–28 (1999)
29. Petit, C., Lauter, K.E.: Hard and easy problems for supersingular isogeny graphs. IACR Cryptol. ePrint Arch. 2017, 962 (2017). http://eprint.iacr.org/2017/962
30. Rostovtsev, A., Stolbunov, A.: Public-key cryptosystem based on isogenies. IACR Cryptology ePrint Archive **2006**, 145 (2006)
31. Seres, I.A., Horváth, M., Burcsi, P.: The legendre pseudorandom function as a multivariate quadratic cryptosystem: Security and applications. IACR Cryptol. ePrint Arch. 2021, 182 (2021). https://eprint.iacr.org/2021/182
32. Silverman, J.H.: The Arithmetic of Elliptic Curves. GTM, vol. 106. Springer, New York (2009). https://doi.org/10.1007/978-0-387-09494-6
33. Sullivan, N., Krawczyk, D.H., Friel, O., Barnes, R.: OPAQUE with TLS 1.3. Internet-Draft draft-sullivan-tls-opaque-01, Internet Engineering Task Force (2021), work in Progress

Symmetric-Key Cryptanalysis

A Practical Key-Recovery Attack on 805-Round Trivium

Chen-Dong Ye and Tian Tian$^{(\boxtimes)}$

PLA Strategic Support Force Information Engineering University,
Zhengzhou 450001, China

Abstract. The cube attack is one of the most important cryptanalytic techniques against Trivium. Many key-recovery attacks based on cube attacks have been established. However, few attacks can recover the 80-bit full key information practically. In particular, the previous best practical key-recovery attack was on 784-round Trivium proposed by Fouque and Vannet at FSE 2013. To mount practical key-recovery attacks, it requires a sufficient number of low-degree superpolies. It is difficult both for experimental cube attacks and division property based cube attacks with randomly selected cubes due to lack of efficiency. In this paper, we give a new algorithm to construct candidate cubes targeting linear superpolies. Our experiments show that the success probability is 100% for finding linear superpolies using the constructed cubes. We obtain over 1000 linear superpolies for 805-round Trivium. With 42 independent linear superpolies, we mount a practical key-recovery attack on 805-round Trivium, which increases the number of attacked rounds by 21. The complexity of our attack is $2^{41.40}$, which could be carried out on a PC with a GTX-1080 GPU in several hours.

Keywords: Cube attacks · Key-recovery attacks · Trivium · Heuristic algorithm · Möbius transformation

1 Introduction

Trivium [2] is a bit-oriented synchronous stream cipher designed by De Cannière and Preneel, which is one of the eSTREAM hardware-oriented finalists and an International Standard under ISO/IEC 29192-3:2012. Due to the simple structure and high level security, Trivium attracts a lot of attention.

The cube attack, first proposed by Dinur and Shamir in [4], is a powerful key-recovery attack against Trivium. There are two main phases in a cube attack. In the first phase, called the preprocessing phase, one needs to find appropriate cubes and recover their superpolies which are generally low-degree polynomials in key variables. In the second phase, called the on-line phase, by querying the encryption oracle, one could evaluate the superpolies under the real key and so

Supported by the National Natural Science Foundations of China under grant nos. 61672533.

© International Association for Cryptologic Research 2021
M. Tibouchi and H. Wang (Eds.): ASIACRYPT 2021, LNCS 13090, pp. 187–213, 2021.
https://doi.org/10.1007/978-3-030-92062-3_7

obtain a system of equations in key variables. Then, by solving the obtained system of equations, some bits of information in key or even the whole key could be recovered. Since proposed, many improvements have been established on cube attacks such as cube testers [1], dynamic cube attacks [3,5,17], conditional cube attacks [10,13], division property based cube attacks [8,9,21,22,24,25,28] and correlation cube attacks [15].

Most of the previous work tried to recover the ANFs of the superpolies such that the number of initialization rounds as large as possible. Some attacks could only recover one or two key bits and some attacks have very marginal online complexities. For example, in [7–9], cubes of sizes over 74 were used to recover key bits for 840-, 841- and 842-round Trivium. In these cases, one to three key bits could be recovered with the superpolies. Then, it needs at least 2^{77} requests to exhaustively search the remaining key bits. Thus, the total complexity is very close to that of the brute-force attack using these large cubes.

Those attacks targeting a large number of rounds do not immediately imply a practical attack. A practical key-recovery attack on Trivium is also an important security evaluation of Trivium and a measure of the improvement of cube attacks. Considering a practical key-recovery attack against Trivium, the difficulty lies in finding a sufficient number of useful superpolies. To randomly search cubes with linear superpolies for the round-reduced Trivium with over 800 rounds is almost impossible. Currently, for Trivium, the number of initialization rounds that could be reached by cube attacks with a practical complexity is 784.

How to construct useful cubes in cube attacks has long been a difficult problem. In [4] and [6], the authors provided some ideas for finding cubes with linear superpolies. More specifically, in [4], the authors proposed the random walk method. This method starts with a randomly chosen set I of cube variables. Then, an IV variable is removed randomly from I if the corresponding superpoly is constant and a randomly chosen IV variable is added to I if the corresponding superpoly is nonlinear. This process is repeated to find cubes which pass through a sufficient number of linearity tests. If it fails, then the process restarted with another initial I. With this method, for 767-round Trivium, 35 linear superpolies were found. In [6], the authors proposed to construct a candidate large cube by disjoint union of two subcubes yielding 12 zero polynomials on some specific internal state bits determined by the recursive relation of the six bits involved in the output function. As a result, for 784-round Trivium, they found 42 linear superpolies. Furthermore, for 799-round Trivium, the authors declared that the only way linear superpolies have been found was using this method to construct cubes.

Besides, the idea of Greedy algorithm has been found useful in constructing cube distinguishers. In [19], the authors first proposed the GreedyBitSet algorithm to construct cube distinguishers and nonrandomness detectors. Later, in [18], based on the work in [19], the authors studied the state biases as well as keystream biases. As a result, they obtained cube distinguishers for 829-round Trivium and 850-round TriviA-SC. In [12], combining the GreedyBit-Set algorithm with the degree evaluation method proposed in [14], the authors improved the work in [18]. As a result, they found good distinguishers on Trivium, Kreyvium and ACORN. In particular, they provided a zero-sum distinguisher on 842-round Trivium and a significant non-randomness up to 850-round Trivium.

1.1 Our Contributions

This paper is devoted to practical key-recovery attacks against 805-round Trivium. To achieve this goal, the key problem is to find lots of cubes with linear superpolies. As mentioned above, this is quite difficult when the number of round is over 800. Our main contribution is to propose a new method to construct cubes, which is experimentally verified to be quite effective. It consists of the following three aspects.

A Heuristic Algorithm to Construct Candidate Cubes. By combining the GreedyBitSet algorithm with the division property, we propose a new algorithm to construct cubes targeting linear superpolies. The new algorithm begins with a small set of cube variables and then extends it iteratively. More specifically, there are mainly two stages in our algorithm. During the first stage, we select an IV variable (called 'steep IV variable' in this paper) which could decrease the degrees of the superpolies as fast as possible in each iteration. If we fail in the first stage, then we step into the second stage, where we pick up IV variables (called 'gentle IV variables' in this paper) which decrease the degrees of the superpolies as slowly as possible. Benefited from this two-stage algorithm, we could successfully construct cubes such that degrees of the superpolies are close to 1. Note that, the idea of this algorithm is also applicable to other NFSR-based stream ciphers.

The Preference Bit and an Algorithm to Predict It. Note that all known linear superpolies of Trivium are very sparse, and the output bit function of Trivium is the XOR of six internal state bits. It is thought that a linear superpoly probably comes from a single internal state bit. Hence, to determine a proper starting set of the above new algorithm, we propose the concept of the preference bit. Based on the structure analysis of Trivium, an iterative algorithm is provided to roughly predict the preference bit of r-round Trivium. The experimental results show that our algorithm could predict the preference bit with a success probability 75.3%.

The Improved Möbius Transformation. In cube attacks, the Möbius transformation is a powerful tool which could be used to test all the subcubes of a large cube simultaneously. However, its memory complexity is very large. To reduce the memory complexity, we divide the original Möbius transformation into two stages. Let $f(x_0, x_1, \ldots, x_{n-1})$ be a Boolean function on $x_0, x_1, \ldots, x_{n-1}$. Let q be a positive integer less than $n - 1$. In the first stage, the Möbius transformations of $f(x_0, \ldots, x_{n-q-1}, 0, 0, \ldots, 0)$, $f(x_0, \ldots, x_{n-q-1}, 1, 0, \ldots, 0)$, $\ldots$, $f(x_0, \ldots, x_{n-q-1}, 1, 1, \ldots, 1)$ are calculated and only a part of each Möbius transformation is stored. In the second stage, based on these partly stored transformations, we could recover a part of the ANF of f with a method similar to the

Möbius transformation of a q-variable Boolean function. With this technique, the memory complexity could be decreased from 2^n bits to about 2^{n-q} bits. When it comes to practical cube attacks, this method enables us to test a large number of subcubes of a large cube set at once with a reasonable memory complexity. For instance, we could simultaneously test $2^{32.28}$ subcubes of a cube set of size 43 with less than 9 GBs memory, while testing such a cube with the original Möbius transformation requires 2^{43} bits (1024 GBs) memory.

Fig. 1. The sketch of our idea

As an illustration, we apply our methods, whose sketch is shown in Fig. 1, to 805-round Trivium. As a result, we obtain more than 1000 cubes with linear superpolies for 805-round Trivium. Among these linear superpolies, there are 38 linearly independent superpolies. Besides, by sliding some cubes of 805-round Trivium to 806-round Trivium, we easily obtain several linear superpolies for 806-round Trivium. Based on the linear superpolies of 805- and 806-round Trivium, 42 key bits could be recovered for 805-round Trivium with $2^{41.25}$ requests. By adding a brute-force attack, the 80-bit key could be recovered within $2^{41.40}$ requests, which could be practically implemented by a PC with a NVIDIA GTX-1080 GPU in several hours. This attack on 805-round Trivium improves the previous best practical cube attacks by 21 more rounds, and it is the first practical attack for Trivium variants with more than 800 initialization rounds. As a comparison, we summarize the cube attacks based key-recovery attacks against the round-reduced Trivium in Table 1. Furthermore, to show the effectiveness of the heuristic algorithm to construct candidate cubes, we also applied our method to 810-round Trivium. By only testing one 43-dimensional cube, we find two 42-dimensional cubes with linear superpolies. Since it is almost impossible to find a linear superpoly for 810-round Trivium by random walk algorithm in [4] and the disjoint union method in [6], it is shown that the new heuristic algorithm to construct candidate cubes is powerful.

1.2 Organisation

The rest of this paper is organized as follows. In Sect. 2, we give some basic definitions and concepts. In Sect. 3, we show an algorithm to construct cubes which are potential to have linear superpolies. In Sect. 4, we propose an improved Möbius transformation which enables us to test a large mount of subcubes of

Table 1. A summary of key-recovery attacks on Trivium

Attack type	# of rounds	Off-line phase		On-line phase	Total time	Ref.
		Cube size	# of key bits			
Practical	672	12	63	2^{17}	$2^{18.56}$	[4]
	709	22-23	79	<2	$2^{29.14}$	[16]
	767	28-31	35	2^{45}	$2^{45.00}$	[4]
	784	30-33	42	2^{38}	2^{39}	[6]
	805	32-38	42	2^{38}	$2^{41.40}$	Sect. 5
Not practical	799	32-37	18	2^{62}	$2^{62.00}$	[6]
	802	34-37	8	2^{72}	$2^{72.00}$	[27]
	805	28	7	2^{73}	$2^{73.00}$	[15]
	806	34-37	16	2^{64}	2^{64}	Sect. 5
	835	35	5	2^{75}	$2^{75.00}$	[15]
	832	72	1	2^{79}	$2^{79.01}$	[21, 22, 25]
	832	72	>1	2^{79}	$<2^{79.01}$	[29]
	840	78	1	2^{79}	$2^{79.58}$	[8]
	840	75	3	2^{77}	$2^{77.32}$	[9]
	841	78	1	2^{79}	$2^{79.58}$	[8]
	841	76	2	2^{78}	$2^{78.58}$	[9]
	842	78	1	2^{79}	$2^{79.58}$	[7]
	842	76	2	2^{79}	$2^{78.58}$	[9]

a large cube simultaneously with a reasonable memory complexity. In Sect. 5, we apply our method to round-reduced Trivium and establish a practical cube attack on 805-round Trivium. Finally, Sect. 6 concludes the paper.

2 Preliminaries

In this section, we introduce some related concepts and definitions.

2.1 Specification of Trivium

Trivium is a bit-oriented synchronous stream cipher which was one of eSTREAM hardware-oriented finalists. The main building block of Trivium is a 288-bit nonlinear feedback shift register. For every clock cycle there are three bits of the internal state updated by quadratic feedback functions and all the remaining bits of the internal state are updated by shifting. The internal state of Trivium is initialized by loading an 80-bit secret key and an 80-bit IV into the registers, and setting all the remaining bits to 0 except for the last three bits of the third register. Then, after 1152 initialization rounds, the key stream bits are generated by XORing six internal state bits. Algorithm 1 describes the pseudo-code of Trivium. For more details, please refer to [2].

Algorithm 1. Pseudo-code of Trivium

1: $(s_1, s_2, \ldots, s_{93}) \leftarrow (x_1, x_2, \ldots, x_{80}, 0, \ldots, 0)$;
2: $(s_{94}, s_{95}, \ldots, s_{177}) \leftarrow (v_1, v_2, \ldots, v_{80}, 0, \ldots, 0)$;
3: $(s_{178}, s_{179}, \ldots, s_{288}) \leftarrow (0, \ldots, 0, 1, 1, 1)$;
4: **for** i from 1 to N **do**
5:     $t_1 \leftarrow s_{66} \oplus s_{93} \oplus s_{91}s_{92} \oplus s_{171}$;
6:     $t_2 \leftarrow s_{162} \oplus s_{177} \oplus s_{175}s_{176} \oplus s_{264}$;
7:     $t_3 \leftarrow s_{243} \oplus s_{288} \oplus s_{286}s_{287} \oplus s_{69}$;
8:     **if** $i > 1152$ **then**
9:         $z_{i-1152} \leftarrow s_{66} \oplus s_{93} \oplus s_{162} \oplus s_{177} \oplus s_{243} \oplus s_{288}$;
10:    **end if**
11:    $(s_1, s_2, \ldots, s_{93}) \leftarrow (t_3, s_1, \ldots, s_{92})$;
12:    $(s_{94}, s_{95}, \ldots, s_{177}) \leftarrow (t_1, s_{94}, \ldots, s_{176})$;
13:    $(s_{178}, s_{179}, \ldots, s_{288}) \leftarrow (t_2, s_{178}, \ldots, s_{287})$;
14: **end for**

2.2 Cube Attacks

The idea of cube attacks was first proposed by Dinur and Shamir in [4]. In a cube attack against stream ciphers, an output bit z is described as a Boolean function f in key variables $\boldsymbol{k} = (k_0, k_1, \ldots, k_{n-1})$ and public IV variables $\boldsymbol{v} = (v_0, v_1 \ldots, v_{m-1})$, i.e., $z = f(\boldsymbol{k}, \boldsymbol{v})$. Let $I = \{v_{i_1}, v_{i_2}, \ldots, v_{i_d}\}$ be a subset of IV variables. Then f can be rewritten as

$$f(\boldsymbol{k}, \boldsymbol{v}) = t_I \cdot p_I(\boldsymbol{k}, \boldsymbol{v}) \oplus q_I(\boldsymbol{k}, \boldsymbol{v}),$$

where $t_I = \prod_{v \in I} v$, p_I does not contain any variable in I, and each term in q_I is not divisible by t_I. It can be seen that the summation of the 2^d functions derived from f by assigning all the possible values to d variables in I equals to p_I, that is,

$$\bigoplus_{(v_{i_1}, v_{i_2}, \ldots, v_{i_d}) \in \mathbb{F}_2^d} f(\boldsymbol{k}, \boldsymbol{v}) = p_I(\boldsymbol{k}, \boldsymbol{v}).$$

The public variables in I are called *cube variables*, while the remaining IV variables are called non-cube variables. The set C_I of all 2^d possible assignments of the cube variables is called a *d-dimensional cube*, and the polynomial p_I is called the *superpoly* of C_I in f. For the sake of convenience, we also call p_I the superpoly of I in f. It is worth noting that the superpoly of I in f is a polynomial in key variables when all the non-cube variables are set to constant. In the following paper, we set the non-cube variables to 0's in default.

A cube attack consists of the preprocessing phase and the on-line phase.

- **Off-line Phase.** The attacker should find cubes whose superpolies in the output bit are low-degree polynomials.
- **On-line Phase.** For each cube obtained in the off-line phase, the attacker inquires the encryption oracle to get the cube summation under the real key. With the obtained cube summations corresponding to the previously found

cubes, a system of low-degree equations in key variables could be set up. Then, by solving this system of equations, some key bits could be recovered. Finally, by adding a brute-force attack (if there are some key bits remaining unknown), the whole key could be recovered.

2.3 The Bit-Based Division Property and a Degree Evaluation Algorithm Based on It

In [23], the authors proposed the conventional bit-based division property whose definition is as follows.

Definition 1 (Bit-Based Division Property [23]). *Let $\mathbb{X}$ be a multi-set whose elements take a value of $\mathbb{F}_2^n$. Let $\mathbb{K}$ be a set whose elements take an n-dimensional bit vector. When the multi-set $\mathbb{X}$ has the division property $D_{\mathbb{K}}^{1^n}$, it fulfills the following conditions:*

$$\bigoplus_{x \in \mathbb{X}} x^u = \begin{cases} unknown & \textit{if there exists } \alpha \textit{ in } \mathbb{K} \textit{ s.t. } u \succeq \alpha, \\ 0 & \textit{otherwise,} \end{cases}$$

where $u \succeq \alpha$ if and only if $u_i \geq k_i$ for all i and $x^u = \prod_{i=0}^{n-1} x_i^{u_i}$.

Due to the high memory complexity, the bit-based division property was confined to be applied to small block ciphers such as SIMON32 and Simeck32 [23]. To avoid such a high memory complexity, in [26], the authors applied the mixed integer linear programming (MILP) methods to the bit-based division property. They first introduced the concept of division trails, which is defined as follows.

Definition 2 (Division Trail [26]). *Let us consider the propagation of the division property $\{\alpha\} = \mathbb{K}_0 \to \mathbb{K}_1 \to \mathbb{K}_2 \cdots \to \mathbb{K}_r$. Moreover, for any vector $\alpha_{i+1}^* \in \mathbb{K}_{i+1}$, there exist a vector $\alpha_i^* \in \mathbb{K}_i$ such that α_i^* can propagate to α_{i+1}^* by the propagation rules of division property. Furthermore, for $(\alpha_0, \alpha_1, \ldots, \alpha_r) \in \mathbb{K}_0 \times \mathbb{K}_1 \times \cdots \times \mathbb{K}_r$ if α_i can propagate to α_{i+1} for $i \in \{0, 1, \ldots, r-1\}$, we call $\alpha_0 \to \alpha_1 \to \cdots \to \alpha_r$ an r-round division trail.*

In [26], the authors described the propagation rules for AND, COPY and XOR with MILP models, see [26] for the details. Therefore, they could build an MILP model to cover all the possible division trails generated during the propagation. Besides, in [20,21], the authors simplified those MILP models in [26]. In particular, in [21], the division property based cube attacks were proposed for the first time and were applied to attacking Trivium, Grain-128 and Acorn successfully. Later, to improve the work of [21], in [24], the authors proposed a degree evaluation algorithm which was based on the following proposition.

Proposition 1 ([24]). *Let $f(x, v)$ be a polynomial, where x and v denote the secret and public variables, respectively. For a set of indices $I = \{i_1, i_2, \ldots, i_{|I|}\} \subset \{1, 2, \ldots, m\}$, let C_I be a set of $2^{|I|}$ values where the variables in $\{v_{i_1}, v_{i_2}, \ldots, v_{i_{|I|}}\}$ are taking all possible combinations of values. Let k_I*

be an m-dimensional bit vector such that $\boldsymbol{v}^{I} = t_I = v_{i_1} v_{i_2} \cdots v_{i_{|I|}}$. Let $\boldsymbol{k}_\Lambda$ be an n-dimensional bit vector. If there is no division trail such that $(\boldsymbol{k}_\Lambda \| \boldsymbol{k}_I) \xrightarrow{f} 1$, then the monomial $x^{\boldsymbol{k}_\Lambda}$ is not involved in the superpoly of the cube C_I.

If there is $d \geq 0$ such that for all $\boldsymbol{k}_\Lambda$ of Hamming Weight $hw(\boldsymbol{k}_\Lambda) > d$, the division trail $x^{\boldsymbol{k}_\Lambda}$ does not exist, then it can be seen that d is an upper bound of the algebraic degree of the superpoly. With the MILP method, this d can be naturally modeled as the maximum of the objective function $\sum_{j=1}^{n} x_j$. Therefore, for a given set of cube variables, by solving MILP models, an upper bound of the degree of the superpoly could be obtained. For more details, please refer to Sect. 4 of [24]. In the following paper, we shall combine this algorithm with some greedy strategies to find cubes with linear superpolies.

2.4 The Möbius Transformation

In [5], Dinur and Shamir suggested using the Möbius transformation to compute all possible subcubes of a large cube at once. Later, in [6], the author showed some ways to use the Möbius transformation in cube attacks on Trivium.

Let f be a polynomial in $\mathbb{F}_2[x_0, x_1, \ldots, x_{n-1}]$, whose algebraic normal form is given by

$$f(x_0, \ldots, x_{n-1}) = \bigoplus_{c = (c_0, \ldots, c_{n-1}) \in \mathbb{F}_2^n} g(c_0, \ldots, c_{n-1}) \prod_{i=0}^{n-1} x_i^{c_i},$$

where the function g giving the coefficient of each term $\prod_{i=0}^{n-1} x_i^{c_i}$ is the Möbius transformation of f. With the knowledge of the truth table of f, one could calculate the ANF of f by using the Möbius transform, see Algorithm 2.

Algorithm 2. The Möbius transformation algorithm

Require: Truth Table S of f with 2^n entries
1: **for** i from 0 to $n - 1$ **do**
2:    Let $Sz \leftarrow 2^i$, $Pos \leftarrow 0$
3:    **while** $Pos < 2^n$ **do**
4:       **for** $j = 0$ to $Sz - 1$ **do**
5:          $S[Pos + Sz + j] \leftarrow S[Pos + j] \oplus S[Pos + Sz + j]$
6:       **end for**
7:       Let $Pos \leftarrow Pos + 2 \cdot Sz$
8:    **end while**
9: **end for**

For Algorithm 2, it can be found that it needs to store the whole truth table of f and so a large mount of memory is needed. Specifically, for an n-variable polynomial f, it requires 2^n bits of memory. Furthermore, the computational complexity of Algorithm 2 is $n \cdot 2^n$ basic operations, since the innermost loop is executed $n \cdot 2^{n-1}$ times, which consists of a single assignment and a XOR operation. It is worth noting that Algorithm 2 could be accelerated. For instance, a 32-bit implementation is presented in [11] which performs roughly 32 times less operations, and so has a complexity of $n \cdot 2^{n-5}$ operations.

Now we consider the application of the Möbius transformation to cube attacks. Assume that $f(k_0, k_1, \ldots, k_{n-1}, v_0, v_1 \ldots, v_{m-1})$ is the output bit of a cipher in key variables $k_0, k_1, \ldots, k_{n-1}$ and IV variables $v_0, v_1 \ldots, v_{m-1}$. Let $I = \{v_{i_1}, v_{i_2}, \ldots, v_{i_d}\}$ be a set of cube variables. When all the other variables are set to constants, the output bit function f is reduced to a polynomial f' on cube variables in I only. Given the truth table of f', by using the Möbius transformation, the ANF of f' could be recovered. Note that, for a subset I' of I, the coefficient of the term $\prod_{v \in I'} v$ is the value of $p_{I'}$ when the variables in $I \setminus I'$ are set to 0's, where $p_{I'}$ is the superpoly of I' in f. Based on this fact, with the Möbius transformation, experimental tests such as linearity tests and quadratic tests could be done at once for all the subcubes of a large set of cube variables. It can be seen that the Möbius transformation makes finding linear/quadratic superpolies easier and so improves the efficiency of cube attacks.

3 Construct Potentially Good Cubes

Finding cubes which could be used to mount key-recovery attacks is a tough task in cube attacks. Collecting enough such cubes to establish practical attacks is even more difficult. In this section, combining the idea of GreedyBitSet algorithm with division property, we first devote to constructing cubes which are potential to have linear superpolies[1] through extending a starting cube set iteratively. Then, to obtain a proper starting cube set, we propose the concept of the preference bit and present an algorithm to predict the preference bit based on a structural analysis of Trivium. Combining these ideas, we could construct potentially good cubes successfully.

3.1 A Heuristic Algorithm of Constructing Cubes

In cube attacks, linear superpolies are of significance since linear equations in key variables could be set up based on linear superpolies. To construct cubes which potentially have linear superpolies, we combine the division property with heuristic algorithms to extend a small set of cube variables iteratively. Before illustrating our idea, we shall first give the following definitions.

Definition 3 (Steep IV Variable). *Let $I = \{v_{i_1}, v_{i_2}, \ldots, v_{i_\ell}\}$ be a set containing ℓ cube variables. Then, an IV variable $b \in B = \{v_0, v_1, \ldots, v_{m-1}\} \setminus I$ is called a steep IV variable of I if $ds(I \cup \{b\}) = \min\{ds(I \cup \{v\}) | v \in B\}$, where $ds(I)$ is the degree of the superpoly of I in key variables.*

---

[1] Constant polynomials are also linear. However, key bits could not be recovered from constant superpolies directly. Hence, in this paper, when talking about linear superploies, we do not take the constant linear into consideration.

Let I be a starting set of cube variables, which is a small set. It can be seen that a steep IV variable of I is exactly the one which makes the degree of the superpoly decrease most. To construct a cube with a linear superpoly from I, a natural idea is to extend I iteratively, where a steep IV variable is added to the current set I in each iteration. With this strategy, the degree of superpoly could be decreased fast. However, decreasing the degree of the superpoly too fast sometimes brings troubles to constructing cubes with linear superpolies. Assume that I' is constructed from I after several iterations, where a steep IV variable is added in each iteration. Let v be a steep IV variable of I'. It is possible that $ds(I' \cup v) = 0$, while $ds(I') > 5$. It indicates that adding a steep IV variable could make the degree of the superpoly decrease to 0 suddenly. Hence, it may fail to construct cubes with linear superpolies by only adding steep IV variables. We perform experiments on Trivium and the results show that this phenomenon happens frequently. We provide a concrete example happening in the case of 805-round Trivium, see Example 1.

Example 1. For 805-round Trivium, we try to construct a good cube by extending $\{v_4, v_6, v_{10}, v_{11}, v_{15}, v_{17}, v_{19}, v_{21}, v_{25}, v_{29}, v_{32}, v_{34}, v_{36}, v_{39}, v_{41}, v_{43}, v_{50}\}$. After 16 iterations, we obtain the set

$$I' = \{v_4, v_6, v_{10}, v_{11}, v_{15}, v_{17}, v_{19}, v_{21}, v_{25}, v_{29}, v_{32}, v_{34}, v_{36}, v_{39}, v_{41}, v_{43}, v_{50},$$
$$v_2, v_{69}, v_{79}, v_8, v_{27}, v_0, v_1, v_{28}, v_{71}, v_{13}, v_{45}, v_{23}, v_{26}, v_{38}, v_{76}, v_{47}\}$$

by adding a steep IV variable in each iteration. The degree of $p_{I'}$ is upper bounded by 9. For I', v_{56} is a steep IV variable. However, after adding v_{56} to I', the degree of $p_{I' \cup \{v_{56}\}}$ is 0. Namely, v_{56} decreases the degree of the superpoly from 9 to 0 suddenly. It indicates that we fail to construct a cube with a linear superpoly in the output of 805-round Trivium by only adding steep IV variables.

Recall that our aim is to construct cubes with linear superpolies rather than those with zero-constant superpolies. From Example 1, it can be seen that always adding a steep IV variable does make our aim break sometimes. To solve this problem, we propose the concept of gentle IV variables which decrease the degree of the superpoly slowly. We formally describe the definition of the gentle IV variable in Definition 4.

Definition 4 (Gentle IV Variable). *Let $I = \{v_{i_1}, v_{i_2}, \ldots, v_{i_\ell}\}$ be a set containing ℓ cube variables. Then, an IV variable $b \in B$ is called a gentle IV variable of I if $ds(I \cup \{b\}) = \max\{ds(I \cup \{v\}) | ds(I \cup \{v\}) \leq ds(I), v \in B\}$, where $B = \{v_0, v_1, \ldots, v_{m-1}\} \setminus I$ and $ds(I)$ is the degree of the superpoly of I.*

It can be seen from Definition 4 that a gentle IV variable of I is exactly the one which could decrease the degree of the superpoly as slowly as possible. With gentle IV variables, the above phenomenon could be avoided by adding gentle IV variables instead of steep IV variables to I', where I' is obtained by adding steep IV variables to I after several iterations.

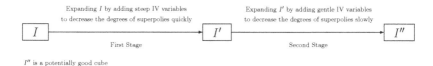

Expanding I by adding steep IV variables
to decrease the degrees of superpolies quickly

Expanding I' by adding gentle IV variables
to decrease the degrees of superpolies slowly

I ⟶ I' ⟶ I''

First Stage   Second Stage

I'' is a potentially good cube

Fig. 2. The sketch of our idea

Based on the above ideas, we propose a new heuristic algorithm to construct cubes with linear superpolies. The sketch of our idea is shown in Fig. 2. Algorithm 3 describes the details of our idea. In Algorithm 3, similar to the GreedyBitSet algorithm proposed in [19], we start with a small starting set of cube variables. Then, there are two stages in Algorithm 3. During the first stage, a steep IV variable is added to the current set I of cube variables so that the degree of the superpoly could be decreased as fast as possible. To determine the steep IV variable of I, we use the degree evaluation method based on division property, which was proposed in [24], to calculate the upper bound of $ds(I \cup v)$ for each IV variable which is not in I. As illustrated above, if only steep IV variables are added, the degree of the superpoly may be decreased to 0 suddenly and so constructing cubes with linear superpolies fails. If so, Algorithm 3 would step into the second stage, where we hope to decrease the degree of the superpoly slowly. During the second stage, we add the first gentle IV variable into the current cube set in each iteration. To determine the gentle IV variables, the same method in stage one is used. By gradually adding gentle IV variables, which make the degree of the superpoly decrease slowly, it is more hopeful to construct cubes with linear superpolies.

Remark 1. In the second stage of Algorithm 3, for I, it may encounter the case that $ds(I \cup \{v\}) > ds(I)$ or $ds(I \cup \{v\}) = 0$ holds for each $v \in B$, i.e., the gentle IV variable of I may do not exist. In this case, we select the cube variable b such that $ds(I \cup \{b\}) = \min\{ds(I \cup \{v\}) > ds(I) | v \in B\}$ to update I.

Construct A Mother Cube. Note that the superpoly of the cube obtained with Algorithm 3 may be not linear still, since the division property based method only returns an upper bound of the degree of the superpoly. To make it more possible to find linear superpolies, we attempt to construct a large cube, called a mother cube in the following paper, and then use the Möbius transformation to test its subcubes simultaneously. Such a mother cube is constructed by jointing some cubes obtained in the last iteration.

Let I be the set of cube variables before the last iteration. When selecting cubes, we prefer to choose those cubes such that the degree of the corresponding superpolies are low. More specifically, for j starting from 1 incrementally, we gradually update the set I as follows until a mother cube with a desired size is obtained

$$I \leftarrow I \cup \{v \in B | \text{ the upper bound of } ds(I \cup v) = j\},$$

where $B = \{v_0, v_1, \ldots, v_{m-1}\} \setminus I$. We offer a concrete example of constructing a mother cube in Subsect. 5.2.

Algorithm 3. The algorithm of constructing cubes with linear superpolies
***

Require: a set of cube variables $I = \{v_{i_1}, \ldots, v_{i_c}\}$ of size c and the target round r
1: $B \leftarrow \{v_0, v_1, \ldots, v_{m-1}\} \setminus I$;
2: $d \leftarrow +\infty$;
    /* The first stage */
3: **while** $d > 1$ and $|I|$ is less than a given bound **do**
4:     **for** $v \in B$ **do**
5:         Estimate the upper bound of $\mathrm{ds}(I \cup \{v\})$ using the division property based method;
6:     **end for**
7:     $I \leftarrow I \cup \{v\}$, where v is the first steep IV variable of I;
8:     $B \leftarrow B \setminus v$;
9:     $d \leftarrow DS(I \cup \{v\})$, where $DS(I \cup \{v\})$ is the upper bound of $\mathrm{ds}(I \cup \{v\})$
10: **end while**
11: **if** $d(I) == 1$ **then**
12:     **return** I
13: **end if**
    /* The second stage */
14: **if** $d(I) == 0$ **then**
15:     $I \leftarrow I \setminus \{v\}$, where v is the steep IV variable added in the last iteration of the first stage.
16:     $I \leftarrow I \cup \{v'\}$, where $DS(I \cup \{v'\})$ attains minimum except 0 in the last iteration of the first stage.
17:     $B \leftarrow \{v_0, v_1, \ldots, v_{m-1}\} \setminus I$;
18:     **while** $d > 1$ and $|I|$ is less than a given bound **do**
19:         **for** $v \in B$ **do**
20:             Estimate the upper bound of $\mathrm{ds}(I \cup \{v\})$ using the division property based method;
21:         **end for**
22:         $I \leftarrow I \cup \{v\}$, where v is the first gentle IV variable
23:         $B \leftarrow B \setminus v$;
24:         $d \leftarrow DS(I \cup \{v\})$
25:     **end while**
26: **end if**
***

3.2   Determine Starting Cube Sets

One critical point of Algorithm 3 is that it requires a small set of cube variables as its input. In this subsection, based on careful analysis of the structure of Trivium, we shall present a method to determine a proper starting set of cube variables to make Algorithm 3 work well.

Recall that the output function of r-round Trivium is the linear combination of six internal state bits, i.e., $z_r = \bigoplus_{j=1}^6 s_{\lambda_j}^{(r)}$, where $\{\lambda_1, \lambda_2, \lambda_3, \lambda_4, \lambda_5, \lambda_6\} = \{66, 93, 162, 177, 243, 288\}$.

It is worth noting that all the known linear superpolies of Trivium are sparse, and most of them contain only a single key variable. It is very likely that there exists some $j \in \{1, 2, 3, 4, 5, 6\}$ such that $p_I = p_{\lambda_j}$ and $p_{i_\ell} = 0$ for $\ell \neq j$, where p_{λ_ℓ} is the superpoly of I in $s_{\lambda_\ell}^{(r)}$ for $\ell \in \{1, 2, 3, 4, 5, 6\}$. In this paper, for a set of cube variables I, if there exists some $j \in \{1, 2, 3, 4, 5, 6\}$ such that $p_I = p_{\lambda_j}$ and $p_{\lambda_\ell} = 0$ for $\ell \neq j$ then we say that the superpoly p_I comes from $s_{\lambda_j}^{(r)}$. The following is an illustrative example.

Example 2. For 769-round Trivium, the superpoly of

$$I = \{v_1, v_3, v_5, v_7, v_{10}, v_{12}, v_{14}, v_{16}, v_{18}, v_{20}, v_{23}, v_{26}, v_{30}, v_{39}, v_{41},$$
$$v_{42}, v_{43}, v_{47}, v_{50}, v_{52}, v_{53}, v_{55}, v_{58}, v_{60}, v_{61}, v_{64}, v_{69}, v_{71}, v_{78}\}$$

in the output bit z_{769} is $p_I = k_{22}$. We figure out the superpolies of I in $s_{66}^{(769)}$, $s_{93}^{(769)}, s_{162}^{(769)}, s_{177}^{(769)}, s_{243}^{(769)}, s_{288}^{(769)}$, respectively. The results show that only $p_{66} = k_{22}$ is linear and the rest five superpolies are 0's . Namely, the linear superpoly k_{22} comes from $s_{66}^{(769)}$.

Determine a Proper Set of Cube Variables. Inspired by the phenomenon mentioned above, when constructing cubes with linear superpolies, we could focus on only one of the six internal state bits in the output function. In the following, we shall illustrate how to determine a proper set of cube variables. Assume that $s_\lambda^{(r)}$ is the chosen target for r-round Trivium. First, according to the update function of Trivium, $s_\lambda^{(r)}$ could be written as

$$s_\lambda^{(r)} = s_{j_1^\lambda}^{(r-\lambda)} \cdot s_{j_2^\lambda}^{(r-\lambda)} \oplus s_{j_3^\lambda}^{(r-\lambda)} \oplus s_{j_4^\lambda}^{(r-\lambda)} \oplus s_{j_5^\lambda}^{(r-\lambda)}. \tag{1}$$

Then, we choose a set I of cube variables and search all its subcubes to find those cubes having linear superpolies in $s_{j_1^\lambda}^{(r-\lambda)}$ or $s_{j_2^\lambda}^{(r-\lambda)}$ with the Möbius transformation. If such subcubes are found, then we randomly choose one of them to be the starting set of Algorithm 3.

Assume that the superpoly $p_{I'}$ of $I' = \{v_{l_1}, v_{l_2}, \ldots, v_{l_u}\} \subseteq I$ in $s_{j_1^\lambda}^{(r-\lambda)}$ is linear. Then, $s_{j_1^\lambda}^{(r-\lambda)}$ could be rewritten as

$$s_{j_1^\lambda}^{(r-\lambda)}(\boldsymbol{k}, \boldsymbol{v}) = g(\boldsymbol{k}, \boldsymbol{v}) \cdot t_{I'} \cdot p_{I'}(\boldsymbol{k}) \oplus q_{I'}(\boldsymbol{k}, \boldsymbol{v}),$$

where $t_{I'} = \prod_{i=1}^u v_{l_i}$. Since $s_{j_1^\lambda}^{(r-\lambda)} \cdot s_{j_2^\lambda}^{(r-\lambda)}$ is the only term of degree 2 in Eq. (1), it is hopeful that we could extend I' to I whose superpoly in $s_\lambda^{(r)}$ is linear. Due to the above phenomenon, it is hopeful that the superpoly of I in the output bit is linear as well. The following is an illustrative example.

Example 3. In the case of 805-round Trivium, the superpoly of

$$I = \{v_4, v_6, v_{10}, v_{11}, v_{15}, v_{17}, v_{19}, v_{21}, v_{25}, v_{29}, v_{32}, v_{34}, v_{36}, v_{39}, v_{41}, v_{43}, v_{50}\}$$

in $s_{286}^{(739)}$ is k_{56}. Furthermore, we find that the superpoly of

$$\begin{aligned} I'' = \{&v_1, v_2, v_4, v_6, v_8, v_{10}, v_{11}, v_{13}, v_{15}, v_{17}, v_{19}, v_{21}, v_{23}, \\ &v_{25}, v_{26}, v_{27}, v_{29}, v_{32}, v_{34}, v_{36}, v_{38}, v_{39}, v_{41}, v_{42}, v_{43}, \\ &v_{45}, v_{47}, v_{48}, v_{50}, v_{52}, v_{57}, v_{59}, v_{69}, v_{71}, v_{76}, v_{79}\} \end{aligned}$$

is also k_{56} in the output of 805-round Trivium. Note that I'' contains all the cube variables in I. This indicates that it is reasonable to construct cubes with linear superpolies in the output bit by extending a starting cube selected in the way illustrated above.

The Preference Bit. Now, for r-round Trivium, the key point is which internal state bit in the output function should be chosen so that we could construct cubes with linear superpolies with a high success probability by extending a small set I of cube variables.

To study the difference of the six internal state bits in the output function with respect to constructing linear superpolies, we perform dedicated experiments on Trivium variants with from 400 to 699 initialization rounds. For each variant, we collect thousands of linear superpolies and check which internal state bit each linear superpoly comes from. The results show that there exists significant difference among six internal state bits in the output function with respect to where a linear superpoly comes from. For example, among the 2953 collected linear superpolies of 699-round Trivium, 2366 linear superpolies come from $s_{243}^{(699)}$, i.e., over 80% of the linear superpolies come from $s_{243}^{(699)}$. Table 2 shows the number of linear supeprolies comes from each internal state bit.

Table 2. The number of linear supeprolies coming from each internal state bit

Internal state bit	$s_{66}^{(699)}$	$s_{93}^{(699)}$	$s_{162}^{(699)}$	$s_{177}^{(699)}$	$s_{243}^{(699)}$	$s_{288}^{(699)}$
Number of linear superpolies	162	0	182	246	2366	0

For 699-round Trivium, linear superpolies come from $s_{243}^{(699)}$ most frequently. Let r be a positive integer. For r-round Trivium, the internal state bit $s_{\lambda_j}^{(r)}$ in the output function such that linear superpolies come from it most frequently is called the *preference bit* of r-round Trivium. For these 300 Trivium variants, there are 230 variants such that more than 40% of the collected linear superpolies come from the preference bit. It can be seen that the preference bit has a significant advantage over the other five internal state bits with respect to where a linear superpoly may come from. In other words, for r-round Trivium, it is more likely to construct cubes with linear superpolies when targeting the preference bit than the other internal state bits in the output function.

An Iterative Algorithm to Predict the Preference Bit. According to the above discussions, if we target the preference bit, then it is more likely to construct cubes with linear superpolies. In this subsection, we design an algorithm to pick up the preference bit among the six ones. Our algorithm is based on the following lemma.

Lemma 1. *Let $I = \{v_{i_1}, v_{i_2}, \ldots, v_{i_d}\}$ be a set of cube variables. If the superpoly of I in $f(\mathbf{k}, \mathbf{v})$ is linear in key variables, then there is a term in the form of $\prod_{v \in I} v \cdot t_v \cdot k_j$ in the ANF of f, where t_v is 1 or a product of some non-cube variables.*

Proof. Since the superpoly of I in f is linear in key variables, then there is a term in the form of $t_v \cdot k_j$ in the ANF of p_I, where t_v is 1 or the product of some non-cube variables. Hence, there is a term in the form of $\prod_{v \in I} v \cdot t_v \cdot k_j$ in the ANF of f.

According to Lemma 1, a necessary condition that a linear superpoly comes from $s_{\lambda_j}^{(r)}$ is that $s_{\lambda_j}^{(r)}$ has a term in the form of $T_v \cdot k_j$ in its ANF, where T_v is a product of some IV variables. In the rest of this paper, such kind of term is called a VK-term for simplicity. Note that a VK-term does not always lead to a linear superpoly. For example, let $\prod_{i=1}^{u} v_{j_i} \cdot k_l$ be a VK-term. If $\prod_{i=1}^{u} v_{j_i} \cdot k_l \cdot k_h$ is in the ANF of z_r, then the superpoliy of $\{v_{j_1}, v_{j_2}, \ldots, v_{j_l}\}$ would be nonlinear, i.e. the VK-term $\prod_{i=1}^{u} v_{j_i} \cdot k_l$ does not lead to a linear superpoly. In other words, it is reasonable that the more VK-terms an internal state bit has, the more linear superpolies come from it. Thus, it is reasonable to assume that the preference bit contains the largest number of VK-terms.

However, it is impossible to accurately calculate the number of VK-terms by the ANF of an internal state bit when the number of initialization rounds is high. To solve this problem, we propose an iterative algorithm whose results could reflect the number of VK-terms in each internal state bit at a high level. With this algorithm, we could predict the preference bit for an arbitrary number of initialization rounds with a very low computing complexity.

Let $s^{(t)} = (s_1^{(t)}, s_2^{(t)}, \ldots, s_{288}^{(t)})$ be the internal state of Trivium after t rounds. Note that each internal state bit $s_j^{(t)} (1 \leq j \leq 288)$ is a polynomial in key variables and IV variables. Denote by $NVK_j^{(t)}$ the number of VK-terms in the ANF of $s_j^{(t)}$. Let $NV_j^{(t)}$ be the number of terms in the form of T_v, which are called V-terms for simplicity, in $s_j^{(t)}$, where T_v is a product of some IV variables. In the following, we take $s_{94}^{(t+1)}$ as an example to illustrate how our algorithm works. According to the update function of Trivium, $s_{94}^{(t+1)}$ is updated as $s_{94}^{(t+1)} = s_{91}^{(t)} \cdot s_{92}^{(t)} \oplus s_{93}^{(t)} \oplus s_{66}^{(t)} \oplus s_{171}^{(t)}$. In $s_{91}^{(t)} \cdot s_{92}^{(t)}$, there are three ways to generate a VK-term which are shown as follows.

- $s_{91}^{(t)}$ provides a V-term (or constant 1) and $s_{92}^{(t)}$ provides a VK-term;
- $s_{91}^{(t)}$ provides a VK-term and $s_{92}^{(t)}$ provides a V-term (or constant 1);
- $s_{91}^{(t)}$ and $s_{92}^{(t)}$ both provide VK-terms, where the key variable in these two VK-terms are the same.

Generally, the VK-terms formed in the third way are much fewer than those formed in the first two ways. Besides, the VK-terms obtained by multiplying constant 1 with VK-terms are also much fewer than those obtained by multiplying a V-term and a VK-term. Hence, in our algorithm, we regard $NV_{91}^{(t)} \cdot NVK_{92}^{(t)} + NV_{92}^{(t)} \cdot NVK_{91}^{(t)}$ as the number of VK-terms in $s_{91}^{(t)} \cdot s_{92}^{(t)}$ which is denoted by $NVK(s_{91}^{(t)} \cdot s_{92}^{(t)})$. Namely, $NVK(s_{91}^{(t)} \cdot s_{92}^{(t)})$ is set as

$$NVK(s_{91}^{(t)} \cdot s_{92}^{(t)}) \leftarrow NV_{91}^{(t)} \cdot NVK_{92}^{(t)} + NV_{92}^{(t)} \cdot NVK_{91}^{(t)}.$$

^{2}Consequently, $NVK_{94}^{(t+1)}$ is set as

$$NVK_{94}^{(t+1)} \leftarrow NVK(s_{91}^{(t)} \cdot s_{92}^{(t)}) + NVK_{93}^{(t)} + NVK_{66}^{(t)} + NVK_{171}^{(t)}.$$

Note that, to calculate $NVK_{94}^{(t+1)}$, it needs to know $NV_{91}^{(t)}$ and $NV_{92}^{(t)}$. Hence, it is necessary to calculate $NV_{94}^{(t+1)}$ as well. According to the update function, $NV_{94}^{(t+1)}$ could be set as

$$NV_{94}^{(t+1)} \leftarrow NV_{91}^{(t)} \cdot NV_{92}^{(t)} + NV_{93}^{(t)} + NV_{66}^{(t)} + NV_{171}^{(t)},$$

since the number of V-terms in $s_{91}^{(t)} \cdot s_{92}^{(t)}$ is dominated by those formed from multiplying two V-terms together.

Moreover, $NVK_1^{(t+1)}, NV_1^{(t+1)}, NVK_{178}^{(t+1)}, NV_{178}^{(t+1)}$ could be calculated in a similar way. Thus, we could update $NVK^{(t+1)}, NV^{(t+1)}$ from $NVK^{(t)}, NV^{(t)}$, where $NVK^{(t)} = (NVK_1^{(t)}, \ldots, NVK_{288}^{(t)})$, and $NV^{(t)} = (NV_1^{(t)}, \ldots, NV_{288}^{(t)})$.

Now, the remaining problem is how to initialize $NVK^{(0)}$ and $NV^{(0)}$. To obtain a more accurate result, we initialize $NVK^{(280)}$ and $NV^{(280)}$ by calculating the ANFs of $s_1^{(280)}, s_2^{(280)}, \ldots, s_{288}^{(280)}$. With the above method, we could figure out $NVK_j^{(r)}$ for $1 \leq j \leq 288$ gradually. Finally, the bit indexed by $j \in \{66, 93, 162, 177, 243, 288\}$ such that

$$NVK_j^{(r)} = \max\{NVK_\lambda^{(r)} | \lambda \in \{66, 93, 162, 177, 243, 288\}\}$$

is predicted as the preference bit. We formally describe our idea in Algorithm 4.

Algorithm 4. The algorithm of predicting the preference bit

1: Calculate the ANFs of $s_i^{(280)}$ to initialise $NVK^{(280)}$ and $NV^{(280)}$;
2: **for** $280 \leq t \leq r - 1$ **do**
3:     $NVK_{t_1} \leftarrow NV_{91}^{(t)} \cdot NVK_{92}^{(t)} + NV_{92}^{(t)} \cdot NVK_{91}^{(t)} + NVK_{93}^{(t)} + NVK_{66}^{(t)} + NVK_{171}^{(t)}$;
4:     $NV_{t_1} \leftarrow NV_{91}^{(t)} \cdot NV_{92}^{(t)} + NV_{93}^{(t)} + NV_{66}^{(t)} + NV_{171}^{(t)}$;
5:     $NVK_{t_2} \leftarrow NV_{175}^{(t)} \cdot NVK_{176}^{(t)} + NV_{176}^{(t)} \cdot NVK_{175}^{(t)} + NVK_{177}^{(t)} + NVK_{162}^{(t)} + NVK_{264}^{(t)}$;
6:     $NV_{t_2} \leftarrow NV_{175}^{(t)} \cdot NV_{176}^{(t)} + NV_{177}^{(t)} + NV_{162}^{(t)} + NV_{264}^{(t)}$;
7:     $NVK_{t_3} \leftarrow NV_{286}^{(t)} \cdot NVK_{287}^{(t)} + NV_{287}^{(t)} \cdot NVK_{286}^{(t)} + NVK_{288}^{(t)} + NVK_{243}^{(t)} + NVK_{69}^{(t)}$;
8:     $NV_{t_3} \leftarrow NV_{286}^{(t)} \cdot NV_{287}^{(t)} + NV_{288}^{(t)} + NV_{243}^{(t)} + NV_{69}^{(t)}$;
9:     **for** $288 \geq j \geq 2$ **do**
10:         $NVK_j^{(t)} \leftarrow NVK_{j-1}^{(t)}$;
11:         $NV_j^{(t)} \leftarrow NV_{j-1}^{(t)}$;
12:     **end for**
13:     $NV_{94}^{(t)} \leftarrow NV_{t_1}; NV_{178}^{(t)} \leftarrow NV_{t_2}; NV_1^{(t)} \leftarrow NV_{t_3}$;
14:     $NVK_{94}^{(t)} \leftarrow NVK_{t_1}; NVK_{178}^{(t)} \leftarrow NVK_{t_2}; NVK_1^{(t)} \leftarrow NVK_{t_3}$;
15: **end for**
16: Choose the bit $s_b^{(t)}$ such that

$$NVK_b^{(t)} = \max\{NVK_\lambda^{(t)} | \lambda \in \{66, 93, 162, 171, 243, 288\}\}$$

as the preference bit, where $b \in \{66, 93, 162, 171, 243, 288\}$;

---

^{2} Here, we only consider the VK-terms formed in the first two ways and do not take the terms which are eliminated by the XOR operation into consideration.

4   An Improved Möbius Transformation

The Möbius transformation is a powerful tool which could be used to search all the subcubes of a large cube at once. It improves the efficiency of cube attacks a lot. Note that, for Trivium variants with more than 800 initialization rounds, the sizes of all known cubes with linear superpolies are larger than 30. Hence, to find linear superpolies, for a large cube set I, it is not necessary to test its subcubes of small sizes, and only subcubes of large sizes should be taken into consideration. However, in the original Möbius transformation, to test all the subcubes of I, the memory complexity is $O(2^{|I|})$ which expands exponentially as $|I|$ increases. In this section, we shall present an improved Möbius transformation which could recover a part of ANF of $f(x_0, x_1, \ldots, x_{n-1})$ according to the truth table of $f(x_0, x_1, \ldots, x_{n-1})$. With the improved Möbius transformation, we could test a large number of subcubes of I simultaneously with a reasonable memory complexity.

Let $f(x_0, x_1, \ldots, x_{n-1})$ be a Boolean function on $x_0, x_1, \ldots, x_{n-1}$. The ANF of f is obtained by writing

$$f = \bigoplus_{(c_0, c_1, \ldots, c_{n-1}) \in \mathbb{F}_2^n} g(c_0, c_1, \ldots, c_{n-1}) \prod_{i=0}^{n-1} x_i^{c_i}.$$

Recall that the function g is the Möbius transformation of f. It can be seen that the Möbius transformation g is actually a Boolean function on n variables. Furthermore, the Möbius transformations of $f(x_0, \ldots, x_{n-1})$, $f(x_0, \ldots, x_{n-2}, 0)$, and $f(x_0, \ldots, x_{n-2}, 1)$ are closely related, i.e. the Möbius transformation of $f(x_0, x_1, \ldots, x_{n-1})$ could be obtained from the Möbius transformations of $f(x_0, x_1, \ldots, x_{n-2}, 0)$ and $f(x_0, x_1, \ldots, x_{n-2}, 1)$, see Chap. 9.2 of [11] for details. Actually, it could be generalised, see Corollary 1.

Corollary 1. *Let $f(x_0, x_1, \ldots, x_{n-1})$ be a Boolean function on $x_0, x_1, \ldots, x_{n-1}$. Assume that $g_0, g_1, \ldots, g_{2^q-1}$ are the Möbius transformations of $f(x_0, \ldots, x_{n-q-1}, 0, \ldots, 0), f(x_0, \ldots, x_{n-q-1}, 1, \ldots, 0), \ldots, f(x_0, \ldots, x_{n-q-1}, 1, \ldots, 1)$. Then, the Möbius transformation g of f could be determined with the knowledge of $g_0, g_1, \ldots, g_{2^q-1}$.*

Proof. According to Chap. 9.2 of [11], it is sufficient to calculate the Möbius transformation of f with the Möbius transformations of $f(x_0, x_1, \ldots, x_{n-2}, 0)$ and $f(x_0, x_1, \ldots, x_{n-2}, 1)$. Similarly, with the knowledge of the Möbius transformations of $f(x_0, x_1, \ldots, x_{n-3}, 0, 0)$ and $f(x_0, x_1, \ldots, x_{n-3}, 1, 0)$, the Möbius transformation of $f(x_0, x_1, \ldots, x_{n-2}, 0)$ could be deduced. Recursively, for x_{n-q}, $x_{n-q+1}, \ldots, x_{n-1}$, the Möbius transformation g of f could be determined with the Möbius transformations of $f(x_0, \ldots, x_{n-q-1}, 0, \ldots, 0), f(x_0, \ldots, x_{n-q-1}, 1, \ldots, 0), \cdots, f(x_0, x_1, \ldots, x_{n-q-1}, 1, \ldots, 1)$.

Note that it requires $2^q \times 2^{n-q} = 2^n$ bits memory to store $g_0, g_1, \ldots, g_{2^q-1}$. When n is large, a huge amount of bits memory are required. To reduce the memory complexity, one natural idea is to store only a part values of $g_0, g_1, \ldots, g_{2^q-1}$.

In fact, by storing a part values of $g_0, g_1, \ldots, g_{2^q-1}$, a part of the ANF of f could still be recovered. We formally describe this fact in Proposition 2.

Proposition 2. *Let $f, g_0, g_1, \ldots, g_{2^q-1}$ be defined as Corollary 1. Assume that $\boldsymbol{c} = (c_0, c_1, \ldots, c_{n-q-1})$ is an arbitrary element in $\mathbb{F}_2^{n-q}$. With the knowledge of $g_0(\boldsymbol{c}), g_1(\boldsymbol{c}), \ldots, g_{2^q-1}(\boldsymbol{c})$, we could obtain the coefficients of $\prod_{i=0}^{n-q-1} x_i^{c_i}, x_{n-q} \cdot \prod_{i=0}^{n-q-1} x_i^{c_i}, \ldots, x_{n-q} \cdot x_{n-q+1} \cdots x_{n-1} \cdot \prod_{i=0}^{n-q-1} x_i^{c_i}$. in the ANF of f.*

Proof. Assume that $(b_{n-q}, b_{n-q+1}, \ldots, b_{n-1})$ takes an arbitrary value of $\mathbb{F}_2^q$. Following the proof of Corollary 1, $g(c_0, \ldots, c_{n-q-1}, b_{n-q}, \ldots, b_{n-1})$ could be determined by

$$h_0(c_0, \ldots, c_{n-q-1}, b_{n-q}, \ldots, b_{n-2}) \text{ and } h_1(c_0, \ldots, c_{n-q-1}, b_{n-q}, \ldots, b_{n-2}),$$

where h_0 and h_1 are the Möbius transformations of $f(x_0, x_1, \ldots, x_{n-2}, 0)$ and $f(x_0, x_1, \ldots, x_{n-2}, 1)$ respectively. Furthermore, the value of $h_0(c_0, \ldots, c_{n-q-1}, b_{n-q}, \ldots, b_{n-2})$ can be deduced from

$$h_{0,0}(c_0, \ldots, c_{n-q-1}, b_{n-q}, \ldots, b_{n-3}) \text{ and } h_{0,1}(c_0, \ldots, c_{n-q-1}, b_{n-q}, \ldots, b_{n-3}),$$

where $h_{0,0}$ and $h_{0,1}$ are the Möbius transformations of $f(x_0, \ldots, x_{n-3}, 0, 0)$ and $f(x_0, \ldots, x_{n-3}, 1, 0)$ respectively. Recursively, it is sufficient to calculate $g(c_0, \ldots, c_{n-q-1}, b_{n-q}, \ldots, b_{n-1})$ with the knowledge of $g_0(\boldsymbol{c}), g_1(\boldsymbol{c}), \ldots, g_{2^q-1}(\boldsymbol{c})$. Since $(b_{n-q}, b_{n-q+1}, \ldots, b_{n-1})$ takes an arbitrary value in $\mathbb{F}_2^q$, it indicates that $g(c_0, \ldots, c_{n-q-1}, 0, 0, \ldots, 0)$, $g(c_0, \ldots, c_{n-q-1}, 1, 0, \ldots, 0), \ldots, g(c_0, \ldots, c_{n-q-1}, 1, 1, \ldots, 1)$ could be obtained. Namely, we could recover the coefficients of

$$\prod_{i=0}^{n-q-1} x_i^{c_i}, \quad x_{n-q} \cdot \prod_{i=0}^{n-q-1} x_i^{c_i}, \ldots, \quad x_{n-q} \cdots x_{n-1} \cdot \prod_{i=0}^{n-q-1} x_i^{c_i}$$

in the ANF of f.

Based on Proposition 2, we propose an improved Möbius transformation by breaking the original Möbius transformation into two stages and only store a part of the results during the first stage to reduce the memory complexity. We formally describe the improved Möbius transformation in Algorithm 5. During the first stage of Algorithm 5, for each $0 \leq j \leq 2^q-1$, the Möbius transformation of g_j is calculated one by one so that the memory could be used repeatedly. Furthermore, for each g_j, only the values g_j under elements whose Hamming Weights are not smaller than ω is stored, where ω is a given bound. Then, during the second stage, by using a way similar to calculate the Möbius transformation of a q-variable polynomial, a part of the ANF of f could be recovered.

The Memory Complexity. The memory needed in Algorithm 5 consists of two parts.

– The size of S is 2^{n-q}, and so it costs 2^{n-q} bits memory.
– For each j, the size of $FS[j]$ is t, and so it requires $2^q \times t$ bits memory totally.

To sum up, it requires $2^q \times t + 2^{n-q}$ bits in Algorithm 5. If $t \lll 2^{n-q}$, then $2^q \times t + 2^{n-q} \lll 2^n$ which indicates that the memory could be decreased to about 2^{n-q} bits from 2^n bits.

Algorithm 5. An Improved Möbius Transformation

Require: A Boolean function f, the parameter q, the bound ω

    /* the first stage */

1: **for** $(c_0, c_1, \ldots, c_{q-1})$ from $(0, 0, \ldots, 0)$ to $(1, 1, \ldots, 1)$ **do**
2:    $S \leftarrow$ the truth table of $f(x_0, x_1, \ldots, x_{n-q-1}, c_0, c_1, \ldots, c_{q-1})$;
3:    Call Algorithm 2 to do Möbius transformation on S;
4:    $t \leftarrow 0, j \leftarrow \sum_{l=0}^{q-1} 2^l c_l$;
5:    **for** i from 0 to $2^{n-q} - 1$ **do**
6:       $tmp \leftarrow (b_0, b_1, \ldots, b_{n-q-1})$, where $i = \sum_{l=0}^{n-q-1} b_l \cdot 2^l$;
7:       **if** $wt(tmp) \geq \omega$ **then**
8:          $FS[j][t] \leftarrow S[i]$;
9:          $t \leftarrow t + 1$;
10:      **end if**
11:    **end for**
12: **end for**

    /* the second stage */

13: **for** i from 1 to q **do**
14:    $Sz \leftarrow 2^i, Pos \leftarrow 1$;
15:    **while** $Pos < 2^q$ **do**
16:       **for** b from 0 to $Sz - 1$ **do**
17:          **for** a from 0 to $t - 1$ **do**
18:             $FS[Pos + Sz + b][a] \leftarrow FS[Pos + Sz + b][a] \oplus FS[Pos + b][a]$;
19:          **end for**
20:       **end for**
21:       $Pos \leftarrow Pos + 2 \times Sz$;
22:    **end while**
23: **end for**

---

5 Experimental Results

In this section, we first perform experiments to illustrate the effect of Algorithm 4. Then, utilising the starting sets determined with the method described in Sect. 3.2, we attempt to find linear superpolies for Trivium variants with at least 805 initialization rounds. As a result, we find over 1000 linear superpolies for 805-round Trivium as well as several linear superpolies for 806-round Trivium and 810-round Trivium. Based on the found linear superpolies, we establish a practical attack on 805-round Trivium.

5.1 The Effect of Algorithm 4

To verify the effect of Algorithm 4, we perform extensive experiments on r-round Trivium with $400 \leq r \leq 699$. As mentioned in Sect. 3.2, for r-round Trivium, we collect thousands of linear superpolies and test which internal state bit each linear superpoly comes from, where r ranges from 400 to 699. Thus, we could determine the preference bit of each Trivium variant experimentally. As a comparison, we predict the preference bit of r-round Trivium by Algorithm 4. The results show that the preference bits are correctly predicted for 226 variants of Trivium out of the total 300 variants. This indicates that the preference bit could be predicted with a success probability 75.3% by Algorithm 4. Furthermore, in the experiment on 400- to 699-round Trivium, the success rate increases as the number of initialization rounds increases. More specifically, for 600- to 699-round Trivium, we could predict the preference bit with a success probability around 84% which is higher than the average value 75.3%, and for 634- to 699-round

Trivium the success probability is 100%. Hence for a higher number of rounds, say 805 or more, the probability probably will not drop. Moreover, based on the preference bit predicted by our method, we practically found a large number of cubes with linear superpolies for the 805-round Trivium. This indicates that our method could predict the preference bit with a good success probability for a higher round.

Remark 2. In the formula of computing $NVK(s_{91} \cdot s_{92})$, we dropped the terms of the form $(\prod_{v \in I} v \cdot k_j)(\prod_{v \in J} v \cdot k_j)$, that is, the key variables in the two VK-terms of s_{91} and s_{92} are the same. Because this number is very small compared with other cases. To verify this, we performed experiments which take the dropped terms into consideration in our formula. For the 300 Trivium variants from 400 to 699 initialization rounds, the result showed that only one of the 300 predicted preference bits was changed.

5.2 A Practical Key-Recovery Attack on 805-Round Trivium

In this subsection, we target 805-round Trivium. We first predict the preference bit of 805-round Trivium. Then, aiming at the preference bit, we determine some proper starting sets of Algorithm 3. For each proper starting set, we construct a potentially good cube with Algorithm 3. Finally, to find linear superpolies, we simultaneously test a large number of subcubes of the potentially good cube with the improved Möbius transformation.

Determine Proper Starting Sets. To determine a proper starting set, we first need to predict the preference bit of 805-round Trivium. With Algorithm 4, we have that the predicted preference bit is $s_{66}^{(805)}$. Since $s_{66}^{(805)} = s_{286}^{(739)} \cdot s_{287}^{(739)} \oplus s_{243}^{(739)} \oplus s_{288}^{(739)} \oplus s_{69}^{(739)}$, we choose cubes of sizes 22 and use the Möbius transformation to search all the subcubes to find proper cubes whose superpolies in $s_{286}^{(739)}$ are linear. Finally, we select some subcubes with linear superpolies to be the starting sets of Algorithm 3. In the following, we take

$$I_1 = \{v_2, v_4, v_6, v_8, v_{10}, v_{11}, v_{15}, v_{17}, v_{19}, v_{21}, v_{23}, v_{25},$$
$$v_{29}, v_{30}, v_{32}, v_{34}, v_{36}, v_{39}, v_{41}, v_{43}, v_{45}, v_{50}\}$$

as an example to illustrate how to determine a proper starting set in details. First, we search all its subcubes to find cubes with linear superpolies in $s_{286}^{(739)}$ and hundreds of such cubes are obtained. When choosing a starting set from these cubes, we prefer to choose cubes with relatively large sizes. Among these cubes, there are two cubes of size 17 and the others have smaller sizes. Among these two cubes, we randomly choose

$$I_2 = \{v_4, v_6, v_{10}, v_{11}, v_{15}, v_{17}, v_{19}, v_{21}, v_{25}, v_{29}, v_{32}, v_{34}, v_{36}, v_{39}, v_{41}, v_{43}, v_{50}\}$$

as a proper starting set. With similar procedure, we determine some other starting sets of Algorithm 3.

Table 3. The chosen cube variables in the last iteration

Chosen cube	$I_5 \cup \{v_{48}\}$	$I_5 \cup \{v_{59}\}$	$I_5 \cup \{v_{58}\}$	$I_5 \cup \{v_{63}\}$
Upper bound of the degree of superpolies	1	1	2	3

Construct Candidate Cubes. There are two main stages of constructing a potentially good cube in Algorithm 3. We take I_2 as an example to make an illustration. In the first stage, Algorithm 3 adds steep IV variables to decrease the degree of the superpoly as quickly as possible. For I_2, the first stage of Algorithm 3 terminates after 17 iterations, since the superpoly p_{I_3} is zero-constant, where

$$I_3 = \{v_4, v_6, v_{10}, v_{11}, v_{15}, v_{17}, v_{19}, v_{21}, v_{25}, v_{29}, v_{32}, v_{34}, v_{36}, v_{39}, v_{41}, v_{43}, v_{50},$$
$$v_2, v_{69}, v_{79}, v_8, v_{27}, v_0, v_1, v_{28}, v_{71}, v_{13}, v_{45}, v_{23}, v_{26}, v_{38}, v_{76}, v_{47}, v_{56}\}.$$

Then, the second phase is started with

$$I_4 = \{v_4, v_6, v_{10}, v_{11}, v_{15}, v_{17}, v_{19}, v_{21}, v_{25}, v_{29}, v_{32}, v_{34}, v_{36}, v_{39}, v_{41}, v_{43}, v_{50},$$
$$v_2, v_{69}, v_{79}, v_8, v_{27}, v_0, v_1, v_{28}, v_{71}, v_{13}, v_{45}, v_{23}, v_{26}, v_{38}, v_{76}, v_{47}, v_{52}\},$$

since the upper bound of the degree of p_{I_4} attains minimum expect 0 among all the cubes obtained after 17 iterations. In this stage, our aim is to decrease the degree of the superpoly slowly to obtain cube with linear superpolies instead of zero-sum distinguishers. After three iterations, we obtain two cubes such that the degree of their superpolies are upper bounded by 1. Besides, we also obtain several cubes such that the degree of their superpolies are not larger than 3. By jointing 4 cubes, we constructed a potentially good cube of size 40. Table 3 shows the cubes and the upper bounds of the degrees of their superpolies, where

$$I_5 = \{v_4, v_6, v_{10}, v_{11}, v_{15}, v_{17}, v_{19}, v_{21}, v_{25}, v_{29}, v_{32}, v_{34}, v_{36}, v_{39}, v_{41}, v_{43}, v_{50}, v_2,$$
$$v_{69}, v_{79}, v_8, v_{27}, v_0, v_1, v_{28}, v_{71}, v_{13}, v_{45}, v_{23}, v_{26}, v_{38}, v_{76}, v_{47}, v_{52}, v_{57}, v_{42}\}.$$

Finally, the potentially good cube I_6 constructed from I_2 is as follows,

$$I_6 = I_5 \cup \{v_{48}, v_{58}, v_{59}, v_{63}\}.$$

Linear Superpolies for 805-Round Trivium. After obtaining a potentially good cube, we use the improved Möbius transformation to search its subcubes which miss few cube variables. For instance, in the case of I_6, we set the parameter $q = 7$ and $\omega = 26$ in the improved Möbius transformation, and we find 201 subcubes with linear superpolies eventually. Among these 201 linear superpolies, there are 22 linear superpolies which are linearly independent. Together with some other candidate cubes, we find more than 1000 cubes with linear superpolies in the output of 805-round Trivium. Among these cubes, we could pick up 38 cubes whose superpolies are linearly independent, see Table 4.

Table 4. Linear superpolies for 805-round Trivium

Cube indices	Superpoly
0,1,2,4,6,8,11,13,15,17,19,21,23,26,27,28,29,32,34, 36,38,39,41,42,45,47,48,50,52,53,57,69,71,75,76,79	$1 \oplus k_2 \oplus k_{65}$
0,1,2,4,6,8,10,11,12,13,15,16,19,21,23,25,26,27,29, 31,34,36,38,39,40,43,45,47,49,62,64,70,74,77,79	$1 \oplus k_3$
0,1,2,4,6,8,10,11,13,15,17,19,21,23,26,27,29,31, 34,36,38,39,40,41,43,45,47,49,58,62,64,77,79	$k_4 \oplus k_{19} \oplus k_{34}$
0,1,2,4,6,8,10,13,15,17,19,21,23,25,26,27,28,29,32,34, 36,38,39,41,42,43,47,48,50,52,57,59,69,71,75,76,79	k_{14}
0,1,2,4,6,8,10,11,13,15,17,19,21,23,25,26,27,29,32,34, 36,38,39,41,42,43,47,48,50,52,53,57,59,69,71,76,79	k_{15}
0,1,2,4,6,8,10,13,15,17,19,21,23,25,26,27,28,29,32, 34,36,38,39,41,42,43,47,48,50,52,59,69,71,75,76,79	$1 \oplus k_{16}$
0,1,2,4,6,8,10,11,13,15,17,19,21,23,25,26,27,28,29,32, 34,36,38,39,41,42,43,45,47,48,50,53,57,69,71,75,76,79	$1 \oplus k_{17}$
0,1,2,4,6,8,10,11,12,13,15,16,19,21,23,25,27,28, 29,34,36,38,40,41,43,45,47,49,50,64,70,74,77,79	k_{18}
0,1,2,4,6,8,10,11,12,13,15,16,19,23,25,27,28,31,34, 36,38,39,40,41,43,45,47,49,50,58,62,64,74,77,79	$1 \oplus k_{19} \oplus k_{34} \oplus k_{51}$
0,2,4,6,8,10,12,13,15,17,19,21,23,25,26,27,28,29,31, 34,38,39,40,41,43,45,47,49,50,58,62,64,70,74,77,79	k_{21}
1,2,4,6,8,10,11,12,13,15,17,19,21,23,25,26,27,28,29, 31,34,36,38,39,40,41,43,47,49,50,58,62,70,74,77,79	$1 \oplus k_{29}$
0,1,2,4,6,8,10,11,13,15,17,19,21,23,25,26,27,29,32,34, 36,38,39,42,43,45,47,48,50,52,53,57,59,71,75,76,79	$k_{31} \oplus k_{46} \oplus k_{56}$
0,1,2,4,6,8,10,13,15,17,19,21,23,25,26,28,29,32,34, 36,38,39,41,42,45,47,48,50,52,57,59,69,71,75,76,79	$k_{17} \oplus k_{32}$
0,1,2,4,6,8,10,11,13,15,17,19,21,23,25,26,27,29,32,34, 36,38,39,42,43,45,47,48,50,52,53,57,59,69,71,76,79	$1 \oplus k_{33}$
0,1,2,4,6,8,10,11,13,15,17,19,21,23,25,26,27,29,32, 34,36,39,41,42,43,45,47,48,50,52,57,59,69,71,76,79	k_{34}
0,1,2,4,6,8,10,11,13,15,17,19,21,23,25,26,27,29,32, 34,36,38,39,41,42,43,45,47,50,52,53,57,69,71,75,79	k_{36}
0,1,2,4,6,8,10,12,13,15,17,19,21,23,25,26,27,28, 29,31,34,36,39,40,41,43,47,49,50,62,64,70,77,79	k_{40}
0,1,2,4,6,8,10,11,13,15,17,19,21,23,26,27,28,31, 34,36,38,40,41,43,45,47,49,50,58,62,64,70,77,79	k_{42}
0,1,2,4,6,8,10,11,13,15,16,19,21,23,26,27,28,29,31, 34,36,38,39,41,43,45,47,49,50,58,62,64,74,77,79	k_{43}
0,1,2,4,6,8,10,11,13,15,17,19,21,23,25,27,29,32, 34,36,38,42,45,47,48,50,53,57,59,69,71,75,76,79	k_{44}
0,1,2,4,6,8,10,11,13,15,17,19,21,23,25,27,28,29, 32,34,36,38,41,42,43,45,47,50,53,59,69,71,76,79	$1 \oplus k_{45}$
0,1,2,4,6,8,10,11,13,15,17,19,21,23,25,27,28,29,32, 34,36,38,39,42,43,45,48,50,52,57,59,69,71,75,76,79	$k_{46} \oplus k_{56}$
0,1,2,4,6,8,10,11,13,15,17,19,21,23,25,27,29,32,34, 36,38,39,41,42,43,45,47,48,50,57,59,69,71,76,79	$1 \oplus k_{47}$
0,1,2,4,6,8,11,13,15,17,19,21,23,26,27,28,29, 34,36,38,41,43,45,47,49,50,62,64,70,74,77,79	k_{49}
0,1,2,4,6,8,11,13,15,17,19,21,23,25,27,28,29,32,34, 36,38,39,41,42,43,45,47,52,53,57,69,71,75,76,79	k_{51}
0,2,4,6,8,10,11,12,13,15,16,19,21,23,25,26,27,28,29, 31,34,36,38,39,41,43,47,49,58,62,64,70,74,77,79	k_{53}
0,1,4,6,8,10,11,13,15,17,19,21,23,25,26,28,29,32,34,36, 38,39,41,42,43,45,47,48,50,52,53,57,59,69,71,75,76,79	k_{54}
0,1,2,4,6,8,10,11,13,15,17,19,21,23,25,27,29,32,34, 36,38,39,42,43,45,47,48,50,53,57,59,69,71,75,79	k_{56}
0,1,2,4,6,8,10,11,12,13,15,17,19,21,23,25,26,27,28, 29,31,34,36,38,39,40,41,45,47,49,58,62,64,70,79	$k_{57} \oplus k_{59}$
0,1,2,4,6,8,10,13,15,17,19,21,23,25,27,28,29,32, 34,36,38,39,42,43,45,47,48,53,57,59,69,71,75,79	k_{58}
0,1,2,4,6,8,10,11,13,15,17,19,21,23,25,26,27,28,29, 32,34,36,38,39,41,42,43,45,47,50,53,57,59,69,76,79	$1 \oplus k_{47} \oplus k_{60}$
0,1,2,4,6,8,10,11,13,15,17,19,21,23,25,27,28,29,32, 34,36,38,39,41,42,43,45,47,48,50,59,69,71,75,76,79	k_{60}
0,1,2,4,6,8,10,11,13,15,17,19,21,23,25,27,28,29,32, 34,36,38,39,41,42,43,45,47,48,50,52,59,71,76,79	k_{61}
0,2,4,6,8,10,11,12,13,15,16,19,21,23,25,26,27,28,31, 34,36,38,39,40,41,43,45,47,49,50,58,62,64,77,79	k_{62}
0,1,2,4,6,8,10,11,13,15,16,19,21,23,25,27,28,29,31, 34,36,39,41,43,45,47,49,62,64,70,74,77,79	k_{63}
0,1,4,6,8,10,11,12,13,15,17,19,21,23,25,26,27,28,29, 34,36,38,39,41,43,45,47,49,58,62,64,70,74,77,79	k_{64}
0,2,4,6,8,10,11,13,15,17,19,21,23,25,26,27,28,29,32, 34,36,39,41,43,45,47,48,50,52,57,59,69,71,76,79	k_{65}
0,1,2,4,6,8,11,12,13,15,17,19,21,23,25,27,28,29,31, 34,36,39,40,41,43,45,47,49,50,62,64,70,74,77,79	k_{68}

Linear Superpolies for 806-Round Trivium. For the cubes found for 805-round Trivium, we slide some of them, i.e. decrease the index of each cube variables by 1, to find cubes with linear superpolies for 806-round Trivium. Finally, we find several cubes whose superpolies in the output bit of 806- round Trivium, see Table 5.

Table 5. Linear superpolies for 806-round Trivium

Cube indices	Superpoly
$0,1,3,5,7,9,10,11,12,14,15,18,20,22,24,27,28,30,33,35,37,39,40,42,44,46,48,49,57,61,63,73,76,78$	$k_{14} \oplus k_{44}$
$0,1,3,5,7,9,10,11,12,14,15,18,20,22,24,26,28,30,33,35,37,39,40,42,44,46,48,49,57,61,63,73,76,78$	k_{15}
$0,1,3,5,7,9,10,11,12,14,15,18,20,22,24,26,28,30,33,35,37,39,40,42,44,46,48,49,57,61,63,76,78$	$1 \oplus k_{17}$
$0,1,3,5,7,9,10,11,12,14,16,18,20,22,24,25,26,27,28,30,33,35,37,38,39,40,42,46,48,49,57,61,69,73,76,78$	$1 \oplus k_{28}$
$0,1,3,5,7,9,10,11,12,14,15,16,18,20,22,24,25,26,27,28,30,33,35,37,38,39,40,42,46,48,49,57,61,63,76,78$	k_{32}
$0,1,3,5,7,9,10,11,12,14,15,18,20,22,24,26,27,28,33,35,37,39,40,42,44,46,48,49,57,61,63,73,76,78$	k_{33}
$0,3,5,7,9,11,14,15,18,20,22,24,25,26,27,30,33,35,37,39,40,42,44,46,48,49,57,61,63,69,73,76,78$	k_{41}
$0,1,3,5,7,9,10,11,12,14,15,18,20,22,24,26,27,28,30,33,35,37,40,42,44,46,48,49,57,61,63,73,76,78$	k_{42}
$1,3,5,7,9,10,11,12,14,16,18,20,22,24,25,26,27,28,30,33,35,37,38,39,40,42,46,48,49,57,61,63,73,76,78$	k_{44}
$0,1,3,5,7,9,10,12,14,16,18,20,22,24,26,27,28,30,33,35,37,38,40,42,44,46,48,57,61,63,73,76,78$	k_{46}
$0,1,3,5,7,9,10,11,12,14,16,18,20,22,24,26,27,28,30,33,35,37,39,40,42,44,46,48,49,57,61,63,76,78$	k_{52}
$0,1,3,5,9,10,11,12,14,16,18,20,22,24,26,27,28,30,33,35,37,38,40,42,44,46,48,49,57,61,63,69,73,76,78$	k_{55}
$0,1,3,5,7,9,10,11,12,14,16,18,20,22,24,26,27,28,30,33,35,37,38,42,44,46,48,49,57,61,63,69,76,78$	k_{58}
$0,1,3,5,7,9,10,11,12,14,15,18,20,22,24,25,26,27,28,30,33,35,37,38,39,40,42,46,48,57,61,63,69,76,78$	k_{59}
$0,1,3,5,7,9,11,12,14,15,16,18,20,22,24,25,26,27,28,30,33,35,37,38,40,42,44,46,48,49,57,61,63,69,73,76,78$	k_{63}
$0,3,5,7,9,10,11,12,14,15,18,20,22,24,25,26,27,28,33,35,37,38,39,40,42,44,46,48,57,61,63,69,73,76,78$	k_{65}

A Practical Key-Recovery Attack on 805-Round Trivium. Based on the linear superpolies of 805- and 806-round Trivium, we could recover 42 key bits for 805-round Trivium. The sizes of the chosen cubes are from 32 to 38, and 42 key bits could be recovered with $2^{41.25}$ requests. By adding a brute-force attack, the remaining 38 key bits could be recovered within 2^{38} requests. Consequently, to recover the whole key for 805-round Trivium, the on-line complexity is not larger than $2^{41.40}$ requests. Under a PC with a GTX-1080 GPU, we could recover 42 key bits in several hours. For remaining key bits, they could be recovered in less than 2^{38} requests which is much easier. Consequently, our attack on 805-round Trivium is practical.

5.3   Experimental Results on 810-Round Trivium

We do the similar experiments on 810-round Trivium. In this case, the preference bit is $s_{66}^{(810)}$ as well. We perform experiments on the starting cube set

$$I_7 = \{v_2, v_6, v_8, v_{10}, v_{11}, v_{15}, v_{19}, v_{21}, v_{25}, v_{29}, v_{30}, v_{32}, v_{34}, v_{36}, v_{39}, v_{41}, v_{43}, v_{45}, v_{50}\}.$$

With Algorithm 3, we finally get a cube I_8 given by

$$I_8 = \{v_2, v_6, v_8, v_{10}, v_{11}, v_{15}, v_{19}, v_{21}, v_{25}, v_{29}, v_{30}, v_{32},$$
$$v_{34}, v_{36}, v_{39}, v_{41}, v_{43}, v_{45}, v_{50}, v_0, v_{75}, v_{12}, v_{22},$$
$$v_{16}, v_{27}, v_{23}, v_{72}, v_4, v_{14}, v_{20}, v_{52}, v_{55}, v_{60}, v_{37},$$
$$v_{79}, v_{62}, v_{64}, v_{47}, v_{54}, v_{69}, v_{51}, v_{71}, v_{18}, v_{53}\}.$$

The size of I_8 is 44. Because it is too time consuming to perform linearity tests, we try to remove some cube variables from I_8 to obtain a smaller cube with low-degree superpolies. Finally, we obtain the cube I_9 of size 43, where

$$
\begin{aligned}
I_9 = \{ & v_2, v_6, v_8, v_{10}, v_{11}, v_{15}, v_{19}, v_{21}, v_{25}, v_{29}, v_{30}, v_{32}, \\
& v_{34}, v_{36}, v_{39}, v_{41}, v_{43}, v_{45}, v_{50}, v_0, v_{75}, v_{12}, v_{22}, \\
& v_{16}, v_{27}, v_{23}, v_{72}, v_4, v_{14}, v_{20}, v_{52}, v_{55}, v_{60}, \\
& v_{37}, v_{79}, v_{62}, v_{64}, v_{47}, v_{54}, v_{69}, v_{71}, v_{18}, v_{53} \}.
\end{aligned}
$$

and the degree of the superpoly of I_9 is upper bounded by 2. By using a computer with four NVIDIA V100 GPUs, we search a part of subcubes which only misses few cube variables in I_9. With the original Möbius transformation, to search subcubes of a 43-dimensional cubes, it needs 2^{43} bits memory. Benefited from the improved Möbius transformation, we could perform linearity tests on $2^{32.28}$ subcubes of I_9 with several GBs memory which is much less than the memory (1024 GB) required by the original Möbius transformation. Finally, we find 2 different cubes with linear superpolies, which are listed in Table 6.

Table 6. Linear superpolies for 810-round Trivium

Cube indices	Superpoly
0, 2, 4, 6, 8, 10, 11, 12, 14, 15, 16, 18, 19, 20, 21, 22, 23, 25, 27, 29, 30, 32, 34, 36, 37, 39, 41, 43, 45, 47, 50, 53, 54, 55, 60, 62, 64, 69, 71, 72, 75, 79	k_{62}
0, 2, 4, 6, 8, 10, 11, 12, 14, 15, 16, 18, 19, 20, 21, 22, 23, 25, 27, 29, 30, 32, 34, 36, 37, 39, 41, 43, 45, 47, 50, 51, 53, 54, 60, 62, 64, 69, 71, 72, 75, 79	k_{62}

Remark 3. We put our codes and all the found superpolies on https://github. com/YT92/Practical-Cube-Attacks.

6   Conclusion

In this paper, we focus on practical full key-recovery attacks on Trivium. We design a new framework for finding linear superpolies in cube attacks by presenting a new algorithm to construct cubes which potentially yield linear superpolies. With this new framework, we find sufficiently many linear superpolies and establish a practical full key-recovery attack on 805-round Trivium. To show the effectiveness of our algorithm for constructing cubes, we also tried 810-round Trivium. As a result, by constructing one 43-dimensional cube, we find two subcubes of size 42 with linear superpolies for 810-round Trivium. So far the success rate of our algorithm for finding linear superpolies is 100%. The 805-round Trivium is just chosen for an example. We believe that the new algorithm could also be applicable to Trivium up to 810 rounds with a bit more time since cube sizes increases a little. Since we use linearity test and Moebius transformation to recover superpolies, large cube sizes could not be explored. Recently, Hao et al. at EUROCRYPT 2020 proposed a new MILP modeling method for the three-subset division property which could be used to recover the exact super-poly for a given cube. Combing our new algorithm for selecting cubes with the three-subset division property to recover low-degree superpolies for large cubes will be one subject of our future work.

References

1. Aumasson, J.-P., Dinur, I., Meier, W., Shamir, A.: Cube testers and key recovery attacks on reduced-round MD6 and Trivium. In: Dunkelman, O. (ed.) FSE 2009. LNCS, vol. 5665, pp. 1–22. Springer, Heidelberg (2009). https://doi.org/10.1007/978-3-642-03317-9_1

2. De Cannière, C., Preneel, B.: TRIVIUM. In: Robshaw, M., Billet, O. (eds.) New Stream Cipher Designs. LNCS, vol. 4986, pp. 244–266. Springer, Heidelberg (2008). https://doi.org/10.1007/978-3-540-68351-3_18

3. Dinur, I., Güneysu, T., Paar, C., Shamir, A., Zimmermann, R.: An experimentally verified attack on full Grain-128 using dedicated reconfigurable hardware. In: Lee, D.H., Wang, X. (eds.) ASIACRYPT 2011. LNCS, vol. 7073, pp. 327–343. Springer, Heidelberg (2011). https://doi.org/10.1007/978-3-642-25385-0_18

4. Dinur, I., Shamir, A.: Cube attacks on tweakable black box polynomials. In: Joux, A. (ed.) EUROCRYPT 2009. LNCS, vol. 5479, pp. 278–299. Springer, Heidelberg (2009). https://doi.org/10.1007/978-3-642-01001-9_16

5. Dinur, I., Shamir, A.: Breaking Grain-128 with dynamic cube attacks. In: Joux, A. (ed.) FSE 2011. LNCS, vol. 6733, pp. 167–187. Springer, Heidelberg (2011). https://doi.org/10.1007/978-3-642-21702-9_10

6. Fouque, P.-A., Vannet, T.: Improving key recovery to 784 and 799 rounds of Trivium using optimized cube attacks. In: Moriai, S. (ed.) FSE 2013. LNCS, vol. 8424, pp. 502–517. Springer, Heidelberg (2014). https://doi.org/10.1007/978-3-662-43933-3_26

7. Hao, Y., Leander, G., Meier, W., Todo, Y., Wang, Q.: Modeling for three-subset division property without unknown subset. IACR Cryptol. ePrint Arch. **2020**, 441 (2020)

8. Hao, Y., Leander, G., Meier, W., Todo, Y., Wang, Q.: Modeling for three-subset division property without unknown subset. In: Canteaut, A., Ishai, Y. (eds.) EUROCRYPT 2020. LNCS, vol. 12105, pp. 466–495. Springer, Cham (2020). https://doi.org/10.1007/978-3-030-45721-1_17

9. Hu, K., Sun, S., Wang, M., Wang, Q.: An algebraic formulation of the division property: revisiting degree evaluations, cube attacks, and key-independent sums. In: Moriai, S., Wang, H. (eds.) ASIACRYPT 2020. LNCS, vol. 12491, pp. 446–476. Springer, Cham (2020). https://doi.org/10.1007/978-3-030-64837-4_15

10. Huang, S., Wang, X., Xu, G., Wang, M., Zhao, J.: Conditional cube attack on reduced-round Keccak sponge function. In: Coron, J.-S., Nielsen, J.B. (eds.) EUROCRYPT 2017. LNCS, vol. 10211, pp. 259–288. Springer, Cham (2017). https://doi.org/10.1007/978-3-319-56614-6_9

11. Joux, A.: Algorithmic Cryptanalysis, 1st edn. Chapman & Hall/CRC Cryptography and Network Security Series. Chapman and Hall/CRC (2009)

12. Kesarwani, A., Roy, D., Sarkar, S., Meier, W.: New cube distinguishers on NFSR-based stream ciphers. Des. Codes Cryptogr. **88**(1), 173–199 (2020)

13. Li, Z., Bi, W., Dong, X., Wang, X.: Improved conditional cube attacks on Keccak keyed modes with MILP method. In: Takagi, T., Peyrin, T. (eds.) ASIACRYPT 2017. LNCS, vol. 10624, pp. 99–127. Springer, Cham (2017). https://doi.org/10.1007/978-3-319-70694-8_4

14. Liu, M.: Degree evaluation of NFSR-based cryptosystems. In: Katz, J., Shacham, H. (eds.) CRYPTO 2017. LNCS, vol. 10403, pp. 227–249. Springer, Cham (2017). https://doi.org/10.1007/978-3-319-63697-9_8

15. Liu, M., Yang, J., Wang, W., Lin, D.: Correlation cube attacks: from weak-key distinguisher to key recovery. In: Nielsen, J.B., Rijmen, V. (eds.) EUROCRYPT 2018. LNCS, vol. 10821, pp. 715–744. Springer, Cham (2018). https://doi.org/10.1007/978-3-319-78375-8_23

16. Mroczkowski, P., Szmidt, J.: Corrigendum to: the cube attack on stream cipher Trivium and quadraticity tests. IACR Cryptol. ePrint Arch. **2011**, 32 (2011)

17. Rahimi, M., Barmshory, M., Mansouri, M.H., Aref, M.R.: Dynamic cube attack on Grain-v1. IET Inf. Secur. **10**(4), 165–172 (2016)

18. Sarkar, S., Maitra, S., Baksi, A.: Observing biases in the state: case studies with Trivium and Trivia-SC. Des. Codes Crypt. **82**(1), 351–375 (2016). https://doi.org/10.1007/s10623-016-0211-x

19. Stankovski, P.: Greedy distinguishers and nonrandomness detectors. In: Gong, G., Gupta, K.C. (eds.) INDOCRYPT 2010. LNCS, vol. 6498, pp. 210–226. Springer, Heidelberg (2010). https://doi.org/10.1007/978-3-642-17401-8_16

20. Sun, L., Wang, W., Wang, M.: MILP-aided bit-based division property for primitives with non-bit-permutation linear layers. Cryptology ePrint Archive, Report 2016/811 (2016)

21. Todo, Y., Isobe, T., Hao, Y., Meier, W.: Cube attacks on non-blackbox polynomials based on division property. In: Katz, J., Shacham, H. (eds.) CRYPTO 2017. LNCS, vol. 10403, pp. 250–279. Springer, Cham (2017). https://doi.org/10.1007/978-3-319-63697-9_9

22. Todo, Y., Isobe, T., Hao, Y., Meier, W.: Cube attacks on non-blackbox polynomials based on division property. IEEE Trans. Comput. **67**(12), 1720–1736 (2018)

23. Todo, Y., Morii, M.: Bit-based division property and application to SIMON family. In: Peyrin, T. (ed.) FSE 2016. LNCS, vol. 9783, pp. 357–377. Springer, Heidelberg (2016). https://doi.org/10.1007/978-3-662-52993-5_18

24. Wang, Q., Hao, Y., Todo, Y., Li, C., Isobe, T., Meier, W.: improved division property based cube attacks exploiting algebraic properties of superpoly. In: Shacham, H., Boldyreva, A. (eds.) CRYPTO 2018. LNCS, vol. 10991, pp. 275–305. Springer, Cham (2018). https://doi.org/10.1007/978-3-319-96884-1_10

25. Wang, S., Hu, B., Guan, J., Zhang, K., Shi, T.: MILP-aided method of searching division property using three subsets and applications. In: Galbraith, S.D., Moriai, S. (eds.) ASIACRYPT 2019. LNCS, vol. 11923, pp. 398–427. Springer, Cham (2019). https://doi.org/10.1007/978-3-030-34618-8_14

26. Xiang, Z., Zhang, W., Bao, Z., Lin, D.: Applying MILP method to searching integral distinguishers based on division property for 6 lightweight block ciphers. In: Cheon, J.H., Takagi, T. (eds.) ASIACRYPT 2016. LNCS, vol. 10031, pp. 648–678. Springer, Heidelberg (2016). https://doi.org/10.1007/978-3-662-53887-6_24

27. Ye, C., Tian, T.: A new framework for finding nonlinear superpolies in cube attacks against Trivium-like ciphers. In: Susilo, W., Yang, G. (eds.) ACISP 2018. LNCS, vol. 10946, pp. 172–187. Springer, Cham (2018). https://doi.org/10.1007/978-3-319-93638-3_11

28. Ye, C.-D., Tian, T.: Revisit division property based cube attacks: key-recovery or distinguishing attacks? IACR Trans. Symmetric Cryptol. **2019**(3), 81–102 (2019)
29. Ye, C.-D., Tian, T.: Algebraic method to recover superpolies in cube attacks. IET Inf. Secur. **14**(4), 430–441 (2020)

Algebraic Attacks on Rasta and Dasta Using Low-Degree Equations

Fukang Liu[1(✉)], Santanu Sarkar[4,6], Willi Meier[5],
and Takanori Isobe[1,2,3]

[1] University of Hyogo, Hyogo, Japan
liufukangs@163.com, takanori.isobe@ai.u-hyogo.ac.jp
[2] National Institute of Information and Communications Technology, Tokyo, Japan
[3] PRESTO, Japan Science and Technology Agency, Tokyo, Japan
[4] Indian Institute of Technology Madras, Chennai, India
santanu@iitm.ac.in
[5] FHNW, Windisch, Switzerland
willi.meier@fhnw.ch
[6] Ruhr-University Bochum, Bochum, Germany

Abstract. Rasta and Dasta are two fully homomorphic encryption friendly symmetric-key primitives proposed at CRYPTO 2018 and ToSC 2020, respectively. We point out that the designers of Rasta and Dasta neglected an important property of the χ operation. Combined with the special structure of Rasta and Dasta, this property directly leads to significantly improved algebraic cryptanalysis. Especially, it enables us to theoretically break 2 out of 3 instances of full Agrasta, which is the aggressive version of Rasta with the block size only slightly larger than the security level in bits. We further reveal that Dasta is more vulnerable against our attacks than Rasta for its usage of a linear layer composed of an ever-changing bit permutation and a deterministic linear transform. Based on our cryptanalysis, the security margins of Dasta and Rasta parameterized with $(n, \kappa, r) \in \{(327, 80, 4), (1877, 128, 4), (3545, 256, 5)\}$ are reduced to only 1 round, where n, κ and r denote the block size, the claimed security level and the number of rounds, respectively. These parameters are of particular interest as the corresponding ANDdepth is the lowest among those that can be implemented in reasonable time and target the same claimed security level.

Keywords: Rasta · Dasta · Agrasta · χ operation · Linearization · Algebraic attack

1 Introduction

Since the pioneering work [5] of Albrecht et al. on designs of ciphers friendly to secure multi-party computation (MPC), fully homomorphic encryption (FHE) and zero-knowledge proofs (ZK), an increasing number of MPC-, FHE- and ZK-friendly symmetric-key primitives have been proposed, including LowMC [5],

© International Association for Cryptologic Research 2021
M. Tibouchi and H. Wang (Eds.): ASIACRYPT 2021, LNCS 13090, pp. 214–240, 2021.
https://doi.org/10.1007/978-3-030-92062-3_8

Kreyvrium [15], FLIP [40], Rasta [23], MiMC [4], GMiMC [3], Jarvis [9], Hades [34], Poseidon [33], Vision [7], Rescue [7] and Ciminion [25]. As designing symmetric-key primitives in this domain is relatively new and not well-understood, the designers may be prone to make mistakes in their innovative proposals. Four concrete examples come from the cryptanalysis of LowMC [5], the preliminary version of FLIP [40], the initial version of MARVELlous [9] and MiMC [29].

In the case of LowMC, new higher-order differential cryptanalysis [24] and the optimized interpolation attack [22] revealed that the original parameters of LowMC were too optimistic, which directly made LowMC move to LowMC v2. However, the so-called difference enumeration attack [41] in the low-data setting could still violate the security of some parameters in LowMC v2. As a countermeasure, the formula to calculate the secure number of rounds is updated and this version is called LowMC v3. However, it has been recently demonstrated in [38] that some parameters in LowMC v3 are still insecure when new algebraic techniques and the difference enumeration attack are combined. In addition, a very recent generic method [20] to solve multivariate equation systems over $GF(2)$ also shows that some parameters of LowMC v3 in the Picnic3 [37] setting are insecure.

In the case of the preliminary version of FLIP, Duval, Lallemand and Rotella revealed some weaknesses in its filter function and exploited them to devise an efficient full key recovery attack based on guess-and-determine techniques [27]. This result directly leads to a more conservative design of FLIP.

In the case of MARVELlous [9], Albrecht et al. described a clever way [2] to express the primitive as a set of low-degree equations with the introduction of intermediate variables. On the other hand, as MARVELlous works on a large field, the total number of variables in the equation system is still small even though there are intermediate variables. These directly lead to powerful Gröbner basis attacks as the Gröbner basis of such a set of polynomials can be efficiently computed in time less than that of the brute-force attack.

In the case of MiMC [4] proposed at ASIACRYPT 2016, the key-recovery attack on the full-round versions over $\mathbb{F}_{2^n}$ was presented at ASIACRYPT 2020 [29], mainly owing to a careful study of the evolution of the algebraic degree, though it is only slightly faster than the brute-force attack.

Such a trend in designing symmetric-key primitives for advanced protocols also motivates the cryptographers to generalize several cryptanalytic techniques to fields of odd characteristic [11]. As a consequence, some undesirable properties have been reported for GMiMC and Poseidon.

From the perspective of design, there are two common metrics for these primitives, i.e. the multiplicative complexity (MC) and the multiplicative depth of the circuit. In the context of Rasta [23], MC refers to the total number of AND gates and the multiplicative depth of the circuit refers to the number of rounds (called ANDdepth in Rasta [23]). The aim of Rasta is to provide a design strategy achieving d ANDdepth and d ANDs per bit at the same time. The designers proposed several parameters for the block/key size n, the ANDdepth d and the targeted security level κ. To make d as small as possible and keep its practical usage, $d \in \{4, 5, 6\}$ is recommended. Since generating the affine layers in each encryption is quite time-consuming in Rasta, Hebborn and Leander proposed Dasta [36] where the linear layer is replaced with an ever-changing bit permutation and a deterministic linear transform. Such a construction has made Dasta hundreds times faster than Rasta in the offline settings.

A feature in Rasta and Dasta is that n is much larger than κ and there is indeed no generic attack matching the claimed security level κ. To encourage more cryptanalysis, the designers of Rasta also proposed an aggressive version called Agrasta with $n = \kappa + 1$. The currently best key-recovery attack [26] on Agrasta in the single-plaintext setting is based on a brute-force approach and only 3 rounds can be covered. Moreover, no nontrivial third-party attacks have been published for Rasta or Dasta. It should be emphasized the same key can be used to encrypt many different plaintext blocks for Rasta, Dasta and Agrasta and hence the attacks should not be limited to the single-plaintext setting. Indeed, it has been shown in [23,36] that given the capability to collect many plaintext-ciphertext pairs under the same key, the attackers still cannot break any of the three proposals.

Algebraic Attacks. Algebraic attacks are potential threats to aforementioned primitives, as can be observed from the analysis of LowMC, FLIP, MARVEL-lous, MiMC, GMiMC and Poseidon. A crucial step to improve the efficiency of an algebraic attack is to construct a suitable equation system that can be efficiently solved with techniques like linearization, guess-and-determine, F4/F5 algorithms [30,31] (computing Gröbner basis) or XL algorithm [17]. How to construct useful equations is nontrivial and dominates the effectiveness of algebraic attacks. For methods to solve equations, the linearization technique is the simplest one, which is to treat each different monomial in the equations as an independent new variable. The drawback is hence obvious as the attacker needs to collect sufficiently many equations in order to solve it with Gaussian elimination. In addition, as the degree of the equations increases, the number of monomials will become very large and the cost of Gaussian elimination may even exceed the generic attack. For the guess-and-determine technique, its performance fully depends on the structure of the original equation system. Finding a clever guess-and-determine strategy is nontrivial. Especially, when the equation system tends to be random, the effect of such a strategy seems to be limited. For advanced algorithms like F4/F5 algorithms and the XL algorithm to solve multivariate polynomial equations, their complexity is hard to bound when the system is much over-defined. If only a portion of equations are taken into account, though the time complexity can be bounded, the resulting complexity may turn to be very high and exceeds the generic attack.

Our Contributions. We observed the feasibility to derive exploitable low-degree equations from the raw definition of the χ operation, which seems to be neglected by the designers for the high degree of the inverse of the large-scale χ operation. As a result, we could construct a system of equations of much lower degree than expected by the designers to describe the primitives. Specifically, r_0 rounds of Rasta can be represented as a system of equations of degree upper bounded by $2^{r_0-1} + 1$ rather than 2^{r_0}. For Dasta, by guessing only 1-bit secret information, we even could extract a system of equations of degree upper bounded by 2^{r_0-1} from many different plaintext-ciphertext pairs for r_0 rounds, which is mainly due to the usage of a deterministic linear transform following a bit permutation in the last linear layer.

It should be emphasized that constructing low-degree equations based on high-degree equations is not new in symmetric-key cryptanalysis. The underlying idea was first utilized in the algebraic attack [18] and fast algebraic attack [16] on several LFSR-based stream ciphers. A common notion in these attacks is the algebraic immunity of the filter function or the augmented function, which has been studied in several papers [8,32]. It should be mentioned that the resistance against these attack vectors has been taken into account in the design of FLIP [40] as it is very similar to an LFSR-based design, though the register is no longer updated by means of the LFSR, but with pseudorandom bit permutations.

However, Rasta is completely different from the LFSR-based stream cipher and it is more like a block cipher, which can explain why the designers ruled out the above attack vectors as they have not been successfully applied to block ciphers. We emphasize that this is mainly because common block ciphers always have a large number of rounds and hence the degree after a certain number of rounds is very high. However, this is not the case of Rasta, which has only a small number of rounds. Although our attack is based on low-degree equations, its feasibility indeed also much relies on our observation on the key feed-forward operation in Dasta and Rasta, i.e. the feature of the construction.

In a sense, our basic idea can be viewed as exploiting the algebraic immunity of the augmented function, which is the large-scale χ operation in Rasta and Dasta. As far as we know, there is no efficient method to compute the algebraic immunity of a huge S-box, which may be another reason why the designers did not take it into account. Understanding our attacks requires no knowledge of the algebraic immunity of the augmented function, though. In a nutshell, we reveal that the last nonlinear layer is ineffective to significantly increase the degree for the usage of a simple key feed-forward operation, whatever the last linear layer is.

On the Complexity of Gaussian Elimination. Denote the exponent of Gaussian elimination by ω. A naive implementation of Gaussian elimination leads to $\omega = 3$. Due to Strassen's divide-and-conquer algorithm [42], the upper bound of ω is updated as $\log_2 7$ and the algorithm has been practically implemented in [1]. Although there exists a more efficient algorithm [6] to perform the matrix multiplication and the upper bound can be further updated as $\omega < 2.3728596$, it is in practice useless for its hidden huge constant factor. In the preliminary analysis, the designers of Rasta [23] adopted $\omega = 2.8$ to compute the time complexity of algebraic attacks on reduced-round Agrasta and compared it with the required number of binary operations to encrypt a plaintext. The designers of Dasta [36] instead chose $\omega = 2.37$ to evaluate the resistance against algebraic attacks in order to explicitly understand the security margins of Dasta and Rasta. Therefore, in this paper, we provide the time complexity under both cases, i.e. $\omega = 2.8$ and $\omega = 2.37$. It should be emphasized that the former one is reasonable in practice.

Our Results. According to the Rasta paper [23], performing r rounds of Rasta with block size n requires about $(r+1)n^2$ binary operations caused by the linear layers. In our algebraic attacks, the number of equations is always kept the same with the number of variables and it is denoted by U, even though we are able to collect more equations. When evaluating the time complexity with $\omega = 2.8$, we adopt the formula $U^\omega / ((r+1)n^2)$ as in [23]. When $\omega = 2.37$ is used, we directly compute the time complexity with the formula U^ω as in [36]. The corresponding memory complexity is obvious, i.e. U^2. Our results are summarized in Table 1.

Organization. We briefly introduce Rasta, Dasta and the trivial linearization attack in Sect. 2. Then, we describe how to construct exploitable low-degree equations from the raw definition of the χ operation in Sect. 3. The application of these low-degree equations to the cryptanalysis of Rasta and Dasta will be explained in Sect. 4. Before concluding the paper in Sect. 6, we will also discuss in Sect. 5 why our attacks are overlooked, the application of others techniques such as the polynomial-based method [20] and the optimized exhaustive search [14], and the experimental results.

2   Preliminaries

In this section, we briefly describe the overall structure of Rasta and Dasta. Since several instances are specified, they will be distinguished with the notations Rasta-κ-r and Dasta-κ-r, where κ and r denote the claimed security level and the total number of rounds, respectively. In addition, throughout this paper, n denotes the block size, $rank(M)$ denotes the rank of the matrix M, M^{-1} denotes the inverse of the matrix M, a_i denotes the i-th bit of the vector a, $Deg(f)$ denotes the degree of the function f. In addition, we define

$$max(p,q) = \begin{cases} p & (p \geq q), \\ q & (p < q). \end{cases}$$

2.1   Description of Rasta

Rasta is a stream cipher based design where the nonlinear layer is deterministic while the linear layer is randomly generated during the encryption phase. Specifically, its input consists of a key $K \in \mathbb{F}_2^n$, a nonce N, a counter C and a message block $m \in \mathbb{F}_2^n$. To encrypt m, Rasta first randomly generates a concrete instance with SHAKE-256 [28] taking (N, C) as input. Then this instance is utilized to encrypt K to generate the keystream $Z \in \mathbb{F}_2^n$. Finally, $c = m \oplus Z$ is corresponding ciphertext block.

Formally, the keystream Z can be defined in the following way:

$$Z = (A_{r,N,C} \circ S \circ A_{r-1,N,C} \circ S \circ \ldots \circ A_{1,N,C} \circ S \circ A_{0,N,C}(K)) \oplus K,$$

Table 1. Summary of the attacks on Rasta, Dasta and Agrasta, where R, D, M and T denote the number of attacked rounds, data complexity, memory complexity and time complexity, respectively. The number of rounds marked with ⋆ means that the corresponding time complexity exceeds the claimed security level. We recomputed the time/data complexity of the trivial linearization attacks in [36] to keep consistent with our calculations and the results only slightly differ.

Target	Methods	n	R	$\log_2 D$	$\log_2 M$	$\log_2 T$	$\log_2 U$	ω	Reference
Agrasta-128-4	Brute-force	129	3	0	25	124.2	–	–	[26]
	Linearization	129	3	0	14	125.76	7	2.8	[23]
	Linearization	129	4	35.7	90	**110**	45	**2.8**	This paper
Agrasta-256-5	Brute-force	257	3	0	25	252.2	–	–	[26]
	Linearization	257	3	0	16	253.5	8	2.8	[23]
	Linearization	257	5	76.7	174	**225.1**	87	**2.8**	This paper
Rasta/Dasta-80-6	Linearization	219	2	19.3	54	64	27	2.37	[36]
Rasta-80-6		219	3	22	64	75.9	32	2.37	This paper
Dasta-80-6		219	3	27	54	65	27	2.37	This paper
Rasta-80-6		219	3	22	64	**72.1**	32	**2.8**	This paper
Dasta-80-6		219	3	27	54	**59.1**	27	**2.8**	This paper
Rasta/Dasta-80-4	Linearization	327	2	20.7	58	68.8	29	2.37	[36]
Rasta-80-4		327	3⋆	24.4	70	83	35	2.37	This paper
Dasta-80-4		327	3	29	58	69.8	29	2.37	This paper
Rasta-80-4		327	3	24.4	70	**79.3**	35	**2.8**	This paper
Dasta-80-4		327	3	29	58	**62.5**	29	**2.8**	This paper
Rasta/Dasta-128-6	Linearization	351	3	44.6	106	125.6	53	2.37	[36]
Rasta-128-6		351	4⋆	47.3	116	137.5	58	2.37	This paper
Dasta-128-6		351	4	53	106	126.6	53	2.37	This paper
Rasta/Dasta-128-5	Linearization	525	2	23	64	75.9	32	2.37	[36]
Rasta-128-5		525	3	27.7	78	92.5	39	2.37	This paper
Dasta-128-5		525	3	32	64	76.9	32	2.37	This paper
Rasta-128-5		525	3	27.7	78	**89.2**	39	**2.8**	This paper
Dasta-128-5		525	3	32	64	**70.6**	32	**2.8**	This paper
Rasta/Dasta-128-4	Linearization	1877	2	28.2	78	92.5	39	2.37	[36]
Rasta-128-4		1877	3	34.9	96	113.8	48	2.37	This paper
Dasta-128-4		1877	3	39	78	93.5	39	2.37	This paper
Rasta-128-4		1877	3	34.9	96	**111.4**	48	**2.8**	This paper
Dasta-128-4		1877	3	39	78	**87.2**	39	**2.8**	This paper
Rasta/Dasta-256-6	Linearization	703	4	97.6	214	253.6	107	2.37	[36]
Rasta-256-6		703	5⋆	101.3	226	267.9	113	2.37	This paper
Dasta-256-6		703	5	107	214	254.6	107	2.37	This paper
Rasta/Dasta-256-5	Linearization	3545	3	68.3	160	189.7	80	2.37	[36]
Rasta-256-5		3545	4	73.9	176	208.6	88	2.37	This paper
Dasta-256-5		3545	4	80	160	190.7	80	2.37	This paper
Rasta-256-5		3545	4	73.9	176	**221.4**	88	**2.8**	This paper
Dasta-256-5		3545	4	80	160	**200**	80	**2.8**	This paper

where $A_{i,N,C}$ is an affine mapping and S is the large-scale χ operation. The corresponding illustration can be referred to Fig. 1.

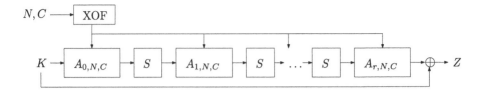

Fig. 1. Illustration of r rounds of Rasta

Nonlinear Layer $y = S(x)$. Denote the input and output of the nonlinear layer by $x = (x_0, x_1, \ldots, x_{n-1}) \in \mathbb{F}_2^n$ and $y = (y_0, y_1, \ldots, y_{n-1}) \in \mathbb{F}_2^n$, respectively. In this way, $y = S(x)$ can be specified as follows:

$$y_i = x_i \oplus \overline{x_{i+1}} x_{i+2},$$

where $0 \leq i \leq n - 1$ and the indices are considered within modulo n. For convenience, such a function $y = S(x)$ is defined as **the n-bit χ operation**. To make $y = S(x)$ bijective, n must be odd. It is also known that the degree of the inverse of the n-bit χ operation is $(n - 1)/2 + 1$. It should be mentioned that the 5-bit χ operation is the S-box used in the Keccak round function [10].

Affine Layers $u = A_{i,N,C}(v)$. Denote the input and output of the affine layers by $v \in \mathbb{F}_2^n$ and $u \in \mathbb{F}_2^n$, respectively. The affine mapping $u = A_{i,N,C}(v)$ is a binary multiplication of an $n \times n$ matrix $M_{r,N,C}$ with the n-bit input v, followed by the addition of an n-bit round constant $RC_{i,N,C}$, i.e.

$$u = M_{i,N,C} \cdot v \oplus RC_{i,N,C}.$$

A feature of Rasta is that both $M_{i,N,C}$ and $RC_{i,N,C}$ are not specified in advance. Instead, when a message block has to be encrypted, the corresponding message block counter C and a nonce N are taken as the input of SHAKE-256 [28] and the output of SHAKE-256 will be used to construct $M_{i,N,C}$ and $RC_{i,N,C}$ such that $rank(M_{i,N,C}) = n$ $(0 \leq i \leq r)$.

The Data Limit. To resist against algebraic attacks, it is explicitly specified in [23] that the largest number of n-bit message blocks that can be encrypted under the same key is $\sqrt{2^\kappa}/n$ for the instance parameterized with (n, κ, r).

The Instances. The designers have recommended several instances that can be implemented in practical time in [23], as shown in Table 2.

In addition to the above recommended instances, the authors also proposed aggressive versions called Agrasta with $n = \kappa + 1$, as listed in Table 3. For simplicity, Agrasta parameterized with (κ, r) is denoted by Agrasta-κ-r. From the following statement by the designers, it is easy to see that the data limit remains the same for Agrasta, i.e. $\sqrt{2^\kappa}/n$. We will give a detailed explanation later.

"[23] Agrasta has a block size of 81-bit for 80-bit security having 4 rounds, 129-bit for 128-bit security having 4 rounds and 257-bits for 256-bit security having 5 rounds (in this case trivial linearization would work for 4 rounds)."

Table 2. Parameters of Rasta

κ	n	r
	327	4
80	327	5
	219	6
	1877	4
128	525	5
	351	6
	445939	4
256	3545	5
	703	6

Table 3. Parameters of Agrasta

κ	n	r
80	81	4
128	129	4
256	257	5

2.2 Description of Dasta

Dasta is in general the same with Rasta and we therefore do not distinguish the used notations. Formally, the keystream Z of Dasta is defined as follows:

$$Z = (L \circ P_{r,C} \circ S \circ L \circ P_{r-1,C} \circ S \circ \ldots \circ L \circ P_{1,C} \circ S \circ L \circ P_{0,C}(K)) \oplus K,$$

where L is a fixed $n \times n$ binary matrix while $P_{i,C}$ ($0 \leq i \leq r$) is an ever-changing bit permutation parameterized with (i, C) and a fixed bit permutation P. The construction of Dasta is depicted in Fig. 2.

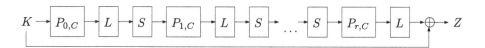

Fig. 2. Illustration of r rounds of Dasta

Our attacks are irrelevant to the details of L and $P_{i,C}$ and hence their details are omitted. The only thing we would like to emphasize is that $P_{i,C}$ is continuously changing, but it is always a bit permutation.

Differences Between Rasta and Dasta. One difference is that there is no constant addition operation in Dasta. Therefore, the encryption will output failure when K is 0. Another difference is that the linear layer is composed of an ever-changing bit permutation and a deterministic linear transform. Such a way to construct linear layers will obviously significantly improve the performance of

Rasta as there is no need to use SHAKE-256 to generate a random $n \times n$ full-rank binary matrix, which is quite time-consuming. Finally, Dasta only specifies 7 instances as shown below:

$$(n, \kappa, r) \in \{(327, 80, 4), (219, 80, 6),$$
$$(1877, 128, 4), (525, 128, 5), (351, 128, 6),$$
$$(3545, 256, 5), (703, 256, 6)\}.$$

The parameter $(n, \kappa, r) = (445939, 256, 4)$ is not taken into account in Dasta for its huge matrix size. For this reason, the attack on Rasta with such a parameter is not included in our results, though it is trivial to derive it based on our analysis.

2.3   Trivial Linearization Attacks

Due to the special construction of Dasta and Rasta, the conventional cryptanalysis techniques such as differential attacks, higher-order differential attacks, cube attacks and integral attacks immediately become infeasible as they all require the attackers to collect a sufficiently large number of plaintext-ciphertext pairs under the same key for a fixed concrete instance. Notice that when encrypting different message blocks under the same key, both primitives behave like moving targets, i.e. different message blocks are encrypted with different concrete instances.

Consequently, the designers of Rasta [23] made a comprehensive study on a more potential threat, namely the algebraic attack. However, all the reported results derived from the linearization attack, guess-and-determine attack and Gröbner basis attack are negative. In the Dasta document [36], the designers clearly described the number of rounds that the algebraic attacks can reach, as already mentioned in Table 1. As the time complexity of the Gröbner basis attack cannot be well estimated once the equation system becomes much overdefined, it is not surprising that the resistance against the linearization attack whose time complexity can be easily computed become a main concern of the designers. Indeed, the parameters of Rasta are chosen based on the resistance against the linearization attack, though the designers estimate the complexity to solve a large-scale linear equation system in a very conservative way, i.e. $O(1)$.

Since our results are indeed based on the linearization attack, it is necessary to describe how the designers performed such an attack on Dasta and Rasta. Due to the high degree of the inverse of the χ operation, the designers only considered the nonlinear equations in terms of the key in the forward direction. Specifically, if the total number of rounds is reduced to r_0 rounds, according to the keystream $Z = (z_0, z_1, \ldots, z_{n-1})$, the attackers are able to collect the following n nonlinear equations in terms of the key $K = (k_0, k_1, \ldots, k_{n-1})$:

$$\begin{cases} F_0(k_0, k_1, \ldots, k_{n-1}) \oplus z_0 = 0, \\ F_1(k_0, k_1, \ldots, k_{n-1}) \oplus z_1 = 0, \\ \quad \cdots \\ F_{n-1}(k_0, k_1, \ldots, k_{n-1}) \oplus z_{n-1} = 0. \end{cases} \tag{1}$$

The generic upper bound of $Deg(F_i)$ is $Deg(F_i) \leq 2^{r_0}$ $(0 \leq i \leq n-1)$ as the degree of the χ operation is 2. Although an attacker cannot collect many plaintext-ciphertext pairs under the same key for a fixed concrete instance in both primitives, he is able to collect many such pairs under the same key for many different instances and the number of such pairs is upper bounded by the data limit $\sqrt{2^\kappa}/n$.

A trivial linearization attack is to collect $\sum_{i=0}^{2^{r_0}} \binom{n}{i}$ such equations. Then, by renaming all the high-degree terms as new variables, the attacker indeed could construct $\sum_{i=0}^{2^{r_0}} \binom{n}{i}$ linear equations in terms of $\sum_{i=0}^{2^{r_0}} \binom{n}{i}$ variables. Solving such an equation system requires time complexity

$$T(n, r_0, \omega) = \left(\sum_{i=0}^{2^{r_0}} \binom{n}{i} \right)^\omega .$$

The designers of Rasta also mentioned a guess-and-determine attack. Specifically, after guessing υ key bits, the attacker only needs to collect

$$\sum_{i=0}^{2^{r_0}} \binom{n-\upsilon}{i}$$

equations. Solving such an equation system would require time complexity

$$2^\upsilon \cdot \left(\sum_{i=0}^{2^{r_0}} \binom{n-\upsilon}{i} \right)^\omega .$$

It is not difficult to observe that guessing variables is not a clever choice if taking the algebra constant ω into account as

$$2^\upsilon \cdot \left(\sum_{i=0}^{2^{r_0}} \binom{n-\upsilon}{i} \right)^\omega$$

tends to increase as υ increases when n is large and 2^{r_0} is small, which is indeed the case of Rasta, Dasta and Agrasta.

The effect of the trivial linearization attack on Rasta and Dasta has been discussed in [36] with $\omega = 2.37$, as displayed in Table 1. To show that Agrasta also resists against this attack vector, we simply calculate the corresponding time complexity with $\omega \in \{2.8, 2.37\}$, as shown below:

$$T(81, 4, 2.8) = 2^{153.72} , T(81, 4, 2.37) = 2^{130.113}$$
$$T(129, 4, 2.8) = 2^{186.2} , T(129, 4, 2.37) = 2^{157.605}$$
$$T(257, 5, 2.8) = 2^{379.68} , T(257, 5, 2.37) = 2^{321.372}.$$

Even if taking the time to perform the encryption into account, the attack cannot be better than the brute force. As stated by the designers [23], there exists a trivial linearization attack on Agrasta parameterized with $(n, \kappa, r) = (257, 256, 4)$. Indeed, we have

$$T(257, 4, 2.8) = 2^{232.68} ,$$

which means this parameter is insecure. However, it also implies that the data limit $\sqrt{2^\kappa}/n$ also works for Agrasta.

To better understand the data limit, we repeat the designers' description to determine the claimed security level. The attacker can collect at most $\sqrt{2^\kappa}/n \times n = \sqrt{2^\kappa}$ equations. In addition, there are in total

$$\sum_{i=0}^{2^r} \binom{n-\kappa}{i}$$

variables after linearization. It can be found that

$$\sum_{i=0}^{2^r} \binom{n-\kappa}{i} > 2^\kappa$$

for the parameters of Rasta displayed in Table 2. This also shows that the designers made a very conservative estimation of the complexity of Gaussian elimination, i.e. in time $O(1)$, even though that attacker are still unable to collect sufficiently many equations under the data limit.

3   Low-Degree Equations Hidden in the χ Operation

Both the designers of Rasta and Dasta expect that the degree of the equations that the attacker can collect is upper bounded by 2^{r_0} when the number of rounds is reduced to r_0. The main reason is that the inverse of the χ operation is too costly and they directly gave up in this direction. In the following, we demonstrate that there exist exploitable low-degree equations if relating the input and output of the χ operation in a more clever way.

Low-Degree Exploitable Equations. Denote the input and output of the χ operation by $(x_0, x_1, \ldots, x_{n-1})$ and $(y_0, y_1, \ldots, y_{n-1})$, respectively. Consider two consecutive output bits (y_i, y_{i+1}), as shown below:

$$y_i = x_i \oplus \overline{x_{i+1}} x_{i+2},$$
$$y_{i+1} = x_{i+1} \oplus \overline{x_{i+2}} x_{i+3}.$$

It can be derived that

$$y_{i+1}(y_i \oplus x_i) = 0. \tag{2}$$

Proof. As $y_i \oplus x_i = \overline{x_{i+1}} x_{i+2}$, we have

$$y_{i+1}(y_i \oplus x_i) = y_{i+1}\overline{x_{i+1}} x_{i+2} = (x_{i+1} \oplus \overline{x_{i+2}} x_{i+3})\overline{x_{i+1}} x_{i+2} = 0.$$

This completes the proof of Eq. 2.

Another very similar useful low-degree equation has been discussed in [35] to mount preimage attacks on reduced-round Keccak, as shown below:

$$y_i \oplus x_i = (y_{i+1} \oplus 1)x_{i+2}. \tag{3}$$

Indeed, Eq. 2 can also be derived from Eq. 3 if both sides of Eq. 3 are multiplied by y_{i+1}.

In addition, we further observed an exploitable cubic boolean equation from our experiments on the small-scale χ operation (e.g. $n \in \{7, 9\}$) with sagemath, as shown in Eq. 4. How to perform the experiments will be explained in Sect. 5.

$$y_{i+3}(y_{i+2}y_{i+1} \oplus y_{i+2} \oplus y_i \oplus x_i) = 0. \tag{4}$$

Proof. From the definition of the χ operation, we have

$$
\begin{aligned}
y_{i+2}y_{i+1} \oplus y_{i+2} \oplus y_i \oplus x_i &= y_{i+2}\overline{y_{i+1}} \oplus \overline{x_{i+1}}x_{i+2} \\
&= (x_{i+2} \oplus \overline{x_{i+3}}x_{i+4})(\overline{x_{i+1}} \oplus \overline{x_{i+2}}x_{i+3}) \oplus \overline{x_{i+1}}x_{i+2} \\
&= x_{i+2}\overline{x_{i+1}} \oplus \overline{x_{i+1}}x_{i+4}\overline{x_{i+3}} \oplus \overline{x_{i+1}}x_{i+2} \\
&= \overline{x_{i+1}}x_{i+4}\overline{x_{i+3}}.
\end{aligned}
$$

Hence,

$$y_{i+3}(y_{i+2}y_{i+1} \oplus y_{i+2} \oplus y_i \oplus x_i) = (x_{i+3} \oplus \overline{x_{i+4}}x_{i+5})\overline{x_{i+1}}x_{i+4}\overline{x_{i+3}} = 0.$$

This completes the proof.

$$
\begin{cases}
y_1 y_0 \oplus y_1 x_0 = 0, \\
y_1 x_2 \oplus y_0 \oplus x_0 \oplus x_2 = 0, \\
y_1(y_0 y_{n-1} \oplus y_0 \oplus y_{n-2} \oplus x_{n-2}) = 0, \\
y_2 y_1 \oplus y_2 x_1 = 0, \\
y_2 x_3 \oplus y_2 \oplus x_2 \oplus x_3 = 0, \\
y_2(y_1 y_0 \oplus y_1 \oplus y_{n-1} \oplus x_{n-1}) = 0, \\
\quad \cdots \\
y_{i+1} y_i \oplus y_{i+1} x_i = 0, \\
y_{i+1} x_{i+2} \oplus y_i \oplus x_i \oplus x_{i+2} = 0, \\
y_{i+1}(y_i y_{i-1} \oplus y_i \oplus y_{i-2} \oplus x_{i-2}) = 0, \\
\quad \cdots \\
y_{n-1} y_{n-2} \oplus y_{n-1} x_{n-2} = 0, \\
y_{n-1} x_0 \oplus y_{n-2} \oplus x_{n-2} \oplus x_0 = 0, \\
y_{n-1}(y_{n-2} y_{n-3} \oplus y_{n-2} \oplus y_{n-4} \oplus x_{n-4}) = 0, \\
y_0 y_{n-1} \oplus y_0 x_{n-1} = 0, \\
y_0 x_1 \oplus y_0 \oplus x_0 \oplus x_1 = 0, \\
y_0(y_{n-1} y_{n-2} \oplus y_{n-1} \oplus y_{n-3} \oplus x_{n-3}) = 0.
\end{cases}
\tag{5}
$$

***The Total Number of Exploitable Equations of Degree Upper Bounded
by 3.*** If treating $y_{i+1}x_{i+2}$, $y_{i+1}x_i$, $y_{i+1}y_i$, $y_{i+3}y_i$, $y_{i+3}x_i$ and $y_{i+3}y_{i+2}y_{i+1}$ as new
variables, we can say that Eq. 2, Eq. 3 and Eq. 4 are linearly independent. Taking
all the input bits into account, we obtain the equation system (5).

It is not difficult to observe that these $3n$ equations are linearly independent if
the high-degree terms are treated as new variables. This is because each equation
contains one high-degree term that never appears in other equations.

What benefits can be brought by such a system of equations? Imagine the
case when the degree of the boolean expressions of the input $x = (x_0, \ldots, x_{n-1})$
and output $y = (y_0, \ldots, y_{n-1})$ of the χ operation in terms of the key bits are
upper bounded by $\mathcal{D}_x$ and $\mathcal{D}_y$, respectively. If only the raw definition of the χ
operation is taken into account, i.e. the equations are constructed based on

$$y_i = x_i \oplus \overline{x_{i+1}}x_{i+2},$$

the degree of the collected equations will be upper bounded by

$$max(2\mathcal{D}_x, \mathcal{D}_y).$$

However, the equation system (5) can also be utilized to describe the relations
between x and y. Moreover, the degree of the equations in the equation system
(5) is upper bounded by

$$max(\mathcal{D}_x + \mathcal{D}_y, 3\mathcal{D}_y).$$

If we can know $\mathcal{D}_y = 1$ and $\mathcal{D}_x \geq 2$, there will be

$$max(\mathcal{D}_x + \mathcal{D}_y, 3\mathcal{D}_y) = \mathcal{D}_x + 1 < 2\mathcal{D}_x = max(2\mathcal{D}_x, \mathcal{D}_y).$$

In other words, we could construct equations of much lower degree based on
the equation system (5). As the degree of the equations is reduced, the number
of all possible monomials in the equations will be reduced to $\sum_{i=0}^{\mathcal{D}_x+1} \binom{n}{i}$ from
$\sum_{i=0}^{2\mathcal{D}_x} \binom{n}{i}$, which will be extremely useful to improve the trivial linearization
attack where the equations are derived only based on $y_i = x_i \oplus \overline{x_{i+1}}x_{i+2}$.

3.1   A General Approach to Search for Exploitable Equations

The above 3 equations are found manually or by performing experiments on the
small-scale χ operation, which are sufficient to devise the attacks in this paper.
However, it is still possible to miss similar equations and more equations can
be utilized to reduce the data complexity. Therefore, we are motivated to find a
more general approach to search for such useful equations. For this purpose, we
introduce the notion of **exploitable equation**.

Definition 1. *An exploitable equation is defined as an equation where the input
bits of the χ operation are only allowed to form linear terms or quadratic terms
with the output bits.*

Now we discuss our general idea to identify more exploitable equations. Consider the vectorial Boolean function $S : \mathbb{F}_2^n \to \mathbb{F}_2^n$. Suppose $(x_0, x_1, \ldots, x_{n-1})$ be the input of S and $(y_0, y_1, \ldots, y_{n-1})$ be the corresponding output. We aim to find equations involving input variables and output variables of the function S. Suppose our target is to bound the degree of input variables as 1 and degree of the output variables as ℓ. In other words, for any input $(x_0, x_1, \ldots, x_{n-1})$ and output $(y_0, y_1, \ldots, y_{n-1})$, the following relation should hold:

$$a^0 \oplus \sum_{0 \leq i < n} b_i^1 x_i \oplus \sum_{0 \leq i, j_1 < n} b_{i,j_1}^2 x_i y_{j_1} \oplus \sum_{0 \leq j_1 < n} c_{j_1}^1 y_{j_1} \oplus$$

$$\sum_{0 \leq j_1 < j_2 < n} c^2{}_{j_1, j_2} y_{j_1} y_{j_2} \oplus \cdots \oplus \sum_{0 \leq j_1 < j_2 < \cdots < j_\ell < n} c^\ell{}_{j_1, j_2, \ldots, j_\ell} y_{j_1} y_{j_2} \cdots y_{j_\ell} = 0, \quad (6)$$

where $a^0, b_i^1, b_{i,j_1}^2, c_{j_1}^1, \ldots, c_{j_1, j_2, \ldots, j_\ell}^\ell$ denote coefficients and are in $\mathbb{F}_2$.

Our aim is to identify these coefficients and they are treated as unknown variables. Thus, there are $t = n + n^2 + \sum_{i=0}^\ell \binom{n}{i}$ many unknown variables. If $\ell \ll n$, we have $t < 2^n$. Our procedure is to first fix some small odd number n. Next, we generate $t' > t$ many random input $(x_0, x_1, \ldots, x_{n-1})$ output $(y_0, y_1, \ldots, y_{n-1})$ pairs and put these values in Eq. 6. Thus we have t' linear equations over $GF(2)$. Each solution of the linear equation system gives a possible option of an exploitable equation. We then generate few more random input-output pairs and check the validity of the expression. If the expression is still valid, we can assume the expression to be valid for any input-output pair. From this expression, we try to estimate the expression for any odd number n. Thus our approach is based on interpolation-guess technique.

From Eq. (5), we know there are $3n$ linearly independent exploitable equations. First, we construct a set $\mathcal{S} = \{\psi_1, \psi_2, \ldots, \psi_{3n}\}$ where each ψ_i denotes a different equation among the $3n$ equations. Let $\mathcal{M}$ be the union of monomials of the polynomials of $\mathcal{S}$. Now if a new equation ψ' is generated using our interpolation-guess technique and contains at least one monomial outside $\mathcal{M}$, we include ψ' in $\mathcal{S}$ and update $\mathcal{M}$. We continue this process for each possible expression using our interpolation-guess technique.

In our interpolation-guess idea[1], we take $\ell = 5$ and $n = 11$. Hence, we are searching for $t = 11 + 11^2 + \sum_{i=0}^5 \binom{11}{i} = 1156$ many binary variables. From the results, we found the following two simple polynomials:

$$\psi_1^i = y_{i+5}\left(x_i \oplus x_{i+2} \oplus y_i \oplus y_{i+1} y_{i+2} \oplus y_{i+1} \overline{y_{i+3}} y_{i+4}\right), \quad (7)$$

$$\psi_2^i = y_{i+7}\left(x_i \oplus y_i \oplus \overline{y_{i+1}} y_{i+2} \oplus \overline{y_{i+1}}(y_{i+4} \oplus \overline{y_{i+5}} y_{i+6})\overline{y_{i+3}}\right). \quad (8)$$

Let $f_i = y_i \oplus x_i \oplus \overline{y_{i+1}} x_{i+2}$ for $0 \leq i \leq n-1$. Then we have $\psi_1^i = y_{i+5}(f_i \oplus y_{i+1} f_{i+2} \oplus y_{i+1} \overline{y_{i+3}} f_{i+4})$, $\psi_2^i = y_{i+7}(f_i \oplus \overline{y_{i+1}} f_{i+2} \oplus \overline{y_{i+1}} \, \overline{y_{i+3}} f_{i+4} \oplus \overline{y_{i+1}} \, \overline{y_{i+3}} \, \overline{y_{i+5}} f_{i+6})$. From 3, we know $f_i = 0$. Thus we have $2n$ extra relations:

$$y_{i+5}\left(x_i \oplus x_{i+2} \oplus y_i \oplus y_{i+1} y_{i+2} \oplus y_{i+1} \overline{y_{i+3}} y_{i+4}\right) = 0, \quad (9)$$

---

[1] Obviously, all the $3n$ equations in the equation system (5) can also be detected with this technique if it starts from an empty set $\mathcal{S}$.

$$y_{i+7}\big(x_i \oplus y_i \oplus \overline{y_{i+1}}y_{i+2} \oplus \overline{y_{i+1}}(y_{i+4} \oplus \overline{y_{i+5}}y_{i+6})\overline{y_{i+3}}\big) = 0. \tag{10}$$

Consider the ideal $\mathcal{I} = \langle f_0, \ldots, f_{n-1} \rangle$. It is further found that

$$\psi_1^i \in \mathcal{I}, \psi_2^i \in \mathcal{I},$$
$$y_{i+1}(y_i \oplus x_i) = y_{i+1}(y_i \oplus x_i \oplus \overline{y_{i+1}}x_{i+2}) \in \mathcal{I},$$
$$y_{i+3}(y_{i+2}y_{i+1} \oplus y_{i+2} \oplus y_i \oplus x_i)$$
$$= y_{i+3}(y_i \oplus x_i \oplus \overline{y_{i+1}}x_{i+2}) \oplus y_{i+3}\overline{y_{i+1}}(y_{i+2} \oplus x_{i+2} \oplus \overline{y_{i+3}}x_{i+4}) \in \mathcal{I}.$$

Thus, all the $5n$ useful relations are in $\mathcal{I}$.

Remark. Apart from $5n$ such relations, we obtained many other useful relations for $n = 11, \ell = 5$. However, these expressions are too complicated. Hence, we do not try to generalize them. One interesting observation is that these relations are also in $\mathcal{I}$. We emphasize that our algorithm is very similar to the algorithm proposed by Fischer and Meier at FSE 2007, which is used to compute the algebraic immunity of S-boxes and augmented functions [32]. However, as most similar algorithms [12,19] to search for quadratic boolean functions of a certain S-box based on Gaussian elimination, the algorithm [32] soon becomes impractical for a huge S-box, i.e. the large-scale χ operation. This is because as the size of the S-box increases, the number of possible monomials, i.e. the number of to-be-determined coefficients, will become very large, which will result in high costs of Gaussian elimination. The feasibility of our algorithm contributes to our critical observation that some forms of exploitable equations holding for the small-scale χ operation (with small n) might also apply to the large-scale χ operation (with large n). This directly allows to first search for exploitable equations for the small-scale χ operation, and then to check whether they also hold for the large-scale one.

4   Algebraic Cryptanalysis of Rasta and Dasta

Notice that there exists a key feed-forward phase just before computing the final keystream Z in Rasta and Dasta. This special construction together with the above low-degree exploitable equations will lead to significantly improved linearization attacks.

For simplicity, denote the state after $A_{i,N,C}$ by α^i and the state before $A_{i,N,C}$ by β^i. In this way, the state transitions in Rasta can be described as follows:

$$K = \beta^0 \xrightarrow{A_{0,N,C}} \alpha^0 \xrightarrow{S} \beta^1 \xrightarrow{A_{1,N,C}} \alpha^1 \xrightarrow{S} \ldots \xrightarrow{A_{r-1,N,C}} \alpha^{r-1} \xrightarrow{S} \beta^r \xrightarrow{A_{r,N,C}} \alpha^r.$$

For Dasta, similarly, denote the state after $P_{i,C}$ by ρ^i, the state after L by π^i and the state before $P_{i,C}$ by λ^i. In this way, the state transitions in Dasta can be expressed as follows:

$$\lambda^0 \xrightarrow{P_{0,C}} \rho^0 \xrightarrow{L} \pi^0 \xrightarrow{S} \lambda^1 \xrightarrow{P_{1,C}} \rho^1 \xrightarrow{L} \pi^1 \xrightarrow{S} \ldots \xrightarrow{L} \pi^{r-1} \xrightarrow{S} \lambda^r \xrightarrow{P_{r,C}} \rho^r \xrightarrow{L} \pi^r,$$

where $K = \lambda^0$.

4.1 Constructing Low-Degree Equations for Rasta

First of all, we discuss the attacks on r_0 rounds of Rasta. In the forward direction, α^{r_0-1} can be written as boolean expressions in terms of the key. Denote the expression of $\alpha_i^{r_0-1}$ $(0 \le i \le n-1)$ in terms of $K = (k_0, k_1, \ldots, k_{n-1})$ by $g_i(k_0, k_1, \ldots, k_{n-1})$, i.e.

$$\alpha_i^{r_0-1} = g_i(k_0, k_1, \ldots, k_{n-1}).$$

As the degree of the χ operation is 2, we have

$$Deg(g_i) \le 2^{r_0-1}. \tag{11}$$

According to the plaintext-ciphertext pair (m, c), the corresponding keystream Z can be computed with $Z = m \oplus c$. Since

$$\alpha^{r_0} = Z \oplus K,$$
$$\alpha^{r_0} = M_{r_0,N,C} \cdot \beta^{r_0} \oplus RC_{r_0,N,C},$$

we have

$$\beta^{r_0} = M_{r_0,N,C}^{-1} \cdot (m \oplus c \oplus K \oplus RC_{r_0,N,C}).$$

In other words, in the backward direction, β^{r_0} can be written as linear expressions in terms of K. For simplicity, denote the corresponding linear expression of $\beta_i^{r_0}$ $(0 \le i \le n-1)$ by $h_i(k_0, k_1, \ldots, k_{n-1})$, i.e.

$$\beta_i^{r_0} = h_i(k_0, k_1, \ldots, k_{n-1}).$$

Hence, we have

$$Deg(h_i) = 1. \tag{12}$$

Notice that

$$\beta^{r_0} = S(\alpha^{r_0-1}).$$

Hence, according to Eq. 2, Eq. 3, Eq. 4, Eq. 9 and Eq. 10, the following low-degree equations can be derived:

$$h_{i+1} \cdot h_i \oplus h_{i+1} \cdot g_i = 0,$$
$$h_i \oplus g_i \oplus h_{i+1} \cdot g_{i+2} \oplus g_{i+2} = 0,$$
$$h_{i+3}(h_{i+2}h_{i+1} \oplus h_{i+2} \oplus h_i \oplus g_i) = 0,$$
$$h_{i+5}\left(g_i \oplus g_{i+2} \oplus h_i \oplus h_{i+1}h_{i+2} \oplus h_{i+1}\overline{h_{i+3}}h_{i+4}\right) = 0,$$
$$h_{i+7}\left(g_i \oplus h_i \oplus \overline{h_{i+1}}h_{i+2} \oplus \overline{h_{i+1}}(h_{i+4} \oplus \overline{h_{i+5}}h_{i+6})\overline{h_{i+3}}\right) = 0,$$

where the indices are considered within modulo n. Based on Eq. 11 and Eq. 12, it can be found that the degree of the above 5 equations is upper bounded by

$$\mathcal{D} = max(Deg(g_i) + Deg(h_i), 5Deg(h_i)) = max(2^{r_0-1} + 1, 5).$$

When $r_0 \geq 3$, which is the case in our attacks[2], we have

$$\mathcal{D} = 2^{r_0-1} + 1. \tag{13}$$

As h_i is linearly independent from each other and g_i can also be viewed as linearly independent from each other once all high-degree monomials are renamed with new variables, we can then construct $5n$ linearly independent equations in terms of the key K for each pair (m, c). Different from the designers' analysis, the degree of our $5n$ equations is upper bounded by $2^{r_0-1} + 1$ rather than 2^{r_0}. This is a great reduction in the number of all possible monomials, i.e. reduced from $\sum_{i=0}^{2^{r_0}} \binom{n}{i}$ to $\sum_{i=0}^{2^{r_0-1}+1} \binom{n}{i}$. Obviously, such a reduction contributes to our clever way to utilize the low-degree equations discussed in Sect. 3.

Linearization Attacks on Reduced-Round Rasta. The attacks are now quite straightforward. Specifically, the attacker collects sufficiently many plaintext-ciphertext pairs. For each pair, $5n$ equations in terms of K can be constructed and the degree of these equations is upper bounded by $\mathcal{D}$ (Eq. 13). To solve this equation system, the linearization technique is applied. As a result, the time complexity T_0 and data complexity D_0 of our attacks on r_0 rounds of Rasta can be formalized as follows, where U denotes the maximal number of possible monomials.

$$U = \sum_{i=0}^{2^{r_0-1}+1} \binom{n}{i}, T_0 = U^{\omega}, D_0 = U/(5n).$$

As the maximal number of message blocks that can be encrypted under the same key is $\sqrt{2^{\kappa}}/n$, we need to ensure

$$D_0 = \left(\sum_{i=0}^{2^{r_0-1}+1} \binom{n}{i} \right) /(5n) < \sqrt{2^{\kappa}}/n \to \left(\sum_{i=0}^{2^{r_0-1}+1} \binom{n}{i} \right) < 5\sqrt{2^{\kappa}}. \tag{14}$$

In addition, as mentioned before, when the time complexity is evaluated with the algebra constant $\omega = 2.8$, the final time complexity will be computed with Eq. 15, i.e. the time to encrypt a plaintext requires about $(r_0 + 1)n^2$ binary operations for r_0 rounds of Rasta.

$$T_0' = \left(\sum_{i=0}^{2^{r_0-1}+1} \binom{n}{i} \right)^{2.8} / \left((r_0 + 1)n^2 \right) \tag{15}$$

When the time complexity is evaluated with $\omega = 2.37$ as in [36], the time complexity will be directly computed with

$$T_0 = \left(\sum_{i=0}^{2^{r_0-1}+1} \binom{n}{i} \right)^{2.37}. \tag{16}$$

---

[2] For $r_0 = 2$, we then only use Eq. 2, Eq. 3 and Eq. 4.

To violate the claimed security levels, it is essential to require

$$T_0' < 2^\kappa \tag{17}$$

when $\omega = 2.8$ or

$$T_0 < 2^\kappa \tag{18}$$

when $\omega = 2.37$.

Based on the formulas Eq. 15, Eq. 17 and Eq. 14, we directly break 2 out of 3 instances of Agrasta. In addition, the trivial linearization attacks on Rasta taking the parameters

$$(n, \kappa, r) \in \{(327, 80, 4), (1877, 128, 4), (3545, 256, 5)\}$$

are significantly improved, which directly reduces the security margins of these instances to only 1 round.

If evaluating the complexity with Eq. 16 and Eq. 14 as in [23], under the constraint Eq. 18, almost all linearization attacks described in [23] are improved by one round. All the results are summarized in Table 1.

Remark. For the high-degree nonlinear function, the designers should make a careful investigation of whether low-degree equations exist. For Rasta, the degree of the inverse of the χ operation is very high. However, this does not mean that we cannot derive useful low-degree equations if considering the relations between the input bits and output bits in a more careful way, which is obviously neglected by the designers. Especially, when the design has an additional structure, the neglected useful equations will become potential threats to the security.

4.2 Constructing Low-Degree Equations for Dasta

The above results can be trivially applied to Dasta. However, we further observe that the last linear layer of Dasta is constructed in the way to apply a bit permutation followed by a fixed linear transform. In the following, we describe how to exploit this feature to further obtain nonlinear equations of lower degree.

Based on similar analysis, when the target is r_0 rounds of Dasta, from the forward direction, π^{r_0-1} can be written as expressions in terms of K and the degree of these equations is upper bounded by 2^{r_0-1}. In the backward direction, both λ^{r_0} and ρ^{r_0} can be written as linear expressions in terms of K.

Firstly, focus on the expressions of ρ^{r_0}. It can be derived that

$$\rho^{r_0} = L^{-1} \cdot (m \oplus c \oplus K) = L^{-1} \cdot (m \oplus c) \oplus L^{-1} \cdot K.$$

Let

$$\sigma = L^{-1} \cdot K. \tag{19}$$

It can be found that the expressions of σ_i $(0 \le i \le n - 1)$ remain invariant due to the usage of a fixed linear transform L. As

$$\rho^{r_0} = L^{-1} \cdot (m \oplus c) \oplus \sigma,$$

under different (m, c), the expressions of ρ^{r_0} only vary in the constant parts. As λ^{r_0} is just a bit permutation on ρ^{r_0}, we have that the set of expressions of λ^{r_0} also only vary in the constant parts that only depend on (m, c).

In other words, if guessing one bit of σ, we can always find a bit of λ^{r_0} that can be uniquely determined based on this guess. More specifically, since the bit permutation may change when different message blocks are encrypted, a fixed guessed bit of σ will always lead to a computable bit of λ^{r_0} whose bit position is not fixed. How to exploit this fact to improve the attacks on Dasta is detailed as follows.

Linearization Attacks on Reduced-Round Dasta. Denote the expression of $\lambda_i^{r_0}$ by $h_i'(k_0, k_1, \ldots, k_{n-1})$ and the expression of $\pi_i^{r_0-1}$ by $g_i'(k_0, k_1, \ldots, k_{n-1})$ $(0 \le i \le n - 1)$. Similarly, we have

$$Deg(h_i') = 1, Deg(g_i') \le 2^{r_0-1}.$$

Based on the above analysis, guessing a fixed bit of σ will lead to a determined bit of λ^{r_0}, though its position is not fixed and is indeed a moving position. However, we can always find a bit λ^{r_0} that can be determined. Since

$$\lambda^{r_0} = S(\pi^{r_0-1}),$$

according to Eq. 3, we can deduce that

$$h_i' \oplus g_i' = (h_{i+1}' \oplus 1)g_{i+2}'. \tag{20}$$

Based on Eq. 4, we have

$$h_{i+1}'(h_i'h_{i-1}' \oplus h_i' \oplus h_{i-2}' \oplus g_{i-2}') = 0. \tag{21}$$

In addition, based on Eq. 9 and Eq. 10, we further have

$$h_{i+1}'\left(g_{i-4}' \oplus g_{i-2}' \oplus h_{i-4}' \oplus h_{i-3}'h_{i-2}' \oplus h_{i-3}'\overline{h_{i-1}'h_i'}\right) = 0. \tag{22}$$

$$h_{i+1}'\left(g_{i-6}' \oplus h_{i-6}' \oplus \overline{h_{i-5}'}h_{i-4}' \oplus \overline{h_{i-5}'}(h_{i-2}' \oplus \overline{h_{i-1}'h_i'})\overline{h_{i-3}'}\right) = 0. \tag{23}$$

Therefore, if the value of the expression h_{i+1}' is known, an equation of degree upper bounded by 2^{r_0-1} can be constructed based on Eq. 20, further reducing the degree by 1. If $h_{i+1}' = 1$, three more equations of degree upper bounded by 2^{r_0-1} can be derived from Eq. 21, Eq. 22 and Eq. 23 given that $r_0 \ge 3$.

As mentioned several times, once a fixed bit of σ is guessed, there always exists a bit of λ^{r_0} that can be uniquely determined. In other words, we can always find an expression h_{i+1}' whose value can be uniquely calculated based on the guessed bit. However, different from the attacks on Rasta, the number of useful equations of degree upper bounded by 2^{r_0-1} is 4 for each plaintext-ciphertext pair. Among the 4 equations, one can always be constructed, while whether the remaining three equations can be constructed will depend on the collected plaintext-ciphertext pair. Therefore, to make our results more convincing, we only use the probability-1 equation derived from Eq. 20. Therefore, the data complexity of our attack on Dasta is just an upper bound.

The attacks now become quite straightforward. Specifically, denote the data complexity and time complexity by D_1 and T_1, respectively. As we only aim at equations of degree upper bounded by 2^{r_0-1}, the maximal number of possible monomials is

$$U = \sum_{i=0}^{2^{r_0-1}} \binom{n-1}{i}.$$

Since only 1 equation is useful for a pair (m, c), we have

$$D_1 = \sum_{i=0}^{2^{r_0-1}} \binom{n-1}{i}.$$

As we need to guess a bit of σ, the time complexity is computed as follows:

$$T_1 = 2 \times \left(\sum_{i=0}^{2^{r_0-1}} \binom{n-1}{i} \right)^{\omega}.$$

Again, when $\omega = 2.8$, the time complexity is refined as

$$T_1' = 2 \times \left(\sum_{i=0}^{2^{r_0-1}} \binom{n-1}{i} \right)^{2.8} / \left((r_0 + 1)n^2 \right).$$

The time complexity should not exceed the claimed security level. The data complexity cannot exceed the data limit. Under the two constraints, we can significantly improve the linearization attacks on reduced-round Dasta, as shown in Table 1. It is not surprising to find that the attacks become more powerful as the degree decreases.

Countermeasures. A countermeasure to keep Dasta as secure as Rasta is to swap the bit permutation and linear transform in the last linear layer. In addition, the bit permutation should always be different when different message blocks are encrypted under the same key, which is indeed the strategy used in the first linear layer of Dasta. In this case, under different (m, c), the attacker needs to guess different bits in order to collect one equation of degree upper bounded by 2^{r_0-1}, which is obviously more time-consuming than the attacks based on equations of degree upper bounded by $2^{r_0-1} + 1$.

5   Discussions

The presented attack is surprisingly simple and can be treated as a generic attack on Rasta-like constructions. It should be emphasized that such a simple generic attack has remained undiscovered since the publication of Rasta [23] at CRYPTO 2018 and that designing and analyzing symmetric-key primitives for advanced protocols is an active field in recent years. Especially, Eq. 3 has been frequently exploited to mount preimage attacks on reduced-round Keccak [10] since the linear structure of Keccak was proposed at ASIACRYPT 2016 [35], though it is always interpreted in another way due to the sponge construction. Specifically, as the 5-bit χ operation is adopted in Keccak, Eq. 3 is always interpreted as follows in the context of preimage attacks:

Observation 1 *[35] When l $(1 < l < 5)$ consecutive output bits of the 5-bit S-box are known, there exist $l - 1$ linear equations **only in terms of the input bits** holding with probability 1.*

The reason to construct equations only in terms of the input bits is that some output bits of the 5-bit S-box are unknown to adversaries and the degree of their expressions in terms of the message bits is very high. Therefore, equations like

$$y_{i+1}(y_i \oplus x_i) = 0,$$
$$y_i \oplus x_i \oplus (y_{i+1} \oplus 1)x_{i+2} = 0,$$
$$y_{i+3}(y_{i+2}y_{i+1} \oplus y_{i+2} \oplus y_i \oplus x_i) = 0$$

are not friendly to attacks when only y_i is known to adversaries. Otherwise, the involved equations will contain more unknown variables (e.g. y_{i+1}) or the degree of the constructed equations in terms of the message bits will increase, both of which will have negative influences on the preimage attacks.

Based on the above fact, it is imaginable why the presented attack in this paper is overlooked. Specifically, due to the key feed-forward operation in Rasta, none of the output bits of the last χ operation is known, even though it is very easy to observe that these output bits are linear in the key bits in the backward direction. Hence, the above widely-used observation does not apply anymore as it requires known output bits of the χ operation and guessing output bits is too costly for Rasta.

Our simple attacks also demonstrate that the designers should make a thorough study on the new components in their innovative proposals, e.g. the large-scale χ operation in Rasta and Dasta. Indeed, finding a set of quadratic boolean equations satisfying a given S-box in terms of the input and output bits is well-known since the algebraic attack on AES [19], though our attacks require some special equations where the input bits are only allowed to form linear terms or quadratic terms with the output bits. We could only imagine that the large-scale χ operation is too large to handle, thus making the exploitable low-degree equations neglected.

However, dealing with a small-scale χ operation is sufficient and such equations can be easily observed. Indeed, there is an interface[3] in sagemath to compute the reduced Gröbner basis of the quadratic polynomials satisfying a given

---

[3] https://doc.sagemath.org/html/en/reference/cryptography/sage/crypto/sbox. html.

S-box, i.e. `sbox.polynomials(groebner=True)`. This function first computes a set of polynomials of degree upper bounded by 2 satisfying a given S-box with the method in [12] and then computes the reduced Gröbner basis for the obtained polynomials. We tested the 7-bit and 9-bit χ operations and observed Eq. 4. We argue that this is not a general method and we may miss some exploitable equations[4]. We recommend to use the dedicated approach discussed in Sect. 3 to search for more exploitable equations, which is also based on the idea to detect equations in the small-scale χ operation and then to further verify them for the large-scale χ operation.

Indeed, Eq. 2, Eq. 3 and Eq. 4 are sufficient to mount attacks on full Agrasta, Rasta and Dasta. With the general approach to search for more complicated exploitable equations, the data complexity can be reduced as more equations can be constructed based on a plaintext-ciphertext pair. However, the final time complexity and memory complexity of the linearization attack will remain the same. Moreover, it seems that the number of exploitable equations of degree upper bounded by a certain value is still small and the data complexity cannot be significantly reduced.

5.1 On the Polynomial Method [20]

Recently, based on the polynomial method [13, 21, 39], an improved generic method to solve multivariate equation systems over $GF(2)$ is proposed [20]. The conclusion is that the time complexity and memory complexity of solving systems of equations in terms of $\mathcal{N}$ variables are $\mathcal{N}^2 \cdot 2^{(1-1/2.7D)\mathcal{N}}$ bit operations and $\mathcal{N}^2 \cdot 2^{(1-1/1.35D)\mathcal{N}}$ bits, respectively, where D represents the upper bound of the degree of the equations. A disadvantage of such a generic method is that it cannot benefit from an overdefined system of equations.

When such a method is applied to Agrasta-128-4 and Agrasta-256-5, based on our way to construct low-degree equations, the memory complexity of the corresponding attacks is $129 \times 129 \times 2^{118.4} \approx 2^{132.4}$ and $257 \times 257 \times 2^{245.8} \approx 2^{261.8}$ bits, respectively. Thus, it is not better than the generic attack and requires much more memory than ours. In addition, as mentioned in [20], an optimized exhaustive search algorithm [14] for solving polynomial systems of degree D over $GF(2)$ requires $2D\log_2\mathcal{N} \cdot 2^{\mathcal{N}}$ bit operations. In other words, based on our way to construct low-degree equations, the optimized exhaustive search for Agrasta-128-4 and Agrasta-256-5 requires at least 2^{136} and 2^{265} bit operations, respectively. For the technique in [20], without guessing key bits, it requires $2^{137.7}$ and 2^{267} bit operations, respectively. Guessing key bits will increase the time complexity and hence the technique in [20] will not be faster than the optimized exhaustive search. If counting the number of bit operations for our linearization attacks on Agrasta-128-4 and Agrasta-256-5, we need about $2^{45 \times 2.8} = 2^{126}$ and

---

[4] One reviewer of Asiacrypt 2021 recommended to try different monomial orderings. Although we did get some new exploitable equations, the degree-4 and degree-5 equations described in this paper still do not appear in the computed Gröbner basis. We recommend the interested readers to try this by themselves.

$2^{87 \times 2.8} = 2^{243.6}$ bit operations, respectively, which are still significantly below that of the optimized exhaustive search.

For attacks on reduced-round Rasta and Dasta based on the proposed polynomial method [20] or the optimized exhaustive search [14], even with our method to construct low-degree equations, the corresponding memory complexity and time complexity will be much higher than the claimed security level because n is much larger than κ. This shows the advantage of the linearization attacks which can greatly benefit from an over-defined system of equations.

5.2   Experimental Verification

The main concern of the linearization attack is whether the constructed equations are indeed linearly independent. To address it, we performed some experiments[5] on the small-state Rasta with small n for $r_0 \in \{2, 3\}$. Notice that the number of possible monomials increases very fast as the number of rounds increases. Consequently, the experiments are performed on 2 and 3 rounds of Rasta for efficiency. We are aware that the linearization attacks on such instances may not be competitive to the pure brute-force attack. However, we emphasize that the experiments are mainly used to check whether the constructed equations with our method are indeed linearly independent.

For the experiments on 2-round attack, only Eq. 2, Eq. 3 and Eq. 4 will be considered, while Eq. 9 and Eq. 10 will be included in the 3-round attack. This is because the degree of Eq. 9 and Eq. 10 is upper bounded by 4 and 5, respectively.

The aim of our experiments is to compute the number of linearly independent equations after Gaussian elimination, which is denoted by EQA, i.e. the rank of the coefficient matrix. If it is almost the same with the total number of equations before Gaussian elimination, which is denoted by EQB, our assumption on the linear independence between the equations is reasonable. We performed 100

Table 4. Experimental results on small-state versions, where $\#(= i)$ represents the number of tests when $EQB - EQA = i$ among the 100 tests.

r_0	n	EQB	EQB − EQA			
			$\#(= 0)$	$\#(= 1)$	$\#(= 2)$	$\#(= 3)$
2	21	1561	29	54	17	0
2	23	2047	38	55	7	0
2	25	2625	32	51	17	0
2	27	3303	25	63	12	0
2	29	4089	27	56	16	1
3	9	381	25	67	7	1
3	11	1023	27	61	12	0
3	13	2379	25	56	19	0

---

[5] The source code can be found at https://github.com/LFKOKAMI/AlgebraicAttackOnRasta.git.

random tests for each small instance, it was found that

$$0 \leq EQB - EQA \leq 3, \tag{24}$$

which indicates that our assumption is reasonable. The experimental results are displayed in Table 4.

6 Conclusion

While fully inverting the large-scale χ operation will make the linearization attack worse for its high degree, by carefully studying the relations between its input bits and output bits, we find that there exist some hidden low-degree equations where the input bits are only allowed to form linear terms or quadratic terms with the output bits. Combined with the key feed-forward operation in Dasta and Rasta, these hidden equations can be utilized to significantly improve the linearization attacks on reduced-round Rasta and Dasta. Especially, the improvement directly allows us to theoretically break 2 out of 3 instances of Agrasta. Based on our analysis, some recommended parameters of Dasta and Rasta seem to be aggressive for their small security margins. Our cryptanalysis also implies that the last nonlinear layer in Rasta and Dasta cannot effectively increase the degree in a fast way as expected by the designers.

Acknowledgement. We thank the reviewers of Asiacrypt 2021 for their insightful comments. Especially, we thank one reviewer for suggesting we try different monomial orderings to compute the reduced Gröbner basis for the small-scale χ operation. Fukang Liu is supported by the Invitation Programs for Foreigner-based Researchers of NICT. Santanu Sarkar acknowledges experienced researchers fellowship from Alexander von Humboldt Foundation. Takanori Isobe is supported by JST, PRESTO Grant Number JPMJPR2031, Grant-in-Aid for Scientific Research (B) (KAKENHI 19H02141) for Japan Society for the Promotion of Science, and SECOM science and technology foundation.

References

1. Albrecht, M., Bard, G.: The M4RI Library. The M4RI Team (2021). http://m4ri.sagemath.org
2. Albrecht, M.R., et al.: Algebraic cryptanalysis of STARK-friendly designs: application to MARVELLOus and MiMC. In: Galbraith, S.D., Moriai, S. (eds.) ASIACRYPT 2019, Part III. LNCS, vol. 11923, pp. 371–397. Springer, Cham (2019). https://doi.org/10.1007/978-3-030-34618-8_13
3. Albrecht, M.R., et al.: Feistel structures for MPC, and more. In: Sako, K., Schneider, S., Ryan, P.Y.A. (eds.) ESORICS 2019, Part II. LNCS, vol. 11736, pp. 151–171. Springer, Cham (2019). https://doi.org/10.1007/978-3-030-29962-0_8
4. Albrecht, M., Grassi, L., Rechberger, C., Roy, A., Tiessen, T.: MiMC: efficient encryption and cryptographic hashing with minimal multiplicative complexity. In: Cheon, J.H., Takagi, T. (eds.) ASIACRYPT 2016, Part I. LNCS, vol. 10031, pp. 191–219. Springer, Heidelberg (2016). https://doi.org/10.1007/978-3-662-53887-6_7

5. Albrecht, M.R., Rechberger, C., Schneider, T., Tiessen, T., Zohner, M.: Ciphers for MPC and FHE. In: Oswald, E., Fischlin, M. (eds.) EUROCRYPT 2015, Part I. LNCS, vol. 9056, pp. 430–454. Springer, Heidelberg (2015). https://doi.org/10.1007/978-3-662-46800-5_17

6. Alman, J., Williams, V.V.: A refined laser method and faster matrix multiplication. In: Marx, D. (ed.) Proceedings of the 2021 ACM-SIAM Symposium on Discrete Algorithms, SODA 2021, Virtual Conference, 10–13 January 2021, pp. 522–539. SIAM (2021)

7. Aly, A., Ashur, T., Ben-Sasson, E., Dhooghe, S., Szepieniec, A.: Design of symmetric-key primitives for advanced cryptographic protocols. IACR Trans. Symmetric Cryptol. **2020**(3), 1–45 (2020)

8. Armknecht, F., Carlet, C., Gaborit, P., Künzli, S., Meier, W., Ruatta, O.: Efficient computation of algebraic immunity for algebraic and fast algebraic attacks. In: Vaudenay, S. (ed.) EUROCRYPT 2006. LNCS, vol. 4004, pp. 147–164. Springer, Heidelberg (2006). https://doi.org/10.1007/11761679_10

9. Ashur, T., Dhooghe, S.: MARVELlous: a STARK-friendly family of cryptographic primitives. Cryptology ePrint Archive, Report 2018/1098 (2018). https://eprint.iacr.org/2018/1098

10. Bertoni, G., Daemen, J., Peeters, M., Van Assche, G.: Keccak. In: Johansson, T., Nguyen, P.Q. (eds.) EUROCRYPT 2013. LNCS, vol. 7881, pp. 313–314. Springer, Heidelberg (2013). https://doi.org/10.1007/978-3-642-38348-9_19

11. Beyne, T., et al.: Out of oddity – new cryptanalytic techniques against symmetric primitives optimized for integrity proof systems. In: Micciancio, D., Ristenpart, T. (eds.) CRYPTO 2020, Part III. LNCS, vol. 12172, pp. 299–328. Springer, Cham (2020). https://doi.org/10.1007/978-3-030-56877-1_11

12. Biryukov, A., De Cannière, C.: Block ciphers and systems of quadratic equations. In: Johansson, T. (ed.) FSE 2003. LNCS, vol. 2887, pp. 274–289. Springer, Heidelberg (2003). https://doi.org/10.1007/978-3-540-39887-5_21

13. Björklund, A., Kaski, P., Williams, R.: Solving systems of polynomial equations over GF(2) by a parity-counting self-reduction. In: Baier, C., Chatzigiannakis, I., Flocchini, P., Leonardi, S. (eds.) 46th International Colloquium on Automata, Languages, and Programming, ICALP 2019, Patras, Greece, 9–12 July 2019. LIPIcs, vol. 132, pp. 26:1–26:13. Schloss Dagstuhl - Leibniz-Zentrum für Informatik (2019)

14. Bouillaguet, C., et al.: Fast exhaustive search for polynomial systems in $\mathbb{F}_2$. In: Mangard, S., Standaert, F.-X. (eds.) CHES 2010. LNCS, vol. 6225, pp. 203–218. Springer, Heidelberg (2010). https://doi.org/10.1007/978-3-642-15031-9_14

15. Canteaut, A., et al.: Stream ciphers: a practical solution for efficient homomorphic-ciphertext compression. In: Peyrin, T. (ed.) FSE 2016. LNCS, vol. 9783, pp. 313–333. Springer, Heidelberg (2016). https://doi.org/10.1007/978-3-662-52993-5_16

16. Courtois, N.T.: Fast algebraic attacks on stream ciphers with linear feedback. In: Boneh, D. (ed.) CRYPTO 2003. LNCS, vol. 2729, pp. 176–194. Springer, Heidelberg (2003). https://doi.org/10.1007/978-3-540-45146-4_11

17. Courtois, N., Klimov, A., Patarin, J., Shamir, A.: Efficient algorithms for solving overdefined systems of multivariate polynomial equations. In: Preneel, B. (ed.) EUROCRYPT 2000. LNCS, vol. 1807, pp. 392–407. Springer, Heidelberg (2000). https://doi.org/10.1007/3-540-45539-6_27

18. Courtois, N.T., Meier, W.: Algebraic attacks on stream ciphers with linear feedback. In: Biham, E. (ed.) EUROCRYPT 2003. LNCS, vol. 2656, pp. 345–359. Springer, Heidelberg (2003). https://doi.org/10.1007/3-540-39200-9_21

19. Courtois, N.T., Pieprzyk, J.: Cryptanalysis of block ciphers with overdefined systems of equations. In: Zheng, Y. (ed.) ASIACRYPT 2002. LNCS, vol. 2501, pp. 267–287. Springer, Heidelberg (2002). https://doi.org/10.1007/3-540-36178-2_17

20. Dinur, I.: Cryptanalytic applications of the polynomial method for solving multivariate equation systems over GF(2). Cryptology ePrint Archive, Report 2021/578 (2021). https://eprint.iacr.org/2021/578

21. Dinur, I.: Improved algorithms for solving polynomial systems over GF(2) by multiple parity-counting. In: Marx, D. (ed.) Proceedings of the 2021 ACM-SIAM Symposium on Discrete Algorithms, SODA 2021, Virtual Conference, 10–13 January 2021, pp. 2550–2564. SIAM (2021)

22. Dinur, I., Liu, Y., Meier, W., Wang, Q.: Optimized interpolation attacks on LowMC. In: Iwata, T., Cheon, J.H. (eds.) ASIACRYPT 2015, Part II. LNCS, vol. 9453, pp. 535–560. Springer, Heidelberg (2015). https://doi.org/10.1007/978-3-662-48800-3_22

23. Dobraunig, C., et al.: Rasta: a cipher with low ANDdepth and few ANDs per bit. In: Shacham, H., Boldyreva, A. (eds.) CRYPTO 2018, Part I. LNCS, vol. 10991, pp. 662–692. Springer, Cham (2018). https://doi.org/10.1007/978-3-319-96884-1_22

24. Dobraunig, C., Eichlseder, M., Mendel, F.: Higher-order cryptanalysis of LowMC. In: Kwon, S., Yun, A. (eds.) ICISC 2015. LNCS, vol. 9558, pp. 87–101. Springer, Cham (2016). https://doi.org/10.1007/978-3-319-30840-1_6

25. Dobraunig, C., Grassi, L., Guinet, A., Kuijsters, D.: Ciminion: symmetric encryption based on Toffoli-Gates over large finite fields. Cryptology ePrint Archive, Report 2021/267 (2021). https://eprint.iacr.org/2021/267

26. Dobraunig, C., Moazami, F., Rechberger, C., Soleimany, H.: Framework for faster key search using related-key higher-order differential properties: applications to Agrasta. IET Inf. Secur. **14**(2), 202–209 (2020)

27. Duval, S., Lallemand, V., Rotella, Y.: Cryptanalysis of the FLIP family of stream ciphers. In: Robshaw, M., Katz, J. (eds.) CRYPTO 2016, Part I. LNCS, vol. 9814, pp. 457–475. Springer, Heidelberg (2016). https://doi.org/10.1007/978-3-662-53018-4_17

28. Dworkin, M.: SHA-3 Standard: Permutation-Based Hash and Extendable-Output Functions, 04 August 2015

29. Eichlseder, M., et al.: An algebraic attack on ciphers with low-degree round functions: application to full MiMC. In: Moriai, S., Wang, H. (eds.) ASIACRYPT 2020, Part I. LNCS, vol. 12491, pp. 477–506. Springer, Cham (2020). https://doi.org/10.1007/978-3-030-64837-4_16

30. Faugère, J.-C.: A new efficient algorithm for computing Gröbner bases (F4). J. Pure Appl. Algebra **139**(1–3), 61–88 (1999)

31. Faugère, J.-C.: A new efficient algorithm for computing Gröbner bases without reduction to zero F5. In: International Symposium on Symbolic and Algebraic Computation Symposium - ISSAC 2002, Villeneuve d'Ascq, France, July 2002, pp. 75–83. ACM. Colloque avec actes et comité de lecture. internationale (2002)

32. Fischer, S., Meier, W.: Algebraic immunity of S-boxes and augmented functions. In: Biryukov, A. (ed.) FSE 2007. LNCS, vol. 4593, pp. 366–381. Springer, Heidelberg (2007). https://doi.org/10.1007/978-3-540-74619-5_23

33. Grassi, L., Kales, D., Khovratovich, D., Roy, A., Rechberger, C., Schofnegger, M.: Starkad and Poseidon: new hash functions for zero knowledge proof systems. IACR Cryptology ePrint Archive 2019:458 (2019)

34. Grassi, L., Lüftenegger, R., Rechberger, C., Rotaru, D., Schofnegger, M.: On a generalization of substitution-permutation networks: the HADES design strategy. In: Canteaut, A., Ishai, Y. (eds.) EUROCRYPT 2020, Part II. LNCS, vol. 12106, pp. 674–704. Springer, Cham (2020). https://doi.org/10.1007/978-3-030-45724-2_23

35. Guo, J., Liu, M., Song, L.: Linear structures: applications to cryptanalysis of round-reduced KECCAK. In: Cheon, J.H., Takagi, T. (eds.) ASIACRYPT 2016, Part I. LNCS, vol. 10031, pp. 249–274. Springer, Heidelberg (2016). https://doi.org/10.1007/978-3-662-53887-6_9

36. Hebborn, P., Leander, G.: Dasta - alternative linear layer for Rasta. IACR Trans. Symmetric Cryptol. **2020**(3), 46–86 (2020)

37. Kales, D., Zaverucha, G.: Improving the performance of the picnic signature scheme. IACR Trans. Cryptogr. Hardw. Embed. Syst. **2020**(4), 154–188 (2020)

38. Liu, F., Isobe, T., Meier, W.: Cryptanalysis of full LowMC and LowMC-M with algebraic techniques. In: Malkin, T., Peikert, C. (eds.) CRYPTO 2021, Part III. LNCS, vol. 12827, pp. 368–401. Springer, Cham (2021). https://doi.org/10.1007/978-3-030-84252-9_13

39. Lokshtanov, D., Paturi, R., Tamaki, S., Williams, R.R., Yu, H.: Beating Brute force for systems of polynomial equations over finite fields. In: Klein, P.N. (ed.) Proceedings of the Twenty-Eighth Annual ACM-SIAM Symposium on Discrete Algorithms, SODA 2017, Barcelona, Spain, Hotel Porta Fira, 16–19 January, pp. 2190–2202. SIAM (2017)

40. Méaux, P., Journault, A., Standaert, F.-X., Carlet, C.: Towards stream ciphers for efficient FHE with low-noise ciphertexts. In: Fischlin, M., Coron, J.-S. (eds.) EUROCRYPT 2016, Part I. LNCS, vol. 9665, pp. 311–343. Springer, Heidelberg (2016). https://doi.org/10.1007/978-3-662-49890-3_13

41. Rechberger, C., Soleimany, H., Tiessen, T.: Cryptanalysis of low-data instances of full LowMCv2. IACR Trans. Symmetric Cryptol. **2018**(3), 163–181 (2018)

42. Strassen, V.: Gaussian elimination is not optimal. Numer. Math. **13**, 354–356 (1969)

Automatic Classical and Quantum Rebound Attacks on AES-Like Hashing by Exploiting Related-Key Differentials

Xiaoyang Dong[1], Zhiyu Zhang[3,4], Siwei Sun[2,5(✉)], Congming Wei[1],
Xiaoyun Wang[1,6,7], and Lei Hu[3,4]

[1] Institute for Advanced Study, BNRist, Tsinghua University, Beijing, China
{xiaoyangdong,wcm16,xiaoyunwang}@tsinghua.edu.cn
[2] School of Cryptology, University of Chinese Academy of Sciences,
Beijing, China
sunsiwei@ucas.ac.cn
[3] State Key Laboratory of Information Security, Institute of Information
Engineering, Chinese Academy of Sciences, Beijing, China
{zhangzhiyu,hulei}@iie.ac.cn
[4] School of Cyber Security, University of Chinese Academy of Sciences,
Beijing, China
[5] State Key Laboratory of Cryptology, P.O. Box 5159, Beijing 100878, China
[6] Key Laboratory of Cryptologic Technology and Information Security,
Ministry of Education, Shandong University, Jinan, China
[7] School of Cyber Science and Technology, Shandong University, Qingdao, China

Abstract. Collision attacks on AES-like hashing (hash functions constructed by plugging AES-like ciphers or permutations into the famous PGV modes or their variants) can be reduced to the problem of finding a pair of inputs respecting a differential of the underlying AES-like primitive whose input and output differences are the same. The rebound attack due to Mendel et al. is a powerful tool for achieving this goal, whose quantum version was first considered by Hosoyamada and Sasaki at EURO-CRYPT 2020. In this work, we automate the process of searching for the configurations of rebound attacks by taking related-key differentials of the underlying block cipher into account with the MILP-based approach. In the quantum setting, our model guide the search towards characteristics that minimize the resources (e.g., QRAM) and complexities of the resulting rebound attacks. We apply our method to `Saturnin-hash`, `SKINNY`, and `Whirlpool` and improved results are obtained.

Keywords: Quantum computation · Collision attacks · Rebound attacks · `Saturnin` · `SKINNY` · `Whirlpool` · MILP

1 Introduction

A cryptographic hash function is a primitive that maps a binary string of arbitrary length into a short fixed-length digest, enjoying collision resistance,

---

The full version of the paper is available at https://eprint.iacr.org/2021/1119.

© International Association for Cryptologic Research 2021
M. Tibouchi and H. Wang (Eds.): ASIACRYPT 2021, LNCS 13090, pp. 241–271, 2021.
https://doi.org/10.1007/978-3-030-92062-3_9

preimage resistance, and second-preimage resistance. One popular approach for building a cryptographic hash function is to plug a secure block cipher into one of the twelve secure PGV modes [46] to build the compression function, and then iterate it with the Merkle-Damgård paradigm [13,41]. In this work, we focus on the collision resistance of hash functions constructed in this way with AES-like ciphers (named as AES-like hashing) in both the classical and quantum setting.

The differential attack plays an important role in analyzing the collision resistance of a hash function H, since a successful collision attack implies a pair of inputs x and x' with nonzero difference $x \oplus x'$ such that the output difference $H(x) \oplus H(x')$ is zero. In the context of AES-like hashing, due to the feed-forward mechanism of the PGV modes, a collision means the identification of a pair of different inputs conforming a differential of the underlying block cipher whose input and output differences are the same. To be more concrete, let us consider the MMO mode (one of the twelve secure PGV modes) shown in Fig. 1: $H(x) \oplus H(x') = 0$ implies $(m \oplus E_K(m)) \oplus (m \oplus \Delta \oplus E_K(m \oplus \Delta)) = 0$ or $E_K(m) \oplus E_K(m \oplus \Delta) = \Delta$. Therefore, finding a collision is equivalent to finding a pair conforming a differential of the underlying block cipher whose input and output differences are of the same value. One method for achieving this goal is the rebound attack [39], which is the main technique involved in this work.

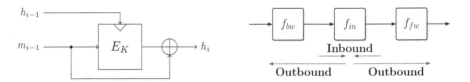

Fig. 1. (MMO) Matyas-Meyer-Oseas   Fig. 2. The rebound attack

1.1 The Rebound Attack

The rebound attack was first introduced by Mendel et al. at FSE 2009 [39]. Essentially, it is a technique for generating a pair of inputs fulfilling a differential $\delta \to \Delta$ for a block cipher. In the rebound attack, the targeted primitive with a truncated differential trail whose input and output differences share a common pattern is divided into three parts as shown in Fig. 2. Then, the attacker generates a lot of pairs (named as starting points in the literature) conforming the inbound differential. Finally, the starting points are propagated forward and backward to identify data pairs fulfilling the outbound differentials and the additional constraint that the input and output differences of the whole trail should be equal.

To increase the number of rounds covered by the inbound differential for AES-like ciphers, the super S-box technique was introduced independently by Gilbert et al. [21] and Lamberger et al. [38], where two consecutive AES-like rounds are considered as a whole with several super S-boxes. Later, Sasaki et al. [48]

showed that the memory complexity of the rebound attack can be significantly reduced by exploiting the differential property of non-full-active Super S-boxes. At CRYPTO 2011, Naya-Plasencia further improved the rebound attack by using better algorithms for merging large lists and finding solutions of the underlying differential trail [43]. The rebound attack has become a basic technique for collision attacks [16,30–32,40,49] and distinguishing attacks on various hash functions. It even finds applications in the context of DS-MITM attacks [14,15].

The Role of the Key Expansions. In rebound attacks, the generation of the starting points relies on the degrees of freedom from the encryption data path of the underlying block cipher. A natural idea is to utilize the degrees of freedom from the key-schedule algorithm if we do not require the key to be a prefixed value (e.g., the IV). For the sake of simplicity, let us consider the MMO mode with a single message block (see Fig. 1). A standard collision message pair (m, m') satisfies $H(IV, m) = H(IV, m')$, where the master key of the underlying block cipher is fixed and thus no degrees of freedom from the key-schedule algorithm can be used. However, for a semi-free-start collision $H(u, m) = H(u, m')$ ($u \neq IV$) or a free-start collision $H(v, m) = H(v', m')$ ($v \neq v'$), the key is allowed to be changed and thus the degrees of freedom from the key-schedule algorithm may be utilized. At ASIACRYPT 2009, Lamberger et al. presented the semi-free-start collision attacks on reduced `Whirlpool` by exploiting the degrees of freedom from the key schedule algorithm [38]. Since there is no difference in the key material, this type of attack can be modeled with the MILP-based method presented in [18,26]. At ASIACRYPT 2012, Sasaki et al. [49] applied the rebound attack on `Whirlpool` with an 8-round related-key truncated differential trail and find an 8-round free-start collision attack. To the best of our knowledge, no automatic method is available to find such free-start collisions based on the rebound attack. Finally, we would like to emphasize the importance of free-start collision attacks: The Merkle-Damgård security reduction assumes that any type of collision for the compression function should be intractable for the attacker, including free-start collisions.

1.2 Collision Attacks with Quantum Computing

For a long time, it was believed that quantum computing would have a limited impact on symmetric ciphers due to the quadratic speedup of an exhaustive search attack based on Grover's algorithm [25]. In ISIT 2010, Kuwakado and Morii showed how to break some provable secure schemes in the quantum setting [36], and this naive view started to change. Some follow-up works break more constructions [34,37]. However, a key step in these attacks involving the application of Simon's algorithm on a function with a hidden period related to the secret key, which requires the access to the keyed quantum oracle of the target. This is a strong requirement whose practical relevance is questioned. Hence, quantum attacks with higher complexities are still meaningful if they do not need to make online queries to superposition oracles of keyed primitives [6,7,24,28,29,35,44].

As keyless primitives, hash functions can be quantumly implemented offline and the thus attackers can freely make quantum superposition queries. For a hash function with n-bit output, classical algorithms find collisions with time complexity $O(2^{n/2})$. In the quantum setting, we have the following bounds induced by generic quantum attacks on hash functions.

- The BHT algorithm [8] equipped with a qRAM with size S finds a collision with a time complexity $T = \frac{2^{n/2}}{\sqrt{S}}$. It achieves optimal tradeoff when $T = 2^{n/3}$ and $S = 2^{n/3}$.
- Since the existence of large qRAM is still doubtful [22,23], there is a time-space tradeoff attack without qRAM, namely the quantum version of parallel rho's algorithm [4,26,50]. It achieves a time complexity of $T = \frac{2^{n/2}}{S}$ with S processors.
- The CNS algorithm [10] finds a collision with time complexity $T = 2^{2n/5}$ requiring a classical memory of size $2^{n/5}$ and $O(n)$ qubits.

At EUROCRYPT 2020, Hosoyamada and Sasaki [26] introduced the first dedicated quantum attack on hash functions (a quantum version of the rebound attack), which reveals that a differential trail whose probability is too low to be used in the classical setting may be exploitable in quantum attacks. However, the presented attacks are inferior to the CNS attack when there is no large qRAMs. At ASIACRYPT 2020, Dong et al. [18] reduced or even avoid the use of qRAM in the quantum rebound attacks by leveraging the non-full-active Super S-box technique. Recently, Hosoyamada and Sasaki [27] converted the classical semi-free-start collision attack on reduced SHA-2 into quantum collision attack and significantly improved the number of rounds attacked. At ToSC 2021, Chauhan et al. [11] found quantum collisions on reduced `AES-256` in double block length hashing. Ni et al. [45] investigated the quantum collision attacks on reduced `Simpira v2` in hashing modes.

1.3   Our Contribution

In this paper, we introduce an automatic tool to determine the related-key differentials, which are optimized for rebound attacks. More concretely, we focus on the free-start collision attacks based on rebound attack technique.

The main task is to increase the probability of the differential trail of the outbound part by properly consuming the degrees of freedom of the key. In addition, we have to deal with the *linear incompatibility*, which are frequently encountered in various automatic tools about related-key differential on AES-like ciphers, such as [5,12,20]. At CRYPTO 2013, Fouque et al. [20] find that the difference cancellation between the AES-128's key state and the round state in some round imposes some linear relationship between the key and state differences. Hence, difference cancellation in a different round cannot be independently simulated.

On ciphers with linear key schedule, Cid et al. [12] described an MILP model to search the related-key differentials, i.e., `Deoxys-BC` [33]. Since the relationship between Deoxys-BC's round keys are somewhat weakened by the LFSRs, they do not need to consider incompatibilities between many rounds. In this paper, we study a more complex case, i.e., Saturnin [9], a round 2 candidate of NIST LWC competition, proposed by Canteaut et al. In Saturnin, the round keys are identical for the even or odd rounds, respectively, and the round key in the odd rounds are derived by shifting the key in even round by 5 cells. Hence, the relationships between the round keys in Saturnin are stronger, and Cid et al.'s model may lead to many incompatible solutions for Saturnin. To deal with the problem, we build an efficient method to fast abandon the incompatible solutions, where the incompatibilities come from many rounds, for example, contradictions between the truncated differentials in round 0 and round 6. In addition, we also model the inbound phase with key differences, where both the 2-round and 3-round inbound phases are considered. We build a uniform objective function on the time complexity to perform the rebound attack, that takes the complexity of solving the inbound phase and the probability of the outbound phase as a whole. Thereafter, we find an 8-round trail for the rebound attacks and generate an 8-round quantum free-start collision attack on the compression function of Saturnin-hash. In addition, we also identify a 7-round quantum collision attack on Saturnin-hash based on a 7-round single-key rebound attack trail.

We also apply the automatic model to SKINNY-128-384 [3]. Since SKINNY adopts non-MDS matrix, we build a dedicated method to solve the super S-box with non-MDS matrix. Compared to the usual super S-box with MDS matrix, our method explores the details of the non-MDS matrix of SKINNY and decomposes the super S-box into a sequence of small S-boxes. Our super S-box technique with non-MDS matrix does not need to precompute the differential distribution of the super S-box even in the full active case, which works efficiently in quantum attack without qRAM and large classic memory. Concretely, about $\sqrt{2^c}$ time is needed to solve the full active super S-box with non-MDS matrix quantumly without qRAM, while the time is $\sqrt{2^{dc}}$ for full active super S-box with MDS matrix, where $d = 4$ for SKINNY and AES. Thereafter, we give the 16-round free-start quantum collision attacks on the hashing modes with SKINNY-128-384.

On ciphers with nonlinear key schedule, we study the compression function of ISO standard hash function, Whirlpool [2]. In the automatic model, we place the 3-round inbound phase in both the key schedule path and data encryption path (we do not find better trail with the two-round inbound phases). In its quantum attack, we nest multiple Grover's algorithms to solve several local searching problems. For Saturnin, the role of the consumption of degrees of freedom for key schedule is mainly to increase the probability of the outbound phase of the encryption data path. However, for Whirlpool, we have to consume the degrees of freedom of the key to increase the probabilities of the outbound phases in both the key schedule and the encryption data path. Finally, we introduce a 9-round quantum free-start collision attack on the compression function of Whirlpool, while the best previous attack is 8-round in classical setting [49]. The results are summarized in Table 1. Our quantum attacks do not need qRAM or classical memories, which perform better than the generic quantum collision attacks by parallel rho's algorithm [4,26,50]. However, certain time complexities may be inferior to the quantum attacks equipped with large classical memory by Chailloux, Naya-Plasencia, and Schrottenloher's algorithm [10].

Table 1. A summary of the results.

Whirlpool							
Target	Attack	Rounds	Time	C-Mem	qRAM	Setting	Ref.
Hash function	Collision	4/10	2^{120}	2^{16}	–	Classic	[39]
		5/10	2^{120}	2^{64}	–	Classic	[21,38]
		6/10	2^{228}	–	–	Quantum	[26]
		6/10	2^{248}	2^{248}		Classic	[17]
	Preimage	5/10	2^{504}	2^8	–	Classic	[47]
		6/10	2^{481}	2^{256}	–		[49]
		7/10	2^{497}	2^{128}			[1]
Compression function	Semi-free-start	5/10	2^{120}	2^{16}	–	Classic	[39]
	Semi-free-start	7/10	2^{184}	2^8	–	Classic	[38]
	Free-start	8/10	2^{120}	2^8	–	Classic	[49]
	Free-start	9/10	$2^{220.5}$	–	–	Quantum	Sect. 6
	Any	Any	2^{256}	–	–	Quantum	[4,26,50]
	any	any	$2^{170.7}$	–	$2^{170.7}$	Quantum	[8]
	Any	Any	$2^{204.8}$	$2^{102.4}$	–	Quantum	[10]
Saturnin-hash							
Hash	Collision	5/16	2^{64}	2^{66}	–	Classic	Full Ver. [19]
		7/16	$2^{113.5}$	–	–	Quantum	Full Ver. [19]
	Preimage	7/16	2^{232}	2^{48}	–	Classic	[17]
Compression function	Free-start	6/16	2^{80}	2^{66}	–	Classic	Full Ver. [19]
	Semi-free	7/16	$2^{90.99}$	–	–	Quantum	Full Ver. [19]
	Free-start	8/16	$2^{122.5}$	–	–	Quantum	Sect. 4
	Any	Any	2^{128}	–	–	Quantum	[4,26,50]
	Any	Any	$2^{85.3}$	–	$2^{85.3}$	Quantum	[8]
	Any	Any	$2^{102.4}$	$2^{51.2}$	–	Quantum	[10]
SKINNY-128-384-MMO/MP							
Compression func.	Free-start	16	$2^{59.8}$	–	–	Quantum	Sect. 5
	Any	Any	2^{64}	–	–	Quantum	[4,26,50]
	Any	Any	$2^{42.7}$	–	$2^{42.7}$	Quantum	[8]
	Any	Any	$2^{51.2}$	$2^{25.6}$	-	Quantum	[10]

2 Preliminaries

2.1 Quantum Computation and Quantum RAM

The state space of an n-qubit quantum system is the set of all unit vectors in $\mathbb{C}^{2^n}$ under the orthonormal basis $\{|0\cdots00\rangle, |0\cdots01\rangle, \cdots, |1\cdots11\rangle\}$, alternatively written as $\{|i\rangle : 0 \leq i < 2^n\}$. Quantum computation is achieved by manipulating the state of an n-qubit system by a sequence of unitary transformations and measurements.

Superposition Oracles for Classical Circuit. The superposition oracle of a Boolean function $f : \mathbb{F}_2^n \to \mathbb{F}_2$ is the unitary transformation $\mathcal{U}_f$ acting on an $(n+1)$-qubit system with the following functionality

$$\mathcal{U}_f \left(\sum_{x \in \mathbb{F}_2^n} a_i |x\rangle |y\rangle \right) = \sum_{x \in \mathbb{F}_2^n} a_i |x\rangle |y \oplus f(x)\rangle.$$

Grover's Algorithm. Given a quantum black-box access to a Boolean function $f : \mathbb{F}_2^n \to \mathbb{F}_2$ with $0 < f^{-1}(1) \ll 2^n$. Grover's algorithm finds an element $x \in \mathbf{F}_2^n$ such that $f(x) = 1$ with $O(\sqrt{2^n/|f^{-1}(1)|})$ calls to the quantum oracle $\mathcal{U}_f$ that outputs $\sum_x a_x |x\rangle |y \oplus f(x)\rangle$ upon input of $\sum_x a_x |x\rangle |y\rangle$. To be more specific, Grover's algorithm iteratively apply the unitary transformation $(2|\psi\rangle\langle\psi| - I)\mathcal{U}_f$ to the uniform superposition $|\psi\rangle = \frac{1}{\sqrt{2^n}} \sum_{x \in \mathbb{F}_2^n} |x\rangle$ of all basis vectors produced by applying the Hadamard transformation $H^{\otimes n}$ to $|0\rangle^{\otimes n}$. During this process, the amplitudes of those values x with $f(x) = 1$ are amplified. Then, a final measurement gives a value x of interest with an overwhelming probability [25].

Quantum Random Access Memories (qRAM). A quantum random access memory (qRAM) uses n-qubit to address any quantum superposition of 2^n memory cells. For a list of classical data $L = \{x_0, \cdots, x_{2^n-1}\}$ with $x_i \in \mathbb{F}_2^m$, the qRAM for L is modeled as an unitary transformation $\mathcal{U}_{\mathsf{qRAM}}^L$ such that

$$\mathcal{U}_{\mathsf{qRAM}}^L \left(\sum_i a_i |i\rangle \otimes |y\rangle \right) = \sum_i a_i |i\rangle \otimes |y \oplus x_i\rangle.$$

Currently, it is unknown how a large qRAM can be built. Therefore, quantum algorithms using less or no qRAM are preferred.

2.2 The Full-Active and Non-full-Active Super S-Box Technique

The super S-box technique proposed by Gilbert et al. [21] and Lamberger et al. [38] extends the Mendel et al.'s [39] inbound part into 2 S-box layers, by identifying four non-interfering $\mathbb{F}_2^{32} \to \mathbb{F}_2^{32}$ permutations across two consecutive AES rounds and regarding them as four super S-boxes as shown in Fig. 3(a). In [48], Sasaki et al. further reduced the the memory complexity by considering non-full-active super S-boxes as shown in Fig. 3(b).

Full-Active Super S-Box. We consider a more general scenario that the internal state of the cipher is a $d \times d$ matrix of c-bit cells. As shown in Fig. 3(a) with $d = 4$, for the ith super S-box SSB_i and given input difference $\Delta X_1^{(i)}$, we compute $\Delta Y_2^{(i)} = \mathsf{SSB}_i(x \oplus \Delta X_1^{(i)}) \oplus \mathsf{SSB}_i(x)$ for $x \in \mathbb{F}_2^{dc}$. Store the pair $(x, x \oplus \Delta X_1^{(i)})$ in a table $\mathbb{L}^{(i)}[\Delta Y_2^{(i)}]$. In the inbound phase, given $\Delta_{in} = \Delta Z_0$, we compute $\Delta X_1^{(i)}$ for $0 \leq i \leq d - 1$, then we compute the d tables $\mathbb{L}^{(0)}, \mathbb{L}^{(1)}, ..., \mathbb{L}^{(d-1)}$.

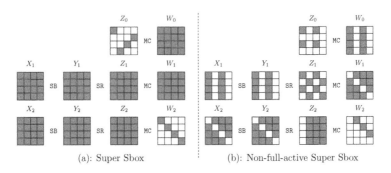

Fig. 3. A differential with non-full-active super S-box

For each $\Delta_{out} = \Delta W_2 \in \mathbb{F}_2^{dc}$, compute $\Delta Y_2^{(i)}$ with $0 \leq i \leq d-1$ to access the table $\mathbb{L}^{(i)}[\Delta Y_2^{(i)}]$ to generate a pair conforming the truncated differential of the inbound part. Hence, for given Δ_{in}, we need $d \times 2^{dc}$ memory to store the four tables, and will generate $|\Delta_{out}| = 2^{dc}$ pairs on average satisfying the inbound part.

At EUROCRYPT 2020, Hosoyamada and Sasaki [26] converted the classical super S-box technique into a quantum one. They introduced two quantum ways. The first one is to use the qRAM to replace the classical memory to store the super S-box, which needs a exponential size of qRAM. The second one is to apply the Grover's algorithm to search a conforming pair for a given input-output difference $(\Delta X_1^{(i)}, \Delta Y_2^{(i)})$ of SSB_i. This method needs about $2^{dc/2}$ super S-box computations to find the right pair.

Non-full-Active Super S-Box. For the non-full-active super S-box in Fig. 3(b), the Property 1 of MDS in MC is used. Look at $\Delta W_1 = \mathrm{MC}(\Delta Z_1)$, suppose there are totally s non-active cells ($s < d$) and $2d - s$ active cells in ΔZ_1 and ΔW_1 ($s = 3$ in Fig. 3(b)), then by guessing the differences of $d - s$ active cells, we can determine other differences according to Property 1. Then, for a fixed input-output differences $(\Delta X_1^{(i)}, \Delta Y_2^{(i)})$ of SSB_i, we can deduce all the input-output differences for the $2d - s$ active cells of two S-box layers for each guess and then deduce their values by accessing the differential distribution table (DDT) of the S-box. Now, for the equation $W_1 = \mathrm{MC}(Z_1)$, we have $2d - s$ known cells in W_1 and Z_1, hence it acts of probability $2^{-(2d-s-d)c} = 2^{(s-d)c}$. Hence, for a fixed $(\Delta X_1^{(i)}, \Delta Y_2^{(i)})$, we get $2^{(d-s)c} \cdot 2^{(s-d)c} = 1$ conforming pair on average. The time complexity is $2^{(d-s)c}$. The memory is 2^{2c} to store the DDT of S-box.

Property 1. $\mathrm{MC} \cdot (Z[1], Z[2], \cdots, Z[d])^T = (W[1], W[2], \cdots W[d])^T$ can be used to fully determine the remaining unknowns if any d cells of Z, W are known.

In the quantum setting, Dong et al. [18] converted the non-full-active super S-box technique into a quantum one by searching the $2^{(d-s)c}$ differences with Grover's algorithm, which gains a square root speedup. Both in quantum and classical setting, the complexity is determined by the number of inactive cells in $(\Delta X_1^{(i)}, \Delta Y_2^{(i)})$, i.e., s.

2.3 Inbound Part with Three Full Rounds

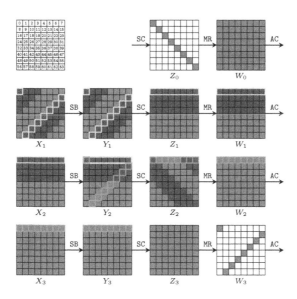

Fig. 4. Details in inbound phase covering 3 rounds (Color figure online)

As shown in Fig. 4, given fixed differences ΔZ_0 and ΔW_3, Jean et al. [30] introduced an algorithm to find the pairs of conforming to the 3-round differential. At EUROCRYPT 2020, Hosoyamada and Sasaki [26] introduced a memoryless algorithm (see Algorithm 9 of our full version paper). The time complexity is $2^{d^2 c/2 + dc}$ and there expects one conforming pair. Hosoyamada and Sasaki [26] also introduced the quantum variant shown in Sect. 6.

3 Modeling Rebound Attacks in the Related-Key Setting

In the related-key setting, taken MMO mode as an example in Fig. 1, we construct free-start collisions using related-key truncated differential trail of E_K, which meets Eq. (1):

$$(m \oplus E_K(m)) \oplus (m \oplus \Delta m \oplus E_{K \oplus \Delta K}(m \oplus \Delta m)) = \Delta m \oplus \Delta m = 0. \quad (1)$$

The procedures of the related-key rebound attack are:

1. Find a related-key truncated differential for E_K,
2. Choose a key pair (K, K') which meets the differential in the key-schedule,
3. Perform the rebound attack in the encryption data path with (K, K').

The Outbound Phase. In the single-key setting, previous works [18,26] consider the probability of the truncated differential, which is mainly due to the cancellations of MC operation. In the related-key setting, we try to use similar method directly, i.e., calculating the probability of differential transition by counting the number of inactive cells in the output of linear operations (e.g. MC, AK etc.) whose input is active. We use the round function of AES as an example without the SR. In Fig. 5(a), the four cells in first column of Y_i are active which are the input to the MC operation. The first column of Z_i has one inactive cell. Assume the differences in all active cells are independent uniform random, then $Prob(Y_i \to Z_i) \approx 2^{-c}$ (one cell of the state is of c bits). Similarly, $Prob(Z_i \to W_i) \approx 2^{-c}$. Thus the probability of the truncated differential trail in Fig. 5(a) is about 2^{-2c}.

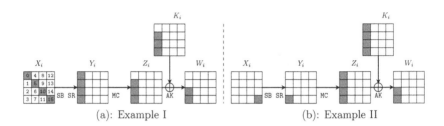

(a): Example I   (b): Example II

Fig. 5. AES rounds in forward outbound phase.

The method borrowed from single-key rebound attack seems to work well, but in related-key setting, this method may lead to a lower probability than the reality. For example, in Fig. 5(b), two active cells are cancelled by AK operation. Using the above method, we can calculate the probability of the trail is about 2^{-2c}. Note that in the related-key rebound attack, the key pair is first determined, then perform the rebound attack in the encryption data path, where key materials act as constants. Hence, the probability of the outbound phase in the encryption data path is computed under a fixed key difference. Therefore, $\Delta K_i[0,1] = \Delta Z_i[0,1]$ and $\Delta Z_i[0,1]$ is fixed. Due to Property 1, all other active cells of differences in Y_i and Z_i are determined. Hence, the probability of the differential is determined by the differential propagation of the S-box, i.e., $Prob(\Delta X_i[15] \xrightarrow{\text{S-box}} \Delta Y_i[3]) > 2^{-c}$ with DDT, which is bigger than 2^{-2c}. In detail, we derive the relationship between the first column of Y_i and Z_i from MC as shown in Eq. (2).

$$\begin{bmatrix} \Delta Z_i[0] \\ \Delta Z_i[1] \\ \Delta Z_i[2] \\ \Delta Z_i[3] \end{bmatrix} = \begin{bmatrix} 02\ 03\ 01\ 01 \\ 01\ 02\ 03\ 01 \\ 01\ 01\ 02\ 03 \\ 03\ 01\ 01\ 02 \end{bmatrix} \times \begin{bmatrix} \Delta Y_i[0] \\ \Delta Y_i[1] \\ \Delta Y_i[2] \\ \Delta Y_i[3] \end{bmatrix}. \tag{2}$$

As 3 cells in the 1st column of ΔY_i are 0 and $\Delta Z_i[0,1] = \Delta K_i[0,1]$, we have

$$\begin{bmatrix} \Delta K_i[0] \\ \Delta K_i[1] \\ \Delta Z_i[2] \\ \Delta Z_i[3] \end{bmatrix} = \begin{bmatrix} 02\ 03\ 01\ 01 \\ 01\ 02\ 03\ 01 \\ 01\ 01\ 02\ 03 \\ 03\ 01\ 01\ 02 \end{bmatrix} \times \begin{bmatrix} 0 \\ 0 \\ 0 \\ \Delta Y_i[3] \end{bmatrix},$$

which shows that $\Delta Y_i[3] = \Delta K_i[0] = \Delta K_i[1]$. Hence, $\Delta K_i[0]$ and $\Delta K_i[1]$ are related to each other. We call the number of cells in key, whose differences can be chosen independent randomly, the *degree of freedom* in the key differential states. In Fig. 5(b), key states have four active cells, among them two cells meet the condition $\Delta K_i[0] = \Delta K_i[1]$ that consumes one-cell degree of freedom. Hence, the degrees of freedom in the key differential states are $4 - 1 = 3$ in Fig. 5(b). Therefore, the degree of freedom in K is reduced to increase the probability of the trail in Fig. 5(b) from 2^{-2c} to about 2^{-c}. The consumption of freedom in the whole differential trail should not be higher than the number of active cells in key. Note that similar technique has already been used by Cid et al. [12] in the cryptanalysis of Deoxys against related-key differential attack. We apply the technique to the rebound attack by taking the features of rebound attack into the model.

Degree of Freedom. For a target with linear key schedule algorithms (e.g. Saturnin [9] and SKINNY [3]), we formulate its degree of freedom in the following. Taking Saturnin as an example, if there are t active cells in the master key, then we say that the initial degree of freedom for the key difference is t-cell (denoted by DoK $= t$), since there are about $(2^c)^t$ different choices for the key difference. However, as discussed previously, in rebound attacks exploiting related-key differentials, we may constrain the key difference by a system of linear equations with the active cells in the master key as variables to increase the probability of the outbound differentials. Assuming we have l independent linear equations, then l-cell degree of freedom is consumed (denoted by DoK$^- = l$). Therefore, to ensure there is at least one solution for the master key difference, we require DoK $\geq$ DoK$^-$. Otherwise, we have an over-defined system of equations for the active cells of the master key, which may have some conflicts.

Besides the degree of freedom from the master key difference, another source of degree of freedom should be considered. For a given master key difference, we can form $(2^c)^{\bar{n}}$ key pairs satisfying the given difference, where the key is of $\bar{n}$ c-bit cells. Taking the encryption data path into account and supposing that for a given $(\Delta_{in}, \Delta_{out})$ and key pair (K, K'), there is one solution for the inbound part in the data encryption path on average, then we can generate $(2^c)^{\text{DoK}-\text{DoK}^-+\bar{n}}(|\Delta_{in}| \cdot |\Delta_{out}|)$ starting points as $(K, M, K'M')$, which is called the degrees of freedom for the rebound attack [39] (denoted by DoA). To expect one solution fulfilling the outbound differential with probability p, we require that $(2^c)^{\text{DoA}} = (2^c)^{\text{DoK}-\text{DoK}^-+\bar{n}}(|\Delta_{in}| \cdot |\Delta_{out}|) \geq \frac{1}{p}$.

3.1   Dedicated Modelings and Case Study on Saturnin-hash

Saturnin is a suite of lightweight symmetric algorithms proposed by Canteaut et al. [9]. It is among the 2nd round candidates of the NIST LWC. Based on a 256-bit AES-like block cipher with 256-bit key, two authenticated ciphers and a hash function are designed. In this section, we focus on its hash function, called Saturnin-Hash. The round function only consists of AK, SB layer and linear layer, where MixRows (MR) and MixColumns (MC) are applied alternatively in even or odd number of round. The key schedule is linear and simple. In even round, K is used and in odd round the K is rotated by 5 cells (denoted as $\tilde{K}$).

Related-Key Truncated Differential Model. For an R-round primitive, we use several binary variables $x_r^{i,j}$ and $y_r^{i,j}$ to represent the state before and after the MR (or MC) operations in the r-th round, where i and j mean that the cell is in i-th row and j-th column. These variables are 1 if and only if the corresponding cell is active. For the key states, we use $K^{i,j}$ and $\tilde{K}^{i,j}$ to represent the rotated key and the master key in the same way.

Without loss of generality, we only consider MR operation now. To model the MR operations (similar constraints are also applied to MC), we use binary variables b_r^i to express MR operations are active or not in the i-th row of r-th round, and use branch number to generate constraints just like Mouha et al.'s model [42].

Another operation is key addition. The constraint of key addition are quite like constraint of XOR, except the result of two active cells addition can be active or inactive.

The Outbound Phase. As shown in Fig. 5(b), the number of cancelled cells could not show the real probability in a related-key model. Hence, the constraints in our model are different from single-key models. We use $Prob_r^i$ to represent the probability of the i-th row in round r.

In forward part of the outbound phase, we use c_r^i to represent the number of cells cancelled after the r-th round MR operation in row i, and $\tilde{c}_r^i$ to represent the number of cells cancelled after the next key addition operation in row i. If $\sum_{j=0}^{j\leq 3} x_r^{i,j} \geq c_r^i + \tilde{c}_r^i$ (like the trail in Fig. 5(a)), then the probability of this MR operation in this row is estimated by $c_r^i + \tilde{c}_r^i$ (to show the connection of probabilities and variables in our MILP model, the probabilities are taken in $-log_{2^c}$). If $\sum_{j=0}^{j\leq 3} x_r^{i,j} < c_r^i + \tilde{c}_r^i$ (like the trail in Fig. 5(b)), then the probability is $\sum_{j=0}^{j\leq 3} x_r^{i,j}$, and the degree of freedom in key states is consumed $c_r^i + \tilde{c}_r^i - \sum_{j=0}^{j\leq 3} x_r^{i,j}$. Thus, $Prob_r^i = \min(c_r^i + \tilde{c}_r^i, \sum_{j=0}^{j\leq 3} x_r^{i,j})$.

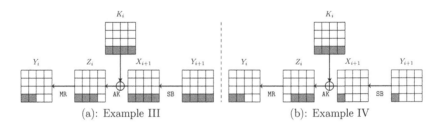

Fig. 6. Saturnin rounds in backward outbound phase.

Similar to forward part, in backward part, we also use c_r^i to represent the number of cells that are cancelled by the r-th round MR^{-1} operation in row i, and $\tilde{c}_r^i$ to represent the number of cells are cancelled before the next key addition operation in row i. If $\sum_{j=0}^{j\leq 3} x_{r+1}^{i,j} \geq c_r^i$ (like the trail in Fig. 6(a)), then the probability of this MR operation in this row is $c_r^i + \tilde{c}_r^i$. If $\sum_{j=0}^{j\leq 3} x_{r+1}^{i,j} < c_r^i$ (like the trail in Fig. 6(b)), then the cancellation of this MR operation in this row is $\sum_{j=0}^{j\leq 3} x_{r+1}^{i,j}$, and the degree of freedom in key states is consumed $c_r^i - \sum_{j=0}^{j\leq 3} x_r^{i,j}$. Thus, $Prob_r^i = \min(c_r^i + \tilde{c}_r^i, \sum_{j=0}^{j\leq 3} x_{r+1}^{i,j})$.

To limit the consumption of freedom, we add the following constraint

$$\underbrace{\sum (c_r^i + \tilde{c}_r^i - Prob_r^i)}_{Forward} + \underbrace{\sum (c_r^i - Prob_r^i)}_{Backward} \leq \sum_{0 \leq i,j \leq 3} K^{i,j}.$$

The Inbound Phase. We use a variable l to determine the inbound part and outbound part, and the inbound part includes r_{in} rounds. Thus round $l + 1$ to $l + r_{in}$ are inbound part, while other rounds are outbound parts. If $r_{in} = 2$, we use the super S-box techniques to solve the inbound part. In classical setting, it usually does not increase the overall time complexity, and only need some memories as shown in Sect. 2.2. However, in quantum setting without qRAM, the overall time complexity is also affected by the super S-box technique. As shown by Dong et al. [18], if the super S-boxes are not fully active, the time for quantum attack may be reduced. Following the notations in Sect. 2.2, the number of inactive S-boxes in the i-th super S-box SSB_i is denoted as s^i. Then the quantum time to solve the inbound part is about $\sqrt{2^{d-\min\{s^0,s^1,s^2,s^3\}}}$ according to Dong et al. [18], where d is the number of cells in each row, and $d = 4$ for Saturnin. In related-key setting, some cells in super S-boxes can be determined by key difference. As we shown in Algorithm 2 of Sect. 4, cells with known difference play the same role as inactive cells in non-full active super S-boxes technique. Thus s_i denote the number of cells whose difference is fixed before or after the MR or MC operation in the middle of a super S-box.

When $r_{in} = 3$, the inbound phase in solved by the methods of Jean et al. [30] classically or Hosoyamada et al. [26] quantumly. Both the time complexities are fixed and independent to the rebound attack trails as shown in Sect. 2.3. We will give more details in the attack on Whirlpool, whose rebound trail includes a 3-round inbound part in both the key schedule and encryption data path.

Time Complexity and Objective Function. In quantum setting without qRAM, we have two time complexities according to r_{in}:

▶ $r_{in} = 2$, the time complexity is about $\sqrt{2^{(\sum Prob_r^i + \sum x_0^{i,j} + d - \min\{s^0,s^1,s^2,s^3\})}}$, where $\sum Prob_r^i$ corresponds to the probability of the truncated difference of the outbound phase, $\sum x_0^{i,j}$ are the number of active cells to be collided for the plaintext and ciphertext, $d - \min\{s^0, s^1, s^2, s^3\}$ corresponds to the time to solve the inbound part. Hence, when $r_{in} = 2$, the objective function is to minimize $\sum Prob_r^i + \sum x_0^{i,j} + d - \min\{s^0, s^1, s^2, s^3\}$.

▶ $r_{in} = 3$, the objective function is $\sum Prob_r^i + \sum x_0^{i,j}$.

The Incompatibilities Within Many Rounds. Cid et al. [12] described an MILP model to search the related-key differentials on ciphers with linear key schedule, e.g., Deoxys-BC [33]. Since the relationship between Deoxys-BC's round keys are somewhat weakened by the LFSRs, they do not need to consider incompatibilities between many rounds. In `Saturnin`, the round keys are identical for many rounds, which lead to strong relationship on the round keys. Though we limit the consumption of degree of freedom in our MILP model, a trail can be incompatible when the same key cell needs to satisfy two different relationships in different rounds. For example, in Fig. 7, from Y_2 to X_3 we have $(\Delta Z_2[2], \Delta k_{11}, \Delta k_{15}, \Delta k_0) = \mathtt{MR}(\Delta Y_2[2], 0, 0, 0)$. From Y_4 to X_5 we have $(\Delta k_7, \Delta k_{11}, \Delta k_{15}, \Delta k_0) = \mathtt{MR}(\Delta Y_4[2], 0, 0, 0)$. The above two linear equations have 6 same cells., Due to Property 1, $\Delta Z_2[2] = \Delta k_7$, then $\Delta X_3[2]$ should be 0, which is a contradiction.

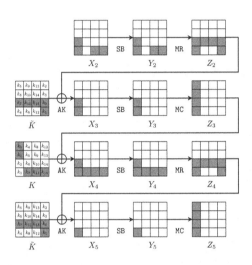

Fig. 7. An incompatible trail of `Saturnin`

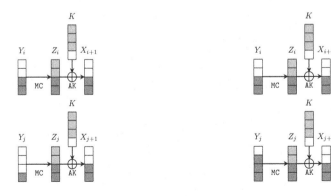

Fig. 8. An incompatible trail (Color figure online)

Fig. 9. A compatible trail (Color figure online)

Adding more constraints to remove this kind of contradictions in MILP model is quite hard. According to Property 1, a set of equations of MC (or MR) operation has 8 cells of variables, and if two sets of equations have at least 4 same cells, then all cells of variables in the two sets of equations should be same. We use this property to fast delete the incompatible trails. Figure 8 and Fig. 9 show examples of incompatible and compatible trails. The inactive cells are in white and active cells are in gray and green, and the difference in green cells are determined by key difference. We can encode the truncated difference in Y and Z to a 8-dimensional vector $\mathbb{S} = (y_0, y_1, y_2, y_3, z_0, z_1, z_2, z_3)$, where $y_m = 1$ if $\Delta Y[m]$ is inactive with $0 \leq m \leq 3$, else $y_m = 0$; $z_m = 1$ if $\Delta Z[m]$ is 0 or equals to key differences, else $z_m = 0$. For example, in Fig. 8, we have $\mathbb{S}_i = (1, 1, 0, 0, 1, 1, 0, 0)$ for round i and $\mathbb{S}_i = (1, 1, 1, 0, 1, 1, 0, 0)$ for round j with the same K. The dot product of two vectors $\mathbb{S}_i$ and $\mathbb{S}_j$ is the number of same cells of two sets of equations of MC (or MR) operations. For example, $\langle \mathbb{S}_i, \mathbb{S}_j \rangle = 4$ in Fig. 8, hence, due to Property 1, all the cells of differences in Y_i and Y_j (also for Z_i, Z_j and X_{i+1}, X_{j+1}) should be the same. However, $Y_i[2]$ is active but $Y_j[2]$ is inactive, which leads to contradiction and Fig. 8 is an incompatible trail. In Fig. 9, we have $\mathbb{S}_i = (1, 1, 0, 0, 1, 1, 0, 0)$ and $\mathbb{S}_j = (1, 0, 0, 0, 1, 1, 0, 0)$ with $\langle \mathbb{S}_i, \mathbb{S}_j \rangle = 3 < 4$, hence the trail is compatible.

Since we can derive the vector $\mathbb{S}_i$ from the solutions of our MILP model, we use the PoolSearchMode of Gurobi to get many solutions for our MILP model and then check if one of the solutions does not have this kind of contradiction. For 8-round Saturnin with $l \geq 1$ and $r_{in} = 2$, we get thousands of different truncated differentials from our MILP model through the PoolSearchMode and after checking them with the above method, none of them are left; for 8-round Saturnin with $l = 0$ and $r_{in} = 2$, we get a hundred of different truncated differentials and most of them are compatible. For those left solutions, we pick one trail to launch our rebound attacks. See supplementary materials for the source code of constructing MILP model and detecting contradiction. We have put the source code for the automatic model of Saturnin-hash in a public domain at https://github.com/rebound-rk/rebound-rk.

4   Free-Start Collision on 8-Round Saturnin-hash

By applying the MILP model, we find an 8-round truncated differential on Saturnin as shown in Fig. 10(a). We perform the quantum collision attack based on the truncated differential. The inbound phase covers from Y_0 to X_3, including two SB layers. The two outbound phases are from Y_0 to the plaintext and X_3 to the ciphertext. In the inbound phase, there are four parallel non-full active super S-boxes. The input difference $\Delta_{in} = \Delta X_1$ is determined by ΔY_0. At round 2 and 3, from $MR(\Delta Y_2) \oplus \Delta \tilde{K} = \Delta X_3$, at the 3rd row, we get

$$MR^{-1}(\Delta k_7, \Delta k_{11}, \Delta k_{15}, \Delta k_0) = (\Delta Y_2[2], 0, 0, 0). \tag{3}$$

For row 3 of the computation from ΔY_4 to ΔX_5, and from ΔY_6 to ΔX_7, the same requirement of Eq. (3) is also applied, since the subkeys are all $\tilde{K}$ and the truncated form are the same.

At round 3 to 4, in the first column of the computation from ΔY_3 to ΔX_4, we have $\Delta Z_3[0] = \Delta k_0$ and $\Delta Z_3[1] = \Delta k_1$. Further, we get

$$\mathrm{MC}^{-1}\left(\Delta k_0, \Delta k_1, \Delta Z_3[2], \Delta Z_3[3]\right)^{\mathrm{T}} = \left(0, 0, 0, \Delta Y_3[3]\right)^{\mathrm{T}}. \tag{4}$$

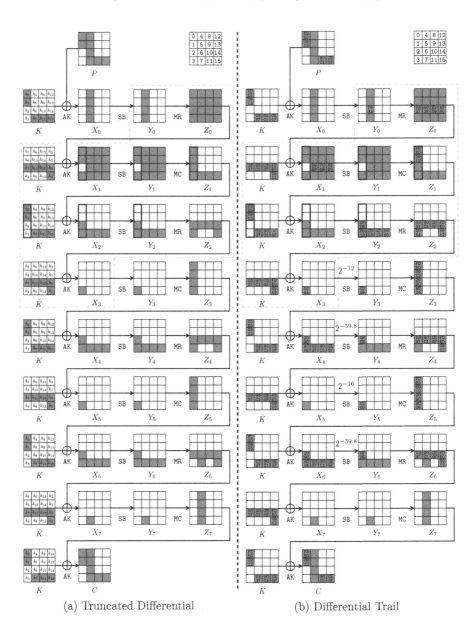

(a) Truncated Differential   (b) Differential Trail

Fig. 10. 8-round related-key rebound-attack trail on `Saturnin-hash`

The condition of Eq. (4) also applies to the computation from ΔY_5 to ΔX_6. Hence, for Eq. (4) and (3), if we fixed Δk_0, then Δk_7, Δk_{11}, Δk_{15}, and Δk_1 are determined by Property 1. As shown in Fig. 10(a), at Round 0 and 1, $\Delta X_1[2] = \Delta k_7 \oplus \Delta Z_0[2] = 0$, so $\Delta Z_0[2] = \Delta k_7$. From $\Delta Z_0 = \text{MR}(\Delta Y_0)$, for the third row, we have $\Delta Y_0[2, 10, 14] = 0$ and $\Delta Z_0[2] = \Delta k_7$ and Eq. (5) is derived. Hence, if Δk_7 is fixed, all other differences in the active cells of ΔY_0 and ΔZ_0 in row 3 are deduce by Property 1.

$$\text{MR}^{-1}(\Delta k_7, \Delta Z_0[6], \Delta Z_0[10], \Delta Z_0[14]) = (0, \Delta Y_0[6], 0, 0). \tag{5}$$

Algorithm 1: Determine the Differences From the Truncated Form

---

1 **for** $\Delta k_0 \in \mathbb{F}_2^{16}$ **do**
2   Deduce Δk_7, Δk_{11}, Δk_{15}, Δk_1 by Equation (4) and (3) and Property 1
3   /* All the differences in the key schedule are determined.   */
4   Round 2: Deduce $\Delta Z_2[2, 6, 10, 14]$, $\Delta Y_2[2]$
5   Round 3: Deduce $\Delta Y_3[3]$ by Equation (4) and Property 1. Then $Z_3[0, 1, 2, 3]$ and $X_4[2, 3]$ are fixed.
6   Round 4: Similar to Round 2 to get $\Delta Z_4[2, 6, 10, 14]$, $\Delta Y_4[2]$. In addition, we have $\Delta Z_4[15] = \Delta k_1$
7   Round 5: Similar to Round 3 to get $\Delta Y_5[3]$, $Z_5[0, 1, 2, 3]$ and $X_6[2, 3]$
8   Round 6: Similar to Round 2 to get $\Delta Z_6[2, 6, 10, 14]$, $\Delta Y_6[2]$. In addition, we have $\Delta Z_6[15] = \Delta k_1$
9   Round 0: With Equation (5), we deduce $\Delta Z_0[6, 10, 14]$ and $\Delta Y_0[6]$. Then $\Delta X_1[6, 10, 14]$ are determined.
10   Round 1: Since $\Delta Z_1[0] = \Delta k_0$ and $\Delta Z_1[1] = \Delta k_1$, $\Delta Z_1[0]$ and $\Delta Z_1[1]$ is fixed.
11   Round 7: In **Saturnin-hash** (MMO hashing mode), the plaintext is XORed into the ciphertext of the internal block cipher to output the digest. We have $T = P \oplus C = X_0 \oplus K \oplus Z_7 \oplus K = X_0 \oplus Z_7$. Then, if two message collide, we have $\Delta T = 0 = \Delta X_0 \oplus \Delta Z_7$.
12   As shown in Figure 10(b), from ΔX_4 to ΔY_5, multiple differential trails are taken into account.

We derive an 8-round rebound-attack characteristic in Fig. 10(b) from the truncated form in Fig. 10(a) by Algorithm 1. By traversing $\Delta k_0 \in \mathbb{F}_2^{16}$ in Algorithm 1, we find characteristic with as higher probability as possible. The best trail is given in Fig. 10(b), whose total probability of the outbound phase is $2^{-(12+59.8+16+59.8+64)} = 2^{-211.6}$ including the probability of $\Delta X_0 = \Delta Z_7$. In round 4, $2^{-59.8}$ is the total probability of a cluster differential trails from ΔX_4 to ΔZ_4. The same happens to round 6.

As shown in Fig. 10(b), the 2nd, 3rd and 4th super S-boxes are typical non-full-active super S-boxes, where there are only 5 active cells among the 8 input-ouput cells between MC in round 1 in each super S-box. However, the first super S-box is not a typical one. In fact, between MC in round 1 in the first Super-Sbox, there are one non-active cell and two cells with fixed differences. However, we can regard the two cells with fixed differences as another two "non-active" cells to perform the quantum version of non-full active super S-box technique [18] whose details will be given in Algorithm 2.

For the ith ($i = 0, 1, 2, 3$) non-full-active super S-box, we define $G^{(i)} : \mathbb{F}_2^{16} \times \mathbb{F}_2^3 \mapsto \mathbb{F}_2$ as $G^{(i)}(K, K', \Delta X_1^{(i)}, \Delta Y_2^{(i)}; x, \beta)$, where $x = X_1^{(i)}[0] \in \mathbb{F}_2^{16}$ and $\beta = \beta_0 \| \beta_1 \| \beta_2 \in \mathbb{F}_2^3$. $G^{(i)}(K, K', \Delta X_1^{(i)}, \Delta Y_2^{(i)}; x, \beta) = 1$ if and only if (x, β) leads to a valid connection of $(\Delta X_1^{(i)}, \Delta Y_2^{(i)})$ under the key pair (K, K'). The quantum implementation of $\mathcal{U}_{G^{(0)}}$ is given in Algorithm 2.

Complexity of $\mathcal{U}_{G^{(0)}}$ Is Given in Algorithm 2. The time is bounded by Line 7 to Line 9 of Algorithm 2, which is about (including uncomputing) $3 \times \frac{\pi}{4} \cdot \sqrt{2^{16}} \cdot 2 \cdot 2 = 2^{11.24}$ Sbox evaluations.

Algorithm 2: Implementation of $\mathcal{U}_{G^{(0)}}$ without using qRAMs

---

Input: $|K, K', \Delta X_1^{(0)}, \Delta Y_2^{(0)}; X_1^{(0)}[0], \beta\rangle|y\rangle$ with $\beta = (\beta_0, \beta_1, \beta_2) \in \mathbb{F}_2^3$
Output: $|K, K', \Delta X_1^{(0)}, \Delta Y_2^{(0)}; X_1^{(0)}[0], \beta\rangle|y \oplus G^{(0)}(K, K', \Delta X_1^{(0)}, \Delta Y_2^{(0)}; X_1^{(0)}[0], \beta)\rangle$

1 /* Please focus on the super Sbox marked by blue box in Fig. 10   */
2 $Y_1^{(0)}[0] \leftarrow S(X_1^{(0)}[0])$
3 $\Delta Y_1^{(0)}[0] \leftarrow S(X_1^{(0)}[0] \oplus \Delta X_1^{(0)}[0]) \oplus S(X_1^{(0)}[0])$

4 Solving the system of equations $MC(\Delta Y_1^{(0)}) = \Delta Z_1^{(0)}$ with the knowledge of $\Delta Z_1^{(0)}[0] = \text{0xFDE0}$, $\Delta Z_1^{(0)}[1] = \text{0x0912}$ and $\Delta Y_1^{(0)}[2] = 0$
5 /* All differences of cells in $\Delta Y_1^{(0)}$, $\Delta Z_1^{(0)}$ are known   */

6 Let $g_j : \mathbb{F}_2^{16} \to \mathbb{F}_2$ be a Boolean function such that $g_j(\delta_{in}, \delta_{out}, \beta_j = 0; x) = 1$ if and only if $S(x) \oplus S(x \oplus \delta_{in}) = \delta_{out}$ and $x \leq x \oplus \delta_{in}$, and $g_j(\delta_{in}, \delta_{out}, \beta_j = 1, x) = 1$ if and only if $S(x) \oplus S(x \oplus \delta_{in}) = \delta_{out}$, and $x > x \oplus \delta_{in}$.

7 Run the Grover search on the function $g_0(\Delta X_1^{(0)}[1], \Delta Y_1^{(0)}[1], \beta_0; \cdot) : \mathbb{F}_2^{16} \to \mathbb{F}_2$. Let $X_1^{(0)}[1]$ be the output.
8 Run the Grover search on the function $g_1(\Delta X_1^{(0)}[3], \Delta Y_1^{(0)}[3], \beta_1; \cdot) : \mathbb{F}_2^{16} \to \mathbb{F}_2$. Let $X_1^{(0)}[3]$ be the output.
9 Run the Grover search on the function $g_2(\Delta X_2^{(0)}[3], \Delta Y_2^{(0)}[3], \beta_2; \cdot) : \mathbb{F}_2^{16} \to \mathbb{F}_2$. Let $X_2^{(0)}[3]$ be the output.

10 Compute $Y_1^{(0)}[1]$, $Y_1^{(0)}[3]$ and $Z_1^{(0)}[3]$;   /* $Y_1^{(0)}[0]$ is known */
11 Solve the equation $MC(Y_1^{(0)}) = Z_1^{(0)}$ for other unknown cells, i.e., $Y_1^{(0)}[2]$, $Z_1^{(0)}[0, 1, 2]$, and $X_1^{(0)}$
12 /* the value $Y_1^{(0)}$ is known   */

13 **if** $S(Z_1^{(0)}[2] \oplus \Delta Z_1^{(0)}[2] \oplus K'[2]) \oplus S(Z_1^{(0)}[2] \oplus K[2]) = \Delta Y_2^{(0)}[2]$ **then**
14 | **return** $|K, K', \Delta X_1^{(0)}, \Delta Y_2^{(0)}; X_1^{(0)}[0], \beta\rangle |y \oplus 1\rangle$
15 **else**
16 | **return** $|K, K', \Delta X_1^{(0)}, \Delta Y_2^{(0)}; X_1^{(0)}[0], \beta\rangle |y\rangle$

Since the probability of the outbound phase is $2^{-211.6}$, after traversing $2^{211.6}$ starting points computed by the inbound phase, it is expected to find one collision. Given the key difference $\Delta K = K \oplus K'$, there are 2^{256} valid key pairs

(K, K'). Hence, we have enough degrees of freedom to find the collision. For simplicity, we just fix the input difference ΔX_1 of the inbound phase and compute the starting points by traversing a 212-bit K to find the collision. Define $F : \mathbb{F}_2^{212} \times \mathbb{F}_2^3 \mapsto \mathbb{F}_2$ as $F(\Delta K, \Delta X_1, \Delta Y_2; x, \alpha)$, where $x = K \in \mathbb{F}_2^{212}$ and $\alpha = \alpha_0 \| \alpha_1 \| \alpha_2 \in \mathbb{F}_2^3$. $F(\Delta K, \Delta X_1, \Delta Y_2; x, \alpha) = 1$ if and only if $(\Delta K, \Delta X_1, \Delta Y_2; x, \alpha)$ leads a collision. The implementation of $\mathcal{U}_F$ is given in Algorithm 3.

Algorithm 3: Implementation of $\mathcal{U}_F$ without using qRAMs

---

Input: $|\Delta K, \Delta X_1, \Delta Y_2; K, \alpha\rangle |y\rangle$ with $\alpha = (\alpha_0, \alpha_1, \alpha_2) \in \mathbb{F}_2^3$
Output: $|\Delta K, \Delta X_1, \Delta Y_2; K, \alpha\rangle |y \oplus F(\Delta K, \Delta X_1, \Delta Y_2; K, \alpha)\rangle$

1 Compute $K' = K \oplus \Delta K$
2 **for** $i \in \{0, 1, 2\}$ **do**
3   Derive the $\Delta X_1^{(i)}$ and $\Delta Y_2^{(i)}$ for SSB$^{(i)}$ from the ΔX_1 and ΔY_2
4   Run Grover search on the function $G^{(i)}(K, K', \Delta X_1^{(i)}, \Delta Y_2^{(i)}; \cdot) : \mathbb{F}_2^{19} \mapsto \mathbb{F}_2$.
     Let $X_1^{(i)}[0] \in \mathbb{F}_2^{16}$, $\beta^{(i)} \in \mathbb{F}_2^3$ be the output.
5   Run Line 2 to Line 11 of Algorithm 2 with $X_1^{(i)}[0] \in \mathbb{F}_2^{16}$, $\beta^{(i)} \in \mathbb{F}_2^3$ as input.
     Let $X_1^{(i)}$ as ouput.
6   Let $\tilde{X}_1^{(i)} = \max\{X_1^{(i)}, X_1^{(i)} \oplus \Delta X_1^{(i)}\}$ if $\alpha_i = 0$, else
     $\tilde{X}_1^{(i)} = \min\{X_1^{(i)}, X_1^{(i)} \oplus \Delta X_1^{(i)}\}$
7 Derive the $\Delta X_1^{(3)}$ and $\Delta Y_2^{(3)}$ for SSB$^{(3)}$ from the ΔX_1 and ΔY_2
8 Run Grover search on the function $G^{(3)}(K, K', \Delta X_1^{(3)}, \Delta Y_2^{(3)}; \cdot) : \mathbb{F}_2^{19} \mapsto \mathbb{F}_2$. Let
     $X_1^{(3)}[0] \in \mathbb{F}_2^{16}$, $\beta^{(3)} \in \mathbb{F}_2^3$ be the output.
9 Run Line 2 to Line 11 of Algorithm 2 with $X_1^{(3)}[0] \in \mathbb{F}_2^{16}$, $\beta^{(3)} \in \mathbb{F}_2^3$ as input.
     Let $X_1^{(3)}$ as ouput.
10 Let $\tilde{X}_1^{(3)} = \max\{X_1^{(i)}, X_1^{(i)} \oplus \Delta X_1^{(i)}\}$
11 /* Create the starting point (K, X_1) with $(\Delta K, \Delta X_1, \Delta Y_2)$ */
12 $X_1 \leftarrow (\tilde{X}_1^{(0)}, \tilde{X}_1^{(1)}, \tilde{X}_1^{(2)}, \tilde{X}_1^{(3)})$
13 $X_1' \leftarrow X_1 \oplus \Delta X_1$
14 Compute forward and backward to the beginning and ending of the 8-round trail from (X_1, X_1') with (K, K')
15 **if** (X_1, X_1') and (K, K') *lead to a collision* **then**
16   return $|\Delta K, \Delta X_1, \Delta Y_2; K, \alpha\rangle |y \oplus 1\rangle$
17 **else**
18   return $|\Delta K, \Delta X_1, \Delta Y_2; K, \alpha\rangle |y\rangle$

Complexity of $\mathcal{U}_F$ in Algorithm 3. There are four Grover searches on $G^{(i)}$ in Line 4 and 8. There are four calls of Algorithm 2 in Line 5 and Line 9. Those procedures bound the time complexity of $\mathcal{U}_F$ as $4 \cdot \frac{\pi}{4} \cdot \sqrt{2^{19}} \cdot 2^{11.24} + 4 \cdot 2^{11.24} = 2^{22.39}$ S-box evaluations.

To find the collision on 8-round Saturnin-hash, we apply Grover search on $F(\Delta K, \Delta X_1, \Delta Y_2; \cdot) : \mathbb{F}_2^{212+3} \mapsto \mathbb{F}_2$ with $\mathcal{U}_F$ in Algorithm 3, which costs

$$\frac{\pi}{4} \cdot \sqrt{2^{212+3}} \cdot 2^{22.39} = 2^{129.54} \quad \text{S-box evaluations.}$$

Since there are $16 \times 8 = 128$ Sbox applications, the time complexity to find the collision is about $2^{129.54}/128 = 2^{122.54}$ 8-round Saturnin-hash.

In our full version paper, we also present a 7-round quantum collision attack, a 5-round classical collision attack and a 6-round classical free-start collision attack, and a 7-round quantum semi-free-start collision on Saturnin-hash.

5   Free-Start Collision on Reduced SKINNY-n-$3n$-MMO/MP

SKINNY is a family of lightweight block ciphers designed by Beierle et al. [3]. In this section, we apply our method to SKINNY-n-$3n$. Please find the structure of SKINNY-n-$3n$ in [3] or our full version paper. The MC operation is non-MDS:

$$\text{MC} \begin{pmatrix} a \\ b \\ c \\ d \end{pmatrix} = \begin{pmatrix} a \oplus c \oplus d \\ a \\ b \oplus c \\ a \oplus c \end{pmatrix} \quad \text{and} \quad \text{MC}^{-1} \begin{pmatrix} \alpha \\ \beta \\ \gamma \\ \delta \end{pmatrix} = \begin{pmatrix} \beta \\ \beta \oplus \gamma \oplus \delta \\ \beta \oplus \delta \\ \alpha \oplus \delta \end{pmatrix}. \tag{6}$$

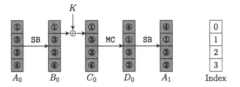

Fig. 11. Super S-box with SKINNY's non-MDS matrix

Since SKINNY applies non-MDS matrix in MC, we will adapt the method of super S-box technique for SKINNY. Different from the super S-box technique with MDS matrix [21,38], we do not need to an exponential memory to store the differential distribution of the super S-box, which is friendly to quantum attacks.

5.1   Super S-Box with Non-MDS Matrix

As shown in Fig. 11 (SR is omitted), the circled numbers indicate the computation sequence. When computing the super S-box, the key pair is fixed, i.e., K and K' are known.

1. In step ①, we have $D_0[1] = C_0[0]$ due to Eq. (6), then we have

$$\begin{aligned} \Delta A_1[1] &= \text{S}(D_0[1]) \oplus \text{S}(D_0'[1]) \\ &= \text{S}(C_0[0]) \oplus \text{S}(C_0'[0]) = \text{S}(\text{S}(A_0[0]) \oplus K[0]) \oplus \text{S}(\text{S}(A_0'[6]) \oplus K'[0]) \\ &= \text{S}(\text{S}(A_0[0]) \oplus K[0]) \oplus \text{S}(\text{S}(A_0[0] \oplus \Delta A_0[0]) \oplus K'[0]). \end{aligned} \tag{7}$$

Hence, given input-output differences $(\Delta A_0[0], \Delta A_1[1])$, we compute one conforming value of $A_0[0]$ that satisfy Eq. (7) by traversing a space of 2^c for $A_0[0]$. After that, all cells marked by "①" are determined.

2. In step ②, we have $D_0[3] = C_0[0] \oplus C_0[2]$ due to Eq. (6), then we have

$$
\begin{aligned}
\Delta A_1[3] &= \mathsf{S}(D_0[3]) \oplus \mathsf{S}(D_0'[3]) = \mathsf{S}(C_0[0] \oplus C_0[2]) \oplus \mathsf{S}(C_0'[0] \oplus C_0'[2]) \\
&= \mathsf{S}(\mathsf{S}(A_0[0]) \oplus K[0] \oplus \mathsf{S}(A_0[2])) \oplus \mathsf{S}(\mathsf{S}(A_0'[0]) \oplus K'[0] \oplus \mathsf{S}(A_0'[2])) \\
&= \mathsf{S}(\mathsf{S}(A_0[0]) \oplus K[0] \oplus \mathsf{S}(A_0[2])) \oplus \mathsf{S}(\mathsf{S}(A_0[0] \oplus \Delta A_0[0]) \oplus K'[0] \oplus \mathsf{S}(A_0[2] \oplus \Delta A_0[2])).
\end{aligned} \tag{8}
$$

Since all the input-output differences of the super S-box and the pair of K are fixed, and $A_0[0]$ is determined by in step ①, only $A_0[2]$ is unfixed. We search $A_0[2]$ in a space of 2^8 to find the right one that make Eq. (8) holds. All cells marked by "②" are fixed.

3. In step ③, we have $D_0[2] = C_0[1] \oplus C_0[2]$ due to Eq. (6), then we have

$$
\begin{aligned}
\Delta A_1[2] &= \mathsf{S}(D_0[2]) \oplus \mathsf{S}(D_0'[2]) \\
&= \mathsf{S}(C_0[1] \oplus C_0[2]) \oplus \mathsf{S}(C_0'[1] \oplus C_0'[2]) \\
&= \mathsf{S}(\mathsf{S}(A_0[1]) \oplus K[1] \oplus \mathsf{S}(A_0[2])) \oplus \mathsf{S}(\mathsf{S}(A_0'[1]) \oplus K'[1] \oplus \mathsf{S}(A_0'[2])) \\
&= \mathsf{S}(\mathsf{S}(A_0[1]) \oplus K[1] \oplus \mathsf{S}(A_0[2])) \oplus \mathsf{S}(\mathsf{S}(A_0[1] \oplus \Delta A_0[1]) \oplus K'[1] \oplus \mathsf{S}(A_0[2] \oplus \Delta A_0[2])).
\end{aligned} \tag{9}
$$

Since all the input-output differences of the super S-box and the pair of K are fixed, and $A_0[2]$ is determined by in step ②, only $A_0[1]$ is unfixed. We search $A_0[1]$ in a space of 2^8 to find the right one that make Eq. (9) holds. All cells marked by "③" are fixed.

4. In step ④, we have $D_0[0] = C_0[0] \oplus C_0[2] \oplus C_0[3]$ due to Equation (6), then we have

$$
\begin{aligned}
\Delta A_1[0] &= \mathsf{S}(D_0[0]) \oplus \mathsf{S}(D_0'[0]) \\
&= \mathsf{S}(C_0[0] \oplus C_0[2] \oplus C_0[3]) \oplus \mathsf{S}(C_0'[0] \oplus C_0'[2] \oplus C_0'[3]) \\
&= \mathsf{S}(\mathsf{S}(A_0[0]) \oplus K[0] \oplus \mathsf{S}(A_0[2]) \oplus \mathsf{S}(A_0[3])) \oplus \mathsf{S}(\mathsf{S}(A_0'[0]) \oplus K'[0] \oplus \mathsf{S}(A_0'[2]) \oplus \mathsf{S}(A_0'[3])) \\
&= \mathsf{S}(\mathsf{S}(A_0[0]) \oplus K[0] \oplus \mathsf{S}(A_0[2]) \oplus \mathsf{S}(A_0[3])) \oplus \\
&\quad \mathsf{S}(\mathsf{S}(A_0[0] \oplus \Delta A_0[0]) \oplus K'[0] \oplus \mathsf{S}(A_0[2] \oplus \Delta A_0[2]) \oplus \mathsf{S}(A_0[3] \oplus \Delta A_0[3])).
\end{aligned}
$$

Since all the input-output differences of the super S-box and the pair of K are fixed, and $A_0[0]$ and $A_0[2]$ are already determined by in step ② and ③, only $A_0[3]$ is unfixed. We search $A_0[3]$ in a space of 2^8 to find the right one that make Eq. (9) holds. All cells marked by "④" are fixed.

Following the above computing order, given an input-output difference $(\Delta A_0, \Delta A_1)$ with fixed key pair, we find the conforming pair for the full active super S-box in time complexity of about 2^8 two-round computations without any memory. Note that if the MC operation adopts MDS matrix, without memory, we need 2^{32} classical time to find a conforming pair for full active super S-box.

5.2   Collision on Hashing Modes with Reduced SKINNY-128-384

By applying the model given in Sect. 3, we find 16-round rebound trail for SKINNY-128-384 (see Fig. 19 in our full version paper). The inbound phase covers round 11 and round 12. The probability of the outbound phase is 2^{-112}. We apply similar technique of super S-box with non-MDS matrix to the inbound phase of the 16-round rebound trail, whose quantum time complexity is about $2^{8.65}$ S-box evaluations. To be more clear, we list the details for solving the inbound phase in Section D in our full version paper.

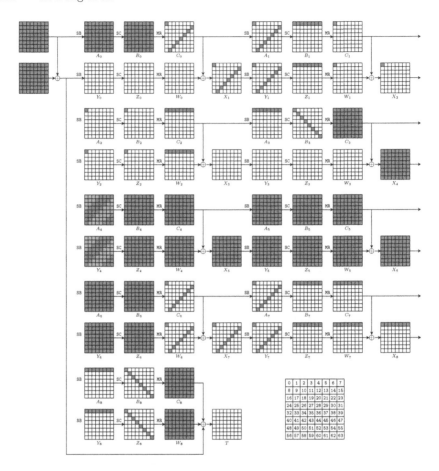

Fig. 12. Free-start collision attack on 9-round `Whirlpool`

Define $F : \mathbb{F}_2^{112} \times \mathbb{F}_2^3 \mapsto \mathbb{F}_2$ as $F(\Delta K, \Delta X_{11}, \Delta Y_{12}; x, \alpha)$, where $x = K \in \mathbb{F}_2^{112}$ and $\alpha = \alpha_0 \| \alpha_1 \| \alpha_2 \in \mathbb{F}_2^3$. $F(\Delta K, \Delta X_{11}, \Delta Y_{12}; x, \alpha) = 1$ if and only if $(\Delta K, \Delta X_{11}, \Delta Y_{12}; x, \alpha)$ leads a collision. The overall time complexity is

$$\frac{\pi}{4} \cdot \sqrt{2^{112+3}} \cdot 4 \cdot 2^{8.65} = 2^{67.8} \quad \text{S-box evaluations,}$$

which is about $2^{67.8}/256 = 2^{59.8}$ 16-round `SKINNY-128-384`, since there are 256 S-boxes in the 16-round `SKINNY-128-384`.

6   Free-Start Collision Attack on 9-Round `Whirlpool`

Different from `Saturnin` and `SKINNY`, the key schedule of `Whirlpool` is nonlinear. Hence, we have to tweak the automatic tool in Sect. 3 which targets on linear key schedule ciphers. For `Whirlpool`, we place the rebound attacks in both the encryption data path and the key schedule path just like Sasaki et al.'s work [49]. For the inbound part of the key schedule path, we only have input and output differences Δ_{in}^K and Δ_{out}^K that act as the degrees of freedom to preform the rebound attack in the key. We expect to get $|\Delta_{in}^K| \cdot |\Delta_{out}^K|$ key pairs conforming to the inbound part of key schedule path. For each key pair, we will get $|\Delta_{in}^E| \cdot |\Delta_{out}^E|$ pairs conforming to the inbound part of the encryption data path. Suppose the total probability of outbound paths in the key and encryption path is p, then the condition $|\Delta_{in}^K| \cdot |\Delta_{out}^K| \cdot |\Delta_{in}^E| \cdot |\Delta_{out}^E| \geq 1/p$ should be satisfied to finally find a key pair and data pair fulfilling the whole trails in the key schedule and the encryption data path. We embed the 2-round full/non-full active super S-box technique [21,48] or 3-round-inbound technique [30] in the inbound part. The inbound phase in related-key setting is quite similar to the single-key setting. A slight different point is to deal with the operation of XOR the key difference into the internal state, where the constraint [42] for truncated differential in XOR operation is applied. The outbound phase is also similar to single-key setting, where only propagations of truncated differential are constrained with MILP.

At ASIACRYPT 2012, Sasaki et al. [49] introduced a free-start collision attack on 8-round `Whirlpool`. In this section, we find a new 9-round rebound characteristic in Fig. 12, and based on it, we give the quantum free-start collision on 9-round `Whirlpool`.

6.1   Comparison Between Sasaki et al's Trail and Ours

The number of active S-boxes in Sasaki et al.'s 8-round trail is shown below:

$$\begin{cases} Key: 64 \xrightarrow{1^{st}R} 8 \xrightarrow{2^{nd}R} 1 \xrightarrow{3^{rd}R} 8 \xrightarrow{4^{th}R} 8 \xrightarrow{5^{th}R} 64 \xrightarrow{6^{th}R} 8 \xrightarrow{7^{th}R} 8 \xrightarrow{8^{th}R} 64, \\ Data: 0 \xrightarrow{1^{st}R} 8 \xrightarrow{2^{nd}R} 1 \xrightarrow{3^{rd}R} 8 \xrightarrow{4^{th}R} 0 \xrightarrow{5^{th}R} 8 \xrightarrow{6^{th}R} 1 \xrightarrow{7^{th}R} 8 \xrightarrow{8^{th}R} 64. \end{cases}$$

The number of active S-boxes in our 9-round trail is shown below:

$$\begin{cases} Key: 64 \xrightarrow{1^{st}R} 8 \xrightarrow{2^{nd}R} 1 \xrightarrow{3^{rd}R} 8 \xrightarrow{4^{th}R} 64 \xrightarrow{5^{th}R} 64 \xrightarrow{6^{th}R} 64 \xrightarrow{7^{th}R} 8 \xrightarrow{8^{th}R} 8 \xrightarrow{9^{th}R} 64, \\ Data: 0 \xrightarrow{1^{st}R} 8 \xrightarrow{2^{nd}R} 1 \xrightarrow{3^{rd}R} 0 \xrightarrow{4^{th}R} 64 \xrightarrow{5^{th}R} 64 \xrightarrow{6^{th}R} 64 \xrightarrow{7^{th}R} 8 \xrightarrow{8^{th}R} 8 \xrightarrow{9^{th}R} 64. \end{cases}$$

In the key schedule, Sasaki et al.'s inbound phase "$8 \xrightarrow{4^{th}R} 64 \xrightarrow{5^{th}R} 8$" is replaced by a longer inbound phase "$8 \xrightarrow{4^{th}R} 64 \xrightarrow{5^{th}R} 64 \xrightarrow{6^{th}R} 64 \xrightarrow{7^{th}R} 8$" in our trail, namely we gain a 2-round extension in the inbound phase. In the meantime, Sasaki et al.'s outbound part "$8 \xrightarrow{6^{th}R} 1 \xrightarrow{7^{th}R} 8 \xrightarrow{6^{th}R} 64$" is shortened to "$8 \xrightarrow{8^{th}R} 8 \xrightarrow{9^{th}R} 64$" to gain enough degrees of freedom. In Sasaki et al.'s 8-round trail, the full active state to match in the inbound phase only happens to the key schedule data path. In the inbound part of the encryption data path, many cells are inactive, so that one can assign arbitrary values. Hence, we do not worry about the degree of freedom for Sasaki et al.'s trail. However, in our 9-round trail, both the key and data path adopt full state active inbound part, so that the internal states are fully determined by a match-in-the-middle approach and the degree of freedoms only comes from the possible input and output differences of the inbound part. Hence, the outbound phase is different to gain enough degrees of freedom for the collision attack.

In the key schedule path, the inbound part covers from ΔB_3 to ΔC_6 that includes 3 SB layers. We apply Jean et al.'s [30] 3-round-inbound technique and their quantum version by Hosoyamada and Sasaki [26] to perform the attack. We first define G in Algorithm 4 which marks the compatible ■ cells in Fig. 4 for (X_1, X_1') for a given input difference ΔX_1 and output difference ΔY_3.

Complexity of $\mathcal{U}_G$ in Algorithm 4. Taken uncomputing into account, there are $32 \times 2 \times 2 \times 2 = 128$ S-boxes operations in Line 3. In Line 5 to Line 8, we need $8 \cdot \frac{\pi}{4} \cdot \sqrt{2^{64}} \cdot 16 \times 2 = 2^{39.65}$ S-boxes operations.

In Line 10 of Algorithm 4, only the ■ cells are needed to compute backward to X_1, hence, $32 \times 2 \times 2 \times 2 = 128$ S-boxes operations are needed. Totally, we need about $2^{39.65}$ S-boxes operations to implement $\mathcal{U}_G$.

Given $(\Delta X_1, \Delta Y_3)$, run Grover's algorithm on $\mathcal{U}_G$ to find the correct ■ cells for (X_1, X_1') in Fig. 4. $\mathcal{U}_G$ outputs 1 with probability of 2^{-256}. Hence, the time complexity to find the correct value with Grover's algorithm is

$$\frac{\pi}{4} \cdot \sqrt{2^{256}} \cdot 2^{39.65} = 2^{167.3} \text{ S-boxes operations.} \tag{10}$$

6.2   Free-Start Collision on 9-Round Whirlpool

Classical Analysis on the 9-Round Rebound Trail. As shown in Fig. 12, in the key schedule part, given an input-output difference ΔB_3 and ΔC_6 of the inbound part, we have one conforming pair on average. In the outbound phase of the key schedule, the probability that the truncated differential ΔC_2 propogates to ΔB_2 is 2^{-56}. Hence, there will be $2^{64 \times 2 - 56} = 2^{72}$ valid key pairs that meet the truncated differential in the key schedule path. For each valid key pair, we look at the encryption data path. ΔX_4 is fixed by ΔC_3, and there are 2^{64} possible differences in ΔW_6. There is also a 3-round inbound phase in the encryption data path with input difference ΔX_4 and output difference ΔW_6. With a given $(\Delta X_4, \Delta W_6)$, it is expected to find one data pair (X_4, X_4'). Together with the key pair, we compute backward with the data pair (X_4, X_4'). Since $\Delta W_2 = \Delta C_2$ and $\Delta B_2 = \text{MR}^{-1}(\Delta C_2)$ whose row 0 is of $(*, 0, 0, 0, 0, 0, 0, 0)$, ΔZ_2 is also of the truncated form $(*, 0, 0, 0, 0, 0, 0, 0)$ with probability 1. At round 0, $\Delta W_0 = \Delta C_0 \oplus \Delta X_1 = 0$ holds with probability of 2^{-64}. At the last round, $\Delta B_8 = \Delta Z_8$ holds with probability 2^{-64}, which finally leads to a collision. The total degrees of freedom are derived from ΔB_3, ΔC_6 and ΔW_6, which consists of 2^{192} possible differences (24-byte). The probability to generate a collision is $2^{-56-128} = 2^{-184}$. The classical time complexity to solve the 3-round inbound phase is about 2^{320}. Obviously, the classical complexity will be much larger that a generic birthday attack, which only needs 2^{256} time to find the 512-bit collision.

Quantum Free-Start Collision Attack on 9-Round Whirlpool. In the key schedule path, for given $C_6[\mathbb{U}]$ with $\mathbb{U} = \{0, 15, 22, 29, 36, 43, 50, 57\}$ positions of

---

Algorithm 4: Implementation of $\mathcal{U}_G$ without using qRAMs

---

Input: $|\Delta X_1, \Delta Y_3; X_1[\blacksquare]\rangle |y\rangle$
Output: $|\Delta X_1, \Delta Y_3; X_1[\blacksquare]\rangle |y \oplus G(\Delta X_1, \Delta Y_3; X_1[\blacksquare])\rangle$

1 /* $X_1[\blacksquare]$ means the value of 32 $\blacksquare$ cells in state X_1 shown in Figure 4, and $X_1'[\blacksquare]$ is for state X_1' */

2 Compute $X_1'[\blacksquare] = \Delta X_1 \oplus X_1[\blacksquare]$

3 Compute $Z_2[\blacksquare]$ and $Z_2'[\blacksquare]$ by $X_1[\blacksquare]$ and $X_1'[\blacksquare]$, respectively

4 Define $g_j : \mathbb{F}_2^{8\times8} \mapsto \mathbb{F}_2$ for row $j = 0, 1, 2..., 7$ of Z_2. E.g., for row 0, define $g_0(Z_2[\blacksquare], Z_2'[\blacksquare]; x)$, where x is the $\blacksquare$ cells of Z_2 and Z_2' in row 0, i.e., $x = Z_2[1, 2, 3, 4] \| Z_2'[1, 2, 3, 4] \in \mathbb{F}_2^{8\times8}$. $g_0(Z_2[\blacksquare], Z_2'[\blacksquare]; x) = 1$ if and only if $\text{SB}(\text{MR}(Z_2[0, 1, ..., 7])) \oplus \text{SB}(\text{MR}(Z_2'[0, 1, ..., 7])) = \Delta Y_3[0, 1, ..., 7]$. Similar property holds for other g_j

5 Run the Grover search on $g_0(Z_2[\blacksquare], Z_2'[\blacksquare]; \cdot) : \mathbb{F}_2^{8\times8} \mapsto \mathbb{F}_2$. Let $Z_2[1, 2, 3, 4] \| Z_2'[1, 2, 3, 4]$ be the output.

6 Run the Grover search on $g_1(Z_2[\blacksquare], Z_2'[\blacksquare]; \cdot) : \mathbb{F}_2^{8\times8} \mapsto \mathbb{F}_2$. Let $Z_2[10, 11, 12, 13] \| Z_2'[10, 11, 12, 13]$ be the output.

7 $\vdots$

8 Run the Grover search on $g_7(Z_2[\blacksquare], Z_2'[\blacksquare]; \cdot) : \mathbb{F}_2^{8\times8} \mapsto \mathbb{F}_2$. Let $Z_2[19, 20, 21, 22] \| Z_2'[19, 20, 21, 22]$ be the output.

9 /* Now the whole states Z_2 and Z_2' are fixed.   */

10 Compute backward from Z_2 and Z_2' to X_1 and X_1'

11 if $X_1[\blacksquare] \oplus X_1'[\blacksquare] = \Delta X_1[\blacksquare]$ then

12 | return $|\Delta X_1, \Delta Y_3; X_1[\blacksquare]\rangle |y \oplus 1\rangle$

13 else

14 | return $|\Delta X_1, \Delta Y_3; X_1[\blacksquare]\rangle |y\rangle$

---

active cells in C_6, we define $f : \mathbb{F}_2^{8\times8} \mapsto \mathbb{F}_2$ as $f(\Delta C_6[\mathbb{U}]; x)$, where $x = \Delta B_3[\mathbb{V}] \in \mathbb{F}_2^{8\times8}$ with $\mathbb{V} = \{0, 9, 18, 27, 36, 45, 54, 63\}$. $f(\Delta C_6[\mathbb{U}]; x) = 1$ if and only if the key pair derived by solving the 3-round inbound satisfies the truncated differential from ΔC_2 to ΔB_2. The implementation of $\mathcal{U}_f$ is given in Algorithm 5.

Complexity of $\mathcal{U}_f$. The time is bounded by Line 2 of Algorithm 5, which is about $2^{167.3}$ S-boxes operations according to Eq. (10).

Run Grover's algorithm on $f(\Delta C_6[\mathbb{U}]; \cdot)$, we will find a key pair (K, K') that conforms to the truncated differential in Fig. 12. In encryption data path, for the computed key pair (K, K'), we define $\tilde{f} : \mathbb{F}_2^{8\times8} \mapsto \mathbb{F}_2$ as $\tilde{f}(K, K'; x)$, where $x = \Delta W_6[\mathbb{U}] \in \mathbb{F}_2^{8\times8}$. $\tilde{f}(K, K'; x) = 1$ if and only if a collision occurs in the digest that happens with probability of 2^{-128}. The implementation of $\mathcal{U}_{\tilde{f}}$ is given in Algorithm 6.

Complexity of $\mathcal{U}_{\tilde{f}}$. The time complexity is bounded by Line 3 of Algorithm 6, which is also $2^{167.3}$ S-boxes operations according to Eq. (10).

We define $F : \mathbb{F}_2^{8\times8} \mapsto \mathbb{F}_2$ as $F(x)$, where $x = \Delta C_6[\mathbb{U}] \in \mathbb{F}_2^{8\times8}$ with $\mathbb{U} = \{0, 15, 22, 29, 36, 43, 50, 57\}$. $F(x) = 1$ if and only if the digests of two messages collide. The implementation of $\mathcal{U}_F$ is given in Algorithm 7.

Algorithm 5: $\mathcal{U}_f$ of the quantum attack on 9-round `Whirlpool`

Input: $|\Delta C_6[\mathbb{U}]; \Delta B_3[\mathbb{V}]\rangle |y\rangle$
Output: $|\Delta C_6[\mathbb{U}]; \Delta B_3[\mathbb{V}]\rangle |y \oplus f(\Delta C_6[\mathbb{U}]; \Delta B_3[\mathbb{V}])\rangle$

1 Compute ΔC_3 and ΔA_6 from $\Delta B_3[\mathbb{V}]$ and $\Delta C_6[\mathbb{U}]$
2 Run Grover's algorithm on $G(\Delta C_3, \Delta A_6; \cdot)$ with $\mathcal{U}_G$ implemented in Algorithm 4. Let $A_4[\blacksquare]$ be the output
3 /* $A_4[\blacksquare]$ are the $\blacksquare$ cells in A_4 in Figure 12   */
4 Run Line 2 to Line 10 of Algorithm 4 with input $(\Delta C_3, \Delta A_6; A_4[\blacksquare])$. Let (C_3, C_3') be the output
5 Compute backward from (C_3, C_3') to (B_2, B_2')
6 **if** *row 0 of ΔB is of the truncated form* $(*, 0, 0, 0, 0, 0, 0, 0)$ **then**
7 | return $|\Delta C_6[\mathbb{U}]; \Delta B_3[\mathbb{V}]\rangle |y \oplus 1\rangle$
8 **else**
9 |_   return $|\Delta C_6[\mathbb{U}]; \Delta B_3[\mathbb{V}]\rangle |y\rangle$

Algorithm 6: $\mathcal{U}_{\tilde{f}}$ of the quantum attack on 9-round `Whirlpool`

Input: $|K, K'; \Delta W_6[\mathbb{U}]\rangle |y\rangle$
Output: $|K, K'; \Delta W_6[\mathbb{U}]\rangle |y \oplus \tilde{f}(K, K'; \Delta W_6[\mathbb{U}])\rangle$

1 Compute ΔX_4 from (K, K')
2 Compute ΔY_6 from $\Delta W_6[\mathbb{U}]$
3 Run Grover's algorithm on $G(\Delta X_4, \Delta Y_6; \cdot)$ with $\mathcal{U}_G$ implemented in Algorithm 4. Let $Y_4[\blacksquare]$ be the output
4 /* $Y_4[\blacksquare]$ are the $\blacksquare$ cells in Y_4 in Figure 12   */
5 Run Line 2 to Line 10 of Algorithm 4 with input $(\Delta X_4, \Delta Y_6, Y_4[\blacksquare])$. Let (X_4, X_4') be output
6 Together with (K, K'), compute backward from (X_4, X_4') to (X_1, X_1') and forward to (W_8, W_8')
7 Compute (C_0, C_0') and (C_8, C_8') by (K, K')
8 **if** $\Delta X_1 = \Delta C_0$ *and* $\Delta W_8 = \Delta C_8$ **then**
9 | return $|K, K'; \Delta W_6[\mathbb{U}]\rangle |y \oplus 1\rangle$
10 **else**
11 |_   return $|K, K'; \Delta W_6[\mathbb{U}]\rangle |y\rangle$

Complexity of $\mathcal{U}_F$. The time complexity of the implementation of $\mathcal{U}_F$ in Algorithm 7 is bounded by Line 1 and Line 4, which is $\frac{\pi}{4} \cdot \sqrt{2^{64-8}} \cdot 2^{167.3} + \frac{\pi}{4} \cdot \sqrt{2^{64}} \cdot 2^{167.3} = 2^{199.04}$ S-boxes operations.

. $\mathcal{U}_F$ returns $|\Delta C_6[\mathbb{U}]\rangle|y \oplus 1\rangle$ with probability of $2^{64-128} = 2^{-64}$. Hence, applying Grover's algorithm on $F(x)$ will finally find the collision. Since only the correct state $\Delta C_6[\mathbb{U}]$ is output, we have to re-run Line 1 to Line 6 of Algorithm 7 to finally find the collision. The total time complexity is bounded by the step of applying Grover's algorithm on $F(x)$, which is

$$\frac{\pi}{4} \cdot \sqrt{2^{64}} \cdot 2^{199.04} = 2^{230.7} \quad \text{S-boxes operations.}$$

Since there are $128 \times 9 = 1152$ S-boxes operations in the 9-round `Whirlpool`, the total time complexity of the attack is $2^{230.7}/1152 = 2^{220.5}$ 9-round `Whirlpool`.

Algorithm 7: $\mathcal{U}_F$ of the quantum attack on 9-round `Whirlpool`

Input: $|\Delta C_6[\mathbb{U}]\rangle |y\rangle$

Output: $|\Delta C_6[\mathbb{U}]\rangle |y \oplus F(\Delta C_6[\mathbb{U}])\rangle$

1 Run Grover's algorithm on $f(\Delta C_6[\mathbb{U}]; \cdot)$ with implementation of $\mathcal{U}_f$ in Algorithm 5. Let $\Delta B_3[\mathbb{V}]$ as output

2 /* Note that the truncated differential ΔC_2 to ΔB_2 holds with probability of 2^{-56}, hence, about $\frac{\pi}{4}\sqrt{2^{56}}$ Grover iterations on $f(\Delta C_6[\mathbb{U}]; \cdot)$ are needed to find a good one.   */

3 Run Line 1 to Line 5 of Algorithm 5 to get (C_3, C_3'), then compute the key pair (K, K')

4 Run Grover's algorithm on $\tilde{f}(K, K'; \cdot)$ with implementation of $\mathcal{U}_{\tilde{f}}$ in Algorithm 6. Let $\Delta W_6[\mathbb{U}]$ as output

5 /* Note that since $\mathcal{U}_{\tilde{f}}$ returns 1 with probability of 2^{-128}, however, the size of its domain is 2^{64}. Then after 2^{32} Grover iterations, if a right $\Delta W_6[\mathbb{U}]$ is in the domain, then it will output. If all the $\Delta W_6[\mathbb{U}]$ are wrong, then a random $\Delta W_6[\mathbb{U}]$ will output.   */

6 Run Line 1 to Line 7 of Algorithm 6 to get (X_1, X_1'), then compute the message pair (M, M') with (K, K')

7 **if** (M, K)'s digest collides with (M', K')'s **then**

8 $\quad$ **return** $|\Delta C_6[\mathbb{U}]\rangle |y \oplus 1\rangle$

9 **else**

10 $\quad$ **return** $|\Delta C_6[\mathbb{U}]\rangle |y\rangle$

---

7 Conclusion

By taking the degrees of freedom of the key materials into consideration, we build the automatic tools for the so-called related-key rebound attack, where the degrees of freedom are used to increase the probability of the outbound phase. We develop the new technique to deal with the incompatibilities when searching rebound-attack trails on `Saturnin`, whose subkeys have very strong relationships. Besides the automatic model, we build new super S-box technique with non-MDS matrix for `SKINNY`, which is not seen before. For `Whirlpool`, multiple nested Grover's algorithms are applied to deal with the complex case that both the key schedule path and encryption path adopt rebound attacks. All in all, we achieve certain best free-start collision attacks.

Acknowledgments. This work is supported by National Key R&D Program of China (2018YFA0704701, 2018YFA0704704), the Major Program of Guangdong Basic and Applied Research (2019B030302008), Major Scientific and Technological Innovation Project of Shandong Province, China (2019JZZY010133), Natural Science Foundation of China (61902207, 61772519, 62072270) and the Chinese Major Program of National Cryptography Development Foundation (MMJJ20180101, MMJJ20180102).

References

1. Bao, Z., Guo, J., Shi, D., Yi, T.: MITM meets guess-and-determine: further improved preimage attacks against AES-like hashing. IACR Cryptology ePrint Archive 2021:575 (2021)
2. Barreto, P.S.L.M., Rijmen, V.: The WHIRLPOOL hashing function, Submitted to NESSIE (2000)
3. Beierle, C., et al.: The SKINNY family of block ciphers and its low-latency variant MANTIS. In: Robshaw, M., Katz, J. (eds.) CRYPTO 2016, Part II. LNCS, vol. 9815, pp. 123–153. Springer, Heidelberg (2016). https://doi.org/10.1007/978-3-662-53008-5_5
4. Bernstein, D.J.: Cost analysis of hash collisions: will quantum computers make SHARCS obsolete. In: SHARCS, vol. 9, p. 105 (2009)
5. Biryukov, A., Nikolić, I.: Automatic search for related-key differential characteristics in byte-oriented block ciphers: application to AES, Camellia, Khazad and others. In: Gilbert, H. (ed.) EUROCRYPT 2010. LNCS, vol. 6110, pp. 322–344. Springer, Heidelberg (2010). https://doi.org/10.1007/978-3-642-13190-5_17
6. Bonnetain, X., Hosoyamada, A., Naya-Plasencia, M., Sasaki, Yu., Schrottenloher, A.: Quantum attacks without superposition queries: the offline Simon's algorithm. In: Galbraith, S.D., Moriai, S. (eds.) ASIACRYPT 2019, Part I. LNCS, vol. 11921, pp. 552–583. Springer, Cham (2019). https://doi.org/10.1007/978-3-030-34578-5_20
7. Bonnetain, X., Naya-Plasencia, M., Schrottenloher, A.: Quantum security analysis of AES. IACR Trans. Symmetric Cryptol. 2019(2), 55–93 (2019)
8. Brassard, G., HØyer, P., Tapp, A.: Quantum cryptanalysis of hash and claw-free functions. In: Lucchesi, C.L., Moura, A.V. (eds.) LATIN 1998. LNCS, vol. 1380, pp. 163–169. Springer, Heidelberg (1998). https://doi.org/10.1007/BFb0054319
9. Canteaut, A., et al.: Saturnin: a suite of lightweight symmetric algorithms for post-quantum security. IACR Trans. Symmetric Cryptol. 2020(S1), 160–207 (2020)
10. Chailloux, A., Naya-Plasencia, M., Schrottenloher, A.: An efficient quantum collision search algorithm and implications on symmetric cryptography. In: Takagi, T., Peyrin, T. (eds.) ASIACRYPT 2017, Part II. LNCS, vol. 10625, pp. 211–240. Springer, Cham (2017). https://doi.org/10.1007/978-3-319-70697-9_8
11. Chauhan, A.K., Kumar, A., Sanadhya, S.K.: Quantum free-start collision attacks on double block length hashing with round-reduced AES-256. IACR Trans. Symmetric Cryptol. 2021(1), 316–336 (2021)
12. Cid, C., Huang, T., Peyrin, T., Sasaki, Y., Song, L.: A security analysis of Deoxys and its internal tweakable block ciphers. IACR Trans. Symmetric Cryptol. 2017(3), 73–107 (2017)
13. Damgård, I.B.: A design principle for hash functions. In: Brassard, G. (ed.) CRYPTO 1989. LNCS, vol. 435, pp. 416–427. Springer, New York (1990). https://doi.org/10.1007/0-387-34805-0_39
14. Derbez, P., Fouque, P.-A.: Automatic search of meet-in-the-middle and impossible differential attacks. In: Robshaw, M., Katz, J. (eds.) CRYPTO 2016, Part II. LNCS, vol. 9815, pp. 157–184. Springer, Heidelberg (2016). https://doi.org/10.1007/978-3-662-53008-5_6

15. Derbez, P., Fouque, P.-A., Jean, J.: Improved key recovery attacks on reduced-round AES in the single-key setting. In: Johansson, T., Nguyen, P.Q. (eds.) EURO-CRYPT 2013. LNCS, vol. 7881, pp. 371–387. Springer, Heidelberg (2013). https://doi.org/10.1007/978-3-642-38348-9_23

16. Derbez, P., Huynh, P., Lallemand, V., Naya-Plasencia, M., Perrin, L., Schrottenloher, A.: Cryptanalysis results on spook. In: Micciancio, D., Ristenpart, T. (eds.) CRYPTO 2020, Part III. LNCS, vol. 12172, pp. 359–388. Springer, Cham (2020). https://doi.org/10.1007/978-3-030-56877-1_13

17. Dong, X., Hua, J., Sun, S., Li, Z., Wang, X., Hu, L.: Meet-in-the-middle attacks revisited: key-recovery, collision, and preimage attacks. In: Malkin, T., Peikert, C. (eds.) CRYPTO 2021, Part III. LNCS, vol. 12827, pp. 278–308. Springer, Cham (2021). https://doi.org/10.1007/978-3-030-84252-9_10

18. Dong, X., Sun, S., Shi, D., Gao, F., Wang, X., Hu, L.: Quantum collision attacks on AES-like hashing with low quantum random access memories. In: Moriai, S., Wang, H. (eds.) ASIACRYPT 2020, Part II. LNCS, vol. 12492, pp. 727–757. Springer, Cham (2020). https://doi.org/10.1007/978-3-030-64834-3_25

19. Dong, X., Zhang, Z., Sun, S., Wei, C., Wang, X., Hu, L.: Automatic classical and quantum rebound attacks on AES-like hashing by exploiting related-key differentials. Cryptology ePrint Archive, Report 2021/1119 (2021)

20. Fouque, P.-A., Jean, J., Peyrin, T.: Structural evaluation of AES and chosen-key distinguisher of 9-round. In: Canetti, R., Garay, J.A. (eds.) CRYPTO 2013, Part I. LNCS, vol. 8042, pp. 183–203. Springer, Heidelberg (2013). https://doi.org/10.1007/978-3-642-40041-4_11

21. Gilbert, H., Peyrin, T.: Super-Sbox cryptanalysis: improved attacks for AES-like permutations. In: Hong, S., Iwata, T. (eds.) FSE 2010. LNCS, vol. 6147, pp. 365–383. Springer, Heidelberg (2010). https://doi.org/10.1007/978-3-642-13858-4_21

22. Giovannetti, V., Lloyd, S., Maccone, L.: Architectures for a quantum random access memory. Phys. Rev. A **78**(5), 052310 (2008)

23. Giovannetti, V., Lloyd, S., Maccone, L.: Quantum random access memory. Phys. Rev. Lett. **100**(16), 160501 (2008)

24. Grassi, L., Naya-Plasencia, M., Schrottenloher, A.: Quantum algorithms for the k-xor problem. In: Peyrin, T., Galbraith, S. (eds.) ASIACRYPT 2018, Part I. LNCS, vol. 11272, pp. 527–559. Springer, Cham (2018). https://doi.org/10.1007/978-3-030-03326-2_18

25. Grover, L.K.: A fast quantum mechanical algorithm for database search. In: Proceedings of the Twenty-Eighth Annual ACM Symposium on the Theory of Computing, Philadelphia, Pennsylvania, USA, 22–24 May 1996, pp. 212–219 (1996)

26. Hosoyamada, A., Sasaki, Yu.: Finding hash collisions with quantum computers by using differential trails with smaller probability than birthday bound. In: Canteaut, A., Ishai, Y. (eds.) EUROCRYPT 2020, Part II. LNCS, vol. 12106, pp. 249–279. Springer, Cham (2020). https://doi.org/10.1007/978-3-030-45724-2_9

27. Hosoyamada, A., Sasaki, Yu.: Quantum collision attacks on reduced SHA-256 and SHA-512. In: Malkin, T., Peikert, C. (eds.) CRYPTO 2021, Part I. LNCS, vol. 12825, pp. 616–646. Springer, Cham (2021). https://doi.org/10.1007/978-3-030-84242-0_22

28. Hosoyamada, A., Sasaki, Yu.: Cryptanalysis against symmetric-key schemes with online classical queries and offline quantum computations. In: Smart, N.P. (ed.) CT-RSA 2018. LNCS, vol. 10808, pp. 198–218. Springer, Cham (2018). https://doi.org/10.1007/978-3-319-76953-0_11

29. Hosoyamada, A., Sasaki, Yu.: Quantum Demiric-Selçuk meet-in-the-middle attacks: applications to 6-round generic Feistel constructions. In: Catalano, D., De Prisco, R. (eds.) SCN 2018. LNCS, vol. 11035, pp. 386–403. Springer, Cham (2018). https://doi.org/10.1007/978-3-319-98113-0_21

30. Jean, J., Naya-Plasencia, M., Peyrin, T.: Improved rebound attack on the finalist Grøstl. In: Canteaut, A. (ed.) FSE 2012. LNCS, vol. 7549, pp. 110–126. Springer, Heidelberg (2012). https://doi.org/10.1007/978-3-642-34047-5_7

31. Jean, J., Naya-Plasencia, M., Peyrin, T.: Multiple limited-birthday distinguishers and applications. In: Lange, T., Lauter, K., Lisoněk, P. (eds.) SAC 2013. LNCS, vol. 8282, pp. 533–550. Springer, Heidelberg (2014). https://doi.org/10.1007/978-3-662-43414-7_27

32. Jean, J., Naya-Plasencia, M., Schläffer, M.: Improved analysis of ECHO-256. In: Miri, A., Vaudenay, S. (eds.) SAC 2011. LNCS, vol. 7118, pp. 19–36. Springer, Heidelberg (2012). https://doi.org/10.1007/978-3-642-28496-0_2

33. Jean, J., Nikolić, I., Peyrin, T., Seurin, Y.: Submission to CAESAR: Deoxys v1.41, October 2016

34. Kaplan, M., Leurent, G., Leverrier, A., Naya-Plasencia, M.: Breaking symmetric cryptosystems using quantum period finding. In: CRYPTO 2016, Santa Barbara, CA, USA, 14–18 August 2016, Proceedings, Part II, pp. 207–237 (2016). https://doi.org/10.1007/978-3-662-53008-5_8

35. Kaplan, M., Leurent, G., Leverrier, A., Naya-Plasencia, M.: Quantum differential and linear cryptanalysis. IACR Trans. Symmetric Cryptol. **2016**(1), 71–94 (2016)

36. Kuwakado, H., Morii, M.: Quantum distinguisher between the 3-round Feistel cipher and the random permutation. In: ISIT 2010, Austin, Texas, USA, 13–18 June 2010, Proceedings, pp. 2682–2685 (2010)

37. Kuwakado, H., Morii, M.: Security on the quantum-type Even-Mansour cipher. In: ISITA 2012, Honolulu, HI, USA, 28–31 October 2012, pp. 312–316 (2012)

38. Lamberger, M., Mendel, F., Rechberger, C., Rijmen, V., Schläffer, M.: Rebound distinguishers: results on the full whirlpool compression function. In: Matsui, M. (ed.) ASIACRYPT 2009. LNCS, vol. 5912, pp. 126–143. Springer, Heidelberg (2009). https://doi.org/10.1007/978-3-642-10366-7_8

39. Mendel, F., Rechberger, C., Schläffer, M., Thomsen, S.S.: The rebound attack: cryptanalysis of reduced whirlpool and. In: Dunkelman, O. (ed.) FSE 2009. LNCS, vol. 5665, pp. 260–276. Springer, Heidelberg (2009). https://doi.org/10.1007/978-3-642-03317-9_16

40. Mendel, F., Rijmen, V., Schläffer, M.: Collision attack on 5 rounds of Grøstl. In: Cid, C., Rechberger, C. (eds.) FSE 2014. LNCS, vol. 8540, pp. 509–521. Springer, Heidelberg (2015). https://doi.org/10.1007/978-3-662-46706-0_26

41. Merkle, R.C.: One way hash functions and DES. In: Brassard, G. (ed.) CRYPTO 1989. LNCS, vol. 435, pp. 428–446. Springer, New York (1990). https://doi.org/10.1007/0-387-34805-0_40

42. Mouha, N., Wang, Q., Gu, D., Preneel, B.: Differential and linear cryptanalysis using mixed-integer linear programming. In: Wu, C.-K., Yung, M., Lin, D. (eds.) Inscrypt 2011. LNCS, vol. 7537, pp. 57–76. Springer, Heidelberg (2012). https://doi.org/10.1007/978-3-642-34704-7_5

43. Naya-Plasencia, M.: How to improve rebound attacks. In: Rogaway, P. (ed.) CRYPTO 2011. LNCS, vol. 6841, pp. 188–205. Springer, Heidelberg (2011). https://doi.org/10.1007/978-3-642-22792-9_11

44. Naya-Plasencia, M., Schrottenloher, A.: Optimal merging in quantum k-xor and k-sum algorithms. In: Canteaut, A., Ishai, Y. (eds.) EUROCRYPT 2020, Part II. LNCS, vol. 12106, pp. 311–340. Springer, Cham (2020). https://doi.org/10.1007/978-3-030-45724-2_11

45. Ni, B., Dong, X., Jia, K., You, Q.: (Quantum) collision attacks on reduced simpira v2. IACR Trans. Symmetric Cryptol. **2021**(2), 222–248 (2021)

46. Preneel, B., Govaerts, R., Vandewalle, J.: Hash functions based on block ciphers: a synthetic approach. In: Stinson, D.R. (ed.) CRYPTO 1993. LNCS, vol. 773, pp. 368–378. Springer, Heidelberg (1994). https://doi.org/10.1007/3-540-48329-2_31

47. Sasaki, Yu.: Meet-in-the-middle preimage attacks on AES hashing modes and an application to whirlpool. In: Joux, A. (ed.) FSE 2011. LNCS, vol. 6733, pp. 378–396. Springer, Heidelberg (2011). https://doi.org/10.1007/978-3-642-21702-9_22

48. Sasaki, Yu., Li, Y., Wang, L., Sakiyama, K., Ohta, K.: Non-full-active Super-Sbox analysis: applications to ECHO and Grøstl. In: Abe, M. (ed.) ASIACRYPT 2010. LNCS, vol. 6477, pp. 38–55. Springer, Heidelberg (2010). https://doi.org/10.1007/978-3-642-17373-8_3

49. Sasaki, Yu., Wang, L., Wu, S., Wu, W.: Investigating fundamental security requirements on whirlpool: improved preimage and collision attacks. In: Wang, X., Sako, K. (eds.) ASIACRYPT 2012. LNCS, vol. 7658, pp. 562–579. Springer, Heidelberg (2012). https://doi.org/10.1007/978-3-642-34961-4_34

50. van Oorschot, P.C., Wiener, M.J.: Parallel collision search with cryptanalytic applications. J. Cryptol. **12**(1), 1–28 (1999)

Clustering Effect in SIMON and SIMECK

Gaëtan Leurent[1(✉)], Clara Pernot[1(✉)], and André Schrottenloher[2(✉)]

[1] Inria, Paris, France
{gaetan.leurent,clara.pernot}@inria.fr
[2] Cryptology Group, CWI, Amsterdam, The Netherlands
andre.schrottenloher@m4x.org

Abstract. SIMON and SIMECK are two lightweight block ciphers with a simple round function using only word rotations and a bit-wise AND operation. Previous work has shown a strong clustering effect for differential and linear cryptanalysis, due to the existence of many trails with the same inputs and outputs.

In this paper, we explore this clustering effect by exhibiting a class of high probability differential and linear trails where the active bits stay in a fixed window of w bits. Instead of enumerating a set of good trails contributing to a differential or a linear approximation, we compute the probability distribution over this space, including all trails in the class.

This results in stronger distinguishers than previously proposed, and we describe key recovery attacks against SIMON and SIMECK improving the previous results by up to 7 rounds. In particular, we obtain an attack against 42-round SIMECK64, leaving only two rounds of security margin, and an attack against 45-round SIMON96/144, reducing the security margin from 16 rounds to 9 rounds.

Keywords: Lightweight cipher · SIMON · SIMECK · Differential cryptanalysis · Linear cryptanalysis · Clustering effect

1 Introduction

SIMON and SIMECK are two lightweight block ciphers with a simple round function and very good hardware and software performances. SIMON [5] was designed by Beaulieu, Shors, Smith, Treatman-Clark, Weeks and Wingers and published without a rationale, but has been considered for ISO standardisation. It follows a Feistel structure with a very simple round function:

$$f(x) = ((x \lll 8) \wedge (x \lll 1)) \oplus (x \lll 2).$$

SIMECK is an academic variant of SIMON designed by Yang, Zhu, Suder, Aagaard and Gong, and published at CHES 2015 [28]. It has the same number of rounds, and the same round function as SIMON, but with different rotation amounts:

$$f(x) = ((x \lll 5) \wedge x) \oplus (x \lll 1).$$

© International Association for Cryptologic Research 2021
M. Tibouchi and H. Wang (Eds.): ASIACRYPT 2021, LNCS 13090, pp. 272–302, 2021.
https://doi.org/10.1007/978-3-030-92062-3_10

The key schedule of SIMECK is also modified to reuse the function f.

Previous work has shown that the best attacks against these ciphers use differential cryptanalysis or linear cryptanalysis [1,9,12,18,24], and has provided a detailed analysis of differential paths and linear trails using various techniques and tools [6,17,21,27]. Moreover they show a strong clustering effect for differential characteristics and linear trails. There exist many trails with the same input and output, and the probability of a differential (respectively the potential of a linear approximation) is significantly higher than the probability of the best characteristic (respectively the best linear trail). In order to estimate the probability of a differential or the potential of a linear approximation, we have to combine the effect of as many trails as possible with the corresponding input/output. This generates a lower bound on the quality of the differential or linear approximation. For instance, the best differential characteristic for 27-round SIMECK64 has probability 2^{-70} [18], but a 27-round differential $(0, 11) \rightarrow (5, 2)$ with probability $2^{-60.75}$ was given in [16].

Our Contribution. In this work, we explore this clustering effect in a more systematic way. Instead of building a list of trails with a given input/output, we consider a class of high probability trails where the active bits stay in a fixed window of w bits. In particular, we observe that the differentials and linear hulls used in most previous attacks fit in this framework.

Using properties of the round function, we compute efficiently the probability distribution over this space by multiplication of the differential transition matrix, or the linear correlation matrix. This provides a tighter lower bound on the probability of the differential (or the potential of the linear approximation) than used in previous works, because we implicitly consider *all* trails with intermediate states fitting in the window. Concretely, the 27-round differential $(0, 11) \rightarrow (5, 2)$ has probability at least $2^{-56.06}$ for SIMECK64. In general, we obtain a good understanding of the propagation of differences and linear masks in this class: there is a high probability to stay in the class because of the slow diffusion of SIMON and SIMECK.

We observe that this class includes many high quality distinguishers with input/output that are independent of the number of rounds targeted by the attacks. In particular, we use distinguishers with a single active bit in the input and output, because we can add more rounds of key-recovery than when using distinguishers with multiple active bits. Concretely, for SIMECK64, the differential $(0, 1) \rightarrow (1, 0)$ has probability at least $2^{-54.72}$ over 27 rounds, and $2^{-60.41}$ over 30 rounds.

Finally, we use the distinguishers to build key-recovery attacks, using dynamic key-guessing [24,26] for differential attacks, and the Fast Walsh Transform approach of [15] for linear cryptanalysis. We observe that SIMON and SIMECK are rotation-invariant, so that any differential or linear attack can be repeated several times using rotations of the original distinguisher. In particular, we can exploit attack parameters with low success rates, and repeat them several times to increase the success rate. We compare our results with the best previous analysis in Table 1.

Table 1. Summary of previous and new attacks against SIMON and SIMECK. Attacks marked with † recover information about subkey bits, but the advantage is too low to attack the cipher. Attacks marked with ‡ use the duality between linear and differential distinguishers, which is not exact.

Cipher	Rounds	Attacked	Data	Time	Ref	Note
SIMECK48/96	36	30	$2^{47.66}$	$2^{88.04}$	[25]	Linear † ‡
		32	2^{47}	$2^{90.9}$	**New**	Linear
SIMECK64/128	44	37	$2^{63.09}$	$2^{121.25}$	[25]	Linear † ‡
		42	$2^{63.5}$	$2^{123.9}$	**New**	Linear
SIMON96/96	52	37	2^{95}	$2^{87.2}$	[26]	Differential
		43	2^{94}	$2^{89.6}$	**New**	Linear
SIMON96/144	54	38	$2^{95.2}$	2^{136}	[12]	Linear
		45	2^{95}	$2^{136.5}$	**New**	Linear
SIMON128/128	68	50	2^{127}	$2^{119.2}$	[26]	Differential
		53	2^{127}	2^{121}	**New**	Linear
SIMON128/192	69	51	2^{127}	$2^{183.2}$	[26]	Differential
		55	2^{127}	$2^{185.2}$	**New**	Linear
SIMON128/256	72	53	$2^{127.6}$	2^{249}	[12]	Linear
		56	2^{126}	2^{249}	**New**	Linear

Outline. We begin with preliminaries about differential and linear cryptanalysis in general in Sect. 2. Then we apply them to SIMON-like ciphers in Sect. 3, starting with previous results and explaining our main contribution. We explain in detail how to apply these ideas to SIMECK with differential cryptanalysis (Sect. 4) and linear cryptanalysis (Sect. 5). We apply the same techniques to SIMON in Sect. 6, and conclude in Sect. 7.

The code used to compute the probabilities of differentials and linear approximations (Table 4), as well as the success probability of linear attacks (Sect. 5), is available at https://github.com/Clustering-Simon.

1.1   Notations

The following notations are used in this paper:

n/κ block size and key size
$x^{(i)}$ left part of the input of round i
x_j j-th bit of x
r number of rounds
P/C plaintext and ciphertext
$\tilde{P}/\tilde{C}$ plaintext after the first round the ciphertext before the last round
D data complexity
C_1 time complexity to run an attack a single time
F_W/F_R probability distribution function for a wrong/right key guess
P_S success probability of an attack
a, b, c rotation constants: $f(x) = ((x \lll a) \wedge (x \lll b)) \oplus (x \lll c)$

1.2   Description of SIMON and SIMECK

SIMONn/κ and SIMECKn/κ are Feistel block ciphers with block size $n \in \{32, 48, 64, 96, 128\}$ and key size $\kappa \in \{n, 1.5n, 2n\}$. There are 10 versions of SIMON, with the following parameters:

n	32		48		64		96		128		
κ	64	72	96	96	128	96	144	128	192	256	
r	32*	36	36*	42	44*	52	54	68	69	72	

There are 3 versions of SIMECK, using a subset of the SIMON parameters marked with *; in particular, SIMECK has $\kappa = 2n$, and we often omit the κ parameter. The plaintext P is divided in two parts of $n/2$ bits named $x^{(0)}$ and $x^{(-1)}$, which correspond to the initialization of the left and the right parts of our Feistel network. For the round i, we denote by $x^{(i)}$ and $x^{(i-1)}$ the left and the right part of the input of this round. The round function is (Fig. 1):

$$x^{(i+1)} = x^{(i-1)} \oplus f(x^{(i)}) \oplus k^{(i)}, \qquad \text{with}$$
$$f(x) = ((x \lll a) \wedge (x \lll b)) \oplus (x \lll c).$$

We denote by $x \lll d$ the cyclic rotation of d bits by left, $\wedge$ the bitwise AND, and $\oplus$ the bitwise exclusive or (XOR). The j-th bit of x is noted x_j where the index j is taken modulo $n/2$. The rotations of SIMON are defined as $(a, b, c) = (1, 8, 2)$, while those of SIMECK are defined as $(a, b, c) = (0, 5, 1)$ (the rotation amounts are independent of the block size).

Since there is no whitening key, the first and last round functions do not depend on the key. We define $\tilde{P}$ as the plaintext after the first round, $\tilde{C}$ as the ciphertext before the last round, and we use them as input for our analysis:

$$P = (x^{(0)}, x^{(-1)}) \quad \tilde{P} = (x^{(-1)} \oplus f(x^{(0)}), x^{(0)})$$
$$C = (x^{(r)}, x^{(r-1)}) \quad \tilde{C} = (x^{(r-1)}, x^{(r)} \oplus f(x^{(r-1)}))$$

The input of round 1 corresponds to $\tilde{P} \oplus (k^{(0)} \| 0^{n/2})$ (see Fig. 5).

The key schedule allows to derive the subkeys $k^{(i)}$ for $0 \leq i < r$ from the master key k. First, the master key is divided into $2\kappa/n$ words $(k^{(2\kappa/n-1)}, \ldots, k^{(1)}, k^{(0)})$. Then, the subkeys $k^{(i)}$ for $i \geq 2\kappa/n$ are obtained using a recursion formula. For SIMECK, the recursion is defined as

$$k^{(i+4)} = k^{(i)} \oplus f(k^{(i+1)}) \oplus C \oplus z^{(i)},$$

with C and $z^{(i)}$ constants depending on the block size and f is the same function as used in the data path. SIMON uses a different key schedule, that is linear. We omit further details because our analysis does not exploit them.

2   Differential and Linear Cryptanalysis

We begin with some preliminaries on differential and linear cryptanalysis.

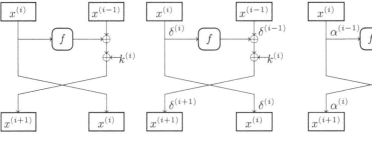

Fig. 1. Round function of SIMON and SIMECK.

Fig. 2. Differential characteristic with probability $\Pr_x[\delta^{(i)} \xrightarrow{f} \delta^{(i-1)} \oplus \delta^{(i+1)}]$

Fig. 3. Linear trail with correlation $c(\alpha^{(i-1)} \oplus \alpha^{(i+1)} \xrightarrow{f} \alpha^{(i)})$

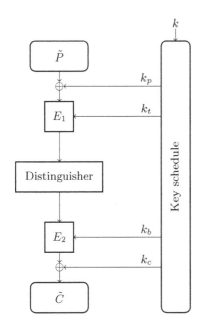

Fig. 4. General description of a cipher.

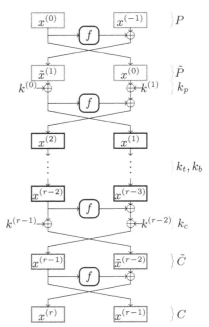

Fig. 5. SIMON/SIMECK with our notations: $\tilde{x}^{(1)}$ and $\tilde{x}^{(r-2)}$ respectively stand for $x^{(-1)} \oplus f(x^{(0)})$ and $x^{(r)} \oplus f(x^{(r-1)})$.

2.1 Differential Cryptanalysis

Differential cryptanalysis is a technique introduced by Biham and Shamir [7, 8], exploiting the propagation of differences in (reduced versions of) a cipher. Starting from a well-chosen difference δ, the distribution of $E_k(x) \oplus E_k(x \oplus \delta)$ is non-uniform, and there exist differences δ' such that $\Pr_{k,x}[E_k(x) \oplus E_k(x \oplus \delta) = \delta']$ is high (significantly higher than 2^{-n}). Such a pair (δ, δ') is called a *differential*.

In practice, we use the notion of *differential characteristic* (or trail) to estimate the probability of a differential. A differential characteristic $(\delta_0, \delta_1, \ldots, \delta_r)$ specifies the intermediate state difference after each round of the function. Therefore, we can easily compute the probability that each round follows the characteristic, and we estimate the probability of the differential as the product of the probability of each round, assuming that they are independent.

More formally, we use the following notations for the probability of the round function, the probability of a characteristic, and the probability of a differential, where R denotes the round function of a cipher, and $E_k^{(r)}$ is a reduced version of the cipher with r rounds:

$$\Pr[\delta \rightarrow \delta'] = \Pr_x[R(x) \oplus R(x \oplus \delta) = \delta']$$

$$\Pr[\delta_0 \rightarrow \delta_1 \rightarrow \ldots \rightarrow \delta_r] = \Pr_{k,x}[E_k^{(i)}(x) \oplus E_k^{(i)}(x \oplus \delta_0) = \delta_i, \forall i \leq r]$$

$$\Pr[\delta \overset{r}{\rightsquigarrow} \delta'] = \Pr_{k,x}[E_k^{(r)}(x) \oplus E_k^{(r)}(x \oplus \delta) = \delta']$$

Lai, Massey and Murphy have defined the notion of a Markov cipher (Simon and Simeck with independent round keys are Markov ciphers), where the probability of a characteristic is the product of the probabilities of the round function transitions [19]:

$$\Pr[\delta_0 \rightarrow \delta_1 \rightarrow \ldots \rightarrow \delta_r] = \prod_{i=1}^{r} \Pr[\delta_{i-1} \rightarrow \delta_i] .$$

When there is a dominant characteristic, it can be used as an approximation of the probability of the differential. In general, the probability of a differential is the sum over all compatible characteristics:

$$\Pr[\delta_0 \overset{r}{\rightsquigarrow} \delta_r] = \sum_{\delta_1, \delta_2, \ldots \delta_{r-1}} \prod_{i=1}^{r} \Pr[\delta_{i-1} \rightarrow \delta_i] .$$

If we write all the transition probabilities $\Pr[\delta \rightarrow \delta']$ in a differential transition matrix A, the probabilities of all r-round differentials are given by A^r, as shown by [19]. Computing A^r is infeasible for practical ciphers, but this approach can be applied to a set of predetermined characteristics, and provide a good approximation of the probability of a differential.

Differential Distinguisher. In order to distinguish a cipher with a high probability differential (δ, δ') from a random permutation, we collect D ciphertexts corresponding to pairs of plaintexts $(P, P \oplus \delta)$, and we compute the number of pairs following the differential:

$$Q = \#\{P : E(P) \oplus E(P \oplus \delta) = \delta'\} .$$

The expected value of Q is $D \times \Pr[\delta \rightsquigarrow \delta']$ for the cipher, and $D \times 2^{-n}$ for a random permutation; therefore the distinguisher succeeds with high probability when $D = \mathcal{O}(1/\Pr[\delta \rightsquigarrow \delta'])$.

2.2   Linear Cryptanalysis

Linear cryptanalysis was introduced by Matsui [22]; it uses linear approximations of the round function in order to obtain a biased approximation of the (reduced) cipher. A *linear approximation* is a pair of masks (α, α') such that the distribution of $x \cdot \alpha \oplus E_k(x) \cdot \alpha'$ is biased ($|\Pr_x[x \cdot \alpha = E_k(x) \cdot \alpha'] - 1/2| \gg 2^{-n/2}$ for most keys k), where $x \cdot y = \bigoplus_i x_i y_i$ denotes the dot product. Since the correlation is expected to be zero when averaged over all keys, we define the key-dependent correlation as follows:

$$c_k(\alpha \overset{r}{\leadsto} \alpha') = 2 \Pr_x[x \cdot \alpha = E_k^{(r)}(x) \cdot \alpha'] - 1 \ .$$

In practice, we use *linear trails* where a mask is specified for each intermediate state. For an iterative cipher $E_k = R_k^{(r)} \circ \cdots \circ R_k^{(2)} \circ R_k^{(1)}$, we can express the correlation $c_k(\alpha_0 \overset{r}{\leadsto} \alpha_r)$ as the sum of the correlation over all corresponding linear trails by defining the correlation of the keyed round function $R_k^{(i)}$ [14]:

$$c_k(\alpha_0 \overset{r}{\leadsto} \alpha_r) = \sum_{\alpha_1, \alpha_2, \ldots \alpha_{r-1}} \prod_{i=1}^{r} c_k^{(i)}(\alpha_{i-1} \to \alpha_i)$$

$$c_k^{(i)}(\alpha_{i-1} \to \alpha_i) = 2 \Pr_x[x \cdot \alpha = R_k^{(i)}(x) \cdot \alpha'] - 1 \ .$$

If the cipher is a key-alternating cipher with independent round keys, the correlation of the keyed round function can be expressed in terms of the correlation of the unkeyed round function:

$$c_k(\alpha_0 \overset{r}{\leadsto} \alpha_r) = \sum_{\alpha_1, \alpha_2, \ldots \alpha_{r-1}} (-1)^{\oplus_i k_i \cdot \alpha_i} \prod_{i=1}^{r} c(\alpha_{i-1} \to \alpha_i)$$

$$c(\alpha \to \alpha') = 2 \Pr_x[x \cdot \alpha = R(x) \cdot \alpha'] - 1 \ .$$

Therefore, the correlation of a linear approximation is the sum of the correlations over all linear trails, with signs that depend on the key. When there is a single dominant trail, we can approximate the correlation of the linear approximation as the correlation of the trail, up to a change of sign. However when there are several dominant trails, they can interact constructively or destructively depending on the key.

Nyberg [23] defined the expected linear potential as the expected value of the square correlation for a random key, and showed that it is equal to the sum of the squared correlation over all linear trails (assuming a key-alternating cipher with independent keys):

$$\mathrm{ELP}(\alpha_0 \overset{r}{\leadsto} \alpha_r) = \mathrm{Exp}_k(c_k^2(\alpha_0 \overset{r}{\leadsto} \alpha_r))$$

$$= \sum_{\alpha_1, \alpha_2, \ldots \alpha_{r-1}} \prod_{i=1}^{r} c^2(\alpha_{i-1} \to \alpha_i) \ .$$

Similarly to the differential case, we can compute the expected linear potential for all linear approximations by computing the powers of a correlation matrix C with coefficients $c^2(\alpha \to \alpha')$.

Linear Distinguisher. In order to distinguish a cipher with a biased linear approximation (α, α') from a random permutation, we collect D known plaintexts/ciphertexts, and we evaluate the experimental correlation

$$Q = (\# \{P, C : P \cdot \alpha \oplus C \cdot \alpha' = 0\} - \# \{P, C : P \cdot \alpha \oplus C \cdot \alpha' = 1\})/D$$

The expected value of Q is larger (in absolute value) for the cipher than for a random permutation, and this can be detected with high probability when $D = \mathcal{O}(\text{ELP}[\alpha \rightsquigarrow \alpha']^{-1})$ (see Sect. 5.2 for more details).

2.3   Last-Round Key Recovery

In order to turn a statistical distinguisher (differential or linear) into a key recovery attack, we add a few rounds at the top and/or bottom, and partially encrypt/decrypt the available data to evaluate the statistical property. We denote the statistic used by the distinguisher as Q, and we assume that it can be evaluated by guessing only a subset of the key, shown as (k_p, k_t, k_b, k_c) in Fig. 4. We let $\kappa_g = \kappa_p + \kappa_t + \kappa_b + \kappa_c$ denote the corresponding number of key bits. We denote the value obtained for key candidate k as $Q(k)$, and consider it as a random variable (depending on the choice of the encryption key, and the data set). We evaluate $Q(k)$ for all key candidates; in a naive approach, this requires $D \times 2^{\kappa_g}$ operations. However, this can often be reduced to roughly $D + 2^{\kappa_g}$ operations using algorithmic tricks (details are given in the next sections).

By analysing the theoretical behaviour of the distinguisher, we can predict the distribution of the random variables. We denote the probability distribution function of the statistic for the right key as F_R, and for wrong keys as F_W. We rank the key candidates according to $Q(k)$, and expect that the correct key will be in the top candidates if the distinguisher is strong enough (w.l.o.g., we assume that the statistic used gives a higher value for the right key).

More precisely, we aim to have the correct key among the top $2^{\kappa_g - a}$ candidates, where a is called the advantage (in bits). If the key schedule of the cipher is simple enough, the attacker can reconstruct the $2^{\kappa - a}$ master keys corresponding to these candidates and exhaustively test them. In particular, the key schedule of SIMON is linear, so that master key candidates can be constructed from any subkey bits using linear algebra. The complexity of this type of attack is roughly:

$$T = D + 2^{\kappa_g} + 2^{\kappa - a} \ .$$

In order to keep a fraction 2^{-a} of the key candidates, we set a threshold of $s = F_W^{-1}(1 - 2^{-a})$ and keep all keys with $Q(k) \geq s$. The attack succeeds if the value of Q corresponding to the right key is higher than the threshold, this happens with probability:

$$P_S = 1 - F_R(s) = 1 - F_R(F_W^{-1}(1 - 2^{-a})) \ . \tag{1}$$

As a first condition, the parameters must satisfy:

$$D \leq 2^n \qquad D \ll 2^\kappa \qquad 2^{\kappa_g} \ll 2^\kappa \qquad 2^a \gg 1 \qquad P_S \gg 0 \tag{2}$$

Complex Key Schedules. When the key schedule is complex and non-linear, reconstructing the master key candidates corresponding to the κ_g recovered bits can be an issue. In particular when adding rounds on both sides of the distinguisher, the attacker recovers candidates for keys bits in the first and last rounds, but it is not possible to efficiently build the corresponding candidates for the master key. In particular, some previous attacks on SIMECK [16,24,25] use a small advantage a and compute the time complexity as $2^{\kappa-a}$, but the key recovery would actually have a complexity higher than 2^{κ} with the parameters used. Instead the attacker can focus on the recovered bits on a single side of the distinguisher, and exhaustively search the missing bits, with a cost of $2^{\kappa-a+\min\{\kappa_p+\kappa_t,\kappa_b+\kappa_c\}}$.

3   Analysis of SIMON-Like Ciphers

Since the round function of SIMON-like ciphers is quadratic, we can efficiently compute the exact probability of a differential or linear transition through the function f. This was explored in details by Kölbl, Leander and Tiessen [17]:

– For a given α, there is an affine space U_α such that

$$\Pr_{x}[f(\alpha \oplus x) \oplus f(x) = \beta] = \begin{cases} 2^{-\dim(U_\alpha)} & \text{if } \beta \in U_\alpha \\ 0 & \text{otherwise} \end{cases}$$

U_α is a coset of the image of a linear function:

$$U_\alpha = \mathrm{Img}\big(x \mapsto f(x) \oplus f(x \oplus \alpha) \oplus f(\alpha)\big) \oplus f(\alpha)$$

Given the Feistel structure of the round function (Fig. 2), we deduce

$$\Pr[(\delta_L, \delta_R) \to (\delta'_L, \delta'_R)] = \begin{cases} 2^{-\dim(U_{\delta_L})} & \text{if } \delta_L = \delta'_R \text{ and } \delta_R \oplus \delta'_L \in U_{\delta_L} \\ 0 & \text{otherwise} \end{cases}$$

– For a given β, there is an affine space V_β such that

$$c(x \cdot \alpha, f(x) \cdot \beta)^2 = \begin{cases} 2^{-\dim(V_\beta)} & \text{if } \alpha \in V_\beta \\ 0 & \text{otherwise} \end{cases}$$

V_β is a coset of the image of a linear function:

$$V_\beta = \mathrm{Img}\Big(x \mapsto \big((\beta \wedge (x \lll a - b)) \oplus ((\beta \wedge x) \ggg a - b)\big) \ggg b\Big) \oplus (\beta \ggg c)$$

For the Feistel-based round function (Fig. 3), this implies

$$c((\alpha_L, \alpha_R) \to (\alpha'_L, \alpha'_R))^2 = \begin{cases} 2^{-\dim(V_{\alpha_R})} & \text{if } \alpha_R = \alpha'_L \text{ and } \alpha_L \oplus \alpha'_R \in V_{\alpha_R} \\ 0 & \text{otherwise} \end{cases}$$

This provides an efficient representation of the differential transition matrix A and of the squared correlation matrix C. However, computing the transitions over the full space is still infeasible for $n > 32$, because we need at least to store a vector with 2^n elements.

Table 2. An example of 12-round iterative trail (differential and linear) for SIMECK. We show a list of active bits.

i	0	1	2	3	4	5	6	7	8	9	10	11	12	13
δ_i	$\varnothing$	0	1	0,2	3	0,2,3,4	1,2	0,2,4	3	0,2	1	0	$\varnothing$	0
α_i	$\varnothing$	4	3	4,2	1	4,2,1,0	3,2	4,2,0	1	4,2	3	4	$\varnothing$	4

3.1 A Class of High Probability Trails

In this work we consider a class of trails that are only active in a window of w bits of each word (e.g., the w least significant bits). Several previous works have already shown that there exist iterative trails in this class for SIMECK [3, 24,25] and SIMON [21]; we give an example in Table 2. More generally, SIMON and SIMECK have a relatively slow diffusion. If a difference is restricted to the w least significant bits, it will stay on the $w + 5$ (for SIMECK) or $w + 8$ (for SIMON) least significant bits after one round. Moreover, the diffusion to bit $w + 5$ (respectively $w + 8$) is non-linear; if it is absorbed then the difference stays on $w + 1$ (respectively $w + 2$) bits only. Therefore, we expect many high probability trails in this class. We detail our results on SIMECK in this section, and we discuss SIMON in Sect. 6.

Let $w \le n/2$ and Δ_w be the vector space of differences active only in the w least significant bits (LSBs) of a word. Let Δ_w^2 be the product $\Delta_w \times \Delta_w$ where the two words are considered. For a given $\delta_0, \delta_r \in \Delta_w$, we can compute a lower bound of the probability of the differential $\delta_0 \to \delta_r$ by summing over all characteristics with intermediate differences in Δ_w^2:

$$\Pr[\delta_0 \xrightarrow[w]{r} \delta_r] = \sum_{\delta_1, \delta_2, \dots \delta_{r-1} \in \Delta_w^2} \prod_{i=1}^{r} \Pr[\delta_{i-1} \to \delta_i] \le \Pr[\delta_0 \xrightarrow{r} \delta_r]$$

As mentioned in Sect. 2.1, we can compute these values by evaluating A_w^r where the coefficients of the matrix A_w are the probabilities of transition $\Pr[\delta \to \delta']$ for all $\delta, \delta' \in \Delta_w^2$. In order to reduce the memory requirement, we do not explicitly build the matrix A_w but we use the properties of the previous section to compute it on the fly. Moreover, we focus on the probabilities $\Pr[\delta_0 \xrightarrow[w]{r} \delta']$ for a fixed δ_0, i.e., a single line of A_w^r. Indeed, we can evaluate $A_w^r \times e_{\delta_0}$ (where e_{δ_0} is the basis vector corresponding to δ_0) using iterated matrix-vector products.

This is shown as Algorithm 1: we use a vector X to represent the probability distribution of the differences, and we update it iteratively. The complexity of the algorithm is bounded by $r \times 2^{2w} \times \max_{\alpha \in \Delta_w} |U_\alpha|$ elementary operations. By increasing w, the lower bound is refined but the complexity increases, as seen in Fig. 6. Our results show that the lower bounds grows very slowly after $w = 16$, therefore we expect to have a rather tight approximation. Moreover, we have performed experiments on 20-round distinguishers that closely match the prediction (Fig. 7 and Fig. 8). In practice, it takes about a week to run the algorithm with $w = 18$ and $r = 30$ using 1TB of RAM on a 48-core machine.

We have used this approach to evaluate the probability of differentials used in previous attacks against SIMECK, and we find that the probability is significantly better than estimated in previous works (See Table 3). In particular, our approach covers a huge number of trails than cannot be listed individually (See Table 4).

For large numbers of rounds, the best characteristics we have identified with this search are a set of 64 characteristics with essentially the same probability, of the form (using a hexadecimal notation to represent the value in Δ_w)

$$\{(1,2),(1,3),(1,22),(1,23),(2,5),(2,7),(2,45),(2,47)\}$$
$$\rightarrow$$
$$\{(2,1),(3,1),(22,1),(23,1),(5,2),(7,2),(45,2),(47,2)\}$$

However, we note that the characteristic $(0,1) \rightarrow (1,0)$ is almost as good and will lead to a more efficient key-recovery (because it has fewer active bits). Therefore, we focus on this characteristic in the following. The corresponding probabilities are given in Table 4.

3.2   Links Between Linear and Differential Trails

Alizadeh et al. have shown a duality between differential and linear trails in SIMON [2], that also applies to SIMECK. Given a differential trail with probability p:

$$(\alpha_0, \beta_0) \rightarrow (\alpha_1, \beta_1) \rightarrow \ldots \rightarrow (\alpha_r, \beta_r)$$

we can convert it into a linear trail:

$$(\overleftarrow{\beta}_0, \overleftarrow{\alpha}_0) \rightarrow (\overleftarrow{\beta}_1, \overleftarrow{\alpha}_1) \rightarrow \ldots \rightarrow (\overleftarrow{\beta}_r, \overleftarrow{\alpha}_r)$$

where $\overleftarrow{x}$ denotes bit-reversed x. If all the non-linear gates are independent, the linear trail has squared correlation p. This explains that linear distinguishers and differential distinguishers of SIMON-like ciphers are very similar. However they are not equivalent: when trails are more dense, there are dependencies when two different AND gates share an input, and the probabilities of the linear and differential trail are not the same.

Since our approach applies almost identically to differential cryptanalysis and linear cryptanalysis, we have also applied it to linear cryptanalysis. We consider masks in the set Λ_w^2 active only in the w least significant bits, and we compute a lower bound on the ELP by summing over trails with intermediate masks in the set Λ_w^2. Since the diffusion of linear masks goes from most significant bits to least significant bits, the highest-bias trail with a single active bit is $(2^{w-1}, 0) \rightarrow (0, 2^{w-1})$. For simplicity, we rotate the trail by $w - 1$ bits and display it as $(1,0) \rightarrow (0,1)$. We obtain a set of 64 (almost) optimal trails, corresponding to the bit-reversed versions of the optimal differential characteristics. We represent

Table 3. Comparison of our lower bound on the differential probability for SIMECK (with $w = 18$), and estimates used in previous attacks.

Rounds	Differential	Proba (previous)	Ref	Proba (new)
26	$(0, 11) \rightarrow (22, 1)$	$2^{-60.02}$	[18]	$2^{-54.16}$
26	$(0, 11) \rightarrow (2, 1)$	$2^{-60.09}$	[25]	$2^{-54.16}$
27	$(0, 11) \rightarrow (5, 2)$	$2^{-61.49}$	[21]	$2^{-56.06}$
27	$(0, 11) \rightarrow (5, 2)$	$2^{-60.75}$	[16]	"
28	$(0, 11) \rightarrow (A8, 5)$	$2^{-63.91}$	[16]	$2^{-59.16}$

Algorithm 1. Computation of $\Pr[(\delta_L, \delta_R) \overset{r}{\underset{w}{\rightsquigarrow}} (\delta'_L, \delta'_R)]$

$X \leftarrow [0 \text{ for } i \in \Delta_w^2]$
$X[\delta_L, \delta_R] \leftarrow 1$
for $0 \leq i < r$ **do**
   $Y \leftarrow [0 \text{ for } i \in \Delta_w^2]$
   for $\alpha \in \Delta_w$ **do**
      for $\beta \in \Delta_w$ **do**
         for $\gamma \in U_\alpha$ **do**
            $Y[\beta \oplus \gamma, \alpha] = Y[\beta \oplus \gamma, \alpha] + 2^{-\dim(U_\alpha)} X[\alpha, \beta]$
   $X \leftarrow Y$
return $X[\delta'_L, \delta'_R]$

them after a rotation of $w - 7$ bits for simplicity:

$$\{(20, 40), (22, 40), (60, 40), (62, 40), (50, 20), (51, 20), (70, 20), (71, 20)\}$$

$$\rightarrow$$

$$\{(40, 20), (40, 22), (40, 60), (40, 62), (20, 50), (20, 51), (20, 70), (20, 71)\}$$

Our results are given in Table 4 (where the trail $(1, 2) \rightarrow (2, 1)$ corresponds to $(20, 40) \rightarrow (40, 20)$), and show that the results obtained for linear cryptanalysis and differential cryptanalysis are very close, but not identical.

3.3   Key Bits for Last-Round Key Recovery

When a differential or linear distinguisher is extended into a key recovery attack, we have to study what are the key bits necessary to evaluate the statistical property after a few rounds. We denote the required key as k_p, k_t on the plaintext side, and k_b, k_c on the ciphertext side (see Fig. 4), and the corresponding number of bits as κ_p, κ_t (respectively κ_b, κ_c). The total number of required key bits is denoted as $\kappa_g = \kappa_p + \kappa_t + \kappa_b + \kappa_c$. For simplicity, we focus on distinguishers with a single active bit, as used in this work.

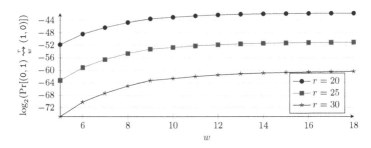

Fig. 6. Effect of w on the probability of SIMECK differentials.

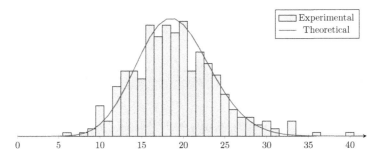

Fig. 7. Experimental verification of the 20-round differential distinguisher $(0, 1) \to (1, 0)$ for SIMECK64. We take 336 random keys with 2^{46} random plaintext pairs each, and we count the number of pairs following the differential. The theoretical curve is a Poisson distribution with parameter $\lambda = 2^{46} \times 2^{-41.75}$. We have 6408 good pairs in total, which gives an experimental probability of $2^{-41.75}$, matching our analysis.

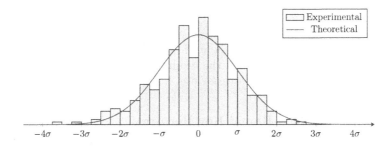

Fig. 8. Experimental verification of the 20-round linear distinguisher $(1, 0) \to (0, 1)$ for SIMECK64. We take 336 random keys with 2^{48} random plaintexts each, and we measure the experimental correlation over the available plaintexts. The theoretical curve is a normal distribution with parameter $\sigma^2 = \text{ELP} + B/N \approx 2^{-41.74} + 2^{-48} \approx 2^{-41.72}$. The average square correlation observed is $2^{-41.7}$, matching the analysis.

Table 4. Comparison of the probability of differentials and the linear potential of linear approximations for SIMECK ($\log_2$, computed with $w = 18$). We also give the total number of trails included in the bound in parenthesis ($\log_2$)

Rounds	Differential			Linear		
	$(0,1) \to (1,0)$		$(1,2) \to (2,1)$	$(1,0) \to (0,1)$		$(1,2) \to (2,1)$
1	0	(0)	$-\infty$	0	(0)	$-\infty$
2	$-\infty$		-4.00	$-\infty$		-4.000
3	$-\infty$		-4.00	$-\infty$		-4.000
4	$-\infty$		$-\infty$	$-\infty$		$-\infty$
5	$-\infty$		$-\infty$	$-\infty$		$-\infty$
6	$-\infty$		$-\infty$	$-\infty$		$-\infty$
7	$-\infty$		$-\infty$	$-\infty$		$-\infty$
8	$-\infty$		$-\infty$	$-\infty$		$-\infty$
9	$-\infty$		$-\infty$	$-\infty$		$-\infty$
10	$-\infty$		$-\infty$	$-\infty$		$-\infty$
11	-23.25	(28.0)	-27.25	-23.81	(23.9)	-27.81
12	-26.40	(36.2)	-26.17	-26.39	(31.7)	-26.68
13	-28.02	(47.2)	-26.90	-27.98	(42.0)	-27.31
14	-30.06	(58.2)	-29.59	-29.95	(52.5)	-29.56
15	-31.93	(70.8)	-31.37	-31.86	(64.9)	-31.29
16	-33.96	(83.0)	-33.35	-33.76	(77.0)	-33.24
17	-35.48	(95.2)	-35.25	-35.09	(88.8)	-35.12
18	-37.95	(107.5)	-37.12	-37.94	(100.7)	-36.85
19	-39.92	(119.7)	-38.97	-39.93	(112.6)	-38.67
20	-41.75	(131.9)	-41.26	-41.74	(124.5)	-41.25
21	-43.47	(144.1)	-43.17	-43.56	(136.4)	-43.17
22	-45.42	(156.3)	-44.97	-45.45	(148.4)	-44.99
23	-47.27	(168.5)	-46.77	-47.30	(160.3)	-46.83
24	-49.14	(180.7)	-48.68	-49.14	(172.2)	-48.71
25	-51.01	(192.9)	-50.54	-51.00	(184.1)	-50.56
26	-52.88	(205.2)	-52.41	-52.86	(196.0)	-52.40
27	-54.72	(217.4)	-54.28	-54.68	(207.9)	-54.26
28	-56.64	(229.6)	-56.15	-56.59	(219.8)	-56.11
29	-58.53	(241.8)	-58.02	-58.47	(231.7)	-57.96
30	-60.41	(254.0)	-59.92	-60.36	(243.6)	-59.86
31	-62.29	(266.2)	-61.81	-62.24	(255.5)	-61.75
32	-64.17	(278.4)	-63.69	-64.12	(267.4)	-63.63
33	-66.05	(290.6)	-65.57	-66.00	(279.3)	-65.51
34	-67.93	(302.9)	-67.45	-67.90	(291.2)	-67.40
35	-69.81	(315.1)	-69.33	-69.78	(303.1)	-69.28
36	-71.69	(327.3)	-71.21	-71.65	(315.0)	-71.17
37	-73.57	(339.5)	-73.09	-73.53	(326.9)	-73.05
38	-75.45	(351.7)	-74.97	-75.40	(338.8)	-74.92

Linear Cryptanalysis. For linear cryptanalysis, we have to compute an internal bit $x_j^{(i)}$ from the plaintext (or from the ciphertext). We compute recursively the necessary key bits following the expression of the round function. In the case of SIMECK (see Algorithm 3 in the full version [20]), the formula is:

$$x_j^{(i)} = (x_j^{(i-1)} \wedge x_{j+5}^{(i-1)}) \oplus x_{j+1}^{(i-1)} \oplus x_j^{(i-2)} \oplus k_j^{(i-1)} \ . \tag{3}$$

The algorithm returns the key bits that $x_j^{(i)}$ depends on: a list of (linear combinations of) key bits with a linear effect on $x_j^{(i)}$, and a list of (linear combinations of) key bits with non-linear effect.

Differential Cryptanalysis. For differential cryptanalysis, we have to determine whether a pair of plaintexts (or ciphertexts) P, P' reaches a specific internal state difference $\Delta x^{(i)} = x^{(i)} \oplus x'^{(i)}$ after a few rounds. However, the plaintexts are not chosen randomly. Instead they have a specific pattern of differences that is fixed in advance, and known to potentially reach the target difference.

More precisely, we follow the approach of [24,26] to track the propagation of differences in the additional rounds, assuming that a pair follows the differential. We use the rule that the output difference of an AND operator is 0 if and only if its input differences are $(0,0)$ and we identify bits with a fixed difference (0 or 1) and those with an unknown difference ($*$), as shown in Table 6. The number of bits with a fixed difference for round i is denoted ℓ_i.

Next, we determine sufficient bit conditions for pairs following the input and output constraints of the extended path: a small set of bit conditions that ensure that we get the desired difference at the input and output of our differential when they are satisfied. The other differences are automatically satisfied if the bit conditions of the external rounds have already been checked. To determine the sufficient bit conditions, we proceed round by round, from the outer to the inner rounds. For each bit with a fixed output difference (0 or 1, not $*$), we look at the input of the associated AND operator, and if they are different from $(0,0)$, then we add the condition corresponding to this output difference to the set of sufficient bit conditions.

Finally, for each sufficient bit condition, we compute the set of subkey bits required to check the condition. The goal is to determine which subkey bits are needed to compute a difference $\Delta x_j^{(i)}$. For SIMECK, we use the following relation:

$$\Delta x_j^{(i)} = (\Delta x_j^{(i-1)} \wedge x_{j+5}^{(i-1)}) \oplus (\Delta x_{j+5}^{(i-1)} \wedge x_j^{(i-1)}) \oplus (\Delta x_j^{(i-1)} \wedge \Delta x_{j+5}^{(i-1)})$$
$$\oplus \Delta x_{j+1}^{(i-1)} \oplus \Delta x_j^{(i-2)}. \tag{4}$$

The resulting algorithm for the upper part is given in the full version [20].

Comparison. Table 5 shows the number of key bits to guess for a linear or differential attack on SIMECK with a single active bit, depending on the number of rounds. (Similar tables for SIMON are given in the full version [20]). The

Table 5. Comparison of key recovery rounds for differential and linear attacks against SIMECK64/128.

Key bits	Differential		Linear	
Rounds	Total	Independent	Total	Independent
1	0	0	0	0
2	2	2	2	2
3	9	9	7	7
4	27	27	16	16
5	56	56	30	30
6	88	88	50	48
7	120	114	75	68
8			104	88

list of bits returned by the previous algorithms is simplified in order to keep only linearly independent combinations of bits. Moreover, we report the number of independent bits after removing bits that can be computed using the key schedule. We see that linear cryptanalysis requires a lower number of key bits to guess.

We now explain in detail key-recovery attacks against SIMECK based on those distinguishers. We consider differential attacks in Sect. 4, and linear attacks in Sect. 5.

4   Key-Recovery Attacks Using Differential Cryptanalysis

In this section, we detail differential key-recovery attacks on SIMECK. We explain the dynamic key-guessing technique [24, 26] in Sect. 4.1 and we give our results in Sect. 4.2.

4.1   The Dynamic Key-Guessing Technique

Offline Phase. Starting from a differential $\Delta_i \rightarrow \Delta_o$ covering R rounds, we append r_0 rounds before and r_1 rounds after and we build the extended differential as explained in Sect. 3.3. Then we identify sufficient bit conditions as shown in Table 6, and we identify the key bits required to check whether a pair reaches the difference specified by the distinguisher.

Online Phase. Here we describe how the attack takes place from the construction of the pairs to the recovery of the possible master keys. First, we build structures of plaintexts such that the bits with a fixed difference in round 1 are identical for all the plaintexts in each structure. Each structure is composed of $2^{n-\ell_1}$ plaintexts and if D denotes the data complexity, there are $D \times 2^{\ell_1-n}$ structures. The structures are associated in pairs such that the differences between the two structures for bits with a fixed difference in round 1 correspond to the desired difference in the extended path. For each structure, the corresponding ciphertexts are saved in a table according to their value in the bits with fixed difference in $\tilde{C}$. This allows to filter the pairs at the output and $2^{2(n-\ell_1)-\ell_r-1}$ pairs remains in each pair of structures.

Our goal is to associate partial key guesses to each of these pairs, such that they validate the internal differential. We proceed in a dynamic way. Round by round and for each sufficient bit condition, we associate to each pair the possible combinations of key bits that lead to the desired difference in the input and output of the distinguisher, according to the extended path. Some pairs and/or combinations of key guesses are progressively eliminated when they create an incompatibility with the required differential path. For each pair, when a combination of key bits that leads to Δ_i and Δ_o is found, we increment the counter corresponding to this combination of key bits. In total, at the end of the procedure we have incremented $\lambda_W \times 2^{\kappa_g}$ counters on average, with λ_W the average value of a counter for a wrong key guess. This process is partially compatible with the use of key schedule relations on one side of the distinguisher. Indeed, we guess key bits independently, and filter the combinations of bits which do not verify the relations given by the key schedule afterwards. The details of the attack (round by round) must be considered to calculate the time complexity of the attack.

When all pairs have been processed, we set a threshold s, and for each counter greater than s, we have to find the corresponding master keys. The information given by the κ_g key bits is separated into 2 parts: we have bits of information on the first subkeys, and others on the last subkeys. Due to the non-linear key-schedule of SIMECK, we cannot directly combine this information and do an exhaustive search on the $\kappa - \kappa_g$ missing bits. Instead, we use only the side for which we have the most information bits, and then we do an exhaustive search on the missing bits.

Complexity and Success Probability. In order to compute the complexity and the success probability of this attack, we need to estimate the average value of the counters for the right key and for wrong key guesses: we denote those values λ_R and λ_W.

As explained before, structures are associated in pairs. Let S_1 and S_2 denote two structures that form a pair. For each plaintext $\tilde{P}_1$ in S_1 and for each key guess, we compute $\tilde{P}_2 = E_1^{-1}(E_1(\tilde{P}_1) \oplus \Delta_i)$ such that we have the relation $E_1(\tilde{P}_1) \oplus E_1(\tilde{P}_2) = \Delta_i$. $\tilde{P}_2$ necessarily belongs to S_2, due to structures construction. So, if D denotes the data complexity of the attack, for each key guess we have $D/2$ pairs with the desired difference at the input of our distinguisher.

For the right key guess, if our differential occurs with probability p, we have $\lambda_R = p \times D/2$ pairs that satisfy Δ_o. By construction, all these pairs belong to the structures and pass the filters. On the other hand, for wrong key guesses, $\tilde{P}_1$ and $\tilde{P}_2$ don't actually have a difference Δ_i at the input of the distinguisher with the real encryption key, so the probability that they have a fixed difference Δ_o

at the output is $1/2^n$. The value of the counter for wrong key guesses is expected to be $\lambda_W = D/2^{n+1}$ on average[1].

We model the counter associated to the right key guess and a wrong key guess as a Poisson distribution with parameters λ_R and λ_W. We denote the cumulative distributive function as F_R and F_W. The probability that a counter associated to a wrong key guess is greater than a threshold s is $1 - F_W(s)$, and the expected number of counters greater than s is $2^{\kappa_g} \cdot (1 - F_W(s))$.

Let $\kappa_{\min}$ and $\kappa_{\max}$ be the minimum and the maximum of $\kappa_p + \kappa_t$ and $\kappa_b + \kappa_c$. The cost of reconstructing the master keys from the remaining combinations is $2^{\kappa_g} \cdot (1 - F_W(s)) \times 2^{\kappa - \kappa_{\max}} = 2^{\kappa + \kappa_{\min}} \cdot (1 - F_W(s))$. The time complexity is therefore determined by this term, but also by the data and the time required to scan all the counters at the end of the key-recovery: 2^{κ_g}. Knowing that most of the counters are at 0, this term could be reduced to the number of remaining pairs: $2^{\kappa_g} \cdot \lambda_W$. The time complexity and success probability are:

$$C_1 = D + 2^{\kappa_g} \cdot \lambda_W + 2^{\kappa + \kappa_{\min}} \cdot (1 - F_W(s))$$

$$P_S = 1 - F_R(s)$$

4.2   40-Round Key-Recovery on SIMECK64/128

We apply the methods described in the previous subsection with the differential $(0, 1)$ to $(1, 0)$ covering 30 rounds with probability $p = 2^{-60.41}$. We append 3 rounds before and 7 rounds after. The extended path is given in Table 6 and the details of the bits to guess round by round are given in the full version [20] (Table 12). Round by round, we use the sufficient bit conditions from Table 6 to guess the key bits that lead to the desired differences. When possible, we filter using the relations of the key schedule. In the rightmost column, we detail the time complexity of each step starting from 2^t pairs. To compute this complexity more precisely, we split the round 33 in two parts corresponding to the two sufficient bit conditions. In total, the complexity of guessing the key bits leading to Δ_i and Δ_o, and incrementing the corresponding counters is 2^{t+71}. During this step, $\kappa_{\min} = 9$ bits from the first subkeys and $\kappa_{\max} = 114$ from the last subkeys are guessed.

Attack Parameters. If all the codebook $(D = 2^{64})$ is taken, knowing that $\ell_1 = 57$ and $\ell_{39} = 19$, we split the data into 2^{57} structures of 2^7 plaintexts and after constructing our pairs of structures and filtering the ciphertexts $\tilde{C}$, there remain $2^{57-1} \times 2^{7 \times 2}/2^{19} = 2^{51}$ pairs. So $t = 51$ and the time complexity for the counter incrementing part is $2^{t+71} = 2^{122}$. The average value for the counter of the right key guess is $\lambda_R = p \times D/2 = 2^{2.59}$. And for a bad key guess, we expect the counter to be close to $\lambda_W = D/2^{64-1} = 2^{-1}$. So, if we choose to set

---

[1] The same result can be obtained using the formulas in [24] and the code provided by the authors of this paper.

Table 6. Extended path for 40 rounds of SIMECK64/128. Red bold bits represent the sufficient bit conditions.

r	Differential path		ℓ_i
0	00000000000000000000*000**001**	000000000000000*000**00***01***	50
1	0000000000000000000000000*0001*	000000000000000000*000**001**	57
2	000000000000000000000000000000001	00000000000000000000000000*0001*	62
3	00000000000000000000000000000000	00000000000000000000000000000001	64
	30-round differential (3 → 33)		
33	00000000000000000000000000000001	00000000000000000000000000000000	64
34	0000000000000000000000000*0001*	00000000000000000000000000000001	62
35	0000000000000000000*000**001**	00000000000000000000000000*0001*	57
36	000000000000000*000**00***01***	000000000000000000*000**001**	50
37	0000000000*000**00***0****1****	0000000000000*000**00***01***	41
38	000000*000**00***0**************	0000000000*000**00***0****1****	30
39	0*000**00***0******************	000000*000**00***0*************	19
40	**00***0**********************	0*000**00***0******************	10

Table 7. Attack parameters for differential attacks on SIMECK. C_1 is the time complexity to run the attack a single time, and the corresponding success probability is P_S. The average time is obtained as C_1/P_S, by assuming that the attack is repeated until it succeeds, using rotations of the initial differential.

Cipher	Rounds	$\kappa_{\min}$	$\kappa_{\max}$	D	λ_R	λ_W	s	C_1	P_S	Time
SIMECK64/128	$40 = 3 + 30 + 7$	9	114	2^{64}	$2^{2.59}$	2^{-1}	6	$2^{122} + 2^{117.07}$	0.40	$2^{123.4}$
SIMECK64/128	$40 = 3 + 30 + 7$	9	114	2^{64}	$2^{2.59}$	2^{-1}	5	$2^{122} + 2^{120.89}$	0.55	$2^{123.4}$
SIMECK64/128	$40 = 3 + 30 + 7$	9	114	2^{63}	$2^{1.59}$	2^{-2}	4	$2^{121} + 2^{119.79}$	0.19	$2^{123.9}$
SIMECK48/96	$30 = 2 + 22 + 6$	2	74	2^{48}	$2^{1.58}$	2^{-1}	5	$2^{75} + 2^{81.9}$	0.08	$2^{85.5}$
SIMECK48/96	$30 = 2 + 22 + 6$	2	74	2^{47}	$2^{0.58}$	2^{-2}	3	$2^{74} + 2^{85.1}$	0.06	$2^{89.1}$
SIMECK32/64	$22 = 3 + 13 + 6$	8	51	2^{32}	$2^{2.98}$	2^{-1}	5	$2^{58} + 2^{55.9}$	0.80	$2^{58.6}$
SIMECK32/64	$22 = 3 + 13 + 6$	8	51	2^{31}	$2^{1.98}$	2^{-2}	4	$2^{57} + 2^{54.8}$	0.36	$2^{58.8}$

the threshold s at 5, the complexity is $2^{120.89} + 2^{122} = 2^{122.54}$ with a success probability of 55%.

We show parameters with different time/data trade-offs, as well as parameters for other variants of SIMECK in Table 7.

5   Key-Recovery Attacks Using Linear Cryptanalysis

The first description of a last-round key recovery attack using linear cryptanalysis was given by Matsui's Algorithm 2 [22]. We consider a biased linear approximation $P' \cdot \alpha \oplus C' \cdot \beta$ with P' and C' intermediate values after a few rounds of encryption/decryption. Given a set of D known plaintexts/ciphertexts pair (P, C), we can compute the intermediate values P' and C' for each partial key guess $k_g = (k_p, k_t, k_c, k_b)$ for the first and/or last rounds, and compute the experimental correlation of the linear approximation:

$$q(k_p, k_t, k_c, k_b) = \frac{1}{D}\left(\# \{P, C : P' \cdot \alpha = C' \cdot \beta\} - \# \{P, C : P' \cdot \alpha \neq C' \cdot \beta\}\right)$$

$$= \frac{1}{D} \sum_{P,C} (-1)^{P' \cdot \alpha \oplus C' \cdot \beta}$$

$P' \cdot \alpha$ and $C' \cdot \beta$ are computed as a function of the partial key and some bits of the plaintexts/ciphertexts denoted as $\chi_c(C)$ and $\chi_p(P)$ respectively (we assume that the bit positions correspond to the key bits in k_p and k_c):

$$P' \cdot \alpha = f(k_t, k_p \oplus \chi_p(P))$$
$$C' \cdot \beta = g(k_b, k_c \oplus \chi_c(C))$$

5.1   The FWT Approach of [13, 15]

The time complexity of the attack is dominated by the time necessary to compute the statistic for all key candidates. Several tricks have been introduced to make this step more efficient. Since the values of $P' \cdot \alpha$ and $C' \cdot \beta$ do not depend on the full plaintext/ciphertext, we can "compress" the dataset using a distillation phase where we only count how many plaintext/ciphertext pairs reach each value of those bits [22]:

$$q(k_p, k_t, k_c, k_b)$$

$$= \frac{1}{D} \sum_{P,C} (-1)^{f(k_t, k_p \oplus \chi_p(P)) \oplus g(k_b, k_c \oplus \chi_c(C))}$$

$$= \frac{1}{D} \sum_{i \in \mathbb{F}_2^{\kappa_p}} \sum_{j \in \mathbb{F}_2^{\kappa_c}} \# \{P, C : \chi_p(P) = i, \chi_c(C) = j\} \times (-1)^{f(k_t, k_p \oplus i) \oplus g(k_b, k_c \oplus j)}$$

We remark that the previous expression is actually a convolution:

$$= \frac{1}{D} \sum_{i,j} \phi(i, j) \times \psi_{k_t, k_b}(k_p \oplus i, k_c \oplus j) = \frac{1}{D}(\phi * \psi_{k_t, k_b})(k_p, k_c),$$

with

$$\phi(x, y) = \# \{P, C : \chi_p(P) = x, \chi_c(C) = y\}$$
$$\psi_{k_t, k_b}(x, y) = (-1)^{f(k_t, x) \oplus g(k_b, y)}$$

Therefore, for a given k_t, k_b, we can evaluate $q(k_p, k_t, k_c, k_b)$ for all k_p, k_c with complexity $\tilde{\mathcal{O}}(2^{\kappa_p + \kappa_c})$ using a Fast Walsh Transform. This was first observed in [13] (with additional rounds on one side only), and then generalized in [15]. The time complexity of the analysis is reduced to $\tilde{\mathcal{O}}(D + 2^{\kappa_g})$.

5.2   Statistical Models to Estimate the Success Probability

We follow the analysis of Blondeau and Nyberg [10,11], taking into account the impact of the variance of the correlation due to the random key, and the sampling model with a factor B depending on the type of attack: $B = 1$ if the plaintexts are randomly chosen with repetition, and $B = (2^n - D)/(2^n - 1)$ if they are distinct (in the following, we assume distinct plaintexts).

Single Dominant Characteristic. When there is a single dominant characteristic with absolute bias ε, the correlation of the approximation is either ε or $-\varepsilon$ depending of the key. The empirical correlation for the right key follows one of two possible normal distributions, with parameters

$$\mu_R = \pm\varepsilon \qquad\qquad \sigma_R^2 = B/D + 2^{-n}.$$

When the key guess is wrong, we assume that the computed statistic follows the correlation of a random permutation; it follows a normal distribution with parameters

$$\mu_W = 0 \qquad\qquad \sigma_W^2 = B/D + 2^{-n}.$$

Since there are two possible distributions for the right key, we have to slightly modify the analysis of (1). For an attack with gain a, we set a threshold $s = F_W^{-1}(1 - 2^{-a-1}) = \sigma_W \Phi^{-1}(1 - 2^{-a-1})$ and keep key candidates with $|q| \geq s$. The attack succeeds with probability $P_S = 1 - F_R(s)$ when $\mu_R > 0$, and $P_S = F_R(-s)$ otherwise:

$$P_S = \Phi\left(\frac{|\varepsilon| - \sigma_W \Phi^{-1}(1 - 2^{-a-1})}{\sigma_R}\right),$$

where Φ is the cumulative distribution function of the standard normal distribution.

Single Approximation with Many Trails. When using a single linear hull with many high correlation trails (rather than a dominant trail), the correlations for the right and wrong keys follow normal distributions with parameters:

$$\mu_R = 0 \qquad\qquad \sigma_R^2 = B/D + \text{ELP}$$
$$\mu_W = 0 \qquad\qquad \sigma_W^2 = B/D + 2^{-n},$$

Following [10], we estimate the expected linear potential ELP using the correlations ε_τ for characteristics τ in a set $\mathcal{S}$ of dominating characteristics:

$$\text{ELP} \approx 2^{-n} + \sum_{\tau \in \mathcal{S}} \varepsilon_\tau^2,$$

using the results of Sect. 3.1 to compute $\sum_{\tau \in \mathcal{S}} \varepsilon_\tau^2$ with $\mathcal{S}$ the set of characteristics with masks in Λ_w.

The distributions are both centered on zero, but since the variance is larger for the right key, we can sort the keys according to the absolute value of the measured correlation, and we expect a larger value for the right key than for wrong keys. More precisely, using a threshold $s = \sigma_W \Phi^{-1}(1 - 2^{-a-1})$ on the absolute value of the correlation, the success rate is given by [10, Theorem 2]:

$$P_S = 2 - 2\Phi\left(\frac{\sigma_W}{\sigma_R}\Phi^{-1}(1 - 2^{-a-1})\right).$$

Equivalently, we can consider the squared correlation, which follows a χ^2 distribution with one degree of freedom, and use the generic formula (1) with the following distributions:

$$F_R/\sigma_R \sim \chi_1^2 \qquad\qquad F_W/\sigma_W \sim \chi_1^2$$

Multiple Approximations. When using M linear approximations, there are different ways to exploit the information to rank the keys. Again, we follow the analysis of [10], and we rank the keys according to

$$Q(k) = \sum q_i(k)^2$$

According to [10], we can model the statistics for the right key as a Gaussian distribution with parameters

$$\sigma_R^2 = 2B^2 M + 4BD \sum_i \mathrm{ELP}_i + 2D^2 \sum_i \mathrm{ELP}_i^2$$

$$\mu_R = BM + D \sum_i \mathrm{ELP}_i$$

On the other hand the statistic for the wrong key is proportional to a χ^2 distribution with M degrees of freedom:

$$F_W/(B + D2^{-n}) \sim \chi_M^2$$

In our analysis, we consider either a single approximation $(1,0) \rightarrow (0,1)$, or the approximation $(1,0) \rightarrow (0,1)$ combined with lower quality approximations that can be used with the same key bits.

5.3   12-Round Key-Recovery

We apply the previous techniques to SIMECK64, starting from the linear approximation $(0,1) \rightarrow (0,1)$, and adding 8 rounds on the plaintext side and 4 rounds on the ciphertext side. Following Eq. 3, $x_0^{(8)}$ can be computed from $\kappa_p = 54$ bits of $\tilde{P}$, $\kappa_p = 54$ bits of the whitening key $k_p = k^{(0)} \| k^{(1)}$, and $\kappa_t = 50$ additional key bits. Similarly, $x_0^{(r-5)}$ can be computed from $\kappa_c = 14$ bits of $\tilde{C}$, $\kappa_c = 14$ bits of the whitening key $k^{(r-1)} \| k^{(r-2)}$, and $\kappa_b = 2$ additional key bits:

$$k_p = k^{(0)}_{[0,-1,\ldots,-23,-25,-26,-27,-30,-31]}, k^{(1)}_{[0,-1,\ldots,-18,-20,-21,-22,-25,-26,-30]}$$

$$k_t = k^{(2)}_{[0,-1,\ldots,-13,-15,-16,-17,-20,-21,-25]},$$

$$k^{(3)}_{[0,-1,-2,-3,-5,-6,-7,-8,-10,-11,-12,-15,-16,-20]},$$

$$k^{(4)}_{[0,-1,-2,-5,-6,-7,-10,-11,-15]}, k^{(5)}_{[0,-1,-5,-6,-10]}, k^{(6)}_{[0,-5]}$$

$$k_b = k^{(r-3)}_{[0,-5]}$$

$$k_c = k^{(r-1)}_{[0,-1,-2,-5,-6,-7,-10,-11,-15]}, k^{(r-2)}_{[0,-1,-5,-6,-10]}$$

We ignore bits that have a linear effect because they only flip the sign of the imbalance. Moreover, we can use key schedule relations to reduce κ_t by 2:

$$k_0^{(6)} = k_0^{(2)} \oplus k_{-1}^{(3)} \oplus k_0^{(3)} \wedge k_{-5}^{(3)} \oplus c_0^{(6)}$$

$$k_{-5}^{(6)} = k_{-5}^{(2)} \oplus k_{-6}^{(3)} \oplus k_{-5}^{(3)} \wedge k_{-10}^{(3)} \oplus c_{-5}^{(6)}$$

There are 14 additional relations between bits of κ_t and κ_p.

The attack is decomposed in three phases:

Distillation phase. Compute $\phi(x,y) = \#\{P, C : \chi_p(P) = x, \chi_c(C) = y\}$ for $0 \leq x < 2^{\kappa_p}$, $0 \leq y < 2^{\kappa_c}$.
This only requires to set up $2^{\kappa_p + \kappa_c}$ counters, and to iterate over the D available plaintext/ciphertext pairs.

Analysis phase. For each guess of k_t, k_b, for all $0 \leq x < 2^{\kappa_p}$, $0 \leq y < 2^{\kappa_c}$, compute $\psi_{k_t,k_b}(x,y) = (-1)^{f(k_t,x) \oplus g(k_b,y)}$, then evaluate the convolution $\phi * \psi_{k_t,k_b}$ using the Fast Walsh Transform.
For each k_t, k_b, this requires $2^{\kappa_p + \kappa_c}$ evaluations of f and g to generate ψ_{k_t,k_b}, and $3(\kappa_p + \kappa_c)2^{\kappa_p + \kappa_c}$ additions and $2^{\kappa_p + \kappa_c}$ multiplications to evaluate the convolution. Assuming that the cost of $\kappa_p + \kappa_c$ additions and the cost of a multiplication are comparable to the cost of an encryption call, the total complexity of the analysis phase is $\mathcal{O}(2^{\kappa_g})$ using a memory of size $2^{\kappa_p + \kappa_c}$.

Search phase. For all keys with $q(k_p, k_t, k_c, k_b) \geq s$, exhaustively try all master keys corresponding to k_p, k_t, k_c, k_b.
With a threshold $s = F_W^{-1}(1 - 2^{-a})$ we expect a fraction 2^{-a} of the keys to remain. We iterate over 2^{88+16} candidates k_p, k_t, k_c, k_b that satisfy the 14 key schedule equations between k_t and k_p, keep only the 88 independent bits of k_p, k_t for keys meeting the threshold, and exhaustively search the remaining 40 bits, with a complexity of $2^{88+16-a} \times 2^{40} = 2^{144-a}$.

With our parameters, we have $\kappa_g = 118$ (after removing the two relations between bits of k_t). Using the Walsh transform pruning technique of [15] (and partially precomputing the Walsh transform of ψ), the complexity of the analysis phase is reduced to[2]:

$$68\rho_A 2^{68} + 2\rho_M 2^{118} + \rho_A 2^{64}(2^{54} + 39 \times 2^{40}) + \rho_A 2^{90}(2^{14} + 13 \times 2^{14}) \approx 2\rho_M 2^{118}$$

with ρ_A the cost of an addition, and ρ_M the cost of a multiplication. Assuming that 2 multiplications correspond to roughly one evaluation of the cipher, we end up with a complexity of 2^{κ_g}. This variant uses a memory of $2^{\kappa_p + \kappa_c} + 2^{\kappa_p + \kappa_t} + 2^{\kappa_c + \kappa_b} = 2^{68} + 2^{102} + 2^{16} \approx 2^{102}$ elements.

5.4   Attack Parameters

We use this attack to target 41 or 42 rounds of SIMECK64, and smaller variants of SIMECK, with various time/data trade-offs summarized in Table 8. We explain two attacks in detail here and include others in the full version [20] (Appendix B).

42-Round SIMECK64 with $2^{63.5}$ Plaintexts. The ELP of the linear approximation $(1,0) \rightarrow (0,1)$ over 30 rounds is $2^{-64} + 2^{-60.36} = 2^{-60.25}$. The complexity of the analysis phase is 2^{118}. With an advantage of $a = 24$, the complexity of the search phase is 2^{120} and the success probability is $P_S = 8.3\%$.

Since SIMECK is rotation-invariant, we can repeat the attack 32 times by rotating the linear approximation used. On average we expect the attack to succeed after $1/P_S = 12$ attempts, leading to an average complexity of $2^{123.9}$. If we fix this as the maximum complexity, we expect a success rate of roughly $1 - 1/e \approx 63\%$.

41-Round SIMECK64 with 2^{63} Plaintexts. Alternatively, we can use multiple linear approximations to reduce the time complexity of a 41-round attack. We use the following 29-round linear approximations:

$$(1,0) \rightarrow (0,1) : \text{ELP} = 2^{-64} + 2^{-58.47}$$
$$(1,0) \rightarrow (1,0) : \text{ELP} = 2^{-64} + 2^{-60.36}$$
$$(1,0) \rightarrow (1,1) : \text{ELP} = 2^{-64} + 2^{-60.36}$$
$$(0,1) \rightarrow (0,1) : \text{ELP} = 2^{-64} + 2^{-60.36}$$
$$(1,1) \rightarrow (0,1) : \text{ELP} = 2^{-64} + 2^{-60.36}$$

The extra approximations have been chosen because the corresponding masks can be computed from the same keys bits as the main approximation $(1,0) \rightarrow (0,1)$; they have a combined capacity of $2^{-57.39}$. Thanks to the higher capacity, we can aim for a higher advantage $a = 52$, and obtain a success rate of 23% with 2^{63} plaintexts. Therefore, we split the key recovery rounds as 7 rounds on the plaintext side and 5 on the ciphertext side (rather than 8 and 4), leading to parameters $\kappa_p = 45$, $\kappa_t = 30$, $\kappa_c = 23$, $\kappa_b = 7$; this reduces the complexity of the analysis phase to 5×2^{105}, while the search phase has a complexity of $2^{128+23+7-52} = 2^{106}$.

---

[2] With their notations, we have $k_0 = 54$, $k_1 = 50$, $k_2 = 2$, $k_3 = 14$, $l_{12} = 2$, $l_0 = 14$, $l_3 = 0$.

Table 8. Attack parameters for linear attacks on SIMECK. C_1 is the time complexity to run the attack a single time, and the corresponding success probability is P_S. The average time is obtained as C_1/P_S.

Cipher	Rounds	#app.	Capacity	D	Adv.	C_1	P_S	Time
SIMECK64	$41 = 7+29+5$	5	$2^{-57.34}$	2^{63}	52	$5 \times 2^{105} + 2^{106}$	0.23	2^{110}
	$41 = 8+29+4$	1	$2^{-58.44}$	2^{62}	26	$2^{118} + 2^{118}$	0.11	$2^{122.2}$
	$42 = 8+30+4$	1	$2^{-60.25}$	$2^{63.5}$	24	$2^{118} + 2^{120}$	0.08	$2^{123.9}$
	$42 = 8+30+4$	1	$2^{-60.25}$	2^{64}	29	$2^{118} + 2^{115}$	0.10	$2^{121.5}$
SIMECK48	$32 = 7+21+4$	1	$2^{-43.50}$	2^{47}	26	$2^{87} + 2^{86}$	0.10	$2^{90.9}$
SIMECK32	$23 = 5+13+5$	1	$2^{-27.68}$	$2^{31.5}$	37	$2^{58} + 2^{56}$	0.07	$2^{62.2}$

5.5 Experimentations

We have performed experimentations to verify the theory leading to the probabilities of success P_S. To do this, we take a set of D plaintext/ciphertext pairs and we compute the experimental correlation $Q(k)$ for the right key and for a random sample of wrong keys. We choose an advantage a and we consider that a success is obtained when the correlation of the right key is among the 2^{-a} highest correlations. This experiment was repeated 1000 times with random keys to compute an experimental success probability. Our results are presented in Table 9. We compare attacks with a single approximation $(1,0) \rightarrow (0,1)$ and attacks with five approximations $(1,0) \rightarrow (0,1)$, $(1,0) \rightarrow (0,1)$, $(1,0) \rightarrow (0,1)$, $(1,0) \rightarrow (0,1)$, $(1,0) \rightarrow (0,1)$, as used in the 41-round attack with 2^{63} plaintexts. The experimental probability of success is close to the prediction, confirming that both the model for the success probability, and our estimation of the ELP are accurate.

For SIMECK32, we compute the exact ELP of the linear approximation using our algorithm with $w = 16$; we obtain an ELP of $2^{-30.73}$ over 15 rounds for $(1,0) \rightarrow (0,1)$ and $2^{-31.59}$ for the four other approximations.

Table 9. Comparison of the theoretical (P_S) and experimental success probability for linear attacks. We perform 1000 experiments, taking D pairs of plaintext/ciphertext and testing whether the correlation associated to the right key is among the 2^{-a} highest correlations with a sample of random wrong keys.

Cipher	Rounds	D	# app.	capacity	# wrong keys	Adv.	Success	P_S
SIMECK32/64	15	2^{31}	1	$2^{-30.73}$	2^8	5	7.4%	9.9%
SIMECK32/64	15	2^{31}	5	$2^{-29.05}$	2^8	5	9%	7.4%
SIMECK32/64	16	2^{31}	1	$2^{-31.59}$	2^8	5	4.9%	4.5%
SIMECK32/64	16	2^{31}	5	$2^{-29.44}$	2^8	5	3.6%	2.3%
SIMECK64/128	12	2^{28}	1	$2^{-26.39}$	2^{12}	10	9.9%	10.1%
SIMECK64/128	12	2^{28}	5	$2^{-25.17}$	2^{12}	10	14.8%	14.8%

6   Application to SIMON

Similarly to SIMECK, previous results [21] have shown the existence of iterative trails for SIMON with a single active bit in the input and output, where all intermediate states fit in a small window of active bits. This makes SIMON an interesting target for our analysis, just like SIMECK. In this section we focus on linear cryptanalysis, and we obtain improved attack against SIMON96 and SIMON128, gaining between 3 and 7 rounds compared to previous attacks.

Previous works have shown that SIMON offers a higher security against differential and linear cryptanalysis than SIMECK. In particular, iterative trails have a higher weight, and require a larger window of active bits. Moreover, we notice that the trail $(1, 0) \to (0, 1)$ is only possible for round numbers of the form $4r+1$, because some bits have a linear update when the trail is limited to a window smaller than the word size. More precisely, for linear trails, the high order bits follow a pattern

$$(10*\ldots, 0*0\ldots) \to (0*0\ldots, 10*\ldots) \to (10*\ldots, 0*1\ldots) \to (0*1\ldots, 10*\ldots) \to (10*\ldots, 0*0\ldots)$$

Since the transition matrix is sparser than for SIMECK we can run our analysis with larger values of w. The lower bound on the ELP that we obtain for the trail $(1, 0) \to (0, 1)$ is given in Table 11. The bounds show a smaller linear potential (and differential probability) for SIMON than for SIMECK. However, we see in Fig. 9 that the linear potential still increases significantly with the window size w; this indicates that our bound is not as tight as on SIMECK. Further work is needed to capture the full clustering effect on SIMON, and this could further reduce the security margin of the cipher.

The approximations $(1, 0) \to (0, 1)$ can be extended by one round on either side with correlation 2^{-2}, leading to two active bits. After rotating the approximation by two bits to $(4, 0) \overset{r}{\to} (0, 4)$ with ELP c, the extended approximations are $(4, 0) \overset{r+1}{\to} (4, 1)$ and $(1, 4) \overset{r+1}{\to} (0, 4)$ with ELP $2^{-2}c$, and $(1, 4) \overset{r+2}{\to} (4, 1)$ with ELP $2^{-4}c$.

We summarize the parameters of the best attacks we have identified against SIMON96 and SIMON128 in Table 10; our analysis does not seem to improve previous results on SIMON32, SIMON48 and SIMON64. As shown in the full version [20] (Table 13 and 14), we don't have any key-schedule relation between bits of k_t or k_b, but we have relations between k_t and k_p or between k_b and k_c. Therefore we can use the Walsh transform pruning technique of [15], as in the SIMECK attacks. We explain two attacks in detail below.

56-Rounds SIMON128/256. We use the 41-round linear approximation $(1, 0) \to (0, 1)$ with ELP lower bound of $2^{-123.07} + 2^{-128}$. We add 8 rounds on the plaintext side, and 7 rounds on the ciphertext side, obtaining parameters $\kappa_p = 80$, $\kappa_t = 65$, $\kappa_c = 64$, $\kappa_b = 37$. The complexity of the analysis phase is about 2^{246}. With 2^{126} data, and an advantage $a = 10$, we have a success probability of 26% and the search phase has a complexity of 2^{246}. Finally we obtain an average complexity of $(2^{246} + 2^{246})/0.26 \approx 2^{249}$.

Table 10. Attack parameters for linear cryptanalysis of SIMON.

Cipher	Rounds	$\kappa_p, \kappa_t, \kappa_c, \kappa_b$	D	a	C_1	P_S	Time	Approx
S128/256	$56 = 8{+}41{+}7$	80, 65, 64, 37	2^{126}	10	$2^{246} + 2^{246}$	0.26	2^{249}	$(1,0) \to (0,1)$
S128/192	$55 = 7{+}42{+}6$	64, 37, 56, 23	2^{127}	10	$2^{180} + 2^{182}$	0.13	$2^{185.2}$	$(4,0) \to (4,1)$
S128/128	$53 = 6{+}42{+}5$	47, 18, 38, 9	2^{127}	10	$2^{112} + 2^{118}$	0.13	2^{121}	$(4,0) \to (4,1)$
S96/144	$45 = 6{+}33{+}6$	47, 18, 47, 18	2^{95}	10	$2^{130} + 2^{134}$	0.19	$2^{136.5}$	$(1,0) \to (0,1)$
S96/96	$43 = 5{+}33{+}5$	30, 7, 30, 7	2^{94}	10	$2^{74} + 2^{86}$	0.08	$2^{89.6}$	$(1,0) \to (0,1)$

Table 11. ELP of the linear approximation $(1,0) \to (0,1)$ and probability of the differential $(0,1) \to (1,0)$ for SIMON ($\log_2$, computed with $w = 19$)

r	13	17	21	25	29	33	37	41	45
ELP	−41.99	−46.30	−67.87	−77.90	−87.25	−92.60	−113.06	−123.07	−132.95
Pr	−40.68	−47.31	−67.56	−78.08	−86.96	−94.62	−113.67	−124.22	−133.66

55-Rounds SIMON128/192. For SIMON128/192, we use the 42-round linear approximation $(4,0) \to (4,1)$ with an ELP lower bound of $2^{-125.07} + 2^{-128}$. We add 7 rounds on the plaintext side, and 6 rounds on the ciphertext side, obtaining parameters $\kappa_p = 64$, $\kappa_t = 37$, $\kappa_c = 56$, $\kappa_b = 23$. The complexity of the analysis phase is about 2^{180}. With 2^{127} data, and an advantage $a = 10$, we have a success probability of 13% and the search phase has a complexity of 2^{182}. Finally we obtain an average complexity of $(2^{180} + 2^{182})/0.13 \approx 2^{185.2}$.

45-Rounds SIMON96/144. We use the 33-round linear approximation $(1,0) \to (0,1)$ with an ELP lower bound of $2^{-93.57} + 2^{-96}$. We add 6 rounds on each side, obtaining parameters $\kappa_p = 47$, $\kappa_t = 18$, $\kappa_c = 47$, $\kappa_b = 18$. The complexity of the analysis phase is about 2^{130}. With 2^{95} data, and an advantage $a = 10$, we have a success probability of 19% and the search phase has a complexity of 2^{134}. Finally we obtain an average complexity of $(2^{130} + 2^{134})/0.19 \approx 2^{136.5}$.

7   Perspectives

Our work provides the first attack against 42-round SIMECK64, showing that the security margin is very slim (the full version has 44 rounds). Moreover, if the designers of SIMECK had proposed a 128-bit variant with the same number of rounds as SIMON128, the full version would be broken by our analysis.

We also improve significantly previous attacks on SIMON. In particular we show that SIMON96/144 only has 17% of the rounds as security margin, while the designers wrote [4]:

> *"After almost 4 years of concerted effort by academic researchers, the various versions of Simon and Speck retain a margin averaging around 30%, and in every case over 25%. The design team's analysis when making stepping decisions was consistent with these numbers."*

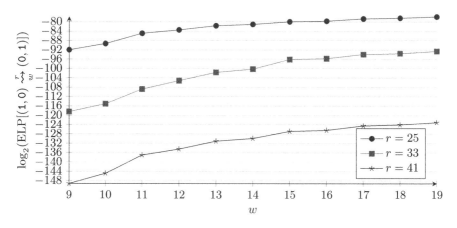

Fig. 9. Effect of w on the probability of Simon linear hulls.

Comparison of Differential and Linear Cryptanalysis. Our work shows that differential and linear attacks against Simon and Simeck are very similar. The differential characteristics and linear approximations are almost equivalent; we use trails with a single input/output bit in both cases, and the differential probability p is almost the same as the linear potential ELP (See Table 4). Using advanced techniques (dynamic key-guessing and Fast Walsh Transform respectively), both attacks have a complexity that is essentially $D + 2^{\kappa_g}$ (with $D = \mathcal{O}(1/p)$ or $D = \mathcal{O}(1/\text{ELP})$ respectively).

However, there is an important difference in the key-recovery part. As seen in Table 5, we have to guess more key bits for differential cryptanalysis than for linear cryptanalysis (for the same number of additional rounds). This explains why linear cryptanalysis is more efficient than differential cryptanalysis on those ciphers, as shown by previous analysis.

Impact of the Rotations. The main difference between Simeck and Simon is the value of the rotations of the round function. In order to find which combinations of the rotation constants a, b and c would be a bad or a good choice, we reuse Algorithm 1 to obtain a lower bound for the probability of a differential for several values of a, b and c. We set the following parameters: $w = 13$, $r = 30$, and $0 \leq a, b, c \leq 10$. A lower bound of the probability of all the differentials with input $(\delta_L, \delta_R) = (0, 1)$ is computed, and this allows to confirm that the following trivial conditions must be verified: a, b and c must all be different, c must be different from 0, and a, b and c must be of different parity: the three shifts must not be all even or all odd.

We also notice that (a, b, c) must not be of the form $(i, 2j - i, j)$ or $(2j - i, i, j)$ and that the bias we observe strongly decreases when c increases. However, this does not allow us to conclude that taking a large value of c ensures a better security since it is possible that there exists other differentials with high bias. Our approach does not allow to conclude when a and b are smaller than c because in this case, the difference cannot remain in a fixed window after a large number of rounds. This is due to the fact that the difference generated by the linear part can never cancel out with the difference of the non-linear part.

Alternative Class. Instead of using differences or masks in a fixed window of w bits, we could consider low-weight values. Indeed, this class also includes the iterative trails given in previous works, and should contain many high-probability trails. We have implemented the search algorithm with this alternative class, using 32-bit words of weight at most 5 (a set of $2^{17.9}$ values).

In terms of resources, this requires roughly the same amount of memory as with a window of size $w = 18$, but it runs about 50 times faster, because there are fewer possible transitions at each round: the probability to reach a value with weight lower than 5 is smaller than the probability to stay in a fixed window. However, the bounds given with this class on SIMECK and SIMON are not competitive with those obtained with a fixed window. On SIMECK, using words of weight 5 gives probabilities comparable to using a window with $w = 9$, largely below $w = 18$. On SIMON, the gap is smaller: we obtain results similar to using a window of size $w = 15$. In both cases, using a fixed window requires fewer resources (time and memory) to achieve the same quality of results.

Acknowledgements. The second author is funded by a grant from Région Ile-de-France. and the third author by ERC ADG 740972 (ALGSTRONGCRYPTO). This work was also supported by ANR grant ANR-20-CE48-0017 (SELECT).

References

1. Abed, F., List, E., Lucks, S., Wenzel, J.: Differential cryptanalysis of round-reduced SIMON and SPECK. In: Cid, C., Rechberger, C. (eds.) FSE 2014. LNCS, vol. 8540, pp. 525–545. Springer, Heidelberg (2015). https://doi.org/10.1007/978-3-662-46706-0_27

2. Alizadeh, J., et al.: Cryptanalysis of SIMON variants with connections. In: Saxena, N., Sadeghi, A.-R. (eds.) RFIDSec 2014. LNCS, vol. 8651, pp. 90–107. Springer, Cham (2014). https://doi.org/10.1007/978-3-319-13066-8_6

3. Bagheri, N.: Linear cryptanalysis of reduced-round SIMECK variants. In: Biryukov, A., Goyal, V. (eds.) INDOCRYPT 2015. LNCS, vol. 9462, pp. 140–152. Springer, Cham (2015). https://doi.org/10.1007/978-3-319-26617-6_8

4. Beaulieu, R., Shors, D., Smith, J., Treatman-Clark, S., Weeks, B., Wingers, L.: Notes on the design and analysis of SIMON and SPECK. Cryptology ePrint Archive, Report 2017/560 (2017). http://eprint.iacr.org/2017/560

5. Beaulieu, R., Treatman-Clark, S., Shors, D., Weeks, B., Smith, J., Wingers, L.: The simon and speck lightweight block ciphers. In: 2015 52nd ACM/EDAC/IEEE Design Automation Conference (DAC), pp. 1–6 (2015)

6. Beierle, C.: Pen and paper arguments for SIMON and SIMON-like designs. In: Zikas, V., De Prisco, R. (eds.) SCN 2016. LNCS, vol. 9841, pp. 431–446. Springer, Cham (2016). https://doi.org/10.1007/978-3-319-44618-9_23

7. Biham, E., Shamir, A.: Differential cryptanalysis of DES-like cryptosystems. In: Menezes, A.J., Vanstone, S.A. (eds.) CRYPTO 1990. LNCS, vol. 537, pp. 2–21. Springer, Heidelberg (1991). https://doi.org/10.1007/3-540-38424-3_1

8. Biham, E., Shamir, A.: Differential cryptanalysis of DES-like cryptosystems. J. Cryptol. **4**(1), 3–72 (1991)
9. Biryukov, A., Roy, A., Velichkov, V.: Differential analysis of block ciphers SIMON and SPECK. In: Cid, C., Rechberger, C. (eds.) FSE 2014. LNCS, vol. 8540, pp. 546–570. Springer, Heidelberg (2015). https://doi.org/10.1007/978-3-662-46706-0_28
10. Blondeau, C., Nyberg, K.: Improved parameter estimates for correlation and capacity deviates in linear cryptanalysis. IACR Trans. Symm. Cryptol. **2016**(2), 162–191 (2016). http://tosc.iacr.org/index.php/ToSC/article/view/570
11. Blondeau, C., Nyberg, K.: Joint data and key distribution of simple, multiple, and multidimensional linear cryptanalysis test statistic and its impact to data complexity. Des. Codes Cryptogr. **82**(1–2), 319–349 (2017)
12. Chen, H., Wang, X.: Improved linear hull attack on round-reduced SIMON with dynamic key-guessing techniques. In: Peyrin, T. (ed.) FSE 2016. LNCS, vol. 9783, pp. 428–449. Springer, Heidelberg (2016). https://doi.org/10.1007/978-3-662-52993-5_22
13. Collard, B., Standaert, F.-X., Quisquater, J.-J.: Improving the time complexity of Matsui's linear cryptanalysis. In: Nam, K.-H., Rhee, G. (eds.) ICISC 2007. LNCS, vol. 4817, pp. 77–88. Springer, Heidelberg (2007). https://doi.org/10.1007/978-3-540-76788-6_7
14. Daemen, J., Govaerts, R., Vandewalle, J.: Correlation matrices. In: Preneel, B. (ed.) FSE 1994. LNCS, vol. 1008, pp. 275–285. Springer, Heidelberg (1995). https://doi.org/10.1007/3-540-60590-8_21
15. Flórez-Gutiérrez, A., Naya-Plasencia, M.: Improving key-recovery in linear attacks: application to 28-round PRESENT. In: Canteaut, A., Ishai, Y. (eds.) EUROCRYPT 2020. LNCS, vol. 12105, pp. 221–249. Springer, Cham (2020). https://doi.org/10.1007/978-3-030-45721-1_9
16. Huang, M., Wang, L., Zhang, Y.: Improved automatic search algorithm for differential and linear cryptanalysis on SIMECK and the applications. In: Naccache, D. et al. (eds.) ICICS 2018. LNCS, vol. 11149, pp. 664–681. Springer, Cham (2018). https://doi.org/10.1007/978-3-030-01950-1_39
17. Kölbl, S., Leander, G., Tiessen, T.: Observations on the SIMON block cipher family. In: Gennaro, R., Robshaw, M. (eds.) CRYPTO 2015. LNCS, vol. 9215, pp. 161–185. Springer, Heidelberg (2015). https://doi.org/10.1007/978-3-662-47989-6_8
18. Kölbl, S., Roy, A.: A brief comparison of SIMON and SIMECK. In: Bogdanov, A. (ed.) LightSec 2016. LNCS, vol. 10098, pp. 69–88. Springer, Cham (2017). https://doi.org/10.1007/978-3-319-55714-4_6
19. Lai, X., Massey, J.L., Murphy, S.: Markov ciphers and differential cryptanalysis. In: Davies, D.W. (ed.) EUROCRYPT 1991. LNCS, vol. 547, pp. 17–38. Springer, Heidelberg (1991). https://doi.org/10.1007/3-540-46416-6_2
20. Leurent, G., Pernot, C., Schrottenloher, A.: Clustering effect in simon and simeck. Cryptology ePrint Archive, Report 2021/1198 (2021). https://ia.cr/2021/1198
21. Liu, Z., Li, Y., Wang, M.: Optimal differential trails in SIMON-like ciphers. IACR Trans. Symm. Cryptol. **2017**(1), 358–379 (2017)
22. Matsui, M.: Linear cryptanalysis method for DES cipher. In: Helleseth, T. (ed.) EUROCRYPT 1993. LNCS, vol. 765, pp. 386–397. Springer, Heidelberg (1994). https://doi.org/10.1007/3-540-48285-7_33
23. Nyberg, K.: Linear approximation of block ciphers (rump session). In: Santis, A.D. (ed.) EUROCRYPT'94. LNCS, vol. 950, pp. 439–444. Springer, Heidelberg (1995)

24. Qiao, K., Hu, L., Sun, S.: Differential security evaluation of simeck with dynamic key-guessing techniques. In: Camp, O., Furnell, S., Mori, P. (eds.) Proceedings of the 2nd International Conference on Information Systems Security and Privacy, ICISSP 2016, Rome, Italy, 19–21 February, 2016, pp. 74–84. SciTePress (2016)
25. Qin, L., Chen, H., Wang, X.: Linear hull attack on round-reduced simeck with dynamic key-guessing techniques. In: Liu, J.K., Steinfeld, R. (eds.) ACISP 2016. LNCS, vol. 9723, pp. 409–424. Springer, Cham (2016). https://doi.org/10.1007/978-3-319-40367-0_26
26. Wang, N., Wang, X., Jia, K., Zhao, J.: Differential attacks on reduced SIMON versions with dynamic key-guessing techniques. Sci. China Inf. Sci. **61**(9), 098103:1–098103:3 (2018)
27. Wang, X., Wu, B., Hou, L., Lin, D.: Automatic search for related-key differential trails in SIMON-like block ciphers based on MILP. In: Chen, L., Manulis, M., Schneider, S. (eds.) ISC 2018. LNCS, vol. 11060, pp. 116–131. Springer, Cham (2018). https://doi.org/10.1007/978-3-319-99136-8_7
28. Yang, G., Zhu, B., Suder, V., Aagaard, M.D., Gong, G.: The Simeck family of lightweight block ciphers. In: Güneysu, T., Handschuh, H. (eds.) CHES 2015. LNCS, vol. 9293, pp. 307–329. Springer, Heidelberg (2015). https://doi.org/10.1007/978-3-662-48324-4_16

New Attacks on LowMC Instances with a Single Plaintext/Ciphertext Pair

Subhadeep Banik$^{(\boxtimes)}$, Khashayar Barooti, Serge Vaudenay, and Hailun Yan

LASEC, École Polytechnique Fédérale de Lausanne, Lausanne, Switzerland
{subhadeep.banik,khashayar.barooti,serge.vaudenay,hailun.yan}@epfl.ch

Abstract. Cryptanalysis of the LowMC block cipher when the attacker has access to a single known plaintext/ciphertext pair is a mathematically challenging problem. This is because the attacker is unable to employ most of the standard techniques in symmetric cryptography like linear and differential cryptanalysis. This scenario is particularly relevant while arguing the security of the PICNIC digital signature scheme in which the plaintext/ciphertext pair generated by the LowMC block cipher serves as the public (verification) key and the corresponding LowMC encryption key also serves as the secret (signing) key of the signature scheme. In the paper by Banik et al. (IACR ToSC 2020:4), the authors used a linearization technique of the LowMC S-box to mount attacks on some instances of the block cipher. In this paper, we first make a more precise complexity analysis of the linearization attack. Then, we show how to perform a 2-stage MITM attack on LowMC. The first stage reduces the key candidates corresponding to a fraction of key bits of the master key. The second MITM stage between this reduced candidate set and the remaining fraction of key bits successfully recovers the master key. We show that the combined computational complexity of both these stages is significantly lower than those reported in the ToSC paper by Banik et al.

1 Introduction

The LowMC family of block ciphers was first proposed by Albrecht et al. in [ARS+15] and was designed specifically for use in FHE and MPC applications due to its low multiplicative complexity. The block cipher uses a 3-bit S-box which is the only non-linear transformation in the construction. Both the linear layers and round key generation are done by multiplying with full rank matrices over $GF(2)$ of appropriate dimensions. The designers propose several instances of the block cipher, some of which have partial non-linear layers i.e. in which the S-boxes are not applied over the entire internal state of the cipher.

Recently, LowMC has been used in the PICNIC digital signature scheme in the following way. Let $E(K, pt)$ be the LowMC encryption of the plaintext pt using the key K. The plaintext/ciphertext pair $(pt, ct = E(K, pt))$ is used as the public key of the signature scheme (verification key) and encryption key K is used as the secret key (signing key). If an adversary can recover the encryption

© International Association for Cryptologic Research 2021
M. Tibouchi and H. Wang (Eds.): ASIACRYPT 2021, LNCS 13090, pp. 303–331, 2021.
https://doi.org/10.1007/978-3-030-92062-3_11

key given only a single plaintext/ciphertext pair (pt, ct) i.e. the public key of the signature scheme, then in effect he computes the secret signing key. This allows him to forge a signature by following exactly the honest prover protocol with the recovered signing key. This demonstrates that a data complexity one key recovery attack on LowMC block cipher leads to a signature forgery on PICNIC.

1.1 Previous Work

In ICISC 2015 Dobraunig et al. [DEM15] proposed an attack on LowMC family of block ciphers, based on cube attack strategies. The authors proposed an algorithm which successfully recovers the key of the round reduced version of the cipher, aiming for 80-bit security. Dinur et al. [DLMW15] showed that around 2^{-38} fraction of its 80-bit key instances could be broken 2^{23} times faster than exhaustive search. Moreover, all instances that claimed to provide 128-bit security could be broken about 1000 times faster. In [DKP+19], the authors showed that for the LowMC instances that employs partial linear layers, each instance belonged to a large class of equivalent instances that differ in their linear layers. This led to a more efficient implementation of the cipher that required reduces the evaluation time and storage of computing the linear layers. In FSE 2018, Rechberger et al. [RST18] proposed a meet-in-the-middle style attack, based on possible output differentials, given an input differential, which affects the security of the variants of LowMCv2 with partial S-box layers drastically. In [LIM20] some results on LowMC were reported building on the techniques of [RST18], albeit with higher data complexities, which naturally do not apply to the PIC-NIC scenario. In [DN19] the authors proposed multi-target attacks on the PICNIC signature scheme. For a survey of key recovery attacks on LowMC, readers may check the survey done by Rechberger et al. [GKRS]. As mentioned, one of the main use cases of LowMC, is the PICNIC post quantum signature scheme. Due to PICNIC's algebraic composition, the scheme would be trivially forged by a key recovery attack on LowMC that uses only a single pair of plaintext/ciphertext. In other words only attacks with data complexity one directly affect the security of the signature scheme.

The LowMC cryptanalysis challenge asked for cryptanalysis of several instances of LowMC (in which the blocksize and keysize are equal), with both partial and complete non-linear layers given only one plaintext and ciphertext pair. In [BBDV20], some instances of the challenge were successfully solved. The authors used the fact that after guessing the value of any balanced quadratic Boolean function on the inputs of the LowMC S-box, the transformation becomes completely linear. The authors chose the 3-variable majority function for this purpose, but they show that any balanced quadratic function can be used. Using this fact, they showed various attacks on

A 2-round LowMC with complete non-linear layers.

B $0.8 \cdot \lfloor \frac{n}{s} \rfloor$-round LowMC with partial non-linear layers. Here n denotes the blocksize of the LowMC instance, and s denotes the number of S-boxes in each round.

The authors in [BBDV20] report attack complexities in number of linear/quadratic expression evaluations. However it is always preferable to have computational complexity reported in terms of number of encryptions. We actually show in this paper that the best complexity of these attacks are equivalent to $\frac{n}{2r} \times 2^{rs}$ encryptions (r denotes the number of rounds used in the encryption), as will be discussed later in this paper. In [BBDV20], the authors then presented a speedup of a factor of 8 over the MITM attack by using the 3-xor problem.

In [Din], the authors showed an ingenious method of finding roots of multiple polynomial systems over $GF(2)$. The n variables of the equation system are partitioned into two disjoint sets $y = y_0, y_1, \ldots, y_{m-1}$ and $z = z_0, z_1, \ldots, z_{p-1}$ (with $n = m + p$). It is argued that any random linear combination of the polynomials in the original equation system, has an isolated solution with high probability, i.e. if $(\hat{y}, \hat{z})$ is an isolated solution then $(\hat{y}, z')$ is not a solution for all $z' \neq \hat{z}$. The authors then observed that all such isolated solutions could be recovered bit-by-bit by computing $p + 1$ partial sums for each candidate solution $\hat{y} \in \{0, 1\}^m$. The first step is to randomly combine the original equation system into a system with smaller number of equations whose solutions can be found by brute force. These solutions are then used to compute partial sums and construct a candidate solution of the original equation system. This generic method of solving equations works quite well if the algebraic degree of the system is small and so it was applied to attack 3, 4 and 5 round LowMC with complete non-linear layers for some specific block-lengths. However, the method can not be applied to LowMC instances with partial non-linear layers, since the number of rounds in such instances are generally much higher, and the degree of the internal state variables (as a function of the key) doubles every round. [LIM21] reports an algebraic attack on LowMC. However the authors use the $n^{2.8}$ estimate (ignoring constant factors) to solve Gaussian elimination, to report the complexity of their attack. As such it is unclear if the complexity bounds they report are tight.

1.2 Contribution and Organization of the Paper

In this paper we present new improved attacks on LowMC instances that use the linearization technique of the LowMC S-box as a starting point. We first provide a more precise complexity analysis of the linearization attack and of its proof. Then, we present improved attacks on both **a)** the 2 and 3-round complete non-linear layer instance, and **b)** the $0.8 \cdot \lfloor \frac{n}{s} \rfloor$ and $\lfloor \frac{n}{s} \rfloor$-round LowMC instance with partial non-linear layers. We show that the attack complexity can be reduced if we perform the MITM in two separate stages: the first stage reduces the set of possible key candidates of a fraction of key bits to smaller set. A second MITM stage is then performed on this reduced candidate set and the candidates in the remaining fraction of the key bits. The paper shows how to efficiently formulate equations to perform the 2 MITM stages, and proves conclusively that the correct key can be found with certainty. It also shows that the combined computational complexity of the 2 attack stages is significantly lower than the complexities reported in [BBDV20]. Table 1 tabulates in detail the complexities

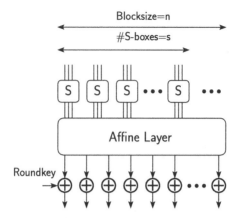

Fig. 1. LowMC Round Function

of the attacks reported in this paper and compares with the corresponding complexities reported in [BBDV20]. Note that in this table, we have recalculated all computational complexities in terms of number of encryptions.

The rest of the paper is organized in the following manner. In Sect. 2, we begin by presenting a mathematical description of LowMC and some information about the LowMC cryptanalysis challenge. In Sect. 3, we list out some of the issues with the computational complexity reported in [BBDV20] and explain how we have tried to compute all complexities in terms of number of encryptions. In Sect. 4, we present our attack on the 2-round and 3-round LowMC instances with complete non-linear layers. In Sect. 5, we present our attack on the $0.8 \cdot \lfloor \frac{n}{s} \rfloor$ and $\lfloor \frac{n}{s} \rfloor$-LowMC instance with partial non-linear layers. In Sect. 6, we present some experimental results on reduced LowMC instances with smaller blocksizes. This is done to prove that the attacks presented in Sects. 4, 5 can indeed be applied to full-size LowMC instances. Section 7 concludes the paper.

2 Preliminaries

The LowMC round function is a typical SPN construction given in Fig. 1. It consists of an n-bit block undergoing either a partial or a complete substitution layer consisting of s 3-bit S-boxes where $3s \leq n$. It is followed by an affine layer which consists of multiplication of the block with an invertible $n \times n$ matrix over $\mathbb{F}_2$ and addition with an n-bit round constant. Finally the block is xored with an n-bit round key. If the master secret key K is of size n-bits (which is true for all the instances in the LowMC challenge), then each round key is obtained by multiplication of K with an $n \times n$ invertible matrix. As in most SPN constructions, a plaintext is first xored with a whitening key which for LowMC is simply the secret key K, and the round functions are executed r times to give the ciphertext. From the point of view of cryptanalysis, we note that the design is completely known to the attacker, i.e. all the matrices and constants

Table 1. Summary of results. Note for the complexity is given in #Encryptions

Instance	n	s	r	Type of Attack	Recalculated Complexity	Reference
Full S-box layer	129	43	2	Linearization	2^{91}	[BBDV20]*
	192	64			2^{134}	
	255	85			2^{176}	
Partial S-box layer	128	1	$0.8 \times \lfloor \frac{n}{s} \rfloor$	Linearization	2^{102}	[BBDV20]*
	192	1			2^{153}	
	256	1			2^{204}	
Partial S-box layer	128	10	$0.8 \times \lfloor \frac{n}{s} \rfloor$	Linearization	2^{103}	[BBDV20]*
	192	10			2^{163}	
	256	10			2^{203}	
Full S-box layer	129	43	2	Equation solving	2^{102}	[Din]**
			3		2^{108}	
			4		2^{113}	
Full S-box layer	192	64	2	Equation solving	2^{153}	[Din]**
			3		2^{162}	
			4		2^{170}	
			5		2^{175}	
Full S-box layer	255	85	2	Equation solving	2^{204}	[Din]**
			3		2^{216}	
			4		2^{226}	
			5		2^{232}	
Full S-box layer	129	43	2	2-Stage MITM	$\mathbf{2^{81}}$	Sec 4
	192	64			$\mathbf{2^{122}}$	
	255	85			$\mathbf{2^{164}}$	
Full S-box layer	129	43	3	2-Stage MITM	$\mathbf{2^{123}}$	Sec 4
	192	64			$\mathbf{2^{186}}$	
	255	85			$\mathbf{2^{248}}$	
Partial S-box layer	128	1	$0.8 \times \lfloor \frac{n}{s} \rfloor$	2-Stage MITM	$\mathbf{2^{101}}$	Sec 5
	192	1			$\mathbf{2^{151}}$	
	256	1			$\mathbf{2^{202}}$	
Partial S-box layer	128	1	$\lfloor \frac{n}{s} \rfloor$	2-Stage MITM	$\mathbf{2^{125}}$	Sec 5
	192	1			$\mathbf{2^{189}}$	
	256	1			$\mathbf{2^{253}}$	
Partial S-box layer	128	10	$0.8 \times \lfloor \frac{n}{s} \rfloor$	2-Stage MITM	$\mathbf{2^{91}}$	Sec 5
	192	10			$\mathbf{2^{149}}$	
	256	10			$\mathbf{2^{188}}$	
Partial S-box layer	128	10	$\lfloor \frac{n}{s} \rfloor$	2-Stage MITM	$\mathbf{2^{111}}$	Sec 5
	192	10			$\mathbf{2^{179}}$	
	256	10			$\mathbf{2^{238}}$	

*Complexities recalculated and do not always match those reported in [BBDV20]

**[Din] reports complexities in bit operations. We recalculate them in number of encryptions.

used in the round function and key update are known. Note that in general instantiations of LowMC, the key size and block size are not the same. The whitening key and all the round keys are extracted by multiplying the master key with full rank matrices over $GF(2)$. However for all the instances of LowMC used in the LowMC challenge the block size and key size are the same. This being so, the lengths of the master key, whitening key and all the subsequent round keys are the same. Effectively, this makes all these keys related to each other by multiplication with an invertible matrix over $GF(2)$. Thus all round keys can be extracted by multiplying the whitening key with an invertible matrix. So for all practical purposes used in this paper, the whitening key can also be seen as the master secret key. This is true since given any candidate whitening key, all round keys can be generated from it, and thus given any known plaintext-ciphertext pair, it is possible to verify if that particular candidate key has been used to generate the corresponding plaintext/ciphertext pair. As such we use the terms master key/whitening key interchangeably.

The LowMC challenge specifies 9 challenge scenarios for key recovery given only 1 plaintext-ciphertext pair, i.e. the data complexity $d = 1$.

- **1.** $[n = 128, \ s = 1]$ **2.** $[n = 128, \ s = 10]$ **3.** $[n = 129, \ s = 43]$
- **4.** $[n = 192, \ s = 1]$ **5.** $[n = 192, \ s = 10]$ **6.** $[n = 192, \ s = 64]$
- **7.** $[n = 256, \ s = 1]$ **8.** $[n = 256, \ s = 10]$ **9.** $[n = 255, \ s = 85]$

The number of rounds r for instances with the full S-box layer is either 2, 3, or 4 and for instances with a partial S-box layer can vary between $0.8 \times \lfloor \frac{n}{s} \rfloor$, $\lfloor \frac{n}{s} \rfloor$ and $1.2 \times \lfloor \frac{n}{s} \rfloor$. When these are not integers, the number of rounds is taken as the next higher integer. The key length k for all instances is n bits. PICNIC v3.0 [Zav] incidentally uses LowMC instances with the parameter sets $[n, s, r]$ given by $[128, 10, 20]$, $[192, 10, 30]$, $[256, 10, 38]$ (partial S-box layer) and $[129, 43, 4]$, $[192, 64, 4]$, $[255, 85, 4]$ (complete S-box layer) for use under different security levels.

3   Linearization Attack

The starting point of the attack in [BBDV20] was the following lemma that helps linearize the LowMC S-box by guessing only one balanced quadratic expression on its input bits.

Lemma 1. *[BBDV20] Consider the LowMC S-box S defined over the input bits x_0, x_1, x_2. If we guess the value of any 3-variable quadratic Boolean function f which is balanced over the input bits of the S-box, then it is possible to re-write the S-box as affine function of its input bits.*

The authors used the majority function $f = x_0 x_1 + x_1 x_2 + x_0 x_2$ for this purpose which is both quadratic and balanced. This is true since the LowMC S-box output bits can be written as:

$$s_0 = x_0 + x_1 \cdot x_2 \qquad\qquad = f \cdot (x_1 + x_2 + 1) + x_0,$$
$$s_1 = x_0 + x_1 + x_0 \cdot x_2 \qquad = f \cdot (x_0 + x_2 + 1) + x_0 + x_1,$$
$$s_2 = x_0 + x_1 + x_2 + x_0 \cdot x_1 \qquad = f \cdot (x_0 + x_1 + 1) + x_0 + x_1 + x_2.$$

The same is true for the inverse LowMC S-box (which is incidentally affine equivalent to the forward S-box):

$$t_0 = x_0 + x_1 + x_1 \cdot x_2 \qquad = f \cdot (x_1 + x_2 + 1) + x_0 + x_1,$$
$$t_1 = x_1 + x_0 \cdot x_2 \qquad\qquad = f \cdot (x_0 + x_2 + 1) + x_1,$$
$$t_2 = x_0 + x_1 + x_2 + x_0 \cdot x_1 \qquad = f \cdot (x_0 + x_1 + 1) + x_0 + x_1 + x_2.$$

Using the above fact, the first attack proposed in [BBDV20] used only the linearization technique to obtain affine equations relating plaintext and ciphertext. The idea is as follows. The values of the majority function at the input of all the S-boxes in the encryption circuit were guessed: this made expression relating the plaintext and ciphertext completely linear in the key variables, i.e. of the form:

$$A \cdot [k_0, k_1, \ldots, k_{n-1}]^T = const, \tag{1}$$

where A is an $n \times n$ matrix over $GF(2)$. Thereafter the key could be found by using Gaussian elimination. A wrong key found by this method could be discarded by recalculating the encryption and checking if the given plaintext mapped to the given ciphertext.

The above method would work if the total number of S-boxes in the encryption circuit is strictly less than the size of the key in bits. This happens for **a)** 2-round LowMC with complete non-linear layers and **b)** $0.8 \times \lfloor \frac{n}{s} \rfloor$-round LowMC with partial non-linear layers. However the authors pointed out 2 issues in this approach:

1. If the total number of S-boxes in the encryption circuit is t, then the algorithm requires in the worst case requires at least 2^t computations of the encryption function (for the verification of each computed candidate key). It additionally requires 2^t Gaussian elimination calculations. For large blocksizes, the authors claimed this could prove to be a significant bottleneck.
2. For any guess of the majority values, the matrix A computed above may not necessarily be invertible. If the dimension of the kernel of the matrix A is d_A, then we can see that $O(2^{d_A})$ keys would satisfy any equation of the form $A \cdot K = const$. Thus the verification would require running the verification for 2^{d_A} candidate keys.

The authors could not find a closed form for the value of d_A and so could not assign a tight bound on the computational complexity incurred in this approach. However we find that some of these issues can be resolved to get a closed form expression of the complexity of the linearization algorithm. First of all, the expected number of solutions for the system $A \cdot [k_0, k_1, \ldots, k_{n-1}]^T = const$ is 1 if the system is random. If $const$ lies in the image of the linear transformation defined by A then the system has 2^{d_A} solutions, and it has 0 solutions otherwise. Now the probability that $const$ lies in the image of A is exactly 2^{-d_A} and so the average number of solutions by Bayes theorem is $2^{d_A} \cdot 2^{-d_A} + (1 - 2^{-d_A}) \cdot 0 = 1$, and testing this solution costs us one encryption.

Note that multiplying an $n \times n$ matrix with an n-bit column vector requires n^2 bit operations. Every LowMC round therefore requires at least $2n^2$ bit operations (n^2 for computing the affine layer and another n^2 for generating the round key). Assuming calculation of the S-box layer can be done in linear time using a lookup table and also since key xor with state also takes linear time, the sum total of all the other bit operations in the round are linear in n. Suppressing these, the total bit operations required in performing a LowMC encryption is around $2rn^2$. Solving a system of linear equations by Gaussian elimination (GE) costs around n^3 bit operations which is equivalent to $\frac{n^3}{2rn^2} = \frac{n}{2r}$ encryptions.

Also note the computational complexity required to formulate the linear system $A \cdot [k_0, k_1, \ldots, k_{n-1}]^T = const$. We argue that this is equivalent to n encryptions. After guessing the majority bits, the system becomes completely linear. Therefore finding the i-th column of A and the i-th bit of $const$ is equivalent to performing one encryption with the basis key vector $[0, 0, \ldots, k_i, \ldots, 0, 0]$. Hence the result follows. Therefore the total computational complexity required to perform the attack using only linearization in terms of number of encryptions is

$$2^{rs} \text{ (Guessing majority bits)} \times [\, n \text{ (Formulating the linear system)} +$$
$$\frac{n}{2r} \text{ (Solving the linear system)} +$$
$$1 \text{ (Testing one solution on average)}].$$

We can simplify this to $n \cdot 2^{rs}$ encryptions. Also note that 2^{rs} is the worst case complexity for guessing rs bits. The average case complexity is 2^{rs-1}. However since we want to compare this complexity to the complexity of exhaustive search 2^n which is also a worst case complexity we use 2^{rs} for all our complexity estimations.

3.1 Improving Complexity Using Gray-Code Based Approach

The above complexity can be significantly improved if one were to make the majority guesses in a Gray-code like manner. Recall that the encoding is defined as follows: **Graycode**$(i) = i \oplus (i \gg 1)$. Note that hamming difference between **Graycode**(i) and **Graycode**$(i + 1)$ is always 1 for all values of i. The idea is instead of ordering the majority guesses in lexicographic order, we use the order defined by the Gray-code, i.e. in the i-th step the majority guess sequence is the binary string defined by the bits of **Graycode**(i). When this is done the matrix A defined above, changes very little from iteration i to $i + 1$. Thus having already constructed A in the i-th iteration, the corresponding construction in the $i+1$-th iteration can be done much faster and so the cost of formulating the linear system of equations defined by Eq. (1) can be amortized over all the majority guesses.

Let us state the algorithm formally. Let $M = m_0, m_1, \ldots, m_{s-1}, \; m_s, m_{s+1},$ $\ldots, m_{2s-1}, \ldots, m_{(r-1)s}, m_{(r-1)s+1}, \ldots, m_{rs-1}$ be the rs majority guesses for the s number of S-boxes in each of the r rounds. Let M_i denote the value of the string M at the i-th iteration which we want to be equal to **Graycode**(i). Let the linearized system of equations at the i-th iteration be denoted as $A_i \cdot k = c_i$. We want to determine how A_{i+1}, c_{i+1} relate with respect to A_i, c_i. Let $x \to Tx \oplus v$ be the linear map from $\{0,1\}^n \to \{0,1\}^n$ that is obtained as a result of linearizing the S-boxes in any single round with the majority value string Str (note that T is an $n \times n$ matrix and v is a n-element vector). Let $x \to T'x + v'$ be the corresponding map when the majority string is $Str \oplus \mathbf{e}_t$ (here $\mathbf{e}_t$ denotes the t-th unit vector of length s and $0 \le t < s$). Then we define $\Delta_t = T \oplus T'$ and $\lambda_t = v \oplus v'$, so that $\Delta_t x + \lambda_t$ denotes the change of linear map when the majority guess changes at the t-th S-box.

Let L_a denote the $n \times n$ matrix used in the linear layer in the a-th round (with $1 \le a \le r$). Also, let **Graycode**$(i) \oplus$ **Graycode**$(i+1) = \mathbf{e}_j$ for some j (by slight abuse of notation $\mathbf{e}_j$ here denotes the j-th unit vector of length rs). If $j < s$, then it can be deduced that $A_i \oplus A_{i+1} = (\prod_{a=1}^r L_a) \cdot \Delta_j := B_j$ (say) and $c_i \oplus c_{i+1} = (\prod_{a=1}^r L_a) \cdot \lambda_j := b_j$. If $j \in [(u-1)s, us-1]$, which means that the change of majority guess occurs in the u-th round, then denote $j' = j - (u-1)s$. B_j is now defined as $A_i \oplus A_{i+1} = (\prod_{a=u}^r L_a) \cdot \Delta_{j'}$ and $b_j = (\prod_{a=u}^r L_a) \cdot \lambda_{j'}$. Note that it is thus possible to precompute for all $j \in [0, rs-1]$ the matrix-vector pair (B_j, b_j) before the linearization step begins. Thus the linearization attack can be restated as follows:

1. For all $j \in [0, rs-1]$ precompute the matrix-vector pair (B_j, b_j).
2. Compute A_0, c_0 and try to solve the system $A_0 \cdot k = c_0$ using GE.
3. For $i = 1 \to 2^n - 1$ do
   - The majority guess is $M_i = $ **Graycode**(i).
   - Let **Graycode**$(i) \oplus$ **Graycode**$(i-1) = \mathbf{e}_j$.
   - Calculate $A_i = A_{i-1} \oplus B_j$ and $c_i = c_{i-1} \oplus b_j$.
   - Try to solve the system $A_i \cdot k = c_i$ using GE.

Note that since none of the B_j's are sparse matrices, we can not devise a quicker method of doing GE on A_i from the knowledge of steps involved in the GE of A_{i-1}. The additional complexity of constructing A_i, c_i at each step is given by a matrix and vector addition and so equal to $n^2 + n$ bit operations which roughly corresponds to $\frac{n^2+n}{2rn^2} \approx \frac{1}{2r}$ encryption operations. Thus if P denotes the cost involved in pre-computation (which is at most a polynomial in rs) then the total complexity of the method can be written as $P + 2^{rs} \cdot (\frac{n}{2r} + 1 + \frac{1}{2r}) \approx \frac{n}{2r} \cdot 2^{rs}$ encryptions which gives us an improvement of a factor of $2r$ over the naive linearization method of the previous subsection. We have recalculated the complexities in Table 1 using this expression.

4   Attacking Instances with Complete S-Box Layers

4.1   MITM Attack on 2-Round LowMC in [BBDV20]

Before we present our attack, let us summarize the attack in [BBDV20] for better understanding of the process. The attack is summarized in Fig. 2. The idea is as follows: let us denote $K = [k_0, k_1, \ldots, k_{n-1}]$ to be the whitening key or the master key. Let us split the key into two parts $K_1 = [k_0, \ldots, k_{t-1}]^T$ and $K_2 = [k_t, \ldots, k_{n-1}]^T$, each of around $t \approx \frac{n}{2}$ bits. We denote by R_1, R_2 the first and second round functions i.e. $R_1(pt + K, RK_1) = x$ and $R_2(x, RK_2) = ct$, where x denotes the n-bit input to the second round and RK_1, RK_2 denotes the first, second round keys, respectively, which are of course linear functions of the whitening key K.

The idea is to formulate equations for the bits of x from both the plaintext and ciphertext side. Let us begin from the plaintext in the forward direction. Note that K_1 and K_2 have to be chosen so that the bits of K_1 and K_2 are never multiplied in the first round function. For example if the number of S-boxes in each round $s = n/3$ is odd, then t can be chosen to be $3(s-1)/2$ (else $t = 3s/2$). This way, K_1 and K_2 both contain close to $n/2$ key bits: the bits of K_1 after whitening are input to the first $(s - 1)/2$ S-boxes and K_2 to the remaining $(s + 1)/2$ S-boxes if s is odd (else both are input to $s/2$ S-boxes each). The

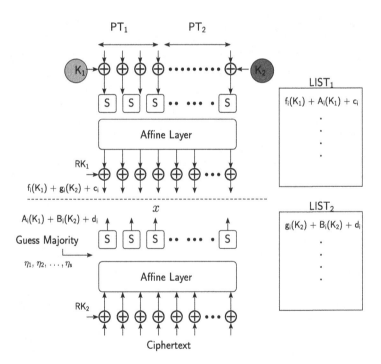

Fig. 2. Meet in the Middle attack in [BBDV20]

only source of non-linearity in the first round are the S-boxes, and each S-box either gets the bits of K_1 or K_2 as inputs and so K_1 and K_2 are not mixed in a multiplicative sense in this round. This being the case, after the affine layer and addition of RK_1, each bit x_i can be written as $f_i(K_1) + g_i(K_2) + c_i$ where each f_i, g_i are at most quadratic functions over K_1, K_2 and c_i is a single bit constant.

Now let us consider the expression for x from the ciphertext side in the backward direction. To do this we first perform the inverse affine function operation on the vector $ct \oplus RK_2$ (where RK_2 is expressed in terms of K_1 and K_2). Thereafter we guess the s majority bits $\eta_1, \ldots, \eta_s$ at the input of the second round inverse S-boxes to linearize R_2. After this, each bit of x can be written as an affine function of the key and the ciphertext. In fact each x_i can be further written as $x_i = A_i(K_1) + B_i(K_2) + d_i$, $\forall\, i \in [0, n-1]$, where each A_i, B_i are linear functions over K_1, K_2 and d_i is a single bit constant. Given the equality $x_i = f_i(K_1) + g_i(K_2) + c_i = A_i(K_1) + B_i(K_2) + d_i$, we can rearrange the terms to get:

$$f_i(K_1) + A_i(K_1) + c_i = g_i(K_2) + B_i(K_2) + d_i, \ \forall\, i \in [0, n-1].$$

Thereafter the attack is straightforward: first the algebraic expressions of f_i, g_i and c_i for all $i \in [0, n-1]$ are calculated. Then for each of the 2^s guesses of the second round majority values:

1. A hash table $LIST_1$ indexed by the n-bit vector $[f_i(K_1) \oplus A_i(K_1) \oplus c_i]$, $\forall\, i \in [0, n-1]$ is created (2^t evaluations). Note that each evaluation is done for only t of the n key variables and costs roughly $\frac{t}{n}$ of a round computation. Hence the computational complexity incurred in this step is $\frac{t}{4n} \cdot 2^t$ encryptions. Let us argue this point more closely. Note that in the above expression the $f_i(K_1)$ terms are always constant and does not change with every new guess of majority values. Thus we do not have to re-calculate it every new majority guess, and so this expression ($\forall\, i \in [0, n-1]$) can be calculated once and stored in a table. The part that varies with every new majority guess is $A_i(K_1) \oplus c_i$: note that calculating the n bit-values $A_i(K_1)$ is equivalent to a matrix-vector multiplication between a $n \times t$ matrix and the t-element vector K_1 and thus takes around nt bit operations. Adding c_i and the precomputed $f_i(K_1)$ requires $2n$ more bit operations and so a total of $nt + 2n$ bit operations are required at every step. Since $2rn^2 = 4n^2$ bit operations are required in a single 2-round LowMC encryption, this corresponds to $\frac{nt+2n}{4n^2} \approx \frac{t}{4n}$ encryptions, and so the result follows.
2. A hash table $LIST_2$ indexed by the n-bit vector $[g_i(K_2) \oplus B_i(K_2) \oplus d_i]$, $\forall\, i \in [0, n-1]$ is created (2^{n-t} evaluations). By following the previous logic this is computationally equivalent to $\frac{n-t}{4n} \cdot 2^{n-t}$ encryptions.

As a final remark, note that the complexity required to formulate the expressions $x_i = A_i(K_1) + B_i(K_2) + d_i$ and hence $f_i(K_1) + A_i(K_1) + c_i$ and $g_i(K_2) + B_i(K_2) + d_i$ is around $O(n)$ encryptions as explained in the previous section. However, this only appears as an additive term along with $\frac{t}{4n} \cdot 2^t$ and $\frac{n-t}{4n} \cdot 2^{n-t}$ and since it is much less as compared to both these terms, it can be ignored for simplicity.

Although, it was not mentioned in [BBDV20], a Gray-code like approach as outlined in Sec 3.1 may be adopted here too, but since the cost of formulating the linear system is not the dominant term in the final complexity estimate, it does not reduce the computational cost significantly.

A collision in the 2 lists gives us a candidate key and there are on average $2^t \cdot 2^{n-t} \cdot 2^{-n} = 1$ collisions in every MITM stage. Then a check is performed to see if the majority bits calculated for this candidate key are consistent with the initial guess $\eta_1, \ldots, \eta_s$. If yes, the attack terminates. The total complexity for the steps inside the iterations is given as $T = 2^s \cdot (\frac{t}{4n} \cdot 2^t + \frac{n-t}{4n} \cdot 2^{n-t})$ encryptions.

The cost for precomputing the values $f_i(K_1)$ and $g_i(K_2)$ over all the points in their input spaces can be done by using Möbius transforms over the respective algebraic forms. Since any t variable Boolean function can be evaluated in $t \cdot 2^{t-1}$ bit operations using this method, the total complexity of evaluating them is around $n \cdot (\frac{t}{2} \cdot 2^t + \frac{(n-t)}{2} \cdot 2^{n-t})$ bit-operations. This is considerably lower than the complexity T of the MITM part. Specifically, for $n = 129$, we can take $t = 63$ and $n - t = 66$. The total complexity of the attack is around $2^{43} \cdot (2^{60} + 2^{63}) \approx 2^{43+63} = 2^{106}$ encryptions.

4.2   2-Stage MITM Attack on 2-Rounds with Full S-Box Layer

After guessing the majority bits of the second round and linearizing it, we have already seen that the algebraic relation between the plaintext and ciphertext can be written as

$$f_i(K_1) + A_i(K_1) + c_i = g_i(K_2) + B_i(K_2) + d_i, \ \forall \ i \in [0, n-1]. \tag{2}$$

Note that the functions A_i, B_i are linear and f_i, g_i are quadratic. It can be seen that for Eq. (2) to hold we need not split K in such a way that K_1 and K_2 have approximately $n/2$ bits. We can, for example, also split K so that K_1 has around $n/3$ and K_2 has around $2n/3$ bits. The only condition that must be satisfied is that the sizes of K_1 and K_2 are chosen so that they are never mixed multiplicatively in the first round. It is easy to see that if we choose $t = |K_1|$ and $n - t = |K_2|$ to be multiples of 3 then this condition is automatically satisfied.

Note that, f_i, g_i can be expressed as affine functions in an extension of the input of double size. This comes from the structure of the Sbox: $S(x_0, x_1, x_2)$ is an affine function on $(x_0, x_1, x_2, x_0 x_1, x_1 x_2, x_2 x_0)$. Let $\overline{f}_i, \overline{g}_i$ be the affine functions associated with f_i, g_i. Therefore the above set of equations can be written as

$$\overline{f}_i(\overline{K}_1) + A_i(\overline{K}_1) + c_i + d_i = g_i(K_2) + B_i(K_2), \ \forall \ i \in [0, n-1], \tag{3}$$

where if $K_1 = [k_0, k_1, k_2, \ldots, k_{3w-3}, k_{3w-2}, k_{3w-1}]$, we define

$$\overline{K}_1 = [k_0, k_1, k_2, k_0 k_1, k_1 k_2, k_2 k_0, \ldots \ldots \ldots, k_{3w-3}, k_{3w-2}, k_{3w-1},$$
$$k_{3w-3} k_{3w-2}, k_{3w-2} k_{3w-1}, k_{3w-1} k_{3w-3}].$$

Since K_1 only has the first $t = 3w$ bits of the master key and so $\overline{K}_1$ is of size $6w$. Since $F_i = \overline{f}_i + A_i$ is an affine function over $\overline{K}_1$, the map $\phi : \overline{K}_1 \rightarrow$

$[F_0, F_1, \ldots, F_{n-1}]$ can be seen as a linear code of length n and dimension $6w$. Let w be such that K_1 contains around $n/3$ key bits i.e. $w \approx n/9$ and hence K_2 contains the remaining $2n/3$ key bits. Since ϕ is seen as a linear code, let $\mathbf{G}$ be the corresponding generator matrix (of size $n \times 6w \approx n \times 2n/3$), which can be efficiently constructed from the algebraic forms of the functions F_i. Let $\mathbf{H}$ be the parity check matrix of the code (of size $(n - 6w) \times n \approx n/3 \times n$). The parity check matrix is essentially obtained from the generator matrix by employing one Gaussian elimination. Define Con to be the vector $[c_0 + d_0, c_1 + d_1, \ldots c_{n-1} + d_{n-1}]^T$. Note that the left side of Eq. (3), when written in matrix notation for all $i = 0, 1, \ldots, n - 1$ is essentially $\phi(\overline{K}_1) + Con$. Therefore we have $\mathbf{H} \cdot [\phi(\overline{K}_1) + Con] = \mathbf{H} \cdot [\mathbf{G}\overline{K}_1 + Con] = \mathbf{H} \cdot Con = e$ (say). This follows from the fact that since $\mathbf{G}$ and $\mathbf{H}$ are the generator and parity check matrices of a linear code, we must have $\mathbf{H} \cdot \mathbf{G} = 0$.

We can split K_2 into two halves K_{21} and K_{22} such that both halves contain approximately $n/3$ key bits each. Let's say $|K_{21}| = 3u$ and $|K_{22}| = n - 3w - 3u$ (our strategy would be to have $3u \approx n - 3w - 3u$ so that the halves are of equal size). We can rewrite $g_i(K_2) + B_i(K_2)$ as $g_i^1(K_{21}) + B_i^1(K_{21}) + g_i^2(K_{22}) + B_i^2(K_{22})$ for all $i \in [0, n-1]$, where g_i^j are quadratic and B_i^j are linear for $j = 1, 2$. Again this is possible if we take $|K_{21}|$ and $|K_{22}|$ to be multiples of 3, so that the bits of K_{21} and K_{22} after xor with the plaintext are input to different S-boxes. Due to the structure of LowMC, the quadratic terms from adjacent S-boxes do not combine multiplicatively after one round and so the separation into the 2 expressions is possible. Define the n-bit vectors:

$$M_1 = [g_0^1(K_{21}) + B_0^1(K_{21}), \ldots, g_{n-1}^1(K_{21}) + B_{n-1}^1(K_{21})]^T, \text{ and}$$
$$M_2 = [g_0^2(K_{22}) + B_0^2(K_{22}), \ldots, g_{n-1}^2(K_{22}) + B_{n-1}^2(K_{22})]^T.$$

Note that if Eq. (3) for $i = 0, 1, \ldots, n - 1$, can be written together as a vector equation. The right hand side of the vector equation is essentially $M_1 + M_2$. We have already seen that the left hand side of the vector equation when multiplied by $\mathbf{H}$ results in the vector $\mathbf{H} \cdot Con = e$. Multiplying the right side of the vector equation by $\mathbf{H}$, we get the matrix equation:

$$\mathbf{H} \cdot (M_1 + M_2) = e, \ \Rightarrow \mathbf{H} \cdot M_1 = \mathbf{H} \cdot M_2 + e.$$

Pre-computation: In this phase we try and compute some expressions that remain constant over different majority guesses. We compute the following vectorial functions over all points over its input space: **(a)** $f_i(K_1)$, $\forall i \in [0, n-1]$ over input space of K_1 i.e. $\{0,1\}^{3w}$, **(b)** $g_i^1(K_{21})$, $\forall i \in [0, n-1]$ over input space of K_{21} i.e. $\{0,1\}^{3u}$ and **(c)** $g_i^2(K_{22})$, $\forall i \in [0, n-1]$ over input space of K_{22} i.e. $\{0,1\}^{n-3u-3w}$. Using Möbius transform the number of bit-operations required are

$$n \cdot \left(\frac{3w}{2} \cdot 2^{3w} + \frac{3u}{2} \cdot 2^{3u} + \frac{n - 3u - 3w}{2} \cdot 2^{n-3u-3w} \right).$$

This follows since any t-variable Boolean polynomial can be evaluated over all its input space using Möbius transform using $t \cdot 2^{t-1}$ bit operations.

1st MITM Stage: Note that M_1 and M_2 only contain expressions on the key bits in the sets K_{21} and K_{22} respectively. Thus we can conduct a first MITM stage in which we create 2 lists L_1, L_2. L_1 contains the $(n - 6w)$, n-bit vector pairs $\mathbf{H} \cdot M_1$, M_1 for all 2^{3u} values of K_{21}. And similarly the list L_2 contains the $(n - 6w), n$-bit vector pairs $\mathbf{H} \cdot M_2 + e, M_2$ for all $2^{n-3w-3u}$ values of K_{22}. We look for a collision in the $n - 6w$ co-ordinates of these lists. We are expected to get around $2^{3u+(n-3w-3u)-(n-6w)} \approx 2^{3w}$ collisions. Thus in the process we get 2^{3w} key values for the key bit set $K_2 = (K_{21}, K_{22})$. For computing each entry in the list L_1 we do the following:

1. Compute the vectorial linear functions $B_0^1, B_1^1, \ldots, B_{n-1}^1$ over a given point k in K_{21}. Each such computation takes $|K_{21}| \cdot n = 3un$ bit operations.
2. Add to the corresponding precomputed vector $g_i^1(k)$, $\forall i \in [0, n - 1]$. This requires n bit operations.
3. Multiply by $\mathbf{H}$. Each such computation takes $(n - 6w) \cdot n$ bit operations.

This is computationally equivalent to $\frac{3un+n+(n-6w)n}{2rn^2} \approx \frac{3u+n-6w}{4n}$ of an encryption for $r = 2$. A similar argument holds for L_2. Hence the total computational cost incurred in this step is $\frac{3u+n-6w}{4n} \cdot 2^{3u} + \frac{2n-9w-3u}{4n} \cdot 2^{n-3w-3u}$ encryptions.

2nd MITM: Let us now turn to Eq. (2). The left side of this equation is defined over approximately the $3w$-bit set K_1 which can have 2^{3w} values in total. And we have just reduced K_2 to a set of 2^{3w} values. Thus the next MITM is making two more lists L_3, L_4 of size 2^{3w} each in the following way. L_3 contains all 2^{3w} n-bit vectors $[f_i(K_1) \oplus A_i(K_1) \oplus c_i \oplus d_i]$, $\forall i \in [0, n-1]$ enumerated for all the 2^{3w} values of K_1. For all the 2^{3w} values of K_2 that have passed the previous MITM step we make the list L_4 containing the n-bit vector $[g_i(K_2) \oplus B_i(K_2)]$, $\forall i \in [0, n - 1]$. We now look for a collision between L_3 and L_4. On average we have $2^{3w+3w-n} = 2^{6w-n} < 1$ collisions. This means that the correct key K will necessarily by the output of one of these MITM steps for the correct guess of majority bits in the second round. For constructing L_3 we need to compute the n linear functions $A_i(K_1)$ over the $3w$-bit variable K_1 which by the previous logic, requires $3wn$ bit operations each and then n bit operations for addition to the precomputed vector $f_i(K_1)$. Populating L_4 requires computing $[g_i(K_2) \oplus B_i(K_2)]$ for all the K_2 that have passed the previous MITM step. However we can compute this vector by simply adding the M_1, M_2 vectors that have collided in the previous MITM stage. This stage therefore requires $\frac{3wn+n}{4n^2} \cdot 2^{3w} + \frac{n}{4n^2} \cdot 2^{3w} \approx \frac{3w}{4n} \cdot 2^{3w}$ encryptions. We are now ready to state the attack formally:

1. Calculate the functional forms of $f_i, g_i, \overline{f}_i, g_i^1, g_i^2$ and c_i for all $i \in [0, n - 1]$.
2. Pre-compute $f_i(K_1)$, $g_i^1(K_{21})$, $g_i^2(K_{22})$, $\forall i \in [0, n - 1]$ over their respective input spaces.
3. Guess the majority values $\eta_1, \ldots, \eta_s$ at the output of 2nd round S-box layer as in the previous attack. This step is done 2^s times in the worst case (note $s = n/3$).
   - Compute A_i, B_i, d_i for all $i \in [0, n - 1]$ using the guessed values.
   - Compute the functions $F_i = \overline{f}_i + A_i$ for all $i \in [0, n - 1]$.

- Using the F_i's, construct the generator matrix $\mathbf{G}$.
- Using Gaussian elimination, construct the parity check matrix $\mathbf{H}$.
- Construct $Con = [c_0 + d_0, c_1 + d_1, \ldots c_{n-1} + d_{n-1}]^T$, and $e = \mathbf{H} \cdot Con$.
- For all possible values of K_{21}, create a hash table L_1 indexed by the $(n - 6w)$-bit vector $\mathbf{H} \cdot M_1$.
- For all possible values of K_{22}, create a hash table L_2 indexed by the $(n - 6w)$-bit vector $\mathbf{H} \cdot M_2 + e$.
- Find all collisions between L_1 and L_2. Store all values of K_{21}, K_{22} extracted from the collision in a list L.
- For all possible values of K_1, create a hash table L_3 indexed by the n-bit vector $[f_i(K_1) \oplus A_i(K_1) \oplus c_i \oplus d_i]$, $\forall\, i \in [0, n-1]$.
- For all values of $K_2 \in L$, create a hash table L_4 indexed by the n-bit vector $[g_i(K_2) \oplus B_i(K_2)]$, $\forall\, i \in [0, n-1]$.
- When a collision is found for K_1 and K_2 check if the majority bits are consistent with the guess of the key. If yes, this key is in fact the encryption key. Otherwise try another guess of $\eta_1, \ldots, \eta_s$.

Complexity Estimation: We first consider the time complexity. For each guess of $2^s = 2^{n/3}$ majority values, we have to perform a Gaussian elimination and 2 MITM steps. The cost of Gaussian elimination and the linear terms required to formulate A_i, B_i, d_i and pre-computation may be ignored in comparison with $2^{n/3}$. Hence the total time complexity for this attack is around

$$2^{n/3} \cdot \left(\frac{3u + n - 6w}{4n} \cdot 2^{3u} + \frac{2n - 9w - 3u}{4n} \cdot 2^{n-3w-3u} + \frac{3w}{4n} \cdot 2^{3w} \right). \quad (4)$$

For $w = u = n/9$, the above evaluates to $2^{n/3} \cdot ((\frac{1}{6} + \frac{1}{6} + \frac{1}{12}) \cdot 2^{n/3}) = \frac{5}{12} \cdot 2^{2n/3} \approx 2^{2n/3 - 1.26}$ encryptions.

Memory Complexity: In the first MITM stage, we created 2 lists L_1, L_2 which contain $(n - 6w)$, n-bit vector pairs for 2^{3u} possible values of K_{21} and $(n - 6w)$, n-bit vector pairs for $2^{n-3w-3u}$ possible values of K_{22}, respectively. Note that in practice, 2 different lists are not necessary. We can instead insert each new vector of L_1 and L_2 into a single hash table. The memory complexity here is $(2n - 6w) \cdot (2^{3u} + 2^{n-3w-3u})$ bits. In the second MITM stage, we create 2 more lists L_3, L_4, both containing 2^{3w} n-bit vectors. By similar logic, memory complexity here is thereby $2n \cdot 2^{3w}$ bits. The pre-computation part generates n-bit vectors over the input spaces of K_1, K_{21}, K_{22}. Hence the memory complexity here is $n \cdot (2^{3w} + 2^{3u} + 2^{n-3u-3w})$ bits. The total memory complexity for this attack is around

$$(2n - 6w) \cdot (2^{3u} + 2^{n-3w-3u}) + 2n \cdot 2^{3w} + n \cdot (2^{3w} + 2^{3u} + 2^{n-3u-3w}) \text{ bits.} \quad (5)$$

If we look at concrete parameters, for $n = 129$ and $s = 43$, we can choose the parameters in the following manner: we can choose $w = u = 14$, which makes $|K_1| = 42$ and $|K_2| = 87$ and hence $|K_{21}| = 42$ and $|K_{22}| = 45$. The parity check matrix $\mathbf{H}$ is of size $(n - 6w) \times n = 45 \times 129$, which makes $\mathbf{H} \cdot M_1$

and $\mathbf{H} \cdot M_2 + e$ both 45-bit vectors. After the first MITM stage the number of remaining candidates for K_2 is $\approx 2^{|K_{21}|+|K_{22}|-45} = 2^{42}$. The complexity of the first MITM stage is thus $\frac{1}{6} \cdot (2^{45} + 2^{42}) \approx \frac{1}{6} \cdot 2^{45} \approx 2^{42.4}$ encryptions. The second MITM stage requires $\frac{1}{12} \cdot 2^{42} = 2^{38.4}$ encryptions. Hence the total attack complexity is $2^s \cdot (2^{42.4} + 2^{38.4}) \approx 2^{85}$ encryptions and around 2^{53} bits of memory. This is lower than the linearization attack by a factor of 2^6 for this LowMC instance.

4.3   Extending Attack to 3-Rounds

The attack can be extended to 3-round LowMC in which we keep the basic character of the algorithm and run it by guessing the majority values of the last 2 rounds and linearizing both of them simultaneously. Hence a total of 2^{2s} values would need to be guessed in stead of 2^s. All other steps remain the same. Thus the computational complexity will be given by:

$$2^{2n/3} \cdot \left(\frac{3u + n - 6w}{6n} \cdot 2^{3u} + \frac{2n - 9w - 3u}{6n} \cdot 2^{n-3w-3u} + \frac{3w}{6n} \cdot 2^{3w} \right).$$

This is so since encryption is now given by $2rn^2 = 6n^2$ bit operations. The memory complexity is essentially the same as in the 2-round attack. For $w = u = n/9$, the above evaluate of computational complexity is $2^{2n/3} \cdot ((\frac{1}{9} + \frac{1}{9} + \frac{1}{18}) \cdot 2^{n/3}) \approx \frac{5}{18} \cdot 2^n$ encryptions, which is better than exhaustive search by a factor equal to approximately 2 bits. For $n = 129$ and $s = 43$, using the values $w = 14$, $|K_1| = 42$, $|K_{21}| = 42$ and $|K_{22}| = 45$, we get $\frac{1}{9} \cdot (2^{45} + 2^{42}) \approx 2^{41.8}$ encryptions for the first MITM. The second MITM requires $\frac{1}{18} \cdot 2^{42} \approx 2^{37.8}$ encryptions. The total complexity is therefore $2^{2s} \cdot (2^{41.8} + 2^{37.8}) \approx 2^{128}$ encryptions.

4.4   Speedup Using Gray-Codes

There are 3 places in the above process where a speed-up may be applied using a Gray-code like approach.

1. By ordering the majority guesses in a Gray-code like manner as in Sec 3.1 so that the affine expressions formed after linearizing the S-boxes can be generated more efficiently. But we have already seen that this does not result in significant speed-up when employed along with MITM.
2. Using a Gray-code like approach to do the pre-computations.
3. Using a Gray-code like approach to generate the values of the expressions that are inserted in the tables in each of the MITM stages. We will see how optimizing this stage results in significant speed-up.

There are several methods of evaluating an n-variable Boolean function over all the 2^n points of its input space, given its algebraic expression. One such method, as we have already seen is the Möbius transform which evaluates the function in-place by performing around $n \cdot 2^{n-1}$ bit operations. However the method we will use for this method is the Gray-code based approach suggested by [BCC+10] which finds all roots of a polynomial over GF(2) by evaluating it over all points of its input space by traversing the space in a Gray-code like manner. We start with the following theorem from [BCC+10].

Theorem 1. *[BCC+10] All the zeroes of a single multivariate polynomial f in n variables of degree d can be found in essentially $d \cdot 2^n$ bit operations (plus a negligible overhead), using n^{d-1} bits of read-write memory, and accessing n^d bits of constants, after an initialization phase of negligible complexity $O(n^{2d})$.*

We present a top-level overview of the approach used in this paper. Consider the derivative $\frac{\delta f}{\delta i} : \mathbf{x} \to f(\mathbf{x} + \mathbf{e}_i) \oplus f(\mathbf{x})$. Then for any vector $\mathbf{x}$, we have $f(\mathbf{x} + \mathbf{e}_i) = f(\mathbf{x}) \oplus \frac{\delta f}{\delta i}(\mathbf{x})$. If the algebraic degree of f is d then $\frac{\delta f}{\delta i}$ is of degree $d - 1$. Thus the idea is to calculate $\frac{\delta f}{\delta i}$ recursively for lower degrees till at the lowest level of recursion $\frac{\delta f}{\delta i}$ is a constant. Since we will only use this method to evaluate linear or quadratic functions, we will use the method outlined in [BCC+10, pg 209, Fig. (b)], that specifically caters to the case when f is of degree less than or equal to 2. When we use this approach to optimize the pre-computation part, we can evaluate each t-variable quadratic Boolean function in 2^{t+1} bit-operations. As a result the pre-computation cost can be brought down to $2n \cdot \left(2^{3w} + 2^{3u} + 2^{n-3u-3w}\right)$ bit-operations. However, note that the pre-computation is not the most dominant term in the total computational cost, and so this gives only a slight improvement.

We now see how we can improve the complexity of the MITM stages by using this approach. Note that we only evaluate linear functions inside the iterations for each majority guess. Since only 2^t bit-operations are required to evaluate any linear function using the Gray-code approach we can accelerate this part considerably. Note that in L_1 we need to store both $\mathbf{H} \cdot M_1$ and M_1. To do this, we begin by computing the quadratic expressions each one of the n bits M_1 and then each of the $(n - 6w)$-bits given by $\mathbf{H} \cdot M_1$. We use the Gray-code approach of [BCC+10], to evaluate these functions over all the points of their input domains. The number of bit operations required are therefore $n \cdot 2^{3u+1} + (n - 6w) \cdot 2^{3u+1} \approx \frac{2n-6w}{2rn^2} \cdot 2^{3u+1}$ encryptions. Similarly the list L_2 would require around $\frac{2n-6w}{2rn^2} \cdot 2^{n-3u-3w+1}$ encryptions.

The lists L_3, L_4 are simpler to construct. For L_3 we need to compute the n linear functions $A_i(K_1)$ which requires $n \cdot 2^{3w}$ bit operations each and then add to the precomputed vector $f_i(K_1)$. Populating L_4, as before can be done by simply adding the M_1, M_2 vectors that have collided in the previous MITM stage. This stage therefore requires $\frac{2n}{2rn^2} \cdot 2^{3w} + \frac{n}{2rn^2} \cdot 2^{3w} \approx \frac{3n}{2rn^2} \cdot 2^{3w}$ encryptions. This reduces the main terms of the computational complexity to

$$T = 2^{\frac{(r-1)n}{3}} \cdot \left(\frac{n - 3w}{rn^2} \cdot 2^{3u+1} + \frac{n - 3w}{rn^2} \cdot 2^{n-3u-3w+1} + \frac{3n}{2rn^2} \cdot 2^{3w}\right) \text{ encryptions}$$

For $n = 129$, $r = 2$ and $u = w = 14$, we have $T = 2^{80.7}$ encryptions. For $n = 129$, $r = 3$ and $u = w = 14$, we have $T = 2^{123.2}$ encryptions. The memory complexity of this attack is the same as the attack in the previous sub-section plus the additional cost for storing tables required for fast Gray-code based evaluations. Using Theorem 1, this additional memory is $(3u)^2 \cdot (2n - 6w) + (n - 3u - 3w)^2 \cdot (2n - 6w) + (3w) \cdot n$ bits which is negligible when compared to the space occupied by the lists.

5   2-Stage MITM Attack on Partial S-Box Layers

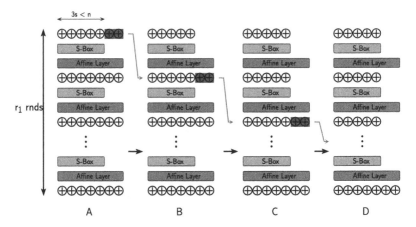

Fig. 3. Transforming the round function in the first r_1 rounds. From A → B, the key material not added to bits input to the S-box in round 1 (shown in orange background) are carried to the next round, through the affine layer and merged with the round key in round 2. B → C → D do the same from the second round onwards. Figure taken from [BBDV20] (Color figure online)

In order to perform a MITM on the partial S-box layer instances of LowMC, we use a trick used in both [BBDV20, RST18] to transform some of the initial and final rounds so that the total number of different key bits involved in these rounds is $3s$ per round. The transformations are shown in Figs. 3, 4 and are similar to the ones used in [RST18]. In fact the transform used in the backward direction (see Fig. 4) is exactly same as the one used in [RST18, Fig. 1]. The idea is that the affine layer and key addition are interchangeable. Since L is a linear function, we have $L(x) + K = L(x + L^{-1}(K))$ and similarly $L(x + K) = L(x) + L(K)$. Hence the key addition can be moved before or after the affine layer as required, by multiplying the round key by the appropriate matrix. Figure 3 further shows how to transform the first r_1 rounds. To mount this attack let us split the LowMC into 4 parts as shown in Fig. 5:

1. First $a + b$ rounds which have been transformed as per Fig. 3.
2. Final c rounds which have been transformed as per Fig. 4.
3. The remaining $d = r - a - b - c$ rounds which lie in between.

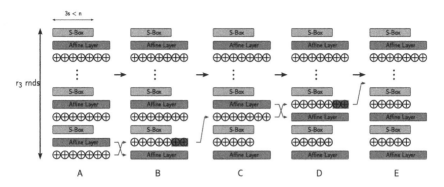

Fig. 4. Transforming the round function in the final r_3 rounds. A $\rightarrow$ B flips the order of the last round Affine layer and round key xor. B $\rightarrow$ C takes the bits of the last round key that are not added to S-box outputs (shown in orange background), and brings them back by 1 round and merges it with the penultimate round key. C $\rightarrow$ D flips the order of the Affine layer and round key of the penultimate round, and D $\rightarrow$ E generalizes the process from this point onwards. Figure taken from [BBDV20] (Color figure online)

Let the set of round key bits in the first a, b and the last c rounds be denoted as

$$K_a = [\kappa_0, \kappa_1, \ldots, \kappa_{3sa-1}], \quad K_b = [\kappa_{3sa}, \kappa_{3sa+1}, \ldots, \kappa_{3sa+3sb-1}], \text{ and}$$
$$K_c = [\kappa_{n-3sc}, \kappa_{n-3sc+1}, \ldots, \kappa_{n-1}].$$

Denote by K_{rem} the remaining $n - 3s(a + b + c)$ key bits such that K_a, K_b, K_c, and K_{rem} are linearly independent expressions of the master key and so any key bit can be expressed as a linear function of them. Note that we implicitly assume here that $n \geq 3s(a + b + c)$.

Let $X = [x_0, x_1, x_2, \ldots, x_{n-1}]$ be the output of the first a rounds, $W = [\omega_0, \omega_1, \ldots, \omega_{n-1}]$ be the output of the first $a+b$ rounds and $Y = [y_0, y_1, \ldots, y_{n-1}]$ be the input to the last c rounds as shown in Fig. 5. Observe the middle b and $d = r - a - b - c$ rounds closely, as seen in Fig. 6. Let us introduce $6b \cdot s$ new variables $U = [u_0, u_1, \ldots, u_{3bs-1}]$ and $Z = [z_0, z_1, \ldots, z_{3bs-1}]$ such that they represent the input and output bits of the $b \cdot s$ S-boxes in the middle b rounds. Our first aim is to find a linear expression relating the x_i's, y_i's and z_i's and the key bits. Let $D = [D_0, D_1, \ldots, D_{n-1}]$ be the output of the first of the b rounds (see Fig. 6). Then we can write $D = \text{Lin}_1(z_0, z_1, \ldots, z_{3s-1}, x_{3s}, x_{3s+1}, \ldots, x_{n-1})$, where Lin_1 denotes a set of n affine functions. Similarly, if $E = [E_0, E_1, \ldots, E_{n-1}]$ is the output of the next round we can write E as a set of linear functions on $(z_{3s}, z_{3s+1}, \ldots, z_{6s-1}, D_{3s}, D_{3s+1}, \ldots, D_{n-1})$ which means that we can write $E = \text{Lin}_2(z_0, z_1, \ldots, z_{6s-1}, x_{3s}, x_{3s+1}, \ldots, x_{n-1})$ as a set of linear functions on X and the first $6s$ z_i's. Iterating upto all the b rounds, it can be seen that W can be written as a set of linear functions on the entire Z and $x_{3s}, x_{3s+1}, \ldots, x_{n-1}$. Now if we guess the majority bits at the inputs of the following d rounds, they become completely linear. In that case Y itself becomes linear in W and K_a, K_b, K_c, K_{rem}

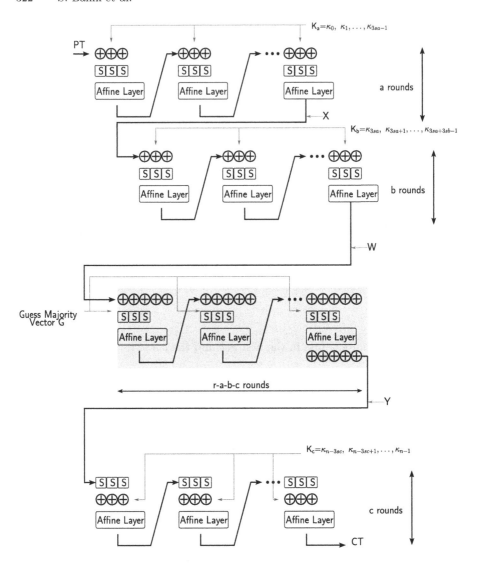

Fig. 5. Splitting LowMC into 4 sections

(since the key bits used in these d rounds can be seen as linear expressions in K_a, K_b, K_c, K_{rem}). Hence we have

$$Y = \mathsf{Lin}(Z, x_{3s}, x_{3s+1}, \ldots, x_{n-1}, K_a, K_b, K_c, K_{rem}). \tag{6}$$

The above equation denotes a system of n affine equations (one for each bit in Y) in all the n bits of the key. Our aim is to get a reduced set of equations by somehow eliminating Z, K_b, K_{rem} from this set. Note that the set $\Lambda = \{Z, K_b, K_{rem}\}$ comprises a total of $\theta = 3sb + 3sb + (n - 3s(a + b + c))$ variables. Consider the system of n equations given in Eq. (6). Apart from the θ variables the system has n (for Y) $+ (n - 3s)$ (for X) $+ (3as + 3cs)$ (for K_a, K_c) $= 2n + 3(a + c - 1)s$ variables. So the above system can be written in matrix notation as $\mathbb{M} \cdot \mathbf{v} = \mathbf{a}$, where $\mathbf{v}$ is the set of $2n + 3(a + c - 1)s + \theta = (3n + 3sb - 3s)$ variables, $\mathbb{M}$ is a matrix over $GF(2)$ of size $n \times (3n + 3sb - 3s)$, and $\mathbf{a}$ is a constant vector. Rearrange $\mathbf{v}$ so that the variables in Λ are the first θ elements of $\mathbf{v}$. Then we use Gaussian elimination to sweep out at least the first θ columns of $\mathbb{M}$. Then the last $n - \theta$ rows of the matrix would then have the entries in the first θ columns all equal to 0 and thus these are the linear equations in K_a, K_c, X, Y that we get from this process. Note we have a total of $n - \theta = 3sa + 3sc - 3sb$ equations of this form.

First MITM: The equations so obtained can be rearranged and written as $\mathbf{Aff}_1(K_a, X) = \mathbf{Aff}_2(K_c, Y)$, where $\mathbf{Aff}_1, \mathbf{Aff}_2$ are the set of $3sa + 3sc - 3sb$ affine functions on K_a, X and K_c, Y respectively, obtained above. We now state the first MITM step: note that if we guess the value of K_a, we can easily obtain the value of X by computing the forward a rounds from the plaintext. If we guess K_c we can similarly compute Y, by computing backward the last c rounds from the ciphertext. Hence for all the 2^{3sa} values of K_a we make the first list L_1 that contains all the $(3sa - 3sb + 3sc)$-bit vectors calculated from $\mathbf{Aff}_1(K_a, X)$. Similarly for all the 2^{3sc} values of K_c we make the second list L_2 that contains all the $3sa - 3sb + 3sc$-bit vectors calculated from $\mathbf{Aff}_2(K_c, Y)$. We look for collisions

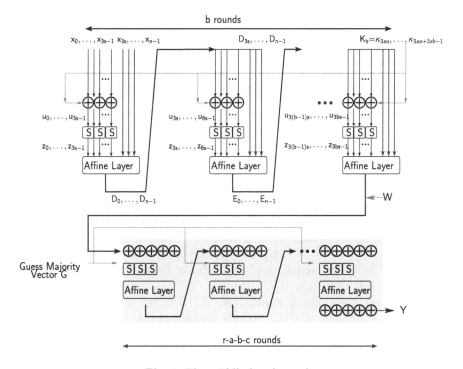

Fig. 6. The middle $b + d$ rounds

in the two lists. We can expect around $2^{3sa+3sc-(3sa-3sb+3sc)} = 2^{3sb}$ collisions. We store all the 2^{3sb} tuples (K_a, K_c) so obtained in a list L.

Second MITM: The second part of the attack focuses on getting an affine relation between U, Z and K_b. From Fig. 6, we can see that $u_i = x_i + \kappa_{3sa+i}$, $\forall i \in [0, 3s - 1]$. For the second round we have

$$u_{3s+i} = D_i + \kappa_{3sa+3s+i}, \ \forall \ i \in [0, 3s - 1]$$
$$= \mathsf{Lin}_{1,i}(z_0, \dots, z_{3s-1}, x_{3s}, \dots, x_{n-1}) + \kappa_{3sa+3s+i}, \ \forall \ i \in [0, 3s - 1]$$

where $\mathsf{Lin}_{1,i}$ is the i-th linear function of Lin_1 described above. The above holds since we have already seen that all D_i's are linear functions in $(z_0, \dots, z_{3s-1}, x_{3s}, \dots, x_{n-1})$. Similarly for the third round we have

$$u_{6s+i} = E_i + \kappa_{3sa+6s+i}, \ \forall \ i \in [0, 3s - 1]$$
$$= \mathsf{Lin}_{2,i}(z_0, \dots, z_{6s-1}, x_{3s}, \dots, x_{n-1}) + \kappa_{3sa+6s+i}, \ \forall \ i \in [0, 3s - 1]$$

where $\mathsf{Lin}_{2,i}$ is similarly the i-th linear function of Lin_2. Iterating over all the b rounds we can write the vector equation, $U = K_b + \mathbf{P}(Z, x_{3s}, \dots, x_{n-1})$, where $\mathbf{P}$ denotes the set of $3bs$ linear expressions obtained by putting together the linear expressions $\mathsf{Lin}_{1,i}, \mathsf{Lin}_{2,i}$ etc. We can now replace K_b in Eq. (6) to get

$$Y = \mathsf{Lin}(Z, x_{3s}, x_{3s+1}, \dots, x_{n-1}, K_a, U + \mathbf{P}(Z, x_{3s}, \dots, x_{n-1}), K_c, K_{rem})$$
$$= \mathsf{Lin}'(Z, x_{3s}, x_{3s+1}, \dots, x_{n-1}, K_a, U, K_c, K_{rem}).$$

This time we eliminate K_{rem} from the above set of linear equations using the same Gaussian elimination method as in the previous stage. There are $n - 3s(a + b + c)$ variables in K_{rem} that we eliminate, which leaves us with $3s(a + b + c)$ equations in $Z, x_{3s}, x_{3s+1}, \dots, x_{n-1}, K_a, U, K_c$. We can rearrange the terms in the equation to get $\mathsf{Aff}_3(Z, U) = \mathsf{Aff}_4(X, K_a, K_c)$, where $\mathsf{Aff}_3, \mathsf{Aff}_4$ are a set of $3s(a + b + c)$ affine functions on Z, U and K_a, K_c, X respectively.

Note that if we guess Z, we can compute U since the S-box is bijective, and we have already seen that guessing K_a lets us compute X by computing the a forward rounds from the plaintext. Thus in the next MITM stage we make 2 lists L_3, L_4. In L_3 we store the $3s(a + b + c)$-bit vector given by the expressions $\mathsf{Aff}_3(Z, U)$ for each of 2^{3bs} values of Z. In L_4 we store the $3s(a+b+c)$-bit vector given by the expressions $\mathsf{Aff}_4(X, K_a, K_c)$ for each of 2^{3bs} values of (K_a, K_c) in L. We again look for collisions in the 2 lists. The expected number of collisions is $2^{3bs+3bs-3s(a+b+c)} = 2^{3sb-3sa-3sc}$. However the correct value of the key K_a, K_c is guaranteed to be the outcome of the collision finding stage for the correct guess of the majority values.

Once we get a candidate solution K_a, K_c, Z, U we can compute the vectors X, Y by computing the a, c rounds forwards/backwards from the plaintext/ciphertext. We can then compute $K_b = U + \mathbf{P}(Z, x_{3s}, \dots, x_{n-1})$. As we know the majority of the inputs of the S-boxes in $r - a - b - c$ middle rounds, we can solve an affine equation of form $\mathsf{Aff}_{rem}(W, K_{rem}) = Y$ to recover the value of K_{rem}, which was the only part of the key which remained unknown.

After this one can check if the key so obtained produces the required majority values guessed at the beginning. If not the attacker can restart the process with another set of majority values. The expected number of such checks is around $2^{s(r-a-b-c)+3sb-3sa-3sc} = 2^{rs-4sa-4sc+2sb}$. We formally state the attack:

1. Separate the first $a + b$ and last c rounds of the cipher
2. Denote the output of the first a rounds by X, the output of the b rounds by W and the input of the last c rounds by Y.
3. Denote the inputs/outputs of the S-boxes in the b rounds by U/Z
4. Guess majority bits of the inputs of the S-boxes of $r - a - b - c$ middle rounds.
5. For every majority guess do:
   First MITM:
   - Compute the relation $Y = \mathsf{Lin}(Z, x_{3s}, \ldots, x_{n-1}, K_a, K_b, K_c, K_{rem})$
   - Eliminate K_b, K_{rem}, Z from the relation and form and equation of form $\mathsf{Aff}_1(K_a, X) = \mathsf{Aff}_2(K_c, Y)$.
   - By exhausting all possible values of K_a keep a list of $\mathsf{Aff}_1(K_a, X)$, where X is computed knowing K_a and plaintext pt.
   - Try all possible values of K_c and find collisions between $\mathsf{Aff}_2(K_c, Y)$ and the list computed in the previous step. Keep a list L of (K_a, K_c) values satisfying the condition.
   Second MITM:
   - Compute the relation $Y = \mathsf{Lin}'(Z, x_{3s}, x_{3s+1}, \ldots, x_{n-1}, K_a, U, K_c, K_{rem})$ by replacing K_b.
   - Eliminate K_b, K_{rem} to get a relation of form $\mathsf{Aff}_3(Z, U) = \mathsf{Aff}_4(X, K_a, K_c)$.
   - For every pair (K_a, K_c) in the list L, compute $\mathsf{Aff}_4(X, K_a, K_c)$.
   - For every possible value of Z, compute $\mathsf{Aff}_3(Z, U)$, where U can be computed efficiently from Z, and look for occurrence with $\mathsf{Aff}_3(Z, U)$ in the list from the previous step.
   - For every (K_a, K_c, Z, U) satisfying the relation, compute K_b, W, Y as shown before.
   - Linearize the middle $r - a - b - c$ rounds using the majority guess and compute K_{rem} from $\mathsf{Aff}_{rem}(K_{rem}, K_a, K_b, K_c, W) = Y$.
   - After the entire key is found, check if they result in the same majority values assumed at the beginning of the attack or else retry with another set of majority values.

Complexity Estimation: Before we state our analysis to calculate the computational complexity, let us state a few observations:

1. Note that the number of variables on the right side of Eq. (6) is $2n + 3sb - 3s$. Hence using the basis vector logic, forming Eq. (6) is equivalent to $2n + 3sb - 3s$ encryptions limited to $r - a - c$ rounds, hence equivalent to $(2n + 3sb - 3s) \cdot \frac{(r-a-c)}{r}$ encryptions.
2. For the first MITM, eliminating $\theta = n - 3s(a - b + c)$ variables in an $n \times (3n + 3sb - 3s)$ matrix using the sweeping out method costs around $\frac{n \cdot \theta \cdot (3n + 3sb - 3s)}{2rn^2}$ encryptions.

3. Computing U from X and K is equivalent to the encryption of $2n$ base vectors (for the n bits of X and the n bits of K) in b rounds instead of r. So, this costs $2n \cdot \frac{b}{r}$ encryptions

4. For the 2nd MITM, eliminating $3sb$ (K_b) and $n - 3s(a+b+c)$ (K_{rem}) variables in a $n \times (3n + 6sb - 3s)$ matrix requires $\frac{(n - 3s(a+c)) \cdot n \cdot (3n + 6sb - 3s)}{2rn^2}$ encryptions.

5. Solve the system of linear equations to get K_{rem} from $\mathbf{Aff}_{rem}(K_{rem}, K_a, K_b, K_c, W) = Y$. This requires one Gaussian Elimination which is equivalent to $\frac{(n - 3s(a+b+c))^3}{2rn^2}$ encryptions.

Both MITM steps should be done for each majority guess for the middle rounds, hence should be repeated $2^{s(r-a-b-c)}$ times. Note that to evaluate $\mathbf{Aff}_1(K_a, X)$ we need to evaluate the first a encryption rounds to get X from the plaintext. Thereafter we evaluate $(3sa - 3sb + 3sc)$ linear expressions in $(3sa + n)$ bits of K_a, X, which requires around $(3sa + 3sb - 3sc) \cdot (3sa + n)$ bit-operations. Similarly to evaluate $\mathbf{Aff}_2(K_c, Y)$ we need to evaluate the last c decryption rounds to get Y from the ciphertext, followed by evaluation of linear expressions that take $(3sa + 3sb - 3sc) \cdot (3sc + n)$ bit-operations. Hence the first MITM takes time equivalent to $T_1 = \left(\frac{a}{r} + \frac{(3sa - 3sb + 3sc) \cdot (3sa + n)}{2rn^2} \right) \cdot 2^{3sa} + \left(\frac{c}{r} + \frac{(3sa - 3sb + 3sc) \cdot (3sc + n)}{2rn^2} \right) \cdot 2^{3sc}$ encryptions. The number of pairs stored in the first MITM is around 2^{3sb} as mentioned before.

Later on we replace K_b in the linear equation and eliminate K_b, K_{rem}, this can also be seen as a matrix multiplication followed by a Gaussian elimination. Next we compute the values of $\mathbf{Aff}_3(Z, U)$ and $\mathbf{Aff}_4(X, K_a, K_c)$ having values of K_a, K_c and Z. Computing the value of U from Z takes time less than required in the b encryption rounds. Thereafter, evaluating $3s(a+b+c)$ linear expressions in $6bs$ bits requires $3s(a+b+c) \cdot 6bs$ bit-operations. Again for $\mathbf{Aff}_4$ computing X from K_a requires evaluating the first a encryption rounds. Then evaluation of linear expressions requires $3s(a + b + c) \cdot (3sa + 3sc + n)$ bit-operations. Hence the 2nd MITM takes $T_2 = \left(\frac{b}{r} + \frac{(3sa + 3sb + 3sc) \cdot (6bs)}{2rn^2} + \frac{a}{r} + \frac{(3sa + 3sb + 3sc) \cdot (3sa + 3sc + n)}{2rn^2} \right) \cdot 2^{3sb}$ encryptions. The expected number of collisions in this procedure is $2^{3sb - 3sa - 3sc}$ which the attacker needs to filter whenever it is greater than 1. Hence the total complexity of the attack is estimated as:

$$2^{s(r-a-b-c)} \times \Bigg[T_1 + T_2 \text{ (The 2 MITMs) } + (2^{3s(b-a-c)}) \text{ (Filter Solutions)}$$

$$+ (2n + 3sb - 3s) \cdot \frac{(r - a - c)}{r} + \frac{n \cdot \theta \cdot (3n + 3sb - 3s)}{2rn^2}$$

$$+ 2n \cdot \frac{b}{r} + \frac{(n - 3s(a + c)) \cdot n \cdot (3n + 6sb - 3s)}{2rn^2}$$

$$+ \frac{(n - 3s(a + b + c))^3}{2rn^2} \Bigg].$$

As n and s go to infinity, the optimal parameters become $a = b = c = 1$ and the asymptotic complexity is equivalent to $\frac{4}{r} * 2^{sr}$, which is an improvement by a factor $n/8$ compared to the linearization attack. When s remains small (e.g.

$s = 1$), the optimal parameters can be larger. With $a = b = c = \frac{\log_2(2n)}{3s}$, the complexity is asymptotically $\frac{4\log_2(n)}{3sr} \cdot 2^{sr}$. If we take $sr = n$, this is better than exhaustive search by a factor $\Omega\left(\frac{n}{\log(n)}\right)$. The memory complexity is dominated by the space required for the 2 MITM stages. It can be seen that the total memory complexity in bits can be computed as

$$(3sa - 3sb + 3sc) \cdot (2^{3as} + 2^{3cs}) + (3sa + 3sb + 3sc) \cdot 2^{3bs+1}.$$

For the $\lfloor \frac{n}{s} \rfloor$-round instances, we get the following results. For $n = 128$, $s = 1, r = 128$, if we take $a = b = c = 5$, we get the total complexity around 2^{125} encryptions with 2^{22} bits of memory. For $n = 128$, $s = 10, r = 12$, if we take $a = b = c = 1$, we get the total complexity around 2^{119} encryptions with 2^{38} bits of memory. For the $0.8 \times \lfloor \frac{n}{s} \rfloor$-round instances, we get the following results. For $n = 128$, $s = 1, r = 103$, if we take $a = b = c = 5$, we get the total complexity around 2^{101} encryptions. For $n = 128$, $s = 10, r = 10$, if we take $a = b = c = 1$, we get the total complexity around 2^{99} encryptions. The memory complexity is the same as the corresponding $\lfloor \frac{n}{s} \rfloor$-round attacks.

5.1   Speed-Up Using Gray-Codes

Note that the technique outlined in [BCC+10] to evaluate a function over all points of its input domain, works best for linear or quadratic functions. As such, it is best to employ the attack when the set of functions for which we want to evaluate over the input space is quadratic/linear. This is only possible if we restrict $a = c = 1$. Let us see why. The first MITM procedure finds collision between two lists using the equation $\mathbf{Aff}_1(K_a, X) = \mathbf{Aff}_2(K_c, Y)$. Note that, thus far, X (rep. Y) has been computed from the plaintext (resp. ciphertext) by guessing K_a (resp. K_c) and evaluating the first a rounds in the forward direction (resp. last c rounds in the backward direction). In order to apply Gray-code based speed-up we need to express X and Y as functions of K_a and K_c. These functions happen to be quadratic only when $a = c = 1$. This condition automatically ensures that in the second MITM equations are also quadratic. This is true since the second MITM essentially equates $\mathbf{Aff}_3(Z, U) = \mathbf{Aff}_4(X, K_a, K_c)$, and we know that the relation between U, Z is quadratic since these are the input-output bits of the LowMC S-box in the middle b rounds. However note that unlike, in the MITM for the complete non-linear layers, there is no pre-computation in the first MITM that helps us reduce the steps in the second MITM. $\mathbf{Aff}_4(X, K_a, K_c)$ needs to be only evaluated for the 2^{3sb} pairs of K_a, K_c that survive the 1st MITM. However to employ Gray-code based speed up we need to evaluate $\mathbf{Aff}_4$ over all points of its input space. We could split $\mathbf{Aff}_4$ into $\mathbf{Aff}_5(K_a, X) + \mathbf{Aff}_6(K_c)$ and then evaluate each of the $\mathbf{Aff}_5$ and $\mathbf{Aff}_6$ separately. Thus the time required for the first MITM would be $T_{G_1} = \frac{3sa - 3sb + 3sc}{2rn^2} \cdot (2^{3as+1} + 2^{3sc+1})$ encryptions. The 2nd MITM requires $T_{G_2} = \frac{3sa + 3sb + 3sc}{2rn^2} \cdot (2^{3bs+1} + 2^{3as+1} + 2^{3sc})$ encryptions.

It only makes sense to employ Gray-codes if $T_{G_1} + T_{G_2} < T_1 + T_2$. For $s = 1$, the optimal values of a, b, c are considerably higher and it does not make sense to

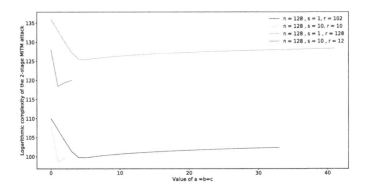

Fig. 7. The base 2 logarithm of the complexity of the 2-stage MITM attack when $n = 128$ and $s = 1, 10$, for $n = 0.8 \times \lfloor \frac{n}{s} \rfloor$, when a, b, c are kept equal and varied.

attempt the Gray-code speed-up using this algorithm. In fact even if we attempt to use this method by forcing $a = b = c = 1$, the complexity is many times higher. Intuitively this makes sense, if a, c and s are both 1 then the lists require exhaustive search over only $3as = 3sc = 3$ variables, for which employing even a non-Gray-code approach would take only 2^3 function evaluations. However when $s = 10$, using such Gray-codes to execute the MITM stages is beneficial. For $n = 128$, $s = 10, r = \lfloor \frac{n}{s} \rfloor = 12$, if we take $a = b = c = 1$, we get the total complexity around $2^{110.6}$ encryptions which is better than the previous estimate by a factor of around 2^9. For $r = 0.8 \times \lfloor \frac{n}{s} \rfloor = 10$ using the same parameters we get the total complexity around $2^{90.8}$ encryptions which again outperforms the previous estimate by a factor of around 2^8.

6   Experimental Results

In this section we present experimental data to showcase how our new attacks stack up in comparison to the attacks proposed in [BBDV20] on instances of LowMC with smaller blocksizes. Our results indicate that for all instances targeted in our paper, there is a significant speedup compared to the previous attacks. Moreover, we provide experimental evidence that our attacks successfully recover the key with a better complexity than exhaustive search for both 3-round with full S-box layer and n/s-round with partial S-box layer variants.

All the attacks and variants of the encryption function were implemented in Sage and ran on an Intel Xeon E5-2680 processor with 256 GB of memory. Each attack was run for several randomly generated instances. The complexity figures are reported by computing the base 2 logarithm of the amount of time taken by the attack, divided by the amount of time one encryption takes.[1]

---

[1] The source code of the attacks can be found at https://gitlab.epfl.ch/barooti/lowmc-challenge-round-3.

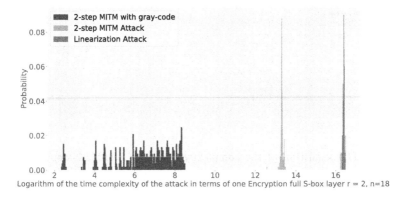

Fig. 8. The histogram of base 2 logarithm of the time complexity of all linearization, 2-stage MITM and 2-stage MITM with gray-code enumeration attacks for $n = 18$, $s = 6$, $r = 2$, in terms of the time it takes to perform a single encryption with the same key, the same affine layers, and the same key update functions.

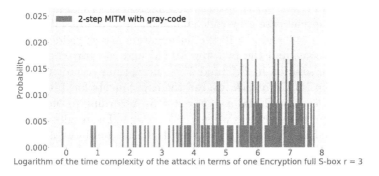

Fig. 9. The histogram of base 2 logarithm of the time complexity of the gray-code enumerated 2-stage MITM attack for $n = 12$, $s = 4$, $r = 3$, in terms of the time it takes to perform a single encryption

Full S-box Layer: For the 2-round full S-box layer variant of the cipher, we implemented all three Linearization, 2-step MITM and 2-step MITM with gray-code enumeration attacks for $n = 18$. The results are presented in Fig. 8. On average, the linearization attack required $2^{16.38}$ encryptions to recover the key, where as the 2-stage MITM, and the gray code enumeration attacks required $2^{13.31}$ and $2^{6.42}$ encryptions to yield a solution respectively.

We also implemented the attack using Gray-code enumeration for 3-round variants of block size 12. Figure 9 show cases the complexity of this attack for several randomly generated samples. Our experimental results indicate that the 3-round variant of this attack yields a solution faster than exhaustive search for all the samples we ran the attack for and the average complexity of our experiments was $2^{5.88}$ encryptions for $n = 12$, $s = 4$, $r = 3$.

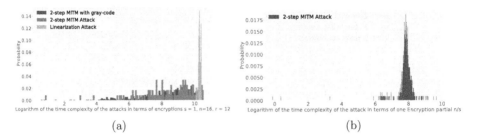

Fig. 10. (a) The logarithm of the complexity of 2-step MITM, 2-step MITM with gray-code enumeration and linearization attacks for the partial S-box layer variant with parameters $n = 16$, $s = 1$ and $r = 12$, (b) The logarithm of the complexity of the two-step MITM attack for $n = 12, s = 1, r = 12$.

Partial Non-Linear Layer: For the partial S-box layer variant of the cipher with number of rounds equal to $r = \lfloor \frac{n}{s} \rfloor \times 0.8$, we implemented the 2-stage MITM attack described in Sect. 5, the linearization method described in [BBDV20] and in addition the special case gray-code enumeration attack described at the end of 5. For $n = 16$, $s = 1$ and $r = 12$ the linearization attack yielded a complexity of $2^{10.29}$ encryptions, and the two-step MITM and the gray-code enumeration attacks yielded a solution in $2^{8.46}$ and $2^{8.50}$ encryptions respectively.

For the 2-step MITM attack, we ran the experiments for 3 instances of $a = b = c = 1$, $a = b = c = 2$ and $a = b = c = 3$. According to our experimental results the best performance was when $a = b = c = 1$. The results of the 3 attacks are demonstrated in Fig. 10a, and it is evident that both our new attacks are significantly faster than the linearization method.

We also experimented the attack for $n = 12$, $s = 1$ and $r = n/s = 12$ and $a = b = c = 1$. According to our experimental results demonstrated in Fig. 10b, this attack had an average complexity of $2^{7.402}$ encryptions, indicating a speed up over exhaustive search.

7   Conclusion

In this paper, we present a 2-stage MITM on several instances of LowMC using only a single plaintext/ciphertext. The first MITM stage reduces the key candidates corresponding to a fraction of key bits of the master key. The second MITM stage between this reduced candidate set and the remaining fraction of key bits successfully recovers the master key. We have shown with experimental evidence on smaller versions of LowMC that the combined computational complexity of both these stages is significantly lower than those reported in [BBDV20].

Acknowledgments. Subhadeep Banik was supported by the Swiss National Science Foundation (SNSF) through the Ambizione Grant PZ00P2_179921.

Khashayar Barooti was supported by the SNSF through the project grant 192364 on Post Quantum Cryptography.

References

[ARS+15] Albrecht, M.R., Rechberger, C., Schneider, T., Tiessen, T., Zohner, M.: Ciphers for MPC and FHE. In: Oswald, E., Fischlin, M. (eds.) EUROCRYPT 2015. LNCS, vol. 9056, pp. 430–454. Springer, Heidelberg (2015). https://doi.org/10.1007/978-3-662-46800-5_17

[BBDV20] Banik, S., Barooti, K., Durak, F.B., Vaudenay, S.: Cryptanalysis of lowmc instances using single plaintext/ciphertext pair. IACR Trans. Symmetric Cryptol. **2020**(4), 130–146 (2020)

[BCC+10] Bouillaguet, C., et al.: Fast exhaustive search for polynomial systems in F_2. In: Cryptographic Hardware and Embedded Systems, CHES 2010, 12th International Workshop, Santa Barbara, CA, USA, 17–20 August, 2010. Proceedings, pp. 203–218 (2010)

[DEM15] Dobraunig, C., Eichlseder, M., Mendel, F.: Higher-order cryptanalysis of LowMC. In: Kwon, S., Yun, A. (eds.) ICISC 2015. LNCS, vol. 9558, pp. 87–101. Springer, Cham (2016). https://doi.org/10.1007/978-3-319-30840-1_6

[Din] Dinur, I.: Cryptanalytic applications of the polynomial method for solving multivariate equation system over gf(2). IACR Cryptology ePrint Archive, 2021/578. https://eprint.iacr.org/2021/578.pdf

[DKP+19] Dinur, I., Kales, D., Promitzer, A., Ramacher, S., Rechberger, C.: Linear equivalence of block ciphers with partial non-linear layers: application to LowMC. In: Ishai, Y., Rijmen, V. (eds.) EUROCRYPT 2019. LNCS, vol. 11476, pp. 343–372. Springer, Cham (2019). https://doi.org/10.1007/978-3-030-17653-2_12

[DLMW15] Dinur, I., Liu, Y., Meier, W., Wang, Q.: Optimized interpolation attacks on LowMC. In: Iwata, T., Cheon, J.H. (eds.) ASIACRYPT 2015. LNCS, vol. 9453, pp. 535–560. Springer, Heidelberg (2015). https://doi.org/10.1007/978-3-662-48800-3_22

[DN19] Dinur, I., Nadler, N.: Multi-target attacks on the picnic signature scheme and related protocols. In: Ishai, Y., Rijmen, V. (eds.) EUROCRYPT 2019. LNCS, vol. 11478, pp. 699–727. Springer, Cham (2019). https://doi.org/10.1007/978-3-030-17659-4_24

[GKRS] Grassi, L., Kales, D., Rechberger, C., Schofnegger, M.: Survey of key-recovery attacks on lowmc in a single plaintext/ciphertext scenario. https://raw.githubusercontent.com/lowmcchallenge/lowmcchallenge-material/master/docs/survey.pdf

[LIM20] Liu, F., Isobe, T., Meier, W.: Cryptanalysis of Full LowMC and LowMC-M with Algebraic Techniques. IACR Cryptol. ePrint Arch. **2020**, 1034 (2020)

[LIM21] Liu, F., Isobe, T., Meier, W.: A simple algebraic attack on 3-round lowmc. IACR Cryptol. ePrint Arch. **2021**, 255 (2021)

[RST18] Rechberger, C., Soleimany, H., Tiessen, T.: Cryptanalysis of low-data instances of full lowmcv2. IACR Trans. Symmetric Cryptol. **2018**(3), 163–181 (2018)

[Zav] Zaverucha, G.: The picnic signaure algorithm specifications, version 3.0. https://github.com/microsoft/Picnic/blob/master/spec/spec-v3.0.pdf

Convexity of Division Property Transitions: Theory, Algorithms and Compact Models

Aleksei Udovenko[(✉)]

CryptoExperts, Paris, France
aleksei@affine.group

Abstract. Integral cryptanalysis is a powerful tool for attacking symmetric primitives, and *division property* is a state-of-the-art framework for finding integral distinguishers.

This work describes new theoretical and practical insights into traditional bit-based division property. We focus on analyzing and exploiting monotonicity/convexity of division property and its relation to the graph indicator. In particular, our investigation leads to a *new compact representation* of propagation, which allows CNF/MILP modeling for larger S-Boxes, such as 16-bit Super-Sboxes of lightweight block ciphers or even 32-bit *random* S-boxes. This solves the challenge posed by Derbez and Fouque (ToSC 2020), who questioned the possibility of SAT/SMT/MILP modeling of 16-bit Super-Sboxes. As a proof-of-concept, we model the Super-Sboxes of the 8-round LED by CNF formulas, which was not feasible by any previous approach.

Our analysis is further supported by an elegant algorithmic framework. We describe simple algorithms for computing division property of a set of n-bit vectors in time $O(n2^n)$, reducing such sets to minimal/maximal elements in time $O(n2^n)$, computing division property propagation table of an $n \times m$-bit S-box and its compact representation in time $O((n + m)2^{n+m})$. In addition, we develop an advanced algorithm tailored to "heavy" bijections, allowing to model, for example, a randomly generated 32-bit S-box.

Keywords: Division property · S-boxes · SAT · CNF · MILP · LED

1 Introduction

With the ongoing surge of lightweight cryptography, the field of cryptanalysis of lightweight symmetric primitives is pressured to evaluate the security as precisely as possible: adding a few extra rounds as a security margin is not affordable in the lightweight setting. Among the most powerful cryptanalysis techniques are linear and differential cryptanalysis, and integral cryptanalysis. For example, the long-standing MISTY1 [24] block cipher was broken recently by integral cryptanalysis [1,32] (based on division property, the topic of this work) with a

© International Association for Cryptologic Research 2021
M. Tibouchi and H. Wang (Eds.): ASIACRYPT 2021, LNCS 13090, pp. 332–361, 2021.
https://doi.org/10.1007/978-3-030-92062-3_12

surprisingly low time complexity 2^{70}. While provable security arguments against linear and differential cryptanalysis exist already since the design of the AES block cipher [10], provable security arguments against integral attacks started to appear only recently [18].

Division property is a state-of-the-art technique for finding integral distinguishers in symmetric ciphers. Since the seminal work of Todo [33] focusing on word/state-based division property, many improvements and variants of the technique were developed. The focus shifted towards bit-based division property [34], followed by a surprisingly effective MILP-based approach [38] (mixed-integer linear programming) of finding division property-based distinguishers via the search of the so-called *division trails*. This line continued with a series of works improving MILP and SAT/SMT-based (satisfiability modulo theories) modeling [14,21,27,31]. Classic (also called *traditional* or *conventional*) division property is *imperfect*: it may miss an integral distinguisher, although it never produces a false positive. A more recent advancement is the development of "perfect" monomial prediction techniques [17,18,20], which require *counting division trails* and so far are computationally feasible only in a few cases. This work focuses on traditional division property, as it remains powerful and the most widely applicable tool for integral cryptanalysis.

From the theory side, following preliminary analysis [15,29], the work of Boura and Canteaut [5] formalized and studied the *state-based* division property in terms of *parity sets*. In particular, they showed that state-based division property of a set is defined by the set's algebraic *degree*. While many of their results about parity sets translate directly into *bit-based* division property, such links were not explicitly stated. To the best of our understanding, the theory behind *bit-based* division property is not fully developed. Furthermore, very recently, Carlet [7] proposed method for bounding the algebraic degree of a composition of function from the degrees of their *graph indicators*. It is a natural question whether division property can be improved by incorporating such bounds. A recent work [9] studied formally relationships between different variants of division property and algebraic degree bounds for composite functions, such as the Boura-Canteaut bound [4]. However, this work did not consider graph indicator-based bounds, leaving this gap open. As a part of this work, we aim to fill the aforementioned gaps and extend the theory, focusing on the monotonicity/convexity aspects of division property and relations with the graphs of the analyzed functions.

The imperfectness of traditional bit-based division property shows up in various ways. Division property analysis can be applied to any Boolean circuit implementation of a cipher (constructed from e.g. AND and XOR gates). However, due to the imperfectness, information gets lost during propagation through the circuit. Considering larger parts of the cipher, such as S-boxes and linear maps, allows to slow down the loss of information. For example, Zhang and Rijmen [39] showed that propagating division property through a linear map via a basic COPY-and-XOR implementation is imperfect. The right way to handle a linear map is to encode all invertible square submatrices of the linear map's matrix. A typical linear layer of a lightweight block cipher operates on at least 16 bits and its matrix may contain a large number of invertible submatrices. Encoding the division property propagation through such a layer in a SAT/MILP instance deemed to be not feasible until recently, when Hu, Wang and Wang [21] proposed a generic SMT-based solution, which is feasible for up to 64-bit linear maps. Lambin, Derbez and Fouque [22] showed that propagation through S-boxes is also fragile: combining an S-Box with a linear map may also result in loss or gain of information.

To battle the imperfectness of traditional division property, Derbez and Fouque [11] proposed to increase its precision by considering a Super-Sbox - a composition of the cipher's linear map with the adjacent S-boxes - as a single propagation unit. For many lightweight block ciphers, Super-Sboxes are 16-bit bijections. The results of [11] shows that this approach increases precision significantly and allows to find new integral distinguishers for 1–2 more rounds for some ciphers. However, SAT/MILP modeling of Super-Sboxes was not feasible by state-of-the-art techniques and the authors of [11] had to develop an ad-hoc search technique. In fact, they challenged the community to develop SAT/MILP modeling of such large mappings: "*We also believe this work will challenge the community in handling such large propagation tables with generic solvers for MILP, SAT or SMT models.*". As a part of this work, we provide a solution to this challenge, based on our theoretical advancement.

Our contribution. This work focuses on theory and practice of *traditional division property*. All other variants, such as three-subset division property [34] (and without the unknown subset [17]), monomial prediction [20], are out of scope of this work. The main contributions of this work are:

1. Development of the theoretic framework behind the classic division property. This includes fine-grained (bit-based) formulations of previous statements about division property, exhibiting convexity of division property and its relation to the recent graph indicator-based bounds by Carlet [7].
2. Compact characterization of division property propagation through a function F by means of the (reduced) division property of its graph. This yields compact constraint systems for MILP/SAT solvers, allowing us to model much larger S-boxes than was previously possible, including 16-bit Super-Sboxes and, as a proof-of-concept, randomly generated 32-bit S-boxes. We also introduce additional techniques for improving modeling efficiency.
3. A framework for manipulation of dense sets of binary vectors. It includes simple algorithms for computing division property of a set of n-bit vectors (complexity $\mathcal{O}(n2^n)$), reducing such sets to minimal/maximal elements (complexity $\mathcal{O}(n2^n)$), computing division property propagation table of an $n \times m$-bit S-box and its compact representation (complexity $\mathcal{O}((n + m)2^{n+m})$). These algorithms improve previous best algorithms by a factor of 2^n. In addition, we develop an advanced algorithm for the compact representation tailored to "heavy" n-bit bijections, for which it runs in time $\tilde{O}(2^n)$ (heuristically).
4. As a proof-of-concept, we apply our techniques to 8-round LED and show that its Super-Sbox model does not yield integral distinguishers (although they might still exist), even with linear masks applied to an input and an

output Super-Sbox. This fills the gap left by [11], as their approach was not feasible for LED.

Our implementations are written in a mix of Python and C++, featuring performance and a convenient API. All the source code will be made publicly available. For details, see:

https://github.com/CryptoExperts/AC21-DivProp-Convexity

Outline. Section 2 provides the necessary background with a focus on the partial order on bit-vectors. In Sect. 3, we briefly reintroduce traditional division property and develop its theory, culminating in a new compact representation. As a byproduct, we exhibit a direct link between division property and graph indicators. The following Sect. 4 focuses on CNF/MILP modeling aspects of the new representation. Section 5 presents our algorithmic framework for manipulating dense sets of binary vectors. Finally, in Sect. 6, we show how our techniques can be applied to model the Super-Sbox representation of LED.

2   Preliminaries

Boolean operations AND, OR, XOR, NOT denoted respectively by $\wedge, \vee, \oplus, \neg$ can be applied to (pairs of) single bits or bitwise to bit-vectors. We use $\underline{1} \in \mathbb{F}_2^n$ (resp. $\underline{0}$) to denote the all-one (resp. all-zero) vector of a dimension n depending on the context. We write $\neg x := x \oplus \underline{1}$ and $\neg X := \{\neg x \mid x \in X\}$, $X \subseteq \mathbb{F}_2^n$, to disambiguate from the set complement $\overline{X} := \{y \in \mathbb{F}_2^n \mid y \notin X\}$. The unit vectors $e_j \in \mathbb{F}_2^n, 0 \leq j < n$, are the vectors with the j-th (0-based) coordinate equal to 1 and all other coordinates equal to 0.

The notation $x^u, u \in \mathbb{F}_2^n$, is used to denote the monomial $\prod_{i=0}^{n-1} x_i^{u_i}$, letting $x_i^0 = 1$. Any Boolean function $f : \mathbb{F}_2^n \to \mathbb{F}_2$ has a unique expression $f(x) = \bigoplus_{u \in \mathbb{F}_2^n} a_u x^u$, where $a_u \in \mathbb{F}_2$. This expression is called the *algebraic normal form* (ANF) of f. We say that f *contains* the monomial x^u if $a_u = 1$ in the ANF of f. The ANF support of f, denoted $\mathrm{Supp}_{\mathrm{ANF}}(f)$, is the set of all exponents u with $a_u = 1$ in the ANF of f.

The indicator vector of a set $X \subseteq \mathbb{F}_2^n$ is the vector $I \in \mathbb{F}_2^{2^n}$ such that $I_x = 1$ if and only if $x \in X$. Here we use the natural identification of $\mathbb{F}_2^n$ with $\{0, \ldots, 2^n - 1\}$. By an abuse of notation, we will identify a set X with its indicator vector implicitly. The indicator function of X is the map $\mathbb{1}_X : \mathbb{F}_2^n \to \mathbb{F}_2 : x \mapsto I_x$.

The *graph* of a function $F : \mathbb{F}_2^n \to \mathbb{F}_2^m$, denoted $\mathbf{\Gamma}_F$, is the set

$$\mathbf{\Gamma}_F = \{(x, y) \mid x \in \mathbb{F}_2^n, y = F(x)\} \subseteq \mathbb{F}_2^n \times \mathbb{F}_2^m.$$

The *graph indicator* of F is the indicator function of its graph $\mathbf{\Gamma}_F$.

2.1 Partial Order

We use the product order on vectors over $\mathbb{F}_2$, which is, for $x, y \in \mathbb{F}_2^n$, $x \preceq y$ if and only if $x_i \leq y_i$ for all i. We write $x \prec y$ if $x \preceq y$ and $x \neq y$.

Definition 1. *The* lower closure *of a set* $X \subseteq \mathbb{F}_2^n$, *denoted by* $\mathrm{LowerClosure}\,(X)$, *is the set of all* $u \in \mathbb{F}_2^n$ *with* $u \preceq x$ *for some* $x \in X$:

$$\mathrm{LowerClosure}\,(X) := \{u \in \mathbb{F}_2^n \mid \exists x \in X : u \preceq x\} = \bigcup_{x \in X} \{u \in \mathbb{F}_2^n \mid u \preceq x\}.$$

The upper closure *of a set* $X \subseteq \mathbb{F}_2^n$, *denoted by* $\mathrm{UpperClosure}\,(X)$, *is the set of all* $u \in \mathbb{F}_2^n$ *with* $x \preceq u$ *for some* $x \in X$:

$$\mathrm{UpperClosure}\,(X) := \{u \in \mathbb{F}_2^n \mid \exists x \in X : u \succeq x\} = \bigcup_{x \in X} \{u \in \mathbb{F}_2^n \mid u \succeq x\}.$$

A set X *is an* upper set *if its upper closure is* X *itself. A set* X *is a* lower set *if its lower closure is* X *itself.*

Remark 1. An intuitive interpretation is as follows. For each vector in X, the upper closure converts positions with the value 0 into a wildcard, whereas the lower closure converts positions with the value 1 into a wildcard.

Example 1. $\mathrm{LowerClosure}(\{110, 001\}) = \{000, 010, 100, 110, 000, 001\}$.

Example 2. $\mathrm{UpperClosure}(\{110, 001\}) = \{001, 011, 101, 110, 111\}$.

Proposition 1. *Let* X, Y *be lower sets (resp. upper sets). Then,* $X \cup Y$ *and* $X \cap Y$ *are lower sets (resp. upper sets);* $\overline{X}$ *is an upper set (resp. a lower set).*

Definition 2. *A subset* $X \subseteq \mathbb{F}_2^n$ *is called* convex, *if for any* $a, b, c \in \mathbb{F}_2^n$, $a \preceq b \preceq c$ *and* $a, c \in X$ *imply* $b \in X$. *An equivalent condition is*

$$X = \mathrm{LowerClosure}\,(X) \cap \mathrm{UpperClosure}\,(X).$$

Definition 3. *The* max-set *of a set* $X \subseteq \mathbb{F}_2^n$, *denoted by* $\mathrm{MaxSet}\,(X)$, *is the set of all maximal elements in* X:

$$\mathrm{MaxSet}\,(X) := \{u \in X \mid \nexists x \in X : x \succ u\}.$$

The min-set *of a set* $X \subseteq \mathbb{F}_2^n$, *denoted by* $\mathrm{MinSet}\,(X)$, *is the set of all minimal elements in* X:

$$\mathrm{MinSet}\,(X) := \{u \in X \mid \nexists x \in X : x \prec u\}.$$

Max-/min-sets are compact representations of lower/upper sets. Max-/min-sets are *antichains* (their elements are pairwise incomparable) and so are convex.

Proposition 2. *The operator* $\neg$ *anti-commutes with* MinSet, MaxSet, $\mathrm{LowerClosure}$, $\mathrm{UpperClosure}$: *for any set* X,

$$\neg\mathrm{MinSet}\,(X) = \mathrm{MaxSet}\,(\neg X), \qquad \neg\mathrm{LowerClosure}\,(X) = \mathrm{UpperClosure}\,(\neg X),$$

$$\neg\mathrm{MaxSet}\,(X) = \mathrm{MinSet}\,(\neg X), \qquad \neg\mathrm{UpperClosure}\,(X) = \mathrm{LowerClosure}\,(\neg X).$$

3   New Insights into Division Property

We start by briefly reformulating the traditional bit-based division property in terms of parity sets in (Subsect. 3.1). Then, we present a complete link with the set indicator (Subsect. 3.2). This link helps us to develop new characterization of transitions (Theorem 1), which in turn leads to a compact representation. Next, Subsect. 3.6 summarizes the observed convex structure of division property transitions, setting the basement for modeling techniques described in Sect. 4. In Subsect. 3.7, we revisit the approach of applying input/output linear masks and reformulate it in our framework. Finally, relationships with recent graph indicator-based degree bounds by Carlet [7] are investigated in Subsect. 3.8.

3.1   Division Property and Parity Sets

Boura and Canteaut [5] introduced the notion of *parity sets* as another view of division property.

Definition 4 (Parity set [5]).   *The* parity set *of a set* $X \subseteq \mathbb{F}_2^n$, *denoted* ParitySet (X), *is the set of all* $u \in \mathbb{F}_2^n$ *such that* $\bigoplus_{x \in X} x^u = 1$.

We reformulate the bit-based division property [33, 34] in terms of parity sets and the partial order framework.

Definition 5 (Bit-based division property).   *A set* $X \subseteq \mathbb{F}_2^n$ *satisfies bit-based division property* $\mathbb{K} \subseteq \mathbb{F}_2^n$, *if*

$$\text{ParitySet}\,(X) \subseteq \text{UpperClosure}\,(\mathbb{K}).$$

We define two special cases of division property mainly to simplify analysis.

Definition 6.   *For any set* $X \subseteq \mathbb{F}_2^n$, *define:*

1. the minimal division property MinDP (X) *of* X *as*

$$\text{MinDP}\,(X) := \text{MinSet}\,(\text{ParitySet}\,(X)),$$

2. the full division property FullDP (X) *of* X *as*

$$\text{FullDP}\,(X) := \text{UpperClosure}\,(\text{ParitySet}\,(X)).$$

Boura   and   Canteaut   developed   distinguishers   based   on UpperClosure (ParitySet (X)), however the link with the bit-based division property was not explicitly established. In fact, they showed [5, Prop. 6] that UpperClosure (ParitySet (X)) is precisely what is preserved when X goes through a constant addition:

$$\text{UpperClosure}\,(\text{ParitySet}\,(X \oplus c)) = \text{UpperClosure}\,(\text{ParitySet}\,(X))$$

for all $c \in \mathbb{F}_2^n$. It follows that bit-based division property is essentially equivalent to parity sets in the presence of key additions.

3.2   Link with the Set Indicator

We first note that the parity set of a set is closely linked to the ANF of the indicator of the set.

Proposition 3. *Parity set's coefficients can be expressed in terms of the ANF (Möbius) transform in the reverse direction:*

$$u \in \text{ParitySet}(X) \quad \Leftrightarrow \quad \bigoplus_{x \succeq u} \mathbb{1}_X(x) = 1 \quad \Leftrightarrow \quad \bigoplus_{x \in \mathbb{F}_2^n} x^u \cdot \mathbb{1}_X(x) = 1.$$

Proof. The elements $x \in X$ contributing to the sum $\bigoplus_{x \in X} x^u = 1$ in Definition 4 are precisely those with $x \succeq u$.   □

Corollary 1. *For any set $X \subseteq \mathbb{F}_2^n$,*

$$\text{ParitySet}(X) = \neg\text{Supp}_{\text{ANF}}(\mathbb{1}_{\neg X}).$$

Several works [3,5,15] established independently the relation between the degree of a set and its state-level division property. Let D_k^n consist of all vectors of $\mathbb{F}_2^n$ of weight at least k. Then, a set $X \subseteq \mathbb{F}_2^n$ satisfies the division property D_k^n if and only if the degree of the indicator $\mathbb{1}_X$ of the set is at most $n - k$. The following proposition generalizes this relation to the case of bit-based division property. Naturally, *minimal vectors* of a bit-based division property define *maximal monomials* that can occur in the ANF of the indicator. As minimal/maximal vectors are compact representations of upper/lower sets, the same fact holds also for the respective closures.

Proposition 4. *Let $X \subseteq \mathbb{F}_2^n$. Then,*

$$\text{MinDP}(X) := \text{MinSet}(\text{ParitySet}(X)) = \neg\text{MaxSet}(\text{Supp}_{\text{ANF}}(\mathbb{1}_X)),$$
$$\text{UpperClosure}(\text{ParitySet}(X)) = \neg\text{LowerClosure}(\text{Supp}_{\text{ANF}}(\mathbb{1}_X)).$$

Proof. Follows from Corollary 1, Proposition 2 and the fact that the set of max-terms in the ANF does not change on adding a constant to the input:

$$\text{MinSet}(\text{ParitySet}(X)) = \text{MinSet}(\neg\text{Supp}_{\text{ANF}}(\mathbb{1}_{\neg X}))$$
$$= \neg\text{MaxSet}(\text{Supp}_{\text{ANF}}(\mathbb{1}_{\neg X})) = \neg\text{MaxSet}(\text{Supp}_{\text{ANF}}(\mathbb{1}_X)).   □$$

3.3   Division Property Propagation

Xiang *et al.* [38] proposed a method to propagate division property through a public function (an S-box). Essentially the same method was described by Boura and Canteaut in terms of parity sets, although not linked to the division property. We define division property transitions based on these methods.

Definition 7 (Division property transition). *Let $S : \mathbb{F}_2^n \to \mathbb{F}_2^m, u \in \mathbb{F}_2^n, v \in \mathbb{F}_2^m$. We say that (u, v) is a valid division property transition for S and write $u \xrightarrow{S} v$ if there exist $u' \succeq u, v' \preceq v$, such that $S^{v'}(x)$ contains the monomial $x^{u'}$. Otherwise, we write $u \xnrightarrow{S} v$.*

The defined kind of transition corresponds to full division property in the output and is useful for analysis. In practice, minimal (reduced) output division property is used as it reduces the search space of trail search algorithms.

Definition 8 (Minimal transition). *Let* $u \xrightarrow{S} v$. *If* v *is minimal such vector, then we say that* $u \xrightarrow{S} v$ *is a* minimal *transition and write* $u \xrightarrow[\text{min.}]{S} v$.

Transitions allow to propagate division property through a public function. Due to monotonicity of division property, the propagation can be done by propagating each element of division property set $\mathbb{K}$ into a set of elements of output division property and taking a union over all such sets. This is a standard "propagation rule" in the division property literature, and was also formulated in terms of parity sets in [5, Prop. 7].

Proposition 5. *Let* $S : \mathbb{F}_2^n \to \mathbb{F}_2^m$ *and let* $X \subseteq \mathbb{F}_2^n$ *satisfy division property* $\mathbb{K} \subseteq \mathbb{F}_2^n$. *Then, the odd-multiplicity elements of* $S(X)$ *satisfy division property* $\mathbb{K}'$, *with*

$$\mathbb{K}' = \bigcup_{u \in \mathbb{K}} \left\{ v \in \mathbb{F}_2^m \mid u \xrightarrow{S} v \right\}.$$

Remark 2. It is sufficient to consider minimal transitions $u \xrightarrow[\text{min.}]{S} v$ instead of all $u \xrightarrow{S} v$, however, even in this case the resulting division property $\mathbb{K}'$ is not guaranteed to be minimal and has to be reduced if required so by search algorithms.

3.4 Core Transitions and Their Characterizations

In this subsection, we describe the key component of our work: a new compact description of the set of division property transitions of a function. This new description is rather natural and turns out to be equivalent to the minimal division property of the graph of the function, or, alternatively, to the set of maximal monomials in the ANF of the graph indicator of the function.

First, we define a new subclass of transitions, called *core* transitions, which are minimal transitions with additional *maximality* restriction of the input division property vector. The idea is that, by Definition 7, a valid transition $u \xrightarrow{S} v$ induces valid transitions $u' \xrightarrow{S} v$ for all $u' \preceq u$. As a result, it is sufficient to store transitions with *maximal* u and *minimal* v. Indeed, any minimal transition $u \xrightarrow{S} v$ can be covered by some maximal u' such that $u' \xrightarrow{S} v$ is a core transition.

Definition 9 (Core transitions). *Let* $u \xrightarrow{S} v$. *If* (u, v) *is* (maximal,minimal) *such pair, then we say that* $u \xrightarrow{S} v$ *is a* core *transition and write* $u \xrightarrow[\text{core}]{S} v$.

Remark 3. Todo and Morii [35] proposed alternative compact structure of division property transitions. Their idea is to group input division property vectors by the output division sets they propagate to. However, the main usage of their compact structure was in an ad-hoc exhaustive trail search. It is not clear if

SAT/MILP-based trail search can profit from such a structure. Our structure, on the contrary, lends itself naturally to compact CNF/DNF/MILP encodings (see Sect. 4).

We now show that core transitions have rich equivalent characterizations in terms of the ANFs of products of outputs bits, in terms of the ANF of the graph indicator and, finally, in terms of the (minimal) division property of the graph of the function.

Lemma 1. *Let* $f : \mathbb{F}_2^n \to \mathbb{F}_2$, $u \in \mathbb{F}_2^n$. *Then,*

$$\bigoplus_{x \in \mathbb{F}_2^n} x^u f(x) = 1 \tag{1}$$

and u *is minimal such vector if and only if the ANF of* f *contains maximal monomial* $x^{\neg u}$.

Proof. Let X be the support of f. By Proposition 3, (1) holds if and only if $u \in \text{ParitySet}(X)$. By Proposition 4, we get that u is minimal in $\text{ParitySet}(X)$ if and only if $\neg u$ is maximal in $\text{Supp}_{\text{ANF}}(\mathbb{1}_X) = \text{Supp}_{\text{ANF}}(f)$. $\square$

Theorem 1. *Let* $S : \mathbb{F}_2^n \to \mathbb{F}_2^m$, $u \in \mathbb{F}_2^n$, $v \in \mathbb{F}_2^m$. *The following statements are equivalent:*

1. $u \xrightarrow[\text{core}]{S} v$ *(i.e.,* (u,v) *is (maximal,minimal) such that* $u \xrightarrow{S} v$*);*
2. (u,v) *is (maximal,minimal) such that* $S^v(x)$ *contains the monomial* x^u;
3. $(\neg u, v)$ *belongs to* $\text{DivCore}_S := \text{MinDP}(\boldsymbol{\Gamma}_S) := \text{MinSet}(\text{ParitySet}(\boldsymbol{\Gamma}_S))$; *(Definition 10 below)*
4. *the graph indicator* $\mathbb{1}_{\boldsymbol{\Gamma}_S}(x,y)$ *contains the maximal monomial* $x^u y^{\neg v}$.

Proof. $(1 \Leftrightarrow 2)$ Observe that $u \xrightarrow[\text{core}]{S} v$ implies that $S^v(x)$ contains the monomial x^u. Conversely, if $S^v(x)$ contains the monomial x^u, then $u \xrightarrow{S} v$. It follows that the extremality is transferred in both directions.

$(2 \Leftrightarrow 3)$ By Definition 4, $(\neg u, v) \in \text{MinSet}(\text{ParitySet}(\boldsymbol{\Gamma}_S))$ if and only if

$$\bigoplus_{(x,y) \in \boldsymbol{\Gamma}_S} x^{\neg u} y^v = \bigoplus_{x \in \mathbb{F}_2^n} x^{\neg u} S^v(x) = 1 \tag{2}$$

and $(\neg u, v)$ is minimal such pair. For any fixed v, by Lemma 1, (2) holds with $\neg u$ minimal if and only if $S^v(x)$ contains the maximal monomial x^u. It follows that the extremality is transferred in both directions.

$(3 \Leftrightarrow 4)$ Follows from Proposition 4 applied to the set $\boldsymbol{\Gamma}_S$. $\square$

Remark 4. While characterizations 1 and 2 are related simply by definition, the other relations are more interesting. Remarkably, $(1 \Leftrightarrow 3)$ identifies division property propagation through S with the (minimal) division property of the graph of S; $(2 \Leftrightarrow 4)$ identifies *extreme* exponents (u,v) such that $S^v(x)$ contains x^u with maximal monomials in the graph indicator of S.

Note that the asymmetry of maximality/minimality of u/v is not present in characterizations 3 and 4: valid division property transitions of both S and S^{-1} (if it exists) are determined by the same set of *minimal* vectors $(\neg u, v) \in$ ParitySet (Γ_S), or, equivalently, by the same set of *maximal* monomials $x^u y^{\neg v}$ in the ANF of the graph indicator of S. This yields the following proposition.

Proposition 6. *Let S be a permutation of $\mathbb{F}_2^n$, $u, v \in \mathbb{F}_2^n$. Then,*

$$u \xrightarrow{S} v \quad \text{if and only if} \quad \neg v \xrightarrow{S^{-1}} \neg u,$$

$$u \xrightarrow[\text{core}]{S} v \quad \text{if and only if} \quad \neg v \xrightarrow[\text{core}]{S^{-1}} \neg u.$$

Proof. If $u \xrightarrow{S} v$, then by Definition 7 there exist $u' \succeq u, v' \preceq v$ such that $u' \xrightarrow[\text{core}]{S} v'$ and then by Theorem 1

$$\bigoplus_{(x,y) \in \Gamma_S} x^{\neg u'} y^{v'} = 1.$$

By swapping roles of x, y, we obtain $\neg v' \xrightarrow{S^{-1}} \neg u'$. Since $\neg u' \preceq \neg u, \neg v' \succeq \neg v$, we get $\neg v \xrightarrow{S^{-1}} \neg u$. Equivalence for core transitions holds because the extremality condition is the same for both directions: $(\neg u, v)$ is minimal. $\square$

Remark 5. This result is an extension of [5, Lemma 3] to the framework of division property transitions and extremality. The cited lemma states that $S^v(x)$ contains x^u if and only if $(\neg S^{-1})^{\neg u}(\neg x)$ contains $x^{\neg v}$. Furthermore, a similar degree-based statement was given by Boura and Canteaut already in [4].

Importantly, this proposition shows a bijection between forward and backward integral distinguishers based on division property. While this relation was known before, it is unfortunately rarely used in the literature to convert discovered forward distinguishers into backward distinguishers.

3.5 Division Core and Its Relation to Transition Classes

From now on, we focus on the studying the set of core transitions. Due to the aforementioned symmetry, it is more convenient to study its characterization as the min-set of the parity set of the graph of S. As we shall use this set extensively, we introduce a new term for brevity.

Definition 10 (Division Core). *Let $S : \mathbb{F}_2^n \to \mathbb{F}_2^m$. Define the division core of S, denoted DivCore_S, as the minimal division property of the graph of S:*

$$\text{DivCore}_S := \text{MinDP}(\Gamma_S) = \text{MinSet}(\text{ParitySet}(\Gamma_S))$$

$$= \text{MinSet}\left(\left\{ (u, v) \in \mathbb{F}_2^n \times \mathbb{F}_2^m \;\middle|\; \bigoplus_{(x,y) \in \Gamma_S} x^u y^v = 1 \right\}\right).$$

We deduce the following characterization of division property transitions *solely from the division core.*

Theorem 2. *Let* $S : \mathbb{F}_2^n \to \mathbb{F}_2^m$. *Then,*

1. $u \xrightarrow{S} v$ *if and only if* $(\neg u, v) \in \text{UpperClosure}\,(\text{DivCore}_S)$;

2. $u \xrightarrow[\text{min.}]{S} v$ *if and only if* $(\neg u, v) \in \text{MinSet}_v(\text{UpperClosure}\,(\text{DivCore}_S))$;

3. $u \xrightarrow[\text{core}]{S} v$ *if and only if* $(\neg u, v) \in \text{DivCore}_S$.

If, in addition, $n = m$ *and* S *is bijective:*

4. $v \xrightarrow{S^{-1}} u$ *if and only if* $(u, \neg v) \in \text{UpperClosure}\,(\text{DivCore}_S)$;

5. $v \xrightarrow[\text{min.}]{S^{-1}} u$ *if and only if* $(u, \neg v) \in \text{MinSet}_u(\text{UpperClosure}\,(\text{DivCore}_S))$;

6. $v \xrightarrow[\text{core}]{S^{-1}} u$ *if and only if* $(u, \neg v) \in \text{DivCore}_S$.

Here, the subscript of MinSet *defines the variable on which the min-set is computed (the vectors are labeled* (u, v)*).*

On the Compactness of Division Core. By Sperner's theorem, the division core, as a min-set, has size bound $\mathcal{O}(2^{n+m}/\sqrt{n+m})$. This might seem as not so "compact" representation. For example, linear functions with domain $\mathbb{F}_2^n$ contain only vectors of weight n (to show this, consider any minimal transition $u \xrightarrow[\text{min.}]{S} v$ and observe that $\mathbf{wt}(\neg u) + \mathbf{wt}(v) = n$). Furthermore, for a random binary matrix $\mathbb{F}_2^{n \times m}$ one can expect a large number of invertible submatrices which translates into a large number of minimal/compact division property transitions (see [21,39]). Perhaps counter-intuitively, it follows that linear maps are the ones that may achieve the largest size of the division core, which could be interpreted as having the most complex division property propagation. On the opposite side, for a random function of full degree, most minimal transitions $u \xrightarrow[\text{min.}]{S} v$ have v of very small weight which translates into small-weight vectors in division core. This in turn makes most vectors of larger weight redundant and so the division core is expected to be a small set. The right intuition is that "heavier" functions tend to have "simpler" division property propagation and this is exactly captured by the division core as a compact representation.

Finally, we describe a new view on division trail composition in terms of the division core. The proof is given in the full version of this paper [36].

Proposition 7. *Let* $F : \mathbb{F}_2^n \to \mathbb{F}_2^m$, $G : \mathbb{F}_2^m \to \mathbb{F}_2^r$, $u \in \mathbb{F}_2^n, w \in \mathbb{F}_2^r$. *Then, there exists a valid division trail*

$$u \xrightarrow{F} v \xrightarrow{G} w$$

if and only if there exist $a \in \mathbb{F}_2^n, b, b' \in \mathbb{F}_2^m, c \in \mathbb{F}_2^r$ *such that*

$$a \preceq \neg u, \quad (a, b) \in \text{DivCore}_F, \quad b \wedge b' = \underline{0}, \quad (b', c) \in \text{DivCore}_G, \quad c \preceq w.$$

3.6   Convex Structure of the Set of Minimal Transitions

In theory, identifying valid transitions (UpperClosure (DivCore$_S$)) is sufficient to identify propagation of division property and resulting integral distinguishers. In practice, it is crucial to also remove redundant transitions to reduce the search space of automated SAT/MILP solvers or ad-hoc search engines such as [11,33,34]. Therefore, we analyze the set of *minimal/reduced* transitions in more details.

Definition 11. *Let $S : \mathbb{F}_2^n \to \mathbb{F}_2^m$. Define the following sets:*

$$\mathcal{I}_S := \left\{ (u,v) \in \mathbb{F}_2^n \times \mathbb{F}_2^m \mid \neg u \overset{S}{\nrightarrow} v \right\},$$

$$\mathcal{M}_S := \left\{ (u,v) \in \mathbb{F}_2^n \times \mathbb{F}_2^m \mid \neg u \overset{S}{\rightarrow} v, \nexists v' \prec v : \neg u \overset{S}{\rightarrow} v' \right\},$$

$$\mathcal{R}_S := \left\{ (u,v) \in \mathbb{F}_2^n \times \mathbb{F}_2^m \mid \neg u \overset{S}{\rightarrow} v, \exists v' \prec v : \neg u \overset{S}{\rightarrow} v' \right\}.$$

Remark 6. These sets contain respectively invalid transitions, minimal transitions and redundant transitions through S. The defining condition of $\mathcal{M}_S$ is equivalent to $\neg u \xrightarrow[\text{min.}]{S} v$.

Proposition 8. *The sets $\mathcal{I}_S, \mathcal{M}_S, \mathcal{R}_S$ form a partition of $\mathbb{F}_2^n \times \mathbb{F}_2^m$. Moreover, $\mathcal{I}_S$ is a lower set, $\mathcal{M}_S$ is a convex set, $\mathcal{R}_S$ is an upper set.*

Proof. The conditions of set generators in the sets' definitions clearly induce a partition of $\mathbb{F}_2^n \times \mathbb{F}_2^m$.

It is clear that $\mathcal{M}_S \cup \mathcal{R}_S = $ UpperClosure (DivCore$_S$) (both from the definitions and the fact that it is the complement of $\mathcal{I}_S$). Since $\mathcal{I}_S$ is the complement of this upper set, it must be a lower set.

The convexity of $\mathcal{M}_S$ follows from the fact that $\mathcal{M}_S = (\mathbb{F}_2^n \times \mathbb{F}_2^m) \setminus \mathcal{R}_S \setminus \mathcal{I}_S$. Indeed, let $a, c \in \mathcal{M}_S$. If there exists $b \notin \mathcal{M}_S$ such that $a \preceq b \preceq c$, then from $b \in \mathcal{I}_S$ it would follow that $a \in \mathcal{I}_S$ and so $a \notin \mathcal{M}_s$. The same argument applies to c and $\mathcal{R}_S$, leading to contradiction.   □

We emphasize that all the three sets $\mathcal{I}_S, \mathcal{M}_S, \mathcal{R}_S$ can be derived from the division core DivCore$_S$, highlighting its universality as a compact representation:

$$\mathcal{I}_S = \overline{\text{UpperClosure (DivCore}_S)},$$
$$\mathcal{M}_S = \text{MinSet}_v(\text{UpperClosure (DivCore}_S)),$$
$$\mathcal{R}_S = \overline{\mathcal{I}_S \cup \mathcal{M}_S}.$$

Remarkably, these sets can themselves be expected to have compact representations in the form of max-set for $\mathcal{I}_S$, min-set for $\mathcal{R}_S$, and both min-set and max-set for $\mathcal{M}_S$. We discuss concrete efficient algorithms for computing these sets in Sect. 5.

Note that the maximal upper-set of removable vectors is given by

$$\mathcal{R}'_S := \overline{\text{LowerClosure}(\mathcal{M}_S)}.$$

Compared to $\mathcal{R}_S$, it may include some extra vectors from $\mathcal{I}_S$ (but it always is a superset of $\mathcal{R}_S$). While its size is not smaller than that of $\mathcal{R}_S$, most often it has a simpler structure resulting in smaller models, as we shall see later on examples (see Table 1 in Sect. 4).

3.7   Linear Combinations at the Input/output

Lambin, Derbez and Fouque [22] noticed that division property is not preserved under a composition of S-boxes with linear maps. One has to consider such maps in order to find integral distinguishers with a non-cube-shaped affine space at the input and/or a balanced linear combination of bits at the output. The authors of [22] exhausted all 4-bit linear maps to be composed with one S-box at the input and one S-box at the output. In [11], Derbez and Fouque showed that exhaustion of linear *maps* is unnecessary and exhaustion of linear *masks* is sufficient, tremendously reducing the complexity.

For the input linear masks, they use the fact that an affine space of dimension $n-1$ can be defined by its 1-dimensional orthogonal complement, i.e. by its single non-zero vector. It is thus sufficient to define a linear bijective map that maps this vector to a single bit (completed arbitrarily), compose its inverse at the input of an S-box in the first round (and recompute the division property propagation through the composition), and assume this bit to be a constant and all other bits to be active in the division trail search.

For the output linear masks, the approach is more straightforward: define a bijective linear map that maps the chosen linear combination to a single bit, compose it at the output of an S-Box in the last round (and recompute the division property propagation through the composition), and, finally, check if this single output bit is balanced.

Formulation in Our Framework. We now formulate this problem and simplify its solution in our framework. For simplicity, we assume that an "S-box" covers the full state. The case when target S-boxes cover only part of the state follows naturally. Our analysis is restricted to using traditional division property to find such distinguishers.

Let $S_{\text{in}} : \mathbb{F}_2^n \to \mathbb{F}_2^n$ be a bijection, $F : \mathbb{F}_2^n \to \mathbb{F}_2^m$, $S_{\text{out}} : \mathbb{F}_2^m \to \mathbb{F}_2^r$. Let $\alpha \in \mathbb{F}_2^n, \beta \in \mathbb{F}_2^r$ be the input and the output linear masks respectively, $\alpha \neq \underline{0}, \beta \neq \underline{0}$. We are interested in the integral (zero-sum) distinguishers of $S_{\text{out}} \circ F \circ S_{\text{in}}$ with the input linear mask α and the output mask β:

$$\bigoplus_{x \in \mathbb{F}_2^n, \langle \alpha, x \rangle = c} \langle \beta, S_{\text{out}} \circ F \circ S_{\text{in}}(x) \rangle = 0, \quad c \in \mathbb{F}_2 \text{ a constant.}$$

The approach of [11, 22] is to search for division trails through each of the three steps of the composition

$$(\langle \beta, S_{\text{out}} \rangle) \circ F \circ (S_{\text{in}} \circ L_\alpha^{-1}),$$

where $L_\alpha \in GL_n(\mathbb{F}_2)$ is any such that the first coordinate of $L_\alpha(x)$ equals to $\langle \alpha, x \rangle$. To ensure the precision, the first and the last step must be propagated as units. The following theorem states an equivalent to the method of [11] sufficient condition of existence of such an integral distinguisher based on division property. As we will show in Subsect. 4.3, this leads to easy and efficient CNF/MILP modeling.

Theorem 3. *Let $L_\alpha \in GL_n(\mathbb{F}_2)$ be such that $L_\alpha(x) = (\langle \alpha, x \rangle, \ldots)$ Then, there exists a division trail*

$$(0, 1, \ldots, 1) \xrightarrow{S_{in} \circ L_\alpha^{-1}} u \xrightarrow{F} v \xrightarrow{\langle \beta, S_{out} \rangle} (1)$$

if and only if $u \xrightarrow{F} v$ and

$$\neg u \in \text{LowerClosure}\left(\text{Supp}_{\text{ANF}} \langle \alpha, S_{in}^{-1} \rangle\right), \tag{3}$$

$$v \in \text{LowerClosure}\left(\text{Supp}_{\text{ANF}} \langle \beta, S_{out} \rangle\right). \tag{4}$$

Proof. The first transition by Proposition 6 is equivalent to $\neg u \xrightarrow{L_\alpha \circ S_{in}^{-1}} (1, 0, \ldots, 0)$, equivalently $\neg u \xrightarrow{\langle \alpha, S_{in}^{-1} \rangle} (1)$, equivalent to (3). The last transition is similarly equivalent to (4). $\qquad \square$

Remark 7. For a non-invertible $S_{in} : \mathbb{F}_2^{n'} \to \mathbb{F}_2^n$, one can replace the Boolean function $y \mapsto \langle \alpha, S_{in}^{-1}(y) \rangle$ by the function

$$y \mapsto \bigoplus_{x \in (S_{in} \circ L_\alpha^{-1})^{-1}(y)} \langle \alpha, x \rangle.$$

3.8   Relationships with Graph Indicator-Based Degree Bounds

Recently, Carlet [7] derived new degree bounds on compositions of functions based on the degrees of the graph indicators of the involved functions. It is a natural question whether these bounds can beat traditional bit-based division property and whether division property can be improved by incorporating these bounds. In this section, we show a close relationship of these bounds with division property propagations, based on the relationship of division property propagation and the graph indicator given by Theorem 1.

   Carlet in [8] gives an elegant expression for the graph indicator of the composition of functions in terms of their graph indicators.

Proposition 9 ([7,8]). *Let $G_i : \mathbb{F}_2^{m_{i-1}} \to \mathbb{F}_2^{m_i}$, $i \in \{1, \ldots, r\}$, let $F = G_r \circ \ldots \circ G_1$. Then,*

$$\mathbb{1}_{\Gamma_F}(x, z) = \bigoplus_{\substack{(y_1, \ldots, y_{r-1}) \\ \in \mathbb{F}_2^{m_1} \times \ldots \times \mathbb{F}_2^{m_{r-1}}}} \mathbb{1}_{\Gamma_{G_1}}(x, y_1) \cdot \mathbb{1}_{\Gamma_{G_2}}(y_1, y_2) \cdot \ldots \cdot \mathbb{1}_{\Gamma_{G_r}}(y_{r-1}, z).$$

Example 3. Let $H : \mathbb{F}_2^n \to \mathbb{F}_2^m, G : \mathbb{F}_2^m \to \mathbb{F}_2^r$. Then,

$$\mathbb{1}_{\Gamma_{G \circ H}}(x, z) = \bigoplus_{y \in \mathbb{F}_2^m} \mathbb{1}_{\Gamma_H}(x, y)\mathbb{1}_{\Gamma_G}(y, z).$$

This expression naturally allows to bound possible monomials in $\mathbb{1}_{\Gamma_F}(x, z)$:
(i) $\mathbb{1}_{\Gamma_F}(x, z)$ does not contain a monomial multiple of $x^u z^{\neg v}$ if and only if (ii)

$$\mathbb{1}_{\Gamma_{G_1}}(x, y_1)\mathbb{1}_{\Gamma_{G_2}}(y_1, y_2) \ldots \mathbb{1}_{\Gamma_{G_r}}(y_{r-1}, z)$$

does not contain a monomial multiple of $x^u y_1^{m_1} y_2^{m_2} \ldots y_{r-1}^{m_{r-1}} z^{\neg v}$. By Theorem 1, the condition (i) is equivalent to: for any $v' \preceq v$, $F^{v'}(x)$ does not contain a monomial multiple of x^u. Sufficient conditions for (ii) can be derived from degree bounds of the involved graph indicators, as done in [7]. In this way, graph indicators' degrees allow to derive upper bounds on monomials occurring in products of outputs of the composition F.

We now show that bit-based division property verifies a stronger condition, which in fact can be seen as a bit-based formulation of the degree-based bounds.

Theorem 4. *Let F, G_i be defined as above. Let I be the formal expansion (i.e., no $\oplus$-cancellations) of*

$$\mathbb{1}_{\Gamma_{G_1}}(x, y_1)\mathbb{1}_{\Gamma_{G_2}}(y_1, y_2) \ldots \mathbb{1}_{\Gamma_{G_r}}(y_{r-1}, z).$$

Then, I contains a monomial multiple of

$$x^u y_1^{m_1} y_2^{m_2} \ldots y_{r-1}^{m_{r-1}} z^{\neg v} \tag{5}$$

if and only if there exists a valid division trail

$$u \xrightarrow{G_1} w_1 \xrightarrow{G_2} \ldots \xrightarrow{G_{r-1}} w_{r-1} \xrightarrow{G_r} v. \tag{6}$$

Proof. By Theorem 1, each link in the trail has an equivalent condition on the monomial multiple in the corresponding graph indicator:

$$u \xrightarrow{G_1} w_1 \quad \Leftrightarrow \quad \mathbb{1}_{\Gamma_{G_1}}(x, y_1) \text{ contains a monomial multiple of } x^u y_1^{\neg w_1},$$

$$w_1 \xrightarrow{G_2} w_2 \quad \Leftrightarrow \quad \mathbb{1}_{\Gamma_{G_2}}(y_1, y_2) \text{ contains a monomial multiple of } y_1^{w_1} y_2^{\neg w_2},$$

$$\ldots$$

$$w_{r-1} \xrightarrow{G_r} v \quad \Leftrightarrow \quad \mathbb{1}_{\Gamma_{G_{r-1}}}(y_{r-1}, z) \text{ contains a monomial multiple of } y_{r-1}^{w_{r-1}} z^{\neg v}.$$

($\Rightarrow$) If I contains a monomial multiple of (5), there exists one monomial per each of $\mathbb{1}_{\Gamma_{G_1}}, \mathbb{1}_{\Gamma_{G_2}}, \ldots$ such that all these monomials multiply to (5). Clearly, there must exist $w_1, \ldots, w_{r-1}$ such that $\mathbb{1}_{\Gamma_{G_1}}(x, y_1)$ contains a monomial multiple of $x^u y_1^{\neg w_1}$, $\mathbb{1}_{\Gamma_{G_2}}(y_1, y_2)$ contains a monomial multiple of $y_1^{w_1} y_2^{\neg w_2}$ (to get $y_1^{m_1}$), etc.

($\Leftarrow$) If there exists a trail of the form (6), then there exist corresponding monomial multiples of $x^u y_1^{\neg w_1}$, $y_1^{w_1} y_2^{\neg w_2}$, etc. that obviously multiply to a monomial multiple of (5). $\qquad\square$

This theorem gives an alternative view on division property trails: a division property trail $u \xrightarrow{G_1} \ldots \xrightarrow{G_r} v$ is equivalent to a chain of monomials, one from each of the graph indicators of the composed functions $G_1, \ldots, G_r$, such that, in their product, all intermediate variables are fully saturated, the input variable has an exponent succeeding u and the output variable has an exponent succeeding $\neg v$. In particular, *division property allows to derive an upper bound on monomials occurring in the graph indicator of the composition.*

While an existence of such a trail/a monomial chain does not mean that $\mathbb{1}_{\Gamma_F}$ in fact *contains* a monomial multiple of $x^u y^{\neg v}$ (due to the possible cancellations), the inverse is true: for $\mathbb{1}_{\Gamma_F}$ to contain such a monomial multiple, there must exist a corresponding division trail.

We conclude that traditional bit-based division property is optimal in determining upper bounds on monomials in $\mathbb{1}_{\Gamma_F}$ *as long as cancellations in the product*

$$\mathbb{1}_{\Gamma_{G_1}}(x, y_1) \mathbb{1}_{\Gamma_{G_2}}(y_1, y_2) \ldots \mathbb{1}_{\Gamma_{G_r}}(y_{r-1}, z)$$

are not considered.

4 CNF Modeling of a Convex Set

In this section, we show that the convex structure of division property transitions from Subsect. 3.6 naturally lends itself to CNF models. We recall that it is sufficient to derive constraints removing the lower set $\mathcal{I}_S$ and the upper set $\mathcal{R}_S$ (or $\mathcal{R}'_S$).

Remark 8. Any CNF formula can be trivially converted to a MILP system, however MILP inequalities are generally more expressive and one can expect a significant reduction in the number of inequalities compared to the number of clauses. Recently, Udovenko [37] developed techniques for constructing smallest MILP models for Boolean functions. In particular, an efficient approach for modeling monotone Boolean functions (lower/upper sets) is given and can be directly applied to remove the lower set $\mathcal{I}_S$ and the upper set $\mathcal{R}_S / \mathcal{R}'_S$ optimally (separately).

Throughout this section, we consider division property transitions in the "directionless" (symmetric) way: for a transition $u \xrightarrow{S} v$, we consider the vector $(\neg u, v)$. This is done for convenience and has no extra cost since the variable negation is free in CNF/MILP models.

4.1 Basic Modeling

A lower set W is called *principal* if it is spanned by a single element: $W =$ LowerClosure $(\{w\})$. Such a lower set can be removed by one CNF clause precisely without removing any other point from the hypercube $\{0, 1\}^n$. In fact, up to negation of the variables, a principal lower set is exactly what can be removed by a single CNF clause. It is thus a building block of general CNF modeling tools such as the Quine-McCluskey algorithm [25, 26].

Proposition 10. *Let $w \in \mathbb{F}_2^n$. Then,*

$$x \notin \text{LowerClosure}(\{w\}) \iff \bigvee_{i:w_i=0} x_i$$

$$x \notin \text{UpperClosure}(\{w\}) \iff \bigvee_{i:w_i=1} \neg x_i.$$

Since a general lower set is a union of principal lower sets by definition, it can be removed by a set of clauses each removing a principal lower set spanned by one of the maximal elements. The case of an upper set is completely analogous.

Corollary 2. *The set $\mathcal{M}_S$ of minimal division property transitions can be modeled by $|\text{MaxSet}(\mathcal{I}_S)| + |\text{MinSet}(\mathcal{R}_S)|$ constraints (CNF clauses or integer inequalities).*

It is also easy to show that such CNF model is *optimal* (in the number of clauses), although *separately* for each of the two sets $\mathcal{I}_S$ and $\mathcal{R}_S$. The proof is omitted due to the page limit.

Proposition 11. *Let $L \subseteq \mathbb{F}_2^n$ be a lower set. If a CNF formula precisely removes L from the hypercube $\{0,1\}^n$, then it contains at least $|\text{MaxSet}(L)|$ clauses.*

We provide the sizes of the relevant sets for a variety of S-boxes in Table 1. For optimal CNF encodings, we used the Quine-McCluskey algorithm together with the open source SCIP optimization suite [13] to find/bound the minimum number of clauses (approach described in [6]).

Example 4. Consider the AES S-Box $S : \mathbb{F}_2^8 \to \mathbb{F}_2^8$ as an example. Its division core DivCore_S contains 122 vectors $(u,v) \in \mathbb{F}_2^8 \times \mathbb{F}_2^8$ with $(\mathbf{wt}(u), \mathbf{wt}(v))$ distributed as follows:

$$(0,8):1, \quad (1,1):25, \quad (1,2):40, \quad (1,3):6,$$
$$(2,1):26, \quad (2,2):4, \quad (3,1):19, \quad (8,0):1.$$

Here, weights $(8,0)$ and $(0,8)$ correspond to the vectors $(\underline{1},\underline{0})$, $(\underline{0},\underline{1})$ which in turn correspond to the division property of the domain and of its image. The set $\text{MaxSet}(\mathcal{I}_S)$ contains 87 maximal invalid vectors, the $\text{MinSet}(\mathcal{R}_S)$ contains 319 minimal redundant vectors. Therefore, minimal transitions through S can be precisely described by 406 CNF clauses (and 87 are sufficient at the cost of allowing redundant transitions). Using the alternative upper bound allows to further reduce the number to $87 + 274 = 361$ clauses.

We compare briefly with other tools/methods. The automated tool Solvatore [12] generates 2921 CNF clauses. A tool from Hu-Wang-Wang [21] uses the STP solver and generates a DNF formula by enumerating all 2001 valid non-redundant trails. Our approach can be easily adapted to compute two DNF formulas with much less clauses: $122 + 119 = 241$. With the Quine-McCluskey algorithm (applied to division property in [14]) we obtain the optimal value of 234 CNF and a heuristic value of ≤ 151 DNF clauses. This is about 2 times better than our result, showing however that our models are close to optimal (in particular, removing invalid and redundant trails separately is done optimally by Proposition 11). Most importantly, Quine-McCluskey is not applicable to larger S-boxes while our method can produce CNF/DNF models of very good quality.

Table 1. Sizes of the convex sets relevant for modeling division property for a variety of S-boxes. $\mathrm{MinDPPT}_S$ is the set of all minimal division property transitions. $\mathrm{DivCore}_S$ is the compact set containing all the information about division property transitions. $\mathrm{MaxSet}(\mathcal{I}_S)$ and one of $\mathrm{MinSet}(\mathcal{R}_S)$, $\mathrm{MinSet}(\mathcal{R}'_S)$ define the number of CNF clauses sufficient for SAT modeling (see Sect. 4). † since MixColumn of Midori-64/Skinny-64 consist of 4 parallel independent 4-bit maps, the optimal CNF was computed from concatenating 4 optimal CNF models (28/21 clauses respectively) of each 4-bit block.

Func. S	n	$|\mathrm{MinDPPT}_S|$	$|\mathrm{DivCore}_S|$	$|\mathrm{MaxSet}(\mathcal{I}_S)|$	$|\mathrm{MinSet}(\mathcal{R}_S)|$	$|\mathrm{MinSet}(\mathcal{R}'_S)|$	CNF (our)	CNF (opt.)
Present	4	47	16	20	24	24	44	26
Knot	4	49	26	32	29	27	59	40
Ascon	5	190	71	83	93	83	166	115
Keccak	5	137	57	45	75	25	70	50
Fides	6	419	188	146	359	254	400	222
Misty S7	7	1779	436	396	1000	967	1363	607
AES	8	2001	122	87	319	274	361	234
Skinny-128	8	2089	611	193	1383	198	391	246
DryGASCON-256	9	7983	631	480	1309	552	1032	475
Misty S9	9	27 623	6755	5120	18 575	16 868	21 988	10403-11819
LED MixColumn	16	177 643 913	177 643 913	33 412	334 974 429	33 061	66 473	–
Midori-64 MixColumn	16	9 834 496	9 834 496	56	39 337 984	56	112	112†
Skinny-64 MixColumn	16	1 185 921	1 185 921	40	6 324 912	44	84	84†
Midori-64 Super-Sbox (all keys)	16	14 714 723	2 380 924	1 912 088	6 277 211	4 317 883	6 229 971	–
LED Super-Sbox (all keys)	16	8 458 909	319 606	321 168	1 119 494	1 261 465	1 440 662	–
LED Super-Sbox (zero key)	16	8 481 417	382 591	388 134	1 215 435	1 317 330	1 603 569	–

4.2 Cardinality Bounds

Cardinality bounds allow to bound the number of bits equal to 1 among a given set of variables. A popular CNF construction for encoding cardinality bounds is due to Sinz [28] and is based on the so-called sequential counters, which encode addition of variables in the unary representation. Although it requires auxiliary variables, it is known to perform well on practice, since it is decided by unit propagation. Cardinality bounds using sequential counters were used recently for differential/linear trail search using SAT-solvers [30].

Cardinality bounds may be particularly helpful for constraining division property transitions, as they can remove a large number of transitions at a very low cost. There are two particular use cases.

The first use is to replace a precise convex upper bound (e.g., $\mathrm{MinSet}(\mathcal{R}_S)$ or $\mathrm{MinSet}(\tilde{\mathcal{R}}_S)$) by a simpler (yet possibly imprecise) cardinality upper bound.

Here, we use the fact that removing precisely all redundant transitions is not necessary: it is usually done as a heuristic aid for SAT solvers to reduce the search space. For a function S, this cardinality constraint is given by $\mathbf{wt}(u||v) \leq h$, where $h := \max_{w \in \mathcal{M}_S} \mathbf{wt}(w)$ and u, v are the division property variables modeling the transition $\neg u \xrightarrow{S} v$.

The second use is to supplement precise bounds to allow faster conflicts during the SAT search. Cardinality bounds allow solvers to quickly skip a large part of invalid transitions, and to process the remaining precise constraints on the remaining smaller search space. In addition to the upper bound described above, a supplementary lower bound is given by $l \leq \mathbf{wt}(u||v)$, where $l := \min_{w \in \mathcal{M}_S} \mathbf{wt}(w)$.

The Case of a Linear Map. We consider the particular case of a linear map $S : \mathbb{F}_2^n \to \mathbb{F}_2^n$. For a minimal transition $\neg u \xrightarrow[\text{min.}]{S} v$ it is known that $\mathbf{wt}(\neg u) = \mathbf{wt}(v)$ is necessary but not sufficient. In the symmetric form (u, v), this constraint becomes

$$n - \mathbf{wt}(u) = \mathbf{wt}(v) \quad \Leftrightarrow \quad \mathbf{wt}(u||v) = n.$$

A redundant transition (u, v) is such that $\mathbf{wt}(v) > \mathbf{wt}(\neg u)$, implying

$$\mathbf{wt}(u||v) > n.$$

It follows that redundant transitions $\mathcal{R}_S$ can be removed with a single cardinality constraint $\mathbf{wt}(u||v) \leq n$.

Proposition 12. *For a linear map $S : \mathbb{F}_2^n \to \mathbb{F}_2^n$, for some $I \subseteq \mathcal{I}_S$, the set $\mathcal{R}_S \cup I$ can be removed with a single cardinality constraint $\mathbf{wt}(u||v) \leq n$, where $(u||v) \in \mathbb{F}_2^{2n}$.*

Remark 9. It is natural to use the more strict constraint $\mathbf{wt}(u||v) = n$, since it may also remove a larger part of $\mathcal{I}_S$.

Remark 10. This constraint is equivalent to $\mathbf{wt}(\neg u) = \mathbf{wt}(v)$ and is basic and well-known in the literature. What is important for our purposes is that it fully removes $\mathcal{R}_S$.

Example 5. Consider the MixColumns matrix of LED [16], $M : \mathbb{F}_2^{16} \to \mathbb{F}_2^{16}$ (see Table 1). It is such that:

$$|\mathcal{M}_M| = 177\,643\,913; \qquad |\text{MinSet}\,(\mathcal{R}_M)| = 334\,974\,429;$$
$$|\text{MaxSet}\,(\mathcal{I}_M)| = 33\,412; \qquad |\text{MinSet}\,(\mathcal{R}'_M)| = 33\,061.$$

Despite a large number of minimal division property transitions (177M), it can be modeled by only 33k CNF clauses plus a cardinality constraint, which adds a negligible amount of clauses and auxiliary variables.

Remark 11. The approach of [21] (using auxiliary variables) allows to model large linear layers (up to 64 bits), by encoding the submatrix invertability condition in the problem, in a way that requires the SMT solver to find the inverse matrix. We remark though that it was only presented in the SMT form, not in pure SAT or MILP.

The advantage of our SAT encoding (which although has a smaller feasible range of about 16-bit linear maps) is its simpler form and the fact that it can be decided by unit propagation: given the input and output mask (u, v), the SAT solver can decide its validity without making further guesses (although at the cost of verifying a possibly large number of clauses).

4.3   Linear Masks at the Input/at the Output

In Subsect. 3.7, we derived simple conditions for applying linear masks at the input and/or at the output. We now show how to model these conditions. We recall that we consider a composition $S_{out} \circ F \circ S_{in}$ with an input linear mask α and an output linear mask β. Theorem 3 provides the following necessary and sufficient conditions (together with the validity of $u \xrightarrow{F} v$):

$$\neg u \in \mathrm{LowerClosure}\left(\mathrm{Supp}_{\mathrm{ANF}}\left\langle \alpha, S_{in}^{-1} \right\rangle\right),$$
$$v \in \mathrm{LowerClosure}\left(\mathrm{Supp}_{\mathrm{ANF}}\left\langle \beta, S_{out} \right\rangle\right).$$

These three conditions can be efficiently modeled by CNF/MILP formulas as was described in Subsect. 4.1.

Moreover, it is sufficient to check if a transition $u \xrightarrow{F} v$ is valid for any of *maximal* exponents $\neg u, v$ in the ANFs of $\left\langle \alpha, S_{in}^{-1} \right\rangle$ and $\left\langle \beta, S_{out} \right\rangle$ respectively. However, the maximality of v can not be guaranteed in practice since the corresponding trail $u \xrightarrow{F} v$ may be redundant, while standard modeling approaches disallow redundant transitions for efficiency reasons.

For the input case, we can restrict the division property mask of the input to F to take values only from $\neg \mathrm{MaxSet}\left(\mathrm{Supp}_{\mathrm{ANF}}\left\langle \alpha, S_{in}^{-1} \right\rangle\right)$, with the goal of reducing the search space. Since a max-set is an antichain, it is convex, and can be modeled by removing the complementary lower and upper bounds. Formally, define

$$U := \mathrm{MaxSet}\left(\mathrm{Supp}_{\mathrm{ANF}}\left\langle \alpha, S_{in}^{-1} \right\rangle\right),$$
$$P := \mathrm{MaxSet}\left(\overline{\mathrm{UpperClosure}\left(U\right)}\right),$$
$$Q := \mathrm{MinSet}\left(\overline{\mathrm{LowerClosure}\left(U\right)}\right).$$

Then, a vector $x \in \mathbb{F}_2^n$ belongs to U (we set $x := \neg u$) if and only if

$$\left(x \notin \mathrm{LowerClosure}\left(P\right)\right) \wedge \left(x \notin \mathrm{UpperClosure}\left(Q\right)\right),$$

which can be encoded by $|P| + |Q|$ CNF clauses (or MILP inequalities).

5   Algorithmic Framework for Dense Sets

5.1   Bitwise Transformations, Lower, Upper, Min-, Max-Sets

We start by introducing a simple yet very generic and powerful tool for manipulating dense subsets of $\mathbb{F}_2^n$ represented by their indicator vectors. This is a straightforward abstraction of well-known algorithms such as the Möbius transform for computing the ANF, the Walsh-Hadamard transform, sum-over-subsets technique, etc. The tool is described in Algorithm 1.

Algorithm 1. Bitwise multidimensional transform

Input: array $X \in A^{2^n}$, transformation map $f : A^2 \to A^2$, mask $I \in \mathbb{F}_2^n$ set to $\underline{1}$ by default
Output: in-place transformed array $X \in A^{2^n}$
Complexity: $\mathcal{O}(\mathbf{wt}(I)2^n) \leq \mathcal{O}(n2^n)$

1: **function** Transform$[f, I](X)$
2:     **for all** $i \in \{0, \ldots, n-1\}$, s.t. I has i-th bit set **do**   ▷ 0-based
3:         **for all** $j \in \{0, \ldots, 2^n - 1\}$, s.t. j has $(n-1-i)$-th bit set **do**   ▷ 0-based
4:             $(X_{j-2^i}, X_j) \leftarrow f(X_{j-2^i}, X_j)$
5:     **return** X

Definition 12. *Define the following maps with the signature* $(\mathbb{F}_2)^2 \to (\mathbb{F}_2)^2$:

$$\text{XOR-up} : (a, b) \mapsto (a, b \oplus a),$$
$$\text{XOR-down} : (a, b) \mapsto (a \oplus b, b),$$
$$\text{OR-up} : (a, b) \mapsto (a, b \vee a),$$
$$\text{OR-down} : (a, b) \mapsto (a \vee b, a),$$
$$\text{LESS-up} : (a, b) \mapsto (a, b \wedge \neg a), \quad equiv.\ b \leftarrow b \wedge [a < b],$$
$$\text{MORE-down} : (a, b) \mapsto (a \wedge \neg b, b), \quad equiv.\ a \leftarrow a \wedge [a > b].$$

Proposition 13. *The defined transformations have the following effects:*

1. Transform[XOR-up] *computes the Möbius transform (involution), i.e. transforms the truth table of a Boolean function into its ANF and vice versa.*
2. Transform[XOR-down] *computes the involution* ParitySet;
3. Transform[OR-up] *computes* UpperClosure.
4. Transform[OR-down] *computes* LowerClosure.
5. Transform[LESS-up] ∘ Transform[OR-up] *computes* MinSet.
6. Transform[MORE-down] ∘ Transform[OR-down] *computes* MaxSet.

Proof. The proofs can be done by induction on the bit-position.   □

Remark 12. The transformations can be efficiently batched in an efficient bitslice fashion, by lifting the set A and operations from $\mathbb{F}_2$ to $\mathbb{F}_2^t$ where t is the number of considered sets.

5.2   Division Property of a Set

Malviya and Tiwari [23] consider the problem of computing the minimal division property of a given (multi)set X. They claim classical complexity $\mathcal{O}(n2^n|X|)$ and quantum complexity $\mathcal{O}(n2^n\sqrt{|X|})$.

The relation between the division property and the set indicator given by Proposition 4 together with the fast MinSet algorithm from the previous subsection lead to a simple and efficient classical algorithm with complexity $\mathcal{O}(n2^n)$ for the problem (see Algorithm 2).

Algorithm 2. Minimal division property of a set

Input: $X \subseteq \mathbb{F}_2^n$
Output: MinDP $(X) \subseteq \mathbb{F}_2^n$
Complexity: $\mathcal{O}(n2^n)$

1: $G \leftarrow$ indicator vector of X $(\in \mathbb{F}_2^{2^n})$
2: $G \leftarrow$ Transform[XOR-down] (G) ▷ parity set of X
3: $G \leftarrow$ Transform[OR-up] (G) ▷ upper set of parity masks
4: $G \leftarrow$ Transform[LESS-up] (G) ▷ min-set of parity masks
5: **return** G ▷ MinDP (X)

5.3   Division Core and Propagation Table

Let $S : \mathbb{F}_2^n \to \mathbb{F}_2^m$. By definition, DivCore$_S := $ MinDP (Γ_S), which can be computed by Algorithm 2. This approach leads to time and memory complexity $\mathcal{O}((n+m)2^{n+m})$. In particular, for bijective S-Boxes we get the time complexity $\mathcal{O}(n2^{2n})$. The complexity is independent of the S-box and of the size of the division core.

Recall that the set of all valid division property transitions through S can be computed as $(\underline{1}, \underline{0}) \oplus$ UpperClosure (DivCore$_S$). To obtain the usual reduced division property propagation table (i.e., all minimal transitions), we can simply compute partial min-set on the second coordinate. See Algorithm 3 for details.

Algorithm 3. Division property propagation table (only minimal transitions)

Input: $S : \mathbb{F}_2^n \to \mathbb{F}_2^m$ as a lookup-table
Output: reduced DPPT of S: $D = \left\{ (u, v) \in \mathbb{F}_2^n \times \mathbb{F}_2^m \mid u \xrightarrow[\text{min.}]{S} v \right\}$
Complexity: $\mathcal{O}((n+m)2^{n+m})$

1: $D \leftarrow$ DivCore$_S$ ▷ Algorithm 2 on Γ_S, without redundant steps 3-4
2: $D \leftarrow$ Transform[OR-up] (D) ▷ full DPPT (up to $\neg u$)
3: $D \leftarrow$ Transform[LESS-up, $(\underline{0}, \underline{1})$] (D) ▷ min-set on v; $= \mathcal{M}_S$ from Definition 11
4: **return** $D \leftarrow (\underline{1}, \underline{0}) \oplus D$ ▷ compute $\neg u$

This in particular achieves "quadratic" complexity $\mathcal{O}(n2^{2n})$, an improvement over the "cubic" complexity $\mathcal{O}(2^{3n})$ claimed in [11] for computing the DPPT using algorithm from [38] (in the case $m = n$).

Finally, from the set $\mathcal{M}_S$ computed by *Algorithm* 3 we can easily compute the necessary min-/max-sets and respective complementary sets required for modeling:

$$\mathcal{I}_S = \overline{\mathrm{UpperClosure}\,(\mathrm{DivCore}_S)},$$
$$\mathcal{R}_S = \overline{\mathcal{I}_S \cup \mathcal{M}_S},$$
$$\mathcal{R'}_S = \overline{\mathrm{LowerClosure}\,(\mathrm{DivCore}_S)}.$$

For the compact CNF modeling (Sect. 4), it is left to compute $\mathrm{MaxSet}\,(\mathcal{I}_S)$ and $\mathrm{MinSet}\,(\mathcal{R}_S)$ (or $\mathrm{MinSet}\,(\mathcal{R'}_S)$).

5.4   Compact Representation (Advanced Algorithm)

In this subsection, we describe a breadth-first search algorithm which performs much better for "heavy" functions, i.e., those having many high-degree monomials in most products of output bits, implying a small size of the division core and a small number of non-trivial invalid transitions. In this algorithm, we assume access to the lookup table of the function and the memory footprint is of the same magnitude, so this approach is limited up to about 32-bit functions on practice.

We restrict the description to the case of a bijective function $S : \mathbb{F}_2^n \to \mathbb{F}_2^n$ for simplicity, as non-bijective functions would require more fine-grained case analysis due to possible degeneracy.

We consider first vectors $(u, v) \in \mathrm{DivCore}_S$ with $u = \underline{0}$ or $v = \underline{0}$. The case of $v = \underline{0}$ corresponds to the minimal division property of the domain which leads exactly to $(\underline{1}, \underline{0}) \in \mathrm{DivCore}_S$. The case of $u = \underline{0}$ can be exhausted by computing the minimal division property of the image of S (more precisely, of the set of its elements with odd multiplicity). For bijective S this case leads to only $(\underline{0}, \underline{1}) \in \mathrm{DivCore}_S$. Note that all predecessors of these vectors define invalid transitions (have parity zero), and should be explicitly excluded to avoid enumeration of the $2 \cdot 2^n$ "trivial" pairs.

We are going to explore all possible nonzero u, v in a breadth-first manner (from low weight to high weight), until we obtain the full division core of S. Given a pair (u, v) of unknown parity, and a promise that all its strictly preceding vectors have parity zero (due to the exploration order), we can compute its parity by computing the parity set of (the support of) S^v or of $(S^{-1})^u$; we choose the one with the minimal weight ($\mathbf{wt}(v)$ or $\mathbf{wt}(u)$). The parity set of, say, S^v, may provide many other vectors $(u', v) \in \mathrm{DivCore}_S$. In particular, we consider all *minimal* u' in the parity set as candidates and save the corresponding pairs (u', v) in a set D. Although D may also include redundant vectors, each vector of $\mathrm{DivCore}_S$ will be present in one of such lists of candidates.

After the main step, if (u, v) has parity one, we add it to the division core (it is guaranteed to be minimal due to the exploration order) and continue with the next pair in the queue. Otherwise, if (u, v) has parity zero, we consider its successors for adding to the exploration queue. However, for each pair, we maintain a counter of its direct predecessors that were visited and have parity zero. The pair is added to the queue only when the counter is full, i.e. when the last direct predecessor is visited. This allows to avoid duplicate processing of (u, v), and, more importantly, ensures that all predecessors have parity zero and the new pair is not redundant. In this way, when a new pair is visited and it belongs to the list D of parity-1 pairs, we know that this pair is minimal and so belongs to the division core.

The algorithm effectively explores full set $\mathcal{I}_S$ and the bordering subset of UpperClosure (DivCore_S) (in fact, among them, only elements of DivCore_S are visited), which is at most $2n$ times larger. Note that all the predecessors of $(\underline{1}, \underline{0})$ and $(\underline{0}, \underline{1})$ are excluded. Let

$$\mathcal{I}_S^\times := \{(u, v) \in \mathcal{I}_S \mid u \neq \underline{0}, v \neq \underline{0}\}.$$

Then, the algorithm performs at most $2n \left| \mathcal{I}_S^\times \right|$ iterations of the algorithm. Each iteration is dominated by an n-bit ParitySet computation together with its min-set (time $n2^n$). The total time complexity is upper bounded by $\mathcal{O}\left(\left| \mathcal{I}_S^\times \right| n^2 2^n\right)$. Note however that, due to maintaining the list D of parity-1 pairs, many visited pairs do not incur a parity set computation. In addition, by storing masks u and v for which the parity sets were already computed, we can avoid recomputing them for many pairs from $\mathcal{I}_S^\times$ as well. We conclude that the algorithm is expected to be much faster on practice.

Due to the page limit, the pseudocode is given in the full version of this paper [36].

Computing complete compact representation. Since the algorithm effectively enumerates full $\mathcal{I}_S^\times$, its max-set can be computed by marking redundant vectors during the enumeration (in addition, we need to manually add direct predecessors of $(\underline{0}, \underline{1})$ and $(\underline{1}, \underline{0})$ to avoid enumerating their exponentially-sized lower sets). For the compact modeling, it is left to compute $\text{MinSet}(\mathcal{R}_S)$. For this purpose, we derive an alternative expression for $\mathcal{R}_S$.

Proposition 14. *Let* $S : \mathbb{F}_2^n \to \mathbb{F}_2^M$. *Then,*

$$\mathcal{R}_S = \bigcup_{(u,v) \in \text{DivCore}_S} \{(u', v') \in \mathbb{F}_2^n \times \mathbb{F}_2^m \mid u' \succeq u, v' \succ v\}.$$

Proof. Each set in the union defines redundant vectors identified by an element $(u, v) \in \text{DivCore}_S$. Conversely, each redundant vector must have an associated irredundant vector from $(u, v) \in \text{DivCore}_S$. □

It follows that $\text{MinSet}(\mathcal{R}_S)$ can be computed from DivCore_S by replacing each vector $(u, v) \in \text{DivCore}_S$ by the set of vectors (u, v'), where v' is taken from direct successors of v (i.e., $v' \succeq v, \mathbf{wt}(v') = \mathbf{wt}(v) + 1$). However, redundant vectors may occur there and a final computation of MinSet is needed. Assuming sparse DivCore_S, it makes sense to use the naive quadratic MinSet algorithm instead of the dense one. The final complexity of computing MinSet $(\mathcal{R}_S)$ is thus upper-bounded by $\mathcal{O}(|\text{DivCore}_S|^2 \cdot n^2)$.

Corollary 3. *Let* $S : \mathbb{F}_2^n \to \mathbb{F}_2^m$. *Then,* $|\text{MinSet}\,(\mathcal{R}_S)| \leq m \cdot |\text{DivCore}_S|$.

Example 6. We ran the algorithm on a randomly generated 32-bit bijective S-box. Together with the generation and inversion, it took less than a core-day on a laptop with 64GB RAM. The resulting numbers are:

$$|\text{DivCore}_S| = 7\,152, \quad |\text{MaxSet}\,(\mathcal{I}_S)| = 2\,958, \quad |\text{MinSet}\,(\mathcal{R}_S)| = 40\,093.$$

These numbers show that it would even be possible to model such an S-box in a cipher. Although it is unlikely that such a cipher would be of interest, this proof-of-concept show the power of the algorithm and of the compact representation to capture the simplicity of "heavy" S-boxes (i.e., the compactness of the maximal sets of monomials).

6   Application to LED

Derbez and Fouque [11] increased precision of traditional division property by two techniques: (1) computing "perfect" division property propagation tables of Super-Sboxes; (2) checking linear combinations of bits (inside Super-Sbox boundaries) at the input and at the output. In addition, the authors designed an ad-hoc search method, since modeling 16-bit S-boxes was not possible with state-of-the-art techniques. They considered lightweight block ciphers with 4-bit S-boxes and 16-bit Super-Sboxes, such as Midori64, Skinny-64, LED [16]. Their approach succeeded for Midori64 and Skinny-64, for which they improved best integral distinguishers by 1–2 rounds. However, the running time during their experiments with LED was not reasonable.

In this section, we apply our new framework to handle this case. The best integral distinguisher for LED is due to Hu, Wang and Wang [21], who managed to model perfectly the MixColumn matrix of LED, which is MDS. The distinguisher covers 7 rounds, with 63 input active bits and full output state balanced. Full balanced state may hint towards possibility of weaker distinguishers (partially balanced state) on 8 or more rounds. We set to evaluate 8 rounds of LED using the two techniques by Derbez and Fouque implemented using our advancements. As we shall see, these two techniques are insufficient to find an 8-round integral distinguisher, if it exists.

All experiments were done on the version of LED with 128-bit key (the key size affects the constants in the Super-Sboxes).

6.1   Structure of LED and Its Model

The structure of LED is particularly convenient for our analysis. Each round consists of four standard operations: AddConstants(AC), SubBytes(SB),

ShiftRows(SR), MixColumns(MC). The state of LED is a 4×4 array of 4-bit nibbles. The key is added only after every 4 rounds (a step).

The 8-round LED has a natural Super-Sbox decomposition: 4 rounds of Super-Sboxes (SB $\to$ MC $\to$ AC$_{2i+1}$ $\to$ SB, applied on columns) with the SR $\to$ MC $\to$ SR linear layers in-between. For example, the following equation describes the Super-Sbox decomposition of the first two rounds (note that SR commutes with SB):

$$AC_0 \to SB \to SR \to MC \to AC_1 \to SB \to SR \to MC$$
$$= AC_0 \to SR \to (SB \to MC \to AC_1 \to SB) \to SR \to MC.$$

The key addition happens outside of the Super-Sboxes and thus does not affect the modeling. However, the constant addition AC does affect Super-Sboxes, and we compute the division property transitions for each Super-Sbox separately, using the actual constant in the middle. In the following subsection, we describe modeling details for the two main components: Super-Sboxes and the MixColumns linear layer.

6.2 Modeling Details

As our theoretical analysis shows that division property can be very naturally modeled by pure CNF formulas, we set to use a bare SAT-solver (not an SMT-solver). We chose Kissat [2], a recent solver which showed strong performance at a recent SAT competition [19]. We modeled 2 Super-Sbox rounds with SR $\circ$ MC $\circ$ SR layers in-between and outside. The missing 2 Super-Sbox rounds are treated by the linear mask analysis (Subsect. 3.7) and by trivial Super-Sbox transitions $1^{16} \to 1^{16}$, $0^{16} \to 0^{16}$. Each such model took less than a few minutes to solve on a laptop with an Intel(R) Core(TM) i5-10210U CPU.

Modeling MixColumn matrix. The MixColumn matrix of LED is an MDS matrix M mapping $\mathbb{F}_{2^4}^4$ to itself. We apply directly our algorithms to compute the complementary lower and upper bounds on division property transitions. The lower bound (removing invalid transitions) consists of 33 412 vectors, the upper bound (removing redundant transitions) contains 334 974 429 vectors, the alternative upper bound contains 33 061 vectors. The total number of minimal transitions is 177 643 913. We observe that 33k clauses is reasonable for the lower bound. However, the upper bound is unnecessarily large. Therefore, we used the cardinality constraint described in Subsect. 4.2 to remove $\mathcal{R}_M$ and used the 33k clauses to remove $\mathcal{I}_M$.

Modeling Super-Sbox. We provide numbers for the case of Super-Sbox with the zero constant; the cases of other constants are similar. The division core contains 382 591 vectors and the number of valid minimal transitions is 8 481 417; the complementary lower and upper bounds contain 388 134 and 1 215 435 vectors respectively. These number are rather large, but still in a feasible range of modern

SAT solvers. We used the 388 134 clauses to remove invalid trails precisely, while we used a cardinality bound to remove a part of redundant trails, to avoid using the 1 215 435 clauses per Super-Sbox for removing all redundant trails.

6.3   Exhausting All Linear Masks

We applied the approach from Subsect. 3.7 to search for distinguishers with linear masks applied to an input and an output Super-Sbox.

Naive approach would be to exhaust all possible linear masks α, β and check the existence of respective distinguishers. However, as noticed by [11], many linear masks are redundant: an absence of distinguishers for one mask may imply absence of distinguishers for others, making them redundant (in case a distinguisher is found, redundant masks may be re-evaluated if needed).

On practice, many linear combinations turn to have the same set of maxterms in the ANF. For example, for the Super-Sbox of LED with the zero constant, the number of unique sets of maxterms among linear combinations of outputs is only 1785 (out of 65 535). The first step is thus to remove masks with duplicate sets of ANF maxterms.

From Theorem 3 it is clear that a mask is redundant if the lower closure of the respective ANF (i.e., that of $\langle \alpha, S_{in}^{-1} \rangle$ or $\langle \beta, S_{out} \rangle$) covers the lower closure of the ANF of another mask. As a result, we only need to consider masks corresponding to *minimal* by inclusion lower closure of the ANF. In the example constant-0 Super-Sbox of LED, the 1785 maxterm-unique ANFs reduce further to 255 (by a pairwise comparison). For the Super-Sbox' inverse, among 2021 maxterm-unique combinations again only 255 are minimal by (lower closure) inclusion.

Still, a straightforward search (as done in [11] for other ciphers) would require solving $16 \times 255 \times 255 \approx 1$ million (4×4 combinations of input and output Super-Sboxes) of search instances. This may be a feasible goal but it would require a significant computational effort. We describe a natural optimization that shows to be particularly helpful in the case of LED.

Reusing trails. Usually, one may expect that many linear combinations of output bits have similar ANFs. Therefore, a trail $\neg u \xrightarrow{F} v$ satisfying conditions of Theorem 3 for a pair of masks (α, β), may satisfy the conditions for some other pairs of masks (α', β') as well, even if both pairs correspond to unique and non-redundant ANFs. This condition can be checked much faster than solving a SAT instance. This suggests the following optimization: before solving the SAT instance for a pair of masks (α, β), check whether any previously found trail satisfies the condition.

This approach works well for the 8-round LED. For each combination of input/output Super-Sbox, about 30 trails are sufficient to show that the Super-Sbox model of 8-round LED does not allow to find integral distinguishers. All computed trails are provided in the code repository of the paper. An example trail is provided in Fig. 1.

```
      1111 1111 1111            1111 1111 1111 1111            1111 1011 1111 1101            0100 0011 1000 1000
1^15  1111 1111 1111  SuperSbox 0010 1111 1111 1111  SR∘MC∘SR 1111 1111 1101 1111  SuperSbox 0001 1111 0100 1111
(α,x)^4 1111 1111 1111          1111 1111 1111 1111            1111 1111 1111 1111            1111 0001 0100 1010
      1111 1111 1111            0110 1111 1111 1111            1101 1111 1101 1111            1111 1111 0110 0100

                                              SR∘MC∘SR

0000 0000 1111 0000            0000 0000 0100 0000            0000 0000 0000 0000                0000 0000 0000
0111 1011 0000 0011  SuperSbox 1010 0000 0000 0100  SR∘MC∘SR 0000 0000 0000 0000  SuperSbox 1^1 0000 0000 0000
1011 1101 1010 1101            0000 0000 0000 0000            1011 0000 0000 0000          (β,x) 0000 0000 0000
0011 1101 0111 0111            0000 0010 0010 0000            0111 0000 0000 0000                0000 0000 0000
```

Fig. 1. Example division trail from the 1st input Super-Sbox to the 1st output Super-Sbox. Covers input masks α such that the ANF of $\langle \alpha, \mathrm{SSB}_{0,0}^{-1}(x) \rangle$ contains a multiple of $x_4 x_5 x_7 x_{12} x_{15}$ (zeroes in the first column after the first Super-Sbox), output masks β such that the ANF of $\langle \beta, \mathrm{SSB}_{3,0}(y) \rangle$ contains a multiple of $y_8 y_{10} y_{11} y_{13} y_{14} y_{15}$ (ones in the first column before the last Super-Sbox).

6.4 Summary

Using the described techniques, we managed to show that integral distinguishers for the 8-round LED (and, by Proposition 6, for its inverse), if any exists, can not be found using traditional bit-based division property even with perfect Super-Sbox modeling and arbitrary linear masks applied to Super-Sboxes at the input and at the output. To do this, we found a small set of division trails through 8-round LED that, together with Theorem 3, proves the claim.

References

1. Bar-On, A., Keller, N.: A 2^{70} attack on the full MISTY1. In: Robshaw, M., Katz, J. (eds.) CRYPTO 2016. LNCS, vol. 9814, pp. 435–456. Springer, Heidelberg (2016). https://doi.org/10.1007/978-3-662-53018-4_16
2. Biere, A., Fazekas, K., Fleury, M., Heisinger, M.: CaDiCaL, Kissat, Paracooba, Plingeling and Treengeling entering the SAT Competition 2020. In: Proceedings of SAT Competition 2020 – Solver and Benchmark Descriptions. Department of Computer Science Report Series b, vol. B-2020-1, pp. 51–53. University of Helsinki (2020)
3. Biryukov, A., Khovratovich, D., Perrin, L.: Multiset-algebraic cryptanalysis of reduced Kuznyechik, Khazad, and secret SPNs. IACR Trans. Symm. Cryptol. **2016**(2), 226–247 (2016)
4. Boura, C., Canteaut, A.: On the influence of the algebraic degree of F^{-1} on the algebraic degree of G ∘ F. IEEE Trans. Inf. Theor. **59**(1), 691–702 (2013)
5. Boura, C., Canteaut, A.: Another view of the division property. In: Robshaw, M., Katz, J. (eds.) CRYPTO 2016. LNCS, vol. 9814, pp. 654–682. Springer, Heidelberg (2016). https://doi.org/10.1007/978-3-662-53018-4_24
6. Boura, C., Coggia, D.: Efficient MILP modelings for Sboxes and linear layers of SPN ciphers. IACR Trans. Symmetric Cryptol. **2020**(3), 327–361 (2020)
7. Carlet, C.: Graph indicators of vectorial functions and bounds on the algebraic degree of composite functions. IEEE Trans. Inf. Theor. **66**(12), 7702–7716 (2020)
8. Carlet, C.: Handling vectorial functions by means of their graph indicators. IEEE Trans. Inf. Theor. **66**(10), 6324–6339 (2020)

9. Chen, S., Xiang, Z., Zeng, X., Zhang, S.: On the relationships between different methods for degree evaluation. IACR Trans. Symmetric Cryptol. **2021**(1), 411–442 (2021)

10. Daemen, J., Rijmen, V.: The Design of Rijndael: AES - The Advanced Encryption Standard. Information Security and Cryptography, Springer, Heidelberg (2002). https://doi.org/10.1007/978-3-662-04722-4

11. Derbez, P., Fouque, P.A.: Increasing precision of division property. IACR Trans. Symmetric Cryptol. **2020**(4), 173–194 (2020)

12. Eskandari, Z., Kidmose, A.B., Kölbl, S., Tiessen, T.: Finding integral distinguishers with ease. In: Cid, C., Jacobson, M., Jr., (eds.) Selected Areas in Cryptography – SAC 2018, SAC 2018. LNCS, vol. 11349. Springer, Cham (2019). https://doi.org/10.1007/978-3-030-10970-7_6

13. Gamrath, G., et al.: The SCIP Optimization Suite 7.0. Technical report, Optimization Online (2020)

14. Fujioka, A., Okamoto, Y., Saito, T.: Security of sequential multiple encryption. In: Abdalla, M., Barreto, P.S.L.M. (eds.) LATINCRYPT 2010. LNCS, vol. 6212, pp. 20–39. Springer, Heidelberg (2010). https://doi.org/10.1007/978-3-642-14712-8_2

15. Göloğlu, F., Rijmen, V., Wang, Q.: On the division property of S-boxes. Cryptology ePrint Archive, Report 2016/188 (2016)

16. Guo, J., Peyrin, T., Poschmann, A., Robshaw, M.: The LED block cipher. In: Preneel, B., Takagi, T. (eds.) CHES 2011. LNCS, vol. 6917, pp. 326–341. Springer, Heidelberg (2011). https://doi.org/10.1007/978-3-642-23951-9_22

17. Hao, Y., Leander, G., Meier, W., Todo, Y., Wang, Q.: Modeling for three-subset division property without unknown subset. In: Canteaut, A., Ishai, Y. (eds.) EUROCRYPT 2020. LNCS, vol. 12105, pp. 466–495. Springer, Cham (2020). https://doi.org/10.1007/978-3-030-45721-1_17

18. Hebborn, P., Lambin, B., Leander, G., Todo, Y.: Lower bounds on the degree of block ciphers. In: Moriai, S., Wang, H. (eds.) ASIACRYPT 2020. LNCS, vol. 12491, pp. 537–566. Springer, Cham (2020). https://doi.org/10.1007/978-3-030-64837-4_18

19. Heule, M., Jarvisalo, M., Suda, M., Iser, M., Balyo, T., Froleyks, N.: SAT Competition 2020 - Results. https://satcompetition.github.io/2020/index.html

20. Hu, K., Sun, S., Wang, M., Wang, Q.: An algebraic formulation of the division property: revisiting degree evaluations, cube attacks, and key-independent sums. In: Moriai, S., Wang, H. (eds.) ASIACRYPT 2020. LNCS, vol. 12491, pp. 446–476. Springer, Cham (2020). https://doi.org/10.1007/978-3-030-64837-4_15

21. Hu, K., Wang, Q., Wang, M.: Finding bit-based division property for ciphers with complex linear layer. IACR Trans. Symm. Cryptol. **2020**(1), 396–424 (2020)

22. Lambin, B., Derbez, P., Fouque, P.-A.: Linearly equivalent S-boxes and the division property. Des. Codes Crypt. **88**(10), 2207–2231 (2020). https://doi.org/10.1007/s10623-020-00773-4

23. Malviya, A.K., Tiwari, N.: Quantum algorithm to identify division property of a multiset. Arab. J. Sci. Eng. **46**(9), 8711–8719 (2021)

24. Matsui, M.: New block encryption algorithm MISTY. In: Biham, E. (ed.) FSE 1997. LNCS, vol. 1267, pp. 54–68. Springer, Heidelberg (1997). https://doi.org/10.1007/BFb0052334

25. McCluskey, E.J.: Minimization of Boolean functions. Bell Syst. Tech. J. **35**(6), 1417–1444 (1956)

26. Quine, W.V.: A way to simplify truth functions. Am. Math. Mon. **62**(9), 627–631 (1955)

27. Sasaki, Yu., Todo, Y.: New algorithm for modeling S-box in MILP based differential and division trail search. In: Farshim, P., Simion, E. (eds.) SecITC 2017. LNCS, vol. 10543, pp. 150–165. Springer, Cham (2017). https://doi.org/10.1007/978-3-319-69284-5_11

28. Sinz, C.: Towards an optimal CNF encoding of Boolean cardinality constraints. In: van Beek, P. (ed.) CP 2005. LNCS, vol. 3709, pp. 827–831. Springer, Heidelberg (2005). https://doi.org/10.1007/11564751_73

29. Sun, B., Hai, X., Zhang, W., Cheng, L., Yang, Z.: New observation on division property. Sci. Chin. Inf. Sci. **60**(9), 1–3 (2016). https://doi.org/10.1007/s11432-015-0376-x

30. Sun, L., Wang, W., Wang, M.: Accelerating the search of differential and linear characteristics with the sat method. IACR Trans. Symmetric Cryptol. **2021**(1), 269–315 (2021)

31. Sun, L., Wang, W., Wang, M.Q.: MILP-aided bit-based division property for primitives with non-bit-permutation linear layers. IET Inf. Secur. **14**(1), 12–20 (2016)

32. Todo, Y.: Integral cryptanalysis on full MISTY1. In: Gennaro, R., Robshaw, M. (eds.) CRYPTO 2015. LNCS, vol. 9215, pp. 413–432. Springer, Heidelberg (2015). https://doi.org/10.1007/978-3-662-47989-6_20

33. Todo, Y.: Structural evaluation by generalized integral property. In: Oswald, E., Fischlin, M. (eds.) EUROCRYPT 2015. LNCS, vol. 9056, pp. 287–314. Springer, Heidelberg (2015). https://doi.org/10.1007/978-3-662-46800-5_12

34. Todo, Y., Morii, M.: Bit-based division property and application to Simon family. In: Peyrin, T. (ed.) FSE 2016. LNCS, vol. 9783, pp. 357–377. Springer, Heidelberg (2016). https://doi.org/10.1007/978-3-662-52993-5_18

35. Todo, Y., Morii, M.: Compact representation for division property. In: Foresti, S., Persiano, G. (eds.) CANS 2016. LNCS, vol. 10052, pp. 19–35. Springer, Cham (2016). https://doi.org/10.1007/978-3-319-48965-0_2

36. Udovenko, A.: Convexity of division property transitions: theory, algorithms and compact models. Cryptology ePrint Archive, Report 2021/1285 (2021). https://ia.cr/2021/1285

37. Udovenko, A.: MILP modeling of Boolean functions by minimum number of inequalities. Cryptology ePrint Archive, Report 2021/1099 (2021)

38. Xiang, Z., Zhang, W., Bao, Z., Lin, D.: Applying MILP method to searching integral distinguishers based on division property for 6 lightweight block ciphers. In: Cheon, J.H., Takagi, T. (eds.) ASIACRYPT 2016. LNCS, vol. 10031, pp. 648–678. Springer, Heidelberg (2016). https://doi.org/10.1007/978-3-662-53887-6_24

39. Zhang, W., Rijmen, V.: Division cryptanalysis of block ciphers with a binary diffusion layer. IET Inf. Secur. **13**(2), 87–95 (2018)

Strong and Tight Security Guarantees Against Integral Distinguishers

Phil Hebborn[1(✉)], Baptiste Lambin[1(✉)], Gregor Leander[1(✉)],
and Yosuke Todo[2(✉)]

[1] Horst Görtz Institute for IT Security, Ruhr University Bochum, Bochum, Germany
{phil.hebborn,gregor.leander}@rub.de, baptiste.lambin@protonmail.com
[2] NTT Social Informatics Laboratories, Tokyo, Japan
yosuke.todo.xt@hco.ntt.co.jp

Abstract. Integral attacks belong to the classical attack vectors against any given block ciphers. However, providing arguments that a given cipher is resistant against those attacks is notoriously difficult. In this paper, based solely on the assumption of independent round keys, we develop significantly stronger arguments than what was possible before: our main result is that we show how to argue that the sum of ciphertexts over any possible subset of plaintext is key-dependent, i.e., the non existence of integral distinguishers.

Keywords: Block cipher · Integral distinguisher

1 Introduction

As symmetric primitives, due to their performance advantages, are a vital part of our security building blocks, being able to assess their security is of great practical importance and theoretical interest. The security of block ciphers, and actually any symmetric primitive in use, is always the security against concrete attacks. Two of the most important attacks are certainly differential and linear attacks. Security arguments with respect to those attacks have been studied for quite some time already, leading to important concepts like the Markov model in [16]. Nowadays, we are usually able to bound, under the assumption of independent round-keys, the probability of a differential characteristic (or the correlation of a linear characteristic). Those are good, but certainly not fully satisfactory security arguments, as we often ignore the differential or linear-hull effect. Stronger arguments, like a bound of the expected differential probability, require a dedicated design, see e.g. [18] and [8].

Another classical attack vector is integral attacks, which can be traced back to high-order differentials by Lai [15], and then exploited by Knudsen to be used in actual attacks [14] as well as the so-called "Square attack" [10]. In a nutshell, given a block cipher E_k, those attacks work by identifying a subset of plaintexts M such that summing over the corresponding ciphertexts results in a constant

© International Association for Cryptologic Research 2021
M. Tibouchi and H. Wang (Eds.): ASIACRYPT 2021, LNCS 13090, pp. 362–391, 2021.
https://doi.org/10.1007/978-3-030-92062-3_13

sum, i.e., $\sum_{x \in M} E_k(x)$ does not depend on the secret key k. Arguments for security against those attacks, i.e. arguments showing that such a set M should not exist for a given cipher, are very difficult to obtain. For most ciphers, we do not have any argument at all and if arguments are given, they only cover very specific sets M.

In most attacks, M is chosen as a subspace and more specifically by fixing some bits in the plaintext to constants. This specific choice of M is not at all necessary for a successful attack, and indeed there are examples of more involved plaintext sets being used for improved attacks. The main reason for this choice is the relation to the algebraic degree of the cipher. Indeed, for a cipher of algebraic degree at most d, taking M as any subspace of dimension larger than d leads to a successful distinguisher, as the sum is zero. Thus, a first step towards arguing the security of a block cipher against integral attacks is to show that its algebraic degree is maximal. However, even this special case was only settled very recently. For a long time, only upper bounds on the algebraic degree have been discussed. At ASIACRYPT'20 in [12], it was shown for the first time how to compute meaningful lower bounds on the degree of round-reduced block ciphers. Technically, this approach is based on recent progress on the division property initially introduced in [20].

While [12] demonstrated how to compute lower bounds on the degree for the first time, several drawbacks remained: It does not allow to exclude integral attacks and its applicability is limited due to a lack of efficiency. Further, only bounds for round-reduced variants could be computed.

Limited Arguments. As outlined above, even if the degree is high, there might still be integral distinguishers and attacks. An integral distinguisher in general makes use of a fixed set $M \subset \mathbb{F}_2^n$ of plaintext values and a bit-mask β such that, for any key k the value of $\sum_{x \in M} \langle \beta, E_k(x) \rangle$ is independent of the key. In [12], this was shown for a natural, but very limited, choice of sets M, where M consists of just fixing bits in the input. While this is, to the best of our knowledge, the best argument against integral attacks so far, it is far from being satisfactory. In particular, it does not capture integral distinguishers where M consists of fixing linear combination in the input, used in [17] or [19]. More generally, it does not capture integral distinguishers where M is not a linear subspace, as in [22].

Limited Number of Rounds. The arguments given in [12] allowed to compute lower bounds on the algebraic degree for a fixed number of rounds. When the number of rounds is increased, computing the bounds quickly becomes infeasible. This is in sharp contrast to the expected result. If r rounds of a given cipher have maximal degree $n - 1$, it is naturally expected that more than r rounds have the same degree. While this intuition is probably true in most cases, it is of course not a sound security argument. Making this argument more precise is non-trivial. It is clear that in general, given F of degree $n - 1$, representing the (fixed-key) first-part of the cipher there always exists a function G such that $G \circ F$ is of lower degree than F. Indeed, the easiest example is to choose G as the inverse of F, in case F is a permutation. One might hope that in the case of a keyed permutation, the situation is less bad, as at least the trivial example above is not applicable anymore. However, even in the keyed case, as we show in Example 4, there exist permutations F and G such that

$$\deg(G \circ (F(x) + k)) < \min(\deg(F), \deg(G)).$$

That is, the degree of the composition is actually smaller than the individual degrees, *for any key k*. This shows that it cannot be excluded simply by assuming independent round keys that the degree (as a keyed function) decreases.

Lack of Efficiency. The proof of the lower bound of degree proposed in [12] strongly ties to the division property [20], which is originally a tool to detect an integral distinguisher. To prove the lower bound, we need to generate a key pattern whose number of division trails is odd, and countable in practical time. As pointed out in [12], it is not easy because the number of trails exponentially increases unless a key pattern is generated in a clever manner. The so-called trail extension was used to generate such a key pattern and enabled to prove lower bounds on the degree (especially the number of rounds so that this lower bound is maximal, i.e. 63), for SKINNY-64, GIFT-64, and PRESENT. On the other hand, the applicability of the trail extension to other block ciphers is an open question. Interestingly, we faced potential difficulties of the trail extension when we tried expanding applications (the tweakable block cipher CRAFT as an example). The number of trails exceeds the practically countable range quickly, and it is unfeasible to prove a lower bound on the degree of CRAFT.

Our Contribution. In this paper we derive strong and tight bounds against integral distinguishers for several block ciphers. The only assumption on which we rely for our bounds is having independent-round key, i.e., independent round keys are XORed with the full state. Our bounds are *strong* as we show that for a cipher E_k, the sum $\sum_{x \in M} \langle \beta, E_k(x) \rangle$ is key-dependent for *any possible set M* (excluding only the whole input space and the empty set) and *any possible non-zero mask β*. We refer to this as the *integral-resistance property*. Our bounds are *tight* as (in most cases) the minimal number of rounds where we can show the non-existence *matches the best known distinguishers*. Our arguments extend to an arbitrary number of rounds greater than that.

First, we fix our notation and recall the basic techniques in Sect. 2. We develop the necessary theory to achieve the strong arguments in Sect. 3. To formalize the strong arguments, which means the guarantee of the non-existence of integral distinguishers under the sole assumption of independent round keys, we introduce the Proposition. We develop the theoretical background to utilize the division property, for not only showing a lower bound of the degree of a cipher as in [12], but to show the Proposition.

In Sect. 4 we study how adding more rounds (separated with a key addition) will affect the algebraic degree, the minimum degree, and the strong argument against integral distinguishers. For the minimum degree and the strong argument, we are able to show that adding (keyed or un-keyed) rounds is never a problem, as the minimum degree never decreases and the strong argument never vanishes when doing so. The algebraic degree on the other hand potentially decreases, as also sketched above. Here we are able to present efficiently computable criteria on the S-box that allow to exclude such undesirable behavior.

The drawback of the lack of efficiency is handled in Sect. 5. We show that, maybe counter-intuitively, a suitable rewriting of the cipher and in particular the S-box, can have a significant effect on the running time of the techniques used in [12]. We present (heuristic) conditions on how to choose a suitable description of the cipher that allows to keep the number of division trails reasonably low - a fact that is crucial as those have to be enumerated.

Finally, in Sect. 6 we apply the theory and tools developed to a set of ciphers. Besides the ciphers treated in [12], and which present a large fraction of the primitives used in the running NIST lightweight competition, we added a discussion of CRAFT [5], which was previously out of reach and a discussion of the ciphers SIMON and Simeck as examples of non-SPN ciphers. We assume independent round keys for all ciphers. Further, for GIFT-64 and SKINNY-64, we assume, contrary to the specification, a key addition on the full state.

For all those applications we are able to show the non-existence of integral distinguishers. Interestingly, except for GIFT-64 and PRESENT, our result matches the best known attacks tightly, as can be seen in Table 1.

We finally emphasize the meaning of our results. Our results guarantee that improving integral distinguishers is impossible under our assumption. This is strong claim compared to heuristic attack failure. For example, for CRAFT, we guarantee no integral distinguisher for 14 rounds and more. Thus any such distinguisher would have to violate our assumptions. In other words, it has to exploit the key scheduling. For SKINNY-64 and GIFT-64 our results are slightly weaker compared to the other applications because here round keys are not XORed with the whole state in both ciphers. Room of improvements still remains without exploiting key scheduling, but it must exploit the fact that the round key is XORed with the half of the state only.

2   Preliminaries

In this section, we are going to recall the definitions and the different notations of degree that are commonly used for Boolean functions. We also recall what was shown in [12] and briefly explain the necessary background on division property to explain how this was done technically.

2.1   Degree of Keyed Functions - Definitions and Results

A block cipher can be seen as a family of (keyed) vectorial boolean permutations, that is, bijective functions $E_k : \mathbb{F}_2^n \to \mathbb{F}_2^n$ with $k \in \mathbb{F}_2^m$. We can represent such functions with their algebraic normal form (ANF)

$$E_k(x) = \sum_{u \in \mathbb{F}_2^n} p_u(k) x^u$$

Table 1. Number of rounds of the best known integral distinguisher (together with a reference for this) vs. the number of rounds we need to ensure the Propositionunder the assumption that independent round keys are XORed to the full state. Numbers in red indicate are tight results.

Cipher	Known integral distinguisher	Integral-resistance property
SKINNY-64	12 [11]	13
CRAFT	13 [5]	14
GIFT-64	10 [2]	12
PRESENT	9 [23]	13
SIMON32	15 [21]	16
SIMON48	16 [23]	17
SIMON64	18 [23]	19
SIMON96	22 [23]	23
SIMON128	26 [23]	27
Simeck32	15 [21]	16
Simeck48	18 [23]	19
Simeck64	21 [23]	22

with $x^u = \prod_i x_i^{u_i}$ and $p_u(k)$ are functions $p_u : \mathbb{F}_2^m \to \mathbb{F}_2^n$ mapping keys to values in $\mathbb{F}_2^n$. We define the *algebraic degree* of E_k as the degree in the input variables x, that is, the algebraic degree $\deg(E_k)$ is defined as

$$\deg(E_k) := \max_u \{ \mathrm{wt}(u) \mid p_u \neq 0 \},$$

where $\mathrm{wt}(u)$ denotes the Hamming weight of u, i.e. the number of non-zero coordinates of u.

The *minimum degree* of E_k, is defined as the minimum degree over all non-zero component functions $\langle \beta, E_k \rangle$

$$\mathrm{minDeg}(E_k) = \min_{\beta \neq 0} \deg(\langle \beta, E_k \rangle).$$

Until recently, getting meaningful lower bounds for both the algebraic degree and the minimum degree was deemed essentially impossible for block ciphers of relevant size (i.e. at least 64-bit block size). However at ASIACRYPT'20, Hebborn et al. [12] managed to obtain such lower bounds at least for round-reduced variants. The main idea is that to show a lower bound d on the algebraic degree of E_k, one "simply" needs to show that there exists a $u \in \mathbb{F}_2^n$ such that $\mathrm{wt}(u) \geq d$ and $p_u \neq 0$. If we denote the coefficients of p_u by $\lambda_{u,v} \in \mathbb{F}_2^n$, that is,

$$E_k(x) = \sum_{u \in \mathbb{F}_2^n, v \in \mathbb{F}_2^m} \lambda_{u,v} x^u k^v,$$

this is the same as finding a $u \in \mathbb{F}_2^n$ with $\mathrm{wt}(u) \geq d$ and $v \in \mathbb{F}_2^m$ such that $\lambda_{u,v} \neq 0$, which is equivalent to $p_u \neq 0$.

Finally, they also introduced an even stronger notion, namely the appearance of *all* maximum-degree monomials, which is that for any given monomial x^u of algebraic degree $n-1$, and for any component function $\langle \beta, F \rangle$, there always exists at least one key k such that the monomial x^u appears in the ANF of $\langle \beta, E_k \rangle$.

However this paper comes with significant limitations. It was shown that having the all maximum-degree monomial property allows to rule out basic integral distinguishers. Indeed, it can only rule out distinguishers constructed with a set of plaintexts M built as an affine space of the form

$$M = \{x \in \mathbb{F}_2^n \text{ s.t. } \forall i \in I, x_i = c_i\},$$

where I is a subset of $\{1, \dots, n\}$ and c_i are fixed constants in $\mathbb{F}_2$. On the other hand, the case presented in [17], where the input set is an affine space with a more convoluted structure, is not. For example, already the affine space

$$M = \{x \in \mathbb{F}_2^n \text{ s.t. } x_0 + x_1 = 0\},$$

is out of scope, not to mention arbitrary subsets.

Despite these limitations, we can use the core idea of their work, which is, after explaining how to compute such a $\lambda_{u,v}$, to decide how to choose these u and v, allowing to actually compute $\lambda_{u,v}$ in practical time so that we can prove the various lower bounds and properties. We give more details about this in Sect. 2.3. Before that, in the next section we first give a high-level overview of the main tool used in their work, that is, division property.

2.2 High-Level Summary of Division Property

After the division property was first proposed in [20], many follow-up works have been proposed [7]. In [12], the various notations, definitions, and theorems about the division property were unified by using the parity set, which was used as another view of the division property in [7]. Here we briefly recall the main definitions and connections with the algebraic normal form.

Definition 1 (Parity Set). *Let* $\mathbb{X} \subseteq \mathbb{F}_2^n$ *be a set. We define the* parity set *of* $\mathbb{X}$ *as*

$$\mathcal{U}(\mathbb{X}) := \left\{ u \in \mathbb{F}_2^n \text{ such that } \sum_{x \in \mathbb{X}} x^u = 1 \right\}.$$

The addition of two subsets $\mathbb{X}, \mathbb{Y} \subseteq \mathbb{F}_2^n$ is defined by

$$\mathbb{X} + \mathbb{Y} := (\mathbb{X} \cup \mathbb{Y}) \setminus (\mathbb{X} \cap \mathbb{Y}).$$

In other words, we view the set of all subsets of $\mathbb{F}_2^n$ as a binary vector space of dimension 2^n, and this addition is isomorphic to adding the binary indicator vectors of the sets. From this perspective, for $\mathbb{X}_i \subseteq \mathbb{F}_2^n$,

$$\mathcal{U}\left(\sum \mathbb{X}_i\right) = \sum \mathcal{U}(\mathbb{X}_i)$$

holds, i.e. $\mathcal{U}$ is a linear mapping. Moreover, it was shown in [7] that there is a one to one correspondence between sets and its parity set. That is the mapping $\mathcal{U} : \mathbb{X} \mapsto \mathcal{U}(\mathbb{X})$ is a bijection and actually its own inverse, i.e., $\mathcal{U}(\mathcal{U}(\mathbb{X})) = \mathbb{X}$.

We next define the propagation as follows.

Definition 2 (Propagation). *Given $F : \mathbb{F}_2^n \to \mathbb{F}_2^m$ and $a \in \mathbb{F}_2^n, b \in \mathbb{F}_2^m$, we say that the division property a propagates to the division property b, denoted by $a \xrightarrow{F} b$ if and only if $b \in \mathcal{U}(F(\mathcal{U}(\{a\})))$.*

Here the image of a set $\mathbb{X}$ under F is defined as

$$F(\mathbb{X}) := \sum_{a \in \mathbb{X}} \{F(a)\},$$

that is again using the addition of sets as defined above. Given $U_1 = \mathcal{U}(\mathbb{X})$, for any function F, $U_2 = \mathcal{U}(F(\mathbb{X}))$ is evaluated as

$$U_2 = \mathcal{U}(F(\mathbb{X})) = \sum_{x \in \mathbb{X}} \mathcal{U}(F(\{x\})) = \sum_{a \in \mathcal{U}(\mathbb{X})} \mathcal{U}(F(\mathcal{U}(\{a\}))) = \sum_{a \in U_1, a \xrightarrow{F} b} \{b\}. \quad (1)$$

To determine U_2 after applying the function F, it is enough to consider what happens with individual elements of U_1 to start with. Again, we emphasize that the sum in Eq. 1 is modulo two, that is, if an element appears an even number of times on the right side, it actually does not appear in U_2. Note that the propagation rules shown in [21] can be proven by assigning concrete operation to F. More generally, the propagation for any function F is described as follows.

Proposition 1 ([12]). *Let $F: \mathbb{F}_2^n \to \mathbb{F}_2^m$ be defined as $F(x) = y$. For $a \in \mathbb{F}_2^n$ and $b \in \mathbb{F}_2^m$, it holds that $a \xrightarrow{F} b$ if and only if y^b contains the monomial x^a.*

We now generalize the definition above to the setting where F is actually given as the composition of many functions as $F = F_R \circ \cdots \circ F_2 \circ F_1$.

Definition 3 (Trail). *Given $F: \mathbb{F}_2^n \to \mathbb{F}_2^n$ as $F = F_R \circ \cdots \circ F_2 \circ F_1$, and $a_0, \ldots, a_R \in \mathbb{F}_2^n$ we call $(a_0, \ldots, a_R)$ a (division) trail for the compositions of F into the F_i if and only if*

$$\forall i \in \{1, \ldots, R\}, a_{i-1} \xrightarrow{F_i} a_i.$$

We denote such a trail by $a_0 \xrightarrow{F_1} a_1 \xrightarrow{F_2} \cdots \xrightarrow{F_R} a_R$.

Using the same considerations as in Eq. 1, we can now state the main reason of why considering trails is useful.

Theorem 1 ([12]). *Given $F: \mathbb{F}_2^n \to \mathbb{F}_2^n$ as $F = F_R \circ \cdots \circ F_2 \circ F_1$, and $\mathbb{X} \subseteq \mathbb{F}_2^n$. Then*

$$\mathcal{U}(F(\mathbb{X})) = \sum_{a_0, \ldots, a_R, a_0 \in \mathcal{U}(\mathbb{X}), a_0 \xrightarrow{F_1} a_1 \xrightarrow{F_2} \cdots \xrightarrow{F_R} a_R} \{a_R\}$$

Finally, we show the link between the division property and the ANF.

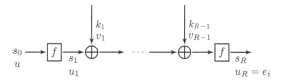

Fig. 1. Notations for the trails of a key-alternating block cipher, where the terms in red are the parity-set vector of the corresponding state

Corollary 1 ([12]). *Let* $F : \mathbb{F}_2^n \to \mathbb{F}_2^n$ *be a function with algebraic normal form*

$$F(x) = \sum_{u \in \mathbb{F}_2^n} \lambda_u x^u$$

where $\lambda_u = (\lambda_u^{(1)}, \ldots, \lambda_u^{(n)}) \in \mathbb{F}_2^n$. *Furthermore, let* $\mathbb{X}$ *be the set such that* $\mathcal{U}(\mathbb{X}) = \{\ell\}$. *Then*

$$\lambda_\ell^{(i)} = 1 \Leftrightarrow e_i \in \mathcal{U}(F(\mathbb{X})) \Leftrightarrow \#\{a_1, \ldots, a_{R-1} | \ell \xrightarrow{F_1} a_1 \xrightarrow{F_2} \cdots \xrightarrow{F_R} e_i\} = 1 \bmod 2$$

2.3 Proof of a Lower Bound on the Degree and Finding Key Patterns

Now that we are equipped with the results from the previous section, we can give more details about the work from [12] where the authors gave lower bounds on the algebraic degree and minimum degree of block ciphers, as the techniques we use in the next section to give strong arguments against integral distinguishers strongly rely on their results. We put ourselves in the context of key-alternating block ciphers, depicted in Fig. 1. We assume that we have a round function f, and the block cipher E is built by alternating applications of f with a round key addition (with an XOR) between them. As in [12], we assume that the round keys are independent from each other. The internal states are thus denoted by $s_0, \ldots, s_R$, where R is the number of rounds, s_0 is the input (plaintext) of the block cipher and s_R the output (ciphertext). The round keys are denoted by $k_1, \ldots, k_{r-1}$. The key length m is $(r-1)n$.

As mentioned in Sect. 2.1, showing a lower bound d on the algebraic degree of a block cipher is equivalent to exhibiting vectors $u \in \mathbb{F}_2^n$ of weight at least d and $v \in \mathbb{F}_2^m$ (where m is the key length) so that $\lambda_{u,v}$ is non-zero, which in particular means that one coordinate $\lambda_{u,v}^{(i)}$ is equal to 1. As each round key is independent, we can write v as $(v_1, \ldots, v_{R-1})$ so that $k^v = k_1^{v_1} k_2^{v_2} \ldots k_{R-1}^{v_{R-1}}$.

According to the previous section, proving that $\lambda_{u,v}^{(i)} = 1$ is equivalent to showing that the number of trails $(u, v) \xrightarrow{E} e_i$ is odd. We take the same denomination as in [12], and call u the *input pattern*, v the *key pattern* and $u_R = e_i$ the *output pattern*. As mentioned in Sect. 2.1, to get lower bounds on the minimum degree, instead of showing that a single $\lambda_{u,v}^{(i)}$ is equal to 1, we now need to compute the value of several of these $\lambda_{u,v}^{(i)}$ so that we end up with a set of $\lambda_{u,v}$ which spans a vector space of dimension n.

In both cases, the main goal is to find (several) u and v so that we can compute the coefficients $\lambda_{u,v}^{(i)}$ in practical time, which according to the previous section, means being able to enumerate all corresponding trails. The core of the work in [12] is thus to give a (heuristic) algorithm to determine which u and v to choose so that we can actually enumerate all of these trails in a reasonable time. As we also need to compute such $\lambda_{u,v}^{(i)}$ for our results, we give a quick overview of their algorithm and refer the reader to the full paper for more details. Their main observation is that having a key pattern with a high weight tends to lower the resulting number of trails, which is quite interesting since the lower this number is, the easier (and quicker) enumerating them should be. However, the naive idea of simply maximizing the weight of the key pattern is not enough, and thus they used the following strategy. We start by fixing the input pattern u and output pattern $u_R = e_i$, and focus on finding $v = (v_1, \ldots, v_{R-1})$ so that the number of trails is reasonably low. Starting from u_R, we first search for a (partial) key pattern v_{R-1} so that the number of trails $(u_{R-1}, v_{R-1}) \rightarrow e_i$ is odd and low (optimally, only one trail), maximizing the weight of the (partial) key pattern v_{R-1} as it should help minimize the number of trails. After finding such a v_{R-1}, we now search in the same way for a partial key pattern v_{R-2} so that again, the number of trails $(u_{R-2}, v_{R-2}, v_{R-1}) \rightarrow e_i$ is odd and low (again, optimally, only one trail). The authors observed that this "local optimization" strategy seems to fail if we keep going too close to the first round. Thus, we only keep doing this up to some round "in the middle" R_{mid}, leading us to a partial key pattern $(v_{R_{mid}}, \ldots, v_{R-1})$ so that the number of trails from $(u_{R_{mid}}, v_{R_{mid}}, \ldots, v_{R-1})$ to e_i is odd and low. After that, we directly search for the remaining parts of the key pattern $(v_1, \ldots, v_{R_{mid}-1})$ so that the number of trails from $(u, v_1, \ldots, v_{R_{mid}-1})$ to $u_{R_{mid}}$ is odd and low, and finally verify that the number of trails $(u, v_1, \ldots, v_{R-1}) \rightarrow e_i$ is still odd. If so, we proved that $\lambda_{u,v}^{(i)} = 1$ and keep using the same strategy until we found enough (u, v) as we need. One limitation is that for various technical reasons, the authors of [12] were limited to SPN block ciphers, so that they were able to exploit Super S-box representations, making ciphers like Feistel networks out of reach, and some ciphers (e.g. CRAFT) did not have a favorable behavior regarding the trail extension technique that we just summarized. Nonetheless, we actually managed to get results for the Feistel networks ciphers SIMON and Simeck, as shown in Sect. 6.5, as well as getting results on CRAFT with new techniques in Sect. 5.

In summary, from [12], we can efficiently compute the value of some coefficients $\lambda_{u,v}$, which we will use in the upcoming sections to prove our results.

3   Strong Arguments Against Integral Distinguishers

Here, we are going to derive necessary and sufficient conditions on when integral distinguishers are not possible. More precisely, we aim at conditions such that we can conclude that, for a cipher E_k, the sum

$$\sum_{x \in M} \langle \beta, E_k(x) \rangle$$

is key-dependent for *any possible set* M (excluding only the whole input space and the empty set) and *any possible non-zero mask* β. Note that this covers a much larger set of possible integral distinguishers than commonly used in previous works. Indeed, most classical integral distinguishers build the set M as an affine space by fixing some bits to a constant value, while the other bits take all possible values. Some recent works [11,17] extended this further and built M still as an affine space, but now using constant *linear combinations* of bits instead of single bits. What we aim to show here is the most general case as we are considering *any* possible set M, including sets without an affine structure.

Before stating the general results and explaining how to verify those efficiently for specific ciphers (under the assumption of independent round keys), we are going to consider simple examples to clarify the approach beforehand.

For this, we consider Boolean functions only, i.e. only a single output bit. This can be thought of as investigating a single fixed β. All the examples will be key-dependent with a key consisting of the three-bit key $k = (k_0, k_1, k_2)$.

Example 1 (Missing High-Degree Terms). As a first example, let $f_k : \mathbb{F}_2^3 \to \mathbb{F}_2$ be given as

$$f_k(x_0, x_1, x_2) = k_1 x_0 x_1 + k_1 x_0 + x_1 + (k_1 k_2 + k_3) x_2$$

While this function reaches the maximal degree (for a balanced function), it clearly does not satisfy the condition that $\sum_{x \in M} f_k(x)$ is key-dependent for any non-trivial M. Indeed, considering simply $M = \{000\}$ leads to a key-independent sum, simply as the constant term of f_k is key-independent. When considering a version of f_k using an additional whitening key $h = (h_0, h_1, h_2)$ defined as $f_{h,k}(x) = f_k(x + h)$, we get the polynomial expression

$$\begin{aligned} f_{h,k}(x) = {} & k_1 x_0 x_1 + (k_1 h_1 + k_1) x_0 + (k_1 h_0 + 1) x_1 \\ & + (k_1 k_2 + k_3) x_2 + (k_1 k_2 h_2 + k_1 h_0 h_1 + k_1 h_0 + k_3 h_2 + h_1) \end{aligned}$$

which now does contain a key-dependent constant term, but choosing M as $M' = \{000, 001, 100, 101\}$ leads to $\sum_{x \in M'} f_{h,k}(x) = 0$ again. So while lower degree integral attacks might be avoided by adding whitening keys, high degree attacks remain unchanged. This is due to the fact that whitening keys do not affect the coefficients of monomials of maximal degree.

Example 2 (Linearly Dependent High-Degree Terms). Consider now g_k as

$$g_k(x_0, x_1, x_2) = k_0 x_0 x_1 + k_1 x_0 x_2 + (k_0 + k_1) x_1 x_2.$$

Now, all quadratic terms are present. While for g_k itself, there are key-independent coefficients, e.g. the constant term, this is not the case for $g_{h,k}$ defined as $g_{h,k}(x) = g_k(x + h)$. The corresponding expression is

$$g_{h,k}(x) = \sum_u \lambda_u(k)$$
$$= k_0 x_0 x_1 + k_1 x_0 x_2 + (k_0 h_1 + k_1 h_2)x_0 + (k_0 + k_1)x_1 x_2$$
$$+ (k_0 h_0 + k_0 h_2 + k_1 h_2)x_1 + (k_0 h_1 + k_1 h_0 + k_1 h_1)x_2$$
$$+ k_0 h_0 h_1 + k_0 h_1 h_2 + k_1 h_0 h_2 + k_1 h_1 h_2$$

and contains every monomial of degree smaller than n with a key-dependent coefficient. However, there are still sets M such that the corresponding sum is key-independent. For this example, there are exactly two non-trivial sets namely

$$M_0 = \{000, 110, 011, 101\} \text{ and } M_1 = \mathbb{F}_2^3 \setminus M_0$$

which yield to constant sums. Concretely we have

$$\sum_{x \in M_0} g_{h,k}(x) = \sum_{x \in M_1} g_{h,k}(x) = 0.$$

The reason for this is that the coefficients of g_k (and thus of $g_{h,k}$) of the monomials $x_0 x_1$, $x_0 x_2$ and $x_1 x_2$ are linearly dependent polynomials. Indeed, the set can be written as $M_0 = \mathcal{U}(\{110, 101, 011\})$. Thus, the sum can be written as

$$\sum_{x \in \mathcal{U}(\{110,101,011\})} g_{h,k}(x) = \sum_{u \in \{110,101,011\}} \lambda_u(k) = k_0 + k_1 + (k_0 + k_1),$$

that is the sum of the linearly dependent coefficients.

Example 3 (Linearly Independent High-Degree Terms). A slight modification of the second example is given by

$$\ell_k(x) = k_0 x_0 x_1 + k_1 x_0 x_2 + k_0 k_1 x_1 x_2$$

and the version with whitening keys leads to

$$\ell_{h,k}(x) = k_0 x_0 x_1 + k_1 x_0 x_2 + (k_0 h_1 + k_1 h_2)x_0 + k_0 k_1 x_1 x_2 + (k_0 k_1 h_2 + k_0 h_0)x_1$$
$$+ (k_0 k_1 h_1 + k_1 h_0)x_2 + k_0 k_1 h_1 h_2 + k_0 h_0 h_1 + k_1 h_0 h_2.$$

As can be checked by running through all possible non-empty sets of size less than eight, none of the corresponding sums will be key-independent.

The reason why the last example does not lead to any integral distinguishers is, as we will elaborate in general next, that $\ell_k(x)$ (i) contains all monomials of degree $n - 1$ and (ii) the corresponding coefficients are linearly independent polynomials.

Considering a Single Output Bit. For two vectors $u, v \in \mathbb{F}_2^n$, we define (as usually in this context)

$$u \succeq v \quad \Leftrightarrow \quad (v_i = 1 \Rightarrow u_i = 1).$$

Lemma 1. *Let* $f_k : \mathbb{F}_2^n \rightarrow \mathbb{F}_2$ *be a family of functions with ANF*

$$f_k(x) = \sum_{u \in \mathbb{F}_2^n} p_u(k) x^u$$

and consider a version of f_k *with an additional pre-whitening key* k_0, *i.e.*

$$f_{k,k_0}(x) := f_k(x + k_0) = \sum_{v \in \mathbb{F}_2^n} q_v(k, k_0) x^v$$

Then we have

$$q_v(k, k_0) = \sum_{u \succeq v} p_u(k) k_0^{u \oplus v}$$

Proof. We express $q_v(k, k_0)$ in terms of p_u. We get

$$f_{k,k_0}(x) = f_k(x + k_0) = \sum_{u \in \mathbb{F}_2^n} p_u(k) (x + k_0)^u$$

$$= \sum_{u \in \mathbb{F}_2^n} p_u(k) \left(\sum_{v \preceq u} x^v k_0^{u \oplus v} \right) = \sum_{v \in \mathbb{F}_2^n} \left(\sum_{u \succeq v} p_u(k) k_0^{u \oplus v} \right) x^v$$

$\square$

Next, we show a sufficient criterion to ensure that all the polynomials $q_v(k, k_0)$ are linearly independent (for $v \neq (1, \ldots, 1)$). For this, we denote by u_i the vector in $\mathbb{F}_2^n$ of weight $n - 1$ such that its ith position is zero. That is, u_i is the bitwise complement of the ith unit vector.

Theorem 2. *Let* f_k *and* f_{k,k_0} *be defined as above. If the polynomials* $p_{u_i}(k)$ *are linearly independent and* $p_{(1,\ldots,1)}(k) = 0$, *then all polynomials*

$$\{q_v(k, k_0) \mid v \in \mathbb{F}_2^n \setminus \{1\}\}$$

are linearly independent.

Proof. Assume there are coefficients $\alpha_v \in \mathbb{F}_2$ such that

$$T = \sum_{v \in \mathbb{F}_2^n \setminus \{1\}} \alpha_v q_v(k, k_0) = 0.$$

We have to show that this implies $\alpha_v = 0$ for all v. We first rewrite this as

$$T = \sum_{v \in \mathbb{F}_2^n \setminus \{1\}} \alpha_v q_v(k, k_0) = \sum_{v \in \mathbb{F}_2^n \setminus \{1\}} \alpha_v \left(\sum_{u \succeq v} p_u(k) k_0^{u \oplus v} \right)$$

$$= \sum_{v \in \mathbb{F}_2^n \setminus \{1\}} \alpha_v \left(\sum_{v \oplus w \succeq v} p_{v \oplus w}(k) k_0^w \right) = \sum_{v \in \mathbb{F}_2^n \setminus \{1\}} \alpha_v \left(\sum_{\substack{w \in \mathbb{F}_2^n \\ \mathrm{Sup}(w) \cap \mathrm{Sup}(v) = \emptyset}} p_{v \oplus w}(k) k_0^w \right)$$

$$= \sum_{w \in \mathbb{F}_2^n} \left(\sum_{\substack{v \in \mathbb{F}_2^n \setminus \{1\} \\ \mathrm{Sup}(w) \cap \mathrm{Sup}(v) = \emptyset}} \alpha_v p_{v \oplus w}(k) \right) k_0^w$$

Here, we denote by $\mathrm{Sup}(x)$ the set of non-zero bit positions, that is

$$\mathrm{Sup}(x) = \{i \mid x^{(i)} = 1\}.$$

The above implies that $T = 0$ if and only if for all $w \in \mathbb{F}_2^n$, we have

$$T(w) := \sum_{\substack{v \in \mathbb{F}_2^n \setminus \{1\} \\ \mathrm{Sup}(w) \cap \mathrm{Sup}(v) = \emptyset}} \alpha_v p_{v \oplus w}(k) = 0.$$

We show that this implies $\alpha_v = 0$ by induction on the weight of v.

For $\mathrm{wt}(v) = 0$, that is v being the all-zero vector, consider a vector w with $\mathrm{wt}(w) = n - 1$. That is, w is one of the vectors u_i. The set of vectors v such that $\mathrm{Sup}(w) \cap \mathrm{Sup}(v) = \emptyset$ contains only the all-zero vector and e_i. We thus get,

$$T((1, \ldots, 1)) = \alpha_{(0,\ldots,0)} p_{u_i}(k) + \alpha_{e_i} p_{((1\ldots,1))}(k) = 0.$$

By assumption $p_{((1\ldots,1))}(k)$ is zero, while $p_{u_i}(k)$ is not, thus $\alpha_{(0,\ldots,0)} = 0$.

$\mathrm{wt}(v) = t \leq n - 2$: We now assume by induction that $\alpha_v = 0$ for all v of weight smaller than t. We consider a vector w of weight $\mathrm{wt}(w) = n - (t + 1)$. Then, the set of vectors such that $\mathrm{Sup}(w) \cap \mathrm{Sup}(v) = \emptyset$ contains one vector of weight $t + 1$, vectors of weight exactly t, and vectors of weight smaller than t. We split $T(w)$ accordingly as follows

$$T(w) = \sum_{\substack{\mathrm{wt}(v) = t+1 \\ \mathrm{Sup}(w) \cap \mathrm{Sup}(v) = \emptyset}} \alpha_v p_{v \oplus w}(k) + \sum_{\substack{\mathrm{wt}(v) = t \\ \mathrm{Sup}(w) \cap \mathrm{Sup}(v) = \emptyset}} \alpha_v p_{v \oplus w}(k) + \sum_{\substack{\mathrm{wt}(v) < t \\ \mathrm{Sup}(w) \cap \mathrm{Sup}(v) = \emptyset}} \alpha_v p_{v \oplus w}(k)$$

By the induction hypothesis, the last part is zero, as $\alpha_v = 0$ for $\mathrm{wt}(v) < t$. Furthermore, the first part is zero as here $v \oplus w = (1, \ldots, 1)$ and $p_{((1\ldots,1))}(k)$ is zero, which implies

$$T(w) = \sum_{\substack{\mathrm{wt}(v) = t \\ \mathrm{Sup}(w) \cap \mathrm{Sup}(v) = \emptyset}} \alpha_v p_{v \oplus w}(k) = 0.$$

Now here $v \oplus w$ is of weight $n - 1$ and thus is one of the vectors u_i. By assumption, the polynomials p_{u_i} are linearly independent and thus $T(w) = 0$ implies $\alpha_v = 0$ for all v of weight t such that $\mathrm{Sup}(w) \cap \mathrm{Sup}(v) = \emptyset$. As w was arbitrary of weight $n - (t + 1)$ this means that $\alpha_v = 0$ for all v of weight t. □

This finally implies, as a corollary, that there are no key-independent integral distinguishers in a very general sense. Any sum of output values, except for the empty sum and summing all outputs, is key-dependent. More precisely,

Corollary 2. *Let f_k and f_{k,k_0} be defined as above and assume that the polynomials $p_{u_i}(k)$ are non-constant linearly independent, and $p_{(1,\ldots,1)}(k) = 0$. Then, for any proper non-empty subset $M \subset \mathbb{F}_2^n$ the sum*

$$\sum_{x \in M} f_{k,k_0}(x)$$

depends on the value of the key (k, k_0).

Proof. It holds that

$$\sum_{x \in M} f_{k,k_0}(x) = \sum_{\ell \in \mathcal{U}(M)} \left(\sum_{x \preceq \ell} f_{k,k_0}(x) \right) = \sum_{\ell \in \mathcal{U}(M)} q_\ell(k, k_0).$$

As M is non-empty and not the full space, $\mathcal{U}(M)$ contains elements of weight less than n. Then, the theorem above implies that the sum is non-zero viewed as a polynomial in k and k_0 and thus key-dependent as claimed. □

We like to remark that this property is not only sufficient but also necessary. Indeed, if the polynomials p_{u_i} are linearly dependent, there exist a linear combination that is constant zero. As the whitening key does not influence the value of the monomials of degree $n - 1$, this directly leads to a set M corresponding to a constant, i.e. key-independent, sum.

Linear Combinations of Output Bits. Let us next consider a family of vectorial Boolean functions E_k, with the most important example being a block cipher. We want to extend the previous arguments to this case. Here, we want to guarantee that any non-trivial linear combination of output bits is key dependent. This can be done as follows.

Consider $E_k \colon \mathbb{F}_2^n \to \mathbb{F}_2^n$ be a family of functions with ANF

$$E_k(x) = \sum_{u \in \mathbb{F}_2^n} P_u(k) x^u$$

where now $P_u(k)$ is a vector in $\mathbb{F}_2^n$. A linear combination of output bits is specified by fixing a $\beta \in \mathbb{F}_2^n$ and considering

$$\langle \beta, E_k(x) \rangle = \langle \beta, \sum_{u \in \mathbb{F}_2^n} P_u(k) x^u \rangle = \sum_{u \in \mathbb{F}_2^n} \langle \beta, P_u(k) \rangle x^u$$

If we can ensure that, for each fixed non-zero β, the polynomials $\langle \beta, P_u(k) \rangle$ fulfill the conditions of Corollary 2, we ensured that no integral distinguisher is possible on any linear combination of output bits.

So, for any non-zero β, the polynomials $\langle \beta, P_{u_i}(k) \rangle$ should be linearly independent and $\langle \beta, P_{(1,\ldots,1)}(k) \rangle = 0$. The latter is true if and only if $P_{(1,\ldots,1)}(k) = 0$. Note that in the case of a block cipher, since we need the block cipher to be invertible, it can be at most of degree $n - 1$ and thus we are guaranteed to have $P_{(1,\ldots,1)}(k) = 0$. For the former, we require that

$$\sum_i \alpha_i \langle \beta, P_{u_i}(k) \rangle = 0 \ , \ \alpha_i \in \mathbb{F}_2$$

implies that all α_i are equal to zero. This can be rewritten as

$$0 = \sum_i \alpha_i \langle \beta, P_{u_i}(k) \rangle = \sum_i \alpha_i \sum_j \beta^{(j)} P_{u_i}^{(j)}(k)$$

$$= \sum_{i,j} \alpha_i \beta^{(j)} P_{u_i}^{(j)}(k) = \sum_{i,j} \gamma_{i,j} P_{u_i}^{(j)}(k)$$

with $\gamma_{i,j} = \alpha_i \beta^{(j)} \in \mathbb{F}_2$. One way to simplify this equation is to require something (potentially significantly) stronger, namely that all $n \times n$ polynomials

$$p_{i,j}(k) := P_{u_i}^{(j)}$$

are linearly independent.

On Key-Patterns and Matrices. Asking that all the polynomials $p_{i,j}$ are linearly independent can be put into the following context for input-, output- and key-pattern. Consider the polynomials in its ANF

$$p_{i,j}(k) := P_{u_i}^{(j)} = \sum_{v \in \mathbb{F}_2^\ell} \lambda_{u_i,v}^{(j)} k^v.$$

The values of $\lambda_{u_i,v}^{(j)}$ are equal to the parity of the number of trails $(u_i, v) \to e_j$, that is trails with input pattern u_i, key-pattern v and output pattern e_j. If we want to show that all those polynomials are linearly independent, it is sufficient (and actually necessary) to find a set of key-patterns $v_1, \ldots v_s$, with $s \geq n^2$ such that the *integral-resistance matrix*

$$\mathcal{I}(E) = \begin{pmatrix} \lambda_{u_1,v_1}^{(1)} & \lambda_{u_1,v_1}^{(2)} & & \lambda_{u_1,v_1}^{(n)} & \lambda_{u_2,v_1}^{(1)} & \lambda_{u_2,v_1}^{(2)} & & \lambda_{u_i,v_1}^{(j)} & & \lambda_{u_n,v_1}^{(n-1)} & \lambda_{u_n,v_1}^{(n)} \\ \lambda_{u_1,v_2}^{(1)} & \lambda_{u_1,v_2}^{(2)} & \cdots & \lambda_{u_1,v_2}^{(n)} & \lambda_{u_2,v_2}^{(1)} & \lambda_{u_2,v_2}^{(2)} & \cdots & \lambda_{u_i,v_2}^{(j)} & \cdots & \lambda_{u_n,v_2}^{(n-1)} & \lambda_{u_n,v_2}^{(n)} \\ \vdots & \vdots & & \vdots & \vdots & \vdots & & \vdots & & \vdots & \vdots \\ \lambda_{u_1,v_s}^{(1)} & \lambda_{u_1,v_s}^{(2)} & & \lambda_{u_1,v_s}^{(n)} & \lambda_{u_2,v_s}^{(1)} & \lambda_{u_2,v_s}^{(2)} & & \lambda_{u_i,v_s}^{(j)} & & \lambda_{u_n,v_s}^{(n-1)} & \lambda_{u_n,v_s}^{(n)} \end{pmatrix}$$

has full rank. This brings us to the following proposition which we apply in Sect. 6.

Proposition 2 (Integral-resistance property). *Let $E \colon \mathbb{F}_2^n \times \mathbb{F}_2^m \to \mathbb{F}_2^n$ be a block cipher and $\mathcal{I}(E)$ be a corresponding integral-resistance matrix. If $\mathcal{I}(E)$ has full rank and k_0 is an independent whitening key, $E_k(x + k_0)$ fulfills the Proposition, i.e. for every proper subset $M \subset \mathbb{F}_2^n$ and output mask $\beta \in \mathbb{F}_2^n$ the sum*

$$\sum_{x \in M} \langle \beta, E_k(x + k_0) \rangle$$

is key-dependent.

4   Guarantee for More Rounds

Even if the lower bound on the degree of an R-round block cipher is d, it is not clear that $R+1$ rounds have a degree at least d. Indeed, the next example shows that this is not only non-trivial but simply wrong in general.

Example 4. Let $F, G \colon \mathbb{F}_2^3 \to \mathbb{F}_2^3$ be permutations of degree 2 defined as follows:

$$F(x_1, x_2, x_3) := \begin{pmatrix} x_1 x_2 + x_3 \\ x_1 \\ x_2 \end{pmatrix}, \qquad G(x_1, x_2, x_3) := \begin{pmatrix} x_1 + x_2 x_3 \\ x_2 \\ x_3 \end{pmatrix}.$$

Then we can write the composition of F and G with a key addition in the middle as

$$G(F(x) + k) = G \begin{pmatrix} x_1 x_2 + x_3 + k_1 \\ x_1 + k_2 \\ x_2 + k_3 \end{pmatrix} = \begin{pmatrix} x_3 + x_1 k_3 + x_2 k_2 + k_1 + k_2 k_3 \\ x_1 + k_2 \\ x_2 + k_3 \end{pmatrix},$$

which has only degree 1 in x.

Thus, the algebraic degree can decrease if the highest-degree monomials are cancelled out by applying an additional one round. Although it is nontrivial in general, for some block ciphers (with independent round key assumption), we show that we can guarantee that the algebraic degree does not decrease. Intriguingly, as we will see in this section, this argument does not work for all choices of S-boxes. The case of minimal degree and for the strong arguments against integral distinguishers, the situation is more clear: Here, as we will detail later in this section, adding additional rounds never allows to decrease the minimal degree nor invalidates the strong argument.

4.1   More Rounds for the Algebraic Degree

We split the discussion of how to argue about the algebraic degree into parts, dealing step by step with the linear layer, a single Boolean function, and finally an entire round.

The linear layer does not change anything as both the algebraic degree as well as the minimal-degree are invariant under affine equivalence (see e.g. [9]).

Lemma 2. *Let $F \colon \mathbb{F}_2^n \to \mathbb{F}_2^n$ be any function and $A \colon \mathbb{F}_2^n \to \mathbb{F}_2^n$ be an affine, invertible function, then it holds that*

$$\deg(F \circ A) = \deg(A \circ F) = \deg(F),$$
$$\mathrm{minDeg}(F \circ A) = \mathrm{minDeg}(A \circ F) = \mathrm{minDeg}(F).$$

To cover a layer of S-boxes, we consider the general situation of a parallel application of functions. Since the algebraic degree is the maximum degree of all output bits, it is enough to look at each output bit separately. Therefore, it is sufficient to consider the influence of an isolated S-box on the algebraic degree.

As a next step, the following theorem gives efficient to verify conditions on when appending a single Boolean function does not decrease the algebraic degree.

Theorem 3. *Let a Boolean function $f : \mathbb{F}_2^m \to \mathbb{F}_2$ be given and consider a round key $k \in \mathbb{F}_2^m$. Consider the algebraic normal form of the function*

$$f_k : \mathbb{F}_2^m \to \mathbb{F}_2, \quad f_k(x) = f(x + k)$$

be given as

$$f_k(x) = \sum_{u \in \mathbb{F}_2^m} p_u(k) x^u.$$

Assume that

$$p_{e_i}(k) \notin \operatorname{span}\{p_u(k) \mid u \neq e_i \text{ and } u \neq 0\},$$

that is p_{e_i} is not linearly dependent on the other coefficients when viewed as a polynomial in k. Then it holds that $\deg(f_k \circ F) \geq \deg(F_i)$ for any function $F : \mathbb{F}_2^n \to \mathbb{F}_2^m$. That is, the degree of the ith coordinate of F is a lower bound of the algebraic degree of the composition of F with f_k.

Proof. We denote the algebraic normal form of F_i by

$$F_i(y) = \sum_{v \in \mathbb{F}_2^n} \lambda_v y^v$$

Let the degree of F_i be d. Then, there exists a vector w of weight d such that $\lambda_w = 1$. We now get

$$f_k(F(y)) = \sum_{u \in \mathbb{F}_2^m} p_u(k) F(y)^u = p_{e_i}(k) F_i(y) + \sum_{u \neq e_i} p_u(k) F(y)^u$$

$$= p_{e_i}(k) \left(\sum_{v \in \mathbb{F}_2^n} \lambda_v y^v \right) + \sum_{u \neq e_i} p_u(k) F(y)^u$$

$$= p_{e_i}(k) \lambda_w y^w + \sum_{v \neq w} p_{e_i}(k) \lambda_v y^v + \sum_{u \neq e_i} p_u(k) F(y)^u.$$

By expanding the expression of $F(y)^u$, the last sum can be rearranged into $\sum_{\ell \in \mathbb{F}_2^n} q_\ell(k) y^\ell$, where each $q_\ell(k)$ corresponds to a linear combination of the $p_u(k)$ for $u \neq e_i$.

$$f_k(F(y)) = p_{e_i}(k) \lambda_w y^w + \sum_{v \neq w} p_{e_i}(k) \lambda_v y^v + \sum_{\ell \in \mathbb{F}_2^n} q_\ell(k) y^\ell$$

$$= (p_{e_i}(k) \lambda_w + q_w(k)) y^w + \sum_{v \neq w} (p_{e_i}(k) \lambda_v + q_v) y^v.$$

As $p_{e_i}(k)$ is linearly independent from the $p_u(k)$ for $u \neq e_i$ and q_w corresponds to such a sum, the key-dependent coefficient of y^w is non-zero. As $\operatorname{wt}(w)$ equals d we conclude that $\deg(f_k \circ F) \geq d$. $\qquad \square$

If a given Boolean function f fulfills the conditions of the above theorem, we say that f *preserves the degree of its ith input component.*

Example 5. Consider the Boolean function

$$f(x) = x_0 x_1 x_2 + x_0 x_1 + x_0 x_2 + x_0 + x_1 x_2 + x_2 x_3 + x_3 + 1.$$

Then

$$\begin{aligned}
f_k(x) = {} & x_0 x_1 x_2 + (k_2 + 1)x_0 x_1 + (k_1 + 1)x_0 x_2 + (k_1 k_2 + k_1 + k_2 + 1)x_0 \\
& + (k_0 + 1)x_1 x_2 + (k_0 k_2 + k_0 + k_2)x_1 + x_2 x_3 + (k_0 k_1 + k_0 + k_1 + k_3)x_2 \\
& + (k_2 + 1)x_3 + k_0 k_1 k_2 + k_0 k_1 + k_0 k_2 + k_0 + k_1 k_2 + k_2 k_3 + k_3 + 1.
\end{aligned}$$

The non-zero non constant coefficients to consider are

$$\begin{array}{lll}
p_{1110}(k) = 1 & p_{1100}(k) = k_2 + 1 & p_{1010}(k) = k_1 + 1 \\
p_{0110}(k) = k_0 + 1 & p_{1000}(k) = k_1 k_2 + k_1 + k_2 + 1 & p_{0100}(k) = k_0 k_2 + k_0 + k_2 \\
p_{0011}(k) = 1 & p_{0010}(k) = k_0 k_1 + k_0 + k_1 + k_3 & p_{0001}(k) = k_2 + 1.
\end{array}$$

While $p_{1000}, p_{0100}, p_{0010}$ cannot be expressed as linear combination of the others (as the quadratic term is unique in the non-constant terms) p_{0001} actually can (as it is simply equal to p_{1100}). So in this case we get that

$$\deg(f_k \circ F) \geq \max\{\deg(F_0), \deg(F_1), \deg(F_2)\},$$

and thus f preserves the degree of its first (x_0), second (x_1) and third (x_2) input. However, it does not always preserve the degree of its last input. Indeed, consider F on four inputs y_0, y_1, y_2, y_3 such that

$$x_0 = F_0 = y_0 y_1 \quad x_1 = F_1 = y_2 y_3 \quad x_2 = F_2 = y_2 \quad x_3 = F_3 = y_0 y_1 y_2 y_3.$$

Then $\deg(F) = 4$ while $\deg(f_k \circ F) = 2$.

Now, this theorem can be used to bound the algebraic degree as summarized in the next corollary. For this, we denote by $\mathbb{S}_k^{(r)}$ an S-box layer (the r-fold parallel application of S) together with an independent round key addition k, i.e.

$$\mathbb{S}_k(x_1, \ldots, x_r) = (S(x_1 + k_1), \ldots, S(x_r + k_r)).$$

Corollary 3. *Consider an S-box $S \colon \mathbb{F}_2^m \to \mathbb{F}_2^m$. If, for each $1 \leq i \leq m$ there exists a coordinate function S_j such that S_j preserves the degree of its ith input, then for all functions $F \colon \mathbb{F}_2^{mr} \to \mathbb{F}_2^{mr}$, we have $\deg(\mathbb{S}_k^{(r)} \circ F) \geq \deg(F)$.*

Results. Based on Corollary 3, we computed which S-boxes preserve the degree. For a single S-box, that can be checked efficiently for all practical relevant values of n. The sage code that automatically checks the properties is given in the full version. Especially, if we go through all 302 representatives of all affine equivalence classes for 4-bit bijective S-boxes, there are 244 such S-boxes that preserve the algebraic degree, while 58 do not. Some specific examples are that the S-box of GIFT and PRESENT preserve the algebraic degree, while it is not the case for the S-box of CRAFT, SKINNY-64 and SKINNY-128. We also tested the inverse mapping over $\mathbb{F}_{2^n}$ for $n = 3$ to $n = 8$ (e.g. the AES S-box), and each of them also preserves the algebraic degree. So in particular we see that any bound on the algebraic degree of the AES implies the same bound for the full AES.

4.2 More Rounds for the Minimal Degree

To bound the algebraic degree, we had to show that for any input bit i, there is at least on output bit that preserves the degree of its ith input. For the minimal degree, the situation is different in two ways. On the one hand, we have to ensure more. As we want to bound the minimal degree, we have to bound the degree of any linear combination of output bits. On the other hand, as we are going to assume that F has a given minimal degree, we know that preserving the degree of any linear combination of its input is sufficient. Finally, there is no direct equivalence to Corollary 3 for minimal degree. However, the next theorem (and its proof) shows that this can be dealt with. Indeed the case for minimal degree is significantly easier.

Theorem 4. *Let* $F \colon \mathbb{F}_2^n \to \mathbb{F}_2^m$ *be a function and* $S \colon \mathbb{F}_2^m \to \mathbb{F}_2^t$ *be a function such that for any non-zero* $\beta \in \mathbb{F}_2^t$ *the component function* $\langle \beta, S \rangle$ *is non-constant. If we denote by* S_k *the function* $S_k(x) = S(x + k)$ *parameterized by a key* $k \in \mathbb{F}_2^m$ *then the minimal degree never decreases, that is*

$$\mathrm{minDeg}(S_k \circ F) \geq \mathrm{minDeg}(F).$$

Proof. Let $\beta \in \mathbb{F}_2^t$ be a non-zero vector. We consider the component function $f(x) = \langle \beta, S(x) \rangle$ and show that the minimal degree of $f_k \circ F$ is at least the minimal degree of F. For this, consider a monomial of maximal degree in the algebraic normal form of f, without loss of generality $x_0 \cdots x_{d-1}$. For f_k, this will in particular generate the term $k_1 \cdots k_{d-1} x_0$. This key-monomial $k_1 \ldots k_{d-1}$ could also appear as part of the coefficients of *different linear* monomials x_i, but not in coefficients of non-linear monomials. Thus f_k can be written as

$$f_k(x) = k_1 \cdots k_{t-1} \langle \gamma, x \rangle + g_k(x)$$

with a non-zero $\gamma \in \mathbb{F}_2^m$ and a polynomial g such that $k_1 \cdots k_{t-1}$ cannot be expressed as a linear combination of its coefficients. That is, the term $k_1 \cdots k_{t-1} \langle \gamma, x \rangle$ cannot cancel in the algebraic normal form of $f_k \circ F$. Finally the degree of $\langle \gamma, x \rangle = \langle \gamma, F(y) \rangle$ is bounded by the minimal degree of F by definition. $\square$

4.3 More Rounds for Strong Arguments

The strong arguments extends to more rounds automatically without any additional requirements. Indeed, consider the composition $E_k \circ F$ where E_k fulfills the strong arguments and F is a fixed permutation. Note that if F is actually key-dependent (using an independent key-value), the same argument applies. Considering any non-empty set $M \subset \mathbb{F}_2^n$, and any β, we get

$$\sum_{x \in M} \langle \beta, E_k(F(x)) \rangle = \sum_{y \in F(M)} \langle \beta, E_k(y) \rangle,$$

which depends on k as any sum does for E_k. Note that in the context of block ciphers where the round function is (most of the time) identical for each round

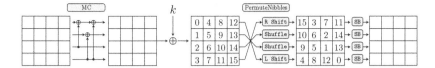

Fig. 2. Round function of CRAFT.

(assuming independent round keys and thus absorbing round constants), even though this arguments is valid when adding an arbitrary amount of rounds before E_k, it also includes the case where we add an arbitrary amount of rounds *after* E_k. Indeed in this context, $F^r \circ E_k = E_{k'} \circ F^r$, where F is the round function. If the previous arguments hold for $E_k \circ F^r$, it thus automatically holds for $F^r \circ E_k$, i.e. any sum $\sum_{x \in M} \langle \beta, F^r(E_k(x)) \rangle$ is key-dependent.

5 Improvements of Efficiency by Using Equivalent S-Boxes

The core part to guarantee the lower bound of degrees is to find a key pattern where the number of division trails from a plaintext to a ciphertext is odd. To find such a key pattern, the trail extension technique was proposed in [12]. A key pattern is generated from the ciphertext side round by round as outlined in Sect. 2.3. In the end, lower bounds on the (minimum) degree for round-reduced variants of SKINNY-64, GIFT-64, and PRESENT could be efficiently computed. On the other hand, it is open whether the trail extension technique can find such key patterns for other ciphers. We used the tool provided in [12] and modified it for the block cipher CRAFT. As a result, we failed to find key patterns in spite of the similarity to SKINNY. This is because the round function of CRAFT has fundamental problems to disturb trail extensions. In practice, the round function of SKINNY-64 or GIFT-64 is significantly suited to the trail extension, and the trail extension is unlikely succeeded in general.

We are only interested in the parity of the number of trails for a fixed pattern, but in practice, we cannot know the parity unless all trails are enumerated. Therefore, the feasibility highly depends on the number of trails, which we try to keep significantly small. When the key pattern is sequentially generated in the trail extension, the number of trails must be kept small throughout all iterations.

Let us focus on the CRAFT round function (see Fig. 2), in particular, a super S-box, which consists of four 4-bit S-boxes, MixColumns, and four 4-bit S-boxes. Let u, v, and w be the input, key, and output patterns on the super S-box, and the trail extension technique generates (u, v) from w such that the Hamming weights of u and v are as high as possible. As an example, we enumerated all (u, v) that can propagate to $w = $ 0x1200, where the two S-boxes and one MixColumns are independently evaluated. Then, $wt(u) + wt(v) = 13$ is the maximum choice, e.g., $(u = $ 0x7777$, v = $ 0x2000$)$ can propagate to $w = $ 0x1200. Unfortunately, this trail is not available because there are 4 different trails satisfying $(u, v) \to w$.

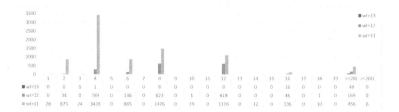

	1	2	3	4	5	6	7	8	9	10	11	12	13	14	15	16	17	18	19	>=20E	>=20O
wt=13	0	0	0	1	0	0	0	8	0	0	0	8	0	0	0	16	0	0	0	48	0
wt=12	0	34	0	789	0	136	0	623	0	1	0	618	0	0	0	46	0	1	0	169	0
wt=11	28	873	24	3428	0	885	0	1476	0	19	0	1116	0	12	0	136	0	10	0	456	6

Fig. 3. The number of (u, v) and their numbers of trails, output pattern is $\texttt{0x1200}$. For example, when $wt(u) + wt(v) = 11$, there are 3428 (u, v) whose number of trails is 4. When the number of trails exceeds 20, the labels $\geq 20E$ and $\geq 20O$ are used for even parity and odd parity, respectively.

Figure 3 summarizes the number of (u, v) and their numbers of trails when $w = \texttt{0x1200}$. The numbers of (u, v) with $wt(u) + wt(v) = 13$ and $wt(u) + wt(v) = 12$ are 81 and 1917, respectively, but there is no (u, v) whose number of trails is odd. When $wt(u) + wt(v) = 11$, there are 28 (u, v) whose number of trails is 1, but the number is very few. In other words, the choice of the trail extension is very limited among all trails. Even if such a rare propagation is adopted, after several rounds, it is unlikely to restrict the number of trails to a size that is able to handle in practice. This trend is not limited to $w = \texttt{0x1200}$. Indeed, a preferable propagation is very rare for many output pattern. This is our heuristic explanation why the trail extension cannot find a key pattern for $\texttt{CRAFT}$.

5.1 Replacement to Equivalent S-Box

We tackle the problem to expand the class of ciphers that we can prove a lower bound on the degree. The core of the problem is having too many trails. Therefore, we propose a new method to decrease the number of trails fundamentally. Generally, this method is based on rewriting the ciphers specification (potentially up to a linear change of plaintext and ciphertext and a different key-scheduling). We call such ciphers equivalent. More specifically, we replace the S-box in such a way that we get the exact same cipher. Thus, while we keep the cipher identical, its behaviour with respect to division trails might well change.

The first important remark is that even constant addition changes the propagation table of the division property unlike the differential distribution table or linear approximation table. Under the key-alternating ciphers, constant addition before/after S-boxes results in a different representation of the original cipher because such constant addition can be included in the round key addition.

Proposition 3 (Equivalent S-box for key-alternating ciphers). *Replacing an S-box S in a key-alternating cipher with an S-box $S' : S'(x) = S(x \oplus c_{in}) \oplus c_{out}$ results in an equivalent cipher under the independent round key.*

To demonstrate the effect of the equivalent S-box, we use the $\texttt{CRAFT}$ S-box as an example. There are 76 possible transitions in the propagation table (see the left one in Table 2). On the other hand, in $S'(x) = S(x \oplus \text{0x7}) \oplus \text{0x7}$, there are only 56 possible transitions. The total number of trails decreases from 76 to 56. We can expect that the use of S' instead of S decreases the number of trails from a plaintext to a ciphertext.

For ciphers whose linear layer consists of word-wise XOR and word-wise shuffle such as CRAFT or SKINNY, there is a more wide equivalent class.

Proposition 4 (Equivalent S-box for ciphers with word-wise linear layer). *Replacing an S-box S in a key-alternating cipher whose linear layer consists of word-wise XOR and word-wise shuffle with an S-box $S' : S'(x) = A^{-1} \times S(A \times (x \oplus c_{in})) \oplus c_{out}$ results in an equivalent cipher under the independent round key.*

An invertible linear transformation, denoted by $A \times x$, is applied before the S-box, and its inverse A^{-1} is multiplied after the S-box. Unlike in the generally studied affine-equivalent class, we limit the second linear transformation to the inverse of the former linear transformation. Since multiplication of A^{-1} and word-wise XOR/shuffle are commutative, the multiplication of A^{-1} can be moved at the beginning of the next round. Then, as $A \times A^{-1}$ is the identity, we see that the ciphers are indeed equivalent.

The number of linear transformations is 20160 for 4-bit S-boxes. Therefore, there are (at most) $20160 \times 2^4 \times 2^4 \approx 2^{22.23}$ equivalent S-boxes, and we can choose a preferable S-box to prove the lower bound. Note that the target cipher also changes to the cipher whose plaintext and ciphertext is linearly transformed, but it never affects the algebraic degree, the minimum degree, and of course, the claim of no integral distinguisher[1].

5.2 Choice of Preferable Equivalent S-Boxes

The most important problem is how to choose a preferable S-box from the equivalent class. Intuitively, the lower number of possible trails, the better. However, as far as we tried, this problem is not so simple, and choosing an S-box whose propagation table has the following property is better. In the following, let u and v be an input pattern and an output pattern, respectively.

- For any u with $wt(u) = n - 1$, the possible output pattern v is uniquely determined when $wt(u) - wt(v)$ is maximized.
- For any v with $wt(v) = 1$, the possible input pattern u is uniquely determined when $wt(u) - wt(v)$ is maximized.
- The number of possible transitions is as small as possible.

Note that these conditions are heuristically found, and whether adopting these conditions is optimal or not is an open question. As a consequence, the use of S-boxes satisfying these conditions allows us to prove the lower bound of CRAFT.

---

[1] Similar technique is already known in [11,17], but there is significant difference. In previous works, a linear transformation is applied to S-boxes in the first and the last rounds only. In our proposal, it is applied to all S-boxes in the middle rounds.

Table 2. Propagation table for the CRAFT S-box. The left is the table of the original S-box. The right is the table of the equivalent S-box described in Example 6

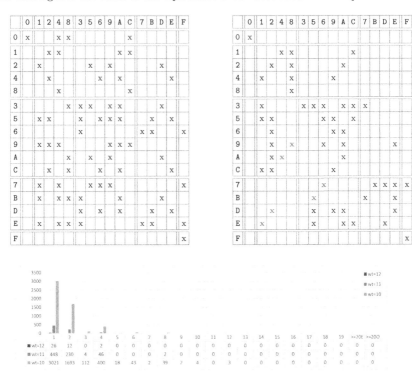

Fig. 4. The number of (u, v) and their numbers of trails in the CRAFT super S-box using the equivalent S-box described in Example 6. Output pattern is 0x1200.

Example 6. The following S-box

$$S' : \text{0x0, 0xC, 0xA, 0x7, 0x9, 0x6, 0x1, 0xF, 0x8, 0xE, 0x4, 0x3, 0x2, 0x5, 0xD, 0xB}$$

is equivalent to the original S-box of CRAFT and satisfies the three conditions. Note that S' is generated from the original S-box S as follows:

$$S'(x) = A^{-1} \times S(A \times (x \oplus \text{0x5})) \oplus \text{0xD}, \qquad A = \begin{pmatrix} 1 & 0 & 1 & 1 \\ 0 & 0 & 0 & 1 \\ 0 & 1 & 0 & 0 \\ 1 & 0 & 0 & 1 \end{pmatrix},$$

where $x = x_4\|x_3\|x_2\|x_1$ is identical to the transpose of (x_4, x_3, x_2, x_1), i.e., $(x_4, x_3, x_2, x_1)^T$. Table 2 shows the comparison between the propagation tables of the original S-box and the equivalent S-box. The table of the equivalent S-box is more sparse than that of the original one. Six propagations labeled in red color correspond to the first and second conditions. For example, when $v = \text{0x4}$, u with maximum Hamming weight is uniquely determined to 0xA. As another example, when $u = \text{0xD}$, v with minimum Hamming weight is uniquely determined to 0x2.

Finally, we test the same experiment using the super S-box, i.e., we enumerate all (u, v) that can propagate to $w = \texttt{0x1200}$. Figure 4 summarizes the number of (u, v) and their numbers of trails. Unlike the original one shown in Fig. 3, the majority of possible propagations has only one trail.

6 Applications

In this section we are going to apply our results, i.e. how to give stronger arguments to a set of ciphers. For each cipher, we briefly explain some specific observations and improvements. The results for all ciphers are given in Table 1.

In all ciphers whose block length is n, we need n^2 key patterns to guarantee no integral distinguisher, and the integral-resistance matrix has n^4 entries, i.e., 2^{24} and 2^{28} on 64-bit and 128-bit block ciphers, respectively. To compute these entries efficiently, we use a key pattern in which key patterns for the 1st and last rounds are non-zero if it is possible. Then, almost all entries in the integral-resistance matrix must be 0, and the integral-resistance matrix has the form of a diagonal block matrix. When all block matrices have full rank, the integral-resistance matrix has full rank. Another important remark is that even if some entries are not determined, we can still prove that the integral-resistance matrix has full rank. For example, since the following matrix

$$\begin{pmatrix} 1 & 0 & \star \\ 0 & 1 & 0 \\ 0 & 0 & 1 \end{pmatrix},$$

has full rank independent of $\star$, we do not need to determine the entry $\star$. Note that [1] observed that using the Convex Hull technique to modelize S-boxes [23] in MILP can sometimes leads to inconsistencies. We double checked and made sure that this phenomenon does not happen for the S-boxes that we use.

6.1 Applications to CRAFT

CRAFT is a lightweight tweakable block cipher published in ToSC 2019 [5]. The block length is 64 bits, and 4-bit S-boxes are used as the nonlinear operation. On our proof, we assume independent tweakeys each round.

The designers of CRAFT showed an 13-round integral distinguisher [5] in the single tweak-key setting. For the tightness of results, our goal is therefore to show that 14 rounds (and more) do not have any integral distinguisher under the independent-tweakey assumption.

Figure 2 shows the round function of CRAFT. The propagation of the division property for the SB and MixColumns are independently modeled, where MixColumns is regarded as 16 parallel applications of 4-bit to 4-bit linear transformation. Moreover, the first round consists of the SB only. As shown in Sect. 5, we use an equivalent S-box instead of the original S-box to improve the efficiency. Note that using the original S-box did neither allow to extend trails nor to find key patterns whose number of trails is odd. Therefore, our new proposal using an equivalent S-box is necessary to handle CRAFT.

We start with the proof of having no integral distinguisher in 14 rounds. To prove it, we need at least 4096 key patterns whose corresponding 4096×4096 integral-resistance matrix has full rank. Generating 4096 key patterns is time consuming. Besides, it is unlikely that the integral-resistance matrix becomes full rank when 4096 key patterns are generated without care. A systematic strategy is required to efficiently generate such key patterns.

As a first improvement, we exploit the symmetry property of CRAFT. Denote

$$T\left(\begin{pmatrix} s_0 & s_4 & s_8 & s_{12} \\ s_1 & s_5 & s_9 & s_{13} \\ s_2 & s_6 & s_{10} & s_{14} \\ s_3 & s_7 & s_{11} & s_{15} \end{pmatrix}\right) = \begin{pmatrix} s_8 & s_{12} & s_0 & s_4 \\ s_9 & s_{13} & s_1 & s_5 \\ s_{10} & s_{14} & s_2 & s_6 \\ s_{11} & s_{15} & s_3 & s_7 \end{pmatrix},$$

then the round function R of CRAFT (excluding constant and tweakey additions) fulfills $R(T(s)) = T(R(s))$. As we can ignore the impact of keys and constant addition under the independent tweakey assumption, rotating by two columns is thus invariant for the computation of key patterns. Therefore, once we find a key pattern, the key pattern transformed by the symmetry property is also available. Thanks to this property, $4096/2 = 2048$ key patterns are enough.

As a second improvement, we use key patterns that share the same division trail in the middle part. Concretely, we first construct 12-round input/key/output patterns whose number of trails is odd, and then, the trail is systematically extended both forward and backward direction by 1 round, respectively. Then, we can generate 2048 key patterns only from 32 12-round patterns. As a consequence, we can generate 4096 key patterns whose corresponding integral-resistance matrix has full rank. As shown in Sect. 4.3, once we can generate an integral-resistance matrix of full rank for 14 rounds, it also guarantees no integral distinguisher in 14 rounds and higher.

6.2   Applications to SKINNY-64

SKINNY is a lightweight block cipher published at CRYPTO'16 [4]. There are two different version of SKINNY (64-bit block SKINNY-64 and 128-bit block SKINNY-128).

In [12], the lower bounds of the algebraic degree and the minimum degree reach the maximum, i.e., 63, in 10-round SKINNY-64 and 11-round SKINNY-64, respectively. It also shows that 13-round SKINNY-64 has 64 maximum degree monomials. On the contrary, the best integral distinguisher reaches 11 rounds [11][2]. Note that SKINNY does not have the pre-whitening key, the 11-round integral distinguisher can be extended to a 12-round one for free.

Our goal is to show that 13 rounds and more never have integral distinguishers under the assumption that each round-tweakey is independent and they are

---

[2] In the 11-round distinguisher shown in [11], each tweakey is not XORed to the full state. However, we confirmed that there are 11-round distinguishers even when each tweakey is XORed to the full state.

XORed to the full state. Again, SKINNY does not have a pre-whitening key. Therefore, to prove no integral distinguisher in 13 rounds, we need to construct a full-rank integral-resistance matrix for 12 rounds.

Similarly to CRAFT, the SC and MixColumns are independently modeled, where MixColumns is regarded as 16 parallel applications of 4-bit to 4-bit linear transformation. Moreover, the last round consists of the SC only. Unlike the CRAFT S-box, the division property table of the SKINNY-64 S-box is relatively sparse. Therefore, the trail extension is possible without the equivalent S-box technique [12]. However, using the equivalent S-box technique increases the efficiency significantly. The following S-box

$$S' : \text{0x1, 0xA, 0x2, 0xB, 0x3, 0xC, 0x4, 0x9, 0x6, 0xE, 0x5, 0xF, 0x8, 0x0, 0xD, 0x7}$$

is equivalent to the original S-box of SKINNY-64 and satisfies the three conditions shown in Sect. 5. We also use two improvements which are similar to CRAFT to generate a full-rank integral-resistance matrix efficiently. The first improvement is the so-called *column rotation equivalence* [12]. Once we find a key pattern, three key patterns whose columns are rotated by 1, 2, and 3 are also available. Thanks to this property, $4096/4 = 1024$ key patterns are enough.

The second improvement used for CRAFT, i.e., to first generate division trails which cover only 10 rounds and then extend it to 12 rounds, is also applicable here. Unfortunately, we cannot use this trick for all of 1024 key patterns because there is no 10-round division trail from specific input pattern to specific output pattern. For key patterns where this is not possible, we need to generate key patterns for 12 rounds directly.

As a consequence, we can generate 4096 key patterns whose corresponding integral-resistance matrix has full rank. Again, once we generate a full rank integral-resistance matrix for 12 rounds, it also guarantees that there is no integral distinguisher for 12 rounds and more.

6.3   Applications to GIFT-64

GIFT is a lightweight block cipher published as CHES'17 by Banik et al. [2], with a 128-bit key and two variants depending on the block size : GIFT-64 and GIFT-128 for 64-bit and 128-bit block size respectively. Its round function is very simple and only consists of the key-addition, an S-box layer with 4-bit S-boxes and a bit permutation layer. Note that in the original design, the round key is only added to half of the state. As in [12] we are here considering a slightly different variant where the round key is added to the full state, as well as assuming that each round key is independent (as in the rest of this paper).

We reused the key patterns given by [12] for their proof of the "all maximal degree monomial" property, leading to key patterns $v_1, \ldots, v_s$ with $s = n^2 = 4096$ for 11 rounds. Note that these key patterns already have the special property mentioned at the start of Sect. 6.

We set a time limit of one minute for the computation of each coefficient in the integral-resistance matrix. That is, if we could not compute the total number

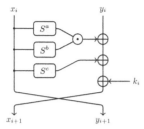

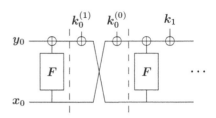

Fig. 5. SIMON/Simeck round function [13].

Fig. 6. SIMON/Simeck one round extension for pre-whitening key.

of trails in less than one minute, we replace the coefficient by $\star$. By doing this we are still able to compute enough coefficients so that we can prove that the matrix is always full rank. Note that since GIFT doesn't have a whitening key, having the integral-resistance matrix at full rank for 11 rounds means that we prove the resistance against integral distinguishers for 12 rounds (as in the case of SKINNY-64). Thus with this, and assuming independent round keys, we were able to prove that 12 rounds and higher of GIFT64 has no integral distinguisher, according to Corollary 2.

6.4 Applications to PRESENT

PRESENT is another lightweight block cipher, published at CHES'07 [6], with a 64-bit block size and the option between 80-bit and 128-bit key. Its round function is also very simple, built with only a key addition, S-box layer of 4-bit S-boxes and a bit permutation. Similarly to CRAFT, we first build input/output/key-patterns leading to an odd number of trails for 11 rounds, and extend them by one round both in the forward and backward direction using affine equivalent S-boxes for the first and last round. In the end this allowed us to prove that 13 rounds and higher of PRESENT, assuming independent round keys, does not have any integral distinguisher, according to Corollary 2.

6.5 Applications to SIMON/Simeck

SIMON is a Feistel cipher which was published in 2013 [3]. Figure 5 shows the round function where S^i is the left circular shift by i positions. The shift constants for SIMON are $a = 8$, $b = 1$, and $c = 2$. While the cipher operates on n-bit words, the block length is $2n$. SIMON supports the block lengths 32, 48, 64, 96, and 128. The cipher Simeck [24] is very similar, it just replaces the shifts constants by $a = 0$, $b = 5$, $c = 1$ (to allow an even more efficient implementation) and supports the block lengths 32, 48, and 64.

For the division property of SIMON/Simeck we can observe the following *word rotation equivalence*: let $F(x_i, y_i, k_i) = (x_{i+1}, y_{i+1})$ be one round of SIMON/Simeck. Then the round function is shift invariant, that is, for all $0 \leq l < n$

$$(a_1, a_2, a_3) \xrightarrow{F} (b_1, b_2) \Leftrightarrow (S^l(a_1), S^l(a_2), S^l(a_3)) \xrightarrow{F} (S^l(b_1), S^l(b_2)).$$

Showing the Proposition for SIMON and Simeck requires, with a naive app-roach, $4n^2$ key patterns. Based on the word rotation equivalence, we can reduce this number down to $4n$. Finding a key pattern where only one combination of a monomial and an output bit leads to an odd number of trails and all other combinations to an even number of trails leads to a unit vector as a column in the integral-resistance matrix. In this row where the unit vector has the 1 entry, we do not need to count the number of trails for other key pattern and just insert a 0 there. If the number of trails is odd for the specific monomial/output bit combination for another key pattern, we can just add the unit vector to this column to create a 0 entry there. Unlike the other block ciphers examined in this paper, the trail extension was not used, we simply maximized the weight of the key patterns.

We iterated over all monomial/output bit combinations and try to find a key pattern, so that the number of trails is odd. We parallelized the search of key patterns, which leads to a program behaviour where for "easy" monomi-al/output bit combinations key patterns are found very fast and often give unit vectors. When the program found key patterns for "complicated" monomial/out-put bit combinations, for many positions in the column the trail counting can be omitted, which drastically improves the performance.

When we can compute the integral-resistance matrix of full rank for r rounds of SIMON resp. Simeck, we still need a pre-whitening key on the full state to ensure the Proposition. For that we add one additional round in the beginning (see Fig. 6). As we already assume independent round keys, we can (virtually, similarly to masking or secret sharing) split the second round key in two indepen-dent parts (k_1 and $k_0^{(0)}$), and add $k_0^{(0)}$ on the right word. Then $(k_0^{(0)}, k_0^{(1)})$ is our pre-whitening key on the full state. The application of F before does not change the Proposition as shown in Sect. 4.3. This leads to a proof of the Proposition for $r + 1$ rounds.

The best known integral distinguishers for SIMON32 and Simeck32 cover 15 rounds [21]. We can show that the Proposition holds for 16 rounds of both ciphers which is tight in terms of number of rounds. The integral distinguishers shown in [23] for SIMON48/64/96/128 and SIMECK48/64 can be extended by one round with the technique shown in [22]. Adding another round gives our bounds in Table 1 where we show the Proposition.

7   Conclusion and Future Work

In this paper, we were able to show strong security arguments against integral distinguishers for several block ciphers following the SPN and Feistel designs. Although these are the best security guarantees against integral distinguishers so far, in theory, it could still be that it is easy to mount integral attacks. Our result shows that any sum is key-dependent, however, this does not exclude the case where the sum is simply one key bit, which could be exploited in an attack.

A wider application to more (block) ciphers would be interesting, especially under the aspect of more automatization and less optimization by hand. We see further research directions in closing the gap for GIFT-64 and PRESENT between the best known integral distinguisher and the Proposition, and a more intuitive understanding of what allows the degree to be extended to more rounds. For the question of covering more rounds, in the case of an algebraic degree, it would be interesting to better understand which S-boxes, or family of S-boxes, allow to preserve the degree for more rounds.

Our results are inherently non applicable to cryptographic permutations because (i) the key addition is crucial for our results and to reduce the complexity of the MILP models and (ii) the conditions for the integral distinguisher cannot be fulfilled. Deriving similar results for permutations or permutation based schemes would be interesting.

Acknowledgments. This work was partially funded by the DFG, (German Research Foundation) under Germany's Excellence Strategy - EXC 2092 CASA – 390781972 and within the project Analysis and Protection of Lightweight Cryptographic Algorithms (432878529).

References

1. Baksi, A.: New insights on differential and linear bounds using mixed integer linear programming. In: Maimut, D., Oprina, A.-G., Sauveron, D. (eds.) SecITC 2020. LNCS, vol. 12596, pp. 41–54. Springer, Cham (2021). https://doi.org/10.1007/978-3-030-69255-1_4
2. Banik, S., Pandey, S.K., Peyrin, T., Sasaki, Yu., Sim, S.M., Todo, Y.: GIFT: a small present. In: Fischer, W., Homma, N. (eds.) CHES 2017. LNCS, vol. 10529, pp. 321–345. Springer, Cham (2017). https://doi.org/10.1007/978-3-319-66787-4_16
3. Beaulieu, R., Shors, D., Smith, J., Treatman-Clark, S., Weeks, B., Wingers, L.: The SIMON and SPECK families of lightweight block ciphers. IACR Cryptol. ePrint Arch. **2013**, 404 (2013)
4. Beierle, C., et al.: The SKINNY family of block ciphers and its low-latency variant MANTIS. In: Robshaw, M., Katz, J. (eds.) CRYPTO 2016. LNCS, vol. 9815, pp. 123–153. Springer, Heidelberg (2016). https://doi.org/10.1007/978-3-662-53008-5_5
5. Beierle, C., Leander, G., Moradi, A., Rasoolzadeh, S.: CRAFT: lightweight tweakable block cipher with efficient protection against DFA attacks. IACR Trans. Symmetric Cryptol. **2019**(1), 5–45 (2019). https://doi.org/10.13154/tosc.v2019.i1.5-45
6. Bogdanov, A., et al.: PRESENT: an ultra-lightweight block cipher. In: Paillier, P., Verbauwhede, I. (eds.) CHES 2007. LNCS, vol. 4727, pp. 450–466. Springer, Heidelberg (2007). https://doi.org/10.1007/978-3-540-74735-2_31
7. Boura, C., Canteaut, A.: Another view of the division property. In: Robshaw, M., Katz, J. (eds.) CRYPTO 2016. LNCS, vol. 9814, pp. 654–682. Springer, Heidelberg (2016). https://doi.org/10.1007/978-3-662-53018-4_24
8. Canteaut, A., Lallemand, V., Leander, G., Neumann, P., Wiemer, F.: BISON instantiating the whitened swap-or-not construction. In: Ishai, Y., Rijmen, V. (eds.) EUROCRYPT 2019. LNCS, vol. 11478, pp. 585–616. Springer, Cham (2019). https://doi.org/10.1007/978-3-030-17659-4_20

9. Carlet, C., Crama, Y., Hammer, P.L.: Vectorial Boolean functions for cryptography. In: Crama, Y., Hammer, P.L. (eds.) Boolean Models and Methods in Mathematics, Computer Science, and Engineering, pp. 398–470. Cambridge University Press (2010). https://doi.org/10.1017/cbo9780511780448.012

10. Daemen, J., Knudsen, L., Rijmen, V.: The block cipher square. In: Biham, E. (ed.) FSE 1997. LNCS, vol. 1267, pp. 149–165. Springer, Heidelberg (1997). https://doi.org/10.1007/BFb0052343

11. Derbez, P., Fouque, P.: Increasing precision of division property. IACR Trans. Symmetric Cryptol. **2020**(4), 173–194 (2020). https://doi.org/10.46586/tosc.v2020.i4.173-194

12. Hebborn, P., Lambin, B., Leander, G., Todo, Y.: Lower bounds on the degree of block ciphers. In: Moriai, S., Wang, H. (eds.) ASIACRYPT 2020. LNCS, vol. 12491, pp. 537–566. Springer, Cham (2020). https://doi.org/10.1007/978-3-030-64837-4_18

13. Jean, J.: TikZ for cryptographers (2016). https://www.iacr.org/authors/tikz/

14. Knudsen, L.R.: Truncated and higher order differentials. In: Preneel, B. (ed.) FSE 1994. LNCS, vol. 1008, pp. 196–211. Springer, Heidelberg (1995). https://doi.org/10.1007/3-540-60590-8_16

15. Lai, X.: Higher order derivatives and differential cryptanalysis. In: Blahut, R.E., Costello, D.J., Maurer, U., Mittelholzer, T. (eds.) Communications and Cryptography. The Springer International Series in Engineering and Computer Science (Communications and Information Theory), vol. 276. Springer, Boston (1994). https://doi.org/10.1007/978-1-4615-2694-0_23

16. Lai, X., Massey, J.L., Murphy, S.: Markov ciphers and differential cryptanalysis. In: Davies, D.W. (ed.) EUROCRYPT 1991. LNCS, vol. 547, pp. 17–38. Springer, Heidelberg (1991). https://doi.org/10.1007/3-540-46416-6_2

17. Lambin, B., Derbez, P., Fouque, P.-A.: Linearly equivalent S-boxes and the division property. Des. Codes Crypt. **88**(10), 2207–2231 (2020). https://doi.org/10.1007/s10623-020-00773-4

18. Nyberg, K., Knudsen, L.R.: Provable security against a differential attack. J. Cryptol. **8**(1), 27–37 (1995). https://doi.org/10.1007/BF00204800

19. Shibayama, N., Kaneko, T.: A new higher order differential of CLEFIA. IEICE Trans. Fundam. Electron. Commun. Comput. Sci. **97–A**(1), 118–126 (2014). https://doi.org/10.1587/transfun.E97.A.118

20. Todo, Y.: Structural evaluation by generalized integral property. In: Oswald, E., Fischlin, M. (eds.) EUROCRYPT 2015. LNCS, vol. 9056, pp. 287–314. Springer, Heidelberg (2015). https://doi.org/10.1007/978-3-662-46800-5_12

21. Todo, Y., Morii, M.: Bit-based division property and application to SIMON family. In: Peyrin, T. (ed.) FSE 2016. LNCS, vol. 9783, pp. 357–377. Springer, Heidelberg (2016). https://doi.org/10.1007/978-3-662-52993-5_18

22. Wang, Q., Liu, Z., Varıcı, K., Sasaki, Yu., Rijmen, V., Todo, Y.: Cryptanalysis of reduced-round SIMON32 and SIMON48. In: Meier, W., Mukhopadhyay, D. (eds.) INDOCRYPT 2014. LNCS, vol. 8885, pp. 143–160. Springer, Cham (2014). https://doi.org/10.1007/978-3-319-13039-2_9

23. Xiang, Z., Zhang, W., Bao, Z., Lin, D.: Applying MILP method to searching integral distinguishers based on division property for 6 lightweight block ciphers. In: Cheon, J.H., Takagi, T. (eds.) ASIACRYPT 2016. LNCS, vol. 10031, pp. 648–678. Springer, Heidelberg (2016). https://doi.org/10.1007/978-3-662-53887-6_24

24. Yang, G., Zhu, B., Suder, V., Aagaard, M.D., Gong, G.: The Simeck family of lightweight block ciphers. IACR Cryptol. ePrint Arch. **2015**, 612 (2015)

Massive Superpoly Recovery with Nested Monomial Predictions

Kai Hu[1,5], Siwei Sun[2], Yosuke Todo[3], Meiqin Wang[1,5(✉)],
and Qingju Wang[1,4,5]

[1] School of Cyber Science and Technology, Shandong University, Qingdao,
Shandong, China
hukai@mail.sdu.edu.cn, mqwang@sdu.edu.cn
[2] School of Cryptology, University of Chinese Academy of Sciences, Beijing, China
[3] NTT Social Informatics Laboratories, Tokyo, Japan
[4] SnT, University of Luxembourg, Luxembourg City, Luxembourg
yosuke.todo.xt@hco.ntt.co.jp
[5] Key Laboratory of Cryptologic Technology and Information Security,
Ministry of Education, Shandong University, Qingdao, Shandong, China

Abstract. Determining the exact algebraic structure or some partial information of the superpoly for a given cube is a necessary step in the cube attack – a generic cryptanalytic technique for symmetric-key primitives with some secret and public tweakable inputs. Currently, the division property based approach is the most powerful tool for exact superpoly recovery. However, as the algebraic normal form (ANF) of the targeted output bit gets increasingly complicated as the number of rounds grows, existing methods for superpoly recovery quickly hit their bottlenecks. For example, previous method stuck at round 842, 190, and 892 for TRIVIUM, Grain-128AEAD, and Kreyvium, respectively. In this paper, we propose a new framework for recovering the exact ANFs of massive superpolies based on the monomial prediction technique (ASIACRYPT 2020, an alternative language for the division property). In this framework, the targeted output bit is first expressed as a polynomial of the bits of some intermediate states. For each term appearing in the polynomial, the monomial prediction technique is applied to determine its superpoly if the corresponding MILP model can be solved within a preset time limit. Terms unresolved within the time limit are further expanded as polynomials of the bits of some deeper intermediate states with symbolic computation, whose terms are again processed with monomial predictions. The above procedure is iterated until all terms are resolved. Finally, all the sub-superpolies are collected and assembled into the superpoly of the targeted bit. We apply the new framework to TRIVIUM, Grain-128AEAD, and Kreyvium. As a result, the exact ANFs of the superpolies for 843-, 844- and 845-round TRIVIUM, 191-round Grain-128AEAD and 894-round Kreyvium are recovered. Moreover, with help of the Möbius transform, we present a novel key-recovery technique based on superpolies involving *all* key bits by exploiting the sparse structures, which leads to the best key-recovery attacks on the targets considered.

Due to the page limit, the appendix of this paper are included in the full version [23].

© International Association for Cryptologic Research 2021
M. Tibouchi and H. Wang (Eds.): ASIACRYPT 2021, LNCS 13090, pp. 392–421, 2021.
https://doi.org/10.1007/978-3-030-92062-3_14

Keywords: Cube attack · Superpoly · TRIVIUM · Grain-128AEAD · Kreyvium · Division property · Monomial prediction

1 Introduction

The cube attack was proposed by Dinur and Shamir at EUROCRYPT 2009 against symmetric-key primitives with a secret key and a public input [16]. For a cipher with a secret key $k \in \mathbb{F}_2^m$ and a public input $x \in \mathbb{F}_2^n$, any output bit of the cipher can be regarded as a Boolean function in k and x, denoted as $f(x, k)$. For a constant $u \in \mathbb{F}_2^n$, let $x^u = \prod_{u_i=1} x_i$ where u_i and x_i are the ith coordinate of u and x, respectively. Then $f(x, k)$ can be written uniquely as

$$f(x, k) = p \cdot x^u + q(x, k),$$

where each term of $q(x, k)$ misses at least one variable in $\{x_i : u_i = 1\}$. Let $\mathbb{C}_u = \{x \in \mathbb{F}_2^n : x \preceq u\}$, where $x \preceq u$ means $x_i \leq u_i$ for all $0 \leq i \leq n-1$. Then, we have

$$\bigoplus_{x \in \mathbb{C}_u} f(x, k) = \bigoplus_{x \in \mathbb{C}_u} (p \cdot x^u + q(x, k)) = p. \tag{1}$$

We call p the superpoly of the cube term x^u or the cube $\mathbb{C}_u$. Note that p is a Boolean function in k and $x[\bar{u}] = \{x_i : u_i = 0\}$, thus sometimes this fact is signaled by the notation $p(x[\bar{u}], k)$.

Typically, in the cube attack, the attacker first recovers the superpoly in the offline phase, and then queries the cipher oracle over the cube to compute the summation given by Eq. (1), i.e., the value of the superpoly. Information of the secret keys can be obtained from the equation of the superpoly and its value. Hence recovering superpolies is a crucial step in the cube attack.

In early applications of cube attacks [16,17,33,47], the target ciphers are regarded as black boxes and the superpoly recovery is achieved by experimental test. Hence, superpolies recovered in this way have to be extremely simple (typically linear or quadratic functions). In [39], the conventional bit-based division property [41] was first introduced to probe the structure of the superpoly, which allows us to identify some key bits that do not appear in the superpoly. This is the first time that the targeted cipher is regarded as a non-black box object in performing the cube attacks. By setting the key bits that are not involved in the superpoly to arbitrary constants and varying the remaining l key bits, one can obtain the truth table of the superpoly for a subsequent key-recovery attack with complexity $2^{|I|+l}$, where $I = \{i : u_i = 1\}$ is the so-called cube indices. The complexity of recovering the superpoly could be further improved by computing the upper bound on the algebraic degree of the superpoly [42].

At ASIACRYPT 2019, Wang et al. took the three-subset bit-based division property model with the pruning technique to recover the exact superpoly for the first time [43]. However, as the method needs to test every possible monomial in the superpoly, its usage is practically limited when the superpoly is dense. In [44], Ye and Tian introduced a division property-aided algebraic method to recover the exact superpolies by recursively expressing the output of a cipher as the bits of intermediate states and discarding those terms that have no contribution to the superpoly. They found out that several superpolies recovered in [42] were actually constants, based on which we can only perform distinguishing attacks rather than key-recovery attacks. In [19,20], Hao et al. proposed the three-subset division property without unknown subsets (3SDPwoU) and utilized the Gurobi `PoolSearchMode` to enumerate all possible three-subset trails. By counting the number of trails, they could recover the exact superpolies. In [24], Hu et al. proposed the *monomial prediction* technique aided by the divide-and-conquer strategy to speed up the enumeration of the monomial trials, and more superpolies have been recovered. Besides, Ye and Tian also introduced a pure algebraic method in [48]. By representing the output bit in a polynomial of the intermediate states, the superpoly can be recovered for some so-called useful cubes directly. Recently, Sun claimed that a superpoly of a 78-dimensional cube for 843-round TRIVIUM can be recovered [36] without describing details of the method employed.

Contribution. As the number of rounds grows, the superpolies for certain cubes become increasingly complex. Existing methods for superpoly recovery quickly hit their bottlenecks [19,20,24,43,48,50]. Motivated by this fact, we propose a new framework with nested monomial predictions which scales well for massive superpoly recovery. In this framework, the targeted output bit is first expressed as a polynomial of the bits of some intermediate state. For each term appearing in the polynomial, the monomial prediction technique is applied to determine its superpoly if the corresponding MILP model can be solved within a given time limit. Terms unresolved within the time limit are further expanded as polynomials of the bits of some deeper intermediate states with symbolic computation, whose terms are again processed with monomial predictions. The above procedure is iterated until all terms are resolved. Finally, all the sub-superpolies are collected and assembled into the superpoly of the targeted bit. All the source codes of our framework is available in the public domain https://github.com/hukaisdu/massive_superpoly_recovery.git.

We apply the framework to some important symmetric-key ciphers, including TRIVIUM (ISO/IEC standard), Grain-128AEAD (one of the ten Finalists of the NIST lightweight cryptography standardization process), and Kreyvium (designed for fully Homomorphic encryption). For TRIVIUM, we are the first to obtain superpolies for up to 845-round TRIVIUM. For Grain-128AEAD, we recover two 191-round superpolies, while the previous best results reach only 190 rounds. For Kreyvium, we recover a 894-round superpoly, penetrating two more rounds than the best previous results. The details of the superpolies recovered by the new framework and the previous ones are shown in Table 1.

To perform key-recovery attacks based on these superpolies, we face a difficulty that makes existing key-recovery techniques inferior to exhaustive key search: the superpolies are too complicated whose ANFs involve all secret key bits. With help of the Möbius transformation, we present a novel key-recovery technique based on superpolies involving all key bits exploiting the disjoint

Table 1. Summary of the exact superpolies recovered practically for round-reduced TRIVIUM, Grain-128AEAD, and Kreyvium.

Cipher	Rounds	Dim	# Term	Degree	Balancedness¶	Method	Ref.
	818	35	189,540	22	$2^{-11.8}$	Algberaic§	[48]
	835	37	471,120	23	$2^{-10.0}$	Algberaic§	[48]
	837	37	5,011,664	26	$2^{-8.0}$	Algberaic§	[48]
	832	72	3	3	0.375	Pruning & GE†	[39,43,50]
	838	37	2,877,096	25	$2^{-8.3}$	Algberaic§	[48]
	840	78	67	4	0.5	3SDP/u	[19,20]
	840	75	41	4	0.5	Mon. Pred	[24]
	840	76	6	3	0.5	Mon. Pred	[24]
	840	76	4	2	0.5	Mon. Pred	[24]
	840	47	390,899	20	0.02	Nested	[23, App. C.1]
	840	49	357,989	20	0.08	Nested	[23, App. C.1]
	840	42	31,647	17	0.14	Nested	[23, App. C.1]
	840	53	116,145	17	0.26	Nested	[23, App. C.1]
	840	56	7,549	14	0.30	Nested	[23, App. C.1]
	840	62	1,253	12	0.44	Nested	[23, App. C.1]
	841	78	53	5	0.5	3SDP/u	[19,20]
TRIVIUM	841	76	3,632	9	0.5	Mon. Pred	[24]
	841	77	11,161	8	0.5	Mon. Pred	[24]
	841	56	20,485	16	0.48	Nested	[23, App. C.2]
	842	78	975	6	0.5	3SDP/u	[20]
	842	76	5,147	8	0.5	Mon. Pred	[24]
	842	77	4,174	8	0.5	Mon. Pred	[24]
	842	56	343,000	17	0.50	Nested	[23, App. C.3]
	843	78	16,561	8	0.5	–‡	[36]
	843	56	1,671,492	17	0.50	Nested	Sect. 5.1
	843	57	7,985,786	19	0.50	Nested	Sect. 5.1
	843	55	359,466	17	0.49	Nested	Sect. 5.1
	843	54	628,607	18	0.50	Nested	Sect. 5.1
	843	76	38,021	18	0.50	Nested	Sect. 5.1
	844	55	1,770,734	19	0.50	Nested	Sect. 5.1
	844	54	917,468	17	0.49	Nested	Sect. 5.1
	845	55	19,967,968	22	0.50	Nested	Sect. 5.1
	845	54	12,040,654	21	0.50	Nested	Sect. 5.1
	190*	95	178 ∼ 18,958	19 ∼ 24	0.012 ∼ 0.196	3SDP/u	[19,20]
Grain-128AEAD	190	96	1,097	21	0.032	3SDP/u	[19,20]
	191	95	3,053,028	27	0.312	Nested	Sect. 5.2
	191	96	2,398,450	27	0.293	Nested	Sect. 5.2
	892	115	6	1	0.5	3SDP/u	[20]
Kreyvium	893	118	5⋆	1	0.5	3SDP/u	[20]
	894	119	191	4	0.5	Nested	Sect. 5.3

¶: The balancedness is measured by the probability that the superpoly is 1.
§: In [48], the complete ANFs are not given. We take our framework to recover them.
†: In [40], Todo et al. showed this superpoly could be recovered in 2^{77} by the conventional bit-based division property. In [43,50], the superpoly was recovered practically by the method of three subset division property with a pruning technique and the recursively-expressing method.
‡: In [36], Sun claimed they recovered a superpoly for 843-round TRIVIUM but no details of their technique was present.
*: In [19], the authors recovered superpolies for 15 different 95-dimensional cubes.
⋆: In [20], there is an extra term pre-computed offline with 2^{118} time complexity.

properties. Applying this technique with the recovered superpolies leads to the best key-recovery attacks on the targets considered (see Table 2).

Table 2. A summary of the key-recovery attacks on TRIVIUM, Grain-128AEAD, and Kreyvium. Here we do not consider the key recovery attacks under the weak-key seeting such as the works in [30, 48].

Cipher	Rounds	Type	Data	Time	Ref.
	672	Cube	$2^{18.6}$	2^{17}	[16]
	709	Cube	2^{23}	$2^{29.14}$	[33]
	767	Cube	2^{31}	2^{45}	[16]
	784	Cube	2^{33}	2^{39}	[17]
	799	Cube	2^{38}	2^{62}	[17]
	802	Cube	2^{37}	2^{72}	[47]
	805	Corr. Cube	2^{28}	2^{73}	[31]
	805	Cube	2^{38}	$2^{41.4}$	[49]
	806	Cube	2^{16}	2^{64}	[49]
	832	Cube	2^{72}	2^{79}	[40, 43, 50]
	835	Corr. Cube	2^{35}	2^{75}	[31]
TRIVIUM	840	Cube	2^{78}	$2^{79.6}$	[19, 20]
	840	Cube	$2^{76.6}$	$2^{77.8}$	[24]
	840	**Cube**	$\mathbf{2^{62}}$	$\mathbf{2^{76.32}}$	[23, App. C.1]
	841	Cube	2^{78}	$2^{79.6}$	[24]
	841	Cube	2^{77}	$2^{78.6}$	[24]
	841	**Cube**	$\mathbf{2^{56}}$	$\mathbf{2^{78}}$	[23, App. C.2]
	842	Cube	2^{78}	$2^{79.6}$	[24]
	842	Cube	2^{77}	$2^{78.6}$	[24]
	842	**Cube**	$\mathbf{2^{56}}$	$\mathbf{2^{78}}$	[23, App. C.3]
	843	Cube	2^{78}	$2^{79.6}$	[36]
	843	**Cube**	$\mathbf{2^{56}}$	$\mathbf{2^{77}}$	Sect. 6.2
	844	**Cube**	$\mathbf{2^{56}}$	$\mathbf{2^{78}}$	Sect. 6.2
	845	**Cube**	$\mathbf{2^{56}}$	$\mathbf{2^{78}}$	Sect. 6.2
	169	Condit. Diff	2^{47}	small	[30]
	182	Cube	2^{88}	2^{129}	[39, 40]
Grain-128a†	182	Cube	2^{88}	2^{127}	[39, 40, 42]
	183	Cube	2^{92}	2^{127}	[42]
	183	Cube	2^{95}	2^{127}	[42]
	190	Cube	2^{96}	2^{123}	[19, 20]
Grain-128AEAD	–	State Recovery	–	Practical*	[12]
	191	**Cube**	$\mathbf{2^{96}}$	$\mathbf{2^{126.26}}$	Sect. 6.2
	849	Cube	2^{61}	2^{127}	[40, 42]
	872	Cube	2^{85}	2^{127}	[40, 42]
Kreyvium	891	Cube	2^{113}	2^{127}	[19, 20]
	892	Cube	2^{115}	2^{127}	[18–20]
	893	Cube	2^{118}	2^{119}	[20]
	894	**Cube**	$\mathbf{2^{119}}$	$\mathbf{2^{127}}$	Sect. 6.2

†: Since in our assumption, the Grain-128AEAD is the same as Grain-128a, we provided the results for Grain-128a for a better comparison.
∗: In [12], the authors showed that if the state after the initialization ($t = 384$) is known, then the secret key can be recovered in practical time.

2   Division Property and Monomial Prediction

The division property [38] was proposed by Todo initially as generalized integral attacks [28] (a.k.a. Square attacks [13] or higher-order differential attacks [27,29]). The division property was successfully applied to many primitives. In particular, it was employed to break the full MISTY1 block cipher [32], which undoubtedly demonstrates its powerfulness [6,37].

At the early stage, the division property works in a word-oriented app-roach, and the propagation of the division properties only considers the alge-braic degrees of the local components. Subsequently, by considering the divi-sion property at the bit level, Todo and Morii [41] introduced the bit-based division property [7]. With a deeper understanding of the propagation of the bit-based division properties for local components [8], Xiang et al. introduced a MILP-based method to search for the conventional (a.k.a. two-subset) bit-based division properties automatically [46].

From then on, a series of researches on extending the application scope or increasing the accuracy of the algorithms for detecting division properties were conducted [14,15,25,26]. To capture not only balanced but also constant output bits as well as some cancellation characteristics ignored by the conventional bit-based division property, the so-called three-subset bit-based division property was proposed [41]. In [43,45], Wang et al. presented the automated methods for detecting the three-subset bit-based division properties. In [19,20], Hao et al. proposed the three-subset bit-based division property without unknown subsets (3SDPwoU). Eventually, we arrive at methods for detecting division properties with perfect accuracy.

The monomial prediction is another language for describing the division prop-erties from a pure polynomial viewpoint [24]. They are equivalent although they start from different perspectives. In this paper, we mainly take the conceptions of the monomial prediction to interpret our new framework, so in the remaining of this section, we introduce some basic language of the monomial prediction.

2.1 Notations and Definitions

We use bold italic lowercase letters to represent bit vectors. For an n-bit vector $\boldsymbol{u} = (u_0, \cdots, u_{n-1}) \in \mathbb{F}_2^n$, its complementary vector is denoted by $\bar{\boldsymbol{u}}$, where $u_i \oplus \bar{u}_i = 1$ for $0 \leq i < n$. The Hamming weight of $\boldsymbol{u}$ is $wt(\boldsymbol{u}) = \sum_{i=0}^{n-1} u_i$. For $\boldsymbol{u}, \boldsymbol{x} \in \mathbb{F}_2^n$, $\boldsymbol{x}[\boldsymbol{u}]$ denotes a sub-vector of $\boldsymbol{x}$ with respect to $\boldsymbol{u}$ as $\boldsymbol{x}[\boldsymbol{u}] = (x_{i_0}, x_{i_1}, \ldots, x_{i_{wt(\boldsymbol{u})-1}}) \in \mathbb{F}_2^{wt(\boldsymbol{u})}$, where $i_j \in \{0 \leq i \leq n-1 : u_i = 1\}$. For any n-bit vectors $\boldsymbol{u}$ and $\boldsymbol{u}'$, we define $\boldsymbol{u} \succeq \boldsymbol{u}'$ if $u_i \geq u_i'$ for all i. Similarly, we define $\boldsymbol{u} \preceq \boldsymbol{u}'$ if $u_i \leq u_i'$ for all i.

Boolean Function. Let $f : \mathbb{F}_2^n \to \mathbb{F}_2$ be a Boolean function whose *algebraic normal form* (ANF) is

$$f(\boldsymbol{x}) = f(x_0, x_1, \ldots, x_{n-1}) = \bigoplus_{\boldsymbol{u} \in \mathbb{F}_2^n} a_{\boldsymbol{u}} \prod_{i=0}^{n-1} x_i^{u_i},$$

where $a_{\boldsymbol{u}} \in \mathbb{F}_2$, and

$$\boldsymbol{x}^{\boldsymbol{u}} = \pi_{\boldsymbol{u}}(\boldsymbol{x}) = \prod_{i=0}^{n-1} x_i^{u_i} \text{ with } x_i^{u_i} = \begin{cases} x_i, & \text{if } u_i = 1, \\ 1, & \text{if } u_i = 0, \end{cases}$$

is called a monomial. We use the notation $\boldsymbol{x}^{\boldsymbol{u}} \to f$ to indicate that the coefficient of $\boldsymbol{x}^{\boldsymbol{u}}$ in f is 1, i.e., $\boldsymbol{x}^{\boldsymbol{u}}$ appears in f. Otherwise, $\boldsymbol{x}^{\boldsymbol{u}} \nrightarrow f$. In this work, we will use $\boldsymbol{x^u}$ and $\pi_{\boldsymbol{u}}(\boldsymbol{x})$ interchangeably to avoid using the awkward notation $\boldsymbol{x}^{(i)\boldsymbol{u}^{(j)}}$ when both $\boldsymbol{x}$ and $\boldsymbol{u}$ have superscripts.

Vectorial Boolean Function. Let $\boldsymbol{f} : \mathbb{F}_2^m \to \mathbb{F}_2^n$ be a vectorial Boolean function with $\boldsymbol{y} = (y_0, y_1, \ldots, y_{m-1}) = \boldsymbol{f}(\boldsymbol{x}) = (f_0(\boldsymbol{x}), f_1(\boldsymbol{x}), \ldots, f_{n-1}(\boldsymbol{x}))$. For $\boldsymbol{v} \in \mathbb{F}_2^n$, we use $\boldsymbol{y^v}$ to denote the product of some coordinates of $\boldsymbol{y}$:

$$\boldsymbol{y^v} = \prod_{i=0}^{m-1} y_i^{v_i} = \prod_{i=0}^{m-1} (f_i(\boldsymbol{x}))^{v_i},$$

which is a Boolean function in $\boldsymbol{x}$.

2.2   Monomial Prediction

Let $\boldsymbol{f} : \mathbb{F}_2^{n_0} \to \mathbb{F}_2^{n_r}$ be a composite vectorial Boolean function of a sequence of r smaller function $\boldsymbol{f}^{(i)} : \mathbb{F}_2^{n_i} \to \mathbb{F}_2^{n_{i+1}}, 0 \le i \le r - 1$ as

$$\boldsymbol{f} = \boldsymbol{f}^{(r-1)} \circ \boldsymbol{f}^{(r-1)} \circ \cdots \circ \boldsymbol{f}^{(0)}. \tag{2}$$

For $0 \le i \le r - 1$, suppose $\boldsymbol{x}^{(i)} \in \mathbb{F}_2^{n_i}$ and $\boldsymbol{x}^{(i+1)} \in \mathbb{F}_2^{n_{i+1}}$ are the input and output of the ith component function $\boldsymbol{f}^{(i)}$. Considering a monomial of $\boldsymbol{x}^{(0)}$, say $\pi_{\boldsymbol{u}^{(0)}}(\boldsymbol{x}^{(0)})$, it is easy to find all the monomials of $\pi_{\boldsymbol{u}^{(1)}}(\boldsymbol{x}^{(1)})$ that contain $\pi_{\boldsymbol{u}^{(0)}}(\boldsymbol{x}^{(0)})$, i.e., $\pi_{\boldsymbol{u}^{(0)}}(\boldsymbol{x}^{(0)}) \to \pi_{\boldsymbol{u}^{(1)}}(\boldsymbol{x}^{(1)})$; for every such $\pi_{\boldsymbol{u}^{(1)}}(\boldsymbol{x}^{(1)})$, we then find all the $\pi_{\boldsymbol{u}^{(2)}}(\boldsymbol{x}^{(2)})$ satisfying $\pi_{\boldsymbol{u}^{(1)}}(\boldsymbol{x}^{(1)}) \to \pi_{\boldsymbol{u}^{(2)}}(\boldsymbol{x}^{(2)})$; finally, if we are interested in whether $\pi_{\boldsymbol{u}^{(0)}}(\boldsymbol{x}^{(0)}) \to \pi_{\boldsymbol{u}^{(r)}}(\boldsymbol{x}^{(r)})$, we may collect some transitions from $\pi_{\boldsymbol{u}^{(0)}}(\boldsymbol{x}^{(0)})$ to $\pi_{\boldsymbol{u}^{(r)}}(\boldsymbol{x}^{(r)})$ as

$$\pi_{\boldsymbol{u}^{(0)}}(\boldsymbol{x}^{(0)}) \to \pi_{\boldsymbol{u}^{(1)}}(\boldsymbol{x}^{(1)}) \to \cdots \to \pi_{\boldsymbol{u}^{(r)}}(\boldsymbol{x}^{(r)}).$$

Every such transition is called a monomial trail from $\pi_{\boldsymbol{u}^{(0)}}(\boldsymbol{x}^{(0)})$ to $\pi_{\boldsymbol{u}^{(r)}}(\boldsymbol{x}^{(r)})$, denoted by $\pi_{\boldsymbol{u}^{(0)}}(\boldsymbol{x}^{(0)}) \rightsquigarrow \pi_{\boldsymbol{u}^{(r)}}(\boldsymbol{x}^{(r)})$. All the trails from $\pi_{\boldsymbol{u}^{(0)}}(\boldsymbol{x}^{(0)})$ to $\pi_{\boldsymbol{u}^{(r)}}(\boldsymbol{x}^{(r)})$ are denoted by $\pi_{\boldsymbol{u}^{(0)}}(\boldsymbol{x}^{(0)}) \bowtie \pi_{\boldsymbol{u}^{(r)}}(\boldsymbol{x}^{(r)})$, which is the set of all trails. Then whether $\pi_{\boldsymbol{u}^{(0)}}(\boldsymbol{x}^{(0)}) \to \pi_{\boldsymbol{u}^{(r)}}(\boldsymbol{x}^{(r)})$ is determined by the size of $\pi_{\boldsymbol{u}^{(0)}}(\boldsymbol{x}^{(0)}) \bowtie \pi_{\boldsymbol{u}^{(r)}}(\boldsymbol{x}^{(r)})$, represented as $|\pi_{\boldsymbol{u}^{(0)}}(\boldsymbol{x}^{(0)}) \bowtie \pi_{\boldsymbol{u}^{(r)}}(\boldsymbol{x}^{(r)})|$. If there is no trail from $\pi_{\boldsymbol{u}^{(0)}}(\boldsymbol{x}^{(0)})$ to $\pi_{\boldsymbol{u}^{(r)}}(\boldsymbol{x}^{(r)})$, we say $\pi_{\boldsymbol{u}^{(0)}}(\boldsymbol{x}^{(0)}) \not\rightsquigarrow \pi_{\boldsymbol{u}^{(r)}}(\boldsymbol{x}^{(r)})$ and accordingly $|\pi_{\boldsymbol{u}^{(0)}}(\boldsymbol{x}^{(0)}) \bowtie \pi_{\boldsymbol{u}^{(r)}}(\boldsymbol{x}^{(r)})| = 0$.

Theorem 1. (Integrated from [19–21,24]). Let $\boldsymbol{f} = \boldsymbol{f}^{(r-1)} \circ \boldsymbol{f}^{(r-1)} \circ \cdots \circ \boldsymbol{f}^{(0)}$ defined as above. $\pi_{\boldsymbol{u}^{(0)}}(\boldsymbol{x}^{(0)}) \to \pi_{\boldsymbol{u}^{(r)}}(\boldsymbol{x}^{(r)})$ if and only if

$$|\pi_{\boldsymbol{u}^{(0)}}(\boldsymbol{x}^{(0)}) \bowtie \pi_{\boldsymbol{u}^{(r)}}(\boldsymbol{x}^{(r)})| \equiv 1 \pmod{2}.$$

Propagation Rules for the Monomial Trail and the MILP Model. Any component of a symmetric cipher can be regarded as a vectorial Boolean function as $\boldsymbol{f} : \mathbb{F}_2^n \to \mathbb{F}_2^m, \boldsymbol{y} = \boldsymbol{f}(\boldsymbol{x})$. According to the definition of the monomial prediction [24], the propagation rule for $\boldsymbol{f}$ can be described by a set of tuples generated with [23, Algorithm 5], which in turn can be described with a set linear inequalities [9, 34, 35] and thus modeled with MILP. Since any symmetric primitive can be represented as a sequence of basic operations such as XOR, AND and COPY, it suffices to give the propagation rules for these basic functions. We provide their concrete propagation rules and MILP models in [23, App. A].

Gurobi Solver and PoolSearchMode. In this paper, we choose the Gurobi solver [2] as our MILP tool to trace the propagation trails. Gurobi supports a special mode called `PoolSearchMode`, which is useful to extract all possible solutions of a model. In [19, 20, 24], this mode has been successfully used to enumerate all the trails. In this paper, we use the notation

$$\mathcal{M}.\text{PoolSearchMode} \leftarrow 1$$

to signal that the `PoolSearchMode` is turned on. For more on Gurobi and the `PoolSearchMode`, readers are requested to refer to the Gurobi manual [3].

3 Cube Attack and Superpoly Recovery

In the context of the symmetric-key cryptanalysis, we typically regard each output bit of a primitive as a parameterized Boolean function $f : \mathbb{F}_2^n \to \mathbb{F}_2$ whose algebraic normal form is

$$f_{\boldsymbol{k}}(\boldsymbol{x}) = \bigoplus_{\boldsymbol{u} \in \mathbb{F}_2^n} a_{\boldsymbol{u}}(\boldsymbol{k}) \boldsymbol{x}^{\boldsymbol{u}}, \boldsymbol{x} \in \mathbb{F}_2^n, \boldsymbol{k} \in \mathbb{F}_2^m,$$

where the coefficient $a_{\boldsymbol{u}}(\boldsymbol{k})$ of the monomial $\boldsymbol{x}^{\boldsymbol{u}}$ can be regarded as a Boolean function of $\boldsymbol{k}$. In this paper, we denote the coefficient of $\boldsymbol{x}^{\boldsymbol{u}}$ in f by $a_{\boldsymbol{u}}(\boldsymbol{k}) = \text{Coe}(f, \boldsymbol{x}^{\boldsymbol{u}})$. Since the function mapping $(\boldsymbol{x}, \boldsymbol{k})$ to $f_{\boldsymbol{k}}(\boldsymbol{x})$ can be expressed as a Boolean function from $\mathbb{F}_2^{n+m}$ to $\mathbb{F}_2$, we may use $f(\boldsymbol{x}, \boldsymbol{k})$ to denote the parameterized Boolean function $f_{\boldsymbol{k}}(\boldsymbol{x})$ when there is no confusion.

3.1 Cube Attack

Let $f(\boldsymbol{x}, \boldsymbol{k})$ be a parameterized Boolean function from $\mathbb{F}_2^{n+m}$ to $\mathbb{F}_2$, and $\boldsymbol{u}$ be a constant vector. $f(\boldsymbol{x}, \boldsymbol{k})$ can be represented uniquely as

$$f(\boldsymbol{x}, \boldsymbol{k}) = p(\boldsymbol{x}[\bar{\boldsymbol{u}}], \boldsymbol{k}) \cdot \boldsymbol{x}^{\boldsymbol{u}} + q(\boldsymbol{x}, \boldsymbol{k}),$$

where each term of $q(\boldsymbol{x}, \boldsymbol{k})$ is not divisible by $\boldsymbol{x}^{\boldsymbol{u}}$. $\boldsymbol{x}^{\boldsymbol{u}}$ is called a *cube term*, and $\mathbb{C}_{\boldsymbol{u}} = \{\boldsymbol{x} \in \mathbb{F}_2^n : \boldsymbol{x} \preceq \boldsymbol{u}\}$ is called a *cube*. The cube we use is sometimes represented by its *cube indices* $I = \{0 \le i \le n-1 : u_i = 1\} \subseteq \{0, 1, \ldots, n-1\}$, and the cube is also denoted by $\mathbb{C}_I$. If we compute the sum of f over $\mathbb{C}_{\boldsymbol{u}}$, we have

$$\bigoplus_{x \in \mathbb{C}_{\boldsymbol{u}}} f(\boldsymbol{x}, \boldsymbol{k}) = \bigoplus_{x \in \mathbb{C}_{\boldsymbol{u}}} (p(\boldsymbol{x}[\bar{\boldsymbol{u}}], \boldsymbol{k}) \cdot \boldsymbol{x}^{\boldsymbol{u}} \oplus q(\boldsymbol{x}, \boldsymbol{k})) = p(\boldsymbol{x}[\bar{\boldsymbol{u}}], \boldsymbol{k}).$$

where $p(\boldsymbol{x}[\bar{\boldsymbol{u}}], \boldsymbol{k})$ is called the *superpoly* of $\mathbb{C}_{\boldsymbol{u}}$. It is easy to check that the superpoly of $\mathbb{C}_{\boldsymbol{u}}$ is just the coefficient of $\boldsymbol{x}^{\boldsymbol{u}}$ in the parameterized Boolean function $f(\boldsymbol{x}, \boldsymbol{k})$, i.e.,

$$p(\boldsymbol{x}[\bar{\boldsymbol{u}}], \boldsymbol{k}) = \mathsf{Coe}\,(f(\boldsymbol{x}, \boldsymbol{k}), \boldsymbol{x}^{\boldsymbol{u}})\,.$$

If we set the variables in $\boldsymbol{x}[\bar{\boldsymbol{u}}]$ to some fixed constants, the superpoly $p(\boldsymbol{x}[\bar{\boldsymbol{u}}], \boldsymbol{k}) = \mathsf{Coe}\,(f, \boldsymbol{x}^{\boldsymbol{u}})$ is a Boolean function of $\boldsymbol{k}$. In this paper, $\boldsymbol{x}[\bar{\boldsymbol{u}}]$ will be always fixed as $\boldsymbol{0}$.

As mentioned, in the cube attack the superpoly recovery plays a critical role. If the attacker manages to recover the superpoly in the offline phase, then in the online phase, he queries the encryption oracle with the cube and gets the value of the superpoly (0 or 1). Then the attacker obtains an equation of some key bits. By solving this equation, some key information can be extracted. The remaining key bits can be recovered by exhaustive search.

3.2   Superpoly Recovery Based on the 3SDPwoU/Monomial Prediction

To our best knowledge, currently there are four kinds of methods of recovering the exact superpolies for a non-blackbox cipher. A brief introduction to the four methods is provided in [23, App. B]. In this subsection, we recall some details about the MILP model for recovering the exact superpoly based on the 3SDPwoU [19,20] or the monomial prediction [24].

As we mentioned, any cipher output bit can be decomposed into a sequence of small vectorial Boolean functions. Then by constructing the MILP models for the propagation rules of these small functions in the way shown in [23, Algorithm 5], we can construct the whole MILP model whose solutions are all valid monomial trails. If we want to recover the superpoly of a cube term $\boldsymbol{x}^{\boldsymbol{u}}$, then we use $\boldsymbol{u}$ to assign the public input variables (plaintext, IV or tweak) in the MILP model. For the secret input (secret key), we just leave them as free variables. And for those constant values of the input, if they are zero, the MILP variable corresponding to the variables are also assigned by zero, while for those constant one input, we let them be free variables.

After the model is constructed, every solution will be a valid monomial trail like the form $\boldsymbol{k}^{\boldsymbol{v}}\boldsymbol{x}^{\boldsymbol{u}} \rightsquigarrow f$. By calling the Gurobi solver with the `PoolSearchMode` on, we can obtain all solutions of the MILP model. Once we collect all the monomials from $\boldsymbol{k}^{\boldsymbol{v}}\boldsymbol{x}^{\boldsymbol{u}}$ for f for any $\boldsymbol{v} \in \mathbb{F}_2^m$, we can compute the superpoly of $\boldsymbol{x}^{\boldsymbol{u}}$ as

$$\mathsf{Coe}\,(f, \boldsymbol{x}^{\boldsymbol{u}}) = \mathsf{Coe}\left(\bigoplus_{|\boldsymbol{k}^{\boldsymbol{v}}\boldsymbol{x}^{\boldsymbol{u}} \bowtie f| \equiv 1 \pmod 2} \boldsymbol{k}^{\boldsymbol{v}}\boldsymbol{x}^{\boldsymbol{u}}, \boldsymbol{x}^{\boldsymbol{u}}\right) = \bigoplus_{|\boldsymbol{k}^{\boldsymbol{v}}\boldsymbol{x}^{\boldsymbol{u}} \bowtie f| \equiv 1 \pmod 2} \mathsf{Coe}\,(\boldsymbol{k}^{\boldsymbol{v}}\boldsymbol{x}^{\boldsymbol{u}}, \boldsymbol{x}^{\boldsymbol{u}})\,.$$

In [24], Hu et al. observed that for the composite function f, where

$$f = f^{(r-1)} \circ \boldsymbol{f}^{(r-2)} \circ \cdots \circ \boldsymbol{f}^{(0)},$$

if $\pi_{\boldsymbol{u}^{(0)}}(\boldsymbol{x}^{(0)}) \rightsquigarrow f$, then for $0 < i < r$,

$$|\pi_{\boldsymbol{u}^{(0)}}(\boldsymbol{x}^{(0)}) \bowtie f| \equiv \sum_{\pi_{\boldsymbol{u}^{(r-i)}}(\boldsymbol{x}^{(r-i)}) \to f} \left|\pi_{\boldsymbol{u}^{(0)}}(\boldsymbol{x}^{(0)}) \bowtie \pi_{\boldsymbol{u}^{(r-i)}}(\boldsymbol{x}^{(r-i)})\right| \quad (\mathrm{mod}\ 2).$$

Since computing $|\pi_{\boldsymbol{u}^{(0)}}(\boldsymbol{x}^{(0)}) \bowtie \pi_{\boldsymbol{u}^{(r-i)}}(\boldsymbol{x}^{(r-i)})|$ one by one is much easier than computing $|\pi_{\boldsymbol{u}^{(0)}}(\boldsymbol{x}^{(0)}) \bowtie f|$ when i is significantly smaller than r, such a divide-and-conquer strategy helps to speed up the search significantly.

4   Superpoly Recovery with Nested Monomial Predictions

In this section, we introduce a new framework for superpoly recovery that scales well for massive superpolies. In some sense, the new framework is a hybrid of the four previous methods described in [23, App. B]. First, we describe the new framework in detail, and then a comprehensive comparison will be made with existing methods.

4.1   The Nested Framework

Given a parameterized Boolean function which consists of a sequence of simple vectorial Boolean functions as

$$f(\boldsymbol{x}, \boldsymbol{k}) = f^{(r-1)} \circ \boldsymbol{f}^{(r-2)} \circ \cdots \circ \boldsymbol{f}^{(0)}(\boldsymbol{x}, \boldsymbol{k}),$$

let the output of $\boldsymbol{f}^{(i)}$ is $\boldsymbol{s}^{(i+1)}$. For simplicity, we always let the dimension of $\boldsymbol{s}^{(i+1)}$ be n. Then we choose a proper positive number (we will elaborate on how to choose it later) r_0 and express f in a polynomial of $\boldsymbol{s}^{(r-r_0)} \in \mathbb{F}_2^n$, i.e.,

$$f(\boldsymbol{x}, \boldsymbol{k}) = \bigoplus_{\substack{\boldsymbol{t}^{(r-r_0)} \in \mathbb{F}_2^n \\ \pi_{\boldsymbol{t}^{(r-r_0)}}(\boldsymbol{s}^{(r-r_0)}) \in \mathbb{S}^{(r-r_0)}}} \pi_{\boldsymbol{t}^{(r-r_0)}}(\boldsymbol{s}^{(r-r_0)}),$$

where $\mathbb{S}^{(r-r_0)} = \{\pi_{\boldsymbol{t}^{(r-r_0)}}(\boldsymbol{s}^{(r-r_0)}) : \pi_{\boldsymbol{t}^{(r-r_0)}}(\boldsymbol{s}^{(r-r_0)}) \to f\}$. Suppose the cube term is $\boldsymbol{x}^{\boldsymbol{u}}$, we need to compute $\mathsf{Coe}\left(\pi_{\boldsymbol{t}^{(r-r_0)}}(\boldsymbol{s}^{(r-r_0)}), \boldsymbol{x}^{\boldsymbol{u}}\right)$ for each element in $\mathbb{S}^{(r-r_0)}$.

Compute $\mathsf{Coe}\left(\pi_{\boldsymbol{t}^{(r-r_0)}}(\boldsymbol{s}^{(r-r_0)}), \boldsymbol{x}^{\boldsymbol{u}}\right)$. According to the definition, $\boldsymbol{s}^{(r-r_0)}$ is the output vector of a new composite vectorial Boolean function as

$$\boldsymbol{s}^{(r-r_0)} = \boldsymbol{f}^{(r-r_0-1)} \circ \boldsymbol{f}^{(r-r_0-2)} \circ \cdots \circ \boldsymbol{f}^{(0)},$$

then $\pi_{\boldsymbol{t}^{(r-r_0)}}(\boldsymbol{s}^{(r-r_0)})$ is a polynomial of $(\boldsymbol{x}, \boldsymbol{k})$. Hence we can construct the MILP model to enumerate all feasible trails representing $\boldsymbol{k}^{\boldsymbol{v}}\boldsymbol{x}^{\boldsymbol{u}} \rightsquigarrow \pi_{\boldsymbol{t}^{(r-r_0)}}(\boldsymbol{s}^{(r-r_0)})$ to compute $\mathsf{Coe}\left(\pi_{\boldsymbol{t}^{(r-r_0)}}(\boldsymbol{s}^{(r-r_0)}), \boldsymbol{x}^{\boldsymbol{u}}\right)$ just like [19,20,24]. Different from the previous methods, we set a time limit $\tau^{(r-r_0)}$ for the MILP model. For a MILP model $\mathcal{M}$, we use

$$\mathcal{M}.\mathrm{TimeLimit} \leftarrow \tau^{(r-r_0)}$$

to denote it. We refer the readers to, e.g., the Gurobi manual [3, p. 591] for more details about the TimeLimit. If the solver hasn't stopped when the time is up, the procedure will be forcibly terminated. For each element in $\mathbb{S}^{(r-r_0)}$, the model of enumerating the trails will end up with three different kinds of status,

1. The model is solved and infeasible, then $\mathsf{Coe}\left(\pi_{t^{(r-r_0)}}(s^{(r-r_0)}), x^u\right) = 0$;
2. The model is solved and feasible, and all the solutions has been enumerated, then $\mathsf{Coe}\left(\pi_{t^{(r-r_0)}}(s^{(r-r_0)}), x^u\right)$ are obtained [19,20,24];
3. The model is not solved in the time limit $\tau^{(r-r_0)}$.

According to the three different results, we partition $\mathbb{S}^{(r-r_0)}$ into three parts in sequence, say

$$\mathbb{S}^{(r-r_0)} = \mathbb{S}_0^{(r-r_0)} \bigcup \mathbb{S}_p^{(r-r_0)} \bigcup \mathbb{S}_u^{(r-r_0)},$$

where $\mathbb{S}_0^{(r-r_0)}$ is called a *solved-0 set* that contains the elements of case 1, $\mathbb{S}_p^{(r-r_0)}$ is called a *solved-p set* containing the elements of case 2, and $\mathbb{S}_u^{(r-r_0)}$ is called an *undecided set* containing the elements of case 3. The intersection of any two sets among $\mathbb{S}_0^{(r-r_0)}, \mathbb{S}_p^{(r-r_0)}$ and $\mathbb{S}_u^{(r-r_0)}$ is empty.

The solved-0 set is discarded naturally since the elements in it have no contribution to $\mathsf{Coe}\,(f, x^u)$. For the solved-p set,

$$p^{(r-r_0)} = \bigoplus_{\pi_{t^{(r-r_0)}}(s^{(r-r_0)}) \in \mathbb{S}_p^{(r-r_0)}} \mathsf{Coe}\left(\pi_{t^{(r-r_0)}}(s^{(r-r_0)}), x^u\right)$$

is collected as a part of the whole superpoly $\mathsf{Coe}\,(f, x^u)$. The undecided set is the only one we proceed with.

To deal with the monomials in the undecided set $\mathbb{S}_u^{(r-r_0)}$, we choose another positive r_1 and expand each monomial in $\mathbb{S}_u^{(r-r_0)}$ in a polynomial of $s^{(r-r_0-r_1)}$. All the monomials from the expression are inserted into the $\mathbb{S}^{(r-r_0-r_1)}$, i.e.,

$$\mathbb{S}^{(r-r_0-r_1)} = \{\pi_{t^{(r-r_0-r_1)}}(s^{(r-r_0-r_1)}) : \pi_{t^{(r-r_0-r_1)}}(s^{(r-r_0-r_1)}) \to \pi_{t^{(r-r_0)}}(s^{(r-r_0)}),$$
$$\pi_{t^{(r-r_0)}}(s^{(r-r_0)}) \in \mathbb{S}_u^{(r-r_0)}\}$$

Note that if even-number monomials $\pi_{t^{(r-r_0-r_1)}}(s^{(r-r_0-r_1)})$ are inserted into $\mathbb{S}^{(r-r_0-r_1)}$, they should cancel each other by combining the similar terms. Only those occurring odd-number times should be held. Then we repeat the process of dealing with $\mathbb{S}^{(r-r_0)}$, and keep going to reduce r.

As r reduces, there are two possible results of the whole procedure, the first is for some $r' = r - r_0 - r_1 - \cdots - r_i, i > 0$, $\mathbb{S}_u^{(r')}$ is an empty set. Then we obtain

$$\mathsf{Coe}\,(f, x^u) = p^{(r-r_0)} \oplus p^{(r-r_0-r_1)} \oplus \cdots \oplus p^{(r')},$$

the superpoly is recovered. The second result is we finally get $\mathbb{S}^{(0)}$, it is natural to get the partial superpoly from monomials in $\mathbb{S}^{(0)}$. In this case, we also say $\mathbb{S}_u^{(0)}$ is empty. Hence the superpoly is also recovered.

The nested framework can be illustrated by Fig. 1 and the procedure superpolyRecFramework in Algorithm 1. The procedure superpoly

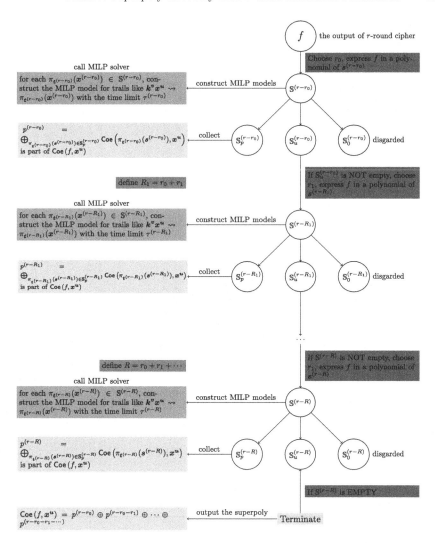

Fig. 1. The nested framework of the superpoly recovery for the cube term x^u for r-round cipher f, i.e., $\mathsf{Coe}\,(f, x^u)$.

`RecFramework` accepts four inputs: the first stands for the function of the output bit of our target; the second is the round number we are interested in; the third is the cube indices related to the cube term x^u; and the fourth is a MILP model constructor for computing $\mathsf{Coe}\left(\pi_{u^{(r')}}(x^{(r')}), x^u\right)$ based on works in [19,20,24], which is given when we introduce the concrete application. For example, when we target TRIVIUM, the fourth parameter should be `ModelTrivium` in Algorithm 2.

Algorithm 1: A framework for the superpoly recovery

---

1 **Procedure** SuperpolyRecFramework($f(x, k)$, r, I, *ModelX*):

2   Prepare a polynomial $p = 0$

3   Initialize $\mathbb{S}_u^{(r)} = \{f\}$

4   Prepare a hash table J whose key is the key monomial and the values is an integer

5   **while** $\mathbb{S}_u^{(r)} \neq \emptyset$ **do**

6        $r' = r - \texttt{ChooseRiX}(\mathbb{S}_u^{(r)}, r)$

7   **for** $\pi_{t^{(r)}}(s^{(r)}) \in \mathbb{S}_u^{(r)}$ **do**

          /* Express $\pi_{t^{(r)}}(s^{(r)})$ in a polynomial of $s^{(r')}$ */

8           $\mathbb{S}^{(r')} \leftarrow \texttt{Express}(\pi_{t^{(r)}}(s^{(r)}), r, r')$

9   Remove the elements occurring even-number times in $\mathbb{S}^{(r')}$

10   **for** $\pi_{t^{(r')}}(s^{(r')}) \in \mathbb{S}^{(r')}$ **do**

11           $\mathcal{M} \leftarrow \texttt{ModelX}(r', \pi_{t^{(r')}}(s^{(r')}), I)$

12           $\tau^{(r')} = \texttt{ChooseTiX}(r')$

13           $\mathcal{M}$.PoolSearchMode $\leftarrow 1$

14           $\mathcal{M}$.TimeLimit $\leftarrow \tau^{(r')}$

15   Solve $\mathcal{M}$

16   **if** $\mathcal{M}$ *is solved and all the solutions are extracted* **then**

17   Extract k^v in every found solution

18   Increase $J[k^v]$ by 1

19   Prepare $p^{(r')} = 0$

20   **for** k^v *whose* $J[k^v]$ *is an odd number* **do**

21                 $p^{(r')} = p^{(r')} \oplus k^v$

22              $p = p \oplus p^{(r')}$

23   **else if** $\mathcal{M}$ *is not solved within* $\tau^{(r')}$ **then**

24              $\mathbb{S}_u^{(r')} \leftarrow \pi_{t^{(r')}}(s^{(r')})$

25   **return** p

The Choices of r_i and $\tau^{(r_i)}$. The choices of r_i and $\tau^{(r_i)}$ play important roles in the whole algorithm since they affect the efficiency directly. When r_i is big, it is sometimes difficult to express $\pi_{t^{(r-r_0-\cdots-r_{i-1})}}(s^{(r-r_0-\cdots-r_{i-1})})$ in $s^{(r-r_0-\cdots-r_i)}$ especially when $r - r_0 - \ldots - r_{i-1}$ has been close to 0. On the contrary, if r_i is too small, the size of $\mathbb{S}^{(r-r_0-\cdots-r_i)}$ will be small, too, then the program is also not efficient, because we have to repeat more times of the expression. Generally speaking, the choice of r_i is heavily related to the position in the life cycle of the nested framework. So we take a dynamic way to decide it. Given $\mathbb{S}^{(r-r_0-\cdots-r_{i-1})}$, we choose that r_i which makes the size of $\mathbb{S}^{(r-r_0-\cdots-r_i)}$ become larger than a given number N for the first time. In our application, we usually choose $N = 10,000$ or $100,000$. In Algorithm 1, the choice of r_i is represented by `ChooseRiX` function, X stands for the concrete instance.

The choice of $\tau^{(r_i)}$ affects the efficiency, too, as well as the memory consumption. For a monomial $\pi_{t^{(r-r_0-\cdots-r_i)}}(s^{(r-r_0-\cdots-r_i)})$ that is hard or even impossible to compute out $\mathsf{Coe}\left(\pi_{t^{(r-r_0-\cdots-r_i)}}(s^{(r-r_0-\cdots-r_i)}), x^u\right)$, a large $\tau^{(r_i)}$ is pure waste. However, if $\mathsf{Coe}\left(\pi_{t^{(r-r_0-\cdots-r_i)}}(s^{(r-r_0-\cdots-r_i)}), x^u\right)$ can be obtained in, e.g., $100\,\mathrm{s}$, while we set $\tau^{(r_i)} = 50\,\mathrm{s}$, then $\pi_{t^{(r-r_0-\cdots-r_i)}}(s^{(r-r_0-\cdots-r_i)})$ will be pushed into the undecided set $\mathbb{S}_u^{(r-r_0-\cdots-r_i)}$ and wait to be expressed. Then the $50\,\mathrm{s}$ is also waste. It is indeed a tough task to choose a proper $\tau^{(r_i)}$. We can only provide some principles and the $\tau^{(r_i)}$ should be obtained according to the concrete instance.

When $r - r_0 - \cdots - r_i$ is closer to r, $\tau^{(i)}$ should be smaller since it is more likely that the model for computing $\mathsf{Coe}\left(\pi_{t^{(r-r_0-\cdots-r_i)}}(s^{(r-r_0-\cdots-r_i)}), x^u\right)$ needs an unbearable amount of the time to solve or even impossible to solve. While $r - r_0 - \cdots - r_i$ is closer to 0, the model is more likely to be solved in a limited time and expressing $\pi_{t^{(r-r_0-\cdots-r_i)}}(s^{(r-r_0-\cdots-r_i)})$ in $\pi_{t^{(r-r_0-\cdots-r_{i+1})}}(s^{(r-r_0-\cdots-r_{i+1})})$ is more difficult and will spawn thousands of new monomials. Therefore, we prefer to choose a larger $\tau^{(i)}$. The concrete $\tau^{(i)}$ we use for our applications will be given on the spot, i.e., we will give `ChooseRiX` function when discussing the concrete cipher.

4.2   A Comparison with Existing Methods

At first glance, the nested framework is similar to Ye and Tian's recursively-expressing method [50], as we need to express the polynomials in intermediate states, too. However, there is one critical difference between the new framework and the recursively-expressing method. In each step, we partition $\mathbb{S}^{(r')}$ into three parts, say solved-0, solved-p and undecided sets while the recursively-expressing method partitions it into two parts, in the same language with ours, solved-0 and undecided sets. Some parts of the superpoly could be computed out by MILP model when we process the solved-1 set, whereas the recursively-expressing method simply pushes all monomials that should have been in solved-1 set into the undecided set. As a result, the size of the undecided set may become larger and larger. Every such monomial is potential to spawn thousands of new monomials in the next expression. Especially when the superpoly is massive, the size may explode in an exponential way. This is the main reason why their method is not suitable to a large superpoly recovery and longer rounds of TRIVIUM.

The 3SDPwoU and the monomial prediction are embedded in our nested framework as a sub-procedure. However, we use the MILP model in an restrained way rather than totally relying on the MILP solver as done in [19,20,24]. This is important because the internal mechanisms of the MILP solver are unknown. The time consumption is hard to predict beforehand. In some extreme cases, the MILP model is even impossible to be solved but we have no measures to deal with it at all. While in our framework, each MILP model is small and under control by setting the time limit. Besides, since the superpoly is computed in the offline phase, we only need to calculate it once. It is natural for us to resort more computation resources to compute it. Although some solvers like Gurobi support the multithreading property, however, the improvement of the efficiency is not always proportional to the number of threads we use in the experiments. Whereas in the new framework, the program is naturally parallel when processing the monomials in the undecided set, then the efficiency will be proportional to the number of the threads we use. Hence, it is smooth for us to take a multithreading strategy to speed up the search.

As discussed in [23, App. B], Ye and Tian's algebraic methods is potential for massive superpolies but it only works when we find the useful cubes so it has many restrictions when dealing with a casual cube. Most importantly, such requirements for useful cubes are hard to meet when the number of rounds increases. Our method is more general and has no such limitations.

Since Wang's et al. pruning method needs to test every possible monomial of the polynomial one by one, it is meaningful more in theory rather than practice. Our new framework focuses more on the practical recovery of the massive superpolies.

5   Massive Superpoly Recovery

In this section, we apply the new framework to TRIVIUM, Grain-128AEAD, and Kreyvium. As a result, the exact ANFs of the superpolies for 843-, 844- and 845-round TRIVIUM, 191-round Grain-128AEAD and 894-round Kreyvium are recovered, though they are extraordinarily massive. All the experiments are conducted by Gurobi Solver (version 9.1.1) on a work station with 2×AMD EPYC 7302 16-core (32 siblings) Processor 3.3 GHz, (totally 64 threads), 256G RAM, and Ubuntu 20.10. In our platform, the superpolies for 843- and 844-round Trivium are obtained less than two weeks, while the results for 845-round Trivium consume less than three weeks. It costs 31 days to recovery the superpoly for 894-round Kreyvium (who looks quite simple though). The two results for Grain-128AEAD cost 3 and 5 days, respectively. The source codes (as well as the superpolies we recovered) are available in our git repository.

5.1   Superpoly Recovery for TRIVIUM up to 845 Rounds

TRIVIUM is a hardware oriented stream cipher designed by De Cannière and Preneel [10]. It has been selected as part of the eSTREAM portfolio [1] and specified as an International Standard under ISO/IEC 29192-3 [4]. At the initialization phase, an 80-bit key and an 80-bit IV are loaded into the 288-bit initial state $(s_0, s_1, \ldots, s_{287})$. Then the state is updated through 1152 rounds. This process is summarized by the following pseudo-code:

$$(s_0, s_1, \ldots, s_{92}) \leftarrow (K_0, K_1, \ldots, K_{79}, 0, \ldots, 0)$$
$$(s_{93}, s_{95}, \ldots, s_{177}) \leftarrow (IV_0, IV_1, \ldots, IV_{79}, 0, \ldots, 0)$$
$$(s_{177}, s_{179}, \ldots, s_{287}) \leftarrow (0, \ldots, 0, 1, 1, 1)$$
for $i = 0$ to 1151 **do**

$$t_1 \leftarrow s_{65} \oplus s_{90} \cdot s_{91} \oplus s_{92} \oplus s_{170}$$

$$t_2 \leftarrow s_{161} \oplus s_{174} \cdot s_{175} \oplus s_{176} \oplus s_{263}$$

$$t_3 \leftarrow s_{242} \oplus s_{285} \cdot s_{286} \oplus s_{287} \oplus s_{68}$$

$$(s_0, s_1, \ldots, s_{92}) \leftarrow (t_3, s_0, s_1, \ldots, s_{91})$$

$$(s_{93}, s_{95}, \ldots, s_{177} \leftarrow (t_1, s_{93}, s_{94}, \ldots, s_{175})$$

$$(s_{177}, s_{179}, \ldots, s_{287}) \leftarrow (t_2, s_{177}, s_{178} \ldots, s_{286})$$

end for

After the initialization phase, one key stream bit is generated by $z = s_{65} \oplus s_{92} \oplus s_{161} \oplus s_{176} \oplus s_{242} \oplus s_{287}$. When we say r-round TRIVIUM, we mean after r times of updates in the initialization phase, one key bit denoted by z_r is generated. We assume that an attacker has the right to access z_r.

In [19,20,24], the MILP model of TRIVIUM for tracing the three-subset division/monomial trails are proposed. In this paper, we slightly adjust their model to make them suitable to the nested framework. The `TriviumCore` in Algorithm 2 generates the MILP constraints for all the monomial trails of the update function, which is directly borrowed from [19,20]. The procedure `ModelTrivium` generates a model $\mathcal{M}$ as the input of Algorithm 1. All feasible solutions of $\mathcal{M}$ cover all $\boldsymbol{k}^v \boldsymbol{x}^u \rightsquigarrow \pi_{t^{(R)}}(\boldsymbol{s}^{(R)})$ where $\boldsymbol{v} \in \mathbb{F}_2^{80}$ and $\boldsymbol{x}^u$ is the cube term. The functions that produce the sequences of $r_0, r_1, \ldots, r_i$ and $\tau^{(r-r_0)}, \tau^{(r-r_0-r_1)}, \ldots, \tau^{(r-r_0-\cdots-r_i)}$ for TRIVIUM used in Algorithm 1, i.e., `ChooseRiTrivium` and `ChooseTiTrivium` are given in Algorithm 3.

Superpoly Recovery for 843-Round TRIVIUM. Currently, there is no optimal method of choosing a good cube, so we construct new cubes heuristically as shown in Table 3. It is worth noting that we took the method in [24] to recover the superpoly for I_4, the program had not ended for more than one month and we had to give up. Taking our nested framework, the superpoly for I_4 could be recovered in less than 12 days. Since the superpolies for $I_0, I_1, \ldots, I_4$ are too complicated to present here, we provide them in the git repository. We here only give some information of the five superpolies in Table 4. Since the superpolies are too complicated, the balancedness of each superpoly is tested by 2^{15} random keys.

Superpoly Recovery for 844- and 845-Round Trivium. From Table 3, we know the number of monomial trails and the terms in the superpoly for I_2 is the minimum. We heuristically choose I_2 for 844- and 845-round TRIVIUM and recover the superpolies. The information of the two superpolies are listed in Table 5. Since the superpolies are too complicated, the balancedness of each superpoly is tested by 2^{15} random keys.

5.2   Superpoly Recovery for 191-Round Grain-128AEAD

Grain-128AEAD [22] is an authenticated encryption algorithm with support for associated data, which has recently been selected as the one of the ten finalist candidates of the NIST lightweight cryptography standardization process. The

---

Algorithm 2: Model for the propagation trails of R-round TRIVIUM

---

1 **Procedure** TriviumCore($\mathcal{M}, x_0, x_1, \ldots, x_{287}, i_1, i_2, i_3, i_4, i_5$):

2      $\mathcal{M}.var \leftarrow y_{i_1}, y_{i_2}, y_{i_3}, y_{i_4}, y_{i_5}, z_1, z_2, z_3, z_4, a$ as binary

3      $\mathcal{M}.con \leftarrow x_{i_j} = y_{i_j} \vee z_j$ for all $j \in \{1, 2, 3, 4\}$

4      $\mathcal{M}.con \leftarrow a = z_3$

5      $\mathcal{M}.con \leftarrow a = z_4$

6      $\mathcal{M}.con \leftarrow y_{i_5} = x_{i_5} + a + z_1 + z_2$

7   **for** $i \in \{0, 1, \ldots, 287\}$ w/o i_1, i_2, i_3, i_4, i_5 **do** $y_i = x_i$

8   **return** $(\mathcal{M}, y_0, y_1, \ldots, y_{287})$

9 **Procedure** ModelTrivium($round\ R,\ \pi_{t^{(R)}}(s^{(R)}),\ I$):

10   Prepare empty MILP Model $\mathcal{M}$

11      $\mathcal{M}.var \leftarrow s_i^0$ for $i \in \{0, 1, \ldots, 287\}$

12   **for** $i = 80$ to 92 and $i = 93 + 80$ to 284 **do** $\mathcal{M}.con \leftarrow s_i^0 = 0$

13   **for** $i = 93$ to 172 **do**

14          $\mathcal{M}.con \leftarrow s_i^0 = 1 \ \forall\ i - 93 \in I$

15          $\mathcal{M}.con \leftarrow s_i^0 = 0 \ \forall\ i - 93 \notin I$

16   **for** $r = 0$ to $R - 1$ **do**

17          $(\mathcal{M}, x_0, \ldots, x_{287}) = \text{TriviumCore}(\mathcal{M}, s_1^r, \ldots, s_{288}^r, 65, 170, 90, 91, 92)$

18          $(\mathcal{M}, y_0, \ldots, y_{287}) = \text{TriviumCore}(\mathcal{M}, x_1, \ldots, x_{288}, 161, 263, 174, 175, 176)$

19          $(\mathcal{M}, z_0, \ldots, z_{287}) = \text{TriviumCore}(\mathcal{M}, y_1, \ldots, y_{288}, 242, 68, 285, 286, 287)$

20          $(s_0^{r+1}, \ldots, s_{287}^{r+1}) = (z_{287}, z_0, \ldots, z_{286})$

21   **for** $i = 0$ to 287 **do**

22          $\mathcal{M}.con \leftarrow s_i^r = t_i^{(R)}$ // $t^{(R)} = (t_0, t_1, \ldots, t_{287})$

23   **return** $\mathcal{M}$

Algorithm 3: ChooseRiTrivium and ChooseTiTrivium

---

1 **Procedure** ChooseRiTrivium($\mathbb{S}, r$):

2      $r' = 0$

3   **while** $|\mathbb{S}'| < 100,000$ and $r - r' > 0$ **do**

4          $r' = r' + 1$

5          $\mathbb{S}' = \emptyset$

6   **for** $s \in \mathbb{S}$ **do** $\mathbb{S}' = \mathbb{S}' \cup \text{Express}(s, r, r')$

7   **return** r'

8 **Procedure** ChooseTiTrivium(r):

9   **if** $r \geq 600$ **then** $\tau = 60\,\text{s}$

10   **else if** $r \geq 500$ **then** $\tau = 120\,\text{s}$

11   **else if** $r \geq 400$ **then** $\tau = 180\,\text{s}$

12   **else if** $r \geq 300$ **then** $\tau = 360\,\text{s}$

13   **else if** $r \geq 200$ **then** $\tau = 720\,\text{s}$

14   **else if** $r \geq 100$ **then** $\tau = 1200\,\text{s}$

15   **else if** $r \geq 20$ **then** $\tau = 3600\,\text{s}$

16   **else if** $r \geq 0$ **then** $\tau = \infty$

17   **return** τ

Table 3. Cube indices we use for the superpoly recovery of 843-round TRIVIUM

I	$|I|$	Indices
I_0	56	0, 1, 2, 3, 4, 5, 6, 7, 8, 9, 10, 11, 12, 13, 14, 15, 16, 17, 18, 19, 20, 21, 22, 23, 24, 25, 26, 27, 28, 29, 30, 31, 32, 33, 34, 36, 38, 40, 42, 45, 47, 49, 51, 53, 55, 57, 60, 62, 64, 66, 68, 70, 72, 77, 75, 79
I_1	57	0, 1, 2, 3, 4, 5, 6, 7, 8, 9, 10, 11, 12, 13, 14, 15, 16, 17, 18, 19, 20, 21, 22, 23, 24, 25, 26, 27, 28, 29, 30, 31, 32, 33, 34, 35, 36, 38, 40, 42, 45, 47, 49, 51, 53, 55, 57, 60, 62, 64, 66, 68, 70, 72, 77, 75, 79
I_2	55	0, 1, 2, 3, 4, 5, 6, 7, 8, 9, 10, 11, 12, 13, 14, 15, 16, 17, 18, 19, 20, 21, 22, 23, 24, 25, 26, 27, 28, 29, 30, 31, 32, 34, 36, 38, 40, 42, 45, 47, 49, 51, 53, 55, 57, 60, 62, 64, 66, 68, 70, 72, 77, 75, 79
I_3	54	0, 1, 2, 3, 4, 5, 6, 7, 8, 9, 10, 11, 12, 13, 14, 15, 16, 17, 18, 19, 20, 21, 22, 23, 24, 25, 26, 27, 28, 29, 30, 32, 34, 36, 38, 40, 42, 45, 47, 49, 51, 53, 55, 57, 60, 62, 64, 66, 68, 70, 72, 77, 75, 79
I_4	76	0, 1, 2, 3, 4, 5, 6, 7, 8, 9, 10, 11, 12, 13, 14, 15, 16, 17, 18, 19, 20, 21, 22, 23, 24, 25, 26, 27, 28, 29, 30, 31, 32, 34, 35, 36, 37, 38, 39, 40, 41, 42, 43, 44, 45, 46, 47, 48, 49, 50, 51, 52, 53, 54, 55, 56, 57, 58, 59, 60, 61, 62, 63, 64, 65, 66, 67, 68, 69, 70, 71, 73, 75, 77, 79

Table 4. Details related to the Superpoly of $\mathbb{C}_I$ for 843-round TRIVIUM. The concrete ANFs for them are provided in the git repository.

I	# Trails	# Monomials	# Involved key bits	Degree	Balancedness
I_0	44,586,510	1,671,492	80	17	0.50
I_1	217,694,326	7,985,786	80	19	0.50
I_2	6,124,212	359,466	80	17	0.49
I_3	15,587,645	628,607	80	18	0.50
I_4	1,977,228,919	38,021	80	10	0.50

design of Grain-128AEAD is closely based on the Grain-128a [5] which was introduced in 2011. Before the pre-output bits are used for encryption, a 64-bit shift register and a 64-bit accumulator are also initialized to generate the authentication tag later. In [19,20], Hao et al. assumed that the first pre-output bit could be observed, then the Grain-128AEAD is actually the same as Grain-128a. In this work, we also analyze Grain-128AEAD under this setting.

The internal state of Grain-128AEAD is represented by two 128-bit states as $\boldsymbol{b} = (b_0, b_1, \ldots, b_{127})$ and $\boldsymbol{s} = (s_0, s_1, \ldots, s_{127})$. The 128-bit key is loaded to the first register $\boldsymbol{b}$, and the 96-bit nonce (the initialization vector for Grain128a) is loaded to the second register $\boldsymbol{s}$. The other state bits are set to 1 except the least one bit in the second register. Namely, the initial state bits are represented as

$$(b_0, b_1, \ldots, b_{127}) = (K_0, K_1, \ldots, K_{127}),$$
$$(s_0, s_1, \ldots, s_{127}) = (N_0, N_1, \ldots, N_{95}, 1, \ldots, 1, 0).$$

Table 5. Details related to the Superpoly for I_2 for 844- and 845-round TRIVIUM. The concrete ANFs of them are available in the git repository.

I	Round	# Trails	# Monomials	# Involved key bits	Degree	Balancedness
I_2	844	186,128,078	1,770,734	80	19	0.50
I_3	844	55,152,796	917,468	80	17	0.49
I_2	845	4,731,073,108	19,967,968	80	22	0.50
I_3	845	1,362,323,454	12,040,654	80	21	0.50

The pseudo code of the update function in the initialization is given as follows.

$$g \leftarrow b_0 \oplus b_{26} \oplus b_{56} \oplus b_{91} \oplus b_{96} \oplus b_3 b_{67} \oplus b_{11} b_{13} \oplus b_{17} b_{18} \oplus b_{27} b_{59} \oplus b_{40} b_{48}$$
$$\oplus b_{61} b_{65} \oplus b_{68} b_{84} \oplus b_{88} b_{92} b_{93} b_{95} \oplus b_{22} b_{24} b_{25} \oplus b_{70} b_{78} b_{82},$$
$$f \leftarrow s_0 \oplus s_7 \oplus s_{38} \oplus s_{70} \oplus s_{81} \oplus s_{96},$$
$$h \leftarrow b_{12} s_8 \oplus s_{13} s_{20} \oplus b_{95} s_{42} \oplus s_{60} s_{79} \oplus b_{12} b_{95} s_{94},$$
$$z \leftarrow h \oplus s_{93} \oplus b_2 \oplus b_{15} \oplus b_{36} \oplus b_{45} \oplus b_{64} \oplus b_{73} \oplus b_{89},$$
$$(b_0, b_1, \ldots, b_{127}) \leftarrow (b_1, \ldots, b_{127}, g \oplus s_0 \oplus z),$$
$$(s_0, s_1, \ldots, s_{127}) \leftarrow (s_1, \ldots, s_{127}, f \oplus z).$$

In the initialization, the state is updated 256 times without producing an output. After the initialization, the update function is tweaked such that z is not fed to the state, and z is used as a pre-output key stream.

MILP Model. ModelGrain-128AEAD in [23, Algorithm 6] produces the MILP model as the fourth input of Algorithm 1. The MILP model is used to enumerate all trails like $\boldsymbol{k}^v \boldsymbol{x}^u \rightsquigarrow \pi_{t(R)}(\boldsymbol{s}^{(R)})$ where $\boldsymbol{v} \in \mathbb{F}_2^{128}$, and $\boldsymbol{x}^u$ is the cube term we are interested in. [23, Algorithm 6] is slightly adapted from [19,20], the supporting functions such as funcZ, funcG and funcF are directly borrowed ([23, Algorithm 8]). The functions that produce the sequences of $r_0, r_1, \ldots, r_i$ and $\tau^{(r-r_0)}, \tau^{(r-r_0-r_1)}, \ldots, \tau^{(r-r_0-\cdots-r_i)}$ for Grain-128AEAD used in Algorithm 1, i.e., ChooseRiGrain-128AEAD and ChooseTiGrain-128AEAD are also given in [23, Algorithm 7]. Due to the page limits, all the algorithms are presented in [23, App. D].

Superpoly Recovery for 191-Round Grain-128AEAD. For 191-round Grain-128AEAD, we apply the nested framework to two cubes. The first is $I_0 = \{0, 1, 2, \ldots, 95\}$, where all nonce bits are active. The second is $I_1 = \{0, 1, 2, \ldots, 95\} \backslash \{30\}$, where all IV bits except the 30th are active. The information of the two superpolies are shown in Table 6.

Table 6. Details related to the Superpoly of I_0 and I_1 for 191-round Grain-128AEAD. The concrete ANFs of them are available in the git repository.

I	# Trails	$ Monomials	# Involved key bits	Degree	Balancedness
I_0	58,442,962	2,398,450	80	27	0.31
I_1	123,946,062	3,053,028	80	27	0.30

5.3 Superpoly Recovery for 894-Round Kreyvium

Kreyvium is a stream cipher which was designed for the use of the fully Homomorphic encryption [11]. As a variant of TRIVIUM, Kreyvium shares the same internal structure but allows for bigger keys of 128 bits. The main advantage of Kreyvium over TRIVIUM is that it provides 128-bit security (instead of 80-bit) with the same multiplicative depth, and inherits the same security arguments. Kreyvium supports 128-bit IV and consists of five registers, two of them are LFSRs denoted by K^* and IV^*, respectively. Each one of these two registers is rotated independently from the rest of the cipher when updated. The remaining three registers are NFSRs which are identical to those of TRIVIUM. The five registers are initialized as

$$(s_0, s_1, \ldots, s_{92}) \leftarrow (K_0, K_1, \ldots, K_{92})$$
$$(s_{93}, s_{95}, \ldots, s_{176} \leftarrow (IV_0, IV_1, \ldots, IV_{83})$$
$$(s_{177}, s_{179}, \ldots, s_{287}) \leftarrow (IV_{85}, \ldots, IV_{127}, 1, \ldots, 1, 0)$$
$$(IV^*_{127}, \ldots, IV^*_0) \leftarrow (IV_{127}, \ldots, IV_0)$$
$$(K^*_{127}, \ldots, K^*_0) \leftarrow (K_{127}, \ldots, K_0)$$

Then, the state is updated over 1152 rounds, which is also identical with TRIVIUM. The update function is as follows,

for $i = 0$ to 1151 **do**

$\quad t_1 \leftarrow s_{65} \oplus s_{92}, \quad t_2 \leftarrow s_{161} \oplus s_{176}, \quad t_3 \leftarrow s_{242} \oplus s_{287} \oplus K^*_0$

$\quad z_i \leftarrow t_1 \oplus t_2 \oplus t_3$

$\quad t_1 \leftarrow t_1 \oplus s_{90}s_{91} \oplus s_{170} \oplus IV^*_0$

$\quad t_2 \leftarrow t_2 \oplus s_{174}s_{175} \oplus s_{263}$

$\quad t_3 \leftarrow t_3 \oplus s_{285}s_{286} \oplus s_{68}$

$\quad t_4 \leftarrow K^*_0, \ t_5 \leftarrow IV^*_0$

$\quad (s_0, s_1, \ldots, s_{92}) \leftarrow (t_3, s_0, s_1, \ldots, s_{91})$

$\quad (s_{92}, s_{93}, \ldots, s_{176}) \leftarrow (t_1, s_{93}, s_{94}, \ldots, s_{175})$

$\quad (s_{177}, s_{178}, \ldots, s_{287}) \leftarrow (t_2, s_{177}, s_{178}, \ldots, s_{286})$

$\quad (K^*_{127}, K^*_{126}, \ldots, K^*_0) \leftarrow (t_4, K^*_{127}, K^*_{126}, \ldots, K^*_1)$

$\quad (IV^*_{127}, IV^*_{126}, \ldots, IV^*_0) \leftarrow (t_5, IV^*_{127}, IV^*_{126}, \ldots, IV^*_1)$

end for

Only after the initialization finishes, the key stream bit $z_i, i \geq 1152$ is produced. In this paper, we focus on the variant of Kreyvium whose initialization is reduced to R rounds, where the key stream bit is denoted by z_R.

MILP Model. ModelKreyvium in [23, Algorithm 10] produces the MILP model as the fourth input of Algorithm 1. The MILP model is used to enumerate all trails like $k^v x^u \rightsquigarrow \pi_{t(R)}(s^{(R)})$ where $v \in \mathbb{F}_2^{128}$, and x^u is the cube term we are interested in. [23, Algorithm 10] is slightly adapted from [19,20] and the TriviumCore subroutine is identical to that in Algorithm 2. The functions that produce the sequences of $r_0, r_1, \ldots, r_i$ and $\tau^{(r-r_0)}, \tau^{(r-r_0-r_1)}, \ldots, \tau^{(r-r_0-\cdots-r_i)}$

for Kreyvium in Algorithm 1, i.e., `ChooseRiKreyvium` and `ChooseTiKreyvium` are given in [23, Algorithm 11]. These algorithms are provided in [23, App. E].

Superpoly Recovery for 893- and 894-Round Kreyvium. For 893- and 894-round Kreyvium, we let the 119-dimensional cube indices be

$$I = \{0, 1, \ldots, 127\} \backslash \{6, 66, 72, 73, 78, 101, 106, 109, 110\}.$$

We apply the nested framework to recover the superpolies. For the 893-round Kreyvium, there are 53 trails are obtained. However, only the trails representing the monomial 1 appear odd-number times, i.e., the superpoly of z_{893} is $p_I = 1$.

For 894-round Kreyvium, we get 24,107 trails, and 191 terms are involved in the superpoly in z_{894}. The superpoly is a 4-degree polynomial and involves 77 key bits. Since k_{119} is an independent term, the superpoly is a balance Boolean function. The superpoly is as follows,

6   Key-Recovery Attacks Exploiting Massive Superpolies

Suppose we have recovered the exact ANF of a superpoly $p(\boldsymbol{k})$ for the cube term $\boldsymbol{x}^u$ (the corresponding cube is denoted by $\mathbb{C}_u$). In the online phase, we first call the cipher oracle to encrypt all elements in the cube and get the value of the superpoly with time complexity $2^{wt(u)}$. In this paper, we always use small-dimensional cubes such that the complexity of this step can be ignored. Next, we try to obtain some information of the secret key from the equation:

$$p(\boldsymbol{k}) = \bigoplus_{\boldsymbol{x} \in \mathbb{C}_u} f_{\boldsymbol{k}}(\boldsymbol{x}). \tag{3}$$

Suppose that $p(\boldsymbol{k})$ involves n' bits of the n-bit secret key. In the simplest case where $n' \ll n$, i.e., $p(\boldsymbol{k})$ involves only a small part of the secret key, as the situation in [20,24], we can evaluate $p(\boldsymbol{k})$ for every combination of the involved n' key bits and filter out those incorrect keys that violates Eq. (3).

However, for the case $n' = n$, i.e., $p(\boldsymbol{k})$ involves all the key bits, the method presented above does not work any more. Indeed, the complexity of evaluating Eq. (3) with all possible key values is larger than 2^n, especially for massive superpolies. To tackle this problem, we present a new key-recovery technique with the binary Möbius transforms shown in Algorithm 4 as its fundamental algorithm.

We first introduce a trivial method for the key recovery based on the Möbius transform. It is well known that Möbius transformation is available for the conversion between the ANF and the truth table of any Boolean function. It requires $n \times 2^{n-1}$ 1-bit XORs and 2^n-bit memory complexity. Of course, the complexity is higher than 2^n in $n \geq 2$, but the unit of the complexity is significantly lower. One recovered superpoly can recover at most 1 bit of information, and the exhaustive search is necessary to determine the whole of secret key bits. Considering the difference between each unit of the complexity, the use of the Möbius transformation could be useful already. Although the superpolies we recovered

---

Algorithm 4: Möbius transformation

---

1 **Procedure** MöbiusTransformation($a[i], 0 \leq i \leq 2^n$):
2   **for** $k = 1$ *to* n **do**
3   **for** $i = 0$ *to* 2^{n-k} **do**
4   **for** $j = 0$ *to* $2^{k-1} - 1$ **do**
5                  $a[2^k i + 2^{k-1} + j] = a[2^k i + j] \oplus a[2^k i + 2^{k-1} + j]$

6   **return** a

---

are massive, they are still very sparse when compared with the random polynomials (a random polynomial may contains about 2^{n-1} monomials). Considering the sparse property, in [23, App. G] we give a more efficient algorithm to compute the truth table from the ANF. With the efficient algorithm, the Möbius transformation costs only $n \times 2^{n-2}$ XORs for the superpolies we consider in this paper.

6.1 Divide-and-Conquer Method Using the Disjoint Set

Then, we exploit more detailed structural property of the recovered superpolies to give a delicate key recovery attack on ciphers whose superpolies are massive.

Definition 1 (Disjoint set). *Given a superpoly $p(\boldsymbol{k})$ with n variables, if for $0 \leq i \neq j < n$, k_i and k_j are never multiplied mutually in all monomials of $p(\boldsymbol{k})$, then we say k_i and k_j are disjoint. If for a subset of variables $D \subseteq \{k_0, k_1, \ldots, k_{n-1}\}$, every pair of variables like $k_i, k_j \in D$ are all disjoint, we call D a disjoint set.*

Search for a Disjoint Set of $p(\boldsymbol{k})$. Obviously, there can be many different disjoint sets for $p(\boldsymbol{k})$, while usually we are only interested in the one with the maximum size. To better study the disjoint sets of $p(\boldsymbol{k})$, we introduce the *disjoint matrix*. A matrix $M \in \mathbb{F}_2^n$ is called the disjoint matrix of $p(\boldsymbol{k})$, if $M[i][j] = 0$ when k_i and k_j are disjoint, $M[i][j] = 1$ otherwise, where $M[i][j]$ stands for the value located at the intersection of the ith row and the jth column. Obviously, all the pairs of the disjoint variables can be reflected by the disjoint matrix. Given the disjoint matrix, a locally-optimized disjoint set can be obtained by a greedy algorithm as follows,

1. sort the variables in $\{k_0, k_1, \ldots, k_{n-1}\}$ in certain order, e.g., an increasing order according to the value $\sum_{0 \leq j < n} M[i][j]$ for k_i. The sorted variables are denoted as $\{k'_0, k'_1, \ldots, k'_{n-1}\}$;
2. initialize a set $D = \{k'_0\}$;
3. for $1 \leq i < n$, if k'_i is disjoint with all variables in D, put k'_i into D; otherwise, process the next variable.
4. after all the variables are processed, D is one of the disjoint sets.

Besides the greedy algorithm, noting that every disjoint set is one-to-one mapped to a zero square sub-matrix of M that takes the diagonal of M as the axis of symmetry, then an SAT/SMT model also works for finding a disjoint set with a certain number of variables and sometimes it may find the optimal disjoint set.

We first consider the case where the targeted superpoly is balanced. And later we consider the case where the superpolies are with a significant bias.

Key Recovery Attacks with Single Balanced Superpoly. If the balanced superpoly $p(\mathbf{k})$ has a disjoint set D with m variables and $J = \{k_0, k_1, \ldots, k_{n-1}\}/D$, then $p(\mathbf{k})$ can be written as the form

$$p(k_0, k_1, \ldots, k_{n-1}) = \left(\bigoplus_{0 \leq i < m} k_i \cdot p_i(J) \right) \oplus p_m(J) \tag{4}$$

where $p_i(J)$ is a polynomial of the variables in J.

Every $p_i(J)$ involves at most $n - m$ variables, then we can use the Möbius transform to compute the truth tables of $p_0, p_1, \ldots, p_m$ over all possible values of variables in J. Once we get the $m + 1$ truth tables, we can access them and get the values for every key combination in J, then Eq. (4) will become a linear expression of variables in D. Considering Eq. (3), we get a linear equation of variables in D. For the linear equation, we can remove 1-bit key guessing efficiently after guessing $m - 1$ key bits additionally.

As is pointed out, the complexity of computing the truth table from the ANF of a Boolean function with κ variables by the Möbius transform is $\kappa \times 2^{\kappa-2}$ XORs (see [23, App. G] for more details about the complexity). Hence, if a superpoly has a disjoint set with m variables, the above process costs $(m + 1) \times (n - m) \times 2^{n-m-2}$ XORs to construct the truth tables. For each of the 2^{n-m} combinations of variables in J, we access the $m+1$ truth tables to get the values of $p_i, 1 \leq i \leq m$ and construct a linear equation for the variables in D. Thereafter, with 2^{m-1} guesses for the values of any $m - 1$ variables in the linear equations, the value of the remaining one variable can be determined. Finally we call the cipher oracle to test whether the key candidate is correct.

Key Recovery Attacks with Multiple Balanced Superpolies. Suppose we have recovered N balanced superpolies $p^{(0)}, p^{(1)}, \ldots, p^{(N-1)}$, if D is the disjoint set for all $p^{(i)}, 0 \leq i < N$, we call D their *common disjoint set*. With N superpolies, we may get more linear equations to gain more information of the secret keys. The complexity of the case then consists of

1. constructing the truth tables, which costs $N \times (m + 1) \times (n - m) \times 2^{n-m-2}$ XORs;
2. constructing the linear equations, which is $N \times 2^{n-m} \times (m + 1)$ truth table lookups;
3. guessing the value of $m - N$ (we always let $m > N$) variables, then the remaining N variables can be determined by solving a set of simple linear equations. This step costs $2^{n-m} \times 2^{m-N}$ guesses. For each guess in the third step, call the cipher oracle to verify the key candidate.

The analysis of the complexity actually contains many redundant computations. For example, each sub-polynomial of a superpoly in Eq. (4) at most involves $n - m$ variables, while in practice, some sub-polynomials may involves less key bits. In this case, the complexity of constructing the truth tables and the linear equations can be reduced. What's more, for a superpoly, all linear equations are limited within 2^{m+1} different types. So with a precomputed table containing all the linear equations (and their solutions), the complexity of constructing the linear equations can be improved further. Finally, the dominant part of the complexity is 2^{n-N} cipher calls.

Compared with the previous cube attacks, our method requires considerable memory complexities to store the $N \times (m + 1)$ truth tables. We will provide the memory cost for each concrete case later.

Key Recovery Attacks with Significantly Biased Superpolies. When the superpolies we consider are not balanced, then there are some problems with the above process. For example, when a superpoly p is highly biased towards zero, then its component sub-polynomials are very likely to be zero, too. We may get many identities like $0 = 0$ rather than the useful linear equations about the variables in the disjoint set. The information we gain from the superpolies are also reduced. Fortunately, the information of the secret keys contained in the superpolies can be measured by their entropy. In this line of works, Hao et al. also took the entropy to measure the information we can gain from the superpolies of the 190-round Grain-128AEAD in [19,20].

For N superpolies $p^{(0)}, p^{(1)}, \ldots, p^{(N-1)}$, we are interested in the joint probability distribution of

$$P(p^{(0)} = \nu_0, p^{(1)} = \nu_1, \ldots, p^{(N-1)} = \nu_{N-1}) = P_{(\nu_0, \nu_1, \ldots, \nu_{N-1})}, \ (\nu_0, \nu_1, \ldots, \nu_{N-1}) \in \mathbb{F}_2^N. \tag{5}$$

The distribution can be determined by experiments, e.g., in this paper, we test 2^{15} random keys to observe this distribution. The entropy of this distribution is

$$E = - \sum_{(\nu_0, \nu_1, \ldots, \nu_{N-1}) \in \mathbb{F}_2^N} P_{(\nu_0, \nu_1, \ldots, \nu_{N-1})} \log P_{(\nu_0, \nu_1, \ldots, \nu_{N-1})}, \tag{6}$$

When we know the entropy of the targeted superpolies, the information we gain from the key recovery process are also known. If we have gained E bit of the key information, then the final complexity is approximately 2^{n-E} cipher calls.

6.2   Applications to Trivium, Grain-128AEAD and Kreyvium

Key Recovery Attack on 843-round TRIVIUM. Consider the five superpolies for cubes listed in Table 3, if we choose the superpolies for I_0, I_2 and I_3, denoted by $p^{(0)}, p^{(2)}$ and $p^{(3)}$, one of their common disjoint sets is

$$D = \{k_1, k_{39}, k_{43}, k_{12}, k_{37}\}.$$

Then we can decompose $p^{(0)}, p^{(2)}$ and $p^{(3)}$ as follows,

$$
\begin{cases}
p^{(0)} = k_{37} \cdot p_0^{(0)} \oplus k_{12} \cdot p_1^{(0)} \oplus k_{43} \cdot p_2^{(0)} \oplus k_{39} \cdot p_3^{(0)} \oplus k_1 \cdot p_4^{(0)} \oplus p_5^{(0)} \\
p^{(2)} = k_{37} \cdot p_0^{(2)} \oplus k_{12} \cdot p_1^{(2)} \oplus k_{43} \cdot p_2^{(2)} \oplus k_{39} \cdot p_3^{(2)} \oplus k_1 \cdot p_4^{(2)} \oplus p_5^{(2)} \\
p^{(3)} = k_{37} \cdot p_0^{(3)} \oplus k_{12} \cdot p_1^{(3)} \oplus k_{43} \cdot p_2^{(3)} \oplus k_{39} \cdot p_3^{(3)} \oplus k_1 \cdot p_4^{(3)} \oplus p_5^{(3)}
\end{cases}
$$

The sub-polynomials of $p^{(0)}$, i.e., $p_i^{(0)}, 0 \le i \le 5$ involve respectively 58, 46, 67, 60, 69 and 75 key bits; the sub-polynomials of $p^{(2)}$, i.e., $p_i^{(2)}, 0 \le i \le 5$ involve respectively 54, 18, 51, 33, 32 and 74 key bits; and the sub-polynomials of $p^{(3)}$, i.e., $p_i^{(3)}, 0 \le i \le 5$ involve respectively 65, 40, 65, 47, 45 and 75 key bits. Then it can be seen that comparing with $p_5^{(0)}, p_5^{(2)}$ and $p_5^{(3)}$, other sub-polynomials involves much less key bits, then the complexity of constructing the truth tables and linear equations for them can be neglected. According to Table 4, these three superpolies are almost balanced. Then the complexity consists of (where $n = 80, m = 5, N = 3$):

1. $3 \times 75 \times 2^{73}$ XORs for constructing the truth tables;
2. 3×2^{75} table lookups for constructing the linear equations;
3. $2^2 \times 2^{75}$ guesses to determine the remaining three bits of information of the keys. For each guess, call the 843-round TRIVIUM to verify the key candidate.

Therefore, the final time complexity is slightly more than 2^{77} 843-round TRIVIUM calls to recover all the secret key bits. To store all the truth tables, we need approximately $2^{76.6}$ bits of memory, which is equivalent to 2^{70} 80-bit blocks.

Key Recovery Attack on 844-Round TRIVIUM. Consider the two super-polies for 844-round TRIVIUM of the cube I_2 and I_3, denoted by $p^{(2)}$ and $p^{(3)}$, respectively, one of the common disjoint sets is

$$
D = \{k_1, k_{10}, k_{20}, k_{43}, k_7, k_{22}\}.
$$

Then we can decompose $p^{(2)}$ and $p^{(3)}$ as

$$
\begin{cases}
p^{(2)} = k_{22} \cdot p_0^{(2)} \oplus k_7 \cdot p_1^{(2)} \oplus k_{43} \cdot p_2^{(2)} \oplus k_{20} \cdot p_3^{(2)} \oplus k_{10} \cdot p_4^{(2)} \oplus k_1 \cdot p_5^{(2)} \oplus p_6^{(2)} \\
p^{(3)} = k_{22} \cdot p_0^{(3)} \oplus k_7 \cdot p_1^{(3)} \oplus k_{43} \cdot p_2^{(3)} \oplus k_{20} \cdot p_3^{(3)} \oplus k_{10} \cdot p_4^{(3)} \oplus k_1 \cdot p_5^{(3)} \oplus p_6^{(3)}
\end{cases}
$$

The numbers of involved key bits in $p_0^{(2)}, p_1^{(2)}, \ldots, p_6^{(2)}$ are respectively 69, 68, 67, 69, 64, 61 and 74, while the numbers for subpolies of $p^{(3)}$ are respectively 57, 62, 63, 62, 50, 63, 74. Furthermore, the superpoly is experimentally balanced. Thereafter, the complexity consists of (where $N = 2, n = 80, m = 6$):

1. $2 \times 74 \times 2^{72}$ XORs for constructing the truth tables;
2. 2×2^{74} truth table lookups for constructing the linear equations;
3. $2^4 \times 2^{74}$ guesses to determine two key variables in the linear equation and for each guess, call 844-round TRIVIUM to check the candidate.

Therefore, the final complexity is slightly more than 2^{78} 844-round TRIVIUM calls to recover all the secret key bits. The memory cost is about 2^{75} bits, equivalent to 2^{69} 80-bit blocks.

Key recovery attack on 845-round TRIVIUM. Consider the superpoly $p^{(2)}$ and $p^{(3)}$ for 845-round TRIVIUM of the cubes I_2 and I_3, respectively, the only common disjoint set is

$$D = \{k_1, k_{10}\}.$$

Then we can decompose $p^{(2)}$ and $p^{(3)}$ as

$$\begin{cases} p^{(2)} = k_1 \cdot p_0^{(2)} \oplus k_{10} \cdot p_1^{(2)} \oplus p_2^{(2)} \\ p^{(3)} = k_1 \cdot p_0^{(3)} \oplus k_{10} \cdot p_1^{(3)} \oplus p_2^{(3)} \end{cases}$$

$p_0^{(2)}, p_2^{(2)}, p_1^{(3)}$ and $p_2^{(3)}$ involve 78 key bits while $p_1^{(2)}$ and $p_0^{(3)}$ involves only 77 key bits. Therefore, the complexity consists of (where $N = 2, n = 80, m = 2$):

1. $4 \times 78 \times 2^{76} + 2 \times 77 \times 2^{75}$ XORs for constructing the truth tables;
2. $4 \times 2^{78} + 2 \times 2^{77}$ truth table lookups for constructing the linear equations;
3. Solver the linear equations of k_1 and k_{10} to determine one key variables. For each candidate, call the 845-round TRIVIUM to verify the candidate.

Note the number of kinds of all linear equations of k_1 and k_{10} is 8, so the complexity of constructing the linear equations and solving them is very small. Table lookups to the big tables may cost a lot. However, considering that the values contained in the truth tables are all single bits. So we can construct these tables parally. Then once lookup can obtain all bits that are used to construct the linear equations. Fairly speaking, the final complexity is slightly more than 2^{78} 845-round TRIVIUM calls to recover all the secret key bits. The memory complexity is about 2^{80} bits, which is equivalent to about 2^{74} 80-bit blocks.

Key recovery attack on 191-round Grain-128AEAD. Consider the superpolies $p^{(0)}$ and $p^{(1)}$ for 191-round Grain-128AEAD, one of their common disjoint sets is

$$D = \{k_9, k_6, k_0, k_2, k_7, k_8, k_5, k_4, k_{14}, k_3, k_{11}, k_1\}.$$

Then we can decompose $p^{(0)}$ and $p^{(1)}$ as

$$\begin{cases} p^{(0)} = k_1 \cdot p_0^{(0)} \oplus k_{11} \cdot p_1^{(0)} \oplus \cdots \oplus k_9 \cdot p_{11}^{(0)} \oplus p_{12}^{(0)} \\ p^{(1)} = k_1 \cdot p_0^{(1)} \oplus k_{11} \cdot p_1^{(1)} \oplus \cdots \oplus k_9 \cdot p_{11}^{(1)} \oplus p_{12}^{(1)} \end{cases}$$

The sub-polynomials of $p^{(0)}$, i.e., $p_0^{(0)}, p_1^{(0)}, \ldots, p_{12}^{(0)}$ involves respectively 89, 115, 112, 116, 93, 83, 109, 110, 29, 93, 112, 100, 116 key bits; while the sub-polynomials of $p^{(1)}$, i.e., $p_0^{(1)}, p_1^{(1)}, \ldots, p_{12}^{(1)}$ involves respectively 86, 115, 115, 116, 92, 96, 110, 115, 39, 99, 115, 107, 115 key bits. So for the complexity, it is enough to consider only those superpolies involving at least 115 key bits. Further, since $p^{(0)}$ and $p^{(1)}$ are highly biased, we compute the entropy of them according to Eq. (5) and (6). By taking 2^{15} keys, the entropy contained in the two superpolies is about 1.74. Then the complexity approximately consists of (where $n = 128, m = 12, N = 2$):

1. $3 \times 116 \times 2^{114} + 6 \times 115 \times 2^{113}$ XORs for constructing the truth tables;
2. $3 \times 2^{116} + 6 \times 2^{115}$ table lookups for constructing the linear equations;
3. $2^{10} \times 2^{116}$ guesses to determine two bits of key information.
4. For about $2^{116.26}$ guesses from the previous step, we call 191-round Grain-128AEAD for the verification for the key candidate.

The final complexity is then approximately $2^{116.26}$ 191-round Grain-128AEAD calls to recover all the secret key bits. The memory complexity is about $2^{118.6}$ bits which is equivalent to $2^{117.6}$ 128-bit blocks.

Key recovery attack on 894-round Kreyvium. The superpoly for 894-round TRIVIUM is simple involving only 77 key variables, so we can recover all the secret keys in 2^{127} Kreyvium calls by a normal way as done in [19, 20, 24].

7 Conclusion

In this paper, we propose a nested framework based on the monomial prediction technique for efficiently recovering the massive superpolies. The nested framework iteratively expands the cipher output in the polynomial of intermediate states. For every term in the polynomial, we try to call the MILP solver to recover a part of the superpoly from a smaller MILP model in a limited time. For those terms which cannot be solved in the limited time, we proceed to expand them in deeper intermediate states. Finally, the targeted superpoly can be fully recovered. We apply this new framework to TRIVIUM, Grain-128AEAD and Kreyvium, superpolies for up to 845, 191 and 894 rounds of the three ciphers are recovered. With the disjoint set method taking the sparse property of the variables involved in the superpoly, the key recovery attacks on the corresponding rounds of the three ciphers are improved. However, the disjoint set will take huge memory cost which is a significant weakness. As the number of rounds increases, the superpolies are expected to be more and more massive. Therefore, we put up an open question: how to efficiently recover the secret keys in cube attacks based on massive suoperpolies involving all secret key bits?

Acknowledgments. The authors would like to thank the anonymous reviewers for their valuable comments and suggestions. Kai Hu and Meiqin Wang are supported by the National Natural Science Foundation of China (Grant No. 62002201, Grant No. 62032014), the National Key Research and Development Program of China (Grant No. 2018YFA0704702, 2018YFA0704704), the Major Scientific and Technological Innovation Project of Shandong Province, China (Grant No. 2019JZZY010133), the Major Basic Research Project of Natural Science Foundation of Shandong Province, China (Grant No. ZR202010220025). Siwei Sun is supported by the National Natural Science Foundation of China (61772519) and the Chinese Major Program of National Cryptography Development Foundation (MMJJ20180102). Qingju Wang is funded by Huawei Technologies Co., Ltd., (Agreement No.: YBN2020035184). The scientific calculations in this paper have been done on the HPC Cloud Platform of Shandong University.

References

1. eSTREAM: the ECRYPT stream cipher project (2018). https://www.ecrypt.eu.org/stream/. Accessed 23 Mar 2021
2. Gorubi Optimization. https://www.gurobi.com
3. Gorubi Optimization Reference Manual. https://www.gurobi.com/wp-content/plugins/hd_documentations/documentation/9.1/refman.pdf
4. ISO/IEC 29192-3:2012: Information technology - Security techniques - Lightweight cryptography - part 3: Stream ciphers. https://www.iso.org/standard/56426.html
5. Ågren, M., Hell, M., Johansson, T., Meier, W.: Grain-128a: a new version of Grain-128 with optional authentication. Int. J. Wirel. Mob. Comput. **5**(1), 48–59 (2011)
6. Bar-On, A., Keller, N.: A 2^{70} attack on the full MISTY1. In: Robshaw, M., Katz, J. (eds.) CRYPTO 2016. LNCS, vol. 9814, pp. 435–456. Springer, Heidelberg (2016). https://doi.org/10.1007/978-3-662-53018-4_16
7. Beaulieu, R., Shors, D., Smith, J., Treatman-Clark, S., Weeks, B., Wingers, L.: The SIMON and SPECK lightweight block ciphers. In: DAC 2015, pp. 175:1–175:6. ACM (2015)
8. Boura, C., Canteaut, A.: Another view of the division property. In: Robshaw, M., Katz, J. (eds.) CRYPTO 2016. LNCS, vol. 9814, pp. 654–682. Springer, Heidelberg (2016). https://doi.org/10.1007/978-3-662-53018-4_24
9. Boura, C., Coggia, D.: Efficient MILP modelings for sboxes and linear layers of SPN ciphers. IACR Trans. Symmetric Cryptol. **2020**(3), 327–361 (2020)
10. De Cannière, C., Preneel, B.: TRIVIUM. In: Robshaw, M., Billet, O. (eds.) New Stream Cipher Designs. LNCS, vol. 4986, pp. 244–266. Springer, Heidelberg (2008). https://doi.org/10.1007/978-3-540-68351-3_18
11. Canteaut, A., et al.: Stream ciphers: a practical solution for efficient homomorphic-ciphertext compression. J. Cryptol. **31**(3), 885–916 (2018)
12. Chang, D., Turan, M.S.: Recovering the key from the internal state of Grain-128AEAD. IACR Cryptol. ePrint Arch. **2021**, 439 (2021)
13. Daemen, J., Knudsen, L., Rijmen, V.: The block cipher square. In: Biham, E. (ed.) FSE 1997. LNCS, vol. 1267, pp. 149–165. Springer, Heidelberg (1997). https://doi.org/10.1007/BFb0052343
14. Derbez, P., Fouque, P.-A.: Increasing precision of division property. IACR Trans. Symmetric Cryptol. **2020**(4), 173–194 (2020)
15. Derbez, P., Fouque, P.-A., Lambin, B.: Linearly equivalent S-boxes and the division property. IACR Cryptol. ePrint Arch. **2019**, 97 (2019)
16. Dinur, I., Shamir, A.: Cube attacks on tweakable black box polynomials. In: Joux, A. (ed.) EUROCRYPT 2009. LNCS, vol. 5479, pp. 278–299. Springer, Heidelberg (2009). https://doi.org/10.1007/978-3-642-01001-9_16
17. Fouque, P.-A., Vannet, T.: Improving key recovery to 784 and 799 rounds of trivium using optimized cube attacks. In: Moriai, S. (ed.) FSE 2013. LNCS, vol. 8424, pp. 502–517. Springer, Heidelberg (2014). https://doi.org/10.1007/978-3-662-43933-3_26
18. Hao, Y., Jiao, L., Li, C., Meier, W., Todo, Y., Wang, Q.: Links between division property and other cube attack variants. IACR Trans. Symmetric Cryptol. **2020**(1), 363–395 (2020)
19. Hao, Y., Leander, G., Meier, W., Todo, Y., Wang, Q.: Modeling for three-subset division property without unknown subset. Improved cube attacks against Trivium and Grain-128AEAD. In: Canteaut, A., Ishai, Y. (eds.) EUROCRYPT 2020. LNCS, vol. 12105, pp. 466–495. Springer, Cham (2020). https://doi.org/10.1007/978-3-030-45721-1_17

20. Hao, Y., Leander, G., Meier, W., Todo, Y., Wang, Q.: Modeling for three-subset division property without unknown subset. J. Cryptol. **34**(3), 22 (2021)

21. Hebborn, P., Lambin, B., Leander, G., Todo, Y.: Lower bounds on the degree of block ciphers. In: Moriai, S., Wang, H. (eds.) ASIACRYPT 2020. LNCS, vol. 12491, pp. 537–566. Springer, Cham (2020). https://doi.org/10.1007/978-3-030-64837-4_18

22. Hell, M., Johansson, T., Meier, W., Sönnerup, J., Yoshida, H.: Grain-128AEAD - a lightweight AEAD stream cipher. In: NIST Lightweight Cryptography, Round, 3 (2019)

23. Hu, K., Sun, S., Todo, Y., Wang, M., Wang, Q.: Massive superpoly recovery with nested monomial predictions. Cryptology ePrint Archive, Report 2021/1225 (2021). https://ia.cr/2021/1225

24. Hu, K., Sun, S., Wang, M., Wang, Q.: An algebraic formulation of the division property: revisiting degree evaluations, cube attacks, and key-independent sums. In: Moriai, S., Wang, H. (eds.) ASIACRYPT 2020. LNCS, vol. 12491, pp. 446–476. Springer, Cham (2020). https://doi.org/10.1007/978-3-030-64837-4_15

25. Hu, K., Wang, M.: Automatic search for a variant of division property using three subsets. In: Matsui, M. (ed.) CT-RSA 2019. LNCS, vol. 11405, pp. 412–432. Springer, Cham (2019). https://doi.org/10.1007/978-3-030-12612-4_21

26. Kai, H., Wang, Q., Wang, M.: Finding bit-based division property for ciphers with complex linear layers. IACR Trans. Symmetric Cryptol. **2020**(1), 236–263 (2020)

27. Knudsen, L.R.: Truncated and higher order differentials. In: Preneel, B. (ed.) FSE 1994. LNCS, vol. 1008, pp. 196–211. Springer, Heidelberg (1995). https://doi.org/10.1007/3-540-60590-8_16

28. Knudsen, L., Wagner, D.: Integral cryptanalysis. In: Daemen, J., Rijmen, V. (eds.) FSE 2002. LNCS, vol. 2365, pp. 112–127. Springer, Heidelberg (2002). https://doi.org/10.1007/3-540-45661-9_9

29. Lai, X.: Higher order derivatives and differential cryptanalysis. In: Blahut, R.E., Costello, D.J., Maurer, U., Mittelholzer, T. (eds.) Communications and Cryptography. The Springer International Series in Engineering and Computer Science (Communications and Information Theory), vol. 276. Springer, Boston (1994). https://doi.org/10.1007/978-1-4615-2694-0_23

30. Lehmann, M., Meier, W.: Conditional differential cryptanalysis of Grain-128a. In: Pieprzyk, J., Sadeghi, A.-R., Manulis, M. (eds.) CANS 2012. LNCS, vol. 7712, pp. 1–11. Springer, Heidelberg (2012). https://doi.org/10.1007/978-3-642-35404-5_1

31. Liu, M.: Degree evaluation of NFSR-based cryptosystems. In: Katz, J., Shacham, H. (eds.) CRYPTO 2017. LNCS, vol. 10403, pp. 227–249. Springer, Cham (2017). https://doi.org/10.1007/978-3-319-63697-9_8

32. Matsui, M.: New block encryption algorithm MISTY. In: Biham, E. (ed.) FSE 1997. LNCS, vol. 1267, pp. 54–68. Springer, Heidelberg (1997). https://doi.org/10.1007/BFb0052334

33. Mroczkowski, P., Szmidt, J.: The cube attack on stream cipher Trivium and quadraticity tests. Fundam. Informaticae **114**(3–4), 309–318 (2012)

34. Sasaki, Yu., Todo, Y.: New algorithm for modeling S-box in MILP based differential and division trail search. In: Farshim, P., Simion, E. (eds.) SecITC 2017. LNCS, vol. 10543, pp. 150–165. Springer, Cham (2017). https://doi.org/10.1007/978-3-319-69284-5_11

35. Sun, S., Hu, L., Wang, P., Qiao, K., Ma, X., Song, L.: Automatic security evaluation and (related-key) differential characteristic search: application to SIMON, PRESENT, LBlock, DES(L) and other bit-oriented block ciphers. In: Sarkar, P., Iwata, T. (eds.) ASIACRYPT 2014. LNCS, vol. 8873, pp. 158–178. Springer, Heidelberg (2014). https://doi.org/10.1007/978-3-662-45611-8_9

36. Sun, Y.: Cube attack against 843-round Trivium. IACR Cryptol. ePrint Arch. **2021**, 547 (2021)

37. Todo, Y.: Integral cryptanalysis on full MISTY1. In: Gennaro, R., Robshaw, M. (eds.) CRYPTO 2015. LNCS, vol. 9215, pp. 413–432. Springer, Heidelberg (2015). https://doi.org/10.1007/978-3-662-47989-6_20

38. Todo, Y.: Structural evaluation by generalized integral property. In: Oswald, E., Fischlin, M. (eds.) EUROCRYPT 2015. LNCS, vol. 9056, pp. 287–314. Springer, Heidelberg (2015). https://doi.org/10.1007/978-3-662-46800-5_12

39. Todo, Y., Isobe, T., Hao, Y., Meier, W.: Cube attacks on non-blackbox polynomials based on division property. In: Katz, J., Shacham, H. (eds.) CRYPTO 2017. LNCS, vol. 10403, pp. 250–279. Springer, Cham (2017). https://doi.org/10.1007/978-3-319-63697-9_9

40. Todo, Y., Isobe, T., Hao, Y., Meier, W.: Cube attacks on non-blackbox polynomials based on division property. IACR Cryptol. ePrint Arch. **2017**, 306 (2017)

41. Todo, Y., Morii, M.: Bit-based division property and application to SIMON family. In: Peyrin, T. (ed.) FSE 2016. LNCS, vol. 9783, pp. 357–377. Springer, Heidelberg (2016). https://doi.org/10.1007/978-3-662-52993-5_18

42. Wang, Q., Hao, Y., Todo, Y., Li, C., Isobe, T., Meier, W.: Improved division property based cube attacks exploiting algebraic properties of superpoly. In: Shacham, H., Boldyreva, A. (eds.) CRYPTO 2018. LNCS, vol. 10991, pp. 275–305. Springer, Cham (2018). https://doi.org/10.1007/978-3-319-96884-1_10

43. Wang, S., Hu, B., Guan, J., Zhang, K., Shi, T.: MILP-aided method of searching division property using three subsets and applications. In: Galbraith, S.D., Moriai, S. (eds.) ASIACRYPT 2019. LNCS, vol. 11923, pp. 398–427. Springer, Cham (2019). https://doi.org/10.1007/978-3-030-34618-8_14

44. Wang, S.P., Bin, H., Guan, J., Zhang, K., Shi, T.: A practical method to recover exact superpoly in cube attack. IACR Cryptology ePrint Archive **2019**, 259 (2019)

45. Wang, S., Bin, H., Guan, J., Zhang, K., Shi, T.: Exploring secret keys in searching integral distinguishers based on division property. IACR Trans. Symmetric Cryptol. **2020**(3), 288–304 (2020)

46. Xiang, Z., Zhang, W., Bao, Z., Lin, D.: Applying MILP method to searching integral distinguishers based on division property for 6 lightweight block ciphers. In: Cheon, J.H., Takagi, T. (eds.) ASIACRYPT 2016. LNCS, vol. 10031, pp. 648–678. Springer, Heidelberg (2016). https://doi.org/10.1007/978-3-662-53887-6_24

47. Ye, C., Tian, T.: A new framework for finding nonlinear superpolies in cube attacks against Trivium-like ciphers. In: Susilo, W., Yang, G. (eds.) ACISP 2018. LNCS, vol. 10946, pp. 172–187. Springer, Cham (2018). https://doi.org/10.1007/978-3-319-93638-3_11

48. Ye, C.-D., Tian, T.: Algebraic method to recover superpolies in cube attacks. IET Inf. Secur. **14**(4), 430–441 (2020)

49. Ye, C.-D., Tian, T.: A practical key-recovery attack on 805-round Trivium. IACR Cryptol. ePrint Arch. **2020**, 1404 (2020)

50. Ye, C., Tian, T.: Revisit division property based cube attacks: key-recovery or distinguishing attacks? IACR Trans. Symmetric Cryptol. **2019**(3), 81–102 (2019)

Quantum Linearization Attacks

Xavier Bonnetain[1,2]([✉]), Gaëtan Leurent[3]([✉]), María Naya-Plasencia[3]([✉]),
and André Schrottenloher[4]([✉])

[1] Institute for Quantum Computing, Department of Combinatorics and
Optimization, University of Waterloo, Waterloo, ON, Canada
[2] Université de Lorraine, CNRS, Inria, Nancy, France
xavier.bonnetain@inria.fr
[3] Inria, Paris, France
{gaetan.leurent,maria.naya_plasencia}@inria.fr
[4] Cryptology Group, CWI, Amsterdam, The Netherlands
andre.schrottenloher@m4x.org

Abstract. Recent works have shown that quantum period-finding can
be used to break many popular constructions (some block ciphers such as
Even-Mansour, multiple MACs and AEs...) in the superposition query
model. So far, all the constructions broken exhibited a strong algebraic
structure, which enables to craft a periodic function of a single input
block. Recovering the secret period allows to recover a key, distinguish,
break the confidentiality or authenticity of these modes.

In this paper, we introduce the *quantum linearization attack*, a new
way of using Simon's algorithm to target MACs in the superposition
query model. Specifically, we use inputs of multiple blocks as an interface to a function hiding a linear structure. Recovering this structure
allows to perform forgeries.

We also present some variants of this attack that use other quantum
algorithms, which are much less common in quantum symmetric cryptanalysis: Deutsch's, Bernstein-Vazirani's, and Shor's. To the best of our
knowledge, this is the first time these algorithms have been used in quantum forgery or key-recovery attacks.

Our attack breaks many parallelizable MACs such as LightMac,
PMAC, and numerous variants with (classical) beyond-birthday-bound
security (LightMAC+, PMAC+) or using tweakable block ciphers
(ZMAC). More generally, it shows that constructing parallelizable
quantum-secure PRFs might be a challenging task.

Keywords: Quantum cryptanalysis · MACs · Superposition query
model · Deutsch's algorithm · Bernstein-Vazirani algorithm · Simon's
algorithm · Shor's algorithm

1 Introduction

The possible emergence of large-scale quantum computing devices in a near
future has prompted a wide move towards *post-quantum security*, which takes

© International Association for Cryptologic Research 2021
M. Tibouchi and H. Wang (Eds.): ASIACRYPT 2021, LNCS 13090, pp. 422–452, 2021.
https://doi.org/10.1007/978-3-030-92062-3_15

into account the new security threats that they pose. In particular, the most popular asymmetric cryptosystems currently in use, such as RSA, can be broken by an adversary capable of successfully implementing Shor's algorithm [58]. An ongoing standardization project led by the NIST [55] has structured the efforts of the (asymmetric) cryptographic community on this question.

As symmetric primitives do not rely on a trapdoor, they seemed for a long time to avoid the cases where quantum computers bring an exponential speedup over the best classical algorithms. In fact, most problems in symmetric cryptography, such as the search for the secret key of a black-box cipher, seem to admit a quadratic speedup at best, given by Grover's quantum search algorithm [29]. Although this speedup is significant, it could be countered by increasing the parameters of symmetric cryptosystems, e.g., doubling the size of secret keys.

However, in the past few years, a series of works have shown the insecurity of some symmetric cryptosystems against quantum adversaries entitled to *superposition queries*. That is, some primitives become broken if they can be queried inside a quantum algorithm. This started with the 3-round Feistel distinguisher proposed by Kuwakado and Morii [44]. Later, they found a polynomial-time key-recovery attack on the Even-Mansour cipher [45], which was the first quantum key-recovery on a classically secure symmetric construction. These results rely crucially on the fact that many popular designs in symmetric cryptography have a strong algebraic structure, as they are built by combining smaller primitives (such as permutations or block ciphers) using cheap operations such as XORs. Kaplan *et al.* [39] showed that many other constructions exhibited a structure exploitable by a quantum adversary, and designed the first forgery attacks on MACs (notably CBC-MAC [11], OMAC [35], PMAC [12]) and authenticated encryption schemes (e.g., OCB3 [43], GCM [49]).

In this paper, we will focus on idealized MAC constructions that authenticate messages of arbitrary size using smaller primitives such as permutations, block ciphers or tweakable block ciphers (TBCs) of block size n. These constructions have classical proofs of security showing either that the MAC behaves as a pseudo-random function, or that it is unforgeable, up to some exponential bound in n. We will exhibit polynomial-time quantum attacks on constructions that were not vulnerable to previous Simon's attacks (like those of [39,57]).

Previous Attacks. Although there have been many of them, all the quantum forgery attacks known so far follow the same paradigm. They query the MAC with a constant number of blocks, using usually a single block of message x in superposition. Inside the MAC, this block of message x is XORed to some unknown value α depending on other blocks: thus, the result is $\mathsf{MAC}(x \oplus \alpha)$. Having two different values α_0, α_1, we then have access to two functions $f(x) = \mathsf{MAC}(x \oplus \alpha_0)$ and $g(x) = \mathsf{MAC}(x \oplus \alpha_1)$, such that $f(x) = g(x \oplus \alpha_0 \oplus \alpha_1)$. From there, we can use Simon's Boolean hidden shift algorithm [59] as a black box. It recovers $\alpha_0 \oplus \alpha_1$ in quantum polynomial time, whereas any classical algorithm would require exponentially many queries to f and g (thus to the MAC). The recovery of the internal shift $\alpha_0 \oplus \alpha_1$ then enables the adversary to forge new messages, and in some cases to recover secret-key material.

Let us point out the following important remark:

If the message blocks are not directly XORed to internal values (keys, offsets, encryption of other blocks...), then the previous attacks based on Simon's algorithm do not apply.

Contributions. In this paper, we present the *quantum linearization attack*, which is a new family of quantum attacks on classically unforgeable MACs when superposition queries are allowed. Thanks to the novelty of our approach, we are able to attack many MACs that resisted previous cryptanalysis, as they do not exhibit the property recalled above (a message block XORed to an internal state value). In particular, our attack usually circumvents the use of TBCs instead of block ciphers. It is also the first case of a quantum polynomial-time attack on MACs with *beyond-birthday* security, where the internal state has a bigger size. As an example, we break LightMAC with a linear number of queries, and we can attack LightMAC+ with only twice as much.

Overview. Our attack starts with the following remark. Consider a function of ℓ blocks $x_1, \ldots, x_\ell$ of the form: $G(x_1, \ldots, x_\ell) = g_1(x_1) \oplus \ldots \oplus g_\ell(x_\ell) \oplus C$, where C is an independent constant, and the g_i are independent random functions to which the adversary *does not have access*. Then classically, this function cannot be distinguished from random with a single query, though as little as four would be enough: we make $x_3, \ldots, x_\ell$ constant, we query for every $x_1 \in \{0,1\}$ and $x_2 \in \{0,1\}$: the XOR of the four results is zero.

Our key idea is to *linearize* the function G by restricting the block inputs so that the output is an affine function. Similarly to the simple classical distinguisher, we make the blocks $x_1, \ldots, x_\ell$ take only one-bit values and emulate a function of an ℓ-bit input: $F(x) = F(b_1 \| \ldots \| b_\ell) = G(0^{n-1} \| b_1, \ldots, 0^{n-1} \| b_\ell)$. Now, we will remark that F is an *affine* function of $b_1, \ldots, b_\ell$. As the g_i are XORed; flipping a bit b_i in the input XORs $g_i(0) \oplus g_i(1)$ to the output.

It is well known that the Bernstein-Vazirani algorithm allows to distinguish an affine function from a random one with a *single* quantum query. This shows that, thanks to a multi-block input, we can access new vulnerabilities of cryptographic constructions. But the power of our attack is clearly demonstrated when we make G go through a new random function:

$$G'(x_1, \ldots, x_\ell) = g(G(x)) = g(g_1(x_1) \oplus \ldots \oplus g_\ell(x_\ell) \oplus C) . \tag{1}$$

All the functions $g_1, \ldots, g_\ell, g$ are unknown to the adversary, so she cannot find the affine structure of the internal G. In fact, this function would be classically secure as a MAC. However, when linearizing, we obtain: $G'(x) = g(F(x))$ where F is an affine function of $x = b_1 \| \ldots \| b_\ell$. Thus, G' embeds a *hidden Boolean period*, and Simon's algorithm can recover it in polynomial time.

Applications. In Sect. 4 and Sect. 5, we detail the applications of our algorithm. We obtain the first polynomial-time attacks against the following MACs:

ΘCB3 [43,56], LightMAC [47], LightMAC+ [53], Deoxys [38], ZMAC [37], PMAC_TBC3k [52], PolyMAC [36], GCM-SIV2 [36]

In addition, we provide attacks on the XOR-MACs of [4], on MACs based on universal hashing (e.g., NMH* [31] and BRW Hashing [7]) and, in Sect. 5.5, a new superposition forgery attack against Poly1305 [6]. A previous quantum attack was given in [18], using a hidden shift structure. Using Shor's algorithm instead, we reduce the number of superposition queries from 2^{38} to about 32.

On Parallelizable MACs. The quantum linearization attack leaves only little space for quantum-secure parallelizable PRFs. Indeed, we are able to break any PRF with extendable domain, where at least $\geq n$ independent input blocks of $\leq n$ bits are processed independently, then XORed. This works as well for any operation that is linear on $(\mathbb{F}_2)^n$. It is still possible to obtain an unforgeable IV- or nonce-based MAC of this form, as shown in [9], but the security then relies on the non-repetition of IVs. We do not know if an attack applies when we use a modular addition instead of a XOR in (1). If this was the case, then it would clearly mean that one has to rely on sequentiality or on nonlinear operations.

Organization. We start in Sect. 2 by reviewing some quantum computing notions, the quantum algorithms used in this paper (Deutsch's algorithm, Bernstein-Vazirani, Simon's algorithm, Shor's algorithm), the Q1/Q2 attack scenarios and notions of quantum unforgeability. In Sect. 3, we detail our new algorithmic ideas. In Sect. 4, we apply our attack to many parallelizable MAC constructions. We dedicate Sect. 5 to MACs based on universal hashing. We discuss the implications of our attacks in Sect. 6 and conclude the paper in Sect. 7.

2 Preliminaries

In this section, we give some preliminaries about quantum computing, quantum attacker models and the well-known quantum algorithms that will be used throughout this paper. We elaborate about the Q2 attacker model and the notion of quantum unforgeability for MACs, with or without IVs. Note that some details of quantum computing will appear in this section. They are intended for the interested reader. In the rest of this paper (with the exception of Sect. 5.5), we will use the algorithms of this section as black boxes.

2.1 Notation

We consider n-bit string values, sometimes as elements of $\mathbb{F}_{2^n}$, sometimes as elements of $\mathbb{F}_2^n$. This shall be clear from context. We let $\oplus$ denote the XOR (addition in $\mathbb{F}_2^n$), $\odot$ denote multiplication in $\mathbb{F}_{2^n}$, and $+$ modular addition. We let $\cdot$ denote the scalar product of bit-strings seen as n-bit vectors.

2.2 On Quantum Computing

Although we choose to present in detail the quantum algorithms that we will use for our attacks, most of our results can be obtained by applying them as black boxes. Thus we stress that our results, similarly as other structural attacks on symmetric cryptosystems [39,45], can be understood from a high-level perspective, and our attacks do not require specific knowledge of quantum computing. Further details are only required to prove the correctness of the algorithms.

A general presentation of the *quantum circuit model* can be found in [54]. The basic computation units are qubits, two-level quantum systems whose state is represented by a *superposition* $\alpha\,|0\rangle + \beta\,|1\rangle$, with amplitudes α and β, which is a normalized vector in $\mathbb{C}^2$ (of norm $|\alpha^2| + |\beta^2| = 1$). The state of an n-qubit system belongs to $\mathbb{C}^{2^n}$, its 2^n basis vectors (in the computational basis) are the 2^n n-bit strings.

A quantum algorithm is a sequence of unitary operators of $\mathbb{C}^{2^n}$, partial measurements, and oracle calls. We say that a function f is queried *in superposition* if the following unitary operator O_f is made available: $|x\rangle\,|y\rangle \mapsto |x\rangle\,|y \oplus f(x)\rangle$. Indeed, this operator allows to query f on any quantum state, thus on any *superposition* of inputs x. This is the *standard* oracle, equivalent to the *phase oracle* $O_{f,\pm}$ which computes $|x\rangle \mapsto (-1)^{f(x)}\,|x\rangle$.

One of the basic unitary operations of the quantum circuit model (*quantum gates*), and actually the most important one in the algorithms of Sect. 2.3, is the Hadamard gate H which maps a single qubit $|b\rangle$ to $\frac{1}{\sqrt{2}}\left(|0\rangle + (-1)^b\,|1\rangle\right)$. By applying Hadamard gates to each individual qubit of an n-bit input, we compute the *Hadamard transform*, a particular example of Quantum Fourier Transform:

$$H^{\otimes n} : |x\rangle \mapsto \frac{1}{2^{n/2}} \sum_{y \in \{0,1\}^n} (-1)^{x \cdot y}\,|y\rangle \ .$$

An important property is that the Hadamard transform is involutive. For better readability, we often omit global amplitude factors such as the $\frac{1}{2^{n/2}}$ above, as quantum states are always normalized.

Given a quantum state of the form $\sum_x \alpha_x\,|x\rangle$, the measurement operation destroys the state and yields an element x with probability $|\alpha_x|^2$. Partially measuring the state *projects* it on a smaller superposition of elements. For a quantum state of the form: $\sum_{x,y} \alpha_{xy}\,|x\rangle\,|y\rangle$, measuring the register $|x\rangle$ yields a value x_0 with probability $\sum_y |\alpha_{x_0 y}|^2$, and projects on the state $\frac{1}{\sqrt{\sum_y |\alpha_{x_0 y}|^2}} \sum_y \alpha_{x_0 y}\,|y\rangle$.

2.3 Quantum Algorithms

Our new attacks are based on well-known quantum algorithms: Deutsch's algorithm [26], which is a single-bit version of the Deutsch-Jozsa algorithm [27], the Bernstein-Vazirani algorithm [8], Simon's algorithm [59] and Shor's algorithm [58]. These algorithms have in common to be based on *Fourier sampling*, a process in which a quantum Fourier transform is applied before and after a single query to a superposition oracle. They are also amongst the earliest quantum algorithms proven to beat any classical algorithm, and as such are often presented in textbooks (see e.g. [54]). However, except for Shor's algorithm, their practical interest remained unclear for a long time.

Algorithm 1. Deutsch's algorithm

1: Start from $|0\rangle$ ▷ $|0\rangle$
2: Apply a Hadamard gate   ▷ $|0\rangle + |1\rangle$
3: Apply $O_{f,\pm}$ ▷ $(-1)^{f(0)}|0\rangle + (-1)^{f(1)}|1\rangle = (-1)^{f(0)}\left(|0\rangle + (-1)^{f(0)\oplus f(1)}|1\rangle\right)$
4: Apply a Hadamard gate   ▷ $(-1)^{f(0)}|f(0) \oplus f(1)\rangle$
5: Measure the state

Algorithm 2. Bernstein-Vazirani algorithm

1: Start from $|0_n\rangle$ ▷ $|0_n\rangle$
2: Apply a Hadamard transform   ▷ $\sum_i |i\rangle$
3: Apply $O_{f,\pm}$ ▷ $\sum_i (-1)^{(a\cdot i)\oplus b}|i\rangle$
4: Apply a Hadamard transform
5: Measure the state   ▷ $(-1)^b H^{\otimes n}\sum_i (-1)^{a\cdot i}|i\rangle = (-1)^b H^{\otimes n}\left(H^{\otimes n}|a\rangle\right) = (-1)^b|a\rangle$

Deutsch's Algorithm. Deutsch's algorithm [26] solves Problem 1 with probability 1 using a single query to O_f, whereas classically, two queries to f are needed for the same success probability. This constant speedup might seem anecdotal, but is crucial when the same function cannot be queried more than once.

Problem 1 (Deutsch's problem). Given access to a quantum oracle O_f for a function $f : \{0,1\} \to \{0,1\}$, decide whether f is *constant* ($f(0) = f(1)$) or *balanced* ($f(0) \neq f(1)$).

Deutsch's algorithm (Algorithm 1) is best presented with a phase oracle $O_{f,\pm}|b\rangle = (-1)^{f(b)}|b\rangle$. It can be seen that upon measurement, the algorithm actually yields the value $f(0) \oplus f(1)$ (although a single query has been made to f) whose knowledge solves Problem 1.

Bernstein-Vazirani Algorithm. The Bernstein-Vazirani algorithm [8] offers a polynomial speedup for finding the slope of an affine function over $\mathbb{F}_2^n$.

Problem 2 (Bernstein-Vazirani). Given access to an oracle O_f for an affine function $f : \{0,1\}^n \to \{0,1\}$, that is, $f(x) = a \cdot x \oplus b$ for a, b unknown, find a.

Upon measurement in Algorithm 2, we obtain the unknown a with certainty, using a single query to $O_{f,\pm}$, while n queries would be needed classically.

Remark 1. This algorithm can be seen as a generalization of Deutsch's algorithm. Indeed, in the case $n = 1$, there are only two types of affine functions: $f(x) = x \oplus b$ ($a = 1$) and $f(x) = b$ ($a = 0$), and Bernstein-Vazirani allows to distinguish them in one query.

Simon's Algorithm. Simon's algorithm [59] solves the problem of distinguishing an injective function from a periodic one. Note that it was the first example of an exponential quantum speedup relatively to an oracle.

Algorithm 3. Simon's algorithm

1: $Y = \emptyset$
2: Choose a number r depending on the required probability of error
3: **Repeat** $n + r$ **times**
4:　　Start from $|0_n 0_n\rangle$
5:　　Apply a Hadamard transform to the first register　　　　　　$\triangleright \sum_x |x\rangle |0\rangle$
6:　　Apply O_f (standard)　　　　　　　　　　　　　　　　　$\triangleright \sum_x |x\rangle |f(x)\rangle$
7:　　Measure the second register, obtain a　　　　　　　　　$\triangleright \sum_{x|f(x)=a} |x\rangle$
8:　　Apply a Hadamard transform　　　$\triangleright \sum_y (\sum_{x|f(x)=a} (-1)^{x \cdot y}) |y\rangle$
9:　　Measure a y, $Y \leftarrow Y \cup \{y\}$
10: **EndRepeat**
11: **if** Y is of full rank **then**
12:　　**return** "injective case"
13: **else if** Y is of rank $n - 1$ **then**
14:　　**return** "periodic case" and the s orthogonal to Y
15: **else**
16:　　**return** "failure"
17: **end if**

Problem 3 (Simon). Given access to a function $f : \{0,1\}^n \to \{0,1\}^n$ for which there exists s such that: $\forall x, y, f(x) = f(y) \iff y \in \{x, x \oplus s\}$, find s.

In Algorithm 3, at Step 9 in the injective case, the value a obtained before has a single preimage x_a. Thus, the current state is $\sum_y ((-1)^{x_a \cdot y}) |y\rangle$ and we sample a uniformly random $y \in \{0,1\}^n$. After $n + r$ such samples, the family Y will grow to a full-rank family. In the periodic case, the value a has exactly two preimages x_a and $x_a \oplus s$ which interfere with each other. The current state is

$$\sum_y ((-1)^{x_a \cdot y} + (-1)^{(x_a \oplus s) \cdot y}) |y\rangle = \sum_y (-1)^{x_a \cdot y} (1 + (-1)^{s \cdot y}) |y\rangle$$

and only the vectors y orthogonal to s have a non-zero amplitude. Thus, the family Y grows to span the euclidean subspace orthogonal to s. Computing the rank of Y allows to detect the period and solving the linear system $Ys = 0_n$ allows to recover it.

Generalizations. Although the original Simon's problem concerns functions without random collisions (that is, we cannot have $f(x) = f(y)$ if $x \oplus y \notin \{0, s\}$), it can be shown that the algorithm works as well for *random functions having a period*, which models the cryptographic problems that we are interested in.

The following simple condition was given in [39]. For Simon's algorithm to run as expected (i.e., with $\mathcal{O}(n)$ queries), it is sufficient for the periodic function f, of period s, to satisfy the following condition:

$$\max_{t \notin \{0,s\}} \Pr_x \left[f(x \oplus t) = f(x) \right] \leq \frac{1}{2} . \tag{2}$$

That is, f should not admit another "unwanted partial period" t. In the examples studied in this paper, the condition (2) will be easy to check.

Note that if we had $f(x \oplus t) = f(x)$ for all x, then t would simply turn the set of periods of f into a vector space of dimension 2. In general, the space of periods could be a vector space of any dimension. An extended version of Simon's algorithm by Brassard and Høyer [20] allows to recover this whole space in polynomial time.

Finally, another important case is when the output set is smaller than the input set. This was studied in [16] for Simon's algorithm and [48] for period-finding in general. The results in [16] show that as long as the functions behave as random (but with the periodicity constraint), then for n input bits, the number of output bits required to run correctly without any cost increase is of order $\log_2 n$. The results in [48] show that the output can be hashed down to a single bit, and the algorithms still work up to a constant increase in queries.

Shor's Algorithm. We will use Shor's algorithm [58] to solve the *abelian hidden period* problem. It will appear in a "black-box" manner in Sect. 5.4, and in Sect. 5.5. We will analyse in detail the behavior of the algorithm on Poly1305.

Problem 4 (Abelian hidden period). Let $(G, +)$ be an abelian group, X a set. Given access to a function $f : G \to X$ which is either injective, or periodic $(\exists s \in G, f(s + \cdot) = f(\cdot))$, then determine the case and/or find the period.

In particular, we consider $G = \mathbb{Z}_{M_1} \times \ldots \times \mathbb{Z}_{M_k}$ the product of multiple cyclic groups of known order. For simplicity, and to prepare for Sect. 5.5, we present the algorithm in the case of $\mathbb{Z}_p^2$ for some prime p. Note that f is also periodic over $\mathbb{Z}_p$ in each of its parameters. This is the typical situation when Shor's algorithm is used to solve the Discrete Logarithm Problem. The periods of f form a two-dimensional integer lattice, which is generated by $(p, 0)$ and $(-1, s)$ for some s. In other words, the value of $f(x, y)$ depends only on the value of $xs + y \bmod p$. We may assume for simplicity that the function $xs + y \bmod p \mapsto f(x, y)$ is injective.

The algorithm only relies on an efficient implementation of the Quantum Fourier Transform over $\mathbb{Z}_p$:

$$|x\rangle \mapsto \sum_{y=0}^{p-1} \exp\left(2i\pi\frac{xy}{p}\right) |y\rangle \ ,$$

which we assume exact. We represent the elements of X on m bits.

In Algorithm 4, at Step 4, we can only measure a vector $|z, t\rangle$ having a nonzero amplitude. This means that we need:

$$\sum_{x=0}^{p-1} \exp\left(2i\pi\frac{(z - st)x}{p}\right) \neq 0 \ ,$$

which happens only when $(z - st) = 0$. In that case, the sum simply gives p. After renormalization, all vectors $|z, t\rangle$ with $(z - st) = 0$ have the same amplitude $\frac{1}{\sqrt{p}}$, and we will measure one of them taken uniformly at random. If $t \neq 0$, we compute s by $s = zt^{-1} \bmod p$. This occurs with probability $1 - \frac{1}{p}$.

2.4   Attack Scenarios

We consider different *attack scenarios* throughout this paper.

Q1 and Q2 Setting. Following [17,33,40], we will adopt the Q1/Q2 terminology to classify quantum attacks on symmetric schemes. Note that these models have alternative names, for example "quantum chosen-plaintext attack" (qCPA) is used for "Q2" in [22,34]. In the Q1 setting, the adversary is given only *classical* encryption or decryption query access to black-boxes. In the Q2 setting, the adversary is given *quantum* or *superposition* access, in the sense that a black-box E_K becomes a quantum oracle O_{E_K}. This is the case for all the attacks of this paper.

Algorithm 4. Shor's algorithm

1: Start from $|0, 0, 0_m\rangle$ ▷ $|0, 0, 0_m\rangle$

2: Apply a Quantum Fourier Transform on both input registers
$$\triangleright \sum_{x,y=0}^{p-1} |x, y\rangle\, |0_m\rangle$$

3: Apply O_f ▷ $\sum_{x,y=0}^{p-1} |x, y\rangle\, |f(x, y)\rangle$

4: Measure the second register. The state collapses on a uniform superposition of all (x, y) such that $xs + y = a \bmod p$ for some unknown a, meaning $y = a - xs \bmod p$:

$$\sum_{x=0}^{p-1} |x\rangle\, |a - xs\rangle \quad .$$

5: Apply a Quantum Fourier Transform again. The state becomes:

$$\sum_{z,t=0}^{p-1} \left(\sum_{x=0}^{p-1} \exp\left(2i\pi \frac{zx + (a - xs)t}{p}\right) \right) |z, t\rangle$$

$$= \sum_{z,t=0}^{p-1} \exp(2i\pi at/p) \left(\sum_{x=0}^{p-1} \exp\left(2i\pi \frac{(z - st)x}{p}\right) \right) |z, t\rangle \quad .$$

6: Measure a $|z, t\rangle$ and return $s = zt^{-1} \bmod p$.

The study of quantum attacks on symmetric schemes in the Q2 setting was sparkled by seminal work of Kuwakado and Morii [44,45], who showed that the 3-round Luby-Rackoff construction and the Even-Mansour cipher became insecure if exposed to superposition queries. More precisely, they can use Simon's algorithm to respectively distinguish the construction and recover the key of the cipher in polynomial time, while classical proofs of security exist.

Attacks Based on Period-Finding. Since these earlier results, many works have extended the reach of Q2 attacks [15,19,28,30,39,46]. However, the attack strategy has remained the same. A hidden structure is embedded in the construction to be attacked, so that $f(E_K(x), x)$ for some choice of combination f, is a periodic function of x; or that a shift exists between $f(E_K(x), x)$ and $g(E_K(x), x)$. The recovery of this hidden period or shift, which is secret material, then leads to a break. We can cite some examples:

Against the Even-Mansour Construction [45]: $E_K(x) = K_2 \oplus \Pi(x \oplus K_1)$ for a random public permutation Π and two keys K_1, K_2. One has:

$$E_K(x) \oplus \Pi(x) = E_K(x \oplus K_1) \oplus \Pi(x \oplus K_1)$$

which leads to a recovery of K_1 in $\mathcal{O}(n)$ queries and $\mathcal{O}(n^3)$ computations.

Against CBC-MAC *with Two Blocks* [39]: It can be defined as:

$$\mathsf{CBC\text{-}MAC}(y, x) = E_{K'} \circ E_K \left(x \oplus E_K(y) \right) ,$$

where K and K' are two keys that will remain unknown to the adversary. Due to the structure of CBC-MAC, one can take two arbitrary values α_0, α_1, and define the function:

$$F : \begin{cases} \{0,1\} \times \{0,1\}^n \mapsto & \{0,1\}^n \\ (b, x) & \to \mathsf{CBC\text{-}MAC}(\alpha_b, x) \end{cases} \tag{3}$$

We have then that $F(b, x) = F(b \oplus 1, x \oplus E_K(\alpha_0) \oplus E_K(\alpha_1))$. Thus F has a hidden boolean period $1 \| E_K(\alpha_0) \oplus E_K(\alpha_1)$. Having obtained the internal value $E_K(\alpha_0) \oplus E_K(\alpha_1)$, we can query the tag of any message starting with block α_0, and then forge a message starting with α_1 with the same tag.

Constructions Based on IVs. We consider two types of constructions with quantum access: some make use of an *initialization value* (IV, sometimes also named a *nonce*) and some do not. In the IV case, we consider that the IV is a classical value, chosen randomly before each oracle query, and not repeated. This model follows from the idea that the IV is not controlled by the adversary, and it can serve as an intermediate between the classical setting and a (much) stronger model in which the adversary would completely (and quantumly) control the IVs.

In fact, the latter case does not seem to have been studied so far in quantum security. Well-known notions such as IND-qCPA [14] rely on classical randomness, and many modes of operation have been proven secure in this model [3,9].

In the classical setting, many MAC constructions have a security that relies on the non-repetition of IVs, for example the MAC of OCB [43]. The same happens in the quantum setting, since the MAC of QCB [9] has been proven secure under quantum queries with classical non-repeated IVs.

Unforgeability. The first notion of quantum unforgeability for MACs was defined by Boneh and Zhandry [13]. We will name it *plus-one unforgeability* (PO), following [1]. The idea is that an adversary making q quantum queries to the construction, where q is polynomial, should not be able to produce q+1 valid {message, tag} pairs. A more recent definition is *blind-unforgeability* (BU), proposed in [1]. It is strictly stronger than PO-unforgeability. In this paper, we will give several quantum forgery attacks that break the PO notion, thereby also breaking BU.

Quantum PRFs. A *quantum pseudorandom function* (qPRF) is a family of functions F_K, indexed by a key space $\mathcal{K}$, such that no quantum adversary making queries to an oracle O_f can distinguish efficiently between a function F_K, with K drawn uniformly at random, and a truly random function. It is shown respectively in [13] and [1] that a qPRF is also a quantum-secure deterministic MAC by the PO and BU definitions. Therefore, any function that is not PO-unforgeable is also not a secure qPRF. To the best of our knowledge, the only classical symmetric construction that has been proven quantum-secure as a deterministic MAC, the Cascade/NMAC/HMAC construction [60], is also a qPRF.

2.5 A Quantum Attack on OCB3

We detail the Q2 attack on the MAC of OCB3 from [39]. As the other previous works recalled above, this attack relies on a Boolean period-finding problem.

Specification. OCB3 is an IV-based mode of authenticated encryption with associated data (AEAD), based on a block cipher [43]. As OCB stands for *offset codebook*, the scheme relies on the definition of *offsets* that are dependent on the key and change between each block. We will focus on the authentication tag of OCB3 (see Fig. 1). Our considerations are independent on the exact value of the offsets, and apply to all versions of OCB, but we use OCB3 as a concrete example.

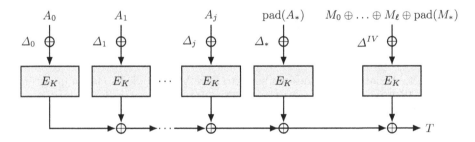

Fig. 1. Computation of the tag in OCB3. Only the offset Δ^{IV} depends on the IV.

Forgery Attack with Simon's Algorithm. Kaplan *et al.* showed in [39] how to forge authentication tags using Simon's algorithm. The idea is to query the tag of an empty message with two AD blocks $A_0, A_1 = x$:

$$x \to E_K(\Delta_{IV}) \oplus E_K(\Delta_0 \oplus x) \oplus E_K(\Delta_1 \oplus x) \ .$$

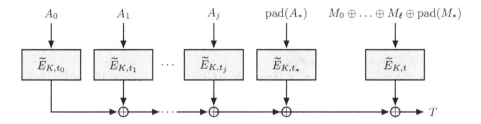

Fig. 2. Computation of the tag in ΘCB3. Only the final tweak t depends on the IV.

One can then remark that this function of x is periodic, of period $\Delta_0 \oplus \Delta_1$, independent of the IV, and only on the secret key K. Although the function changes at each query (since the IV changes), the period is always the same and Simon's algorithm allows to recover it with $\mathcal{O}(n)$ superposition queries. (For the same reason, we could use a non-empty message, and even different messages between the queries.)

Once $\Delta_0 \oplus \Delta_1$ has been obtained, one can then query the tag of any pair of AD blocks A_0, A_1 and forge the tag of A_1, A_0.

Remark 2. It is easy to check that Eq. (2) is satisfied in practice. If it wasn't, then the existence of an unwanted partial period t:

$$\Pr_x \left[f(x \oplus t) = f(x) \right] \geq \frac{1}{2} \ ,$$

would imply a higher-order differential of probability greater than $\frac{1}{2}$ for E_K, which is impossible if E_K is a pseudorandom permutation (in other words, E_K would suffer from a classical break).

3 The Quantum Linearization Attack: Algorithmic Ideas

In this section, we present the algorithmic ideas underlying our new *quantum linearization attack*. To that end, we keep the example of OCB3 [43] introduced in Sect. 2.5. We explain a new way to forge with Q2 queries. The extensions and applications of this new idea will be explored in the next sections.

Note that to the best of our knowledge, this is the first application of the Deutsch and Bernstein-Vazirani algorithms for forgery attacks.

3.1 Attack on ΘCB with Deutsch's Algorithm

The attack of Sect. 2.5 works only because of the offsets. In fact, the existence of a controlled value (here x) XORed to a secret (here the offsets) has been so far a prerequisite of all Q2 attacks.

Here we present a forgery attack against the mode ΘCB3 [43,56], which is a more abstract version of OCB3 in which the block cipher E_K is replaced by a *tweakable* block cipher (a family of independent block ciphers $\widetilde{E}_{K,t}$ indexed by a *tweak* t). This is shown in Fig. 2.

Here, the tweaks $t_0, \ldots, t_j, t_*$ form an arbitrary sequence of distinct values, that depend only on the block index; the tweak t is the only one dependent on the IV. Again, we consider an empty message, but this time a single AD block that is either 0 or 1. We define i functions which truncate the output of such a call to the ith bit:

$$F_i : \begin{array}{ccc} \{0,1\} & \to & \{0,1\} \\ b & \mapsto & \text{Trunc}_i(\widetilde{E}_{K,t_0}(b) \oplus \widetilde{E}_{K,t}(0)) \end{array} \quad .$$

The functions F_i change at each new superposition query (because the IV intervenes in $\widetilde{E}_{K,t}(0)$). Thus we need the ability to compute a query to F_i using a *single* query to the untruncated mode itself. This is fortunately easy to do so using the truncation technique of [33].

With this single query, Deutsch's algorithm allows to recover the value:

$$\text{Trunc}_i(\widetilde{E}_{K,t_0}(0) \oplus \widetilde{E}_{K,t}(0)) \oplus \text{Trunc}_i(\widetilde{E}_{K,t_0}(1) \oplus \widetilde{E}_{K,t}(0))$$
$$= \text{Trunc}_i(\widetilde{E}_{K,t_0}(0) \oplus \widetilde{E}_{K,t_0}(1)) \ ,$$

and within n queries and uses of the algorithm, we can obtain the full value $\widetilde{E}_{K,t_0}(0) \oplus \widetilde{E}_{K,t_0}(1)$.

We can now forge valid messages as follows: we query a message with 0 as the first block, we XOR $\widetilde{E}_{K,t_0}(0) \oplus \widetilde{E}_{K,t_0}(1)$ to the tag, and we have obtained the tag of the same message with 1 replacing the first block. This works for any block and for any pair of messages.

This attack shows that XORing with an IV-dependent value, although it provides sufficient protection against forgeries in the classical setting (since ΘCB has a security proof), does not in the quantum setting.

Interestingly, it is possible to protect against this attack by using the IV in the TBC calls, as done by Bhaumik et al. in [9]. While this simple modification has practically no incidence on the classical security of the mode, it is crucial to obtain unforgeability in the quantum setting.

Another Example: XOR-MACs. In [4], two *XOR-MAC* constructions are defined, which can be attacked with Deutsch's algorithm. They are both based on a pseudorandom function F_K and an IV. The first one, XMACR (*randomized XOR scheme*), considers that the IV is drawn uniformly at random, and the second one, XMACC (*counter-based XOR scheme*) that it is maintained as a counter. Both compute:

$$\text{MAC}(m_1, \ldots, m_\ell; IV) = F_K(0\|IV) \oplus \bigoplus_{1 \le i \le \ell} F_K(1\|i\|m_i) \ .$$

Then, since the contribution of the IV is only XORed, forgeries can be made.

3.2   Using the Bernstein-Vazirani Algorithm

We propose here a generalization of the previous attack, with longer queries. We now consider functions of the form

$$g_1(x_1) \oplus g_2(x_2) \oplus \cdots \oplus g_\ell(x_\ell) \oplus C$$

with, as before, a C that is independent from all x_i. Now, we can choose some arbitrary α_i^0 and α_i^1, and consider the function

$$F_j : \begin{array}{ccc} \{0,1\}^\ell & \to & \{0,1\} \\ (b_1, \ldots, b_\ell) & \mapsto & \mathrm{Trunc}_j \left(\bigoplus_{i=1}^{\ell} g_i(\alpha_i^{b_i}) \oplus C \right) \end{array} ,$$

It is easy to see that this function is affine: indeed, if we change the value of b_i, then we add $\mathrm{Trunc}_j \left(g_i(\alpha_i^0) \oplus g_i(\alpha_i^1) \right)$ to the output.

Hence, if we apply the Berstein-Vazirani algorithm, in one query, we recover the values of the $\mathrm{Trunc}_j \left(g_i(\alpha_i^0) \oplus g_i(\alpha_i^1) \right)$, for all i. Next, it suffices to repeat the algorithm for each bit of the output to obtain the value of all the $g_i(\alpha_i^0) \oplus g_i(\alpha_i^1)$.

This technique can be applied to OCB3/ΘCB3, as the tag is a function of the form

$$\bigoplus_i g_i^k(AD_i) \oplus f_k(IV, M)$$

Hence, we can attack multiple blocks of associated data at once.

3.3   Attacking Any XOR of Permutations

The main limitation of the previous attacks is that they need a direct access to the linear combination of independent blocks. In this section, we overcome this limitation with an attack that leverages linear combinations of permutations in a more intrinsic way, using Simon's algorithm in a novel fashion.

We consider a MAC construction that processes $m > n$ message blocks $x_1, \ldots, x_m$ by pushing the x_i through independent TBC calls $\widetilde{E}_{K,i}$, XORing the result and applying an IV-dependent function afterwards.

$$IV, (x_1, \ldots, x_m) \mapsto f_K \left(IV, \left(\bigoplus_{1 \le i \le m} \widetilde{E}_{K,i}(x_i) \right) \right) .$$

Remark 3. We write the attack with a TBC, i.e., a family of independent block ciphers $\widetilde{E}_{K,T}$ indexed by a secret key K and a public tweak T. This is to emphasize the application of our attack to parallelizable MACs; however, the attack works in the same way if we replace the independent block ciphers by independent functions.

In the case of ΘCB, the definition of f_K is simple, since it only XORs the IV- and the AD-dependent parts. But the attack of Sect. 3.2 does not apply anymore if f_K is a pseudorandom function. This will be the case of our new attack, which is why it will apply to many MAC constructions.

Quantum Attack. First of all, it is easy to see that if the $\widetilde{E}_{K,i}$ are independent block ciphers, and if f_K is a pseudorandom function family, then this construction is a classically unforgeable MAC: this is the security of ΘCB3.

Our attack in the quantum setting starts from the same idea as above (Sect. 3.2): we query the MAC with arbitrary blocks taking two values: $x_1 = b_1 \| 0_{n-1}, \ldots, x_m = b_m \| 0_{n-1}$, where $x = b_1 \ldots b_m$ forms an m-bit input (in the remaining of this paper, we will write the $n-1$ zeroes used for completion as a single 0). We will put x in superposition, and so, there will be only "one superposed bit" in each individual block input.

One then observes that $\widetilde{E}_{K,1}(x_1) \oplus \ldots \oplus \widetilde{E}_{K,m}(x_m)$ is an affine function of x:

$$F(x) := \widetilde{E}_{K,1}(x_1) \oplus \ldots \oplus \widetilde{E}_{K,m}(x_m)$$
$$= \bigoplus_i \left(b_i \odot \left(\widetilde{E}_{K,i}(0) \oplus \widetilde{E}_{K,i}(1) \right) \oplus \widetilde{E}_{K,i}(0) \right) .$$

More precisely, if we identify bit-strings with boolean column vectors, $F(b_1 \ldots b_m)$ is equal to:

$$\underbrace{\left((\widetilde{E}_{K,1}(0) \oplus \widetilde{E}_{K,1}(1)) \cdots (\widetilde{E}_{K,m}(0) \oplus \widetilde{E}_{K,m}(1)) \right)}_{M_m} \times \begin{pmatrix} b_1 \\ \vdots \\ b_m \end{pmatrix} \oplus \bigoplus_i \widetilde{E}_{K,i}(0) .$$

The matrix M_m has n rows and m columns, so when $m \geq n+1$, its kernel is nontrivial. This means there will exist a non-zero m-bit boolean vector α such that:

$$\left((\widetilde{E}_{K,1}(0) \oplus \widetilde{E}_{K,1}(1)) \cdots (\widetilde{E}_{K,m}(0) \oplus \widetilde{E}_{K,m}(1)) \right) \times \alpha = \begin{pmatrix} 0 \\ \vdots \\ 0 \end{pmatrix} ,$$

and for all such vectors α, seen as m-bit strings, we have:

$$F(x \oplus \alpha) = M_m \times (x \oplus \alpha) \oplus \bigoplus_i \widetilde{E}_{K,i}(0) = F(x) .$$

In other words, this function F hides a subgroup of $(\mathbb{F}_2)^m$ generated by all the vectors α satisfying the condition above (it is easy to see that they indeed form a group). Thus, F satisfies the promise of Simon's algorithm: by making a single superposition query, we can find y such that $y \cdot \alpha = 0$ for such an α, and furthermore, as Brassard and Høyer showed [20], we can even recover the full subspace of periods with a polynomial number of quantum queries to F.

However, in our model, we cannot query F directly and we have instead access to: $f_K(IV, F(x))$, where IV changes at each query. The key remark is that the hidden subgroup is unchanged, since F is independent of the IV. This assumption is enough to allow Simon's algorithm and its extensions to work.

Remark 4 (Smaller m). Some period might still arise if $m \leq n$. Indeed, if $m = n$, there will be a non-trivial period with probability around $1 - 1/e$. This quickly decays for smaller m.

Remark 5 (Unwanted collisions). Since the "inner" function F is affine, it does not contain any unwanted collisions. If $F(x \oplus a) = F(x)$ for some a and x, then this holds as well for all x. However, unwanted collisions might occur in $f_K(IV, \cdot)$.

Assuming that M_m is full rank, we can express the probability of unwanted partial periods for $f_K(IV, F(\cdot))$ as the probability of such unwanted collisions for $f_K(IV, \cdot)$:

$$
\begin{aligned}
p &= \max_{t, M_m \times t \neq 0} \Pr_{x \in \{0,1\}^\ell} \left[f_K(IV, F(x \oplus t)) = f_K(IV, F(x)) \right] \\
&= \max_{t, M_m \times t \neq 0} \Pr_{x \in \{0,1\}^\ell} \left[f_K(IV, F(x) \oplus M_m \times t) = f_K(IV, F(x)) \right] \\
&= \max_{u \neq 0} \Pr_{x \in \{0,1\}^\ell} \left[f_K(IV, F(x) \oplus u) = f_K(IV, F(x)) \right] \\
&= \max_{u \neq 0} \Pr_{y \in \{0,1\}^n} \left[f_K(IV, y \oplus u) = f_K(IV, y) \right] .
\end{aligned}
$$

Even if the output is truncated to less than n bits, $p \leq \frac{1}{2}$ follows trivially from the fact that $f_K(IV, \cdot)$ should not admit a differential of such high probability. To conclude, it is precisely the fact that the termination function $f_K(IV, \cdot)$ is a good PRF, and does *not* admit an interfering period, that allows to apply easily Simon's algorithm in our case.

Thus, by making a polynomial number of Q2 queries to the MAC construction, we can obtain such an a. This allows to create forgeries as follows.

Forgeries Without IVs. We first make n queries to find a valid a with Simon's algorithm (with constant probability of success). Then, the knowledge of this a allows us, for each tag x queried, to output a forged tag $x \oplus a$. Thus we can double the number of tags that we produce compared to the number of queries we make. This breaks the PO notion as soon as, making $r + n$ queries, we have $2r \geq r + 1 + n$ tags, thus with $2n + 2$ queries in total. Note that by breaking PO, we are actually showing that the MAC construction is not a qPRF (if it were, it would be PO-secure).

Forgeries with IVs. As long as the IV (or nonce) is used only in the keyed post-processing, we can recover a value a and run the attack as above. We will indeed output more triples $\{IV, \text{message}, \text{tag}\}$ than the number of queries made, although some IVs are repeated in the outputs.

Universal Forgeries. Instead of taking the arbitrary values $b_i \| 0$ in message blocks, we can take any pair of values for each of them. That way, we can even start from any m-block message $y_1, \ldots, y_m$, and then define a function of

$x = b_1 \ldots b_m$ that inputs y_i in block i if $b_i = 1$ and an arbitrary value 0 otherwise. Using Simon's algorithm, we will find a subset of the y_i such that the $\widetilde{E}_{K,i}(y_i)$ have the same XOR as the $\widetilde{E}_{K,i}(0)$. Hence, we can produce a new message having the same tag as $y_1, \ldots, y_m$. This works as soon as $m \geq n$ (there just needs to be enough message blocks for our attack).

4   Applications to Parallelizable MACs

In this section, we apply the quantum linearization attack to many parallelizable MACs of the literature. In particular, we show that the attack can be extended to parallelizable beyond birthday-bound (BBB) MACs, although they have a larger internal state. Here is a summary of MACs attacked in this section (usually in time quadratic in the internal state size n), whose previous best quantum attack was exponential:

LightMAC [47], LightMAC+ [53], Deoxys [38], ZMAC [37],
PMAC_TBC3k [52]

On the contrary, here are some MACs on which, to the best of our knowledge, our attack does not apply: SUM-ECBC [61], 2K-ECBC-Plus [24], 3kf9 [62]. The best Q2 attacks on these remain exponential-time (usually $\widetilde{\mathcal{O}}\left(2^{n/2}\right)$ or $\mathcal{O}\left(2^{k/2}\right)$ where n is the internal block size, and k the key size).

4.1   First Examples

We will consider MAC designs with or without IVs or nonces. When there is no IV, then the attack of Sect. 3.3 breaks them in the PO notion. This also shows that even though they usually yield classical PRFs, these constructions are not quantum-secure PRFs. When there is an IV, the MAC may be insecure as a PRF but still secure as a MAC (since the IV is changed at each query, and not repeated). Despite that, our attack may still yield a break, as we showed in the example of ΘCB above. In that case, the period that is recovered with Simon's algorithm is independent of the IV, and can be reused to forge a new valid (message, tag) pair under any previously queried IV.

LightMAC. LightMAC [47] is based on an n-bit block cipher and separates the message in blocks of $n - s$ bits, where $s \leq n/2$ is some parameter that limits the maximal message size. The function is the following:

$$\mathsf{LightMAC}(m_1, \ldots, m_\ell) = \mathrm{Trunc}_t\left(E_{K_2}\left((m_\ell 10*) \oplus \bigoplus_{i=1}^{\ell-1} E_{K_1}(i_s m_i)\right)\right),$$

where the i_s are s-bit constants. Calling LightMAC with single-bit blocks and using Simon's algorithm, we immediately obtain a sequence of indices $j_1, \ldots, j_v$ such that $E_{K_1}(i_{j_1} 1) \oplus \ldots \oplus E_{K_1}(i_{j_v} 1) = E_{K_1}(i_{j_1} 0) \oplus \ldots \oplus E_{K_1}(i_{j_v} 0)$ and thus, we can produce existential forgeries, and universal forgeries of messages with a linear number of blocks.

Deoxys. Due to the similarity of its MAC with ΘCB, our attack applies to all versions of Deoxys-II [38], one of the finalists of the CAESAR competition (it also applies to Deoxys-I).

Protected Counter Sums. In [5], Bernstein defined the *protected counter sum* construction, which uses a pseudorandom function $f : \{0,1\}^{d+c} \to \{0,1\}^c$ to build a pseudorandom function with message space of at most $2^c - 1$ blocks of length d:
$$f'(m_1, \ldots, m_\ell) = f\left(0\|f(1\|m_1)\right) \oplus \ldots \oplus f(\ell\|m_\ell)) \; .$$
The quantum linearization attack essentially shows that this construction, while classically sound, does not yield a quantum-secure pseudorandom function (even if f itself is a qPRF).

4.2 Attacks on BBB MACs

We consider here a variant of the previous construction typically used to design Beyond Birthday MACs. We focus on deterministic MACs, but as before, the same forgery attacks apply if IVs are used in the final processing of the tag.

In the most generic setting, the input $x_1, \ldots, x_m$ is processed with a TBC $\widetilde{E}_{K,i}$, then combined in two different ways:
$$(x_1, \ldots, x_m) \mapsto f_K\left(\bigoplus_i \widetilde{E}_{K,i}(x_i), \bigoplus_i 2^i \widetilde{E}_{K,i}(x_i)\right) \; .$$

Here f_K is a function whose details are insignificant for our attack.

A similar observation as above applies. By calling the MAC in superposition with messages of the form $x = b_1\|0, \ldots, b_m\|0$, we will obtain a periodic function. Indeed, there are now two matrices M_m and M'_m with n rows and m columns, and two column vectors C, C' such that:
$$F(x) = F(b_1, \ldots, b_m) := f_K\left(M_m \times \begin{pmatrix} b_1 \\ \vdots \\ b_m \end{pmatrix} \oplus C, M'_m \times \begin{pmatrix} b_1 \\ \vdots \\ b_m \end{pmatrix} \oplus C'\right) \; ,$$

where the columns of M_m correspond to $\widetilde{E}_{K,i}(0) \oplus \widetilde{E}_{K,i}(1)$ and the columns of M'_m correspond to $2^i(\widetilde{E}_{K,i}(0) \oplus \widetilde{E}_{K,i}(1))$. Then, as soon as $m \geq 2n+1$, the matrix: $\begin{pmatrix} M_m \\ M'_m \end{pmatrix}$ has $2n$ rows and at least $2n + 1$ columns, and so, it has a non-trivial kernel. There exists a non-zero vector α such that
$$M_m\alpha = M'_m\alpha = \begin{pmatrix} 0 \\ \vdots \\ 0 \end{pmatrix} \; .$$

This α is a boolean period of F, for which $MAC(x \oplus \alpha) = MAC(x)$. Again, the further we increase m, the bigger the subspace of periods will become. This whole space can be recovered using Brassard and Høyer's extension of Simon's algorithm [20] in polynomial time.

Related Works. In [30], Guo, Wang, Hu and Ye used combinations of Simon's algorithm and Grover's algorithm to design forgery attacks on many BBB MACs, in the Q2 setting. With this technique, they found two things. First, state-recovery attacks of complexity $\widetilde{\mathcal{O}}\left(2^{n/2}\right)$ where n is the block size of the underlying block cipher, and the internal state is $2n$ bits in total. This comes from the fact that the same input blocks are processed in two branches separately. The standard use of Simon's algorithm, where a controlled message block x is XORed to an uncontrolled value, allows only to recover this value in one of the branches. The n bits on the other branch have to be guessed with a Grover search, and so, the attack is a Grover-meets-Simon [46] instance. And next, partial key-recovery attacks for parallelizable MACs, of complexity $\mathcal{O}\left(2^{k/2}\right)$, where k is the partial key size (the total key size ranges from $3k$ to $5k$). They consist in guessing part of the key and breaking the MAC by using a symmetry of the branches. To these attacks correspond classical partial key-recoveries of complexity $\mathcal{O}\left(2^{k}\right)$.

Our attack has completely different requirements and offers different results. We need longer messages (of roughly $2n$ blocks in this setting), but when it applies, the complexity is always polynomial. Note that there are constructions targeted by Guo *et al.*, such as SUM-ECBC, that we cannot attack since the blocks are processed sequentially and not linearly in parallel as we require.

LightMAC+. LightMAC+ [53], as its name suggests, is a BBB extension of LightMAC.

As shown in Fig. 3, it processes ℓ message blocks $m_1, \ldots, m_\ell$ as follows:

$$\mathsf{LightMAC+}(m_1, \ldots, m_\ell) = E_{K_1}(E_K(1_s \| m_1) \oplus \ldots \oplus E_K(\ell_s \| m_\ell))$$
$$\oplus E_{K_2}(2^{\ell-1} \odot E_K(1_s \| m_1) \oplus \ldots \oplus 2^0 \odot E_K(\ell_s \| m_\ell)) \ ,$$

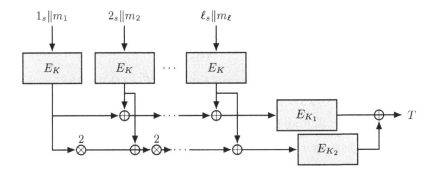

Fig. 3. LightMAC+ with three keys K, K_1, K_2.

where the multiplications are done in the finite field $\mathbb{F}_{2^n}$. This falls into our framework and is thus forgeable in quadratic time (about $2n$ blocks are required to embed a vector space in both branches, and this can then be recovered in a linear number of queries).

PMAC+. It is a double-block hash-then-sum construction similar to LightMAC+, which also falls into our framework. In full generality, there are three keys K_1, K_2, K_3. The message blocks $m_1, \ldots, m_\ell$ are processed as follows: $y_i = m_i \oplus 2^i \odot E_{K_1}(0) \oplus 2^{2i} \odot E_{K_1}(1)$ and then:

$$
\mathsf{PMAC+}(m_1, \ldots, m_\ell) = E_{K_2}\left(E_{K_1}(y_1) \oplus \ldots E_{K_1}(y_\ell)\right)
$$
$$
\oplus E_{K_3}\left(2 \odot E_{K_1}(y_1) \oplus \ldots 2^\ell \odot E_{K_1}(y_\ell)\right) \ .
$$

The masking by $2^i \odot E_{K_1}(0) \oplus 2^{2i} \odot E_{K_1}(1)$ simply makes the processing of each block different, but this is insignificant for our attack. By recovering a period, we can create forgeries and break PMAC+ as a qPRF.

Note that both LightMAC+ and PMAC+ were classically proven secure up to $2^{3n/4}$ queries [41]. Besides, increasing the number of parallel branches may have consequences on the bound, but only increases the complexity of our attack by a constant factor. We considered here three-key versions, but of course, the two- and one-key versions [24,25] are similarly broken.

4.3 Other MACs

LAPMAC. LAPMAC was defined in [50]. The definition depends on some parallelization parameter μ. Successive chunks of μ message blocks will be processed in parallel through the block cipher E_K (except the last one), then some tweak function depending on their index in the chunk. The results are XORed and encrypted again, before being XORed to the next chunk of μ message blocks, etc. When $\mu \geq n$, LAPMAC applied to n message blocks becomes similar to LightMAC or PMAC, and there is sufficient parallelization to perform our attack. Whether a variant of the attack applies for smaller values of μ is an interesting question.

ZMAC. ZMAC [37] is a MAC that uses a TBC. It is based on the ZHASH double-block hash construction followed by a finalization function. We can simply focus on the abstraction ZHASH (see Fig. 5 in [37]):

$$
\mathrm{ZHASH}(X_\ell^1, X_r^1, \ldots, X_\ell^l, X_r^l) = \bigoplus_i 2^{l+1-i} \widetilde{E}_K^{i, X_r^i}(X_\ell^i), \bigoplus_i X_r^i \oplus \bigoplus_i \widetilde{E}_K^{i, X_r^i}(X_\ell^i) \ ,
$$

where $\widetilde{E}_K^t$ is $\widetilde{E}_K$ called with a tweak t. If we make the tweak inputs constant, then the construction is similar to PMAC+ with a TBC, and different random keyed permutations for each block. Our attack applies as well.

PMAC with a TBC. Naito [52] showed that PMAC+ used with a TBC could achieve full PRF security (up to $\mathcal{O}(2^n)$ queries). In this variant, the message blocks are processed independently with different tweaks. This has no consequence on our attack, which requires only $\mathcal{O}(n)$ queries of about $2n$ blocks each.

5   Attacks on MACs Based on Universal Hashing

In this section, we focus on some attacks on MACs based on universal hashing. In particular, we give polynomial-time attacks on PolyMAC [36], GCM-SIV2, and we give a superposition attack on Poly1305 requiring about 32 queries.

5.1   Overview

Universal hash functions were introduced by Carter and Wegman in 1977 [21] in order to build secure MACs, and are now used in many MAC constructions and security proofs. The first proposal by Wegman and Carter was to hash the message and to encrypt the result with a one-time-pad. This defines a MAC with information-theoretic security, but the use of a one-time-pad is impractical, and it was soon suggested to replace it with the output of a PRF, i.e., to replace the one-time-pad by counter-mode encryption. This results in the Wegman-Carter construction used in GCM and Poly1305-AES: $M \mapsto H_{K_1}(M) \oplus F_{K_2}(N)$ where F is a secure pseudorandom function family, and H an almost-XOR-universal hash function family.

5.2   Universal Hash Functions and MAC Constructions

An almost-XOR-universal hash function family is a family of function H from $\{0,1\}^*$ to $\{0,1\}^n$ indexed by a key $K \in \mathcal{K}$ such that:

$$\forall m \neq m', \forall d \in \{0,1\}^n, \#\{K \in \mathcal{K} : H_K(m) \oplus H_K(m') = d\} \leq \varepsilon \# \mathcal{K}$$

The most widely used universal hash function construction is polynomial hashing. The input message is interpreted as the coefficients of a polynomial in a field $\mathbb{F}$, and the polynomial is evaluated on the hash key:

$$\mathsf{PolyHash}_K : \mathbb{F}^\ell \to \mathbb{F} \qquad m_1, m_2, \dots m_\ell \mapsto \sum_{i=1}^{\ell} K^i \odot m_i$$

Block cipher-based constructions such as the OCB3 MAC can also be analysed as universal hashing-based, using $\bigoplus_i E_K(A_i \oplus \Delta_i)$ as a universal hash function.

There are many different ways to turn a universal hash function into a MAC:

One-time-MAC: $H_K(M)$. If the universal hash function satisfies extra properties (it must be strongly universal), it can be used directly as a MAC, if a new key is used for each message. This construction is used in ChaCha20-Poly1305, Grain128A and Grain128AEAD [32].

Wegman-Carter: $H_{K_1}(M) \oplus F_{K_2}(N)$. The Wegman-Carter construction is a nonce-based MAC using a universal hash function H and a PRF F. It authenticates several messages using the same key, as long as the nonce N is not repeated (the security is lost as soon as two different messages are authenticated with the same key). This construction is used in GMAC.

More generally, the construction $H(M) \star F(N)$ with $\star$ a group operation and F almost-$\star$-universal is a secure MAC. This construction is used in Poly1305-AES.

Hash-then-PRF: $F_{K_2}(H_{K_1}(M))$. The hash-then-PRF construction builds a deterministic MAC from a universal hash function H and a PRF F.

The PolyMAC construction discussed below follows this design. More generally, security proofs for several block cipher-based MACs consider the MAC as following the hash-then-PRF construction; in particular this is the case of double-block hash-then-sum constructions [24].

WMAC: $F_{K_2}(H_{K_1}(M)\|N)$. WMAC [10] is a generalization of the hash-then-PRF construction using an additional nonce input N to the PRF. This requires a PRF with a larger input, but provides higher security when nonces are unique, without breaking down when they are repeated.

EWCDM: $E_{K_3}(E_{K_2}(N) \oplus N \oplus H_{K_1}(M))$. The *Encrypted Wegman-Carter with Davies-Meyer* construction [23] is an alternative construction offering high security with a nonce with graceful degradation when nonces are repeated. Instead of using a $2n$-bit PRF as in WMAC, it uses two calls to an n-bit block cipher.

5.3 Attacking Wegman-Carter MACs

All MACs following the Wegman-Carter construction are exposed to the attack using Deutsch's algorithm that we presented in Sect. 3.1. More precisely, an IV-respecting quantum adversary can retrieve the value of $H_{K_1}(M_1) \oplus H_{K_1}(M_2)$ for an arbitrary pair of messages M_1, M_2. He can then repeatedly query the tag of M_1 under new nonces, and produce corresponding valid tags for M_2.

When using the generalization with a group operation $\star$ instead of $\oplus$, this simple attack does not apply. In particular, Poly1305-AES uses a modular addition and cannot be broken with Deutsch's algorithm, but we will show a dedicated attack in Sect. 5.5, using the fact that it is based on polynomial hashing.

5.4 Attacking Algebraic Universal Hash Functions

We can apply our linearization attack to MACs that reuse the same hash key for several messages, whether deterministic (like hash-then-PRF), or nonce-based (like Wegman-Carter, WMAC, and EWCDM). Indeed, it is enough for us to linearize the function H, and the attack applies regardless of the security of the operations that are computed afterwards, even if they involve a nonce.

Many Universal Hash Functions based on algebraic operations have a strong linear structure. In particular, polynomial hashing is a linear function of the message, making it a natural target for Simon's algorithm (in characteristic 2) or Shor's algorithm (in general). We describe concrete attacks against a few constructions.

PolyMAC. PolyMAC [24] is a double block hash-then-sum construction based on polynomial hashing. The generic construction uses two hashing keys K_1, K_2 and two encryption keys K_3, K_4. For an ℓ-block message $m_1, \ldots, m_\ell$, this gives:

$$\mathrm{PolyMAC}(m_1, \ldots, m_\ell) = E_{K_3}\left(K_1 \odot m_\ell \oplus K_1^2 \odot m_{\ell-1} \oplus \ldots \oplus K_1^\ell \odot m_1\right)$$
$$\oplus E_{K_4}\left(K_2 \odot m_\ell \oplus K_2^2 \odot m_{\ell-1} \oplus \ldots \oplus K_2^\ell \odot m_1\right) \ .$$

If a single branch is used, then this looks like the GMAC construction [49] (but without a nonce), using polynomial hashing. GMAC was already attacked in [39] due to its similarities with CBC-MAC, and the fact that the nonce did not influence the embedded hidden shift. However, we can use our attack here. By taking ℓ-block message inputs with blocks 0 or 1, we will recover with Simon's algorithm a period $b_1 \cdots b_\ell$ such that:

$$\bigoplus_i b_i K_1^i = 0 \text{ and } \bigoplus_i b_i K_2^i = 0 \ .$$

This immediately allows a forgery attack, but also, we can recover multiple such periods and solve the corresponding equations to recover K_1 and K_2.

PolyMAC with Modular Additions. Interestingly, our attack applies as well when the polynomial hashing does not use XORs, but modular additions (modulo some value M). However, Simon's algorithm has to be replaced by Shor's algorithm. Note that this is specific to polynomial hashing, and does not apply to LightMAC or PMAC-style constructions in general.

We can define:

$$\mathrm{PolyMAC+}(m_1, \ldots, m_\ell) = E_{K_3}\left(K_1 \odot m_\ell + K_1^2 \odot m_{\ell-1} + \ldots + K_1^\ell \odot m_1 \bmod M\right)$$
$$\oplus E_{K_4}\left(K_2 \odot m_\ell + K_2^2 \odot m_{\ell-1} + \ldots + K_2^\ell \odot m_1 \bmod M\right) \ .$$

In that case, we can remark that there exists periods $a_1, \ldots, a_\ell$ such that:

$$K_1 a_1 + \ldots + K_1^\ell a_\ell \bmod M = 0 \text{ and } K_2 a_1 + \ldots + K_2^\ell a_\ell \bmod M = 0 \ .$$

More precisely, these periods form a lattice in $\mathbb{Z}_M^\ell$, and for all of them, we have:

$$\forall m_1, \ldots, m_\ell, \mathrm{PolyMAC+}(m_1 + a_1, \ldots, m_\ell + a_\ell) = \mathrm{PolyMAC+}(m_1, \ldots, m_\ell) \ .$$

Thus, the generalization by Mosca and Ekert [51] of Shor's algorithm allows to retrieve the full lattice of these periods: we can not only forge, but also recover the internal hashing keys.

GCM-SIV2. This is a double-block variant of GCM-SIV defined in [36]. The tag generation combines two independent polynomial hashes (with two keys K_1, K_2) with a keyed-dependent combination function F_K, of which we shall not study the details. This mode is nonce-based. With an empty associated data, the tag is computed as follows:

$$\mathrm{GCM\text{-}SIV2 - MAC}(N, m_1, \ldots, m_\ell)$$
$$= F_K\left(N \oplus H_{K_1}(m_1, \ldots, m_\ell), N \oplus H_{K_2}(m_1, \ldots, m_\ell)\right) \ ,$$

where H_{K_1} and H_{K_2} are polynomial hashes (this would be similar for the tag of an empty message, replacing M by the associated data). Thus, although the MAC is nonce-dependent, it falls into our framework since the periods of the polynomial hashes remain independent of N.

Other Algebraic Hashing Constructions. There are many alternatives to polynomial hashing based on field operations. Several constructions are linear, such as the dot product construction, and Toeplitz hashing [42].[1]

Some other constructions can be linearized using specially crafted messages.

NMH* [31]. The NMH* universal hash function is defined as:

$$\text{NMH}^*(M) = \sum (m_{2i} + K_{2i})(m_{2i+1} + K_{2i+1}) \bmod p$$

If we consider messages with blocks with an even index set to arbitrary constants, we obtain a linear function of the odd message blocks. Therefore, Shor's algorithm can break MACs based on this hash function that reuse the hash key.

BRW Hashing [7]. The BRW universal hash function is based on a class of polynomials that can be evaluated with $\ell/2$ multiplications with ℓ inputs, using a single key. The construction is defined recursively, depending on the input length:

- $BRW_K() = 0$
- $BRW_K(m_1) = m_1$
- $BRW_K(m_1, m_2) = m_1 \odot K + m_2$
- $BRW_K(m_1, m_2, m_3) = (K + m_1) \odot (K^2 + m_2) + m_3$
- $BRW_K(m_1, m_2, \ldots m_\ell) = BRW_K(m_1, m_2, \ldots m_{t-1}) \odot (K^t + m_t) +$
  $BRW_K(m_{t+1}, m_{t+2}, \ldots m_\ell)$ with t a power of 2, and $4 \leq t \leq n < 2t$.

For instance, with 8 inputs, we obtain

$$\Big(((K+m_1) \odot (K^2+m_2)+m_3) \odot (K^4+m_4) + (K+m_5) \odot (K^2+m_6)+m_7\Big) \odot (K^8+m_8)$$

This construction can also be linearized by setting message blocks with an even index set to arbitrary constants.

5.5   Period-Finding Against Poly1305

Poly1305 [6] is a polynomial MAC with some specific constraints that force a dedicated analysis. It has already been cryptanalysed in [18], where the authors proposed an attack in 2^{38} time and queries. The authors managed to overcome the specific constraints by leveraging a *hidden shift* structure. The attack we propose here is drastically more efficient, and uses a *hidden period* instead.

---

[1] Grain128A and Grain128AEAD [32] use Toeplitz hashing, but we can only attack them in the nonce-misuse setting because they use the one-time-MAC construction.

Poly1305 uses a hashing key r of 124 bits with at most 106 non-zero bits and a 128-bit cipher key K. The MAC of a message $m_1, \ldots, m_\ell$ with the nonce N is computed as:

$$\mathsf{Poly1305}(m_1, \ldots, m_\ell) = (c_1 r^\ell + c_2 r^{\ell-1} + \ldots + c_\ell r^1) \bmod 2^{130} - 5$$
$$+ AES_K(N) \bmod 2^{128} \ ,$$

where $c_1, \ldots, c_\ell$ are the padded message blocks obtained from the message blocks $m_1, \ldots, m_\ell$. When message blocks are full 128-bit blocks, the c_i are simply obtained from the m_i by adding 2^{128}.

Let us assume that we query with two message blocks. We have:

$$\mathsf{Poly1305}(m_1, m_2) = \left((m_1 + 2^{128}) \cdot r^2 + (m_2 + 2^{128}) \cdot r\right) \bmod 2^{130} - 5$$
$$+ AES_K(N) \bmod 2^{128}$$
$$= \left(((m_1 \cdot r + m_2) \cdot r + C_1) \bmod 2^{130} - 5\right) + C_2 \bmod 2^{128} \ ,$$

where C_1, C_2 are constants of our query that depend on r, K, N. Since the computation ends with a reduction modulo 2^{128}, which is smaller than $2^{130} - 5$, we must actually use a *compressed* instance of Shor's algorithm [48]. This increases mildly the number of queries, by less than a factor 2.

Two inputs (m_1, m_2) and (m_1', m_2') lead to the same tag if

$$m_1 r + m_2 = m_1' r + m_2' \bmod 2^{130} - 5$$
$$\Leftrightarrow (m_1 - m_1')r + (m_2 - m_2') = 0 \bmod 2^{130} - 5 \ .$$

Hence, the periods of the function $\mathsf{Poly1305}(m_1, m_2)$ are solutions of $m_1 r + m_2 = 0 \bmod 2^{130} - 5$.

As the period is modulo $2^{130} - 5$ but the input is 128-bit long, we cannot do the query expected by Shor's algorithm. Still, the fraction of inputs we can actually query is large enough so that we can still apply Shor's algorithm with a *partial* query, and recover efficiently the period.

The initial query is:

$$\frac{1}{2^{128}} \sum_{m_1, m_2 = 0}^{2^{128} - 1} |m_1\rangle |m_2\rangle |\mathsf{Poly1305}(m_1, m_2)\rangle$$

$$= \frac{1}{2^{128}} \sum_{m_1, m_2 = 0}^{2^{128} - 1} |m_1\rangle |m_2\rangle |f(m_1 r + m_2)\rangle \ .$$

Here, f is a function that depends on r, K, N. The only relevant point is that it does not depend on m_1, m_2 directly, but only on $m_1 r + m_2$. For simplicity, in the following we assume f is a permutation. We will now apply the QFT over $\mathbb{Z}/(2^{130} - 5)$ on the input registers. We note $p = 2^{130} - 5$. We obtain

$$\frac{1}{p}\frac{1}{2^{128}}\sum_{m_1,m_2=0}^{2^{128}-1}\sum_{x,y=0}^{p-1}\exp\left(2i\pi\frac{xm_1+ym_2}{p}\right)|x\rangle\,|y\rangle\,|f(m_1r+m_2)\rangle\quad.$$

We can rewrite the state by regrouping components with identical m_1r+m_2:

$$\frac{1}{p}\frac{1}{2^{128}}\sum_{x,y=0}^{p-1}\sum_{c=0}^{p-1}\sum_{\substack{m_1,m_2=0\\m_1r+m_2=c}}^{2^{128}-1}\exp\left(2i\pi\frac{xm_1+ym_2}{p}\right)|x\rangle\,|y\rangle\,|f(c)\rangle$$

$$=\frac{1}{p}\frac{1}{2^{128}}\sum_{x,y=0}^{p-1}\sum_{c=0}^{p-1}\sum_{\substack{m_1,m_2=0\\m_1r+m_2=c}}^{2^{128}-1}\exp\left(2i\pi\frac{xm_1+y(c-m_1r)}{p}\right)|x\rangle\,|y\rangle\,|f(c)\rangle$$

$$=\frac{1}{p}\frac{1}{2^{128}}\sum_{x,y=0}^{p-1}\sum_{c=0}^{p-1}\exp\left(2i\pi\frac{yc}{p}\right)\sum_{\substack{m_1,m_2=0\\m_1r+m_2=c}}^{2^{128}-1}\exp\left(2i\pi\frac{m_1(x-yr)}{p}\right)|x\rangle\,|y\rangle\,|f(c)\rangle$$

Now, we can compute the probability to measure a nonzero tuple (x,y) with $x=yr$.

As there are $p-1$ such tuples, the overall probability is

$$\left(\frac{1}{p}\frac{1}{2^{128}}\right)^2(p-1)\sum_{c=0}^{p-1}\left(\sum_{\substack{m_1,m_2=0\\m_1r+m_2=c}}^{2^{128}-1}1\right)^2$$

$$=\frac{p-1}{p^2 2^{256}}\sum_{c=0}^{p-1}\left(\#\{0\le m_1,m_2<2^{128}:m_1r+m_2=c\}\right)^2$$

Now, as $x\mapsto x^2$ is a convex function, we can use Jensen's inequality:

$$\sum_{i=1}^{n}\frac{1}{n}\alpha_i^2\ge\left(\sum_{i=1}^{n}\frac{1}{n}\alpha_i\right)^2\quad.$$

This allows us to lower bound the previous probability by

$$\frac{p-1}{p^2 2^{256}}p\left(\sum_{c=0}^{p-1}\frac{1}{p}\#\{0\le m_1,m_2<2^{128}:m_1r+m_2=c\}\right)^2$$

$$=\frac{p-1}{p^2 2^{256}}\left(\frac{1}{p}\#\{0\le m_1,m_2<2^{128}\}\right)^2=\frac{p-1}{p^2 2^{256}}\left(\frac{2^{256}}{p}\right)^2=\frac{(p-1)2^{256}}{p^3}>\frac{1}{16}\quad.$$

Thus, we measure a tuple $(x,y)\ne(0,0)$ with $x=yr$ with probability at least $1/16$. As $2^{130}-5$ is prime, one such tuple is enough to recover r. Hence, we need at most 16 queries on average to recover r, assuming f is a permutation. Here, as f is a function, we rely on [48] to bound the increase by a factor 2. Note that as we are only a few bits of output short of having a permutation, this is a very loose bound. Overall, the attack will require no more than 32 queries.

6   On Parallelizable Quantum PRFs

Let us take a broader point of view. The deterministic MACs that we attacked in this paper all have common points. Besides allowing inputs of any length (as should be expected of any MAC construction), they • process their input blocks independently; • compute one or more linear functions, *with XORs*, of these processed input blocks; • process the authentication tag from the outputs of these linear functions.

These characteristics are to be expected from any MAC that is: • of average rate one, meaning that there are as many primitive calls as there are blocks; • parallelizable; • having an internal state of size $\mathcal{O}(n)$, independent of the query length. Our attack is easily defeated if the blocks are processed sequentially by calling a compression function, as in the NMAC construction. However, the construction becomes unparallelizable.

It may be possible to obtain a quantum-secure parallelizable qPRF using a tree hashing, where the blocks are placed at the leaves of a binary tree, and each node is computed by calling a (keyed) compression function on its two children. However, such a construction requires an internal state greater than $\mathcal{O}(n)$, and that increases with the amount of data. Typically to traverse the binary tree, we will need to remember $\mathcal{O}(\log m)$ nodes, where m is the number of leaves.

Open Question. If we stand by the characteristics listed above (efficient, parallelizable, constant internal state size), then it seems that the only solution is to use modular additions in place of XORs in the constructions that we attacked. In that case, our attack does not seem to work anymore, due to the fact that modular additions, contrary to XORs, are not involutive. Thus changing one of the blocks in our n-block queries does not modify involutively the result, which breaks the periodicity property that we used with Simon's algorithm.

This makes this option worth investigating, both from a provable security and a cryptanalysis perspective. Note that the situation is different from most attacks with Simon's algorithm, where the replacement of XORs by + changes the attack complexity from polynomial to subexponential (see [2,18]). In our case, it is possible that using + allows an exponential security level.

7   Conclusion

In this paper, we introduced a novel way of using quantum period-finding to break parallelizable MAC constructions in the superposition query model, breaking most of them in this setting. In full generality, our attack makes use of multiple blocks to embed a hidden period, a surprisingly simple idea that might have other applications. We gave new polynomial-time forgery or partial key-recovery attacks on LightMAC, LightMAC+, PolyMAC, Poly1305, GCM-SIV2, Deoxys, ZMAC, PMAC_TBC3k. Our attack is not mitigated by the use of multiple parallel branches (as in double-block hash-then-sum MACs). It can be prevented for IV-based MACs if the non-reused IV intervenes in the processing of all message blocks (as done in [9]).

These results show that we cannot obtain a parallelizable quantum-secure PRF by processing independently the message blocks, XORing the results, and then hashing the output. If modular additions are used instead of XORs, our attack does not apply anymore (except on polynomial hashing, which has a simpler structure). Overcoming this limitation, or on the contrary, proving the security of such a PRF, is an interesting open question.

Acknowledgments. This project has received funding from the European Research Council (ERC) under the European Union's Horizon 2020 research and innovation programme (grant agreement no. 714294 - acronym QUASYModo). A.S. is supported by ERC-ADG-ALGSTRONGCRYPTO (project 740972).

References

1. Alagic, G., Majenz, C., Russell, A., Song, F.: Quantum-access-secure message authentication via blind-unforgeability. In: Canteaut, A., Ishai, Y. (eds.) EUROCRYPT 2020. LNCS, vol. 12107, pp. 788–817. Springer, Cham (2020). https://doi.org/10.1007/978-3-030-45727-3_27
2. Alagic, G., Russell, A.: Quantum-secure symmetric-key cryptography based on hidden shifts. In: Coron, J.-S., Nielsen, J.B. (eds.) EUROCRYPT 2017. LNCS, vol. 10212, pp. 65–93. Springer, Cham (2017). https://doi.org/10.1007/978-3-319-56617-7_3
3. Anand, M.V., Targhi, E.E., Tabia, G.N., Unruh, D.: Post-quantum security of the CBC, CFB, OFB, CTR, and XTS modes of operation. In: Takagi, T. (ed.) PQCrypto 2016. LNCS, vol. 9606, pp. 44–63. Springer, Cham (2016). https://doi.org/10.1007/978-3-319-29360-8_4
4. Bellare, M., Guérin, R., Rogaway, P.: XOR MACs: new methods for message authentication using finite pseudorandom functions. In: Coppersmith, D. (ed.) CRYPTO 1995. LNCS, vol. 963, pp. 15–28. Springer, Heidelberg (1995). https://doi.org/10.1007/3-540-44750-4_2
5. Bernstein, D.J.: How to stretch random functions: the security of protected counter sums. J. Cryptol. **12**(3), 185–192 (1999)
6. Bernstein, D.J.: The Poly1305-AES message-authentication code. In: Gilbert, H., Handschuh, H. (eds.) FSE 2005. LNCS, vol. 3557, pp. 32–49. Springer, Heidelberg (2005). https://doi.org/10.1007/11502760_3
7. Bernstein, D.J.: Polynomial evaluation and message authentication (2007). http://cr.yp.to/papers.html#pema
8. Bernstein, E., Vazirani, U.V.: Quantum complexity theory. SIAM J. Comput. **26**(5), 1411–1473 (1997)
9. Bhaumik, R., et al.: QCB: efficient quantum-secure authenticated encryption. In: Tibouchi, M., Wang, H. (eds.) ASIACRYPT 2021. LNCS, vol. 13090, pp. 668–698. Springer, Cham (2021). https://doi.org/10.1007/978-3-030-92062-3_23
10. Black, J., Cochran, M.: MAC reforgeability. In: Dunkelman, O. (ed.) FSE 2009. LNCS, vol. 5665, pp. 345–362. Springer, Heidelberg (2009). https://doi.org/10.1007/978-3-642-03317-9_21
11. Black, J., Rogaway, P.: CBC MACs for arbitrary-length messages: the three-key constructions. In: Bellare, M. (ed.) CRYPTO 2000. LNCS, vol. 1880, pp. 197–215. Springer, Heidelberg (2000). https://doi.org/10.1007/3-540-44598-6_12

12. Black, J., Rogaway, P.: A block-cipher mode of operation for parallelizable message authentication. In: Knudsen, L.R. (ed.) EUROCRYPT 2002. LNCS, vol. 2332, pp. 384–397. Springer, Heidelberg (2002). https://doi.org/10.1007/3-540-46035-7_25
13. Boneh, D., Zhandry, M.: Quantum-secure message authentication codes. In: Johansson, T., Nguyen, P.Q. (eds.) EUROCRYPT 2013. LNCS, vol. 7881, pp. 592–608. Springer, Heidelberg (2013). https://doi.org/10.1007/978-3-642-38348-9_35
14. Boneh, D., Zhandry, M.: Secure signatures and chosen ciphertext security in a quantum computing world. In: Canetti, R., Garay, J.A. (eds.) CRYPTO 2013. LNCS, vol. 8043, pp. 361–379. Springer, Heidelberg (2013). https://doi.org/10.1007/978-3-642-40084-1_21
15. Bonnetain, X.: Quantum key-recovery on full AEZ. In: Adams, C., Camenisch, J. (eds.) SAC 2017. LNCS, vol. 10719, pp. 394–406. Springer, Cham (2018). https://doi.org/10.1007/978-3-319-72565-9_20
16. Bonnetain, X.: Tight bounds for Simon's algorithm. In: Longa, P., Ràfols, C. (eds.) LATINCRYPT 2021. LNCS, vol. 12912, pp. 3–23. Springer, Cham (2021). https://doi.org/10.1007/978-3-030-88238-9_1
17. Bonnetain, X., Hosoyamada, A., Naya-Plasencia, M., Sasaki, Y., Schrottenloher, A.: Quantum attacks without superposition queries: the offline Simon's algorithm. In: Galbraith, S.D., Moriai, S. (eds.) ASIACRYPT 2019. LNCS, vol. 11921, pp. 552–583. Springer, Cham (2019). https://doi.org/10.1007/978-3-030-34578-5_20
18. Bonnetain, X., Naya-Plasencia, M.: Hidden shift quantum cryptanalysis and implications. In: Peyrin, T., Galbraith, S. (eds.) ASIACRYPT 2018. LNCS, vol. 11272, pp. 560–592. Springer, Cham (2018). https://doi.org/10.1007/978-3-030-03326-2_19
19. Bonnetain, X., Naya-Plasencia, M., Schrottenloher, A.: On quantum slide attacks. In: Paterson, K.G., Stebila, D. (eds.) SAC 2019. LNCS, vol. 11959, pp. 492–519. Springer, Cham (2020). https://doi.org/10.1007/978-3-030-38471-5_20
20. Brassard, G., Høyer, P.: An exact quantum polynomial-time algorithm for Simon's problem. In: ISTCS, pp. 12–23. IEEE Computer Society (1997)
21. Carter, L., Wegman, M.N.: Universal classes of hash functions (extended abstract). In: STOC, pp. 106–112. ACM (1977)
22. Cid, C., Hosoyamada, A., Liu, Y., Sim, S.M.: Quantum cryptanalysis on contracting Feistel structures and observation on related-key settings. In: Bhargavan, K., Oswald, E., Prabhakaran, M. (eds.) INDOCRYPT 2020. LNCS, vol. 12578, pp. 373–394. Springer, Cham (2020). https://doi.org/10.1007/978-3-030-65277-7_17
23. Cogliati, B., Seurin, Y.: EWCDM: an efficient, beyond-birthday secure, nonce-misuse resistant MAC. In: Robshaw, M., Katz, J. (eds.) CRYPTO 2016. LNCS, vol. 9814, pp. 121–149. Springer, Heidelberg (2016). https://doi.org/10.1007/978-3-662-53018-4_5
24. Datta, N., Dutta, A., Nandi, M., Paul, G.: Double-block hash-then-sum: a paradigm for constructing BBB secure PRF. IACR Trans. Symmetric Cryptol. **2018**(3), 36–92 (2018)
25. Datta, N., Dutta, A., Nandi, M., Paul, G., Zhang, L.: Single key variant of PMAC_Plus. IACR Trans. Symmetric Cryptol. **2017**(4), 268–305 (2017)
26. Deutsch, D.: Quantum theory, the Church-Turing principle and the universal quantum computer. Proc. Roy. Soc. Lond. A **400**, 117–197 (1985)
27. Deutsch, D., Jozsa, R.: Rapid solution of problems by quantum computation. Proc. Roy. Soc. Lond. Ser. A Math. Phys. Sci. **439**(1907), 553–558 (1992)
28. Dong, X., Dong, B., Wang, X.: Quantum attacks on some feistel block ciphers. Des. Codes Cryptogr. **88**(6), 1179–1203 (2020)

29. Grover, L.K.: A fast quantum mechanical algorithm for database search. In: STOC, pp. 212–219. ACM (1996)

30. Guo, T., Wang, P., Hu, L., Ye, D.: Attacks on beyond-birthday-bound MACs in the quantum setting. In: Cheon, J.H., Tillich, J.-P. (eds.) PQCrypto 2021 2021. LNCS, vol. 12841, pp. 421–441. Springer, Cham (2021). https://doi.org/10.1007/978-3-030-81293-5_22

31. Halevi, S., Krawczyk, H.: MMH: software message authentication in the Gbit/second rates. In: Biham, E. (ed.) FSE 1997. LNCS, vol. 1267, pp. 172–189. Springer, Heidelberg (1997). https://doi.org/10.1007/BFb0052345

32. Hell, M., Johansson, T., Meier, W., Sönnerup, J., Yoshida, H.: Grain-128 AEAD a lightweight AEAD streamcipher. Submission to NIST-LWC (2nd Round) (2019)

33. Hosoyamada, A., Sasaki, Y.: Quantum Demiric-Selçuk meet-in-the-middle attacks: applications to 6-round generic Feistel constructions. In: Catalano, D., De Prisco, R. (eds.) SCN 2018. LNCS, vol. 11035, pp. 386–403. Springer, Cham (2018). https://doi.org/10.1007/978-3-319-98113-0_21

34. Ito, G., Hosoyamada, A., Matsumoto, R., Sasaki, Y., Iwata, T.: Quantum chosen-ciphertext attacks against Feistel ciphers. In: Matsui, M. (ed.) CT-RSA 2019. LNCS, vol. 11405, pp. 391–411. Springer, Cham (2019). https://doi.org/10.1007/978-3-030-12612-4_20

35. Iwata, T., Kurosawa, K.: OMAC: one-key CBC MAC. In: Johansson, T. (ed.) FSE 2003. LNCS, vol. 2887, pp. 129–153. Springer, Heidelberg (2003). https://doi.org/10.1007/978-3-540-39887-5_11

36. Iwata, T., Minematsu, K.: Stronger security variants of GCM-SIV. IACR Trans. Symmetric Cryptol. **2016**(1), 134–157 (2016)

37. Iwata, T., Minematsu, K., Peyrin, T., Seurin, Y.: ZMAC: a fast tweakable block cipher mode for highly secure message authentication. In: Katz, J., Shacham, H. (eds.) CRYPTO 2017. LNCS, vol. 10403, pp. 34–65. Springer, Cham (2017). https://doi.org/10.1007/978-3-319-63697-9_2

38. Jean, J., Nikolić, I., Peyrin, T., Seurin, Y.: Deoxys v1. 41. Submitted to CAESAR (2016)

39. Kaplan, M., Leurent, G., Leverrier, A., Naya-Plasencia, M.: Breaking symmetric cryptosystems using quantum period finding. In: Robshaw, M., Katz, J. (eds.) CRYPTO 2016. LNCS, vol. 9815, pp. 207–237. Springer, Heidelberg (2016). https://doi.org/10.1007/978-3-662-53008-5_8

40. Kaplan, M., Leurent, G., Leverrier, A., Naya-Plasencia, M.: Quantum differential and linear cryptanalysis. IACR Trans. Symmetric Cryptol. **2016**(1), 71–94 (2016)

41. Kim, S., Lee, B., Lee, J.: Tight security bounds for double-block hash-then-sum MACs. In: Canteaut, A., Ishai, Y. (eds.) EUROCRYPT 2020. LNCS, vol. 12105, pp. 435–465. Springer, Cham (2020). https://doi.org/10.1007/978-3-030-45721-1_16

42. Krawczyk, H.: New hash functions for message authentication. In: Guillou, L.C., Quisquater, J.-J. (eds.) EUROCRYPT 1995. LNCS, vol. 921, pp. 301–310. Springer, Heidelberg (1995). https://doi.org/10.1007/3-540-49264-X_24

43. Krovetz, T., Rogaway, P.: The software performance of authenticated-encryption modes. In: Joux, A. (ed.) FSE 2011. LNCS, vol. 6733, pp. 306–327. Springer, Heidelberg (2011). https://doi.org/10.1007/978-3-642-21702-9_18

44. Kuwakado, H., Morii, M.: Quantum distinguisher between the 3-round Feistel cipher and the random permutation. In: ISIT, pp. 2682–2685. IEEE (2010)

45. Kuwakado, H., Morii, M.: Security on the quantum-type Even-Mansour cipher. In: ISITA, pp. 312–316. IEEE (2012)

46. Leander, G., May, A.: Grover meets Simon – quantumly attacking the FX-construction. In: Takagi, T., Peyrin, T. (eds.) ASIACRYPT 2017. LNCS, vol. 10625, pp. 161–178. Springer, Cham (2017). https://doi.org/10.1007/978-3-319-70697-9_6

47. Luykx, A., Preneel, B., Tischhauser, E., Yasuda, K.: A MAC mode for lightweight block ciphers. In: Peyrin, T. (ed.) FSE 2016. LNCS, vol. 9783, pp. 43–59. Springer, Heidelberg (2016). https://doi.org/10.1007/978-3-662-52993-5_3

48. May, A., Schlieper, L.: Quantum period finding is compression robust. CoRR abs/1905.10074 (2019)

49. McGrew, D.A., Viega, J.: The security and performance of the Galois/Counter Mode (GCM) of operation. In: Canteaut, A., Viswanathan, K. (eds.) INDOCRYPT 2004. LNCS, vol. 3348, pp. 343–355. Springer, Heidelberg (2004). https://doi.org/10.1007/978-3-540-30556-9_27

50. Minematsu, K.: A lightweight alternative to PMAC. In: Paterson, K.G., Stebila, D. (eds.) SAC 2019. LNCS, vol. 11959, pp. 393–417. Springer, Cham (2020). https://doi.org/10.1007/978-3-030-38471-5_16

51. Mosca, M., Ekert, A.: The hidden subgroup problem and eigenvalue estimation on a quantum computer. In: Williams, C.P. (ed.) QCQC 1998. LNCS, vol. 1509, pp. 174–188. Springer, Heidelberg (1999). https://doi.org/10.1007/3-540-49208-9_15

52. Naito, Y.: Full PRF-secure message authentication code based on tweakable block cipher. In: Au, M.-H., Miyaji, A. (eds.) ProvSec 2015. LNCS, vol. 9451, pp. 167–182. Springer, Cham (2015). https://doi.org/10.1007/978-3-319-26059-4_9

53. Naito, Y.: Blockcipher-based MACs: beyond the birthday bound without message length. In: Takagi, T., Peyrin, T. (eds.) ASIACRYPT 2017. LNCS, vol. 10626, pp. 446–470. Springer, Cham (2017). https://doi.org/10.1007/978-3-319-70700-6_16

54. Nielsen, M.A., Chuang, I.L.: Quantum Computation and Quantum Information. Cambridge University Press (2010). https://doi.org/10.1017/CBO9780511976667. ISBN 9781107002173

55. NIST: Submission requirements and evaluation criteria for the post-quantum cryptography standardization process (2016). https://csrc.nist.gov/CSRC/media/Projects/Post-Quantum-Cryptography/documents/call-for-proposals-final-dec-2016.pdf

56. Rogaway, P.: Efficient instantiations of tweakable blockciphers and refinements to modes OCB and PMAC. In: Lee, P.J. (ed.) ASIACRYPT 2004. LNCS, vol. 3329, pp. 16–31. Springer, Heidelberg (2004). https://doi.org/10.1007/978-3-540-30539-2_2

57. Santoli, T., Schaffner, C.: Using Simon's algorithm to attack symmetric-key cryptographic primitives. Quant. Inf. Comput. **17**(1 & 2), 65–78 (2017)

58. Shor, P.W.: Algorithms for quantum computation: discrete logarithms and factoring. In: FOCS, pp. 124–134. IEEE Computer Society (1994)

59. Simon, D.R.: On the power of quantum computation. SIAM J. Comput. **26**(5), 1474–1483 (1997)

60. Song, F., Yun, A.: Quantum security of NMAC and related constructions. In: Katz, J., Shacham, H. (eds.) CRYPTO 2017. LNCS, vol. 10402, pp. 283–309. Springer, Cham (2017). https://doi.org/10.1007/978-3-319-63715-0_10

61. Yasuda, K.: The sum of CBC MACs is a secure PRF. In: Pieprzyk, J. (ed.) CT-RSA 2010. LNCS, vol. 5985, pp. 366–381. Springer, Heidelberg (2010). https://doi.org/10.1007/978-3-642-11925-5_25

62. Zhang, L., Wu, W., Sui, H., Wang, P.: 3kf9: enhancing 3GPP-MAC beyond the birthday bound. In: Wang, X., Sako, K. (eds.) ASIACRYPT 2012. LNCS, vol. 7658, pp. 296–312. Springer, Heidelberg (2012). https://doi.org/10.1007/978-3-642-34961-4_19

Generic Framework for Key-Guessing Improvements

Marek Broll[1]($\boxtimes$), Federico Canale[1]($\boxtimes$), Antonio Flórez-Gutiérrez[2]($\boxtimes$),
Gregor Leander[1]($\boxtimes$), and María Naya-Plasencia[2]($\boxtimes$)

[1] Horst Görtz Institute for IT Security, Ruhr University Bochum, Bochum, Germany
{marek.broll,federico.canale,gregor.leander}@rub.de
[2] Inria, Paris, France
{antonio.florez-gutierrez,maria.naya_plasencia}@inria.fr

Abstract. We propose a general technique to improve the key-guessing step of several attacks on block ciphers. This is achieved by defining and studying some new properties of the associated S-boxes and by representing them as a special type of decision trees that are crucial for finding fine-grained guessing strategies for various attack vectors. We have proposed and implemented the algorithm that efficiently finds such trees, and use it for providing several applications of this approach, which include the best known attacks on NOEKEON, GIFT, and RECTANGLE.

Keywords: Cryptanalysis · S-box · Key-guessing · Affine decision trees

1 Introduction

Literally *all* sensitive data needs to be encrypted, and it is vital to have trustworthy symmetric primitives. The only way to build confidence in these primitives is through a continuous effort to evaluate their security and constantly update their security margin: this is the role of cryptanalysis.

Several different attack families against symmetric ciphers exist. The most important are differential and linear cryptanalysis [3,16,17] and their variants. While the boundary is often blurry (see e.g. [11]), many attacks can usually be separated into two parts: a distinguisher and a key-recovery part.

A distinguisher highlights some non-random behaviour in a part of a cipher, like linear correlation between several states or an output difference occurring unusually often when a specific input difference is introduced.

The key-recovery part usually involves the rounds before and after the distinguisher, and makes use of this non-random behaviour to (partially) recover the secret key. Fundamentally, the attacker guesses some key information from this outer part, and checks if the non-random behaviour occurs with the distinguisher. If the data behaves as expected, the key guess is likely correct. Our work focuses on the key-recovery step.

© International Association for Cryptologic Research 2021
M. Tibouchi and H. Wang (Eds.): ASIACRYPT 2021, LNCS 13090, pp. 453–483, 2021.
https://doi.org/10.1007/978-3-030-92062-3_16

Various commonly-used ideas to improve the efficiency of this part have been proposed, such as reducing the data complexity by using plaintext structures (see e.g. [15] for applications to ARX), improved statistical tools (e.g. [4]), and the use of the Fast Fourier Transform (FFT) in linear cryptanalysis ([9] and the improved [13]).

For SPN ciphers, the key-guessing is often done in a word-oriented fashion in which key-words are guessed in alignment with the S-box layer. The S-box is treated like a black box, and a full key-word is guessed when the attacker needs some information about its output. There are examples of partial improvements to the key-guessing in some specific attacks, albeit never in a generic manner. Some decompose the S-box to either filter wrong pairs (e.g. [12]), avoid unnecessary key guesses [6], or improve filtering in meet-in-the-middle attacks [8].

A comprehensive and focused study of S-box properties with respect to optimal key-guessing strategies is nevertheless missing.

Our Contribution

In this paper we provide this overdue analysis by introducing a unified and generic framework to optimize the key-recovery part of various attacks. Inspired particularly by the techniques used in [6], we aim to reduce the number of key bits guessing to the strict minimum for which the output information is still determined, avoiding unnecessary guesses of full-key words. To this end, we first transform an S-box (or one of its component functions) into a binary decision tree. We then show that all the important optimizations naturally arise as properties of this tree. We find that one of the most important properties is the number of leaves. Consequently, finding tree representations with a minimal number of leaves directly optimizes the attacks.

While their application to cryptanalysis is new, (parity) decision trees for boolean functions themselves are not. For an overview of the theory see [18]. The (asymptotic) size (which we call numLeaves) and approximation of parity decision trees (i.e. decision trees with arbitrary instead of unit vector labels) is subject to research (e.g. [20]). Here, a link to linear structures in the case of vectorial boolean functions is examined.

We first describe this tree representation and discuss some basic properties in Sect. 2. In particular, we show that optimizing the number of leaves automatically considers linear structures, a simple and well-known property. Moreover, we show that equivalence conditions for functions to lead to isomorphic trees, which allows us to classify functions with respect to their optimal trees. In addition, this provides new criteria for choosing good S-boxes with better resistance against attacks which exploit our representation explicitly or implicitly. We also provide a simple yet efficient algorithm which computes an optimal tree for reasonable S-box sizes ($n < 8$), which has been necessary for the applications. An implementation is provided as supplementary material online[1].

---

[1] https://github.com/rub-hgi/ConditionsLib

Before giving several specific application examples, we explain how using trees can improve various generic attack families in a broader sense in Sect. 3.

Concrete applications are detailed in the following sections. In Sect. 4 we explain how to optimize linear attacks by giving the current best attack on NOEKEON [10]. We then focus on differential attacks. We improve the best attack on GIFT that was known at the time of writing ([14], see Sect. 5), a related-key rectangle attack, and decrease its time complexity by a factor of more than 2^{20} and its data complexity by a factor of 2. However, we are confident that an improvement to the new best attack on GIFT [21] is also possible thanks to our techniques. We also attack the cipher RECTANGLE (see Sect. 6) and improve the time complexity of the best attack by a factor larger than 2^{14}. Finally, we explain how meet-in-the-middle or more precisely sieve-in-the-middle attacks can also benefit from our improvements on the example of PRESENT [5] in the extended version of the paper [7]. Our attack provides just a small improvement factor, but shows how our technique can be applied. Our on PRESENT concrete findings are summarized in Table 1.

We expect that follow-up work will use our results for building even better attacks, including attacks on more rounds. Our main aim was to provide applications that underline the usefulness of the framework. For covering more rounds, one should design a whole new attack using our ideas. In particular, we expect that a 19 round attack on RECTANGLE is within reach, due to the fact that the already large margin for the key-guessing complexity can be further improved if one aims at optimization (and not simplicity, as we do in the present work). Furthermore, note that there is nothing fundamental that prevents the framework from being applied to larger S-boxes.

Table 1. Overview of the Applications. The improvements on NOEKEON and RECTANGLE provide the new best known attacks on these ciphers. [14] was the best attack on GIFT at the time of writing. An attack on 26-round GIFT was presented in [21].

Cipher (Block, Key)	Rnds	Type	(Time, Data)-Previous	This paper	Best
NOEKEON-128-128	12	linear	$(2^{124}, 2^{124})$ [10]	$(2^{122.14}, 2^{119})$	yes
GIFT-64-128	25	RK rectangle	$(2^{120.92}, 2^{63.78})$ [14]	$(2^{99.18}, 2^{62.73})$	no
RECTANGLE -64-80	18	differential	$(2^{78.88}, 2^{64})$ [22]	$(2^{64}, 2^{64})$	yes
PRESENT-64-80	8	sieve-in-the-middle	$(2^{73.42}, 2^{6})$ [8]	$(2^{72.91}, 2^{6})$	no

2   Representing Functions as Affine Decision Trees and Applications in Cryptanalysis

In this section, we develop our new, condition-centered representation of S-boxes that is motivated by trying to compute (parts of) the output given only partial information on the inputs.

We denote by $\mathbb{F}_2$ the field with two elements, i.e. a bit, and by $\mathbb{F}_2^n$ the n-dimensional vector space over it. For x, y in $\mathbb{F}_2^n$ we denote the canonical inner product $\sum_i x_i y_i$ by $\langle x, y \rangle$.

An S-box, or more generally, a part of a cipher, is a function

$$S : \mathbb{F}_2^n \to \mathbb{F}_2^m.$$

Such functions are either represented by a simple look-up table or its algebraic normal form.

However, for our purpose of improving the key-recovery part of several attacks, the representation as a look-up table or as a polynomial is not very suitable, as they hide possible short-cuts and finding an optimal solution with them often requires exhaustively trying all the possible restrictions. The basic property we are going to use in all the attacks is that we can deduce information about (parts of) the output even when only partial information on the input is available.

As a first example we consider the NOEKEON S-box S

x	0	1	2	3	4	5	6	7	8	9	a	b	c	d	e	f
$S(x)$	7	a	2	c	4	8	f	0	5	9	1	e	3	d	b	6

In particular, consider the function $f(x)$ that outputs the most significant bit of $S(x)$, which is given as the following look-up table.

x_0	0	1	0	1	0	1	0	1	0	1	0	1	0	1	0	1
x_1	0	0	1	1	0	0	1	1	0	0	1	1	0	0	1	1
x_2	0	0	0	0	1	1	1	1	0	0	0	0	1	1	1	1
x_3	0	0	0	0	0	0	0	0	1	1	1	1	1	1	1	1
$f(x)$	0	1	0	1	0	1	1	0	0	1	0	1	0	1	1	0

A closer look at the table above reveals that the output of f actually does not depend on x_3 at all. This corresponds to the well-known property of a linear structure of a Boolean function and in this example is given by the fact that

$$f(x) + f(x + (0,0,0,1)) = 0 \quad \forall x.$$

This is a first, trivial but very helpful example of the property we are looking for. However, more can be said. To cite another example, in the case of $x_1 = 0$ and $x_0 = 0$ we get $f(x) = 0$ independent of the value of x_2. If $x_1 = 0$ and $x_0 = 1$ we get $f(x) = 1$. In case $x_1 = 1$ knowing a single bit in addition will not be sufficient, however one additional bit of information actually is. Namely if $x_1 = 1$ and $x_0 + x_2 = 0$ we get $f(x) = 0$. Finally, if $x_1 = 1$ and $x_0 + x_2 = 1$, we get $f(x) = 1$.

Now, instead of collecting these conditions in terms of equations, a better way is to present them in terms of graphs which we will define formally below. The example given here translates into the graph shown in Fig. 1. Starting with the root, each node is labeled with a vector corresponding to a linear combination of the inputs. Depending on the value of this linear combination of the inputs, the left or right edge is taken until one ends up in a leaf. Leaves are labeled with the value the function takes on all the inputs fulfilling the conditions corresponding to the path leading there.

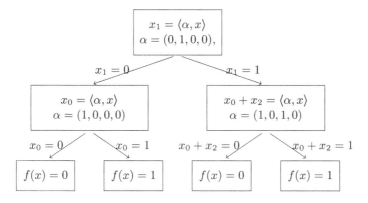

Fig. 1. Graph representation of the conditions for f

Thus, the graph is a representation of the function f that actually captures exactly the conditions we wanted. It can also be thought of as a way of implementing the function. Clearly given a function, the representation of the graph is not unique. Indeed, the graph in Fig. 2 is a graph for the same function, but intuitively (and also formally as we will see later) less helpful. Indeed, except x_3, which we know is not relevant, in order to compute the output, every input bit has to be known in this representation.

Considering $x + k$ as input to f, in order to evaluate the function for some fixed x, we have to obtain (usually by guessing all the possible values) enough bits of k to calculate $\langle \alpha, x+k \rangle$ for inner nodes on the path which is taken during the evaluation of $f(x + k)$.

In the end, for each fixed x, we find that we must consider a different guess of k for each possible evaluation path through the graph, or that is, one guess for each leaf of the tree. Since the number of leaves is at most equal to 2^n (which is the "naïve" number of guesses), we can often reduce the time complexity of the attack, as we will explain below when optimizing the tree towards a minimal number of leaves.

In the remaining part of this section, we explain how to find good graphs automatically, how those related to the linear structures, and how equivalent functions lead to equivalent graphs.

All the guessing strategies we consider can be thought of as guessing one bit at a time and depending on the result of the guess continue on the left branch (in case we guess zero) or in the right branch (in case we guess one).

We assume that, along one path from the source to a leaf, all node labels (the α-values) are independent. Then, at each stage, the linear combination of inputs splits the space into equal parts, a subspace and its complement. Both can be identified with a space again, and this is the space in the next level. The advantage is that this view is very simple, general and recursive.

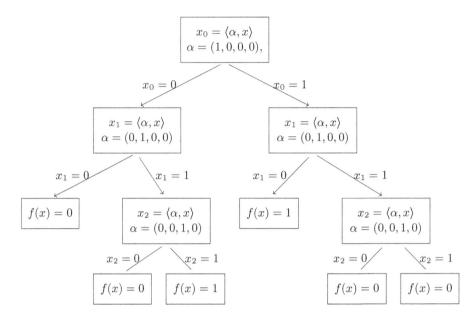

Fig. 2. Alternative Graph representation of the conditions for f

2.1 Formalization

Instead of starting with a function and building a tree in the above manner, it is more convenient to directly start with a tree and discuss the function it corresponds to afterwards. The trees we consider are binary trees, where each node either has two or no children. More formally, we consider trees defined as follows.

Definition 1 (Affine Decision Tree). *An (n,m)-affine decision tree is a regular and binary tree where each node v has a label $v.label$. A node without children is called a* leaf *and has labels in $\mathbb{F}_2^m$. A node v which is not a leaf is called an* inner node *and has labels in $\mathbb{F}_2^n$. Its children are denoted by $v.left$ and $v.right$.*

We identify a tree and its root whenever it simplifies the formulation. For a tree r, we also write $v \in r$ when v is a node of r.

In Fig. 1 the labels for the inner nodes are denoted with α and the nodes for the leafs correspond to the value the function takes on the corresponding inputs.

These trees correspond to maps (generalizing the example above) as follows. We will take the liberty to use the same notation for both the tree and the corresponding map.

Definition 2. *Given an (n,m)-affine decision tree r we can construct an associated map $r : \mathbb{F}_2^n \to \mathbb{F}_2^m$. For $x \in \mathbb{F}_2^n$ we define $r(x)$, the value calculated by an affine decision tree r, recursively:*

1. *If r is a leaf, $r(x) = r.label$.*
2. *If r is an inner node and $\langle r.label, x \rangle = 0$, $r(x) = r.left(x)$.*
3. *If r is an inner node and $\langle r.label, x \rangle = 1$, $r(x) = r.right(x)$.*

Given $f \colon \mathbb{F}_2^n \to \mathbb{F}_2^m$, if $r(x) = f(x)$ for all x, we say that r is a tree for f.

It is clear that for any given function, there can be many possible trees, again see Figs. 1 and 2. However, for the applications considered later, we are interested in trees which lead to a small overhead on attack complexity. In our applications this is mostly achieved for trees with a low number of leaves, which we denote by

$$\mathrm{numLeaves}(r) = \text{ Number of leaves of } r$$

for a tree r.

To give an example, Fig. 1 corresponds to a tree r_1 with $\mathrm{numLeaves}(r_1) = 4$, while Figure 2, implementing the same function, corresponds to a tree r_2 with $\mathrm{numLeaves}(r_2) = 6$.

Especially for linear cryptanalysis, besides the number of leaves, the union of all inner labels $r.label$ that have to be evaluated as $\langle r.label, x \rangle$ when evaluating the function r on all possible inputs is of interest. This is what we call the *actual linear domain* and is formally defined in the next definition.

Definition 3 (domsize, **Actual Linear Domain**). *The* actual linear domain *of r is the space spanned by all inner node labels:*

$$\mathrm{Dom}(r) = \mathrm{span}\{n.label. \; n \text{ is an inner node of } r\}.$$

We call its dimension domsize(r).

In the graph r_1 from Figure 1 the actual linear domain is given by

$$\mathrm{Dom}(r_1) = \mathrm{span}\left\{(1,0,0,0), (0,1,0,0), (1,0,1,0)\right\},$$

which corresponds to all vectors x of the form $x = (*, *, *, 0)$. The actual linear domain of the graph r_2 in Fig. 2 is exactly the same, even though the concrete labels are different. In both cases we get

$$\mathrm{domsize}(r_1) = \mathrm{domsize}(r_2) = 3.$$

For a fixed function, we are interested in the optimal tree with respect to the number of leaves and with respect to the actual linear domain. For a given function $f \colon \mathbb{F}_2^n \to \mathbb{F}_2^m$ we denote the minimal number of leaves of all trees for f by $\mathrm{minLeaves}(f)$. That is

$$\mathrm{minLeaves}(f) = \min_{r : \forall x. r(x) = f(x)} \mathrm{numLeaves}(r).$$

A tree r for f taking on this minimum is called $\mathrm{numLeaves}$-*minimal*.

Similarly, we call the minimal actual linear domain of all trees for f the *optimal actual linear domain size* of f, denoted by domopt(f). More formally,

$$\text{domopt}(f) = \min_{r:\forall x.r(x)=f(x)} \text{domsize}(r).$$

Again, a tree r for f taking on this minimum is called domsize-*minimal*.

We are interested in finding trees which optimise either parameter depending on the application. Luckily, any tree that is optimal with respect to the number of leaves is also optimal with respect to the actual linear domain, as we show now.

Connection Between Linear Structures and Dom(r). In order to see this, it is helpful to have a closer look at all the values $x \in \mathbb{F}_2^n$ that end up at the same leaf N in the tree in the evaluation of $r(x)$. As the evaluation of r for a given input x consists of computing a sequence of inner products $\langle r.label, x \rangle$ along the path from the root to a leaf, the exact values x that end up in the same leaf are characterised by the values of those inner products.

For a node N of a tree r, let us denote by $D(N)$ the set of all labels on the path from the root to that node, excluding N itself.

$$D(N) := \text{span}\{v.label \colon v \text{ is on the path leading from } r \text{ to } N, v \neq N\}$$

Furthermore, again for a given node N we denote by $N.space$ the set of all inputs $x \in \mathbb{F}_2^n$ such that the evaluation path of $r(x)$ contains N.

If N is a node, then $D(N)$ corresponds to the set of inner products which have been evaluated to reach it, while $N.space$ corresponds to the set of inputs which end up in that leaf during the evaluation of $r(x)$. So $N.space$ is an affine subspace of the form

$$N.space = V(N) + a(N),$$

where $V(N) \subseteq \mathbb{F}_2^n$ is a vector subspace and $a(N) \in \mathbb{F}_2^n$ is a translation. In fact, $V(N)$ consists of all vectors v such that $\langle r.label, v \rangle = 0$, for $r.label \in D(N)$. Thus, $V(N)$ is the dual space of the span of $D(N)$:

$$V(N) = D(N)^{\perp}.$$

For example, the left-most leaf N of the tree in Fig. 1 is reached for all elements of $N.space = D(N)^{\perp} + a(N) = \text{span}\{(0,1,0,0),(1,0,0,0)\}^{\perp} + 0 = \text{span}\{(0,0,1,0),(0,0,0,1)\}$. The underlying subspace $V(N)$ of the two leaves of the right subtree is span $\{(1,0,1,0),(0,0,0,1)\}$.

From these considerations we arrive at another interretation of the actual linear domain:

Lemma 1.

$$\text{Dom}(r)^{\perp} = \bigcap_{N \in r} V(N) = \bigcap_{\substack{N \in r \\ N \text{ is a leaf}}} V(N)$$

Proof. We rewrite $\mathrm{Dom}(r)$ in term of the grouped labels $D(N)$:

$$\mathrm{Dom}(r) = \mathrm{span}\left(\bigcup_{N \in r} D(N)\right) = \sum_{N \in r} \mathrm{span}(D(N)),$$

and considering the dual spaces we get

$$\mathrm{Dom}(r)^{\perp} = \bigcap_{N \in r} \mathrm{span}(D(N))^{\perp} = \bigcap_{N \in r} D(N)^{\perp} = \bigcap_{N \in r} V(N).$$

Since $D(N_2) \subseteq D(N_1)$ whenever N_2 is a descendant of N_1, we deduce that $V(L) \subseteq V(N)$ if L is a leaf and N is one of its ancestors. This means that we can restrict the intersection to just the leaves of the tree. □

The domain of the tree in Fig. 1 has already been given, its orthogonal complement is $\mathrm{span}\{(0,0,0,1)\}$. The intersection of the two $V(N)$ occurring in this tree is the same, $\mathrm{span}\{(0,0,1,0),(0,0,0,1)\} \cap \mathrm{span}\{(1,0,1,0),(0,0,0,1)\}$.

Since $\mathrm{Dom}(r)$ consists of all the inner products which may need to be evaluated, inner products v that are not contained in $\mathrm{Dom}(r)$ are never used when computing $r(x)$, and the value of $\langle v, x \rangle$ does not influence the image $r(x)$ for any x. This is a property which resembles the notion of linear structures. Linear structures, see e.g. [12][2], can be thought of as truncated differentials with probability one. More formally, they are defined as follows:

Definition 4 (Linear Structures). *The set of* 0*-linear structures of a function* $f \colon \mathbb{F}_2^n \to \mathbb{F}_2^m$ *is defined as*

$$\mathrm{LS}_0 = \{\alpha : \forall x \in \mathbb{F}_2^n, \ f(x) + f(x + \alpha) = 0\}.$$

It can be easily shown that LS_0 is in fact a vector subspace of $\mathbb{F}_2^n$.

To understand the connection with $\mathrm{Dom}(r)$, consider $\alpha \in \mathrm{Dom}(r)^{\perp}$ and two inputs $x, y \in \mathbb{F}_2^n$ which differ by α, that is, $x + y = \alpha$. Taking Lemma 1 into account, this implies that $x + y \in \bigcap_{N \in r} V(N)$ and thus x and y follow the same evaluation path and map to the same image, $r(x) = r(x + \alpha)$. Thus α is a 0-linear structure of r, and we conclude that

Lemma 2. *For any affine decision tree* r *we have*

$$\mathrm{Dom}(r)^{\perp} \subseteq \mathrm{LS}_0$$

We note that given a funtion f, the space LS_0 is independent of the tree r we choose, and it can be computed directly from f. This allows to efficiently bound the optimal actual linear domain size $\mathrm{domopt}(f)$ of any function simply by computing the dimension of its 0-linear structures.

---

[2] We use a slightly different definition of linear structures for vectorial Boolean functions which suits our purpose better than the original.

Theorem 1. *Let $f : \mathbb{F}_2^n \to \mathbb{F}_2^m$ be a given map and r be an $(n,m)-$affine decision tree for f which is optimal with respect to* numLeaves. *It holds that*

$$\mathrm{LS}_0(f) = \mathrm{Dom}(r)^\perp$$

and consequently

$$\mathrm{domopt}(f) = n - \dim(\mathrm{LS}_0(f)) = \mathrm{domsize}(r).$$

For our purposes, this has two important consequences: (i) any tree that is optimal with respect to the number of leaves is actually optimal with respect to the actual domain size, too, and (ii) computing the 0-linear structures of a target function first allows to compute the optimal tree on the function modulo its 0-linear structures, which provides a computationally less costly reduced input space.

The intuition for proving Theorem 1 is that for any tree evaluations of inner products $\langle \alpha, x \rangle$ can be removed when they correspond to 0-linear structures. We give a formal proof of Theorem 1 in the extended version of the paper [7].

Invariance Under Transformations of the Input and Output. The most important cryptographic criteria, e.g. the algebraic degree, the maximal probability for differential transitions, or the maximal absolute linear correlations, are invariant under affine equivalence. That is to say that, given a function $f : \mathbb{F}_2^n \to \mathbb{F}_2^m$ and two affine permutations $A : \mathbb{F}_2^n \to F_2^n$ and $B : \mathbb{F}_2^m \to \mathbb{F}_2^m$ the function $B \circ f \circ A$ has the same values for these criteria. This is of importance as it in particular (i) allows to classify S-boxes with respect to these criteria and (ii) gives larger freedom to the designer of a new primitive.

We next argue that the optimal number of leaves and the optimal actual linear domain size are invariant under an even larger notion of equivalence.

For this, let $f : \mathbb{F}_2^n \to \mathbb{F}_2^m$ be a function and let r be a tree for f. Consider an arbitrary, not necessarily affine, permutation $\pi : \mathbb{F}_2^m \to \mathbb{F}_2^m$. Replacing the labels of the leafs of r by their images under π, we automatically get a tree for $\pi \circ f$ directly. Moreover, the structure of the tree, and thus the number of leaves, is not affected by this modification. This implies that numLeaves$(B \circ f) = $ numLeaves(f) for any function f and any permutation B.

Next, consider an affine permutation $A : \mathbb{F}_2^n \to \mathbb{F}_2^n$. In order to change r, the tree for f, into a tree for $f \circ A$ two changes are necessary. First, the constant part of A will (potentially) swap the children of a node. Second, the linear part will be taken care of by changing the labels of all inner nodes of the tree (replacing a label α by $A^t \alpha$ in case A is linear). These observations, which are made more precise in the extended version of the paper [7], are summarized in the following.

Theorem 2. *Let r be a tree for a function $f : \mathbb{F}_2^n \to \mathbb{F}_2^m$. Let $A : \mathbb{F}_2^n \to \mathbb{F}_2^n$ be an affine permutation, and $\pi : \mathbb{F}_2^m \to \mathbb{F}_2^m$ be a permutation. It holds that*

$$\mathrm{minLeaves}(f) = \mathrm{minLeaves}(\pi \circ f \circ A)$$

and

$$\mathrm{domopt}(f) = \mathrm{domopt}(\pi \circ f \circ A)$$

We give a formal proof in the extended version of the paper [7].

Remark 1. Note that besides domopt and minLeaves any other criteria computed from the trees that is invariant under graph-isomorphism, behaves as described in Theorem 2. Examples that might be of interest include but are not limited to the number of bits used averaged over all inputs, maximal depth of the tree, and the number of leaves of a certain depth.

2.2   Computing Trees

In this part, we discuss the algorithmic aspects of computing (optimal) trees for a given function $f\colon \mathbb{F}_2^n \to \mathbb{F}_2^m$. Conceptually, it is easy to compute all possible trees recursively by choosing a root label $r.label = \alpha$ and then applying the algorithm recursively to $f|_{\langle \alpha,x \rangle=0}$ and $f|_{\langle \alpha,x \rangle=1}$ until these functions become constant. As we are mainly interested in optimal trees, and in order to (significantly) decrease the run time of the algorithm, several improvements are helpful. Those improvements basically avoid to search for, in a sense, "equivalent" trees and use early abort strategies when searching for a tree with a minimal number of leaves.

Algorithm 1 ListTrees(f, V, W)

Require: $f : \mathbb{F}_2^n \to \mathbb{F}_2^m$
 1: Affine subspaces $V, W \subset \mathbb{F}_2^n$, $V = U + c \subseteq W = Z + c$, where U, Z are subspaces
    and c is a translation in $\mathbb{F}_2^n$
 2: For the initial call we set $V = W = \mathbb{F}_2^n$
Ensure: A list of trees for $f|_V$.
 3: Initialize an empty list L of all trees (generated) for $f|_V$.
 4: **if** f is constant on V **then**
 5:     Add leaf r with label $f(c)$ to L.
 6:     **return** L.
 7: **end if**
 8: Calculate P such that $P \oplus U^\perp = Z$.
 9: **for all** $\alpha \in P \setminus \{0\}$ **do**
10:     $U_0 := \{x \in U : \langle \alpha, x \rangle = 0\}$.
11:     Choose $c' \in U$ such that $\langle c', \alpha \rangle = 1$.   ▷ Exists due to the choice of P.
12:     $b = \langle c, \alpha \rangle$.   ▷ Translating U_0 into V can change the value of $\langle \alpha, \cdot \rangle$.
13:     $V_b := U_0 + c$, $V_{1-b} := U_0 + c' + c$.
14:     Initialize a tree with root r and $r.label = \alpha$.
15:     **for all** $(r.left, r.right) \in \text{ListTrees}(f, V_0, V) \times \text{ListTrees}(f, V_1, V)$ **do**
16:         Add a copy of r to L.
17:     **end for**
18: **end for**
19: **return** L

Improvements. We already stated that, when building a subtree we can omit root labels which are linear combinations of the labels on the path leading to this subtree. That is, in all trees we consider, the labels along a path are linearly independent. Moreover, each label can be chosen up to the space spanned by the labels aready used, i.e. a label for a node N can basically be chosen in $\mathbb{F}_2^n/D(N)$. Algorithmically, this is done by running through a fixed complement space of $D(N)$. A pseudocode for the algorithm including this optimization is given in *Algorithm 1*.

A numLeaves-minimal tree can have at most 2^{n-d} leaves in a subtree of depth d as otherwise it would involve redundant bits of information on a path. This can be used to cut some recursive calls and reduce the run time of the algorithm.

For functions with linear structures in the sense of Definition 4 we can also ignore choices of sister nodes which only differ by a linear structure due to Theorem 1. This is equivalent to finding trees for the function $g \colon \mathbb{F}_2^n/\mathrm{LS}_0 \to \mathbb{F}_2^m$ with $g(x + \mathrm{LS}_0) = f(x)$. This can be done not only for the initial function but also for each sub-tree recursively.

Using these kinds of optimizations we could analyze individual functions up to dimension 7 in a reasonable amount of time. For our experiments we used a standard PC with a 2.3-GHz CPU. For dimension 4 it is usually possible to enumerate all trees using Algorithm 1 without optimizing the costs and filter afterwards. For k-bit Boolean functions chosen uniformly at random computing the optimal tree on a single core takes on average roughly 4 ms for $k = 4$, 190 ms for $k = 5$ and 21 s for $k = 6$. For $k = 7$ we could not test enough to get a reliable run-time estimate, but the program usually takes somewhere around 1.7 h. For $k = 8$ we estimate an average running time of less than three weeks on the above machine.

Analyzing Balanced Boolean Functions in Dimension up to 5. When considering single components of S-boxes, only balanced Boolean functions are of interest. Using Theorem 2 together with Algorithm 1 allows us to classify all possible values for the optimal number of leaves at least for all balanced Boolean functions in small dimensions.

3   Application to Generic Attack Families

The purpose of this section is to illustrate the time complexity improvements which can be obtained by applying the tree descriptions of boolean functions to some of the most widely-used attack families on SPN block ciphers.

The most natural case directly depends on minLeaves(S) which will become the cost of performing the guess, compared to 2^n. This natural case directly applies to linear attacks with no FFT acceleration and to differential attacks with more than one round covered by the key-guessing part, when some values coming from non-active S-boxes are needed after the first round in order to compute the differential transitions of the next rounds, automatically reducing the key-guessing complexity of the latter.

3.1   The Case of Linear Cryptanalysis with FFT Acceleration

Although our generalised approach can often reduce the time complexity of most key-recovery attack families, sometimes other accelerations may provide better results, and a method must be picked. This is the case of linear cryptanalysis when combined with the fairly common FFT acceleration of [9].

Consider a linear attack using a single approximation. The "naïve" implementation consists of counting for how many of the N plaintexts the approximation is zero for each of the 2^k guesses of the key (where k is the number of bits) by processing each combination individually. The time complexity is $O\left(N2^k\right)$.

We now construct a tree for the S-box layer with minLeaves $\leq 2^k$ (this automatically considers things like inactive S-boxes). From each plaintext, we can extract all the information from minLeaves key guesses. However, each leaf is associated to different key guesses depending on the value of the same bits in the plaintext. We thus have to keep a separate set of minLeaves key guess counters for each of these plaintext groupings. When all the data has been processed, we can filter promising partial key guesses (those which exhibit high correlation for part of the plaintexts) and separate them into full guesses until the complete guess with the highest counter can be located. This means we can reduce the time complexity of this kind of attack to $O\left(N \cdot \text{minLeaves}\right)$.

When the data complexity is large, we first distill the data into a table according to the bits which interact with the key (time complexity $O(N)$) and then guess all possible values of the key for each entry (time complexity $O\left(2^{2k}\right)$), as was first shown in [16]. If we apply guessing trees on the S-boxes, we find that for each of the minLeaves guesses of the key, we still have to look up 2^k entries of the table. The distillation table must work for every key guess, so its size can only be reduced to 2^{domopt}. The best time complexity reduction we can achieve on this attack algorithm is thus $O(N) + O\left(\text{minLeaves} \cdot 2^{\text{domopt}}\right)$.

Another common improvement to linear cryptanalysis makes use of the Fast Fourier Transform, and was introduced in [9]. By using the FFT in order to process the distilled data more quickly, the time complexity of the analysis phase can be reduced to $O\left(k2^k\right)$. Since the size of the distilled table cannot be reduced by using decision trees, we can only reduce this complexity to $O\left(\text{domopt}2^{\text{domopt}}\right)$.

The best approach here is to compute minLeaves and domopt for each S-box and find an optimal trade-off between these approaches (as we can use different techniques in each S-box), as we show with an example in the extended version of the paper [7].

3.2   Applications to Differential Cryptanalysis

Intuitively, differential cryptanalysis improvements seem naturally more complex than linear ones, as in addition to possibly determining some values we need to determine some differences, and depending on the cases, several trees should be studied. This also implies that the gain can be quite significant.

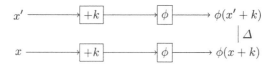

Fig. 3. Finding good pairs over one round of an iterated cipher.

Besides the case presented earlier covered by the natural case, there are other (usually coexistent) cases that often appear[3]: 1) given one plaintext x, determine another one x' that generates a certain difference Δ after the S-box ϕ along with an associated partial guessed key; 2) given pairs of plaintexts (x, x'), determine the ones that might generate a wanted difference Δ after ϕ; 3) given pairs of plaintexts (x, x'), determine the optimal partial key guess that ensures Δ after ϕ; 4) when at least two consecutive rounds are considered in the keyguessing, in any of the above cases we might need to know, in addition, the value of certain bits to verify the differential transition of further rounds; 5) when at least two consecutive rounds are considered, a key guess of a later round can be absorbed by a needed output defined by a linear equation.

We will next show how to use the S-box properties defined in the previous section to propose improvements in each of the 5 cases, while considering the example from Fig. 3 for the three first cases.

Case 1: Input Difference Not Determined. We are interested in determining x' such that $x' = \phi^{-1}(\phi(x + k) + \Delta) + k$. If we let $y = x + k$, the attacker can try to find inexpensive trees for

$$f_\Delta(y) = \phi^{-1}(\phi(y) + \Delta) = x' + k. \tag{1}$$

These trees allow the attacker to cheaply deduce bits of $x' + k$ by guessing a small amount of bits of $x + k$. Since the value of x is considered known, this is equivalent to guessing bits of k (the tree is the same for all values of x but different paths are taken for each value). Using this approach we only get information about $x' + k$ and about some bits of x', which correspond to the bits of k which were guessed.

An important limitation of using f_Δ is that some "evidently useful" relations might be missed, like for example if there is a differential $\delta \to \Delta$ through ϕ with probability 1, then $f_\Delta(y) = y + \delta$: by simply looking at the relations of f_Δ, it would seem that we need to guess all the bits of the key, but no key-guessing is necessary here since $x' = x + \delta$. In other words, decisions based on expressions of the form $\langle \gamma, (x' + k) + (x + k) \rangle$ are "key-free" and this can be incorporated into the search. A way to get trees with cost 0 is to apply the tree search algorithm to $F_\Delta(y) = f_\Delta(y) + y = x' + x$. The resulting trees provide "direct" information about x' (as x is known) and only require guessing the bits of key directly

---

[3] For the sake of simplicity, we will consider in this section that key-guessing rounds are done in the beginning, but everything can be applied similarly in the last rounds.

involved in the decision trees, as well as detecting completely free key guesses like the one described above.

Furthermore, when the key addition is shorter than the S-box size (like for GIFT), decisions on the same path involving only the same bits of the key but also some bits of the unaltered plaintext have no additional cost in the application, as the involved key bits cancel out. To deal with particular cases we simply use our algorithm to generate a list of optimal trees filtered in accordance to the individual requirements of the attack at hand, sometimes considering restricted functions. An application is described in Sect. 5 and an example can be found in the extended version of the paper [7].

Case 2: Preliminary Sieving. Filtering wrong pairs is important as it often allows to reduce the time-complexity (and the noise) in attacks. We know that (x, x') is a wrong pair if $x + x'$ is not in the image of $F_\Delta(x) = f_\Delta(x) + x$. Note that the image of F_Δ is the same as the image of $y \mapsto \phi^{-1}(y) + \phi^{-1}(y + \Delta)$ and thus exactly corresponds to the possible input differences for the given output difference Δ. This idea has already been used in differential cryptanalysis already in the beginning [3] and also more recently like for instance [19], but many recent attacks do not use this despite the ample margin of improvement, as we show for instance in our GIFT applications in Sect. 5, where using this for filtering in the output already allows to reduce the complexity of the best known attacks.

Case 3: Fixed Input Difference. Suppose that we know the value of x (which is the case for external rounds of keyguessing) and that $x' = x \oplus \delta$ for a fixed δ (this is often the case in applications, since the difference of the pair is not key dependent).

Clearly, the possible input differences δ are given by the image of $(F_\Delta)^{-1}$. However, we can say more: a pair $(x \oplus k, x \oplus k \oplus \delta)$ satisfies

$$S(x \oplus k) \oplus S(x \oplus \delta \oplus k) = \Delta \tag{2}$$

with $x = x' \oplus \delta$ if and only if $x \oplus k \in (F_\Delta)^{-1}(\delta)$. Notice that $|(F_\Delta)^{-1}(\delta)|$ is in fact the DDT with input difference δ and output difference Δ.

Let us define the function $g_\Delta^\delta : \mathbb{F}_2^n \to \mathbb{F}_2$ such that $g_\Delta^\delta(x) = 0$ if and only if $x \in (F_\Delta)^{-1}(\delta)$. Our problem has now become equivalent to computing the value of $g_\Delta^\delta(x \oplus k)$ with as little information on k as possible: indeed, the best key-guessing strategy to determine whether a pair is a good pair is the one given by the optimal tree for $g_\Delta^\delta(x \oplus k)$ and the cost of this guess is given by the number of its leaves (minLeaves).

If we use this guessing strategy for each δ, we can drastically decrease the average guessing cost for determining whether a pair is a good pair. As an example, if we wanted to find what are the good pairs for the RECTANGLE S-box and $\Delta = 2$, this technique will allow to do so with an average guessing cost of 3 for each pair, instead of the 16 when using the naïve strategy, where for each possible value of k, one would compute Eq. (2). A detailed example for the slightly more general transition ???? → 00?0 can be found in the extended version of the paper [7].

Case 4: Determining Values in Addition to Good Pairs. If we are mounting an attack with two or more consecutive rounds of key-guessing, then in the first round we do not only want to sieve the good pairs, but we also want to determine the values of one or more output bits of the plaintexts that form those pairs. To retrieve these bits in addition to the difference value we might need less bits than a whole key word.

This can be easily done by looking at the optimal tree of the output bits that we are interested in, where we fixed the first nodes based on what key bits have already been guessed to determine the output difference.

Case 5: Absorbing Next Round Guessing. We can clearly apply the same method to determine the good pairs seen in Case 3 for later rounds in a chained manner. However, we have anticipated that it is actually not always necessary to determine this value for middle rounds, contrary to the previous cases, thanks to the following approach, that we call *key absorption*.

More concretely, consider the case of a two consecutive rounds of key-guessing, where we indicate as k the round key of the first round and κ the round key of the second one. Let $(x \oplus k, x' \oplus k)$ be the pair before going through the S-box layer $\mathcal{S}$ (which is a parallel application of S to each nibble) of the first round, and $(z + \kappa, z' + \kappa)$ be the pair before going through the second S-box layer, i.e. that we want to determine whether it is good or not for this second S-box layer.

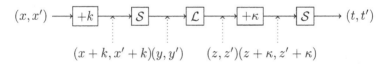

$$(x, x') \longrightarrow \boxed{+k} \longrightarrow \boxed{\mathcal{S}} \longrightarrow \boxed{\mathcal{L}} \longrightarrow \boxed{+\kappa} \longrightarrow \boxed{\mathcal{S}} \longrightarrow (t, t')$$

$$(x + k, x' + k)(y, y') \qquad (z, z')(z + \kappa, z' + \kappa)$$

Suppose for simplicity that, in order to determine the output difference of $S(z + \kappa) + S(z + \kappa)$, following the strategies explained in Cases 1 and 3, we need to determine the first bit

$$z_0 + \kappa_0 = \mathcal{L}_0(y) + \kappa_0 = \langle \alpha, y \rangle + \kappa_0,$$

of $z + \kappa$ only, where α corresponds to the first row of L. Doing a step-by-step guess would require to guess the key-bit κ_0 and compute $\langle \alpha, y \rangle$. Using the trees as explained above, we can make use of the case where $\langle \alpha, y \rangle$ depends linearly on a linear combination $\langle \gamma, k \rangle$ of key-bits of k. Instead of guessing all those key-bits we actually have to guess only their linear combination $\langle \gamma, k \rangle + \kappa_0$, i.e. only a single bit.

A detailed example can be found in the extended version of the paper [7].

3.3   Further Extensions

When several rounds are taken into account in the key-guessing parts, the best interactions between the different trees need to be considered and carefully studied, which complicates the optimization of the application a bit. The automatically generated trees with the algorithm are particularly useful in these cases, which can become quite intricate. Some example of such applications can be found in Sects. 5 and 6. In addition, the previous properties and techniques can be extended to other types of attacks, like for instance:

Differential-Linear Attacks. All the improvements of both differential and linear key-guessing parts will be applicable also to these type of attacks. See for example [6].

Rectangle and Boomerang Attacks. Using the properties of the S-box and of F_Δ for finding good pairs we can reduce the number of key guesses and total complexity. An example can be found in Sect. 5.

Meet-in-the-Middle - Sieve-in-the-Middle. Though the framework is not the same as the attacks based on distinguishers we presented in the beginning, using the S-box properties that we enounced can allow to determine more known bits in the middle and therefore have a higher sieving probability, improving the complexity. To illustrate the principle of this improvement we provide a small improved attacks on 8-round PRESENT. The time complexity of the 8-round sieve-in-the-middle attack on PRESENT from [8] can be reduced from about $2^{73.42}$ to about $2^{72.91}$ full encryptions. We elaborated the details in the extended version of the paper [7]. In short, you can use the trees to derive more bits around the middle round after guessing the key and this decreases the sieving-probability.

4   Application to NOEKEON

In this section we describe the best known linear attacks on 12-round NOEKEON. NOEKEON is a 16-round block cipher which was presented by Daemen et al. ([10]) to the Nessie competition and has a block and key length of 128 bits. A short description of NOEKEON can be found in the extended version of the paper [7]. We denote the linear transformation (including shifts) by $\widehat{\theta}$. We can consider that the key is added to the state either before or after this linear transformation by considering an equivalent key.

Iterative Linear Trails of NOEKEON. Our attacks are based on iterative two-round linear trails with correlation 2^{-14}. Since all the transformations in a NOEKEON round except for the constant and key additions are invariant under rotation, we can obtain new trails from known ones by rotation and round swapping. We have identified four families of trails, shown in Fig. 4.

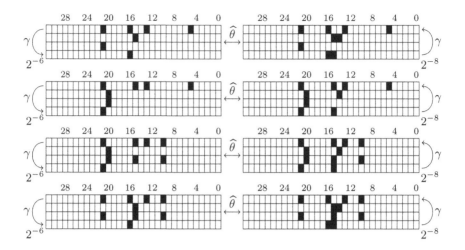

Fig. 4. Four two-round iterative linear trails of NOEKEON.

4.1 Attacks on Reduced-Round NOEKEON (Without Relations)

A 12-round linear attack on NOEKEON is sketched by its designers in [10]. An iterative trail is extended to nine rounds with correlation 2^{-62}. The trail is used as a distinguisher between rounds 1 and 9 to mount a 12-round linear attack with the following key recovery structure:

$$\underbrace{\overbrace{\theta\ \pi_1\ \gamma}^{\text{Round 0}}\ \pi_2\ \overbrace{\theta\ \pi_1\ \gamma\ \pi_2}^{\text{Round 1}}\ \dots\ \overbrace{\theta\ \pi_1\ \gamma\ \pi_2}^{\text{Round 9}}\ \overbrace{\theta\ \pi_1}^{\text{Round 10}}\ \gamma\ \pi_2\ \overbrace{\theta\ \pi_1\ \gamma\ \pi_2}^{\text{Round 11}}}$$

Key rec. — Linear approximation — Key rec. — Peelback

We guess 24 bits of the transformed keys after $\widehat{\theta}$ in round 0 and before $\widehat{\theta}$ in round 11, or 48 in total. The data complexity is around $2^{62\cdot2} = 2^{124}$ known plaintexts. If a distillation table is used as in [16], the time complexity is $2^{124} + 2^{48\cdot2} = 2^{124}$.

4.2 Attacks on Reduced-Round NOEKEON (with Relations)

We propose a 12-round attack which modifies the nine-round distinguisher (using the first iterative linear trail) which will reduce the data complexity to 2^{119}. This improvement in correlation is achieved by modifying the linear trail in two ways:

- In the first round, we remove S-box 15 from the approximation (so that the input mask is "staggered"), increasing the correlation by a factor of 2^2.
- In the last round we substitute the S-box 15 approximation from $2 \to 2$ to $2 \to b$, the correlation changes from 2^{-2} to 2^{-1}.
- We also modify the other transitions in the first and last rounds in order to reduce the number of active S-boxes in the key recovery.

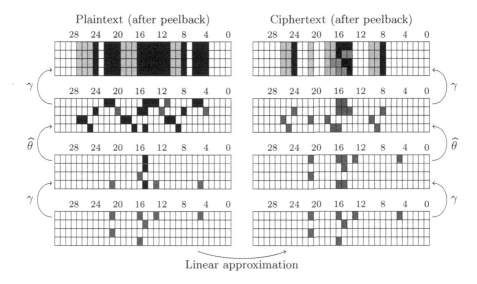

Fig. 5. Attack on 12-round NOEKEON with 2^{119} data and $2^{124.5}$ time complexity.

The correlation of the linear trail increases from 2^{-62} to 2^{-59}. However, in a key recovery attack, we would need to guess 92 key bits in the first round, 4 in the second, and 48 in the last. Even with the FFT techniques of [9] and [13], the time complexity surpasses 2^{144}. We look at the properties of the S-box:

- S-box 15 in the second round: if we only know x_0, x_1 and x_3, y_1 can still be computed with probability $1/2$. We can thus ignore input bit x_2, which doubles the data complexity (we'll reject plaintexts for which x_2 would be used) but reduces the active bits and S-boxes in the first round.
- In the first and last rounds, whenever we need y_2 or y_3 at the output of an S-box, which happens for 8 S-boxes in the first round and 7 in the last, we can reduce the key guess by one bit because domopt $= 3$.

The key guess is now 124 bits. If we apply the FFT algorithm directly, the key recovery cost would be $121 \cdot 2^{124} \simeq 2^{130.9}$ additions. It can be decreased by using Walsh transform pruning as described in [13]. There are three key bits repeated in the first and second rounds, as well as six last round key bits which can be deduced from the first round. The time complexity can thus be reduced to

$$2^3 \cdot \left(2^{121} + (121 - 9)2^{121-9}\right) \simeq 2^{124.29} \text{ additions.}$$

The details of the key recovery are specified in Fig. 5. Blue bits represent the masks of the linear approximation, while the active bits for the key recovery are black. The S-boxes where domopt $= 3$ are in green, while the red bits on the last round can be deduced from the first round key guess.

We must also compare the costs of additions and a 12-round NOEKEON encryptions. A conservative estimate[4] is at least 3840 bit operations for an encryption. An addition of $3 \cdot 128$-bit integers takes around 768 bit operations. Therefore its cost is at most one fifth of the cost of an encryption. The full time complexity is thus $2^{119} + 0.2 \cdot 2^{124.29} \simeq 2^{122.14}$ encryptions.

Overall, the new attack has a data complexity of 2^{119} and a time complexity of $2^{122.14}$, which is as far as we know the best on 12-round NOEKEON. The best attacks without relations have 2^{124} data and time complexity.

5   Application to GIFT

In this section we describe an improved version of the attack presented in [14]. This related-key rectangle attack is the known attack which reaches the most rounds of GIFT-64 (25). We apply our improved key-guessing techniques in order to improve its complexity. The section is structured as follows: We provide a brief description of GIFT, next we present the original attack, and we propose two ways of improving its complexity in the two last subsections.

5.1   Description of GIFT-64

GIFT-64 is a block cipher first introduced in [2] of block size 64 and key length 128. The 64-bit state consists of 16 4-bit nibbles which will be denoted by $b_{63} \ldots b_0 = x_{15} \| \ldots \| x_0$. Each round consists of three steps: the application of a 4-bit S-box, a bit permutation, and the addition of a 32-bit subkey.

The GIFT S-box. The GIFT S-Box is given as a lookup table.

x	0	1	2	3	4	5	6	7	8	9	a	b	c	d	e	f
$S(x)$	1	a	4	c	6	f	3	9	2	d	b	7	5	0	8	e

Bit Permutation and Key Addition. As a linear layer, GIFT uses the permutation

$$P_{64}(i) = 4 \left\lfloor \frac{i}{16} \right\rfloor + 16 \left(\left(3 \left\lfloor \frac{i \bmod 16}{4} \right\rfloor + (i \bmod 4) \right) \bmod 4 \right) + (i \bmod 4).$$

GIFT-64 uses 32-bit round subkeys which are XORed to the bit positions of the state of the form b_{4i}, b_{4i+1}, $i = 0, \ldots, 15$ (that is, the two rightmost bits of each S-box before the non-linear layer). We won't detail the keyschedule as it won't be used in the attack.

5.2   The Best Previous Attack on GIFT-64 ([14])

We now describe the attack on 25-round GIFT-64 from [14], which is a related-key rectangle attack. The 20-round boomerang distinguisher can be found in

---

[4] 128 operations per S-box layer or key addition, 64 operations per linear layer.

Table 2. ([14], Table 5) The related key rectangle attack on 25-round GIFT-64.

Label	State	#
Plaintext	???? ???? ???? ???? ???? ???? ???? ???? ???? ???? ???? ???? ???? ???? ???? ????	#0
R1 After S	??0? 1??0 01?? ?0?? 1?0? ?1?0 0??? ?0?? ??0? ???0 0??? ?0?? ??0? ???0 0??? ?0??	#1
After P, K	???? ???? ???? ???? 0000 0000 0000 0000 11?? ???? ???? ???? ???? 11?? ???? ????	#2
R2 After S	0?01 00?0 000? ?000 0000 0000 0000 0000 0100 00?0 000? ?000 ?000 0100 00?0 000?	#3
After P, K	???? 0000 ?1?? 0000 0000 0000 0000 0000 0000 0000 0000 0000 0000 0000 0000 ?1??	#4
R3 After S	1000 0000 0010 0000 0000 0000 0000 0000 0000 0000 0000 0000 0000 0000 0000 0010	#5
After P	0000 0000 0000 0000 0000 0000 0000 0000 0000 0000 0010 1010 0000 0000 0000 0000	#6
	20-round rectangle distinguisher	
R24 Before S	0000 0100 0000 0000 0000 0000 0000 0000 0001 0010 0000 0001 0000 0000 0000 0000	#7
Before P, K	0000 ???1 0000 0000 0000 0000 0000 0000 0000 ???? ???? 0000 ???? 0000 0000 0000	#8
R25 Before S	00?0 0000 00?? 0?00 0001 0000 ?00? 00?0 ?000 0000 ??00 000? 0?00 0000 0??0 ?000	#9
Before P, K	???? 0000 ???? ???? ???? 0000 ???? ???? ???? 0000 ???? ???? ???? 0000 ???? ????	#10
Ciphertext	??0? ??0? ??0? ??0? ??0? ??0? ??0? ??0? 0??? 0??? 0??? 0??? ?0?? ?0?? ?0?? ?0??	#11

[14]. We just need to know that its probability is $2^{-n}\hat{p}^2\hat{q}^2 = 2^{-64} \cdot 2^{-58.557}$. The key recovery extends the distinguisher by three rounds at the top and two rounds at the bottom and can be found in Table 2.

The authors build a key-recovery attack by applying the model from [23] to the external rounds. We start with the initial difference right before the first key addition, numbered #2 in Table 2. We have $r_b = 44$ (? bits in #2), and $m_b = 30$ (active key bits in the differential transitions of the initial rounds), $r_f = 48$ (? bits in #11), $m_f = 32$ (involved key bits in the differential transitions of the final rounds). Let $s = 2$ be the expected number of good quartets per structure. The attack proceeds as follows:

1. Build $y = \sqrt{s}\dfrac{2^{n/2-r_b}}{\hat{p}\hat{q}} = 2^{17.79}$ structures of $2^{r_b} = 2^{44}$ plaintexts. Encrypt each plaintext four times, using the four keys $K_1 = K$, $K_2 = K \oplus \Delta$, $K_3 = K \oplus \nabla$ and $K_4 = K \oplus \Delta \oplus \nabla$. For each structure j, we obtain four lists L_1^j, L_2^j, L_3^j and L_4^j, which we sort by the r_b active bits in #2.
2. We guess the m_b bits of the first two round subkeys as K_b. For each guess:
   (a) For each structure, we partially encrypt all the plaintexts of L_1^j until #6 using K_b, we add the difference α from the rectangle path, and partially decrypt back to #0 with $K_b \oplus \Delta$. We find the plaintext in L_2^j which matches it. After doing this for all the structures, we obtain a list S_1 which contains $y \cdot 2^{r_b}$ pairs with the right input difference at the distinguisher. We repeat this with lists L_3^j and L_4^j to obtain S_2. We sort S_1 and S_2 according to the non-active bits of the ciphertexts.
   (b) We go through S_1 and S_2 to find all collisions in the non-active bits of the ciphertexts. We obtain a list S_3 of $y^2 \cdot 2^{2r_b+2r_f-2n}$ candidate quartets.
   (c) For each guess of the m_f bits of key K_f, we examine each candidate in S_3 to see how many satisfy the rectangle distinguisher. As we can guess and filter S-box by S-box (detailed in [23]), the cost is negligible.
   (d) Keep the $h = 22$ values of K_f with the most conforming quartets, and find the correct one with an exhaustive search over the rest of the key.

The data complexity of the attack is $D = 4 \cdot y \cdot 2^{r_b} = 2^{63.78}$ chosen plaintexts. The time complexity is

$$T = 4 \cdot y \cdot 2^{r_b} + 2^{m_b} \left(3 \cdot y \cdot 2^{r_b} + y^2 \cdot 2^{2r_b + 2r_f - 2n} \cdot \frac{4}{25} \right) + 2^{k-h} \simeq 2^{120.92}$$

encryptions with a success probability of 74%.

5.3   S-Box Properties in the First Rounds for Better Sieving

We now explain how to gain 6 bits in time complexity and slightly improve the data complexity. The improvement is quite technical, but it can be summarized as modifying the way we build the structures using the S-box properties. The aim of organising the plaintexts in structures is for each one to produce enough rectangle quartets so that we obtain enough in total. By taking all the possible values for the active bits of the plaintext and partially encrypting forwards and backwards, each possible guess of K_b will map one entry of L_1^j to an entry of L_2^j. Each structure thus produces exactly 2^{r_b} pairs which verify the input difference α. As can be seen in the formula of y, this is discounted from the total number of structures. By exploiting the properties of the S-boxes we can reduce the size of the structures as well as the number of key bits m_b, which will allow us to reduce the time complexity, and potentially the data. For computing the new needed number of structures, y', we won't use the same formula as before, as the elements in the lists will have some particularities now, but instead will deduce the new value of y' from the wanted expected number of good quartets, S, and from carefully computing how many potentially good pairs and quartets we keep in each list with the new type of structures.

Finding S-box Properties. We applied the tree search algorithm on $F_\Delta = f_\Delta + x$ for all output differences and filtered them according to two criteria. First, we wanted only one of the two key bits to be involved. We also forced at least one subtree on level 2 not to be of full depth to reduce the search space.

Property of $f_{(0010)_2} + x$. The most interesting tree we obtained was in the case of $f_{(0010)_2} + x$, where the following relation appeared:

$$x_0 = x_3 = 0 \implies F_2(x) = 2.$$

It is useful with transitions of the form ???? → 00?0, which appear in S-boxes 1, 6 and 14 at round 2. In particular, it implies that guessing the key bit added to x_1 is not *a priori* necessary. The aim is to build smaller structures where these properties are verified, and to guess less key bits, which will in turn reduce the time complexity (the number of quartets to try stays the same, but the number of guesses decreases). From now on, we consider that all the data has bit x_3 of the input to S-boxes 1, 6 and 14 at R2 fixed to zero. Intuitively, though the number of structures available is tight, guessing less key bits implies a relaxation of the conditions, and this in turn implies proportionally more kept pairs and quartets.

Reducing the Bits in Round 3. We can also show that it is unnecessary to guess the bit k_1 in the three active S-boxes of round 3. In essence, not all the pairs in S_i will necessarily have this bit determined, which will allow us to keep more quartets while guessing less bits.

The output differences of the three S-boxes can take two values, which in turn affect the input differences of the active S-boxes in the third round (0, 13 and 15). We need to carefully compute how many pairs will verify the input difference α when guessing six less key bits than before. The transitions of S-boxes 0 and 13 in round 3 are $?1X? \rightarrow 0010$, where X depends on the transitions from round 2 where the key guess was reduced, and can thus be active or not. In S-box 15, the transition is $??X? \rightarrow 1000$.

Let us examine how we build the differential pairs from the lists L_i^j. After guessing the key bits associated to all the active S-boxes of round 2 but 1,6 and 14, we can compute, for each plaintext, the three bits x_0, x_2, x_3 at the input to S-boxes 0, 13 and 15. Choosing the value of Δx_1 for each S-box determines the other plaintext so that the pair generates α. A *priori* this should produce 2^3 different plaintexts, but we should note:

- When the input bit x_0 (which is known) of the three round 2 S-boxes 1,6,14 is 0, $F_{(0010)}$ is independent of x_1.
- In order to exploit the property efficiently, we will only consider pairs of plaintexts for which $x_0 = 0$ for S-boxes 1, 6 and 14. The property therefore always holds (as we also have $x_3 = 0$) and we can focus on the active S-boxes in the third round.
- Each element of the list L_i^j will have a different number of associated plaintexts in the other list, and each pair will have determined one additional key bit value per treated transition (so three in total). When looking at just one S-box, for the sake of simplicity, this bit will not be the same for each pair: some will exclusively determine the associated bit from round 3, which are the ones involving a difference value in round 2 or a non difference value but a 0 in the round 2 position 0 S-box, and some will determine the xor of the not-guessed key bit of round 3 with the not-guessed bit from round 2 of the related S-box: when the bit at position 0 of the S-box at round 2 takes a value one, both values 1 or 0 are possible in the output at position 1, while only one value is possible when $x_0 = 0$.

Taking this into account, we can now say that the transitions of round 3 of S-box 0 (or 13 that will behave the same way), for all the possible 2^3 values of the 3 known input bits, 3 cases will imply that no difference exists at position 1 (no matter the value of bit at position 1), 3 cases imply that there is always a difference and two cases imply that depending on the value of the bit at position 1 there will or there will not be a difference.

So for one S-box, for each input pair, we have a number of possible pairs from L_2 to be associated to L_1 that is:

$$1/8(3(1/2 \cdot 2 + 1/2 \cdot 2) + 3(1/2 \cdot 2) + 2(1/2 \cdot 2 + 1/2 \cdot 1)) = 1.5.$$

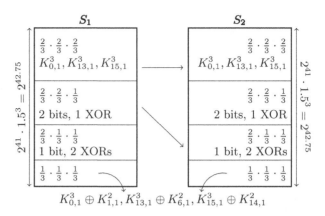

Fig. 6. Representation of the lists S1 and S2 of size $2^{42.75}$ and the distribution of their elements. In each chunk we can see: 1) the proportion of their size (the first for instance has a size of $\frac{2^3}{3^3}2^{42.75}$ as well as 2) the bits that are determined for these pairs from rounds 2 and 3. When two bits are xored, this can be seen as the bits of values $K^3_{0,1}$, $K^3_{13,1}$ and $K^2_{14,1}$ are three absorbed bits: κ_1, κ_2, and κ_3. In order to build list S_3, we consider the subset of the crossproduct of all the elements of each list that verify the output conditions and additionally that has the same value when some identical key bits of information have been determined, as otherwise it would imply and impossible quartet.

The previous amount includes pairs generated when the bit x_0 of the input of the associated S-box of round 2 is 0 or 1. As we saw in the previous facts, that will change the key bits that become implicitly determined from the formed pairs (bit from round 3, or xor of this with the bits from round 2). Let us separate the previous amount regarding this: $1.5 = 1/8(3 + 2 + 3) + 1/8(3 + 1) = 8/8 + 4/8$, which implies that in 2/3's of the cases the bit from round 3 will be determined, and 1/3 it will be the xor of bit, which have no incompatibilities between them.

Regarding the transitions of round 3 of S-box 15 we have a different distribution of the cases, but it is easy to check that we arrive at the same configuration of 2/3 and 1/3.

The lists S_1 and S_2 that we obtain this way are represented in Fig. 6. The structures we build in this new attack will have size of $2^{44-3} = 2^{41}$, as the bit at position 3 of the 3 considered S-boxes are fixed to 0. The size of S_1 and S_2 is given by $2^{41} \cdot 1.5 \cdot 1.5 \cdot 1.5 = 2^{42.75}$. We now just have to compute the exact number of compatible pairs that we can obtain from merging both lists before taking into account the output conditions. This number that we will call P will have to verify later (where $2^{y'}$ will be the new number of structures that we need to compute now):

$$y' = y2^{r_b}/\sqrt{P} = 2^{17.78+44}/\sqrt{P}.$$

By looking at the properties of the different chunks in Fig. 6 and all their possible crossproducts, that will determine how many common key bit conditions that will filter they have, we can compute P as:

$$P = 2^{42.75}[2^3/3^3 \cdot 2^{42.75}(2^3/3^3 \cdot 2^{-3} + 3 \cdot 2^2/3^3 \cdot 2^{-2} + 3 \cdot 2/3^3 \cdot 2^{-1} + 1/3^3) + 3 \cdot$$
$$2^2/3^3 \cdot 2^{42.75}(2^3/3^3 \cdot 2^{-2} + 2^2/3^3 \cdot 2^{-3} = 2 \cdot 2^2/3^3 \cdot 2^{-1} + 2/3^3 + 2^2/3^3 \cdot 2^{-2} + 1/3^3 \cdot$$
$$2^{-1}) + 3 \cdot 2/3^3 \cdot 2^{42.75}(2^3/3^3 \cdot 2^{-1} + 2^2/3^3 + 2 \cdot 2^2/3^3 \cdot 2^{-2} + 2/3^3 \cdot 2^{-3} + 2 \cdot 2/3^3 \cdot$$
$$2^{-1} + 1/3^3 \cdot 2^{-2}) + 1/3^3 \cdot 2^{42.75}(2^3/3^3 + 3 \cdot 2^2/3^3 \cdot 2^{-1} + 3 \cdot 2/3^3 \cdot 2^{-2} + 1/3^3 \cdot 2^{-3})]$$

$$\Rightarrow P = 2^{85.5} \cdot 2^{-9.509} \cdot 2^{8.09} = 2^{84.09}$$

And therefore we can compute the needed y':

$$y' = 2^{17.78+44-(84.09/2)} = 2^{19.73}.$$

We have now an improved data complexity of $D = 4 \cdot 2^{19.73} \cdot 2^{41} = 2^{62.73}$, instead of $2^{63.78}$ previously. Please note that the data limit here is $4 \cdot 2^{64}$, we are encrypting each plaintext with 4 different keys, and that the limit of y is 2^{20}.

The time complexity will become:

$$T = 4y' \cdot 2^{41} + 2^{m_b-6}(3y'2^{41} + 2^{2*19.73}2^{84.09}2^{-2(n-r_f)})2^2/25 = 2^{114.92}$$

instead of $2^{120.92}$ with the same success probability.

5.4   Using S-Box Properties in the Final Rounds for Better Sieving

We use our improved key-guessing techniques to improve the complexity of the previous attack. This idea will improve the overall complexity by reducing the size of r_f, which in turn reduces the size of S_3 and therefore of the quartets to try.

If we now have a look at the final rounds, we can see that the rightmost S-box need to verify a transition of ???? to ?000 through S^{-1}. That means that this input difference can be 0 or 8 at the end of round 24. If the difference is 0, we have 4 additional conditions when building up the quartets and we will sieve more of them, if the difference is 8, then, by looking at the image of $F_8(X_3, X_2, X_1, X_0) = S(S^{-1}(X_3, X_2, X_1, X_0) \oplus (1000)) \oplus (X_3, X_2, X_1, X_0)$, we see it can only take four values : $(3, 7, F, B)$. In total, with the zero difference is a total of 5, that leaves an additional factor of $(4+1)/16 = 2^{-1.67}$. We can do the same with the transitions ???? to 0?00 and ???? to 00?0 (that appear each two times) and add a sieving factor of $(5+1)/16 = 2^{-1.41}$ and of $(6+1)/16 = 2^{-1.19}$ respectively per transition. Transition ???? to ?010 has a factor of $(6+6-4)/16 = 2^{-1}$.

Step 2(c), that before kept $2^{91.56}$ quartets to try, was the bottleneck when multiplied by the 2^{30} complexity of guessing m_b. We will see now how this amount of quartets can be reduced:

$$2^{91.56}(2^{-1.67})^2(2^{-1.41})^4(2^{-1.19})^4(2^{-1})^2 = 2^{91.56-15.74} = 2^{75.82},$$

where the first factor corresponds to the F_8 relations, and it is squared as it has to be verified by both of the pairs that form a quartet, the second factor correspond to the relations of F_4, that appears twice and should also be squared, which gives a power of 4, and the same goes for the third factor from F_2. The fourth one that comes from the relation from transition ???? to ?010 where the non-zero difference is not an option, and needs to be squared because of the two pairs.

This $2^{75.82}$ will be the new cost of this step (multiplied by 2^{30} gives $2^{105.82}$ instead of $2^{121.56}$), as we can directly check the values from S_2 that have a difference that belongs to the image of their corresponding F_i, which means that we have reduced the complexity by a factor $2^{15.74}$. Thanks to the trees of F_i step 2(d) could become slightly smaller than 2^2, but as the gain would be very small we won't detail it here (but we point out to consider this in other scenarios where it could help).

When taking into account the factor of the computations for the attack compared to an encryption we obtain a final complexity of $2^{105.18}$ instead of $2^{120.92}$.

5.5 Combining Both

As both improvements consider independent parts of the attack, they can both be taken into account, generating a new improved time complexity of $2^{114.92-15.74} = 2^{99.18}$ and data complexity of $2^{62.73}$, improving time by a factor bigger than 2^{21}, and data by a factor of 2.

6 Application to RECTANGLE-80

In the present section, we want to improve the best attack on the updated version of the SPN cipher RECTANGLE-80 [22] which, to the best of our knowledge, is the differential attack presented by the authors of the cipher themselves in the same paper.[5]

A description of the cipher can be found in the extended version of the paper [7].

In this section (following the same framework used in [19]), we will indicate the round key i as K_i, the input of the S-box layer at round i as I_i and the output of the S-box layer of round i as O_i. This means that the output of the ShiftRow operation at round i is I_{i+1}. Similarly, we will call $\Delta I_i, \Delta O_i$ the respective differences of the state of a given a pair. We will sometimes indicate a vector of $\mathbb{F}_2^4$ as an hexadecimal number.

---

[5] A differential attack that requires less data is claimed by the authors of [1] thanks to a distinguisher that covers the same number of rounds with better probability. However, no description or time complexity of the attack was given and we could not verify it due to the large time complexity of the key-guessing phase. We believe that, with the techniques presented in this paper, it could be possible to make the attack work, but the time and memory complexity would still be much worse than the attack we present here.

Table 3. The differential attack on 18 rounds of RECTANGLE-80 with the distinguisher from [22]. The $\emptyset$ indicates an active bit with difference 0. The ? indicates an unknown difference value.

$\Delta P = \Delta I_0$	????	0000	0000	????	????	????	0000	0000	????	????	0000	0000	0000	0000	0000	0̸0̸0̸0̸
ΔO_0	?000	0000	0000	000?	01?0	?000	0000	0000	000?	0010	0000	0000	0000	0000	0000	0̸000
ΔI_1	0000	0000	0000	?0̸??	0000	0000	0000	0000	?11?	0000	0000	0000	0000	0000	0000	0000
ΔO_1	0000	0000	0000	0110	0000	0000	0000	0000	0010	0000	0000	0000	0000	0000	0000	0000
ΔI_2	0000	0000	0010	0000	0000	0000	0000	0110	0000	0000	0000	0000	0000	0000	0000	0000
14-round differential distinguisher																
ΔI_{16}	0000	0000	0000	0100	0000	0000	0000	0000	0000	0000	0000	0000	0000	0000	0010	0000
ΔO_{16}	0000	0000	0000	??11	0000	0000	0000	0000	0000	0000	0000	0000	0000	0000	????	0000
ΔI_{17}	0000	?000	0?10	0001	0000	0000	?000	0?00	0000	0000	0000	0000	0000	0?00	000?	0000
ΔO_{17}	0000	????	????	????	0000	0000	????	????	0000	0000	0000	0000	0000	????	????	0000

6.1 Description of the Attack

As already mentioned, we want to improve the best attack on the new variant of RECTANGLE-80, which is a differential attack presented by the authors themselves with time complexity of $2^{78.67}$ 18-round encryptions, data complexity of 2^{64} and memory complexity of 2^{72} key counters [22]. The bottleneck in this attack is given by the large amount of key-guessing needed in the two rounds before and after the distinguisher.

We will show here how to cover these rounds of key-guessing using the framework presented in [19] and how to reduce the complexity of the key-guessing phase by a factor of about 2^{28}, thanks to the techniques introduced in Sect. 3.2.

During the key-guessing phase, we gradually guess the necessary bits of the round key K_i nibble by nibble. We will actually simplify the guessing done to determine good pairs with respect to Case 3 of Sect. 3.2, since this is anyway going to make the key-guessing phase complexity negligible with respect to that of the data collection phase. In particular, any time we have to guess whether a pair $(x \oplus k, x \oplus \delta \oplus k)$ determines an output difference Δ through S, we will not do a gradual guess depending on the value of x using the tree of g_Δ^δ, as would be preferable. Instead, we will simply guess, whatever the value of x, the bits of k given by the inner nodes of g_Δ^δ (or, equivalently, by Dom). The guessing cost, then, will be 2^{domopt} and not numLeaves. An example of this simpler guessing strategy is given in the extended version of the paper [7].

In order for the attack to work, we need to prepare enough pairs of plaintext that can satisfy the desired input difference ΔI_2, so that at least $2^{62.83} = p^{-1}$ such pairs are available to the distinguisher starting at round 2 (see [3] for the heuristic).

To this end, we prepare a number of 2^y of data structures, each containing all possible plaintexts with a fixed value in the non-active bits in ΔI_0. Since the linear layer of RECTANGLE-80 is a permutation of the bits, it is easy to see from Table 3 that the amount of active bits in the first round is 24, i.e. the number of ?. Thanks to the properties of S, we can see that the real number of active bits is actually 23: in fact, for S-box 6 of I_0 we only need to determine the active output bit y_1 of O_0, in addition to the good pairs, and from the trees of y_1 and F_2 we see that their actual domain is generated by the vectors $1, 2$ and 8, implying that the bit at position 4 from S-box 6 of a plaintext won't affect at all the key-guessing, i.e. it is not active.

Therefore, from each data structures we can generate 2^{23} plaintexts, by letting the active bits vary through all the possible values (while keeping fixed the non-active ones) and build a maximum of 2^{45} ordered pairs. In order to determine the necessary number of structures, we see that for a fixed key guess, we expect 2^{y+22} pairs to lead to the desired input difference ΔI_2: this means that we want $y + 22 - 62.83 \geq 0$, i.e. $y = 41$.

However, by looking at the possible values that the states ΔP and ΔO_{17} can take, we can sieve the pairs to use in the key-guessing phase and keep, on average, $2^{5.71}$ pairs for each structure (see the extended version of the paper [7] for details).

Step 1 (guess of K_0 to Determine the Good Pairs of Round 0 and Retrieve Linear Relations for the Active Bits of O_0). We gradually guess nibble by nibble the necessary amount of key material to determine whether each plaintext pair is a good pair and retrieve linear relations that describe the active bits of O_0 in terms of K_0 (the latter are necessary for key absorption). Just as an example, in order to guess the relevant key-material for S-box 7, we can compute both the good pairs and the linear relations for the active output bit y_0 (necessary for the key absorption in Step 2) with an average number of key-guesses of $2 \times 1/8 + 7 \times 7/8 = 2^{2.73}$. In fact, in case the input difference is $\delta = 0$ (which we expect to happen for $1/8$ of the pairs) we only need to guess one key-bit of K_0 to find a linear relation of y_0 (as suggested by the optimal tree for $\langle S(x), 1 \rangle$); if $\delta \neq 0$ (which we expect to happen for $7/8$ of the pairs), we need to make 7 guesses to determine which pairs are good (thanks to the tree for g_1^δ); indeed, these guesses are always enough to also determine a linear relation on y_0 and we need to guess no further. After that, we can sieve all the pairs such that

$$S(x \oplus K_0) \oplus S(x \oplus \Delta + K_0) \neq \{1, 0\},$$

which happens with a probability of $2/8 = 2^{-2}$. Notice that the verification of this condition costs $2 \times 1/18 \times 1/16$ 18-round encryptions for each pair. Overall, this process is applied to each nibble, for a total time complexity of this step is $2^{y+4.90}$ 18-round encryptions.

Step 2 (guesses of K_1, K_0 to determine the pairs that satisfy ΔO_1). In this step, we guess the remaining key bits to ensure the right difference after the first two rounds. First, we notice that we can discard any pair which has not an input difference that could lead to ΔO_1, by looking at F_Δ for S-box 7 and 12, and find out that we can keep only $3/4$ of the remaining pairs so far. Thanks to the key absorption technique of Sect. 3.2, we can jointly guess an average of 2 bits of (K_0, K_1). Notice that deciding whether a pair satisfies the transition of S-box 7 is independent of the third input bit (and therefore of the second output bit of nibble 13 in round 17, as was anticipated), thanks to the fact that F_2 has domopt $= 3$ (i.e. independent of bit 4). This also implies that output bit y_2 of S-box 11 of round 0 does not need to be guessed. The total complexity of this step is then $2^{y+4.52}$ 18-round encryptions.

Step 3 (guess of K_{18} to determine the pairs that satisfy ΔI_{17} and retrieve linear relations for the active input bits of I_{17}). As was done in Step 1, we want to filter the good pairs by gradually guessing the necessary key material for each S-box and retrieve linear relations for the active input bits of I_{17}. In the hypothesis that the values of the active bits of O_{18} are uniformly distributed, we expect an average complexity of this step of $2^{y+8.98}$ 18-round encryptions.

Step 4 (guess of K_{17}, K_{18} to Determine the Pairs that Satisfy ΔI_{16}). As done in Step 2, we first sieve all the pairs whose output difference cannot lead to a good pair, using as before F_Δ, and then do a combined guess of K_{17} and K_{18} with key absorption. As before, we notice that determining good pairs through S-box 12 is independent of the second input bit (and therefore of the second output bit of nibble 13 in round 17) by looking at F_2. The total complexity of this step of $2^{y+7.42}$ 18-round encryptions.

Final Complexity. The time complexity for the key-guessing is about $2^{y+9.50} = 2^{50.50}$ 18-round encryptions, which means that the bottleneck is no longer the key-guessing, as was in the attack of [22]. Together with the data collection phase, the time complexity of the attack is then 2^{64} 18-round encryptions.

7   Conclusion

Using our description of S-boxes as decision trees allows us to improve the best known attacks against NOEKEON, GIFT, and RECTANGLE . These attacks belong to different families, yet our general framework to optimized the key-guessing part has been applied to all of them.

As future work, it might be of interest to attempt to handle larger functions, that is, with more input bits. For now, all the applications shown above require some degree of manual analysis of the trees (e.g. when combining several rounds in the GIFT or RECTANGLE application). A more heuristic search for the trees might produce trees for significantly larger functions, thus analyzing more than one S-box or even more than one round. This would have the potential to automatically include many of the manual improvements.

In addition, understanding the general behaviour of the minimal number of leaves is an interesting problem on its own. A non-trivial upper bound on the minimal number of leaves for an arbitrary (balanced) Boolean function of n bits would be of great interest.

We expect that many other attack scenarios will benefit from our framework for gradually performing the key-guessing using binary trees, improving other attacks complexities, as it is quite generic.

Acknowledgment. This work was partially funded by the DFG, (German Research Foundation) under Germany's Excellence Strategy - EXC 2092 CASA - 390781972 and within the APLICA project. We would further like to thank Shahram Rasoolzadeh for his valuable support. This project has received funding from the European Research Council (ERC) under the European Union's Horizon 2020 research and innovation programme (grant agreement no. 714294 - acronym QUASYModo).

References

1. Ankele, R., Kölbl, S.: Mind the gap - a closer look at the security of block ciphers against differential cryptanalysis. In: Cid, C., Jacobson, Jr. M. (eds.) SAC 2018. LNCS, vol. 11349, pp. 163–190. Springer, Cham (2018). https://doi.org/10.1007/978-3-030-10970-7_8

2. Banik, S., Pandey, S.K., Peyrin, T., Sasaki, Yu., Sim, S.M., Todo, Y.: GIFT: a small present - towards reaching the limit of lightweight encryption. In: Fischer, W., Homma, N. (eds.) CHES 2017. LNCS, vol. 10529, pp. 321–345. Springer, Cham (2017). https://doi.org/10.1007/978-3-319-66787-4_16

3. Biham, E., Shamir, A.: Differential cryptanalysis of DES-like cryptosystems. In: Menezes, A.J., Vanstone, S.A. (eds.) CRYPTO 1990. LNCS, vol. 537, pp. 2–21. Springer, Heidelberg (1991). https://doi.org/10.1007/3-540-38424-3_1

4. Blondeau, C., Gérard, B., Nyberg, K.: [Multiple Differential Cryptanalysis Using , and $?^2$ Statistics]. In: Visconti, I., De Prisco, R. (eds.) SCN 2012. LNCS, vol. 7485, pp. 343–360. Springer, Heidelberg (2012). https://doi.org/10.1007/978-3-642-32928-9_19

5. Bogdanov, A., Knudsen, L.R., Leander, G., Paar, C., Poschmann, A., Robshaw, M.J.B., Seurin, Y., Vikkelsoe, C.: PRESENT: an ultra-lightweight block cipher. In: Paillier, P., Verbauwhede, I. (eds.) CHES 2007. LNCS, vol. 4727, pp. 450–466. Springer, Heidelberg (2007). https://doi.org/10.1007/978-3-540-74735-2_31

6. Broll, M., et al.: Further improving differential-linear attacks: Applications to chaskey and serpent. Cryptology ePrint Archive, Report 2021/820 (2021). https://ia.cr/2021/820

7. Broll, M., Canale, F., Leander, G., Gutiérrez, A.F., Naya-Plasencia, M.: Generic framework for key-guessing improvements. Cryptology ePrint Archive, Report 2021/1238 (2021). https://ia.cr/2021/1238

8. Canteaut, A., Naya-Plasencia, M., Vayssière, B.: Sieve-in-the-middle: improved MITM attacks. In: Canetti, R., Garay, J.A. (eds.) CRYPTO 2013. LNCS, vol. 8042, pp. 222–240. Springer, Heidelberg (2013). https://doi.org/10.1007/978-3-642-40041-4_13

9. Collard, B., Standaert, F.-X., Quisquater, J.-J.: Improving the time complexity of matsui's linear cryptanalysis. In: Nam, K.-H., Rhee, G. (eds.) Improving the time complexity of Matsui's linear cryptanalysis. LNCS, vol. 4817, pp. 77–88. Springer, Heidelberg (2007). https://doi.org/10.1007/978-3-540-76788-6_7

10. Daemen, J., Peeters, M., Assche, G., Rijmen, V.: The NOEKEON block cipher. Nessie proposals (2000)

11. Eichlseder, M., Kales, D.: Clustering related-tweak characteristics: application to MANTIS-6. IACR Trans. Symmetric Cryptol. **2018**(2), 111–132 (2018)

12. Evertse, J.-H.: Linear structures in blockciphers. In: Chaum, D., Price, W.L. (eds.) Linear structures in blockciphers. LNCS, vol. 304, pp. 249–266. Springer, Heidelberg (1988). https://doi.org/10.1007/3-540-39118-5_23

13. Flórez-Gutiérrez, A., Naya-Plasencia, M.: Improving key-recovery in linear attacks: application to 28-round PRESENT. In: Canteaut, A., Ishai, Y. (eds.) Improving key-recovery in linear attacks: Application to 28-round PRESENT. LNCS, vol. 12105, pp. 221–249. Springer, Cham (2020). https://doi.org/10.1007/978-3-030-45721-1_9

14. Ji, F., Zhang, W., Zhou, C., Ding, T.: Improved (related-key) differential cryptanalysis on GIFT. IACR Cryptol. ePrint Arch. 2020, 1242 (2020). https://eprint.iacr.org/2020/1242

15. Leurent, G.: Differential and linear cryptanalysis of ARX with partitioning - application to FEAL and chaskey. IACR Cryptol. ePrint Arch. 2015, 968 (2015). http://eprint.iacr.org/2015/968

16. Matsui, M.: The first experimental cryptanalysis of the data encryption standard. In: Desmedt, Y.G. (ed.) CRYPTO 1994. LNCS, vol. 839, pp. 1–11. Springer, Heidelberg (1994). https://doi.org/10.1007/3-540-48658-5_1

17. Matsui, M., Yamagishi, A.: A new method for known plaintext attack of FEAL cipher. In: Rueppel, R.A. (ed.) A new method for known plaintext attack of FEAL cipher. LNCS, vol. 658, pp. 81–91. Springer, Heidelberg (1993). https://doi.org/10.1007/3-540-47555-9_7

18. O'Donnell, R.: Analysis of Boolean Functions. Cambridge University Press (2014)

19. Shan, J., Hu, L., Song, L., Sun, S., Ma, X.: Related-key differential attack on round reduced RECTANGLE-80. IACR Cryptol. ePrint Arch. 2014, 986 (2014). http://eprint.iacr.org/2014/986

20. Shpilka, A., Tal, A., lee Volk, B.: On the structure of boolean functions with small spectral norm. Comput. Complex. 26(1), 229–273 (2017)

21. Sun, L., Wang, W., Wang, M.: Accelerating the search of differential and linear characteristics with the SAT method. IACR Trans. Symmetric Cryptol. 2021(1), 269–315 (2021)

22. Zhang, W., Bao, Z., Lin, D., Rijmen, V., Yang, B., Verbauwhede, I.: RECTANGLE: a bit-slice lightweight block cipher suitable for multiple platforms. Sci. China Inf. Sci. 58(12), 1–15 (2015)

23. Zhao, B., Dong, X., Jia, K.: New related-tweakey boomerang and rectangle attacks on Deoxys-BC including BDT effect. IACR Trans. Symmetric Cryptol. 2019(3), 121–151 (2019)

Quantum Security

On the Non-tightness
of Measurement-Based Reductions
for Key Encapsulation Mechanism
in the Quantum Random Oracle Model

Haodong Jiang[1,2,3,4], Zhenfeng Zhang[1(✉)], and Zhi Ma[3,4(✉)]

[1] TCA Laboratory, State Key Laboratory of Computer Science,
Institute of Software, Chinese Academy of Sciences, Beijing 100190, China
{haodong2020,zhenfeng}@iscas.ac.cn
[2] State Key Laboratory of Cryptology, P.O. Box 5159, Beijing 100878, China
[3] State Key Laboratory of Mathematical Engineering and Advanced Computing,
Zhengzhou 450001, Henan, China
mazhi@meac-skl.cn
[4] Henan Key Laboratory of Network Cryptography Technology,
Zhengzhou 450001, Henan, China

Abstract. Key encapsulation mechanism (KEM) variants of the Fujisaki-Okamoto (FO) transformation (TCC 2017) that turn a weakly-secure public-key encryption (PKE) into an IND-CCA-secure KEM, were widely used among the KEM submissions to the NIST Post-Quantum Cryptography Standardization Project. Under the standard CPA security assumptions, i.e., OW-CPA and IND-CPA, the security of these variants in the quantum random oracle model (QROM) has been proved by black-box reductions, e.g., Jiang et al. (CRYPTO 2018), and by non-black-box reductions (EUROCRYPT 2020). The non-black-box reductions (EUROCRYPT 2020) have a liner security loss, but can only apply to specific *reversible* adversaries with strict *reversible* implementation. On the contrary, the existing black-box reductions in the literature can apply to an arbitrary adversary with an arbitrary implementation, but suffer a quadratic security loss.

In this paper, for KEM variants of the FO transformation, we first show the tightness limits of the black-box reductions, and prove that a *measurement-based* reduction in the QROM from breaking the standard OW-CPA (or IND-CPA) security of the underlying PKE to breaking the IND-CCA security of the resulting KEM, will *inevitably* incur a quadratic loss of the security, where "measurement-based" means the reduction measures a hash query from the adversary and uses the measurement outcome to break the underlying security of PKE. In particular, most black-box reductions for these FO-like KEM variants are of this type, and our results suggest an explanation for the lack of progress in improving this reduction tightness in terms of the degree of security loss. Then, we further show that the quadratic loss is also unavoidable when one turns a search problem into a decision problem using the one-way to hiding technique in a black-box

© International Association for Cryptologic Research 2021
M. Tibouchi and H. Wang (Eds.): ASIACRYPT 2021, LNCS 13090, pp. 487–517, 2021.
https://doi.org/10.1007/978-3-030-92062-3_17

manner, which has been recognized as an essential technique to prove the security of cryptosystems involving quantum random oracles.

Keywords: Non-tightness · Quantum random oracle model · Key encapsulation mechanism · Fujisaki-okamoto · One-way to hiding

1   Introduction

Indistinguishability against chosen-ciphertext attacks (IND-CCA) [1] has been considered as a standard security notion for a key encapsulation mechanism (KEM) [2]. For designing efficient cryptographic protocols, an idealized model called Random oracle model (ROM) [3] is usually used, where a hash function is idealized to be a publicly accessible random oracle (RO). Generic constructions of an IND-CCA-secure KEM in the ROM were well studied by Dent [4] and Hofheinz, Hövelmanns and Kiltz [5].

Essentially, the generic constructions in [5] can be classified into two categories. One category is the KEM variants of the Fujisaki-Okamoto (FO) transformation [6,7] including $FO^{\perp}$, $FO_m^{\perp}$, $FO^{\not\perp}$, $FO_m^{\not\perp}$, $QFO_m^{\perp}$ and $QFO_m^{\not\perp 1}$, which turn a public-key encryption (PKE) with the standard CPA security (one-wayness against chosen-plaintext attacks (OW-CPA) or indistinguishability against chosen-plaintext attacks (IND-CPA)) into an IND-CCA KEM. The second category is the KEM variants of the REACT/GEM transformation [9,10], including $U^{\not\perp}$, $U^{\perp}$, $U_m^{\not\perp}$, $U_m^{\perp}$, $QU_m^{\not\perp}$ and $QU_m^{\perp}$, which turn a PKE with non-standard security (e.g., OW-PCA, one-way against plaintext checking attack [9,10]) or a deterministic PKE (DPKE, where the encryption algorithm is deterministic) into an IND-CCA-secure KEM. The modular analysis of the FO transformation by Hofheinz et al. [5] suggests that the FO transformation implicitly contains the REACT/GEM transformation at least as far as the proof techniques are concerned. Thus, in what follows, we just call these variants FO-like KEMs for brevity.

In modern cryptography, cryptosystem constructions are usually proposed together with a proof of security. Typically, when proving a security of a cryptographic scheme S under a hardness assumption of an underlying problem P, one usually constructs a reduction algorithm $R^{\mathcal{A}}$ that runs an adversary $\mathcal{A}$ against S as a subroutine to break the underlying hardness assumption of P. Let $(T_{\mathcal{A}}, \epsilon_{\mathcal{A}})$ and (T_R, ϵ_R) denote the running times and advantages of $\mathcal{A}$ and $R^{\mathcal{A}}$, respectively. The reduction is said to be tight if $T_{\mathcal{A}} \approx T_R$ and $\epsilon_{\mathcal{A}} \approx \epsilon_R$. Otherwise, if $T_R \gg T_{\mathcal{A}}$ or $\epsilon_R \ll \epsilon_{\mathcal{A}}$, the reduction is non-tight. Generally, the tightness gap, (informally) defined by $\frac{T_{\mathcal{A}}\epsilon_R}{T_R\epsilon_{\mathcal{A}}}$ [11], is used to measure the quality of a reduction. Tighter reductions with smaller tightness gap are desirable for practical cryptographic applications especially in large-scale scenarios, since the tightness of a reduction determines the strength of the security guarantees provided by

---

[1] Q means an additional Targhi-Unruh hash [8] (a length-preserving hash function) is appended to the ciphertext. m (without m) means $K = H(m)$ ($K = H(m, c)$). $\not\perp(\perp)$ means implicit (explicit) rejection. In implicit (explicit) rejection, a pseudorandom key (an abnormal symbol $\perp$) is returned for an invalid ciphertext.

the security proof. Thus, pursuing tighter reduction has been recognized as a vital goal in cryptographic community.

A reduction is called black-box if it merely uses the adversary's input-output behavior, and does not depend on the internals like the adversary's code (e.g., concrete gate operations). As surveyed by Marc Fischlin [12], black-box reductions are pervasive in cryptography. In contrast, a non-black-box reduction requires knowledge of the adversary's internals. For several cryptographic tasks, e.g., zero-knowledge proofs [13], it can be shown that non-black-box reductions have significantly more power than black-box ones [14]. In particular, this additional power of non-black-box reductions can be used to obtain new results, which were previously proven to be impossible to obtain when using only black-box techniques [14]. However, in some settings, e.g. secure computation, non-black-box reductions may cause high efficiency costs, and are unlikely to be very useful in practice [15]. In addition, as argued by Pass, Tseng and Venkitasubramaniam [16], in the context of basing cryptographic primitives on one another, black-box reductions provide a semantically stronger notion of security than non-black-box reductions, since non-black-box reductions require an explicit description of the adversary's code that might be hard to find in practical attacks. Thus, typically, when proving the security of a cryptosystem, a black-box reduction is always the first choice.

In the ROM, if an adversary queries the random oracle with m, the reduction can see this query and learn m. This is sometimes called extractability. When proving the IND-CCA security of a PKE/KEM under various standard assumptions in the ROM, one usually constructs a *query-based*[2] reduction that uses a hash query from the adversary to break the underlying hard problem, such as when proving the FO transformation [6,7], the REACT/GEM transformation [9,10], the Bellare-Rogaway transformation [3], the OAEP transformation [18,19], and the hashed ElGamal encryption scheme [20]. A query-based reduction is also used in getting a tight security proof for a unique signature [17]. In particular, for FO-like KEMs from standard CPA assumptions (in what follows, standard CPA assumptions refer to OW-CPA and IND-CPA), the currently known security reductions in the ROM [4,5,21] are all query-based.

Recently, post-quantum security of FO-like KEMs has gathered great interest [5,22–29] due to the widespread adoption [23, Table 1] in KEM submissions to the NIST Post-Quantum Cryptography (PQC) Standardization Project [30]. The goal of this project is to standardize new public-key cryptographic algorithms with security against quantum adversaries. Motivated by the fact that quantum adversaries can execute all "offline primitives" such as hash functions on arbitrary superpositions, Boneh et al. [31] introduced quantum random oracle model (QROM), where the adversary can query the random oracle with quantum state, and argued that to prove post-quantum security one needs to prove security in the QROM[3].

Unfortunately, the aforementioned query-based reduction in the ROM can not carry over to the QROM setting offhand due to the fact that the extractability might be problematic when the query is a quantum state which can be a superposition of exponentially many classical states [31]. In a quantum world,

---

[2] This name comes from Guo et al.'s paper [17].

[3] Separations of ROM and QROM were given by [31–33].

measurement allows us to extract classical information from a quantum state and thus is a way that we can "read out" information. Thus, naturally, a QROM version of the aforementioned query-based reduction can be a reduction that measures a hash query from the adversary and uses the measurement outcome to break the underlying hard problem. In this paper, we call this type of reductions a *measurement-based* reduction.

Particularly, for FO-like KEMs from standard CPA assumptions, most black-box reductions[4] (e.g., [5,22–27]) and non-black-box reductions [37] in the QROM are of this type, and have the tightness[5], (1) T_R is about T_A; (2) $\epsilon_R \approx \frac{1}{\kappa}\epsilon_A^\tau$, where κ and τ are respectively called the factor and degree of security loss in the following. Let q be the total number of adversary's queries (including quantum and classical) to various oracles.

- In [5], Hofheinz et al. presented security reductions for $\text{QFO}_m^{\not\perp}$ and $\text{QFO}_m^{\perp}$ from the OW-CPA security of the underlying PKE with $\kappa = O(q^6)$ and $\tau = 4$, for $\text{QU}_m^{\not\perp}$ and $\text{QU}_m^{\perp}$ from the OW-PCA security of the underlying PKE with $\kappa = O(q^2)$ and $\tau = 2$.
- In [22], Saito, Xagawa and Yamakawa presented a tight security reduction (i.e., $\kappa = O(1)$ and $\tau = 1$) for $\text{U}_m^{\not\perp}$ from a new non-standard security called disjoint simulatability (DS) of the underlying DPKE, and also provided a security reduction for a variant of $\text{FO}_m^{\not\perp}$ from the standard IND-CPA security of the underlying PKE with $\kappa = O(q^2)$ and $\tau = 2$.
- In [23], Jiang et al. first presented security reductions for $\text{FO}^{\not\perp}$ and $\text{FO}_m^{\not\perp}$ from the standard OW-CPA security of the underlying PKE with $\kappa = O(q^2)$ and $\tau = 2$. Then, they presented security reductions for $\text{U}^{\not\perp}$ ($\text{U}^{\perp}$, resp.) from the OW-qPCA (OW-qPVCA, resp.) security of the underlying PKE, $\text{U}_m^{\not\perp}$ ($\text{U}_m^{\perp}$, resp.) from the OW-CPA (OW-VA, resp.) security of the underlying DPKE with $\kappa = O(q^2)$ and $\tau = 2$, where OW-qPCA, OW-qPVCA and OW-VA are new non-standard security notions of PKE introduced by [5,23].
- Using the semi-classical oracle technique in [24,25,27,38] improved the tightness of security reductions in [23]. Precisely, under the standard IND-CPA security of the underlying PKE, security reductions with tightness $\kappa = O(q)$ and $\tau = 2$ were given for $\text{FO}^{\not\perp}$, $\text{FO}_m^{\not\perp}$ and their variants with explicit rejection. For $\text{U}^{\not\perp}$, $\text{U}^{\perp}$, $\text{U}_m^{\not\perp}$ and $\text{U}_m^{\perp}$, the reduction tightness was improved to be $\kappa = O(q)$ and $\tau = 2$ under the same security assumptions as in [23].
- In [26], following Zhandry's compressed oracle technique [34], Bindel et al. further gave tighter security reduction for $\text{U}^{\not\perp}$ and its variants with $\kappa = O(1)$ and $\tau = 2$.

---

[4] The reductions in [34–36] that use the compressed oracle technique developed by [34] do not belong to the class of measurement-based reductions, since they access information contained in the adversary's queries in a non-trivially different way than by measurement.

[5] When comparing the tightness of different reductions, we assume perfect correctness of the underlying scheme for brevity.

- In [37], introducing a new technique called "Measure-Rewind-Measure" (MRM), Kuchta et al. first gave non-black-box reductions for FO-like KEMs. In particular, for $U^{\not\perp}$ ($FO^{\not\perp}$, resp.) and its variants, the reduction tightness was improved to be $\kappa = O(q)$ and $\tau = 1$ ($\kappa = O(q^2)$ and $\tau = 1$, resp.).

As we can see, the existing black-box reductions in the QROM for FO-like KEMs from standard CPA assumptions, are far from desirable due to the quadratic security loss (at least). Although this quadratic loss can be avoided by non-black-box reductions [37], as we will show in Sect. 1.4, the non-black-box reductions in [37] can only apply to specific *reversible* adversaries[6] with strict *reversible* implementation (the existing black-box reductions in the literature can cover arbitrary adversaries with arbitrary implementations). These results are quite different from the ones in the ROM setting, where security reductions with linear loss can be achieved in a black-box manner [4,5].

The quadratic loss in these security proofs arises from the usage of the one-way to hiding (OW2H) technique [40], which essentially gives a reduction from an extraction algorithm against the one-wayness-style property (search problem) to a distinguishing adversary against hiding-style property (decision problem) with quadratic loss. Actually, the OW2H technique has been recognized as an essential technique to prove security of various cryptosystems involving quantum random oracles [38,40]. Besides FO-like constructions, the OW2H technique was also used to prove the security of revocable timed-release encryption schemes [40], authenticated key exchange [27], position verification protocol [41], PRF and MACs [42], non-interactive zero-knowledge proof systems and signature schemes [43–45]. Very recently, several works [26,37,38] tried to improve the tightness of the OW2H technique. However, as in the case of the aforementioned proofs for FO-like KEMs, the tightness improvements are only restricted to the factor of reduction loss, and the quadratic loss still exists (except the improvement using a non-black-box reduction for *reversible* distinguishing adversaries in [37]).

Thus, a natural question is that

For FO-like KEMs and the one-way to hiding technique, is the quadratic loss unavoidable for measurement-based black-box reductions?

1.1   Our Contributions

In this paper, we give an affirmative answer for the above question, and show that the current quadratic loss is indeed unavoidable for any measurement-based black-box reduction that runs the adversary once without rewinding[7].

---

[6] In post-quantum setting, most adversaries are irreversible since most oracles (e.g., decapsulation oracle) in the security model can only be classically queried. Thus, a quantum adversary has to measure his quantum query registers to perform a classical query. Moreover, adversaries may also perform a mix of classical (probably irreversible) and quantum algorithm, see the full version [39] for details.

[7] Our impossibility results can also be extended to cover measurement-based reductions with *simple* rewinding (a quantum counterpart of classical sequential rewinding [46]), see Remark 5 and Appendix C.

Given a real p ($0 \leq p \leq 1$) and a FO-like KEM construction,

1. We first construct an unbounded quantum adversary $\mathcal{A}$ that breaks the IND-CCA security of the resulting KEM by querying the random oracle with a well-designed *quantum* state and solving a discrimination problem between two *quantum* states. The advantage of $\mathcal{A}$ is at least $\sqrt{p}$, i.e., $\epsilon_{\mathcal{A}} \gtrsim \sqrt{p}$.
2. Then, using the meta-reduction methodology [47,48], we bound the advantage ϵ_R of a measurement-based reduction $R^{\mathcal{A}}$ that runs above $\mathcal{A}$ as a subroutine to break the OW-CPA (or IND-CPA) security of the underlying PKE. In particular, the advantage ϵ_R can not substantially exceed p, i.e., $\epsilon_R \lesssim p$, unless there exists an algorithm breaking the OW-CPA (or IND-CPA) security of the underlying PKE efficiently.

Therefore, for FO-like KEMs, our results show that a measurement-based black-box reduction in the QROM from breaking the standard OW-CPA (or IND-CPA) security of the underlying PKE to breaking the IND-CCA security of the resulting KEM, will *inevitably* incur a quadratic loss of the security.

Moreover, our impossibility results can also be extended to show that the quadratic loss is also unavoidable when one turns a search problem into a decision problem via the essential OW2H technique in a black-box manner. That is, the black-box OW2H technique [26,38,40] is essentially optimal in terms of the degree of reduction loss.

1.2 The Interest of Our Result

As pointed out by [5, Sect. 1.2], FO-like constructions remain the only known generic constructions from CPA to CCA security. That is, our results cover all the current generic constructions of an IND-CCA-secure KEM based on a CPA-secure PKE. On the other hand, our impossibility results can apply to typical measurement-based reduction, which is a QROM version of the query-based reduction that has been widely used in proving CCA security of a PKE/KEM under various standard assumptions. For FO-like KEMs from a standard CPA PKE, the currently known black-box reductions in [5,22–27] belong to this type. Thus, our results suggest an explanation for the lack of progress in improving the reduction tightness in terms of the degree of security loss in these works [5,22–27].

The tightness of security reductions is important to evaluate the concrete security of a cryptosystem [11]. Our results first give a black-box reduction bound for FO-like KEMs, which can be taken as a baseline for tightness comparison. For example, at TCC 2019, Bindel et al. [26] took this result as a theoretical support for their "tight" reduction (their main contribution) for $\mathsf{U}^{\not\perp}$ and its variants since their black-box reductions essentially match our impossibility bound.

As pointed out by Baecher et al. [49], an impossibility result, which clearly specifies the type of reduction it rules out, enables us to identify the potential leverages to bypass the limits. Fischlin [12] mentioned that the impossibility result can also been viewed as a shortcoming of the proof technique itself, and non-black-box techniques can be used to circumvent a black-box impossibility result. At EUROCRYPT 2020, following our work, Kuchta et al. [37] introduced a new technique called "measure-rewind-measure" (MRM), and proposed a non-black-box reduction that can bypass our black-box impossibility results to achieve a linear loss, see Sect. 1.4 for detailed discussion. Therefore, our impossibility results can be taken as guidance toward a positive answer, and will be a step forward into looking for new approaches to prove security in the QROM.

In NIST PQC standardization process, all the Round-3 KEM candidates use FO-like constructions to achieve the CCA security [30]. For NIST's round-3 evaluations, our results suggest that in order to derive a tight QROM proof, one (especially the NIST submission teams) has to research on developing new proof techniques (particularly for their specific constructions).

1.3   Technique Overview

In FO-like KEMs, the (session) key K is derived by $H(m)$ (or $H(m,c)$) and the ciphertext $c = Enc(pk, m; G(m))$ (or $Enc(pk, m)$ if Enc is deterministic) is the corresponding encapsulation of the key K, where Enc is the encryption algorithm of the underlying PKE, m is uniformly picked at random, G and H are random oracles. In this section, for a concise presentation, we just take KEM $-$ U$_m^{\not\perp}$ (see Fig. 1 for details) as an example, and thus $K = H(m)$ and $c = Enc(pk, m)$. It is easy to extend the techniques here to other FO-like KEMs and the general OW2H technique, see Sects. 5.1 and 6.

Meta-reduction methodology. Since the introduction by Boneh and Venkatesan in [47], the meta-reduction methodology has proven to be a versatile tool in deriving impossibility results and tightness bounds of security proofs for many cryptosystem constructions [46–48,50–57], please see the review [12]. Let R be a reduction that breaks the underlying hard problem P with access to an adversary $\mathcal{A}$ against a scheme S. Roughly speaking, a meta-reduction MR^R simulates the adversarial part $\mathcal{A}$, runs R as a subroutine, and break the underlying hard problem P directly without reference to an allegedly successful adversary. That is, a meta-reduction MR^R treats the reduction R as an adversary itself, and reduces the existence of such a reduction R to a presumably hard problem. Note that the meta-reduction methodology clearly requires the existence of a successful adversary $\mathcal{A}$ against the scheme S in the first place, and such an adversary is usually unbounded [12]. A more detailed description of the meta-reduction methodology can be found in the full version [39].

When attacking the IND-CCA security of KEM $-$ U$_m^{\not\perp}$, an adversary $\mathcal{A}(pk, c^*, K_b)$ needs to distinguish $K_0 = H(m^*)$ from a uniformly random key K_1, where $c^* = Enc(pk, m^*)$ is an encryption of a uniformly random m^*, the coin $b \in \{0,1\}$ is uniformly random. We note that the random oracle H has a useful property that if m^* has not been queried by $\mathcal{A}$, then the value $H(m^*)$ is uniformly random in $\mathcal{A}$'s view. Thus, $\mathcal{A}$'s distinguishing advantage is negligible when $\mathcal{A}$ does not query H with m^*. Intuitively, to achieve a non-negligible distinguishing advantage, $\mathcal{A}$ has to query H with m^*.

In the ROM, $\mathcal{A}$ can only make classical queries to H. For any p ($0 \leq p \leq 1$), if $\mathcal{A}$ makes a query m^* to H with probability p, he will learn $K_0 = H(m^*)$ with probability p and break the IND-CCA security with advantage approximately p by testing whether K_0 is equal to K_b. For a reduction $R^{\mathcal{A}}$ against the OW-CPA security of the underlying DPKE, a natural way is to take $\mathcal{A}$'s query as a return. Then, with probability p, $R^{\mathcal{A}}$ will return the m^* and break the OW-CPA security of the underlying DPKE. That is, the advantages of $R^{\mathcal{A}}$ and $\mathcal{A}$ are approximately equal, which is consistent with the currently known tight reduction in [5].

Unbounded quantum adversary $\mathcal{A}$. In the QROM, a quantum adversary $\mathcal{A}$ makes queries to H with quantum states. Consider the following quantum state

$$|\psi_{-1}\rangle := \sqrt{p}|m^*\rangle|0\rangle + \sqrt{1-p}|m'\rangle|\Sigma\rangle,$$

where $m' \neq m^*$, $|\Sigma\rangle = \sum_{k \in \mathcal{K}} 1/\sqrt{|\mathcal{K}|}|k\rangle$ and $\mathcal{K}$ is the (session) key space. For a quantum query with $|\psi_{-1}\rangle$, the random oracle H will return

$$|\psi_0\rangle := \sqrt{p}|m^*\rangle|K_0\rangle + \sqrt{1-p}|m'\rangle|\Sigma\rangle.$$

We remark that if the adversary $\mathcal{A}$ directly measures $|\psi_0\rangle$ in the standard computational basis, he will obtain K_0 with probability p, and break the IND-CCA security with advantage (approximately) p by testing whether K_0 is equal to K_b as the aforementioned ROM adversary does.

Here, we construct an unbounded quantum adversary $\mathcal{A}(pk, c^*, K_b)$ that first determines m^* such that $c^* = Enc(pk, m^*)$ by exhaustive search (if none is found, $\mathcal{A}$ outputs 1) and randomly selects a uniform m' such that $m' \neq m^*$, then queries H with $|\psi_{-1}\rangle$, lastly guesses b by *testing* whether $|\psi_0\rangle$ is equal to $|\psi_b\rangle$, where

$$|\psi_b\rangle := \sqrt{p}|m^*\rangle|K_b\rangle + \sqrt{1-p}|m'\rangle|\Sigma\rangle.$$

Testing whether $|\psi_0\rangle$ is equal to $|\psi_b\rangle$[8] can be accomplished using the standard state discrimination method (known as Helstrom measurement) [58,59] with advantage (approximately) at least $\sqrt{p}$. Thus, quantum adversary $\mathcal{A}$ can break the IND-CCA security with advantage (approximately) at least $\sqrt{p}$. That is, $\epsilon_{\mathcal{A}} \gtrsim \sqrt{p}$.

In the currently known proofs for KEM $-$ U$_m^{\not\perp}$ in [23], the reduction algorithm $R^{\mathcal{A}}$ against the OW-CPA security of the underlying DPKE *just* randomly measures one of $\mathcal{A}$'s queries to H in the standard computational basis and takes the measurement outcome as a return. The security bound is given by $\epsilon_{\mathcal{A}} \lesssim q\sqrt{\epsilon_R}$. We note that the aforementioned unbounded adversary $\mathcal{A}$ does not query the decapsulation oracle, and just reveals one quantum query $|\psi_{-1}\rangle$ to H and a guessing of b. Thus, the total number of $\mathcal{A}$'s queries to various oracles is one, i.e., $q = 1$. We also note that the advantage of the reduction algorithm $R^{\mathcal{A}}$ in [23] is exactly the probability of the measurement outputting m^*, which is equal to p. That is, $\epsilon_R = p$. Thus, for above unbounded quantum adversary $\mathcal{A}$, the advantage can match the bound $\epsilon_{\mathcal{A}} \lesssim q\sqrt{\epsilon_R}$ in [23].

---

[8] Formally, we need to judge $|\psi_0\rangle\langle\psi_0|$ comes from $|\psi_b\rangle\langle\psi_b|$ or $\mathbb{E}_{K_{1-b}}|\psi_{1-b}\rangle\langle\psi_{1-b}|$ (the the expectation is taken over $K_{1-b} \xleftarrow{\$} \mathcal{K}$), please refer to Sect. 3 for details.

The advantage of a measurement-based reduction. Here, we consider a measurement-based black-box reduction $R^{\mathcal{A}}$ that runs $\mathcal{A}$ once and without rewinding, measures $\mathcal{A}$'s query $|\psi_{-1}\rangle$ and uses the measurement outcome (any further postprocessing is allowed) to break the OW-CPA security of the underlying DPKE. We say a reduction R is efficient if the running time of R (excluding $\mathcal{A}$'s running time) is polynomial in the security parameter. We make a convention that $R^{\mathcal{A}}$ measures $|\psi_{-1}\rangle$ in the standard computational basis[9].

Consider the advantage of $R^{\mathcal{A}}$ in the following three cases, where INE is denoted as the event that the exhaustive search does not return an m^* such that $Enc(pk, m^*) = c^*$, EXI is denoted as the event that such an m^* is found, GOOD is denoted as the event that the measurement outcome is m^*, and BAD is denoted as the event that the measurement outcome is not m^*.

Case 1: INE. In this case, $\mathcal{A}$ just outputs 1 without queries to H. Thus, exhaustive search for m^* in this case is vain, and $\mathcal{A}$ can be replaced by an adversary $\mathcal{A}_1$ that always outputs 1 without the search for m^* and the query to the random oracle H. Therefore, we can easily construct a meta-reduction MR_1^R that simulates $\mathcal{A}_1$ and takes $R^{\mathcal{A}_1}$ as a subroutine to break the OW-CPA security of the underlying DPKE such that the running time of MR_1^R is about the running time of R, and under the condition INE the advantage of MR_1^R is about the advantage of R.

Case 2: EXI $\wedge$ GOOD. Since $\Pr[\text{GOOD}|\text{EXI}] = p$, we can bound the advantage of R in this case by p.

Case 3: EXI $\wedge$ BAD. In this case, R gets $m' \neq m^*$. Let $\mathcal{A}_2$ be an adversary that makes a single query to H with quantum state $\sum_{m,k} 1/\sqrt{|\mathcal{M}| \cdot |\mathcal{K}|}|m\rangle|k\rangle$ and outputs 1 without searching for m^*. Thus, the advantage of R under the condition EXI $\wedge$ BAD remains unchanged when $\mathcal{A}$ is replaced by $\mathcal{A}_2$. As in the case 1, we can also construct a meta-reduction MR_2^R against the underlying OW-CPA security that simulates $\mathcal{A}_2$ and takes $R^{\mathcal{A}_2}$ as a subroutine such that the running time of MR_2^R is about the running time of R, and under the condition EXI $\wedge$ BAD the advantage of MR_2^R is about the advantage of R.

Under the assumption that the advantage of any efficient algorithm breaking the OW-CPA security of the underlying DPKE is negligible, we have that both advantages of MR_1^R and MR_2^R are negligible since the running time is polynomial in the security parameter. Thus, both advantages of R in Case 1 and Case 3 are negligible, which implies that the upper bound of R's advantage is approximately p. That is, the advantage of a measurement-based black-box reduction against the OW-CPA security of the underlying DPKE can not substantially exceed p unless there exists an algorithm that can break the OW-CPA security of the underlying DPKE efficiently.

1.4 Subsequent Work

Observing our constructed quantum state distinguisher, Kuchta et al. [37] found that in one of the measurement basis states, the amplitude of $|m^*\rangle$ has a rela-

---

[9] The discussion on other measurements is given by Sect. 4.

tively high norm. That is, such a measurement basis state essentially encodes m^*, thus measuring this measurement basis state can give m^* with a high probability. In order to extract m^* from adversary's quantum registers, Kuchta et al. [37] developed a novel MRM extractor. In particular, the extractor of m^* first runs the adversary $\mathcal{A}$ until the end, performs the first-measurement on $\mathcal{A}$'s internal outputting registers, and then rewinds $\mathcal{A}$ conditioned on the first-measurement outcome, finally conducts a second-measurement on $\mathcal{A}$'s query registers. Note that above rewinding is done in the end of $\mathcal{A}$'s run by applying the inverses of the quantum gate operations (i.e., codes) that $\mathcal{A}$ has applied earlier, rather by restarting $\mathcal{A}$ in a black-box manner from the very beginning. Thus, the MRM extractor can only apply to *reversible* adversaries. In particular, the MRM extractor must access $\mathcal{A}$ in a non-black-box way since it requires knowledge of $\mathcal{A}$'s internal codes and needs to access $\mathcal{A}$'s internal quantum registers.

Based on the aforementioned MRM extractor, Kuchta et al. [37] gave a new non-black-box version of the OW2H lemma. Modifying the proofs in [26] by replacing the black-box OW2H with this non-black-box one, Kuchta et al. first achieved a linear reduction loss for FO-like KEMs. However, due to fact the MRM extractor can only be used for reversible adversaries, thus the non-black-box proofs [37] can only cover reversible CCA adversaries with reversible implementation. We also note that the prior black-box security proofs, including [5,22–27], can apply to arbitrary adversaries with arbitrary implementation. In particular, the prior black-box OW2H lemmas do not require the underlying adversary $\mathcal{A}$ unitary, e.g., [38, Theorems 1 and 3], see the full version [39].

Unfortunately, most adversaries in post-quantum setting are irreversible since most oracles (e.g., decapsulation oracle) in the security model can only be classically queried. That is, a quantum adversary has to measure his quantum query registers to perform a classical query. There are a well-known generic transform [60, Chap. 3.2.5] that can convert any irreversible adversary into a reversible one, and can be used to extend Kuchta et al.'s non-black-box OW2H to cover arbitrary adversaries with arbitrary implementation. However, on the one hand, such a transform will cost a space overhead linearly increased with the adversary's running time. On the other hand, it requires that the oracles (e.g., decapsulation oracle) accessed by the adversary must be simulated such that the adversary can make quantum queries instead of classical queries considered in the typical post-quantum setting. That is, the MRM OW2H extended by the aforementioned generic transform can only apply to the case where there are efficient quantum simulations for all the oracles accessed by the adversary. We provide a detailed discussion on these issues in the full version [39].

1.5   Other Related Works

Before our work, the meta-reduction methodology was only used to derive a QROM impossibility for Fiat-Shamir signature by Dagdelen, Fischlin, and Gagliardoni [54]. More specifically, they used the meta-reduction technique to show that if the Fiat-Shamir transformation applied to the identification protocol would support a knowledge extractor, then a contradiction to the active security will be obtained. In this paper, we focus on the limits of FO-like KEMs and more general one-way to hiding, and the meta-reduction constructions are totally different from theirs.

At ASIACRYPT 2020, Hosoyamada and Yamakawa [61] also studied black-box impossibility in quantum setting, and showed that there does not exist a quantum black-box reduction from collision-resistant hash functions to one-way permutations (or even trapdoor permutations). In particular, different from our work where the meta-reduction methodology is used, the results in [61] is obtained by using another typical technique called *two-oracle* technique [62] that is also popular in deriving the limitations of black-box reductions.

2   Preliminaries

The cryptographic primitives used in this paper are given by Appendix A. For basics of quantum computation, one can refer to [60].

Symbol description. A security parameter is denoted by λ. We use the standard O-notations: O and ω. The abbreviation PPT stands for probabilistic polynomial time. A function $f(\lambda)$ is said to be *negligible* if $f(\lambda) = \lambda^{-\omega(1)}$. We denote a set of negligible functions by $\mathsf{negl}(\lambda)$. $\mathcal{K}$, $\mathcal{M}$, $\mathcal{C}$ and R are respectively denoted as key space, message space, ciphertext space and randomness space. Given a finite set X, we denote the sampling of a uniformly random element x by $x \overset{\$}{\leftarrow} X$. Denote the sampling from some distribution D by $x \leftarrow D$. $x = ?y$ is denoted as an integer that is 1 if $x = y$, and otherwise 0. Denote deterministic computation of an algorithm A on input x by $y = A(x)$. Probabilistic computation of an algorithm A on input x is denoted by $y \leftarrow A(x)$. If necessary, we also make the used randomness r explicit by writing $y = A(x; r)$. Let $|X|$ be the cardinality of set X. A^H means that the algorithm A gets access to the oracle H. $\mathsf{Time}(R)$ is the running time (computational steps) of an algorithm R. $\mathsf{Time}(R^{\mathcal{A}}) = \mathsf{Time}(R) + k\mathsf{Time}(\mathcal{A})$ is the running time of an algorithm $R^{\mathcal{A}}$ that takes $\mathcal{A}$ as a subroutine[10], where k is the number of times $\mathcal{A}$ is invoked by R.

3   An Unbounded Quantum Adversary Against the IND-CCA Security of KEM

In this section, we will construct an unbounded quantum adversary against the IND-CCA security of KEM $- \mathsf{U}_m^{\not\perp} = \mathsf{U}_m^{\not\perp}[\mathrm{DPKE}, H, f]$ shown by Fig. 1, where $\mathrm{DPKE} = (Gen', Enc', Dec')$, a hash function $H : \mathcal{M} \to \mathcal{K}$, and a pseudorandom function (PRF) f with key space $\mathcal{K}^{prf}$. The IND-CCA game of KEM $- \mathsf{U}_m^{\not\perp}$ is given by Fig. 2.

Let $\mathcal{A}(pk, c^*, K_b; r_1, r_2)$ (r_1 and r_2 are classical randomness) be a quantum adversary against the IND-CCA game of KEM $- \mathsf{U}_m^{\not\perp}$ that does as follows.

---

[10] Here, in this paper, $\mathcal{A}$ is forbidden to call R as a subroutine.

Gen	Encaps(pk)	Decaps(sk', c)
1 : $(pk, sk) \leftarrow Gen'$	1 : $m \xleftarrow{\$} \mathcal{M}$	1 : Parse $sk' = (sk, k)$
2 : $k \xleftarrow{\$} \mathcal{K}^{prf}$	2 : $c := Enc'(pk, m)$	2 : $m' := Dec'(sk, c)$
3 : $sk' := (sk, k)$	3 : $K := H(m)$	3 : **if** $Enc'(pk, m') = c$
4 : **return** (pk, sk')	4 : **return** (K, c)	4 : **return** $K := H(m')$
		5 : **else return** $K := f(k, c)$

Fig. 1. IND-CCA-secure KEM $-$ $U_m^{\not{\perp}} = U_m^{\not{\perp}}[DPKE, H, f]$

IND-CCA game of KEM $-$ $U_m^{\not{\perp}}$	DECAPS $(c \neq c^*)$
1 : $(pk, sk') \leftarrow Gen; H \xleftarrow{\$} \Omega_H$	1 : Parse $sk' = (sk, k)$
2 : $m^* \xleftarrow{\$} \mathcal{M}; c^* := Enc'(pk, m^*)$	2 : $m' := Dec'(sk, c)$
3 : $K_0^* := H(m^*); K_1^* \xleftarrow{\$} \mathcal{K}; b \xleftarrow{\$} \{0, 1\}$	3 : **if** $Enc'(pk, m') = c$
4 : $b' \leftarrow \mathcal{A}^{H, \text{DECAPS}}(pk, c^*, K_b^*)$	4 : **return** $K := H(m')$
5 : **return** $b' = ?b$	5 : **else return** $K := f(k, c)$

Fig. 2. IND-CCA game of KEM $-$ $U_m^{\not{\perp}}$

$\mathcal{A}(pk, c^*, K_b; r_1, r_2)$
1 :   Search a $m^* \in \mathcal{M}$ such that $Enc'(pk, m^*) = c^*$
// If no one (or more than one) is found, output 1 and terminate the procedure.
2 :   Sample a real $p \in [0, 1]$ using randomness r_1
3 :   Sample a uniform m' from $\{m' \in \mathcal{M} : m' \neq m^*\}$ using randomness r_2
4 :   Query H with quantum state $|\psi_{-1}\rangle := \sqrt{p}|m^*\rangle|0\rangle + \sqrt{1-p}|m'\rangle|\Sigma\rangle$
// $|\Sigma\rangle = \sum_{k \in \mathcal{K}} 1/\sqrt{|\mathcal{K}|}|k\rangle$ can be derived by $H^{\otimes \log |\mathcal{K}|}|0\rangle$.
5 :   Perform Helstrom measurement M on $|\psi_0\rangle$ (the state returned by H)
6 :   Return the measurement outcome.

Remark 1. The $|\psi_0\rangle$ returned by H is given by

$$|\psi_0\rangle = \mathcal{O}_H|\psi_{-1}\rangle = \sqrt{p}|m^*\rangle|H(m^*)\rangle + \sqrt{1-p}|m'\rangle|(\sum_{k \in \mathcal{K}} 1/\sqrt{|\mathcal{K}|}|k \oplus H(m')\rangle)$$

$$= \sqrt{p}|m^*\rangle|K_0\rangle + \sqrt{1-p}|m'\rangle|(\sum_{k \in \mathcal{K}} 1/\sqrt{|\mathcal{K}|}|k\rangle)$$

$$= \sqrt{p}|m^*\rangle|K_0\rangle + \sqrt{1-p}|m'\rangle|\Sigma\rangle.$$

Remark 2. Helstrom measurement M is a binary POVM measurement with measurement operators M_1 and $M_0 = I - M_1$. M_1 can be derived by following the standard method in [58,59]. In details, let $\psi_b = |\psi_b\rangle\langle\psi_b|$ and

$\psi_{1-b} = \mathbb{E}_{K_{1-b}} |\psi_{1-b}\rangle\langle\psi_{1-b}|$, where the expectation is taken over $K_{1-b} \xleftarrow{\$} \mathcal{K}$ and $|\psi_b\rangle = \sqrt{p}|m^*\rangle|K_b\rangle + \sqrt{1-p}|m'\rangle|\Sigma\rangle$. Note that $\mathcal{A}$ knows ψ_b and ψ_{1-b} since he gets m^*, p, m' and K_b. Thus, by the spectral decomposition of $\psi_b - \psi_{1-b} = \lambda_+ M_1 - \lambda_- M_0$, $\mathcal{A}$ can easily obtain M_1 and M_0. Theorem 3.1 shows that the adversary $\mathcal{A}$ using Helstrom measurement can break security with advantage at least $\sqrt{p}(1 - 1/|\mathcal{K}|)$. It is well-known that Helstrom measurement has the optimal distinguishing advantage for two state discrimination[11]. But for our specific case, there still exist some alternative measurements that can also be adopted by the adversary to attain advantage at least $\sqrt{p}(1 - 1/|\mathcal{K}|)$ (although they are not optimal). For example, the adversary can adopt the measurement with operators $M_1 = |\Psi\rangle\langle\Psi|$ and $M_0 = I - M_1$, where $|\Psi\rangle = \sin(x)|m^*\rangle|K_b\rangle + \cos(x)|m'\rangle|\Sigma\rangle$ and $x = \frac{1}{2}\arccos(-\frac{\sqrt{p}}{\sqrt{4-3p}})$ ($\sin(2x) \geq 0$). In Appendix B, we will show the adversary with such an alternative measurement can also have advantage at least $\sqrt{p}(1 - 1/|\mathcal{K}|)$.

Theorem 3.1 (The advantage of $\mathcal{A}$ in the QROM). *If the underlying DPKE is perfectly correct, the advantage of $\mathcal{A}$ against the IND-CCA security of* $\mathrm{KEM} - \mathrm{U}_m^{\not\perp}$ *is at least* $\sqrt{p}(1 - 1/|\mathcal{K}|)$.

Proof. In the IND-CCA game of $\mathrm{KEM} - \mathrm{U}_m^{\not\perp}$, $c^* = Enc'(pk, m^*)$, where $m^* \xleftarrow{\$} \mathcal{M}$, thus there exists at least one $m^* \in \mathcal{M}$ such that $Enc'(pk, m^*) = c^*$. Since DPKE is perfectly correct, there are no more than one m^* such that $Enc'(pk, m^*) = c^*$. Thus, the m^* that $\mathcal{A}$ gets is exactly the one chosen by the challenger.

Note that the adversary $\mathcal{A}$ knows nothing about K_{1-b}. Thus, in $\mathcal{A}$'s view, the state $|\psi_0\rangle$ returned by H can be described by a mixed state $\psi_0 = \mathbb{E}_{K_{1-b}} |\psi_0\rangle\langle\psi_0|$, where the expectation is taken over $K_{1-b} \xleftarrow{\$} \mathcal{K}$. It is obvious that ψ_0 is equal to ψ_b if $b = 0$, and ψ_{1-b} if $b = 1$, where ψ_b and ψ_{1-b} are defined in Remark 2. Therefore, we have $\mathbf{Adv}_{\mathrm{KEM}-\mathrm{U}_m^{\not\perp}}^{\mathrm{IND\text{-}CCA}}(\mathcal{A}) = |\Pr[\mathcal{A} \Rightarrow 1|b = 0] - \Pr[\mathcal{A} \Rightarrow 1|b = 1]| = |tr(M_1\psi_b) - tr(M_1\psi_{1-b})|$.

Since $b \xleftarrow{\$} \{0,1\}$ and $\mathcal{A}$ adopts Helstrom (optimal) measurement, $\|tr(M_1\psi_b) - tr(M_1\psi_{1-b})|$ is the optimal advantage of solving the minimum-error state discrimination between ψ_b and ψ_{1-b}. Thus, $|tr(M_1\psi_b) - tr(M_1\psi_{1-b})| = \|\psi_b - \psi_{1-b}\|_1 = |\lambda_+| + |\lambda_-| \geq 2(1 - 1/|\mathcal{K}|)\sqrt{p^2/4 + p(1-p)} = 2(1 - 1/|\mathcal{K}|)\sqrt{p}\sqrt{1 - 3/4p} \geq (1 - 1/|\mathcal{K}|)\sqrt{p} \approx \sqrt{p}$, where λ_+ and λ_- are respectively positive eigenvalue and negative eigenvalue of operator $\psi_b - \psi_{1-b}$. $\square$

In the ROM, $\mathcal{A}$ can only classically query the random oracle H. That is, before querying H, the input state is measured in the standard computational basis. Then, $\mathcal{A}$ will query H on m^* with probability p, and on m' with probability $1 - p$. Accordingly, $H(m^*)$ or $H(m')$ will be returned. Note that classical states (orthogonal quantum states) can be perfectly distinguished. Thus, by testing

---

[11] Optimal quantum state discrimination is in general difficult apart from the case of two state discrimination, see the review [59].

whether the returned hash value is equal to K_b, $\mathcal{A}$ can break the IND-CCA security of $\mathrm{KEM} - \mathrm{U}_m^{\not\perp}$ with advantage $1 - \frac{1}{\mathcal{K}}$ if m^* is queried, and 0 if m' is queried. Thus, in the ROM, the advantage of $\mathcal{A}$ will become $p(1 - \frac{1}{|\mathcal{K}|})$.

4   The Advantage of a Measurement-Based Reduction

In this section, we will bound the advantage of a measurement-based black-box reduction that runs the quantum adversary $\mathcal{A}$ (given by Sect. 3) once without rewinding[12], measures $\mathcal{A}$'s hash query and uses the measurement outcome to break the OW-CPA security of the underlying DPKE. Note that the quantum adversary $\mathcal{A}$ in Sect. 3 just makes a *single* query to the random oracle H and no queries to the DECAPS oracle. Thus, the total number q of $\mathcal{A}$'s queries to various oracles is one, i.e., $q = 1$.

Before giving our general result for a general measurement-based reduction, we first discuss a *simple* measurement-based reduction adopted by the current (black-box) proofs [23]. A *simple* measurement-based reduction $R^{\mathcal{A}}(pk, c^*)$ samples a $K_b \in \mathcal{K}$, runs $\mathcal{A}(pk, c^*, K_b)$, measures $\mathcal{A}$'s query to H in the computational basis, and returns the measurement outcome without any further analysis. It is obvious that the advantage of $R^{\mathcal{A}}(pk, c^*)$ against the OW-CPA security of the underlying DPKE is p, that is $\mathrm{Adv}_{\mathrm{DPKE}}^{\mathrm{OW\text{-}CPA}}(R^{\mathcal{A}}) = p$. Thus, through the adversary $\mathcal{A}$, a simple measurement-based reduction in [23] *inevitably* has a quadratic security loss, $\mathrm{Adv}_{\mathrm{KEM}-\mathrm{U}_m^{\not\perp}}^{\mathrm{IND\text{-}CCA}}(\mathcal{A}) \gtrsim \sqrt{p} = \sqrt{\mathrm{Adv}_{\mathrm{DPKE}}^{\mathrm{OW\text{-}CPA}}(R^{\mathcal{A}})}$, which matches the bound given by [23].

Next, we consider *a general measurement-based (black-box) reduction R* described as follows. Since only one RO-query is revealed by the constructed adversary in Sect. 3, we just need to consider the behaviors of a reduction interacting with an adversary that just makes a single RO-query.

1. Reduction R receives a challenge $inpt_1$ as input, runs a PPT preprocessing (quantum) subalgorithm $(inpt, rand, s) \leftarrow R_1(inpt_1)$, and then launches $\mathcal{A}(inpt; rand)$[13].
2. When $\mathcal{A}$ makes a query to the RO with quantum state ϕ, R measures ϕ in the computational basis[14], and gets the measurement outcome $mest$.
3. Reduction R runs a PPT postprocessing (quantum) subalgorithm $out \leftarrow R_2(s, mest)$, and returns out.

Take the adversary $\mathcal{A}$ in Sect. 3 and a reduction R against the OW-CPA security of DPKE as an example. The reduction $R^{\mathcal{A}}(inpt_1 = (pk_1, c_1^*))$ runs $\mathcal{A}(inpt = (pk, c^*, K_b); rand = (r_1, r_2))$ in a black-box manner (any preprocessing subalgorithm R_1 is allowed and (pk, c^*) is not required to be (pk_1, c_1^*)), measures $\mathcal{A}$'s query in the computational basis, and uses the measurement outcome (any

---

[12] An extension to measurement-based reductions with *simple* sequential rewinding can be found in Appendix C.

[13] Here, $inpt_1$, $inpt$ and $rand$ are classical, and s can be a quantum state.

[14] The reduction R just measures the query input registers.

postprocessing subalgorithm (R_2 or R_3) is allowed) to break the DPKE OW-CPA security.

Remark 3. Performing an additional quantum (unitary) operation on adversary's query before measuring isn't allowed. But, such an additional unitary operation U cannot substantially increase reduction's advantage. The sole RO-query by our adversary in Sect. 3 is $|\psi_{-1}\rangle = \sqrt{p}|m^*\rangle|0\rangle + \sqrt{1-p}|m'\rangle|\Sigma\rangle$, where $|m'\rangle|\Sigma\rangle$ can be efficiently derived without m^*. The direct measurement $P = |m^*\rangle\langle m^*|$ gives advantage p. If U is applied before P, we still have advantage $\|PU|\psi_{-1}\rangle\|^2 \lesssim \|PU\sqrt{p}|m^*\rangle|0\rangle\|^2 \leq p$, since $\|PU|m'\rangle|\Sigma\rangle\|^2$ is negligible (otherwise we can easily construct $|m'\rangle|\Sigma\rangle$, and use U to break the DPKE OW-CPA security without adversary's aid).

Remark 4. The currently known black-box reductions [5,22–27], run the adversary once without rewinding, measure the adversary's queries, and directly take the measurement outcome as a return (without any further postprocessing) to break the underlying assumption. These measurements are standard measurement in computational basis, semi-classical measurement in [38] or the compressed measurement based on Zhandry's compressed oracle technique [26]. Since the adversary's RO query is the superposition of two terms $|m^*\rangle|0\rangle$ and $|m'\rangle|\Sigma\rangle$, the semi-classical measurement and the compressed measurement are equivalent to the standard measurement considered in this paper. In addition, measurement-based reductions do not restrict the simulations of random oracles and other oracles that adversary queries. Thus, our results can cover the black-box reductions in [5,22–27].

Constructing meta-reductions against the OW-CPA security, we bound the advantages of a measurement-based black-box reduction by the advantages of the meta-reductions. In general, the construction and analysis of meta-reductions are complicated since the meta-reductions need to efficiently simulate the unbounded adversary. But, thanks to our well-designed adversary in Sect. 3, the construction of our meta-reductions is concise, and the analysis is generally accessible.

Theorem 4.1. *If the underlying DPKE is perfectly correct, for any above described measurement-based reduction $R^{\mathcal{A}}$ that run the adversary $\mathcal{A}$ once without rewinding, there exist two meta-reductions MR_1^R and MR_2^R against the OW-CPA security of the underlying DPKE such that*

$$\mathrm{Adv}_{\mathrm{DPKE}}^{\mathrm{OW\text{-}CPA}}(R^{\mathcal{A}}) \leq p + \mathrm{Adv}_{\mathrm{DPKE}}^{\mathrm{OW\text{-}CPA}}(MR_1^R) + \frac{|\mathcal{M}|}{|\mathcal{M}| - 1}\mathrm{Adv}_{\mathrm{DPKE}}^{\mathrm{OW\text{-}CPA}}(MR_2^R),$$

and $\mathsf{Time}(R) \approx \mathsf{Time}(MR_1^R) \approx \mathsf{Time}(MR_2^R)$.

Let (pk_1, c_1^*) be the challenge given to $R^{\mathcal{A}}$ against the OW-CPA security of underlying PKE, where $(pk_1, sk_1) \leftarrow Gen'$, $m_1^* \overset{\$}{\leftarrow} \mathcal{M}$, and $c_1^* = Enc'(pk_1, m_1^*)$. Then, $\mathrm{Adv}_{\mathrm{DPKE}}^{\mathrm{OW\text{-}CPA}}(R^{\mathcal{A}}) = \Pr[R^{\mathcal{A}} \Rightarrow m_1^*]$. Let (pk, c^*, K_b) be the input to $\mathcal{A}$ provided by $R^{\mathcal{A}}$. Since the underlying DPKE is perfectly correct, there are no more than one m^* such that $Enc'(pk, m^*) = c^*$. Let EXI be the event that there exists an m^* such that $Enc'(pk, m^*) = c^*$, and INE be the event that such an m^* dose not exist. Thus,

$$
\begin{aligned}
\mathsf{Adv}_{\mathrm{DPKE}}^{\mathrm{OW\text{-}CPA}}(R^{\mathcal{A}}) &= \Pr[R^{\mathcal{A}} \Rightarrow m_1^* \wedge \mathrm{EXI}] + \Pr[R^{\mathcal{A}} \Rightarrow m_1^* \wedge \mathrm{INE}] \\
&\leq \Pr[\mathrm{EXI}] \cdot \Pr[R^{\mathcal{A}} \Rightarrow m_1^* | \mathrm{EXI}] + \Pr[R^{\mathcal{A}} \Rightarrow m_1^* \wedge \mathrm{INE}]. \quad (1)
\end{aligned}
$$

Denote GOOD as the event that the measurement on $\mathcal{A}$'s query returns an m^* such that $Enc(pk, m^*) = c^*$, and BAD as the event that an $m' \neq m^*$ is returned. It's apparent that $\Pr[\mathrm{GOOD}|\mathrm{EXI}] = p$ and $\Pr[\mathrm{BAD}|\mathrm{EXI}] = 1 - p$. Thus, we have

$$
\begin{aligned}
\Pr[R^{\mathcal{A}} \Rightarrow m_1^* | \mathrm{EXI}] &= \Pr[R^{\mathcal{A}} \Rightarrow m_1^* | \mathrm{EXI} \wedge \mathrm{GOOD}] \Pr[\mathrm{GOOD}|\mathrm{EXI}] \\
&\quad + \Pr[R^{\mathcal{A}} \Rightarrow m_1^* | \mathrm{EXI} \wedge \mathrm{BAD}] \Pr[\mathrm{BAD}|\mathrm{EXI}] \\
&\leq p + \Pr[R^{\mathcal{A}} \Rightarrow m_1^* | \mathrm{EXI} \wedge \mathrm{BAD}]. \quad (2)
\end{aligned}
$$

Combining the Eqs. (1) and (2), we have

$$
\mathsf{Adv}_{\mathrm{DPKE}}^{\mathrm{OW\text{-}CPA}}(R^{\mathcal{A}}) \leq p + \Pr[R^{\mathcal{A}} \Rightarrow m_1^* \wedge \mathrm{INE}] + \Pr[\mathrm{EXI}] \cdot \Pr[R^{\mathcal{A}} \Rightarrow m_1^* | \mathrm{EXI} \wedge \mathrm{BAD}].
$$

Then, we give upperbounds of $\Pr[R^{\mathcal{A}} \Rightarrow m^* \wedge \mathrm{INE}]$ and $\Pr[\mathrm{EXI}] \cdot \Pr[R^{\mathcal{A}} \Rightarrow m_1^* | \mathrm{BAD} \wedge \mathrm{EXI}]$ by the following Lemmas 4.1 and 4.2.

Lemma 4.1. *There exists a meta-reduction MR_1^R such that $\Pr[R^{\mathcal{A}} \Rightarrow m^* \wedge \mathrm{INE}] \leq \mathsf{Adv}_{\mathrm{DPKE}}^{\mathrm{OW\text{-}CPA}}(MR_1^R)$, and $\mathsf{Time}(R) \approx \mathsf{Time}(MR_1^R)$.*

Proof. Let $\mathcal{A}_1(pk, c^*, K_b)$ be a trivial adversary against the IND-CCA game of $\mathrm{KEM} - \mathrm{U}_m^{\not\perp}$ that always returns 1 and does nothing else. It is obvious that when INE happens, both $\mathcal{A}$ and $\mathcal{A}_1(pk, c^*, K_b)$ just outputs 1, and $\Pr[R^{\mathcal{A}} \Rightarrow m^* \wedge \mathrm{INE}] = \Pr[R^{\mathcal{A}_1} \Rightarrow m^* \wedge \mathrm{INE}]$.

Let $MR_1^R(pk_1, c_1^*)$ be a meta reduction that simulates $\mathcal{A}_1$, runs $R^{\mathcal{A}_1}(pk_1, c_1^*)$, and returns $R^{\mathcal{A}_1}$'s output. It's obvious that $\mathsf{Adv}_{\mathrm{DPKE}}^{\mathrm{OW\text{-}CPA}}(MR_1^R) = \mathsf{Adv}_{\mathrm{DPKE}}^{\mathrm{OW\text{-}CPA}}(R^{\mathcal{A}_1})$. Since $\mathsf{Adv}_{\mathrm{DPKE}}^{\mathrm{OW\text{-}CPA}}(R^{\mathcal{A}_1}) \geq \Pr[R^{\mathcal{A}_1} \Rightarrow m^* \wedge \mathrm{INE}]$, we have

$$
\Pr[R^{\mathcal{A}} \Rightarrow m^* \wedge \mathrm{INE}] \leq \mathsf{Adv}_{\mathrm{DPKE}}^{\mathrm{OW\text{-}CPA}}(MR_1^R).
$$

Since $\mathsf{Time}(\mathcal{A}_1)$ is negligible, $\mathsf{Time}(MR_1^R) \approx \mathsf{Time}(R) + \mathsf{Time}(\mathcal{A}_1) \approx \mathsf{Time}(R)$. $\square$

Lemma 4.2. *There exists a meta-reduction MR_2^R such that $\Pr[\mathrm{EXI}] \cdot \Pr[R^{\mathcal{A}} \Rightarrow m_1^* | \mathrm{EXI} \wedge \mathrm{BAD}] \leq \frac{|\mathcal{M}|}{|\mathcal{M}|-1} \mathsf{Adv}_{\mathrm{DPKE}}^{\mathrm{OW\text{-}CPA}}(MR_2^R)$, and $\mathsf{Time}(R) \approx \mathsf{Time}(MR_2^R)$.*

Proof. Let $\mathcal{A}_2$ be an adversary against the IND-CCA game of $\mathrm{KEM} - \mathrm{U}_m^{\not\perp}$ which queries the random oracle H with quantum state $\psi'_{-1} = \sum_{m,k} \frac{1}{\sqrt{|\mathcal{M}| \cdot |\mathcal{K}|}} |m\rangle |k\rangle$, and outputs 1 with probability 1 (after the return of the random oracle H).

We note that under the condition $\text{EXI} \wedge \text{BAD}$, both measurement outcomes of $\mathcal{A}$'s query and $\mathcal{A}_2$'s query obey the uniform distribution over $\{m' \in \mathcal{M} : m' \neq m^*\}$. Thus, $\Pr[R^{\mathcal{A}} \Rightarrow m_1^* | \text{EXI} \wedge \text{BAD}] = \Pr[R^{\mathcal{A}_2} \Rightarrow m^* | \text{EXI} \wedge \text{BAD}]$.

Construct a meta reduction $MR_2^R(pk_1, c_1^*)$ against the OW-CPA security of the underlying DPKE that simulates $\mathcal{A}_2$, runs $R^{\mathcal{A}_2}(pk_1, c_1^*)$, and returns $R^{\mathcal{A}_2}$'s output.

It is easy to see that for above $\mathcal{A}_2$ and MR_2^R, $\Pr[\text{GOOD}|\text{EXI}] = \frac{1}{|\mathcal{M}|}$ and $\Pr[\text{BAD}|\text{EXI}] = 1 - \frac{1}{|\mathcal{M}|}$. Then, we have

$$\begin{aligned}
\text{Adv}_{\text{DPKE}}^{\text{OW-CPA}}(MR_2^R) = \text{Adv}_{\text{DPKE}}^{\text{OW-CPA}}(R^{\mathcal{A}_2}) &\geq \Pr[R^{\mathcal{A}_2} \Rightarrow m^* | \text{EXI}] \cdot \Pr[\text{EXI}] \\
&\geq (1 - \frac{1}{|\mathcal{M}|}) \Pr[R^{\mathcal{A}_2} \Rightarrow m^* | \text{EXI} \wedge \text{BAD}] \cdot \Pr[\text{EXI}] \\
&= (1 - \frac{1}{|\mathcal{M}|}) \Pr[R^{\mathcal{A}} \Rightarrow m_1^* | \text{EXI} \wedge \text{BAD}] \cdot \Pr[\text{EXI}]
\end{aligned}$$

as we wanted. Since $\text{Time}(\mathcal{A}_2)$ is negligible, $\text{Time}(MR_2^R) \approx \text{Time}(R) + \text{Time}(\mathcal{A}_2) \approx \text{Time}(R)$. □

5 Impossibility Results for FO-Like KEMs

Combing Theorems 3.1 and 4.1, we can directly obtain the following main Theorem.

Theorem 5.1. *If the underlying DPKE is perfectly correct, there exists a quantum adversary $\mathcal{A}$ against the IND-CCA security of $\text{KEM} - \text{U}_m^{\not\perp}$ such that for any measurement-based black-box reduction $R^{\mathcal{A}}$ that runs $\mathcal{A}$ (once without rewinding), measures $\mathcal{A}$'s query and uses the measurement outcome to break the OW-CPA security of the underlying DPKE, there exist two meta-reductions MR_1^R and MR_2^R which take R as a subroutine to break the OW-CPA security of the underlying DPKE such that $\text{Adv}_{\text{KEM}-\text{U}_m^{\not\perp}}^{\text{IND-CCA}}(\mathcal{A}) \geq$*

$$(1 - \tfrac{1}{|\mathcal{K}|}) \times \sqrt{\text{Adv}_{\text{DPKE}}^{\text{OW-CPA}}(R^{\mathcal{A}}) - \text{Adv}_{\text{DPKE}}^{\text{OW-CPA}}(MR_1^R)} - \tfrac{|\mathcal{M}|}{|\mathcal{M}|-1} \cdot \text{Adv}_{\text{DPKE}}^{\text{OW-CPA}}(MR_2^R)$$

and $\text{Time}(R) \approx \text{Time}(MR_1^R) \approx \text{Time}(MR_2^R)$.

Assuming that no PPT adversary can break the OW-CPA security of the underlying DPKE with non-negligible probability, we must have that $\text{Adv}_{\text{DPKE}}^{\text{OW-CPA}}(MR_1^R) \approx \text{Adv}_{\text{DPKE}}^{\text{OW-CPA}}(MR_2^R) \in \text{negl}(\lambda)$ since $\text{Time}(MR_1^R) \approx \text{Time}(MR_2^R) \approx \text{Time}(R)$ is polynomial[15], and the message space $\mathcal{M}$ is exponentially large due to the brute-force attack. For real-world applications, the key space $\mathcal{K}$ is also exponentially large. Thus, $1 - \frac{1}{|\mathcal{K}|} \approx 1$ and $\frac{|\mathcal{M}|}{|\mathcal{M}|-1} \approx 1$.

---

[15] We remark that $\text{Time}(R^{\mathcal{A}}) = \text{Time}(R) + \text{Time}(\mathcal{A})$ is exponential since $\mathcal{A}$ is an unbounded adversary.

Thus, informally, Theorem 5.1 shows the existence of a quantum adversary $\mathcal{A}$ against the IND-CCA security of $\mathrm{KEM} - \mathrm{U}_m^{\not\perp}$ with advantage $\epsilon_{\mathcal{A}} = \mathrm{Adv}^{\mathrm{IND\text{-}CCA}}_{\mathrm{KEM\text{-}U}_m^{\not\perp}}(\mathcal{A})$ such that for any measurement-based black-box reduction $R^{\mathcal{A}}$ that takes $\mathcal{A}$ as a subroutine to break the OW-CPA security of the underlying DPKE, the advantage $\epsilon_R = \mathrm{Adv}^{\mathrm{OW\text{-}CPA}}_{\mathrm{DPKE}}(R^{\mathcal{A}})$ is approximately at most $\epsilon_{\mathcal{A}}^2$, i.e., $\epsilon_R \lesssim \epsilon_{\mathcal{A}}^2$. Namely, for $\mathrm{KEM} - \mathrm{U}_m^{\not\perp}$ from a OW-CPA-secure DPKE, measurement-based black-box reductions *inevitably* have a quadratic security loss.

As discussed in Sect. 4, the black-box reductions in [22–27] belong to the class of measurement-based reductions considered in this paper. Thus, Theorem 5.1 suggests an explanation for the lack of progress in improving the black-box reduction tightness in terms of the degree of security loss.

Remark 5. The impossibility result in Theorem 5.1 and subsequent generalizations in Sects. 5.1 and 6.2 can be extended to cover measurement-based reductions with *simple* rewinding[16]. The *simple* rewinding here is a quantum counterpart of classical sequential rewinding [46]. In this rewinding, the reduction restarts the adversary with the same input and randomness from the very beginning, which is different from the rewinding in [37] where the reduction applies the inverses of the adversary's quantum operations (that have been applied already) on the adversary's registers from the end of adversary's run. In addition, the adversary is not allowed to use the intrinsic "quantum randomness" or have auxiliary quantum input, which guarantees the reduction can re-create the same quantum query state as before at every interaction point. In Appendix C, we will show that when *simple* rewinding is applied r times ($r \geq 1$), we still have $\epsilon_R \lesssim (r+1)\epsilon_{\mathcal{A}}^2$. Namely, the *simple* rewinding might increase the advantage of R by $r \cdot \epsilon_{\mathcal{A}}^2$, but the running time of R will be accordingly increased by $r \cdot \mathsf{Time}(\mathcal{A})$, where $\mathsf{Time}(\mathcal{A})$ is the running time of $\mathcal{A}$.

5.1 Extension to Other FO-Like KEMs

$\mathrm{U}_m^{\perp}$, $\mathrm{U}^{\perp}$, $\mathrm{U}^{\not\perp}$, $\mathrm{QU}_m^{\not\perp}$ and $\mathrm{QU}_m^{\perp}$ are variants of $\mathrm{U}_m^{\not\perp}$, where m (without m, resp.) means $K = H(m)$ ($K = H(m,c)$, resp.), $\not\perp$ ($\perp$, resp.) means implicit (explicit, resp.) rejection[17] and Q means adding an additional Targhi-Unruh hash to the ciphertext. It is easy to see that our main results for $\mathrm{U}_m^{\not\perp}$ can also apply to above variants from one-wayness security assumption. That is, measurement-based black-box reductions for these variants from one-wayness security assumption will *inevitably* have a quadratic security loss.

$\mathrm{FO}^{\not\perp}$, $\mathrm{FO}^{\perp}$, $\mathrm{FO}_m^{\not\perp}$, $\mathrm{FO}_m^{\perp}$, $\mathrm{QFO}_m^{\not\perp}$ and $\mathrm{QFO}_m^{\perp}$ in [5] are KEM variants of the FO transformation [6,7], and widely used in the NIST KEM submissions. Following

---

[16] In general, the rewinding is challenging when quantum adversaries are considered, see [63].

[17] In implicit (explicit) rejection, a pseudorandom key (an abnormal symbol $\perp$) is returned for an invalid ciphertext.

the same analysis for $\text{KEM} - \text{U}_m^{\not\perp}$, we can also show that for these KEM variants of the FO transformation from standard OW-CPA security (and even IND-CPA security) of the underlying PKE, quadratic security loss is also inevitable for measurement-based black-box reductions.

Gen	Encaps(pk)	Decaps(sk', c)
$1: (pk, sk) \leftarrow Gen'$	$1: m \xleftarrow{\$} \mathcal{M}$	$1:$ Parse $sk' = (sk, k)$
$2: k \xleftarrow{\$} \mathcal{K}^{prf}$	$2: c = Enc'(pk, m; G(m))$	$2: m' := Dec'(sk, c)$
$3: sk' := (sk, k)$	$3: K := H(m)$	$3:$ **if** $Enc'(pk, m'; G(m')) = c$
$4:$ **return** (pk, sk')	$4:$ **return** (K, c)	$4:$ **return** $K := H(m')$
		$5:$ **else return** $K := f(k, c)$

Fig. 3. $\text{KEM} - \text{FO}_m^{\not\perp} = \text{FO}_m^{\not\perp}[\text{PKE,}G\text{,}H\text{,}f]$, where $\text{PKE} = (Gen', Enc', Dec')$ with message space $\mathcal{M}$ and randomness space R, $G : \mathcal{M} \to R$, $H : \mathcal{M} \to \mathcal{K}$ are hash functions, and f is a PRF with key space $\mathcal{K}^{prf}$.

Theorem 5.2. *If the underlying PKE is perfectly correct, there exists a quantum adversary $\mathcal{A}$ against the IND-CCA security of $\text{KEM} - \text{FO}_m^{\not\perp}$ (see Fig. 3) such that for any measurement-based black-box reduction $R^{\mathcal{A}}$ that runs $\mathcal{A}$ (once without rewinding), measures $\mathcal{A}$'s query in the computational basis, and uses the measurement outcome to break the IND-CPA security (OW-CPA security, resp.) of the underlying PKE, there exist two meta-reductions MR_1^R and MR_2^R which take R as a subroutine to break the IND-CPA security (OW-CPA security, resp.) of the underlying PKE such that $\text{Time}(R) \approx \text{Time}(MR_1^R) \approx \text{Time}(MR_2^R)$ and $\text{Adv}_{\text{KEM-FO}_m^{\not\perp}}^{\text{IND-CCA}}(\mathcal{A}) \geq$*

$$(1 - \tfrac{1}{|\mathcal{K}|})\sqrt{\text{Adv}_{\text{PKE}}^{\text{IND-CPA}}(R^{\mathcal{A}}) - \epsilon_1^{\text{IND}} - \tfrac{|\mathcal{M}|}{|\mathcal{M}|-1} \cdot (\epsilon_2^{\text{IND}} + \tfrac{1}{|\mathcal{M}|})}$$

$$((1 - \tfrac{1}{|\mathcal{K}|})\sqrt{\text{Adv}_{\text{PKE}}^{\text{OW-CPA}}(R^{\mathcal{A}}) - \epsilon_1^{\text{OW}} - \tfrac{|\mathcal{M}|}{|\mathcal{M}|-1} \cdot \epsilon_2^{\text{OW}}}, \; resp.),$$

where $\epsilon_1^{\text{IND}} = \text{Adv}_{\text{PKE}}^{\text{IND-CPA}}(MR_1^R)$, $\epsilon_2^{\text{IND}} = \text{Adv}_{\text{PKE}}^{\text{IND-CPA}}(MR_2^R)$, $\epsilon_1^{\text{OW}} = \text{Adv}_{\text{PKE}}^{\text{OW-CPA}}(MR_1^R)$ and $\epsilon_2^{\text{OW}} = \text{Adv}_{\text{PKE}}^{\text{OW-CPA}}(MR_2^R)$.

Remark 6. It is not hard to extend above results to other KEM variants of the FO transformation, including $\text{FO}^{\not\perp}$, $\text{FO}^{\perp}$, $\text{FO}_m^{\perp}$, $\text{QFO}_m^{\not\perp}$ and $\text{QFO}_m^{\perp}$, we just omit them in this paper.

The proof of Theorem 5.2 is similar to the proof of Theorem 5.1. We first construct a quantum adversary $\mathcal{A}$ against the IND-CCA security of $\text{KEM} - \text{FO}_m^{\not\perp}$ with advantage at least $(1 - \tfrac{1}{|\mathcal{K}|})\sqrt{p}$, and then use the meta-reduction methodology to bound the advantage of a measurement-based black-box reduction against the IND-CPA security (OW-CPA security, resp.) of the underlying PKE. The complete proofs are presented in the full version [39].

6 A Generalization of Our Impossibility Results

We note that the quantum adversaries against the IND-CCA security of FO-like KEMs in Sect. 5 make no queries to the decapsulation oracle. Therefore, the distinction between the IND-CPA security and the IND-CCA security of KEM is irrelevant. Thus, the impossibility results in Sect. 5 can be roughly interpreted as the unavoidable quadratic loss incurred by the black-box reduction from a search problem to an indistinguishability-based security.

In this section, we give a generalization of our impossibility results and show that a black-box one-way-to-hiding (OW2H) technique[18] that turns a one-wayness-style (search) problem into a hiding-style (decision) problem via a quantum random oracle, will *inevitably* incur a quadratic reduction loss. Thus, our impossibility results can also be used to explain why the quadratic loss in the black-box OW2H lemmas is unavoidable.

6.1 One-Way to Hiding

Here, the description of one-way to hiding reduction follows [40].

Given a one-way function $f : \{0,1\}^m \rightarrow \{0,1\}^n$ and a random oracle $H : \{0,1\}^m \rightarrow \{0,1\}^{n'}$, a hiding-style problem can be given as follows.

Construct a distinguishing game DIST for an adversary $\mathcal{A}$.

$$
\begin{array}{l}
\mathrm{DIST}(|\psi_0\rangle, |\psi_1\rangle) \\
\hline
b \xleftarrow{\$} \{0,1\}, x \xleftarrow{\$} \{0,1\}^m, K_0 = H(x), K_1 \xleftarrow{\$} \{0,1\}^{n'} \\
b' \leftarrow \mathcal{A}(f(x), K_b), \textbf{return } b' = ?b
\end{array}
$$

Define the advantage of $\mathcal{A}$ against the game DIST as $\mathsf{Adv}_{Hiding}^{\mathrm{DIST}}(\mathcal{A}) :=$

$$
|2\Pr[\mathrm{DIST}_{Hiding}^{\mathcal{A}} = 1] - 1| = |\Pr[\mathcal{A} \Rightarrow 1|b=0] - \Pr[\mathcal{A} \Rightarrow 1|b=1]|.
$$

Such a one-way to hiding technique can be seen as a generalization of FO-like KEMs. In particular, the one-way function f can be instantiated by the encryption algorithm of the underlying PKE, the one-wayness of f is exactly the one-way security of the underlying PKE, and the hardness of solving the hiding-style problem is exactly the indistinguishable security of the resulting KEM.

Query-based reduction in the ROM. We note that $\mathsf{Adv}_{Hiding}^{\mathrm{DIST}}(\mathcal{A})$ can be bounded by the probability of the adversary $\mathcal{A}$ querying H with x. Thus, in the ROM, it is easy to construct a query-based reduction $R^{\mathcal{A}}$ against the one-wayness of f by running $\mathcal{A}$ and taking one of $\mathcal{A}$'s queries to H as a return. Obviously,

$$
\mathsf{Adv}_{Hiding}^{\mathrm{DIST}}(\mathcal{A}) \leq q\mathsf{Adv}_f^{\mathrm{OW}}(R^{\mathcal{A}}).
$$

Thus, the indistinguishability between K_0 and K_1 is reduced to the hardness of inverting $f(x)$.

---

[18] This name follows Unruh's paper [40].

Measurement-based reduction in the QROM. The case in the QROM is complicated since $\mathcal{A}$ may make queries to H with quantum state and it's hard to well define whether x is queried. To circumvent this issue, Unruh [40] gave the following OW2H lemma, which essentially gives a measurement-based black-box reduction from a one-wayness-style property (unpredictability) to a hiding-style property (indistinguishability security) with quadratic loss.

Lemma 6.1. ([40, Lemma 6.2] and [38, Theorem 3] (OW2H)). *Let $S \subseteq X$ be random. Let $G, H : X \to Y$ be random functions satisfying $\forall m \notin S, G(m) = H(m)$. Let z be a random value. (S, G, H, z may have arbitrary joint distribution.) Consider an oracle algorithm A^O (not necessarily reversible[19]) that makes at most q queries to O ($O \in \{G, H\}$). Let B be an oracle algorithm that on input z does the following: pick $i \xleftarrow{\$} \{1, \ldots, q\}$, run $A^H(z)$ until (just before) the i-th query, measure the query input registers in the computational basis, output the set T of measurement outcomes. (When A makes less than i queries, B outputs $\bot \notin X$).*
  Let
$$P_A^1 = \Pr[b' = 1 : b' \leftarrow A^H(z)],$$
$$P_A^2 = \Pr[b' = 1 : b' \leftarrow A^G(z)],$$
$$P_B := \Pr[S \cap T \neq \emptyset : T \leftarrow B^H(z)].$$

Then,
$$|P_A^1 - P_A^2| \leq 2q\sqrt{P_B}.$$

The OW2H lemma can be used to reduce the one-wayness of the function f (search problem) to the hardness of solving the aforementioned distinguishing problem between $K_0 = H(x)$ and a uniformly random K_1 (decision problem) in a black-box manner. Let $X = \{0,1\}^m$, $Y = \{0,1\}^{n'}$, $S = \{x\}$, $H = H$, $G(x) = K_1$ and $z = (f(x), K_1)$. Let $\mathcal{A}^O(z)$ ($O \in \{G, H\}$) be an oracle algorithm that runs $\mathcal{A}^O(z)$, and returns $\mathcal{A}$'s guessing. Then, we have $P_A^1 = \Pr[\mathcal{A} \Rightarrow 1 | b = 1]$ and $P_A^2 = \Pr[\mathcal{A} \Rightarrow 1 | b = 0]$. Let $R^{\mathcal{A}}(f(x))$ be a measurement-based black-box reduction that picks $i \xleftarrow{\$} \{1, \ldots, q\}$ and $y \xleftarrow{\$} \{0,1\}^{n'}$, runs $\mathcal{A}(f(x), y)$ until (just before) the i-th query, measures the query in the computational basis, output the measurement outcome. Thus, $P_B = \mathrm{Adv}_f^{\mathrm{OW}}(R^{\mathcal{A}})$. Applying Lemma 6.1, we have
$$\mathrm{Adv}_{Hiding}^{DIST}(\mathcal{A}) \leq 2q\sqrt{\mathrm{Adv}_f^{\mathrm{OW}}(R^{\mathcal{A}})}.$$

6.2 Impossibility Results for One-Way to Hiding

As we can see, the reduction given by the OW2H lemma (Lemma 6.1) is highly non-tight. The degree of reduction loss is two (i.e., $\tau = 2$), and the factor of reduction loss is about $O(q^2)$ (i.e., $\kappa = O(q^2)$). Very recently, several variants of the OW2H lemma [26,38] are introduced with tighter bounds in some special

---

[19] In [38, Theorem 3], Ambainis et al. state that A^O is not necessarily unitary. Note that a unitary algorithm must be reversible. To make a clear comparison with the non-black-box OW2H in [37], we substitute 'unitary' by 'reversible'.

cases. In particular, using the semi-classical oracle technique, [38] improved the factor of reduction loss κ to be $O(q)$. Following the compressed oracle technique developed by [34] to record adversary's queries, [26] further improved κ to be $O(1)$. However, all these OW2H lemmas still have a quadratic reduction loss. The reductions in [26,38,40] are black-box. In the following, we will show such a quadratic loss is unavoidable for these black-box reductions [26,38,40].

Theorem 6.1. *If the underlying f is injective, there exists a quantum adversary $\mathcal{A}$ solving the hiding-style problem such that for any measurement-based black-box reduction $R^{\mathcal{A}}$ that runs $\mathcal{A}$ (once without rewinding), measures $\mathcal{A}$'s query and uses the measurement outcome to break the one-wayness of the underlying f, there exist two meta-reductions MR_1^R and MR_2^R which take R as a subroutine to break the one-wayness of the underlying f such that* $\mathrm{Adv}_{Hiding}^{\mathrm{DIST}}(\mathcal{A}) \geq$

$$\frac{2^{n'} - 1}{2^{n'}} \sqrt{\mathrm{Adv}_f^{\mathrm{OW}}(R^{\mathcal{A}}) - \mathrm{Adv}_f^{\mathrm{OW}}(MR_1^R) - \frac{2^m}{2^m - 1} \cdot \mathrm{Adv}_f^{\mathrm{OW}}(MR_2^R)},$$

and $\mathsf{Time}(R) \approx \mathsf{Time}(MR_1^R) \approx \mathsf{Time}(MR_2^R)$.

The proof of Theorem 6.1 is essentially the same as the one of Theorem 5.1. We present it in the full version [39].

Assuming f is a one-way function, we have $\mathrm{Adv}_f^{\mathrm{OW}}(MR_1^R) \approx \mathrm{Adv}_f^{\mathrm{OW}}(MR_2^R) \in \mathsf{negl}(\lambda)$ since $\mathsf{Time}(MR_1^R) \approx \mathsf{Time}(MR_2^R) \approx \mathsf{Time}(R)$ is polynomial. Note that $\frac{2^m}{2^m - 1} \leq 2$. Thus, informally, Theorem 6.1 shows the existence of a quantum adversary $\mathcal{A}$ solving the hiding-style problem with advantage $\epsilon_{\mathcal{A}} = \mathrm{Adv}_{Hiding}^{\mathrm{DIST}}(\mathcal{A})$ such that for any measurement-based black-box reduction $R^{\mathcal{A}}$ that takes $\mathcal{A}$ as a subroutine to break the one-wayness of the underlying f, the advantage $\epsilon_R = \mathrm{Adv}_f^{\mathrm{OW}}(R^{\mathcal{A}})$ is approximately at most $\epsilon_{\mathcal{A}}^2$, i.e., $\epsilon_R \lesssim \epsilon_{\mathcal{A}}^2$. Namely, for the one-way to hiding technique, measurement-based black-box reductions *inevitably* have a quadratic loss.

Acknowledgements. We would like to thank anonymous reviewers for their insightful comments and suggestions. Haodong Jiang was supported by the National Key R&D Program of China (No. 2020YFA0309705), and the National Natural Science Foundation of China (Nos. 62002385, 61701539, 61802376). Zhenfeng Zhang was supported by the National Key R&D Program of China (No. 2017YFB0802000). Zhi Ma was supported by the National Natural Science Foundation of China (No. 61972413).

A   Cryptographic Primitives

Definition A.1 (One-way function (OWF)). *We say a function $f : \{0,1\}^n \rightarrow \{0,1\}^m$ is a one way function if for any PPT adversary $\mathcal{A}$, the following advantage function is negligible in λ:* $\mathrm{Adv}_f^{\mathrm{OW}}(\mathcal{A}) := \Pr[x' = x^* : x^* \xleftarrow{\$} \{0,1\}^n; y^* \leftarrow f(x^*); x' \leftarrow \mathcal{A}(1^\lambda, y^*)]$.

Definition A.2 (Public-key encryption). *A public-key encryption scheme* PKE $= (Gen, Enc, Dec)$ *consists of a triple of polynomial time (in the security parameter λ) algorithms and a finite message space $\mathcal{M}$. (1) $Gen(1^\lambda) \rightarrow (pk, sk)$: the key generation algorithm, is a probabilistic algorithm which on input 1^λ outputs a public/secret key-pair (pk, sk). Usually, for brevity, we will omit the input of Gen. (2) $Enc(pk, m) \rightarrow c$: the encryption algorithm Enc, on input pk and a message $m \in \mathcal{M}$, outputs a ciphertext $c \leftarrow Enc(pk, m)$. If necessary, we make the used randomness of encryption explicit by writing $c := Enc(pk, m; r)$, where $r \xleftarrow{\$} R$ (R is the randomness space). (3) $Dec(sk, c) \rightarrow m$: the decryption algorithm Dec, is a deterministic algorithm which on input sk and a ciphertext c outputs a message $m := Dec(sk, c)$ or a rejection symbol $\perp \notin \mathcal{M}$.*

A PKE is deterministic if Enc is deterministic. We denote DPKE to stand for a deterministic PKE.

Definition A.3 (Correctness). *A public-key encryption scheme* PKE *is perfectly correct if for any $(pk, sk) \leftarrow Gen$ and $m \in \mathcal{M}$, we have that $\Pr[Dec(sk, c) = m | c \leftarrow Enc(pk, m)] = 1$.*

Definition A.4 (OW-CPA-secure PKE). *Let* PKE $= (Gen, Enc, Dec)$ *be a public-key encryption scheme with message space $\mathcal{M}$. Define* OW $-$ CPA *game of PKE as in Fig. 4. Define the* OW $-$ CPA *advantage of an adversary $\mathcal{A}$ against PKE as* $\mathsf{Adv}_{\mathrm{PKE}}^{\mathrm{OW\text{-}CPA}}(\mathcal{A}) := \Pr[\text{OW-CPA}_{\mathrm{PKE}}^{\mathcal{A}} = 1]$.

Game OW-CPA	Game IND-CPA
1 : $(pk, sk) \leftarrow Gen; m^* \xleftarrow{\$} \mathcal{M}$	1 : $(pk, sk) \leftarrow Gen; b \leftarrow \{0, 1\}$
2 : $c^* \leftarrow Enc(pk, m^*)$	2 : $(m_0, m_1) \leftarrow \mathcal{A}(pk); c^* \leftarrow Enc(pk, m_b)$
3 : $m' \leftarrow \mathcal{A}(pk, c^*)$	3 : $b' \leftarrow \mathcal{A}(pk, c^*)$
4 : **return** $m' =? m^*$	4 : **return** $b' =? b$

Fig. 4. Game OW-CPA and game IND-CPA for PKE.

Game IND-CCA	$\mathrm{DECAPS}(sk, c)$
1 : $(pk, sk) \leftarrow Gen; b \xleftarrow{\$} \{0, 1\}$	1 : **if** $c = c^*$
2 : $(K_0^*, c^*) \leftarrow Encaps(pk); K_1^* \xleftarrow{\$} \mathcal{K}$	2 : **return** $\perp$
3 : $b' \leftarrow \mathcal{A}^{\mathrm{DECAPS}}(pk, c^*, K_b^*)$	3 : **else return**
4 : **return** $b' =? b$	4 : $K := Decaps(sk, c)$

Fig. 5. Game IND-CCA for KEM.

Definition A.5 (IND-CPA-secure PKE). *Let* PKE $= (Gen, Enc, Dec)$ *be a public-key encryption scheme with message space* $\mathcal{M}$. *Define* IND $-$ CPA *game of PKE as in Fig. 4, where* m_0 *and* m_1 *have the same length. Define the advantage of an adversary* $\mathcal{A}$ *against the* IND $-$ CPA *security of PKE as* $\text{Adv}_{\text{PKE}}^{\text{IND-CPA}}(\mathcal{A}) :=$ $|2\Pr[\text{IND-CPA}_{\text{PKE}}^{\mathcal{A}} = 1] - 1|$.

Definition A.6 (Key encapsulation). *A key encapsulation mechanism KEM consists of three algorithms Gen, Encaps and Decaps. (1) $Gen(1^\lambda) \to (pk, sk)$: the key generation algorithm Gen outputs a key pair (pk, sk). Usually, for brevity, we will omit the input of Gen. (2) $Encaps(pk) \to (K, c)$: the encapsulation algorithm Encaps, on input pk, outputs a tuple (K, c), where $K \in \mathcal{K}$ and c is said to be an encapsulation of the key K. (3) $Decaps(sk, c) \to K$: the deterministic decapsulation algorithm Decaps, on input sk and an encapsulation c, outputs either a key $K := Decaps(sk, c) \in \mathcal{K}$ or a rejection symbol $\perp \notin \mathcal{K}$.*

Definition A.7 (IND-CCA-secure KEM). *We define the* IND $-$ CCA *game as in Fig. 5 and the* IND $-$ CCA *advantage of an adversary* $\mathcal{A}$ *against KEM as* $\text{Adv}_{\text{KEM}}^{\text{IND-CCA}}(\mathcal{A}) := |2\Pr[\text{IND-CCA}_{\text{KEM}}^{\mathcal{A}} = 1] - 1|$.

B   An Alternative Measurement for the Adversary in Sect. 3

In this section, we show that an alternative measurement with operators $M_1 = |\Psi\rangle\langle\Psi|$ and $M_0 = I - M_1$ can also help the adversary in Sect. 3 to achieve advantage at least $\sqrt{p}(1 - 1/|\mathcal{K}|)$, where $|\Psi\rangle = \sin(x)|m^*\rangle|K_b\rangle + \cos(x)|m'\rangle|\Sigma\rangle$ and $x = \frac{1}{2}\arccos(-\frac{\sqrt{p}}{\sqrt{4-3p}})$ $(\sin(2x) \geq 0)$.

Theorem B.1 (The advantage of $\mathcal{A}$ with an alternative measurement). *If the underlying DPKE is perfectly correct, the IND-CCA advantage of $\mathcal{A}$ with the above alternative measurement is at least $\sqrt{p}(1 - \frac{1}{|\mathcal{K}|})$.*

Proof. According to the proof of Theorem 3.1, the m^* that $\mathcal{A}$ gets is exactly the one chosen by the challenger.

Let $|\psi_0\rangle = \sqrt{p}|a\rangle + \sqrt{1-p}|c\rangle$, $|\psi_1\rangle = \sqrt{p}|b\rangle + \sqrt{1-p}|c\rangle$, $|\Psi_0\rangle = \sin(x)|a\rangle + \cos(x)|c\rangle$ and $|\Psi_1\rangle = \sin(x)|b\rangle + \cos(x)|c\rangle$, where $|a\rangle = |m^*\rangle|K_0\rangle$, $|b\rangle = |m^*\rangle|K_1\rangle$, and $|c\rangle = |m'\rangle|\Sigma\rangle$. Then, the probability $\Pr[\mathcal{A} \Rightarrow 1]$ is $|\langle\psi_0|\Psi_0\rangle|^2$ if $b = 0$, and $|\langle\psi_0|\Psi_1\rangle|^2$ if $b = 1$. Thus,

$$\text{Adv}_{\text{KEM}-\text{U}_m^{\not\perp}}^{\text{IND-CCA}}(\mathcal{A}) = ||\langle\psi_0|\Psi_0\rangle|^2 - |\langle\psi_0|\Psi_1\rangle|^2|.$$

When $K_0 = K_1$, $|\Psi_0\rangle = |\Psi_1\rangle$ and the advantage of $\mathcal{A}$ is 0. In the following, we consider the case $K_0 \neq K_1$. It's easy to verify that when $K_0 \neq K_1$, $\langle a|b\rangle = \langle a|c\rangle = \langle b|c\rangle = 0$ since $m^* \neq m'$. Thus, $|\langle\psi_0|\Psi_1\rangle|^2 = |\langle\psi_1|\Psi_0\rangle|^2$. Therefore, the advantage of $\mathcal{A}$ will become

$$\text{Adv}_{\text{KEM}-\text{U}_m^{\not\perp}}^{\text{IND-CCA}}(\mathcal{A}) = ||\langle\psi_0|\Psi_0\rangle|^2 - |\langle\psi_1|\Psi_0\rangle|^2|.$$

Simple calculations show that $||\langle\psi_0|\Psi_0\rangle|^2 - |\langle\psi_1|\Psi_0\rangle|^2| = \sqrt{p}(\frac{\sqrt{p}+\sqrt{4-3p}}{2})$. It is easy to verify that $\sqrt{p} + \sqrt{4 - 3p} \geq 2$ for $0 \leq p \leq 1$. Thus, we can have $||\langle\psi_0|\Psi_0\rangle|^2 - |\langle\psi_1|\Psi_0\rangle|^2| \geq \sqrt{p}$. Note that $K_0 \neq K_1$ with probability $1 - \frac{1}{|\mathcal{K}|}$. Therefore, we have $\mathbf{Adv}^{\text{IND-CCA}}_{\text{KEM}-U_m^{\ell}}(\mathcal{A}) \geq \sqrt{p}(1 - \frac{1}{|\mathcal{K}|}) \approx \sqrt{p}$. $\square$

C   Impossibility Results with Sequential Rewinding

In this section, we show Theorem 5.1 can be extended to cover measurement-based reductions with *simple* rewinding. Similarly, the generalized impossibility results in Secs. 5.1 and 6.2 can be also extended, we just omit them here.

As noted by Remark 5, *simple* rewinding considered here is a simple quantum counterpart of classical sequential rewinding [46]. In particular, quantum adversary $\mathcal{A}$ is not allowed to use intrinsic "quantum randomness" or have auxiliary quantum input. The reduction R can sequentially restart $\mathcal{A}$ with the same input and (classical) randomness used in the first invocation. Thus, $\mathcal{A}$ queries with a fixed quantum state in every invocation. Take the adversary in Sect. 3 as an example. When reduction $R^{\mathcal{A}}$ rewinds $\mathcal{A}$, $R^{\mathcal{A}}$ *restarts* $\mathcal{A}$ with the same input (pk, c^*, K_b) and randomness (r_1, r_2) from the beginning.

Next, we will bound the advantage of a measurement-based black-box reduction with *simple* rewinding, and extend Theorem 4.1 to the following theorem.

Theorem C.1. *If the underlying DPKE is perfectly correct, for any measurement-based black-box reduction $R^{\mathcal{A}}$ that sequentially rewinds the adversary $\mathcal{A}$ at most r $(r \geq 1)$ times, there exist two meta-reductions MR_1^R and MR_2^R against the OW-CPA security of the underlying DPKE such that*

$$\mathbf{Adv}^{\text{OW-CPA}}_{\text{DPKE}}(R^{\mathcal{A}}) \leq (r + 1) \cdot p + \mathbf{Adv}^{\text{OW-CPA}}_{\text{DPKE}}(MR_1^R) + (\frac{|\mathcal{M}|}{|\mathcal{M}| - 1})^{r+1}\mathbf{Adv}^{\text{OW-CPA}}_{\text{DPKE}}(MR_2^R),$$

and $\text{Time}(R) \approx \text{Time}(MR_1^R) \approx \text{Time}(MR_2^R)$.

Proof. The proof of Theorem C.1 has the same skeleton as the one of Theorem 4.1. Let (pk_1, c_1^*) be the challenge given to $R^{\mathcal{A}}$ against the OW-CPA security of underlying PKE, and $\mathbf{Adv}^{\text{OW-CPA}}_{\text{DPKE}}(R^{\mathcal{A}}) = \Pr[R^{\mathcal{A}} \Rightarrow m_1^*]$, where $Enc(pk_1, m_1^*) = c_1^*$. Let (pk, c^*, K_b) be the input to $\mathcal{A}$ provided by $R^{\mathcal{A}}$. We only consider the reduction that rewinds the adversary with the same input and randomness. Thus, (pk, c^*, K_b) and r_1, r_2 are fixed in every rewinding of $\mathcal{A}$. If the event EXI (INE, resp.) happens in the first invocation of $\mathcal{A}$, then the event EXI (INE, resp.) happens in the sequent rewinding with probability 1, where the events EXI and INE are defined as in Sect. 4. Then, define $\overline{\text{INE}}$ ($\overline{\text{EXI}}$, resp.) as the event that INE (EXI, resp.) happens in every invocation of $\mathcal{A}$. Denote $\overline{\text{GOOD}}_i$ $(i \in \{1, \ldots, r + 1\})$ as the event that $\overline{\text{EXI}}$ happens, the measurement of $\mathcal{A}$'s query in the i-th invocation returns m^* such that $Enc(pk, m^*) = c^*$, and all the measurement outputs of $\mathcal{A}$'s queries in the previous $i - 1$ invocations are not

m^*. Denote $\overline{\text{BAD}}$ as the event that $\overline{\text{EXI}}$ happens, and all the the measurement outputs of $\mathcal{A}$'s queries in the $r+1$ invocations are not m^*. Thus, we have

$$\text{Adv}_{\text{DPKE}}^{\text{OW-CPA}}(R^{\mathcal{A}}) = \sum_{i \in [r+1]} \Pr[R^{\mathcal{A}} \Rightarrow m_1^* \wedge \overline{\text{EXI}} \wedge \overline{\text{GOOD}}_i]$$
$$+ \Pr[R^{\mathcal{A}} \Rightarrow m_1^* \wedge \overline{\text{EXI}} \wedge \overline{\text{BAD}}] + \Pr[R^{\mathcal{A}} \Rightarrow m_1^* \wedge \overline{\text{INE}}] \quad (3)$$

Note that for any $i \in \{1, \ldots, r+1\}$, $\Pr[R^{\mathcal{A}} \Rightarrow m_1^* \wedge \overline{\text{EXI}} \wedge \overline{\text{GOOD}}_i]$

$$= \Pr[R^{\mathcal{A}} \Rightarrow m_1^* | \overline{\text{EXI}} \wedge \overline{\text{GOOD}}_i] \Pr[\overline{\text{GOOD}}_i \wedge \overline{\text{EXI}}]$$
$$\leq \Pr[\overline{\text{GOOD}}_i \wedge \overline{\text{EXI}}] = \Pr[\overline{\text{GOOD}}_i | \overline{\text{EXI}}] \Pr[\overline{\text{EXI}}]$$
$$\leq \Pr[\overline{\text{GOOD}}_i | \overline{\text{EXI}}] = (1-p)^{i-1} \cdot p \leq p \quad (4)$$

Thus, combing the Eqs. (3) and (4), we have $\text{Adv}_{\text{DPKE}}^{\text{OW-CPA}}(R^{\mathcal{A}})$

$$\leq (r+1) \cdot p + \Pr[R^{\mathcal{A}} \Rightarrow m_1^* \wedge \overline{\text{EXI}} \wedge \overline{\text{BAD}}] + \Pr[R^{\mathcal{A}} \Rightarrow m_1^* \wedge \overline{\text{INE}}]$$
$$\leq (r+1) \cdot p + \Pr[R^{\mathcal{A}} \Rightarrow m_1^* | \overline{\text{EXI}} \wedge \overline{\text{BAD}}] \cdot \Pr[\overline{\text{EXI}}] + \Pr[R^{\mathcal{A}} \Rightarrow m_1^* \wedge \overline{\text{INE}}] \quad (5)$$

Note that when the event $\overline{\text{INE}}$ happens, $\mathcal{A}$ just outputs 1 for *every* invocation, and can be replaced by a trivial adversary $\mathcal{A}_1$ that always returns 1 and does nothing else. Then, we can construct a meta reduction MR_1^R against the OW-CPA security of DPKE that simulates $\mathcal{A}_1$, runs $R^{\mathcal{A}_1}$ and returns $R^{\mathcal{A}_1}$'s output. Obviously, $\text{Time}(R) \approx \text{Time}(MR_1^R)$. As in Lemma 4.1, we can have

$$\Pr[R^{\mathcal{A}} \Rightarrow m_1^* \wedge \overline{\text{INE}}] \leq \text{Adv}_{\text{DPKE}}^{\text{OW-CPA}}(MR_1^R). \quad (6)$$

Meanwhile, if the event $\overline{\text{EXI}} \wedge \overline{\text{BAD}}$ happens, $\mathcal{A}$ can be substituted with $\mathcal{A}_2$ that queries the random oracle H with $\psi'_{-1} = \sum_{m,k} \frac{1}{\sqrt{|\mathcal{M}| \cdot |\mathcal{K}|}} |m\rangle |k\rangle$, and outputs 1 with probability 1 in every invocation. Then, we can construct a meta reduction MR_2^R against the OW-CPA security of DPKE that simulates $\mathcal{A}_2$, runs $R^{\mathcal{A}_2}$ and returns $R^{\mathcal{A}_2}$'s output. It is easy to see $\text{Time}(R) \approx \text{Time}(MR_2^R)$.

We note that conditioned on $\overline{\text{EXI}} \wedge \overline{\text{BAD}}$, both measurement outcomes of $\mathcal{A}$'s query and $\mathcal{A}_2$'s query obey the uniform distribution over $\{m' \in \mathcal{M} : m' \neq m^*\}$ in every invocation. Thus, $\Pr[R^{\mathcal{A}} \Rightarrow m_1^* | \overline{\text{EXI}} \wedge \overline{\text{BAD}}] = \Pr[R^{\mathcal{A}_2} \Rightarrow m_1^* | \overline{\text{EXI}} \wedge \overline{\text{BAD}}]$. Since $\Pr[\overline{\text{BAD}} | \overline{\text{EXI}}] = (1 - \frac{1}{|\mathcal{M}|})^{r+1}$,

$$\text{Adv}_{\text{DPKE}}^{\text{OW-CPA}}(MR_2^R) = \text{Adv}_{\text{DPKE}}^{\text{OW-CPA}}(R^{\mathcal{A}_2}) \geq \Pr[R^{\mathcal{A}_2} \Rightarrow m_1^* | \overline{\text{EXI}}] \cdot \Pr[\overline{\text{EXI}}]$$
$$\geq (1 - \frac{1}{|\mathcal{M}|})^{r+1} \Pr[R^{\mathcal{A}_2} \Rightarrow m_1^* | \overline{\text{EXI}} \wedge \overline{\text{BAD}}] \cdot \Pr[\overline{\text{EXI}}]$$
$$= (1 - \frac{1}{|\mathcal{M}|})^{r+1} \Pr[R^{\mathcal{A}} \Rightarrow m_1^* | \overline{\text{EXI}} \wedge \overline{\text{BAD}}] \cdot \Pr[\overline{\text{EXI}}]. \quad (7)$$

Combing the Eqs. (5), (6) and (7), we can get the desired bound in Theorem C.1. □

Assuming that no PPT adversary can break the OW-CPA security of the underlying DPKE with non-negligible probability, we have $\mathrm{Adv}_{\mathrm{DPKE}}^{\mathrm{OW\text{-}CPA}}(MR_1^R) \approx \mathrm{Adv}_{\mathrm{DPKE}}^{\mathrm{OW\text{-}CPA}}(MR_2^R) \in \mathsf{negl}(\lambda)$. In addition, $(\frac{|\mathcal{M}|}{|\mathcal{M}|-1})^{r+1} \leq (1 + \frac{1}{|\mathcal{M}|-1})^{|\mathcal{M}|-1} < \exp(1)$ (assuming $r \leq |\mathcal{M}| - 2$). Thus, Theorem C.1 essentially says $\epsilon_R = \mathrm{Adv}_{\mathrm{DPKE}}^{\mathrm{OW\text{-}CPA}}(R^{\mathcal{A}}) \lesssim (r+1) \cdot p$. According to Theorem 3.1, $\epsilon_{\mathcal{A}} = \mathrm{Adv}_{\mathrm{KEM}-\mathrm{U}_m^{\not\perp}}^{\mathrm{IND\text{-}CCA}}(\mathcal{A}) \gtrsim \sqrt{p}$. Thus, for $r \geq 1$ (the reduction rewinds the adversary r times), we have $\epsilon_R \lesssim (r+1) \cdot \epsilon_{\mathcal{A}}^2$. Namely, although the rewinding considered in this paper might increase the advantage of R by $r \cdot \epsilon_{\mathcal{A}}^2$, the running time of R will be accordingly increased by $r \cdot \mathrm{Time}(\mathcal{A})$. Therefore, the current quadratic loss is also unavoidable for any measurement-based black-box reduction with *simple* rewinding.

References

1. Rackoff, C., Simon, D.R.: Non-interactive zero-knowledge proof of knowledge and chosen ciphertext attack. In: Feigenbaum, J. (ed.) CRYPTO 1991. LNCS, vol. 576, pp. 433–444. Springer, Heidelberg (1992). https://doi.org/10.1007/3-540-46766-1_35

2. Cramer, R., Shoup, V.: Design and analysis of practical public-key encryption schemes secure against adaptive chosen ciphertext attack. SIAM J. Comput. **33**(1), 167–226 (2003)

3. Bellare, M., Rogaway, P.: Random oracles are practical: a paradigm for designing efficient protocols. In: Denning, D.E., Pyle, R., Ganesan, R., Sandhu, R.S., Ashby, V., (eds.) Proceedings of the 1st ACM Conference on Computer and Communications Security - CCS 1993, pp. 62–73. ACM (1993)

4. Dent, A.W.: A designer's guide to KEMs. In: Paterson, K.G. (ed.) Cryptography and Coding 2003. LNCS, vol. 2898, pp. 133–151. Springer, Heidelberg (2003). https://doi.org/10.1007/978-3-540-40974-8_12

5. Hofheinz, D., Hövelmanns, K., Kiltz, E.: A modular analysis of the Fujisaki-Okamoto transformation. In: Kalai, Y., Reyzin, L. (eds.) TCC 2017. LNCS, vol. 10677, pp. 341–371. Springer, Cham (2017). https://doi.org/10.1007/978-3-319-70500-2_12

6. Fujisaki, E., Okamoto, T.: Secure integration of asymmetric and symmetric encryption schemes. In: Wiener, M. (ed.) CRYPTO 1999. LNCS, vol. 1666, pp. 537–554. Springer, Heidelberg (1999). https://doi.org/10.1007/3-540-48405-1_34

7. Fujisaki, E., Okamoto, T.: Secure integration of asymmetric and symmetric encryption schemes. J. Cryptology **26**(1), 1–22 (2013)

8. Targhi, E.E., Unruh, D.: Post-quantum security of the Fujisaki-Okamoto and OAEP transforms. In: Hirt, M., Smith, A. (eds.) TCC 2016. LNCS, vol. 9986, pp. 192–216. Springer, Heidelberg (2016). https://doi.org/10.1007/978-3-662-53644-5_8

9. Okamoto, T., Pointcheval, D.: REACT: rapid enhanced-security asymmetric cryptosystem transform. In: Naccache, D. (ed.) CT-RSA 2001. LNCS, vol. 2020, pp. 159–174. Springer, Heidelberg (2000). https://doi.org/10.1007/3-540-45353-9_13

10. Jean-Sébastien, C., Handschuh, H., Joye, M., Paillier, P., Pointcheval, D., Tymen, C.: GEM: a generic chosen-ciphertext secure encryption method. In: Preneel, B. (ed.) CT-RSA 2002. LNCS, vol. 2271, pp. 263–276. Springer, Heidelberg (2002). https://doi.org/10.1007/3-540-45760-7_18

11. Menezes, A.: Another look at provable security. In: Pointcheval, D., Johansson, T. (eds.) EUROCRYPT 2012. LNCS, vol. 7237, pp. 8–8. Springer, Heidelberg (2012). https://doi.org/10.1007/978-3-642-29011-4_2

12. Fischlin, M.: Black-box reductions and separations in cryptography. In: Mitrokotsa, A., Vaudenay, S. (eds.) AFRICACRYPT 2012. LNCS, vol. 7374, pp. 413–422. Springer, Heidelberg (2012). https://doi.org/10.1007/978-3-642-31410-0_26

13. Boaz, B.: How to go beyond the black-box simulation barrier. In: 42nd Annual Symposium on Foundations of Computer Science, FOCS 2001, IEEE Computer Society, pp. 106–115 (2001)

14. Boaz, B.: Non-black-box techniques in cryptography (2004). https://www.boazbarak.org/Papers/thesis.pdf

15. Haitner, I., Ishai, Y., Kushilevitz, E., Lindell, Y., Petrank, E.: Black-box constructions of protocols for secure computation. SIAM J. Comput. 40(2), 225–266 (2011)

16. Pass, R., Tseng, W.-L.D., Venkitasubramaniam, M.: Towards non-black-box lower bounds in cryptography. In: Ishai, Y. (ed.) TCC 2011. LNCS, vol. 6597, pp. 579–596. Springer, Heidelberg (2011). https://doi.org/10.1007/978-3-642-19571-6_35

17. Guo, F., Chen, R., Susilo, W., Lai, J., Yang, G., Mu, Y.: Optimal security reductions for unique signatures: bypassing impossibilities with a counterexample. In: Katz, J., Shacham, H. (eds.) CRYPTO 2017. LNCS, vol. 10402, pp. 517–547. Springer, Cham (2017). https://doi.org/10.1007/978-3-319-63715-0_18

18. Bellare, M., Rogaway, P.: Optimal asymmetric encryption. In: De Santis, A. (ed.) EUROCRYPT 1994. LNCS, vol. 950, pp. 92–111. Springer, Heidelberg (1995). https://doi.org/10.1007/BFb0053428

19. Fujisaki, E., Okamoto, T., Pointcheval, D., Stern, J.: RSA-OAEP is secure under the RSA assumption. In: Kilian, J. (ed.) CRYPTO 2001. LNCS, vol. 2139, pp. 260–274. Springer, Heidelberg (2001). https://doi.org/10.1007/3-540-44647-8_16

20. Abdalla, M., Bellare, M., Rogaway, P.: The oracle Diffie-Hellman assumptions and an analysis of DHIES. In: Naccache, D. (ed.) CT-RSA 2001. LNCS, vol. 2020, pp. 143–158. Springer, Heidelberg (2001). https://doi.org/10.1007/3-540-45353-9_12

21. Bernstein, D.J., Persichetti, E.: Towards KEM unification. Cryptology ePrint Archive, Report 2018/526 (2018). https://eprint.iacr.org/2018/526

22. Saito, T., Xagawa, K., Yamakawa, T.: Tightly-secure key-encapsulation mechanism in the quantum random oracle model. In: Nielsen, J.B., Rijmen, V. (eds.) EURO-CRYPT 2018. LNCS, vol. 10822, pp. 520–551. Springer, Cham (2018). https://doi.org/10.1007/978-3-319-78372-7_17

23. Jiang, H., Zhang, Z., Chen, L., Wang, H., Ma, Z.: IND-CCA-secure key encapsulation mechanism in the quantum random oracle model, revisited. In: Shacham, H., Boldyreva, A. (eds.) CRYPTO 2018. LNCS, vol. 10993, pp. 96–125. Springer, Cham (2018). https://doi.org/10.1007/978-3-319-96878-0_4

24. Jiang, H., Zhang, Z., Ma, Z.: Key encapsulation mechanism with explicit rejection in the quantum random oracle model. In: Lin, D., Sako, K. (eds.) PKC 2019. LNCS, vol. 11443, pp. 618–645. Springer, Cham (2019). https://doi.org/10.1007/978-3-030-17259-6_21

25. Jiang, H., Zhang, Z., Ma, Z.: Tighter security proofs for generic key encapsulation mechanism in the quantum random oracle model. In: Ding, J., Steinwandt, R. (eds.) PQCrypto 2019. LNCS, vol. 11505, pp. 227–248. Springer, Cham (2019). https://doi.org/10.1007/978-3-030-25510-7_13

26. Bindel, N., Hamburg, M., Hövelmanns, K., Hülsing, A., Persichetti, E.: Tighter proofs of CCA security in the quantum random oracle model. In: Hofheinz, D., Rosen, A. (eds.) TCC 2019. LNCS, vol. 11892, pp. 61–90. Springer, Cham (2019). https://doi.org/10.1007/978-3-030-36033-7_3

27. Hövelmanns, K., Kiltz, E., Schäge, S., Unruh, D.: Generic authenticated key exchange in the quantum random oracle model. In: Kiayias, A., Kohlweiss, M., Wallden, P., Zikas, V. (eds.) PKC 2020. LNCS, vol. 12111, pp. 389–422. Springer, Cham (2020). https://doi.org/10.1007/978-3-030-45388-6_14

28. Szepieniec, A., Reyhanitabar, R., Preneel, B.: Key encapsulation from noisy key agreement in the quantum random oracle model. Cryptology ePrint Archive, Report 2018/884 (2018). https://eprint.iacr.org/2018/884

29. Xagawa, K., Yamakawa, T.: (Tightly) QCCA-secure key-encapsulation mechanism in the quantum random oracle model. In: Ding, J., Steinwandt, R. (eds.) PQCrypto 2019. LNCS, vol. 11505, pp. 249–268. Springer, Cham (2019). https://doi.org/10.1007/978-3-030-25510-7_14

30. NIST: National institute for standards and technology. Post quantum crypto project (2017). https://csrc.nist.gov/Projects/post-quantum-cryptography/round-2-submissions

31. Boneh, D., Dagdelen, Ö., Fischlin, M., Lehmann, A., Schaffner, C., Zhandry, M.: Random Oracles in a Quantum World. In: Lee, D.H., Wang, X. (eds.) ASIACRYPT 2011. LNCS, vol. 7073, pp. 41–69. Springer, Heidelberg (2011). https://doi.org/10.1007/978-3-642-25385-0_3

32. Yamakawa, T., Zhandry, M.: Classical vs Quantum random oracles. In: Canteaut, A., Standaert, F.-X. (eds.) EUROCRYPT 2021. LNCS, vol. 12697, pp. 568–597. Springer, Cham (2021). https://doi.org/10.1007/978-3-030-77886-6_20

33. Zhang, J., Yu, Y., Feng, D., Fan, S., Zhang, Z.: On the (quantum) random oracle methodology: New separations and more. Cryptology ePrint Archive, Report 2019/1101 (2019). https://eprint.iacr.org/2019/1101

34. Zhandry, M.: How to record quantum queries, and applications to quantum indifferentiability. In: Boldyreva, A., Micciancio, D. (eds.) CRYPTO 2019. LNCS, vol. 11693, pp. 239–268. Springer, Cham (2019). https://doi.org/10.1007/978-3-030-26951-7_9

35. Katsumata, S., Kwiatkowski, K., Pintore, F., Prest, T.: Scalable ciphertext compression techniques for post-quantum KEMs and their applications. In: Moriai, S., Wang, H. (eds.) ASIACRYPT 2020. LNCS, vol. 12491, pp. 289–320. Springer, Cham (2020). https://doi.org/10.1007/978-3-030-64837-4_10

36. Don, J., Fehr, S., Majenz, C., Schaffner, C.: Online-extractability in the quantum random-oracle model. Cryptology ePrint Archive, Report 2021/280 (2021). https://ia.cr/2021/280

37. Kuchta, V., Sakzad, A., Stehlé, D., Steinfeld, R., Sun, S.-F.: Measure-rewind-measure: tighter quantum random oracle model proofs for one-way to hiding and CCA security. In: Canteaut, A., Ishai, Y. (eds.) EUROCRYPT 2020. LNCS, vol. 12107, pp. 703–728. Springer, Cham (2020). https://doi.org/10.1007/978-3-030-45727-3_24

38. Ambainis, A., Hamburg, M., Unruh, D.: Quantum security proofs using semi-classical oracles. In: Boldyreva, A., Micciancio, D. (eds.) CRYPTO 2019. LNCS, vol. 11693, pp. 269–295. Springer, Cham (2019). https://doi.org/10.1007/978-3-030-26951-7_10

39. Jiang, H., Zhang, Z., Ma, Z.: On the non-tightness of measurement-based reductions for key encapsulation mechanism in the quantum random oracle model (full version). ePrint Archive Report 2019/494 (2019) https://eprint.iacr.org/2019/494.pdf

40. Unruh, D.: Revocable quantum timed-release encryption. J. ACM **62**(6), 49:1–49:76 (2015)

41. Unruh, D.: Quantum position verification in the random oracle model. In: Garay, J.A., Gennaro, R. (eds.) CRYPTO 2014. LNCS, vol. 8617, pp. 1–18. Springer, Heidelberg (2014). https://doi.org/10.1007/978-3-662-44381-1_1

42. Song, F., Yun, A.: Quantum security of NMAC and related constructions. In: Katz, J., Shacham, H. (eds.) CRYPTO 2017. LNCS, vol. 10402, pp. 283–309. Springer, Cham (2017). https://doi.org/10.1007/978-3-319-63715-0_10

43. Unruh, D.: Post-quantum security of fiat-Shamir. In: Takagi, T., Peyrin, T. (eds.) ASIACRYPT 2017. LNCS, vol. 10624, pp. 65–95. Springer, Cham (2017). https://doi.org/10.1007/978-3-319-70694-8_3

44. Unruh, D.: Non-interactive zero-knowledge proofs in the quantum random oracle model. In: Oswald, E., Fischlin, M. (eds.) EUROCRYPT 2015. LNCS, vol. 9057, pp. 755–784. Springer, Heidelberg (2015). https://doi.org/10.1007/978-3-662-46803-6_25

45. Eaton, E.: Leighton-micali hash-based signatures in the quantum random-oracle model. In: Adams, C., Camenisch, J. (eds.) SAC 2017. LNCS, vol. 10719, pp. 263–280. Springer, Cham (2018). https://doi.org/10.1007/978-3-319-72565-9_13

46. Bader, C., Jager, T., Li, Y., Schäge, S.: On the impossibility of tight cryptographic reductions. In: Fischlin, M., Coron, J.-S. (eds.) EUROCRYPT 2016. LNCS, vol. 9666, pp. 273–304. Springer, Heidelberg (2016). https://doi.org/10.1007/978-3-662-49896-5_10

47. Boneh, D., Venkatesan, R.: Breaking RSA may not be equivalent to factoring. In: Nyberg, K. (ed.) EUROCRYPT 1998. LNCS, vol. 1403, pp. 59–71. Springer, Heidelberg (1998). https://doi.org/10.1007/BFb0054117

48. Coron, J.-S.: Optimal security proofs for PSS and other signature schemes. In: Knudsen, L.R. (ed.) EUROCRYPT 2002. LNCS, vol. 2332, pp. 272–287. Springer, Heidelberg (2002). https://doi.org/10.1007/3-540-46035-7_18

49. Baecher, P., Brzuska, C., Fischlin, M.: Notions of black-box reductions, revisited. In: Sako, K., Sarkar, P. (eds.) ASIACRYPT 2013. LNCS, vol. 8269, pp. 296–315. Springer, Heidelberg (2013). https://doi.org/10.1007/978-3-642-42033-7_16

50. Dodis, Y., Oliveira, R., Pietrzak, K.: On the generic insecurity of the full domain hash. In: Shoup, V. (ed.) CRYPTO 2005. LNCS, vol. 3621, pp. 449–466. Springer, Heidelberg (2005). https://doi.org/10.1007/11535218_27

51. Garg, S., Bhaskar, R., Lokam, S.V.: Improved bounds on security reductions for discrete log based signatures. In: Wagner, D. (ed.) CRYPTO 2008. LNCS, vol. 5157, pp. 93–107. Springer, Heidelberg (2008). https://doi.org/10.1007/978-3-540-85174-5_6

52. Seurin, Y.: On the exact security of schnorr-type signatures in the random oracle model. In: Pointcheval, D., Johansson, T. (eds.) EUROCRYPT 2012. LNCS, vol. 7237, pp. 554–571. Springer, Heidelberg (2012). https://doi.org/10.1007/978-3-642-29011-4_33

53. Fischlin, M., Fleischhacker, N.: Limitations of the meta-reduction technique: the case of schnorr signatures. In: Johansson, T., Nguyen, P.Q. (eds.) EUROCRYPT 2013. LNCS, vol. 7881, pp. 444–460. Springer, Heidelberg (2013). https://doi.org/10.1007/978-3-642-38348-9_27

54. Dagdelen, Ö., Fischlin, M., Gagliardoni, T.: The Fiat–Shamir transformation in a quantum world. In: Sako, K., Sarkar, P. (eds.) ASIACRYPT 2013. LNCS, vol. 8270, pp. 62–81. Springer, Heidelberg (2013). https://doi.org/10.1007/978-3-642-42045-0_4

55. Fleischhacker, N., Jager, T., Schröder, D.: On tight security proofs for schnorr signatures. In: Sarkar, P., Iwata, T. (eds.) ASIACRYPT 2014. LNCS, vol. 8873, pp. 512–531. Springer, Heidelberg (2014). https://doi.org/10.1007/978-3-662-45611-8_27

56. Lewko, A., Waters, B.: Why proving HIBE systems secure is difficult. In: Nguyen, P.Q., Oswald, E. (eds.) EUROCRYPT 2014. LNCS, vol. 8441, pp. 58–76. Springer, Heidelberg (2014). https://doi.org/10.1007/978-3-642-55220-5_4

57. Kakvi, S.A., Kiltz, E.: Optimal security proofs for full domain hash, revisited. J. Cryptology **31**(1), 276–306 (2018)

58. Helstrom, C.W.: Quantum detection and estimation theory. J. Stat. Phys. **1**, 231–252 (1969)

59. Bae, J., Kwek, L.C.: Quantum state discrimination and its applications. J. Phys. Math. Theor. **48**(8), 083001 (2015)

60. Nielsen, M.A., Chuang, I.L.: Quantum Computation and Quantum Information. Number 2. Cambridge University Press, Cambridge (2000)

61. Hosoyamada, A., Yamakawa, T.: Finding collisions in a quantum world: quantum black-box separation of collision-resistance and one-wayness. In: Moriai, S., Wang, H. (eds.) ASIACRYPT 2020. LNCS, vol. 12491, pp. 3–32. Springer, Cham (2020). https://doi.org/10.1007/978-3-030-64837-4_1

62. Hsiao, C.-Y., Reyzin, L.: Finding collisions on a public road, or do secure hash functions need secret coins? In: Franklin, M. (ed.) CRYPTO 2004. LNCS, vol. 3152, pp. 92–105. Springer, Heidelberg (2004). https://doi.org/10.1007/978-3-540-28628-8_6

63. Ambainis, A., Rosmanis, A., Unruh, D.: Quantum attacks on classical proof systems: the hardness of quantum rewinding. In: 55th IEEE Annual Symposium on Foundations of Computer Science - FOCS 2014, pp. 474–483. IEEE (2014)

Redeeming Reset Indifferentiability and Applications to Post-quantum Security

Mark Zhandry[1,2](✉)

[1] NTT Research, Palo Alto, USA
mark.zhandry@ntt-research.com
[2] Princeton University, Princeton, USA

Abstract. Indifferentiability is used to analyze the security of constructions of idealized objects, such as random oracles or ideal ciphers. Reset indifferentiability is a strengthening of plain indifferentiability which is applicable in far more scenarios, but has largely been abandoned due to significant impossibility results and a lack of positive results. Our main results are:

– Under *weak* reset indifferentiability, ideal ciphers imply (fixed size) random oracles, and domain shrinkage is possible. We thus show reset indifferentiability is more useful than previously thought.
– We lift our analysis to the quantum setting, showing that ideal ciphers imply random oracles under quantum indifferentiability.
– Despite Shor's algorithm, we observe that generic groups are still meaningful quantumly, showing that they are quantumly (reset) indifferentiable from ideal ciphers; combined with the above, cryptographic groups yield post-quantum *symmetric* key cryptography. In particular, we obtain a plausible post-quantum random oracle that is a subset-product followed by two modular reductions.

1 Introduction

The random oracle model [BR93] (ROM) has become a critical tool for justifying the security cryptosystems, both real-world and theoretical. In the ROM, all parties, including the cryptosystem and adversary, are given oracle access to a function H sampled uniformly from the set of all functions. To actually implement the cryptosystem, H is replaced with a concrete cryptographic hash function, with the hope that there is no way to exploit the structure of a well-designed H to attack the cryptosystem. For many of the most efficient cryptosystems, the random oracle model is the only known justification for security, and constructions in the random oracle model tend to be simpler and require milder computational assumptions than those without random oracles.

Random oracles are members of a larger class of "idealized" objects, where an adversary is modeled as only having black box access. Ideal ciphers are idealizations of block ciphers, modeled as random keyed permutations. Generic

© International Association for Cryptologic Research 2021
M. Tibouchi and H. Wang (Eds.): ASIACRYPT 2021, LNCS 13090, pp. 518–548, 2021.
https://doi.org/10.1007/978-3-030-92062-3_18

groups are idealizations of cryptographic groups, modeled as random embeddings of $\mathbb{Z}_p$ into strings. Idealized objects have been used to design numerous cryptosystems (e.g. [RST01, Des00, BSW07, AY20, CLMQ20]) or justify the security of new computational assumptions (e.g. Diffie-Hellman [Sho97] and its many variants [BBG05, BFF+14, DHZ14, BMZ19]). Ideal objects simplify the task of protocol design and analysis while providing meaningful heuristics for security.

1.1 Indifferentiability

Hash functions and other objects are usually built from lower-level building blocks. If one is not careful, such structure can be exploited in attacks [CDMP05], thus violating the random oracle assumption, even if the lower-level building block is treated ideally. The resolution is the indifferentiability framework of Maurer, Renner, and Holenstein [MRH04], a composable simulation-based definition which captures what it means for a construction to be "as good as" an ideal object, despite its structure, provided the underlying building block is treated ideally. Here, "as good as" applies to a wide array of settings called "single-stage games", capturing most standard cryptographic definitions. Indifferentiability has become a gold standard for analyzing hash function constructions, and numerous positive results are known such as domain extension and the equivalence of random oracles and ideal ciphers [CPS08, HKT11, DS16].

Two Motivations for Reset Indifferentiability. In the more general setting of "multi-stage" games, which capture cases where there are multiple distinct adversary parties, indifferentiability is insufficient [RSS11]. Such games include leakage resilience, deterministic encryption, key-dependent message security, and non-malleability, among others. In order to generically guarantee composition for multi-stage games including these critical applications, one needs a much stronger notion called *reset* indifferentiability, which is equivalent to requiring that the simulator be stateless. Given the limitations of plain indifferentiability, reset indifferentiability *should* be the gold standard, rather than plain indifferentiability.

Unfortunately, reset indifferentiability is subject to significant impossibility results [RSS11, LAMP12, DGHM13, BBM13]; in particular, any sort of domain extension is known to be impossible. Most prior work on reset indifferentiability focuses on a "strong" variant, which requires a single universal simulator to work for any distinguisher; under this variant, even stronger impossibilities are known. In particular, domain *shrinkage* is even impossible, which can in turn be used to prove other impossibilities such as constructing constant-sized ideal ciphers from infinite-sized random oracles, or vice versa [BBM13]. These are surprising and counter-intuitive results, and seem to have been interpreted as implying that reset indifferentiability is *too strong* to be useful. As such, reset indifferentiability seems to have been largely abandoned, with authors instead proposing milder notions of indifferentiability and showing that they apply to restricted classes of games [RSS11, DGHM13, Mit14]. However, reset indifferentiability is *exactly* characterized by general multi-stage games, meaning there will necessarily be applications where such restricted notions cannot be applied. Thus, under these weaker notions, security for a particular game has to be carefully analyzed.

However, we note that, beyond the impossibility of domain extension, not much is actually known about the "weak" variant of reset indifferentiability, where the stateless simulator can depend on the distinguisher. This variant still captures general multi-stage games, meaning any weak reset indifferentiability result implies full applicability of the construction. Even though domain extension is still not possible, the notion may still be useful in many applications. For example, if one is considering public key encryption with fixed-sized messages, then domain extension may not be necessary.

An independent, perhaps unexpected, motivation for reset indifferentiability comes from the threat of quantum computing. The ability of a quantum algorithm to query the idealized object in superposition invalidates most classical results, and certain impossibilities are known [BDF+11,YZ20]. The difficulty is that even a single superposition query "views" the entire oracle; in order to ensure that the simulation of the ideal object is consistent and "looks like" the true ideal object, the approach employed by most works (e.g. [BDF+11,Zha12b,Unr15,TU16]) has been to simulate essentially statelessly, with the simulator usually depending on the distinguisher. In the context of indifferentiability, such an approach would correspond exactly to weak reset indifferentiability. We note that some recent techniques [Zha19,LZ19,CMSZ19, DFMS19,DFM20,KSS+20,YZ20] utilize stateful quantum simulators, and in particular [Zha19] proves the (non-reset) indifferentiability of domain extension for random oracles. However, these techniques are far more complex and require comparatively heavy quantum machinery, making the techniques more difficult to use.

We highlight the specific case of random permutations, which has been particularly challenging with few quantum results and techniques known for the setting where inverse queries are allowed. In fact, we are only aware of two such prior results: [AR16] considers the Even-Mansour cipher, but only considers adversaries with perfect success probability. [Zha16] constructs (non-indifferentiable) quantum-secure PRPs in such a model, but side-steps the issue of quantum queries entirely by having the entire oracle truth table be *statistically* close to a random permutation.

Questions. The prior discussion raises the following natural questions:

- Can weak reset indifferentiability be used to achieve *any* non-trivial result, even domain shrinkage?
- If so, how can one make non-black box use of the distinguisher to design an indifferentiability simulator?
- Can *fixed-size* random oracles be built from ideal ciphers, or vice versa?
- Can random oracles (fixed-size or infinite size) be built from ideal ciphers *quantumly*, even in the single-stage setting? In particular, can anything be said about the Sponge construction?

Making progress on these questions will be the focus of our work.

1.2 Our Results

On Prior Impossibilities. Essentially the main prior impossibility for weak reset indifferentiability is that of domain extension [RSS11, LAMP12, DGHM13, BBM13], with other impossibilities [BBM13] relying crucially on the *strong* reset variant. We first observe that the techniques yielding the impossibility of domain extension apply even in the setting of *query-unbounded* simulators.

In contrast, we prove weak reset indifferentiability for random oracle domain shrinkage, ideal ciphers from random oracles, and vice versa, in such an unbounded simulator setting. More generally, we demonstrate that in*distinguisha*bility against query-unbounded attackers can usually be lifted to reset in*differentia*bility using query-unbounded simulators. The inefficient simulator makes these results rather un-useful for positive results. Nevertheless, it shows that the known techniques for negative results are unlikely to extend to a variety of interesting problems, in the weak reset setting. Combined with the lack of prior positive results for reset indifferentiability, this shows that weak reset indifferentiability is essentially completely open for any application that does not require domain extension. The question then is: how can we achieve an *efficient* simulator in these settings?

Positive Results for Weak Reset Indifferentiability. We first show that domain shrinking *is* possible, under weak reset indifferentiability with an *efficient* simulator. We thus see that random oracles with larger domain are *strictly stronger* that random oracles with smaller domain. This is in sharp contrast to the "duality" of *strong* reset indifferentiability, where any two objects are either *equivalent* or *incomparable*, with most examples being incomparable [BBM13].

We also show how to construct a (fixed-size) random oracle from an ideal cipher under weak reset indifferentiability, again with an efficient simulator. Specifically, we show that a natural pad-and-truncation of an ideal cipher—that is, the Sponge construction for a single-block message—gives a random oracle, for sufficient padding and truncation. An interesting feature of our analysis of pad-and-truncate is that the sum of the input and output sizes must be less than the width of the cipher. We show that this is tight: any larger input/output size will not be weakly reset indifferentiable, thus giving (to the best of our knowledge) the first negative result for weak reset indifferentiability that does not rely on domain extension. This is in contrast to the plain (non-reset) indifferentiability setting, where any non-trivial truncation gives indifferentiability [DRRS09]. Our result may help guide the design of Sponge-based hash functions.

These positive results are obtained by first proving reset indifferentiability in certain *shared randomness* models, which allows the simulator access to some consistent randomness, while still being stateless. We show that, for weak reset indifferentiability and for certain classes of "nice" ideal objects (including random oracles and ideal ciphers), the shared randomness can be removed to get a standard reset indifferentiability result.

Quantum. All of our results extend to the quantum setting. The simulators are identical to their classical counterparts. However, very few prior quantum results handle inverse queries, meaning a handful of new ideas are needed to lift our ideal cipher results to the quantum setting. We thus obtain the first proof of quantum indifferentiability (reset or otherwise) for a random oracle from an ideal cipher—and in particular the sponge construction for single-block messages. This may give some evidence for the post-quantum (non-reset) indifferentiability of SHA3, which is based on the full sponge construction. While we cannot prove indifferentiability for the full Sponge construction[1], we can plug pad-and-truncate into the domain extension result of Zhandry [Zha19], obtaining the first quantum indifferentiability proof of an arbitrary-size random oracle from an ideal cipher, under (plain) indifferentiability.

The Post-quantum Generic Group Model. We observe that Shor's algorithm, by virtue of being generic, is captured by the *generic group model* [Sho97] (GGM), albeit the quantum variant allowing quantum access to the group. Thus, despite Shor's algorithm, the GGM may remain a plausible heuristic in the quantum setting. Shor's algorithm, however, shows that the discrete-logarithm problem is easy in the quantum accessible GGM, so the question is then: what use is it?

We demonstrate that the quantum accessible GGM is equivalent to an ideal publicly-invertible injective function under (reset) indifferentiability. Our above positive results for ideal ciphers extend to the injective function case. In particular, by plugging in the above results, we obtain a quantum indifferentiable random oracle from the generic group model[2]. When instantiating with the multiplicative group over finite fields, the result is a plausible post-quantum hash function that is simply a subset-product, followed by two modular reductions.

1.3   Discussion

We significantly expand the set of techniques and results for reset indifferentiability, both classically and quantumly. We thus show that reset indifferentiability is more useful than suggested by prior works. Perhaps the main open question in the classical setting is whether ideal ciphers can be built from random oracles under reset indifferentiability.

We in particular expand the set of techniques available for analyzing quantum queries to permutation inverses, and in doing so expand the applicability of "old school" quantum simulation techniques, showing for the first time that stateless simulation is capable of achieving non-trivial indifferentiability results. Our hope is that our techniques can be combined with the sophisticated "new school" quantum techniques to aid in additional positive results. For example, can quantum indifferentiable ideal ciphers be built from random oracles?

---

[1] Our techniques work within the framework of reset indifferentiability, which cannot achieve domain extension, and therefore our techniques cannot apply to the full Sponge construction.

[2] [ZZ21] previously suggest building a random oracle from generic groups. Their result however is in the classical setting using stateful simulators, which does not translate to quantum. Our results are required to get a quantum indifferentiability proof.

Our results also show that cryptographic groups remain potentially useful in the quantum setting, just that they are limited to the symmetric key setting. While existing symmetric cryptography appears somewhat resilient to quantum attacks, we believe it is nevertheless important to study alternative techniques for building quantum-resistant symmetric cryptography.

1.4 Concurrent and Independent Work

Currently and independently of our work, Czajkowski [Cza21] prove the (plain) indifferentiability of the full Sponge construction in the quantum setting, necessarily using a stateful quantum simulation technique. In particular, this also justifies the *plain* quantum indifferentiability of the pad-and-truncate construction. The results and techniques are largely incomparable to ours, as we focus on reset indifferentiability.

2 Technical Overview and Discussion

Indifferentiability. Recall the usual notion of *indistinguishability* between two distributions over functions F, G, which says that the functions cannot be distinguished by oracle access. We will denote such indistinguishability as

$$F \approx G.$$

Indistinguishability is sufficient for settings like constructing a PRP from a PRF, as the underlying PRF building block is private and not directly accessible to the adversary. In the settings of length extension for hash functions, building ideal ciphers from random oracles, etc., indistinguishability is not sufficient since the adversary additionally can query the underlying building block, and indifferentiability [MRH04] is required instead. A construction C making oracle queries to an ideal object A (denoted C^A), is *indifferentiable* from an ideal object B if there exists a simulator S making queries to B (denoted S^B) such that

$$(C^A, A) \approx (B, S^B).$$

The above says that an adversary with two query interfaces—an "honest" interface to B and "adversarial" interface to A—cannot distinguish the "Real Word" where B is set to C^A for ideal object A from the "Ideal World" where B is ideal and A is simulated as S^B. For building an ideal cipher from a random oracle, A represents a random oracle and B an ideal cipher, with C^A being a construction of a cipher from a hash function.

Note that, while the expression above appears symmetric between A and B, for plain indifferentiability the notation hides the fact that S can keep state between queries, whereas C is usually considered to be stateless. Reset indifferentiability is a strengthening of indifferentiability to require S to be stateless as well. As discussed above, reset indifferentiability is required in settings known as "multi-stage games." We disambiguate between strong and weak security, were strong requires a universal simulator that works for any potential distinguisher between (C^A, A) and (B, S^B), whereas weak allows for a distinguisher-dependent simulator. Weak reset indifferentiability is sufficient for composition and multi-stage games [RSS11]. Strong reset indifferentiability turns out to fully symmetric, with the roles of C and S being interchangeable [BBM13]. This means that any construction (resp. impossibility) of B from A immediately gives a construct (resp. impossibility) of constructing A from B.

2.1   On Prior Impossibilities

We show that if one relaxes to query-*unbounded* simulation, then *indistinguishability* can be upgraded to weak reset indifferentiability, provided the indistinguishability holds against query-unbounded distinguishers. The idea is that the simulator can query the entire object B, and then sample A conditioned on C^A being functionally identical to B; such sampling is guaranteed by plain indistinguishability against unbounded queries. The difficulty is that there may be many A such that C^A is equivalent to B, and we must ensure that the simulator can consistently choose the same A each time. For this, we show the simulator can basically have a choice of A hard-coded for each separate B. The details are given in Sect. 4.

Query-unbounded indistinguishability follows from known results in various settings. For example, perfect shuffles [GP07] allow for constructing PRPs from random oracles. Indistinguishable domain shrinkage is also trivial. Our general theorem lifts these results to weak reset indifferentiability, albeit with inefficient simulators. Due to the above inefficient simulator, the result is not immediately useful. However, we observe that the impossibility of domain extension holds *even* under such inefficient simulators; for completeness, we give the result in the full version [Zha21]. Since domain extension is the main impossibility known to hold for *weak* reset indifferentiability, this shows that new techniques would be required to rule efficient simulation in settings where inefficient simulation is possible. We thus demonstrate that weak reset indifferentiability is largely open for settings that do not involve domain extension.

2.2   Shared Randomness Indifferentiability

We next discuss a model of indifferentiability, which we call shared randomness reset indifferentiability, that we will use as a stepping-stone to full reset indifferentiability. Here, the simulator S is still stateless, but is allowed to query a random oracle R—independent from A and B—in addition to querying B; we require that:

$$(C^A, A) \approx (B, S^{B,R}).$$

Note that the random oracle breaks the symmetry between A and B. In particular, we note that domain shrinking is trivial in this setting, as the simulator can use R to simulate the parts of A that are ignored by C^A.

In Sect. 6, we also show that shared randomness is sufficient for constructing a fixed-size random oracle h from a (keyless) ideal cipher P, P^{-1}. The construction is the natural one based on truncation:

$$\mathsf{PadTrunc}_{c,d}^{P,P^{-1}}(x) = P(x||0^{(1-c)n})|_{[dn]}.$$

Here, $c, d \in (0, 1)$ are constants, P is an ideal cipher on n-bit inputs, x is cn bits and $y|_{[r]}$ is the first r bits of y. Interestingly, we show that if $c + d > 1$, then the truncation-based construction is actually *not* reset indifferentiable:

Theorem 1 (Informal). *If $c + d > 1$, $\mathsf{PadTrunc}_{c,d}$ is not shared-randomness weakly reset indifferentiable from a random oracle.*

The proof of this theorem is as follows. Consider a distinguisher D with query access to a function H and permutation P, P^{-1}. It first chooses a random $x \in \{0, 1\}^{cn}$ and queries $w||z \leftarrow P(x||0^{(1-c)n})$. It also queries $w' \leftarrow H(x)$, and checks that $w' = w$. Then it queries $x'||y' \leftarrow P^{-1}(w||z)$, and checks that $x' = x, y' = 0^{(1-c)n}$. D outputs 1 if and only if all checks pass. Note that in the "Real world" where $H = \mathsf{PadTrunc}_{c,d}^{P,P^{-1}}$, D outputs 1 always. However, in the "Ideal world" with P, P^{-1} being supposedly simulated by a stateless simulator S^H, we argue that D outputs 0 almost always. Indeed, a stateless simulator must have $w = w'$ to pass the distinguisher's first check. But then to answer the query $P^{-1}(w||z)$, it must somehow come up with the original pre-image x of w. Since the simulator is stateless, it cannot remember x, and so computing x would seem to require inverting H on w, which is impossible for a random oracle H.

This intuition is not quite correct, as the simulator is also given z as input, which can be seen as some side-information about x. However, for $c + d > 1$, z is shorter than x, and therefore there must be some entropy left in x. Since random oracles remain hard to invert even for entropic sources, the inability for the simulator to output x follows.

On the other hand, for $c + d \leq 1$, we show that $\mathsf{PadTrunc}_{c,d}$ actually *is* reset indifferentiable:

Theorem 2 (Informal). *If $c + d \leq 1$, $\mathsf{PadTrunc}_{c,d}$ is (strongly) reset indifferentiable from a random oracle in the shared randomness model.*

Inspired by the impossibility above, we devise a simulator that statelessly encodes x into z so that x can be recovered from z alone. It does this by setting z to be the result of a random injection I applied to x, in the case that $y = 0^{(1-c)n}$. For I to indeed be a random injection, we must have $c + d \leq 1$. The problem is that I represents state, which is not allowed in reset indifferentiability. Fortunately, for *shared randomness* reset indifferentiability, S has access to a random oracle R; it can use this single random oracle to build I. Essentially, it follows typical approaches to building block ciphers from pseudorandom random functions, but instantiating the pseudorandom function using R.

In Sect. 5, we show that shared randomness reset security actually implies standard weak reset security, in many settings:

Theorem 3 (Informal). *Suppose a construction C^A is shared randomness weakly reset indifferentiable from B, and that B has certain nice "extraction" properties. Then C^A is also weakly reset indifferentiable from B, without shared randomness.*

Combining with the above results shows that the ideal cipher model implies random oracles under weak reset indifferentiability.

The theorem is proved in two steps. First, we replace the shared randomness R with a q-wise independent hash function R_q, where q is set sufficiently large relative to the number of queries made by the adversary. The result is perfectly indistinguishable from a truly random R. Next, we use a trick from [BBM13] to compute R_q from the oracle B itself, in a way such that R_q is random and independent from the adversary's view.

We note that our simulator is almost black box, but requires knowledge of the number of queries made by the distinguisher, both to select q and to apply the trick from [BBM13].

2.3 Quantum Distinguishers and Generic Groups

Reset indifferentiability is conveniently amenable to quantum proof techniques, and we show how to upgrade our positive results to the quantum setting. This is not trivial, but we show how to structure the classical proofs in such a way that they can be lifted to the quantum setting by plugging in known quantum query lower bounds in key steps. This requires care, since existing techniques mostly prohibit inverse queries to random permutations, whereas our results require such inverse queries. We thus must carefully embed prior inverse-query-less results into our setting to achieve our results. As a result, we obtain fixed-size random oracles from ideal ciphers quantumly. Generically plugging into the domain extension result of Zhandry [Zha19], we obtain the first proof of quantum indifferentiability of an (arbitrary) size random oracle from an ideal cipher:

Corollary 1. *There exists a construction C of an (arbitrary-size) random oracle from an ideal cipher that is quantum (non-reset) indifferentiable.*

We note that our lower bound on the necessary truncation of ideal ciphers also trivially extend to the quantum setting, since a classical distinguisher is in particular a quantum distinguisher[3].

We next investigate the generic group model, quantumly. It is well known that Shor's quantum discrete log algorithm [Sho94] works on any cryptographic group; another interpretation is that Shor's algorithm works in the quantum-accessible generic group model. This interpretation of the generality of Shor's algorithm is usually seen as a negative, since it means that there is no hope of circumventing the algorithm by using alternate groups. But we interpret this as showing that Shor's algorithm does not fundamentally alter the validity of the generic group model quantumly. It just shows that discrete logarithms are now tractable.

The ability of Shor's algorithm to solve discrete log essentially shows that the generic group gives a random injection, quantumly, which we prove formally

---

[3] There is a slight subtlety here, as quantum (reset) indifferentiability allows for a quantum simulator, whereas classical indifferentiability does not. Thus, quantum and classical indifferentiability are technically *incomparable*. Nevertheless, our impossibility results trivially adapt to the quantum simulator case.

under reset indifferentiability. Our positive results from above readily apply to publicly invertible injections, and therefore give an quantum indifferentiable hash function from generic groups.

If we in particular focus on the case of finite fields, what we get is the hash function $H(x) = (g^x \bmod p) \bmod 2^n$, where $x \in \{0,1\}^n$ for $2n \leq \log p$. By precomputing the various powers of 2, g^x becomes a modular subset-product computation. The overall hash function is then a modular subset product followed by an additional modular reduction that can plausibly be used as a (quantum immune) random oracle.

3   Preliminaries

Unless otherwise noted, all functions, sets, algorithms, adversaries, distinguishers, simulators, and distributions are functions of a security parameter λ. We will often omit the security parameter; for example, when we say that $\mathcal{X}$ is a set, we mean that $\mathcal{X}$ is a family of sets $\{\mathcal{X}_\lambda\}_\lambda$. When we say that a function is polynomial or negligible, we mean polynomial or negligible in λ. When there are multiple functions of λ, we assume all functions use the same λ.

For an algorithm A making queries to another (potentially stateful) algorithm B, we will denote their interaction by A^B.

Ideal Objects. For sets $\mathcal{X}, \mathcal{Y}$, a ideal object is a distribution over functions from $\mathcal{X}$ to $\mathcal{Y}$. Some idealized objects we will consider:

- **Random oracles.** A random oracle is just the uniform distribution over all functions RO from $\mathcal{X}$ to $\mathcal{Y}$. We denote this distribution by $\mathcal{Y}^{\mathcal{X}}$. Note that we will usually think of $\mathcal{X}, \mathcal{Y}$ as finite exponential size. It is also possible to consider an infinite random oracle, in which case $\mathcal{X}$ is infinite.
- **Ideal ciphers.** Let $\mathcal{X} = \{0,1\} \times \mathcal{K} \times \mathcal{Y}$ for exponential-size $\mathcal{Y}$, and $\mathcal{K}$ be another set. An ideal cipher is sampled by choosing a function $P : \mathcal{K} \times \mathcal{Y} \to \mathcal{Y}$, where for each k, the function $P(k, \cdot)$ is a uniformly random permutation. Let $P^{-1}(k, \cdot)$ be the inverse of $P(k, \cdot)$. The oracle is then $\mathsf{IC}(b, k, x) = \begin{cases} P(k, x) & \text{if } b = 0 \\ P^{-1}(k, x) & \text{if } b = 1 \end{cases}$. We note that ideal ciphers are typically modeled as being keyed, which corresponds to an exponential-sized family of independent ideal permutations. It is also possible to consider the keyless setting, where $\mathcal{K} = \{1\}$, and can be omitted.
- **(Keyed) Random Injections.** Let $\mathcal{Y} = \mathcal{Y}' \cup \{\perp\}$, $\mathcal{Z}$ an exponential-sized set such that $|\mathcal{Z}| \leq |\mathcal{Y}'|$, and $\mathcal{K}$ be another set. Then let $\mathcal{X} = (\{0\} \times \mathcal{K} \times \mathcal{Z}) \cup (\{1\} \times \mathcal{K} \times \mathcal{Y}')$. A keyed random injection is sampled by choosing a function $I : \mathcal{K} \times \mathcal{Z} \to \mathcal{Y}'$ where for each k, the function $I(k, \cdot)$ is a uniformly random injection. Let $I^{-1}(k, y)$ be the function that outputs x such that $I(k, x) = y$ if it exists, and otherwise outputs $\perp$. Then $\mathsf{RI}(b, k, x) = \begin{cases} I(k, x) & \text{if } b = 0 \\ I^{-1}(k, x) & \text{if } b = 1 \end{cases}$.

- **Generic groups.** Let p be an exponentially-large prime such that $|\mathcal{Y}| \geq p$, and let L be a random injection from $\mathbb{Z}_p$ to $\mathcal{Y}$. The function GG then maps $x \mapsto L(x)$, and also $(\ell_1, \ell_2) \mapsto L(\ L^{-1}(\ell_1) + L^{-1}(\ell_2)\ )$. Here, if L^{-1} is undefined on an input ℓ, the entire expression outputs $\perp$. Note that the generic group model usually also allows for subtraction, but this is redundant since p is known, and $-1 \equiv p - 1 \bmod p$ can be computed using just the addition operation.

Quantum. We will not need much quantum background in this work. In particular, all of our quantum results basically follow the classical proofs, but with key parts replaced with quantum equivalents.

3.1 Indifferentiability

Let $\mathcal{A}, \mathcal{B}$ be two distributions over functions, and C a polynomial-time oracle-aided circuit. We write $C^{\mathcal{A}}$ to be the distribution over C^A where $A \leftarrow \mathcal{A}$.

Definition 1. $C^{\mathcal{A}}$ *is (strong statistical classical plain) indifferentiable from $\mathcal{B}$ if there exists a polynomial-size, potentially stateful, oracle-aided simulator S such that, for any probabilistic potentially unbounded oracle-added Turing machine D making at most a polynomial number of queries, there is a negligible ϵ such that*

$$\left| \Pr_{A \leftarrow \mathcal{A}}\left[D^{C^A, A}() = 1 \right] - \Pr_{B \leftarrow \mathcal{B}}\left[D^{B, S^B}() = 1 \right] \right| \leq \epsilon.$$

Variants. We now discuss some variants of the indifferentiability definition:

- **Weak vs strong.** Weak indifferentiability allows for S to depend on D, flipping the order of quantifiers.
- **Computational vs statistical vs perfect.** Computational indifferentiability only requires security to hold for polynomial-sized D. Note that in the statistical case, we still bound the number of queries made by D to be polynomial. On the other hand, perfect indifferentiability requires security to hold for unbounded Turing machines, and for ϵ to be 0.
- **Quantum vs classical.** Quantum indifferentiability requires security to hold for quantum distinguishers D which can make *quantum* queries to their oracles, but potentially allows for quantum simulators S which can make quantum queries as well.
- **Reset vs plain.** Reset indifferentiability requires S to be stateless. We note that [RSS11] define reset indifferentiability differently, allowing the simulator to be stateful but allowing the distinguisher to "reset" the simulator to its initial state at any point. The two versions are readily seen to be equivalent, and we prefer the stateless simulator definition for its simplicity.

We note that the four variants above are all orthogonal and any subset can be considered, giving a total of 24 possible notions of indifferentiability. Note that strong implies weak, reset implies plain, and perfect implies statistical implies computational, for any settings of the other variants. Quantum does not *necessarily* imply classical since it could be the case that a quantum simulator can fool a classical distinguisher, but no classical simulator can. However, in all cases we will consider in this work, if the scheme is quantum indifferentiable for some setting of the other variants, it will also be classical indifferentiable for the same variants. Thus, for our purposes, we will treat quantum indifferentiability as being stronger.

4   Lifting Indistinguishability to Indifferentiability in the Unbounded Setting

Here, we show how to lift query-unbounded in*distinguisha*bility into weak reset in*differentia*bility, albeit with query-unbounded simulation.

Theorem 4. *Let $\mathcal{A}, \mathcal{B}$ be distributions and C a construction. Suppose the distributions of truth tables B and C^A for $A \leftarrow \mathcal{A}, B \leftarrow \mathcal{B}$ are statistically close. Suppose further that $\mathcal{B}$ has super-logarithmic min-entropy $H_\infty(\mathcal{B}) := \min_B \log 1/\Pr[B \leftarrow \mathcal{B}]$. Then for any (potentially query unbounded, classical or quantum) distinguisher D, there exists a query unbounded classical simulator S and a negligible ϵ such that:*

$$\left| \Pr_{A \leftarrow \mathcal{A}} \left[D^{C^A, A}() = 1 \right] - \Pr_{B \leftarrow \mathcal{B}} \left[D^{B, S^B}() = 1 \right] \right| \le \epsilon.$$

In other words, if C^A is indistinguishable from $\mathcal{B}$ against unbounded distinguishers, then C^A is also indifferentiable from $\mathcal{B}$, albeit using a query unbounded simulator.

Proof. Fix any distinguisher D. For any B, let Q_B be the distribution over $A \leftarrow \mathcal{A}$, conditioned on C^A being identical to B. Then, by the statistical closeness of C^A and B, we have that there exists a negligible δ such that

$$\left| \Pr_{A \leftarrow \mathcal{A}} \left[D^{C^A, A}() = 1 \right] - \Pr_{B \leftarrow \mathcal{B}, A \leftarrow Q_B} \left[D^{B, A}() = 1 \right] \right| \le \delta$$

Now consider the following distribution $\mathcal{J}$ over functions J: for each B, $J(B)$ is sampled from Q_B, independently from all other inputs. Then we have that

$$\Pr_{B \leftarrow \mathcal{B}, J \leftarrow \mathcal{J}} \left[D^{B, J(B)}() = 1 \right] = \Pr_{B \leftarrow \mathcal{B}, A \leftarrow Q_B} \left[D^{B, A}() = 1 \right]$$

We now describe our simulator S. S will have a J hard-coded. For every query, it will compute the truth table for B in its entirety by making exponentially many queries, and then set $A = J(B)$. It will then answer the query using A. It remains to show how to select J. What we show is that, for any D, a *random J* drawn from $\mathcal{J}$ will do. Concretely, consider the random variable $p := \Pr_{B \leftarrow \mathcal{B}} \left[D^{B, J(B)}() = 1 \right]$, which depends on J. We observe that p is identical to the random variable $\sum_B \Pr[B \leftarrow \mathcal{B}] p_B$, where the $p_B \in [0, 1]$ are independent random variables obtained by sampling $A \leftarrow Q_B$ and outputting $\Pr[D^{B,A}() = 1]$, where the last probability is over any random coins of D. Each p_B is in $[0, 1]$, and the expectation of p is exactly $q := \Pr_{B \leftarrow \mathcal{B}, A \leftarrow Q_B} \left[D^{B,A}() = 1 \right]$.

We apply Hoeffding's inequality to the random variables $\Pr[B \leftarrow \mathcal{B}]p_B$, giving:

$$\Pr[|p - q| \geq \gamma] \leq 2e^{-2\gamma^2 / \sum_B \Pr[B \leftarrow \mathcal{B}]^2}$$

$$\leq 2e^{-2\gamma^2 2^{H_\infty(\mathcal{B})} / \sum_B \Pr[B \leftarrow \mathcal{B}]} = 2e^{-2\gamma^2 2^{H_\infty(\mathcal{B})}} \tag{1}$$

Since $2^{H_\infty(\mathcal{B})}$ is super-polynomial, we can choose γ negligible while still having Line 1 be less than 1. Thus, there is *some* value of p_B for each B (and hence choice of J) such that $| \Pr_{B \leftarrow \mathcal{B}} \left[D^{B,J(B)}() = 1 \right] - p| \leq \gamma$. The simulator therefore uses this choice of J, and we have

$$\left| \Pr_{A \leftarrow \mathcal{A}} \left[D^{C^A, A}() = 1 \right] - \Pr_{B \leftarrow \mathcal{B}} \left[D^{B, S^B}() = 1 \right] \right| \leq \delta + \gamma$$

which is negligible.   □

5   Shared Randomness Indifferentiability

In this section, we present shared randomness models of reset indifferentiability. In this model, the simulator has access to a source of randomness, and the same randomness is used in every invocation of the simulator. We will actually consider two variants, one where the shared randomness is simply a random string, and the other where the shared randomness is a random oracle.

Shared Random String (SRS). This model is equivalent to read-only indifferentiability [BDG20]. The simulator has access to an arbitrary-size random string.

Definition 2. C^A *is (strong statistical classical) reset indifferentiable from $\mathcal{B}$ in the SRS model if there exists set $\mathcal{R}$ and a polynomial-sized stateless oracle-aided simulator S such that, for any probabilistic potentially unbounded oracle-added Turing machine D making at most a polynomial number of queries, there exists a negligible ϵ such that*

$$\left| \Pr_{A \leftarrow \mathcal{A}} \left[D^{C^A, A}() = 1 \right] - \Pr_{B \leftarrow \mathcal{B}, r \leftarrow \mathcal{R}} \left[D^{B, S^B(\cdot \,;\, r)}() = 1 \right] \right| \leq \epsilon.$$

Above, $S^B(\cdot \,;\, r)$ means that queries x to S are answered as $S^B(x \,;\, r)$.

Remark 1. [DGHM13] consider a notion of *resource restricted* indifferentiability, where the simulator's space is bounded but potentially non-zero. While the SRS model can be seen as a form of storage, the model is incomparable: SRS allows for unbounded length random string, but the string must be read-only.

Shared Random Oracle (SRO). Here, the simulator has access to an arbitrary-sized random *oracle*.

Definition 3. C^A *is (strong statistical classical) reset indifferentiable from B in the SRO model if there exists sets X, Y and a polynomial-sized stateless oracle-aided simulator S such that, for any oracle-aided Turing machine D making at most a polynomial number of queries, there exists a negligible ϵ such that*

$$\left| \Pr_{A \leftarrow \mathcal{A}}\left[D^{C^A, A}() = 1 \right] - \Pr_{B \leftarrow \mathcal{B}, H \leftarrow \mathcal{Y}^{\mathcal{X}}}\left[D^{B, S^{B, H}}() = 1 \right] \right| \le \epsilon.$$

Above, $\mathcal{Y}^{\mathcal{X}}$ is the uniform distribution over the set of all functions from $\mathcal{X}$ to $\mathcal{Y}$.

When contrasting SRS or SRO indifferentiability from Definition 1, we call Definition 1 the *standard* model. Strong vs weak, computational vs statistical vs perfect, and quantum vs classical are defined analogously to the setting without shared randomness. Note that the definitions also makes sense in the plain (non-reset) setting. However, the SRS and SRO models are redundant in the plain setting, as shown in the following:

Lemma 1. *Let $\Phi \in \{strong, weak\}$, $\Gamma \in \{computational, statistical, perfectly\}$ and $\Delta \in \{classical, quantum\}$. If C^A is $\Phi\ \Gamma\ \Delta$ plain indifferentiable from B in either the of the SRS or SRO models, then it is also $\Phi\ \Gamma\ \Delta$ plain indifferentiable from B in the standard model.*

Proof. All 12 settings of Φ, Γ, Δ are essentially identical. We first show the SRS case. Given a simulator S for SRS indifferentiability, we can simply create a new simulator which chooses a random string r at the first query, and answers all queries using $S(\cdot\ ;\ r)$. For the SRO case, we can simulate the shared random oracle on the fly. In the classical case, this is done via lazy sampling; in the quantum case, this is done using Zhandry's compressed oracles [Zha19]. $\square$

We note that shared randomness is *not* necessarily redundant in the reset setting since there is no explicit ability to store r in order to maintain consistency between the different executions. Looking forward, our results imply that shared randomness is an extra resource in the strong reset setting (in the sense that it makes the notion weaker), but it is usually redundant in the weak reset setting.

5.1   Domain Shrinkage

To illustrate the utility of the shared randomness models, we show that the SRO model is sufficient for domain shrinkage, even with reset indifferentiability. This is in contrast to strong reset indifferentiability without shared randomness, where [BBM13] show that domain extension *and* shrinkage are impossible.

Our domain shrinker is the obvious one, which just ignores part of the domain. Let X, Y be sets with $A : X \to Y$. Let $X' \subset X$. Then $\mathsf{Shrink}^A : X' \to Y$ is simply defined as $\mathsf{Shrink}^A(x) = A(x)$.

Theorem 5. Shrink^{RO} *is strong perfectly quantum and classical reset indifferentiable from a random oracle, in the SRO model.*

Proof. Let $B : \mathcal{X}' \to \mathcal{Y}$ and $H : \mathcal{X} \to \mathcal{Y}$. Let

$$S^{B,H}(x) = \begin{cases} B(x) & \text{if } x \in \mathcal{X}' \\ H(x) & \text{if } x \notin \mathcal{X}' \end{cases}.$$

First, note that $\mathsf{Shrink}^{S^{B,H}}(x) = B(x)$. Also note that if B, H are random functions, then $S^{B,H}(\cdot)$ is a random function. Thus, for any distinguisher D (quantum or classical, computationally unbounded), we have that $\Pr\left[D^{\mathsf{Shrink}^A, A}() = 1\right] = \Pr\left[D^{B, S^{B,H}}() = 1\right]$. □

In the next few subsections, we will show how to remove the SRO model in the setting of weak reset indifferentiability, ultimately achieving domain shrinkage in the standard model with weak reset indifferentiability.

5.2 SRO Implies Weak SRS

Here, we show that indifferentiability with shared random oracles implies indifferentiability with shared random strings, in the weak indifferentiability setting. The idea is to simulate the random oracle using a k-wise independent hash function, which can be set as the shared random string. We note that [BDG20] employ a similar technique, but use a PRF instead, meaning their results require computational assumptions. Our Theorem 6 shows that such computational assumptions are unnecessary.

Theorem 6. *Let $\Gamma \in \{comp., stat., perfect\}$, $\Delta \in \{classical, quantum\}$. If $C^{\mathcal{A}}$ is weak Γ Δ reset indifferentiable from $\mathcal{B}$ in the SRO model, then it is also weak Γ Δ reset indifferentiable from $\mathcal{B}$ in the SRS model.*

Proof. The computational, statistical, and perfect settings are identical, and will be proved together. We first prove the classical case, the quantum case being a small modification that we describe at the end.

Let D be a supposed distinguisher for reset indifferentiability, which we will interpret as a potential distinguisher in both the SRS and SRO models. By SRO indifferentiability, there exists sets $\mathcal{X}$, $\mathcal{Y}$ and a simulator $S^{B,H}$ satisfying Definition 3, meaning there exists a negligible ϵ such that

$$\left| \Pr_{A \leftarrow \mathcal{A}}\left[D^{C^{\mathcal{A}}, A}() = 1\right] - \Pr_{B \leftarrow \mathcal{B}, H \leftarrow \mathcal{Y}^{\mathcal{X}}}\left[D^{B, S^{B,H}}() = 1\right] \right| \leq \epsilon.$$

Now, let q_0 be an upper bound on the number of queries D makes, and q_1 an upper bound on the number of queries S makes to H on any call to S. Then $D^{B,S^{B,H}}()$ makes at most $k = q_0 q_1$ calls to H. Let $\mathcal{F}$ be a family of k-wise independent functions. Then

$$\Pr_{B \leftarrow \mathcal{B}, H \leftarrow \mathcal{Y}^{\mathcal{X}}} \left[D^{B, S^{B,H}}() = 1 \right] = \Pr_{B \leftarrow \mathcal{B}, f \leftarrow \mathcal{F}} \left[D^{B, S^{B,f}}() = 1 \right]$$

Our new simulator therefore sets $\mathcal{F}$ as the space of random strings, and f the shared randomness. SRS security immediately follows.

For the quantum case, we just set $\mathcal{F}$ to be a family of $2k$-wise independent functions, and security follows from the following Lemma of Zhandry [Zha12b]:

Lemma 2 ([Zha12b]). *Let $\mathcal{F}$ to be a family of $2q$-wise independent functions from $\mathcal{X}$ to $\mathcal{Y}$. Then for any algorithm D making at most q quantum queries, $\Pr_{f \leftarrow \mathcal{F}}[D^f() = 1] = \Pr_{f \leftarrow \mathcal{Y}^{\mathcal{X}}}[D^f() = 1]$.*

This completes the proof of Theorem 6.   □

5.3   SRS Often Implies Standard Weak Indifferentiability

Here, we show that SRS (and therefore SRO) indifferentiability often gives weak indifferentiability in the standard model. The intuition is to use the idealized object $\mathcal{A}$ itself to simulate the random string.

Extractable Distributions. Here, we define a notion of *extractability* for a distribution, which captures the ability to extract randomness from the function.

Definition 4. *A distribution $\mathcal{A}$ over functions $A : \mathcal{X} \rightarrow \mathcal{Y}$ is statistically classically extractable if, for any polynomial ℓ and any computationally unbounded distinguisher D making a polynomial number of classical queries, there exists a deterministic polynomial time oracle-aided Turing machine $\mathsf{Ext}^A()$ which outputs ℓ bit strings, and a negligible function ϵ such that:*

$$\left| \Pr_{A \leftarrow \mathcal{A}, r \leftarrow \{0,1\}^\ell} \left[D^A(r) = 1 \right] - \Pr_{A \leftarrow \mathcal{A}} \left[D^A(\mathsf{Ext}^A()) = 1 \right] \right| \leq \epsilon.$$

In other words, D cannot distinguish the output of Ext^A from random. We define computational, perfect, and quantum extractability analogously.

We expect most idealized models of interest to be extractable. In particular, we demonstrate that random oracles are extractable, as is any idealized model that can build random oracles under *plain* (non-reset) indifferentiability.

Theorem 7. *Random oracles are perfectly classically and quantumly extractable.*

Proof. Our proof follows ideas from [BBM13], who show how to remove ephemeral (per query) randomness from "pseudo-deterministic" simulators. We generate randomness in the same way, but with a different application and additionally prove the quantum case. First, we will assume for simplicity that A has ℓ-bit outputs, which is without loss of generality since we can always trade off input and output length in a random oracle, the result potentially multiplying the number of queries by up to ℓ while being perfectly indifferentiable.

Then we have $\mathsf{Ext}^A()$ work as follows. For a parameter k to be chosen latter, Ext arbitrarily (but deterministically) chooses k distinct points $(x_i)_{i\in[k]}$, and outputs $r = \oplus_{i\in[k]}A(x_i)$. Since we require random oracles to have exponential-sized domains, there will always exist k distinct points. To prove extractability, we first consider the classical case. We set $k = q+1$. Then any q-query algorithm D cannot possibly query all the x_i. As such, at least one of the $A(x_i)$ values will be information-theoretically hidden from D, meaning $r = \oplus_{i\in[k]}A(x_i)$ is information-theoretically hidden. As such, D cannot distinguish r from random.

For the quantum case, more care is required since the distinguisher can query on superpositions of potentially all x_i, meaning we cannot argue any particular $A(x_i)$ is hidden. Instead, we use the following result of Zhandry [Zha15b]:

Lemma 3 ([Zha15b], **Theorem 5.1**). *Let Q be a q-quantum query algorithm to A. Then $\Pr[Q^A() = \oplus_{i\in[k]}A(x_i)] \leq \lfloor k/(k-q)\rfloor/2^\ell$. In particular, if $q < k/2$, then the probability is at most $2^{-\ell}$.*

We now turn the very strong intractability of computing r into the desired indistinguishability. Let $k = 2q + 1$ and let D be a q-query distinguisher. Let p_0 be the probability D outputs 1 when given $\oplus_{i\in[k]}A(x_i)$, and let p_1 be the probability D outputs 1 when given a random $r \neq \oplus_{i\in[k]}A(x_i)$ as input. Suppose $p_0 \neq p_1$. In this case, assume without loss of generality that $p_0 > p_1$, by flipping the output bit of D if necessary.

We construct Q as follows: $Q^A()$ chooses a random r, and runs $b \leftarrow D^A(r)$. If $b = 1$, it outputs r; otherwise it chooses a new random r' and outputs r'.

We now compute the probability $Q^A()$ outputs $\oplus_{i\in[k]}A(x_i)$. Conditioned on $r = \oplus_{i\in[k]}A(x_i)$, then $Q^A()$ outputs r (and is hence correct) with probability p_0; otherwise it outputs a random r', which is correct with probability $2^{-\ell}$. Conditioned on $r \neq \oplus_{i\in[k]}A(x_i)$, $Q^A()$ is only correct if it outputs r' (which happens with probability $1 - p_1$) and r' is correct (which has probability $2^{-\ell}$). Over, the probability $Q^A()$ is correct is then

$$
\begin{aligned}
\Pr[Q^A() = \oplus_{i\in[k]}A(x_i)] &= \frac{1}{2^\ell}\left(p_0 + (1-p_0)\frac{1}{2^\ell}\right) + \frac{2^\ell - 1}{2^\ell}(1-p_1)\frac{1}{2^\ell} \\
&> \frac{1}{2^\ell}\left(p_0 + (1-p_0)\frac{1}{2^\ell}\right) + \frac{2^\ell - 1}{2^\ell}(1-p_0)\frac{1}{2^\ell} \\
&= \frac{1}{2^\ell}p_0 + \frac{1}{2^\ell}(1-p_0) = \frac{1}{2^\ell}
\end{aligned}
$$

thus contradicting Lemma 3.   □

Though not needed for our main results, we would also like to show that ideal ciphers are extractable. Classically, the same Ext from the proof of Theorem 7 also works for ideal ciphers. Quantumly, however, the situation is more difficult, in particular because do not know a suitable analog of Lemma 3 for the ideal cipher setting. While it is possible to directly prove that ideal ciphers are quantum extractable by carefully adapting known techniques, we will prove a more general theorem which shows that any ideal model which implies random oracles under indifferentiability is also extractable.

Theorem 8. *Let* $\Gamma \in \{comp., stat., perfect\}, \Delta \in \{classical, quantum\}$. *Suppose* $\mathcal{A}$ *is a distribution over functions such that there exists a construction* $C^{\mathcal{A}}$ *that is strong* Γ Δ *plain indifferentiable from a random oracle. Then* $\mathcal{A}$ *is* Γ Δ *extractable.*

Proof. We prove the classical statistical case, the quantum, perfect, and computational cases being essentially identical. Let ℓ be a polynomial and D a potential distinguisher for the extractability of $\mathcal{A}$. Let S be the universal simulator guaranteed by the *strong* (plain) indifferentiability of $C^{\mathcal{A}}$. Then consider the distinguisher $D_0^{\mathcal{B}} = D^{S^{\mathcal{B}}}$ for the extractability of the random oracle $\mathcal{B}$. By Theorem 7, there must exist an extraction procedure $\mathsf{Ext}_0^{\mathcal{B}}$ and negligible ϵ with

$$\left| \Pr_{B \leftarrow \mathcal{B}, r \leftarrow \{0,1\}^\ell} \left[D_0^B(r) = 1 \right] - \Pr_{B \leftarrow \mathcal{B}} \left[D_0^B(\mathsf{Ext}_0^B()) = 1 \right] \right| = 0.$$

Remembering that $D_0^{\mathcal{B}} = D^{S^{\mathcal{B}}}$, we interpret $D^{\mathcal{A}}(\mathsf{Ext}_0^B)$ and $D^{\mathcal{A}}(r)$ as indifferentiability distinguishers for $C^{\mathcal{A}}$, meaning there exists a negligible ϵ, ϵ' and

$$\left| \Pr_{B \leftarrow \mathcal{B}} \left[D_0^B(\mathsf{Ext}_0^B()) = 1 \right] - \Pr_{A \leftarrow \mathcal{A}} \left[D^{\mathcal{A}}(\mathsf{Ext}_0^{C^{\mathcal{A}}}()) = 1 \right] \right| \leq \epsilon$$

$$\left| \Pr_{B \leftarrow \mathcal{B}, r \leftarrow \mathcal{X}} \left[D_0^B(r) = 1 \right] - \Pr_{A \leftarrow \mathcal{A}, r \leftarrow \mathcal{X}} \left[D^{\mathcal{A}}(r) = 1 \right] \right| \leq \epsilon'.$$

We now let $\mathsf{Ext}^{\mathcal{A}}() = \mathsf{Ext}^{C^{\mathcal{A}}}()$, and we conclude that

$$\left| \Pr_{A \leftarrow \mathcal{A}, r \leftarrow \{0,1\}^\ell} \left[D^{\mathcal{A}}(r) = 1 \right] - \Pr_{A \leftarrow \mathcal{A}} \left[D^{\mathcal{A}}(\mathsf{Ext}^{\mathcal{A}}()) = 1 \right] \right| < \epsilon + \epsilon'.$$

Thus Ext satisfies Definition 4. □

Looking ahead, in Sect. 6, we will prove that ideal ciphers can be used to construct random oracles that are sufficiently indifferentiable to apply Theorem 8. This means that ideal ciphers are extractable.

Removing Shared Randomness for Extractable Sources. We now show that, if the source is extractable, we can remove shared randomness in the weak indifferentiability setting.

Theorem 9. *Let* $\Gamma \in \{comp., stat., perfect\}, \Delta \in \{classical, quantum\}$. *If* $C^{\mathcal{A}}$ *is weak* Γ Δ *reset indifferentiable from* $\mathcal{B}$ *in the SRS model, and if* $\mathcal{B}$ *is* Γ Δ *extractable, then* $C^{\mathcal{A}}$ *is also weak* Γ Δ *reset indifferentiable from* $\mathcal{B}$ *in the standard model.*

Proof. All six settings are essentially identical, so we prove the statistical classical case. Let D be a supposed distinguisher for reset indifferentiability, which we will interpret as both a potential distinguisher in both the SRS and standard models. By SRS indifferentiability, there exists a set $\mathcal{X}$ and a simulator S^B satisfying Definition 2, meaning there exists a negligible ϵ such that

$$\left| \Pr_{A \leftarrow \mathcal{A}} \left[D^{C^A, A}() = 1 \right] - \Pr_{B \leftarrow \mathcal{B}, r \leftarrow \mathcal{X}} \left[D^{B, S^B(\cdot\,;\,r)}() = 1 \right] \right| \leq \epsilon.$$

Consider the extractability distinguisher $E^B(r) := D^{B,S^B(\cdot\,;\,r)}()$ for $\mathcal{B}$. By the assumed extractability of $\mathcal{B}$, there exists an extraction procedure Ext and negligible δ such that

$$\left| \Pr_{B\leftarrow\mathcal{B},r\leftarrow\mathcal{X}}\left[D^{B,S^B(\cdot\,;\,r)}() = 1\right] - \Pr_{B\leftarrow\mathcal{B}}\left[D^{B,S^B(\cdot\,;\,r)}() = 1 : r = \mathsf{Ext}^B()\right] \right| \leq \delta.$$

We therefore define a new standard-model simulator $T^B(x) = S^B(x\,;\,\mathsf{Ext}^B())$. The result is that

$$\left| \Pr_{A\leftarrow\mathcal{A}}\left[D^{C^A,A}() = 1\right] - \Pr_{A\leftarrow\mathcal{A}}\left[D^{B,T^B}() = 1\right] \right| \leq \epsilon + \delta$$

Thus establishing reset indifferentiability in the standard model.   □

As an immediate corollary, we have:

Corollary 2. *For any $\mathcal{X}' \subseteq \mathcal{X}$, $\mathsf{Shrink}^{\mathsf{RO}}$ is weak statistical (classical and quantum) reset indifferentiable from a random oracle, in the standard model.*

Remark 2. It may seem odd that we can use extractability to prove *reset* indifferentiability, when Theorem 8 only needs *plain* indifferentiability to justify extractability. Note, however, that the actual indifferentiability simulator uses Ext, which is indeed stateless. The simulator used to justify extractability only comes up as a hybrid in the security analysis, where it is okay to keep state.

5.4   Extensions

Here, we consider shared randomness beyond random oracles, namely a generalization to oracle distributions are *constructible* from random oracles.

Definition 5. *We say a distribution $\mathcal{F}$ is statistically classically constructible from $\mathcal{G}$ if there is a deterministic polynomial-time oracle-aided Turing machine C such that, for any computationally unbounded distinguisher D making a polynomial number of classical queries, there exists a negligible ϵ such that*

$$| \Pr_{F\leftarrow\mathcal{F}}[D^F() = 1] - \Pr_{G\leftarrow\mathcal{G}}[D^{C^G}() = 1]| \leq \epsilon$$

We analogously define computational, perfect, and quantum constructibility.

Note that constructibility does not give the distinguisher access to G, meaning plain indistinguishability suffices. Let $\Gamma \in \{\text{computational}, \text{statistical}, \text{perfectly}\}$ and $\Delta \in \{\text{classical}, \text{quantum}\}$. We note that constructibility has some basic composition properties:

- If $\mathcal{F}$ is Γ Δ constructible from $\mathcal{G}$, and $\mathcal{G}$ is Γ Δ constructible from $\mathcal{H}$, then $\mathcal{F}$ is Γ Δ constructible from $\mathcal{H}$.
- Let $\mathcal{F}_1, \ldots, \mathcal{F}_n$ be distributions, and denote $(\mathcal{F}_1, \ldots, \mathcal{F}_n)$ denote the distribution on functions $(i, x) \to F_i(x)$ where $F_i \leftarrow \mathcal{F}_i$. If each $\mathcal{F}_i$ is Γ Δ constructible from $\mathcal{G}_i$ for $i = 1, \ldots, n$, then $(\mathcal{F}_1, \ldots, \mathcal{F}_n)$ is Γ Δ constructible from $(\mathcal{G}_1, \ldots, \mathcal{G}_n)$

– Let $RO_1, \ldots, RO_n$ be independent random oracles. Then $(RO_1, \ldots, RO_n)$ is perfectly classical and quantum constructible from appropriately-sized random oracles, by simple domain separation.

Next, we observe that existing results imply the constructibility of ideal ciphers from random oracles:

Lemma 4. *Ideal ciphers are perfectly quantumly and classically constructible from appropriately-sized random oracles.*

Proof. In the classical statistical case, we can use Luby-Rackoff [LR86]. Quantum Luby-Rackoff unfortunately is unknown since we need to handle inversion queries. Instead, we follow [Zha16], and use perfect shuffles. In particular, [GP07] shows the existence of a perfect random permutation from a random oracle, which therefore achieves perfect constructibility, even under quantum queries.□

Corollary 3. *Keyed random injections are perfectly quantumly and classically constructible from appropriately-sized random oracles.*

Proof. Keyed random injections are perfectly classically and quantumly constructible from keyed ideal ciphers, by simply padding the input. Then composition gives the desired result.   □

Generalizing Shared Randomness. We now give our general definition.

Definition 6. *Let $\mathcal{F}$ be a distribution over functions. $C^{\mathcal{A}}$ is (strong statistical classical) reset indifferentiable from $\mathcal{B}$ in the Shared-$\mathcal{F}$ model if there exists a polynomial-time stateless oracle-aided simulator S such that, for any oracle-aided Turing machine D making at most a polynomial number of queries, there exists a negligible ϵ such that*

$$\left| \Pr_{A \leftarrow \mathcal{A}} \left[D^{C^A, A}() = 1 \right] - \Pr_{B \leftarrow \mathcal{B}, f \leftarrow \mathcal{F}} \left[D^{B, S^{B,f}}() = 1 \right] \right| \leq \epsilon.$$

We similarly define weak, computational, perfect, and quantum Shared-$\mathcal{F}$ models.

Lemma 5. *Let $\Phi \in \{strong, weak\}$, $\Gamma \in \{computational, statistical, perfectly\}$ and $\Delta \in \{classical, quantum\}$. If $C^{\mathcal{A}}$ is $\Phi \ \Gamma \ \Delta$ reset indifferentiable from $\mathcal{B}$ in the Shared-$\mathcal{F}$ model, and $\mathcal{F}$ is $\Gamma \ \Delta$ constructible from $\mathcal{G}$, then $C^{\mathcal{A}}$ is also $\Phi \ \Gamma \ \Delta$ reset indifferentiable from $\mathcal{B}$ in the Shared-$\mathcal{G}$ model.*

6   Random Oracles from Ideal Ciphers

Here, we show how to build random oracles from ideal ciphers using weak reset indifferentiability. Concretely, we prove that an ideal cipher gives a random oracle with *strong* reset indifferentiability in the shared random oracle (SRO) model:

Theorem 10. *Let $\mathcal{A}$ be an ideal cipher. There exists a construction $C^{\mathcal{A}}$ that is strong statistical (classical and quantum) reset indifferentiable from a random oracle in the SRO model.*

We prove Theorem 10 in Sect. 6.1, but first show two corollaries:

Corollary 4. *Ideal ciphers are statistical (classical and quantum) extractable.*

Proof. By Lemma 1, $C^{\mathcal{A}}$ is strong statistical quantum *plain* indifferentiable in the *standard* model. The result then follows from Theorem 8. □

Corollary 5. *Let $\mathcal{A}$ be an ideal cipher. There exists a construction $C^{\mathcal{A}}$ that is* weak *statistical (classical and quantum) reset indifferentiable from a random oracle in the standard model.*

Proof. We apply Theorem 6 to Theorem 10 to get that $C^{\mathcal{A}}$ is weak statistical (classical and quantum) reset indifferentiable in the *SRS* model. Then we use the extractability of random oracles and Theorem 9 to conclude weak statistical (classical and quantum) reset indifferentiability in the standard model. □

6.1 The Pad-and-Truncate Construction

Our construction can be seen as the Sponge construction for 1-block messages. Fix real numbers $c, d \in (0, 1)$. Let $A : \mathcal{K} \times \mathcal{X} \to \mathcal{Y}$ be a keyed injection with inverse A^{-1}. Let $\mathcal{X}' \subseteq \mathcal{X}$ and $\mathcal{Y}' \subseteq \mathcal{Y}$ such that $|\mathcal{X}'| \leq |\mathcal{Y}|^c$ and $|\mathcal{Y}'| \leq |\mathcal{Y}|^d$. Assume for simplicity that $|\mathcal{Y}'|$ divides $|\mathcal{Y}|$, interpret $\mathcal{Y} = \mathcal{Y}' \times \mathcal{Z}$, and define $\mathsf{Proj}(y, z) = y$. Then define $\mathsf{PadTrunc}_{c,d}^{A,A^{-1}} : \mathcal{K} \times \mathcal{X}' \to \mathcal{Y}'$ as $\mathsf{PadTrunc}_{c,d}^{A,A^{-1}}(x) = \mathsf{Proj}(A(x))$. We now restate Theorem 10, using $\mathsf{PadTrunc}$:

Theorem 10. *For any constants $c, d \in (0, 1)$ such that $c + d \leq 1$, $\mathsf{PadTrunc}_{c,d}^{\mathsf{IC}}$ is strongly shared randomness statistically (classically and quantumly) reset indifferentiable from a random oracle.*

6.2 The Simulator

In order to be consistent with $\mathsf{PadTrunc}_{c,d}$, our simulator needs to answer queries to $A(k, x)$ with $(B(k, x), z)$ for some z. At the same time, it needs to be able to answer queries to $A^{-1}(k, (B(k, x), z))$ with $x \in \mathcal{X}'$. For all other queries, the simulator needs to answer in a way that "looks like" a random keyed injection.

The central difficulty is that, by virtue of having a stateless simulator, we cannot answer these queries lazily, and we cannot "remember" how previous queries were answered. This particularly represents a problem for answering $A^{-1}(k, (B(k, x), z))$ queries, since we somehow have to recover x, even though B is a random oracle which would hide x. Our solution is to do the following. Following Lemma 5, it suffices to have our simulator work in the Shared-$(\mathsf{RI}, \mathsf{RI})$ model, having access to random keyed injections $I : \mathcal{K} \times \mathcal{X}' \to \mathcal{Z}, Q : \mathcal{K} \times \mathcal{X} \to \mathcal{Y}$, and their inverses I^{-1}, Q^{-1}. The simulator $S^{B,I,Q}$ answers A and A^{-1} queries as P and P^{-1} respectively, where:

$$P(k, x) = \begin{cases} (B(k, x), I(k, x)) & \text{if } x \in \mathcal{X}' \\ Q(k, x) & \text{otherwise} \end{cases} \tag{2}$$

$$P^{-1}(k, (w, z)) = \begin{cases} x & \text{if } w = B(k, x) \text{ where } x = I^{-1}(k, z) \\ Q^{-1}(k, (w, z)) & \text{otherwise} \end{cases} \tag{3}$$

6.3 Indifferentiability Proof

We now need to prove that this simulator is indistinguishable from the case where A, A^{-1} are uniformly random permutations, and $B = \mathsf{PadTrunc}_{c,d}^{A,A^{-1}}$.

First, we show that without loss of generality we can focus on the key-less case ($|\mathcal{K}| = 1$). This follows immediately from a generalization of a result of Zhandry [Zha12a], which we prove in the full version [Zha21]:

Lemma 6. *Let D_0, D_1 be distributions over oracles from $\mathcal{X}$ to $\mathcal{Y}$. Let O_1, O_2 be distributions on oracles from $\mathcal{K} \times \mathcal{X}$ to $\mathcal{Y}$, where for each k, $O_b(k, \cdot)$ is sampled from D_b. Suppose there exists a q quantum query algorithm A with access to an oracle O_0 or O_1 such that $|\Pr[A^{O_0}() = 1] - \Pr[A^{O_1}() = 1]| = \epsilon$. Then there is a quantum algorithm B such that $|\Pr[B^{D_0} = 1] - \Pr[B^{D_1} = 1]| \geq \Omega(\epsilon^2/q^3)$.*

Now let D be a (potentially quantum) distinguisher making polynomially-many queries in the keyless case, and define several hybrid experiments:

- **Hybrid 0.** This is the "Ideal World" where B is a random oracle and A, A^{-1} are set to P, P^{-1} as defined in our simulator in Lines 2 and 3, with I, Q being random (key-less) injections. Let p_0 be the probability D outputs 1.
- **Hybrid 1.** This is the same as **Hybrid 0**, except that we replace D's queries to $B(x)$ with $\mathsf{PadTrunc}_{c,d}^{P,P^{-1}}(x)$. Let p_1 be the probability D outputs 1. Note that $\mathsf{PadTrunc}$ only makes A queries on inputs $x \in \mathcal{X}'$, which S answers as $(B(x), I(x))$. Thus $\mathsf{PadTrunc}_{c,d}^{P,P^{-1}}(x) = B(x)$, and therefore the distribution of oracles seen by D is identical in **Hybrids 0 and 1**. Thus $p_0 = p_1$.
- **Hybrid 2.** This is the "Real World", where A, A^{-1} are a random (keyed) injection and its inverse, and $B(k, x) = \mathsf{PadTrunc}_{c,d}^{A,A^{-1}}(x)$. Equivalently, **Hybrid 2** is the same as **Hybrid 1**, except that P, P^{-1} in Eqs. 2 and 3 are replaced by a random keyed injection A and its inverse A^{-1}. Let p_2 be the probability D outputs 1.

It remains to show that $|p_2 - p_1|$ is negligible, which constitutes the bulk of the indifferentiability proof. For this, the following claim suffices:

Lemma 7. *For any distinguisher E making at most a polynomial number of classical or quantum queries, we have that $|\Pr[E^{P,P^{-1}}() = 1] - \Pr[E^{A,A^{-1}}() = 1]|$ is negligible, where A, A^{-1} are a random (keyless) injection and its inverse, and P, P^{-1} are as in Eqs. 2 and 3, with I, Q are random keyed injections.*

Lemma 7 proves Theorem 10 by letting $E^{A,A^{-1}}() = D^{\mathsf{PadTrunc}_{c,d}^{A,A^{-1}},A,A^{-1}}()$. We now prove Lemma 7.

Proof. Classically, proving this is possible using lazy sampling. However, ultimately we will also want to prove the indistinguishability under quantum queries. This is somewhat more challenging, and requires a more careful proof, given limitations of known techniques. We will therefore structure the proof in a way that allows us to prove both classical and quantum indistinguishability.

Let E be a potential distinguisher. We prove the indistinguishability through another sequence of hybrids:

- **Hybrid α.** Here we give E the oracles A, A^{-1} that are a uniformly random (keyless) injection and its inverse. Define p_α as the probability E outputs 1.
- **Hybrid β.** Here, we sample a uniformly random injection $J : \mathcal{X}' \to \mathcal{Y}$. We give E the oracles A_β, A_β^{-1}, where

$$A_\beta(x) = \begin{cases} A(\ J^{-1}(\ A(x)\ )\ ) & \text{if } A(x) \in \mathsf{Img}(J), x \notin \mathcal{X}' \\ A(x) & \text{otherwise} \end{cases}$$

$$A_\beta^{-1}(y) = \begin{cases} A^{-1}(J^{-1}(A^{-1}(y))) & \text{if } y \in \mathsf{Img}(J), A^{-1}(y) \notin \mathcal{X}' \\ A^{-1}(y) & \text{otherwise} \end{cases}$$

Here, $\mathsf{Img}(J)$ is the set of images of J. Note the J^{-1} in both the definition of A_β and A_β^{-1}. Let p_β be the probability E outputs 1.

Note that A_β, A_β^{-1} are identical to A, A^{-1}, except on points determined by the sparse image of J. Since J is random, these points should be hidden from the view of E. Indeed, it is straightforward that, in the classical case, such points will only be queried with negligible probability, and in the absence of querying these points the distributions are identical.

In the quantum case, we have to work slightly harder. We prove the following in the full version [Zha21], which follows from known quantum techniques:

Lemma 8. *Let D be a distribution over subsets V of $\mathcal{X}$ such that each element in $\mathcal{X}$ is placed in V with probability ϵ (not necessarily independently). Consider any quantum algorithm E making q queries to an oracle O with domain $\mathcal{X}$, and let p_0 be the probability $E^O()$ outputs 1. Let O' that is identical to O, except that on a set V sampled from D, O' is changed arbitrarily. Let p_1 be the probability $E^{O'}()$ outputs 1. Then $|p_0 - p_1| < O(q\sqrt{\epsilon})$.*

The random injection J defines such a set V where each input to A or A^{-1} is placed in the changed set with probability $|\mathcal{X}'|/|\mathcal{Y}| = |\mathcal{Y}|^{-(1-c)}$. Therefore $|p_\beta - p_\alpha| < O(q|\mathcal{Y}|^{-(1-c)/2})$, which is negligible.

- **Hybrid γ.** Here, we sample $J, A, A^{-1}, A_\beta, A_\beta^{-1}$ as in **Hybrid β**. Let $K : \mathcal{X}' \to \mathcal{Y}$ be the restriction of A to $\mathcal{X}'$: $K(x) = A(x)$. Also define $Q(x) = A_\beta(x)$ for $x \notin \mathcal{X}'$. The values $Q(k, x)$ for $x \in \mathcal{X}'$ are random and distinct values from the set $\mathcal{Y} \setminus \{A_\beta(x) : x \notin \mathcal{X}'\}$. Plugging in the definition of A_β, K, this gives

$$Q(x) = \begin{cases} K(J^{-1}(A(x))) & \text{if } A(x) \in \mathsf{Img}(J), x \notin \mathcal{X}' \\ A(x) & \text{if } A(x) \notin \mathsf{Img}(J), x \notin \mathcal{X}' \end{cases}.$$

We then give the adversary the oracles A_γ, A_γ^{-1} defined as

$$A_\gamma(x) = \begin{cases} K(x) & \text{if } x \in \mathcal{X}' \\ Q(x) & \text{otherwise} \end{cases}$$

$$A_\gamma^{-1}(y) = \begin{cases} K^{-1}(y) & \text{if } y \in \mathsf{Img}(K(\cdot)) \\ Q^{-1}(y) & \text{otherwise} \end{cases}$$

Let p_γ be the probability E outputs 1. Plugging in the definitions of Q, K, we see that $A_\gamma = A_\beta, A_\gamma^{-1} = A_\beta^{-1}$. Therefore, $p_\gamma = p_\beta$.

Note that in **Hybrid** γ, Q is a uniformly random keyless permutation, and K is a uniformly random keyless injection.

- **Hybrid** δ. Now give E the oracles A_γ, A_γ^{-1}, except where K is chosen as $K(x) = (B(x), I(x))$, B is a random function, and $I(x)$ is a random keyless injection. Note that the result is equivalent to the oracles P, P^{-1} defined as in Eqs. 2 and 3. Let p_δ be the probability E outputs 1.

It remains to show that p_γ is close to p_δ. Since Q is identically distributed in both hybrids, it suffices to prove that the distribution over K in the two hybrids is indistinguishable:

Lemma 9. *Fix $c, d \in (0, 1)$, and let $\mathcal{X}', \mathcal{Y}', \mathcal{Z}, \mathcal{Y}$, $\mathcal{Y} = \mathcal{Y}' \times \mathcal{Z}$, be sets such that $|\mathcal{X}| \le |\mathcal{Y}|^c$ and $|\mathcal{Y}'| \le |\mathcal{Y}|^d$. Write $K : \mathcal{X}' \to \mathcal{Y}$ as $K(x) = (B(x), I(x))$ for $B : \mathcal{X}' \to \mathcal{Y}'$ and $I : \mathcal{X}' \to \mathcal{Z}$. Then for any adversary making q classical or quantum queries to K and its inverse, the following two distributions are indistinguishable:*

- *K is chosen as a random keyless injection*
- *I is a random keyless injection, and B is a random function.*

Proof. In the classical case, this is straightforward: the only way an adversary can distinguish is by finding x_0, x_1 such that $I(x_0) = I(x_1)$, which cannot happen in the case where I is injective. To prove that such tuples are infeasible to find, we rely on the fact that the adversary cannot make inverse queries on valid images (whp), except on values that were the result of prior forward queries.

In the quantum setting, what makes proving this non-trivial is that the attacker has query access to both K and K^{-1}, whereas the vast majority of the quantum literature does not consider inversion queries. In order to prove security, then, we carefully embed an instance of a problem that does *not* use inversion queries, and then rely on known quantum complexity techniques to prove the hardness of the inversion-less problem.

We first consider the case where $c < d$. The reason this case is easier is that we can switch from using $I(x)$ to recover x to using $B(x)$ to recover x. Then since we do not need to query I^{-1}, we can rely on known quantum query lower bound techniques to switch to I being random.

To prove indistinguishability in the $c < d$ case, we define a few more hybrids.

- **Hybrid i.** This hybrid sets $K : \mathcal{X}' \to \mathcal{Y}$ to be a uniformly random (keyless) injection. Let p_i be the probability of outputting 1.
- **Hybrid ii.** This hybrid sets K to be a random *function*. The problem with K being a uniformly random function is that there might be collisions, meaning the inverse is not well defined. We define $K^{-1}(y)$ to be x is there is a *unique* x such that $K(x) = y$. Otherwise, if there are 0 or ≥ 2 solutions, $K^{-1}(y) = \perp$. Let p_{ii} be the probability of outputting 1.

  Since $c < d$ and $c+d \leq 1$, we have that $2c < 1$. As such, a random function is an injection with overwhelming probability by a union bound. Thus $|p_i - p_{ii}| \leq O(|\mathcal{Y}|^{-(1-2c)})$.

  Note here that if we write $K(x) = (B(x), I(x))$, then B, I are independent uniform random functions.
- **Hybrid iii.** Here, we change how we answer $K^{-1}(w, z)$ queries. Rather than directly computing the inverse (supposing it exists and is unique), we instead compute $L_w := \{x : B(x) = w\}$, and then for each $x \in L_w$, we check if $I(x) = z$ by querying I. To bound the number of queries to I, we abort if $|L_w| > r$, for some parameter r. Let p_{iii} be the probability of outputting 1.

  By standard balls-and-bins arguments, for each $w \in \mathcal{Y}'$, L_w is at most r, except with probability $\binom{|\mathcal{X}'|}{r}|\mathcal{Y}'|^{-r} \leq |\mathcal{Y}|^{-(d-c)}$. Union bounding over all w gives that $\max_w |L_w| \leq r$ except with probability $\leq |\mathcal{Y}|^{d-(d-c)r}$. Setting $r = O(1)$, this bound becomes $|\mathcal{Y}|^{-1}$. In the case all L_w have size at most r, there are no aborts and inverse procedure outputs the same value as in **Hybrid ii**. Thus $|p_{ii} - p_{iii}| \leq |\mathcal{Y}|^{-1}$. Moreover, the number of queries made to I for each K^{-1} query is at most a polynomial.
- **Hybrid iv.** Here, we change I to be a keyless injection, and let p_{iv} be the probability of outputting 1. If the adversary makes q queries, we ultimately make $O(q)$ queries to I (and no queries to I^{-1}). We can use the indistinguishability of random functions from random injections [AS04,Zha15a] to bound $|p_{iii} - p_{iv}| \leq O(q^3/|\mathcal{Z}|) = O(q^3/|\mathcal{Y}|^{1-d})$, which is negligible.

This completes the case $c < d$. We now extend to all $c, d > 0$ such that $c + d \leq 1$. The problem with the above proof is that the output of B is no longer large enough to uniquely decode x. Nevertheless, we show how to embed an instance of the problem for $c' < d'$ into the general case, thereby proving security.

Let $c', d' \in (0, 1)$ be constants to be chosen later. Write $\mathcal{X}' = \mathcal{W} \times \mathcal{X}''$ and $\mathcal{Z} = \mathcal{W} \times \mathcal{Z}'$ for $|\mathcal{X}''| = |\mathcal{Y}|^{c'd/d'}, |\mathcal{W}| = |\mathcal{Y}|^{c-c'd/d'}, |\mathcal{Z}'| = |\mathcal{Y}|^{d/d'-d}$. Since $\mathcal{Z} = \mathcal{W} \times \mathcal{Z}'$, we must have $d' = d(1 - c')/(1 - c)$. Moreover, for the sizes of the sets involved to be non-negative, we must have $c' \leq c$, which implies $d' \geq d$.

We will sample K as follows:

- First choose random keyless permutations $W, W' : (\mathcal{W} \times \mathcal{Z}') \to (\mathcal{W} \times \mathcal{Z}')$.
- Next, choose a *keyed* function $K' : \mathcal{W} \times \mathcal{X}'' \to \mathcal{Y}' \times \mathcal{Z}'$
- Set $K(x)$ to be the following: Let $x' = W'(x)$ and write $x' = (\eta, \mu) \in \mathcal{W} \times \mathcal{X}''$. Then compute $(\zeta, \tau) \leftarrow K'(\eta, \mu) \in \mathcal{Y}' \times \mathcal{Z}'$. Then output $(\zeta, W(\eta, \tau))$.

It is straightforward that, if K' is a random keyed injection, then K is a random keyed injection. On the other hand, suppose for any η, the mapping under K'

of $\mu \mapsto \tau$ was a random injection whereas the mapping $\mu \mapsto \zeta$ was a random function. Then it is straightforward that K satisfies the distribution for **Hybrid iv**. Thus, proving the indistinguishability for the two cases of K reduces to proving the indistinguishability for the two cases of K'. By applying Lemma 6, we can further reduce to the keyless case and ignore η. Since the range of K' has size $|\mathcal{Y}|^{d/d'}$, we have that K' is an instance of Lemma 9 with parameters c', d'. Choose an arbitrary $c' \leq c$ such that $d' = d(1 - c')/(1 - c) > c'$, which is equivalent to $c' < d/(1 + d - c)$. We can then invoke the $c < d$ case of Lemma 9 as proved above on K', obtaining the indistinguishability of the two settings. $\square$

This completes the proof of Lemma 7. Putting everything together, this completes the proof of Theorem 10. $\square$

6.4   On Necessary Shrinkage

Our positive result works for any $c + d \leq 1$. Here, we show that this is tight.

Theorem 11. *For any constants $c, d > 0$ such that $c + d > 1$, if A is a random permutation, then* $\mathsf{PadTrunc}_{c,d}^{A,A^{-1}}$ *is not even weak computational (classical or quantum) reset indifferentiable from a random oracle.*

Proof. For simplicity, we focus on the keyless case ($s = 0$), which is without loss of generality. The intuition behind the proof is that the simulator, when answering queries of the form $A^{-1}(B(x), z)$, cannot invert B to recover x. It must therefore recover x from z. But this is only possible if $|z| \geq |x|$.

Consider the distinguisher D, which chooses a random $x \in \mathcal{X}'$, and runs $(w, z) \leftarrow A(x) \in \mathcal{Y}' \times \mathcal{Z}$. Then it runs $x' \leftarrow A^{-1}(w, z)$ and $w' \leftarrow B(x')$ (assuming $x' \in \mathcal{X}'$), and outputs 1 if and only if $w' = w, x' = x$. Consider a supposed simulator S^B for D, where we write S_0^B, S_1^B for the simulator's responses to A and A^{-1} queries, respectively. We have that there exists a negligible ϵ such that

$$\Pr\left[D^{B,S_0^B,S_1^B}() = 1\right] \geq 1 - \epsilon.$$

We turn S^B into an algorithm $U^B(w)$, which finds an x such that $B(x) = w$. $U^B(w)$ works as follows: choose a random $z^* \in \mathcal{Z}$, and output $x \leftarrow S_1^B(w, z^*)$.

Claim. For a random $x \in \mathcal{X}'$, $\Pr[U^B(B(x)) = x] \geq (1 - \epsilon)/|\mathcal{Y}|^{1 - \max(c,d)}$.

Proof. Imagine running D on a random $x \in \mathcal{X}'$. We therefore know that, with probability at least $1 - \epsilon$, the following are both true: (1) $S_0^B(x)$ outputs $(B(x), z)$ for some z, and (2) $S_1^B(z, w) = x \in \mathcal{X}'$. We will therefore say that x is "good" if the above both hold; there are at least $(1 - \epsilon)|\mathcal{X}'|$ good x. In the case $c \leq d$, suppose that x is good. Then $U^B(B(x))$ will successfully invert provided $z^* = z$, which occurs with probability $|\mathcal{Y}|^{-(1-d)}$.

In the case $c > d$, then there will be multiple good x for each w. Consider the set of good $x' \in \mathcal{X}'$ such that $B(x') = w$, and let z' be the associated value outputted by $S_0^B(x')$. Let p_w be the number of such x'. Then as long as z^* is equal to *any* z' for a good x', $U^B(w)$ will output x', a pre-image of w. Thus, the probability of success for a given w is at least $p_w|\mathcal{Y}|^{-(1-d)}$. Since the total number of good x' is $(1-\epsilon)|\mathcal{X}'|$, the expectation of p_w is $(1-\epsilon)|\mathcal{X}'|/|\mathcal{Y}'| = (1-\epsilon)|\mathcal{Y}|^{c-d}$, meaning B succeeds with probability $(1-\epsilon)|\mathcal{Y}|^{-(1-c)}$.   □

We now contrast Claim 6.4 with the (quantum) hardness of pre-image search:

Lemma 10 ([BBBV97]). *For any q quantum query algorithm A making queries to a random function $O : |\mathcal{X}| \to |\mathcal{Y}|$, $\Pr_{x \leftarrow \mathcal{X}}[O(\ A^O(\ O(x)\ )\ ) = O(x)] \leq O(q^2/\min(|\mathcal{X}|, |\mathcal{Y}|))$. In other words, a random oracle is quantum one-way*[4].

This shows that no q-query (quantum) algorithm can invert B except with probability at most $O(q^2|\mathcal{Y}|^{-\min(c,d)})$. We thus have $q^2 \geq \Omega(|\mathcal{Y}|^{\min(c,d)+\max(c,d)-1}) = \Omega(|\mathcal{Y}|^{c+d-1}) = |\mathcal{Y}|^{\Omega(1)}$ (since $c+d > 1$), which is exponential.   □

7   Post-quantum Groups

Here, we demonstrate that generic groups are strongly reset indifferentiability from random injections in the quantum setting.

Theorem 12. *Let GG be a generic group of order p and label space $\{0,1\}^n$. Then the labeling function for GG, namely L, is strongly statistical quantum reset indifferentiable from a (keyless) random injection $I : \{0,1\}^{\log p} \to \{0,1\}^n$.*

Proof. We use Shor's algorithm [Sho94] to invert the labeling function. We can simulate the group operations by inverting the labeling function, performing the group operation in $\mathbb{Z}_p$, and then re-applying the labeling function.   □

7.1   Instantiations and Applications

We can instantiate the generic group using either subgroups of the multiplicative group of finite fields, or over elliptic curves. Then, applying the pad-and-truncate construction, we obtain a plausible post-quantum random oracle. We briefly discuss the case of finite fields. Let q be a prime and g an element generating a large subgroup of $\mathbb{Z}_q^*$. As we do not need discrete logarithms to be hard, the order of g does not seem to matter, and g can even be a generator of $\mathbb{Z}_q^*$. Let $g_i = g^{2^i} \bmod q$. Then $g^a \bmod q = \prod_{i=0}^{n-1} g_i^{a_i}$, where a_i is the ith binary bit of a. Our pad-and-truncate construction is then $a \mapsto (\prod_{i=0}^{n-1} g_i^{a_i} \bmod q) \bmod r$, for some sufficiently small r, giving a simple plausible a post-quantum random oracle.

---

[4] Note that [BBBV97] phrase their result as finding a marked item in a list. Nevertheless, the statement of their result and its proof can be rephrased as in Lemma 10.

Key-Less Classical Permutations. One limitation of the above is that the generic group is only *quantumly* equivalent to a key-less injection, requiring Shor's algorithm to perform inverses. However, an easy fix is to make the discrete log classically easy, by having the group order be smooth. Let q be such that $q - 1$ has all small prime factors. Then computing discrete logs in $\mathbb{Z}_q^*$ is even classically easy by solving discrete log mod each of the factors of $q - 1$, and then Chinese Remaindering. Our labeling function maps $\mathbb{Z}_{q-1} \to \mathbb{Z}_q^*$; this can be turned into a permutation by simply subtracting 1 from the final result.

References

[AR16] Alagic, G., Russell, A.: Quantum-secure symmetric-key cryptography based on hidden shifts. Cryptology ePrint Archive, Report 2016/960 (2016). http://eprint.iacr.org/2016/960

[AS04] Aaronson, S., Shi, Y.: Quantum lower bounds for the collision and the element distinctness problems. J. ACM **51**(4), 595–605 (2004)

[AY20] Agrawal, S., Yamada, S.: Optimal broadcast encryption from pairings and LWE. In: Canteaut, A., Ishai, Y. (eds.) EUROCRYPT 2020. LNCS, vol. 12105, pp. 13–43. Springer, Cham (2020). https://doi.org/10.1007/978-3-030-45721-1_2

[BBBV97] Bennett, C.H., Bernstein, E., Brassard, G., Vazirani, U.: Strengths and weaknesses of quantum computing. SIAM J. Comput. **26**(5), 1510–1523 (1997)

[BBG05] Boneh, D., Boyen, X., Goh, E.-J.: Hierarchical identity based encryption with constant size ciphertext. In: Cramer, R. (ed.) EUROCRYPT 2005. LNCS, vol. 3494, pp. 440–456. Springer, Heidelberg (2005). https://doi.org/10.1007/11426639_26

[BBM13] Baecher, P., Brzuska, C., Mittelbach, A.: Reset indifferentiability and its consequences. In: Sako, K., Sarkar, P. (eds.) ASIACRYPT 2013. LNCS, vol. 8269, pp. 154–173. Springer, Heidelberg (2013). https://doi.org/10.1007/978-3-642-42033-7_9

[BDF+11] Boneh, D., Dagdelen, Ö., Fischlin, M., Lehmann, A., Schaffner, C., Zhandry, M.: Random oracles in a quantum world. In: Lee, D.H., Wang, X. (eds.) ASIACRYPT 2011. LNCS, vol. 7073, pp. 41–69. Springer, Heidelberg (2011). https://doi.org/10.1007/978-3-642-25385-0_3

[BDG20] Bellare, M., Davis, H., Günther, F.: Separate your domains: NIST PQC KEMs, oracle cloning and read-only indifferentiability. In: Canteaut, A., Ishai, Y. (eds.) EUROCRYPT 2020. LNCS, vol. 12106, pp. 3–32. Springer, Cham (2020). https://doi.org/10.1007/978-3-030-45724-2_1

[BFF+14] Barthe, G., Fagerholm, E., Fiore, D., Mitchell, J., Scedrov, A., Schmidt, B.: Automated analysis of cryptographic assumptions in generic group models. In: Garay, J.A., Gennaro, R. (eds.) CRYPTO 2014. LNCS, vol. 8616, pp. 95–112. Springer, Heidelberg (2014). https://doi.org/10.1007/978-3-662-44371-2_6

[BMZ19] Bartusek, J., Ma, F., Zhandry, M.: The distinction between fixed and random generators in group-based assumptions. In: Boldyreva, A., Micciancio, D. (eds.) CRYPTO 2019. LNCS, vol. 11693, pp. 801–830. Springer, Cham (2019). https://doi.org/10.1007/978-3-030-26951-7_27

[BR93] Bellare, M., Rogaway, P.: Random oracles are practical: a paradigm for designing efficient protocols. In: Denning, D.E., Pyle, R., Ganesan, R., Sandhu, R.S., Ashby, V. (eds.) ACM CCS 1993, pp. 62–73. ACM Press, November 1993

[BSW07] Bethencourt, J., Sahai, A., Waters, B.: Ciphertext-policy attribute-based encryption. In: 2007 IEEE Symposium on Security and Privacy, pp. 321–334. IEEE Computer Society Press, May 2007

[CDMP05] Coron, J.-S., Dodis, Y., Malinaud, C., Puniya, P.: Merkle-Damgård revisited: how to construct a hash function. In: Shoup, V. (ed.) CRYPTO 2005. LNCS, vol. 3621, pp. 430–448. Springer, Heidelberg (2005). https://doi.org/10.1007/11535218_26

[CLMQ20] Chen, Y., Lombardi, A., Ma, F., Quach, W.: Does Fiat-Shamir require a cryptographic hash function? Cryptology ePrint Archive, Report 2020/915 (2020). https://eprint.iacr.org/2020/915

[CMSZ19] Czajkowski, J., Majenz, C., Schaffner, C., Zur, S.: Quantum lazy sampling and game-playing proofs for quantum indifferentiability. Cryptology ePrint Archive, Report 2019/428 (2019). https://eprint.iacr.org/2019/428

[CPS08] Coron, J.-S., Patarin, J., Seurin, Y.: The random oracle model and the ideal cipher model are equivalent. In: Wagner, D. (ed.) CRYPTO 2008. LNCS, vol. 5157, pp. 1–20. Springer, Heidelberg (2008). https://doi.org/10.1007/978-3-540-85174-5_1

[Cza21] Czajkowski, J.: Quantum indifferentiability of SHA-3. Cryptology ePrint Archive, Report 2021/192 (2021). https://eprint.iacr.org/2021/192

[Des00] Desai, A.: The security of all-or-nothing encryption: protecting against exhaustive key search. In: Bellare, M. (ed.) CRYPTO 2000. LNCS, vol. 1880, pp. 359–375. Springer, Heidelberg (2000). https://doi.org/10.1007/3-540-44598-6_23

[DFM20] Don, J., Fehr, S., Majenz, C.: The measure-and-reprogram technique 2.0: multi-round Fiat-Shamir and more. In: Micciancio, D., Ristenpart, T. (eds.) CRYPTO 2020. LNCS, vol. 12172, pp. 602–631. Springer, Cham (2020). https://doi.org/10.1007/978-3-030-56877-1_21

[DFMS19] Don, J., Fehr, S., Majenz, C., Schaffner, C.: Security of the Fiat-Shamir transformation in the quantum random-oracle model. In: Boldyreva, A., Micciancio, D. (eds.) CRYPTO 2019. LNCS, vol. 11693, pp. 356–383. Springer, Cham (2019). https://doi.org/10.1007/978-3-030-26951-7_13

[DGHM13] Demay, G., Gaži, P., Hirt, M., Maurer, U.: Resource-restricted indifferentiability. In: Johansson, T., Nguyen, P.Q. (eds.) EUROCRYPT 2013. LNCS, vol. 7881, pp. 664–683. Springer, Heidelberg (2013). https://doi.org/10.1007/978-3-642-38348-9_39

[DHZ14] Damgård, I., Hazay, C., Zottarel, A.: Short paper on the generic hardness of DDH-II (2014)

[DRRS09] Dodis, Y., Reyzin, L., Rivest, R.L., Shen, E.: Indifferentiability of permutation-based compression functions and tree-based modes of operation, with applications to MD6. In: Dunkelman, O. (ed.) FSE 2009. LNCS, vol. 5665, pp. 104–121. Springer, Heidelberg (2009). https://doi.org/10.1007/978-3-642-03317-9_7

[DS16] Dai, Y., Steinberger, J.: Indifferentiability of 8-round Feistel networks. In: Robshaw, M., Katz, J. (eds.) CRYPTO 2016. LNCS, vol. 9814, pp. 95–120. Springer, Heidelberg (2016). https://doi.org/10.1007/978-3-662-53018-4_4

[GP07] Granboulan, L., Pornin, T.: Perfect block ciphers with small blocks. In: Biryukov, A. (ed.) FSE 2007. LNCS, vol. 4593, pp. 452–465. Springer, Heidelberg (2007). https://doi.org/10.1007/978-3-540-74619-5_28

[HKT11] Holenstein, T., Künzler, R., Tessaro, S.: The equivalence of the random oracle model and the ideal cipher model, revisited. In: Fortnow, L., Vadhan, S.P. (eds.) 43rd ACM STOC, pp. 89–98. ACM Press, June 2011

[KSS+20] Kuchta, V., Sakzad, A., Stehlé, D., Steinfeld, R., Sun, S.-F.: Measure-rewind-measure: tighter quantum random oracle model proofs for one-way to hiding and CCA security. In: Canteaut, A., Ishai, Y. (eds.) EURO-CRYPT 2020. LNCS, vol. 12107, pp. 703–728. Springer, Cham (2020). https://doi.org/10.1007/978-3-030-45727-3_24

[LAMP12] Luykx, A., Andreeva, E., Mennink, B., Preneel, B.: Impossibility results for indifferentiability with resets. Cryptology ePrint Archive, Report 2012/644 (2012). http://eprint.iacr.org/2012/644

[LR86] Luby, M., Rackoff, C.: How to construct pseudo-random permutations from pseudo-random functions. In: Williams, H.C. (ed.) CRYPTO 1985. LNCS, vol. 218, pp. 447–447. Springer, Heidelberg (1986). https://doi.org/10.1007/3-540-39799-X_34

[LZ19] Liu, Q., Zhandry, M.: Revisiting post-quantum Fiat-Shamir. In: Boldyreva, A., Micciancio, D. (eds.) CRYPTO 2019. LNCS, vol. 11693, pp. 326–355. Springer, Cham (2019). https://doi.org/10.1007/978-3-030-26951-7_12

[Mit14] Mittelbach, A.: Salvaging indifferentiability in a multi-stage setting. In: Nguyen, P.Q., Oswald, E. (eds.) EUROCRYPT 2014. LNCS, vol. 8441, pp. 603–621. Springer, Heidelberg (2014). https://doi.org/10.1007/978-3-642-55220-5_33

[MRH04] Maurer, U., Renner, R., Holenstein, C.: Indifferentiability, impossibility results on reductions, and applications to the random oracle methodology. In: Naor, M. (ed.) TCC 2004. LNCS, vol. 2951, pp. 21–39. Springer, Heidelberg (2004). https://doi.org/10.1007/978-3-540-24638-1_2

[RSS11] Ristenpart, T., Shacham, H., Shrimpton, T.: Careful with composition: limitations of the indifferentiability framework. In: Paterson, K.G. (ed.) EUROCRYPT 2011. LNCS, vol. 6632, pp. 487–506. Springer, Heidelberg (2011). https://doi.org/10.1007/978-3-642-20465-4_27

[RST01] Rivest, R.L., Shamir, A., Tauman, Y.: How to leak a secret. In: Boyd, C. (ed.) ASIACRYPT 2001. LNCS, vol. 2248, pp. 552–565. Springer, Heidelberg (2001). https://doi.org/10.1007/3-540-45682-1_32

[Sho94] Shor, P.W.: Algorithms for quantum computation: discrete logarithms and factoring. In: 35th FOCS, pp. 124–134. IEEE Computer Society Press, November 1994

[Sho97] Shoup, V.: Lower bounds for discrete logarithms and related problems. In: Fumy, W. (ed.) EUROCRYPT 1997. LNCS, vol. 1233, pp. 256–266. Springer, Heidelberg (1997). https://doi.org/10.1007/3-540-69053-0_18

[TU16] Targhi, E.E., Unruh, D.: Post-quantum security of the Fujisaki-Okamoto and OAEP transforms. In: Hirt, M., Smith, A. (eds.) TCC 2016. LNCS, vol. 9986, pp. 192–216. Springer, Heidelberg (2016). https://doi.org/10.1007/978-3-662-53644-5_8

[Unr15] Unruh, D.: Non-interactive zero-knowledge proofs in the quantum random oracle model. In: Oswald, E., Fischlin, M. (eds.) EUROCRYPT 2015. LNCS, vol. 9057, pp. 755–784. Springer, Heidelberg (2015). https://doi.org/10.1007/978-3-662-46803-6_25

[YZ20]   Yamakawa, T., Zhandry, M.: Classical vs quantum random oracles. Cryptology ePrint Archive, Report 2020/1270 (2020). https://eprint.iacr.org/2020/1270

[Zha12a] Zhandry, M.: How to construct quantum random functions. In: 53rd FOCS, pp. 679–687. IEEE Computer Society Press, October 2012

[Zha12b] Zhandry, M.: Secure identity-based encryption in the quantum random oracle model. In: Safavi-Naini, R., Canetti, R. (eds.) CRYPTO 2012. LNCS, vol. 7417, pp. 758–775. Springer, Heidelberg (2012). https://doi.org/10.1007/978-3-642-32009-5_44

[Zha15a] Zhandry, M.: A note on the quantum collision and set equality problems. Quantum Info. Comput. **15**(7–8), 557–567 (2015)

[Zha15b] Zhandry, M.: Quantum oracle classification - the case of group structure (2015)

[Zha16]   Zhandry, M.: A note on quantum-secure PRPs. Cryptology ePrint Archive, Report 2016/1076 (2016). http://eprint.iacr.org/2016/1076

[Zha19]   Zhandry, M.: How to record quantum queries, and applications to quantum indifferentiability. In: Boldyreva, A., Micciancio, D. (eds.) CRYPTO 2019. LNCS, vol. 11693, pp. 239–268. Springer, Cham (2019). https://doi.org/10.1007/978-3-030-26951-7_9

[Zha21]   Zhandry, M.: Redeeming reset indifferentiability and applications to post-quantum security. Cryptology ePrint Archive, Report 2021/288 (2021). https://eprint.iacr.org/2021/288

[ZZ21]   Zhandry, M., Zhang, C.: The relationship between idealized models under computationally bounded adversaries. Cryptology ePrint Archive, Report 2021/240 (2021). https://eprint.iacr.org/2021/240

Franchised Quantum Money

Bhaskar Roberts[1]($\boxtimes$) and Mark Zhandry[2,3]($\boxtimes$)

[1] UC Berkeley, Berkeley, USA
bhaskarr@eecs.berkeley.edu
[2] Princeton University, Princeton, USA
mzhandry@princeton.edu
[3] NTT Research, Sunnyvale, USA

Abstract. The construction of public key quantum money based on standard cryptographic assumptions is a longstanding open question. Here we introduce franchised quantum money, an alternative form of quantum money that is easier to construct. Franchised quantum money retains the features of a useful quantum money scheme, namely unforgeability and local verification: anyone can verify banknotes without communicating with the bank. In franchised quantum money, every user gets a unique secret verification key, and the scheme is secure against counterfeiting and sabotage, a new security notion that appears in the franchised model. Finally, we construct franchised quantum money and prove security assuming one-way functions.

1 Introduction

The application of quantum information to unforgeable currency was first envisioned by Wiesner [Wie83], and these early ideas laid the foundation for the field of quantum cryptography. However, Wiesner's scheme for quantum money has a major drawback: verifying that a banknote is valid requires a classical description of the state, so the banknote must be sent back to the bank for verification.

The key properties that make cash (paper bills) useful are that anyone can verify banknotes *locally*, without communicating with the bank, and the banknotes are hard to counterfeit. In a classical world, digital currency cannot hope to achieve these properties because any classical bitstring can be duplicated. In a quantum world, we have hope for uncounterfeitable money because of the no-cloning theorem.

Recent works [Aar09, FGH+12, AC12, Zha19] have sought a *public* test to verify banknotes. A scheme with such a test is called public key quantum money (or PKQM). Unfortunately, a convincing construction of public key quantum money has been notoriously elusive. Most proposals have been based on new ad hoc complexity assumptions, and in many cases those assumptions were broken [FGH+12, PFP15, Aar16]. Recently, Zhandry [Zha19] showed that the [AC12] scheme can be instantiated using recent indistinguishability obfuscators. However, the quantum security of such obfuscators is currently unclear. Zhandry

© International Association for Cryptologic Research 2021
M. Tibouchi and H. Wang (Eds.): ASIACRYPT 2021, LNCS 13090, pp. 549–574, 2021.
https://doi.org/10.1007/978-3-030-92062-3_19

also proposed a new quantum money scheme in [Zha19], but the security of his scheme was also called into question [Rob21].

Franchised Quantum Money: In this work, we introduce franchised quantum money (FQM), which is useful as a currency system, easier to construct than public key quantum money, and potentially a stepping stone to PKQM. In franchised quantum money, every user receives a unique secret verification key. With their key, a user can verify banknotes locally, but they cannot create counterfeit money that would fool another user. Our main result is to show how to realize franchised quantum money under essentially minimal assumptions, namely one-way functions.

Franchised quantum money is a secret key scheme that approximates the functionality of a public key scheme. In particular, franchised quantum money achieves local verification[1].

The franchised verification model is broadly useful for approximating the security guarantees of public key verification. Building off of an earlier, unpublished version of this paper, [KNY21] proposed a franchised verification model for quantum lightning, and combined with a lattice assumption that we also proposed, they constructed a scheme for secure software leasing.

The central feature of franchised quantum money is that each user has a unique secret key. Furthermore, we only require that an adversary cannot trick a *different* user into accepting a counterfeit banknote.

The difficulty with PKQM is that if the adversary knows the verification key, they know what properties of the state will be tested during verification. It is hard to design a verification procedure that reveals just enough information to verify banknotes, without giving enough information to create fake banknotes that fool the verifier.

Franchised quantum money does not have this issue. The adversary does not know any other user's key, so they don't know what properties the other user will test during verification. Therefore it is hard for the adversary to trick the other user into accepting a counterfeit banknote.

1.1   Technical Details

Definition of Franchised Quantum Money: In franchised quantum money, there is a trusted party, called the bank, that administers the currency system by generating verification keys and banknotes. A banknote is valid if it was generated by the bank.

The other participants in the system are untrusted users, who send and receive banknotes among each other. Each user can request a unique secret

---

[1] [BS20] also propose a quantum money scheme that tries to approximate the functionality of PKQM. However, their scheme does not achieve local verification: their banknotes must be periodically sent back to the bank for verification. Furthermore, the way they define security is hard to justify.

verification key from the bank. The key allows the user to verify any banknote they receive, and valid banknotes are accepted by verification with overwhelming probability.

Some users (the adversaries) are malicious and try to trick other users into accepting invalid banknotes. However it's hard for an adversary to create invalid banknotes that another user would accept.

Security: In order to be considered secure, a franchised quantum money scheme must be secure against both counterfeiting and sabotage.

Security Against Counterfeiting: We say that the scheme is *secure against counterfeiting* if it is hard for an adversary with m valid banknotes to get any other users to accept $m + 1$ banknotes. The key difference from public key quantum money lies in the word *other*. We don't care if the adversary can produce $m + 1$ banknotes that they themself would accept.

In fact in our construction, it's easy for the adversary to "trick themself" into accepting invalid banknotes, because if they know what key will be used in verification, they can create invalid banknotes that will be accepted. However, a different user with a key that is unknown to the adversary will recognize these banknotes as invalid.

Security Against Sabotage: Because each user has a different key, there is a second kind of security we need to consider. We don't want one user to accept an invalid banknote that another user would reject.

We call this attack sabotage:[2] the adversary takes a valid banknote and modifies it. Then they give it to one user, who accepts it even though the banknote is invalid. But when the first user tries to spend the banknote with a second user, the second user rejects the banknote.

How could sabotage be possible if the scheme is secure against counterfeiting? The adversary does not need to spend more banknotes than they received in order to succeed at sabotage.

A scheme is *secure against sabotage* if the adversary cannot produce a banknote that one other user accepts but which a second other user rejects.

Remark 1. We note that sabotage attacks are also a potential concern for public key quantum money schemes. Even though all users run the same verification procedure, technically two successive runs of the procedure may not output the same result. However, this problem can always be avoided by implementing verification as a projective measurement.

Furthermore, in practice, decoherence between runs may cause successive runs to behave differently. In this case too, sabotage attacks may be relevant.

To the best of our knowledge, this is the first work to point out these potential problems.

---

[2] We borrow this name from [BS20].

If an FQM scheme is secure against counterfeiting and sabotage, then it is practically useful as currency. This is because users can trust that any banknote they accept will be accepted by all other users, and the money supply will not increase unless the bank produces more banknotes. Therefore, these banknotes can hold monetary value. Quantum money does not need to be public key in order to be useful as a currency system.

Construction from Hidden Subspaces: Our construction of FQM is based on [AC12]'s proposal for PKQM from black-box subspace oracles. Below is a simplified version of our construction. A less-simplified version is given in Sect. 4, and the full version is given in Sect. 5.

Banknote: The banknote is an n-qubit quantum state. We can think of its computational basis states as vectors in $\mathbb{Z}_2^n$. The banknote $|A\rangle$ is a superposition over some random subspace $A \leq \mathbb{Z}_2^n$ such that $dim(A) = dim(A^\perp) = n/2$. We call this state a subspace state.

$$|A\rangle = \frac{1}{\sqrt{|A|}} \sum_{\mathbf{x} \in A} |\mathbf{x}\rangle$$

Verification Key: For a given banknote $|A\rangle$, each verification key is a pair of random subspaces (V, W). $V \leq A$ and $W \leq A^\perp$, and the dimension of V and W is $t := \Theta(\sqrt{n})$. Each verifier gets an independently random (V, W).

Verification: To verify a banknote, the verifier performs two tests, one in the computational basis, and one in the Fourier basis.

First we test that the classical basis states of $|A\rangle$ are in $W^\perp$.

Then we take the quantum Fourier transform of the banknote. If the banknote is valid, the resulting state, $\widetilde{|A\rangle}$, is a superposition over $A^\perp$ ([AC12]):

$$\widetilde{|A\rangle} = |A^\perp\rangle = \frac{1}{\sqrt{|A^\perp|}} \sum_{\mathbf{y} \in A^\perp} |\mathbf{y}\rangle$$

Next, in the Fourier basis, we test that the vectors in $\widetilde{|A\rangle}$'s superposition are in $V^\perp$. Finally we take the inverse quantum Fourier transform, and return the resulting state. We accept the banknote if both tests passed. If the banknote was valid, the final state is the same as the initial one.

Discussion: A verifier will accept any subspace state $|B\rangle$ where $V \leq B \leq W^\perp$. Note that the adversary can easily construct a $|B\rangle$ based on their key (V, W) that they themself would accept.

However, an adversary cannot trick other users into accepting an invalid banknote. With probability overwhelming in n, the other user's (V, W) include dimensions of A and $A^\perp$, respectively, that are unknown to the adversary. Any banknote the adversary tries to produce, other than an honest banknote, will almost certainly get "caught" by these other dimensions and rejected.

Multiple Banknotes. In the simplified construction above, one verification key (V, W) cannot verify multiple banknotes. Each banknote uses a different subspace A, and (V, W) depend on the choice of A.

However in the full construction, one verification key needs to verify every banknote the user receives. To achieve this, we assume the existence of one-way functions, which implies CPA-secure encryption. First, (V, W) are encrypted and appended to the banknote as a classical ciphertext. Then the decryption key serves as the verification key – the verifier decrypts the ciphertext to get (V, W), which they use to verify the banknote.

It is straightforward to see that *some* computational assumptions are necessary for franchised quantum money, since given an unlimited number of banknotes, the bank's master secret key is information-theoretically determined. So our construction of franchised quantum money uses essentially minimal assumptions.

Franchised vs. Obfuscated Verification: The franchised verification model allows us to avoid using obfuscation when constructing quantum money, and the model may be useful beyond quantum money as a way to avoid obfuscation.

[AC12, Zha19]'s construction of PKQM relies on strong forms of obfuscation, such as post-quantum-secure iO, for which we have no convincing construction. The PKQM construction is like our FQM construction, except every verifier uses $V = A$ and $W = A^\perp$. We call this *full* verification, in contrast to franchised verification. Additionally, the oracles checking membership in A and $A^\perp$ are obfuscated so the adversary can't learn A.

In the franchised model, there is no need for obfuscation. The adversary only gets query access to the verifier, and they do not know the other users' verification keys. It is therefore feasible to construct FQM from assumptions weaker than obfuscation.

Finally, the franchised verifiers enjoy essentially the same security as full verifiers. We will show that the adversary cannot distinguish whether they're interacting with a full verifier or a franchised verifier, so our FQM construction inherits the security guarantees of the PKQM construction.

Colluding Adversaries: As we defined FQM above, each user receives one verification key. But in the real world, it's possible that multiple adversaries collude: they pool their verification keys to gain more counterfeiting or sabotage power.

In our construction, each key gives a small number of dimensions of A and $A^\perp$. If the adversary has unlimited verification keys, then they can learn all of A and $A^\perp$ and produce as many copies of $|A\rangle$ as they want. So we will impose a collusion bound: no more than $C = \frac{n}{4t}$ adversaries can work together. This means no adversary learns more than $n/4$ dimensions of A (or $A^\perp$). With this collusion bound, the scheme is secure.

Although our scheme needs large banknotes to handle a large collusion bound, this may be reasonable in any scenario where the number of users is small – for example, in markets for certain financial securities, event tickets, etc.[3]

Additionally, collusion bounds are commonplace in cryptography, for example in traitor tracing. Our construction is analogous to the early days of traitor tracing, where the initial schemes [CFN94] had ciphertexts with size linear in the collusion bound, and the main goal became to shrink the ciphertext size. Eventually, [GKW18] essentially removed the collusion bound, giving a construction that is secure against exponentially many colluding adversaries, as a function of the ciphertext size.

Finally, we expect that any FQM scheme will require a collusion bound of some kind or else it would likely yield PKQM. See Sect. 1.2 for more detail.

1.2   Next Steps

Increase the Collusion Bound: The main open problem is to increase the collusion bound, while maintaining small banknotes and verification keys. In our construction of FQM, the size of the banknotes (n) grows faster than the collusion bound $(C = \Theta(\sqrt{n}))$. A reasonable next step is to construct a scheme whose banknote size grows slower than the collusion bound.

Here are two possible approaches: first, we might use LWE or similar assumptions to add noise to the verification keys. Given many noisy keys, an adversary would hopefully be unable to learn the secret information needed for counterfeiting. LWE has been used in traitor tracing [GKW18] to increase the collusion bound while achieving short ciphertexts and secret keys (which are analogous to banknotes and verification keys).

Second, we can use combinatorial techniques, such as those used for traitor tracing in [BN08]. [BN08]'s techniques have resulted in optimally short ciphertexts and might be used to achieve short banknotes. However, combinatorial techniques in traitor tracing usually come at the cost of much larger secret keys, and we might expect something similar for franchised quantum money.

Work Up to Public Key Quantum Money: Franchised quantum money is a potential stepping stone to PKQM. Intuitively, the larger the collusion bound, the more the scheme behaves like PKQM, and we expect that PKQM can be easily constructed from an FQM construction that has unbounded collusion.

Hypothetically, how would we prove security for an FQM scheme with unbounded collusion? The reduction would have to generate the adversary's verification keys, and somehow use the adversary's forgery for honest keys to break some underlying hard problem. But if the reduction could generate new verification keys for itself, then the construction might also be able to generate these new keys. If this were the case, we would easily get a public key quantum money scheme: to verify a banknote, generate a new verification key for yourself, and use that key.

---

[3] We thank an anonymous reviewer for suggesting these applications.

Franchised Semi-quantum Money: We can make the mint in our scheme entirely classical, similar to the semi-quantum money scheme of [RS19], which is a secret key scheme. This follows from the fact that anyone can create new (un-signed) banknotes. To create and send a new banknote to a recipient, the recipient will generate a new un-signed banknote $|\$\rangle$ with serial number $\mathbf{y}$ on its own. It will then send $\mathbf{y}$ to the mint, who will sign $\mathbf{y}$ with a classical signature scheme.

2   Preliminaries

Subspaces

- For any subspace $A \leq \mathbb{Z}_2^n$, A will also refer to a matrix whose columns are a basis of the subspace A. The matrix serves as a description of the subspace.
- Let $A^\perp = \{\mathbf{x} \in \mathbb{Z}_2^n \,|\, \forall \mathbf{a} \in A, \langle \mathbf{x}, \mathbf{a} \rangle = 0\}$ be the orthogonal complement of A.
- Let $|A\rangle = \frac{1}{\sqrt{|A|}} \sum_{\mathbf{x} \in A} |\mathbf{x}\rangle$
- Let $O_A : \mathbb{Z}_2^n \to \{0,1\}$ decide membership in A. That is, $\forall \mathbf{x} \in \mathbb{Z}_2^n$:

$$O_A(\mathbf{x}) = \mathbb{1}_{\mathbf{x} \in A}$$

Given a basis B of $A^\perp$, we can compute O_A as follows:

$$O_A(\mathbf{x}) = \mathbb{1}_{B^T \cdot \mathbf{x} = 0}$$

Quantum Computation

Here we recall the basics of quantum computation, and refer to Nielsen and Chuang [NC00] for a more detailed overview.

A quantum system is a Hilbert space $\mathcal{H}$ and an associated inner product $\langle \cdot | \cdot \rangle$. The state of the system is given by a complex unit vector $|\psi\rangle$. Given quantum systems $\mathcal{H}_1$ and $\mathcal{H}_2$, the joint quantum system is given by the tensor product $\mathcal{H}_1 \otimes \mathcal{H}_2$. Given $|\psi_1\rangle \in \mathcal{H}_1$ and $|\psi_2\rangle \in \mathcal{H}_2$, we denote the product state by $|\psi_1\rangle|\psi_2\rangle \in \mathcal{H}_1 \otimes \mathcal{H}_2$. A quantum state $|\psi\rangle$ can be "measured" in an orthonormal basis $B = \{|b_0\rangle, ..., |b_{d-1}\rangle\}$ for $\mathcal{H}$, which gives value i with probability $|\langle b_i | \psi \rangle|^2$. The quantum state then collapses to the basis element $|b_i\rangle$.

For a state over a joint system $\mathcal{H}_1 \otimes \mathcal{H}_2$, we can also perform a partial measurement over just, say, $\mathcal{H}_1$. Let $\{|a_0\rangle, ...\rangle\}$ be a basis for $\mathcal{H}_1$ and $\{|b_0\rangle, ...\rangle\}$ a basis for $\mathcal{H}_2$. Then for a general state $|\psi\rangle = \sum_{i,j} \alpha_{i,j} |a_i\rangle |b_j\rangle$, measuring in $\mathcal{H}_1$ will give the outcome i with probability $p_i = \sum_j |\alpha_{i,j}|^2$. In this case, the state collapses to $\sqrt{1/p_i} \sum_j \alpha_{i,j} |a_i\rangle |b_j\rangle$.

Operations on quantum states are given by unitary transformations over $\mathcal{H}$. An efficient quantum algorithm is a unitary U that can be decomposed into a polynomial-sized circuit, consisting of unitary matrices from some finite set.

Miscellaneous

A function $f(\lambda)$ is *negligible*, written as $f(\lambda) = \mathsf{negl}(\lambda)$, if $f(\lambda) = o(\lambda^{-c})$ for any constant c. $\mathsf{poly}(\lambda)$ is a generic polynomial in λ. A probability p is *overwhelming* if $1 - p = \mathsf{negl}(\lambda)$. Finally $[\lambda] = \{1, \ldots, \lambda\}$, for any $\lambda \in \mathbb{N}$. Numbers are assumed to be in $\mathbb{N}$ unless otherwise stated.

3   Definition of Franchised Quantum Money

Here we'll define franchised quantum money and its notions of security in detail.

Definition 1 (Main Variables).

- *Let $\lambda \in \mathbb{N}$ be the security parameter.*
- *Let $N \in \mathbb{N}$ be the number of verification keys that the bank distributes. $N = O(\mathsf{poly}(\lambda))$ in the security game because the adversary cannot query more than polynomially-many users.*
- *Let $C \in [N]$ be the collusion bound, the maximum number of verification keys that the adversary can receive.*
- *Let msk be the master secret key, known only by the bank.*
- *Let svk be a secret verification key given to a user.*
- *Let $|\$\rangle$ be a valid banknote. Let $|P\rangle$ be a purported banknote, which may or may not be valid.*
- *After verification, $|\$\rangle$ becomes $|\$'\rangle$, and $|P\rangle$ becomes $|P'\rangle$.*

Definition 2. *A **franchised quantum money scheme** $\mathcal{F}$ comprises four polynomial-time quantum algorithms: Setup, Franchise, Mint, and Ver.*

1. **Setup***: The bank runs Setup to initialize the FQM scheme.*

$$msk \leftarrow \mathsf{Setup}(1^\lambda)$$

2. **Franchise***: The bank runs Franchise whenever a user requests a secret verification key. Then the bank sends svk to the user.*

$$svk \leftarrow \mathsf{Franchise}(msk)$$

3. **Mint***: The bank runs Mint to create a new banknote $|\$\rangle$. Then the bank gives $|\$\rangle$ to someone who wants to spend it.*

$$|\$\rangle \leftarrow \mathsf{Mint}(msk)$$

4. **Ver***: Any user with a secret verification key can run Ver to check whether a purported banknote $|P\rangle$ is valid. Ver accepts $|P\rangle$ ($b = 1$) or rejects $|P\rangle$ ($b = 0$). Finally, $|P\rangle$ becomes $|P'\rangle$ after it is processed by Ver.*

$$b, |P'\rangle \leftarrow \mathsf{Ver}(svk, |P\rangle)$$

In order to function as money, $|\$\rangle$ should be accepted by Ver with overwhelming probability, and $|\$'\rangle$ should be close to $|\$\rangle$. This way, we can verify the state in future transactions. The following definition, for correctness, achieves these properties.

Definition 3. $\mathcal{F}$ *is* **correct** *if for any* $svk \leftarrow$ Franchise(msk), *any* $|\$\rangle \leftarrow$ Mint(msk), *and any* N *and* C *that are polynomial in* λ,

1. Ver$(svk, |\$\rangle)$ *accepts with probability overwhelming in* λ, *and*
2. *The trace distance between* $|\$\rangle$ *and* $|\$'\rangle$ *is* $\mathsf{negl}(\lambda)$.

Next, franchised quantum money needs two forms of security: security against counterfeiting and sabotage. Security against counterfeiting, defined below, means that an adversary given m banknotes cannot produce $m + 1$ banknotes that pass verification, except with $\mathsf{negl}(\lambda)$ probability.

Definition 4. $\mathcal{F}$ *is* **secure against counterfeiting** *if for any polynomial-time quantum adversary, the probability that the adversary wins the following security game is* $\mathsf{negl}(\lambda)$:

1. **Setup:** *The challenger is given* λ, N, *and* C, *where* $N, C = \mathsf{poly}(\lambda)$. *Then the challenger runs* Setup(1^λ) *to get* msk, *and finally creates* N *verification keys* $(svk_1, \ldots, svk_N)$ *by running* Franchise(msk) N *times.*
2. **Queries:** *The adversary makes any number of franchise, mint, and verify queries, in any order:*
   - **Franchise:** *the challenger sends a previously unused key to the adversary. By convention, let the last* C *keys be sent to the adversary:* $svk_{N-C+1}, \ldots, svk_N$.
   - **Mint:** *The challenger samples* $|\$\rangle \leftarrow$ Mint(msk) *and sends* $|\$\rangle$ *to the adversary.*
   - **Verify:** *The adversary sends a state* $|P\rangle$ *and an index* $id \in [N - C]$ *to the challenger. The challenger runs* Ver$(svk_{id}, |P\rangle)$, *and sends the results* $(b, |P'\rangle)$ *back to the adversary.*

   Let m *be the number of mint queries made, which represents the number of valid banknotes the adversary receives.*
3. **Challenge:** *The adversary tries to spend* $m + 1$ *banknotes. The adversary sends to the challenger* $u > m$ *purported banknotes, possibly entangled, each with an* $id \in [N - c]$:

$$(id_1, |P\rangle_1), (id_2, |P\rangle_2), \ldots, (id_u, |P\rangle_u)$$

Then for each purported banknote $|P\rangle_k$, *the challenger runs* Ver:

$$b_k, |P'\rangle_k \leftarrow \text{Ver}(svk_{id_k}, |P\rangle_k)$$

The adversary wins the game if at least $m + 1$ *of the purported banknotes are accepted.*

The second form of security is security against sabotage. Sabotage is when the adversary tricks one user into accepting an invalid banknote that is then rejected by a second user.

Definition 5. $\mathcal{F}$ *is **secure against sabotage** if for any polynomial-time quantum adversary, the probability that the adversary wins the following security game is* negl(λ):

1. **Setup:** *same as in Definition 4*
2. **Queries:** *same as in Definition 4*
3. **Challenge:** *The adversary sends to the challenger a banknote* $|P\rangle$ *and two distinct indices* $id_1, id_2 \in [N - c]$.
   The challenger runs Ver *using* svk_{id_1}, *then* svk_{id_2}:

$$b_1, |P'\rangle \leftarrow \mathsf{Ver}(svk_{id_1}, |P\rangle)$$
$$b_2, |P''\rangle \leftarrow \mathsf{Ver}(svk_{id_2}, |P'\rangle)$$

The adversary wins the game if the first verification accepts ($b_1 = 1$) *and the second verification rejects* ($b_2 = 0$).

4   Simple Construction

Here we give a simpler version of our construction of FQM in order to illustrate the main ideas. The simple construction is correct and secure, but only if the adversary gets just one banknote. The full construction of FQM is given in Sect. 5.

Variables and Parameters

- ○ Let N be any poly(λ).
- ○ Let $n = \Omega(\lambda)$ be the dimension of the ambient vector space: $\mathbb{Z}_2^n$.
- ○ Let $A < \mathbb{Z}_2^n$ be a subspace, and let $dim(A) = dim(A^\perp) = n/2$.
- ○ Let $V \leq A$ and $W \leq A^\perp$ be two subspaces given by an svk.
- ○ Let $t = \Theta(\sqrt{n})$ be an upper bound on the dimension of V and W.
- ○ Let $C = \frac{n}{4t}$.

Setup
Input: 1^λ

1. Choose values for N, n, and t.
2. Sample $A \leq \mathbb{Z}_2^n$ such that $dim(A) = dim(A^\perp) = n/2$.
3. For each $id \in [N]$: sample t indices uniformly and independently from $[n/2]$. Call this set I_{id}. Then sample another set called J_{id} from the same distribution.
4. Sample $\mathbf{v}_1, \ldots, \mathbf{v}_{n/2} \in A$ independently and uniformly at random.
   Sample $\mathbf{w}_1, \ldots, \mathbf{w}_{n/2} \in A^\perp$ independently and uniformly at random.

5.
$$\text{Let } msk = \left(A, \{\mathbf{v}_i\}_{i\in[n/2]}, \{\mathbf{w}_j\}_{j\in[n/2]}, \{I_{id}, J_{id}\}_{id\in[N]}\right)$$

and **output** msk.

Franchise
Input: msk

1. Choose an $id \in [N]$ that hasn't been chosen before.
2. Let $svk_{id} = \left(I_{id}, J_{id}, \{\mathbf{v}_i\}_{i\in I_{id}}, \{\mathbf{w}_j\}_{j\in J_{id}}\right)$, and **output** svk_{id}.

Mint
Input: msk

1. Generate and **output** $|\$\rangle = |A\rangle$.

Ver
Input: $svk, |P\rangle$

Let $svk = \left(I, J, \{\mathbf{v}_i\}_{i\in I}, \{\mathbf{w}_j\}_{j\in J}\right)$. Then let

$$V := span(\{\mathbf{v}_i\}_{i\in I}) \text{ and } W = span(\{\mathbf{w}_j\}_{j\in J})$$

1. **Computational basis test:** Check that $O_{W^\perp}(|P\rangle) = 1$. Now $|P\rangle$ becomes $|P_1\rangle$.
2. Take the quantum Fourier transform of $|P_1\rangle$ to get $|\widetilde{P_1}\rangle$.
3. **Fourier basis test:** Check that $O_{V^\perp}(|\widetilde{P_1}\rangle) = 1$. Now $|\widetilde{P_1}\rangle$ becomes $|\widetilde{P_2}\rangle$.
4. Take the inverse quantum Fourier transform of $|\widetilde{P_2}\rangle$ to get $|P_2\rangle$. Let $|P'\rangle = |P_2\rangle$. **Output** 1 (accept) if both tests pass, and 0 (reject) otherwise. Also output $|P'\rangle$.

Proofs of Correctness and Security

Theorem 1. *The simple FQM construction is correct.*

Proof. We will show that for any valid banknote $|\$\rangle = |A\rangle$, Ver$(svk, |\$\rangle)$ outputs $(1, |\$\rangle)$ with probability 1.

1. The computational basis test passes with probability 1. $W \le A^\perp$, so $A \le W^\perp$, and $O_{W^\perp}(|A\rangle) = 1$ with probability 1. Also the banknote is unchanged by this test.
2. The quantum Fourier transform of the banknote is $|A^\perp\rangle$ ([AC12]).
3. The Fourier basis test also passes with probability 1. Since $V \le A$, then $A^\perp \le V^\perp$, and $O_{V^\perp}(|A^\perp\rangle) = 1$ with probability 1. The banknote is also unchanged by this test.
4. Finally, the inverse quantum Fourier transform restores the banknote to its initial state $|A\rangle$, and the banknote is accepted by Ver with probability 1.

$\square$

Theorem 2. *The simple FQM construction is secure against counterfeiting if the adversary receives only $m = 1$ banknote.*

Proof.

1) Preliminaries

Let's say without loss of generality that the adversary receives C verification keys, which correspond to the last C identities: $id \in \{N - C + 1, \ldots, N\}$. Then they receive 1 banknote, and then they make any polynomial number of verification queries. Finally, they attempt the counterfeiting challenge.

We can define the subspaces $V_{adv} \leq A$ and $W_{adv} \leq A^{\perp}$ as the subspaces known to the adversary. We also define V_{id} and W_{id} analogously for each $id \in [N]$:

Definition 6.

  ○ *Let $I_{adv} = \bigcup_{id > N-C} I_{id}$ and $J_{adv} = \bigcup_{id > N-C} J_{id}$.*
  ○ *For any $id \in [N]$, let $V_{id} = span(\{\mathbf{v}_i\}_{i \in I_{id}})$. Let W_{id}, V_{adv}, and W_{adv} be defined analogously.*

Let's assume for simplicity that

$$dim(V_{adv}) = dim(W_{adv}) =: d$$

where d is fixed. This assumption isn't necessary for proving security, but it does make the proof simpler. Also note that $d \leq n/4$.

2) We'll use a hybrid argument to reduce the counterfeiting game to [AC12]'s security game for secret key quantum money:

  ○ **h0** is the counterfeiting security game for the simple FQM construction. In particular, the adversary receives one banknote $|A\rangle$, along with C franchised verification keys.
  ○ **h1** is the same as h0, except the challenger simulates full verifiers: whenever the adversary makes a verification query $(id, |P\rangle)$, the challenger verifies the state using O_A and $O_{A^{\perp}}$ instead of $O_{W_{id}^{\perp}}$ and $O_{V_{id}^{\perp}}$.
  ○ **h2** is essentially [AC12]'s security game for secret key quantum money: let $A \leq \mathbb{Z}_2^{n-2d}$ be a uniformly random subspace such that $dim(A) = dim(A^{\perp}) = n/2 - d$. Next, the adversary gets a banknote $|A\rangle$ but no verification keys. They can make verification queries, and the challenger will run Ver using full verifiers: $(O_A$ and $O_{A^{\perp}})$.

Lemma 1. *For any polynomial-time adversary $\mathcal{A}$, their success probabilities in h0 and in h1 differ by a $\mathsf{negl}(\lambda)$ function.*

We'll defer the proof of Lemma 1 to Sect. 6.

Lemma 2. *If $\mathcal{A}$ is a polynomial-time adversary with non-negligible success probability in h1, then there is a polynomial-time adversary $\mathcal{A}'$ with non-negligible success probability in h2.*

Proof. We can reduce the security game in $h2$ to the security game in $h1$. Let $\mathcal{A}'$ be given an $h2$ banknote $|A\rangle$, where $A \leq \mathbb{Z}_2^{n-2d}$ and $dim(A) = dim(A^\perp) = n/2 - d$. We will turn $|A\rangle$ into an $h1$ banknote $|B\rangle$, where $B \leq \mathbb{Z}_2^n$, and $dim(B) = dim(B^\perp) = n/2$:

1. Prepend $|A\rangle$ with $|0\rangle^{\otimes d}|+\rangle^{\otimes d}$:

$$\text{Let } |A'\rangle = |0\rangle^{\otimes d}|+\rangle^{\otimes d}|A\rangle$$

   $|A'\rangle$ is a subspace state, a uniform superposition over the subspace

$$A' := span[\hat{e}_{d+1}, \ldots, \hat{e}_{2d}, (0^{\times 2d} \times A)]$$

   where $0^{\times 2d} \times A$ is all vectors in $\mathbb{Z}_2^n$ for which the first $2d$ bits are 0 and the rest form a vector in A. Also, $dim(A') = dim(A'^\perp) = n/2$.

2. Sample an invertible matrix $M \in \mathbb{Z}_2^{n \times n}$ uniformly at random. Then apply M to $|A'\rangle$:

$$\text{Let } B = M \cdot A' \text{ and } |B\rangle = M(|A'\rangle)$$

   Observe that $|B\rangle$ is a uniformly random $h1$ banknote.

   Additionally, the adversary knows d dimensions of B and d dimensions of $B^\perp$:

$$V_{adv} = M \cdot span(\hat{e}_{d+1}, \ldots, \hat{e}_{2d})$$
$$W_{adv} = M \cdot span(\hat{e}_1, \ldots, \hat{e}_d)$$

$\mathcal{A}'$ derives C $h1$-verification keys whose vectors span V_{adv} and W_{adv}. Finally, $\mathcal{A}'$ runs $\mathcal{A}$, giving it the banknote $|B\rangle$ along with the verification keys.

When $\mathcal{A}$ makes a verification query $(id, |P\rangle)$, $\mathcal{A}'$ simulates the $h1$ challenger's response as follows, by converting $|P\rangle$ into an $h2$ banknote:

1. Let $|P'\rangle = M^{-1}(|P\rangle)$.
2. Check that the first $2d$ qubits of $|P'\rangle$ are $|0\rangle^{\otimes d}|+\rangle^{\otimes d}$.
3. Query the $h2$ challenger with the remaining $n - 2d$ qubits of $|P'\rangle$. Let $|P''\rangle$ be the state returned by the challenger. Accept the banknote if and only if the first $2d$ qubits passed their test, and the challenger accepted as well.
4. Return $M(|0\rangle^{\otimes d}|+\rangle^{\otimes d}|P''\rangle)$ to the $h1$ adversary.

This procedure simulates $h1$ for $\mathcal{A}$. Also, note that the probability that $|P'\rangle$ passes $h2$ verification is at least the probability that $|P\rangle$ passes $h1$ verification.

Finally, when $\mathcal{A}$ attempts to win the challenge by outputting several purported $h1$ banknotes, $\mathcal{A}'$ converts these into $h2$ banknotes. If $\mathcal{A}$ wins in $h1$ with non-negligible probability, then $\mathcal{A}'$ wins in $h2$ with at least that probability. $\square$

Lemma 3. *In $h2$, any polynomial-time adversary has negligible success probability.*

Proof. [AC12]'s security game is similar to $h2$, except the adversary can query both O_A and $O_{A^\perp}$. They proved the following:

Theorem 3 ([AC12], **Theorem 25**). *Let the adversary get $|A\rangle$, a random n'-qubit banknote, along with quantum query access to O_A and $O_{A^\perp}$. If the adversary prepares two possibly entangled banknotes that both pass verification with probability $\geq \varepsilon$, for all $1/\varepsilon = o(2^{n'/2})$, then they make at least $\Omega(\sqrt{\varepsilon}2^{n'/4})$ oracle queries.*

Let $n' = n - 2d$, the size of the banknote in $h2$. Note that $n' \geq n/2$. Next, let $\varepsilon = 2^{-n'/3}$. Note that $\varepsilon = \mathsf{negl}(\lambda)$. Finally, the number of queries needed to win with probability $\geq \epsilon$ is

$$\Omega(\sqrt{\varepsilon}2^{n'/4}) = \Omega(2^{n'/4-n'/6}) = \Omega(2^{n'/12})$$

Any polynomial-time adversary makes fewer than that many queries, so no polynomial-time adversary can win with non-negligible probability.   □

Putting together Lemmas 1, 2, 3, we get that any polynomial-time adversary has negligible probability of winning the counterfeiting security game for the simple construction of FQM.   □

Theorem 4. *The simple FQM construction is secure against sabotage if the adversary receives only $m = 1$ banknote.*

Proof. The proof of this theorem follows the proof of 2, except at the end. We need to show that in $h2$, any polynomial-time adversary has negligible probability of succeeding at sabotage. To show this, we need the following lemma:

Lemma 4 ([AC12], **Lemma 21**). *In $h2$, Ver projects $|P\rangle$ onto $|A\rangle$ if it accepts and onto a state orthogonal to $|A\rangle$ if it rejects.*

That means that if a purported banknote is verified twice, it is either accepted both times or rejected both times. Therefore, sabotage is not possible in $h2$.

Again, by Lemmas 1 and 2, any polynomial-time adversary has negligible probability of winning the sabotage security game for the simple construction of FQM.   □

5   Full Construction

The full construction of FQM adds a signature scheme and a secret key encryption scheme, which let us hand out the subspaces V_{id}, W_{id} as part of the banknote. As a result, a user can verify many banknotes, each for a different subspace A, without needing to call Franchise for each banknote.

The signature and encryption schemes have the following syntax.

Definition 7 ([KL14], *Definition 12.1*). *A **signature scheme** comprises the following three probabilistic polynomial-time algorithms:*

- SigKeyGen *takes a security parameter λ, and returns (sig_pk, sig_sk), the public and secret keys.*

$$sig\_pk, sig\_sk \leftarrow \mathsf{SigKeyGen}(1^\lambda)$$

- Sign *takes a message msg $\in \{0,1\}^*$ and the secret key and produces σ, the signature for msg.*

$$\sigma \leftarrow \mathsf{Sign}(sig\_sk, msg)$$

- SigVer *takes msg, σ, and the public key, and outputs a bit b to indicate the decision to accept (b = 1) or reject (b = 0) the signature-message pair. Also,* SigVer *is deterministic.*

$$b := \mathsf{SigVer}(sig\_pk, msg, \sigma)$$

The signature scheme is *existentially unforgeable under an adaptive chosen-message attack.* Such a signature scheme can be constructed from one-way functions ([KL14]).

Definition 8 *([KL14], Definition 3.7). A **secret key encryption scheme** comprises the following three probabilistic polynomial-time algorithms:*

- EncKeyGen *takes a security parameter λ and produces a secret key enc_k.*

$$enc\_k \leftarrow \mathsf{EncKeyGen}(1^\lambda)$$

- Enc *encrypts a message msg $\in \{0,1\}^*$ using the key enc_k to produce a cyphertext c.*

$$c \leftarrow \mathsf{Enc}(enc\_k, msg)$$

- Dec *decrypts c, again using enc_k.* Dec *is deterministic, so for any enc_k produced by* EncKeyGen, Dec *always decrpyts c correctly.*

$$msg := \mathsf{Dec}(enc\_k, c)$$

The secret key encryption is *CPA-secure*, and it can also be constructed from one-way functions ([KL14]).

Variables

- Let $|\$\rangle$, a valid banknote, comprise a quantum state $|\Sigma\rangle$ and some classical bits.
- Let $|P\rangle$, a purported banknote, comprise a quantum state $|\Pi\rangle$ and some classical bits.

setup

Input: 1^λ

1. Choose values for the parameters: $n = \Omega(\lambda), t = \Theta(\sqrt{n})$.
2. Set up one signature scheme and n encryption schemes by computing:

$$(sig\_pk, sig\_sk) \leftarrow \mathsf{SigKeyGen}(1^\lambda)$$
$$(enc\_k_1, \ldots, enc\_k_n) \leftarrow \mathsf{EncKeyGen}(1^\lambda), \ldots, \mathsf{EncKeyGen}(1^\lambda)$$

3. Let $msk = (sig\_pk, sig\_sk, enc\_k_1, \ldots, enc\_k_n)$, and then **output** msk.

Franchise

Input: msk

1. Sample t indices uniformly and independently from $[n/2]$. Call this set I. Then sample another set called J from the same distribution.
2. Let $svk = (sig\_pk, I, J, \{enc\_k_i\}_{i \in I}, \{enc\_k_{j+n/2}\}_{j \in J})$, and then **output** svk.

Mint

Input: msk

1. Sample a subspace $A < \mathbb{Z}_2^n$ such that $dim(A) = dim(A^\perp) = n/2$, uniformly at random.
2. Create the subspace state for A, and let $|\Sigma\rangle = |A\rangle$.
3. Sample $n/2$ random vectors in A: $\{\mathbf{v}_1, \ldots, \mathbf{v}_{n/2}\} \in_R A$. And sample $n/2$ random vectors in $A^\perp$: $\{\mathbf{w}_1, \ldots, \mathbf{w}_{n/2}\} \in_R A^\perp$.
4. Encrypt the $\mathbf{v}$s and $\mathbf{w}$s, each with a different enc_k:

$$\text{Let } c_1, \ldots, c_{\frac{n}{2}} = \left[\mathsf{Enc}(enc\_k_1, \mathbf{v}_1), \ldots, \mathsf{Enc}(enc\_k_{\frac{n}{2}}, \mathbf{v}_{\frac{n}{2}}) \right]$$
$$c_{\frac{n}{2}+1}, \ldots, c_n = \left[\mathsf{Enc}(enc\_k_{\frac{n}{2}+1}, \mathbf{w}_1), \ldots, \mathsf{Enc}(enc\_k_n, \mathbf{w}_{\frac{n}{2}}) \right]$$

5. Sign the ciphertexts. Let $\sigma \leftarrow \mathsf{Sign}[sig\_sk, (c_1, \ldots, c_n)]$.
6. Construct the banknote. Let $|\$\rangle = (|\Sigma\rangle, c_1, \ldots, c_n, \sigma)$. Finally, **output** $|\$\rangle$.

Ver

Inputs: $svk_{id}, |P\rangle$

1. Check the signature: $\mathsf{SigVer}(sig\_pk, (c_1, \ldots, c_n), \sigma)$.
2. Decrypt any ciphertexts for which the key is available. For every $i \in I_{id}$ compute $\mathbf{v}_i = \mathsf{Dec}(enc\_k_i, c_i)$, and for every $j \in J_{id}$, compute $\mathbf{w}_j = \mathsf{Dec}(enc\_k_{j+n/2}, c_{j+n/2})$.
   Additionally, define two subspaces, V_{id}, W_{id}:

$$V_{id} := span(\{\mathbf{v}_i\}_{i \in I_{id}})$$
$$W_{id} := span(\{\mathbf{w}_j\}_{j \in J_{id}})$$

3. Recall that $|P\rangle$ comprises a quantum state $|\Pi\rangle$ and some classical bits.
   Computational basis test: Check that $O_{W_{id}^\perp}(|\Pi\rangle) = 1$. After this step, $|\Pi\rangle$ becomes $|\Pi_1\rangle$.
4. Take the quantum Fourier transform of $|\Pi_1\rangle$ to get $|\widetilde{\Pi_1}\rangle$.
5. **Fourier basis test:** Check that $O_{V_{id}^\perp}(|\widetilde{\Pi_1}\rangle) = 1$. After this step, $|\widetilde{\Pi_1}\rangle$ becomes $|\widetilde{\Pi_2}\rangle$.
6. Take the inverse quantum Fourier transform of $|\widetilde{\Pi_2}\rangle$ to get $|\Pi_2\rangle$.
   Let $|P'\rangle$ be the state that $|P\rangle$ has become, with $|\Pi\rangle$ replaced with $|\Pi_2\rangle$.
   Output 1 (accept) if both tests pass, and 0 (reject) otherwise. Also output $|P'\rangle$.

Proofs of Correctness and Security

Theorem 5. *The full construction of franchised quantum money is correct.*

Proof. In steps 1 and 2 of Ver, we check the signature and decrypt the ciphertexts. With probability 1, the signature check passes, and the ciphertexts are correctly decrypted. This follows from the correctness of the signature and encryption schemes.

After the first two steps, Ver is the same as it was in the simple construction. Because the simple construction is correct, the full construction is correct as well.   □

Theorem 6. *The full construction of franchised quantum money is secure against counterfeiting and sabotage.*

Proof. We will use a hybrid argument to show that the adversary's success probability at counterfeiting or sabotage with the full construction is close to what it is with the simple construction. Since the simple construction is secure against counterfeiting and sabotage, the full construction is secure as well.

1) Preliminaries
Without loss of generality, let us say that the adversary receives C $svks$, then receives m valid banknotes from the challenger, and finally makes multiple Ver queries.

Furthermore, let the challenger keep a record of all the banknotes and $svks$ it generated. Finally let the ciphertexts $(c_1, \ldots, c_n)$ of each valid banknote be unique. This occurs with overwhelming probability.

2) Next, we'll use a sequence of hybrids to simplify the situation and remove the need for the signature and encryption schemes.

- **h0** uses the full FQM construction in the counterfeiting or sabotage security game.
- **h1** is the same as $h0$, except Ver only accepts a purported banknote if its ciphertexts $(c_1, \ldots, c_n)$ match those of one of the m valid banknotes given to the adversary.
- **h2** is the same as $h1$, except for any ciphertext c_i for which the adversary does not have the decryption key, c_i is replaced with junk: the encryption under enc_k_i of a random message.

The adversary has $\mathsf{negl}(\lambda)$ advantage in distinguishing $h0$ and $h1$. The signature scheme is existentially unforgeable under an adaptive chosen-message attack, so except with $\mathsf{negl}(\lambda)$ probability, any banknote that passed Ver in $h0$ had ciphertexts that matched one of the m valid banknotes.

The adversary has $\mathsf{negl}(\lambda)$ advantage in distinguishing $h1$ and $h2$ because the encryption scheme is CPA-secure. For any i for which the adversary does not have the decryption key, the adversary receives either m ciphertexts of random messages or m ciphertexts of potentially useful messages. CPA security is equivalent to left-or-right security ([KL14]), which implies that the adversary cannot distinguish these two cases.

3) Next, we'll use another set of hybrids to relate the full construction with the simple construction.

  ○ **h3** is the same as $h2$, except we do not use the signature or encryption schemes. Each valid banknote comprises a subspace state $|\psi_A\rangle$ and a set of plaintext $\mathbf{v}$ vectors in A and $\mathbf{w}$ vectors in $A^\perp$. Finally, to verify a purported banknote, the challenger checks that the $\mathbf{v}$ and $\mathbf{w}$ vectors associated with a purported banknote match those of a valid banknote. Then they use whatever svks were recorded along with the valid banknote to verify the subspace state.
  ○ **h4** is the simple FQM construction with just one banknote. This is the same as $h3$, except the adversary receives only 1 valid banknote, and the $\mathbf{v}$ and $\mathbf{w}$ vectors are given by Franchise and are not included with the banknote.

The adversary's best success probability is the same in h2 and h3 because the signature and encryption schemes were not necessary in h2, so h3 presents essentially the same security game to the adversary.

Lemma 5. *The best success probability for an adversary in h3 is at most m times the best success probability in h4.*

Proof. Given any $h3$ adversary $\mathcal{A}$, there is an $h4$ adversary $\mathcal{A}'$ that simulates $\mathcal{A}$. $\mathcal{A}'$ receives one valid banknote and generates $m-1$ other banknotes. Then $\mathcal{A}'$ runs $\mathcal{A}$ with the m banknotes. When $\mathcal{A}$ makes a verification query, $\mathcal{A}'$ simulates the verifier for the $m-1$ banknotes it generated and queries the $h4$ verifier for the banknote that it received. Finally, $\mathcal{A}$ outputs some purported banknotes at the challenge step, which $\mathcal{A}'$ outputs as well.

If $\mathcal{A}$ wins in $h3$, then there are at least $m+1$ purported banknotes that pass verification, and at least two of them have the same $\mathbf{v}$ and $\mathbf{w}$ vectors. $\mathcal{A}'$ wins in $h4$ if the two banknotes with matching vectors also match the vectors of the banknote given to $\mathcal{A}'$. This happens with probability $\frac{1}{m}$, by the symmetry of the m banknotes. Therefore, $\mathcal{A}'$'s success probability is $\frac{1}{m}$ times $\mathcal{A}$'s. □

4) In $h4$, the adversary has negligible probability of winning the counterfeiting or sabotage games, by Theorems 2 and 4. Since $m = O(\mathsf{poly}(\lambda))$, for any polynomial-time adversary, then any polynomial-time adversary has negligible probability of winning the counterfeiting or security games for the full FQM construction. □

6   Distinguishing Game

In order to prove Lemma 1, we will use the adversary method of [Amb02]. We will study the *distinguishing game*, in which an adversary that is more powerful than the one in Lemma 1 tries to distinguish full and franchised verifiers. Then we show that the more-powerful adversary still has negligible advantage.

In the distinguishing game, the adversary is given a classical description of A, along with other information that is more than what they receive in the security game. However, one piece of information remains hidden to them: the verification keys used by the franchised verifiers. More formally, we say the adversary is given the msk, which includes every (V_{id}, W_{id}). But the verifiers will actually use $(M \cdot V_{id}, M \cdot W_{id})$ for some random matrix M. The next two definitions make this precise.

Definition 9. *Let $\mathcal{M}(A)$ be the set of all matrices $M \in \mathbb{Z}_2^{n \times n}$ such that:*

- M *is invertible*
- *If $\mathbf{x} \in A$, then $M^T \mathbf{x} \in A$, and if $\mathbf{x} \in A^\perp$, then $M^T \mathbf{x} \in A^\perp$.*

Definition 10. *For any $M \in \mathcal{M}(A)$, we also treat M as a function mapping one master secret key to another. Essentially, M is applied to every $\mathbf{v}$ or $\mathbf{w}$ vector that the adversary did not receive. More formally, for any msk:*

$$M(msk) = \left(A, \{\mathbf{v}_i\}_{i \in I_{adv}}, \{M \cdot \mathbf{v}_i\}_{i \notin I_{adv}}, \{\mathbf{w}_j\}_{j \in J_{adv}}, \{M \cdot \mathbf{w}_j\}_{j \notin J_{adv}}, \{I_{id}, J_{id}\}_{id \in [N]} \right)$$

Let $msk' = M(msk)$, and let $V'_{adv}, W'_{adv}, V'_{id}$, and W'_{id} be defined analogously. Then $V'_{adv} = V_{adv}$ and $W'_{adv} = W_{adv}$ because the adversary's $\mathbf{v}$ and $\mathbf{w}$ vectors are not changed by M. Therefore, in the counterfeiting and sabotage security games, the adversary receives the same information, whether the master secret key is msk or msk'.

Next, the adversary in the distinguishing game can also query $O_{W_{id}^\perp}$ and $O_{V_{id}^\perp}$, rather than just Ver. The following definitions bundle together the oracles that the adversary can query.

Definition 11. *The **franchised verification oracle** for a given msk is $O_{Fran}[msk]$. It takes as input an $id \in [N - C]$, a selection bit $s \in \{0,1\}$, and a vector $\mathbf{x} \in \mathbb{Z}_2^n$. Then*

$$O_{Fran}[msk](id, s, \mathbf{x}) = \begin{cases} O_{W_{id}^\perp}(\mathbf{x}) & s = 0 \\ O_{V_{id}^\perp}(\mathbf{x}) & s = 1 \end{cases}$$

Definition 12. *The **full verification oracle** for a given msk is $O_{Full}[msk]$ or $O_{Full}[A]$. It takes as input $id \in [N - C]$, $s \in \{0,1\}$, and $\mathbf{x} \in \mathbb{Z}_2^n$. Then*

$$O_{Full}[A](id, s, \mathbf{x}) = \begin{cases} O_A(\mathbf{x}) & s = 0 \\ O_{A^\perp}(\mathbf{x}) & s = 1 \end{cases}$$

Now we can define the distinguishing game precisely.

Definition 13. *The **distinguishing game** takes as input an msk, which is given to the challenger and the adversary. Then:*

1. *The challenger samples $b \in_R \{0,1\}$ and $M \in_R \mathcal{M}(A)$.*
2. *The adversary makes quantum queries to the challenger. If $b = 0$, the challenger uses $O_{Full}[A]$ to answer the queries; if $b = 1$, the challenger uses $O_{Fran}[M(msk)]$.*
3. *The adversary outputs a bit b', and they win if and only if $b' = b$.*

Theorem 7. *Any polynomial-time quantum adversary $\mathcal{A}$ has negligible advantage in the distinguishing game. That is:*

$$\left| P[\mathcal{A} = 1|b = 0] - P[\mathcal{A} = 1|b = 1] \right| \leq \mathsf{negl}(\lambda)$$

where the probabilities are over the choice of $M \in \mathcal{M}(A)$ and $\mathcal{A}$'s randomness.

We'll prove Theorem 7 later using the adversary method, but assuming Theorem 7 for now, we can prove Lemma 1.

Proof of Lemma 1

We want to show that for any polynomial-time adversary $\mathcal{A}$, their success probabilities in $h0$ and in $h1$ differ by a $\mathsf{negl}(\lambda)$ function. Recall that $h0$ uses franchised verifiers, whereas $h1$ uses full verifiers.

Assume toward contradiction that $\mathcal{A}$'s success probabilities in $h0$ and $h1$ differ by a non-negligible amount. Then we can construct an adversary $\mathcal{A}'$ that has non-negligible advantage in the distinguishing game.

$\mathcal{A}'$ simulates the counterfeiting security game and runs $\mathcal{A}$ on it. Given msk, $\mathcal{A}'$ constructs $|A\rangle$ and the C franchised verification keys. When $\mathcal{A}$ queries a verifier, $\mathcal{A}'$ simulates this by querying either $O_{Full}[A]$ (if we're in $h1$) or $O_{Fran}[M(msk)]$ (if we're in $h0$). $\mathcal{A}'$ can even simulate the counterfeiting challenge, checking if $\mathcal{A}$ successfully counterfeited. Finally, $\mathcal{A}'$ outputs 1 if $\mathcal{A}$ won the security game, and 0 otherwise. $h0$ and $h1$ for the counterfeiting game correspond to $b = 1$ and $b = 0$ in the distinguishing game, so $\mathcal{A}'$ has non-negligible advantage in the distinguishing game.

This is a contradiction, by Theorem 7, so in fact, the success probabilities of $\mathcal{A}$ in the two hybrids must be negligibly close.

The Adversary Method

Now we'll prove Theorem 7 using the adversary method[4]. First, we'll define the scenario that [Amb02] considered, which is an abstract version of the distinguishing game, and then we'll state their main theorem.

Definition 14. *Let $\mathcal{O}$ be a set of oracles, each of which has range $\{0,1\}$. Let $f : \mathcal{O} \to \{0,1\}$ be a predicate that takes an oracle as input. Let X, Y partition $\mathcal{O}$ such that $f(O_x) = 0$, for all $O_x \in X$, and $f(O_y) = 1$, for all $O_y \in Y$.*

---

[4] Our proof is inspired by [AC12].

Next, the adversary will try to compute f on every input, so it must distinguish oracles in X from oracles in Y.

Definition 15. *Let $\mathcal{A}^O$ be a quantum algorithm with query access to an $O \in \mathcal{O}$. We say that $\mathcal{A}$ **approximately computes** f if for every $O \in \mathcal{O}$, $P[\mathcal{A}^O = f(O)] \geq 2/3$.*

Definition 16. *Let u, u' be upper bounds that satisfy:*

- *For any $O_x \in X$ and any input i to O_x, $P_{O_y \in Y}[O_x(i) \neq O_y(i)] \leq u$.*
- *For any $O_y \in Y$ and any input i to O_y, $P_{O_x \in X}[O_x(i) \neq O_y(i)] \leq u'$.*

Theorem 8 ([Amb02], **Thm. 2**). *If $\mathcal{A}$ approximately computes f, then $\mathcal{A}$ makes at least $\Omega\left(\frac{1}{\sqrt{u \cdot u'}}\right)$ queries to O.*

Proof of Theorem 7

The distinguishing game's format matches the format considered by the adversary method. For a given msk, let X comprise only the full verification oracle, $\{O_{Full}[A]\}$. Let Y comprise all possible franchised verification oracles: $Y = \{O_{Fran}[M(msk)]|M \in \mathcal{M}(A)\}$. And let $\mathcal{O} = X \bigcup Y$. Then f equals b from the distinguishing game.

Next, we will assume that each honest verifier gets at least $t/4$ dimensions of V_{id} and $t/4$ dimensions of W_{id} that are unknown to the adversary. As a result, each verifier accepts a negligible fraction of the vectors in $\mathbb{Z}_2^n$. So it is hard for the adversary to find an $\mathbf{x} \in \mathbb{Z}_2^n$ on which the full and franchised oracles behave differently, which makes distinguishing them hard. The next definition and next two lemmas expand on this argument.

Definition 17. *An $msk \leftarrow Setup(1^\lambda)$ is **good** if for every $id \in [N - C]$,*

- $dim[span(V_{adv}, V_{id})] \geq dim(V_{adv}) + t/4$
- $dim[span(W_{adv}, W_{id})] \geq dim(W_{adv}) + t/4$

Lemma 6. *With overwhelming probability in λ, $msk \leftarrow Setup(1^\lambda)$ is good.*

Proof. 1) With overwhelming probability, $|I_{id} \backslash I_{adv}| \geq t/4$ for all $id \in [N - C]$. First, $|I_{adv}| \leq Ct = n/4$, so the probability that a uniformly random $i \in [n/2]$ is in I_{adv} is $\leq 1/2$. Then

$$\text{Let } \mu = \mathbb{E}_{I_{id}}[|I_{id} \backslash I_{adv}|] \geq t/2$$

Next we use the multiplicative Chernoff bound:

$$P[|I_{id} \backslash I_{adv}| \leq t/4] \leq P[|I_{id} \backslash I_{adv}| \leq \mu/2]$$
$$< \left(\frac{e^{-1/2}}{(1/2)^{1/2}}\right)^\mu = \left(\frac{2}{e}\right)^{\mu/2} \leq \left(\frac{2}{e}\right)^{t/4}$$
$$= \left(\frac{2}{e}\right)^{\Theta(\sqrt{n})} = \mathsf{negl}(\lambda)$$

Then by the union bound, the probability that $|I_{id}\backslash I_{adv}| \geq t/4$ for all $id \in [N - C]$ is $1 - (N - C) \cdot \mathsf{negl}(\lambda) = 1 - \mathsf{negl}(\lambda)$.

2) For convenience, let's say that $I_{id}\backslash I_{adv} = \big[|I_{id}\backslash I_{adv}|\big]$. Given that $|I_{id}\backslash I_{adv}| \geq t/4$, the following event E occurs with overwhelming probability:

$$E: \quad dim\big[span(V_{adv}, \mathbf{v}_1, \ldots, \mathbf{v}_{t/4})\big] = dim(V_{adv}) + t/4$$

$$
\begin{aligned}
P_{\{v_i\}_{i \in [t/4]}}(E) &\geq 1 - P(\mathbf{v}_1 \in V_{adv}) - \ldots - P[\mathbf{v}_{t/4} \in span(V_{adv}, \mathbf{v}_1, \ldots, \mathbf{v}_{t/4-1})] \\
&\geq 1 - 2^{n/4-n/2} - \ldots - 2^{n/4+t/4-1-n/2} \\
&\geq 1 - \frac{t}{4} \cdot 2^{(t/4-n/4)} = 1 - 2^{-\Theta(n)} = 1 - \mathsf{negl}(\lambda)
\end{aligned}
$$

3) Putting together steps 1 and 2, we have that with overwhelming probability in λ,

$$dim\big[span(V_{adv}, V_{id})\big] \geq dim(V_{adv}) + t/4$$

□

Lemma 7. *Let msk be good, let $M \in_R \mathcal{M}(A)$, and let $msk' = M(msk)$. Then for any $id \in [N - C]$ and any $\mathbf{x} \in \mathbb{Z}_2^n$,*

- *If $\mathbf{x} \notin A$, then $P\big(\mathbf{x} \in W_{id}'^{\perp}\big) = 2^{-\Omega(\sqrt{n})}$.*
- *If $\mathbf{x} \notin A^{\perp}$, then $P\big(\mathbf{x} \in V_{id}'^{\perp}\big) = 2^{-\Omega(\sqrt{n})}$.*

The probability is over the choice of $M \in_R \mathcal{M}(A)$.

Proof. We'll prove the first claim – the second claim's proof is similar.

1) Let $S = span(\{w_j\}_{j \in J_{id}\backslash J_{adv}})$. This is the random subspace that verifier id has that the adversary cannot predict. We know from Lemma 6 that $dim(S) \geq t/4$. Also $M \cdot S \leq W_{id}'$, so $W_{id}'^{\perp} \leq (M \cdot S)^{\perp}$. Then:

$$P_M\big(\mathbf{x} \in W_{id}'\big) \leq P_M\big(\mathbf{x} \in (M \cdot S)^{\perp}\big) = P_M\big(\mathbf{x}^T \cdot M \cdot S = \mathbf{0}\big)$$

2) $M^T\mathbf{x}$ is a random vector satisfying $M^T\mathbf{x} \notin A$. First, M^T maps A to A and $A^{\perp}$ to $A^{\perp}$. Since $\mathbf{x} \notin A$, $\mathbf{x}$ has a non-zero component in $A^{\perp}$, which M^T maps to a non-zero component in $A^{\perp}$. Therefore, $M^T\mathbf{x} \notin A$.

$$
\begin{aligned}
P_M\big(\mathbf{x}^T \cdot M \cdot S = \mathbf{0}\big) = P_M\big(M^T\mathbf{x} \in S^{\perp}\big) &\leq \frac{|S^{\perp}|}{|\mathbb{Z}_2^n\backslash A|} \\
= \frac{2^{dim(S^{\perp})}}{2^n - 2^{n/2}} &\leq \frac{2^{n-t/4}}{2^{n-1}} = 2^{1-t/4} = 2^{-\Omega(\sqrt{n})}
\end{aligned}
$$

□

Lemma 8. *If msk is good, then any quantum algorithm that approximately computes f needs at least $2^{\Omega(\sqrt{n})}$ oracle queries.*

Proof. 1) If O_{Full} and O_{Fran} differ on an input, then O_{Full} rejects the input, and O_{Fran} accepts it.

For any input $(id, s, \mathbf{x})$ to an oracle, if $O_{Full}[A](id, s, \mathbf{x}) = 1$, then $O_{Fran}[M(msk)](id, s, \mathbf{x}) = 1$ as well. When $s = 0$, O_{Full} accepts iff $\mathbf{x} \in A$. Since $A \leq W_{id}^{\frac{1}{4}}$, O_{Fran} accepts as well. Similar reasoning shows that when $s = 1$, if O_{Full} accepts, then O_{Fran} accepts as well.

Therefore, the only way for O_{Full} and O_{Fran} to give different responses to an input is if:

$$O_{Full}[A](id, s, \mathbf{x}) = 0, \text{ and } O_{Fran}[M(msk)](id, s, \mathbf{x}) = 1$$

2) Lemma 7 says that if $O_{Full}[A](id, s, \mathbf{x}) = 0$, then

$$P_{M \leftarrow \mathcal{M}(A)}\left(O_{Fran}[M(msk)](id, s, \mathbf{x}) = 1\right) = 2^{-\Omega(\sqrt{n})}$$

so we can set $u = 2^{-\Omega(\sqrt{n})}$. Also, we can set $u' = 1$ because 1 is greater than or equal to any probability.

Finally, in order to approximately compute f, the number of oracle queries needed is $\Omega\left(\frac{1}{\sqrt{u \cdot u'}}\right) = 2^{\Omega(\sqrt{n})}$. □

Lemma 9. *For any polynomial-time quantum algorithm $\mathcal{A}$, and any good msk, there exists an $M \in \mathcal{M}(A)$ such that:*

$$\left| P(\mathcal{A}^{O_{Full}[A]} = 1) - P(\mathcal{A}^{O_{Fran}[M(msk)]} = 1) \right| \leq 2^{-\Theta(\sqrt[3]{n})}$$

Proof.
1) Let Δ be the minimum value of

$$\left| P(\mathcal{A}^{O_{Full}[A]} = 1) - P(\mathcal{A}^{O_{Fran}[M(msk)]} = 1) \right|$$

over all M, and let $p = P(\mathcal{A}^{O_{Full}[A]} = 1)$.

Next, assume toward contradiction that there is some polynomial-time algorithm $\mathcal{A}$ and some good msk such that $\Delta > 2^{-\Theta(\sqrt[3]{n})}$. Then we'll construct an algorithm $\mathcal{A}'$ that approximately computes f using $2^{\Theta(\sqrt[3]{n})}$ queries (by Lemma 8, we know this is not possible).

$\mathcal{A}'$ runs $4n/\Delta^2$ independent iterations of $\mathcal{A}$ and averages the outputs. Let $\bar{p}$ be the average number of iterations of $\mathcal{A}$ that output 1. Next, $\mathcal{A}'$ outputs 0 if $|\bar{p} - p| \leq \Delta/2$ and outputs 1 otherwise.

2) $\mathcal{A}'$ gives the incorrect value for f if:

1. $|\bar{p} - p| \leq \Delta/2$, but the oracle is franchised.
2. $|\bar{p} - p| > \Delta/2$, but the oracle is full.

In the first case, $\left|\mathbb{E}[\bar{p}] - p\right| > \Delta$, so $\left|\bar{p} - \mathbb{E}[\bar{p}]\right| \geq \Delta/2$. In the second case as well, $\left|\bar{p} - \mathbb{E}[\bar{p}]\right| \geq \Delta/2$.

The probability of an error is bounded by the Hoeffding inequality:

$$P\left(\left|\bar{p} - \mathbb{E}[\bar{p}]\right| \geq \Delta/2\right) \leq 2e^{-2(\Delta/2)^2 \cdot (4n/\Delta^2)} = 2e^{-2n}$$

Next, $\mathcal{A}'$ approximately computes f because for any $O \in \mathcal{O}$, $\mathcal{A}'$ computes $f(O)$ with probability $\geq 1 - 2e^{-2n} > 2/3$.

3) Finally, $\mathcal{A}'$ makes $2^{\Theta(\sqrt[3]{n})}$ queries. First, $\mathcal{A}$ makes $2^{O(\log n)}$ queries because it runs in polynomial time. So the number of queries that $\mathcal{A}'$ makes is:

$$\frac{4n}{\Delta^2} \cdot 2^{O(\log n)} = 2^{O(\log n) + O(\sqrt[3]{n})} = 2^{O(\sqrt[3]{n})}$$

Since no algorithm can approximately compute f using $2^{O(\sqrt[3]{n})}$ queries, this is a contradiction. So for any polynomial-time $\mathcal{A}$, and any good msk, there exists an M such that

$$\left|P(\mathcal{A}^{O_{Full}[A]} = 1) - P(\mathcal{A}^{O_{Fran}[M(msk)]} = 1)\right| \leq 2^{-\Theta(\sqrt[3]{n})}$$

□

Lemma 10. *For any polynomial-time quantum algorithm $\mathcal{A}$, any good msk, and a uniformly random $M \in_R \mathcal{M}(A)$,*

$$\left|P(\mathcal{A}^{O_{Full}[A]} = 1) - P(\mathcal{A}^{O_{Fran}[M(msk)]} = 1)\right| \leq 2^{-\Theta(\sqrt[3]{n})}$$

The probability is over $\mathcal{A}$'s randomness and the choice of M.

Note that Lemma 10 is equivalent to Theorem 7.

Proof. The problem of distinguishing full and franchised oracles is random self-reducible. Since Lemma 9 says the algorithm's distinguishing advantage is negligible in the worst case, then their advantage is also negligible in the average case.

Assume toward contradiction that there exists a polynomial-time quantum algorithm $\mathcal{A}$ such that for a uniformly random $M \in_R \mathcal{M}(A)$,

$$\delta := \left|P(\mathcal{A}^{O_{Full}[A]} = 1) - P(\mathcal{A}^{O_{Fran}[M(msk)]} = 1)\right| = 2^{-o(\sqrt[3]{n})}$$

Then we'll construct a polynomial-time algorithm $\mathcal{A}'$ that runs $\mathcal{A}$ as a subroutine and achieves $\delta = 2^{-o(\sqrt[3]{n})}$ for all M (by Lemma 9, this is impossible).

Given any $M \in \mathcal{M}(A)$, $\mathcal{A}'$ samples a uniformly random $R \in_R \mathcal{M}(A)$. Then $R[M(msk)]$ is an "average-case" master secret key in the sense that $R[M(msk)] = (R \cdot M)(msk)$, and $R' := R \cdot M$ is uniformly random in $\mathcal{M}(A)$.

$\mathcal{A}'$ gives msk to $\mathcal{A}$ and simulates the distinguishing game in which the franchised verifiers are using $R[M(msk)]$. Whenever $\mathcal{A}$ queries the oracle, $\mathcal{A}'$ uses R as a change-of-basis for the query before forwarding it to the challenger. In $\mathcal{A}$'s view, it is dealing with a uniformly random $R' \in \mathcal{M}(A)$, so $\mathcal{A}$ has distinguishing advantage δ. Therefore, $\mathcal{A}'$ has the same advantage $\delta = 2^{-o(\sqrt[3]{n})}$, but for every M. This contradicts Lemma 9, so in fact, Lemma 10's claim is true. □

Lemma 10 proves Theorem 7.

Acknowledgements. This work is supported in part by NSF. Any opinions, findings and conclusions or recommendations expressed in this material are those of the author(s) and do not necessarily reflect the views of NSF.

This work is also supported by MURI Grant FA9550-18-1-0161 and ONR award N00014-17-1-3025.

We thank Zeph Landau, Umesh Vazirani, and the Princeton Writing Center for helpful feedback on various drafts of this paper.

References

[Aar09] Aaronson, S.: Quantum copy-protection and quantum money. In: Proceedings of the 2009 24th Annual IEEE Conference on Computational Complexity, CCC '09, Washington, DC, USA, pp. 229–242. IEEE Computer Society (2009)

[Aar16] Aaronson, S.: (2016). http://www.scottaaronson.com/blog/?p=2854

[AC12] Aaronson, S., Christiano, P.: Quantum money from hidden subspaces. In: Proceedings of the Annual ACM Symposium on Theory of Computing (2012)

[Amb02] Ambainis, A.: Quantum lower bounds by quantum arguments. J. Comput. Syst. Sci. **64**(4), 750–767 (2002)

[BN08] Boneh, D., Naor, M.: Traitor tracing with constant size ciphertext. In: Proceedings of the 15th ACM Conference on Computer and Communications Security, CCS '08, New York, NY, USA, pp. 501–510. Association for Computing Machinery (2008)

[BS20] Behera, A., Sattath, O.: Almost public quantum coins (2020)

[CFN94] Chor, B., Fiat, A., Naor, M.: Tracing traitors. In: Desmedt, Y.G. (ed.) CRYPTO 1994. LNCS, vol. 839, pp. 257–270. Springer, Heidelberg (1994). https://doi.org/10.1007/3-540-48658-5_25

[FGH+12] Farhi, E., Gosset, D., Hassidim, A., Lutomirski, A., Shor, P.: Quantum money from knots. In: Proceedings of the 3rd Innovations in Theoretical Computer Science Conference, ITCS '12, New York, NY, USA, pp. 276–289. Association for Computing Machinery (2012)

[GKW18] Goyal, R., Koppula, V., Waters, B.: Collusion resistant traitor tracing from learning with errors. In: Proceedings of the 50th Annual ACM SIGACT Symposium on Theory of Computing, STOC 2018, New York, NY, USA, pp. 660–670. Association for Computing Machinery (2018)

[KL14] Katz, J., Lindell, Y.: Introduction to Modern Cryptography, 2nd edn. Chapman & Htall/CRC, Boca Raton (2014)

[KNY21] Kitagawa, F., Nishimaki, R., Yamakawa, T.: Secure software leasing from standard assumptions (2021)

[NC00]   Nielsen, M.A., Chuang, I.: Quantum computation and quantum information. Am. J. Phys. **70**(5), 558 (2000)

[PFP15] Pena, M.C., Faugère, J.-C., Perret, L.: Algebraic cryptanalysis of a quantum money scheme the noise-free case. In: Katz, J. (ed.) PKC 2015. LNCS, vol. 9020, pp. 194–213. Springer, Heidelberg (2015). https://doi.org/10.1007/978-3-662-46447-2_9

[Rob21] Roberts, B.: Security analysis of quantum lightning. In: Canteaut, A., Standaert, F.-X. (eds.) EUROCRYPT 2021. LNCS, vol. 12697, pp. 562–567. Springer, Cham (2021). https://doi.org/10.1007/978-3-030-77886-6_19

[RS19]   Radian, R., Sattath.: Semi-quantum money. In: Proceedings of the 1st ACM Conference on Advances in Financial Technologies, AFT '19, pp. 132–146. Association for Computing Machinery (2019)

[Wie83] Wiesner, S.: Conjugate coding. SIGACT News **15**(1), 78–88 (1983)

[Zha19] Zhandry, M.: Quantum lightning never strikes the same state twice. In: Ishai, Y., Rijmen, V. (eds.) EUROCRYPT 2019. LNCS, vol. 11478, pp. 408–438. Springer, Cham (2019). https://doi.org/10.1007/978-3-030-17659-4_14

Quantum Computationally Predicate-Binding Commitments with Application in Quantum Zero-Knowledge Arguments for NP

Jun Yan[✉]

Jinan University, Guangzhou, China
tjunyan@jnu.edu.cn

Abstract. A quantum bit commitment scheme is to realize bit (rather than qubit) commitment by exploiting quantum communication and quantum computation. In this work, we study the binding property of the quantum *string* commitment scheme obtained by composing a *generic* quantum perfectly(resp. statistically)-hiding *computationally-binding* bit commitment scheme (which can be realized based on quantum-secure one-way permutations(resp. functions)) *in parallel*. We show that the resulting scheme satisfies a stronger quantum computational binding property, which we will call *predicate-binding*, than the trivial honest-binding. Intuitively and very roughly, the predicate-binding property guarantees that given any *inconsistent* predicate pair over a set of strings (i.e. no strings in this set can satisfy both predicates), if a (claimed) quantum commitment can be opened so that the revealed string satisfies one predicate with certainty, then the same commitment cannot be opened so that the revealed string satisfies the other predicate (except for a negligible probability).

As an application, we plug a generic quantum perfectly(resp. statistically)-hiding computationally-binding bit commitment scheme in Blum's zero-knowledge protocol for the **NP**-complete language Hamiltonian Cycle. This will give rise to the first quantum perfect(resp. statistical) zero-knowledge *argument* system (with soundness error 1/2) for all **NP** languages based solely on *quantum-secure one-way permutations(resp. functions)*. The quantum computational soundness of this system will follow immediately from the quantum computational predicate-binding property of commitments.

Keywords: Cryptographic protocols · Quantum bit commitment · Quantum computational binding · Parallel composition · Quantum zero-knowledge argument

---

The full version of this paper is referred to [35].

© International Association for Cryptologic Research 2021
M. Tibouchi and H. Wang (Eds.): ASIACRYPT 2021, LNCS 13090, pp. 575–605, 2021.
https://doi.org/10.1007/978-3-030-92062-3_20

1 Introduction

Bit commitment is an important cryptographic primitive; it can be viewed as an electronic realization of a locked box [16]. Roughly speaking, a bit commitment scheme is a two-stage (consisting of a commit stage and a reveal stage) interactive protocol between a sender and a receiver, providing two security guarantees: hiding and binding. Intuitively, the hiding property states that the commitment to 0 and that to 1 are indistinguishable (to the receiver) in the commit stage, whereas the binding property states that any (claimed) bit commitment cannot be opened (by the sender) as both 0 and 1 (except for a negligible probability) later in the reveal stage. Unfortunately, hiding and binding properties cannot be satisfied information-theoretically at the same time; one of them has to be *conditional*, e.g. based on complexity assumptions such as the existence of one-way functions.

Turning to the quantum setting, there are two *different* meanings of quantum bit commitment in the literature (depending on the context). The *first* refers to the *classical* realization of bit commitment that is secure against *quantum* attacks, or the post-quantum secure (classical) bit commitment [1,31,32]. The *second* refers to a realization of bit commitment by exploiting *quantum* features [4,7,8,10,11,14,15,23,24,34,36]; that is, now the honest parties are allowed to be quantum computers and exchange quantum messages. (But it is still a classical bit that is secured.) Clearly, the first meaning of quantum bit commitment can be viewed as a special case of the second one. In this paper, the term "quantum bit commitment" will be reserved for the second, more general meaning, which will also be the focus of this work.

The concept of quantum bit commitment is natural and sounds exciting. Though *unconditional* quantum bit commitment is still impossible [25,27], as a compromise we may consider quantum bit commitment based on complexity assumptions like in the classical cryptography. Somewhat counter-intuitive at the first glance, but the binding property of a *general* quantum bit commitment is inherently *weaker* than the classical binding property (that is guaranteed by a classical bit commitment secure against classical attacks, which roughly states that any claimed bit commitment is bound to a unique bit that is typically referred to as the *committed value*). In more detail, this weakness of the general quantum binding property comes from the possible superposition attack of the sender of the quantum bit commitment, who may commit to an arbitrary *superposition* of bits 0 and 1, and later open the commitment as this superposition (rather than a classical 0 or 1) successfully with certainty [10,14]. By this kind of quantum superposition attack, a fixed quantum bit commitment is no longer bound to a unique classical bit any more. The quantum binding property that can be guaranteed by a general quantum bit commitment is often referred to as *sum-binding* (named after [31]).

Difficulties in Basing Security on Quantum Binding. It is natural to ask what happen if we replace classical bit commitment with quantum bit commitment in cryptographic applications. Due to the weakness of the general quantum binding property as aforementioned, the security based on the classical binding property may deteriorate after the replacement.

In greater detail, note that in applications we typically commit to a binary string by committing it in a *bitwise* fashion; later, a *subset* of bit commitments may be opened for some verification. For example, it is helpful to keep GMW-type zero-knowledge protocols [5,17] in one's mind. When quantum bit commitments are used, we can no longer say that a claimed quantum commitment to an m-bit string is really bound to some m-bit string; instead, the committed value of such a quantum string commitment could be a superposition of a bunch of m-bit strings of the form $\sum_{s \in \{0,1\}^m} \alpha_s |s\rangle$, where the integer $m \geq 1$ and complex coefficients α_s's satisfy $\sum_{s \in \{0,1\}^m} |\alpha_s|^2 = 1$. One may tend to argue in security analysis that this superposition behaves similar to its induced probability distribution $(|\alpha_s|^2)_{s \in \{0,1\}^m}$: if this is true, then the classical security analysis extend to the quantum setting straightforwardly. Unfortunately, this argument is not necessarily true, because a superposition is generally *not* equivalent to its induced probability distribution; in fact, this is usually where the quantum advantage comes from in algorithm design. Actually, if one goes into detail of the security analysis, one will find that a malicious quantum sender of commitments may attack by making the opening information (which is entangled with quantum commitments and their decommitments) about *which* bit commitments will be opened as *what* value in an arbitrary superposition. By tuning this superposition, the sender may adjust the receiver's acceptance probabilities in different verifications. This kind of superposition attack will make the security analysis based on the general quantum binding property (if possible) much harder than that based on the classical binding property.

Why Quantum Bit Commitment Is Interesting? Besides the weakness as well as technical difficulties in security analysis mentioned above, another shortcoming of quantum bit commitment is that by today's quantum technology, the physical realization of a general quantum bit commitment scheme is still far beyond our reach. In spite of this, quantum bit commitment still interests us for several reasons. First, since as early as 2000 researchers have come to realize that merely based on quantum-secure one-way functions/permutations, one can construct *non-interactive* quantum bit commitments of both flavors (i.e. statistical binding and statistical hiding), whose commit and reveal stages consist of just a single *quantum* message from the sender to the receiver [14,23,24,34]. It turns out that these constructions are not coincidences: recently, Yan [34] has shown that any (interactive) quantum bit commitment scheme can be converted into a non-interactive one of a *generic* form[1] (whose informal definition is referred to the first graph of "Notations" in Subsect. 1.3, and formal definition to Definition 2). This is in contrast to the constant [26] or even polynomial [20] number of rounds in the commit stage by classical constructions of bit

---

[1] Actually, it is shown in [34] a much stronger result that any quantum bit commitment schemes just secure against the *purification attack* can be converted into a non-interactive one of the generic form. For this reason, in this paper we can focus on this generic form without loss of generality. At a very high level, the basis idea of how such a quantum round-collapse is possible is similar to the old idea of converting any *non-interactive* quantum bit commitment scheme into the generic form [15,36].

commitment. Thus, using quantum bit commitments instead of the classical ones in applications can potentially reduce the number of rounds of the interaction[2] while keeping the complexity assumption to the minimum.

More interestingly, Fang, Unruh, Yan and Zhou [15] and Yan [34] also observe that the (either statistical or computational) binding of a *generic* non-interactive quantum bit commitment scheme is automatically *information-theoretically strict*[3]. Here, the strictness of the quantum binding extends the one in [30] for a classical construction of bit commitment, which roughly states that not only the revealed value but also the *decommitment state* used in opening a quantum bit commitment are "unique". We highlight that this strictness of the quantum binding originates from the *entanglement* between the commitment and its decommitment, as opposed to the *classical correlation* in the definition of the classical strict-binding [30]. We also stress that even the quantum computational binding can be information-theoretically strict simultaneously (which may sound contradictory as it appears)[4]. This is in contrast to the computational binding of a classical bit commitment, which is impossible to be information-theoretically strict: though it may be computationally hard to find an alternative opening, there actually *exist* a bunch of them! It turns out that this strictness of the quantum binding can play an important role in applications; in particular, it can help circumvent existing barriers only known for classical constructions, as confirmed in [15] and this paper (Theorem 1).

Overall, if we are optimistic about the development of quantum technology and believe that general quantum computation and communication will be available in future, then *the application of quantum bit commitment as a primitive in quantum cryptography* is worthy of study.

Progress and Perspective Towards Basing Security on Quantum Binding. In the past two decades, there were only few works studying the security based on the binding property of a *general* quantum bit commitment [36]. Recently, some *generic* techniques to cope with the quantum *perfect/statistical* binding property are developed in [15], by which in many cases the security based on the *classical* statistical binding property can be lifted to the quantum setting. Unfortunately, when it comes to the question of the security based on the quantum *computational* binding property, the answer remains elusive. To the best of our knowledge, we are aware of no such results before. In our opinion, the perhaps most important open question towards using quantum bit commitment as a primitive in quantum cryptography is:

Can we base quantum security on the computational binding property of a general quantum bit commitment?

---

[2] The round complexity of any cryptographic task might be one of the most important parameters.

[3] We do not claim that this holds w.r.t. a general quantum bit commitment. But any quantum bit commitment scheme can be converted to the generic form [34], as aforementioned.

[4] All mentioned above about the strictness of the quantum binding will become clear once one reads Definition 2, which is quite simple and intuitive.

Based on the state-of-the-art knowledge, the answer to the question above is unclear. On one hand, intuitively it will be true if we can view the *superposition* of strings underlying quantum bit commitments as its induced *probability distribution* (as aforementioned). Actually, this motivates Unruh [31,32] to introduce (computationally) *collapse-binding* commitments. Unfortunately, general quantum commitments *cannot* be collapse-binding [34]. In spite of this, it turns out that by some tricks this intuitive strategy is enabled to work (in many cases) when perfectly/statistically-binding quantum bit commitments are used [15]. More positive evidences come from the success in various security analysis in the quantum random oracle model, in which adversaries can query a random oracle in an arbitrary superposition [6].

On the other hand, however, after a first attempt towards the security analysis, it turns out that for a naive analysis (r.f. Subsect. 1.3) to work it requires that the binding error be *sub-exponentially* or even *exponentially* small, rather than *negligiblly* small as typical in cryptography. We will refer to this technical difficulty as "exponential curse", which arises from the fact that polynomial number of qubits could be in a superposition of exponentially many basis states. Moreover, the impossibility of the general quantum rewinding [18], as well as other related impossibility results on classical constructions of bit commitment secure against quantum attacks [2], may suggest a *negative* answer to the open question above.

One motivation of this work is to explore the application of *general* quantum computationally-binding bit commitments[5] in cryptographic applications, notably in constructing quantum zero-knowledge arguments for **NP** languages.

1.1   Our Contribution

In spite of the technical difficulty and negative evidences just mentioned, we make some progress towards answering the main open question *affirmatively* in this work. Interestingly, our security analysis will use a more straightforward strategy that is completely *different* from that of viewing the superposition of strings underlying quantum bit commitments as its induced probability distribution.

Specifically, our contribution is two-fold.

1. A *quantum* construction of perfect/statistical zero-knowledge *argument* system (with soundness error 1/2) for all NP languages

We prove the following main theorem of this paper:

Theorem 1. *Plugging a generic quantum perfectly(resp. statistically)-hiding computationally-binding bit commitment scheme (Definition 2) in Blum's protocol [5] gives rise to a three-round public-coin quantum perfect(resp. statistical) zero-knowledge argument system for the **NP**-complete language* Hamiltonian Cycle, *with perfect completeness and soundness error* $1/2$.

---

[5] Though we will actually focus on quantum bit commitment schemes of the generic form (Definition 2) in this paper (as will become clear later), this restriction does not lose any generality due to [34], as aforementioned.

Following [14,23,24,34], since a generic quantum perfectly(resp. statistically)-hiding computationally-binding bit commitment scheme can be constructed from quantum-secure one-way permutations(resp. functions), the theorem above gives the *first* quantum perfect(resp. statistical) zero-knowledge argument for all **NP** languages based on the same assumption.

Compared with classical GMW-type statistical zero-knowledge arguments secure against classical attacks for **NP** [21,28], our *quantum* construction reduces the rounds of the interaction *from polynomial to three*, thanks to the *non-interactivity* of a generic quantum computationally-binding bit commitment scheme. Compared with the classical statistical zero-knowledge argument for **NP** secure against quantum attacks given in [31,32], which assumes collapsing hash functions, our quantum construction relies on a weaker (perhaps minimum) complexity assumption without setup.

We highlight that our proof of Theorem 1 relies heavily on (though implicitly) that the (computational) binding of a generic quantum bit commitment scheme is information-theoretically *strict* (as aforementioned). It is this strict-binding property that enables a simple quantum rewinding [15,36] to work even in our quantum *computational* soundness analysis. This circumvents a barrier which is only known for classical constructions [2].

As a final remark, in this work we only study *stand-alone* Blum's protocol. But we believe it should be meaningful as a first step toward using non-interactive computationally-binding quantum bit commitments in more general protocols. Some remarks on the sequential and the parallel compositions of Blum's atomic protocol is referred to the end of Sect. 4.

2. A non-trivial computational binding property of the quantum *string* commitment scheme obtained by composing a generic quantum bit commitment scheme in parallel

A natural way to construct a string commitment is to compose a bit commitment scheme in *parallel*, i.e. committing a string in a bitwise fashion. For the purpose of proving Theorem 1, we introduce a new binding property of quantum *string* commitments which we call "predicate-binding". And we show that the parallel composition of a generic quantum computationally-binding bit commitment scheme gives rise to a quantum computationally predicate-binding string commitment scheme. When we instantiate Blum's protocol with a generic quantum computationally-binding bit commitment scheme, the quantum computational soundness of the protocol (which is required towards establishing Theorem 1) can be easily based on the predicate-binding property of quantum string commitments.

In more detail, we first formalize a kind of predicates which we will call "pattern-predicates" (Definition 3): informally speaking, for a string to satisfy a pattern-predicate, it should exhibit a certain "pattern" somewhere. The *intuition* underlying our definition is that in typical applications of bit commitments, the receiver (of commitments) will check whether the value of the opened commitments will cause it to accept. For example, in Blum's protocol the (honest) verifier's verification corresponding to each challenge naturally induces a pattern-predicate.

With our definition of pattern-predicate, the *predicate-binding* property (Definition 4, or fomally Definition 5) guarantees that given an arbitrary pair of *inconsistent* pattern-predicates on a set of strings of the same length (i.e. no strings in this set can satisfy both predicates), if a (claimed) quantum commitment can be opened such that the revealed string[6] satisfies one predicate with *certainty*, then the same commitment cannot be opened so as to satisfy the other predicate (except for a negligible probability)[7].

The proof of predicate-binding is the main technical contribution of this work, which is highly non-trivial; in particular, the trivial reduction (via a simple hybrid argument) from string binding to bit binding in the classical setting will fail completely here. Actually, for a technical reason we did *not* prove the *full* predicate-binding property (i.e. w.r.t. the most general inconsistent pattern-predicate pairs) in this work; rather, we can only show predicate-binding such that one predicate is allowed to be of the general form, whereas the other is subject to the restriction that it only depends on a *fixed* portion of the string (Thereom 2, or formally Theorem 3). In spite of this restriction, the predicate-binding property we obtain is more than enough to prove Theorem 1. Any extension of our result is left as an open problem. We believe that quantum predicate-binding string commitments could be of independent interest and will be found useful elsewhere.

A Comparison with Existing Quantum Computational String Binding Properties. The parallel composition of a generic quantum bit commitment scheme trivially gives a quantum *honest-binding* string commitment scheme [36]. Roughly speaking, the honest-binding states that the honest commitment to a string cannot be opened as any other string (except for a negligible probability). Unfortunately, this binding property seems too weak to be useful in applications. This is because a malicious sender may not commit honestly.

In [10], a so-called computational f-*binding* property w.r.t. a function $f : \{0,1\}^m \rightarrow \{0,1\}^l$ for quantum string commitments is proposed, where integers $l \leq m$. Unfortunately, no constructions for quantum f-*binding* commitments are provided in [10]. Our predicate-binding implies the f-binding w.r.t. to any efficiently computable function f whose image is just the set $\{0,1\}$ (i.e. $l = 1$), if we view preimages mapped to 0 as inducing one predicate while preimages mapped to 1 as inducing the other.

Damgård, Fehr and Salvail [12] introduced the so-called Q-*binding* property for classical commitments secure against quantum attacks, which can be extended to quantum commitments in a straightforward way. Here, the "Q"

---

[6] Generally, the revealed value of a quantum string commitment could be a probability distribution over this set of strings.

[7] We note that the parallel composition of *classical* bit commitments secure against classical attacks gives a string commitment that is trivially predicate-binding secure against classical attacks. This is simply because the resulting string commitment (by the parallel composition) is bound to a *unique* classical string.

stands for an arbitrary predicate whose form is close to our pattern-predicate[8]: very roughly, this predicate Q can be viewed as combining various pattern-predicates into one by introducing a "choice" parameter u, and the predicate-binding we establish here can also be viewed as the Q-binding w.r.t. the predicate Q of a special form such that $|U| = 2$ and $p_{\mathrm{IDEAL}} = 1$ (in the notation used in [12]). The general framework for constructing Q-binding (classical) commitments in [12] requires a setup and relies on much stronger assumptions than quantum-secure one-way functions; in particular, one crucial assumption[9] on which it relies has a similar structure as the security game in defining Q-binding, which makes the security proof for Q-binding there much more straightforward than ours for predicate-binding here.

Unruh [31,32] introduced computational collapse-binding *classical* commitments secure against quantum attacks. However, a straightforward extension of collapse-binding to *quantum* commitments cannot hold generally, as aforementioned; more detail is referred to [34].

1.2   A Comparison with Two Recent Works

In two concurrent and independent recent works, statistically-hiding [3] (resp. computationally-hiding [19]) computationally-binding quantum bit commitments that additionally satisfy two nice properties called *extractable* and *equivocal* properties are constructed, also based solely on quantum-secure one-way functions. Compared with our scheme used in this work, i.e. the generic statistically-hiding computationally-binding quantum bit commitment scheme (Definition 2), theirs are more *advantageous* in the following aspects:

1. Their schemes satisfy both *extractable* and *equivocal* properties simultaneously, whereas ours is generally unlikely to satisfy.
2. The *committed value* of the commitments by running the commit stage of their schemes is a *probability distribution* over the set $\{0,1\}$[10], rather than a *superposition* as our scheme. This makes the quantum (computational) binding property of their schemes almost as strong as the classical binding property. As such, their schemes are likely to be more versatile in applications than ours; and the corresponding security analysis with their commitments should be easier, too. In this regard, we believe that plugging their commitments in Blum's protocol will yield a quantum zero-knowledge argument-of-knowledge (rather than just argument as achieved in this paper) system for **NP**, whose security analysis can be adapted from the classical one in a straightforward way (avoiding the issue arisen from the general quantum binding as studied in this paper).

---

[8] As communicated by the authors of [12] recently [13], the definition of Q-binding in the conference version of [12] has a flaw: it misses an additional information z as another input of the predicate Q to make it *efficiently computable*, and the sentence "We do not require Q to be efficiently computable" there should be removed.

[9] Namely, the third assumption in [12, section "A General Framework"].

[10] This can be seen from the *extractability* of their commitments.

3. Both their schemes and ours use quantum communication. But theirs only send (and receive) BB84 states, in contrast to arbitrary quantum states that might be sent by our scheme.

In spite of the above, we stress that commitments in [3,19] achieve better properties (than ours) at the cost of the extremely *high round complexity*: they need *polynomial* (in the security parameter) rounds of the interaction at least in the commit stage[11], which makes them almost impractical even when quantum computation and communication are realized one day. This is in sharp contrast to the *non-interactivity* of both the commit and the reveal stages of our scheme.

1.3   Technical Overview

We sketch the soundness analysis of Blum's protocol instantiated with a generic quantum computationally-binding bit commitment scheme, which is the key step towards establishing Theorem 1. Our goal is to reduce the soundness of the resulting protocol to the predicate-binding property of quantum string commitment (Lemma 3).

We assume that readers are familar with Blum's protocol [5], which is also sketched in Subsect. 2.3. In its soundness analysis, the (possibly cheating) prover's first message constitutes a (claimed) quantum string commitment. The (honest) verifier's acceptance conditions corresponding to challenges 0 and 1 induce two predicates on graphs with the same number of vertices as the input graph. When the input graph is not Hamiltonian, these two predicates will become *inconsistent*, in that no single graph can satisfy both of them simultaneously. Technically, at the heart of the reduction from the soundness of Blum's protocol to the predicate-binding property of the quantum string commitment lies a simple quantum rewinding technique (Lemma 1) that extends from ones used in [15,36] but for the quantum statistical binding setting. We remark that though this extension is technically trivial, conceptually why it is possible relies heavily on that a generic quantum computationally-binding bit commitment scheme is *information-theoretical* strict-binding.

We are then left with showing that the parallel composition of a generic quantum computationally-binding *bit* commitment scheme indeed gives rise to a quantum computationally predicate-binding *string* commitment scheme (a special case in Lemma 2 and a more general case in Theorem 3). This is the main technical part of the paper. In the below, we first explain a technical difficulty towards this goal by a naive try, and then sketch at a high level how to overcome it. But before doing this, we first set up some notations that are necessary for our exposition.

Notations. A generic quantum bit commitment commitment scheme can be represented by a quantum circuit pair[12] (Q_0, Q_1) performing on quantum registers (C, R). To commit a bit $b \in \{0, 1\}$, in the commit stage the sender performs

---

[11] It appears that even the reveal stage of the commitment scheme given in [19] also needs polynomial rounds of the interaction.

[12] For the moment, we drop the security parameter to simplify the notation.

the quantum circuit Q_b on quantum registers (C, R) initialized in the state $|0\rangle$, and then sends the *commitment* register C to the receiver; later in the reveal stage, the sender sends the bit b together with the *decommitment* register R to the receiver, who then does the reversible computation (i.e. performing the quantum circuit $Q_b^\dagger$) to decide whether to accept or not (i.e. checking whether the registers (C, R) return to the all $|0\rangle$ state). Informally, we say that the quantum bit commitment scheme (Q_0, Q_1) is *computationally binding* if for any polynomial-time realizable unitary transformation U performing on the register R, the inner product $\left| \langle 0| Q_1^\dagger U Q_0 |0\rangle \right|$ is negligible; that is, unit vectors $U Q_0 |0\rangle$ and $Q_1 |0\rangle$ are almost orthogonal[13].

To commit a string of length m, we commit it in a *bitwise* fashion using the scheme (Q_0, Q_1). Let Q_s denote the corresponding quantum circuit used to commit the string s; that is, $Q_s = \bigotimes_{i=1}^m Q_{s_i}$, which performs on m copies of the quantum registers (C, R).

Let P_1, P_2 be two (pattern-)*predicates*[14] on all m-bit strings. We use $s \in P_1$ (resp. P_2) to denote that the string $s \in \{0,1\}^m$ satisfies the predicate P_1 (resp. P_2). We say that two predicates P_1, P_2 are *inconsistent* if no string $s \in \{0,1\}^m$ can satisfy both P_1 and P_2. More details about the formalization of predicates are referred to Subsect. 3.1.

A Technical Difficulty: Exponential Curse. We first consider the *simplest* scenario, in which an m-bit string is firstly committed and later *all* (bit) commitments will be opened. Note that a cheating sender can first prepare an arbitrary superposition of the form $\sum_{s \in P_1} \alpha_s |s\rangle^D (Q_s |0\rangle)^{C^{\otimes m} R^{\otimes m}}$ (resp. $\sum_{s \in P_2} \beta_s |s\rangle Q_s |0\rangle$) in registers $(\mathsf{D}, \mathsf{C}^{\otimes m}, \mathsf{R}^{\otimes m})$, and then send all commitment registers $\mathsf{C}^{\otimes m}$ to the receiver in the commit stage[15]. Later in the reveal stage, the sender sends the register D (which is supposed to contain the classical information about what string is to reveal), together with all decommitment registers $\mathsf{R}^{\otimes m}$, to the receiver. By this strategy, the sender can open all commitments successfully with *certainty* as a *distribution* (which is determined by coefficients α_s's (resp. β_s's)) of strings that satisfy the predicate P_1 (resp. P_2). To show predicate-binding, it is sufficient to show that up to any *polynomial-time* realizable unitary transformation U that does not touch commitment registers $\mathsf{C}^{\otimes m}$ (which represents the sender's strategy in opening commitments), any two superpositions $\sum_{s \in P_1} \alpha_s |s\rangle Q_s |0\rangle$ and $\sum_{s \in P_2} \beta_s |s\rangle Q_s |0\rangle$ are almost *orthogonal*, i.e. their inner product is negligible, w.r.t. any inconsistent predicate pair (P_1, P_2). A technical difficulty in showing this lies in that a potential exponential blow-up may occur in bounding this inner product. This difficulty is referred to as the *exponential curse* in [15,36], which we believe is universal when one tries to base

---

[13] The formal definitions of a generic quantum bit commitment scheme and its computational binding propery are referred to Definition 2. Here for simplification, we neglect the auxiliary input state that the cheating sender may receive.

[14] For the moment, we can think of them as efficiently computable predicates in the common sense for simplicity.

[15] The tensor product m in superscripts indicates that there are m copies of the corresponding quantum register.

security on quantum binding; a similar difficulty also appears in [10]. Now let us go into some detail in the below.

By the computational binding property of the quantum bit commitment scheme (Q_0, Q_1), the inner product $|\langle 0| Q_{s'}^\dagger U Q_s |0\rangle|$ where $s \neq s'$ can be bounded by its binding error, which is negligible (as typical in cryptography). Thus, a naive way to bound the inner product

$$\left| \sum_{s \in P_1} \alpha_s^* \langle s| (\langle 0| Q_s^\dagger) U \sum_{s' \in P_2} \beta_{s'} |s'\rangle (Q_{s'} |0\rangle) \right|$$

is first to expand it and bound each term indexed by (s, s') using the binding error bound (while neglecting its coefficient that can be bounded by 1), and then apply the triangle inequality. However, when there are *super-polynomial* (typically exponentially many) strings $s \in P_1$ or $s' \in P_2$, this naive approach will fail.

Actually, whether the inner product above could really be bounded by some negligible quantity is questionable a prior. This is because generally, two superpositions of the form $\sum_x \alpha_x |\phi_x\rangle$ and $\sum_y \beta_y |\xi_y\rangle$, where $\{|\phi_x\rangle\}_x$ and $\{|\xi_y\rangle\}_y$ are two orthonormal bases, are *not* necessarily almost orthogonal, even when $|\phi_x\rangle$ and $|\xi_y\rangle$ are almost orthogonal for each (x, y) pair. To see this, consider the following simple example. The Hilbert space is induced by m qubits, where $\{|x\rangle\}_{x \in \{0,1\}^m}$ is the standard basis and $\{H^{\otimes m} |y\rangle\}_{y \in \{0,1\}^m}$ is the Hadamard basis. Then consider an arbitrary vector in this space, which can be written as a superposition of basis vectors either in the standard basis or the Hadamard basis. Clearly, these two superpositions are actually the same vector, so that their inner product is one. But the inner product between $|x\rangle$ and $H^{\otimes m} |y\rangle$ for arbitrary $x, y \in \{0,1\}^m$ is exponentially small! This example tells us that to bound the inner product aforementioned, we need to exploit the *structures* of the two superpositions (which are induced by the structures of predicates P_1 and P_2).

The similar technical difficulty also appears in the quantum statistical binding setting, where two generic techniques were invented to overcome this exponential curse: *perturbation* and *hypothetical commitment measurement* [15,36]. Unfortunately, neither of them extend to the quantum computational binding setting straightforwardly. Reasons are as below. We note that the *fundamental difference* between these two settings lies in that in the quantum statistical binding setting, the bit commitment to 0 and that to 1 (stored in the commitment register C) themselves are already *almost orthogonal*, and which will *never* be touched by the (possibly cheating) sender *after* they are sent. Thus, we can assume that commitments will *collapse* immediately by hypothetical commitment measurements at the moment they are sent; after the collapse, everything will be similar to that in the *classical* perfect binding setting. However, in case of quantum computational binding, the commitment to 0 and that to 1 could be *close or even identical*, where we are only guaranteed that in the reveal stage the *joint* states of the commitment register C and the decommitment register R are almost orthogonal. But the state of the decommitment register R can be affected by the sender's operation *after* the commitment stage. As such, the hypothetical-collapse trick to handle quantum statistically-binding commitments [15] fails completely here.

In summary, new techniques are needed to establish the quantum computational predicate-binding property (if possible).

Our Approach. For the ease of the exposition, instead of considering the aforementioned inner product, now let us equivalently consider the *projection* of an arbitrary superposition of the form $\sum_{s \in P_1} \alpha_s |s\rangle Q_s |0\rangle$ on the subspace $\sum_{s \in P_2} |s\rangle \langle s| \otimes (Q_s |0\rangle \langle 0| Q_s^\dagger)$, up to any polynomial-time realizable unitary transformation U that does not touch commitment registers $\mathsf{C}^{\otimes m}$. We overload the notation and denote this projection also by P_2 for simplicity. Our goal then becomes to show that this projection is negligible (in the security parameter which we have dropped to simplify the notation; see footnote 12). Our idea is based on the following *key observation*: when the predicate P_1 is *sparse*, i.e. the number of the m-bit strings satisfying it is *polynomially* bounded, then combining a new *perturbation* technique (which looks similar but is inherently different from the one developed in the quantum statistical binding setting [15,36]) and the triangle inequality, we can bound the aforementioned projection by a negligible quantity. However, to remove this sparsity requirement, we still need to overcome the exponential curse. To this end, we need to take into account of the *coefficients* of the superposition, and make an essential use of the following *structure* of predicates P_1 and P_2: to check whether a string satisfies P_1 or P_2, *all* its bits are to examine.

For more technical details, we are to bound the norm

$$\left\| \sum_{s \in P_1} \alpha_s P_2 U \left(|s\rangle Q_s |0\rangle \right) \right\|,$$

where in the summation there could be exponentially many terms. At a high level, our *trick* is to order these terms properly in such a way that they can be treated as *leaves of a binary tree*, whose internal nodes will correspond to the summation of leaves of the subtree it determines; in particular, the root of the tree will correspond to the summation of all leaves, whose norm is just what we want to bound. We will actually bound norms of all internal nodes, including the root, in a *bottom-up* fashion. The formal proof (of Lemma 2) is by induction on the depth of internal nodes. Within the induction step, we will use the triangle inequality. It turns out that the accumulated error will grow only *linearly* in the *depth* of the tree, which is just m.

Extension. However, the (simplest) scenario (i.e. all commitments will be opened) considered above is usually *not* sufficient for applications. This is because in many cases where bit commitments are used in a larger protocol, *not* all bit commitments will be opened for a verification. Even worse, positions of which bit commitments will be opened may not even be fixed: they might depend on the party who plays the role of the (cheating) sender. For example, consider an execution of Blum's protocol in which a Hamiltonian cycle is challenged to open.

Fortunately, we can extend the predicate-binding property established in the simplest case to a more general case in which it holds that for at least one predicate (P_1 or P_2), the positions of which bit commitments will be opened for its verification are fixed, while the other predicate could be arbitrary (Theorem 3). It turns out that this extension already suffices for our purpose of establishing Theorem 1.

For the formal proof of such an extension, there are more technical issues we need to handle.

Organization. We first give preliminaries in Sect. 2. In Sect. 3, we formally introduce and establish the computational predicate-binding property of the quantum string commitment scheme that is obtained by composing a generic quantum computationally-binding bit commitment scheme in parallel. As an application of predicate-binding, in Sect. 4 we show that Blum's zero-knowledge protocol for the **NP**-complete language Hamiltonian Cycle with a generic quantum computationally-binding bit commitment scheme plugged in is sound against any quantum computationally bounded prover. We conclude with Sect. 5.

2   Preliminaries

A quantum system or register induces a Hilbert space. A quantum operation performing on a quantum system induces an operator acting on the Hilbert space associated with the system. In particular, a unitary operation induces a unitary transformation, and a binary projective measurement induces a projector (corresponding to the outcome one). We will *interchangeably* use quantum system and its induced Hilbert space, quantum operation and its induced operator. For example, we may say that a unitary transformation or a projector perform on or do not touch a quantum register.

Notations. We will explicitly write quantum register(s) as a *superscript* of an operator to indicate or highlight on which register(s) this operator performs. Similarly, we will also explicitly write quantum register(s) as a *superscript* of a quantum state to indicate or highlight in which register(s) this quantum state is stored. For example, let A be a quantum register. Then we may write U^A, $|\psi\rangle^A$ (resp. ρ^A), to indicate that the operator U performs on the register A, the quantum pure (resp. mixed) state $|\psi\rangle$ (resp. ρ) is stored in the register A, respectively. We may also write $U \otimes \mathbb{1}^A$ to highlight that the operation U does *not* touch the register A. But when it is clear from the context, we often drop such superscripts or the tensor product with the identity to simplify the notation; this in particular happens in many of derivations within our proofs, where we often write out registers as superscripts or the tensor product with the identity explicitly in the first step, while dropping them subsequently. When there are m copies of the register A, for a subset $T \subseteq \{1, 2, \ldots, m\}$, we write $A^{\otimes T}$ to refer to the copies of the register A indexed by the subset T; when the subset T is the whole set, we may just write $A^{\otimes m}$.

Efficiently Realizable Quantum Computation. In this work, without loss of generality, we restrict to consider the following quantum computational model:

1. Quantum systems or registers are constituted of *qubits*.
2. There are only two kinds of quantum operations: *unitary* transformation and *projective* measurement.

We also need to formalize *efficiently realizable* quantum operations. By [37], any efficiently realizable quantum algorithm or unitary transformation can be formalized by a family of quantum circuits $\{Q_n\}_{n \geq 1}$ such that:

1. Each gate of the quantum circuit Q_n comes from a pre-fixed finite, unitary, and universal quantum gate set, e.g. {Hadamard, phase, CNOT, $\pi/8$} [29].
2. Quantum circuit Q_n is of *polynomial* size (w.r.t. the index n).
3. The quantum circuit family $\{Q_n\}_{n \geq 1}$ can be uniformly generated, i.e. there exists a polynomial-time classical algorithm A which on input 1^n outputs the description of the quantum circuit Q_n.

Since any *projective* measurement can be realized by first performing a unitary transformation, followed by a measurement of all qubits in the *standard* basis, we say that a projective measurement is *efficiently realizable* if the corresponding unitary transformation is efficiently realizable.

Any projector Π induces a binary measurement $\{\Pi, \mathbb{1} - \Pi\}$, which produces the outcome 1 (resp. 0) when the quantum state collapses into the subspace induced the projector Π (resp. $\mathbb{1} - \Pi$). We say that the projector Π is *efficient realizable* if its induced binary measurement is efficiently realizable.

Quantum Rewinding. A quantum rewinding technique as stated in the lemma below is adapted from the one given in [15] directly, whereas now we restrict to consider projectors and unitary transformations that are *efficiently realizable*. In spite of this, its proof follows the same line as the one in [15].

Lemma 1 (A quantum rewinding). *Let $\mathcal{X}$ and $\mathcal{Y}$ be two Hilbert spaces. Unit vector $|\psi\rangle \in \mathcal{X} \otimes \mathcal{Y}$. Efficiently realizable projectors $\Gamma_1, \ldots, \Gamma_k$ perform on the space $\mathcal{X} \otimes \mathcal{Y}$, and efficiently realizable unitary transformations $U_1, \ldots, U_k$ perform on the space $\mathcal{Y}$. If $1/k \cdot \sum_{i=1}^{k} \left\| \Gamma_i(U_i \otimes \mathbb{1}^X) |\psi\rangle \right\|^2 \geq 1 - \eta$, where $0 \leq \eta \leq 1$, then*

$$\left\| (U_k^\dagger \otimes \mathbb{1}^X) \Gamma_k (U_k \otimes \mathbb{1}^X) \cdots (U_1^\dagger \otimes \mathbb{1}^X) \Gamma_1 (U_1 \otimes \mathbb{1}^X) |\psi\rangle \right\| \geq 1 - \sqrt{k\eta}. \quad (1)$$

2.1 A Generic Quantum Bit Commitment Scheme

We first need to define quantum *(in)distinguishability* based on the efficiently realizable quantum computation we fixed above. Our definition follows [33].

Definition 1 ((In)distinguishability of quantum state ensembles). *Two quantum state ensembles $\{\rho_n\}_{n \geq 1}$ and $\{\xi_n\}_{n \geq 1}$ are quantum statistically (resp. computationally) indistinguishable if for any quantum state ensemble $\{\sigma_n\}_{n \geq 1}$*

and any unbounded (resp. efficiently realizable) quantum algorithm D which outputs a single qubit that will be measured in the standard basis, it holds that

$$|\Pr[D(1^n, \rho_n \otimes \sigma_n) = 1] - \Pr[D(1^n, \xi_n \otimes \sigma_n) = 1]| < negl(n)$$

for sufficiently large n, where $negl(\cdot)$ is some negligible function.

Following Yan [34], the definition of a generic quantum computationally-binding bit commitment scheme is given as below.

Definition 2 (A generic computationally-binding quantum bit commitment scheme). *A generic computationally-binding quantum bit commitment scheme is a two-party, two-stage protocol. It can be represented by an ensemble of polynomial-time uniformly generated quantum circuit pair $\{(Q_0(n), Q_1(n))\}_{n \geq 1}$. Specifically,*

- *The scheme involves two parties, a sender and a receiver, proceeding in two stages: a commit stage followed by a reveal stage.*
- *In the commit stage, to commit bit $b \in \{0, 1\}$, the sender performs the quantum circuit $Q_b(n)$ on quantum registers (C, R) initialized in all $|0\rangle$'s state[16]. Then the sender sends the commitment register C, whose state at this moment denoted by $\rho_b(n)$, to the receiver.*
- *In the (canonical) reveal stage, the sender announces b, and sends the decommitment register R to the receiver. The receiver then performs $Q_b(n)^\dagger$ on the registers (C, R), accepting if (C, R) return to all $|0\rangle$'s state. (This can be done by a measurement in the computational basis on each qubit that belongs to the registers (C, R).)*

We are next to define the hiding (or concealing) and the binding properties of the scheme $\{(Q_0(n), Q_1(n))\}_{n \geq 1}$.

- **Statistically hiding.** *We say that the scheme is statistically hiding if the quantum state ensembles $\{\rho_0(n)\}_{n \geq 1}$ and $\{\rho_1(n)\}_{n \geq 1}$ are quantum statistically indistinguishable.*
- **Computationally $\epsilon(n)$-binding.** *We say that the scheme is quantum computationally $\epsilon(n)$-binding if for any state $|\psi\rangle$ in auxiliary register Z, and any efficiently realizable unitary transformation U performing on (R, Z),*

$$\left\| (Q_1 |0\rangle \langle 0| Q_1^\dagger)^{CR} U^{RZ} \left((Q_0 |0\rangle)^{CR} |\psi\rangle^Z \right) \right\| < \epsilon(n), \tag{2}$$

By the reversibility of quantum computation, the binding property can also be equivalently defined by swapping the roles of Q_0 and Q_1 in the above. Then the inequality (2) becomes

$$\left\| (Q_0 |0\rangle \langle 0| Q_0^\dagger)^{CR} U^{RZ} \left((Q_1 |0\rangle)^{CR} |\psi\rangle^Z \right) \right\| < \epsilon(n), \tag{3}$$

We call $\epsilon(n)$ the binding error. When $\epsilon(n)$ is some negligible function, we usually drop it and just say that the scheme is computationally binding.

---

[16] The number of qubits in the state $|0\rangle$ that are needed depends on the quantum circuit $Q_0(n)$ (or $Q_1(n)$).

Remark

1. The (computational) binding property stated in the definition above is actually the *honest-binding*, which is equivalent to the sum-binding w.r.t. a generic quantum bit commitment scheme [34].
2. On instantiations of non-interactive computationally-bindng quantum bit commitments of the generic form based on quantum-secure one-way functions/permutations, one is referred to [34] for the details. Briefly, it is argued in [34] that any *interactive* quantum bit commitment schemes (including both classical and quantum constructions) secure against the *purification attack*[17], which in particular include schemes proposed in [11,14,24,28], can be converted into a non-interactive one of the generic form with the same flavors of hiding and binding properties.

In the sequel, to simplify the notation we often drop the security parameter n and just write (Q_0, Q_1) to denote a generic quantum computationally-binding bit commitment scheme.

We will use the scheme (Q_0, Q_1) to commit a binary string in a bitwise fashion. Namely, the quantum circuit to commit a string $s = s_1 s_2 \cdots s_m \in \{0, 1\}^m$ is given by

$$Q_s \overset{def}{=} \bigotimes_{i=1}^{m} Q_{s_i}, \qquad (4)$$

which performs on m copies of the quantum register pair (C, R).

2.2   Modeling an Attack of the Sender of Quantum Commitments

Consider a running of a larger two-party protocol in which a generic quantum bit commitment scheme is used and the sender of quantum commitments is *malicious*. The other party who will be referred to as the receiver is *honest*. The sender is supposed to commit to a string in $\{0, 1\}^m$ in a bitwise fashion at some moment, and later try to open the commitments in a way as determined by the larger protocol. Then the behavior of the sender can be modeled by $(U, |\psi\rangle)$ such that:

1. The sender prepares the system $(\mathsf{C}^{\otimes m}, \mathsf{R}^{\otimes m}, \mathsf{D}, \mathsf{Z})$ in the quantum state $|\psi\rangle$ at the *end* of the commit stage, and sends the commitment registers $\mathsf{C}^{\otimes m}$ to the receiver.
2. In the reveal stage, the sender first performs the *unitary* transformation U on the system $(\mathsf{R}^{\otimes m}, \mathsf{D}, \mathsf{Z})$, and then sends registers $(\mathsf{R}^{\otimes m}, \mathsf{D})$ to the receiver. The register D is supposed to contain the classical information indicating *which* quantum bit commitments will be opened as *what* value, and $\mathsf{R}^{\otimes m}$ are decommitment registers.

We have two remarks about the modeling as above:

---

[17] Informally speaking, this is a kind of security that turns out to be just slightly stronger than the semi-honest security yet much weaker than the full security.

1. We note that there might be other operations performed by both the sender and the receiver *between* the end of the commit stage and the beginning of the reveal stage within the larger protocol. But in many cases, this can be simulated by absorbing these operations and auxiliary states introduced into the operation U and the state $|\psi\rangle$, respectively. Anyway, in this work we just restrict to consider the modeling as above for simplicity.
2. In the second item above, we assume without loss of generality that *all* decommitment registers $\mathsf{R}^{\otimes m}$ are sent to the receiver in the reveal stage, though sometimes only a proper subset of commitments will be opened[18]. We can do this because the receiver is *honest*; sending all decommitment registers will not affect the security against the sender.

2.3 Blum's Zero-Knowledge Protocol for Hamiltonian Cycle

Basically, Blum's protocol [5] proceeds as follows: on input a graph G (assuming it is represented by its adjacency matrix) with n vertices:

1. The prover first chooses a random permutation $\Pi \in S_n$, where S_n consists of all permutations over the set $\{1, 2, \ldots, n\}$. Then it commits to the graph $\pi(G)$, sending all n^2 (quantum) bit commitments to the verifier.
2. Upon receiving the prover's commitments, the verifier tosses a random coin to obtain the challenge bit $b \in \{0, 1\}$ and sends it to the prover.
3. If the challenge $b = 0$, then the prover sends the permutation π together with the decommitment registers for *all* bit commitments to the verifier. If the challenge $b = 1$, then the prover sends the location of a Hamiltonian cycle H together with the decommitment registers for the commitments of all edges of the cycle H to the verifier.
4. If the challenge $b = 0$, then the verifier accepts if all bit commitments are opened as $\pi(G)$ successfully. If the challenge $b = 1$, then the verifier accepts if the H is a possible location of a Hamiltonian cycle and all commitments to the edges of H are opened as 1 successfully.

3 The Predicate-Binding Property of Quantum String Commitments

In this section, we first introduce the notion of pattern-predicate and then the predicate-binding property of quantum string commitments. Next, we show that the parallel composition of a generic quantum computationally-binding bit commitment scheme gives rise to a quantum string commitment scheme that is predicate-binding w.r.t. a pair of inconsistent pattern-predicates of a special form. Last, we extend this predicate-binding property to a setting that is sufficient for our application, i.e. quantum zero-knowledge arguments for **NP**.

---

[18] For example, consider a running of Blum's zero-knowledge protocol for the language Hamiltonian Cycle in which the cheating prover responds to the challenge 1 of the verifier.

3.1 Pattern-Predicate

Informally, the pattern-predicate defined in the below states that for a string to satisfy some predicate, it should exhibit a certain "pattern" somewhere. The intuition underlying our definition is that in typical applications of bit commitments, the receiver will check whether the value of the opened commitments will cause it to accept.

Definition 3 (Pattern-predicate). *A pattern-predicate P on binary strings $\{0,1\}^m$ ($m \geq 1$) can be represented by a triplet of functions $(\mathsf{val}(\cdot), T(\cdot), s(\cdot))$, where given a candidate witness $w \in \{0,1\}^{poly(m)}$ as input: $\mathsf{val}(w) = 1$ if w is a valid witness, and 0 otherwise[19]; $T(w)$ is a subset of $\{1, 2, \ldots, m\}$; $s(w)$ is a string of length $|T(w)|$; all three functions $\mathsf{val}(\cdot)$, $T(\cdot)$, and $s(\cdot)$ can be computed in $poly(m)$ time. A string $str \in \{0,1\}^m$ satisfies the predicate P if there exists a (valid) witness $w \in \{0,1\}^{poly(m)}$ satisfying $\mathsf{val}(w) = 1$ and $str[T(w)] = s(w)$, where $str[T(w)]$ denotes the substring obtained from the string str by projecting it on coordinates in the subset $T(w)$.*

Remark. Intuitively, a *valid* witness w for a string *str* guides us to find a pattern $s(w)$ locating at positions specified by $T(w)$ efficiently. This pattern will certify that the string *str* satisies the pattern-predicate P. However, it might be *computationally hard* to find a valid witness for a given string *str*.

   In this work, for simplicity we often drop the prefix "pattern" and just write "predicate" to refer to a pattern-predicate. For a predicate P, it induces a subset P (by abusing the notation) of strings in $\{0,1\}^m$ such that a string $s \in P$ if and only if it *satisfies* the predicate P; we will identify a predicate as the subset induced by it. We say that two predicates P_1, P_2 on the set $\{0,1\}^m$ are *inconsistent* if $P_1 \cap P_2 = \emptyset$; that is, no strings in $\{0,1\}^m$ can satisfy both P_1 and P_2 simultaneously.

   In a typical application of commitments within a larger protocol, at some stage of this protocol the party who plays the role of the possibly *cheating* sender of commitments will open commitments, and the party who plays the role of the *honest* receiver of commitments will do some verification. We note that it is this verification that natually induces a pattern-predicate. See the following example.

Example 1. Consider a running of Blum's zero-knowledge protocol for the **NP**-complete language Hamiltonian Cycle, in which the verifier is *honest* while the prover might be *cheating*, and the common input graph G has n vertices. Let $m = n^2$. Each graph with n vertices can be represented by an m-bit string. This running of Blum's protocol induces two predicates on strings over $\{0,1\}^m$, corresponding to the verifier's verifications w.r.t. two possible challenges, respectively. In more detail, when the verifier's challenge is 0, it will check that all bit commitments are opened as a graph that is isomorphic to the input graph. This induces a predicate P_0 which consists of all graphs that are isomorphic to the input

---

[19] Sometimes, it will be more covenient to identify the function $\mathsf{val}(\cdot)$ as an algorithm that decides the validity of a candidate witness.

graph. Formally, the predicate P_0 can be represented by a triplet of functions $(\mathsf{val}(\cdot), T(\cdot), s(\cdot))$ such that: given a claimed permutation π over $\{1, 2, \ldots, n\}$, $\mathsf{val}(\pi) = 1$ if π indeed represents a valid permutation; $T(\cdot) \equiv \{1, 2, \ldots, m\}$, and $s(\pi) = \pi(G)$. When the verifier's challenge is 1, it will check that n (out of n^2) bit commitments are opened as all 1's; moreover, these n positions (of opened bit commitments) should correspond to a possible location of a Hamiltonian cycle. This induces a predicate P_1 which consists of all n-vertices graphs containing a Hamiltonian cycle. Formally, the predicate P_1 can be represented by a triplet of functions $(\mathsf{val}(\cdot), T(\cdot), s(\cdot))$ such that: given a claimed Hamiltonian cycle H, $\mathsf{val}(H) = 1$ if H indeed represents a possible location of a Hamiltonian cycle; $T(H)$ is set of coordinates corresponding to edges of H, and $s(\cdot) \equiv 1^n$. If the input graph is *not* Hamiltonian, then the two predicates P_0 and P_1 are obviously inconsistent.

Another example given below consider a simpler scenario, where a special form of pattern-predicates is introduced. In the sequel, we will study these special pattern-predicates first before more general ones.

Example 2. Consider the following scenario. The sender first commits to a string in a bitwise fashion. Later, *all* (bit) commitments will be opened, and the receiver (of commitments) will check whether the whole revealed string satisfies an efficiently computable predicate P in the *common sense* (i.e. a predicate which can be evaluated on any input string in polynomial time, rather than pattern-predicate introduced in this work). Let $\mathsf{A}(\cdot)$ be an algorithm which runs in time $\mathrm{poly}(m)$ and can decide whether a string $str \in \{0, 1\}^m$ satisies P. We note that the predicate P can also be viewed as a pattern-predicate $(\mathsf{A}(\cdot), T(\cdot), s(\cdot))$ where $T(\cdot) \equiv \{1, 2, \ldots, m\}$ and $s(\cdot)$ is the identity function; any string $str \in P$ itself serves as its witness.

3.2   String Predicate-Binding

We first give an informal definition of the predicate-binding property of a quantum string commitment scheme, and then informally state we have achieved towards predicate-binding by composing a generic computationally-binding quantum bit commitment scheme in parallel. Last, we restate the definition of the predicate-binding w.r.t. the parallization of a generic computationally-binding quantum bit commitment scheme in a formal way for the purpose of proving predicate-binding in the sequel.

Definition 4 (Predicate-binding, informal).   *Let P_1, P_2 be two inconsistent pattern-predicates. We say that a quantum string commitment scheme is predicate-binding w.r.t. (P_1, P_2) if any cheating sender, who can succeed in convincing the receiver that the committed value of the (claimed) quantum string commitment satisfies the predicate P_1 with certainty, will fail to convince the receiver that the committed value satisfies the predicate P_2 (except for a negligible probability). We say that a quantum string commitment scheme is predicate-binding if it is predicate-binding w.r.t. any pair of inconsistent predicates.*

Remark. Classical commitments secure against classical attacks are trivially predicate-binding, simply because there is at most one string (i.e. the committed value) associated with each (claimed) commitment. However, this no longer holds w.r.t. either classical or quantum commitments secure against quantum attacks.

Restricting to consider the quantum string commitment scheme obtained by composing a generic computationally-binding quantum bit commitment scheme (Q_0, Q_1) in parallel, our goal is to show that it is predicate-binding w.r.t. inconsistent pattern-predicates pairs that are general enough for our application (Sect. 4). Informally, we can prove a theorem as below. We highlight (again) that we do not achieve the full predicate-binding, which is left as an interesting open problem.

Theorem 2. *Suppose that the quantum bit commitment scheme (Q_0, Q_1) is computationally binding. Let P_1, P_2 be two inconsistent predicates on the set $\{0, 1\}^m$ such that for (at least) one of them, the verification of whether an m-bit string satisfies it needs to examine the bits at some fixed positions of the string (regardless of the witness provided). Then the parallel composition of the scheme (Q_0, Q_1) gives rise to a quantum string commitment scheme that is computationally predicate-binding w.r.t. (P_1, P_2).*

For the purpose of proving Theorem 2, now let us restate Definition 4 w.r.t. the parallization of a generic computationally-binding quantum bit commitment scheme in a more formal way.

Suppose that a cheating sender who is modeled as in Sect. 2.2 tries to convince the (honest) receiver that the committed value of a (claimed) quantum string commitment satisfies a predicate $P = (\mathsf{val}(\cdot), T(\cdot), s(\cdot))$, i.e. the (claimed) commitment can be opened in such a way that if w is a valid witness, then the bit commitments indexed by the subset $T(w)$ are opened as the string $s(w)$. The predicate P natually induces a *projector* P (also by abusing the notation) whose expression is given by

$$P = \sum_w \left(|w\rangle \langle w| \right)^D \otimes \left(Q_{s(w)} |0\rangle \langle 0| Q_{s(w)}^\dagger \right)^{C^{\otimes T(w)} R^{\otimes T(w)}}. \tag{5}$$

Its explanation follows. The summation is over all valid witnesses[20] for m-bit strings in P_1; the quantum circuit $Q_{s(w)}$ (whose meaning is referred to the equation (4)) performs on the copies of the quantum register pair (C, R) indexed by the subset $T(w)$; in the reveal stage, the receiver will perform the *binary measurement* $\{P, \mathbb{1} - P\}$ on its system to decide whether to accept or not. Hence, the sender's success probability of convincing the receiver to accept is given by $\|PU |\psi\rangle\|^2$, where recall that $|\psi\rangle$ is the quantum state of the whole system at the end of the commit stage and U is the sender's operation in the reveal stage. We also note that the projector P is *efficiently realizable*, since all functions $\mathsf{val}(\cdot)$, $T(\cdot)$ and $s(\cdot)$ are efficiently computable.

Based on the expression (5), we can formalize the predicate-binding property of the parallelization of a generic quantum bit commitment scheme as follows.

---

[20] We point out that a string in P_1 may have *multiple* witnesses.

Definition 5 (Predicate-binding w.r.t. the parallel composition of QBC). *Let P_1, P_2 be two inconsistent pattern-predicates. We say that the quantum string commitment scheme obtained by composing a generic quantum bit commitment scheme (Q_0, Q_1) in parallel is predicate-binding w.r.t. (P_1, P_2) if $\|P_2 U P_1 |\psi\rangle\|^2$ is negligible, where $|\psi\rangle$ is an arbitrary state of registers $(C^{\otimes m}, R^{\otimes m}, D, Z)$, and U could be any efficiently realizable unitary transformations that do not touch the quantum commitment (i.e. the commitment registers $C^{\otimes m}$). We say that this quantum string commitment scheme is predicate-binding if it is predicate-binding w.r.t. any pair of inconsistent pattern-predicates.*

In the subsequent two subsections, we will prove Theorem 2. We will first establish predicate-binding w.r.t. a special form of inconsistent pattern-predicate pair (as formalized in Lemma 2), and then extend it to a general case (as formalized in Theorem 3).

3.3   Towards Predicate-Binding: A Special Case

We first restrict to consider pattern-predicates arising in Example 2 in Subsect. 3.1, and try to establish predicate-binding w.r.t. such a pair of inconsistent predicates.

By instantiating the predicate P in the Eq. (5) with the predicate of the form introduced in Example 2, the expression of the projector P will become

$$P = \sum_{s \in P} \left(|s\rangle \langle s| \right)^D \otimes \left(Q_s |0\rangle \langle 0| Q_s^\dagger \right)^{C^{\otimes m} R^{\otimes m}}. \tag{6}$$

For any inconsistent predicate pair (P_1, P_2) whose corresponding projectors P_1 and P_2 are both of the form (6), we can prove the following main technical lemma of this work.

Lemma 2. *Suppose that the scheme (Q_0, Q_1) is computationally ϵ-binding for some arbitrary negligible function $\epsilon(\cdot)$. Both predicates P_1 and P_2 are of the form given by the expression (6). Then for any quantum state $|\psi\rangle$ of registers $(C^{\otimes m}, R^{\otimes m}, D, Z)$, and any efficiently realizable unitary transformation U that does not touch the commitment registers $C^{\otimes m}$, we have $\|P_2 U P_1 |\psi\rangle\|^2 \leq m^2 \epsilon^2 + 2m\epsilon$.*

Proof. According to the expression (6), we can write

$$P_1 |\psi\rangle = \sum_{s \in P_1} \alpha_s |s\rangle^D \otimes Q_s |0\rangle^{C^{\otimes m} R^{\otimes m}} \otimes |\phi_s\rangle^Z \tag{7}$$

$$= \sum_{s \in \{0,1\}^m} \alpha_s |s\rangle^D \otimes Q_s |0\rangle^{C^{\otimes m} R^{\otimes m}} \otimes |\phi_s\rangle^Z, \tag{8}$$

where for each $s \notin P_1$, we let $\alpha_s = 0$ and $|\phi_s\rangle$ be arbitrary[21]; moreover, the complex coefficients α_s's satisfy $\sum_{s \in \{0,1\}^m} |\alpha_s|^2 \leq 1$. For convenience, we introduce the shorthand

$$|\psi_s\rangle \overset{def}{=} |s\rangle \otimes Q_s |0\rangle \otimes |\phi_s\rangle \tag{9}$$

for each $s \in \{0,1\}^m$. With these notations, our goal becomes to show

$$\left\| P_2 U \sum_{s \in \{0,1\}^m} \alpha_s |\psi_s\rangle \right\|^2 \leq m^2 \epsilon^2 + 2 m \epsilon. \tag{10}$$

We will actually prove a strengthening of the inequality (10) by induction. Specifically, we will prove that for each k ($0 \leq k \leq m$) and each string $x \in \{0,1\}^{m-k}$, it holds that

$$\left\| P_2 U \sum_{s \in \{0,1\}^k \circ x} \alpha_s |\psi_s\rangle \right\|^2 \leq (m^2 \epsilon^2 + 2k\epsilon) \sum_{s \in \{0,1\}^k \circ x} |\alpha_s|^2, \tag{11}$$

where $\{0,1\}^k \circ x$ denotes the set of all m-bit strings with a suffix x of length $m - k$. For each $x \in \{0,1\}^{m-k}$ where $0 \leq k \leq m$, if we view it as inducing an internal node/leaf of a binarty tree which corresponds to the summation $P_2 U \sum_{s \in \{0,1\}^k \circ x} \alpha_s |\psi_s\rangle$, then we will bound the (squared) norm of each internal node in a bottom-up way. Thus, the root of the tree will correspond to the case where $k = m$ (then x becomes an empty string), i.e. l.h.s. of the inequality (10) without the squared norm. If we can prove the inequality (11), then plugging in $k = m$ and the inequality $\sum_{s \in \{0,1\}^m} |\alpha_s|^2 \leq 1$, we will arrive at the inequality (10).

Now we are ready to prove the inequality (11) by induction on k, where $0 \leq k \leq m$.

Base. We show that the inequality (11) holds when $k = 0$. In this case, x is a string of length m. Since the coefficient $\alpha_x = 0$ for $x \notin P_1$, in which case the inequality (11) holds trivially, it suffices to fix an arbitrary $x \in P_1$ and show that $\|P_2 U |\psi_x\rangle\| \leq m\epsilon$. To this end, our technique is the *perturbation* that is similar to the quantum statistical binding setting [15]. Specifically, we will first show that the unit vector $U |\psi_x\rangle$ is *negligibly close* to the (unnormalized) vector

$$|\tilde{\psi}_x\rangle \overset{def}{=} \bigotimes_{i=1}^m \left(\mathbb{1} - (Q_{\bar{x}_i} |0\rangle \langle 0| Q_{\bar{x}_i}^\dagger) \right) U |\psi_x\rangle, \tag{12}$$

where $\bar{x}_i = 1 - x_i$, and the projector $Q_{\bar{x}_i} |0\rangle \langle 0| Q_{\bar{x}_i}^\dagger$ performs on the i-the copy of the register pair (C, R). Second, we show that from the inconsistency of the predicate pair (P_1, P_2), it follows that the vector $|\tilde{\psi}_x\rangle$ is *orthogonal* to the subspace

---

[21] Here, our purpose of introducing α_s and $|\phi_s\rangle$ for $s \notin P_1$ is mainly for a cleaner way of writing the proof; it will *not* affect the places in the subsequent proof where the quantum computational binding property is applied.

P_2. Combining these two facts, we know that $\|P_2 U |\psi_x\rangle\|$ is negligible. Detail follows.

We first show that $\||U |\psi_x\rangle - |\tilde{\psi}_x\rangle\| < m\epsilon$ via a simple hybrid argument. Specifically, we introduce hybrids for each $0 \leq j \leq m$ such that $\mathsf{H}_j \overset{def}{=} \bigotimes_{i=1}^{j} (\mathbb{1} - Q_{\bar{x}_i} |0\rangle \langle 0| Q_{\bar{x}_i}^{\dagger}) U |\psi_x\rangle$; then $U |\psi_x\rangle = \mathsf{H}_0$ and $|\tilde{\psi}_x\rangle = \mathsf{H}_m$. It suffices to show that any two adjacent hybrids are negligibly close: if this is true, then applying the triangle inequality of the operator norm m times will yield the desired bound.

Indeed, for each $1 \leq j \leq m$,

$$
\|\mathsf{H}_j - \mathsf{H}_{j-1}\|
$$
$$
= \left\| \bigotimes_{i=1}^{j} (\mathbb{1} - Q_{\bar{x}_i} |0\rangle \langle 0| Q_{\bar{x}_i}^{\dagger}) U |\psi_x\rangle - \bigotimes_{i=1}^{j-1} (\mathbb{1} - Q_{\bar{x}_i} |0\rangle \langle 0| Q_{\bar{x}_i}^{\dagger}) U |\psi_x\rangle \right\|
$$
$$
\leq \left\| (\mathbb{1} - Q_{\bar{x}_j} |0\rangle \langle 0| Q_{\bar{x}_j}^{\dagger}) U |\psi_x\rangle - U |\psi_x\rangle \right\|
$$
$$
= \left\| (Q_{\bar{x}_j} |0\rangle \langle 0| Q_{\bar{x}_j}^{\dagger}) U(|x\rangle Q_x |0\rangle |\phi_x\rangle) \right\|
$$
$$
< \epsilon,
$$

where the last "$<$" follows from the quantum computational binding property by considering the j-th quantum bit commitment.

We then show that the (unnormalized) vector $|\tilde{\psi}_x\rangle$ is orthogonal to the subspace P_2, i.e. $\|P_2|\tilde{\psi}_x\rangle\| = 0$. This follows straightforwardly from the assumption that the predicate P_2 is *inconsistent* with the predicate P_1. In greater detail, for each $s \in P_2$, we know that it is *different* from the string $x \in P_1$; that is, there exists some index j ($1 \leq j \leq m$) such that $s_j = \bar{x}_j$. Combining this with the Eq. (12), it follows that

$$
\left\| (|s\rangle \langle s| \otimes Q_s |0\rangle \langle 0| Q_s^{\dagger}) |\tilde{\psi}_x\rangle \right\| \leq \left\| (Q_s |0\rangle \langle 0| Q_s^{\dagger}) |\tilde{\psi}_x\rangle \right\|
$$
$$
\leq \left\| (Q_{\bar{x}_j} |0\rangle \langle 0| Q_{\bar{x}_j}^{\dagger}) \left(\bigotimes_{i=1}^{m} (\mathbb{1} - (Q_{\bar{x}_i} |0\rangle \langle 0| Q_{\bar{x}_i}^{\dagger})) U |\psi_x\rangle \right) \right\|
$$
$$
= 0.
$$

Then summing over all $s \in P_2$, we obtain

$$
\left\| \sum_{s \in P_2} (|s\rangle \langle s| \otimes Q_s |0\rangle \langle 0| Q_s^{\dagger}) |\tilde{\psi}_x\rangle \right\| = \|P_2|\tilde{\psi}_x\rangle\| = 0.
$$

Combining $\||U |\psi_x\rangle - |\tilde{\psi}_x\rangle\| < m\epsilon$ with $\|P_2|\tilde{\psi}_x\rangle\| = 0$, we arrive at $\|P_2 U |\psi_x\rangle\| \leq m\epsilon$.

Induction. Now suppose that the inequality (11) holds for $k - 1$ and each binary string x of length $m - (k - 1)$. We are to show that it also holds for k and an arbitrary binary string x of length of $m - k$.

For an arbitrary $x \in \{0,1\}^{m-k}$, we first expand the l.h.s. of the inequality (11):

$$\left\| P_2 U \sum_{s \in \{0,1\}^k \circ x} \alpha_s |\psi_s\rangle \right\|^2 = \left\| P_2 U \sum_{s \in \{0,1\}^{k-1} \circ 0x} \alpha_s |\psi_s\rangle + P_2 U \sum_{s' \in \{0,1\}^{k-1} \circ 1x} \alpha_{s'} |\psi_{s'}\rangle \right\|^2$$

$$\leq \left\| P_2 U \sum_{s \in \{0,1\}^{k-1} \circ 0x} \alpha_s |\psi_s\rangle \right\|^2 + \left\| P_2 U \sum_{s' \in \{0,1\}^{k-1} \circ 1x} \alpha_{s'} |\psi_{s'}\rangle \right\|^2 \qquad (13)$$

$$+2 \left| \sum_{s \in \{0,1\}^{k-1} \circ 0x} \alpha_s \langle \psi_s | \cdot U^\dagger P_2 U \cdot \sum_{s' \in \{0,1\}^{k-1} \circ 1x} \alpha_{s'} |\psi_{s'}\rangle \right|.$$

For convenience, we introduce shorthands

$$\alpha_{0x}^2 \stackrel{def}{=} \sum_{s \in \{0,1\}^{k-1} \circ 0x} |\alpha_s|^2, \qquad \alpha_{1x}^2 \stackrel{def}{=} \sum_{s' \in \{0,1\}^{k-1} \circ 1x} |\alpha_{s'}|^2, \qquad \alpha_x^2 \stackrel{def}{=} \alpha_{0x}^2 + \alpha_{1x}^2.$$

Without loss of generality, we can assume that all $\alpha_{0x}, \alpha_{1x}, \alpha_x \geq 0$. With these notations, our goal (i.e. inequality (11)) becomes to show

$$\left\| P_2 U \sum_{s \in \{0,1\}^k \circ x} \alpha_s |\psi_s\rangle \right\|^2 \leq \alpha_x^2 (m^2 \epsilon^2 + 2k\epsilon),$$

and the induction hypothesis implies

$$\left\| P_2 U \sum_{s \in \{0,1\}^{k-1} \circ 0x} \alpha_s |\psi_s\rangle \right\|^2 \leq \alpha_{0x}^2 (m^2 \epsilon^2 + 2(k-1)\epsilon),$$

$$\left\| P_2 U \sum_{s \in \{0,1\}^{k-1} \circ 1x} \alpha_s |\psi_s\rangle \right\|^2 \leq \alpha_{1x}^2 (m^2 \epsilon^2 + 2(k-1)\epsilon).$$

The remainder of the analysis splits into two cases.

$\underline{\text{Case 1}}$: either $\alpha_{0x} = 0$ or $\alpha_{1x} = 0$. Without loss of generality, we can assume that $\alpha_{1x} = 0$. This implies that $\alpha_{s'} = 0$ for each $s' \in \{0,1\}^{k-1} \circ 1x$. Thus,

$$\left\| P_2 U \sum_{s \in \{0,1\}^k \circ x} \alpha_s |\psi_s\rangle \right\|^2 = \left\| P_2 U \sum_{s \in \{0,1\}^{k-1} \circ 0x} \alpha_s |\psi_s\rangle \right\|^2 \leq \alpha_{0x}^2 (m^2 \epsilon^2 + 2(k-1)\epsilon) \leq \alpha_x^2 (m^2 \epsilon^2 + 2k\epsilon),$$

where the first "$\leq$" uses the induction hypothesis.

$\underline{\text{Case 2}}$: both $\alpha_{0x} > 0$ and $\alpha_{1x} > 0$. Following the inequality (13) and using the induction hypothesis, we have

$$\left\| P_2 U \sum_{s \in \{0,1\}^k \circ x} \alpha_s |\psi_s\rangle \right\|^2 \leq \alpha_{0x}^2 (m^2 \epsilon^2 + (k-1)\epsilon) + \alpha_{1x}^2 (m^2 \epsilon^2 + 2(k-1)\epsilon)$$

$$+ 2\alpha_{0x}\alpha_{1x} \cdot \underbrace{\left| \frac{1}{\alpha_{0x}} \sum_{s \in \{0,1\}^{k-1} \circ 0x} \alpha_s \langle \psi_s | \cdot U^\dagger P_2 U \cdot \frac{1}{\alpha_{1x}} \sum_{s' \in \{0,1\}^{k-1} \circ 1x} \alpha_{s'} |\psi_{s'}\rangle \right|}_{(*)}.$$

We claim (refer to Claim 1 in the below) that the absolute value $(*)$ in the above can be bounded by 2ϵ. Then

$$\left\| P_2 U \sum_{s \in \{0,1\}^k \circ x} \alpha_s |\psi_s\rangle \right\|^2 \le (\alpha_{0x}^2 + \alpha_{1x}^2)(m^2\epsilon^2 + 2(k-1)\epsilon) + 2\alpha_{0x}\alpha_{1x} \cdot 2\epsilon$$

$$\le (\alpha_{0x}^2 + \alpha_{1x}^2)(m^2\epsilon^2 + 2(k-1)\epsilon) + (\alpha_{0x}^2 + \alpha_{1x}^2) \cdot 2\epsilon$$

$$= \alpha_x^2(m^2\epsilon^2 + 2k\epsilon).$$

The induction step is thus completed in both cases.
We finish the proof the inequality (11), and in turn the whole lemma.

We are left to prove the following claim, whose proof is referred to the full version of this paper [35].

Claim 1. The absolute value $(*)$ is less than 2ϵ.

3.4   Extension

By slightly adapting its proof, we can extend Lemma 2 so that it holds w.r.t. more general inconsistent predicate pairs (and thus could be useful in cryptographic applications). Specifically, we can prove Theorem 2. Now let us restate Theorem 2 in a more formal way.

Suppose that (P_1, P_2) is an inconsistent pattern-predicate pair such that the predicate P_2 is of the *most general* form as described by the Eq. (5). The predicate P_1 is restricted to be such that the verification of whether an m-bit string satisfies it only needs to examine the bits at some *fixed* positions of the string (regardless of the witness provided). Formally, let T_1 be the fixed subset that prescribes which bits are to examine for the verification of P_1, and $l = |T_1|$. Then whether a string $str \in \{0,1\}^m$ satisfies the predicate P_1 actually only depends on its substring $str[T_1]$. The predicate P_1 in turn induces a predicate $P_1[T_1]$ on the set $\{0,1\}^l$ which consists of strings obtained by projecting strings in P_1 on positions prescribed by the subset T_1. Specifically, $P_1 = (\text{val}(\cdot), T(\cdot), s(\cdot))$, where $T(\cdot) \equiv T_1$ and $|s(\cdot)| \equiv l$. Following the equation (5), the projector P_1 can be written as

$$P_1 = \sum_w \left(|w\rangle\langle w|\right)^D \otimes \left(Q_{s(w)}|0\rangle\langle 0| Q_{s(w)}^\dagger\right)^{C \otimes T_1 R \otimes T_1} \tag{14}$$

$$= \sum_{str \in P_1[T_1]} \sum_{w:s(w)=str} \left(|w\rangle\langle w|\right)^D \otimes \left(Q_{str}|0\rangle\langle 0| Q_{str}^\dagger\right)^{C \otimes T_1 R \otimes T_1}. \tag{15}$$

Then Theorem 2 can be restated as follows formally.

Theorem 3. *Suppose that the scheme (Q_0, Q_1) is computationally ϵ-binding. Let P_1, P_2 be two inconsistent predicates on the set $\{0,1\}^m$, which induce* *two projectors of the form (15) and (5), respectively. Then for any quantum state $|\psi\rangle$ of registers $(C^{\otimes m}, R^{\otimes m}, D, Z)$, and any efficiently realizable unitary transformation U that does not touch the commitment registers $C^{\otimes m}$, we have $\|P_2 U P_1 |\psi\rangle\|^2 \leq m^2 \epsilon^2 + 3m\epsilon$.*

Due to the space limitation, an informal discussion on why such an extension as described in Theorem 2 (or formally Theorem 3) is possible, as well as the proof of Theorem 3 is referred to the full version of this paper [35].

4   Application: Quantum Zero-Knowledge Argument

In this section, we give an application of the quantum computationally predicate-binding string commitment scheme as shown in the proceeding section. Specifically, we show that Blum's protocol for the **NP**-complete language Hamiltonian Cycle [5] with a generic quantum computationally-binding bit commitment scheme plugged in gives rise to a quantum zero-knowledge *argument* system. While its quantum (perfect or statistical) zero-knowledge property can be obtained by a straightforward application of Watrous's quantum rewinding technique[22] [30,32,33,36], its quantum computational soundness is established by Lemma 3 as stated below. Combing them we arrive at Theorem 1.

Lemma 3. *Blum's protocol for the language* Hamiltonian Cycle *with a generic quantum computationally-binding bit commitment scheme* (Q_0, Q_1) *plugged in is sound against any quantum provers who are polynomial-time bounded, with soundness error* $1/2 + negl(\cdot)$.

Proof. This can be proved by instantiating Theorem 3 with proper predicates induced by Blum's protocol. Detail follows.

Suppose that the binding error of the scheme (Q_0, Q_1) is $\epsilon(\cdot)$, which is a negligible function. We inherit notations as introduced in Subsect. 2.3. Following Subsect. 2.2, we can model a generic attack of the prover of Blum's protocol in the following way. The combined (quantum) system of the (cheating) prover and the (honest) verifier is given by $(P, D, C^{\otimes n^2}, R^{\otimes n^2})$, where the n^2 copies of the register pair (C, R) are used for (in total n^2) quantum bit commitments; the register D will hold the classical information of the prover's response (i.e. the permutation π when the challenge $b = 0$ or the location of a Hamiltonian cycle H when $b = 1$); the register P is the prover's (private) workspace. Suppose that the whole system is initialized in the state $|\psi\rangle$. The prover sends the quantum register $C^{\otimes n^2}$ to the verifier as its first message. Then depending on the challenge b, the prover will perform some polynomial-time realizable unitary transformation U_b

---

[22] We highlight that in the literature we cite, various quantum zero-knowledge properties are based on *different* hiding properties of (classical or quantum) commitments (secure against quantum attacks) than the one considered in this work. However, their proofs extend to our setting straightforwardly, especially the proof of quantum zero-knowledge in [36].

on the registers $(\mathsf{P}, \mathsf{D}, \mathsf{R}^{\otimes n^2})$. After receiving the prover's response, the verifier will perform some binary measurement, which also depends on the challenge b (as prescribed in the below), to decide to whether accept or not.

Formally, depending on the challenge b, the verifier's accepting conditions induce two pattern-predicates, which in turn induces two efficiently realizable projectors/binary measurements as follows:

1. The projector corresponding to $b = 0$ is given by

$$
P_0 = \sum_{\pi \in S_n} \left(|\pi\rangle \langle \pi| \right)^D \otimes \left(Q_{\pi(G)} |0\rangle \langle 0| Q_{\pi(G)}^\dagger \right)^{C^{\otimes n^2} R^{\otimes n^2}}
$$

$$
= \sum_{\substack{s \in \{0,1\}^{n^2}: \\ \exists \pi \in S_n, \pi(G) = s}} \sum_{\pi \in S_n : \pi(G) = s} \left(|\pi\rangle \langle \pi| \right)^D \otimes \left(Q_s |0\rangle \langle 0| Q_s^\dagger \right)^{C^{\otimes n^2} R^{\otimes n^2}}.
$$

2. The projector corresponding to $b = 1$ is given by

$$
P_1 = \sum_{H : n \text{ cycle}} \left(|H\rangle \langle H| \right)^D \otimes \left(Q_{1^n} |0\rangle \langle 0| Q_{1^n}^\dagger \right)^{C^{\otimes H} R^{\otimes H}},
$$

where the projector $Q_{1^n} |0\rangle \langle 0| Q_{1^n}^\dagger$ performs on the n copies of the register pair (C, R) that are determined by the location of the Hamiltonian cycle H.

We highlight that here we implicitly assume that the verifier just performs a big binary measurement (induced by either P_0 or P_1) to decide whether to accept or not; it in particular does not measure the register D to extract any classical information. It is easy to see that whether measuring the register D or not will not change the verifier's acceptance probability. But by doing this, we are then allowed to apply the quantum rewinding lemma (Lemma 1).

Now we are ready to argue the quantum computational soundness of Blum's protocol. Suppose for contradiction that there exists a efficiently realizable cheating prover given by $(|\psi\rangle, U_0, U_1)$ as aforementioned who can break the quantum computational soundness. Namely,

$$
\frac{1}{2} \sum_{b \in \{0,1\}} \| P_b U_b |\psi\rangle \|^2 > \frac{1}{2} + n^{-c},
$$

where c is some constant. Then applying the quantum rewinding lemma (Lemma 1), it follows that

$$
\left\| P_1 U_1 U_0^\dagger P_0 U_0 |\psi\rangle \right\| > n^{-c}. \tag{16}
$$

On the other hand, we invoke Theorem 3 by doing the replacements as summarized in the following table:

Theorem 3	Blum's protocol
m	n^2
Registers $(\mathsf{C}^{\otimes m}, \mathsf{R}^{\otimes m})$	Registers $(\mathsf{C}^{\otimes m}, \mathsf{R}^{\otimes m})$
Register D	Register D
Register Z	Register P
Projector P_1	Projector P_0
Projector P_2	Projector P_1
Quantum state $|\psi\rangle$	Quantum state $U_0 |\psi\rangle$
Unitary transformation U	Unitary transformation $U_1 U_0^\dagger$

In case that the input graph G is not Hamiltonian, the two predicates P_0 and P_1 are inconsistent. Applying Theorem 3 will yield an upper bound $n^4 \epsilon^2 + 3n^2 \epsilon$ of the squared norm $\left\| P_1 U_1 U_0^\dagger P_0 U_0 |\psi\rangle \right\|^2$, which is negligible. But this contradicts with the inequality (16).

We finish the proof of the lemma.

On Compositions. In this section, we only consider the *stand-alone* Blum's protocol, whose soundness error is not tolerable in practice. It is not hard to see that if we compose it *in sequence*, it gives rise to a quantum perfect or statistical zero-knowledge arguments for **NP** with *negligible* soundness error (but at the cost of a significant increase of the round complexity). We may also consider composing Blum's atomic protocol *in parallel*, which we believe can reduce the soundness error to be negligible[23], too However, we do not known whether the parallelization preserves the quantum zero-knowledge property. Actually, the same problem is notorious hard w.r.t. classical zero-knowledge secure against quantum attacks [9,22].

5   Conclusion

In this work, we show that the parallel composition of a generic quantum computationally-binding bit commitment scheme gives rise to a quantum *string* commitment scheme that is computationally predicate-binding, which is nontrivial and turns out to be useful in constructing quantum zero-knowledge arguments for **NP** languages. The main technical part of this work lies in establishing this quantum computational predicate-binding property.

Acknowledgements. We thank Dominique Unruh for helpful and inspiring discussions on the strictness of the quantum binding property and the possibility of basing

---

[23] This can be done by combining the predicate-binding of quantum commitments with a different quantum rewinding lemma (say the one used in [30] to cope with Σ-protocol) than ours (i.e. Lemma 1).

quantum zero-knowledge argument for **NP** on computationally-binding quantum bit commitments at an early stage of this work. We are also grateful to the anonymous referees of Crypto 2021, QCrypt 2021, and Asiacrypt 2021 for their corrections and useful suggestions for the presentation of this paper.

This work was supported by the National Natural Science Foundation of China (Grant No. 61602208, No. 61932019, No. 61772521, No. 62171202, No. 61771222, and No. 61772522), by the PhD Start-up Fund of Natural Science Foundation of Guangdong Province, China (Grant No. 2014A030310333), by the Key Research Program of Frontier Sciences, CAS (Grant No. QYZDB-SSW-SYS035), and by the Open Project Program of the State Key Laboratory of Information Security, IIE, CAS (Grant No. 2015-MS-08).

References

1. Adcock, M., Cleve, R.: A quantum Goldreich-Levin theorem with cryptographic applications. In: Alt, H., Ferreira, A. (eds.) STACS 2002. LNCS, vol. 2285, pp. 323–334. Springer, Heidelberg (2002). https://doi.org/10.1007/3-540-45841-7_26

2. Ambainis, A., Rosmanis, A., Unruh, D.: Quantum attacks on classical proof systems: the hardness of quantum rewinding. In: FOCS, pp. 474–483 (2014)

3. Bartusek, J., Coladangelo, A., Khurana, D., Ma, F.: One-way functions imply secure computation in a quantum world. In: Malkin, T., Peikert, C. (eds.) CRYPTO 2021. LNCS, vol. 12825, pp. 467–496. Springer, Cham (2021). https://doi.org/10.1007/978-3-030-84242-0_17

4. Bennett, C.H., Brassard, G.: Quantum cryptography: Public key distribution and coin tossing. In: Proceedings of IEEE International Conference on Computers, Systems and Signal Processing, vol. 175 (1984)

5. Blum, M.: How to prove a theorem so no one else can claim it. In: Proceedings of the International Congress of Mathematicians, vol. 1, p. 2 (1986)

6. Boneh, D., Dagdelen, Ö., Fischlin, M., Lehmann, A., Schaffner, C., Zhandry, M.: Random oracles in a quantum world. In: Lee, D.H., Wang, X. (eds.) ASIACRYPT 2011. LNCS, vol. 7073, pp. 41–69. Springer, Heidelberg (2011). https://doi.org/10.1007/978-3-642-25385-0_3

7. Brassard, G., Crépeau, C.: Quantum bit commitment and coin tossing protocols. In: Menezes, A.J., Vanstone, S.A. (eds.) CRYPTO 1990. LNCS, vol. 537, pp. 49–61. Springer, Heidelberg (1991). https://doi.org/10.1007/3-540-38424-3_4

8. Chailloux, A., Kerenidis, I., Rosgen, B.: Quantum commitments from complexity assumptions. In: ICALP, no. 1, pp. 73–85 (2011)

9. Chia, N., Chung, K., Liu, Q., Yamakawa, T.: On the impossibility of post-quantum black-box zero-knowledge in constant rounds (2021). CoRR abs/2103.11244, https://arxiv.org/abs/2103.11244

10. Crépeau, C., Dumais, P., Mayers, D., Salvail, L.: Computational collapse of quantum state with application to oblivious transfer. In: Naor, M. (ed.) TCC 2004. LNCS, vol. 2951, pp. 374–393. Springer, Heidelberg (2004). https://doi.org/10.1007/978-3-540-24638-1_21

11. Crépeau, C., Légaré, F., Salvail, L.: How to convert the flavor of a quantum bit commitment. In: Pfitzmann, B. (ed.) EUROCRYPT 2001. LNCS, vol. 2045, pp. 60–77. Springer, Heidelberg (2001). https://doi.org/10.1007/3-540-44987-6_5

12. Damgård, I., Fehr, S., Salvail, L.: Zero-knowledge proofs and string commitments withstanding quantum attacks. In: Franklin, M. (ed.) CRYPTO 2004. LNCS, vol. 3152, pp. 254–272. Springer, Heidelberg (2004). https://doi.org/10.1007/978-3-540-28628-8_16

13. Damgård, I., Fehr, S., Salvail, L.: Private communication (2021)

14. Dumais, P., Mayers, D., Salvail, L.: Perfectly concealing quantum bit commitment from any quantum one-way permutation. In: Preneel, B. (ed.) EUROCRYPT 2000. LNCS, vol. 1807, pp. 300–315. Springer, Heidelberg (2000). https://doi.org/10.1007/3-540-45539-6_21

15. Fang, J., Unruh, D., Yan, J., Zhou, D.: How to base security on the perfect/statistical binding property of quantum bit commitment? (2020). https://eprint.iacr.org/2020/621

16. Goldreich, O.: Foundations of Cryptography, Basic Tools, vol. I. Cambridge University Press, Cambridge (2001)

17. Goldreich, O., Micali, S., Wigderson, A.: Proofs that yield nothing but their validity or all languages in NP have zero-knowledge proof systems. J. ACM **38**(3), 691–729 (1991)

18. van de Graaf, J.: Towards a formal definition of security for quantum protocols. PhD thesis, Université de Montréal (1997)

19. Grilo, A.B., Lin, H., Song, F., Vaikuntanathan, V.: Oblivious transfer is in MiniQCrypt. In: Canteaut, A., Standaert, F.-X. (eds.) EUROCRYPT 2021. LNCS, vol. 12697, pp. 531–561. Springer, Cham (2021). https://doi.org/10.1007/978-3-030-77886-6_18

20. Haitner, I., Hoch, J.J., Reingold, O., Segev, G.: Finding collisions in interactive protocols - a tight lower bound on the round complexity of statistically-hiding commitments. In: FOCS, pp. 669–679 (2007)

21. Haitner, I., Nguyen, M.H., Ong, S.J., Reingold, O., Vadhan, S.P.: Statistically hiding commitments and statistical zero-knowledge arguments from any one-way function. SIAM J. Comput. **39**(3), 1153–1218 (2009)

22. Jain, R., Kolla, A., Midrijanis, G., Reichardt, B.W.: On parallel composition of zero-knowledge proofs with black-box quantum simulators. Quant. Inf. Comput. **9**(5), 513–532 (2009)

23. Koshiba, T., Odaira, T.: Statistically-hiding quantum bit commitment from approximable-preimage-size quantum one-way function. In: Childs, A., Mosca, M. (eds.) TQC 2009. LNCS, vol. 5906, pp. 33–46. Springer, Heidelberg (2009). https://doi.org/10.1007/978-3-642-10698-9_4

24. Koshiba, T., Odaira, T.: Non-interactive statistically-hiding quantum bit commitment from any quantum one-way function (2011). arXiv:1102.3441

25. Lo, H.K., Chau, H.F.: Why quantum bit commitment and ideal quantum coin tossing are impossible. Physica D Nonlinear Phenom. **120**(1), 177–187 (1998)

26. Mahmoody, M., Pass, R.: The curious case of non-interactive commitments – on the power of black-box vs. non-black-box use of primitives. In: Safavi-Naini, R., Canetti, R. (eds.) CRYPTO 2012. LNCS, vol. 7417, pp. 701–718. Springer, Heidelberg (2012). https://doi.org/10.1007/978-3-642-32009-5_41

27. Mayers, D.: Unconditionally secure quantum bit commitment is impossible. Phys. Rev. Lett. **78**(17), 3414–3417 (1997)

28. Naor, M., Ostrovsky, R., Venkatesan, R., Yung, M.: Perfect zero-knowledge arguments for NP using any one-way permutation. J. Cryptol. **11**(2), 87–108 (1998)

29. Nielsen, M.A., Chuang, I.L.: Quantum Computation and Quantum Informatioin. Cambridge University Press, Cambridge (2000)

30. Unruh, D.: Quantum proofs of knowledge. In: Pointcheval, D., Johansson, T. (eds.) EUROCRYPT 2012. LNCS, vol. 7237, pp. 135–152. Springer, Heidelberg (2012). https://doi.org/10.1007/978-3-642-29011-4_10

31. Unruh, D.: Collapse-binding quantum commitments without random oracles. In: Cheon, J.H., Takagi, T. (eds.) ASIACRYPT 2016. LNCS, vol. 10032, pp. 166–195. Springer, Heidelberg (2016). https://doi.org/10.1007/978-3-662-53890-6_6

32. Unruh, D.: Computationally binding quantum commitments. In: Fischlin, M., Coron, J.-S. (eds.) EUROCRYPT 2016. LNCS, vol. 9666, pp. 497–527. Springer, Heidelberg (2016). https://doi.org/10.1007/978-3-662-49896-5_18

33. Watrous, J.: Zero-knowledge against quantum attacks. SIAM J. Comput. **39**(1), 25–58 (2009)

34. Yan, J.: General properties of quantum bit commitments (2020). https://eprint.iacr.org/2020/1488

35. Yan, J.: Quantum computationally predicate-binding commitment with application in quantum zero-knowledge argument for np. Cryptology ePrint Archive, Report 2020/1510 (2020). https://eprint.iacr.org/2020/1510

36. Yan, J., Weng, J., Lin, D., Quan, Y.: Quantum bit commitment with application in quantum zero-knowledge proof (extended abstract). In: Elbassioni, K., Makino, K. (eds.) ISAAC 2015. LNCS, vol. 9472, pp. 555–565. Springer, Heidelberg (2015). https://doi.org/10.1007/978-3-662-48971-0_47

37. Yao, A.C.C.: Quantum circuit complexity. In: FOCS, pp. 352–361 (1993)

Quantum Encryption with Certified Deletion, Revisited: Public Key, Attribute-Based, and Classical Communication

Taiga Hiroka[1]($\boxtimes$), Tomoyuki Morimae[1,2]($\boxtimes$), Ryo Nishimaki[3]($\boxtimes$), and Takashi Yamakawa[3]($\boxtimes$)

[1] Yukawa Institute for Theoretical Physics, Kyoto University, Kyoto, Japan
{taiga.hiroka,tomoyuki.morimae}@yukawa.kyoto-u.ac.jp
[2] PRESTO, JST, Saitama, Japan
[3] NTT Corporation, Tokyo, Japan
{ryo.nishimaki.zk,takashi.yamakawa.ga}@hco.ntt.co.jp

Abstract. Broadbent and Islam (TCC '20) proposed a quantum cryptographic primitive called *quantum encryption with certified deletion*. In this primitive, a receiver in possession of a quantum ciphertext can generate a classical certificate that the encrypted message has been deleted. Although their construction is information-theoretically secure, it is limited to the setting of one-time symmetric key encryption (SKE), where a sender and receiver have to share a common key in advance and the key can be used only once. Moreover, the sender has to generate a quantum state and send it to the receiver over a quantum channel in their construction. Deletion certificates are privately verifiable, which means a verification key for a certificate must be kept secret, in the definition by Broadbent and Islam. However, we can also consider public verifiability. In this work, we present various constructions of encryption with certified deletion.

- Quantum communication case: We achieve (reusable-key) public key encryption (PKE) and attribute-based encryption (ABE) with certified deletion. Our PKE scheme with certified deletion is constructed assuming the existence of IND-CPA secure PKE, and our ABE scheme with certified deletion is constructed assuming the existence of indistinguishability obfuscation and one-way functions. These two schemes are privately verifiable.
- Classical communication case: We also achieve interactive encryption with certified deletion that uses only classical communication. We give two schemes, a privately verifiable one and a publicly verifiable one. The former is constructed assuming the LWE assumption in the quantum random oracle model. The latter is constructed assuming the existence of one-shot signatures and extractable witness encryption.

© International Association for Cryptologic Research 2021
M. Tibouchi and H. Wang (Eds.): ASIACRYPT 2021, LNCS 13090, pp. 606–636, 2021.
https://doi.org/10.1007/978-3-030-92062-3_21

1   Introduction

The no-cloning theorem, which states that an unknown quantum state cannot be copied in general, is one of the most fundamental principles in quantum physics. As any classical information can be trivially copied, this indicates a fundamental difference between classical and quantum information. The no-cloning theorem has been the basis of many quantum cryptographic protocols, including quantum money [Wie83] and quantum key distribution [BB84].

Broadbent and Islam [BI20] used the principle to construct *quantum encryption with certified deletion*. In this primitive, a sender encrypts a classical message to generate a quantum ciphertext. A receiver in possession of the quantum ciphertext and a classical decryption key can either decrypt the ciphertext or "delete" the encrypted message by generating a classical certificate. After generating a valid certificate of deletion, no adversary can recover the message *even if the decryption key is given*.[1] We remark that this functionality is classically impossible to achieve since one can copy a classical ciphertext and keep it so that s/he can decrypt it at any later time. They prove the security of their construction without relying on any computational assumption, which ensures information-theoretical security. Although they achieved the exciting new functionality, their construction is limited to the one-time symmetric key encryption (SKE) setting. A sender and receiver have to share a common key in advance in one-time SKE, and the key can be used only once.

A possible application scenario of quantum encryption with certified deletion is the following. A user uploads encrypted data on a quantum cloud server. Whenever the user wishes to delete the data, the cloud generates a deletion certificate and sends it to the user. After the user verifies the validity of the certificate, s/he is convinced that the data cannot be recovered even if the decryption key accidentally leaks later. Such quantum encryption could prevent data retention and help to implement the right to be forgotten [GDP16]. In this scenario, one-time SKE is quite inconvenient. By the one-time restriction, the user has to locally keep as many decryption keys as the number of encrypted data in the cloud, in which case there seems to be no advantage of uploading the data to the cloud server: If the user has such large storage, s/he could have just locally kept the messages rather than uploading encryption of them to the cloud. Also, in some cases, a party other than the decryptor may want to upload data to the cloud. This usage would be possible if we can extend the quantum encryption with certified deletion to public key encryption (PKE). We remark that the one-time restriction is automatically resolved for PKE by a simple hybrid argument. Even more flexibly, a single encrypted data on the cloud may be supposed to be decrypted by multiple users according to some access control policy. Attribute-based encryption (ABE) [SW05, GPSW06] realizes such an access control in

---

[1] We note that if the adversary is given the decryption key before the deletion, it can decrypt the ciphertext to obtain the message and keep it even after the deletion, but such an "attack" is unavoidable.

classical cryptography. Thus, it would be useful if we have ABE with certified deletion. Our first question in this work is:

Can we achieve PKE and ABE with certified deletion?

Moreover, a sender needs to send quantum states (random BB84 states [BB84]) over a quantum channel in the construction by Broadbent and Islam [BI20]. Although generating and sending random BB84 states are not difficult tasks (and they are already possible with current technologies), a classical sender and communication over only a classical channel are much easier. Besides, communicating over a classical channel is desirable in the application scenario above since many parties want to upload data to a cloud. In addition to these practical motivations, achieving classical channel certified deletion is also an interesting theoretical research direction given the fact that many quantum cryptographic protocols have been "dequantized" recently [Mah18, CCKW19, RS19, AGKZ20, KNY20]. Thus, our second question in this work is:

Can we achieve encryption with certified deletion, a classical sender, and classical communication?

In the definition by Broadbent and Islam [BI20], a verification key for a deletion certificate must be kept secret (privately verifiable). If the verification key is revealed, the security is no longer guaranteed in their scheme. We can also consider public verifiability, which means the security holds even if a verification key is revealed to adversaries. Broadbent and Islam left the following question as an open problem:

Is publicly verifiable encryption with certified deletion possible?

1.1 Our Result

We solve the three questions above affirmatively in this work.

PKE and ABE with Certified Deletion and Quantum Communication. We present formal definitions of PKE and ABE with certified deletion, and present constructions of them:

- We construct a PKE scheme with certified deletion assuming the existence of (classical) IND-CPA secure PKE. We also observe that essentially the same construction gives a reusable SKE scheme with certified deletion if we use IND-CPA secure SKE, which exists under the existence of one-way function (OWF), instead of PKE.
- We construct a (public-key) ABE scheme with certified deletion assuming the existence of indistinguishability obfuscation (iO) [BGI+12] and OWF. This construction satisfies collusion resistance and adaptive security, i.e., it is secure against adversaries that adaptively select a target attribute and obtain arbitrarily many decryption keys.

All building blocks above are post-quantum secure in this work. We note that our constructions rely on computational assumptions and thus are not information-theoretically secure, unlike the construction in [BI20]. This is unavoidable since even plain PKE or ABE cannot be information-theoretically secure. We also note that the constructions above are privately verifiable as the definition of one-time SKE by Broadbent and Islam [BI20].

Our main technical insight is that we can combine the one-time secure SKE with certified deletion of [BI20] and plain PKE to construct PKE with certified deletion by a simple hybrid encryption technique if the latter satisfies *receiver non-committing* (RNC) security [CFGN96, JL00, CHK05]. Since it is known that PKE/SKE with RNC security can be constructed from any IND-CPA secure PKE/SKE [CHK05, KNTY19], our first result follows.

For the second result, we first give a suitable definition of RNC security for ABE that suffices for our purpose. Then we construct an ABE scheme with RNC security based on the existence of iO and OWF. By combining this with one-time SKE with certified deletion by hybrid encryption, we obtain an ABE scheme with certified deletion.

Interactive Encryption with Certified Deletion, a Classical Sender, and Classical Communication. We also present formal definitions of PKE with certified deletion and classical communication, and present two constructions:

- We construct an interactive encryption scheme with privately verifiable certified deletion and classical communication in the quantum random oracle model (QROM) [BDF+11]. Our construction is secure under the LWE assumption in the QROM.
- We construct an interactive encryption scheme with publicly verifiable certified deletion and classical communication. Our construction uses one-shot signatures [AGKZ20] and extractable witness encryption [GGSW13, GKP+13]. This solves the open problem by Broadbent and Islam [BI20].

A sender is a classical algorithm in both constructions but needs to interact with a receiver during ciphertext generation.

An encryption algorithm must be interactive in the classical communication case even if we consider computationally bounded adversaries (and even in the QROM). The reason is that a malicious QPT receiver can generate two copies of a quantum ciphertext from classical messages sent from a sender. One is used for generating a deletion certificate, and the other is used for decryption.

Moreover, both constructions rely on computational assumptions and thus are not information-theoretically secure, unlike the construction by Broadbent and Islam [BI20]. This is unavoidable even if an encryption algorithm is interactive (and even in the QROM). The reason is that a computationally unbounded malicious receiver can classically simulate its honest behavior to get a classical description of the quantum ciphertext.

For the first construction, we use a new property of noisy trapdoor claw-free (NTCF) functions, *the cut-and-choose adaptive hardcore property* (Lemma 4.1), which we introduce in this work. We prove that the cut-and-choose adaptive hardcore property is reduced to the adaptive hardcore bit property [BCM+18] and injective invariance [Mah18]. Those properties hold under the LWE assumption [BCM+18, Mah18]. This new technique is of independent interest. The idea of the second construction is to encrypt a plaintext by witness encryption so that a valid witness is a one-shot signature for bit 0. We use a valid one-shot signature for bit 1 as a deletion certificate. The one-shot property of one-shot signatures prevents decryption of witness encryption after issuing a valid deletion certificate. Georgiou and Zhandry [GZ20] used a similar combination of one-shot signatures and witness encryption to construct unclonable decryption keys.

1.2 Related Work

Before the work by Broadbent and Islam [BI20], Fu and Miller [FM18] and Coiteux-Roy and Wolf [CRW19] also studied the concept of certifying deletion of information in different settings. (See [BI20] for the comparison with these works.)

The quantum encryption scheme with certified deletion by Broadbent and Islam [BI20] is based on Wiesner's conjugate coding, which is the backbone of quantum money [Wie83] and quantum key distribution [BB84]. A similar idea has been used in many constructions in quantum cryptography that include (but are not limited to) revocable quantum timed-release encryption [Unr15], uncloneable quantum encryption [BL20], single-decryptor encryption [GZ20], and copy protection/secure software leasing [CMP20]. Among them, revocable quantum timed-release encryption is conceptually similar to quantum encryption with certified deletion. In this primitive, a receiver can decrypt a quantum ciphertext only after spending a certain amount of time T. The receiver can also choose to return the ciphertext before the time T is over, in which case it is ensured that the message can no longer be recovered. As observed by Broadbent and Islam [BI20], an essential difference from quantum encryption with certified deletion is that the revocable quantum timed-release encryption does not have a mechanism to generate a *classical* certificate of deletion. Moreover, the construction by Unruh [Unr15] heavily relies on the random oracle heuristic [BR97, BDF+11], and there is no known construction without random oracles.

Kundu and Tan [KT20] constructed (one-time symmetric key) quantum encryption with certified deletion with the device-independent security, i.e., the security holds even if quantum devices are untrusted. Moreover, they show that their construction satisfies composable security.

The notion of NTCF functions was first introduced by Brakerski et al. [BCM+18], and further extended to construct a classical verification of quantum computing by Mahadev [Mah18]. (See also a related primitive so-called QFactory [CCKW19].) The adaptive hardcore bit property of NTCF functions was also used for semi-quantum money [RS19] and secure software leasing with classical communication [KNY20].

Ananth and Kaleoglu concurrently and independently present reusable secret key and public key uncloneable encryption schemes [AK21]. Uncloneable encryption [BL20] is related to but different from quantum encryption with certified deletion. Uncloneable encryption prevents adversaries from creating multiple ciphertexts whose plaintext is the same as that of the original ciphertext. Their constructions are based on a similar idea to one of our main ideas. Specifically, their construction is obtained by combining one-time secret key uncloneable encryption and standard SKE/PKE with the "fake-key property", which is similar to the RNC security.

1.3   Technical Overview Part I: Quantum Communication Case

We provide an overview of how to achieve PKE and ABE with certified deletion using quantum communication in this section. To explain our idea, we introduce the definition of PKE with certified deletion.

Definition of Quantum Encryption with Certified Deletion. A PKE with certified deletion consists of the following algorithms.

KeyGen(1^λ) → (pk, sk): This is a key generation algorithm that generates a pair of public and secret keys.

Enc(pk, m) → (vk, CT): This is an encryption algorithm that generates a ciphertext of plaintext and a verification key for this ciphertext.

Dec(sk, CT) → m': This is a decryption algorithm that decrypts a ciphertext.

Del(CT) → cert: This is a deletion algorithm that generates a certificate to guarantee that the ciphertext CT was deleted.

Vrfy(vk, cert) → ⊤ or ⊥: This is a verification algorithm that checks the validity of a certificate cert by using a verification key. As correctness, we require that this algorithm returns ⊤ (i.e., it accepts) if cert was honestly generated by Del(CT) and (vk, CT) was honestly generated by Enc.

Roughly speaking, certified deletion security requires that no quantum polynomial time (QPT) adversary given pk and CT can obtain any information about the plaintext in CT *even if* sk *is given after a valid certificate* cert ← Del(CT) *is generated.* The difference between PKE and reusable SKE with certified deletion is that, in reusable SKE, KeyGen outputs only sk. In the one-time SKE case by Broadbent and Islam [BI20], Enc does not output vk and Vrfy uses sk instead of vk.

Our Idea for PKE. We use the construction of one-time SKE with certified deletion by Broadbent and Islam [BI20]. However, we do not need to know the detail of the SKE scheme since we use it in a black-box way in our PKE scheme. What we need to understand about the SKE scheme are the following abstracted properties: (1) A secret key and a plaintext are classical strings. (2) A ciphertext is a quantum state. (3) The encryption algorithm does not output a verification key since the verification key is equal to the secret key. (4) It satisfies the verification correctness and certified deletion security explained above.

Our idea is to convert the SKE with certified deletion scheme into a PKE with certified deletion scheme by combining with a standard PKE scheme (standard hybrid encryption technique). This conversion is possible since a secret key of the SKE scheme is a classical string. Let PKE.(KeyGen, Enc, Dec) and SKE.(KeyGen, Enc, Dec, Del, Vrfy) be normal PKE and one-time SKE with certified deletion schemes, respectively. Our PKE with certified deletion scheme is described as follows.

KeyGen(1^λ): This outputs (pke.pk, pke.sk) $\leftarrow$ PKE.KeyGen(1^λ).

Enc(pk, m):   This   generates   ske.sk $\leftarrow$ SKE.KeyGen(1^λ), ske.CT $\leftarrow$ SKE.Enc(ske.sk, m), and pke.CT $\leftarrow$ PKE.Enc(pke.pk, ske.sk), and outputs vk := ske.sk and CT := (ske.CT, pke.CT).

Dec(sk, CT): This computes ske.sk$'$ $\leftarrow$ PKE.Dec(pke.sk, pke.CT) and $m' \leftarrow$ SKE.Dec(ske.sk$'$, ske.CT), and outputs m'.

Del(CT): This generates and outputs cert $\leftarrow$ SKE.Del(ske.CT).

Vrfy(vk, cert): This outputs the output of SKE.Vrfy(ske.sk, cert) (note that vk = ske.sk).

At first glance, this naive idea seems to work since even if pke.sk is given to an adversary after a valid cert is generated, ske.CT does not leak information about the plaintext by certified deletion security of the SKE scheme. Note that PKE is used to encrypt ske.sk (not m). One-time SKE is sufficient since ske.sk is freshly generated in Enc. The proof outline is as follows. First, we use IND-CPA security of normal PKE to erase information about ske.sk. Then, we use the one-time certified deletion security of SKE. Unfortunately, we do not know how to prove the first step above because we must give pke.sk to an adversary in a security reduction. In the first step, we need to show that if a distinguisher detects that PKE.Enc(pke.pk, ske.sk) is changed to PKE.Enc(pke.pk, $0^{|\text{ske.sk}|}$), we can break IND-CPA security of the normal PKE. However, to run the distinguisher, we need to give pke.sk to the distinguisher after it sends a valid certificate for deletion. The reduction has no way to give pke.sk to the distinguisher since the reduction is trying to break the PKE scheme!

To solve this problem, we use RNC encryption (RNCE) [JL00,CHK05]. RNCE consists of algorithms (KeyGen, Enc, Dec, Fake, Reveal). The key generation algorithm outputs not only a key pair (pk, sk) but also an auxiliary trapdoor information aux. The fake ciphertext generation algorithm Fake(pk, sk, aux) can generate a fake ciphertext $\widetilde{\text{CT}}$ that does not include information about a plaintext. The reveal algorithm Reveal(pk, sk, aux, $\widetilde{\text{CT}}$, m) can generate a fake secret key that decrypts $\widetilde{\text{CT}}$ to m. The RNC security notion requires that ($\widetilde{\text{CT}}$ = Fake(pk, sk, aux), Reveal(pk, sk, aux, $\widetilde{\text{CT}}$, m)) is computationally indistinguishable from (Enc(pk, m), sk).

RNCE perfectly fits the scenario of certified deletion. We use an RNCE scheme RNCE.(KeyGen, Enc, Dec, Fake, Reveal) instead of a normal PKE in the PKE with certified deletion scheme above. To erase ske.sk, we use the RNC security. We change RNCE.Enc(rnce.pk, ske.sk) and rnce.sk into rnce.$\widetilde{\text{CT}}$ = RNCE.Fake(rnce.pk, rnce.sk, rnce.aux) and RNCE.Reveal(rnce.pk, rnce.sk, rnce.aux, rnce.$\widetilde{\text{CT}}$, ske.sk), respectively. Thus, as long as ske.sk is given after a valid certification is generated, we can simulate the secret key of the PKE with certified deletion scheme. Using RNCE solves the problem above since the reduction obtains both a target ciphertext and a secret key (real or fake) in the RNC security game. To complete the security proof, we use the certified deletion security of SKE. Here, the point is that the reduction can simulate a secret key by Reveal since the reduction is given ske.sk after a valid certificate is sent in the certified deletion security game.

If we use secret key RNCE instead of public key RNCE, we can achieve reusable SKE with certified deletion via the design idea above. Secret/public key RNCE can be constructed from IND-CPA SKE/PKE, respectively [CHK05, KNTY19], and SKE with certified deletion exists unconditionally [BI20]. Thus, we can achieve PKE (resp. reusable SKE) with certified deletion from IND-CPA PKE (resp. OWFs).

Note that the RNCE technique above is the fundamental technique in this work. We use this technique both in the quantum communication case and in the classical communication case.

Our Idea for ABE. We can extend the idea for PKE to the ABE setting. In this work, we focus on key-policy ABE, where a policy (resp. attribute) is embedded in a secret key (resp. ciphertext). The crucial tool is (receiver) non-committing ABE (NCABE), which we introduce in this work.

Although the definition of NCABE is basically a natural extension of that of RNCE, we describe algorithms of NCABE for clarity. It helps readers who are not familiar with normal ABE. The first four algorithms below are algorithms of normal ABE.

Setup(1^λ) $\to$ (pk, msk): This is a setup algorithm that generates a public key and a master secret key.

KeyGen(msk, P) $\to$ sk$_P$: This is a key generation algorithm that generates a secret key for a policy P.

Enc(pk, X, m) $\to$ CT$_X$: This is an encryption algorithm that generates a ciphertext of m under an attribute X.

Dec(sk$_P$, CT$_X$) $\to$ m' or $\perp$: This is a decryption algorithm that decrypts CT$_X$ if $P(X) = \top$. If $P(X) = \perp$, it outputs $\perp$.

FakeSetup(1^λ) $\to$ (pk, aux): This is a fake setup algorithm that generates a public key and a trapdoor auxiliary information aux.

FakeCT(pk, aux, X) $\to$ $\widetilde{\text{CT}}_X$: This is a fake ciphertext generation algorithm that generates a fake ciphertext $\widetilde{\text{CT}}_X$ under an attribute X.

FakeSK(pk, aux, P) $\to$ $\widetilde{\text{sk}}_P$: This is a fake key generation algorithm that generates a fake secret key $\widetilde{\text{sk}}_P$ for P.

Reveal(pk, aux, $\widetilde{\text{CT}}$, m) $\to$ $\widetilde{\text{msk}}$: This is a reveal algorithm that generates a fake master secret key $\widetilde{\text{msk}}$.

Roughly speaking, the NCABE security notion requires that the fake public key, master secret key, ciphertext, and secret keys are computationally indistinguishable from the normal public key, master key, ciphertext, and secret keys. It is easy to see that the hybrid encryption approach works in the ABE setting as well. Thus, the goal is to achieve an NCABE scheme.

Our NCABE construction follows the RNCE construction based on IND-CPA PKE [CHK05, KNTY19]. However, the crucial difference between the PKE and ABE settings is that, in the ABE setting, adversaries are given many secret keys for queried policies (that is, we consider collusion-resistance). There is an obstacle to achieving collusion resistance because secret keys for policies depend on a master secret key. Note that adversaries can send secret key queries *both before and after* the target ciphertext is given.

First, we explain the RNCE scheme from PKE. Although we explain the 1-bit plaintext case, it is easy to extend to the multi-bit case. The idea is the simple double encryption technique by Naor and Yung [NY90], but we do not need non-interactive zero-knowledge (NIZK). We generate two key pairs $(\mathsf{pk}_0, \mathsf{sk}_0)$ and $(\mathsf{pk}_1, \mathsf{sk}_1)$ and set $\mathsf{pk} := (\mathsf{pk}_0, \mathsf{pk}_1)$, $\mathsf{sk} := \mathsf{sk}_z$, and $\mathsf{aux} = (\mathsf{sk}_0, \mathsf{sk}_1, z^*)$ where $z, z^* \leftarrow \{0, 1\}$. A ciphertext consists of $\mathsf{Enc}(\mathsf{pk}_0, b)$ and $\mathsf{Enc}(\mathsf{pk}_1, b)$. We can decrypt the ciphertext by using sk_z. A fake ciphertext $\widetilde{\mathsf{CT}}$ is $(\mathsf{Enc}(\mathsf{pk}_{z^*}, 0), \mathsf{Enc}(\mathsf{pk}_{1-z^*}, 1))$. To generate a fake secret key for a plaintext m^*, the reveal algorithm outputs $\mathsf{sk}_{z^* \oplus m^*}$. It is easy to see that decrypting $\widetilde{\mathsf{CT}}$ with $\mathsf{sk}_{z^* \oplus m^*}$ yields m^*.

Our NCABE is based on the idea above. That is, we use two key pairs $(\mathsf{pk}_0, \mathsf{msk}_0)$ and $(\mathsf{pk}_1, \mathsf{msk}_1)$ of a normal ABE scheme ABE.(Setup, KeyGen, Enc, Dec), and a ciphertext consists of $(\mathsf{ABE}.\mathsf{Enc}(\mathsf{pk}_0, X, b), \mathsf{ABE}.\mathsf{Enc}(\mathsf{pk}_1, X, b))$ where X is an attribute. Our reveal algorithm outputs $\mathsf{msk}_{z^* \oplus m^*}$ for a plaintext m^* as in the PKE case. The problem is a secret key for a policy P. A naive idea is that a key generation algorithm outputs $\mathsf{sk}_P \leftarrow \mathsf{ABE}.\mathsf{KeyGen}(\mathsf{msk}_z, P)$ where $z \leftarrow \{0, 1\}$ is chosen in the setup algorithm, and a fake key generation algorithm outputs $\widetilde{\mathsf{sk}}_P \leftarrow \mathsf{ABE}.\mathsf{KeyGen}(\mathsf{msk}_{z^* \oplus m^*}, P)$. However, this apparently does not work since $\widetilde{\mathsf{sk}}_P$ depends on m^*. Unless $\widetilde{\mathsf{sk}}_P$ is independent of m^*, we cannot use NCABE to achieve ABE with certified deletion because ske.sk of SKE with certified deletion is sent *after* a valid certification is generated (ske.sk would be a plaintext of ABE in the hybrid encryption). To make a fake key generation be independent of m^*, we need to hide which master secret key is used to generate a secret key for P. If a secret key leaks information about which secret key (extracted from msk_0 or msk_1) is used, we cannot adaptively select a fake master secret key in the reveal algorithm.

iO helps us to overcome this hurdle. Our idea is as follows. A key generation algorithm outputs an obfuscated circuit of a circuit $\mathsf{D}[\mathsf{sk}_z]$ that takes a ciphertext $(\mathsf{abe}.\mathsf{CT}_0, \mathsf{abe}.\mathsf{CT}_1) := (\mathsf{ABE}.\mathsf{Enc}(\mathsf{pk}_0, X, b), \mathsf{ABE}.\mathsf{Enc}(\mathsf{pk}_1, X, b))$ and outputs $\mathsf{ABE}.\mathsf{Dec}(\mathsf{sk}_z, \mathsf{abe}.\mathsf{CT}_z)$ where $z \leftarrow \{0, 1\}$ and $\mathsf{sk}_z \leftarrow \mathsf{ABE}.\mathsf{KeyGen}(\mathsf{msk}_z, P)$ is hard-coded in D. A fake key generation algorithm outputs an obfuscated circuit of a circuit $\mathsf{D}_0[\mathsf{sk}_0]$ that takes $(\mathsf{abe}.\mathsf{CT}_0, \mathsf{abe}.\mathsf{CT}_1)$ and outputs $\mathsf{ABE}.\mathsf{Dec}(\mathsf{sk}_0, \mathsf{abe}.\mathsf{CT}_0)$ where $\mathsf{sk}_0 \leftarrow \mathsf{ABE}.\mathsf{KeyGen}(\mathsf{msk}_0, P)$ is hard-coded in D_0. Note that the fake secret key cannot be used to decrypt a fake ciphertext $(\mathsf{abe}.\mathsf{CT}_{z^*}, \mathsf{abe}.\mathsf{CT}_{1-z^*}) := (\mathsf{ABE}.\mathsf{Enc}(\mathsf{pk}_{z^*}, X, 0), \mathsf{ABE}.\mathsf{Enc}(\mathsf{pk}_{1-z^*}, X, 1))$ where $z^* \leftarrow \{0, 1\}$ since $P(X) = \bot$ must hold by the requirement on ABE security.

Since the decryption circuits D and D_0 are obfuscated, adversaries have no idea about which secret key (sk_0 or sk_1) is used for decryption. This idea is inspired by the functional encryption (FE) scheme by Garg et al. [GGH+16].

The final issue is that adversaries can detect whether a secret key is real or fake if they use an invalid ciphertext $(\mathsf{ABE.Enc}(pk_0, b), \mathsf{ABE.Enc}(pk_1, 1 - b))$ as an input to the obfuscated circuits. To prevent this attack, we use statistically sound NIZK to check the consistency of double encryption as the FE scheme by Garg et al. [GGH+16]. By the statistical soundness of NIZK, we can guarantee that the obfuscated decryption circuit does not accept invalid ciphertexts, and D and D_0 are functionally equivalent. Note that a secret key for policy P outputs $\perp$ for the target ciphertext since a target attribute X^* in the target ciphertext satisfies $P(X) = \perp$. We do not need the simulation-soundness, unlike the FE scheme by Garg et al. due to the following reason. In the FE scheme, plain PKE schemes are used for the double encryption technique and a secret key sk_0 or sk_1 is hard-coded in a functional decryption key. Before we use PKE security under pk_b, we need to switch the decryption key from sk_b to sk_{1-b} by iO security. During this phase, we need to use a fake simulated proof of NIZK. Thus, the simulation-soundness is required. However, in our ABE setting, a secret key for P (not the master secret keys msk_0, msk_1) is hard-coded in D (or D_0) above. Thanks to the ABE key oracle, sk_0 and sk_1 for P are always available in reductions. We can first use iO security to switch from D to D_0. After that, we change a real NIZK proof into a fake one. Thus, our NCABE scheme does not need the simulation-soundness. This observation enables us to achieve the adaptive security rather than the selective security, unlike the FE scheme by Garg et al.[2] Thus, we can achieve NCABE from iO and OWFs since adaptively secure standard ABE can be constructed from iO and OWFs.

1.4   Technical Overview Part II: Classical Communication Case

We provide an overview of how to achieve privately verifiable and publicly verifiable interactive encryption with certified deletion using classical communication in this section. We note that both of them rely on interactive encryption algorithms.

Privately Verifiable Construction. For realizing a privately verifiable construction with classical communication, we rely on *NTCF functions* [BCM+18, Mah18]. In this overview, we consider an ideal version, noise-free claw-free permutations for simplicity. A trapdoor claw-free permutation is $f : \{0,1\} \times \{0,1\}^w \to \{0,1\}^w$ such that (1) $f(0,\cdot)$ and $f(1,\cdot)$ are permutations over $\{0,1\}^w$, (2) given the description of f, it is hard to find x_0 and x_1 such that $f(0,x_0) = f(1,x_1)$, and (3) there is a trapdoor td that enables one to efficiently find x_0 and x_1 such that $f(0,x_0) = f(1,x_1) = y$ for any y. In addition, the existing work showed that (a noisy version of) it satisfies a property

---

[2] In the initial version of this work [NY21], we achieve only the selective security because we use statistical simulation-sound NIZK as the FE scheme by Garg et al. [GGH+16]. We improve the result.

called the *adaptive hardcore bit property* under the LWE assumption [BCM+18]. To explain this, suppose that one generates the state $\sum_{b,x} |b\rangle |x\rangle |f(b,x)\rangle$, and measures the third register in the computational basis to get a result y. Then the first and second registers collapse to the state $\frac{1}{\sqrt{2}} (|0\rangle |x_0\rangle + |1\rangle |x_1\rangle)$ with $f(0, x_0) = f(1, x_1) = y$. If one measures the state in the computational basis, the measurement outcome is $(0, x_0)$ or $(1, x_1)$. If, on the other hand, one measures the state in the Hadamard basis, the measurement outcome is (e, d) such that $e = d \cdot (x_0 \oplus x_1)$. The adaptive hardcore bit property roughly means that once one gets $(0, x_0)$ or $(1, x_1)$, it cannot output (e, d) such that $d \neq 0$ and $e = d \cdot (x_0 \oplus x_1)$ with probability better than $1/2 + \mathsf{negl}(\lambda)$. Note that this is a tight bound since $e = d \cdot (x_0 \oplus x_1)$ holds with probability $1/2$ if we randomly choose e. Existing works showed that this property can be amplified by parallel repetition [RS19, KNY20]: Specifically, let $(0, x_{i,0})$ and $(1, x_{i,1})$ be the preimages of y_i under f_i for $i \in [n]$ where $n = \omega(\log \lambda)$. Then once one gets a sequence $\{b_i, x_{i,b_i}\}_{i \in [n]}$ for some $b_1 \| ... \| b_n \in \{0,1\}^n$, it can get a sequence $\{e_i, d_i\}_{i \in [n]}$ such that $d_i \neq 0$ and $e_i = d_i \cdot (x_{i,0} \oplus x_{i,1})$ only with negligible probability.

We use this property to construct an encryption scheme with certified deletion. A natural idea would be as follows: The sender sends n functions $\{f_i\}_{i \in [n]}$ to the receiver, the receiver generates $\{y_i\}_{i \in [n]}$ along with states $\{\frac{1}{\sqrt{2}} (|0\rangle |x_{i,0}\rangle + |1\rangle |x_{i,1}\rangle)\}_{i \in [n]}$ as above and sends $\{y_i\}_{i \in [n]}$ to the sender, and the sender sends receiver a ciphertext CT decryptable only when $\{b_i, x_{i,b_i}\}_{i \in [n]}$ for some $b_1 \| ... \| b_n \in \{0,1\}^n$ is available. We discuss how to implement such a ciphertext later. We use $\{e_i, d_i\}_{i \in [n]}$ such that $e_i = d_i \cdot (x_{i,0} \oplus x_{i,1})$ as a deletion certificate. The receiver can decrypt the ciphertext by measuring the states in the computational basis, and once it outputs a valid deletion certificate, it must "forget" preimages by the amplified adaptive hardcore property and thus cannot decrypt the ciphertext. This idea can be implemented in a straightforward manner if we generate CT by (extractable) witness encryption [GGSW13, GKP+13] under the corresponding **NP** language. However, since witness encryption is a strong assumption, we want to avoid this. Indeed, we can find the following candidate construction using a hash function H modeled as a random oracle. We set the ciphertext as $\mathsf{CT} := \{\mathsf{CT}_{i,b}\}_{i \in [n], b \in \{0,1\}}$ where $\{m_i\}_{i \in [n]}$ is an n-out-of-n secret sharing of the message m and $\mathsf{CT}_{i,b} := m_i \oplus H(b \| x_{i,b})$. The intuition is that an adversary has to get m_i for all $i \in [n]$ to get m and it has to know $(0, x_{i,0})$ or $(1, x_{i,1})$ to know m_i. Therefore, it seems that any adversary that gets any information of m can be used to extract a sequence $\{b_i, x_{i,b_i}\}_{i \in [n]}$ for some $b_1 \| ... \| b_n \in \{0,1\}^n$. If this is shown, it is straightforward to prove that the adversary can get no information of m once it submits a valid deletion certificate by the amplified adaptive hardcore property as explained above. However, turning this intuition into a formal proof seems difficult. A common technique to extract information from adversary's random oracle queries is the one-way to hiding lemma [Unr15, AHU19]. The lemma roughly claims that if the adversary distinguishes $H(X)$ from random, then we would get X with non-negligible probability by measuring a randomly chosen query. Here, a problem is that we have to extract n strings $\{b_i, x_{i,b_i}\}_{i \in [n]}$ simultaneously. On the other hand, the extraction by the one-way to hiding lemma disturbs adversary's state by a measurement, and thus we cannot use this technique sequentially.[3]

The difficulty above comes from the fact that the sender cannot know which of $(0, x_{i,0})$ and $(1, x_{i,1})$ the receiver will get, and thus it has to send a ciphertext that can be decrypted in either case. To resolve this issue, we rely on the injective invariance, which roughly says that there is an injective function g that is computationally indistinguishable from f [Mah18]. First, suppose that we just use g instead of f in the above idea. Since g is injective, there is a unique preimage (b_i, x_i) of y_i, in which case the sender knows that the receiver will get $\{(b_i, x_i)\}_{i \in [n]}$ by the standard basis measurement. In this case, the aforementioned problem can be easily resolved by setting $\mathsf{CT} := m \oplus H(b_1 \| x_1 \| ... \| b_n \| x_n)$ as the ciphertext. In this case, it is easy to prove that we can extract $\{b_i, x_i\}_{i \in [n]}$ if an adversary obtains some information of m by applying the standard one-way to hiding lemma. However, the obvious problem is that the deletion certificate no longer works for g since the receiver's state collapses to a classical state after the measurement of $\{y_i\}_{i \in [n]}$ and thus the Hadamard basis measurement results in just uniform bits.

Our idea is to take advantages of both of them. Specifically, the sender sends functions $\{\eta_i\}_{i \in [n]}$, where η_i is the g-type function for $i \in S$ and it is the f-type function for $i \in [n] \setminus S$ with a certain set $S \subset [n]$. The receiver generates a set of states. Each state is a superposition of two preimages of a f-type function or a state encoding the unique preimage of a g-type function. The preimages of g-type functions are used for encryption/decryption, and the Hadamard measurement results are used for deletion certificate, whose validity is only checked on positions where f-type functions are used. We also include a ciphertext of the description of the subset S in the ciphertext. The ciphertext enables a legitimate receiver to know which position should be used in the decryption. More precisely, we set $\mathsf{CT} := (\mathsf{Enc}(S), m \oplus H(\{b_i, x_i\}_{i \in [S]}))$ where Enc is a PKE scheme with the RNC security.[4,5] A deletion certificate $\{e_i, d_i\}_{i \in [n]}$ is valid if we have $d_i \neq 0$ and $e_i = d_i \cdot (x_{i,0} \oplus x_{i,1})$ for all $i \in [n] \setminus S$. For the security proof of this construction, the amplified adaptive hardcore property cannot be directly used, because it is a property about f-type functions whereas the above construction mixes f-type functions and g-type functions, and what we want to have is the mutually-exclusive property between preimages of g-type functions and deletion certificates of f-type functions. To solve the problem, we introduce a new property which we call *the cut-and-choose adaptive hardcore property* (Lemma 4.1).

---

[3] A recent work by Coladangelo, Majenz, and Poremba [CMP20] studied what is called "simultaneous one-way to hiding lemma", but their setting is different from ours and their lemma cannot be used in our setting.

[4] We require Enc to satisfy the RNC security due to a similar reason to that in Sect. 1.3, which we omit to explain here.

[5] In the actual construction, there is an additional component that is needed for preventing an adversary from decrypting the ciphertext *before* outputting a valid deletion certificate without the decryption key. This is just a security as standard PKE and can be added easily. Thus, we omit this and focus on the security *after* outputting a valid deletion certificate.

The cut-and-choose adaptive hardcore property intuitively means that once the receiver issues a deletion certificate $\{e_i, d_i\}_{i \in [n]}$ that is valid for all $i \in [n] \setminus S$ before knowing S, it can no longer generate correct preimages $\{b_i, x_i\}_{i \in [S]}$ even if it receives S later. Intuitively, this holds because the only way to obtain such $\{e_i, d_i\}_{i \in [n]}$ before knowing S would be to measure the states in the Hadamard basis for all $i \in [n]$, in which case the receiver should forget all preimages. We show that the cut-and-choose adaptive hardcore property can be reduced to the adaptive hardcore bit property and injective invariance. The new property we show itself is of independent interest, and we believe it will be useful in many other applications of quantum cryptography.

Because the only known construction of NTCF functions [BCM+18, Mah18] assumes the LWE assumption, our construction of the interactive encryption with privately verifiable certified deletion with classical communication is also based on the LWE assumption, and our security proof is done in the QROM. We note that the construction only achieves private verification because verification of deletion certificates requires both of two preimages of f-type functions, which cannot be made public.

Publicly Verifiable Construction. The above construction is not publicly verifiable because the verification of the validity of (e_i, d_i) requires both preimages $x_{i,0}$ and $x_{i,1}$, which cannot be made public. One might notice that the validity check of the preimage can be done publicly, and might suggest the following construction: preimages are used for deletion certificate, and Hadamard measurement outcomes $\{e_i, d_i\}_{i \in [n]}$ are used as the decryption key of the encryption. Because a valid $\{e_i, d_i\}_{i \in [n]}$ is a witness of an **NP** statement, we could use (extractable) witness encryption [GGSW13, GKP+13] to ensure that a receiver can decrypt the message only if it knows a valid $\{e_i, d_i\}_{i \in [n]}$. However, this idea does not work because the statement of the witness encryption contains private information (i.e., preimages), and witness encryption ensures nothing about privacy of the statement under which a message is encrypted.

Our idea to solve the problem is to use the one-shot signature [AGKZ20]. Roughly speaking, one-shot signatures (with a message space $\{0, 1\}$) enable one to generate a classical public key pk along with a quantum secret key sk, which can be used to generate either of a signature σ_0 for message 0 or σ_1 for message 1, but not both. We note that a signature can be verified publicly.

We combine one-shot signatures with extractable witness encryption.[6] The encryption $\mathsf{Enc}(m)$ of a message m in our construction is a ciphertext of witness encryption of message m under the statement corresponding to the verification of one-shot signature for message 0. The deletion certificate is, on the other hand, a one-shot signature for message 1. Once a valid signature of 1 is issued, a valid signature of 0, which is a decryption key of our witness encryption, is no longer possible to generate due to the security of the one-shot signature. This intuitively

---

[6] We note that a combination of one-shot signatures and extractable witness encryption appeared in the work of Georgiou and Zhandry [GZ20] in a related but different context.

ensures the certified deletion security of our construction. Because signatures are publicly verifiable, the verification of our construction is also publicly verifiable. In the actual construction, in order to prevent an adversary from decrypting the ciphertext before issuing the deletion certificate, we add an additional layer of encryption, for which we use RNCE due to a similar reason to that in Sect. 1.3.

Unfortunately, the only known construction of the one-shot signature needs classical oracles. Thus, the security proof of existing one-shot signature constructions is a heuristic. Our publicly verifiable construction assumes the existence of provably secure one-shot signatures. It is an open question whether we can construct an interactive encryption with publicly verifiable certified deletion with classical communication based on only standard assumptions such as the LWE assumption.

2 Preliminaries

2.1 Notations and Mathematical Tools

We introduce basic notations and mathematical tools used in this paper.

In this paper, $x \leftarrow X$ denotes selecting an element from a finite set X uniformly at random, and $y \leftarrow \mathsf{A}(x)$ denotes assigning to y the output of a probabilistic or deterministic algorithm A on an input x. When we explicitly show that A uses randomness r, we write $y \leftarrow \mathsf{A}(x; r)$. When D is a distribution, $x \leftarrow D$ denotes sampling an element from D. Let $[\ell]$ denote the set of integers $\{1, \cdots, \ell\}$, λ denote a security parameter, and $y := z$ denote that y is set, defined, or substituted by z. For a string $s \in \{0,1\}^\ell$, $s[i]$ denotes i-th bit of s. QPT stands for quantum polynomial time. PPT stands for (classical) probabilistic polynomial time. For a subset $S \subseteq W$ of a set W, $\overline{S}$ is the complement of S, i.e., $\overline{S} := W \setminus S$.

A function $f : \mathbb{N} \to \mathbb{R}$ is a negligible function if for any constant c, there exists $\lambda_0 \in \mathbb{N}$ such that for any $\lambda > \lambda_0$, $f(\lambda) < \lambda^{-c}$. We write $f(\lambda) \leq \mathsf{negl}(\lambda)$ to denote $f(\lambda)$ being a negligible function. A function $g : \mathbb{N} \to \mathbb{R}$ is a noticeable function if there exist constants c and λ_0 such that for any $\lambda \geq \lambda_0$, $g(\lambda) \geq \lambda^{-c}$. The trace distance between two states ρ and σ is given by $\|\rho - \sigma\|_{\mathrm{tr}}$, where $\|A\|_{\mathrm{tr}} := \mathrm{Tr}\sqrt{A^\dagger A}$ is the trace norm. We call a function f a density on X if $f : X \to [0,1]$ such that $\sum_{x \in X} f(x) = 1$. For two densities f_0 and f_1 over the same finite domain X, the Hellinger distance between f_0 and f_1 is $\mathsf{H}^2(f_0, f_1) := 1 - \sum_{x \in X} \sqrt{f_0(x)f_1(x)}$.

2.2 Cryptographic Tools

In this section, we review cryptographic tools used in this paper. Some explanations are omitted, and given in the full version.

Encryption with Certified Deletion. Broadbent and Islam introduced the notion of encryption with certified deletion [BI20]. Their notion is for secret key encryption (SKE). They consider a setting where a secret key is used only once (that is, one-time SKE). Although it is easy to extend the definition to the reusable secret key setting, we describe the definition for the one-time setting in this section. We provide a definition that is accommodated to the reusable setting in the full version.

Definition 2.1 (One-Time SKE with Certified Deletion (Syntax)). *A one-time secret key encryption scheme with certified deletion is a tuple of QPT algorithms* (KeyGen, Enc, Dec, Del, Vrfy) *with plaintext space* $\mathcal{M}$ *and key space* $\mathcal{K}$.

KeyGen(1^λ) → sk: *The key generation algorithm takes as input the security parameter* 1^λ *and outputs a secret key* sk $\in \mathcal{K}$.

Enc(sk, m) → CT: *The encryption algorithm takes as input* sk *and a plaintext* $m \in \mathcal{M}$ *and outputs a ciphertext* CT.

Dec(sk, CT) → m' **or** ⊥: *The decryption algorithm takes as input* sk *and* CT *and outputs a plaintext* $m' \in \mathcal{M}$ *or* ⊥.

Del(CT) → cert: *The deletion algorithm takes as input* CT *and outputs a certification* cert.

Vrfy(sk, cert) → ⊤ **or** ⊥: *The verification algorithm takes* sk *and* cert *and outputs* ⊤ *or* ⊥.

Definition 2.2 (Correctness for One-Time SKE with Certified Deletion). *There are two types of correctness. One is decryption correctness and the other is verification correctness.*

Decryption Correctness: *There exists a negligible function* negl *such that for any* $\lambda \in \mathbb{N}$, $m \in \mathcal{M}$,

$$\Pr\left[\mathsf{Dec}(\mathsf{sk}, \mathsf{CT}) \neq m \, \middle| \, \begin{array}{l} \mathsf{sk} \leftarrow \mathsf{KeyGen}(1^\lambda) \\ \mathsf{CT} \leftarrow \mathsf{Enc}(\mathsf{sk}, m) \end{array}\right] \leq \mathsf{negl}(\lambda).$$

Verification Correctness: *There exists a negligible function* negl *such that for any* $\lambda \in \mathbb{N}$, $m \in \mathcal{M}$,

$$\Pr\left[\mathsf{Vrfy}(\mathsf{sk}, \mathsf{cert}) = \bot \, \middle| \, \begin{array}{l} \mathsf{sk} \leftarrow \mathsf{KeyGen}(1^\lambda) \\ \mathsf{CT} \leftarrow \mathsf{Enc}(\mathsf{sk}, m) \\ \mathsf{cert} \leftarrow \mathsf{Del}(\mathsf{CT}) \end{array}\right] \leq \mathsf{negl}(\lambda).$$

Definition 2.3 (Certified Deletion Security for One-Time SKE). *Let* $\Sigma = $ (KeyGen, Enc, Dec, Del, Vrfy) *be a secret key encryption with certified deletion. We consider the following security experiment* $\mathsf{Exp}_{\Sigma,\mathcal{A}}^{\mathsf{otsk\text{-}cert\text{-}del}}(\lambda, b)$.

1. *The challenger computes* sk $\leftarrow$ KeyGen(1^λ).
2. $\mathcal{A}$ *sends* $(m_0, m_1) \in \mathcal{M}^2$ *to the challenger.*
3. *The challenger computes* $\mathsf{CT}_b \leftarrow \mathsf{Enc}(\mathsf{sk}, m_b)$ *and sends* CT_b *to* $\mathcal{A}$.
4. $\mathcal{A}$ *sends* cert *to the challenger.*
5. *The challenger computes* Vrfy(sk, cert). *If the output is* ⊥, *the challenger sends* ⊥ *to* $\mathcal{A}$. *If the output is* ⊤, *the challenger sends* sk *to* $\mathcal{A}$.
6. $\mathcal{A}$ *outputs* $b' \in \{0, 1\}$.

We say that the Σ is OT-CD secure if for any QPT $\mathcal{A}$, it holds that

$$\mathsf{Adv}_{\Sigma,\mathcal{A}}^{\mathsf{otsk\text{-}cert\text{-}del}}(\lambda) := \left| \Pr\left[\mathsf{Exp}_{\Sigma,\mathcal{A}}^{\mathsf{otsk\text{-}cert\text{-}del}}(\lambda, 0) = 1\right] - \Pr\left[\mathsf{Exp}_{\Sigma,\mathcal{A}}^{\mathsf{otsk\text{-}cert\text{-}del}}(\lambda, 1) = 1\right] \right| \le \mathsf{negl}(\lambda).$$

We sometimes call it one-time SKE with certified deletion if it satisfies OT-CD security.

Remark 2.1. Definition 2.3 intuitively means that once the valid certificate is issued, decrypting the ciphertext becomes impossible. One might think that it would also be possible to define the inverse: once the ciphertext is decrypted, the valid certificate can no longer be issued. However, this property is impossible to achieve due to the decryption correctness (Definition 2.2). In fact, if the quantum decryption algorithm Dec on a quantum ciphertext CT succeeds with probability at least $1 - \mathsf{negl}(\lambda)$, then the gentle measurement lemma guarantees that CT is only negligibly disturbed, from which the valid certificate can be issued.

Remark 2.2. We modified the security definition of certified deletion due to the following reason. Broadbent and Islam [BI20] require ciphertext indistinguishability, which is security as a normal one-time SKE, in addition to the certified deletion security. We observe that these two security notions can be captured in a single security game if we allow the adversary to make a guess even if the deletion certificate is invalid.

We emphasize that in the existing construction of SKE with certified deletion, a secret key is a classical string though a ciphertext must be a quantum state. Broadbent and Islam prove the following theorem.

Theorem 2.1 (*[BI20]*)**.** *There exists OT-CD secure SKE with certified deletion with $\mathcal{M} = \{0,1\}^{\ell_m}$ and $\mathcal{K} = \{0,1\}^{\ell_k}$ where ℓ_m and ℓ_k are some polynomials, unconditionally.*

Receiver Non-committing Encryption. We introduce the notion of (public key) receiver non-committing encryption (RNCE) [CFGN96, JL00, CHK05], which is used in Sects. 3.2 and 4.3. See the full version for the definition of secret key RNCE.

Definition 2.4 (RNCE (Syntax)). *An RNCE scheme is a tuple of PPT algorithms* (KeyGen, Enc, Dec, Fake, Reveal) *with plaintext space $\mathcal{M}$.*

KeyGen$(1^\lambda) \to$ (pk, sk, aux): *The key generation algorithm takes as input the security parameter 1^λ and outputs a key pair* (pk, sk) *and an auxiliary information* aux.

Enc$($pk$, m) \to$ CT: *The encryption algorithm takes as input* pk *and a plaintext $m \in \mathcal{M}$ and outputs a ciphertext* CT.

Dec$($sk, CT$) \to m'$ **or** $\bot$: *The decryption algorithm takes as input* sk *and* CT *and outputs a plaintext m' or $\bot$.*

Fake$($pk, sk, aux$) \to \widetilde{\mathsf{CT}}$: *The fake encryption algorithm takes* pk, sk *and* aux, *and outputs a fake ciphertext $\widetilde{\mathsf{CT}}$.*

Reveal(pk, sk, aux, $\widetilde{\mathsf{CT}}, m) \to \widetilde{\mathsf{sk}}$: *The reveal algorithm takes* pk, sk, aux, $\widetilde{\mathsf{CT}}$ *and* m, *and outputs a fake secret key* $\widetilde{\mathsf{sk}}$.

Correctness is the same as that of PKE.

Definition 2.5 (Receiver Non-Committing (RNC) Security). *An RNCE scheme is RNC secure if it satisfies the following. Let* Σ = (KeyGen, Enc, Dec, Fake, Reveal) *be an RNCE scheme. We consider the following security experiment* $\mathsf{Exp}^{\mathsf{rec\text{-}nc}}_{\Sigma, \mathcal{A}}(\lambda, b)$.

1. *The challenger computes* (pk, sk, aux) $\leftarrow$ KeyGen(1^λ) *and sends* pk *to* $\mathcal{A}$.
2. $\mathcal{A}$ *sends a query* $m \in \mathcal{M}$ *to the challenger.*
3. *The challenger does the following.*
   - *If* $b = 0$, *the challenger generates* CT $\leftarrow$ Enc(pk, m) *and returns* (CT, sk) *to* $\mathcal{A}$.
   - *If* $b = 1$, *the challenger generates* $\widetilde{\mathsf{CT}}$ $\leftarrow$ Fake(pk, sk, aux) *and* $\widetilde{\mathsf{sk}}$ $\leftarrow$ Reveal(pk, sk, aux, $\widetilde{\mathsf{CT}}, m$) *and returns* ($\widetilde{\mathsf{CT}}, \widetilde{\mathsf{sk}}$) *to* $\mathcal{A}$.
4. $\mathcal{A}$ *outputs* $b' \in \{0, 1\}$.

Let $\mathsf{Adv}^{\mathsf{rec\text{-}nc}}_{\Sigma, \mathcal{A}}(\lambda)$ *be the advantage of the experiment above. We say that the* Σ *is RNC secure if for any QPT adversary, it holds that*

$$\mathsf{Adv}^{\mathsf{rec\text{-}nc}}_{\Sigma, \mathcal{A}}(\lambda) := \left| \Pr\left[\mathsf{Exp}^{\mathsf{rec\text{-}nc}}_{\Sigma, \mathcal{A}}(\lambda, 0) = 1\right] - \Pr\left[\mathsf{Exp}^{\mathsf{rec\text{-}nc}}_{\Sigma, \mathcal{A}}(\lambda, 1) = 1\right] \right| \leq \mathsf{negl}(\lambda).$$

Theorem 2.2 ([KNTY19], Sect. 7.2 in the eprint version). *If there exists an IND-CPA secure SKE/PKE scheme (against QPT adversaries), there exists an RNC secure secret/public key RNCE scheme (against QPT adversaries) with plaintext space* $\{0, 1\}^\ell$, *where* ℓ *is some polynomial, respectively.*

Note that Kitagawa, Nishimaki, Tanaka, and Yamakawa [KNTY19] prove the theorem above for the SKE case in the classical setting, but it is easy to extend their theorem to the post-quantum PKE setting by using post-quantum PKE schemes as building blocks. We also note that the core idea of Kitagawa et al. is based on the observation by Canetti, Halevi, and Katz [CHK05].

3   Public Key Encryption with Certified Deletion

In this section, we define the notion of PKE with certified deletion, which is a natural extension of SKE with certified deletion and present how to achieve PKE with certified deletion from OT-CD secure SKE and IND-CPA secure (standard) PKE.

3.1   Definition of PKE with Certified Deletion

The definition of PKE with certified deletion is an extension of SKE with certified deletion. Note that a verification key for verifying a certificate is generated in the encryption algorithm.

Definition 3.1 (PKE with Certified Deletion (Syntax)). *A PKE with certified deletion is a tuple of QPT algorithms* (KeyGen, Enc, Dec, Del, Vrfy) *with plaintext space* $\mathcal{M}$.

KeyGen$(1^\lambda) \to$ (pk, sk): *The key generation algorithm takes as input the security parameter* 1^λ *and outputs a classical key pair* (pk, sk).

Enc(pk, m) $\to$ (vk, CT): *The encryption algorithm takes as input the public key* pk *and a plaintext* $m \in \mathcal{M}$ *and outputs a classical verification key* vk *and a quantum ciphertext* CT.

Dec(sk, CT) $\to m'$ **or** $\perp$: *The decryption algorithm takes as input the secret key* sk *and the ciphertext* CT, *and outputs a classical plaintext* m' *or* $\perp$.

Del(CT) $\to$ cert: *The deletion algorithm takes as input the ciphertext* CT *and outputs a classical certificate* cert.

Vrfy(vk, cert) $\to \top$ **or** $\perp$: *The verification algorithm takes the verification key* vk *and the certificate* cert, *and outputs* $\top$ *or* $\perp$.

Definition 3.2 (Correctness for PKE with Certified Deletion). *There are two types of correctness. One is decryption correctness and the other is verification correctness.*

Decryption Correctness: *There exists a negligible function* negl *such that for any* $\lambda \in \mathbb{N}$, $m \in \mathcal{M}$,

$$\Pr\left[\text{Dec(sk, CT)} \neq m \;\middle|\; \begin{array}{l} (\text{pk, sk}) \leftarrow \text{KeyGen}(1^\lambda) \\ (\text{vk, CT}) \leftarrow \text{Enc(pk, }m) \end{array}\right] \leq \text{negl}(\lambda).$$

Verification Correctness: *There exists a negligible function* negl *such that for any* $\lambda \in \mathbb{N}$, $m \in \mathcal{M}$,

$$\Pr\left[\text{Vrfy(vk, cert)} = \perp \;\middle|\; \begin{array}{l} (\text{pk, sk}) \leftarrow \text{KeyGen}(1^\lambda) \\ (\text{vk, CT}) \leftarrow \text{Enc(pk, }m) \\ \text{cert} \leftarrow \text{Del(CT)} \end{array}\right] \leq \text{negl}(\lambda).$$

Definition 3.3 (Certified Deletion Security for PKE). *Let* Σ = (KeyGen, Enc, Dec, Del, Vrfy) *be a PKE with certified deletion scheme. We consider the following security experiment* $\text{Exp}_{\Sigma,\mathcal{A}}^{\text{pk-cert-del}}(\lambda, b)$.

1. *The challenger computes* (pk, sk) $\leftarrow$ KeyGen(1^λ) *and sends* pk *to* $\mathcal{A}$.
2. $\mathcal{A}$ *sends* $(m_0, m_1) \in \mathcal{M}^2$ *to the challenger.*
3. *The challenger computes* $(\text{vk}_b, \text{CT}_b) \leftarrow$ Enc(pk, m_b) *and sends* CT_b *to* $\mathcal{A}$.
4. *At some point,* $\mathcal{A}$ *sends* cert *to the challenger.*
5. *The challenger computes* Vrfy$(\text{vk}_b, \text{cert})$. *If the output is* $\perp$, *it sends* $\perp$ *to* $\mathcal{A}$. *If the output is* $\top$, *it sends* sk *to* $\mathcal{A}$.
6. $\mathcal{A}$ *outputs its guess* $b' \in \{0, 1\}$.

Let $\text{Adv}_{\Sigma,\mathcal{A}}^{\text{pk-cert-del}}(\lambda)$ *be the advantage of the experiment above. We say that the* Σ *is IND-CPA-CD secure if for any QPT adversary* $\mathcal{A}$, *it holds that*

$$\text{Adv}_{\mathcal{E},\mathcal{A}}^{\text{pk-cert-del}}(\lambda) := \left| \Pr\left[\text{Exp}_{\Sigma,\mathcal{A}}^{\text{pk-cert-del}}(\lambda, 0) = 1\right] - \Pr\left[\text{Exp}_{\Sigma,\mathcal{A}}^{\text{pk-cert-del}}(\lambda, 1) = 1\right] \right| \leq \text{negl}(\lambda).$$

3.2   PKE with Certified Deletion from PKE and SKE with Certified Deletion

In this section, we present how to construct a PKE scheme with certified deletion from an SKE scheme with certified deletion and an RNCE scheme, which can be constructed from standard IND-CPA PKE schemes.

Our PKE Scheme. We construct $\Sigma_{pkcd} = (KeyGen, Enc, Dec, Del, Vrfy)$ with plaintext space $\mathcal{M}$ from an SKE with certified deletion scheme $\Sigma_{skcd} = SKE.(Gen, Enc, Dec, Del, Vrfy)$ with plaintext space $\mathcal{M}$ and key space $\mathcal{K}$ and a public key RNCE scheme $\Sigma_{rnce} = RNCE.(KeyGen, Enc, Dec, Fake, Reveal)$ with plaintext space $\mathcal{K}$.

$KeyGen(1^\lambda)$:
- Generate $(rnce.pk, rnce.sk, rnce.aux) \leftarrow RNCE.KeyGen(1^\lambda)$ and output $(pk, sk) := (rnce.pk, rnce.sk)$.

$Enc(pk, m)$:
- Parse $pk = rnce.pk$.
- Generate $ske.sk \leftarrow SKE.Gen(1^\lambda)$.
- Compute $rnce.CT \leftarrow RNCE.Enc(rnce.pk, ske.sk)$ and $ske.CT \leftarrow SKE.Enc(ske.sk, m)$.
- Output $CT := (rnce.CT, ske.CT)$ and $vk := ske.sk$.

$Dec(sk, CT)$:
- Parse $sk = rnce.sk$ and $CT = (rnce.CT, ske.CT)$.
- Compute $sk' \leftarrow RNCE.Dec(rnce.sk, rnce.CT)$.
- Compute and output $m' \leftarrow SKE.Dec(sk', ske.CT)$.

$Del(CT)$:
- Parse $CT = (rnce.CT, ske.CT)$.
- Generate $ske.cert \leftarrow SKE.Del(ske.CT)$.
- Output $cert := ske.cert$.

$Vrfy(vk, cert)$:
- Parse $vk = ske.sk$ and $cert = ske.cert$.
- Output $b \leftarrow SKE.Vrfy(ske.sk, ske.cert)$.

Correctness. The decryption and verification correctness easily follow from the correctness of Σ_{rnce} and Σ_{skcd}.

Security. We prove the following theorem.

Theorem 3.1 *If Σ_{rnce} is RNC secure and Σ_{skcd} is OT-CD secure, Σ_{pkcd} is IND-CPA-CD secure.*

Proof of Theorem 3.1 Let $\mathcal{A}$ be a QPT adversary and $b \in \{0, 1\}$ be a bit. We define the following hybrid game $Hyb(b)$.

Hyb(b): This is the same as $\mathsf{Exp}^{\mathsf{pk\text{-}cert\text{-}del}}_{\Sigma_{\mathsf{pkcd}},\mathcal{A}}(\lambda,b)$ except that the challenger generate the target ciphertext as follows. It generates $\mathsf{ske.sk} \leftarrow \mathsf{SKE.Gen}(1^\lambda)$ and computes $\mathsf{rnce.CT}^* \leftarrow \mathsf{RNCE.Fake}(\mathsf{rnce.pk}, \mathsf{rnce.sk}, \mathsf{rnce.aux})$ and $\mathsf{ske.CT}^* \leftarrow \mathsf{SKE.Enc}(\mathsf{ske.sk}, m_b)$. The target ciphertext is $\mathsf{CT}^* := (\mathsf{rnce.CT}^*, \mathsf{ske.CT}^*)$. In addition, we reveal $\widetilde{\mathsf{sk}} \leftarrow \mathsf{Reveal}(\mathsf{rnce.pk}, \mathsf{rnce.sk}, \mathsf{rnce.aux}, \mathsf{rnce.CT}^*, \mathsf{ske.sk})$ instead of $\mathsf{rnce.sk}$.

$\square$

Proposition 3.1. *If Σ_{rnce} is RNC secure,* $\left| \Pr\left[\mathsf{Exp}^{\mathsf{pk\text{-}cert\text{-}del}}_{\Sigma_{\mathsf{pkcd}},\mathcal{A}}(\lambda,b) = 1 \right] - \Pr[\mathsf{Hyb}(b) = 1] \right| \leq$ $\mathsf{negl}(\lambda)$.

Proof of Proposition 3.1. We construct an adversary $\mathcal{B}_{\mathsf{rnce}}$ that breaks the RNC security of Σ_{rnce} by assuming that $\mathcal{A}$ distinguishes these two experiments. First, $\mathcal{B}_{\mathsf{rnce}}$ is given $\mathsf{rnce.pk}$ from the challenger of $\mathsf{Exp}^{\mathsf{rec\text{-}nc}}_{\Sigma_{\mathsf{rnce}},\mathcal{B}_{\mathsf{rnce}}}(\lambda,b')$ for $b' \in \{0,1\}$. $\mathcal{B}_{\mathsf{rnce}}$ generates $\mathsf{ske.sk} \leftarrow \mathsf{SKE.Gen}(1^\lambda)$ and sends $\mathsf{rnce.pk}$ to $\mathcal{A}$. When $\mathcal{A}$ sends (m_0, m_1), $\mathcal{B}_{\mathsf{rnce}}$ sends $\mathsf{ske.sk}$ to the challenger of $\mathsf{Exp}^{\mathsf{rec\text{-}nc}}_{\Sigma_{\mathsf{rnce}},\mathcal{B}_{\mathsf{rnce}}}(\lambda,b')$, receives $(\mathsf{rnce.CT}^*, \widetilde{\mathsf{sk}})$, and generates $\mathsf{ske.CT} \leftarrow \mathsf{SKE.Enc}(\mathsf{ske.sk}, m_b)$. $\mathcal{B}_{\mathsf{rnce}}$ sends $(\mathsf{rnce.CT}^*, \mathsf{ske.CT})$ to $\mathcal{A}$ as the challenge ciphertext. At some point, $\mathcal{A}$ outputs cert. If $\mathsf{SKE.Vrfy}(\mathsf{ske.sk}, \mathsf{cert}) = \top$, $\mathcal{B}_{\mathsf{rnce}}$ sends $\widetilde{\mathsf{sk}}$ to $\mathcal{A}$. Otherwise, $\mathcal{B}_{\mathsf{rnce}}$ sends $\bot$ to $\mathcal{A}$. Finally, $\mathcal{B}_{\mathsf{rnce}}$ outputs whatever $\mathcal{A}$ outputs.

- If $b' = 0$, i.e., $(\mathsf{rnce.CT}^*, \widetilde{\mathsf{sk}}) = (\mathsf{RNCE.Enc}(\mathsf{rnce.pk}, \mathsf{ske.sk}), \mathsf{rnce.sk})$, $\mathcal{B}_{\mathsf{rnce}}$ perfectly simulates $\mathsf{Exp}^{\mathsf{pk\text{-}cert\text{-}del}}_{\Sigma_{\mathsf{pkcd}},\mathcal{A}}(\lambda,b)$.
- If $b' = 1$, i.e., $(\mathsf{rnce.CT}^*, \widetilde{\mathsf{sk}}) = (\mathsf{RNCE.Fake}(\mathsf{rnce.pk}, \mathsf{rnce.sk}, \mathsf{rnce.aux}), \mathsf{RNCE.Reveal}(\mathsf{rnce.pk}, \mathsf{rnce.sk}, \mathsf{rnce.aux}, \mathsf{rnce.CT}^*, \mathsf{ske.sk}))$, $\mathcal{B}_{\mathsf{rnce}}$ perfectly simulates $\mathsf{Hyb}(b)$.

Thus, if $\mathcal{A}$ distinguishes the two experiments, $\mathcal{B}_{\mathsf{rnce}}$ breaks the RNC security of Σ_{rnce}. This completes the proof. $\square$

Proposition 3.2. *If Σ_{skcd} is OT-CD secure,* $|\Pr[\mathsf{Hyb}(0) = 1] - \Pr[\mathsf{Hyb}(1) = 1]| \leq \mathsf{negl}(\lambda)$.

Proof. of Proposition 3.2. We construct an adversary $\mathcal{B}_{\mathsf{skcd}}$ that breaks the OT-CD security of Σ_{skcd} assuming that $\mathcal{A}$ distinguishes these two experiments. $\mathcal{B}_{\mathsf{skcd}}$ plays the experiment $\mathsf{Exp}^{\mathsf{otsk\text{-}cert\text{-}del}}_{\Sigma_{\mathsf{skcd}},\mathcal{B}_{\mathsf{skcd}}}(\lambda,b')$ for some $b' \in \{0,1\}$. First, $\mathcal{B}_{\mathsf{skcd}}$ generates $(\mathsf{rnce.pk}, \mathsf{rnce.sk}, \mathsf{rnce.aux}) \leftarrow \mathsf{RNCE.KeyGen}(1^\lambda)$ and sends $\mathsf{rnce.pk}$ to $\mathcal{A}$. When $\mathcal{A}$ sends (m_0, m_1), $\mathcal{B}_{\mathsf{skcd}}$ sends (m_0, m_1) to the challenger of $\mathsf{Exp}^{\mathsf{otsk\text{-}cert\text{-}del}}_{\Sigma_{\mathsf{skcd}},\mathcal{B}_{\mathsf{skcd}}}(\lambda,b')$, receives $\mathsf{ske.CT}^*$, and generates $\widetilde{\mathsf{rnce.CT}} \leftarrow \mathsf{RNCE.Fake}(\mathsf{rnce.pk}, \mathsf{rnce.sk}, \mathsf{rnce.aux})$. $\mathcal{B}_{\mathsf{skcd}}$ sends $(\widetilde{\mathsf{rnce.CT}}, \mathsf{ske.CT}^*)$ to $\mathcal{A}$ as the challenge ciphertext. At some point, $\mathcal{A}$ outputs cert. $\mathcal{B}_{\mathsf{skcd}}$ passes cert to the challenger of OT-CD SKE. If the challenger returns $\mathsf{ske.sk}$, $\mathcal{B}_{\mathsf{skcd}}$ generates $\widetilde{\mathsf{sk}} \leftarrow \mathsf{RNCE.Reveal}(\mathsf{rnce.pk}, \mathsf{rnce.sk}, \mathsf{rnce.aux}, \widetilde{\mathsf{rnce.CT}}, \mathsf{ske.sk})$ and sends $\widetilde{\mathsf{sk}}$ to $\mathcal{A}$. Otherwise, $\mathcal{B}_{\mathsf{skcd}}$ sends $\bot$ to $\mathcal{A}$. Finally, $\mathcal{B}_{\mathsf{skcd}}$ outputs whatever $\mathcal{A}$ outputs.

- If $b' = 0$, i.e., $\mathsf{ske.CT}^* = \mathsf{SKE.Enc}(\mathsf{ske.sk}, m_0)$, $\mathcal{B}_{\mathsf{skcd}}$ perfectly simulates $\mathsf{Hyb}(0)$.

- If $b' = 1$, i.e., $\mathsf{ske.CT}^* = \mathsf{SKE.Enc}(\mathsf{ske.sk}, m_1)$, $\mathcal{B}_{\mathsf{skcd}}$ perfectly simulates $\mathsf{Hyb}(1)$.

Thus, if $\mathcal{A}$ distinguishes the two experiments, $\mathcal{B}_{\mathsf{skcd}}$ breaks the OT-CD security. This completes the proof. $\square$

By Propositions 3.1 and 3.2, we immediately obtain Theorem 3.1.

$\square$

By Theorems 2.1, 2.2 and 3.1, we immediately obtain the following corollary.

Corollary 3.1. *If there exists IND-CPA secure PKE against QPT adversaries, there exists IND-CPA-CD secure PKE with certified deletion.*

Reusable SKE with Certified Deletion. We can construct a secret key variant of Σ_{pkcd} above (that is, reusable SKE with certified deletion) by replacing Σ_{rnce} with a secret key RNCE scheme. We omit the proof since it is almost the same as that of Theorem 3.1. By Theorem 2.2 and the fact that OWFs imply (reusable) SKE [HILL99, GGM86], we also obtain the following theorem.

Theorem 3.2. *If there exists OWF against QPT adversaries, there exists IND-CPA-CD secure SKE with certified deletion.*

See the full version for the definition and construction of reusable SKE with certified deletion.

3.3   Attribute-Based Encryption with Certified Deletion

By extending the idea in the previous subsections, we construct ABE with certified deletion based on indistinguishability obfuscation and one-way functions. See the full version for details.

4   Interactive Encryption with Certified Deletion and Classical Communication

In this section, we define the notion of interactive encryption with certified deletion and classical communication, and construct it from the LWE assumption in the QROM. In Sect. 4.1, we present the definition of the interactive encryption with certified deletion and classical communication. In Sect. 4.2, we introduce what we call the *cut-and-choose adaptive hardcore property*, which is used in the security proof of the interactive encryption with certified deletion and classical communication. In Sect. 4.3, we construct an interactive encryption with certified deletion and classical communication, and show its security.

4.1 Definition of Interactive Encryption with Certified Deletion and Classical Communication

We define interactive encryption with certified deletion and classical communication. Note that the encryption algorithm of an interactive encryption with certified deletion and classical communication is interactive unlike PKE with certified deletion and quantum communication as defined in Definition 3.1. It is easy to see that the interaction is necessary if we only allow classical communication.

Definition 4.1 (Interactive Encryption with Certified Deletion and Classical Communication (Syntax)). *An interactive encryption scheme with certified deletion and classical communication is a tuple of quantum algorithms* (KeyGen, Enc, Dec, Del, Vrfy) *with plaintext space* $\mathcal{M}$.

KeyGen(1^λ) $\rightarrow$ (pk, sk): *The key generation algorithm takes as input the security parameter* 1^λ *and outputs a classical key pair* (pk, sk).

Enc⟨$\mathcal{S}$(pk, m), $\mathcal{R}$⟩ $\rightarrow$ (vk, CT): *This is an interactive process between a classical sender* $\mathcal{S}$ *with input* pk *and a plaintext* $m \in \mathcal{M}$, *and a quantum receiver* $\mathcal{R}$ *without input. After exchanging classical messages,* $\mathcal{S}$ *outputs a classical verification key* vk *and* $\mathcal{R}$ *outputs a quantum ciphertext* CT.

Dec(sk, CT) $\rightarrow$ m' **or** $\perp$: *The decryption algorithm takes as input the secret key* sk *and the ciphertext* CT, *and outputs a plaintext* m' *or* $\perp$.

Del(CT) $\rightarrow$ cert: *The deletion algorithm takes as input the ciphertext* CT *and outputs a classical certificate* cert.

Vrfy(vk, cert) $\rightarrow$ $\top$ **or** $\perp$: *The verification algorithm takes the verification key* vk *and the certificate* CT, *and outputs* $\top$ *or* $\perp$.

Definition 4.2 (Correctness for Interactive Encryption with Certified Deletion and Classical Communication). *There are two types of correctness. One is decryption correctness and the other is verification correctness.*

Decryption Correctness: *For any* $\lambda \in \mathbb{N}$, $m \in \mathcal{M}$,

$$\Pr\left[\mathsf{Dec}(\mathsf{sk}, \mathsf{CT}) \neq m \,\middle|\, \begin{array}{l} (\mathsf{pk}, \mathsf{sk}) \leftarrow \mathsf{KeyGen}(1^\lambda) \\ (\mathsf{vk}, \mathsf{CT}) \leftarrow \mathsf{Enc}\langle \mathcal{S}(\mathsf{pk}, m), \mathcal{R}\rangle \end{array}\right] \leq \mathsf{negl}(\lambda).$$

Verification Correctness: *For any* $\lambda \in \mathbb{N}$, $m \in \mathcal{M}$,

$$\Pr\left[\mathsf{Vrfy}(\mathsf{vk}, \mathsf{cert}) = \perp \,\middle|\, \begin{array}{l} (\mathsf{pk}, \mathsf{sk}) \leftarrow \mathsf{KeyGen}(1^\lambda) \\ (\mathsf{vk}, \mathsf{CT}) \leftarrow \mathsf{Enc}\langle \mathcal{S}(\mathsf{pk}, m), \mathcal{R}\rangle \\ \mathsf{cert} \leftarrow \mathsf{Del}(\mathsf{CT}) \end{array}\right] \leq \mathsf{negl}(\lambda).$$

Definition 4.3 (Certified Deletion Security for Interactive Encryption with Classical Communication). *Let* $\Sigma = $ (KeyGen, Enc, Dec, Del, Vrfy) *be a PKE scheme with certified deletion and classical communication. We consider the following security experiment* $\mathsf{Exp}_{\Sigma, \mathcal{A}}^{\mathsf{ccpk\text{-}cert\text{-}del}}(\lambda, b)$.

1. *The challenger computes* (pk, sk) $\leftarrow$ KeyGen(1^λ) *and sends* pk *to* $\mathcal{A}$.

2. $\mathcal{A}$ sends $(m_0, m_1) \in \mathcal{M}^2$ to the challenger.
3. The challenger and $\mathcal{A}$ jointly execute $(\mathsf{vk}_b, \mathsf{CT}_b) \leftarrow \mathsf{Enc}\langle \mathcal{S}(\mathsf{pk}, m_b), \mathcal{A}(\mathsf{pk})\rangle$ where the challenger plays the role of the sender and $\mathcal{A}$ plays the role of the receiver.
4. At some point, $\mathcal{A}$ sends cert to the challenger.
5. The challenger computes $\mathsf{Vrfy}(\mathsf{vk}_b, \mathsf{cert})$. If the output is $\perp$, the challenger sends $\perp$ to $\mathcal{A}$. If the output is $\top$, the challenger sends sk to $\mathcal{A}$.
6. $\mathcal{A}$ outputs its guess $b' \in \{0, 1\}$.

Let $\mathsf{Adv}^{\mathsf{ccpk\text{-}cert\text{-}del}}_{\Sigma, \mathcal{A}}(\lambda)$ be the advantage of the experiment above. We say that the Σ is IND-CPA-CD secure if for any QPT adversary $\mathcal{A}$, it holds that

$$\mathsf{Adv}^{\mathsf{ccpk\text{-}cert\text{-}del}}_{\Sigma, \mathcal{A}}(\lambda) := \left| \Pr\left[\mathsf{Exp}^{\mathsf{ccpk\text{-}cert\text{-}del}}_{\Sigma, \mathcal{A}}(\lambda, 0) = 1\right] - \Pr\left[\mathsf{Exp}^{\mathsf{ccpk\text{-}cert\text{-}del}}_{\Sigma, \mathcal{A}}(\lambda, 1) = 1\right] \right| \leq \mathsf{negl}(\lambda).$$

4.2 Preparation: Cut-and-Choose Adaptive Hardcore Property

We prove that any injective invariant NTCF family satisfies a property which we call the *cut-and-choose adaptive hardcore property*, which is used in the security proof of our interactive encryption with certified deletion with classical communication.

Lemma 4.1 (Cut-and-Choose Adaptive Hardcore Property). *Let $\mathcal{F}$ be an injective invariant NTCF family and $\mathcal{G}$ be the corresponding trapdoor injective family. Then $\mathcal{F}$ and $\mathcal{G}$ satisfy what we call the* cut-and-choose adaptive hardcore *property defined below. For a QPT adversary $\mathcal{A}$ and a positive integer n, we consider the following experiment $\mathsf{Exp}^{\mathsf{cut\text{-}and\text{-}choose}}_{(\mathcal{F}, \mathcal{G}), \mathcal{A}}(\lambda, n)$.*

1. *The challenger chooses a uniform subset $S \subseteq [4n]$ such that $|S| = 2n$.[7]*
2. *The challenger generates $(\mathsf{k}_i, \mathsf{td}_i) \leftarrow \mathsf{Gen}_{\mathcal{G}}(1^\lambda)$ for all $i \in S$ and $(\mathsf{k}_i, \mathsf{td}_i) \leftarrow \mathsf{Gen}_{\mathcal{F}}(1^\lambda)$ for all $i \in \overline{S}$ and sends $\{\mathsf{k}_i\}_{i \in [4n]}$ to $\mathcal{A}$.*
3. *$\mathcal{A}$ sends $\{y_i, d_i, e_i\}_{i \in [4n]}$ to the challenger.*
4. *The challenger computes $x_{i,\beta} \leftarrow \mathsf{Inv}_{\mathcal{F}}(\mathsf{td}_i, \beta, y_i)$ for all $(i, \beta) \in \overline{S} \times \{0, 1\}$ and checks if $d_i \in G_{\mathsf{k}_i, 0, x_{i,0}} \cap G_{\mathsf{k}_i, 1, x_{i,1}}$ and $e_i = d_i \cdot (J(x_{i,0}) \oplus J(x_{i,1}))$ hold for all $i \in \overline{S}$. If they do not hold for some $i \in \overline{S}$, the challenger immediately aborts and the experiment returns 0.*
5. *The challenger sends S to $\mathcal{A}$.*
6. *$\mathcal{A}$ sends $\{b_i, x_i\}_{i \in S}$ to the challenger.*
7. *The challenger checks if $\mathsf{Chk}_{\mathcal{G}}(\mathsf{k}_i, b_i, x_i, y_i) = 1$ holds for all $i \in S$. If this holds for all $i \in S$, the experiment returns 1. Otherwise, it returns 0.*

Then for any n such that $n \leq \mathsf{poly}(\lambda)$ and $n = \omega(\log \lambda)$, it holds that

$$\mathsf{Adv}^{\mathsf{cut\text{-}and\text{-}choose}}_{(\mathcal{F}, \mathcal{G}), \mathcal{A}}(\lambda, n) := \Pr\left[\mathsf{Exp}^{\mathsf{cut\text{-}and\text{-}choose}}_{(\mathcal{F}, \mathcal{G}), \mathcal{A}}(\lambda, n) = 1\right] \leq \mathsf{negl}(\lambda).$$

Its proof is given in the full version.

---

[7] We can also take $S \subseteq [2n]$ such that $|S| = n$, but we do as above just for convenience in the proof.

4.3 Construction

We construct an interactive encryption scheme with certified deletion and classical communication $\Sigma_{cccd} = (\mathsf{KeyGen}, \mathsf{Enc}, \mathsf{Dec}, \mathsf{Del}, \mathsf{Vrfy})$ with plaintext space $\mathcal{M} = \{0,1\}^\ell$ from an NTCF family $\mathcal{F}$ with the corresponding trapdoor injective family $\mathcal{G}$ for which we use similar notations as in [Mah18], a public key RNCE scheme $\Sigma_{rnce} = \mathsf{RNCE}.(\mathsf{KeyGen}, \mathsf{Enc}, \mathsf{Dec}, \mathsf{Fake}, \mathsf{Reveal})$ with plaintext space $\{S \subseteq [4n] : |S| = 2n\}$ where n is a positive integer such that $n \leq \mathrm{poly}(\lambda)$ and $n = \omega(\log \lambda)$ and we just write S to mean the description of the set S by abuse of notation, a OW-CPA secure PKE scheme $\Sigma_{ow} = \mathsf{OW}.(\mathsf{KeyGen}, \mathsf{Enc}, \mathsf{Dec})$ with plaintext space $\{0,1\}^\lambda$, and a hash function H from $\{0,1\}^\lambda \times (\{0,1\} \times \mathcal{X})^{2n}$ to $\{0,1\}^\ell$ modeled as a quantumly-accessible random oracle.

$\mathsf{KeyGen}(1^\lambda)$:
- Generate
  $(\mathsf{rnce.pk}, \mathsf{rnce.sk}, \mathsf{rnce.aux}) \leftarrow \mathsf{RNCE}.\mathsf{KeyGen}(1^\lambda)$ and $(\mathsf{ow.pk}, \mathsf{ow.sk}) \leftarrow \mathsf{OW}.\mathsf{KeyGen}(1^\lambda)$ and output $(\mathsf{pk}, \mathsf{sk}) := ((\mathsf{rnce.pk}, \mathsf{ow.pk}), (\mathsf{rnce.sk}, \mathsf{ow.sk}))$.

$\mathsf{Enc}\langle \mathcal{S}(\mathsf{pk}, m), \mathcal{R}\rangle$: This is an interactive protocol between a sender $\mathcal{S}$ with input (pk, m) and a receiver $\mathcal{R}$ without input that works as follows.
- $\mathcal{S}$ parses $\mathsf{pk} = (\mathsf{rnce.pk}, \mathsf{ow.pk})$.
- $\mathcal{S}$ chooses a uniformly random subset $S \subseteq [4n]$ such that $|S| = 2n$, generates

$$(k_i, td_i) \leftarrow \begin{cases} \mathsf{Gen}_\mathcal{G}(1^\lambda) & i \in S \\ \mathsf{Gen}_\mathcal{F}(1^\lambda) & i \in \overline{S} \end{cases}$$

for $i \in [4n]$, and sends $\{k_i\}_{i \in [4n]}$ to $\mathcal{R}$.
- For $i \in [4n]$, $\mathcal{R}$ generates a quantum state

$$|\psi_i'\rangle = \begin{cases} \frac{1}{\sqrt{|\mathcal{X}|}} \sum_{x \in \mathcal{X}, y \in \mathcal{Y}, b \in \{0,1\}} \sqrt{(g_{k_i,b}(x))(y)} |b, x\rangle |y\rangle & (i \in S) \\ \frac{1}{\sqrt{|\mathcal{X}|}} \sum_{x \in \mathcal{X}, y \in \mathcal{Y}, b \in \{0,1\}} \sqrt{(f_{k_i,b}'(x))(y)} |b, x\rangle |y\rangle & (i \in \overline{S}) \end{cases}$$

by using Samp, measure the last register to obtain $y_i \in \mathcal{Y}$, and let $|\phi_i'\rangle$ be the post-measurement state where the measured register is discarded. Note that this can be done without knowing S since $\mathsf{Samp}_\mathcal{F} = \mathsf{Samp}_\mathcal{G}$, which is just denoted by Samp. Then, we can see that for all $i \in [4n]$, $|\phi_i'\rangle$ has a negligible trace distance from the following state:

$$|\phi_i\rangle = \begin{cases} |b_i\rangle |x_i\rangle & (i \in S) \\ \frac{1}{\sqrt{2}} (|0\rangle |x_{i,0}\rangle + |1\rangle |x_{i,1}\rangle) & (i \in \overline{S}) \end{cases}$$

where $(x_i, b_i) \leftarrow \mathsf{Inv}_\mathcal{G}(td_i, y_i)$ for $i \in S$ and $x_{i,\beta} \leftarrow \mathsf{Inv}_\mathcal{F}(td_i, \beta, y_i)$ for $(i, \beta) \in \overline{S} \times \{0,1\}$.[8] $\mathcal{R}$ sends $\{y_i\}_{i \in [4n]}$ to $\mathcal{S}$ and keeps $\{|\phi_i'\rangle\}_{i \in [4n]}$.

---

[8] Indeed, $|\phi_i'\rangle = |\phi_i\rangle$ for $i \in S$.

- S chooses $K \leftarrow \{0,1\}^\lambda$ and computes $(b_i, x_i) \leftarrow \mathsf{Inv}_{\mathcal{G}}(\mathsf{td}_i, y_i)$ for all $i \in S$. If $\mathsf{Chk}_{\mathcal{G}}(k_i, b_i, x_i, y_i) = 0$ for some $i \in S$, S returns $\perp$ to $\mathcal{R}$. Otherwise, let $i_1, ..., i_{2n}$ be the elements of S in the ascending order. S sets $Z := (K, (b_{i_1}, x_{i_1}), (b_{i_2}, x_{i_2}), ..., (b_{i_{2n}}, x_{i_{2n}}))$, computes

$$\mathsf{rnce.CT} \leftarrow \mathsf{RNCE.Enc}(\mathsf{rnce.pk}, S),$$
$$\mathsf{ow.CT} \leftarrow \mathsf{OW.Enc}(\mathsf{ow.pk}, K),$$
$$\mathsf{CT_{msg}} := m \oplus H(Z),$$

  and sends $(\mathsf{rnce.CT}, \mathsf{ow.CT}, \mathsf{CT_{msg}})$ to $\mathcal{R}$.
- S outputs $\mathsf{vk} := \{\mathsf{td}_i, y_i\}_{i \in \overline{S}}$ and $\mathcal{R}$ outputs $\mathsf{CT} := (\{|\phi'_i\rangle\}_{i \in [4n]}, \mathsf{rnce.CT}, \mathsf{ow.CT}, \mathsf{CT_{msg}})$.

$\mathsf{Dec}(\mathsf{sk}, \mathsf{CT})$:
- Parse $\mathsf{sk} = (\mathsf{rnce.sk}, \mathsf{ow.sk})$ and $\mathsf{CT} = (\{|\phi'_i\rangle\}_{i \in [4n]}, \mathsf{rnce.CT}, \mathsf{ow.CT}, \mathsf{CT_{msg}})$.
- Compute $S' \leftarrow \mathsf{RNCE.Dec}(\mathsf{rnce.sk}, \mathsf{rnce.CT})$.
- Compute $K' \leftarrow \mathsf{OW.Dec}(\mathsf{ow.sk}, \mathsf{ow.CT})$.
- For all $i \in S'$, measure $|\phi'_i\rangle$ in the computational basis and let (b'_i, x'_i) be the outcome.
- Compute and output $m' := \mathsf{CT_{msg}} \oplus H(K', (b'_{i_1}, x'_{i_1}), (b'_{i_2}, x'_{i_2}), ..., (b'_{i_{2n}}, x'_{i_{2n}}))$ where $i_1, ..., i_{2n}$ are the elements of S' in the ascending order.[9]

$\mathsf{Del}(\mathsf{CT})$:
- Parse $\mathsf{CT} = (\{|\phi'_i\rangle\}_{i \in [4n]}, \mathsf{rnce.CT}, \mathsf{ow.CT}, \mathsf{CT_{msg}})$.
- For all $i \in [4n]$, evaluate the function J on the second register of $|\phi'_i\rangle$. That is, apply an isometry that maps $|b, x\rangle$ to $|b, J(x)\rangle$ to $|\phi'_i\rangle$. (Note that this can be done efficiently since J is injective and efficiently invertible.) Let $|\phi''_i\rangle$ be the resulting state.
- For all $i \in [4n]$, measure $|\phi''_i\rangle$ in the Hadamard basis and let (e_i, d_i) be the outcome.
- Output $\mathsf{cert} := \{(e_i, d_i)\}_{i \in [4n]}$.

$\mathsf{Vrfy}(\mathsf{vk}, \mathsf{cert})$:
- Parse $\mathsf{vk} = \{\mathsf{td}_i, y_i\}_{i \in \overline{S}}$ and $\mathsf{cert} = \{(e_i, d_i)\}_{i \in [4n]}$.
- Compute $x_{i,\beta} \leftarrow \mathsf{Inv}_{\mathcal{F}}(\mathsf{td}_i, \beta, y_i)$ for all $(i, \beta) \in \overline{S} \times \{0,1\}$.
- Output $\top$ if $d_i \in G_{k_i, 0, x_{i,0}} \cap G_{k_i, 1, x_{i,1}}$ and $e_i = d_i \cdot (J(x_{i,0}) \oplus J(x_{i,1}))$ hold for all $i \in \overline{S}$ and output $\perp$ otherwise.

Correctness. As observed in the description, $|\phi'_i\rangle$ in the ciphertext has a negligible trace distance from $|\phi_i\rangle$. Therefore, it suffices to prove correctness assuming that $|\phi'_i\rangle$ is replaced with $|\phi_i\rangle$. After this replacement, decryption correctness clearly holds assuming correctness of Σ_{rnce} and Σ_{ow}.

---

[9] If $S' = \perp$ or $K' = \perp$, output $\perp$.

We prove verification correctness below. For $i \in \overline{S}$, if we apply J to the second register of $|\phi_i\rangle$ and then apply Hadamard transform for both registers as in Del, then the resulting state can be written as

$$2^{-\frac{w+2}{2}} \sum_{d,b,e} (-1)^{d \cdot J(x_{i,b}) \oplus eb} |e\rangle |d\rangle$$

$$= 2^{-\frac{w}{2}} \sum_{d \in \{0,1\}^w} (-1)^{d \cdot J(x_{i,0})} |d \cdot (J(x_{i,0}) \oplus J(x_{i,1}))\rangle |d\rangle .$$

Therefore, the measurement result is (e_i, d_i) such that $e_i = d_i \cdot (J(x_{i,0}) \oplus J(x_{i,1}))$ for a uniform $d_i \leftarrow \{0,1\}^w$. By the definition of an NTCF family [Mah18], it holds that $d_i \in G_{k_i,0,x_{i,0}} \cap G_{k_i,1,x_{i,1}}$ except for a negligible probability. Therefore, the certificate $\mathsf{cert} = \{(e_i, d_i)\}_{i \in [4n]}$ passes the verification by Vrfy with overwhelming probability.

Security. We prove the following theorem.

Theorem 4.1. *If Σ_{rnce} is RNC secure, Σ_{ow} is OW-CPA secure, and $\mathcal{F}$ is an injective invariant NTCF family with the corresponding injective trapdoor family $\mathcal{G}$, Σ_{cccd} is IND-CPA-CD secure in the QROM where H is modeled as a quantumly-accessible random oracle.*

Proof of Theorem 4.1. What we need to prove is that for any QPT adversary $\mathcal{A}$, it holds that

$$\mathsf{Adv}_{\Sigma_{\mathsf{cccd}},\mathcal{A}}^{\mathsf{ccpk\text{-}cert\text{-}del}}(\lambda) := \left| \Pr\left[\mathsf{Exp}_{\Sigma_{\mathsf{cccd}},\mathcal{A}}^{\mathsf{ccpk\text{-}cert\text{-}del}}(\lambda, 0) = 1 \right] - \Pr\left[\mathsf{Exp}_{\Sigma_{\mathsf{cccd}},\mathcal{A}}^{\mathsf{ccpk\text{-}cert\text{-}del}}(\lambda, 1) = 1 \right] \right| \le \mathsf{negl}(\lambda).$$

Let $q = \mathsf{poly}(\lambda)$ be the maximum number of $\mathcal{A}$'s random oracle queries. For clarity, we describe how $\mathsf{Exp}_{\Sigma_{\mathsf{cccd}},\mathcal{A}}^{\mathsf{ccpk\text{-}cert\text{-}del}}(\lambda, b)$ works below.

1. A uniformly random function H from $\{0,1\}^\lambda \times (\{0,1\} \times \mathcal{X})^{2n}$ to $\{0,1\}^\ell$ is chosen, and $\mathcal{A}$ can make arbitrarily many quantum queries to H at any time in the experiment.
2. The challenger generates $(\mathsf{rnce.pk}, \mathsf{rnce.sk}, \mathsf{rnce.aux}) \leftarrow \mathsf{RNCE.KeyGen}(1^\lambda)$ and $(\mathsf{ow.pk}, \mathsf{ow.sk}) \leftarrow \mathsf{OW.KeyGen}(1^\lambda)$ and sends $\mathsf{pk} := (\mathsf{rnce.pk}, \mathsf{ow.pk})$ to $\mathcal{A}$.
3. $\mathcal{A}$ sends $(m_0, m_1) \in \mathcal{M}^2$ to the challenger.
4. The challenger chooses a uniform subset $S \subseteq [4n]$ such that $|S| = 2n$, generates

$$(k_i, td_i) \leftarrow \begin{cases} \mathsf{Gen}_{\mathcal{G}}(1^\lambda) & i \in S \\ \mathsf{Gen}_{\mathcal{F}}(1^\lambda) & i \in \overline{S} \end{cases}$$

for $i \in [4n]$, and sends $\{k_i\}_{i \in [4n]}$ to $\mathcal{A}$.
5. $\mathcal{A}$ sends $\{y_i\}_{i \in [4n]}$ to the challenger.
6. The challenger chooses $K \leftarrow \{0,1\}^\lambda$ and computes $(b_i, x_i) \leftarrow \mathsf{Inv}_{\mathcal{G}}(td_i, y_i)$ for all $i \in S$. If $\mathsf{Chk}_{\mathcal{G}}(k_i, b_i, x_i, y_i) = 0$ for some $i \in S$, the challenger sets $Z := \mathsf{null}$

and returns $\perp$ to $\mathcal{A}$ where null is a special symbol indicating that Z is undefined. Otherwise, let $i_1, \ldots, i_{2n}$ be the elements of S in the ascending order. The challenger sets $Z := (K, (b_{i_1}, x_{i_1}), (b_{i_2}, x_{i_2}), \ldots, (b_{i_{2n}}, x_{i_{2n}}))$, computes

$$\mathsf{rnce.CT} \leftarrow \mathsf{RNCE.Enc}(\mathsf{rnce.pk}, S),$$
$$\mathsf{ow.CT} \leftarrow \mathsf{OW.Enc}(\mathsf{ow.pk}, K),$$
$$\mathsf{CT}_{\mathsf{msg}} := m_b \oplus H(Z),$$

and sends $(\mathsf{rnce.CT}, \mathsf{ow.CT}, \mathsf{CT}_{\mathsf{msg}})$ to $\mathcal{A}$.

7. $\mathcal{A}$ sends $\mathsf{cert} = \{(e_i, d_i)\}_{i \in [4n]}$ to the challenger.
8. The challenger computes $x_{i,\beta} \leftarrow \mathsf{Inv}_{\mathcal{F}}(\mathsf{td}_i, \beta, y_i)$ for all $(i, \beta) \in \overline{S} \times \{0, 1\}$. If $d_i \in G_{\mathsf{k}_i, 0, x_{i,0}} \cap G_{\mathsf{k}_i, 1, x_{i,1}}$ and $e_i = d_i \cdot (J(x_{i,0}) \oplus J(x_{i,1}))$ hold for all $i \in \overline{S}$, sends $\mathsf{sk} := (\mathsf{rnce.sk}, \mathsf{ow.sk})$ to $\mathcal{A}$, and otherwise sends $\perp$ to $\mathcal{A}$.
9. $\mathcal{A}$ outputs b'. The output of the experiment is b'.

We define the following sequence of hybrids.

$\mathsf{Hyb}_1(b)$: Let $\mathsf{Reveal}_{\mathsf{sk}}$ be the event that the challenger sends sk in Step 8. $\mathsf{Hyb}_1(b)$ is identical to $\mathsf{Exp}^{\mathsf{ccpk\text{-}cert\text{-}del}}_{\Sigma_{\mathsf{cccd}}, \mathcal{A}}(\lambda, b)$ except that K is chosen at the beginning and the oracle given to $\mathcal{A}$ before $\mathsf{Reveal}_{\mathsf{sk}}$ occurs is replaced with $H_{K\|* \to H'}$, which is H reprogrammed according to H' on inputs whose first entry is K where H' is another independent random function. More formally, $H_{K\|* \to H'}$ is defined by

$$H_{K\|* \to H'}(K', (b_1, x_1), \ldots, (b_{2n}, x_{2n}))$$
$$:= \begin{cases} H(K', (b_1, x_1), \ldots, (b_{2n}, x_{2n})) & (K' \neq K) \\ H'(K', (b_1, x_1), \ldots, (b_{2n}, x_{2n})) & (K' = K) \end{cases}.$$

We note that the challenger still uses H to generate $\mathsf{CT}_{\mathsf{msg}}$ and the oracle after $\mathsf{Reveal}_{\mathsf{sk}}$ occurs is still H similarly to the real experiment. On the other hand, if $\mathsf{Reveal}_{\mathsf{sk}}$ does not occur, the oracle $H_{K\|* \to H'}$ is used throughout the experiment except for the generation of $\mathsf{CT}_{\mathsf{msg}}$.

$\mathsf{Hyb}_2(b)$: This is identical to $\mathsf{Hyb}_1(b)$ except that $\mathsf{rnce.CT}$ and $\mathsf{rnce.sk}$ that may be sent to $\mathcal{A}$ in Step 6 and 8 are replaced by

$$\widetilde{\mathsf{rnce.CT}} \leftarrow \mathsf{RNCE.Fake}(\mathsf{rnce.pk}, \mathsf{rnce.sk}, \mathsf{rnce.aux}),$$
$$\widetilde{\mathsf{rnce.sk}} \leftarrow \mathsf{RNCE.Reveal}(\mathsf{rnce.pk}, \mathsf{rnce.sk}, \mathsf{rnce.aux}, \widetilde{\mathsf{rnce.CT}}, S).$$

$\mathsf{Hyb}_3(b)$: This is identical to $\mathsf{Hyb}_2(b)$ except that the oracle given to $\mathcal{A}$ after $\mathsf{Reveal}_{\mathsf{sk}}$ occurs is replaced with $H_{Z \to r}$, which is H reprogrammed to output r on input $Z = (K, (b_{i_1}, x_{i_1}), \ldots, (b_{i_{2n}}, x_{i_{2n}}))$ where r is an independently random ℓ-bit string. More formally, $H_{Z \to r}$ is defined by

$$H_{Z \to r}(Z') := \begin{cases} H(Z') & (Z' \neq Z) \\ r & (Z' = Z) \end{cases}.$$

Note that we have $H_{Z \to r} = H$ if $Z = \mathsf{null}$, i.e., if $\mathsf{Chk}_{\mathcal{G}}(\mathsf{k}_i, b_i, x_i, y_i) = 0$ for some $i \in S$ in Step 6.

Proposition 4.1. *If Σ_{ow} is OW-CPA secure,* $\left| \Pr\left[\text{Exp}_{\Sigma_{\text{cccd}},\mathcal{A}}^{\text{ccpk-cert-del}}(\lambda, b) = 1 \right] - \Pr[\text{Hyb}_1(b) = 1] \right| \leq \text{negl}(\lambda)$.

The only difference between $\text{Exp}_{\Sigma_{\text{cccd}},\mathcal{A}}^{\text{ccpk-cert-del}}(\lambda, b)$ and $\text{Hyb}_1(b)$ is that the random oracle is reprogrammed on inputs with prefix K before $\text{Reveal}_{\text{sk}}$ occurs. By applying the one-way to hiding lemma [AHU19], if $\mathcal{A}$ distinguishes these two games, then we can use it to extract K before $\text{Reveal}_{\text{sk}}$ occurs. This contradicts the OW-CPA security of Σ_{ow}. Therefore, these two games are indistinguishable. The full proof is given in the full version.

Proposition 4.2. *If Σ_{rnce} is RNC secure,* $|\Pr[\text{Hyb}_1(b) = 1] - \Pr[\text{Hyb}_2(b) = 1]| \leq \text{negl}(\lambda)$.

This can be reduced to the RNC security of Σ_{rnce} in a similar manner to that in Proposition 3.1. The full proof is given in the full version.

Proposition 4.3. *If $\mathcal{F}$ and $\mathcal{G}$ satisfy the cut-and-choose adaptive hardcore property described in Lemma 4.1,* $|\Pr[\text{Hyb}_2(b) = 1] - \Pr[\text{Hyb}_3(b) = 1]| \leq \text{negl}(\lambda)$.

The only difference between $\text{Hyb}_2(b)$ and $\text{Hyb}_3(b)$ is that the random oracle is reprogrammed on $Z = (K, (b_{i_1}, x_{i_1}), ..., (b_{i_{2n}}, x_{i_{2n}}))$ after $\text{Reveal}_{\text{sk}}$ occurs. By applying the one-way to hiding lemma [AHU19], if $\mathcal{A}$ distinguishes these two games, then we can use it to extract $Z = (K, (b_{i_1}, x_{i_1}), ..., (b_{i_{2n}}, x_{i_{2n}}))$ after $\text{Reveal}_{\text{sk}}$ occurs. This can be used to break the cut-and-choose adaptive hardcore property of $(\mathcal{F}, \mathcal{G})$. Therefore, these two games are indistinguishable. The full proof is given in the full version.

Proposition 4.4. *It holds that* $\Pr[\text{Hyb}_3(0) = 1] = \Pr[\text{Hyb}_3(1) = 1]$.

Proof of Proposition 4.4. In Hyb_3, the challenger queries H while the adversary queries $H_{K\|*\to H'}$ or $H_{Z\to r}$. Therefore, $H(Z)$ is used only for generating CT_{msg} in Hyb_3 and thus CT_{msg} is an independently uniform string regardless of b from the view of the adversary. Therefore Proposition 4.4 holds. □

By combining Propositions 4.1 to 4.4 Theorem 4.1 is proven. □

4.4 Publicly Verifiable Construction

The scheme given in the previous subsection is privately verifiable. We construct publicly verifiable interactive encryption with certified deletion and classical communication based on extractable witness encryption and one-shot signatures. See the full version for details.

Acknowledgements. TM is supported by the Moonshot R&D JPMJMS2061-5-1-1, MEXT Q-LEAP, JST FOREST, JST PRESTO No. JPMJPR176A, and the Grant-in-Aid for Scientific Research (B) No. JP19H04066 of JSPS.

References

[AGKZ20] Amos, R., Georgiou, M., Kiayias, A., Zhandry, M.: One-shot signatures and applications to hybrid quantum/classical authentication. In: 52nd ACM STOC, pp. 255–268 (2020)

[AHU19] Ambainis, A., Hamburg, M., Unruh, D.: Quantum security proofs using semi-classical Oracles. In: Boldyreva, A., Micciancio, D. (eds.) CRYPTO 2019. LNCS, vol. 11693, pp. 269–295. Springer, Cham (2019). https://doi.org/10.1007/978-3-030-26951-7_10

[AK21] Ananth, P., Kaleoglu, F.: Uncloneable encryption. Revisited. IACR Cryptol. ePrint Arch. **2021**, 412 (2021)

[BB84] Bennett, C.H., Brassard, G.: Quantum cryptography: public key distribution and coin tossing. In: IEEE International Conference on Computers Systems and Signal Processing, pp. 175–179. IEEE (1984)

[BCM+18] Brakerski, Z., Christiano, P., Mahadev, U., Vazirani, U.V., Vidick, T.: A cryptographic test of quantumness and certifiable randomness from a single quantum device. In: 59th FOCS, pp. 320–331 (2018)

[BDF+11] Boneh, D., Dagdelen, Ö., Fischlin, M., Lehmann, A., Schaffner, C., Zhandry, M.: Random Oracles in a quantum world. In: Lee, D.H., Wang, X. (eds.) ASIACRYPT 2011. LNCS, vol. 7073, pp. 41–69. Springer, Heidelberg (2011). https://doi.org/10.1007/978-3-642-25385-0_3

[BGI+12] Barak, B., et al.: On the (im)possibility of obfuscating programs. J. ACM **59**(2), 6:1–6:48 (2012)

[BI20] Broadbent, A., Islam, R.: Quantum encryption with certified deletion. In: Pass, R., Pietrzak, K. (eds.) TCC 2020. LNCS, vol. 12552, pp. 92–122. Springer, Cham (2020). https://doi.org/10.1007/978-3-030-64381-2_4

[BL20] Broadbent, A., Lord, S.: Uncloneable quantum encryption via Oracles. In: 15th Conference on the Theory of Quantum Computation, Communication and Cryptography, TQC 2020, 9–12 June 2020, Riga, Latvia, volume 158 of LIPIcs, pp. 4:1–4:22 (2020)

[BR97] Bellare, M., Rogaway, P.: Collision-resistant hashing: towards making UOWHFs practical. In: Kaliski, B.S. (ed.) CRYPTO 1997. LNCS, vol. 1294, pp. 470–484. Springer, Heidelberg (1997). https://doi.org/10.1007/BFb0052256

[CCKW19] Cojocaru, A., Colisson, L., Kashefi, E., Wallden, P.: QFactory: classically-instructed remote secret qubits preparation. In: Galbraith, S.D., Moriai, S. (eds.) ASIACRYPT 2019. LNCS, vol. 11921, pp. 615–645. Springer, Cham (2019). https://doi.org/10.1007/978-3-030-34578-5_22

[CFGN96] Canetti, R., Feige, U., Goldreich, O., Naor, M.: Adaptively secure multiparty computation. In: 28th ACM STOC, pp. 639–648 (1996)

[CHK05] Canetti, R., Halevi, S., Katz, J.: Adaptively-secure, non-interactive public-key encryption. In: Kilian, J. (ed.) TCC 2005. LNCS, vol. 3378, pp. 150–168. Springer, Heidelberg (2005). https://doi.org/10.1007/978-3-540-30576-7_9

[CMP20] Coladangelo, A., Majenz, C., Poremba, A.: Quantum copy-protection of compute-and-compare programs in the Quantum Random Oracle model. arXiv arXiv:2009.13865 (2020)

[CRW19] Coiteux-Roy, X., Wolf, S.: Proving erasure. In: 2019 IEEE International Symposium on Information Theory (ISIT) (2019)

[FM18] Fu, H., Miller, C.A.: Local randomness: examples and application. Phys. Rev. A **97**(3), 032324 (2018)

[GDP16] Regulation (eu) 2016/679 of the European parliament and of the council of 27 April 2016 on the protection of natural persons with regard to the processing of personal data and on the free movement of such data, and repealing directive 95/46 (general data protection regulation). Off. J. Eur. Union (OJ), 1–88 (2016)

[GGH+16] Garg, S., Gentry, C., Halevi, S., Raykova, M., Sahai, A., Waters, B.: Candidate indistinguishability obfuscation and functional encryption for all circuits. SIAM J. Comput. **45**(3), 882–929 (2016)

[GGM86] Goldreich, O., Goldwasser, S., Micali, S.: How to construct random functions. J. ACM **33**(4), 792–807 (1986)

[GGSW13] Garg, S., Gentry, C., Sahai, A., Waters, B.: Witness encryption and its applications. In: 45th ACM STOC, pp. 467–476 (2013)

[GKP+13] Goldwasser, S., Kalai, Y.T., Popa, R.A., Vaikuntanathan, V., Zeldovich, N.: How to run Turing machines on encrypted data. In: Canetti, R., Garay, J.A. (eds.) CRYPTO 2013. LNCS, vol. 8043, pp. 536–553. Springer, Heidelberg (2013). https://doi.org/10.1007/978-3-642-40084-1_30

[GPSW06] Goyal, V., Pandey, O., Sahai, A., Waters, B.: Attribute-based encryption for fine-grained access control of encrypted data. In: ACM CCS 2006, pp. 89–98 (2006). Available as Cryptology ePrint Archive Report 2006/309

[GZ20] Georgiou, M., Zhandry, M.: Unclonable decryption keys. Cryptology ePrint Archive, Report 2020/877 (2020). https://eprint.iacr.org/2020/877

[HILL99] Håstad, J., Impagliazzo, R., Levin, L.A., Luby, M.: A pseudorandom generator from any one-way function. SIAM J. Comput. **28**(4), 1364–1396 (1999)

[JL00] Jarecki, S., Lysyanskaya, A.: Adaptively secure threshold cryptography: introducing concurrency, removing erasures. In: Preneel, B. (ed.) EUROCRYPT 2000. LNCS, vol. 1807, pp. 221–242. Springer, Heidelberg (2000). https://doi.org/10.1007/3-540-45539-6_16

[KNTY19] Kitagawa, F., Nishimaki, R., Tanaka, K., Yamakawa, T.: Adaptively secure and succinct functional encryption: improving security and efficiency, simultaneously. In: Boldyreva, A., Micciancio, D. (eds.) CRYPTO 2019. LNCS, vol. 11694, pp. 521–551. Springer, Cham (2019). https://doi.org/10.1007/978-3-030-26954-8_17

[KNY20] Kitagawa, F., Nishimaki, R., Yamakawa, T.: Secure software leasing from standard assumptions. Cryptology ePrint Archive, Report 2020/1314 (2020). https://eprint.iacr.org/2020/1314

[KT20] Kundu, S., Tan, E.: Composably secure device-independent encryption with certified deletion. arXiv arXiv:2011.12704 (2020)

[Mah18] Mahadev, U.: Classical verification of quantum computations. In: 59th FOCS, pp. 259–267 (2018)

[NY90] Naor, M., Yung, M.: Public-key cryptosystems provably secure against chosen ciphertext attacks. In: 22nd ACM STOC, pp. 427–437 (1990)

[NY21] Nishimaki, R., Yamakawa, T.: Quantum encryption with certified deletion: public key and attribute-based. IACR Cryptol. ePrint Arch. **2021**, 394 (2021)

[RS19] Radian, R., Sattath, O.: Semi-quantum money. arXiv arXiv:abs/1908.08889 (2019)

[SW05] Sahai, A., Waters, B.: Fuzzy identity-based encryption. In: Cramer, R. (ed.) EUROCRYPT 2005. LNCS, vol. 3494, pp. 457–473. Springer, Heidelberg (2005). https://doi.org/10.1007/11426639_27

[Unr15] Unruh, D.: Revocable quantum timed-release encryption. J. ACM **62**(6), 49:1-49:76 (2015)

[Wie83] Wiesner, S.: Conjugate coding. SIGACT News **15**(1), 78–88 (1983)

Tight Adaptive Reprogramming
in the QROM

Alex B. Grilo[1][(✉)], Kathrin Hövelmanns[2,3][(✉)], Andreas Hülsing[3][(✉)],
and Christian Majenz[4,5][(✉)]

[1] Sorbonne Université, CNRS, LIP6, Paris, France
`Alex.Bredariol-Grilo@lip6.fr`
[2] Ruhr-Universität Bochum, Bochum, Germany
`kathrin@hoevelmanns.net`
[3] Eindhoven University of Technology, Eindhoven, The Netherlands
`andreas@huelsing.net`
[4] Technical University of Denmark, Lyngby, Denmark
`christian.majenz@cwi.nl`
[5] Centrum Wiskunde & Informatica and QuSoft, Amsterdam, The Netherlands

Abstract. The random oracle model (ROM) enjoys widespread popularity, mostly because it tends to allow for *tight* and *conceptually simple* proofs where provable security in the standard model is elusive or costly. While being the adequate replacement of the ROM in the post-quantum security setting, the quantum-accessible random oracle model (QROM) has thus far failed to provide these advantages in many settings. In this work, we focus on *adaptive reprogrammability*, a feature of the ROM enabling tight and simple proofs in many settings. We show that the straightforward quantum-accessible generalization of adaptive reprogramming is feasible by proving a bound on the adversarial advantage in distinguishing whether a random oracle has been reprogrammed or not. We show that our bound is tight by providing a matching attack. We go on to demonstrate that our technique recovers the mentioned advantages of the ROM in three QROM applications: 1) We give a tighter proof of security of the message compression routine as used by XMSS. 2) We show that the standard ROM proof of chosen-message security for Fiat-Shamir signatures can be lifted to the QROM, straightforwardly, achieving a tighter reduction than previously known. 3) We give the first QROM proof of security against fault injection and nonce attacks for the hedged Fiat-Shamir transform.

Keywords: Post-quantum security · QROM · Adaptive reprogramming · Digital signature · Fiat-Shamir transform · Hedged Fiat-Shamir · XMSS

1 Introduction

Since its introduction, the Random oracle model (ROM) has allowed cryptographers to prove efficient practical cryptosystems secure for which proofs in the

ⓒ International Association for Cryptologic Research 2021
M. Tibouchi and H. Wang (Eds.): ASIACRYPT 2021, LNCS 13090, pp. 637–667, 2021.
https://doi.org/10.1007/978-3-030-92062-3_22

standard model have been elusive. In general, the ROM allows for proofs that are conceptually simpler and often tighter than standard model security proofs.

With the advent of post-quantum cryptography, and the introduction of quantum adversaries, the ROM had to be generalized: In this scenario, a quantum adversary interacts with a non-quantum network, meaning that "online" primitives (like signing) stay classical, while the adversary can compute all "offline" primitives (like hash functions) on its own, and hence, in superposition. To account for these stronger capabilities, the quantum-accessible ROM (QROM) was introduced [8]. While successfully fixing the definitional gap, the QROM does not generally come with the advantages of its classical counterpart:

- *Lack of conceptual simplicity.* QROM proofs are extremely complex for various reasons. One reason is that they require some understanding of quantum information theory. More important, however, is the fact that many of the useful properties of the ROM (like preimage awareness and adaptive programmability) are not known to translate directly to the QROM.
- *Tightness.* Many primitives that come with tight security proofs in the ROM are not known to be supported by tight proofs in the QROM. For example, there has been an ongoing effort [7,21,24,25,27,33] to give tighter QROM proofs for the well-known Fujisaki-Okamoto transformation [18,19], which is proven tightly secure in the ROM as long as the underlying scheme fulfills IND-CPA security [20].

In many cases, we expect certain generic attacks to only differ from the ROM counterparts by a square-root factor in the required number of queries if the attack involves a search problem, or no significant factor in the case of guessing. Hence, it was conjectured that it might be sufficient to prove security in the ROM, and then add a square-root factor for search problems. However, recent results [38] demonstrate a separation of ROM and QROM, showing that this conjecture does not hold true in general, as there exist schemes which are provably secure in the ROM and insecure in the QROM. As a consequence, a QROM proof is crucial to establish confidence in a post-quantum cryptosystem.[1]

ADAPTIVE PROGRAMMABILITY. A desirable property of the (classical) ROM is that any oracle value $O(x)$ can be chosen when O is queried on x for the first time (lazy-sampling). This fact is often exploited by a reduction simulating a security game without knowledge of some secret information. Here, an adversary A will not recognize the reprogramming of $O(x)$ as long as the new value is uniformly distributed and consistent with the rest of A's view. This property is called *adaptive programmability*.

The ability to query an oracle in superposition renders this formerly simple approach more involved, similar to the difficulties arising from the question how to extract classical preimages from a quantum query (preimage awareness) [4, 7,10,14,16,27,28,35,39]. Intuitively, a query in superposition can be viewed as a query that might contain all input values at once. Already the first answer of O might hence contain information about every value $O(x)$ that might need to be reprogrammed as the game proceeds. It hence was not clear whether it is

---

[1] Unless, of course, a standard model proof is available.

possible to adaptively reprogram a quantum random oracle without causing a change in the adversary's view.

Until recently, both properties only had extremely non-tight variants in the QROM. For preimage awareness, it was essentially necessary to randomly guess the right query and measure it (with an unavoidable loss of at least $1/q$ for q queries, and the additional disadvantage of potentially rendering the adversary's output unusable due to measurement disturbance). In a recent breakthrough result, Zhandry developed the compressed oracle technique that provides preimage awareness [39] in many settings. For adaptive reprogramming, variants of Unruh's one-way-to-hiding lemma allowed to prove bounds but only with a square-root loss in the entropy of the reprogramming position [17,23,34,36].

In some cases [8,21,26,33], reprogramming could even be avoided by giving a proof that rendered the oracle "a-priori consistent", which is also called a "history-free" proof: In this approach, the oracle is completely redefined in a way such that it is enforced to be *a priori* consistent with the rest of an adversary's view, meaning that it is redefined before execution of the adversary, and on *all* possible input values. Unfortunately, it is not always clear whether it is possible to lift a classical proof to the QROM with this strategy. Even if it is, the "a-priori" approach usually leads to conceptually more complicated proofs. More importantly, it can even lead to reductions that are non-tight with respect to runtime, and may necessitate stronger or additional requirements like, e.g., the statistical counterpart of a property that was only used in its computational variant in the ROM. One example are history-free proofs of CMA security for Fiat-Shamir signatures as e.g. given in [37] and later in [26].

Hence, in this work we are interested in the question:

Can we *tightly* prove that adaptive reprogramming can also be done in the quantum random oracle model?

Our contribution. For common use cases in the context of post-quantum cryptography, this work answers the question above in the affirmative. In more detail, we present a tool for adaptive reprogramming that comes with a tight bound, supposing that the reprogramming positions hold sufficiently large entropy, and reprogramming is triggered by classical queries to an oracle that is provided by the security game (e.g., a signing oracle). These preconditions are usually met in (Q)ROM reductions: The reprogramming is usually triggered by adversarial signature or decryption queries, which remain classical in the post-quantum setting, as the oracles represent honest users.

While we prove a very general lemma, using the simplest variant of the superposition oracle technique [39], we present two corollaries, tailored to cases like a) hash-and-sign with randomized hashing and b) Fiat-Shamir signatures. (Note that we do not have to give a full proof for Fiat-Shamir: We only tend to proving that UF-KOA implies UF-CMA security, as UF-KOA security has already been covered by [16,26,37].) In both cases, reprogramming occurs at a position of which one part is an adversarially chosen string. For a), the other part is a random string z, sampled by the reduction (simulating the signer). For b), the other part is a commitment w chosen from a distribution with sufficient min-entropy, together with additional side-information. In both cases, we manage to bound the distinguishing advantage of any adversary that makes q_s signing and q_H random oracle queries by

$$1.5 \cdot q_s \sqrt{q_H \cdot 2^{-r}} \; ,$$

where r is the length of z for a), and the min-entropy of w for b). We note that it might be possible to alternatively prove a less general adaptive reprogramming lemma covering the special cases a) and b) above by generalizing the semi-classical O2H lemma from [4].

We then demonstrate the applicability of our tool, by giving

– a tighter proof for hash-and-sign applications leading to a tighter proof for message-compression as used by the hash-based signature scheme XMSS in RFC 8391 [22] as a special case,
– a runtime-tight reduction of unforgeability under adaptive chosen message attacks (UF-CMA) to plain unforgeability (UF-CMA$_0$, sometimes denoted UF-KOA or UF-NMA) for Fiat Shamir signatures.
– the first proof of fault resistance for the hedged Fiat-Shamir transform, recently proposed in [5], in the post-quantum setting.

HASH-AND-SIGN. As a first motivating and mostly self-contained application we analyze the hash-and-sign construction that takes a fixed-message-length signature scheme SIG and turns it into a variable-message-length signature scheme SIG′ by first compressing the message using a hash function. We show that if SIG is secure under random message attacks (UF-RMA), SIG′ is secure under adaptively chosen message attacks (UF-CMA). Then we show that along the same lines, we can tighten a recent security proof [9] for message-compression as described for XMSS [11] in RFC 8391. Our new bound shows that one can use random strings of half the length to randomize the message compression in a provably secure way.

THE FIAT-SHAMIR TRANSFORM. In Sect. 4.1, we show that if an identification scheme ID is Honest-Verifier Zero-Knowledge (HVZK), and if the resulting Fiat-Shamir signature scheme SIG := FS[ID, H] furthermore possesses UF-CMA$_0$ security, then SIG is also UF-CMA secure, in the quantum random oracle model. Here, UF-CMA$_0$ denotes the security notion in which the adversary only obtains the public key and has to forge a valid signature without access to a signing oracle. While this statement was already proven in [26], we want to point out several advantages of our proof strategy and the resulting bounds.

Conceptual simplicity. A well-known proof strategy for HVZK, UF-CMA$_0$ ⇒ UF-CMA in the random oracle model (implicitly contained in [1]) is to replace honest transcripts with simulated ones, and to render H *a-posteriori* consistent with the signing oracle during the proceedings of the game. I.e., H(w, m) is patched *after* oracle SIGN was queried on m. Applying our lemma, we observe that this approach actually works in the quantum setting as well. We obtain a very simple QROM proof that is congruent with its ROM counterpart.

In [26], the issue of reprogramming quantum random oracle H was circumvented by giving a history-free proof: In the proof, messages are tied to potential transcripts by generating the latter with message-dependent randomness, *a priori*, and H is patched accordingly, right from the beginning of the game. During each computation of $H(w, m)$, the reduction therefore has to keep H a-priori consistent by going over all transcript candidates (w_i, c_i, z_i) belonging to m, and returning c_i if $w = w_i$.

Applicability to a broader class of signature schemes. To achieve a-priori consistency, [26] crucially relies on *statistical* HVZK. Furthermore, they require that the HVZK simulator outputs transcripts such that the challenge c is uniformly distributed. We are able to drop the requirement on c altogether, and to only require *computational* HVZK. As a practical example, alternate NIST candidate Picnic [12] satisfies only *computational* HVZK: here, we give the first QROM reduction from chosen-message security, i.e. UF-CMA, to plain unforgeability, i.e. UF-CMA$_0$.[2]

Tightness with regards to running time. Our reduction B has about the running time of the adversary A, as it can simply sample simulated transcripts and reprogram H, accordingly. The reduction in [26] suffers from a quadratic blow-up in its running time: They have running time $\mathrm{Time}(B) \approx \mathrm{Time}(A) + q_H q_S$, as the reduction has to execute q_S computations upon each query to H in order to keep it a-priori consistent. As they observe, this quadratic blow-up renders the reduction non-tight in all practical aspects. On the other hand, our upper bound comes with a bigger disruption in terms of commitment entropy (the min-entropy of the first message (the *commitment*) in the identification scheme). While the source of non-tightness in [26] can not be balanced out, however, we offer a trade-off: If needed, the commitment entropy can be increased by appending a random string to the commitment.[3]

ROBUSTNESS OF THE HEDGED FIAT-SHAMIR TRANSFORM AGAINST FAULT ATTACKS. When it comes to real-world implementations, the assessment of a signature scheme will not solely take into consideration whether an adversary could forge a fresh signature as formalized by the UF-CMA game, as UF-CMA does not capture all avenues of real-world attacks. For instance, an adversary interacting

---

[2] As a matter of fact, the inapplicability of the history-free reduction from [26], that was used in [16] to give a full reduction for Fiat Shamir signatures (starting with a quantum-extractable identification scheme) was initially overlooked by the Picnic Team. The Picnic team has acknowledged that, and is working on a revision of the Picnic submission to the NIST standardization process for post-quantum cryptographic schemes that will use our reduction.

[3] While this increases the signature size, the increase is mild in typical post-quantum Fiat-Shamir based digital signature schemes. As an example, suppose Dilithium-1024x768, which has a signature size of 2044 bytes, had zero commitment entropy (it actually has quite some, see remarks in [26]). To ensure that about 2^{128} hash queries are necessary to make the term in our security bound that depends on the commitment entropy equal 1, about 32 bytes would need to be added, an increase of about 1.6% (assuming 2^{64} signing queries).

with hardware that realizes a cryptosystem can try to induce a hardware malfunction, also called fault injection, in order to derail the key generation or signing process. Although it might not always be straightforward to predict where exactly a triggered malfunction will affect the execution, it is well understood that even a low-precision malfunction can seriously injure a schemes' security. In the context of the ongoing effort to standardize post-quantum secure primitives [31], it hence made sense to affirm [32] that desirable additional security features include, amongst others, resistance against fault attacks and randomness generation that has some bias.

Recently [5], the hedged Fiat-Shamir construction was proven secure against biased nonces and several types of fault injections, in the ROM. This result can for example be used to argue that alternate NIST candidate Picnic [12] is robust against many types of fault injections. We revisit the hedged Fiat-Shamir construction in Sect. 4.2 and lift the result of [5] to the QROM. In particular, we thereby obtain that Picnic is resistant against many fault types, even when attacked by an adversary with quantum capabilities.

We considered to generalize the result further by replacing the standard Fiat-Shamir transform with the Fiat–Shamir with aborts transform [26,29]. While our security statements can be extended in a straightforward manner, we decided not to further complicate our proof with the required modifications. For Dilithium, the implications are limited anyway, as several types of faults are only proven ineffective if the underlying scheme is subset-revealing, which Dilithium is not.[4]

OPTIMALITY OF OUR BOUND. We also show that our lower bound is tight for the given setting, presenting a quantum attack that matches our bound, up to a constant factor. Let us restrict our attention to the simple case where $H : \{0,1\}^n \to \{0,1\}^k$ is a random function, which is potentially reprogrammed at a random position x^* resulting in a new oracle H'. Consider an attacker that is allowed $2q$ queries to the random oracle.

A classical attack that matches the classical bound for the success probability, $O(q \cdot 2^{-n})$, is the following: pick values $x_1, ..., x_q$ and compute the XOR of the outputs $H(x_i)$. After the oracle is potentially reprogrammed, the attacker outputs 0 iff the checksum computed before is unchanged.

In order to match the quantum lower bound, we use the same attack, but on a superposition of tuples of inputs: the attacker queries H with the superposition of all possible inputs, and then applies a cyclic permutation σ on the input register. This process is repeated $q - 1$ times (on the same state). After the potential reprogramming, we repeat the same process, but now applying the permutation σ^{-1} and querying H'. Using techniques from [2], we show how to distinguish the two cases with advantage $\Omega\left(\sqrt{\frac{q}{2^n}}\right)$ in time $\mathsf{poly}(q, n)$.

---

[4] Intuitively, an identification scheme is called subset-revealing if its responses do not depend on the secret key. Dilithium computes its responses as $z := y + c \cdot s_1$, where s_1 is part of the secret key.

2   Adaptive Reprogramming: The Toolbox

Before we describe our adaptive reprogramming theorem, let us quickly recall how we usually model adversaries with quantum access to a random oracle: As established in [6,8], we model quantum access to a random oracle $O : X \times Y$ via oracle access to a unitary U_O, which is defined as the linear completion of $|x\rangle_X |y\rangle_Y \mapsto |x\rangle_X |y \oplus O(x)\rangle_Y$, and adversaries A with quantum access to O as a sequence of unitaries, interleaved with applications of U_O. We write $A^{|O\rangle}$ to indicate that O is quantum-accessible.

As a warm-up, we will first present our reprogramming lemma in the simplest setting. Say we reprogram an oracle R many times, where the position is partially controlled by the adversary, and partially picked at random. More formally, let X_1 and X_2 be two finite sets, where X_1 specifies the domain from which the random portions are picked, and X_2 specifies the domain of the adversarially controlled portions. We will now formalize what it means to distinguish a random oracle $O_0 : X_1 \times X_2 \to Y$ from its reprogrammed version O_1. Consider the two REPRO games, given in Fig. 1: In games REPRO$_b$, the distinguisher has quantum access to oracle O_b (see line 03) that is either the original random oracle O_0 (if $b = 0$), or the oracle O_1 which gets reprogrammed adaptively ($b = 1$). To model the actual reprogramming, we endow the distinguisher with (classical) access to a reprogramming oracle REPROGRAM. Given a value $x_2 \in X_2$, oracle REPROGRAM samples random values x_1 and y, and programs the random oracle to map $x_1 \| x_2$ to y (see line 06). Note that apart from already knowing x_2, the adversary even learns the part x_1 of the position at which O_1 was reprogrammed.

GAME REPRO$_b$	REPROGRAM(x_2)
01 $O_0 \leftarrow_\$ Y^{X_1 \times X_2}$	05 $(x_1, y) \leftarrow_\$ X_1 \times Y$
02 $O_1 := O_0$	06 $O_1 := O_1^{(x_1 \| x_2) \mapsto y}$
03 $b' \leftarrow A^{|O_b\rangle, \text{REPROGRAM}}$	07 **return** x_1
04 **return** b'	

Fig. 1. Adaptive reprogramming games REPRO$_b$ for bit $b \in \{0, 1\}$ in the most basic setting.

Proposition 1. *Let X_1, X_2 and Y be finite sets, and let A be any algorithm issuing R many calls to* REPROGRAM *and q many (quantum) queries to O_b as defined in Fig. 1. Then the distinguishing advantage of A is bounded by*

$$|\Pr[\text{REPRO}_1^A \Rightarrow 1] - \Pr[\text{REPRO}_0^A \Rightarrow 1]| \leq \frac{3R}{2} \sqrt{\frac{q}{|X_1|}}. \tag{1}$$

The above theorem constitutes a significant improvement over previous bounds. In [34] and [17], a bound proportional to $q|X_1|^{-1/2}$ for the distinguishing advantage in similar settings, but for $R = 1$, was given. In [23], a bound proportional to $q^2|X_1|^{-1}$ is claimed, but that seems to have resulted from a "translation mistake" from [17] and should be similar to the bounds from [17,34]. What is more, we show in Sect. 6 that the above bound, and therefore also its generalizations, are tight, by presenting a distinguisher that achieves an advantage equal to the right hand side of Eq. (1) for trivial X_1, up to a constant factor.

In fact, we prove something more general than Proposition 1: We prove that an adversary will not behave significantly different, even if

– the adversary does not only control a portion x_2, but instead it even controls the distributions according to which the whole positions $x := (x_1, x_2)$ are sampled at which O_1 is reprogrammed,
– it can additionally pick different distributions, adaptively, and
– the distributions produce some additional side information x' which the adversary also obtains,

as long as the reprogramming positions x hold enough entropy.

Overloading notation, we formalize this generalization by games REPRO, given in Fig. 2: Reprogramming oracle REPROGRAM now takes as input the description of a distribution p that generates a whole reprogramming position x, together with side information x'. REPROGRAM samples x and x' according to p, programs the random oracle to map x to a random value y, and returns (x, x').

GAME REPRO_b	$\text{REPROGRAM}(p)$
01 $O_0 \leftarrow_\$ Y^X$	05 $(x, x') \leftarrow p$
02 $O_1 := O_0$	06 $y \leftarrow_\$ Y$
03 $b' \leftarrow D^{|O_b\rangle, \text{REPROGRAM}}$	07 $O_1 := O_1^{x \mapsto y}$
04 **return** b'	08 **return** (x, x')

Fig. 2. Adaptive reprogramming games REPRO_b for bit $b \in \{0, 1\}$.

We are now ready to present our main Theorem 1. On a high level, the only difference between the statement of Proposition 1 and Theorem 1 is that we now have to consider R many (possibly different) joint distributions on $X \times X'$, and to replace $\frac{1}{|X_1|}$ (the probability of the uncontrolled reprogramming portion) with the highest likelihood of any of those distributions generating a position x.

Theorem 1 ("Adaptive reprogramming" (AR)). *Let X, X', Y be some finite sets, and let D be any distinguisher, issuing R many reprogramming instructions and q many (quantum) queries to O. Let q_r denote the number of queries to O that are issued inbetween the $(r-1)$-th and the r-th query to REPROGRAM. Furthermore, let $p^{(r)}$ denote the rth distribution that REPROGRAM is queried on. By $p_X^{(r)}$ we will denote the marginal distribution of X, according to $p^{(r)}$, and define*

$$p_{\max}^{(r)} := \mathbb{E} \max_x p_X^{(r)}(x),$$

where the expectation is taken over D's behaviour until its rth query to REPROGRAM.

$$|\Pr[\text{REPRO}_1^D \Rightarrow 1] - \Pr[\text{REPRO}_0^D \Rightarrow 1]| \leq \sum_{r=1}^R \left(\sqrt{\hat{q}_r p_{\max}^{(r)}} + \frac{1}{2} \hat{q}_r p_{\max}^{(r)} \right), \quad (2)$$

where $\hat{q}_r := \sum_{i=0}^{r-1} q_i$.

For $R = 1$ and without additional side information output x', the proof of Theorem 1 is given in Sect. 5. The extension to general R is proven in the full version via a standard hybrid argument. Finally, all our bounds are information-theoretical, i.e. they hold against arbitrary query bounded adversaries. The additional output x' can therefore be sampled by the adversary.

We will now quickly discuss how to simplify the bound given in Eq. (2) for our applications, and in particular, how we can derive Eq. (1) from Theorem 1: Throughout Sects. 3 and 4, we will only have to consider reprogramming instructions that occur on positions $x = (x_1, x_2)$ such that

- x_1 is drawn according to the same distribution p for each reprogramming instruction, and
- x_2 represents a message that is already fixed by the adversary.

To be more precise, x_1 will represent a uniformly random string z in 3, and no side information x' has to be considered. In Sect. 4, (x_1, x') will represent a tuple (w, st) that is drawn according to $\text{Commit}(sk)$.

In the language of Theorem 1, the marginal distribution $p_X^{(r)}$ will always be the same distribution p, apart from the already fixed part x_2. We can hence upper bound $p_{\max}^{(r)}$ by $p_{\max} := \max_{x_1} p(x_1)$, and $\hat{q}_r$ by q, to obtain that $\hat{q}_r p_{\max}^{(r)} < q p_{\max}$ for all $1 \leq r \leq R$.

In our applications, we will always require that p holds sufficiently large entropy. To be more precise, we will assume that $p_{\max} < \frac{1}{q}$. In this case, we have that $q p_{\max} < 1$, and that we can upper bound $q p_{\max}$ by $\sqrt{q p_{\max}}$ to obtain

Proposition 2. *Let X_1, X_2, X' and Y be some finite sets, and let p be a distribution on $X_1 \times X'$. Let D be any distinguisher, issuing q many (quantum) queries to O and R many reprogramming instructions such that each instruction consists of a value x_2, together with the fixed distribution p. Then*

$$|\Pr[\text{REPRO}_1^\mathsf{D} \Rightarrow 1] - \Pr[\text{REPRO}_0^\mathsf{D} \Rightarrow 1]| \leq \frac{3R}{2} \sqrt{q p_{\max}} \ ,$$

where $p_{\max} := \max_{x_1} p(x_1)$.

From this we obtain Proposition 1 setting $p_{max} = |X_1|^{-1}$.

3   Basic Applications

In this section, we present two motivating examples that benefit from the most basic version of our bound as stated in Proposition 1. As a first example we chose the canonical hash-and-sign construction when used to achieve security under adaptive chosen message attacks (UF-CMA) from a scheme that is secure under random message attacks (UF-RMA). It is mostly self-contained and similar to our second example. The second example is a tighter bound for the security of hash-and-sign as used in RFC 8391, the recently published standard for the stateful hash-based signature scheme XMSS.

3.1   From RMA to CMA Security via Hash-and-Sign

In the following, we present a conceptually easy proof with a tighter bound for the canonical UF-RMA to UF-CMA transform using hash-and-sign $\mathsf{SIG}' = \mathsf{HaS}[\mathsf{SIG}, \mathsf{H}]$, in the QROM (which additionally allows for arbitrary message space expansion). Recall that $\mathsf{Sign}'(sk, m')$ first samples a uniformly random bitstring $z \leftarrow_\$ Z$, computes $\sigma \leftarrow \mathsf{Sign}(sk, \mathsf{H}(z\|m'))$ and returns the pair (z, σ). Vrfy' accordingly first computes $m := \mathsf{H}(z\|m')$ and then calls $\mathsf{Vrfy}(pk, m, \sigma)$.

The reduction M from UF-RMA to UF-CMA in this case works as follows: First, we have to handle collision attacks. We show that an adversary which finds a forgery for SIG' that contains no forgery for SIG breaks the multi-target version of extended target collision resistance (M-eTCR) of H, and give a QROM bound for this property. Having dealt with collision attacks leaves us with the case where A generates a forgery that contains a forgery for SIG. The challenge in this case is how to simulate the signing oracle SIGN. Our respective reduction M against UF-RMA proceeds as follows: Collect the q_s many message-signature pairs $\{(m_i, \sigma_i)\}_{1 \le i \le q_s}$, provided by the UF-RMA game. When A queries $\mathrm{SIGN}(m'_i)$ for the ith time, sample a random z_i, reprogram $\mathsf{H}(z_i\|m'_i) := m_i$, and return (z_i, σ_i). See also Fig. 5 below.

In the QROM, this reduction has previously required q_s applications of the O2H Lemma in two steps, loosing an additive $\mathcal{O}(q_s \cdot q / \sqrt{|Z|})$ term. In contrast, we only loose a $\mathcal{O}(q_s \sqrt{q/|Z|})$ (both constants hidden by the $\mathcal{O}$ are small):

Theorem 2. *For any (quantum) UF-CMA adversary A issuing at most q_s (classical) queries to the signing oracle SIGN and at most q_H quantum queries to H, there exists an UF-RMA adversary M such that*

$$\mathrm{Succ}^{\mathsf{UF\text{-}CMA}}_{\mathsf{SIG}'}(\mathsf{A}) \le \mathrm{Succ}^{\mathsf{UF\text{-}RMA}}_{\mathsf{SIG}}(\mathsf{M}) + \frac{8q_s(q_s + q_\mathsf{H} + 2)^2}{|\mathcal{M}'|} + 3q_s \sqrt{\frac{q_\mathsf{H} + q_s + 1}{|Z|}} \ ,$$

and the running time of M is about that of A.

The second term accounts for the complexity to find a second preimage for one of the messages m_i, which is an unavoidable generic attack. The third term is the result of $2q_s$ reprogrammings. Half of them are used in the QROM bound for M-eTCR, the other half in the reduction M. This term accounts for an attack that correctly guesses the random bitstring used by the signing oracle for one of the queries (such an attack still would have to find a collision for this part but this is inherently not reflected in the used proof technique).

Proof. We now relate the UF-CMA security of SIG' to the UF-RMA security of SIG via a sequence of games.

GAME G_0. We begin with the original UF-CMA game for SIG' in game G_0. The success probability of A in this game is $\mathrm{Adv}^{\mathsf{UF\text{-}CMA}}_{\mathsf{SIG}'}(\mathsf{A})$ per definition.

GAME G_1. We obtain game G_1 from game G_0 by adding an additional condition. Namely, game G_1 returns 0 if there exists an $0 < i \le q_s$ such that $\mathsf{H}(z^*\|m'^*) =$

$H(z_i\|m_i')$, where z^* is the random element in the forgery signature, and z_i is the random element in the signature returned by $\mathrm{SIGN}(m_i')$ as the answer to the ith query. We will now argue that

$$|\Pr[G_0^A \Rightarrow 1] - \Pr[G_1^A \Rightarrow 1]| \leq \frac{8q_s(q_s + q_H + 2)^2}{|\mathcal{M}'|} + \frac{3q_s}{2}\sqrt{\frac{q_H + q_s + 1}{|Z|}} \,.$$

Towards this end, we give a reduction B in Fig. 3, that breaks the M-eTCR security of H whenever the additional condition is triggered, making $q_s + q_H + 1$ queries to its random oracle. B simulates the UF-CMA game for SIG', using H and an instance of SIG. Clearly, B runs in about the same time as game G_0^A, and succeeds whenever A succeeds and the additional condition is triggered. To complete this step, it hence remains to show that the success probability of any such $(q_s + q_H + 1)$-query adversary is

$$\mathrm{Succ}_H^{\mathsf{M\text{-}eTCR}}(B, q_s) \leq \frac{8q_s(q_s + q_H + 2)^2}{|\mathcal{M}'|} + \frac{3q_s}{2}\sqrt{\frac{q_H + q_s + 1}{|Z|}} \,. \tag{3}$$

We delay the proof of Eq. (3) until the end.

```
B^{Box,|H⟩}()                              SIGN(m_i')
01  (pk, sk) ← KG                          08  z_i ← Box(m_i')
02  (m'^*, σ'^*) = A^{SIGN,|H⟩}(pk)        09  σ_i ← Sign(sk, H(z_i, m_i'))
03  Parse σ'^* as (z^*, σ^*)               10  return (z_i, σ_i)
04  if ∃j : H(z^*‖m'^*) = H(z_j‖m_j')
05      i := j
06  else i ←$ [1, q_s]
07  return (m'^*, z^*, i)
```

Fig. 3. Reduction B breaking M-eTCR. Here, Box is the M-eTCR challenge oracle.

GAME G_2. The next game differs from G_1 in the way the signing oracle works. In game G_2 (see Fig. 4), the ith query to SIGN is answered by first sampling a random value z_i, as well as a random message m_i, and programming $\mathsf{H}' := \mathsf{H}'^{(z_i\|m_i') \mapsto m_i}$. Then m_i is signed using the secret key. We will now show that

$$|\Pr[G_1^A \Rightarrow 1] - \Pr[G_2^A \Rightarrow 1]| \leq \frac{3q_s}{2}\sqrt{\frac{q_H + q_s + 1}{|Z|}} \,.$$

Consider a reduction C that simulates game G_2 for A to distinguish the REPRO_b game. Accordingly, C forwards access to its own oracle O_b to A instead of H. Instead of sampling z_i, m_i itself in line 08 and programming H in line 09, C obtains $z_i \leftarrow \mathrm{REPROGRAM}(m_i')$ from its own oracle and computes $m_i := O_b(z_i\|m_i')$ as the output of its random oracle. Now, if C plays in REPRO_0 it perfectly simulates G_1 for A, as the oracle remains unchanged. If C plays in

REPRO_1 it perfectly simulates G_2, as can be seen by inlining REPROGRAM and removing doubled calls used to recompute m_i. Consequently,

$$|\Pr[G_1^A \Rightarrow 1] - \Pr[G_2^A \Rightarrow 1]|$$

$$= |\Pr[\text{REPRO}_0^{C^A} \Rightarrow 1] - \Pr[\text{REPRO}_1^{C^A} \Rightarrow 1]| \leq \frac{3q_s}{2}\sqrt{\frac{q_H + q_s + 1}{|Z|}} \ .$$

Game G_2	SIGN(m_i')
01 $i := 1$	08 $z_i \leftarrow_\$ Z, m_i \leftarrow_\$ \mathcal{M}$
02 $(pk, sk) \leftarrow \text{KG}()$	09 $H := H^{(z_i\|m_i')\mapsto m_i}$
03 $(m'^*, \sigma'^*) = A^{\text{SIGN},\|H\rangle}(pk)$	10 $\sigma_i \leftarrow \text{Sign}(sk, m_i)$
04 Parse σ'^* as (z^*, σ^*)	11 $i := i + 1$
05 if $\exists 1 \leq i \leq q_s : H(z^*\|m'^*) = H(z_i\|m_i')$	12 return (z_i, σ_i)
06 return 0	
07 return $\text{Vrfy}(pk, m'^*, \sigma^*) \wedge m'^* \notin \{m_i'\}_{i=1}^{q_s}$	

Fig. 4. Game G_2.

$M^{A,\|H\rangle}(pk, \{(m_i, \sigma_i)\}_{1 \leq i \leq q_s})$	SIGN(m_i')
01 $H' := H; i := 1$	05 $z_i \leftarrow_\$ Z$
02 $(m'^*, \sigma'^*) = A^{\text{SIGN},\|H'\rangle}(pk)$	06 if $\exists \hat{m}_i$ s. th. $(z_i\|m_i', \hat{m}_i) \in \mathfrak{L}_{H'}$
03 Parse σ'^* as (z^*, σ^*)	07 $\mathfrak{L}_{H'} := \mathfrak{L}_{H'} \setminus \{(z_i\|m_i', \hat{m}_i)\}$
04 return $(H(z^*\|m'^*), \sigma)$	08 $\mathfrak{L}_{H'} := \mathfrak{L}_{H'} \cup \{(z_i\|m_i', m_i)\}$
	09 $i := i + 1$
	10 return (z_i, σ_i)
	$H'(z\|m')$
	11 if $\exists m$ s. th. $(z\|m', m) \in \mathfrak{L}_{H'}$
	12 return m
	13 else return $H(z\|m')$

Fig. 5. Reduction M reducing UF-RMA to UF-CMA.

To conclude our main argument, we will now argue that

$$\Pr[G_2^A \Rightarrow 1] = \text{Adv}_{\text{SIG}}^{\text{UF-RMA}}(M) \ ,$$

where reduction M is given in Fig. 5. Since reprogramming is done a-posteriori in game G_2, M can simulate a reprogrammed oracle H' via access to its own oracle H and an initial table look-up: M keeps track of the (classical) values on which H' has to be reprogrammed (see line 08) and tweaks A's oracle H', accordingly. The latter means that, given the table $\mathfrak{L}_{H'}$ of pairs $(z_i\|m_i', m_i)$ that were already defined in previous signing queries, controlled on the query input being equal to $z_i\|m_i'$ output m_i, and controlled on the input not being equal to any $z_i\|m_i'$, forward the query to M's own oracle H. If needed, M reprograms values (see line 07) by adding an entry to its look-up table. Given quantum access to H, M can implement this as a quantum circuit, allowing quantum access to H′.

Hence, M perfectly simulates game G_2 towards A. The only differences are that M neither samples the m_i itself, nor computes the signatures for them. Both are given to M by the UF-RMA game. However, they follow the same distribution as in game G_2. Lastly, whenever A would win in game G_2, M succeeds in its UF-RMA game as it can extract a valid forgery for SIG on a new message. This is enforced with the condition we added in game G_1.

The final bound of the theorem follows from collecting the bounds above, and it remains to prove the bound on M-eTCR claimed in Eq. (3). We improve a bound from [23], in which it was shown that for a small constant c,[5]

$$\text{Succ}_{\text{H}}^{\text{M-eTCR}}(\text{B}, q_s) \leq \frac{8q_s(q_{\text{H}} + 1)^2}{|\mathcal{M}'|} + c\frac{q_s q_{\text{H}}}{\sqrt{|Z|}} .$$

Their proof of this bound is explicitly given for the single target step. It is then argued that the multi-target step can be easily obtained, which was recently confirmed in [9]. The proof proceeds in two steps. The authors construct a reduction that generates a random function from an instance of an average-case search problem which requires to find a 1 in a boolean function f. The function has the property that all preimages of a randomly picked point m in the image correspond to 1s of f. When A makes its query to Box, the reduction picks a random z and programs $\text{H}^{(z\|m')\mapsto m}$. An extended target collision for $(z\|m')$ hence is a 1 in f by design. This gives the first term in the above bound, which is known to be optimal.

The second term in the bound is the result of above reprogramming. I.e., it is a bound on the difference in success probability of A when playing the real game or when run by the reduction. More precisely, the bound is the result of analyzing the distinguishing advantage between the following two games (which we rephrased to match our notation):

GAME G_a. A gets access to H. In phase 1, after making at most q_1 queries to H, A outputs a message $m' \in \mathcal{M}'$. Then a random $z \leftarrow_\$ Z$ is sampled and $(z, \text{H}(z\|m'))$ is handed to A. A continues to the second phase and makes at most q_2 queries. A outputs $b \in \{0, 1\}$ at the end.

GAME G_b. A gets access to H. After making at most q_1 queries to H, A outputs a message $m' \in \mathcal{M}'$. Then a random $z \leftarrow_\$ Z$ is sampled as well as a random range element $m \leftarrow_\$ \mathcal{M}$. Program $\text{H} := \text{H}^{(z\|m')\mapsto m}$. A receives $(z, m = \text{H}(z\|m'))$ and proceeds to the second phase. After making at most q_2 queries, A outputs $b \in \{0, 1\}$ at the end.

The authors of [23] showed that for a small constant c (see Footnote 5),

$$|\Pr[G_b^{\text{A}} \Rightarrow 1] - \Pr[G_a^{\text{A}} \Rightarrow 1]| \leq c\frac{q_{\text{H}}}{\sqrt{|Z|}} .$$

---

[5] This is a corrected bound from [23], see discussion in Sect. 2.

A straightforward application of Proposition 1 shows that

$$| \Pr[G_b^A \Rightarrow 1] - \Pr[G_a^A \Rightarrow 1]| \leq \frac{3}{2}\sqrt{\frac{q_H + 1}{|Z|}}.$$

as the games above virtually describe the games REPRO_b with the exception that in REPRO_b the oracle REPROGRAM only returns z and not $H(z\|m'))$. Hence, a reduction needs one additional query per reprogramming.

When applying this to the q_s-target case, a hybrid argument shows that the bound becomes $3q_s/2\sqrt{q_H+1/|Z|}$. Combining this with the reduction of [23] and taking into account that B makes $(q_s + q_H + 1)$ queries confirms the bound claimed in Eq. (3).

3.2   Tight Security for Message Hashing of RFC 8391

Another extremely similar application of our basic bound is for another case of the hash-and-sign construction, used to turn a fixed message length UF-CMA-secure signature scheme SIG into a variable input length one SIG'. This case is essentially covered already by Sect. 3.1: A proof can omit game G_2 and state a simple reduction that simulates game G_1 to extract a forgery. The bound changes accordingly, requiring one reprogramming bound less and becoming $\text{Succ}_{\text{SIG'}}^{\text{UF-CMA}}(A) \leq \text{Succ}_{\text{SIG}}^{\text{UF-CMA}}(M) + 8q_s(q_s+q_H)^2/|\mathcal{M}'| + 1.5q_s\sqrt{q_H+q_s/|Z|}$.

In [22] , it was suggested that for stateful hash-based signature schemes like XMSS [22], the multi-target attacks which cause the first occurrence of q_s in the bound could be avoided. This was recently formally proven in [9]. The idea is to exploit the property of hash-based signature schemes that every signature has an index which binds the signature to a one-time public key. Including this index into the hash forces an adversary to also include it in a collision to make it useful for a forgery. Even more, the index is different for every signature and therefore for every target hash.

Summarizing, the authors of [9] showed that there exists a tight standard model proof for the hash-and-sign construction, as used by XMSS in RFC 8391, if the used hash function is q_s-target extended target-collision resistant with nonce (nM-eTCR, an extension of M-eTCR that considers the index.

To demonstrate the relevance of this result, the authors analyzed the nM-eTCR-security of hash functions under generic attacks, proving a bound for nM-eTCR-security in the QROM in the same way as outlined for M-eTCR above. So far, this bound was suboptimal, as it included a bound on distinguishing variants of games G_a and G_b above in which H takes an additional, externally given index as input). Hence, the bound was $\text{Succ}_H^{\text{nM-eTCR}}(A, p) \leq 8(q_s+q_H)^2/|\mathcal{M}'| + 32q_sq_H^2/|Z|$. Due to the translation error, we believe that the second term needs to be updated to $32q_s \cdot \alpha$, where $\alpha = q_H/\sqrt{|Z|}$, instead of $32q_s \cdot \alpha^2$. In [9], it was conjectured that in α, a factor of $\sqrt{q_H}$ can be removed. We can confirm this conjecture. As in the case above, Proposition 1 can be directly applied to the distinguishing bound for games G_a and G_b. A reduction would simply treat the index as part of the message sent to REPROGRAM. Plugging this into the proof in [9] leads to the bound

$$\text{Succ}_{\text{H}}^{\text{nM-eTCR}}(A, p) \leq \frac{8(q_s + q_{\text{H}})^2}{|\mathcal{M}'|} + 1.5 q_s \sqrt{\frac{q_{\text{H}} + q_s}{|Z|}} .$$

4 Applications to the Fiat-Shamir Transform

For the sake of completeness, we include all used definitions for identification and signature schemes in the full version . The only non-standard (albeit straightforward) definition is computational HVZK for multiple transcripts, which we give below.

(SPECIAL) HVZK SIMULATOR. We first recall the notion of an HVZK simulator. Our definition comes in two flavours: While a standard HVZK simulator generates transcripts relative to the public key, a *special* HVZK simulator generates transcripts relative to (the public key and) a particular challenge.

Definition 1 ((Special) HVZK simulator). *An* HVZK *simulator is an algorithm* Sim *that takes as input the public key pk and outputs a transcript* (w, c, z). *A* special *HVZK simulator is an algorithm* Sim *that takes as input the public key pk and a challenge c and outputs a transcript* (w, c, z).

COMPUTATIONAL HVZK FOR MULTIPLE TRANSCRIPTS. In our security proofs, we will have to argue that collections of honestly generated transcripts are indistinguishable from collections of simulated ones. Since it is not always clear whether computational HVZK implies computational HVZK for *multiple* transcripts, we extend our definition, accordingly: In the multi-HVZK game, the adversary obtains a collection of transcripts (rather than a single one). Similarly, we extend the definition of *special* computational HVZK from [5].

Definition 2 ((Special) computational multi-HVZK). *Assume that* ID *comes with an* HVZK *simulator* Sim. *We define multi-HVZK games t-HVZK as in Fig. 6, and the multi-HVZK advantage function of an adversary* A *against* ID *as*

$$\text{Adv}_{\text{ID}}^{t\text{-HVZK}}(A) := \left| \Pr[t\text{-HVZK}_{1\,\text{ID}}^{A} \Rightarrow 1] - \Pr[t\text{-HVZK}_{0\,\text{ID}}^{A} \Rightarrow 1] \right| .$$

To define special multi-HVZK, assume that ID *comes with a special* HVZK *simulator* Sim. *We define multi-sHVZK games as in Fig. 6, and the multi-sHVZK advantage function of an adversary* A *against* ID *as*

$$\text{Adv}_{\text{ID}}^{t\text{-sHVZK}}(A) := \left| \Pr[t\text{-sHVZK}_{1\,\text{ID}}^{A} \Rightarrow 1] - \Pr[t\text{-sHVZK}_{0\,\text{ID}}^{A} \Rightarrow 1] \right| .$$

STATISTICAL HVZK. Unlike computational HVZK, *statistical* HVZK can be generalized generically, we therefore do not need to deviate from known statistical definitions.

We denote the respective upper bound for (special) statistical HVZK by Δ_{HVZK} (Δ_{sHVZK}).

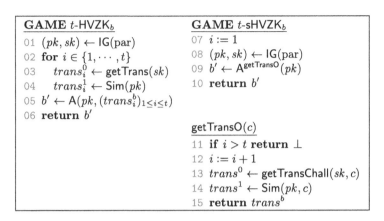

Fig. 6. Multi-HVZK game and multi-sHVZK game for ID. Both games are defined relative to bit $b \in \{0, 1\}$, and to the number t of transcripts the adversary is given.

4.1   Revisiting the Fiat-Shamir Transform

In this section, we show that if an identification scheme ID is HVZK, and if SIG := FS[ID, H] possesses UF-CMA$_0$ security (also known as UF-KOA security), then SIG is also UF-CMA secure, in the QROM. Note that our theorem makes no assumptions on how UF-CMA$_0$ is proven. For arbitrary ID schemes this can be done using a general reduction for the Fiat-Shamir transform [16], incurring a q_H^2 multiplicative loss that is, in general, unavoidable [15]. For a *lossy* ID scheme ID, UF-CMA$_0$ of FS[ID, H] can be reduced tightly to the extractability of ID in the QROM [26]. In addition, while we focus on the standard Fiat-Shamir transform for ease of presentation, the following theorem generalizes to signatures constructed using the multi-round generalization of the Fiat-Shamir transform like, e.g., MQDSS [13].

Theorem 3. *For any (quantum) UF-CMA adversary A issuing at most q_s (classical) queries to the signing oracle SIGN and at most q_H quantum queries to H, there exists a UF-CMA$_0$ adversary B and a multi-HVZK adversary C such that*

$$\mathrm{Succ}_{\mathsf{FS[ID,H]}}^{\mathsf{UF\text{-}CMA}}(\mathsf{A}) \le \mathrm{Succ}_{\mathsf{FS[ID,H]}}^{\mathsf{UF\text{-}CMA_0}}(\mathsf{B}) + \mathrm{Adv}_{\mathsf{ID}}^{q_s-\mathsf{HVZK}}(\mathsf{C}) \tag{4}$$

$$+ \frac{3q_s}{2}\sqrt{(q_H + q_s + 1) \cdot \gamma(\mathsf{Commit})} \ , \tag{5}$$

and the running time of B and C is about that of A. The bound given in Eq. (4) also holds for the modified Fiat-Shamir transform that defines challenges by letting $c := \mathsf{H}(w, m, pk)$ instead of letting $c := \mathsf{H}(w, m)$.

Note that if ID is statistically HVZK, we can replace $\mathrm{Adv}_{\mathsf{ID}}^{q_s-\mathsf{HVZK}}(\mathsf{C})$ with $q_s \cdot \Delta_{\mathsf{HVZK}}$.

Proof. Consider the sequence of games given in Fig. 7.

GAME G_0. Since game G_0 is the original UF-CMA game,

$$\mathrm{Succ}_{\mathsf{FS[ID,H]}}^{\mathsf{UF\text{-}CMA}}(\mathsf{A}) = \Pr[G_0^{\mathsf{A}} \Rightarrow 1] \ .$$

GAMES G_0 - G_2	SIGN(m)	getTrans(m) //G_0-G_1
01 $(pk, sk) \leftarrow$ IG(par)	07 $\mathfrak{L}_{\mathcal{M}} := \mathfrak{L}_{\mathcal{M}} \cup \{m\}$	12 $(w, st) \leftarrow$ Commit(sk)
02 $(m^*, \sigma^*) \leftarrow A^{\text{SIGN},|H\rangle}(pk)$	08 $(w, c, z) \leftarrow$ getTrans(m) //G_0-G_1	13 $c := H(w, m)$ //G_0
03 if $m^* \in \mathfrak{L}_{\mathcal{M}}$ return 0	09 $(w, c, z) \leftarrow$ Sim(pk) //G_2	14 $c' \leftarrow_\$ C$ //G_1
04 Parse $(w^*, z^*) := \sigma^*$	10 $H := H^{(w,m) \mapsto c}$ //G_1 -G_2	15 $z \leftarrow$ Respond(sk, w, c, st)
05 $c^* := H(w^*, m^*)$	11 return $\sigma := (w, z)$	16 return (w, c, z)
06 return $V(pk, w^*, c^*, z^*)$		

Fig. 7. Games G_0 - G_2 for the proof of Theorem 3.

GAME G_1. In game G_1, we change the game twofold: First, the transcript is now drawn according to the underlying ID scheme, i.e., it is drawn uniformly at random as opposed to letting $c := H(w, m)$, see line 14. Second, we reprogram the random oracle H in line 10 such that it is rendered a-posteriori-consistent with this transcript, i.e., we reprogram H such that $H(w, m) = c$.

To upper bound the game distance, we construct a quantum distinguisher D in Fig. 8 that is run in the adaptive reprogramming games $\text{REPRO}_{R,b}$ with $R := q_S$ many reprogramming instances. We identify reprogramming position x with (w, m), additional input x' with st, and y with c. Hence, the distribution p consists of the constant distribution that always returns m (as m was already chosen by A), together with the distribution Commit(sk). Since D perfectly simulates game G_b if run in its respective game REPRO_b, we have

$$| \Pr[G_0^A = 1] - \Pr[G_1^A = 1]| = | \Pr[\text{REPRO}_1^D \Rightarrow 1] - \Pr[\text{REPRO}_0^D \Rightarrow 1]| \ .$$

Since D issues q_S reprogramming instructions and $(q_H + q_S + 1)$ many queries to H, Proposition 2 yields

$$| \Pr[\text{REPRO}_1^D \Rightarrow 1] - \Pr[\text{REPRO}_0^D \Rightarrow 1]| \leq \frac{3q_S}{2} \sqrt{(q_H + q_S + 1) \cdot p_{\max}} \ , \quad (6)$$

where $p_{\max} = \mathbb{E}_{\text{IG}} \max_w \Pr_{W,\text{ST} \leftarrow \text{Commit}(sk)}[W = w] = \gamma(\text{Commit})$.

Distinguisher $D^{|H\rangle}$	SIGN(m)
01 $(pk, sk) \leftarrow$ IG(par)	07 $\mathfrak{L}_{\mathcal{M}} := \mathfrak{L}_{\mathcal{M}} \cup \{m\}$
02 $(m^*, \sigma^*) \leftarrow A^{\text{SIGN},|H\rangle}(pk)$	08 $(w, st) \leftarrow$ REPROGRAM(m, Commit(sk))
03 if $m^* \in \mathfrak{L}_{\mathcal{M}}$ return 0	09 $c := H(w, m)$
04 Parse $(w^*, z^*) := \sigma^*$	10 $z \leftarrow$ Respond(sk, w, c, st)
05 $c^* := H(w^*, m^*)$	11 return $\sigma := (w, z)$
06 return $V(pk, w^*, c^*, z^*)$	

Fig. 8. Reprogramming distinguisher D for the proof of Theorem 3.

GAME G_2. In game G_2, we change the game such that the signing algorithm does not make use of the secret key any more: Instead of being defined relative to the honestly generated transcripts, signatures are now defined relative to the simulator's transcripts. We will now upper bound $| \Pr[G_1^A = 1] - \Pr[G_2^A = 1]|$ via computational multi-HVZK. Consider multi-HVZK adversary C in Fig. 9. C takes as input a list of q_s many transcripts, which are either all honest transcripts or simulated ones. Since reprogramming is done a-posteriori in game G_1, C can simulate it via an initial table look-up, like the reduction M that was given in Sect. 3.1 (see the description on p. 13). C perfectly simulates game G_1 if run on honest transcripts, and game G_2 if run on simulated ones, hence

$$|\Pr[G_1^A = 1] - \Pr[G_2^A = 1]| \leq \mathrm{Adv}_{\mathrm{ID}}^{q_S - \mathrm{HVZK}}(C) .$$

Adversary $C^{|H\rangle}(pk, ((w_i, c_i, z_i)_{i \in \{1,\cdots,q_s\}})$	$\mathrm{SIGN}(m)$	$H'(w, m)$
01 $i := 0$	08 $i{+}{+}$	15 **if** $\exists c$ s. th. $(w, m, c) \in \mathfrak{L}_{H'}$
02 $\mathfrak{L}_{H'} := \emptyset$	09 $\mathfrak{L}_{\mathcal{M}} := \mathfrak{L}_{\mathcal{M}} \cup \{m\}$	16 **return** c
03 $(m^*, \sigma^*) \leftarrow A^{\mathrm{SIGN},|H'\rangle}(pk)$	10 $(w, c, z) := (w_i, c_i, z_i)$	17 **else return** $H(w, m)$
04 **if** $m^* \in \mathfrak{L}_{\mathcal{M}}$ **return** 0	11 **if** $\exists c'$ s. th. $(w, m, c') \in$	
05 Parse $(w^*, z^*) := \sigma^*$	$\mathfrak{L}_{H'}$	
06 $c^* := H(w^*, m^*)$	12 $\mathfrak{L}_{H'} := \mathfrak{L}_{H'} \setminus \{(w, m, c')\}$	
07 **return** $V(pk, w^*, c^*, z^*)$	13 $\mathfrak{L}_{H'} := \mathfrak{L}_{H'} \cup \{(w, m, c)\}$	
	14 **return** $\sigma := (w, z)$	

Fig. 9. HVZK adversary C for the proof of Theorem 3.

It remains to upper bound $\Pr[G_2^A \Rightarrow 1]$. Consider adversary B, given in Fig. 10. B is run in game $\mathrm{UF\text{-}CMA}_0$ and perfectly simulates game G_2 to A. If A wins in game G_2, it cannot have queried SIGN on m^*. Therefore, H' is not reprogrammed on (m^*, w^*) and hence, σ^* is a valid signature in B's $\mathrm{UF\text{-}CMA}_0$ game.

$$\Pr[G_2^A \Rightarrow 1] \leq \mathrm{Succ}_{\mathrm{FS[ID,H]}}^{\mathrm{UF\text{-}CMA}_0}(B) .$$

Collecting the probabilities yields the desired bound.

Adversary $B^{|H\rangle}(pk)$	$\mathrm{SIGN}(m)$	$H'(w, m)$
01 $\mathfrak{L}_{H'} := \emptyset$	05 $\mathfrak{L}_{\mathcal{M}} := \mathfrak{L}_{\mathcal{M}} \cup \{m\}$	11 **if** $\exists c$ s. th. $(w, m, c) \in$
02 $(m^*, \sigma^*) \leftarrow A^{\mathrm{SIGN},|H'\rangle}(pk)$	06 $(w, c, z) \leftarrow \mathrm{Sim}(pk)$	$\mathfrak{L}_{H'}$
03 **if** $m^* \in \mathfrak{L}_{\mathcal{M}}$ ABORT	07 **if** $\exists c'$ s. th. $(w, m, c') \in \mathfrak{L}_{H'}$	12 **return** c
04 **return** (m^*, σ^*)	08 $\mathfrak{L}_{H'} := \mathfrak{L}_{H'} \setminus \{(w, m, c')\}$	13 **else**
	09 $\mathfrak{L}_{H'} := \mathfrak{L}_{H'} \cup \{(w, m, c)\}$	14 **return** $H(w, m)$
	10 **return** $\sigma := (w, z)$	

Fig. 10. Adversary B for the proof of Theorem 3.

It remains to show that the bound also holds if challenges are derived by letting $c := H(w, m, pk)$. To that end, we revisit the sequence of games given in Fig. 7: We replace $c := H(w, m)$ (and $c^* := H(w^*, m^*)$) with $c := H(w, m, pk)$ (and $c^* := H(w^*, m^*, pk)$) in line 13 (line 05), and change the reprogram instruction in line 10, accordingly. Since pk is public, we can easily adapt both distinguisher D and adversaries B and C to account for these changes. In particular, D will simply include pk as a (fixed) part of the probability distribution that is forwarded to its reprogramming oracle. Since the public key holds no entropy once that it is fixed by the game, this change does not affect the upper bound given in Eq. (6).

4.2 Revisiting the Hedged Fiat-Shamir Transform

In this section, we show how Theorem 1 can be used to extend the results of [5] to the quantum random oracle model: We show that the Fiat-Shamir transform is robust against several types of one-bit fault injections, even in the quantum random oracle model, and that the hedged Fiat-Shamir transform is as robust, even if an attacker is in control of the nonce that is used to generate the signing randomness. In this section, we follow [5] and consider the modified Fiat-Shamir transform that includes the public key into the hash when generating challenges. We consider the following one-bit tampering functions:

flip-bit$_i(x)$: Does a logical negation of the i-th bit of x.
set-bit$_i(x, b)$: Sets the i-th bit of x to b.

HEDGED SIGNATURE SCHEMES. Let $\mathcal{N}$ be any nonce space. With a signature scheme SIG = (KG, Sign, Vrfy) with secret key space $\mathcal{SK}$ and signing randomness space $\mathcal{R}_{\mathsf{Sign}}$, and random oracle $\mathsf{G} : \mathcal{SK} \times \mathcal{M} \times \mathcal{N} \to \mathcal{R}_{\mathsf{Sign}}$, we associate

$$\mathsf{R2H}[\mathsf{SIG}, \mathsf{G}] := \mathsf{SIG}' := (\mathsf{KG}, \mathsf{Sign}', \mathsf{Vrfy}) \ ,$$

where the signing algorithm Sign$'$ of SIG$'$ takes as input (sk, m, n), deterministically computes $r := \mathsf{G}(sk, m, n)$, and returns $\sigma := \mathsf{Sign}(sk, m; r)$.

SECURITY OF (HEDGED) FIAT-SHAMIR AGAINST FAULT INJECTIONS AND NONCE ATTACKS. Next, we define UnForgeability in the presence of Faults, under Chosen Message Attacks (UF-F-CMA), for Fiat-Shamir transformed schemes. In game UF-F-CMA, the adversary has access to a faulty signing oracle FAULTSIGN which returns signatures that were created relative to an injected fault. To be more precise, game UF-F$_{\mathcal{F}}$-CMA is defined relative to a set $\mathcal{F}$ of indices, and the indices $i \in \mathcal{F}$ specify at which point during the signing procedure exactly the faults are allowed to occur. An overview is given in Fig. 11.

For the hedged Fiat-Shamir construction, we further define UnForgeability, with control over the used Nonces and in the presence of Faults, under Chosen Message Attacks (UF-N-F-CMA). In game UF-N-F-CMA, the adversary is even allowed to control the nonce n that is used to derive the internal randomness of algorithm Commit. We therefore denote the respective oracle by N-FAULTSIGN. Our definitions slightly simplify the one of [5]: While [5] also considered fault attacks on the input of algorithm Commit (with corresponding indices 2 and 3), they showed that the hedged construction can not be proven robust against these faults, in general. We therefore omitted them from our games, but adhered to the numbering for comparability.

The hedged Fiat-Shamir scheme derandomizes the signing procedure by replacing the signing randomness by $r := \mathsf{G}(sk, m, n)$. Hence, game UF-N-F-CMA

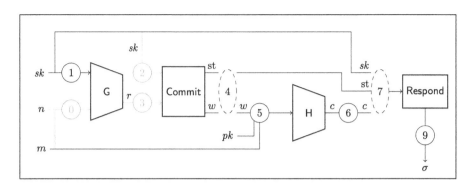

Fig. 11. Faulting a (hedged) Fiat-Shamir signature. Circles represent faults, and their numbers are the respective fault indices $i \in \mathcal{F}$ (following [5], for the formal definition see Fig. 12). Greyed out fault wires indicate that the hedged construction can not be proven robust against these faults, in general. Dashed fault nodes indicate that the Fiat-Shamir construction is robust against these faults if the scheme is subset-revealing.

considers two additional faults: An attacker can fault the input of G, i.e., either the secret key (fault index 1), or the tuple (m, n) (fault index 0). As shown in [5], the hedged construction can not be proven robust against faults on (m, n), in general, therefore we only consider index 1.

Furthermore, we do not formalize derivation/serialisation and drop the corresponding indices 8 and 10 to not overly complicate our application example. A generalization of our result that also considers derivation/serialisation, however, is straightforward.

Definition 3. *(UF-F-CMA and UF-N-F-CMA) For any subset $\mathcal{F} \subset \{4, \cdots, 9\}$, we define the UF-F$_\mathcal{F}$-CMA game as in Fig. 12, and the UF-F$_\mathcal{F}$-CMA success probability of a quantum adversary A against FS[ID, H] as*

$$\mathrm{Succ}_{\mathsf{FS[ID,H]}}^{\mathsf{UF\text{-}F\text{-}}\mathcal{F}\text{-}\mathsf{CMA}}(\mathsf{A}) := \Pr[\mathsf{UF\text{-}F}_\mathcal{F}\text{-}\mathsf{CMA}_{\mathsf{FS[ID,H]}}^{\mathsf{A}} \Rightarrow 1] \ .$$

Furthermore, we define the UF-N-F$_\mathcal{F}$-CMA game (also in Fig. 12) for any subset $\mathcal{F} \subset \{1, 4, \cdots, 9\}$, and the UF-N-F$_\mathcal{F}$-CMA success probability of a quantum adversary A against SIG' := R2H[FS[ID, H], G] as

$$\mathrm{Succ}_{\mathsf{SIG'}}^{\mathsf{UF\text{-}N\text{-}F\text{-}}\mathcal{F}\text{-}\mathsf{CMA}}(\mathsf{A}) := \Pr[\mathsf{UF\text{-}N\text{-}F}_\mathcal{F}\text{-}\mathsf{CMA}_{\mathsf{SIG'}}^{\mathsf{A}} \Rightarrow 1] \ .$$

FROM UF-CMA$_0$ TO UF-F-CMA. First, we generalize [5, Lemma 5] to the quantum random oracle model. The proof is given in the full version .

Theorem 4. *Assume ID to be validity aware . If SIG := FS[ID, H] is UF-CMA$_0$ secure, then SIG is also UF-F$_\mathcal{F}$-CMA secure for $\mathcal{F} := \{5, 6, 9\}$, in the quantum random oracle model. Concretely, for any adversary A against the UF-F$_\mathcal{F}$-CMA security of SIG, issuing at most q_S (classical) queries to FAULTSIGN and q_H*

Game	UF-F$_\mathcal{F}$-CMA	UF-N-F$_\mathcal{F}$-CMA	FAULTSIGN$(m, i \in \mathcal{F}, \phi)$	N-FAULTSIGN$(m, n, i \in \mathcal{F}, \phi)$
01	$(pk, sk) \leftarrow \mathsf{IG}(par)$		08 $f_i := \phi$ and $f_j := \mathrm{id} \; \forall \, j \neq i$	17 $f_i := \phi$ and $f_j := \mathrm{id} \; \forall \, j \neq i$
02	$(m^*, \sigma^*) \leftarrow \mathsf{A}^{\mathsf{FAULTSIGN}, |\mathsf{H}\rangle}(pk)$		09	18 $r := \mathsf{G}(f_1(sk), m, n)$
			10 $(w, st) \leftarrow \mathsf{Commit}(sk)$	19 $(w, st) \leftarrow \mathsf{Commit}(sk; r)$
03		$(m^*, \sigma^*) \leftarrow \mathsf{A}^{\mathsf{N\text{-}FAULTSIGN}, |\mathsf{H}\rangle, |\mathsf{G}\rangle}(pk)$	11 $(w, st) := f_4(w, st)$	20 $(w, st) := f_4(w, st)$
04	**if** $m^* \in \mathfrak{L}_\mathcal{M}$ **return** 0		12 $(\hat{w}, \hat{m}, \hat{pk}) := f_5(w, m, pk)$	21 $(\hat{w}, \hat{m}, \hat{pk}) := f_5(w, m, pk)$
05	Parse $(w^*, z^*) := \sigma^*$		13 $c := f_6(\mathsf{H}(\hat{w}, \hat{m}, \hat{pk}))$	22 $c := f_6(\mathsf{H}(\hat{w}, \hat{m}, \hat{pk}))$
06	$c^* := \mathsf{H}(w^*, m^*)$		14 $z \leftarrow \mathsf{Respond}(f_7(sk, c, st))$	23 $z \leftarrow \mathsf{Respond}(f_7(sk, c, st))$
07	**return** $\mathsf{V}(pk, w^*, c^*, z^*)$		15 $\mathfrak{L}_\mathcal{M} := \mathfrak{L}_\mathcal{M} \cup \{\hat{m}\}$	24 $\mathfrak{L}_\mathcal{M} := \mathfrak{L}_\mathcal{M} \cup \{\hat{m}\}$
			16 **return** $\sigma := f_9(w, z)$	25 **return** $\sigma := f_9(w, z)$

Fig. 12. Left: Game UF-F$_\mathcal{F}$-CMA for SIG $=$ FS[ID, H], and game UF-N-F$_\mathcal{F}$-CMA for the hedged Fiat-Shamir construction SIG$'$ $:=$ R2H[FS[ID, H], G], both defined relative to a set $\mathcal{F}$ of allowed fault index positions. ϕ denotes the fault function, which either negates one particular bit of its input, sets one particular bit of its input to 0 or 1, or does nothing. We implicitly require fault index i to be contained in $\mathcal{F}$, i.e., we make the convention that both faulty signing oracles return $\perp$ if $i \notin \mathcal{F}$.

(quantum) queries to H, *there exists an* UF-CMA$_0$ *adversary* B *and a multi-*sHVZK *adversary* C *such that*

$$\mathsf{Succ}_{\mathsf{SIG}}^{\mathsf{UF\text{-}F}_{\{5,6,9\}}\text{-}\mathsf{CMA}}(\mathsf{A}) \leq \mathsf{Succ}_{\mathsf{SIG}}^{\mathsf{UF\text{-}CMA}_0}(\mathsf{B}) + \mathsf{Adv}_{\mathsf{ID}}^{q_s-\mathsf{sHVZK}}(\mathsf{C})$$
$$+ \frac{3q_S}{2}\sqrt{2 \cdot (q_H + q_S + 1) \cdot \gamma(\mathsf{Commit})} \; . \qquad (7)$$

and B *and* C *have about the running time of* A.

If we assume that ID *is subset-revealing, then* SIG *is even* UF-F$_{\mathcal{F}'}$-CMA *secure for* $\mathcal{F}' := \mathcal{F} \cup \{4, 7\}$. *Concretely, the bound of Eq. (7) then holds also for* $\mathcal{F}' = \{4, 5, 6, 7, 9\}$.

FROM UF-F-CMA TO UF-N-F-CMA. Second, we generalize [5, Lemma 4] to the QROM. The proof is given in the full version.

Theorem 5. *If* SIG $:=$ FS[ID, H] *is* UF-F$_\mathcal{F}$-CMA *secure for a fault index set* $\mathcal{F}$, *then* SIG$'$ $:=$ R2H[SIG, G] *is* UF-N-F$_{\mathcal{F}'}$-CMA *secure for* $\mathcal{F}' := \mathcal{F} \cup \{1\}$, *in the quantum random oracle model, against any adversary that issues no query* (m, n) *to* N-FAULTSIGN *more than once. Concretely, for any adversary* A *against the* UF-N-F$_\mathcal{F}$-CMA *security of* SIG$'$ *for* $\mathcal{F}'$, *issuing at most* q_S *queries to* N-FAULTSIGN, *at most* q_H *queries to* H, *and at most* q_G *queries to* G, *there exist* UF-F$_\mathcal{F}$-CMA *adversaries* B$_1$ B$_2$ *such that*

$$\mathsf{Succ}_{\mathsf{SIG}'}^{\mathsf{UF\text{-}N\text{-}F}_{\mathcal{F}'}\text{-}\mathsf{CMA}}(\mathsf{A}) \leq \mathsf{Succ}_{\mathsf{SIG}}^{\mathsf{UF\text{-}F}_\mathcal{F}\text{-}\mathsf{CMA}}(\mathsf{B}_1) + 2q_G \cdot \sqrt{\mathsf{Succ}_{\mathsf{SIG}}^{\mathsf{UF\text{-}F}_\mathcal{F}\text{-}\mathsf{CMA}}(\mathsf{B}_2)} \; ,$$

and B$_1$ *has about the running time of* A, *while* B$_2$ *has a running time of roughly* Time(B$_2$) $\approx$ Time(A) $+ |sk| \cdot$ (Time(Sign) + Time(Vrfy)), *where* $|sk|$ *denotes the length of* sk.

With regards to the reduction's advantage, this proof is not as tight as the one in [5]: R2H[SIG, G] derives the commitment randomness as $r := \mathsf{G}(sk, m, n)$.

During our proof, we need to decouple r from the secret key. In the ROM, it is straightforward how to turn any adversary noticing this change into an extractor that returns the secret key. In the QROM, however, all currently known extraction techniques still come with a quadratic loss in the extraction probability. On the other hand, our reduction is tighter with regards to running time, which we reduce by a factor of q_G when compared to [5]. If we hedge with an independent seed s of length ℓ (instead of sk), it can be shown with a multi-instance generalization of [33, Lem. 2.2] that

$$\text{Succ}_{\text{SIG}'}^{\text{UF-N-F}_{\mathcal{F}}\text{-CMA}}(\mathsf{A}) \leq \text{Succ}_{\text{SIG}}^{\text{UF-F}_{\mathcal{F}}\text{-CMA}}(\mathsf{B}) + (\ell + 1) \cdot (q_S + q_G) \cdot \sqrt{1/2^{\ell-1}} \ .$$

5   Adaptive Reprogramming: Proofs

We will now give the proof for our main Theorem 1, which can be broken down into three steps: In this section, we consider the simple special case in which only a single reprogramming instance occurs, and where no additional input x' is provided to the adversary. The generalisation to multiple reprogramming instances follows from a standard hybrid argument. The generalisation that considers additional input is also straightforward, as the achieved bounds are information-theoretical and a reduction can hence compute marginal and conditioned distributions on its own. For the sake of completeness, we include the generalisation steps in the full version .

In this and the following sections, we need quantum theory. We stick to the common notation as introduced in, e.g. [30]. Nevertheless we introduce some of the most important basics and notational choices we make. For a vector $|\psi\rangle \in \mathcal{H}$ in a complex Euclidean space $\mathcal{H}$, we denote the standard Euclidean norm by $\| \, |\psi\rangle \, \|$. We use a subscript to indicate that a vector $|\psi\rangle$ is the state of a quantum register A with Hilbert space $\mathcal{H}$, i.e. $|\psi\rangle_A$. Similarly, M_A indicates that a matrix M acting on $\mathcal{H}$ is considered as acting on register A. The joint Hilbert space of multiple registers is given by the tensor product of the single-register Hilbert spaces. Where it helps simplify notation, we take the liberty to reorder registers, keeping track of them using register subscripts. The only other norm we will require is the trace norm. For a matrix M acting on $\mathcal{H}$, the trace norm $\|M\|_1$ is defined as the sum of the singular values of M. An important quantum gate is the quantum extension of the classical CNOT gate. This quantum gate is a unitary matrix CNOT acting on two qubits, i.e. on the vector space $\mathbb{C}^2 \otimes \mathbb{C}^2$, as $\text{CNOT}|b_1\rangle|b_2\rangle = |b_1\rangle|b_2 \oplus b_1\rangle$. We sometimes subscript a CNOT gate with control register A and target register B with $A : B$, and extend this notation to the case where many CNOT gates are applied, i.e. $\text{CNOT}_{A:B}^{\otimes n}$ means a CNOT gate is applied to the i-th qubit of the n-qubit registers A and B for each $i = 1, ..., n$ with the qubits in A being the controls and the ones in B the targets.

5.1   The Superposition Oracle

For proving the main result of this section, we will use the (simplest version of the) superposition oracle introduced in [39]. In the following, we introduce that technique, striving to keep this explanation accessible even to readers with minimal knowledge about quantum theory.

Superposition oracles are perfectly correct methods for simulating a quantum-accessible random oracle $O : \{0,1\}^n \rightarrow \{0,1\}^m$. Different variants of the superposition oracle have different additional features that make them more useful than the quantum-accessible random oracle itself. We will use the fact that in the superposition oracle formalism, the reprogramming can be directly implemented by replacing a part of the quantum state held by the oracle, instead of using a simulator that sits between the original oracle and the querying algorithm. Notice that for this, we only need the simplest version of the superposition oracle from [39].[6] In that basic form, there are only three relatively simple conceptual steps underlying the construction of the superposition oracle, with the third one being key to its usefulness in analyses:

- For each $x \in \{0,1\}^n$, $O(x)$ is a random variable uniformly distributed on $\{0,1\}^m$. This random variable can, of course, be sampled using a *quantum measurement*, more precisely a computational basis measurement of the state

$$|\phi_0\rangle = 2^{-m/2} \sum_{y \in \{0,1\}^m} |y\rangle.$$

- For a function $o : \{0,1\}^n \rightarrow \{0,1\}^m$, we can store the string $o(x)$ in a quantum register F_x. In fact, to sample $O(x)$, we can prepare a register F_x in state $|\phi_0\rangle$, perform a computational basis measurement and keep the *collapsed* so-called *post-measurement state*. Outcome y of the measurement corresponds to the projector $|y\rangle\langle y|$, and a post-measurement state proportional to

$$|y\rangle\langle y| \, |\phi_0\rangle = 2^{-\frac{m}{2}} |y\rangle.$$

Now a query with input $|x\rangle_X |\psi\rangle_Y$ can be answered using CNOT gates, i.e. we can answer queries with a superposition oracle unitary O acting on input registers X, Y and an oracle register $F = F_{0^m} F_{0^{m-1}1} ... F_{1^m}$ such that

$$O_{XYF} |x\rangle\langle x|_X = |x\rangle\langle x|_X \otimes \left(\mathrm{CNOT}^{\otimes m}\right)_{F_x : Y}.$$

- Since the matrices $|y\rangle\langle y|_{F_x}$ and $\left(\mathrm{CNOT}^{\otimes m}\right)_{F_x : Y}$ commute, we can delay the measurement that performs the sampling of the random oracle until the end of the runtime of the querying algorithm. Queries are hence answered using the unitary O, but acting on oracle registers F_x that are all initialized in the uniform superposition state $|\phi_0\rangle$, and only after the querying algorithm has finished, the register F is measured to obtain the concrete random function O.

A quantum-accessible oracle for a random function $O : \{0,1\}^n \rightarrow \{0,1\}^m$ is thus implemented as follows:

---

[6] Note that this basic superposition oracle does not provide an *efficient* simulation of a quantum-accessible random oracle, which is fine for proving a query lower bound that holds without assumptions about time complexity.

– Initialize: Prepare the initial state

$$|\Phi\rangle_F = \bigotimes_{x \in \{0,1\}^n} |\phi_0\rangle_{F_x}.$$

– Oracle: A quantum query on registers X and Y is answered using O_{XYF}

– Post-processing: Register F is measured to obtain a random function O. The last step can be (partially) omitted whenever the function O is not needed for evaluation of the success or failure of the algorithm. In the following, the querying algorithm is, e.g. tasked with distinguishing two oracles, a setting where the final sampling measurement can be omitted.

Note that it is straightforward to implement the operation of reprogramming a random oracle to a fresh random value on a certain input x: just discard the contents of register F_x and replace them with a freshly prepared state $|\phi_0\rangle$. In addition, we need the following lemma

Lemma 1 (Lemma 2 in [3], reformulated). *Let $|\psi_q\rangle_{AF}$ be the joint adversary-oracle state after an adversary has made q queries to the superposition oracle with register F. Then this state can be written as*

$$|\psi_q\rangle_{AF} = \sum_{\substack{S \subset \{0,1\}^n \\ |S| \leq q}} |\psi_q^{(S)}\rangle_{AF_S} \otimes \left(|\phi_0\rangle^{\otimes(2^n - |S|)}\right)_{F_{S^c}},$$

where for any set $R = \{x_1, x_2, ..., x_{|R|}\} \subset \{0,1\}^n$ we have defined $F_R = F_{x_1} F_{x_2} ... F_{x_{|R|}}$ and $|\psi_q^{(S)}\rangle_{AF_S}$ are vectors such that $\langle \phi_0|_{F_x} |\psi_q^{(S)}\rangle_{AF_S} = 0$ for all $x \in S$.

5.2   Reprogramming Once

We are now ready to study our simple special case. Suppose a random oracle O is reprogrammed at a single input $x^* \in \{0,1\}^n$, sampled according to some probability distribution p, to a fresh random output $y^* \leftarrow \{0,1\}^m$. We set $O_0 = O$ and define O_1 by $O_1(x^*) = y$ and $O_1(x) = O(x)$ for $x \neq x^*$. We will show that if x^* has sufficient min-entropy given O, such reprogramming is hard to detect.

More formally, consider a two-stage distinguisher $D = (D_0, D_1)$. The first stage D_0 has trivial input, makes q quantum queries to O and outputs a quantum state $|\psi_{int}\rangle$ and a sampling algorithm for a probability distribution p on $\{0,1\}^n$. The second stage D_1 gets $x^* \leftarrow p$ and $|\psi_{int}\rangle$ as input, has arbitrary quantum query access to O_b and outputs a bit b' with the goal that $b' = b$. We prove the following.

Theorem 6. *The success probability for any distinguisher D as defined above is bounded by*

$$\Pr[b = b'] \leq \frac{1}{2} + \frac{1}{2}\sqrt{q p_{\max}^D} + \frac{1}{4} q p_{\max}^D,$$

where the probability is taken over $b \leftarrow \{0,1\}, (|\psi_{int}\rangle, p) \leftarrow \mathsf{D}_0^{\mathsf{O}}(1^n)$ *and* $b' \leftarrow \mathsf{D}_1^{\mathsf{O}_b}(x^*, |\psi_{int}\rangle)$, *and* $p_{\max}^{\mathsf{D}} = \mathbb{E}_{(|\psi_{int}\rangle, p) \leftarrow \mathsf{D}_0^{\mathsf{O}_0}(1^n)} \max_x p(x)$.

Proof. We implement $\mathsf{O} = \mathsf{O}_0$ as a superposition oracle. Without loss of generality[7], we can assume that D proceeds by performing a unitary quantum computation, followed by a measurement to produce the classical output p and the discarding of a working register G. Let $|\gamma\rangle_{RGF}$ be the algorithm-oracle-state after the unitary part of D_0 and the measurement have been performed, conditioned on its second output being a fixed probability distribution p. R contains D_0's first output .

Define $\varepsilon_x = 1 - \left\| \langle\phi_0|_{F_x} |\gamma\rangle_{RGF} \right\|^2$, a measure of how far the contents of register F_x are from the uniform superposition. Intuitively, this is the 'probability' that the distinguisher knows $\mathsf{O}(x)$, and should be small in expectation over $x \leftarrow p$. We therefore begin by bounding the distinguishing advantage in terms of this quantity. For a fixed x, we can write the density matrix $\rho^{(0)} = |\gamma\rangle\langle\gamma|$ as

$$\rho_{RGF}^{(0)} = \langle\phi_0|_{F_x} \rho_{RGF}^{(0)} |\phi_0\rangle_{F_x} \otimes |\phi_0\rangle\langle\phi_0|_{F_x} + \rho_{RGF}^{(0)} \left(\mathbb{1} - |\phi_0\rangle\langle\phi_0|_{F_x}\right)$$
$$+ \left(\mathbb{1} - |\phi_0\rangle\langle\phi_0|_{F_x}\right) \rho_{RGF}^{(0)} |\phi_0\rangle\langle\phi_0|_{F_x} . \tag{8}$$

The density matrix $\rho_{RGF}^{(1,x)}$ for the algorithm-oracle-state after D_0 has finished and the oracle has been reprogrammed at x (i.e. $b = 1$) is[8]

$$\rho_{RGF}^{(1,x)} = \mathrm{Tr}_{F_x}[\rho_{RGF}^{(1,x)}] \otimes |\phi_0\rangle\langle\phi_0|_{F_x} = \langle\phi_0|_{F_x} \rho_{RGF}^{(0)} |\phi_0\rangle_{F_x} \otimes |\phi_0\rangle\langle\phi_0|_{F_x}$$
$$+ \mathrm{Tr}_{F_x}[(\mathbb{1} - |\phi_0\rangle\langle\phi_0|_{F_x})\rho_{RGF}^{(0)}] \otimes |\phi_0\rangle\langle\phi_0|_{F_x}^{12} , \tag{9}$$

where the second equality is immediate when computing the partial trace in an orthonormal basis containing $|\phi_0\rangle$.

We analyze the success probability of D. In the following, set $x^* = x$. The second stage, D_1, has arbitrary query access to the oracle O_b. In the superposition oracle framework, that means D_1 can apply arbitrary unitary operations on its registers R and G, and the oracle unitary O to some sub-register registers XY of G and the oracle register F. We bound the success probability by allowing arbitrary operations on F, thus reducing the oracle distinguishing task to the task of distinguishing the quantum states $\rho_{RF}^{(b,x)} = \mathrm{Tr}_G \rho_{RGF}^{(b,x)}$ for $b = 0, 1$, where $\rho^{(0,x)} := \rho^{(0)}$. By the bound relating distinguishing advantage and trace distance,

$$\Pr[b = b'|x^* = x] \leq \frac{1}{2} + \frac{1}{4}\left\|\rho_{RF}^{(0)} - \rho_{RF}^{(1,x)}\right\|_1 \leq \frac{1}{2} + \frac{1}{4}\left\|\rho_{RGF}^{(0)} - \rho_{RGF}^{(1,x)}\right\|_1, \tag{10}$$

---

[7] This can be seen by employing the Stinespring dilation theorem, or by using standard techniques to delay measurement and discard operations until the end of a quantum algorithm.

[8] Note that the partial trace expression yields a positive semidefinite matrix due to the cyclicity of the trace and the fact that $\mathbb{1} - |\phi_0\rangle\langle\phi_0|_{F_x}$ is a projector and hence Hermitian.

where the probability is taken over $b \leftarrow \{0,1\}, |\psi_{int}\rangle \leftarrow \mathsf{D}_0^{O_0}(1^n)$ and $b' \leftarrow \mathsf{D}_1^{O_b}(x, |\psi_{int}\rangle)$, and we have used that the trace distance is non-increasing under partial trace. Using Eqs. (8) and (9), we bound

$$\left\| \rho_{RGF}^{(0)} - \rho_{RGF}^{(1,x)} \right\|_1$$
$$\leq \left\| \rho_{RGF}^{(0)} \left(\mathbb{1} - |\phi_0\rangle\langle\phi_0|_{F_x} \right) + \left(\mathbb{1} - |\phi_0\rangle\langle\phi_0|_{F_x} \right) \rho_{RGF}^{(0)} |\phi_0\rangle\langle\phi_0|_{F_x} \right.$$
$$\left. - \mathrm{Tr}_{F_x}[(\mathbb{1} - |\phi_0\rangle\langle\phi_0|_{F_x})\rho_{RGF}^{(0)}] \otimes |\phi_0\rangle\langle\phi_0|_{F_x} \right\|_1$$
$$\leq \left\| \rho_{RGF}^{(0)} \left(\mathbb{1} - |\phi_0\rangle\langle\phi_0|_{F_x} \right) \right\|_1 + \left\| \left(\mathbb{1} - |\phi_0\rangle\langle\phi_0|_{F_x} \right) \rho_{RGF}^{(0)} |\phi_0\rangle\langle\phi_0|_{F_x} \right\|_1$$
$$+ \left\| \mathrm{Tr}_{F_x}[(\mathbb{1} - |\phi_0\rangle\langle\phi_0|_{F_x})\rho_{RGF}^{(0)}] \otimes |\phi_0\rangle\langle\phi_0|_{F_x} \right\|_1,$$

Where the last line is the triangle inequality. The trace norm of a positive semidefinite matrix is equal to its trace, so the last term can be simplified as

$$\left\| \mathrm{Tr}_{F_x}[(\mathbb{1} - |\phi_0\rangle\langle\phi_0|_{F_x})\rho_{RGF}^{(0)}] \otimes |\phi_0\rangle\langle\phi_0|_{F_x} \right\|_1$$
$$= \mathrm{Tr}[(\mathbb{1} - |\phi_0\rangle\langle\phi_0|_{F_x}) |\gamma\rangle\langle\gamma|_{RGF}] = \varepsilon_x.$$

The second term is upper-bounded by the first via Hölder's inequality, which simplifies as

$$\left\| \rho_{RGF}^{(0)} \left(\mathbb{1} - |\phi_0\rangle\langle\phi_0|_{F_x} \right) \right\|_1 = \left\| |\gamma\rangle\langle\gamma|_{RGF} \left(\mathbb{1} - |\phi_0\rangle\langle\phi_0|_{F_x} \right) \right\|_1$$
$$= \left\| \left(\mathbb{1} - |\phi_0\rangle\langle\phi_0|_{F_x} \right) |\gamma\rangle_{RGF} \right\|_2 = \sqrt{\varepsilon_x}$$

where the second equality uses that $|\gamma\rangle$ is normalized. In summary we have

$$\left\| \rho_{RGF}^{(0)} - \rho_{RGF}^{(1,x)} \right\|_1 \leq 2\sqrt{\varepsilon_x} + \varepsilon_x. \tag{11}$$

It remains to bound ε_x in expectation over $x \leftarrow p$. To this end, we prove

$$\mathbb{E}_{x^* \leftarrow p} \left[\left\| \langle\phi_0|_{F_{x^*}} |\gamma\rangle_{RGF} \right\|^2 \right] \geq 1 - q p_{\max}, \tag{12}$$

where $p_{\max} = \max_x p(x)$. In the following, sums over S are taken over $S \subset \{0,1\}^n : |S| \leq q$, with additional restrictions explicitly mentioned. We have

$$\mathbb{E}_{x^* \leftarrow p} \left[\left\| \langle\phi_0|_{F_{x^*}} |\gamma\rangle_{RGF} \right\|^2 \right] = \sum_{x^* \in \{0,1\}^n} p(x^*) \left\| \langle\phi_0|_{F_{x^*}} |\gamma\rangle_{RGF} \right\|^2$$
$$= \sum_{x^* \in \{0,1\}^n} p(x^*) \left\| \sum_S \langle\phi_0|_{F_{x^*}} |\psi_q^{(S)}\rangle_{RGF_S} \otimes \left(|\phi_0\rangle^{\otimes(2^n - |S|)} \right)_{F_{S^c}} \right\|^2,$$

where we have used Lemma 1 as well as the notation $|\psi_q^{(S)}\rangle$ from there. (Lemma 1 clearly also holds after the projector corresponding to second output equaling

p is applied). Using $\langle \phi_0|_{F_x} |\psi_q^{(S)}\rangle_{RGF_S} = 0$ for all $x \in S$ we simplify

$$\sum_{x^* \in \{0,1\}^n} p(x^*)\Big\| \sum_S \langle \phi_0|_{F_{x^*}} |\psi_q^{(S)}\rangle_{RGF_S} \otimes \left(|\phi_0\rangle^{\otimes(2^n-|S|)}\right)_{F_{S^c}} \Big\|^2$$

$$= \sum_{x^* \in \{0,1\}^n} p(x^*)\Big\| \sum_{S \not\ni x^*} |\psi_q^{(S)}\rangle_{RGF_S} \otimes \left(|\phi_0\rangle^{\otimes(2^n-|S|-1)}\right)_{F_{S^c \setminus \{x^*\}}} \Big\|^2.$$

The summands in the second sum are pairwise orthogonal, so

$$\sum_{x^* \in \{0,1\}^n} p(x^*)\Big\| \sum_{S \not\ni x^*} |\psi_q^{(S)}\rangle_{RGF_S} \otimes \left(|\phi_0\rangle^{\otimes(2^n-|S|-1)}\right)_{F_{S^c \setminus \{x^*\}}} \Big\|^2$$

$$= \sum_{x^* \in \{0,1\}^n} p(x^*) \sum_{S \not\ni x^*} \Big\| |\psi_q^{(S)}\rangle_{RGF_S} \otimes \left(|\phi_0\rangle^{\otimes(2^n-|S|-1)}\right)_{F_{S^c \setminus \{x^*\}}} \Big\|^2$$

$$= \sum_S \sum_{x^* \in S^c} p(x^*)\Big\| |\psi_q^{(S)}\rangle_{RGF_S} \otimes \left(|\phi_0\rangle^{\otimes(2^n-|S|-1)}\right)_{F_{S^c \setminus \{x^*\}}} \Big\|^2$$

$$= \sum_S \sum_{x^* \in S^c} p(x^*)\Big\| |\psi_q^{(S)}\rangle_{RGF_S} \otimes \left(|\phi_0\rangle^{\otimes(2^n-|S|)}\right)_{F_{S^c}} \Big\|^2$$

where we have used the fact that the state $|\phi_0\rangle$ is normalized in the last line. But for any $S \subset \{0,1\}^n$ we have

$$\sum_{x^* \in S^c} p(x^*) = 1 - \sum_{x^* \in S} p(x^*) \geq 1 - |S| p_{\max},$$

where here, $p_{\max} = \max_x p(x)$. We hence obtain

$$\sum_S \sum_{x^* \in S^c} p(x^*)\Big\| |\psi_q^{(S)}\rangle_{RGF_S} \otimes \left(|\phi_0\rangle^{\otimes(2^n-|S|)}\right)_{F_{S^c}} \Big\|^2$$

$$\geq \sum_S (1 - |S| p_{\max})\Big\| |\psi_q^{(S)}\rangle_{RGF_S} \otimes \left(|\phi_0\rangle^{\otimes(2^n-|S|)}\right)_{F_{S^c}} \Big\|^2$$

$$\geq (1 - q p_{\max}) \sum_S \Big\| |\psi_q^{(S)}\rangle_{RGF_S} \otimes \left(|\phi_0\rangle^{\otimes(2^n-|S|)}\right)_{F_{S^c}} \Big\|^2 = 1 - q p_{\max},$$

where we have used the normalization of $|\gamma\rangle_{RGF}$ in the last equality. Combining the above equations proves Eq. (12). Putting everything together, we bound

$$\Pr[b = b'] = \mathbb{E}_p \mathbb{E}_x \Pr[b = b'|p,x] \leq \frac{1}{2} + \frac{1}{4}\mathbb{E}_p\mathbb{E}_x[2\sqrt{\varepsilon_x} + \varepsilon_x]$$

$$\leq \frac{1}{2} + \frac{1}{4}\mathbb{E}_p[2\sqrt{q p_{\max}} + q p_{\max}] \leq \frac{1}{2} + \frac{1}{2}\sqrt{q p_{\max}^D} + q p_{\max}^D.$$

Here, the inequalities are due to Eq. (10) and Eq. (11), Eq. (12) and Jensen's inequality, and another Jensen's inequality, respectively.   □

6   A Matching Attack

We now describe an attack matching the bound presented in Theorem 6. For simplicity, we restrict our attention to the case where just one point is (potentially) reprogrammed.

Our distinguisher makes q queries to O, the oracle before the potential reprogramming, and q queries to O', the oracle after the potential reprogramming. In our attack, we fix an arbitrary cyclic permutation σ on $[2^n]$, and for the fixed reprogrammed point x^*, we define $S = \{x^*, \sigma^{-1}(x^*), ..., \sigma^{-q+1}(x^*)\}$, $\overline{S} = \{0,1\}^n \setminus S$, $\Pi_0 = \frac{1}{2}\left(|S\rangle + |\overline{S}\rangle\right)\left(\langle S| + \langle \overline{S}|\right)$ and $\Pi_1 = I - \Pi_0$.[9] The distinguisher D is defined in Fig. 13.

Before potential reprogramming:	After potential reprogramming:
01 Prepare registers XY in $\frac{1}{\sqrt{2^n}}\sum_{x\in[2^n]}|x,0\rangle_{XY}$	06 Query O' using using registers XY
02 Query O using registers XY	07 **for** $i = q - 2, ..., 0$:
03 **for** $i = 0, ..., q - 2$:	08 Apply σ^{-1} on register X
04 Apply σ on register X	09 Query O' using registers XY
05 Query O using registers XY	10 Measure X according to $\{\Pi_0, \Pi_1\}$
	11 Output b if the state projects onto Π_b.

Fig. 13. Distinguisher for a single reprogrammed point.

Theorem 7. *For every $1 \le q < 2^{n-3}$, the attack described in Fig. 13 can be implemented in quantum polynomial-time. Performing q queries each before and after the potential reprogramming, it detects the reprogramming of a random oracle $\mathsf{O} : \{0,1\}^n \to \{0,1\}^m$ at a single point with probability at least $\Omega\left(\sqrt{\frac{q}{2^n}}\right)$.*

Proof (sketch). We can analyze the state of the distinguisher before its measurement. If the oracle is not reprogrammed, then its state is

$$\frac{1}{\sqrt{2^n}}\sum_x |x\rangle|0\rangle,$$

whereas if the reprogramming happens, its state is

$$\sum_{x\in S}|x\rangle|\mathsf{O}(x^*)\oplus\mathsf{O}'(x^*)\rangle + \sum_{x\in\overline{S}}|x\rangle|0\rangle,$$

where $\mathsf{O}(x^*)\oplus\mathsf{O}'(x^*)$ is a uniformly random value. The advantage follows by calculating the probability that these states project onto Π_0.

For the efficiency of our distinguisher, we can use the tools provided in [2] to efficiently implement Π_0 and Π_1, which are the only non-trivial operations of the attack.

Due to space restrictions, we refer to the full version , where we give the full proof of Theorem 7 and discuss its extension to multiple reprogrammed points.

---

[9] Formally, S, Π_0 and Π_1 are functions of x^* but we omit this dependence for simplicity, since we can assume that x^* is fixed.

References

1. Abdalla, M., Fouque, P.-A., Lyubashevsky, V., Tibouchi, M.: Tightly-secure signatures from lossy identification schemes. In: Pointcheval, D., Johansson, T. (eds.) EUROCRYPT 2012. LNCS, vol. 7237, pp. 572–590. Springer, Heidelberg (2012). https://doi.org/10.1007/978-3-642-29011-4_34

2. Alagic, G., Majenz, C., Russell, A.: Efficient simulation of random states and random unitaries. In: Canteaut, A., Ishai, Y. (eds.) EUROCRYPT 2020. LNCS, vol. 12107, pp. 759–787. Springer, Cham (2020). https://doi.org/10.1007/978-3-030-45727-3_26

3. Alagic, G., Majenz, C., Russell, A., Song, F.: Quantum-access-secure message authentication via blind-unforgeability. In: Canteaut, A., Ishai, Y. (eds.) EURO-CRYPT 2020. LNCS, vol. 12107, pp. 788–817. Springer, Cham (2020). https://doi.org/10.1007/978-3-030-45727-3_27

4. Ambainis, A., Hamburg, M., Unruh, D.: Quantum security proofs using semi-classical oracles. In: Boldyreva, A., Micciancio, D. (eds.) CRYPTO 2019. LNCS, vol. 11693, pp. 269–295. Springer, Cham (2019). https://doi.org/10.1007/978-3-030-26951-7_10

5. Aranha, D.F., Orlandi, C., Takahashi, A., Zaverucha, G.: Security of hedged Fiat–Shamir signatures under fault attacks. In: Canteaut, A., Ishai, Y. (eds.) EURO-CRYPT 2020. LNCS, vol. 12105, pp. 644–674. Springer, Cham (2020). https://doi.org/10.1007/978-3-030-45721-1_23

6. Beals, R., Buhrman, H., Cleve, R., Mosca, M., Wolf, R.: Quantum lower bounds by polynomials. In: 39th FOCS, pp. 352–361 (1998)

7. Bindel, N., Hamburg, M., Hövelmanns, K., Hülsing, A., Persichetti, E.: Tighter proofs of CCA security in the quantum random oracle model. In: Hofheinz, D., Rosen, A. (eds.) TCC 2019. LNCS, vol. 11892, pp. 61–90. Springer, Cham (2019). https://doi.org/10.1007/978-3-030-36033-7_3

8. Boneh, D., Dagdelen, Ö., Fischlin, M., Lehmann, A., Schaffner, C., Zhandry, M.: Random oracles in a quantum world. In: Lee, D.H., Wang, X. (eds.) ASIACRYPT 2011. LNCS, vol. 7073, pp. 41–69. Springer, Heidelberg (2011). https://doi.org/10.1007/978-3-642-25385-0_3

9. Bos, J.W., Hülsing, A., Renes, J., van Vredendaal, C.: Rapidly Verifiable XMSS Signatures. Cryptology ePrint Archive, Report 2020/898 (2020). https://eprint.iacr.org/2020/898

10. Broadbent, A., Lord, S.: Uncloneable quantum encryption via oracles. In: Flammia, S.T. (ed.) TQC 2020, LIPIcs, pp. 4:1–4:22. Dagstuhl, Germany (2020)

11. Buchmann, J., Dahmen, E., Hülsing, A.: XMSS - a practical forward secure signature scheme based on minimal security assumptions. In: Yang, B.-Y. (ed.) PQCrypto 2011. LNCS, vol. 7071, pp. 117–129. Springer, Heidelberg (2011). https://doi.org/10.1007/978-3-642-25405-5_8

12. Chase, M., et al.: Post-quantum zero-knowledge and signatures from symmetric-key primitives. In: Proceedings of the 2017 ACM SIGSAC Conference on Computer and Communications Security, CCS 2017, pp. 1825–1842. Association for Computing Machinery, New York (2017)

13. Chen, M.-S., Hülsing, A., Rijneveld, J., Samardjiska, S., Schwabe, P.: From 5-Pass $\mathcal{MQ}$-based identification to $\mathcal{MQ}$-based signatures. In: Cheon, J.H., Takagi, T. (eds.) ASIACRYPT 2016. LNCS, vol. 10032, pp. 135–165. Springer, Heidelberg (2016). https://doi.org/10.1007/978-3-662-53890-6_5

14. Coladangelo, A., Majenz, C., Poremba, A.: Quantum copy-protection of compute-and-compare programs in the quantum random oracle model. arXiv:2009.13865 (2020)
15. Don, J., Fehr, S., Majenz, C.: The measure-and-reprogram technique 2.0: multi-round Fiat-Shamir and more. In: Micciancio, D., Ristenpart, T. (eds.) CRYPTO 2020. LNCS, vol. 12172, pp. 602–631. Springer, Cham (2020). https://doi.org/10.1007/978-3-030-56877-1_21
16. Don, J., Fehr, S., Majenz, C., Schaffner, C.: Security of the Fiat-Shamir transformation in the quantum random-oracle model. In: Boldyreva, A., Micciancio, D. (eds.) CRYPTO 2019. LNCS, vol. 11693, pp. 356–383. Springer, Cham (2019). https://doi.org/10.1007/978-3-030-26951-7_13
17. Eaton, E., Song, F.: Making existential-unforgeable signatures strongly unforgeable in the quantum random-oracle model. In: TQC 2015, LIPIcs (2015)
18. Fujisaki, E., Okamoto, T.: Secure integration of asymmetric and symmetric encryption schemes. In: Wiener, M. (ed.) CRYPTO 1999. LNCS, vol. 1666, pp. 537–554. Springer, Heidelberg (1999). https://doi.org/10.1007/3-540-48405-1_34
19. Fujisaki, E., Okamoto, T.: Secure integration of asymmetric and symmetric encryption schemes. J. Cryptol. **26**(1), 80–101 (2013)
20. Hofheinz, D., Hövelmanns, K., Kiltz, E.: A modular analysis of the Fujisaki-Okamoto transformation. In: Kalai, Y., Reyzin, L. (eds.) TCC 2017. LNCS, vol. 10677, pp. 341–371. Springer, Cham (2017). https://doi.org/10.1007/978-3-319-70500-2_12
21. Hövelmanns, K., Kiltz, E., Schäge, S., Unruh, D.: Generic authenticated key exchange in the quantum random oracle model. In: Kiayias, A., Kohlweiss, M., Wallden, P., Zikas, V. (eds.) PKC 2020. LNCS, vol. 12111, pp. 389–422. Springer, Cham (2020). https://doi.org/10.1007/978-3-030-45388-6_14
22. Hülsing, A., Butin, D., Gazdag, S.-L., Rijneveld, J., Mohaisen, A.: XMSS: Extended Hash-Based Signatures. RFC 8391 (2018)
23. Hülsing, A., Rijneveld, J., Song, F.: Mitigating multi-target attacks in hash-based signatures. In: Cheng, C.-M., Chung, K.-M., Persiano, G., Yang, B.-Y. (eds.) PKC 2016. LNCS, vol. 9614, pp. 387–416. Springer, Heidelberg (2016). https://doi.org/10.1007/978-3-662-49384-7_15
24. Jiang, H., Zhang, Z., Chen, L., Wang, H., Ma, Z.: IND-CCA-secure key encapsulation mechanism in the quantum random oracle model, revisited. In: Shacham, H., Boldyreva, A. (eds.) CRYPTO 2018. LNCS, vol. 10993, pp. 96–125. Springer, Cham (2018). https://doi.org/10.1007/978-3-319-96878-0_4
25. Jiang, H., Zhang, Z., Ma, Z.: Key encapsulation mechanism with explicit rejection in the quantum random oracle model. In: Lin, D., Sako, K. (eds.) PKC 2019. LNCS, vol. 11443, pp. 618–645. Springer, Cham (2019). https://doi.org/10.1007/978-3-030-17259-6_21
26. Kiltz, E., Lyubashevsky, V., Schaffner, C.: A concrete treatment of Fiat-Shamir signatures in the quantum random-oracle model. In: Nielsen, J.B., Rijmen, V. (eds.) EUROCRYPT 2018. LNCS, vol. 10822, pp. 552–586. Springer, Cham (2018). https://doi.org/10.1007/978-3-319-78372-7_18
27. Kuchta, V., Sakzad, A., Stehlé, D., Steinfeld, R., Sun, S.-F.: Measure-rewind-measure: tighter quantum random oracle model proofs for one-way to hiding and CCA security. In: Canteaut, A., Ishai, Y. (eds.) EUROCRYPT 2020. LNCS, vol. 12107, pp. 703–728. Springer, Cham (2020). https://doi.org/10.1007/978-3-030-45727-3_24

28. Liu, Q., Zhandry, M.: Revisiting post-quantum Fiat-Shamir. In: Boldyreva, A., Micciancio, D. (eds.) CRYPTO 2019. LNCS, vol. 11693, pp. 326–355. Springer, Cham (2019). https://doi.org/10.1007/978-3-030-26951-7_12

29. Lyubashevsky, V.: Fiat-Shamir with aborts: applications to lattice and factoring-based signatures. In: Matsui, M. (ed.) ASIACRYPT 2009. LNCS, vol. 5912, pp. 598–616. Springer, Heidelberg (2009). https://doi.org/10.1007/978-3-642-10366-7_35

30. Nielsen, M.A., Chuang, I.L.: Quantum Computation and Quantum Information, 10th Anniversary edn. Cambridge University Press, Cambridge (2010)

31. NIST. National institute for standards and technology. postquantum crypto project (2017). http://csrc.nist.gov/groups/ST/post-quantum-crypto/

32. NIST. Status report on the second round of the NIST post-quantum cryptography standardization process. NISTIR 8309 (2020). https://doi.org/10.6028/NIST.IR.8309

33. Saito, T., Xagawa, K., Yamakawa, T.: Tightly-secure key-encapsulation mechanism in the quantum random oracle model. In: Nielsen, J.B., Rijmen, V. (eds.) EUROCRYPT 2018. LNCS, vol. 10822, pp. 520–551. Springer, Cham (2018). https://doi.org/10.1007/978-3-319-78372-7_17

34. Unruh, D.: Quantum position verification in the random oracle model. In: Garay, J.A., Gennaro, R. (eds.) CRYPTO 2014. LNCS, vol. 8617, pp. 1–18. Springer, Heidelberg (2014). https://doi.org/10.1007/978-3-662-44381-1_1

35. Unruh, D.: Revocable quantum timed-release encryption. In: Nguyen, P.Q., Oswald, E. (eds.) EUROCRYPT 2014. LNCS, vol. 8441, pp. 129–146. Springer, Heidelberg (2014). https://doi.org/10.1007/978-3-642-55220-5_8

36. Unruh, D.: Non-interactive zero-knowledge proofs in the quantum random oracle model. In: Oswald, E., Fischlin, M. (eds.) EUROCRYPT 2015. LNCS, vol. 9057, pp. 755–784. Springer, Heidelberg (2015). https://doi.org/10.1007/978-3-662-46803-6_25

37. Unruh, D.: Post-quantum security of Fiat-Shamir. In: Takagi, T., Peyrin, T. (eds.) ASIACRYPT 2017. LNCS, vol. 10624, pp. 65–95. Springer, Cham (2017). https://doi.org/10.1007/978-3-319-70694-8_3

38. Yamakawa, T., Zhandry, M.: A note on separating classical and quantum random oracles. Cryptology ePrint Archive, Report 2020/787 (2020). https://eprint.iacr.org/2020/787

39. Zhandry, M.: How to record quantum queries, and applications to quantum indifferentiability. In: Boldyreva, A., Micciancio, D. (eds.) CRYPTO 2019. LNCS, vol. 11693, pp. 239–268. Springer, Cham (2019). https://doi.org/10.1007/978-3-030-26951-7_9

QCB: Efficient Quantum-Secure Authenticated Encryption

Ritam Bhaumik[1][✉], Xavier Bonnetain[2,3][✉], André Chailloux[1][✉], Gaëtan Leurent[1][✉], María Naya-Plasencia[1][✉], André Schrottenloher[4][✉], and Yannick Seurin[5][✉]

[1] Inria, Paris, France
{ritam.bhaumik,xavier.bonnetain,andre.chailloux,
gaetan.leurent,maria.naya_plasencia}@inria.fr
[2] Institute for Quantum Computing, Department of Combinatorics and Optimization, University of Waterloo, Waterloo, Canada
xbonnetain@uwaterloo.ca
[3] Université de Lorraine, CNRS, Inria, Nancy, France
[4] Cryptology Group, CWI, Amsterdam, The Netherlands
andre.schrottenloher@m4x.org
[5] ANSSI, Paris, France
yannick.seurin@m4x.org

Abstract. It was long thought that symmetric cryptography was only mildly affected by quantum attacks, and that doubling the key length was sufficient to restore security. However, recent works have shown that Simon's quantum period finding algorithm breaks a large number of MAC and authenticated encryption algorithms when the adversary can query the MAC/encryption oracle with a quantum superposition of messages. In particular, the OCB authenticated encryption mode is broken in this setting, and no quantum-secure mode is known with the same efficiency (rate-one and parallelizable).

In this paper we generalize the previous attacks, show that a large class of OCB-like schemes is unsafe against superposition queries, and discuss the quantum security notions for authenticated encryption modes. We propose a new rate-one parallelizable mode named QCB inspired by TAE and OCB and prove its security against quantum superposition queries.

Keywords: Authenticated encryption · Lightweight cryptography · QCB · Post-quantum cryptography · Provable security · Tweakable block ciphers

1 Introduction

The cryptographic community has launched many competitions and standardization efforts recently. The most recent ones are the CAESAR competition for authenticated encryption (AE) and the NIST standardization processes for

© International Association for Cryptologic Research 2021
M. Tibouchi and H. Wang (Eds.): ASIACRYPT 2021, LNCS 13090, pp. 668–698, 2021.
https://doi.org/10.1007/978-3-030-92062-3_23

post-quantum public-key primitives (PQC) [26] and lightweight cryptography (LWC) [27]. While these competitions have attracted a lot of attention, they have represented rather disjoint efforts: the PQC process focuses on public key cryptography, and post-quantum security has remained out of the scope of most schemes submitted to the LWC process and to the CAESAR competition. A few exceptions exist, like the LWC second-round candidate SATURNIN [15] for instance, which proposes a block cipher and an AE mode aiming at post-quantum security. This is understandable because the impact of quantum computers on symmetric cryptography is expected to be quite limited, and doubling the key length is usually considered a sufficient measure to resist quantum attacks (such as exhaustive key search with Grover's algorithm).

Security in the Superposition Model. However, recent works [21,31] have shown that many MAC and AE modes are broken in the superposition model using Simon's quantum period finding algorithm [32]. In this model, the adversary is capable of accessing a quantum encryption oracle, and of encrypting quantum states. Though the practical significance of attacks in this model is an unsettled issue in the community and opinions might differ, there is a clear consensus on the importance of having provable security in this scenario. First of all, this model is non-trivial, meaning that there exist secure schemes in this model.[1] It also offers better composability, even if we are interested only in quantum adversaries making classical queries. Finally, it captures intermediate scenarios with some level of quantum interaction between the attacker and the oracle and covers the scenarios of obfuscation or white-box encryption.

Though lightness and security against quantum adversaries are two very different topics, let us remark that they are not orthogonal. In particular, SATURNIN is a submission to the LWC effort claiming security in the superposition model, based on a block cipher. But its authenticated encryption mode is not parallelizable and requires two encryption calls per message block. More precisely, it uses the encrypt-then-MAC construction and combines a quantum-secure mode of encryption (the Counter Mode) with a quantum-secure MAC similar to HMAC/NMAC.

Towards a Quantum-Safe Rate-One AE Mode. OCB [22] is one of the most influential authenticated encryption modes. OCB3 is parallelizable, and is a rate-one scheme, using just one block cipher call per block of message. It is proven secure in the classical setting provided that its underlying block cipher is a strong PRP [9]. Nevertheless, several attacks using Simon's algorithm [32] were proposed in [21], with a complexity that is linear in the size of the state. These attacks, that we recall in Sect. 3, can efficiently recover a hidden secret period if the attacker is allowed to query messages in superposition.

Our work started with the idea to make OCB post-quantum secure: we wanted to identify its weaknesses, correct them and obtain a proof of quantum security. The main contribution of this paper is to fill this gap and to propose such a mode together with a proof of security.

---

[1] For example, indistinguishability under quantum encryption queries can be achieved by the Counter Mode from a classical PRP assumption [3].

Results and Organization of the Paper. In Sect. 2, we recall some standard definitions and technical material for our quantum security proofs and attacks. Note
that contrary to most of the recent works on this topic, we shall not require
Zhandry's random oracle recording technique [34] and we will use instead simpler proof arguments, that we introduce here. We also introduce an extension
of Hosoyamada and Sasaki's truncation technique [19] that allows to compose
any linear function with a quantum oracle and compute it with a single query.
In Sect. 3, we define an OCB-like mode with more complex *offsets*. The previous
quantum attack on OCB used the fact that the difference between some offsets
was independent of the nonce. We show how to attack this modified OCB with
a *single* quantum query, yielding an attack that can be applied regardless of the
nonce dependence. In Sect. 4, we define quantum-secure tweakable block ciphers.
We are interested in adversaries making queries with classical tweaks and a superposition of messages, a setting which corresponds to the attacks on OCB. In this
setting, we propose the *key-tweak insertion* TBC, which requires a related-key
secure block cipher. In Sect. 5 we define the new rate-one parallelizable quantum safe mode, QCB, and propose two instances: one using SATURNIN with the
key-tweak insertion TBC and one using the dedicated TBC TRAX-L-17 [4]. We
prove in Sect. 6 the security of QCB if it is used with a secure TBC. We use two
notions: IND-qCPA [11] and BZ-unforgeability [10]. We discuss other possible
definitions in Sect. 7.

2   Preliminaries

We open this section with standard notations for permutations, block ciphers
and AEAD schemes. We also define the quantum oracle access that will be given
to such a scheme in our proof. We recall some standard results and definitions
related to quantum provable security. Finally, we introduce our new *linear post-
processing* lemma (Lemma 2) that we will use in Sect. 3 and Sect. 7.

2.1   Definitions and Notations

We let $\mathcal{P}_n$ denote the set of permutations acting on $\{0,1\}^n$. By $x \xleftarrow{\$} S$ we mean
that x is taken uniformly at random from the set S. We let $\mathcal{A}^{f(\cdot)} \Rightarrow b$ (resp.
$\mathcal{A}^{f(\odot)} \Rightarrow b$) denote an algorithm that performs classical queries to oracle f
(resp. quantum queries to f) and outputs b. We write $\mathcal{A}^{f^{\pm}(\cdot \text{ or } \odot)}$ when $\mathcal{A}$ has
access to the f and the f^{-1} oracle, which we blend into a single oracle $f^{\pm}$.

Block Ciphers. A block cipher with key space $\{0,1\}^k$ and message space $\{0,1\}^n$ is
a map $E \colon \{0,1\}^k \times \{0,1\}^n \to \{0,1\}^n$ such that for every key $K \in \{0,1\}^k$, $M \mapsto
E(K,M)$ is a permutation on $\{0,1\}^n$. We let E_K denote the map $M \mapsto E(K,M)$.
If E is a block cipher then its inverse is the map $E^{-1} \colon \{0,1\}^k \times \{0,1\}^n \to \{0,1\}^n$
defined by $E^{-1}(K,C) = E_K^{-1}(C)$.

AEADs. An authenticated encryption scheme with associated data (AEAD) is specified by a tuple of sets $(\mathcal{K}, \mathcal{IV}, \mathcal{A}, \mathcal{M}, \mathcal{C})$ where $\mathcal{K}$ is the key space, $\mathcal{IV}$ is the IV space, $\mathcal{A}$ is the associated data space, $\mathcal{M}$ is the message space, and $\mathcal{C}$ is the ciphertext space, and a pair of deterministic algorithms (Enc, Dec) with signatures

$$\text{Enc}: \mathcal{K} \times \mathcal{IV} \times \mathcal{A} \times \mathcal{M} \to \mathcal{C}$$
$$\text{Dec}: \mathcal{K} \times \mathcal{IV} \times \mathcal{A} \times \mathcal{C} \to \mathcal{M} \cup \{\bot\}.$$

We require an AEAD scheme to be correct, *i.e.*, for all $(K, IV, A, M) \in \mathcal{K} \times \mathcal{IV} \times \mathcal{A} \times \mathcal{M}$,

$$\text{Dec}\,(K, IV, A, \text{Enc}\,(K, IV, A, M)) = M.$$

We write $\text{Enc}_K\,(IV, A, M)$ for $\text{Enc}\,(K, IV, A, M)$ and similarly $\text{Dec}_K\,(IV, A, C)$. Note that this is the most generic definition of an AEAD, but in our case, we will replace the ciphertext space $\mathcal{C}$ by $\mathcal{C} \times \mathcal{T}$, and the scheme will output a ciphertext C of variable length and an authentication tag $T \in \mathcal{T}$ of fixed size. As we consider AEADs based on block ciphers, C and M will be parsed into *blocks* that we index $M_0, \ldots, M_\ell$ (resp. $C_0, \ldots, C_\ell$) where ℓ is the block length of M (resp. of C).

Quantum Computing. In this paper, an *adversary* is a quantum algorithm that accesses one or more oracles. We use the quantum circuit model, whose basics can be found in [28]. A quantum algorithm is initiated with a set of m qubits (two-level quantum systems) in a fixed state $|0\rangle$. The state of the algorithm lies in a Hilbert space of dimension 2^m, with a canonical basis $\{|i\rangle, 0 \le i \le 2^m - 1\}$. Basic unitary operators, called *quantum gates* (drawn from a universal gate set), are applied on the qubits. These computations are interleaved with oracle calls and *partial measurements*, which transform a *pure state* (an element of the Hilbert space) into a *mixed state* (a probability distribution of pure states). For ease of notation, we often omit normalization factors from quantum states (e.g., $\frac{1}{\sqrt{2}}(|0\rangle + |1\rangle)$ can be written $|0\rangle + |1\rangle$).

2.2 Quantum Oracles and Query Model

We model *quantum oracle access* to any function $f : \mathcal{X} \to \mathcal{Y}$ as a unitary operation: $|x\rangle\,|y\rangle \mapsto |x\rangle\,|y \oplus f(x)\rangle$ (this is the *standard oracle*) or as $|x\rangle\,|y\rangle \mapsto (-1)^{y \cdot f(x)}\,|x\rangle\,|y\rangle$ (this is the *phase oracle*). Standard and phase oracles are well-known to be equivalent.

Choice of IVs. In the classical setting, the security of IV-based AEADs draws on the fact that the IVs of successive queries are distinct and/or randomly chosen. So far, all security notions defined in the quantum setting have followed this setting [3,11,16], by considering randomness-based modes where the random IV is chosen at each new (quantum) query. Although a non-trivial extension to *superposition IVs* might be possible, it remains out of scope of our work.

In this paper, we will use classical and distinct IVs, but relax the randomness assumption. In the security games for AEAD defined and used in Sect. 6, we start the game by an initialization phase in which the adversary declares the IVs that he is going to query. This makes our reasoning easier and (as we will justify in Sect. 6) it includes the cases where IVs are generated at random, or with a stateful counter.

Quantum Query Model. The input plaintext and AD will be in superposition. Furthermore, the bit-length of the message, AD and ciphertext have to be chosen classically and cannot differ within a query; that is, we encrypt a superposition of messages of a fixed length. We let the adversary choose the bit-length of the message and AD in the queries between 0 and $n\ell$ for a fixed ℓ (which determines the maximal number of blocks to be queried). Thus, ℓ will intervene as a parameter in our bounds, together with the number of queries q.

Hence, our encryption and decryption oracles are actually families of unitary operators, indexed by these lengths and by the IV choice. As the ciphertext will be longer than the plaintext, we consider that the encryption oracles for messages of m bits output $c(m) > m$ bits. Conversely, messages of distinct lengths may be encrypted to ciphertexts of the same length. Hence, the decryption oracle of a ciphertext of c bits writes a canonical encoding of either the message or $\bot$ on c bits. We write these oracles $O_{\mathsf{Enc}_K}^{m,a,IV}$ and $O_{\mathsf{Dec}_K}^{c,a,IV}$ respectively, with $0 \le m, a \le \ell n$.

The encryption $O_{\mathsf{Enc}_K}^{m,a,IV}$ is a standard oracle for Enc_K with messages of length m, AD of length a and a fixed $IV \in \mathcal{IV}$:

$$\underbrace{|A\rangle}_{a \text{ qubits}} \quad \underbrace{|M\rangle}_{m \text{ qubits}} \quad \underbrace{|X\rangle}_{\substack{c(m) \\ \text{qubits}}} \quad \mapsto |A\rangle |M\rangle \underbrace{|X \oplus \mathsf{Enc}_K(IV, A, M)\rangle}_{c(m) \text{ qubits}} \ .$$

The decryption $O_{\mathsf{Dec}_K}^{c,a,IV}$ is a standard oracle for Dec_K with ciphertexts of length c, AD of length a and a fixed IV:

$$\underbrace{|A\rangle}_{a \text{ qubits}} \quad \underbrace{|C\rangle}_{c \text{ qubits}} \quad \underbrace{|Y\rangle}_{c \text{ qubits}} \quad \mapsto \begin{cases} |A\rangle |C\rangle \left| Y \oplus \widehat{M} \right\rangle & \text{if } C = \mathsf{Enc}_K(IV, A, M) \\ |A\rangle |C\rangle \left| Y \oplus \widehat{\bot} \right\rangle & \text{otherwise} \end{cases}$$

with $\widehat{M}$ the encoding of M and $\widehat{\bot}$ the encoding of $\bot$.

Counting Data, Time and Memory. While the oracles authorize messages, AD and ciphertexts to take any number of bits, the modes that we will consider are built on block ciphers with a fixed block size n. Hence, we can count the data complexity in the number of blocks queried: a query to Enc_K or to O_{Enc_K} with ℓ blocks costs ℓ data. We count the time complexity either in the number of quantum gates, or in the number of block cipher calls, as a quantum standard oracle. We consider the cost of a single block cipher call to be marginal with respect to the other terms, as it is polynomial in n, making these definitions equivalent. The memory will also be counted in n-bit registers, either classical or quantum.

2.3   Distances

Usually, in game-based definitions, the adversary's advantage is a difference in probabilities to output 1 or 0. However, since our adversaries are quantum, their final state is a quantum state. It is well-known that the *Euclidean distance* between quantum states is related to the distance between the distributions that result from measuring these states. Thus, the probabilistic interpretation of the adversary's result (measuring 0 or 1) can be replaced by a Euclidean distance.

Definition 1 (Euclidean distance). *The Euclidean distance between* $|\phi\rangle = \sum \alpha_i |i\rangle$ *and* $|\psi\rangle = \sum \beta_i |i\rangle$ *is given by:* $\| |\phi\rangle - |\psi\rangle \| = \sqrt{\sum_i |\alpha_i - \beta_i|^2}$.

Two quantum states $|\phi\rangle = \sum \alpha_i |i\rangle$ and $|\psi\rangle = \sum \beta_i |i\rangle$, obtained after running an adversary in two different scenarios, incur two distributions $\mathcal{D}$ and $\mathcal{D}'$ over the states in the computational basis (we could also take another basis, without any change, since composing by a unitary operator leaves the distance unchanged). These distributions are such that $\mathcal{D}(i) = |\alpha_i|^2$ and $\mathcal{D}'(i) = |\beta_i|^2$. The *total variation distance* between $\mathcal{D}$ and $\mathcal{D}'$ is defined as $\sum_i |\mathcal{D}(i) - \mathcal{D}'(i)|$ and equal to $\sum_i ||\alpha_i|^2 - |\beta_i|^2|$. From Lemma 3.6 in [7], we obtain: $\sum_i ||\alpha_i|^2 - |\beta_i|^2| \leq 4\| |\phi\rangle - |\psi\rangle \|$.

The decision of a quantum adversary to output 0 or 1 is conditioned only on its final state. Thus, if two adversaries have similar end states, they can only win with similar probabilities.

Lemma 1. *Let $\mathcal{A}$ be a quantum adversary that outputs a bit b. Let $\mathcal{B}$ be another adversary that also outputs a bit b, and let $|\psi\rangle$ and $|\phi\rangle$ be their respective states after the last oracle query, before measuring their output in the computational basis. Then:*

$$| \Pr[\mathcal{A}(\cdot) = 1] - \Pr[\mathcal{B}(\cdot) = 1] | \leq 4\| |\psi\rangle - |\phi\rangle \|.$$

In practice, we will consider a game in which some parameter is selected at random (e.g., the key K), then the game runs and the final state of the adversary depends on K. We are interested in the quantity $| \Pr_{K \xleftarrow{\$} \mathcal{K}}[\mathcal{A}(\cdot) = 1] - \Pr_{K \xleftarrow{\$} \mathcal{K}}[\mathcal{B}(\cdot) = 1] |$ which determines the difference in advantage between the two adversaries. We have: $\Pr_{K \xleftarrow{\$} \mathcal{K}}[\mathcal{A}(\cdot) = 1] = \sum_{k \in \mathcal{K}} \Pr[K = k] \Pr[\mathcal{A}(\cdot) = 1 | K = k]$. That is, we can write:

$$\begin{aligned}
&| \Pr_{K \xleftarrow{\$} \mathcal{K}}[\mathcal{A}(\cdot) = 1] - \Pr_{K \xleftarrow{\$} \mathcal{K}}[\mathcal{B}(\cdot) = 1] | \\
&\leq \frac{1}{|\mathcal{K}|} \sum_{k \in \mathcal{K}} | \Pr[\mathcal{A}(\cdot) = 1 | K = k] - \Pr[\mathcal{B}(\cdot) = 1 | K = k] | \\
&\leq \frac{4}{|\mathcal{K}|} \sum_{k} \| |\psi_k\rangle - |\phi_k\rangle \|,
\end{aligned}$$

where $|\psi_k\rangle$ and $|\phi_k\rangle$ are the final states conditioned on the fact that the selected key is k. So in practice, we will fix all the random parameters, compute the euclidean distance between the end states and take the average.

2.4   Query Magnitude

We will use a "query magnitude" argument, taken from [6]. Considering an oracle O with arbitrarily defined input and output registers, we modify O on a subset D of its inputs to make the oracle O'. If an algorithm asks queries to O, but puts only "low amplitude" on the inputs of D, then changing O into O' does not have any significant impact on the final state.

Theorem 1 (Adapted from [6], Theorem 3.3). *Let $\mathcal{A}$ be a quantum algorithm that makes q queries to an oracle O and let $|\psi_0\rangle$, ..., $|\psi_q\rangle$ be the current state before each query ($|\psi_q\rangle$ is the final state). Let O' be an oracle that is the same as O, except on some subset D of its inputs, $\mathcal{A}'$ be the same as $\mathcal{A}$, except that every query to O is replaced by a query to O', and $|\psi_i'\rangle$ the state of $\mathcal{A}'$. At each step of the circuit computation, we let $|x\rangle |y\rangle |a\rangle$ denote the basis states, where $|x\rangle$ is the input to O (or O'), $|y\rangle$ is the output register and $|a\rangle$ the rest of the qubits. Let P_D be the projector on the basis states such that $x \in D$. Then:*

$$\| \, |\psi_q\rangle - |\psi_q'\rangle \, \| \leq 2 \sum_i |P_D(|\psi_i\rangle)|.$$

2.5   On Random Functions and Permutations

We will use the following results from the literature. First of all, as shown by Zhandry, it is impossible to distinguish a random function with n-bit domain from a random permutation with probability bigger than $\mathcal{O}\left(\frac{q^3}{2^n}\right)$ with q queries (where the constant in the $\mathcal{O}$ is fixed by the theorem); and conversely. We refer to this statement as *PRF-PRP switching*.

Theorem 2 ([33], Theorem 3.1). *Let $h : \{0,1\}^n \to \{0,1\}^m$ be a random function. Any quantum algorithm making q quantum queries to h can only find a collision with probability at most $\mathcal{O}\left(\frac{q^3}{2^m}\right)$. If $n \leq m$, then any quantum algorithm making q queries cannot distinguish h from a random injective function except with probability $\mathcal{O}\left(\frac{q^3}{2^m}\right)$.*

Second, we use a theorem by Boneh and Zhandry that shows that a quantum algorithm making q queries to a random oracle with a domain of exponential size can only output $q + 1$ valid {input, output} pairs with negligible probability.

Theorem 3 ([10], Theorem 4.1). *Let $\mathcal{A}$ be a quantum algorithm making q queries to a random oracle $h : \{0,1\}^n \to \{0,1\}^m$, and producing $k > q$ pairs $(x_i, y_i) \in \{0,1\}^n \times \{0,1\}^m$. The probability that the x_i are distinct and $y_i = h(x_i)$ for all $1 \leq i \leq k$ is at most: $\frac{1}{2^{mk}} \sum_{r=0}^{q} \binom{k}{r} (2^m - 1)^r$. If $k = q + 1$ then the adversary succeeds with probability at most $\frac{q+1}{2^m}$.*

We will use the terminology "$(q, q+1)$ security game" to refer to the game in which $\mathcal{A}$ accesses O_h q times and must produce $q + 1$ valid pairs. An alternative proof of Theorem 3 for the $q, q + 1$ case can be found in the full version of [1]. By combining this theorem with Theorem 2, we obtain a similar statement for random permutations.

Corollary 1. *There exists a constant c such that, if $\mathcal{A}$ is a quantum algorithm making q queries to a random permutation Π $: \{0, 1\}^n \to \{0, 1\}^n$ and trying to produce $q + 1$ valid input-output pairs, then $\mathcal{A}$ can only succeed with probability at most: $c \frac{q^3}{2^n}$.*

The term in Corollary 1 is simply the sum of the PRP-PRF distinguishing advantage and the $(q, q + 1)$ advantage. The former grows much faster with q, but we will mostly use Corollary 1 with a single query, where both terms are $\mathcal{O}\left(2^{-n}\right)$.

2.6   Computing a Linear Function of a Quantum Oracle

In [19] Hosoyamada and Sasaki show that given access to a standard oracle O_f for a function f, it is possible to make a quantum query to $\mathsf{Trunc}(f(x))$, the *truncation* of the output $f(x)$ to some bits, using only one quantum query to f. We now extend this result, and show that it is possible to compute *any linear function* of the output using only one quantum query. This is especially important with the oracles we will be using, since they involve IVs that are changed at each new quantum query.

The core observation in [19] is simple: the state $|0\rangle + |1\rangle$ is invariant whether we XOR a 0 or a 1 on it. Hence, before the query, in the output register, we can set the qubits we want to drop to $|0\rangle + |1\rangle$ and the qubits we want to keep to $|0\rangle$. We will now extend this result, with the following lemma:

Lemma 2 (Computing a linear function of a quantum oracle). *Let f : $\{0, 1\}^n \to \{0, 1\}^m$ be a function, $O_f : |x\rangle |y\rangle \mapsto |x\rangle |y \oplus f(x)\rangle$. Let $g : \{0, 1\}^m \to \{0, 1\}^o$ be an $\mathbb{F}_2$-linear function. Then it is possible to construct the oracle $O_{g \circ f}$: $|x\rangle |y\rangle \mapsto |x\rangle |y \oplus (g \circ f)(x)\rangle$ using two queries to O_g and a single query to O_f.*

Proof. Let O_g be a quantum oracle that implements g, assume we are given the quantum state $|x\rangle |y\rangle$. We first add an ancilla register containing the uniform superposition on m bits. We then have the state $|x\rangle |y\rangle \sum_{z=0}^{2^m-1} |z\rangle$. Then, we apply O_g with register z as input and y as output, and we get

$$|x\rangle \sum_{z=0}^{2^m-1} |y \oplus g(z)\rangle |z\rangle .$$

Then, we apply O_f with register x as input and z as output. We get

$$|x\rangle \sum_{z=0}^{2^m-1} |y \oplus g(z)\rangle |z \oplus f(x)\rangle .$$

Finally, we reapply O_g with register z as input and y as output. We get

$$|x\rangle \sum_{z=0}^{2^m-1} |y \oplus g(z) \oplus g(z \oplus f(x))\rangle\, |z \oplus f(x)\rangle.$$

As g is linear, we have $g(z) \oplus g(z \oplus f(x)) = g(f(x))$. Hence, the state can be rewritten as

$$|x\rangle\, |y \oplus g(f(x))\rangle \sum_{z=0}^{2^m-1} |z \oplus f(x)\rangle.$$

This state can then be simplified, as the z register contains the uniform superposition over m bits, independently of the value of $f(x)$, to

$$|x\rangle\, |y \oplus g(f(x))\rangle \sum_{z=0}^{2^m-1} |z\rangle.$$

We can now remove the z register, as it is not entangled with the others, and obtain the quantum state we wanted.   □

Remark 1. Lemma 2 can also be applied if the quantum oracle to f uses a group law different from $\oplus$ to update its output register. In that case, g shall be a linear function for the corresponding group law.

3   Offsets Don't Work

In this section we start by recalling the superposition attacks on OCB from [21]. We will next present a first attempt to repair it, that consists of tweaking the value of the *offsets*, along with a new original superposition attack that shows that any offset-based variant can be broken using Simon's algorithm.

3.1   Attack with Simon's Algorithm on OCB

OCB[2] [22] is one of the most influential authenticated modes. OCB3 is represented in Fig. 1, with $\Delta_i = \text{gray}(i) \cdot E_K(0^n)$ (using a finite field multiplication) and $\Delta_i^{IV} = \Delta_i \oplus F_K(IV)$, with F a simple function of K and IV and $\text{gray}(i)$ the gray encoding of i.

OCB3 is classically proven secure if its underlying cipher is a strong PRP.

Simon's Algorithm. Simon's algorithm, proposed in [32] allows to solve efficiently, with a complexity of $\mathcal{O}(n)$, the following problem when we are allowed to ask superposition queries to $\mathcal{F}$:

Given a Boolean function $\mathcal{F}$ on n bits and the promise that there exists s such that, for any $x \neq y$, $\mathcal{F}(x) = \mathcal{F}(y) \iff x = y \oplus s$, find s.

---

[2] Three versions of OCB have been proposed. We focus here on the last one, OCB3, while all three suffer from similar superposition attacks.

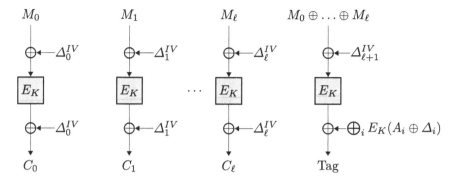

Fig. 1. OCB3. (M_i) is the message, (A_i) is the associated data.

Simon's algorithm recovers a vector orthogonal to the period with a single quantum query; with $\mathcal{O}(n)$ queries, the period is deduced with linear algebra. As shown in [21], a sufficient condition on $\mathcal{F}$ is that there exists no "unwanted period" $t \neq s$ such that $\mathcal{F}(x \oplus t) = \mathcal{F}(x)$ holds with probability $\geq \frac{1}{2}$. For comparison, classically, the best algorithm requires $\Omega\left(\sqrt{2^n}\right)$ queries.

Quantum Superposition Attacks on OCB. Two polynomial-time attacks against OCB that require quantum superposition queries to the construction were proposed in [21]. They both use Simon's algorithm[3].

The main weakness of OCB is that the nonce only influences the construction through the value Δ, which is XORed to the internal state. The scenario of the attack considers that the attacker has access to a superposition oracle that given a superposition of messages as input, returns the superposition of their encryption. The key is a secret value and the IV is different for each query.

The first attack considers an empty message, and two variable identical blocks x of associated data. The output is then

$$E_K(F_K(IV)) \oplus E_K(x \oplus \Delta_1) \oplus E_K(x \oplus \Delta_2).$$

This function is periodic, of period $\Delta_1 \oplus \Delta_2$. It is IV-dependent, but the period is not. This allows to use Simon's algorithm to recover the period.

The second attack uses the same idea, but attacks the encryption part and not the authentication. Its core idea is to consider the XOR of two distinct blocks i and j that encrypt the same message block. This is equal to $f_{i,j}(x) = E_K(\Delta_i^{IV} \oplus x) \oplus E_K(\Delta_j^{IV} \oplus x) \oplus \Delta_i^{IV} \oplus \Delta_j^{IV}$.

This function is periodic, of period $\Delta_i^{IV} \oplus \Delta_j^{IV} = (\text{gray}(i) \oplus \text{gray}(j)) \cdot E_K(0^n)$. We can then use Simon's algorithm, and this time we need to use Lemma 2 to compute the XOR of two blocks using only one query.

---

[3] One attack on OCB presented in [21] was partial, as it assumed without any mention the use of Lemma 2.

Both attacks recover the difference of two offsets, which is sufficient to make some forgeries. Note that in both cases, the existence of an unwanted period t would imply a high-probability higher-order differential of E_K, which would result in a classical break.

3.2   A First (Failed) Attempt to Fix OCB

To protect a mode vulnerable to Simon's algorithm, Alagic and Russell [2] proposed to replace the XOR by modular addition. However, this merely increases the attack complexity from polynomial to subexponential [14], which does not give acceptable security levels for standard block sizes (e.g., 256 bits).

In order to make OCB quantum-resistant, we will rather try to avoid these attacks entirely. Our first idea is to avoid having an IV-independent period, by making the influence of $E_K(IV)$ different for each block. For instance, Δ_i could be changed to a multiple of $E_K(IV)$: $\Delta_i = i \cdot E_K(IV)$. (The multiplication is still done in the finite field, like in OCB's offsets). This way, the previous attack could only recover one bit of $E_K(IV)$ at a time, which is useless if the IV changes for each query.

New Superposition Attack for Any Nonce-Based Solution. Actually, the previous proposal is still unsafe, but it requires a new more advanced attack that we present here. This evolved attack is inspired by the multiple-period attacks from [12]. Its core idea is to leverage the possibility to encrypt a long message to construct multiple copies of the periodic function, in such a way that one query will likely be enough to recover all the bits of the period.

Let g be the function that maps the sequence $(x_1, x_2, \ldots, x_{2n-1}, x_{2n})$ to $(x_1 \oplus x_2, x_3 \oplus x_4, \ldots, x_{2n-1} \oplus x_{2n})$.

We consider the function

$$f(x_1, \ldots, x_n) = g \circ \mathrm{OCB}(x_1, x_1, x_2, x_2, \ldots, x_n, x_n)$$

Reusing the notation $f_{i,j}(x) = E_K(\Delta_i \oplus x) \oplus E_K(\Delta_j \oplus x) \oplus \Delta_i \oplus \Delta_j$, we have

$$f(x_1, \ldots, x_n) = (f_{1,2}(x_1), f_{3,4}(x_2), \ldots f_{2n-1,2n}(x_n))$$

This function is periodic, of period:

$$s = \Delta_1 \oplus \Delta_2, \ldots, \Delta_{2n-1} \oplus \Delta_{2n} = (1 \oplus 2) \cdot E_K(IV), \ldots, ((2n-1) \oplus (2n)) \cdot E_K(IV)$$

We can also bound the probability of unwanted collisions. If f admits an unwanted period t with probability greater than $\frac{1}{2}$, then one of the $f_{i,j}$ would also admit an unwanted period $t_{i,j}$ with probability greater than $\frac{1}{2n}$. As before, this is impossible if E_K does not admit a high-probability higher-order differential.

Hence, Simon's algorithm allows us to sample one vector orthogonal to each of the periods of the involved $f_{i,j}$. As these periods are linearly dependent, this is enough to recover completely the value $E_K(IV)$, assuming n is large enough.

Conclusion. This attack shows that a solution based on offsets is unlikely to work. After this failed attempt, we decided to move one step backwards. OCB can be seen as an instantiation of the mode TAE or ΘCB, which is defined with a *Tweakable Block Cipher* (TBC). The TBC used in OCB is the LRW mode [24], which builds upon a block cipher, and is quantumly broken [21]. The attacks that we gave all seem to stem from the TBC itself, not the mode.

4   Quantum-Secure Tweakable Block Ciphers

In this section, we define quantum-secure tweakable block ciphers (TBCs). We give a TBC construction based on a block cipher in the *ideal cipher model*, which we will recall below, and explicitly provide its security guarantees.

4.1   Definitions

Definition 2. *Let E be a block cipher. Let $\mathcal{A}$ be an oracle algorithm (making either classical or quantum queries depending on the case) which outputs a bit. The advantage of $\mathcal{A}$ against the PRP and Strong PRP (SPRP) security of E is defined as:*

$$\mathbf{Adv}_{E(*)}^{\mathrm{PRP}}(\mathcal{A}) := \left| \Pr_{K \xleftarrow{\$} \{0,1\}^k} [\mathcal{A}^{E_K(*)} \Rightarrow 1] - \Pr_{\Pi \xleftarrow{\$} \mathcal{P}_n} [\mathcal{A}^{\Pi(*)} \Rightarrow 1] \right|$$

$$\mathbf{Adv}_{E(*)}^{\mathrm{SPRP}}(\mathcal{A}) := \left| \Pr_{K \xleftarrow{\$} \{0,1\}^k} [\mathcal{A}^{E_K^{\pm}(*)} \Rightarrow 1] - \Pr_{\Pi \xleftarrow{\$} \mathcal{P}_n} [\mathcal{A}^{\Pi^{\pm}(*)} \Rightarrow 1] \right| .$$

Depending on the access that the adversary has (classical or quantum) to the messages, we replace the $*$ symbol by $\cdot$ (classical) or $\odot$ (quantum).

Tweakable Block Ciphers. A *tweakable block cipher (TBC)* with key space $\{0,1\}^k$, tweak space $\{0,1\}^t$, and message space $\{0,1\}^n$ is a map $\widetilde{E} \colon \{0,1\}^k \times \{0,1\}^t \times \{0,1\}^n \to \{0,1\}^n$ such that for every key $K \in \{0,1\}^k$ and every tweak $T \in \{0,1\}^t$, $M \mapsto \widetilde{E}(K,T,M)$ is a permutation of $\{0,1\}^n$. We let $\widetilde{E}_K$ denote the map $(T,M) \mapsto \widetilde{E}(K,T,M)$. If $\widetilde{E}$ is a TBC then its inverse is the map $\widetilde{E}^{-1} \colon \{0,1\}^k \times \{0,1\}^t \times \{0,1\}^n \to \{0,1\}^n$ defined by $\widetilde{E}^{-1}(K,T,C)$ being the unique M such that $\widetilde{E}(K,T,M) = C$. A *tweakable permutation* with tweak space $\{0,1\}^t$ and message space $\{0,1\}^n$ is a map $\widetilde{\Pi} \colon \{0,1\}^t \times \{0,1\}^n \to \{0,1\}^n$ such that for every tweak $T \in \{0,1\}^t$, $M \mapsto \widetilde{\Pi}(T,M)$ is a permutation of $\{0,1\}^n$. We let $\widetilde{\mathcal{P}}_{t,n}$ denote the set of all tweakable permutations with tweak space $\{0,1\}^t$ and message space $\{0,1\}^n$.

Definition 3. *Let $\mathcal{A}$ be an oracle algorithm making (classical or quantum) queries and which outputs a bit. The advantage of $\mathcal{A}$ against the TPRP, resp. strong TPRP (STPRP) security of $\widetilde{E}$ is defined as*

$$\mathbf{Adv}^{\mathrm{TPRP}}_{\widetilde{E}(*,*)}(\mathcal{A}) := \left| \Pr_{K \xleftarrow{\$} \{0,1\}^k} [\mathcal{A}^{\widetilde{E}_K(*,*)} \Rightarrow 1] - \Pr_{\widetilde{\Pi} \xleftarrow{\$} \widetilde{\mathcal{P}}_{t,n}} [\mathcal{A}^{\widetilde{\Pi}(*,*)} \Rightarrow 1] \right|$$

$$\mathbf{Adv}^{\mathrm{STPRP}}_{\widetilde{E}(*,*)}(\mathcal{A}) := \left| \Pr_{K \xleftarrow{\$} \{0,1\}^k} [\mathcal{A}^{\widetilde{E}^{\pm}_K(*,*)} \Rightarrow 1] - \Pr_{\widetilde{\Pi} \xleftarrow{\$} \widetilde{\mathcal{P}}_{t,n}} [\mathcal{A}^{\widetilde{\Pi}^{\pm}(*,*)} \Rightarrow 1] \right|.$$

Depending on the access that the adversary has (classical or quantum) to the messages and to the tweaks, we replace the $*$ symbols by $\cdot$ (classical) or $\odot$ (quantum).

The Modified (S)TPRP Game. In the proofs of this section, we consider an adversary $\mathcal{A}$ playing a modified (S)TPRP game that consists of three phases:

- *Pre-Declaration Phase:* In the first phase, $\mathcal{A}$ declares a set of m tweaks $\{T_1, \ldots, T_m\}$.
- *Quantum Phase:* In the second phase, $\mathcal{A}$ gets access to a standard oracle implementing either $\widetilde{E}^{(\pm)}_K$ or $\widetilde{\Pi}^{(\pm)}$, and can make q_1 quantum queries with *classical* tweaks, subject to the restriction that the tweak is always chosen from the set of pre-declared tweaks $\{T_1, \ldots, T_m\}$, then measures its final state and outputs s_0 classical bits;
- *Classical Phase:* In the final phase, $\mathcal{A}$ makes an additional q_2 classical queries to the oracle, this time with no restriction on the set of tweaks that can be queried, such that the queries are deterministic functions of the s_0 classical bits output at the end of the previous phase.

Thus, the bounds that we will obtain will depend on the number of pre-declared tweaks m, the number of quantum queries q_1 made by $\mathcal{A}$, the number of classical bits s_0 output at the end of the quantum phase, and the number of classical queries q_2 made by $\mathcal{A}$. Note that in the quantum phase some of the pre-declared tweaks may be used multiple times, and some can be ignored entirely. We use the notation $\mathbf{Adv}^{\mathrm{(S)TPRP}}_{\widetilde{E}(\cdot,\odot)}(\mathcal{A})$ for this restricted case.

TBCs from Block Ciphers. In this section, we will construct a TBC from a block cipher, and prove security in the *ideal cipher model*. In the quantum setting, this model was previously considered by Hosoyamada and Yasuda [20] to analyze the Davies-Meyer and Merkle-Damgard constructions. This means that the underlying block cipher E is chosen uniformly at random from the set $\mathcal{BC}_{k,n}$ of all block ciphers with key space $\{0,1\}^k$ and message space $\{0,1\}^n$ at the beginning of the (S)TPRP distinguishing game and the adversary is allowed to make quantum queries to $E^\pm$ (specifying the key and the plaintext/ciphertext). The advantage is then defined as

$$\mathbf{Adv}_{\widetilde{E}}^{(\mathrm{S})\mathrm{TPRP}}(\mathcal{A}) := \left| \Pr_{\substack{K \xleftarrow{\$} \{0,1\}^k \\ E \xleftarrow{\$} \mathcal{BC}_{k,n}}}[\mathcal{A}^{\widetilde{E}_K^{(\pm)}(*,*),E_{\odot}^\pm(\odot)} \Rightarrow 1] - \Pr_{\substack{\widetilde{\Pi} \xleftarrow{\$} \widetilde{\mathcal{P}}_{t,n} \\ E \xleftarrow{\$} \mathcal{BC}_{k,n}}}[\mathcal{A}^{\widetilde{\Pi}^{(\pm)}(*,*),E_{\odot}^\pm(\odot)} \Rightarrow 1] \right|.$$

(Note that the adversary has access to $E^\pm$ even in the non-strong TPRP definition.)

4.2 Impossibility Results

In order to illustrate the difficulties of building a quantum-secure TBC, even in a weak sense, let us first consider a few examples.

LRW. The LRW mode [24] uses an almost 2-XOR universal hash function family $\mathcal{H}$ and adds $h \in \mathcal{H}$ to the key:

$$\widetilde{E}_{K,h}(T,x) = E_K(h(T) \oplus x) \oplus h(T).$$

An ϵ-almost 2-XOR universal hash function family $\mathcal{H}$ is such that for all x, y, z with $x \neq y$, the probability of $h(x) \oplus h(y) = z$ is small (less than ϵ) when h is chosen at random. Classically, LRW is a strong TBC.

However, the LRW mode is not a quantum-secure TBC even if we allow only classical queries to the tweaks. This was shown in [21], with an attack that is close to the OCB attacks: by querying only two classical tweaks T_0, T_1, one can build a function: $f(x) = E_k(h(T_0) \oplus x) \oplus h(T_0) \oplus E_k(h(T_1) \oplus x) \oplus h(T_1)$ which is periodic, of period $h(T_0) \oplus h(T_1)$. Using Simon's algorithm, we can recover the period of this function in $\mathcal{O}(n)$ queries. This provides a powerful distinguisher, as this property is extremely unlikely with random permutations. Note that this distinguisher still applies for any function h, even if it is an unknown qPRF.

Key-Tweak Insertion. We will consider the *key-tweak insertion TBC*, built from a block cipher E as: $\widetilde{E}_K(T,M) = E_{K \oplus T}(M)$. It admits a simple distinguisher based on Simon's algorithm if the tweaks are queried in superposition: this is the *quantum related-key attack* of [30]. Indeed, the function $f(\odot) = E_{K \oplus \odot}(0) \oplus E_{\odot}(0)$ admits K as a period, and so we can use Simon's algorithm again.

4.3 Proof of Security for the Key-Tweak Insertion TBC

Let $\widetilde{E}_K^\pm(T,x) = E_{K \oplus T}^\pm(x)$ denote the key-tweak insertion TBC. The following proposition shows the STPRP security of this TBC in the ideal cipher model against an adversary playing the modified STPRP game described earlier. We give its proof in the full version of the paper [8].

Proposition 1. *Let $\mathcal{A}$ be an adversary who makes q_1 quantum queries to an oracle implementing $\widetilde{E}_K^{\pm}$ or $\widetilde{\Pi}^{\pm}$ with a pre-declared set of tweaks of size m, and q' queries to $E^{\pm}$, followed by outputting s_0 bits and making q_2 classical queries to the same oracle. Then:*

$$\left| \Pr_{K \xleftarrow{\$} \mathcal{K}} [\mathcal{A}^{\widetilde{E}_K^{\pm}(\cdot,\odot),E_{\odot}^{\pm}(\odot)} \Rightarrow 1] - \Pr_{\{\Pi_T\} \xleftarrow{\$} \mathcal{P}_n} [\mathcal{A}^{\Pi^{\pm}(\cdot,\odot),E_{\odot}^{\pm}(\odot)} \Rightarrow 1] \right|$$
$$\leq 8\sqrt{\frac{mq'^2}{2^k}} + \sqrt{\frac{q_2 s_0}{2 \cdot 2^k}}.$$

Notice that the above bound depends on m but not on q_1 which is reminiscent of the classical security bound of this TBC (see [5], Theorem 6.3 and Corollary 6.5) that depends on the number of different tweaks used and not on the number of queries to $\widetilde{E}^{\pm}$.[4]

We do not explicit how this set of tweaks is determined. It could for example be chosen by the adversary. In that case of course we should not allow him to have a complete control over the size of this set, i.e., the choice of m, or else he could choose m extremely large which would make the above bound useless.

This proposition implies the security when the adversary queries non-adaptive tweaks (so they are predetermined from the start) in which case $m = q_1$, but also allows some adaptivity from a predefined set of tweaks for which we can control the size.

When proving the quantum security of QCB in Sect. 6, we will use the above proposition, but we will be able to control the value of m which will not be significantly larger than q_1.

4.4   Other Directions

Quantum-secure TBCs have been independently considered by Hosoyamada and Iwata in [18]. They used a stronger notion of security where *tweaks can be queried in superposition*, and showed how to construct such a TBC from a block cipher. Their TBC (LRWQ) does not use the ideal cipher model, and only requires the block cipher to be secure as a qPRP. However, they use three block cipher calls for each TBC call, one to process the tweak, and two for the plaintext (before and after XORing the encrypted tweak). Thus, this construction cannot achieve the efficiency that we target. Note that they bound the adversary's advantage, after q queries, by $\mathcal{O}(\sqrt{q^6/2^n})$, compared to a classical $\mathcal{O}(\sqrt{q^2/2^n})$ (assuming respectively that the cipher behaves as a qPRP, and a PRP).

5   Definition of QCB

In this section, we describe the QCB mode, an AEAD based on a Tweakable Block Cipher. It is similar to the TAE mode [23,24] and to ΘCB [22,29]. Throughout this section, $\widetilde{E}_{K,t}$ will denote a TBC used with key K and tweak t, of block

---

[4] Theorem 6.3 in [5] is about related-key attacks, but this implies a corresponding result for the key-tweak insertion TBC, see Theorem 7.1 of the same paper.

Algorithm 1. QCB

Input: message M, associated data A, IV, key K
Requirements: Initialization vectors should not be reused
Output: ciphertext C, tag T

1: Pad the initialization vector if necessary
2: Split M into full blocks $M_0, M_1, \ldots M_\ell$ and a final block M_* (partial or empty)
3: Split A into $A_0, A_1, \ldots A_j, A_*$
4: **for all** $i = 0$ to ℓ **do**
5: $\quad C_i \leftarrow \widetilde{E}_{K,(0,IV,i)}(M_i)$ $\hfill \triangleright$ Encryption of block i
6: **end for**
7: $C_* \leftarrow \widetilde{E}_{K,(1,IV,\ell)}(\mathrm{pad}(M_*))$ $\hfill \triangleright$ Encryption of the final block
8: $T \leftarrow 0$
9: **for all** $i = 0$ to j **do**
10: $\quad T \leftarrow T \oplus \widetilde{E}_{K,(2,IV,i)}(A_i)$ $\hfill \triangleright$ Absorb AD block i
11: **end for**
12: $T \leftarrow T \oplus \widetilde{E}_{K,(3,IV,j)}(\mathrm{pad}(A_*))$ $\hfill \triangleright$ Absorb the final AD block
13: $T \leftarrow T \oplus \widetilde{E}_{K,(4,IV,\ell)}(M_0 \oplus \ldots \oplus M_\ell \oplus \mathrm{pad}(M_*))$
14: **return** $C = (C_0 \| C_1 \| \ldots \| C_\ell \| C_*), T$

---

size n. We separate the tweak space in a cartesian product: $\mathcal{T} = \mathcal{D} \times \mathcal{IV} \times \mathcal{L}$. Thus, tweaks are triples (D, IV, j) where D is a *domain separator*, IV will be an IV, and j will be a block index. Only 5 values of domain separator need to be used.

The mode is defined in Algorithm 1 and represented in Fig. 2 and Fig. 3. When the message and AD are cut in blocks, the last block (M_* and a_* respectively) may be empty. We define the padding scheme $\mathrm{pad}(M_*)$ as appending $10*$ (a 1 followed by as many zeroes as necessary to fill the block). Note that due to the padding and structure of QCB, the ciphertext C is always longer than the plaintext M (by n bits at most).

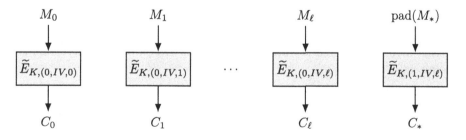

Fig. 2. QCB, encryption.

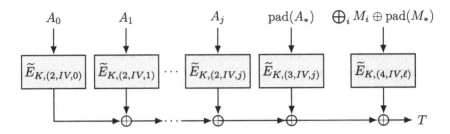

Fig. 3. QCB, processing of the associated data and computation of the tag.

Avoiding Quantum Attacks. It is important to include the IV in the tweak when processing the AD. Otherwise, there is a quantum forgery attack based on Deutsch's algorithm [13]. In Sect. 6, we will prove that QCB is secure assuming a weak quantum-secure TBC. We will use the following property, which follows from its definition.

Proposition 2 (Number of tweaks (informal)). *For a given IV, there exists a set of tweaks $T(IV)$ of size $|T(IV)| = 5(\ell + 1)$ such that any QCB query comprised of at most ℓn (included) bits of AD and ℓn bits of message can only reach tweaks in the set $T(IV)$.*

Proof. The tweaks are of the form (d, IV, i) where i is a block number between 0 and ℓ (included) and d a domain separator that takes 5 values.   □

Instantiation with Saturnin: Saturnin-QCB. We propose to instantiate QCB with the block cipher SATURNIN [15], a second-round candidate of the NIST LWC process [27]. SATURNIN has 256-bit blocks and keys. In addition, the cipher admits a *domain separator D* of 4 bits. The other modes of operation of the SATURNIN submission use values from 0 to 8 included, so we use $D = 9, 10, 11, 12$ and 13 in Algorithm 1. More precisely, the authors of [15] define a variant of SATURNIN with 16 *Super-rounds* aiming at an increased security margin in the related-key scenario, denoted SATURNIN_{16}. We define: $\widetilde{E}_{k,(D,IV,i)}(x) = \text{SATURNIN}_{16}^{D}(k \oplus (IV\|i), x)$, where we use the key-tweak insertion construction of Sect. 4 to turn SATURNIN_{16}^{D} into a TBC with 256-bit tweaks. The IV and the block number are simply concatenated. We use IVs of at most 160 bits and authorize up to 2^{95} blocks of data. This construction motivates further inquiry of related-key attacks, as it needs SATURNIN_{16} to be related-key secure.

Instantiation with a Dedicated TBC: TRAX-QCB. Block ciphers of 256 bits seem more convenient for post-quantum security. However, they are relatively rare (for example, SATURNIN is the only such one in the LWC standardization process). Fortunately, it is possible to instantiate QCB with a dedicated TBC with 256-bit blocks, the TRAX-L-17 cipher of [4]. It has smaller tweaks of 128 bits, contrary to the key-tweak-insertion TBC with SATURNIN, but it has the advantage of being a dedicated design, with possibly a better security than the tight bound for the key-tweak-insertion. 128 bits allow to fit the 3 bits required for domain separation, 80 bits of IV and 45 bits of block numbering. Thus we can encrypt at most $2^{45} - 1$ blocks of plaintext and AD.

6 Security of QCB

We show that, if the underlying TBC is secure under classical tweak queries:

- QCB is IND-qCPA secure (Sect. 6.2): an adversary making quantum encryption queries cannot distinguish between the encryptions of two classical challenge messages;
- QCB is BZ-unforgeable (Sect. 6.3): an adversary making q quantum encryption queries cannot output $q + 1$ valid IV/AD/ciphertext/tag quadruples.

We discuss other possible (and impossible) security definitions in Sect. 7.

6.1 Definitions

In all our definitions, the adversary makes q superposition queries with distinct pre-declared IVs. The messages and ADs both have a *maximal* length of ℓ complete blocks, but the exact length of queries can be chosen adaptively. We will bound the advantage depending only on q and ℓ. We will use superscripts for separate queries, and subscripts for individual blocks within a query.

IND-qCPA. First of all, we recall the definition of the IND-qCPA security game from [11]. In [11], each call to the encryption oracle contains randomness. We extend slightly this definition by making the adversary capable of choosing his IVs. However, we request this choice to be non-adaptive. Thus, the adversary specifies at the start of the game the sequence of IVs that she is going to use.

IND-qCPA game

Key generation: $K \xleftarrow{\$} \mathcal{K}, b \xleftarrow{\$} \{0,1\}$.
Initialization: $\mathcal{A}$ sends to the challenger a sequence of distinct IVs: $(IV^1, \dots, IV^q)$, one for each subsequent query.

- -

$\mathcal{A}$ can perform $q - 1$ encryption queries and one challenge query (at the very end or somewhere in between). For the kth query, the current IV is IV^k.

Encryption queries: $\mathcal{A}$ chooses a message and AD pair (M, A), the encryption oracle encrypts (IV, M, A) with the current IV and returns the output (C, T) to $\mathcal{A}$. Queries can be in superposition.

Challenge query: $\mathcal{A}$ chooses two classical message/AD pairs (M^0, A^0), (M^1, A^1) of the same length and sends them to the challenger. The challenger encrypts (IV, M^b, A^b) with the current IV and returns the output (C^b, T^b).

Guess: $\mathcal{A}$ outputs a bit b' and wins if $b = b'$.

For each query, the message and AD length are chosen between 0 and ℓn bits for a fixed ℓ (superposed messages must have the same length).

The IND-qCPA advantage of an adversary $\mathcal{A}$ against an AEAD E is:

$$\mathbf{Adv}_E^{\text{IND-qCPA}}(\mathcal{A}) = \left| \Pr\left[\mathcal{A} \text{ succeeds}\right] - \frac{1}{2} \right|.$$

BZ. We define our "Boneh-Zhandry" (BZ) unforgeability game, which is analogous to the definition of unforgeability for MACs of [10].

BZ game

Key generation: $K \xleftarrow{\$} \mathcal{K}$.

Initialization: $\mathcal{A}$ sends to the challenger a sequence of distinct IVs: $(IV^1, \ldots, IV^q)$, one for each subsequent query.

- -

Encryption queries: $\mathcal{A}$ chooses a message and AD pair (M, A), the encryption oracle encrypts (IV, M, A) with the current IV and returns the output (C, T) to $\mathcal{A}$. Queries can be in superposition.

Forgeries: $\mathcal{A}$ produces $q+1$ quadruples (A, IV, C, T) with any IVs of her choice and succeeds if all these quadruples are valid, that is, for each quadruple, there exists an M such that the encryption of (IV, M, A) is (C, T).

Note that verifying the forgery attempts requires additional queries. Since we assumed a limit on the message and AD lengths of ℓ blocks at most, we will also impose this limit on the forgery attempts of the adversary.

In practice, IVs are often either specified by a counter or chosen at random. We argue here that our security definitions are stronger than these 2 scenarios:

- If the challenger chooses at random IV^i for each encryption query. Then, he could as well generate all the possible $IV^1, \ldots, IV^q$ from the start. In our model, an adversary can generate $IV^1, \ldots, IV^q$ at random and send them to the challenger. The security is the same as before except that the adversary knows the different IVs. This can only help the adversary so being secure in our model implies security in the model where the IVs are chosen at random by the challenger.

- If the IVs are determined by a counter controlled by the challenger. The adversary can decide when he starts the attack and even assume he has control over the first IV which we call IV_1, then the set of IVs will be $\{IV_1, IV_1 + 1, \ldots, IV_1 + (q-1)\}$. In our model, an adversary can do that by declaring this set so again, our model is stronger[5].

In the IND-qCPA and BZ definitions above, the adversary chooses a sequence of distinct IVs: $(IV^1, \ldots, IV^q)$. When proving the security of QCB with oracle access to a tweakable block cipher $\widetilde{E}$, this immediately implies that the set T of possible tweaks to $\widetilde{E}$ is $T = \cup_{i=1}^q T(IV^i)$ hence $|T| \leq 5(\ell+1)q$ where ℓ is the maximal block length of encryption queries. This control on the size of T allows us to use Proposition 1 in a meaningful way.

6.2   IND-qCPA Security

Theorem 4. *Let* $\mathsf{QCB}[\widetilde{E}]$ *denote the QCB function with oracle access to the tweakable blockcipher* $\widetilde{E}$. *We consider adversaries making q queries of block length $\leq \ell$ to* $\mathsf{QCB}[\widetilde{E}]$, *then we have:*

$$\mathbf{Adv}_{\mathsf{QCB}[\widetilde{E}]}^{\text{Ind-qCPA}}(\mathcal{A}) \leq \mathbf{Adv}_{\widetilde{E}(\cdot,\odot)}^{\text{TPRP}}(5(\ell+1)q), \tag{1}$$

where the right-hand term is the maximal advantage over all adversaries querying $\widetilde{E}(\cdot,\odot)$ *with at most $5(\ell+1)q$ pre-declared tweaks.*

Proof. Suppose $\mathcal{A}$ is an adversary trying to break the IND-qCPA security of $\mathsf{QCB}[\widetilde{E}]$. $\mathcal{A}$ performs q encryption or challenge queries of maximum block length ℓ (the exact bit length of the queries can be chosen freely in the range $0, \ldots, n\ell$). Consider the query number i made to QCB (encryption or challenge). From Proposition 2, in this query, the tweakable block cipher $\widetilde{E}$ is queried with tweaks in the set $T(IV^i)$ having a fixed size $|T(IV^i)| = 5(\ell+1)$.

We can therefore see $\mathcal{A}$ as an algorithm performing at most $q(2\ell+3)$ queries to $\widetilde{E}$, with each tweak lying in the fixed set $T = \cup_{i=1}^q T(IV^i)$ with $|T| \leq 5q(\ell+1)$ (each query contains at most ℓ message and AD blocks, padding blocks and a final checksum block). If we replace $\widetilde{E}$ with $\widetilde{\Pi}$ for a random $\widetilde{\Pi}$, we get:

$$\left| \mathbf{Adv}_{\mathsf{QCB}[\widetilde{E}]}^{\text{Ind-qCPA}}(\mathcal{A}) - \mathbf{Adv}_{\mathsf{QCB}[\widetilde{\Pi}]}^{\text{Ind-qCPA}}(\mathcal{A}) \right| \leq \mathbf{Adv}_{\widetilde{E}(\cdot,\odot)}^{\text{TPRP}}(5(\ell+1)q). \tag{2}$$

Finally, consider an adversary $\mathcal{A}$ playing an IND-qCPA game with $\mathsf{QCB}[\widetilde{\Pi}]$. Recall that in the challenge phase, $\mathcal{A}$ picks two classical plaintext/AD pairs (M^0, A^0) and (M^1, A^1) of the same length, after which the challenger picks a

---

[5] There is only one case in which the use of a counter may enable an adversary to choose his IVs adaptively: he may wait for the counter to increase in order to reach a wanted IV. But the IV increases only when a message is encrypted so waiting for an IV increase should be essentially considered as costly as performing a query, which implies that the IVs that will be used will be in $\{IV_1, \ldots, IV_1 + (q-1)\}$.

random bit b and gives (C^b, T^b)—the encryption (and tag) of (M^b, A^b)—to $\mathcal{A}$. Since the tweaks used for computing this encryption are all different from all the tweaks used during the query phase, and since $\widetilde{\Pi}$ is an ideal tweakable random permutation, the distribution of (C^b, T^b) is independent of the distribution of the responses received by $\mathcal{A}$ during the query phase. Since b is a random bit, if b' is the bit output by $\mathcal{A}$, the probability that $b = b'$ is always $1/2$. Furthermore, this holds irrespective of the choice of $\mathcal{A}$. Thus,

$$\mathbf{Adv}^{\text{Ind-qCPA}}_{\text{QCB}[\widetilde{\Pi}]}(\mathcal{A}) = 0. \tag{3}$$

Our result follows directly by putting this equality into Eq. 2.   □

Theorem 4 is the only result required if we use a dedicated TBC. If we want to use a block cipher, we can replace $\widetilde{E}$ by the key-tweak insertion TBC of Sect. 4. The security will then hold in the ideal cipher model. We use Proposition 1 in the special case where $s_0 = 0$ (in the reduction, there is no second phase of classical queries).

Corollary 2. *In the case of the key-tweak insertion TBC of Sect. 4, we consider adversaries making also q' queries to $E^{\pm}$ and we have:*

$$\mathbf{Adv}^{\text{Ind-qCPA}}_{\text{QCB}[\widetilde{E}]}(\mathcal{A}) \leq \mathbf{Adv}^{\text{TPRP}}_{\widetilde{E}(\cdot,\odot),E_\odot(\odot)}(5(\ell+1)q, q') \leq 8\sqrt{\frac{5(\ell+1)qq'^2}{2^n}}. \tag{4}$$

6.3 Unforgeability

Now, we prove that QCB is BZ-unforgeable. Again, the first statement holds in the standard model, the second in the ideal cipher model.

Theorem 5. *Let $\mathcal{A}$ be an adversary making q superposition queries to QCB, of maximally ℓ blocks each (message and AD), and q' queries to E. Let $\mathcal{A}$ succeed if it outputs $q + 1$ valid quadruples (A, IV, C, T). Then the success probability of $\mathcal{A}$ is upper bounded as:*

$$\Pr\left[\mathcal{A} \text{ succeeds}\right] \leq \mathbf{Adv}^{\text{STPRP}}_{\widetilde{E}^{\pm}(\cdot,\odot)}(\mathcal{B}) + \frac{3+c}{2^n},$$

where c is the constant from Corollary 1 and $\mathcal{B}$ an adversary playing the modified STPRP game against $\widetilde{E}^{\pm}$, who uses at most $5q\ell$ pre-declared tweaks, makes at most $q\ell$ queries in the quantum phase, saves at most $(q + 1)(2\ell + 4)n$ classical bits to carry on to the next phase, and makes at most $(q + 1)(2\ell + 2)$ queries in the classical phase.

In the case of the key-tweak insertion TBC of Sect. 4, we consider adversaries making also q' queries to $E^{\pm}$ and we have:

$$\Pr\left[\mathcal{A} \text{ succeeds}\right] \leq 8\sqrt{\frac{5\ell qq'^2}{2^n}} + 3\sqrt{\frac{\ell^2 nq^2}{2^n}}.$$

Proof. Let G_0 be the original BZ game in which $\mathcal{A}$ interacts with QCB, instantiated with the TBC $\widetilde{E}$ and a randomly selected key k. Let G_1 be the game in which $\widetilde{E}$ is replaced by a family of independent random permutations Π_t for all tweaks t. We first show the following lemma, where $\mathcal{B}$ is as described in the theorem statement.

Lemma 3. $\Pr_{G_0}[\mathcal{A}\ succeeds] \leq \Pr_{G_1}[\mathcal{A}\ succeeds] + \mathbf{Adv}^{\mathrm{STPRP}}_{\widetilde{E}^{\pm}(\cdot,\odot)}(\mathcal{B})$.

Proof. The proof of this lemma is similar, but not equivalent to the proof of Theorem 4. In G_0, $\mathcal{A}$ performs q encryption queries of block length at most ℓ. Consider the ith query. From Proposition 2, in this query, the tweakable block cipher $\widetilde{E}$ is queried with tweaks in the set $T(IV^i)$ having a fixed size $|T(IV^i)| = 5(\ell+1)$.

We can therefore use $\mathcal{A}$ to create a strong TPRP adversary $\mathcal{B}$ for our modified game. $\mathcal{B}$ first declares the tweak-set $T = \cup^q_{i=1} T(IV^i)$ with $|T| \leq 5q(\ell+1)$, and then runs $\mathcal{A}$, performing at most $q\ell$ queries to $\widetilde{E}$, with each tweak lying in T. $\mathcal{A}$ outputs $q+1$ quadruples, which $\mathcal{B}$ stores in s_0 classical bits; since each quadruple has at most $2\ell+4$ n-bit blocks ($\ell+1$ each for A and C, one each for IV and T), $s_0 \leq (q+1)(2\ell+4)n$. Finally, the validity of these quadruples is checked using q_2 non-adaptive classical queries to the TBC (decryption attempts); each quadruple needs at most $2\ell+2$ TBC calls to verify ($\ell+1$ each for A and C), so $q_2 \leq (q+1)(2\ell+2)$.

If we replace $\widetilde{E}$ with $\widetilde{\Pi}$ for a random $\widetilde{\Pi}$, we go from G_0 to G_1. We therefore have

$$\Pr_{G_0}[\mathcal{A}\ succeeds] \leq \Pr_{G_1}[\mathcal{A}\ succeeds] + \mathbf{Adv}^{\mathrm{STPRP}}_{\widetilde{E}^{\pm}(\cdot,\odot)}(\mathcal{B}). \qquad \blacksquare$$

Our goal is now to bound $\Pr_{G_1}[\mathcal{A}\ succeeds]$. We run $\mathcal{A}$. Let $\mathcal{I} = \{IV'^i \mid 1 \leq i \leq q\}$ be the q declared IVs that $\mathcal{A}$ uses during its encryption queries. Let also $\mathcal{S} = \{(A^i, IV^i, C^i, T^i) \mid 1 \leq i \leq q+1\}$ denote the *forge-set*, i.e., the $q+1$ quadruples in $\mathcal{A}$'s output. Finally, let $[[\cdot]]$ denote block-length. We define the following disjoint bad events which correspond to $\mathcal{A}$ winning the game:

- bad-a: For some i, $IV^i \notin \mathcal{I}$.
- bad-b: For some $i, k \neq i$, $IV^i = IV^k \in \mathcal{I}$, and $[[C^i]] \neq [[C^k]]$
- bad-c: For some $i, k \neq i$, $IV^i = IV^k \in \mathcal{I}$, $[[C^i]] = [[C^k]]$, and $[[A^i]] \neq [[A^k]]$.
- bad-d: For some $i, k \neq i$, $IV^i = IV^k \in \mathcal{I}$, $[[C^i]] = [[C^k]]$, and $[[A^i]] = [[A^k]]$.

$\mathcal{A}$ succeeds in G_1 when the $q+1$ quadruples she outputs are valid. As the $q+1$ outputs shall be distinct and $|\mathcal{I}| = q$, this implies that one of the bad events has occurred. We therefore have

$$\Pr_{G_1}[\mathcal{A}\ succeeds] \leq \Pr_{G_1}[\text{bad-a}] + \Pr_{G_1}[\text{bad-b}] + \Pr_{G_1}[\text{bad-c}] + \Pr_{G_1}[\text{bad-d}]. \qquad (5)$$

We bound separately the probability of each bad event in order to conclude. For a quadruple (A, IV, C, T), with $A = (A_0, \ldots, A_j, pad(A_*))$ and $C = (C_1, \ldots, C_\ell, pad(C_*))$, we define $M_i := \Pi^{-1}_{(0,IV,i)}(C_i)$, $pad(M_*) := \Pi^{-1}_{(1,IV,\ell)}(C_*)$ and $M_{CS} := pad(M_*) \oplus \left(\bigoplus_{i=0}^{\ell} M_i \right)$. If the quadruple (A, IV, C, T) is valid in game G_1, this gives us

$$\Pi_{(4,IV,\ell)}(M_{CS}) \oplus \Pi_{(3,IV,j)}(pad(A_*)) \oplus \left(\bigoplus_{i=0}^{j} \Pi_{(2,IV,i)}(A_i) \right) = T. \qquad (6)$$

From there, we have for each $i \in \{0, \ldots, \ell\}$

$$M_i = \Pi^{-1}_{(4,IV,\ell)} \left(T \oplus \Pi_{(3,IV,j)}(pad(A_*)) \oplus \left(\bigoplus_{i=0}^{j} \Pi_{(2,IV,i)}(A_i) \right) \right)$$

$$\oplus pad(M_*) \oplus \left(\bigoplus_{k \neq i} M_k \right). \qquad (7)$$

This means that from a valid quadruple (A, IV, C, T), we can reconstruct each $M_i = \Pi^{-1}_{(0,IV,i)}(C_i)$ without any query to $\Pi_{0,IV,i}$ or $\Pi^{-1}_{0,IV,i}$ (but with access to other Π_t and Π_t^{-1}, in particular to compute $pad(M_*)$ and the M_k for $k \neq i$).

Similarly, for each $i \in \{0, \ldots, j\}$, we have

$$\Pi_{(2,IV,i)}(A_i) = T \oplus \Pi_{(4,IV,\ell)}(M_{CS}) \oplus \Pi_{(3,IV,j)}(pad(A_*)) \oplus \left(\bigoplus_{k \neq i} \Pi_{(2,IV,k)}(A_k) \right). \qquad (8)$$

This means that for a valid quadruple (A, IV, C, T), we can reconstruct each $\Pi_{(2,IV,i)}(A_i)$ without any query to $\Pi_{(2,IV,i)}$ or $\Pi^{-1}_{(2,IV,i)}$ (but with access to other Π_t and Π_t^{-1}).

With these 2 constructions in mind, we can bound the probability of each bad event with the following lemmas.

Lemma 4.

$$\Pr_{G_1}[\mathsf{bad\text{-}a}] \leq \frac{1}{2^n}.$$

Proof. Assume $\mathcal{A}$ outputs a quadruple (A^i, IV^i, C^i, T^i) with $IV^i \notin \mathcal{I}$. Since $IV^i \notin \mathcal{I}$, the permutations $\Pi_{0,IV^i,0}$ and $\Pi^{-1}_{0,IV^i,0}$ have not been queried to compute the quadruple. From the above discussion, if the quadruple is valid, we know how to construct a valid input/output pair $(M_0^i, \Pi_{(0,IV^i,0)}(M_0^i) = C_0^i)$ without any calls to $\Pi_{0,IV^i,0}$ or $\Pi^{-1}_{0,IV^i,0}$. Because $\Pi_{0,IV^i,0}$ is a uniformly random permutation and independent from the others, this happens with probability $\frac{1}{2^n}$. ∎

Lemma 5.

$$\Pr_{G_1}[\text{bad-b}] \leq \frac{1}{2^n}.$$

Proof. Assume $\mathcal{A}$ outputs two quadruples (A^i, IV^i, C^i, T^i) and (A^k, IV^k, C^k, T^k) such that $IV^i = IV^k \in \mathcal{I}$, and $[[C^i]] \neq [[C^k]]$. Without loss of generality, we assume that there exists u such that $IV^i = IV'^u$, and $\ell^i = [[C^i]]$ is different from the output block length ℓ'^u of query number u (which is a fixed value of the query). This property must be true for i or for k. If the adversary succeeds, the quadruple (A^i, IV^i, C^i, T^i) must be valid even though the function Π_{4,IV^i,ℓ^i} has never been queried. Let $j^i = [[A^i]]$. From (A^i, IV^i, C^i, T^i), we define $M_v^i := \Pi_{(0,IV^i,v)}^{-1}(C_v^i)$, $pad(M_*^i) := \Pi_{(1,IV^i,\ell^i)}^{-1}(C_*^i)$ and $M_{CS}^i := pad(M_*^i) \oplus \left(\bigoplus_{u=0}^{\ell^i} M_u^i\right)$. If the quadruple (A^i, IV^i, C^i, T^i) is valid, we have

$$\Pi_{4,IV^i,\ell^i}(M_{CS}^i) = T^i \oplus \Pi_{(3,IV^i,j^i)}(pad(A_*^i)) \oplus \left(\bigoplus_{v=0}^{j^i} \Pi_{(2,IV^i,v)}(A_j^i)\right).$$

This means we can construct a pair $(M_{CS}^i, \Pi_{4,IV^i,\ell^i}(M_{CS}^i))$ without any calls to Π_{4,IV^i,ℓ^i} or Π_{4,IV^i,ℓ^i}^{-1}. Since Π_{4,IV^i,ℓ^i} is a uniformly random permutation and independent from the others, this happens with probability $\frac{1}{2^n}$. ∎

Lemma 6.

$$\Pr_{G_1}[\text{bad-c}] \leq \frac{1}{2^n}.$$

Proof. Assume $\mathcal{A}$ outputs two quadruples (A^i, IV^i, C^i, T^i) and (A^k, IV^k, C^k, T^k) such that $IV^i = IV^k \in \mathcal{I}$, $[[C^i]] = [[C^k]]$ and $[[A^i]] \neq [[A^k]]$. Without loss of generality, we assume that there exists u such that $IV^i = IV'^u$, and $j^i = [[A^i]]$ is different from the AD block length j'^u queried in query u. (This happens either for index i or index k). We focus on this quadruple (A^i, IV^i, C^i, T^i) for which Π_{3,IV^i,j^i} has never been queried. We let $\ell^i = [[C^i]]$. we define $M_u^i := \Pi_{(0,IV^i,u)}^{-1}(C_u^i)$, $pad(M_*^i) := \Pi_{(1,IV^i,\ell^i)}^{-1}(C_*^i)$ and $M_{CS}^i := pad(M_*^i) \oplus \left(\bigoplus_{u=0}^{\ell^i} M_u^i\right)$. If the quadruple is valid, we have

$$\Pi_{(3,IV,j^i)}(pad(A_*^i)) = T^i \oplus \Pi_{4,IV^i,\ell^i}(M_{CS}^i) \oplus \left(\bigoplus_{u=0}^{j^i} \Pi_{(2,IV^i,u)}(A_u^i)\right).$$

This means we can construct a pair $(pad(A_*^i), \Pi_{(3,IV^i,j^i)}(pad(A_*^i)))$ without any calls to $\Pi_{(3,IV^i,j^i)}$ or its inverse. Since it is a uniformly random permutation and independent from the others, this happens with probability $\frac{1}{2^n}$. ∎

Lemma 7. *Let c be the constant of Corollary 1, we have*

$$\Pr_{G_1}[\text{bad-d}] \leq \frac{c}{2^n}.$$

Proof. Assume $\mathcal{A}$ outputs two quadruples (A^i, IV^i, C^i, T^i) and (A^k, IV^k, C^k, T^k) such that $IV^i = IV^k \in \mathcal{I}$, $[[C^i]] = [[C^k]] := \ell$ and $[[A^i]] = [[A^k]] := j$. This means we can write $C^i = (C_0^1, \ldots, C_\ell^i, C_*^i)$, $A^i = (A_0^i, \ldots, A_j^i, pad(A_*^i))$ and similarly for C^k, A^k. Assume the 2 quadruples are valid, we distinguish 2 cases:

- $\exists u, C_u^i \neq C_u^k$. According to the construction following Eq. 7, we can construct two different input/output pairs $(M_u^i, \Pi_{0,IV^i,u}(M_u^i) = C_u^i)$ and $(M_u^k, \Pi_{0,IV^i,u}(M_u^k) = C_u^k)$ without additional queries to $\Pi_{0,IV^i,u}^\pm$. However, there has been only 1 call to $\Pi_{0,IV^i,u}$ during the game (since each IV in the challenge queries is different). Therefore, we have from Corollary 1 that this can happen with probability at most $\frac{c}{2^n}$.
- $\exists u, A_u^i \neq A_u^k$. From the construction following Eq. 7, we can construct two different input/output pairs $(A_u^i, \Pi_{2,IV^i,u}(A_u^i))$ and $(A_u^k, \Pi_{2,IV^i,u}(A_u^k))$ without additional queries to $\Pi_{2,IV^i,u}^\pm$. We conclude using a similar argument as above.

In order to conclude, notice that we have to be in one of the 2 cases above if the 2 quadruples are valid, otherwise they are equal. ∎

The first assertion of the theorem follows from Eq. 5 and Lemmas 3–7. For the second assertion specific to the key-tweak insertion TBC, we use the following additional lemma to bound $\mathbf{Adv}_{\widetilde{E}^\pm(\cdot, \odot)}^{\mathrm{STPRP}}(\mathcal{B})$.

Lemma 8. *When $\mathcal{B}$ plays the modified STPRP game against the key-tweak insertion TBC of Sect. 4 and makes an additional q' queries to $E^\pm$,*

$$\mathbf{Adv}_{\widetilde{E}^\pm(\cdot, \odot)}^{\mathrm{STPRP}}(\mathcal{B}) \leq 8\sqrt{\frac{5\ell q q'^2}{2^n}} + 3\sqrt{\frac{\ell^2 n q^2}{2^n}}.$$

Proof. From Proposition 1 and the definition of $\mathbf{Adv}_{\widetilde{E}^\pm(\cdot, \odot)}^{\mathrm{STPRP}}(\mathcal{B})$, we have

$$\mathbf{Adv}_{\widetilde{E}^\pm(\cdot, \odot)}^{\mathrm{STPRP}}(\mathcal{B}) \leq 8\sqrt{\frac{m q'^2}{2^k}} + \sqrt{\frac{q_2 s_0}{2 \cdot 2^k}},$$

where m, q_1, s_0, q_2 are defined as in Proposition 1. From the description of $\mathcal{B}$ in the theorem statement, we can plug in the bounds

$$m \leq 5q\ell, \qquad\qquad q_1 \leq q\ell,$$
$$s_0 \leq (q+1)(2\ell+4)n, \qquad q_2 \leq (q+1)(2\ell+2),$$

and put $k = n$ to get

$$\mathbf{Adv}_{\widetilde{E}^\pm(\cdot, \odot)}^{\mathrm{STPRP}}(\mathcal{B}) \leq \sqrt{\frac{5\ell q q'^2}{2^k}} + \sqrt{\frac{2(q+1)^2(\ell+1)(\ell+2)n}{2^n}}.$$

Finally to obtain the bound in the lemma we apply the simplification

$$2(q+1)^2(\ell+1)(\ell+2) \leq 9q^2\ell^2$$

which holds for any reasonable choice of q and ℓ (for instance, $q \geq 2, \ell \geq 2$ and $q + \ell \geq 6$). □

Substituting the bound from Lemma 8 in the first inequality of the theorem yields the second inequality, thus completing the proof. □

7   Discussion on Security Notions

In this section, we take a broader viewpoint at suitable notions of quantum security for a combined AEAD mode. In particular, we show an attack that breaks the qIND-qCPA notion [17,25] for all *online* modes (hence all practical AEAD modes). We also discuss the definition of *blind unforgeability* from [1].

7.1   The qIND-qCPA Notion and Attacking All Online Modes

It is well-known that for any mode of encryption that XORs a keystream to the message, IND-CPA security implies IND-qCPA. In other words, a quantum adversary does not benefit from having superposition query access. This comes from the malleability of such a mode.

Lemma 9 ([3], informal). *Define an encryption mode as $E_K(M; IV) = M \oplus f(K, IV)$ where IV is a randomly chosen IV and f is any function. If E_K is IND-CPA, then it is also IND-qCPA.*

Informal. Given a quantum adversary $\mathcal{B}$ that attacks the IND-qCPA security notion, we can construct a (quantum) adversary $\mathcal{A}$ that attacks the IND-CPA security of the mode. $\mathcal{A}$ simulates $\mathcal{B}$. When $\mathcal{B}$ wants a quantum query, $\mathcal{A}$ queries $E_K(0; IV)$ and XORs this value on the input register of $\mathcal{B}$.   □

However, such a mode also admits a well-known quantum distinguishing attack using a *single* superposition query. This attack applies regardless of the function f chosen, and in particular if f is a random oracle (the *one-time pad*).

The qIND-qCPA Notion. In [17], Chevalier, Ebrahimi and Vu propose the "qIND-qCPA" security game where an adversary must distinguish between a quantum oracle for $E_K(M; IV) = M \oplus f(K, IV)$ (with IV selected uniformly at random at each new query) and a random oracle. They use Zhandry's recording technique [34] in the latter case. They also show that certain modes like CFB, OFB and CTR are insecure under this notion. By design, the qIND-qCPA security notion makes the one-time pad attack valid.

We can extend the one-time pad distinguisher in order to attack not only keystream-based modes like CTR, but all "online" modes. By "online" mode, we mean a mode of encryption in which the plaintext blocks are read and encrypted in sequence, so that the first ciphertext block C_0 depends *only* on the first plaintext block M_0, the second ciphertext block C_1 depends only on M_0, M_1, etc.. In fact, it is enough to have *one bit* of the complete ciphertext, say the last one, independent from *one bit* of the complete plaintext, say the first one. For the sake of simplicity, we consider messages of a fixed size (since we make a single query anyway). Note that a similar result was proposed in [16].

Lemma 10. *Let $E_K(M; IV)$ be an encryption function of messages of length m, where the first ciphertext bit is independent of the last plaintext bit. Then there exists a quantum adversary $\mathcal{A}^O$ making a single query to its oracle O and distinguishing $E_K(M; IV)$ ("real world") from a random family of permutations $\Pi_{K,IV}(M)$ ("random world") with probability of success $\frac{3}{4} \geq \frac{1}{2}$.*

Proof. Our distinguisher is based on Deutsch-Jozsa's algorithm and on the post-processing of quantum oracles of Lemma 2. The adversary fixes all the bits of M except the last one to an arbitrary value, say 0, and puts $|0\rangle + |1\rangle$ in the last bit. She queries the oracle and truncates the output to its first bit. Her state becomes: $|0\rangle |f(0)\rangle + |1\rangle |f(1)\rangle$, where f is the first ciphertext bit as a function of the last plaintext bit (after the other bits have been fixed). She then uses Deutsch-Jozsa's algorithm to determine whether f is constant or non-constant. If f is constant, she decides that this is the real world and otherwise, the random world.

- In the random world ($O = \Pi_{K,IV}(M)$), this f should remain a random function. Thus the outputs are equal only with probability $\frac{1}{2}$: the guess is correct with probability $\frac{1}{2}$. • In the real world, f is always constant. The guess is always correct.

Overall, the adversary is correct with probability $\frac{1}{2}\left(1 + \frac{1}{2}\right) = \frac{3}{4}$. Using a full block instead of a mere bit makes the success probability exponentially close to 1 with a single query, as in the one-time pad attack.   □

A consequence of this attack is that, while the qIND-qCPA definition seems nontrivial, it cannot be achieved by an online mode, including e.g. CBC or our proposal QCB. If we require the adversary to distinguish the mode from an *ideal online mode*, instead of a random permutation, our attack should not be applicable anymore. However, the definition and proofs of security may be far more involved, and we leave further exploration of this topic as an open problem.

7.2   Unforgeability for a Combined AEAD Mode

The *Blind Unforgeability* notion was introduced in [1] as a replacement for BZ-unforgeability for MACs. In [1], the authors prove that it is possible to create a BZ-secure MAC scheme (given by a pair Mac_K, Ver_K) such that, after having made q superposition queries to some subset of the message space, one can forge the MAC of another message outside this space.

Note that the example given in [1] is very technical, and relies heavily on the fact that the MAC treats differently different subsets of its input. This is usually not the case for practical constructions (including QCB).

Blind-unforgeability (BU) is a stronger security notion defined with the following game: the adversary is given access to a *blinded* version of Mac_K, that returns $\perp$ on some fraction ϵ of the message space. To win, the adversary has to output a valid forgery in this space. In the game, the uniform random blinding B_ϵ is created by putting every message of the message space with probability ϵ. Alternatively, the adversary could choose her own blinding, but this is equivalent for inverse-polynomial values of ϵ: in [1] (Theorem 2) the authors prove that an adversary capable of outputting a "good" forgery will still do so even if the MAC has been blinded.

BU game

Setup: the adversary selects a parameter $\epsilon < 1$. The challenger picks a random key K, a random blinding B_ϵ which is a fraction of the message space $\mathcal{M}$ of size ϵ.

- -

Forgery: the adversary produces a pair (M, T) and wins if $M \in B_\epsilon$ and $\mathsf{Ver}_K(M, T) = \top$.

MAC queries: the adversary queries the "blinded" MAC:

$$M \mapsto \begin{cases} \bot & \text{if } M \in B_\epsilon, \\ \mathsf{Mac}_K(M) & \text{otherwise.} \end{cases} \tag{9}$$

The following result, together with the example given in [1], shows that BU-unforgeability is a strictly stronger notion than BZ-unforgeability for a MAC.

Theorem 6 ([1], **Theorem 1**). *Any BU-unforgeable MAC is BZ-unforgeable.*

This notion is adapted for a standalone MAC. In our case, we consider a combined AEAD mode, and we would need to adapt the definition. We can propose, for example, to blind the message space. We select a subset B_ϵ of message, AD and IVs (possibly the same pairs of AD and message for all IVs, or selected differently for each one). We give the adversary access to an oracle that encrypts (IV, A, M) if it does not belong to B_ϵ and otherwise, returns $\bot$. The adversary then succeeds if she outputs a valid quadruple (A, IV, C, T) whose corresponding message M is such that $(IV, A, M) \in B_\epsilon$.

The main difference with the original BU definition is that the condition of success relies on the message M, which is not necessarily an output of the forgery (the adversary can forge on an unknown message M). Despite that, we conjecture that this definition is non-trivial and that it might be proven for QCB. This proof would likely be more technical than our original one, and we leave it as an open problem.

8   Conclusion

In this paper, we designed the first AEAD of rate one with quantum security guarantees. With a definition similar to TAE and OCB, our proposal, QCB, retains high security guarantees as soon as it is used with a quantum-secure tweakable block cipher. We explicited this security requirement and proposed a construction based on a block cipher, in the ideal cipher model: the key-tweak insertion of Sect. 4.

In the classical setting, the LRW construction provides a TBC of rate one (one block cipher call per TBC call) from a PRP assumption. Ours requires related-key security for the underlying block cipher. Although we do not rule out the possibility of a rate-one TBC without related-key security, the LRW approach does not seem applicable.

Thus, an interesting open question is whether it is possible to build a post-quantum AEAD of rate one from a block cipher, *with a qPRP assumption only*. It may be possible to obtain directly the security without relying explicitly on a secure TBC, though this was the subject of our first attempt, which failed due to a new attack on OCB with a *single* query.

In our security proofs, we used the IND-qCPA and BZ security notions for indistinguishability and unforgeability. We note that other security definitions have been proposed in the more recent literature and seem worth investigating.

Acknowledgements. We thank the reviewers from EUROCRYPT 2021, CRYPTO 2021 and ASIACRYPT 2021 for their helpful feedback and insights, which helped us improve the paper and correct technical errors. This project has received funding from the European Research Council (ERC) under the European Union's Horizon 2020 research and innovation programme (grant agreement no. 714294 - acronym QUASY-Modo). A. S. is supported by ERC-ADG-ALGSTRONGCRYPTO (project 740972).

References

1. Alagic, G., Majenz, C., Russell, A., Song, F.: Quantum-access-secure message authentication via blind-unforgeability. In: Canteaut, A., Ishai, Y. (eds.) EUROCRYPT 2020. LNCS, vol. 12107, pp. 788–817. Springer, Cham (2020). https://doi.org/10.1007/978-3-030-45727-3_27

2. Alagic, G., Russell, A.: Quantum-secure symmetric-key cryptography based on hidden shifts. In: Coron, J.-S., Nielsen, J.B. (eds.) EUROCRYPT 2017. LNCS, vol. 10212, pp. 65–93. Springer, Cham (2017). https://doi.org/10.1007/978-3-319-56617-7_3

3. Anand, M.V., Targhi, E.E., Tabia, G.N., Unruh, D.: Post-quantum security of the CBC, CFB, OFB, CTR, and XTS modes of operation. In: Takagi, T. (ed.) PQCrypto 2016. LNCS, vol. 9606, pp. 44–63. Springer, Cham (2016). https://doi.org/10.1007/978-3-319-29360-8_4

4. Beierle, C., et al.: Alzette: a 64-Bit ARX-box. In: Micciancio, D., Ristenpart, T. (eds.) CRYPTO 2020. LNCS, vol. 12172, pp. 419–448. Springer, Cham (2020). https://doi.org/10.1007/978-3-030-56877-1_15

5. Bellare, M., Kohno, T.: A theoretical treatment of related-key attacks: RKA-PRPs, RKA-PRFs, and applications. In: Biham, E. (ed.) EUROCRYPT 2003. LNCS, vol. 2656, pp. 491–506. Springer, Heidelberg (2003). https://doi.org/10.1007/3-540-39200-9_31

6. Bennett, C.H., Bernstein, E., Brassard, G., Vazirani, U.V.: Strengths and weaknesses of quantum computing. SIAM J. Comput. **26**(5), 1510–1523 (1997)

7. Bernstein, E., Vazirani, U.V.: Quantum complexity theory. In: STOC, pp. 11–20. ACM (1993)

8. Bhaumik, R., et al.: QCB: efficient quantum-secure authenticated encryption. IACR Cryptol. ePrint Arch, p. 1304 (2020). https://eprint.iacr.org/2020/1304

9. Bhaumik, R., Nandi, M.: Improved security for OCB3. In: Takagi, T., Peyrin, T. (eds.) ASIACRYPT 2017. LNCS, vol. 10625, pp. 638–666. Springer, Cham (2017). https://doi.org/10.1007/978-3-319-70697-9_22

10. Boneh, D., Zhandry, M.: Quantum-secure message authentication codes. In: Johansson, T., Nguyen, P.Q. (eds.) EUROCRYPT 2013. LNCS, vol. 7881, pp. 592–608. Springer, Heidelberg (2013). https://doi.org/10.1007/978-3-642-38348-9_35

11. Boneh, D., Zhandry, M.: Secure signatures and chosen ciphertext security in a quantum computing world. In: Canetti, R., Garay, J.A. (eds.) CRYPTO 2013. LNCS, vol. 8043, pp. 361–379. Springer, Heidelberg (2013). https://doi.org/10.1007/978-3-642-40084-1_21

12. Bonnetain, X.: Quantum key-recovery on full AEZ. In: Adams, C., Camenisch, J. (eds.) SAC 2017. LNCS, vol. 10719, pp. 394–406. Springer, Cham (2018). https://doi.org/10.1007/978-3-319-72565-9_20

13. Bonnetain, X., Leurent, G., Naya-Plasencia, M., Schrottenloher, A.: Quantum linearization attacks. In: The Proceedings of ASIACRYPT (2021)

14. Bonnetain, X., Naya-Plasencia, M.: Hidden shift quantum cryptanalysis and implications. In: Peyrin, T., Galbraith, S. (eds.) ASIACRYPT 2018. LNCS, vol. 11272, pp. 560–592. Springer, Cham (2018). https://doi.org/10.1007/978-3-030-03326-2_19

15. Canteaut, A., et al.: Saturnin: a suite of lightweight symmetric algorithms for post-quantum security. IACR Trans. Symm. Cryptol. **2020**(S1), 160–207 (2020)

16. Carstens, T.V., Ebrahimi, E., Tabia, G., Unruh, D.: On quantum indistinguishability under chosen plaintext attack. Cryptology ePrint Archive, Report 2020/596 (2020). https://eprint.iacr.org/2020/596

17. Chevalier, C., Ebrahimi, E., Vu, Q.H.: On the security notions for encryption in a quantum world. QCrypt 2020 (2020). https://eprint.iacr.org/2020/237

18. Hosoyamada, A., Iwata, T.: Provably quantum-secure tweakable block ciphers. IACR Trans. Symmetric Cryptol. **2021**(1), 337–377 (2021). https://doi.org/10.46586/tosc.v2021.i1.337-377

19. Hosoyamada, A., Sasaki, Y.: Quantum Demiric-Selçuk meet-in-the-middle attacks: applications to 6-round generic Feistel constructions. In: Catalano, D., De Prisco, R. (eds.) SCN 2018. LNCS, vol. 11035, pp. 386–403. Springer, Cham (2018). https://doi.org/10.1007/978-3-319-98113-0_21

20. Hosoyamada, A., Yasuda, K.: Building quantum-one-way functions from block ciphers: Davies-Meyer and Merkle-Damgård constructions. In: Peyrin, T., Galbraith, S. (eds.) ASIACRYPT 2018. LNCS, vol. 11272, pp. 275–304. Springer, Cham (2018). https://doi.org/10.1007/978-3-030-03326-2_10

21. Kaplan, M., Leurent, G., Leverrier, A., Naya-Plasencia, M.: Breaking symmetric cryptosystems using quantum period finding. In: Robshaw, M., Katz, J. (eds.) CRYPTO 2016. LNCS, vol. 9815, pp. 207–237. Springer, Heidelberg (2016). https://doi.org/10.1007/978-3-662-53008-5_8

22. Krovetz, T., Rogaway, P.: The software performance of authenticated-encryption modes. In: Joux, A. (ed.) FSE 2011. LNCS, vol. 6733, pp. 306–327. Springer, Heidelberg, February 2011. https://doi.org/10.1007/978-3-642-21702-9_18

23. Liskov, M., Rivest, R.L., Wagner, D.: Tweakable block ciphers. In: Yung, M. (ed.) CRYPTO 2002. LNCS, vol. 2442, pp. 31–46. Springer, Heidelberg (2002). https://doi.org/10.1007/3-540-45708-9_3

24. Liskov, M., Rivest, R.L., Wagner, D.: Tweakable block ciphers. J. Cryptol. **24**(3), 588–613 (2011)

25. Mossayebi, S., Schack, R.: Concrete security against adversaries with quantum superposition access to encryption and decryption oracles (2016). arxiv.org/1609.03780

26. National Institute of Standards and Technology (NIST): Submission requirements and evaluation criteria for the post-quantum cryptography standardization process, December 2016
27. National Institute of Standards and Technology (NIST): Submission requirements and evaluation criteria for the lightweight cryptography standardization process, August 2018
28. Nielsen, M.A., Chuang, I.L.: Quantum information and quantum computation, vol. 2(8), p. 23. Cambridge University Press, Cambridge (2000)
29. Rogaway, P.: Efficient instantiations of tweakable blockciphers and refinements to modes OCB and PMAC. In: Lee, P.J. (ed.) ASIACRYPT 2004. LNCS, vol. 3329, pp. 16–31. Springer, Heidelberg (2004). https://doi.org/10.1007/978-3-540-30539-2_2
30. Rötteler, M., Steinwandt, R.: A note on quantum related-key attacks. Inf. Process. Lett. **115**(1), 40–44 (2015)
31. Santoli, T., Schaffner, C.: Using Simon's algorithm to attack symmetric-key cryptographic primitives. Quantum Inf. Comput. **17**(1 & 2), 65–78 (2017)
32. Simon, D.R.: On the power of quantum computation. In: 35th FOCS, pp. 116–123. IEEE Computer Society Press, November 1994
33. Zhandry, M.: A note on the quantum collision and set equality problems. Quantum Inf. Comput. **15**(7 & 8), 557–567 (2015)
34. Zhandry, M.: How to record quantum queries, and applications to quantum indifferentiability. In: Boldyreva, A., Micciancio, D. (eds.) CRYPTO 2019. LNCS, vol. 11693, pp. 239–268. Springer, Cham (2019). https://doi.org/10.1007/978-3-030-26951-7_9

Author Index

Printed in the United States
by Baker & Taylor Publisher Services